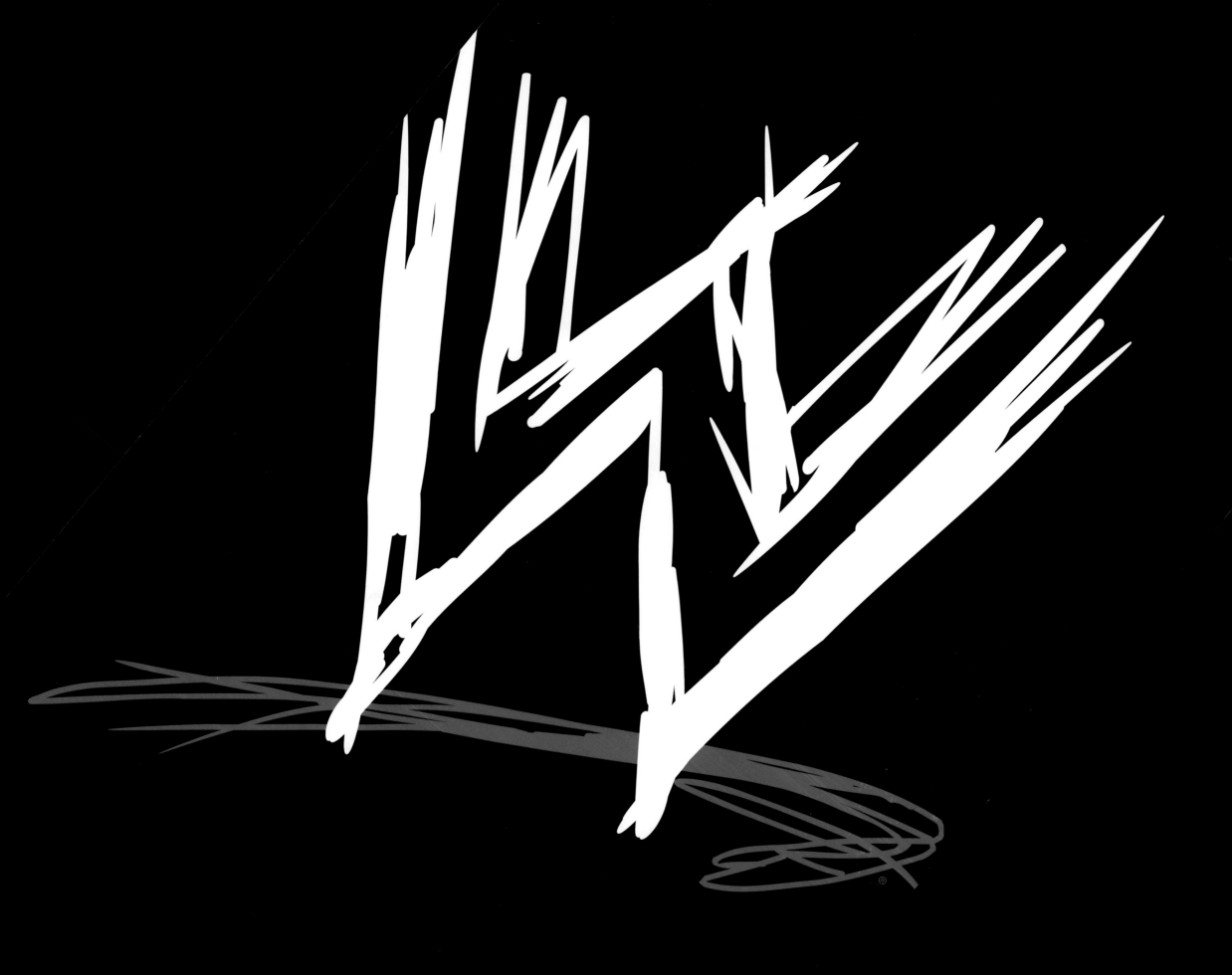

Written by
Brian Shields & Kevin Sullivan

ENCYCLOPEDIA

UPDATED & EXPANDED

THE DEFINITIVE GUIDE TO WWE

TO THE WWE UNIVERSE

I am proud to share with you our updated and expanded encyclopedia detailing the complete history of WWE. The exciting images and dynamic text that bring these pages to life serve as the documented history of the WWE. WWE's unique form of entertainment has translated into an international language, uniting people of all ages, genders, races, colors and creeds. In this all-encompassing work, you will read about our groundbreaking 50 years, and those few who have had the privilege to perform before our audiences to deliver unmatched excitement and drama. I hope you enjoy reading about our incredible history as much as we enjoyed being part of it.

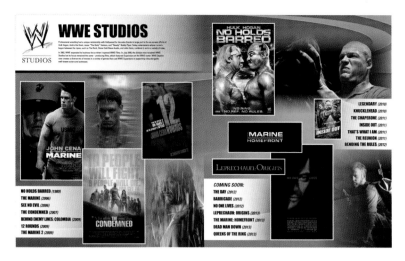

WWE STUDIOS

MERCHANDISE & MEMORABILIA

CONTENTS

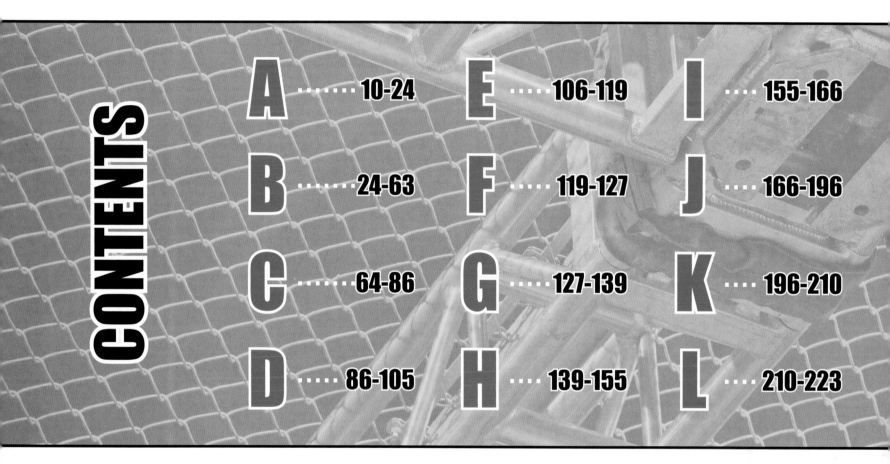

FAN SIGNS

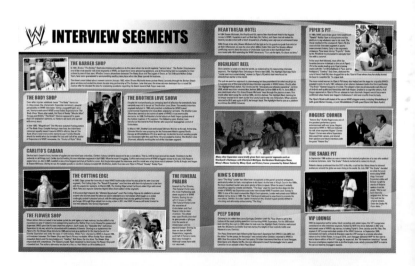

INTERVIEW SEGMENTS

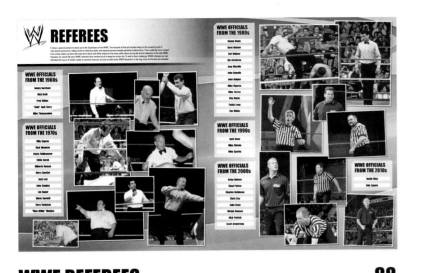

WWE REFEREES

WWE ON TV

WWE HALL OF FAME

20-0: THE STREAK

DK

LONDON, NEW YORK,
MELBOURNE, AND DELHI

Senior Development Editor	**Publisher**	**Marketing Manager**
Ken Schmidt	Mike Degler	Katie Hemlock
Designer	**Editor-In-Chief**	**Operations Manager**
Tracy Wehmeyer	H. Leigh Davis	Stacey Beheler
Cover Designer	**Licensing Manager**	
Franco Malagisi	Christian Sumner	

Published in the United States by DK/BradyGAMES, a division of Penguin Group (USA) Inc.
800 East 96th Street, 3rd Floor
Indianapolis, Indiana 46240

ISBN 978-1-4093-7679-8

Printed by South China

004-WD178-Nov/12

ABOUT THE AUTHORS

BRIAN SHIELDS

Brian Shields's work with the WWE dates back to 1998. After marketing WWE video games, Brian helped create the Legends Program. He co-authored the *New York Times* bestselling *WWE Encyclopedia: The Definitive Guide To World Wrestling Entertainment*. In addition, his writing credits include *Main Event: WWE In The Raging 80's* and *DK Readers: WWE John Cena* and *DK Readers: WWE Triple H*.

Founder of Mighty Pen & Sword, LLC, Brian most recently partnered with WWE licensees Mattel, THQ, and Game On. Brian lectures throughout the United States and writes comedy at the Friars Club in New York City where he enjoys membership.

KEVIN SULLIVAN

Kevin Sullivan is a graduate of Fairfield University in Connecticut, just a few miles north of WWE's Stamford headquarters. In 1998, Sullivan began a decade-long career with both WWE.com and WWE Magazine. In 2008, he left his daily WWE responsibilities, but still works with the worldwide leader in sports-entertainment as an author of nine WWE books. Follow Sullivan on Twitter: @SullivanBooks

Sullivan currently lives in Milford, Connecticut, with his wife, Caryn.

WWE CREDITS

Sr. Coordinator, Home Entertainment & Books

Steve Pantaleo

Vice President, Interactive Licensing & Product Development

Mike Archer

Photo Department

Frank Vitucci, Jamie Piscitelli, Lea Girard, Josh Tottenham, Melissa Halladay, JD Sestito, Mike Moran

Legal

Lauren Dienes-Middlen

Creative Services

John Jones, Diane Udin, Franco Malagisi

ACKNOWLEDGMENTS

KEVIN SULLIVAN

Above all else, I would like to thank my wife for supporting me during this project. Thank you, Caryn. You are the strongest and most beautiful woman I know.

I would also like to thank my parents, Lorraine and Joe, for supporting my WWE addiction while growing up. My mother bought me my first action figure, an LJN version of the Iron Sheik; and my father, who inexplicably loved the Bushwhackers, sacrificed his weekends to take me to live events, including *WrestleMania V* and *X*.

Thank you to my sister, Amy, for using her connections to get me my first job with WWE in 1998.

It's been an honor to work with Ken Schmidt, Mike Degler, Leigh Davis, Tracy Wehmeyer and the entire DK Publishing team. The book you are holding in your hands looks so impressive because of their endless dedication to make it the best it could possibly be.

Thank you to my WWE family. For ten years, I had the honor of being surrounded by the most creative team ever assembled. Special thanks to Mike Archer for mentoring me for all those years; Dean Miller for including me in the first project; Chris Chambers for being so much more than a boss; and Michael Cole for making the twenty-hour workdays a little more enjoyable.

Of course, I would be remiss if I didn't mention the talented team at WWE.com: John Cerilli, Phil Speer, Lucas Swineford, Mike McAvennie, Craig Tello, Zack Zeigler, Bryan Robinson, Ken O'Brien, Jim Monsees, Jennifer Spear and the rest of the gang (Sorry, guys. There are just too many of you to list. It's hard to believe that we all fi t into that .com trailer).

Thank you to the McMahon family for taking a chance on a kid like me and giving me the tools needed to climb the corporate ladder.

Finally, thank you Brian Shields for being an amazing co-author. I'm looking forward to working with you again in the future.

BRIAN SHIELDS

It is a genuine honor to write about something that captured my imagination from the moment I saw *All-Star Wrestling* on television. I will be forever grateful for the opportunity to be part of this amazing work and collaborate with such talented individuals.

To WWE, thank you for allowing me to enter your ring, pen in hand, to trumpet your extraordinary accomplishments as you celebrate 50 years as a sports-entertainment legend. To Dean Miller, thank you for the amazing, once-in-a-lifetime opportunity to be part of your vision. It has been a privilege to work with the dedicated team at DK Publishing, especially Leigh Davis, Ken Schmidt, and Mike Degler. I'm grateful to members of DK for their support following the release of the first Encyclopedia, particularly Michael Vaccaro, Rachel Kempster, Nancy Lambert, and Susan Stockman. To fantastic co-author, Kevin Sullivan, you're an invaluable partner and friend. I can't wait for our next collaboration.

Infinite appreciation goes to Mike Archer for being such a remarkable influence during the past 15 years. Sincere gratitude to Chris Ostuni for his legal expertise and unerring sense of fair play in all things great and small.

To the Breen and Eibeler families, I am forever in your debt for helping set the cornerstone of my career. It all comes back to you. Special recognition to the Alvarado, Borawski, Chiechi, Levi-Minzi, Ma, Ostuni, Papatrefon, Siegel, Utomo, and Wilkins families. Endless thanks to Kevin Brannan, Nique Fajors, Peter Bregman, Lewis Frumkes, Ben Frank, Bonita Pietila, and Andrew Newberg for their endless influence and friendship.

Bravos to my Mighty Pen & Sword team: my sister, Cristiana, and great friends David Skelton, Jack Scalici, James Sewell, Dongwha Lee, Omar Padron, and James McLaughlin as well as the best PR firm in the business, the Highwater Group.

Eternal admiration goes to my mother, Barbara. You remain the guiding light and motivation for our family with a saint's heart and angelic soul. The shining example of what a person should always be, I hope I have made you proud.

To my one-and-only, Amy. I'm truly blessed to have you share my life. Your boundless energy and unfailing optimism make all things possible. Your unconditional love is my inspiration. Thank you for being everything you are and what I strive to be.

WWE

WWE would like to thank Lauren Dienes-Middlen, JD Sestito, Franco Malagisi and John Jones for their tireless efforts to make this book possible. Also, special thanks to Peter Maule, Bernadette Hawks, Kevin Caldwell, and Dean Miller for their contributions.

In an industry defined by larger-than-life personalities performing acts both heinous and heroic, it is a nigh-impossible task to condense almost 50 years of history into any number of pages. however, what you hold in your hands is an attempt to do just that: take the history of World Wrestling Entertainment, from 1963 through *WrestleMania XXVIII*, and catalog the people and events into almost 400 pages.

Not every event in each Superstar's career is covered, but what's inside touches on triumphs and tragedies, rivalries and partnerships, and championship reigns. regardless of whether they were met with cheers or jeers, the men and women on the following pages worked hard to entertain you, the fans, night in and night out, on the road and away from home, hundreds of nights each year.

Superstars are listed by the name for which they are most famous (for example, look in the "R" entries for The Rock instead of Rocky Maivia, and "Hacksaw" Jim Duggan is included with the "H" entries). Those Superstars who are more well-known for tag team accomplishments in WWE than individual accolades appear under the name of their tag team (Arn Anderson and Tully Blanchard are both in the Brain Busters entry, for example).

If you're having trouble finding a specific topic, use the index at the end of this book which lists all the Superstars that appear in these pages, alphabetized by last name (or only name in the case of someone like Yokozuna).

For most Superstars, the background color of their entry indicates the decade in which they first appeared (see the following chart). For the Superstars whose careers helped define the eras in which they competed, they have been given colors that allow them to stand out from the crowd.

❶ 1960-1969   ❷ 1970-1979   ❸ 1980-1989

❹ 1990-1999   ❺ 2000-2009   ❻ 2010-PRESENT

\#

2010-

2000-09

1990-99

1980-89

1970-79

1960-69

ABE "KNUCKLEBALL" SCHWARTZ

HT: 6'0"   **WT:** 240 lbs.   **FROM:** Brooklyn, New York

During the Major League Baseball strike of 1994, WWE did their part in bringing the national pastime to fans when they introduced Abe "Knuckleball" Schwartz (sometimes referred to as MVP). With a baseball painted on his face and sporting a double-zero numbered uniform, he gave fans a piece of that baseball action they were missing.

Accompanied to the ring by a slightly demonic version of "Take Me Out to the Ballgame," Schwartz had big-league aspirations. Unfortunately, however, he struck out when it came to WWE. The closest he came to any fame was competing in a Battle Royal where the two Superstars left standing would face off for the Intercontinental Championship. Schwartz made it halfway through before being eliminated by Owen Hart.

ABRAHAM WASHINGTON

HT: 6'2"   **WT:** 220 lbs.

He may not have matched the thirty-year run of Johnny Carson, but over the course of his seven months on the air, Abraham Washington certainly managed to create a buzz over his late-night talk show. Unfortunately for Washington, however, the buzz wasn't always positive.

As host of *The Abraham Washington Show* on ECW, Washington's self-centered approach to creating compelling conversations continually rubbed audiences the wrong way. As a result of his cocky demeanor, much of what the arrogant host had to say was drowned out by boos, despite Washington pleading for applause on the show's big screen.

With WWE Hall of Famer Tony Atlas as his trusty sidekick, Washington welcomed many of ECW's biggest names to his show, including Tommy Dreamer, Sheamus, and Christian. Nearly every time, Washington's words successfully irritated his guest; but much to the disdain of the Superstars and fans, the big mouth never backed it up in the ring. After ECW went off the air in February 2010, Washington declared himself a free agent. He has yet to be signed.

3-MINUTE WARNING

MEMBERS: Rosey, Jamal
COMBINED WT: 939 lbs.

Even the most casual WWE fan knows that Eric Bischoff abused his authority while serving as *Raw* general manager. To make matters worse, his decisions were oftentimes made just so he could let out a hearty laugh. One of the best (or worst) examples of this is 3-Minute Warning.

In July 2002, Rosey & Jamal made their debut when they jumped the crowd barrier to decimate D'Lo Brown & Shawn Stasiak. The attack opened many eyes and also cured Bischoff's boredom from watching Brown & Stasiak compete. In the months that followed, Bischoff continued to entertain himself by giving Superstars a warning of three minutes before Rosey & Jamal would put a painful end to segments the GM deemed dull.

The most memorable moment of 3-Minute Warning's brief WWE career saw them invade *SmackDown* to crash Billy & Chuck's highly publicized commitment ceremony. Shortly after the invasion, Rosey & Jamal competed in a high-profile Tables Elimination Match at *Survivor Series*. With Rico as their partner, they fell victim to Jeff Hardy, Bubba Ray, and Spike Dudley. The duo never bounced back from the loss, and went their separate ways shortly after.

ADAM BOMB

HT: 6'6"   **WT:** 290 lbs.
FROM: Three Mile Island
SIGNATURE MOVE: The Meltdown

In May 1993, World Wrestling Entertainment faced a nuclear threat. Introduced to fans by Johnny Polo, Adam Bomb was a powerhouse whose intent was to win the coveted WWE Championship. Four months into his career, he relieved Johnny Polo of his managerial duties and replaced him with the ever-slippery Harvey Wippleman.

His relationship with Wippleman soured, however, and Adam Bomb began receiving the support of fans. By August 1995, this apocalyptic threat was diffused as Adam Bomb left WWE. Though he only spent a few years with the organization, Adam Bomb will always be remembered as an unrelenting force in the ring.

"ADORABLE" ADRIAN ADONIS

HT: 5'11"   **WT:** 298 lbs.   **FROM:** New York City
SIGNATURE MOVE: Sleeper Hold

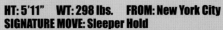

TITLE HISTORY	
WORLD TAG TEAM CHAMPION	*Partnered with Dick Murdoch to defeat Tony Atlas & Rocky Johnson on April 17, 1984*

With a nickname of "Adorable," some might expect Adrian Adonis to be a bit soft in the ring, but those people would be dead wrong. Despite displaying an overtly feminine persona later in his career, Adonis was one of the toughest men of his time.

Adonis arrived in WWE in the early 1980s, alongside his tag team partner Jesse Ventura. When injuries prevented Ventura from competing regularly, Adonis joined forces with fellow tough man Dick Murdoch. Together, Adonis & Murdoch captured the World Tag Team Championship in April 1984. They held the titles for nine months before losing to the U.S. Express (Mike Rotundo & Barry Windham).

Following the loss, Adonis' rugged biker persona gave way to a more flamboyant one. Despite the effeminate makeover, Adonis remained a force in the ring. He proved this right away with a convincing victory over Uncle Elmer at *WrestleMania 2*.

In addition to excelling in the ring, the "Adorable One" also hosted his own interview segment dubbed *The Flower Shop*. Adonis' copycat tactics infuriated Roddy Piper, causing the two Superstars to engage in a memorable rivalry. Their heated rivalry culminated in a Hair vs. Hair Match at *WrestleMania III*, which saw Piper get the win and Adonis get a haircut.

AGUILA

HT: 5'10" **WT:** 184 lbs. **FROM:** Guadalajara, Mexico
SIGNATURE MOVE: Moonsault

Some men spend countless years honing their skills with the hope of one day earning a WWE contract. Not Aguila. In November 1997, the masked man from Mexico made his WWE debut at just 19 years of age. Competing in the first round of the Light Heavyweight Championship tournament, the youngster defeated Super Loco after hitting him with a gravity-defying moonsault.

Aguila's early success earned him a coveted spot on the *WrestleMania XIV* card, where he challenged Taka Michinoku for the Light Heavyweight Title. Despite coming up short in his quest to claim the gold that night, Aguila and his in-ring aerial expertise successfully won over the imaginations of the capacity crowd in Boston and fans watching worldwide on pay-per-view.

Unfortunately for Aguila, he failed to meet the fans' expectations of him following his *WrestleMania* thriller with Michinoku. He competed in a few more *Raw* matches before finally retiring his mask for good in the spring of 1998.

AHMED JOHNSON

HT: 6'2" **WT:** 305 lbs. **FROM:** Pearl River, Michigan
SIGNATURE MOVE: Pearl River Plunge

In 1995 World Wrestling Entertainment was greeted by a powerhouse from the streets of Pearl River. Ahmed Johnson was all business in the ring and during his *Monday Night Raw* debut he showed he

TITLE HISTORY	
INTERCONTINENTAL CHAMPION	Defeated Goldust on June 23, 1996

was for real when he bodyslammed Yokozuna. Ahmed had one of the most impressive starts in WWE history and continued handing opponents quick lessons, including a win over Buddy Landell at *In Your House: Season's Beatings* in under 45 seconds!

At the 1996 *King of the Ring* he made history when he defeated Goldust to become the first African-American Intercontinental Champion. He also formed an alliance with the "Heartbreak Kid" Shawn Michaels and battled Camp Cornette. Unfortunately, a serious kidney injury at the hands of Ron "Faarooq" Simmons forced him to vacate the title. When Ahmed returned to action, he had an on-and-off relationshp with the Nation of Domination.

His WWE career ended in 1998 as a brother in arms to the Legion of Doom and Ken Shamrock. This mountainous Superstar went wherever he pleased and refused to be intimidated by anyone. Ahmed Johnson didn't vanish from the spotlight entirely as in 2001, he appeared in the movie *Too Legit: The MC Hammer Story*.

AIR BOOM

MEMBERS: Kofi Kingston, Evan Bourne
COMBINED WT: 401 lbs.

TITLE HISTORY	
WWE TAG TEAM CHAMPIONS	Defeated David Otunga & Michael McGillicutty on August 22, 2011

Separately, Kofi Kingston and Evan Bourne register a 10 on the excitement scale. Together, however, they are off the charts.

The high-flying duo began teaming together regularly in August 2011. Within weeks of their union, Kingston and Bourne defeated David Otunga & Michael McGillicutty for the WWE Tag Team Championship. With the gold around their waists, Kingston and Bourne breathed a new dynamic energy into the tag division.

Shortly after their championship victory, Kingston and Bourne asked their Twitter followers to submit potential names for their new tag team. Such monikers as Legion of Boom and Fly Guys were suggested. But in the end, the champs chose to go with Air Boom.

Air Boom proudly held the tag titles for five long months, turning back such teams as The Miz & R-Truth and Jack Swagger & Dolph Ziggler. Their reign finally came to an end in January 2012, when they were dethroned by Primo & Epico at a live event in Oakland, California.

AJ

HT: 5'2"
FROM: Union City, New Jersey
SIGNATURE MOVE: The Octopus

A.J. is living proof that perseverance truly does pay off. Growing up in Union City, New Jersey, the future WWE Diva experienced extreme poverty, including homelessness. But she never let her less-than-desirable circumstances hold her down. Instead, she relentlessly battled to break free from the meager surroundings and achieve her ultimate dream of becoming a WWE Diva.

The WWE Universe first laid eyes on A.J. during season three of *WWE NXT*. The spunky Diva hopeful made an immediate impact, teaming with her Pro, Primo, to defeat Aksana and Goldust in tag-team action on the show's premiere. Over the course of the next several weeks, fans couldn't help but fall in love with the perky girl next door. The self-proclaimed "Geek Goddess" made it all the way to the twelfth week before finally being eliminated from competition.

Following her stay on *NXT*, A.J. jumped to *SmackDown* in May 2011. Her sparky personality instantly attracted many members of the Friday night brand, including Daniel Bryan.

A

2010-

2000-09

1990-99

1980-89

1970-79

1960-69

AKSANA

HT: 5'5"
FROM: Alytus, Lithuania

As an accomplished bodybuilder and fitness enthusiast, Aksana possesses many of the attributes necessary to become a successful WWE Diva. But instead of accentuating these positives, which include a victory at the prestigious 2009 Arnold Classic Figure International, Aksana chose to use her sensuality as her ultimate asset.

Behind the power of her voluptuous frame and suggestive Lithuanian accent, Aksana believes she can make any man do anything she wants. The first victim of her aura was her *NXT* Pro, Goldust. While facing deportation from the United States in late 2010, Aksana subliminally convinced Goldust to marry her, thus allowing her to stay in the country. Once the marriage became official, however, the sultry Diva slapped her new husband across the face, revealing that she never had romantic feelings for him.

Following her stay on *NXT*, Aksana debuted on *SmackDown* in August 2011. The new surroundings did little to change the Diva's manipulative mannerisms. Upon arrival, her target of choice was *SmackDown*'s chief decision-maker, General Manager Theodore Long.

AL PEREZ

HT: 6'1" **WT:** 245 lbs. **FROM:** Tampa, Florida
SIGNATURE MOVE: German Suplex

Al Perez began wrestling as an amateur in high school and became one of the top athletes in the state of Florida. Trained by the famous Boris Malenko, he made his pro debut in 1982 and made a name for himself in the mid 1980s as "The Latin Heartthrob" in World Class Championship Wrestling. In 1989, he arrived in WWE. With his amateur background and ring savvy, it looked like Perez was going to be a major championship contender.

He entered the ring against a variety of competitors, including the Brooklyn Brawler, Koko B. Ware, the Red Rooster, and Bret "Hit Man" Hart. In the beginning of 1990, Al left WWE and appeared in WCW. He spent the rest of the decade competing in independent promotions throughout the United States before retiring in 2002.

AL SNOW

HT: 6'1" **WT:** 235 lbs. **FROM:** Lima, Ohio
SIGNATURE MOVE: Snowplow

TITLE HISTORY	
EUROPEAN CHAMPION	*Defeated Perry Saturn on August 31, 2000*
HARDCORE CHAMPION	*6 Times*
WORLD TAG TEAM CHAMPION	*Partnered with Mankind to defeat Crash & Hardcore Holly on November 4, 1999*

Al Snow's quirky persona made him stand out and brought him success. Despite owning impressive in-ring skills, the delusional Superstar's actions oftentimes made fans scratch their heads, especially when he would talk to his Head (his mannequin head, that is).

While competing in ECW, Snow developed a close relationship with a mannequin head named Head. The popularity of Snow and Head eventually caught the attention of WWE. With Head in tow, Snow moved to WWE in 1998 where he became an immediate fixture in the promotion's budding hardcore division.

Using the experience he gained while competing in ECW, Snow went on to capture WWE's Hardcore Championship six times. In November 1999, Snow teamed with the equally deranged Mankind to capture the World Tag Team Championship. While the reign only lasted four days, it remains one of the brightest moments of Snow's career.

The unpredictable Snow is also known for his time spent on the show *Tough Enough*. Working as one of the show's trainers, Snow was responsible for molding many WWE hopefuls into legitimate Superstars. His impressive list of students includes John Morrison, the Miz and Maven.

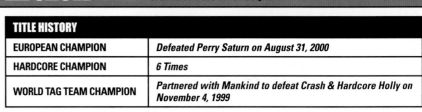

AL WILSON

When Al Wilson went to visit his daughter, former WWE Diva Torrie, at an October 2002 *SmackDown* show, little did he know he'd end up meeting his future bride, as well as his eventual demise.

While backstage, the proud father ran into a bikini-clad Dawn Marie, and despite the enormous age gap separating the two, the meeting proved to be love at first sight for Al. Not long after, the unconventional couple began showing their affection for each other in a very public manner. The uninhibited make-out sessions infuriated Torrie, who stopped at nothing to break up the lovebirds. But there was no stopping Al, who claimed Dawn Marie made him feel "strong, sexy and virile."

After a brief romance, Al and Dawn Marie married in January 2003. Dressed in nothing but their underwear, the newlyweds bolted from the altar and straight to their honeymoon, where they hoped to enjoy the physical pleasures of marriage. Unfortunately for Al, however, Dawn Marie's desire to continually consummate their union eventually stopped his weakened heart.

ALBERT

HT: 6'7"   WT: 331 lbs.   FROM: Boston, Massachusetts
SIGNATURE MOVE: The Baldo Bomb

This former Superstar and NFL player is perhaps best remembered for his body hair and piercings. Albert debuted in WWE in 1999 as Prince Albert. He joined a short-lived trio that went by the name "the Pierced Pals."

TITLE HISTORY

INTERCONTINENTAL CHAMPION	Defeated Kane on June 28, 2001

After the group disbanded, Albert formed a team with Test. Managed by the seductive Trish Stratus, these two big men were known as T & A.

In 2001, Albert formed an alliance with X-Pac and Justin Credible, known as X-Factor. When the group separated, Albert teamed with Scotty 2 Hotty. Dubbed the "Hip-Hop Hippo," the team lasted until April 2002. In late 2002, Albert formed the most powerful alliance of his career. Now billed as A-Train, he was paired with Big Show and Paul Heyman. In singles competition, A-Train faced Undertaker at *SummerSlam 2003,* and continued to appear on *SmackDown* until he was traded to *Monday Night Raw* during the March 2004 Draft Lottery. That November, this pierced powerhouse parted ways with WWE.

ALBERTO DEL RIO

HT: 6'5"   WT: 239 lbs.   FROM: San Luis Potosi, Mexico
SIGNATURE MOVE: Cross Armbreaker

TITLE HISTORY

WWE CHAMPION (2 TIMES)	Defeated CM Punk on August 14, 2011 Defeated CM Punk and John Cena in a Hell In A Cell Triple Threat Match on October 2, 2011

Alberto Del Rio lives by the philosophy "if you've got it, flaunt it." With blood ties to Spanish royals, the Mexican aristocrat has what appears to be an endless supply of funds, as evidenced by his jaw-dropping fleet of luxury vehicles and perfectly-tailored custom suits. Del Rio even employs his own ring announcer, Ricardo Rodriguez.

From the moment Del Rio debuted in the Summer of 2010, the WWE Universe has loathed the sight of him and his elitist attitude. Despite the disdain, however, fans have no choice but to respect his athleticism. After defeating Rey Mysterio in his debut match, the cocky newcomer went on to banish Matt Hardy from the company and shelve Christian, thanks to his debilitating cross armbreaker.

Claiming it was his destiny to become a World Champion, Del Rio outlasted 39 other Superstars to win the 2011 *Royal Rumble* and an opportunity at the World Heavyweight Championship.

Unfortunately for Del Rio, he was unable to unseat champion Edge at *WrestleMania* but that didn't deter Del Rio. Just a few months later, he outdueled seven others to capture the *Raw* Money in the Bank briefcase and a guaranteed WWE Championship Match. Del Rio cashed in his briefcase against CM Punk at *SummerSlam,* following the then-champ's exhausting encounter with John Cena. A few seconds later, Del Rio pinned Punk's shoulders to the mat for the three count, thus claiming his first WWE Championship and finally fulfilling his destiny.

ALDO MONTOYA

HT: 6'1"   WT: 225 lbs.
FROM: Portugal

Clad in his country's colors of green, red and yellow, Aldo Montoya arrived on the WWE scene to much fanfare in late 1994. Dubbed the "Portuguese Man O' War," the proud Superstar from Portugal used his quickness to turn back foes.

A few months after Montoya's debut, Superstars were able to scout his speed and incorporate counters into their game plans. As a result, it wasn't long before he found himself getting tossed around the ring by larger, more skilled opponents like Vader, Goldust and Hunter Hearst-Helmsley. As the losses began to mount, people began to tease Montoya, claiming the mask he wore over his face resembled an athletic supporter. Montoya was never able to attain the level of success many expected from him upon his WWE arrival. By 1997, Montoya began to compete in fewer matches before disappearing from WWE completely.

ALEX RILEY

HT: 6'2"   WT: 251 lbs.
FROM: Washington, D.C.
SIGNATURE MOVE: Implant DDT

Alex Riley has climbed the WWE ladder quicker than most, hitting nearly every rung along the way. In June 2010, he started out as an aspiring Superstar on season two of *NXT*. Fast forward to today and he's one of WWE's top names. Along the way, the charismatic Riley made stops as an apprentice and Vice President of Corporate Communications for The Miz.

As The Miz's right-hand man, Riley's core job responsibility was to ensure his employer retained the WWE Championship, most notably against John Cena at *WrestleMania XXVII*. But when Cena finally secured the gold from Miz at *Extreme Rules*, their working relationship began to sour. Suddenly, Riley became the scapegoat for Miz's title loss.

Rather than sitting back and accepting Miz's verbal assault, Riley struck back, much to the delight of the WWE Universe. Since breaking away from The Miz, Riley has become the successful Superstar many believed he could be. With a newfound confidence, he's picked up several huge victories, including one over The Miz at *Capitol Punishment* in June 2011.

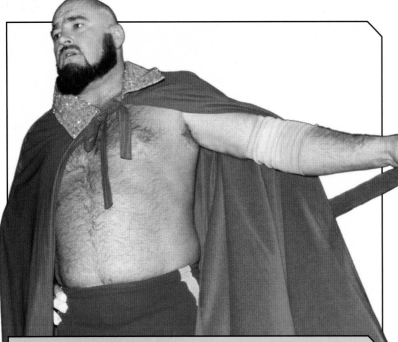

ALEXIS SMIRNOFF

HT: 6'3"   WT: 255 lbs.   FROM: Russia   SIGNATURE MOVE: Heart Punch

Entering WWE in the early 1980s, Alexis Smirnoff used his "Mad Russian" persona to strike fear into audiences nationwide, while his paralyzing Heart Punch instilled terror through WWE locker rooms.

Though his WWE legacy will never equal that of fellow Russians Ivan Koloff and Nikolai Volkoff, Smirnoff will be remembered for setting lofty goals for himself. Upon entering the promotion, he immediately sought out the top stars, which resulted in memorable rivalries with WWE Hall of Famer Rocky Johnson and former World Tag Team Champion Ivan Putski.

ALICIA FOX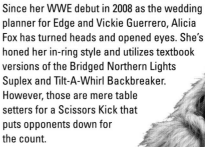

HT: 5'9"   FROM: Ponte Vedra Beach, Florida   SIGNATURE MOVE: Scissors Kick

TITLE HISTORY	
DIVAS CHAMPION	*Won a Fatal 4-Way match on June 20, 2010*

Since her WWE debut in 2008 as the wedding planner for Edge and Vickie Guerrero, Alicia Fox has turned heads and opened eyes. She's honed her in-ring style and utilizes textbook versions of the Bridged Northern Lights Suplex and Tilt-A-Whirl Backbreaker. However, those are mere table setters for a Scissors Kick that puts opponents down for the count.

While she's been aligned with different Divas and Superstars from Michelle McCool to Zack Ryder, A-Fox has displayed time after time she's much more than a walking pin-up. This was evident in the summer of 2010, when she bested three of the top Divas of *Raw*—Eve, Maryse and Gail Kim—to claim her first Divas Championship. Though she lost the championship two months later, she has her sights set on regaining the butterfly-studded championship belt.

THE ALLIANCE

This menagerie came together in July 2001 as members of Shane McMahon's newly acquired World Championship Wrestling came together with the hope of taking over World Wrestling Entertainment. WCW talent like Lance Storm, Hugh Morrus, and Diamond Dallas Page were led by Shane and interrupted WWE broadcasts and events.

On the July 9, 2001 episode of *Monday Night Raw,* WWE was under another attack. This time WWE's flagship program saw the television return of ECW stars Rob Van Dam and Tommy Dreamer as they jumped the guardrail and attacked Kane and Chris Jericho. During the melee, Lance Storm and Mike Awesome suddenly sided with their former hardcore brethren. WWE Superstars rushed the ring and opposed the quartet of Van Dam, Dreamer, Storm, and Awesome. As the stand-off continued, the Superstars suddenly turned around and the odds become 10-on-2. Paul Heyman then left the *Raw* broadcast position and announced to the world the "Invasion" just became extreme.

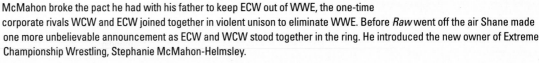

After Shane McMahon broke the pact he had with his father to keep ECW out of WWE, the one-time corporate rivals WCW and ECW joined together in violent unison to eliminate WWE. Before *Raw* went off the air Shane made one more unbelievable announcement as ECW and WCW stood together in the ring. He introduced the new owner of Extreme Championship Wrestling, Stephanie McMahon-Helmsley.

For the next few months, other individuals made their presence felt for both sides and some defected from one entity to go to the other. Superstars also fought for both WWE and WCW championships in numerous battles. Perhaps the most shocking moment in the conflict came at the *Invasion* pay-per-view when Stone Cold Steve Austin turned his back on WWE and became the Alliance leader. The callous trio of Shane, Stephanie, and Paul Heyman devised plans for Austin and his followers to carry out. In November 2001, this war was finally settled at *Survivor Series* as Team WWE defeated Team Alliance in a winner take-all 10-man tag team elimination. Though WWE survived this hostile corporate takeover attempt and continued to prosper, some still bear the scars today from the battles of yesterday.

ALLIED POWERS

MEMBERS: British Bulldog, Lex Luger
COMBINED WT: 525 lbs.

Fate brought these two pillars of strength together during a January 1995 episode of *Monday Night Raw*. History repeated itself as England's British Bulldog and America's Lex Luger combined forces and battled Ted DiBiase's Million Dollar Corporation. The duo became World Tag Team title contenders after an impressive win at *WrestleMania XI* over Jacob & Eli Blu.

Despite heated bouts with then-World Tag Team Champions Owen Hart & Yokozuna, British Bulldog & Lex Luger were unable to win the titles. That August saw a sad turn of events take place during *Monday Night Raw*. When Luger couldn't compete due to a sudden family emergency, Bulldog recruited Diesel to be his partner. After the make-shift duo lost in a valiant effort, British Bulldog turned on Diesel. Unaware of his partner's actions, Luger returned days before *SummerSlam* expecting to reconnect with his partner. To the disappointment of WWE fans all over the world, the Allied Powers were no more. The British Bulldog joined the ranks of Camp Cornette.

ALOISIA

HT: 6'9"

"Who's gonna stop me?"

Those were the words arrogantly uttered by Aloisia in her introduction video for season three of *WWE NXT*. Little did she know that just a few days later, her very own Pro would be the one to stop her before she even got started.

At an astounding 6'9", Aloisia was considered by many as the favorite heading into *WWE NXT*, especially with the cunning Vickie Guerrero serving as her Pro. But in the days leading up to the show's season premiere, the two ladies had a heated behind-the-scenes argument that led to Guerrero dismissing the monstrous Diva wannabe.

Guerrero later revealed Kaitlyn as her new *NXT* Rookie. With *SmackDown*'s official Office Consultant leading the way, the replacement Rookie went on to win *NXT* season three, leaving many to wonder how far Aloisia could have gone if she was never fired by Guerrero. Unfortunately for Aloisia, it's a question to which we'll never have the answer.

ALUNDRA BLAYZE

HT: 5'10"   **FROM:** Tampa, Florida
SIGNATURE MOVE: Bridging German Suplex

TITLE HISTORY	
WOMEN'S CHAMPION (3 TIMES)	*Won a tournament to crown a champion on December 13, 1993* *Defeated Bull Nakano on April 3, 1995* *Defeated Bertha Faye on October 23, 1995*

Alundra Blayze's dangerous combination of athleticism and sex appeal made her the ultimate female force in the ring. When WWE reintroduced its Women's Championship in December 1993, Blayze appeared from out of nowhere to win a tournament to crown the new titleholder. The buxom blonde went on to dominate the division for nearly one year before being toppled by Bull Nakano in November 1994.

Early the next year, Blayze gained her revenge by upending Nakano on *Monday Night Raw* to regain the title. Unfortunately, however, she was derailed by yet another colossal competitor when Bertha Faye defeated her at *SummerSlam 1995*. The loss to Faye proved to be just a blip on the screen, as Blayze quickly recaptured the gold in less than two months.

Blayze held the title until she defected to WCW in December 1995.

AMY WEBER

FROM: Mapleton, Illinois

When Amy Weber was eliminated from the 2004 *Raw* Diva Search, she assumed her dream of one day being in WWE had come to a crashing halt. In reality, though, the elimination was only a temporary derailment for the farm girl from Illinois.

In November 2004—only a few short months after the *Raw* Diva Search—Amy was hired to be the image consultant for *SmackDown*'s John "Bradshaw" Layfield. Realizing that image is everything, the then-WWE Champion relied on Amy to make him look good at all times.

Amy excelled at her job for the first few months. But then in February 2005, she accidentally shot JBL in the face with a tranquilizer gun while he was preparing for a Barbed Wire Steel Cage Match against Big Show. The idiotic act was too much for the image consultant to overcome. The following week, JBL relieved Amy of her duties and she was never heard from again.

ANDRE THE GIANT

HT: 7'4"   **WT:** 540 lbs.   **FROM:** Grenoble, France   **SIGNATURE MOVE:** Sitdown Splash

As Andre Rousimoff played soccer on the streets of Grenoble, France, he never thought one day he'd grow up to be the largest

TITLE HISTORY

WORLD TAG TEAM CHAMPION	*Partnered with Haku to defeat Demolition on December 13, 1989*
WWE CHAMPION	*Defeated Hulk Hogan on February 5, 1988*

professional athlete in the world. In the mid-1960s, a promoter introduced him to then-wrestler and future WWE commentator Lord Alfred Hayes. Audiences were beside themselves at Andre's amazing size, remarkable agility and immeasurable strength. He could even throw dropkicks and leap from the top rope. Since most of his matches lasted a few minutes, he was often showcased in handicap matches against two, three, or four opponents. Soon his fame reached the lights of Paris and he went by the name "Monster" Eiffel Tower. When Andre met Edouard Carpentier after an event, the French-Canadian mega-star saw Andre's natural skill and agreed to train him. Fresh from Carpentier's teachings Andre traveled to Japan in 1969 and frightened everyone as "Monster" Rousimoff.

While there, doctors diagnosed him with Acromegaly, commonly known as "Giantism," an endocrynological disease that causes one to grow at an accelerated rate beyond the age of physical maturity. Andre never told anyone of the diagnosis and remained the fun-loving figure both in and out of the ring.

Worldwide Fame

After his successful Asian tour, Andre connected with his mentor and appeared in French-speaking areas. Though wrestling was broken down into regional territories at the time, Andre quickly became the world's most popular attraction. Now at 7'4" and more than 500 lbs. of awesome power, Andre was referred to as "The Eighth Wonder of the World," a moniker that stayed with him his entire career.

In 1971, Andre met with Vince McMahon, Sr. and was contracted to work in the then-World Wide Wrestling Federation. On March 26, 1973, he debuted in Madison Square Garden and for the first time was called Andre The Giant. Through the 1970's Andre broke into the mainstream. In 1974, he turned down a lucrative contract offer from the National Football League's Washington Redskins to remain in the squared circle. Soon Hollywood knocked on his door and he appeared on television programs including *The Tonight Show, The Merv Griffin Show,* and in 1975 he made his acting debut as Bigfoot on *The Six Million Dollar Man.*

Boxer versus Wrestler

At the 1976 *Showdown At Shea,* he fought the 6'5" "Bayonne Bleeder" Chuck Wepner in a "Boxer vs. Wrestler" contest. Wepner looked like a mere toddler next to Andre and ended up being launched into the third-row seats. In 1980 Andre returned to Shea for another epic showdown against Hulk Hogan, who at the time donned a cape and retained the services of "Classy" Freddie Blassie. In a new decade,

Andre continued to sell out arenas and in 1981 was featured in Sports Illustrated. However, Andre became revered for his interests and accomplishments outside the ring as well. He acted on both the small and silver screens, played and performed music, was a masterful cards player, raised horses at his farm in North Carolina, and amassed one of the largest private cellars in the world as a connoisseur of fine wines.

Andre continued to travel and briefly appeared in the territories of the National Wrestling Alliance, where he held several regional tag team championships. When he returned to World Wrestling Entertainment, the feared Killer Kahn was waiting for him. During their match Kahn jumped from the top rope and broke Andre's ankle, putting him out of action.

Andre recovered and got retribution when he defeated his attacker in a "Mongolian Stretcher Match."

As The Eighth Wonder of the World headed into the mid-80s, a combination of new and familiar faces stood in his path. Andre's rivalry with the Heenan Family began when Big John Studd, Heenan, and Ken Patera schemed to "rape Andre of his dignity," as commentator Vince McMahon famously referred to it, on national television. During a tag match, Patera threw Andre's partner S.D. Jones out of the ring, crashing into the metal guardrail. The two henchmen then ganged up on Andre and beat him unconscious. In an act of humiliation the Heenan Family cut Andre's hair. Fueled by revenge, Andre first took out The Olympic Strongman during a match at Madison Square Garden. His ongoing battle over who was wrestling's true giant culminated at the first WrestleMania. Andre met Big John Studd in a $15,000 Body Slam Challenge. Andre emerged victorious but the victory was somewhat bittersweet when an outraged Bobby "The Brain" Heenan jumped into the ring and took the bag of money from Andre as he threw it to the crowd. Andre's historic undefeated streak continued and he was often referred to as wrestling's "Uncrowned World Champion." At WrestleMania 2, he added another victory to his record-setting number of battle royal wins when he eliminated The Hart Foundation in the 20-man WWE/NFL Battle Royal.

In 1986, Andre again was the focus of a Heenan Family plan when then-President Jack Tunney suspended him for not appearing at matches on WWE cards. As a result of the suspension, Andre was banned from WWE television and live events. However, while he served his suspension under strong protest, a three-man team from Sapporo, Japan called The Machines debuted. Their largest member, Giant Machine, became the target of a witch hunt conceived by Bobby "The Brain" Heenan. After battling with the Heenan Family, the Machines left World Wrestling Entertainment and their identities were never discovered.

Winning A Title by Any Means Necessary

In 1987, Andre returned to Hollywood and co-starred in the hit film The Princess Bride as the gentle giant Fezzik. When he came back to WWE, Andre's appearance and demeanor had changed. He shocked fans worldwide when he appeared on an episode of Piper's Pit with Bobby "The Brain" Heenan at his side. Andre issued a challenge to his longtime friend, Hulk Hogan, to a WWE Championship match at WrestleMania III.

In front of a record-breaking 93,173 fans at the Pontiac Silverdome, the irresistible force met the immovable object. The friendly, warm giant that made fans smile for decades now stood in the ring as a towering, stoic figure dressed in black. In the end, the power of Hulkamania bested Andre the Giant and his fifteen-year undefeated streak was broken. That November, their rivalry carried over to team warfare at the inaugural Survivor Series where Andre was the sole survivor. The momentum from that dominating showing led to a WWE Championship rematch. It was set for February 5, 1988 and was a primetime national television broadcast of The Main Event.

During the bout, Andre suplexed the champion and attempted a pinfall. Referee Dave Hebner made the three-count despite Hulk Hogan raising his left shoulder. As Hogan disputed the outcome, Andre was presented the championship belt with his hand raised. Seconds later, Andre surrendered the title to DiBiase who pronounced himself the new WWE Champion.

The Aftermath

Andre left the ring and taunted a fallen Hulk Hogan when suddenly another referee appeared who looked exactly like Dave Hebner. As the two officials argued, the one who called the match sucker-punched and kicked the man out of the ring who later was identified as the real Dave Hebner. Then-WWE President Jack Tunney ruled that when Andre handed the championship to DiBiase he forfeited the belt. The WWE Championship was considered vacant and a new, undisputed champion would be crowned in a tournament at WrestleMania IV. Andre and Hulk Hogan met in the first match of the second round. With no regard for the rules or themselves, the match ended in a double-countout.

That summer the two Superstars met in the main event of WrestleFest '88 in a Steel Cage match in front of over 25,800 screaming fans. The next major match between them was in the main event of the first-ever SummerSlam. Andre had his partner, "Million Dollar Man" Ted DiBiase, and Hogan had his, then-WWE Champion Randy "Macho Man" Savage.

Redemption in the End

Andre started to team with fellow Heenan Family member Haku and formed the Colossal Connection. On December 13, 1989, Andre and Haku defeated Demolition to capture the WWE World Tag Team Championship. At WrestleMania VI, Ax and Smash regained the titles when a double-team move gone wrong sent Andre into the ropes and Haku was pinned. After the match, a furious Bobby Heenan berated Andre. After venting his frustrations on his now former manager and tag team partner, Andre left the SkyDome to his first WrestleMania ovation in four years. Weeks later he appeared in a sold-out Tokyo Dome for The Wrestling Summit where he teamed with purorseu legend, Giant Baba, against Demolition. Andre continued to appear at WWE events through 1991 as well as in Japan and Mexico. His last in-ring appearance was in 1992 for All-Japan Pro Wrestling. Andre's last television appearance was on Septmeber 2, 1992 at World Championship Wrestling's Clash of Champions XX as he, along with Jim Ross and Gordon Solie, celebrated twenty years of professional wrestling broadcasts on WTBS.

Sadly on January 27, 1993, while back in France for his father's funeral, this amazing human being passed away in his sleep, at the age of forty-six. The disease that was responsible for his size proved to be too much for his body to endure. Shortly after his death, Andre was inducted into the WWE Hall of Fame. The privilege of being the first person acknowledged into sports-entertainment's elite group was fitting for the man who was the industry's first and arguably most recognizable global icon.

2010-
2000-09
1990-99
1980-89
1970-79
1960-69

ANDY LEAVINE

HT: 6'5" **WT:** 270 lbs.
FROM: Brooksville, Florida

Andy Leavine's life changed forever on June 6 2011, when he was declared the champion of *Tough Enough*. As the reality show's winner, the Florida native was awarded a coveted WWE contract. But his career didn't necessarily get off to an astounding start. Just moments after winning, Leavine was slapped by Mr. McMahon, then floored by a Stunner, courtesy of "Stone Cold" Steve Austin.

Prior to claiming his WWE contract, Leavine needed to prove himself to trainers Booker T, Trish Stratus and Bill DeMott. Behind the mystery of his "Silent Rage" persona, Leavine slowly began to impress. Initially, many assumed he lacked the intensity necessary to excel. But it wasn't long before everybody realized Leavine was actually a powder keg waiting to explode. He'd lurk quietly on the sidelines, waiting for the perfect time to unleash the fire that burned inside.

With the win, Leavine joins a short list of Superstars who have earned contracts via *Tough Enough*. Now, it's just a question of whether he can capitalize on his big win.

ANGELO "KING KONG" MOSCA

HT: 6'4" **WT:** 319 lbs. **FROM:** Toronto, Ontario, Canada **SIGNATURE MOVE:** Sleeper

Before his career in the ring, this man played 14 seasons as a defensive tackle in the Canadian Football League and was a five-time Grey Cup winner. A mainstay in the Stampede and Montreal territories, the man who carried the nickname "King Kong" debuted in WWE in 1970. Though he didn't compete full-time until his retirement from football in 1972, Angelo "King Kong" Mosca brutalized opponents in rings all over the globe.

Through the 1970s, Mosca toured the NWA and AWA, winning several singles and tag team titles. "King Kong" returned to WWE in 1981 and battled a new crop of Superstars while contending for both the WWE Championship and Intercontinental Championship. As the mid-1980s approached, Mosca traded in his boots for a microphone and became part of the announce team. In 1985, he dedicated his time to manage the ring career of his son, Angelo Mosca, Jr.

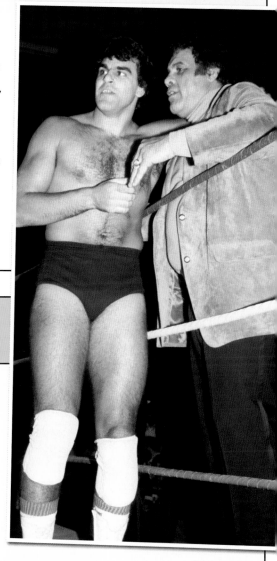

ANGELO MOSCA, JR.

WT: 230 lbs. **FROM:** Boston, Massachusetts
SIGNATURE MOVE: Flying Cross Body

Trained and managed by his legendary father, this second generation Superstar was an incredibly conditioned athlete. He began his career in the early 1980s and first received attention when he defeated "Russian Bear" Ivan Koloff for the Mid-Atlantic Heavyweight Championship.

As his father led the way, Angelo Mosca, Jr. debuted in World Wrestling Entertainment in 1984. With the famous Mosca power and fire, Angelo was also well schooled in mat wrestling and aerial maneuvers. He took on villains and brought fans to their feet until he left the company in April 1985.

ANGELO SALVOLDI   **FROM:** Hoboken, New Jersey

Spending the majority of his career competing at approximately 210 pounds, Angelo Savoldi was a true trailblazer for today's cruiserweights. Savoldi made his professional debut in New York in 1937. Over the next several decades, he competed in main events in Puerto Rico and Boston, but it was in Oklahoma where he attained his greatest notoriety, capturing the National Wrestling Alliance World Junior Heavyweight Championship on three occasions.

Savoldi didn't enter the WWE until the 1970s, which was well after his prime. However, that didn't stop him from being a force within the promotion. Realizing his competitive days were behind him, Savoldi began training many of WWE's younger Superstars. He even became a minority partner in the company, which was owned by Vince J. McMahon at the time.

In 1984, Savoldi and his sons Mario, Joe and Tom formed the Boston-based International Championship Wrestling. The promotion boasted an impressive roster of future WWE Superstars, including Mick Foley, Chris Candido and Tazz.

ANONYMOUS RAW GENERAL MANAGER

Over the course of *Monday Night Raw*'s record-breaking history, some of sports-entertainment's greatest names have steered the ship, including Ric Flair, Eric Bischoff and Stephanie McMahon.

On June 21, 2010, another authority figure was added to the list of *Raw* leaders. However, whether that person possesses the same cache as *Raw*'s prior general managers will never be known, as he/she chose to run the show anonymously.

Ruling from afar, the mysterious GM sent instructions to the show via e-mail, which were then relayed to the audience via Michael Cole. Usually, the announcements were met with a resounding round of boos from the WWE Universe. It was never clear, however, whether the animosity was meant solely for Cole or the Anonymous *Raw* General Manger's rulings.

Throughout the mysterious GM's year-plus reign, he/she made some rather controversial decisions, including hiring all rebel members of *NXT* season one and allowing the most infamous WCW Champion of all time, David Arquette, to compete in a match on *Raw*.

Antonino Rocca (see page 20)

ANTONIO INOKI

HT: 6'2"   WT: 240 lbs.
FROM: Yokohama, Japan

TITLE HISTORY

WORLD MARTIAL ARTS CHAMPION (2 TIMES)	Awarded title on December 18, 1978 Defeated Shota Chochoshivili on May 25, 1989

Antonio Inoki is an iconic figure in Japan's professional wrestling and martial arts scene. What many fans may not realize is that he competed in some of World Wrestling Entertainment's most controversial title matches.

While on tour of Japan in 1979, WWE Champion Bob Backlund lost to Inoki in a shocking upset. The following night, Backlund cashed in his rematch clause and regained the WWE Championship. However, to further complicate matters, outside interference in the rematch caused WWE President Hisashi Shinma to return the title to Inoki. The Japanese legend refused to accept the title in such a manner, resulting in the WWE Championship being briefly vacated. Back in the United States, Backlund won a match to reclaim the vacated WWE Championship. As a result of the controversies surrounding the series of matches, WWE later refused to recognize the title changes.

A few years prior to these Championship matches, the Japanese star gained worldwide exposure when he battled Muhammad Ali in a Boxer vs. Wrestler Match. The restricting rules of the encounter heavily diminished Inoki's offensive arsenal. After fifteen rounds of action (or inaction), the match ended in a draw.

Over the next 22 years, Inoki remained a dominant force in sports- entertainment as the head of New Japan Pro Wrestling. On March 28, 2010 Inoki celebrated the 50th anniversary of his first match and took his place in the WWE Hall of Fame.

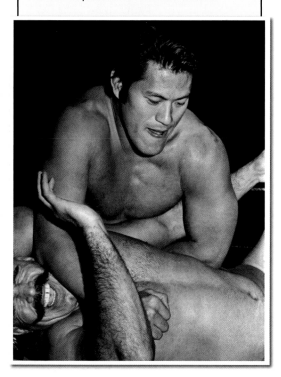

THE APA

MEMBERS: Faarooq & Bradshaw
COMBINED WT: 574 lbs.

TITLE HISTORY

WORLD TAG TEAM CHAMPIONS (3 TIMES)	Defeated Kane & X-Pac on May 31, 1999 Defeated The Hardy Boyz & Michael Hayes on July 25, 1999 Defeated the Dudley Boys on July 9, 2001

These Superstars first came together as members of Hell's Henchmen, but then fell under the spell of Undertaker's Ministry of Darkness. The Acolytes won their first World Tag Team Championship from Kane & X-Pac in May 1999. After they went on their own, they formed the Acolytes Protection Agency, or APA for short.

Their powerful double-team moves, such as the Super Powerbomb, sent foes crashing into the canvas and as their reputation grew so did their business. They were often found in their office puffing on cigars, playing cards and downing beers. If you had the money, they had the time to keep you protected. They held the World Tag Team Championship twice more, and their company motto was simple, "Drink and Fight." Despite being split-up during the 2002 brand extension, supply and demand dictated a reunion in 2003. At *Vengeance,* they hosted a Bar Room Brawl.

Though they continued down separate paths, they have reformed over the years. Most recently, to the delight of all their fans at the *Raw 15th Anniversary,* the APA beat Carlito & Jonathan Coachman at the behest of Hornswoggle. The APA can reform at any time and provide the type of protection you need, for the right price.

ARGENTINA APOLLO

FROM: Buenos Aires, Argentina

TITLE HISTORY

UNITED STATES TAG TEAM CHAMPION	Partnered with Don McClarity to defeat John & Chris Tolos on February 16, 1964

Argentina Apollo's approach to wrestling was unmistakable. Not only did he compete barefoot, but the high-flying Superstar also confused opponents with his dizzying arsenal of moves. This agile Superstar also appeared on the east coast under the name Vittorio Apollo.

Most of his success came in the tag team ranks. He formed a popular union with legend Bruno Sammartino, but it was with Don McClarity that he captured his only WWE title. In February 1964, Apollo & McClarity defeated the famed Tolos Brothers for the United States Tag Team Championship. They successfully defended the titles for four months before finally falling to Dr. Jerry Graham & Luke Graham in Washington, D.C.

Apollo continued to excel in tag team competition after leaving WWE. In April 1970, he teamed with Jose Lothario to claim the National Wrestling Alliance Florida Tag Team Championship. Two years later, he captured the Georgia version of the NWA Tag Team Championship with partner Dick Steinborn.

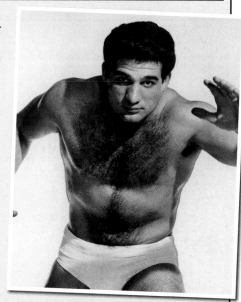

ANTONINO ROCCA

HT: 6'0"   **WT: 224 lbs.**   **FROM: Buenos Aires, Argentina**   **SIGNATURE MOVE: The Argentine Backbreaker**

TITLE HISTORY	
INTERNATIONAL HEAVYWEIGHT CHAMPION	*Defeated Buddy Rogers in July 1959*

Antonino Rocca was one of the most beloved heroes of all-time. His amazing array of maneuvers astounded millions around the world, and his signature repertoire has proven to be timeless. His influence has transcended generations and cultures, which is a testament to the quality of man and the limitless scope of his vision. Rocca is credited with bringing past fans back to professional wrestling and welcoming new ones, as well as being one of the greatest innovators in the history of the art form. He was one of the biggest stars responsible for wrestling's first "Golden Age." His fearless nature in the ring ushered in a new wrestling style that high-flyers of the squared circle will surely study forever.

Born in Trevino, Italy, this trailblazer grew up in Argentina and started his career in professional sports as a soccer player. When a leg injury ended his career, he yearned for another outlet to showcase his charisma, heart, and unparalleled athleticism. Trained by Stanislaus Zbyszko, Rocca received the teachings he needed to succeed in the ultra-competitive world of professional wrestling.

To frustrate opponents and delight fans, Antonino used to slap his opposition in the face with his feet.

He debuted in South America in 1942 and competed as he felt most comfortable: barefoot. Unlike anything ever seen before in the ring, Antonino was in constant motion and beautifully executed exciting maneuvers both in the air and on the mat.

The United States and the NWA

In the late 1940s, Rocca arrived in the United States and started wrestling in Texas, where he was a main event star as the NWA Texas Heavyweight Champion. It was then that promoter Kola Kwariani introduced Antonino to former wrestler and Goldust Trio member Joseph Raymond "Toots" Mondt, the kingpin of wrestling in the Big Apple. Rocca was brought to Manhattan and shared with other promoters in the region, including then-newcomer from Washington, D.C. Vincent J. McMahon.

" ARGENTINA "

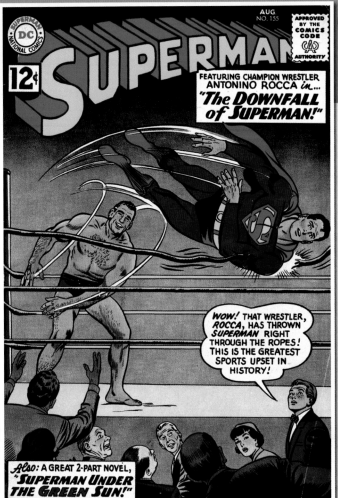

"Superman" #155 © 1962 DC Comics.

The barefoot boy of Argentina was a breath of fresh air. With his elegant balance, showmanship and energetic poise, he put Madison Square Garden back on the map as the ultimate venue for professional wrestling. Hurricanranas, flying dropkicks from any angle, victory rolls and flying body presses dazzled audiences who were accustomed to athletes who never left their feet. His finishing move, the Argentine Backbreaker, brought crowds to a frenzy and dastardly foes to submission as they yelled in incredible pain. From the Empire State Building in New York City to the Grand Olympic Auditorium in Los Angeles and all places in between, "The Amazing Rocca" was king. He was the most dynamic performer the industry had seen to that point and a legitimate phenomenon.

Shows at Madison Square Garden that hosted the NWA Champion saw the Argentine acrobat in the main event. During this period in wrestling history only Gorgeous George was a bigger star. Rocca's ethnicity played a role in his following as well. He was of Italian heritage and hailed from Latin America, which made him a huge attraction for two of the New York area's largest immigrant populations. His fans were so devoted to him, that when Dick The Bruiser split him open during their match in Madison Square Garden, a violent riot ensued. Soon after, an image from the melee taken by a brave photographer was featured on the cover of LIFE Magazine.

Greater Success and Fame

As time went on and Rocca's popularity grew, McMahon convinced him to join his outfit full-time. In 1956 Antonino created a team with Puerto Rican Superstar Miguel Perez, and on March 30, 1957 the duo became the first holders of the United States Tag Team Championship when they defeated Don and Jackie Fargo. During this era, the Argentine Superstar feuded with the likes of Hans Schmidt, The Kangaroos, Eduard Carpentier, Johnny Valentine, Don Leo Jonathan, and Lou Thez. He also took on Gene Kiniski, Skull Murphy, Pampero Firpo, Dr. Jerry Graham, and future WWE Hall of Famers Eddie Graham, Killer Kowalski, Verne Gagne and "Classy" Freddie Blassie. In July 1959, Argentina bested future WWE Hall of Famer "Nature Boy" Buddy Rogers in the tournament finals for the International Heavyweight Championship, which he turned into the longest reign of any International Heavyweight Champion.

Rocca's fame carried him into the early 1960s as his numbers of fans continued to grow. After he graced countless magazine covers, in August 1962, DC Comics featured him on the cover of the Superman #155 comic book throwing The Man of Steel out of the ring. On television, Rocca even grappled with the "King of Late Night" Johnny Carson on The Tonight Show. A Latin music LP by famous artist Billy Mure was released on MGM Records titled, In This Corner, the Musical World of Argentina Rocca and showed the Superstar performing a dropkick on the album cover.

Changing of the Guard

By the time the World Wide Wrestling Federation was independent from the National Wrestling Alliance, Rocca relinquished his title as the company's top Superstar to Bruno Sammartino. In one of his last bouts with the company, he once again stood across the ring from "Nature Boy" Buddy Rogers in a tournament finals. This time, it was in Rio de Janeiro, Brazil for the newly created World Wide Wrestling Federation Championship.

On that evening it was Rogers' turn to lift a gold belt into the air in victory. For the remainder of the decade Argentina wrestled and officiated for the Japanese Pro Wrestling Association. In the early 1970s, he worked for New Japan Pro Wrestling and officiated the classic bout between Antonio Inoki and Karl Gotch. Rocca returned to North America in 1976, and in November of that year he made his silver screen debut in Alice, Sweet Alice starring Brooke Shields.

Over a decade since his last appearance, Antonino Rocca returned to the World Wide Wrestling Federation as an announcer. Each week he called the action with Vince K. McMahon, the legendary promoter's son. On February 25, 1977, he donned the referee's shirt and was the man in the middle of a boxing match that pitted future WWE Hall of Famers Gorilla Monsoon and Andre the Giant at Madison Square Garden. Tragically, on March 15, 1977, this uniquely gifted individual suddenly passed away at Roosevelt Hospital in New York City after complications following an infection.

The greatest honor Antonino Rocca would receive came in 1995, when then-WWE Champion, Diesel posthumously inducted the father of aerial assault into the WWE Hall of Fame, permanently marking his place amongst sports-entertainment's elite figures.

2010-
2000-09
1990-99
1980-89
1970-79
1960-69

ARIEL

With her jet-black hair, blood-red eye shadow and fanged teeth, Ariel possessed a vampire-like quality that scared many. However, her fishnet stockings, knee-high boots, and uncanny ability to hang upside down also made her more than a little sexy.

As Kevin Thorn's bloodthirsty valet in ECW, Ariel could always be found by the side of her man, who she oftentimes kissed mid-match. She also had a penchant for using her signature tarot cards to predict the future. Unfortunately, however, her future did not hold great fortunes. Ariel left WWE in May 2007, less than one year after her debut.

ARMANDO ESTRADA

HT: 6'2" **WT:** 230 lbs.
FROM: Havana, Cuba

Originally a successful Cuban businessman, Armando Estrada came to WWE in April 2006 as the manager of the savage Umaga. Under Estrada's shrewd leadership, the "Samoan Bulldozer" became known as one of the fiercest competitors in all of WWE.

After leading Umaga to the Intercontinental Championship and the famous Battle of the Billionaires Match at *WrestleMania 23*, Estrada left his protégé's side in May 2007. After a brief hiatus, he resurfaced in ECW as the brand's General Manager. As GM, the powerful dictator made life hell for many ECW stars, most notably Colin Delaney.

In June 2008, Estrada was relieved of his GM duties by Theodore Long. Unemployed, the Cuban entrepreneur embarked on a career in the ring. Ironically, he earned his ECW contract after he defeated Tommy Dreamer, with help from rival, Delaney. That November, Armando and WWE parted ways. He returned for one night in May 2011 to manage Tyson Kidd. Though not seen on WWE programming since, you never know when the Cuban industrialist will arrive looking for new business opportunities.

ARMAGEDDON

December 12, 1999
Fort Lauderdale, FL - National Car Rental Center

Main Event: Triple H defeated Mr. McMahon in a No Holds Barred Match

December 10, 2000
Birmingham, AL - Birmingham-Jefferson Civic Center

Main Event: WWE Champion Kurt Angle defeated the Rock, Stone Cold Steve Austin, Rikishi, Triple H, and Undertaker in a 6-Man Armageddon Hell In A Cell Match

December 15, 2002
Fort Lauderdale, FL - Office Depot Center

Main Event: Triple H defeated World Heavyweight Champion Shawn Michaels in Three Stages of Hell (Street Fight, Steel Cage Match, Ladder Match)

December 14, 2003
Orlando, FL - TD Waterhouse Centre

Main Event: Triple H defeated World Heavyweight Champion

December 12, 2004
Atlanta, GA - Gwinnett Center

Main Event: WWE Champion JBL defeated Eddie Guerrero, Booker T, and Undertaker in a Fatal 4-Way Match

December 18, 2005
Providence, RI - Dunkin' Donuts Center

Main Event: Undertaker defeated Randy Orton in a Hell In A Cell Match

December 17, 2006
Richmond, VA - Richmond Coliseum

Main Event: World Heavyweight Champion Batista & WWE Champion John Cena defeated King Booker & Finlay

December 16, 2007
Pittsburgh, PA - Mellon Arena

Main Event: World Heavyweight Champion Batista defeated Edge, and Undertaker in a Triple Threat Match

December 14, 2008
Buffalo, NY - HSBC Arena

Main Event: Jeff Hardy defeated WWE Champion Edge and Triple H in a Triple Threat Match

ARNOLD SKAALAND

HT: 6'0"
WT: 240 lbs.
FROM: White Plains, New York

TITLE HISTORY

UNITED STATES TAG TEAM CHAMPION	*Replaced Antonio Pugliese as Spiros Arion's partner in July 1967*

There was nothing Arnold Skaaland couldn't do. He was an accomplished wrestler, legendary manager, brilliant promoter and cherished friend to countless names within the wrestling industry. This rare combination of greatness lead Skaaland to one of the finest careers in sports-entertainment history.

After representing the U.S. Marines in World War II, Skaaland kept in shape by competing as an amateur boxer. He proved to be a force within the ropes, but never believed he could make a living in the sport. Instead, he focused his efforts on wrestling, an up-and-coming profession that was gaining popularity thanks to television.

Skaaland made his professional debut in 1946, competing mainly in the Northeast. His speed, toughness and overall intelligence quickly earned him the nickname "The Golden Boy." By the early 1960s, he had earned several opportunities at what was then considered the industry's leading title, the National Wrestling Alliance (NWA) Championship.

In 1963, Skaaland began working for Vincent J. McMahon's newly-created WWE. It was here that he gained his greatest success. Not only did Skaaland enjoy a reign as one-half of the United States Tag Team Champions (with Spiros Arion), but he also became a shareholder in McMahon's company. As part owner, Skaaland was responsible handling a great deal of the company's finances.

During this time, Skaaland also made a successful transition into the managerial ranks. Behind his supreme level of wrestling knowledge, he guided Bruno Sammartino and Bob Backlund to three of the most remarkable WWE Championship reigns in history. In fact, aside from ten months in the late 1970s, Skaaland's men held the WWE Championship uninterrupted from December 1973 to December 1983.

Skaaland's managerial career came to an end shortly after he threw in the towel on Backlund's reign in his loss the Iron Sheik in December 1983. From there, he assumed several backstage responsibilities until his retirement in the early 1990s. In 1994, Skaaland's tireless efforts to the sports-entertainment industry were recognized when he was inducted into the WWE Hall of Fame.

ASHLEY

HT: 5'5"
FROM: New York, New York
SIGNATURE MOVE: Starstruck

A bad girl from the Big Apple, this punk chick started to get attention when she was crowned Miss Hawaiian Tropic USA in 2002 and Miss Hawaiian Tropic Canada in 2005. She entered WWE that June when she won the Diva Search contest. From there, she became one of the most popular Superstars on *Raw*.

As she fought off Divas Candice Michelle, Melina and Torrie Wilson, she aligned herself with Trish Stratus and became a tough competitor. She ended her first year in WWE gracing the cover of December's *Flex Magazine*. She started 2006 by stopping the hearts of men everywhere when she appeared in *Maxim*.

As she went from *Raw* to *SmackDown,* Ashley showed her verbal skills behind the broadcast booth. In April 2007, she answered the pleas of men everywhere when she appeared in *Playboy*. She also appeared on an episode of *Smallville* and that summer branched out further as a pop-culture personality and was a contestant on *Survivor: China.*

Ashley and World Wrestling Entertainment parted ways in July 2008. Though her time in WWE was brief, the pierced princess made quite an impact as a Diva.

ASHLEY VALENCE

HT: 5'6"
FROM: Ft. Pierce, Florida

Much like the first season of *WWE NXT*, season two featured eight aspiring Superstars competing to become WWE's next breakout star. This time, though, the beast-like forces battling to become WWE Superstars were delicately complemented by the lovely Ashley Valence.

Alongside fellow *NXT* co-host Matt Striker, Ashley's role was to introduce the Rookies and describe their weekly challenges. When season two of *NXT* came to an end, the beautiful brunette briefly served as a ring announcer for *WWE Superstars* before ultimately leaving WWE in December 2010.

Prior to her brief WWE tenure, Ashley's wide array of interests kept her very busy. In addition to being a former competitive rodeo rider, she was also an emcee for the NBA's Memphis Grizzlies and competed in Miss Florida USA. Ashley continues to model and has made brief appearances on *Jimmy Kimmel Live!* and *The Tonight Show with Jay Leno*. She hopes to one day become a motivational speaker, specializing in sending the correct message to college students.

1960-69
1970-79
1980-89
1990-99
2000-09
2010-

B

2010-
2000-09
1990-99
1980-89
1970-79
1960-69

AVATAR

HT: 6'0" WT: 235 lbs. FROM: Parts Unknown
SIGNATURE MOVE: Frog Splash

This enigmatic competitor combined martial arts with high-flying moves, and made his debut on *Monday Night Raw* in October 1995. Unlike most masked Superstars, he didn't put on a mask until he was in the ring, and removed it after a victory. His version of the Frog Splash was a bit different. To begin, he'd stand on the sternum of his fallen opponent, jump from their body and land on them with a body splash.

Avatar became a fan-favorite as he battled villains like Sycho Sid, Isaac Yankem DDS, Brooklyn Brawler, and Bradshaw. During his stay in WWE, he also formed an exciting tag team with fellow aerialist Aldo Montoya. By March 1997, Avatar vanished from WWE. Even if it was only for a brief period of time, Avatar showcased his talents where only the select few are given the opportunity.

BACKLASH

April 25, 1999
Providence, RI - Providence Civic Center

Main Event: WWE Champion Stone Cold Steve Austin defeated The Rock, Shane McMahon as guest referee

April 30, 2000
Washington, DC - MCI Center

Main Event: The Rock defeated WWE Champion Triple H, Shane McMahon as guest referee

April 29, 2001
Rosemont, IL - Allstate Arena

Main Event: WWE Champion Stone Cold Steve Austin & Intercontinental Champion Triple H defeated World Tag Team Champions Undertaker & Kane

April 21, 2002
Kansas City, MO - Kemper Arena

Main Event: Hulk Hogan defeated WWE Champion Triple H

April 27, 2003
Worcester, MA - Worcester Centrum

Main Event: Goldberg defeated The Rock

April 18, 2004
Edmonton, Alberta, Canada - Rexall Place

Main Event: World Heavyweight Champion Chris Benoit defeated Shawn Michaels and Triple H in a Triple Threat Match

May 1, 2005
Manchester, NH - Verizon Wireless Arena

Main Event: World Heavyweight Champion Batista defeated Triple H

April 30, 2006
Lexington, KY - Rupp Arena

Main Event: WWE Champion John Cena defeated Triple H and Edge in a Triple Threat Match

April 29, 2007
Atlanta, GA - Philips Arena

Main Event: WWE Champion John Cena defeated Randy Orton and Edge and Shawn Michaels in a Fatal 4-Way Match

April 27, 2008
Baltimore, Maryland - 1st Mariner Arena

Main Event: WWE Champion Randy Orton defeated Triple H and John Cena and JBL in a Fatal 4-Way Match

April 26, 2009
Providence, Rhode Island - Dunkin' Donuts Center

Main Event: Edge defeated World Heavyweight Champion John Cena in a Last Man Standing Match

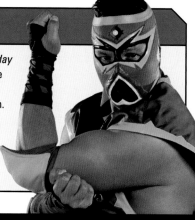

The original *Badd Blood* was an *In Your House* event that featured the very first Hell In A Cell Match and the debut of Kane. *Bad Blood* returned in 2003, but was replaced by *One Night Stand* in 2005.

October 5, 1997
St. Louis, MO - Kiel Center

Main Event: Shawn Michaels defeated Undertaker in a Hell In A Cell Match

June 15, 2003
Houston, TX - Compaq Center

Main Event: World Heavyweight Champion Triple H defeated Kevin Nash in a Hell In A Cell Match with Mick Foley as Special Guest Referee

June 13, 2004
Edmonton, Alberta, Canada - Rexall Place

Main Event: Triple H defeated Shawn Michaels in a Hell In A Cell Match

BAD NEWS BROWN

HT: 6'2" WT: 271 lbs. FROM: Harlen, New York
SIGNATURE MOVE: Ghetto Blaster

In 1977, this Olympic Bronze Medalist in Judo entered the ranks of professional wrestling. Trained by Japanese legend Antonio Inoki, Bad News Brown first made waves in WWE in 1988 and showed why he was one of the meanest, nastiest, most violent Superstars in WWE history. Bad News also showed he could be a persuasive swindler when he double-crossed Bret "Hit Man" Hart and eliminated him to win the Battle Royal at *WrestleMania IV*. Bad News also never hesitated to display his inability to coexist with others when he walked out on teams during the first two *Survivor Series* events. Bad News posed a serious threat to the reign of then-champion Randy "Macho Man" Savage.

In 1990, Bad News vanished from World Wrestling Entertainment after he accosted then-WWE President Jack Tunney on *The Brother Love Show*. He spent the rest of the decade primarily competing in Mexico, Japan and Canada, but when a chronic knee injury intensified, he hung up his boots in 1999. Brown briefly owned and operated his own training facility in his adopted home of Calgary, Alberta in 2005.

Tragically, on March 6, 2007, Bad News Brown passed away. Brown's legacy in amateur athletics and sports-entertainment continues to resonante, as he is widely regarded as one of the toughest men to ever enter the ring.

BALLS MAHONEY

HT: 6'2"   WT: 305 lbs.
FROM: Nutley, New Jersey
SIGNATURE MOVE: Nutcracker Suite

Mahoney started his career in 1987 and toured the United States, Canada and Puerto Rico. Mahoney won numerous singles and tag team championships on the indepenent circuit, and in 1996, Balls Mahoney arrived in ECW. He was quickly embraced by the promotion's demanding fans. Mahoney formed a tag team with another purveyor of pain, Axl Rotten, collectively known as the Chair Swingin' Freaks. When ECW went out of business in early 2001, Mahoney returned to tours of the United States and Asia.

In 2005, he surprised fans everywhere when he appeared at *ECW's One Night Stand* in a brawl with the Blue World Order. Mahoney was the first Extremist signed for the resurrected ECW. While Balls shared the ring with some familiar faces, he faced new challengers as well. Balls even caught the eye of Diva Kelly Kelly. In April 2007, he was an advisor on the Sci-Fi Network's reality show, *Who Wants To Be A Superhero?*

BAM BAM BIGELOW

HT: 6'4"   WT: 390 lbs.   FROM: Asbury Park, New Jersey
SIGNATURE MOVES: Slingshot Splash,
Greetings from Asbury Park

The "Beast From The East" wowed audiences with the agility of a gazelle, forward rolls, cartwheels, and devastating moves off the top rope. His colorful ring attire was topped off with a fireball tattoo that covered his entire skull. In 1987, most WWE managers competed for the employment this powerful newcomer. As the "Battle for Bam Bam" continued, the world stood still when Bam Bam Bigelow selected Sir Oliver Humperdink to guide his career. This fan favorite was tough as nails and selected as a member of Hulk Hogan's team at the first *Survivor Series*. Outnumbered 3-to-1, Bigelow managed to eliminate King Kong Bundy and One Man Gang before finally being eliminated by Andre The Giant. His last appearance of the decade was in the WWE Championship Tournament at *WrestleMania IV*.

Bam Bam returned to WWE in 1992 and later became a member of The Million-Dollar Corporation. In 1995, he made his silver screen debut in *Major Payne*. He then met pro football Hall of Famer Lawrence Taylor in the main event of *WrestleMania XI*. After a stint in Japan, Bam Bam surfaced in Extreme Championship Wrestling and later in WCW. After World Championship Wrestling was purchased by WWE in 2001, Bigelow returned to the independent scene.

On January 19, 2007, Bam Bam Bigelow passed away. Bigelow was considered a physical phenomenon and one of the greatest big men to ever set foot inside the ring. He entertained millions around the world. He commanded an audience, a match, and respect like few others in sports-entertainment. "The Bammer" will be forever missed by those who loved him both in and out of the ring.

BAM NEELY

HT: 6'7"   WT: 275 lbs
FROM: Robbinsdale, Minnesota

Bam Neely comes from a town rich in ring tradition. Hailing from Robbinsdale, Minnesota, the former border patrol agent shares the same zip code as the late, great WWE Legends Rick Rude and Curt Hennig. In the ring, however, Neely shares no likenesses with his renowned predecessors. Instead, he substitutes pure power for their technical ability. His overwhelming strength caught the eye of Chavo Guerrero, who brought Neely in to serve as his bodyguard in April 2008. On occasion, he teamed with his boss and combined a lethal amount of speed and power. This led to Bam's inclusion in the insidious alliance led by Edge known as La Familia. Since he departed from WWE in January 2009, Neely has been in rings on the American independent scene and on the island of Puerto Rico.

B

2010-

2000-09

1990-99

1980-89

1970-79

1960-69

BARBARIAN
HT: 6'2" WT: 300 lbs. FROM: The Isle of Tonga
SIGNATURE MOVE: Kick of Fear

After years of competing as one-half of the intimidating Powers of Pain tag team, the Barbarian washed the paint from his face and went his own way in search of singles success in 1990.

The Barbarian's quest to make it solo began when his manager, Mr. Fuji, sold the big man's contract to Bobby "The Brain" Heenan. Under Heenan's tutelage, the Barbarian altered his image, trading in his leather and chains for a skull-and-antler headdress and warrior-like fur robes. The makeover paid early dividends, as the new-look Barbarian got off to an impressive start, defeating Tito Santana at *WrestleMania VI*.

Unfortunately for the Barbarian, *WrestleMania VI* is where the winning stopped. He spent most of the following year coming up short against the likes of Big Boss Man and Bret "Hit Man" Hart. Realizing a solo career might not yield big benefits, Heenan paired the Barbarian with Haku in hopes of recreating some of the strong man's earlier tag success.

The Barbarian's return to the tag scene proved just as futile as his singles efforts. After his team lost to The Rockers at *WrestleMania VII*, the Barbarian struggled to get back on track. By mid-1992, he left WWE.

BARBARA BUSH (B.B.)

This buxom blonde first appeared as an EMT tending to injured Superstars. For weeks, fans in the crowd suddenly claimed they needed medical attention. She appeared again after the first-ever Gravy Bowl Match on *SmackDown* and got into it with Ivory. Her fights with the then-Women's Champion continued and B.B. participated in the Four-Way Evening Gown Match at *Armageddon 1999*. At the Holiday Topless Top-Rope Match against Terri on *Raw*, she was in Val Venis' corner and Terri in Hardcore Holly's. This match stipulated every time one of the Superstars was thrown over the top rope, his female representative must remove an article of clothing. The first woman to be topless lost the match for "her man." Venis was tossed over twice and Triple H was the judge to make sure she peeled it all off.

B.B. continued to captivate WWE audiences until late 2000, when she left the company. Audiences and Superstars will always remember this energetic EMT who was dedicated to making people feel better.

BARON MIKEL SCICLUNA
HT: 6'3" WT: 256 lbs. FROM: Isle of Malta
SIGNATURE MOVE: Use of Foreign Objects

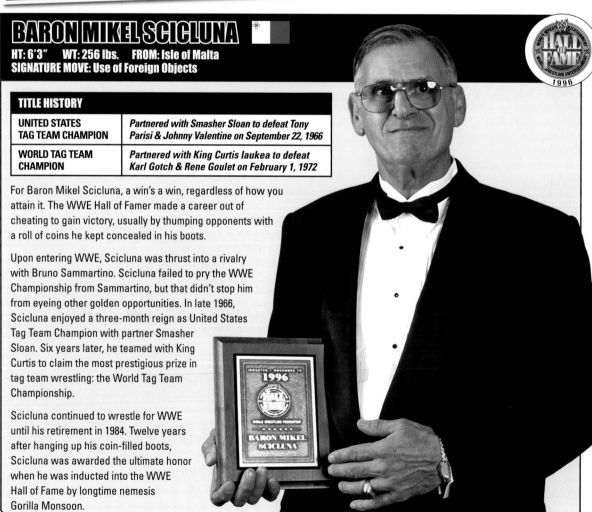

TITLE HISTORY	
UNITED STATES TAG TEAM CHAMPION	*Partnered with Smasher Sloan to defeat Tony Parisi & Johnny Valentine on September 22, 1966*
WORLD TAG TEAM CHAMPION	*Partnered with King Curtis Iaukea to defeat Karl Gotch & Rene Goulet on February 1, 1972*

For Baron Mikel Scicluna, a win's a win, regardless of how you attain it. The WWE Hall of Famer made a career out of cheating to gain victory, usually by thumping opponents with a roll of coins he kept concealed in his boots.

Upon entering WWE, Scicluna was thrust into a rivalry with Bruno Sammartino. Scicluna failed to pry the WWE Championship from Sammartino, but that didn't stop him from eyeing other golden opportunities. In late 1966, Scicluna enjoyed a three-month reign as United States Tag Team Champion with partner Smasher Sloan. Six years later, he teamed with King Curtis to claim the most prestigious prize in tag team wrestling: the World Tag Team Championship.

Scicluna continued to wrestle for WWE until his retirement in 1984. Twelve years after hanging up his coin-filled boots, Scicluna was awarded the ultimate honor when he was inducted into the WWE Hall of Fame by longtime nemesis Gorilla Monsoon.

BARON VON RASCHKE

HT: 6'3" **WT:** 281 lbs.
FROM: The Republic of Germany
SIGNATURE MOVE: Iron Claw

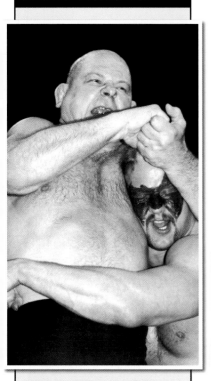

While most of Baron Von Raschke's career was spent competing in the AWA and NWA, news of his devastating Iron Claw made its way to WWE locker rooms, causing many Superstars to fear locking horns with him during one of his rare WWE appearances.

A skilled amateur wrestler, Raschke excelled immediately upon his debut in the mid-1960s. By the mid-1970s, his German goosestep earned him the reputation as one of America's most hated Superstars. Northeast fans feared the worst when Raschke earned an opportunity at Bruno Sammartino's WWE Championship in 1977. Just a few years removed from Ivan Koloff's frightful victory over Sammartino, WWE fans feared another title loss to a hated opponent. Luckily for Sammartino's fans, Raschke's temper got the better of him, as he was disqualified after using a steel chair on the champion.

In 1988, Raschke made a return to WWE as the manager of the Powers of Pain tag team. Known simply as the Baron, he led Barbarian & Warlord to early success before moving over and letting Mr. Fuji take control of the team. Raschke's career began to wind down following his managerial stint in WWE. And though his WWE efforts were minimal, he will long be remembered as one of sports-entertainment's most fear-provoking Superstars.

BARRY HOROWITZ

  HT: 6'0" **WT:** 221 lbs. **FROM:** St. Petersburg, Florida
SIGNATURE MOVE: The Cloverleaf

Barry Horowitz was a touted high school amateur wrestler and later competed collegiately at Florida State. Trained by the legendary Boris Malenko, he made a brief WWE stop in 1983. Barry returned to WWE in 1988, appearing on programs such as *Prime Time Wrestling*, *All-Star Wrestling*, *Superstars of Wrestling* and *Wrestling Challenge*.

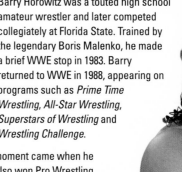

After he recovered from a serious neck injury, Barry's shining moment came when he defeated Bodydonna Skip at *SummerSlam 1995*. That year, he also won Pro Wrestling Illustrated's "Most Inspirational Wrestler of The Year" Award. He maintained a place on WWE cards through 1997, when he moved to WCW, where he stayed until 2000.

One of the most well-traveled ring veterans ever, Barry Horowitz has appeared in promotions all over the world, patting himself on the back each step of the way. In a career that spanned 21 years, Barry is considered by ring aficionados as one of the toughest and technically sound competitors to step inside the ring.

BARRY O

  HT: 6'1" **WT:** 235 lbs.
FROM: Las Vegas, Nevada

With "The Big O," Bob Orton, Sr. as his father, many sports-entertainment insiders forecasted greatness for Barry O. Unfortunately for the younger Orton, those predictions never turned into reality.

Unlike his brother, "Cowboy" Bob Orton, Barry O had a difficult time getting his WWE career off the ground. While brother Bob was competing with the likes of "Rowdy" Roddy Piper and Hulk Hogan, Barry O struggled against opponents like Outback Jack and Corporal Kirschner.

Despite his WWE troubles, Barry O did manage to gain some success while competing for Stu Hart's Stampede Wrestling in Calgary. Competing under a dark mask, Barry O called himself The Zodiac, which was a tribute to his father, who wrestled under the same name during the 1970s. While today's WWE fans may not recognize the name Barry O, they certainly know his nephew, "The Legend Killer" Randy Orton.

BARRY WINDHAM

HT: 6'6" **WT:** 275 lbs. **FROM:** Sweetwater, Texas
SIGNATURE MOVE: The Superplex

TITLE HISTORY

WORLD TAG TEAM CHAMPION (2 TIMES)	Partnered with Mike Rotundo to defeat Adrian Adonis & Dick Murdoch on January 21, 1985 Partnered with Mike Rotundo to defeat Iron Sheik & Nikolai Volkoff on June 17, 1985

WWE fans were first introduced to the son of Blackjack Mulligan as one-half of the incredibly popular US Express. Along with partner Mike Rotundo, Barry Windham entered the first *WrestleMania* as the World Tag Team Champions. Windham left WWE in 1985 but remained active in the NWA for most of the next five years.

In June 1989, Windham returned to WWE as a man who lived by his own laws. Dressed in black and calling himself the Widowmaker, he stalked WWE Superstars, taking his time to take what he wanted. As the Widowmaker, Windham clashed with Superstars such as Koko B. Ware, Paul Roma, Sam Houston, the Red Rooster and Tito Santana. He eventually left WWE again and appeared often in WCW but still popped up in WWE from time to time.

1960-69
1970-79
1980-89
1990-99
2000-09
2010-

BART GUNN

  HT: 6'4"   WT: 275 lbs.   FROM: Austin, Texas

TITLE HISTORY

WORLD TAG TEAM CHAMPION (3 TIMES)	*Partnered with Billy Gunn to defeat 1-2-3 Kid & Bob Holly on January 23, 1995* *Partnered with Billy Gunn to defeat Owen Hart & Yokozuna on September 25, 1995* *Partnered with Billy Gunn to defeat The Godwinns on May 26, 1996*

With his brother Billy by his side, Bart Gunn wrangled up three World Tag Team Championship reigns. His singles efforts, however, were considerably less impressive. Despite his lackluster solo career, though, Bart did manage to attract major mainstream attention in 1999.

After tearing through "Dr. Death" Steve Williams, Bob Holly, The Godfather, and Bradshaw to win the Brawl for All Tournament, Bart legitimized himself as one of WWE's toughest Superstars. With the Brawl for All crown resting comfortably on his mantle, Gunn challenged heavyweight boxer Eric "Butterbean" Esch to a similar-styled contest at *WrestleMania XV*. Just seconds into the match, Butterbean felled his opponent with a devastating right hand. Miraculously, Bart climbed to his feet only to be dropped yet again by a powerful right. The force of the punch knocked Bart straight out of WWE. Later that night, Butterbean's dominance was featured on sportscasts nationwide, including ESPN's *SportsCenter*.

Bart made a cameo appearance at *Raw*'s 15th Anniversary special in December 2007. In a match reminiscent of *WrestleMania X-Seven*'s Gimmick Battle Royal, he competed alongside many other past WWE Superstars, including Al Snow, Bob Backlund and Sgt. Slaughter. Although he failed to win the contest, he did receive a warm ovation from the WWE fans.

BASHAM BROTHERS

MEMBERS: Danny Basham, Doug Basham   COMBINED WT: 495 lbs.   FROM: Columbus, Ohio

TITLE HISTORY

WWE TAG TEAM CHAMPIONS (2 TIMES)	*Defeated Los Guerreros on October 23, 2003* *Defeated Rob Van Dam & Rey Mysterio on January 13, 2005*

Danny & Doug Basham played rough both in the ring and out. Just ask their muscular manager, Shaniqua. Introduced to WWE audiences in May 2003, the Basham Brothers utilized their similar looks to confound opponents. The successful form of trickery eventually lead them to a WWE Tag Team Championship opportunity against Los Guerreros, who they defeated for the titles in October 2003. The brothers held the titles until February 2004.

The Bashams struggled to find their way after losing the titles, but in November 2004, their careers took a positive turn when they joined forces with WWE Champion JBL. As his "Secretaries of Defense," the Bashams enjoyed another reign atop *SmackDown*'s tag team division, but their main job description was to shield JBL from any apparent danger, even if it meant causing themselves harm. In June 2005, the brothers were forced to go their separate ways when Danny was traded to *Raw*. Neither Superstar was able to duplicate the success they achieved as a team. They both left WWE shortly after.

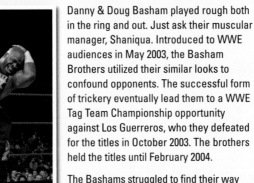

BASTIAN BOOGER

HT: 6'1"   WT: 401 lbs.
FROM: Parts Unknown

Booger arrived in 1994 and had a unique gift of making those around him physically ill. Bastian Booger's repulsive appearance almost equaled his disgusting behavior toward opponents and fans. Vince McMahon once said, "Bastion Booger is the only person I know who refers to his nose as a snack dispenser." One night, Bastian Booger grabbed an ice cream cone from a young child in the crowd, turned to the boy and shoved the entire tasty treat in his mouth. As the boy cried in front of a capacity crowd, the revolting blob laughed all the way to the ring.

Booger had a short-lived alliance with Bam Bam Bigelow, which dissolved on an episode of *Monday Night Raw* when he planted a passionate kiss on Bigelow's valet, Luna Vachon. In early 1995, Booger left WWE and returned to parts unknown. Though some thought he would be dormant forever, he shocked the world when he arrived at the *Raw* 15th Anniversary show, over a decade after his last sickening appearance.

BATISTA

🇺🇸

HT: 6'6" **WT:** 290 lbs.
FROM: Washington, D.C.
SIGNATURE MOVE: Batista Bomb

When WCW officials told him he'd never make it in sports-entertainment, Dave Batista pushed himself to achieve his dream of being a Superstar. In May 2002, he made his debut on *SmackDown* but it wasn't until a move to *Raw* and two victories over Kane that "The Animal" began to make noise in the WWE Universe. The wins impressed Ric Flair and Triple H, who were looking to align themselves with the industry's brightest new stars. After a lengthy search, they identified Randy Orton and Batista. Collectively, the four Superstars became known as Evolution.

TITLE HISTORY	
WORLD HEAVYWEIGHT CHAMPION (4 TIMES)	*Defeated Triple H on April 3, 2005* *Defeated King Booker on November 26, 2006* *Defeated The Great Khali on September 16, 2007* *Defeated Chris Jericho on October 26, 2008*
WORLD TAG TEAM CHAMPION (3 TIMES)	*Partnered with Ric Flair to defeat The Dudley Boys on December 14, 2003* *Partnered with Ric Flair to defeat Booker T & Rob Van Dam on March 22, 2004* *Partnered with John Cena to defeat Ted DiBiase & Cody Rhodes on August 4, 2008*
WWE CHAMPION (2 TIMES)	*Defeated Randy Orton on June 7, 2009* *Defeated John Cena on February 21, 2010*
WWE TAG TEAM CHAMPION	*Partnered with Rey Mysterio to defeat MNM on December 16, 2005*

Batista earned his first championship alongside "The Nature Boy" when the duo captured the WWE Tag Team Championships in December 2003. As Evolution dominated WWE, Batista started to emerge from the shadows of Triple H and Ric Flair. By the time Batista won the 2005 Royal Rumble Match, World Heavyweight Champion Triple H viewed him as a serious threat to his title.

After a triceps injury at the hands of Mark Henry forced Batista to relinquish the title in January 2006, he vowed to return. Batista successfully regained the World Heavyweight Championship at *Survivor Series* in 2006. Four months into his second reign, Batista faced Undertaker at *WrestleMania 23* against the Undertaker. "The Animal" took Undertaker to the limit, but was unable to stop the streak of "The Deadman" at *WrestleMania*. Though disappointed, Batista stayed hungry and always managed to keep himself in the championship hunt for the rest of his career.

At WrestleMania 21, Batista dethroned Triple H for his first World Heavyweight Championship.

At *Bragging Rights* in 2009, Batista shocked the world when he blamed Rey Mysterio for a loss to Undertaker, then attacked his former tag team partner. "The Animal" then became locked in a tense rivalry with another former friend, John Cena, over the WWE Championship. The grueling match at *Over the Limit* led to a wheelchair-bound Batista declaring "I quit!" the following night on *Raw* before fading from the WWE Universe.

BATTLE KAT

HT: 5'10" **WT:** 225 lbs. **From:** Parts Unknown
SIGNATURE MOVE: Moonsault

In October 1990, WWE was introduced to a man with the martial-arts skills of a ninja, the high-flying acrobatics of a gymnast and superior technical wrestling skills. His identity hidden behind a mask, Battle Kat displayed his abilities against the Barbarian, Boris Zhukov, Pez Whatley, and "Playboy" Buddy Rose. Battle Kat disappeared from WWE soon after his debut. Reports at the time speculated that he traveled to Japan to compete there.

Today, the identity of this man remains unknown. Though he was only in WWE for a brief period of time, he will always be remembered as a talented performer.

BATTMAN

HT: 5'10" **WT:** 240 lbs. **FROM:** Gotham City
SIGNATURE MOVE: Abdominal Stretch

TITLE HISTORY	
INTERNATIONAL TAG TEAM CHAMPION	*Partnered with Bruno Sammartino to defeat Prof. Toru Tanaka & Mitsu Arakawa on December 8, 1969*

In 1966, the Battman debuted in Buffalo to the joy of fans and dismay of villains everywhere. Opponents were taken aback by his physical conditioning, wrestling skill, intellect, and his acts of escape artistry. He quickly amassed an impressive win-loss record, and would co-hold the International Tag Team Championship. The first reign saw him hold the belts with then-WWE Champion, Bruno Sammartino. For the second, he teamed with Latin Superstar Victor Rivera. He maintained order across WWE during the turbulent late 1960s and into the next decade.

2010-
2000-09
1990-99
1980-89
1970-79
1960-69

THE BEAST

HT: 5'10" WT: 255 lbs.
FROM: Dorchester, New Brunswick, Canada

With a big, bushy beard and wild hair, The Beast certainly appeared to be well named. He even played the role in between the ropes with his savage in-ring approach. However, behind the wild exterior was a man with close familial ties. Believe it or not, the untamed Superstar is the oldest of four wrestling brothers. His younger, more-refined siblings, Rudy Kay, Bobby Kay and Leo Burke all made a living inside the ring.

The Beast toured the globe seven times during his nearly 40-year career. His undomesticated style attracted huge crowds in Australia, and even landed him in a match against the legendary Giant Baba in front of 45,000 rabid fans in Japan. It was in Canada that The Beast gained his greatest notoriety. In 1966, he defeated Dave Ruhl for Calgary's National Wrestling Alliance Canadian Heavyweight Championship. He also held Toronto's version of the NWA United States Heavyweight Championship for five months after defeating Johnny Valentine in October 1963.

"BEAUTIFUL" BOBBY HARMON

FROM: Cincinnati, Ohio   SIGNATURE MOVE: The Bobby Lock

Known for his flamboyant personality, "Beautiful" Bobby Harmon would oftentimes strut to the squared circle wearing over-the-top satin ring robes, dark sunglasses and kilts. His glitz and gaudiness was only matched by that of his manager, WWE Hall of Famer The Grand Wizard.

Based on appearance alone, fans of the Northeast couldn't stand the sight of "The Beautiful One." Making matters worse, he coupled his extravagant appearance with great conceit and a superior in-ring acumen.

Over the course of his career, Harmon formed several successful tag teams. His partners included the effeminate Magnificent Maurice and WWE Hall of Famers Blackjack Mulligan and "Handsome" Jimmy Valiant. In 1971, Harmon and Valiant started to use entrance music while walking to the ring. Like several other Superstars of the past, Harmon and Valiant claimed to be the first with entrance music. Whether it's true or not, one thing remains certain: "Beautiful" Bobby Harmon was a competitor ahead of his time.

BEAVER CLEAVAGE

HT: 6'0"
WT: 243 lbs.

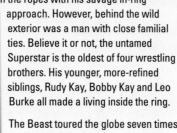

Despite having a shelf life of less than one month, the controversy created by Beaver Cleavage is still being talked about today. In the summer of 1999, Beaver debuted in several black-and-white vignettes filled with double entendres. Fans' jaws hit the floor when the sexy Mrs. Cleavage appeared alongside Beaver. The controversy surrounding Beaver's sexual innuendos failed to prevent him from entering the ring. In June 1999, he defeated Christian in his first in-ring appearance. A few weeks later, he disappeared from WWE television.

BELLA TWINS

NAMES: Brie & Nikki
HT: 5'6" FROM: Scottsdale, Arizona

In August 2008, WWE saw the debut of a delectable Diva who quickly made a name for herself, thanks to her moves on her way to the ring and dizzying ones in it. Brie Bella bested two-time Women's Champion Victoria in her first match on *SmackDown* and proved it was not beginner's luck when she pinned WWE's Black Widow the next week for the second straight time. A few weeks after her debut, Natalya and Victoria uncovered the fact that Brie had a twin sister, named Nikki, who would switch places with her during matches.

Even though the twins lost their underhanded advantage they didn't allow it to slow down their quest for glory in the ring, which hit its high point on April 11, 2011 when Brie captured the Divas Championship. Despite the occasional disagreement, the Bella Twins always back each other up. Whatever the situation, they have a knack for causing mischief, and keeping the cameras focused on them at all times. As their entrance song says, "You can look but you can't touch."

BERTHA FAYE

HT: 5'8"   FROM: Walls, Mississippi   SIGNATURE MOVE: Sit Out Powerbomb

TITLE HISTORY	
WOMEN'S CHAMPION	*Defeated Alundra Blayze on August 27, 1995*

Bertha Faye may not have been the most attractive woman to set foot in the ring, but she may have been the most loved. Despite the fact that she dwarfed him, Harvey Wippleman adored Bertha Faye with every ounce of his being.

Wippleman first introduced fans to Bertha Faye in April 1995 when she attacked Alundra Blayze on an episode of *Monday Night Raw*. As a result of the assault, Blayze suffered a broken nose, which ultimately ignited an intense rivalry between the two competitors. At *SummerSlam 1995*, Bertha Faye flattened her rival with a sit-out powerbomb, enabling her to capture her first-and-only Women's Championship.

Two months after winning the Women's Championship, Bertha Faye found herself on the losing end of a *Monday Night Raw* rematch with Blayze. Shortly after losing the Women's Championship, Bertha Faye was never to be seen in a WWE ring again.

THE BERZERKER

HT: 6'8" **WT:** 323 lbs. **FROM:** Parts Unknown
SIGNATURE MOVE: Big Boot

Unleashed on WWE by Mr. Fuji in 1991, this crazed Superstar was first known as the Viking. However, due to his irregular behavior and spontaneous shouting, this Nordic beast changed his name to something more appropriate. He had an unusual means of communicating with his manager that included unidentifiable hand signals and a dialect that remains untranslatable to this day.

Despite his baffling ring presence, this sword-swinger won many matches by throwing opponents over the top rope, leaving them on the arena floor unable to return to the ring before a ten-count. A consistent championship contender, the Berzerker faced off against Tito Santana, Jimmy "Superfly" Snuka, Bret "Hit Man" Hart, and Greg Valentine.

In early 1993, The Berzerker left WWE and has not been seen since. Today, fans' curiosity is still piqued when archived footage is shown of his matches and interviews. He'll always be remembered as one of the most unique and dangerous personas in WWE history.

BETH PHOENIX

HT: 5'7"
FROM: Buffalo, New York
SIGNATURE MOVE: Glam Slam

Beth Phoenix grew up with a dream to be a part of sports-entertainment. She became the first female amateur wrestler in her high school's history to compete on its varsity team. Beth traveled the country for training necessary to make the transition from amateur wrestling to sports-entertainment.

TITLE HISTORY	
WOMEN'S CHAMPION (3 TIMES)	*Defeated Candice on October 7, 2007* *Defeated Mickie James on August 17, 2008* *Defeated Michelle McCool on April 25, 2010*
DIVAS CHAMPION	*Defeated Kelly Kelly on October 2, 2011*

In May 2006, Phoenix debuted on Raw and assaulted then-Women's Champion Mickie James. As WWE fans searched for more information on her background, Trish Stratus provided some insight on Beth's past with Mickie. Weeks later, Beth was announced as the newest WWE Diva. Unfortunately, she suffered a fractured mandible in a match against Victoria, and was sidelined for over one year.

She returned to *Raw* as a "Glamazon" on the hunt for gold. After unsuccessful attempts at winning the Women's Championship from Candice, Phoenix finally picked up the win in October and ruled for five months. She lost the prize to rival Mickie James, but regained the title in a "Winner Take All Match" at *SummerSlam* 2008.

The Glamazon's dominance continued and she was voted the 2008 "Diva of the Year" by the WWE Universe. She soon became involved with Santino Marella as the one-time rivals ignited a passionate romance. With the "Miracle from Milan" at her side, Beth became known as "Glamarella" and part of many entertaining segments on WWE television. At the 2010 *Royal Rumble*, she became only the second woman ever to compete in the dangerous battle royale, and used all her assets to eliminate the Great Khali. Though a sudden tear of her Anterior Cruciate Ligament (ACL) put her career in jeopardy, she returned at the *Survivor Series* to help friend Natalya topple the tandem of Lay-Cool. On October 2, 2011 Phoenix once again etched her name into WWE history when she craftily captured her first Divas Championship.

THE BEVERLY BROTHERS

MEMBERS: Beau & Blake
COMBINED WT: 514 lbs.

During interview segments that aired in May 1991, the Beverly Brothers proclaimed to WWE, "The Bevs want it all and we'll get it all." The Beverly Brothers, with their deadly finishing move called Shaker Heights Spike, quickly became contenders for the World Tag Team Championship.

After a series of impressive showings, Beau & Blake fought the Natural Disasters for the World Tag Team Championship, but were ultimately unsuccessful in defeating Typhoon & Earthquake. The team disbanded in early 1993 after Blake left WWE.

The Beverly Brothers were another example that a team can emerge onto the scene and shake up the tag team division in short order. No matter who led them to the ring, or who stood across the ring from them, opponents of the Beverlys were in for a long night.

B

2010-
2000-09
1990-99
1980-89
1970-79
1960-69

BIG BOSS MAN

HT: 6'7"   WT: 330 lbs.
FROM: Cobb County, Georgia
SIGNATURE MOVE: Side Slam

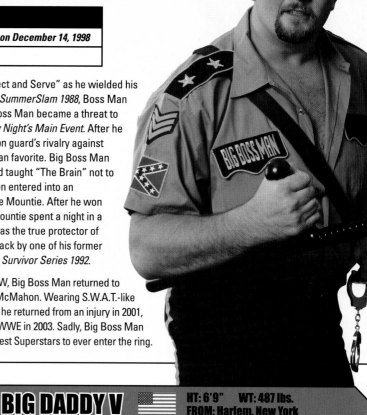

TITLE HISTORY

WORLD TAG TEAM CHAMPION	Partnered with Ken Shamrock to defeat New Age Outlaws on December 14, 1998
HARDCORE CHAMPION	4 Times

Managed by the "Doctor of Style," Slick, Big Boss Man gave new meaning to the term "Protect and Serve" as he wielded his nightstick and destroyed anyone in his path. After a dominating victory over Koko B. Ware at *SummerSlam 1988*, Boss Man teamed with Akeem to form the Twin Towers, one of the largest teams in WWE history. Big Boss Man became a threat to Hulkamania, and on October 1989, they settled their score in a Steel Cage Match on *Saturday Night's Main Event*. After he showed he couldn't be bought, the former prison guard's rivalry against "Million Dollar Man" Ted DiBiase made him a fan favorite. Big Boss Man then battled members of the Heenan Family and taught "The Brain" not to talk bad about people's mothers. Boss Man then entered into an ideological dispute over law and order with The Mountie. After he won their Jailhouse Match at *SummerSlam 1991*, Mountie spent a night in a New York City lockup. Boss Man showed he was the true protector of WWE when he returned to the ring from an attack by one of his former inmates, Nailz, and won a Nightstick Match at *Survivor Series 1992*.

In October 1998, after time overseas and in WCW, Big Boss Man returned to WWE as the head of personal security for Mr. McMahon. Wearing S.W.A.T.-like attire, he happily displayed an updated version of "hard time" suitable for the Attitude Era. After he returned from an injury in 2001, Boss Man formed brief alliances with Bull Buchanan, Booker T, and Mr. Perfect before leaving WWE in 2003. Sadly, Big Boss Man passed away in September 2004. He is remembered as one of the most agile big men and toughest Superstars to ever enter the ring.

BIG BULLY BUSICK

HT: 6'0"   WT: 265 lbs.
FROM: Weirton, West Virginia

Managed by Harvey Wippleman, Big Bully Busick arrived in WWE in the early 1990s with grand plans of pushing around his fellow Superstars. Ironically, however, when it came to his in-ring action, the only Superstar getting bullied around was him. He even lost to perennial loser Brooklyn Brawler.

Realizing he wasn't going to push around the Superstars of WWE, Busick turned his attention to much smaller targets. It wasn't uncommon to see him bullying around ring announcers and kids in the audience. He once went so far as to steal a youngster's balloon. The mean-spirited act turned heartbreaking when he popped the colorful balloon right in front of the little girl.

BIG DADDY V

HT: 6'9"   WT: 487 lbs.
FROM: Harlem, New York

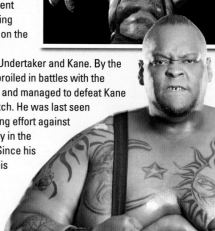

ECW has a way of bringing the extreme out of its Superstars. Covered in curious tattoos, Big Daddy V was brought into ECW to protect Matt Striker from The Boogeyman. After ridding Striker of his worm-eating nemesis, Big Daddy V went inter-promotional, focusing much of his devastation on the bigger Superstars of *SmackDown*, including Undertaker and Kane. By the end of 2007, he was embroiled in battles with the Brothers of Destruction, and managed to defeat Kane in an Extreme Rules Match. He was last seen on ECW in 2008, in a losing effort against CM Punk during a Money in the Bank qualifying match. Since his departure from WWE, this beast has been seen on the independent wrestling circuit and in All-Japan Pro Wrestling.

BIG DICK JOHNSON

"Lock up your daughters, lock up your wives. Lock up the back door and run for your lives…"

Those words come from the revolting exhibitions brought to WWE courtesy of Big Dick Johnson. Appearing when fans least expect it, Big Dick loves prancing around WWE events showing off his finest features. He has appeared on ECW with the Sandman, wished everyone a Merry Christmas at *Armageddon 2006* and at one point was even considered among the possibilities of being Mr. McMahon's illegitimate son.

No matter where you are in the world, when you hear the beat to his familiar theme music, you know who's coming through to give a little something special to all of you: Big Dick Johnson!

THE BIG EVENT

Aug 28 1986 Exhibition Stadium; Toronto, Ontario

With a record 64,000 in attendance, the Big Event pitted Hulk Hogan against "Mr. Wonderful" Paul Orndorff, who lost the match when Bobby Heenan attacked Hogan with a stool.

With nearly a dozen matches on the day, many legendary names made appearances at the show including Junkyard Dog, the Killer Bees, the Funks, and "King" Harley Race. There were two special matches at the event: a Snake Pit match between Ricky Steamboat and Jake Roberts, and a Six-Man Tag Team Match that had Big John Studd, King Kong Bundy & Bobby Heenan face Giant Machine, Super Machine & Lou Albano.

BIG JOHN STUDD

HALL OF FAME 2004

HT: 6'10"   WT: 235 lbs.   FROM: Los Angeles, California

During WWE's magical mainstream renaissance of the 1980s, Big John Studd proved himself as a larger-than-life villain. With an awe-inspiring frame that stood nearly seven-feet tall, he thwarted countless attempts by the fans' heroes to chop him down to size. With each passing conquest, he further cemented his legacy as one of sports-entertainment's greatest giants.

Studd made his professional debut in 1976 after being trained by WWE Hall of Famer Killer Kowalski. In the early 1980s, he started working with WWE. Upon entering the company, he was managed by Freddie Blassie, but quickly switched to Bobby "The Brain" Heenan.

By 1983, Studd began promoting himself as WWE's only true giant. The claim obviously didn't sit well with the 7'4" Andre the Giant. Over the course of the next several years, the two Superstars engaged in a bitter battle designed to crown WWE's elite giant.

Studd gained a favorable advantage in his rivalry with Andre when he cut his foe's hair in December 1984. The stunt eventually lead to a $15,000 Bodyslam Challenge between the big men at the first-ever *WrestleMania*. In the end, it was Andre lifting Studd over his head and slamming him to the ground for the win. After the match, Andre attempted to share his $15,000 with the capacity crowd, but a lightning-quick Heenan swooped in to steal the giant's winnings.

The following year, Studd walked into the *WrestleMania 2* WWE/NFL Battle Royal as one of the favorites. After eliminating William "Refrigerator" Perry, it appeared as though Studd would coast to the end, but "The Fridge" eventually outsmarted Studd when he pulled him out of the ring under the guise of a handshake. Studd left WWE soon after.

Studd made a brief return in late 1988. This time, however, the fans took a liking to the big man after he turned his back on the devious Heenan. His second WWE stint was highlighted by a victory in the 1989 Royal Rumble Match. Big John Studd, one of the greatest giants sports-entertainment has ever seen, was honored with induction into the WWE Hall of Fame in 2004.

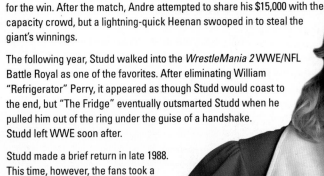

BIG MAN STEEL

HT: 6'3"   WT: 384 lbs.
SIGNATURE MOVE: Bearhug

A protégé of the "Doctor of Style" Slick, this monster of a man appeared in WWE in June 1989. A villain of the most brutal kind, Big Man Steel shook the very foundation of the Convention Center in Niagara Falls just by entering it. When he set foot in the ring during the episode of *Wrestling Challenge,* everyone in attendance watched in awe as he manhandled rugged veteran Tom Horner.

Big Man Steel and his manager had a falling out following the match and what was supposed to be the beginning of an era of dominance, turned out to be a one-time experiment.

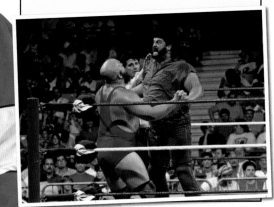

BIG SHOW

HT: 7'0" WT: 441 lbs.
FROM: Tampa, Florida
SIGNATURE MOVE: Chokeslam

" THE WORLD'S LARGEST ATHLETE "

TITLE HISTORY	
ECW CHAMPION	*Defeated Rob Van Dam on July 4, 2006*
HARDCORE CHAMPION	*2 Times*
INTERCONTINENTAL CHAMPION	*Defeated Cody Rhodes on April 1, 2012*
UNITED STATES CHAMPION	*Defeated Eddie Guerrero on October 19, 2003*
WWE CHAMPION (2 TIMES)	*Defeated The Rock and Triple H in a Triple Threat Match on November 14, 1999* *Defeated Brock Lesnar on November 17, 2002*
WORLD TAG TEAM CHAMPION (3 TIMES)	*Partnered with Undertaker to defeat Kane & X-Pac on August 22, 1999* *Partnered with Undertaker to defeat Mankind & The Rock on September 9, 1999* *Partnered with Kane to defeat Lance Cade & Trevor Murdoch on November 1, 2005*
WWE TAG TEAM CHAMPION (3 TIMES)	*Partnered with Chris Jericho when Edge was unable to defend the titles, starting on July 26, 2009* *Partnered with The Miz to defeat D-Generation X on February 8, 2010* *Partnered with Kane to defeat Heath Slater & Justin Gabriel on April 22, 2011*
WORLD HEAVYWEIGHT CHAMPION	*Defeated Mark Henry December 18, 2011*

Just like Andre The Giant and Big John Studd before him, Big Show can inspire fear at first sight. He is the world's largest athlete, with measurements that are astounding: 441 pounds, 7 feet tall, size 22 EEEEE shoes, 22 1/2 ring size, and a 64-inch chest. This man can go wherever he pleases, and do whatever he pleases. If you think you can stop him, try your luck. Odds are the outcome won't be pretty.

This giant was first seen in World Championship Wresting (WCW) in 1995 and quickly became one of its top stars. He held the WCW Championship twice. His dominance garnered attention from sports-entertainment icons, including Hulk Hogan and "Nature Boy" Ric Flair.

However, as he watched sports-entertainment explode from a distance, he knew there was only one place for him to be. In 1999, he made his debut in WWE and manhandled the greats of sports-entertainment. Despite having associates and being a part of factions, Big Show works best as a one-man wrecking crew.

On the July 4, 2006 episode of *ECW on Sci-Fi*, Big Show solidified his place in history when he defeated Rob Van Dam and became the only individual to ever hold the WWE, WCW, and ECW Championships. After over a year away from the ring, Big Show made a stunning WWE return at *No Way Out 2008*. As sports-entertainment was put on notice, this vicious goliath looked to return to annihilating self-professed contenders. He stepped outside of his traditional opponent pool at *WrestleMania XXIV* when he faced boxing great Floyd Mayweather, Jr. in a No Disqualification match.

Back in WWE full time, Big Show added a finishing move to his already expansive list, a devastating right-handed knockout punch that could bring a locomotive to a dead stop. Shortly after, he returned to his rule-breaking ways and was escorted to the ring by Vickie Guerrero. Viewed as the most serious threat to the World Heavyweight Championship, battles ensued with familiar foes including Undertaker, John Cena, Great Khali, and Triple H. The conflict with John Cena was brought to new levels when Big Show interfered in the Last Man Standing match at *Backlash 2009*.

In addition to his singles matches, Big Show captured championships with two of the most contemptuous characters in WWE history. First, he replaced an injured Edge as Chris Jericho's partner, forming a team known as "Jeri-Show." Next up was Sho-Miz, where he and The Miz fought off tandems including Mark Henry & MVP, R-Truth & John Morrison, and the Hart Dynasty. However, the World's Largest Athlete grew tired of the Miz's personality and floored his partner, ending their championship union. The WWE Universe again cheered for Big Show as he took on the Straight Edge Society, Nexus, and the Corre. Each group failed to take out Big Show, but in the process reunited him with Kane, a partnership that resulted in a WWE Tag Team Championship. Big Show added to his collection of championships in the WWE when he defeated Cody Rhodes at *WrestleMania XXVIII* for the Intercontinental Championship.

In a 17-year career that has included more than 20 championships, Big Show remains one of the most recognizable figures in sports-entertainment history. In February 2011, the first-ever official WWE video was released on his career. This three DVD set was titled *Big Show: A Giant's World* and gave fans a glimpse of what things looked like from his eyes.

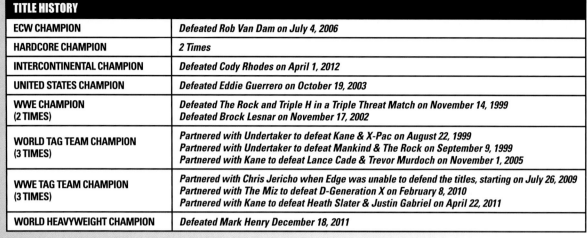

BIG SHOW & KANE COMBINED WT: 767 lbs.

TITLE HISTORY

WORLD TAG TEAM CHAMPIONS	*Defeated Lance Cade & Trevor Murdoch on November 1, 2005*
WWE TAG TEAM CHAMPIONS	*Defeated Heath Slater & Justin Gabriel on April 22, 2011*

Heading into *Taboo Tuesday 2005*, Big Show & Kane found themselves in opposite corners several times throughout their career, but at the annual pay-per-view, the fans' voting forced them to compete as a team. The massive duo instantly clicked, using their size advantage to

dethrone World Tag Team Champions Lance Cade & Trevor Murdoch. The victory gave Kane his ninth reign as World Tag Team Champion; it was Big Show's third.

Over the next several months, Big Show & Kane breezed past WWE's top teams. They even won a Champions vs. Champions Match at *Armageddon*, defeating *SmackDown*'s WWE Tag Team Champions, Batista & Rey Mysterio. After turning back Chris Masters & Carlito at *WrestleMania 22*, Big Show & Kane looked as though there was no WWE duo that could stop them until they signed on to defend against Kenny & Mikey of the Spirit Squad. Unfortunately for the champs, Nicky, Johnny, and Mitch also weaseled their way into the match. The five-on-two disadvantage proved to be too much for Big Show & Kane, as Spirit Squad successfully dethroned the mighty duo.

Following the defeat, the two clashed in matches that put an end to the terrorizing team. The WWE Universe witnessed a brief reunion during WWE's 2009 European tour, but this monstrous duo remained apart until 2011. An unexpected reunion took place when they shared similar interest in dismantling the Corre. At *WrestleMania 27* they teamed with Santino Marella and Kofi Kingston for a convincing victory over the Corre. On April 22, 2011 the massive pairing added the WWE Tag Team Championships to their résumé.

BILL DeMOTT

HT: 6'2"   **WT:** 280 lbs.   **FROM:** Trenton, New Jersey
SIGNATURE MOVE: No Laughing Matter

For years, fans only knew Bill DeMott as the fun-but-dangerous Hugh Morrus. In 2002, the former United States Champion's career took a serious turn when he began training the Superstars of tomorrow on *Tough Enough*. Under his given name, DeMott used fear as his chief teaching technique. His most noteworthy pupils were Matt Cappotelli and John Morrison.

DeMott's in-ring success paled in comparison to the heights he reached as Hugh Morrus. After tearing through many of *SmackDown*'s Superstars, as well as Rikishi, in early 2003, he found himself most often appearing on *Velocity*. After several months, he transitioned from the ring to the announce booth, calling *Velocity* action alongside *Tough Enough* alum Josh Mathews. When *Tough Enough 4* completed production, DeMott left WWE programming to be a full-time trainer in WWE's developmental system. After a four-year hiatus, DeMott returned in 2011 as the head trainer for the revival of *Tough Enough*. Hand-picked by WWE Hall of Famer Stone Cold Steve Austin, the WWE hopefuls quickly learned that training under Demott was no laughing matter.

BILL MILLER

HT: 6'6"   **WT:** 290 lbs.   **FROM:** Fremont, Ohio
SIGNATURE MOVE: Backbreaker

TITLE HISTORY

UNITED STATES TAG TEAM CHAMPION	*Partnered with Dan Miller to defeat Gorilla Monsoon & Cowboy Bill Watts on August 7, 1965*

Before entering the world of sports-entertainment in 1952, this Ohio State Buckeyes alumnus won two Big Ten conference amateur titles. He was also was a letterman in track and football and a member of the 1950 Rose Bowl team. A licensed veterinarian and member of the United States Navy, Dr. Bill Miller started his rounds in the AWA and NWA promotions.

In 1964 the doctor debuted in the World Wide Wrestling Federation and tested his skills against the world's fiercest ring animals, monsters and giants. Often seen in singles and tag team action, he won the U.S. Tag Team Championship, along with his brother Dan, in August, 1965 when they beat the team of Cowboy Bill Watts & Gorilla Monsoon. Miller left the company in 1976 and retired from competition shortly thereafter. In 1997 the Navy veteran passed away. That same year he was inducted into the Hall of Fame of his beloved alma-mater, Ohio State.

BILL WATTS

HT: 6'3"   **WT:** 290 lbs.   **FROM:** Oklahoma
SIGNATURE MOVE: Oklahoma Stampede

TITLE HISTORY

UNITED STATES TAG TEAM CHAMPION	*Partnered with Gorilla Monsoon to defeat Gene Kiniski & Waldo Von Erich on April 8, 1965*

"Cowboy" Bill Watts is one of the few sports-entertainment personalities that can confidently say he was a winner both in the ring and behind the scenes. After debuting in 1963, Watts briefly travelled the territories before settling into a successful WWE pairing with Gorilla Monsoon. In April 1965, the oversized duo defeated Gene Kiniski & Waldo Von Erich for the WWE United States Tag Team Championship. They held the titles for four months before falling to Dan Miller & Dr. Bill Miller. Watts later challenged Bruno Sammartino for the WWE Championship on several occasions. Each time, Sammartino miraculously managed to walk away victorious.

When it came time to hang up the boots, Watts embarked on an impressive career as a promoter. As the leading force behind Mid South Wrestling, the "Cowboy" helped launch the careers of many Hall of Famers, including Junkyard Dog and Ted DiBiase. He later went on to become a WCW executive in the early 1990s. Watts' excellence was recognized in 2009 when he was inducted into the WWE Hall of Fame.

B

2010-

2000-09

1990-99

1980-89

1970-79

1960-69

BILLY & CHUCK

MEMBERS: Billy Gunn, Chuck Palumbo
COMBINED WT: 535 lbs.

With their matching headbands, boy-band entrance theme and touchy-feely affection for each other, the relationship between Billy & Chuck often apppeared to go

TITLE HISTORY

WORLD TAG TEAM CHAMPIONS (2 TIMES)	Defeated Tazz & Spike Dudley on February 21, 2002 Defeated Rico & Rikishi on June 6, 2002

beyond simple tag team partners. With their personal stylist, Rico, in their corner, the duo became two-time World Tag Team Champions.

In September 2002, Chuck presented Billy with a gorgeous ring and asked Billy to be his partner for life. Billy excitedly agreed and the news began to dominate national news. It wasn't long before Billy & Chuck were featured on such major outlets as *The Today Show* and *The New York Times*.

By the time the commitment ceremony rolled around, Billy developed a case of cold feet. Just moments before the actual ceremony took place, the duo put a halt to it and claimed their entire union was nothing but a publicity stunt. Following the shocking revelation, Billy & Chuck soon went their separate ways. While both have enjoyed some measure of success, neither has been able to recreate the same notoriety they enjoyed as the controversial Billy & Chuck.

BILLY GUNN

HT: 6'3"   **WT:** 260 lbs.   **FROM:** Austin, Texas
SIGNATURE MOVE: The Fame-asser

TITLE HISTORY

HARDCORE CHAMPION	2 Times
INTERCONTINENTAL CHAMPION	Defeated Eddie Guerrero on November 23, 2000
WORLD TAG TEAM CHAMPION (10 TIMES)	Partnered with Bart Gunn to defeat 1-2-3 Kid & Bob Holly on January 23, 1995 Partnered with Bart Gunn to defeat Owen Hart & Yokozuna on September 25, 1995 Partnered with Bart Gunn to defeat The Godwinns on May 26, 1996 Partnered with Road Dogg to defeat the Legion of Doom on November 24, 1997 Partnered with Road Dogg to defeat Cactus Jack & Chainsaw Charlie on March 30, 1998 Partnered with Road Dogg to defeat Mankind on August 30, 1998 Partnered with Road Dogg to defeat Mankind & The Rock on September 23, 1999 Partnered with Road Dogg to defeat Mankind & Al Snow on November 8, 1999 Partnered with Chuck Palumbo to defeat Tazz & Spike Dudley on February 21, 2002 Partnered with Chuck Palumbo to defeat Rico & Rikishi on June 6, 2002

World Wrestling Entertainment first saw Billy Gunn in 1993 as part of the Smokin' Gunns. Together with his brother Bart, the team held the World Tag Team Championship three times. In 1997, he traded in his six-shooter for a six string and competed in singles matches. Managed by the Honky Tonk Man, Gunn adopted the identity of a 1950s rocker known as Rockabilly. It was during this period of his career that Gunn first came in contact with Jesse James. While in the midst of a brief rivalry, they decided they were better off forming a tag team, and the WWE Universe was introduced to the New Age Outlaws.

After five World Tag Team Championship reigns and time spent as part of D-Generation X, Billy focused on his singles career. Known as "Mr. Ass," he became a Hardcore Champion for the first time in 1999. Three months later, he defeated X-Pac to become King of the Ring. On November 23, 2000, Gunn defeated Eddie Guerrero for the Intercontinental Championship.

After briefly reforming the New Age Outlaws and rejoining DX, Billy found a new partner in Chuck Palumbo. Billy & Chuck became one of the most controversial teams in sports-entertainment history, as evidenced by their commitment ceremony, but also tasted success once again as WWE Tag Team Champions. In 2003 Billy returned to the singles ranks and drove female fans wild as the ever-popular "Mr. Ass." In November 2004, Gunn's tenure with WWE came to an end.

BILLY JACK HAYNES

HT: 6'3"   **WT:** 246 lbs.   **FROM:** Portland, Oregon
SIGNATURE MOVE: Full Nelson

The pride of Portland, Billy Jack Haynes began his in-ring career in 1982. Over the next few years, he developed a fan following in the Portland, Florida, Mid-Atlantic, and World Class territories. Haynes possessed immense power and an impressive array of mat wrestling moves.

Haynes debuted in WWE in 1986 and was an immediate hit with audiences around the country. His impressive start made him a contender for the Intercontinental Championship, and his matches with Randy "Macho Man" Savage got the attention of the WWE Championship Committee. He is remembered for a violent confrontation with Hercules in a Battle of the Full Nelson Match at *WrestleMania III*.

In 1988, he teamed with fellow Oregonian Ken Patera and battled teams such as Demolition and the Heenan Family. Billy Jack Haynes will be remembered as a master of the Full Nelson and one of WWE's greatest heroes of the 1980s.

BILLY KIDMAN

HT: 5'10" WT: 195 lbs. FROM: Allentown, Pennsylvania
SIGNATURE MOVE: Shooting Star Press

If you passed Billy Kidman in the street, you might not recognize him as a skilled sports-entertainer. He's not overly large, doesn't really wear flashy clothes and isn't very boisterous.

TITLE HISTORY

CRUISIERWEIGHT CHAMPION (4 TIMES)	Defeated Shane Helms on July 5, 2001 Defeated X-Pac on October 11, 2001 Defeated Tajiri on April 4, 2002 Defeated Jamie Noble on November 17, 2002
WWE TAG TEAM CHAMPION	Partnered with Paul London to defeat The Dudley Boys on July 8, 2004

In the ring, however, his talents are undeniable. Kidman came to WWE following the promotion's acquisition of WCW in 2001. He made a strong first impression, upending Gregory Helms to claim the Cruiserweight Championship in his debut match. The win served as a sign of things to come for Kidman, who went on to capture the title three more times while in WWE.

In July 2004, Kidman teamed with Paul London to defeat The Dudley Boys for the WWE Tag Team Championship. It appeared as though things couldn't be going any better for the high-flying Superstar. However, when his signature Shooting Star Press nearly ended the career of Chavo Guerrero, feelings of extreme guilt began to set in on Kidman. It wasn't long before he couldn't bring himself to execute his most powerful weapon. A dejected Kidman even walked away from a September 2004 title defense, leaving his partner to fend for himself.

Kidman later blamed the fans for forcing him to become a more vicious in-ring competitor. The accusations immediately turned fans against the longtime favorite. The following year, Kidman was gone from WWE. This time away from sports-entertainment served him well and in 2006, he returned as a trainer in WWE's development territory, FCW. While there he trained current Superstars Sheamus, Kofi Kingston, and Justin Gabriel and became a student of television production. Today, Billy Kidman is behind the scenes as a producer for *RAW* and *SmackDown*.

BILLY THE KID

Named after the infamous American outlaw, Billy the Kid was one of the South's most renowned midget wrestlers of the 1970s. Clad in a 10-gallon hat and scruffy beard, his cowboy persona helped solidify his status as one of the division's premier attractions.

For much of 1972, Billy the Kid formed a popular tag team with Wee Wee Wilson. In December, they teamed with Darling Dagmar to turn back Little Buiser, Diamond Lil & Johnny Reb in a memorable six-man tag team match. The bout proved to be one of the last times Billy the Kid and Wee Wee Wilson worked as a team, as they soon found themselves engaged in a bitter rivalry.

BILLY WHITE WOLF

HT: 6'0" WT: 245 lbs. FROM: Oklahoma SIGNATURE MOVE: The Indian Deathlock

TITLE HISTORY

WORLD TAG TEAM CHAMPION	Partnered with Chief Jay Strongbow to win a three tag-team tournament on December 7, 1976

Chief Billy White Wolf debuted in the World Wide Wrestling Federation in the late 1960s. This master of the Indian Death Match feuded with the promotion's most dangerous rule-breakers including future WWE Hall of Famer Baron Mikel Scicluna, Bruiser Brody, The Executioners, Stan Hansen and Crusher Blackwell. His great combination of agility, classic mat wrestling, and spirit made him a favorite with fans all over the world.

White Wolf's virtuous path brought him together with another ring great, future WWE Hall of Famer and fellow native Oklahoman, Chief Jay Strongbow. On December 7, 1976 White Wolf and Strongbow defeated The Executioners, and Nikolai Volkoff and Tor Kamata in a three team tournament for the then vacant World Tag Team Championships. The Native Americans held the ultimate tag team prize for eight months until White Wolf suffered a career-ending injury. While his career ended prematurely, Chief Billy White Wolf will always be remembered as a hero to fans all over the world and a pioneer in the sport.

BLACK BART

HT: 6'4" WT: 350 lbs. FROM: Pampa, Texas
SIGNATURE MOVE: Flying Leg Drop

A tough-as-nails Texan, Black Bart left a lasting impression on his opposition literally, as it wasn't uncommon to see him mark his opponents using his trademark "BB" branding iron. Prior to his brief WWE stint in 1989, Black Bart gained notoriety competing in the Southern territories of the United States with his tag team partner, Ron Bass. The duo carried their successful union from state to state before ultimately going their separate ways in 1985.

As a singles competitor, perhaps Black Bart's biggest victory came in September 1986 when he defeated Chris Adams for the World Class Championship Wrestling title. Unfortunately for Bart, however, he lost the title one month later to Kevin Von Erich.

B

2010-
2000-09
1990-99
1980-89
1970-79
1960-69

BLACK TIGER 🇬🇧

HT: 5'8"   WT: 220 lbs.   FROM: England

TITLE HISTORY

JUNIOR HEAVYWEIGHT CHAMPION	*Defeated Gran Hamada on May 6, 1982*

As the name would suggest, Black Tiger concealed his identity by wearing a dark tiger mask to the ring. Once there, however, his in-ring skills were easily recognizable. Despite being a native of Manchester, England, Black Tiger competed mainly in Japan where he was lauded for his hard-hitting aerial style of offense. While competing in front of a capacity crowd in Fukuoka, Japan, the high-flyer defeated Gran Hamada for the now-defunct WWE Junior Heavyweight Championship. This was Black Tiger's first-and-only taste of championship glory in WWE.

Twenty days after topping Hamada in a thrilling contest, Black Tiger lost the Junior Heavyweight Championship to his chief rival, Tiger Mask. Black Tiger's ties to the growing United States promotion began to fade following the heartbreaking loss. For the remainder of the decade, the mysterious masked Superstar continued to compete in the "Land of the Rising Sun," depriving WWE fans in the States of his jaw-dropping skills.

BLACKJACK MULLIGAN 🇺🇸

HT: 6'9"   WT: 300 lbs.
FROM: Eagle Pass, Texas   SIGNATURE MOVE: The Claw

TITLE HISTORY

WORLD TAG TEAM CHAMPION	*Partnered with Blackjack Lanza to defeat Dominic DeNucci & Pat Barrett on August 26, 1975*

Sports-entertainment was introduced to one of its fiercest competitors in the early 1970s. A former Marine and NFL player, Blackjack Mulligan was a merciless force throughout the United States and after graduating from Verne Gagne's wrestling school, he formed a team with Blackjack Lanza. With their black handle-bar mustaches, black ring attire and black hearts, The Blackjacks were reminiscent of outlaws from the ol' Wild West and had the ring mentality of shoot first, ask questions later. In 1975, they arrived in WWE with Capt. Lou

Albano as their manager. On August 26th, they defeated Dominic DeNucci & Pat Barrett for the World Tag Team Championship. During Mulligan's time in WWE, he fought the likes of Bruno Sammartino, Pedro Morales, Haystacks Calhoun and Andre The Giant. That November, he outlasted 19 other competitors and won a $10,000 Battle Royal.

After a brief hiatus, Blackjack returned to WWE in 1983 and soon became a fan favorite. Mulligan's beat 'em and leave 'em style was so popular with WWE audiences that he premiered his own talk show segment *Blackjack's Barbeque* in 1985. Mulligan continued his winning ways until he left the company in 1987. His legacy lived on through his sons Barry and Kendall Windham.

THE BLACKJACKS 🇺🇸

MEMBERS:
Blackjack Mulligan,
Blackjack Lanza
COMBINED WT: 585 lbs.

Hall of Fame 2006

TITLE HISTORY

WORLD TAG TEAM CHAMPIONS	*Defeated Dominic DeNucci & Pat Barrett on August 26, 1975*

A couple of rough and tumble Texans, Blackjack Mulligan & Blackjack Lanza broke nearly every rule in the book on their way to the WWE Hall of Fame.

The Blackjacks first began teaming with each other in the early 1970s. Clad in their signature cowboy hats, leather vests, and black gloves, Mulligan & Lanza captured tag team championships in the World Wrestling Association and National Wrestling Alliance before bringing their game to WWE in the mid-1970s.

The Blackjacks enjoyed a nearly three-month World Tag Team Championship reign in 1975. After losing the titles in November, Mulligan & Lanza failed to reach the same heights, but their amazing legacy would be recreated two decades later.

In 1996, Barry Windham, the son of Blackjack Mulligan, teamed with Blackjack Lanza's nephew, Justin "Hawk" Bradshaw, to form The New Blackjacks. In appearance, the tag team looked identical to the original tandem. Unfortunately, that's where the similarities stopped. After failing to properly represent the legend of the original Blackjacks, Windham & Bradshaw went their separate ways.

In 2006, Blackjack Mulligan & Blackjack Lanza were given the ultimate honor when their efforts in the tag team ranks landed them in the WWE Hall of Fame.

BLU BROTHERS 🇺🇸

MEMBERS: Jacob, Eli   COMBINED WT: 640 lbs.

Identical twins from the mountains of Appalachia, Jacob & Eli Blu were lead to WWE by their Uncle Zebekiah. Their long, flowing hair and bushy beards certainly provided for an unorthodox appearance; but when the bell rang, the Blu Brothers proved to possess a traditional powerhouses approach to tag team wrestling.

Making their WWE debut in January 1995, Jacob & Eli used their identical appearances to confuse opponents, officials and onlookers. Their dastardly tricks, coupled with their immense power, guided them to many victories. After three months of impressing WWE officials, Jacob & Eli earned a spot on the *WrestleMania XI* card. The twin brothers headed into the event with a great deal of momentum, but were unable to stop The Allied Powers, Lex Luger & British Bulldog.

The Blu Brothers' WWE careers cooled after their *WrestleMania* loss. After failing to defeat The Smoking Gunns at *SummerSlam 1995*, Jacob & Eli made a quiet exit from WWE.

BLUE MEANIE 🇺🇸

HT: 6'1"   WT: 323 lbs.
FROM: Atlantic City, New Jersey
SIGNATURE MOVE: Meaniesault

Following a comedic ECW career, Blue Meanie made his WWE debut in late 1998. Originally a member of Al Snow's JOB Squad, the blue-haired Superstar proved to be equally entertaining inside WWE rings.

In early 1999, Meanie resumed the hilarious impersonations that made him so popular in ECW. As Bluedust, he battled Goldust at *St. Valentine's Day Massacre*. Meanie failed in his quest to defeat the original 'Dust, but managed to entertain thousands along the way.

After a five-year absence from WWE, Blue Meanie returned at *One Night Stand* in June 2005 with the rest of the Blue World Order. After a few more appearances, including a win over JBL on *SmackDown*, the Blue Meanie left WWE.

BOB BACKLUND

HT: 6'1" **WT:** 234 lbs.
FROM: Princeton, Minnesota
SIGNATURE MOVE: Crossface Chickenwing

" THAT'S MISTER BACKLUND! "

TITLE HISTORY

WORLD TAG TEAM CHAMPION	*Partnered with Pedro Morales to defeat the Wild Samoans on August 9, 1980*
WWE CHAMPION **(2 TIMES)**	*Defeated "Superstar" Billy Graham on February 20, 1978* *Defeated Bret "Hit Man" Hart on November 23, 1994*

It was always easy to cheer for Bob Backlund during the late 1970s and early 1980s. His boy-next-door looks made him impossible to dislike, while his superior athleticism solidified his lofty in-ring status. Backlund's second stint with WWE, however, was a completely different story. With age, he became more maniacal. By the mid-1990s, he was borderline insane, which makes the Bob Backlund story even more fascinating.

Backlund first made a name for himself within wrestling circles while competing at North Dakota State University, where he captured the NCAA Division II heavyweight wrestling championship. Shortly after college, the successful amateur wrestler took his game to the pro ranks, debuting for his home state's American Wrestling Association (AWA) in 1974. For the next several years, Backlund bounced between various wrestling regions.

The WWE Comes Calling

In the spring of 1977, Backlund received the opportunity of a lifetime when Vincent J. McMahon called to offer him a shot with WWE. He quickly accepted the opportunity, packed his bags and left his small-town life in Minnesota for the bright lights of New York City and WWE. With Arnold Skaaland as his manager, Backlund became an instant hit with WWE fans. His All-American persona gave audiences somebody they could look up to; and within months of his arrival, he was catapulted to the top of the card.

After several unsuccessful attempts to capture the WWE Championship, Backlund finally dethroned "Superstar" Billy Graham in February 1978 despite the champion's leg being on the ropes during the count. His reign will forever go down in history as one of the greatest of all time, lasting nearly six years (second only to Bruno Sammartino's nearly eight-year reign).

In search of more gold, Backlund teamed with Pedro Morales to defeat the Wild Samoans for the World Tag Team Championship at Shea Stadium in August 1980. Unfortunately for Backlund, he was forced to vacate the title due to a WWE rule at the time that prohibited a Superstar from holding more than one championship at any given time.

Backlund's epic WWE Championship reign came to a controversial end in December 1983. While defending against The Iron Sheik, Backlund found himself locked in the challenger's dreaded Camel Clutch. Refusing to submit, he suffered in the submission move for an extended period of time. Finally, in an attempt to prevent permanent damage, manager Arnold Skaaland threw in the towel for Backlund. The popular former champion later suggested that his reign should never have ceased, due to the fact that he didn't give up. The protest proved ineffective and Backlund quickly left WWE soon after.

A New Era, and a New Attitude

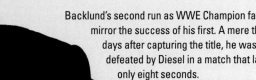

Nearly one decade after vanishing from the sports-entertainment world, Mr. Backlund made a shocking return to WWE in 1992. In his early 40s at the time, WWE fans didn't expect much success from the aging Superstar. They were wrong.

The 1990s version of Bob Backlund proved to be much different from the boy-next-door champion everybody loved in the 1970s and 1980s. This Bob Backlund was a rage-filled, middle-aged maniac who quickly drew the ire of fans with his endless rants and overly verbose vocabulary. Inside the ring, however, he was just as dangerous as ever.

In November 1994, the aging Backlund defied the odds when he defeated Bret Hart for the WWE Championship at *Survivor Series*. Ironically, his second reign began the same way his first one ended when Hart's mother threw in the towel, signifying the end of her son's reign.

Backlund's second run as WWE Champion failed to mirror the success of his first. A mere three days after capturing the title, he was defeated by Diesel in a match that lasted only eight seconds.

The WWE record books will forever recognize Backlund's second reign as one of the shortest of all time. Despite the loss to Diesel, however, his brief time atop WWE capped off one of the most successful returns in sports-entertainment history. It also put a fitting exclamation point on a career that will be remembered as one of the greatest of all time.

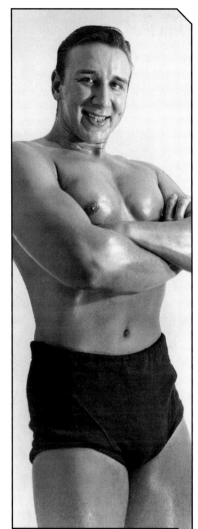

BOB ORTON SR.

HT: 6'2" **WT:** 235 lbs.
FROM: Kansas City, Kansas

Today's sports-entertainment fans recognize Randy Orton as one of the era's most elite Superstars; and they recall the career of Randy's father, WWE Hall of Famer "Cowboy" Bob Orton, with great respect and admiration. But before these two Ortons ruled WWE rings, there was the original Orton: Bob Orton, Sr.

As the patriarch of the legendary Orton family, Bob, Sr. competed mainly in the Florida and Central States territories, where he captured more than fifteen regional NWA titles, including the NWA Florida Tag Team Championship with his son, Bob, Jr.

Orton briefly competed in WWE, where he was billed as Rocky Fitzpatrick. Under the new name, Orton formed a formidable tag team with WWE Hall of Famer Buddy Rogers.

After nearly fifty years in the sports-entertainment industry, "The Big O" finally hung up his boots at the turn of the century, leaving behind an amazing legacy and a long line of Orton family success.

BOBBY DAVIS

When a serious neck injury ended his dreams of becoming a professional wrestler, Bobby Davis didn't walk away from the ring completely. Instead, the persistent youngster shifted his focus from competing in the ring to managing the ring's competitors.

As a manager, the charismatic Davis compiled an impressive stable that included such top names as Johnny Valentine, Dr. Bill Miller, the Graham brothers, Johnny Barend and Magnificent Maurice. But perhaps his most notable client was the first-ever WWE Champion, "Nature Boy" Buddy Rogers.

Together, the arrogant pairing of Rogers and Davis verbally tore down the champ's opposition on a routine basis. Of course, if Rogers ever found himself in trouble at any point during the match, Davis was not above employing some underhanded tactics to ensure his client picked up the win.

BOBBY DUNCUM

HT: 6'7" **WT:** 285 lbs. **FROM:** Austin, Texas
SIGNATURE MOVE: The Sleeperhold

"Cowboy" Bobby Duncum was drafted by the St. Louis Cardinals of the NFL and made his ring debut in 1971. Running into Duncum was like running into a brick wall. The only thing longer than his mean streak was his list of fallen opponents. After victories, Duncum stayed in the ring and attacked his already battered foe adding insult to injury. The Cowboy did things his way, on his terms and if someone didn't like it, they'd get a fist straight to the jaw.

In 1974, Bobby Duncum arrived in WWE and immediately made his presence known when he won a 20-man over-the-top-rope battle royal. He had a series of bloodbaths with Bruno Sammartino, including a Texas Death Match at the Boston Garden with Gorilla Monsoon as special guest referee. After leaving the company in 1975, Duncum won several regional territories titles in the NWA.

In 1979, the Cowboy returned to WWE and was led to the ring by the Grand Wizard, focusing on eliminating then-WWE Champion Bob Backlund. In 1982 the Cowboy from Austin left WWE for good.

"A FRIEND IN NEED IS A PEST."

Bobby Heenan is arguably one of the most gifted minds in the history of sports-entertainment. Heenan was a revolutionary manager to the greatest legends the industry has ever seen. In addition, he was a fearless broadcast journalist who reported the stories that fit his personal agenda. His direction was simple, "Listen to me, you go straight to the top. Don't, you're never heard from again." Strong words from a Weasel!

The first time Bobby Heenan walked into the Indianapolis Coliseum for a wrestling event, he knew what he wanted to do with the rest of his life. Forced to leave school in the seventh grade to care for his family, Bobby Heenan took a job in the profession he loved, selling programs. He made his pro debut in 1965 and in the early 1970s, he appeared as "Pretty Boy" Heenan. When he managed the duo of "Crippler" Ray Stevens and Nick Bockwinkel, he announced that he should be refered to as " The Brain."

BOBBY "THE BRAIN" HEENAN

HT: 5'10" **WT:** 242 lbs. **FROM:** Beverly Hills, California

While wreaking havoc through Minneapolis, Heenan accumulated a collection of outlaws known as "The Heenan Family." The founding members consisted of multiple AWA Champion Bockwinkel, Stevens, Bobby Duncum, Sr., Dick Warren, and Blackjack Lanza. In 1984, the manager extraordinaire debuted in WWE and immediately began his quest to rid sports-entertainment of its most beloved heroes. Heenan's first client was Big John Studd. The massive giant was the cornerstone of Heenan's Family and set his sights on Andre the Giant. As Heenan expanded his strategic assembly of WWE's most feared figures, Superstars were often victim to baseless attacks by the likes of Studd, King Kong Bundy, Ken Patera, and "Mr. Wonderful" Paul Orndorff. During this time, "The Brain" unflaggingly strategized to destroy Hulkamania and employed any tactics in hopes of dethroning the then-World Champion. Heenan's propensity to hit-and-run during matches and interviews earned him the infamous alias "Weasel," which was chanted wherever he went.

Due to his weasel-like ways, the Heenan Family had a constantly changing roster through the decade and he often paid the piper for his dastardly ways. "The Brain's" conniving ways bore their sweetest fruit when he persuaded Andre the Giant to turn his back on best friend Hulk Hogan for a WWE Championship match at

WrestleMania III. Despite his inability to taste championship gold at the Pontiac Silverdome, Heenan continued to recruit talent from all over the world. The year 1989 proved to be an exemplary one for Heenan as he saw his first title in WWE at *WrestleMania V* when "Ravishing" Rick Rude defeated Ultimate Warrior for the Intercontinental title. Success continued when Heenan entered the talk show arena with *The Bobby Heenan Show*. He managed two teams to the World Tag Team Championship in 1989, as the Brain Busters defeated Demolition in July, and The Colossal Connection defeated Demolition in December.

The 1990s saw Heenan become the "Perfect" manager when he led Mr. Perfect to the Intercontinental Championship. Heenan was also instrumental in bringing in multiple time NWA and WCW Champion "Nature Boy" Ric Flair to the company and substantiated Flair's claim that he was the "real" World Champion. Arguably the greatest free-agent acquisition in sports-entertainment history, Flair won the WWE Championship twice with Heenan as a key advisor. As *Monday Night Raw* burst on to cable television, Heenan did anything he could to get on the air. On December 6, 1993, Heenan was given his WWE exit when then-President Gorilla Monsoon tossed him and his belongs out into the cold for good.

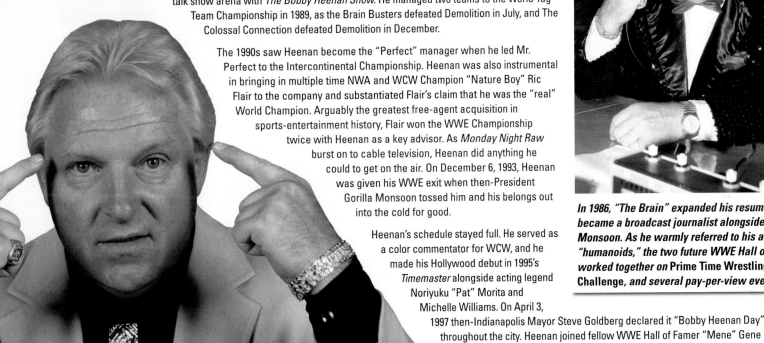

In 1986, "The Brain" expanded his resume and became a broadcast journalist alongside Gorilla Monsoon. As he warmly referred to his audience as "humanoids," the two future WWE Hall of Famers worked together on Prime Time Wrestling, Wrestling Challenge, *and several pay-per-view events.*

Heenan's schedule stayed full. He served as a color commentator for WCW, and he made his Hollywood debut in 1995's *Timemaster* alongside acting legend Noriyuku "Pat" Morita and Michelle Williams. On April 3, 1997 then-Indianapolis Mayor Steve Goldberg declared it "Bobby Heenan Day" throughout the city. Heenan joined fellow WWE Hall of Famer "Mene" Gene Okerlund to call the action at *Wrestlemania X-7's* Gimmick Battle Royal. On March 13, 2004, Bobby Heenan's unparalleled career was honored when he was inducted into the WWE Hall of Fame the night before *WrestleMania XX*.

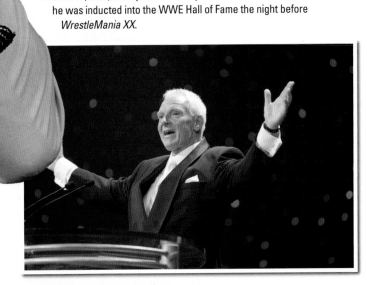

BOBBY LASHLEY

HT: 6'3" **WT:** 273 lbs. **FROM:** Colorado Springs, Colorado
SIGNATURE MOVE: The Dominator

A product of the United States Army, Bobby Lashley is a three-time National Amateur Wrestling Champion, a four-time All-American, a two-time Armed Forces Champion and a Silver Medalist in the 2002 Military World Championships. In September 2005, Bobby debuted on *SmackDown*. Lashley's power and amateur background served him well as he met opponents like Big Vito, Simon Dean, William Regal and Val Venis. Bobby appeared at *WrestleMania 22* in a Money In the Bank Ladder Match. In 2006, he became ECW Champion after surviving the Extreme Elimination Chamber at *December to Dismember*. Bobby reached the pinnacle of his career at *WrestleMania 23* when he was Donald Trump's representative in "The Battle of The Billionaires" and fans saw Mr. McMahon get his head shaved when Bobby Lashley defeated Umaga. When he lost the ECW Championship under questionable circumstances, he regained it at *One Night Stand* in a Street Fight.

As part of WWEs 2007 draft, Bobby competed on *RAW* before he suffered a severe shoulder injury. In early 2008, Lashley left WWE. After briefly appearances in Mexico, he announced he was training for a career in mixed martial arts. In 2011, Lashley debuted in WWE Hall of Famer Antonio Inoki's Inoki Genome Federation in Japan.

TITLE HISTORY

ECW CHAMPION (2 TIMES)	Defeated Big Show on December 3, 2006
	Defeated Mr. McMahon on June 3, 2007
UNITED STATES CHAMPION	Defeated JBL on May 26, 2006

BOBO BRAZIL

HT: 6'6" **WT:** 270 lbs.
FROM: Benton Harbor, Michigan
SIGNATURE MOVE: Coco Butt

The legend of Bobo Brazil goes well beyond wins and losses. As a black man competing during a turbulent time in America, Brazil showed amazing grace while overcoming racial stereotypes and barriers. Along the way, he became recognized as sports-entertainment's Jackie Robinson and one of the industry's most influential figures.

TITLE HISTORY

U.S.A. HEAVYWEIGHT CHAMPION (7 TIMES)	Named as first U.S.A. Heavyweight Champion on April 6, 1963
	Defeated Johnny Barend on July 9, 1963
	Defeated Johnny Barend on September 11, 1963
	Defeated Ray Stevens on August 24, 1967
	Defeated The Sheik on November 25, 1968
	Defeated The Sheik on February 10, 1969
	Named U.S.A Heavyweight Champion on February 15, 1971

Originally named Boo Boo Brazil, the Michigan native made his professional debut in 1951 and competed in the Detroit area. It wasn't until a printing error billed him Bobo that fans began to recognize Brazil under his now-famous name.

It was common practice during this time for African-American competitors to be booked against each other. With that, he spent much of his career battling the likes of Ernie Ladd and Thunderbolt Patterson. However, Brazil's in-ring arsenal, highlighted by the "Coco Butt" head butt, eventually proved to be too valuable for promoters to limit. As a result, he finally battled such legendary opponents as Killer Kowalski and Freddie Blassie. Brazil's fans eventually demanded to see more and more of their hero. His popularity finally forced many promoters to book him in dream matches against several other popular Superstars of the time, such as Andre the Giant and Bruno Sammartino.

After leaving WWE in the late 1960s, Brazil went on to compete throughout Los Angeles, Detroit, and Japan among other locales. During this time, he engaged in a bloody rivalry with The Sheik that saw Brazil capture a version of the United States Championship (not the current WWE title). When Brazil returned to WWE in 1976, the promotion actually announced him as the U.S. Champion, despite the fact that it was not a WWE-recognized title. The act was an enormous sign of respect for the sports-entertainment pioneer.

Bobo Brazil's remarkable career was honored with induction into the WWE Hall of Fame in 1994. The ceremony recognized his amazing in-ring conquests, as well as his tireless civil rights efforts that helped paved the way for those who followed.

THE BODYDONNAS

MEMBERS: Skip, Zip
COMBINED WT: 455 lbs.

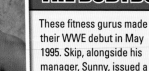

These fitness gurus made their WWE debut in May 1995. Skip, alongside his manager, Sunny, issued a challenge to everyone to get off their butts and get into shape. Skip performed jumping jacks and pushups during his contests. While he started in singles action, he was soon joined by his fraternal twin brother, Zip. The Bodydonnas trio was complete and ready to whip WWE into shape.

TITLE HISTORY

| WORLD TAG TEAM CHAMPIONS | Defeated the Godwinns on March 31, 1996 |

While Sunny made hearts race outside the ring, the Bodydonnas did their damage inside of it. With some help from their manager, Skip & Zip reached the pinnacle when they won a World Tag Team Championship Tournament at *WrestleMania XII*. Unfortunately for the exercise fiends, they lost the titles to the Godwinns, and Sunny followed the gold. The Bodydonnas tried to fill the empty position with a new manager, Kloudy, but this association was short-lived. The fitness fanatics disbanded in 1996 and went their separate ways. The Bodydonnas will be remembered for their fitness vignettes as much as their seamless teamwork in the ring. The message from their manager summed it up best, "You've seen the rest, now see the best."

BOLO MONGOL

HT: 6'3" **WT:** 291 lbs.
FROM: Mongolia

Geto & Bepo Mongol terrorized the tag team ranks during the late 1960s and early 1970s. Collectively known as The Mongols, their unorthodox style lead them to countless victories, including a reign as WWE's International Tag Team Champions. After more than one year with the titles, The Mongols lost the gold to Bruno Sammartino & Dominic DeNucci in June 1971.

The loss failed to set The Mongols back much, as they quickly worked their way back into the win column, but then a freak injury sidelined Bepo. Many thought the injury meant the end of The Mongols, but Geto quickly replaced his partner with the equally unorthodox Bolo Mongol.

Bolo had the signature Mongol look, complete with horns of hair on an otherwise bald head. Together, Bolo & Geto briefly kept the legend of The Mongols alive in the Pittsburgh territory, as well as Japan. Shortly after the new Mongols debuted, Bolo broke away from Geto to form his own identity.

THE BOLSHEVIKS

MEMBERS: Nikolai Volkoff, Boris Zhukov
COMBINED WT: 604 lbs.

These two powerful Superstars joined forces in the name of Mother Russia in the spring of 1988. These men were determined to spark a revolution, with WWE as their battleground. To the disgust of fans and opponents all over the globe, the two came to the ring waiving the Soviet flag and sang the Russian National Anthem before each match.

Nikolai Volkoff & Boris Zhukov specialized in crushing double-team moves and underhanded tactics in their matches. Heading into *SummerSlam 1988,* the Russians were set for a collision with the Powers of Pain. After a string of strong performances, Volkoff & Zhukov earned a match against the Hart Foundation at *WrestleMania VI.* Unfortunately for the Soviets, they were defeated in 19 seconds in front of a capacity SkyDome crowd.

Soon after the loss, the bond that held The Bolsheviks together was irrevocably broken. Volkoff & Zhukov battled across the United States and for the first time in his career, Nikolai Volkoff was a fan favorite. Boris Zhukov remained one of the most hated villains until his departure from WWE in 1991.

BOOGEYMAN

HT: 6'2" **WT:** 260 lbs.
FROM: The Bottomless Pit
SIGNATURE MOVE: Boogeyslam

WWE Superstars are some of the toughest men to walk the planet, but when the lights go out, they all fear the Boogeyman. Hailing from The Bottomless Pit, Boogeyman first started spooking WWE Superstars in October 2005. Despite his unbelievably creepy appearance, he managed to be a tough man to find. Hiding in various backstage locales, Boogeyman would only pop out to frighten fellow Superstars with a disturbing rendition of a classic nursery rhyme.

Boogeyman's in-ring debut came against Simon Dean on a December 2005 edition of *SmackDown.* After pummeling Dean within moments of the opening bell, Boogeyman went on to spook nearly the entire *SmackDown* roster, including former WWE Champion John "Bradshaw" Layfield. At the 2006 *Royal Rumble,* Boogeyman made quick work of JBL, finishing him off with his patented Pump-Handle Slam. After the match, Boogeyman celebrated his first pay-per-view victory with a mouthful of live worms.

After turning back one former World Champion, Boogeyman focused his sinister sights on yet another past titleholder. On the grand stage of *WrestleMania 22,* he defeated the mighty King Booker, but not before planting a worm-filled kiss on Queen Sharmell. Boogeyman's destructive athleticism in the ring, coupled with his unparalleled ability to get inside a man's head, has undoubtedly caused a few WWE Superstars to sleep with the lights on.

1960-69
1970-79
1980-89
1990-99
2000-09
2010-

WWE STUDIOS

Professional wrestling had a unique relationship with Hollywood for decades thanks in large part to the on-screen efforts of Hulk Hogan, Andre the Giant, Jesse "The Body" Ventura, and "Rowdy" Roddy Piper. Today, entertainers whose careers began between the ropes, such as The Rock, Stone Cold Steve Austin, and John Cena, continue to act in a variety of roles.

In 2002, WWE expanded its business focus when it opened WWE Films. In July 2008, the division was renamed WWE Studios but its focus remained the same – producing films, which featured Superstars on the WWE roster. WWE Studios now creates a diverse mix of movies in a variety of genres that cast WWE Superstars in supporting roles alongside well-known actors and actresses

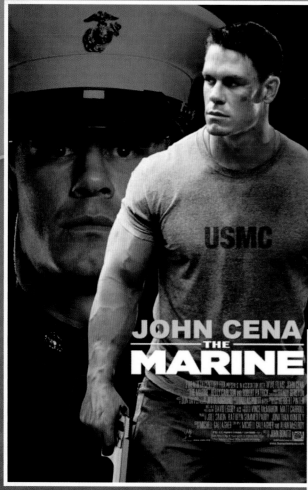

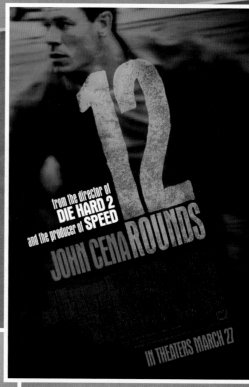

NO HOLDS BARRED *(1989)*

THE MARINE *(2006)*

SEE NO EVIL *(2006)*

THE CONDEMNED *(2007)*

BEHIND ENEMY LINES: COLOMBIA *(2009)*

12 ROUNDS *(2009)*

THE MARINE 2 *(2009)*

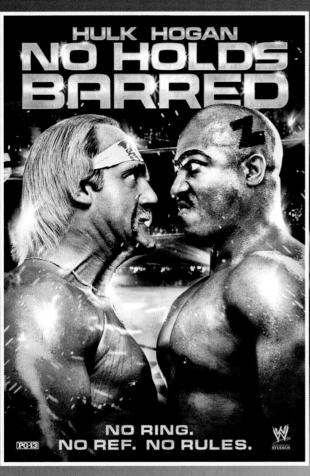

HULK HOGAN
NO HOLDS BARRED

NO RING.
NO REF. NO RULES.

THE MARINE
HOMEFRONT

LEGENDARY *(2010)*
KNUCKLEHEAD *(2010)*
THE CHAPERONE *(2011)*
INSIDE OUT *(2011)*
THAT'S WHAT I AM *(2011)*
THE REUNION *(2011)*
BENDING THE RULES *(2012)*

LEPRECHAUN: ORIGINS

COMING SOON:

THE DAY *(2012)*

BARRICADE *(2012)*

NO ONE LIVES *(2012)*

LEPRECHAUN: ORIGINS *(2013)*

THE MARINE: HOMEFRONT *(2013)*

DEAD MAN DOWN *(2013)*

QUEENS OF THE RING *(2013)*

B
2010-
2000-09
1990-99
1980-89
1970-79
1960-69

BOOKER T

HT: 6'3" **WT:** 253 lbs.
FROM: Houston, Texas
SIGNATURE MOVE: Book End, Scissor Kick

TITLE HISTORY

HARDCORE CHAMPION	*2 Times*
INTERCONTINENTAL CHAMPION	*Defeated Christian on July 7, 2003*
WORLD HEAVYWEIGHT CHAMPION	*Defeated Rey Mysterio on July 23, 2006*
WORLD TAG TEAM CHAMPION (3 TIMES)	*Partnered with Test to defeat The Rock & Chris Jericho on November 1, 2001* *Partnered with Goldust to defeat Christian & Chris Jericho on December 15, 2002* *Partnered with Rob Van Dam to defeat Ric Flair & Batista on February 16, 2004*
UNITED STATES CHAMPION (3 TIMES)	*Defeated Rob Van Dam in an 8-Man Elimination Match on July 29, 2004* *Defeated Chris Benoit on October 21, 2005* *Awarded title when Randy Orton defeated Chris Benoit on January 13, 2006*

Before this five-time WCW Champion was a king, Booker T was arguably the most celebrated tag team competitor in the history of the industry. A ten-time co-holder of the WCW World Tag Team Championship with his brother Stevie Ray as a member of Harlem Heat, the duo dominated the WCW tag team scene in the 1990s. Booker then became a top singles competitor and ended the historic last episode of *WCW Monday Nitro* as WCW Champion. In the weeks that followed WWE's purchase of its one-time rival, Booker T invaded WWE when he attacked Stone Cold Steve Austin at *King of the Ring*. Booker then participated in the first-ever WCW match to be held on WWE programming when he defended his WCW Championship on *Monday Night Raw* against Buff Bagwell. Booker became a key member of The Alliance as they attempted to overthrow WWE. He won the World Tag Team Championship on Nov. 1, 2001 when he & Test defeated The Rock & Chris Jericho on *SmackDown*.

Perhaps Booker's finest moment came when he defeated Rey Mysterio for the World Heavyweight Championship at *The Great American Bash 2006*. For Booker, it was validation that his dominance in WCW could translate over to WWE. He further drove home that point when he won a Champion of Champions Match at *Cyber Sunday 2006*, defeating the reigning WWE Champion, John Cena, and the ECW Champion, Big Show.

After a three year hiatus, the master of the Spin-A-Rooni shocked the WWE Universe when he returned as a participant in the 2011 Royal Rumble. He then put on the headset and brought his signature sounds to the *SmackDown* announce team. Booker's sports-entertainment expertise and more than 30 championships was requested for service by Stone Cold Steve Austin as a trainer for *Tough Enough*. In the ring, behind the microphone, or training Superstar-hopefuls, Booker T is truly in a class by himself. Now can you dig that, sucka?

BOOKER T & GOLDUST

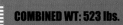

COMBINED WT: 523 lbs.

TITLE HISTORY

WORLD TAG TEAM CHAMPIONS	*Defeated Christian & Chris Jericho on December 15, 2002*

One of the more unlikely tag team pairings in recent memory, these two Superstars came together in 2002 on *Raw* thanks to Goldust showing Booker they could form a great duo. They were able to blend their different ring styles into one and formed an indescribable chemistry. They were also a part of some of the funniest segments in *Raw* history and hosted their own segment "Booker T. & Goldust At The Movies."

On December 15, 2002, they won a Fatal-Four Way Elimination Match for the World Tag Team Championship but lost the titles to Lance Storm & William Regal on *Raw*. After failed attempts to win back the gold, the team split, but the two Superstars remained allies.

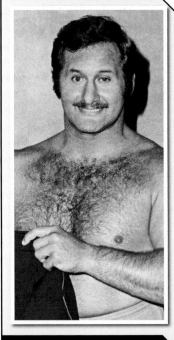

BORIS MALENKO

HT: 5'10" **WT:** 220 lbs.
FROM: Moscow, Russia
SIGNATURE MOVE: Russian Sickle

With the "Red Scare" still lingering in the United States, Boris Malenko used his Russian ancestry to strike fear into both opponents and fans. A master antagonist, Malenko could draw more hatred from audiences than any other Superstar of his time.

Malenko was much more than an ire-inspiring Russian; he was also a brilliant competitor inside the ring. In fact, his amazing abilities earned him the nicknames "The Great Malenko" and "Professor Malenko." Despite possessing superior in-ring skills, however, Malenko was not above cheating to earn a victory. It wasn't uncommon to

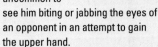

see him biting or jabbing the eyes of an opponent in an attempt to gain the upper hand.

In May 1967, Malenko defeated Wahoo McDaniel to capture the National Wrestling Alliance Florida Heavyweight Championship. It was his first of eleven NWA titles, including seven reigns as the Florida Brass Knuckles Champion. Malenko passed away in 1994, but he left behind an amazing legacy, which includes two sons who also competed in the ring, Joe and Dean Malenko.

BORIS ZHUKOV

HT: 6'2" **WT:** 275 lbs. **FROM:** Siberia, Russia
SIGNATURE MOVE: Flying Clothesline

Boris Zhukov first appeared in World Class Championship Wrestling in 1983 and toured the territories of the Southeastern United States of America. Boris traveled to the AWA in 1985, where he made a name for himself squaring off against foes like Sgt. Slaughter and Jimmy "Superfly" Snuka.

In 1987, the formidable Russian came to WWE and immediately teamed with Nikolai Volkoff to form the Bolsheviks. The two powerhouses were managed by the "Doctor of Style" Slick and were serious threats for the World Tag Team Championship. Boris was also commended for his habits when he won "Best Personal Hygiene" at the 1987 Slammy Awards. Boris returned to singles action after he and Volkoff split until he left WWE in 1991.

Since then, Boris has continued to appear on independent cards all over the world. Fans will never forget the name Boris Zhukov, or the pain he brought opponents throughout his career.

BRADEN WALKER

HT: 6'4" **WT:** 262 lbs. **FROM:** Ft. Wright, Kentucky

"Knock, knock."

"Who's there?"

"Braden Walker, and I'm gonna knock your brains out."

A confident Braden Walker had the above exchange with Armando Estrada during his debut appearance on ECW in July 2008. And just as he prophetically forecasted, the new Superstar defeated Estrada after connecting with a top rope flying cross body. As a member of ECW General Manager Theodore Long's New Superstar Initiative, the future was looking bright for Walker. The big Kentucky native followed up on his debut victory with a win over James Curtis the following month. But with two wins in his back pocket, Walker mysteriously vanished from the sports-entertainment industry in August 2008, never to be seen again. Despite his quick disappearance, Walker's debut knock-knock joke is still referenced by members of the WWE Universe as one of the oddest comments ever uttered.

BRADY BOONE

HT: 5'10" **WT:** 220 lbs. **FROM:** Oregon City, Oregon
SIGNATURE MOVE: Moonsault

Hailing from the state of Oregon, Brady Boone was recognized as one of the top high school gymnasts in the United States before embarking on his sports-entertainment career. In the late 1980s he debuted in WWE displaying his high flying, aerial style as seen on such programs as *Superstars of Wrestling*, *Wrestling Challenge*, and *Wrestling Spotlight*. During this time reports circulated around wrestling that he also donned a mask as the Battle Kat. However, that was never confirmed.

As his in-ring career came to a close, Boone was hired by WCW to serve as a referee. Sadly, on December 18, 1998 Brady Boone's life suddenly ended when he was killed in an automobile accident in Orlando, FL. His high-flying legacy will always be remembered and admired by true mat fans all over the globe.

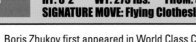

The concept of *Bragging Rights* was simple: matches took place between Superstars from *Raw* and *SmackDown* and the winning brand for the night took home the Bragging Rights Trophy for the year. In its inaugural year the winning brand was decided by the total number of matches won, however, in 2010 the victory went to the winner of a 7-on-7 Interpromotional Elimination Tag Team Match. *SmackDown* took home the trophy both years.

October 25, 2009

Pittsburgh, PA – Mellon Arena

Main Event: John Cena defeated WWE Champion Randy Orton in an Anything Goes Iron Man Match

October 26, 2010

Minneapolis, MN – Target Center

Main Event: Wade Barrett defeated WWE Champion Randy Orton

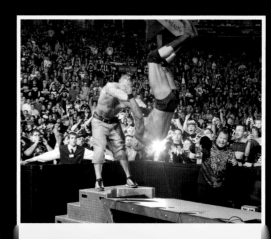

2010-
▲
2000-09
▲
1990-99
▲
1980-89
▲
1970-79
▲
1960-69

BRAIN BUSTERS

MEMBERS: Arn Anderson, Tully Blanchard
COMBINED WT: 475 lbs.

TITLE HISTORY

WORLD TAG TEAM CHAMPIONS	Defeated Demoltion on July 18, 1989

As founding members of the legendary Four Horsemen, Arn Anderson & Tully Blanchard created historic reputations that preceded their WWE debut. Once they arrived in WWE, their impressive teamwork went a long way in proving they were just as good as everybody said they were.

Trading in manager J.J. Dillon for Bobby "The Brain" Heenan, the two-time NWA Tag Team Champions made their way to WWE in 1988. Billed as the Brain Busters (playing off their manager's nickname), Anderson & Blanchard made quick work of WWE's top teams, including The Rockers at *Saturday Night's Main Event* and Strike Force at *WrestleMania V*. Despite their impressive record, it took the team more than seven months to receive their first high-profile World Tag Team Championship opportunity.

In May 1989, the Brain Busters challenged Demolition for the tag titles on *Saturday Night's Main Event*. Anderson & Blanchard walked away with the disqualification victory, but not the championship. Two months later, they finished the job when they beat Demolition in a two-out-of-three falls match. With the titles in their possession, the Brain Busters were finally considered a part of WWE's upper echelon of Superstars.

The Brain Busters left WWE in late 1989. While their stay in the promotion was brief, Anderson & Blanchard used the time to successfully prove to a national audience that they were one of the most intelligent and technically sound tag teams of the 1980s.

BRAKKUS

HT: 6'0"   **WT:** 275 lbs.   **FROM:** Germany
SIGNATURE MOVE: Powerslam

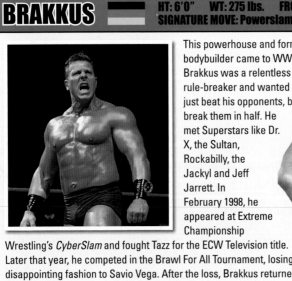

This powerhouse and former professional bodybuilder came to WWE in 1996. Brakkus was a relentless rule-breaker and wanted not to just beat his opponents, but break them in half. He met Superstars like Dr. X, the Sultan, Rockabilly, the Jackyl and Jeff Jarrett. In February 1998, he appeared at Extreme Championship Wrestling's *CyberSlam* and fought Tazz for the ECW Television title. Later that year, he competed in the Brawl For All Tournament, losing in disappointing fashion to Savio Vega. After the loss, Brakkus returned to Europe and has not been seen in WWE since.

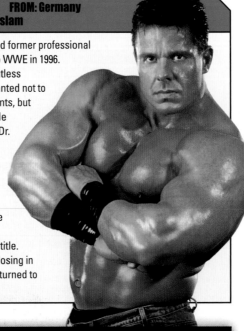

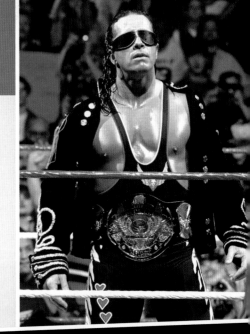

Born into wrestling royalty, Bret Hart was destined to make his living inside the ring. His father, Stu, was well-known as a top competitor and for training many of the biggest names in sports-entertainment. Some of Bret's earliest memories include sitting in the family basement watching his father physically dissect men half his age and twice his size. Bret started building his reputation while competing in his father's Stampede Wrestling promotion. He quickly became one of Calgary's top draws and caught the eye of Vince McMahon. In 1984, rather than trying to lure Bret over to WWE, McMahon simply bought Stampede Wrestling and the rights to its competitors, including Bret.

BRET "HIT MAN" HART

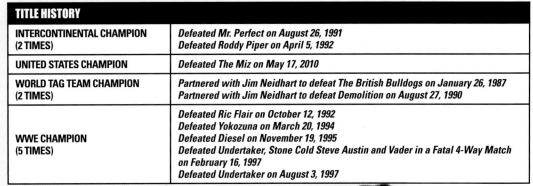

HT: 6'0"   WT: 235 lbs.   FROM: Calgary, Alberta, Canada   SIGNATURE MOVE: Sharpshooter

HALL OF FAME 2006

> " THE BEST THERE IS. THE BEST THERE WAS. THE BEST THERE EVER WILL BE "

The Hart Foundation and World Championships

Bret's career didn't immediately take off south of the border, but he soon teamed with Jim "The Anvil" Neidhart and success soon followed. Dubbed the Hart Foundation, the duo possessed the perfect combination of technical ability and pure power. With Jimmy Hart as their manager, the Hart Foundation captured the World Tag Team Championship on two separate occasions.

After losing the World Tag Team Championship to the Nasty Boys at *WrestleMania VII*, Bret leapt into singles competition. It didn't surprise many when, in a matter of mere months, he won his first major singles title, defeating Mr. Perfect for the Intercontinental Championship at *SummerSlam 1991*. Bret would go on to capture the Intercontinental Championship one more time before setting his sights on the WWE Championship.

On October, 12, 1992, Bret won his first of five WWE Championships. Bret's title reign was derailed at *WrestleMania IX* by Yokozuna, but in typical Bret Hart fashion, he refused to let the loss get him off track. More determined than ever, he turned back Razor Ramon, Mr. Perfect, and Bam Bam Bigelow all in one evening to be crowned the 1993 King of the Ring.

With every major championship and a King of the Ring victory on his resumé, Bret had little left to prove, however he refused to rest on his legendary reputation. Intent on regaining sports-entertainment's ultimate prize, Bret was declared a co-winner of the 1994 *Royal Rumble*. The victory earned him another opportunity at the WWE Championship, which he capitalized on at *WrestleMania X*, defeating Yokozuna to reclaim the title.

Trouble in the Family

Bret Hart will always be remembered as one of the greatest champions in WWE history, but one of his most memorable rivalries revolved around so much more than titles. In 1994, the Harts were a family in crisis. The normally tight-knit clan was nearly torn apart when Bret's younger brother, Owen, attacked the "Hit Man" in a jealous rage. The rivalry resulted in some of the most emotionally-charged encounters to ever take place within a WWE ring. Owen was never able to wrest the WWE Championship away from Bret, but his *WrestleMania X* victory over his older brother went a long way in his attempt to get out from under his legendary shadow.

Unfortunately, Bret's final WWE match in the 1990s was widely recognized as one of the most infamous moments in sports-entertainment history. As a result of what is now commonly referred to as the "Montreal Incident", Bret Hart and Vince McMahon engaged in a bitter war of words that lasted several years. Their differences, however, couldn't stop the "Hit Man" from being honored as one of sports-entertainment's greatest when he was inducted into the WWE Hall of Fame in 2006.

Hart continued to be featured in video packages celebrating WWE history. Then, on January 4, 2010, 12 years removed from his last live appearance on WWE television, the "Hit Man" returned to *Raw*. On that fateful night the five-time WWE Heavyweight Champion was special guest host and engaged in an epic moment of reconciliation when he shook the hand and embraced his greatest rival, Shawn Michaels. While "Hit Man" thought he also made amends with Mr. McMahon, a blind-sided low-blow from the WWE Chairman confirmed time doesn't heal all wounds. This set the stage for the match the WWE Universe longed to see, Hart vs. McMahon in a No Holds Barred match at *WrestleMania XXVI*. It became a family affair, and one which saw Mr. McMahon savagely beaten. Two months later, Hart even won the U.S. Championship—his first WWE title since 1997—when he forced the Miz to submit to the Sharpshooter.

Bret continued to appear on *Raw* and his star shined brighter than ever. His friendship with John Cena led him to join team WWE in the battle against Nexus at *SummerSlam*. Since his triumphant return home to WWE, the "Hit Man" continues to surprise the WWE Universe with appearances on *Raw*, *SmackDown*, pay per views, and live events all over the world.

TITLE HISTORY	
INTERCONTINENTAL CHAMPION (2 TIMES)	*Defeated Mr. Perfect on August 26, 1991* *Defeated Roddy Piper on April 5, 1992*
UNITED STATES CHAMPION	*Defeated The Miz on May 17, 2010*
WORLD TAG TEAM CHAMPION (2 TIMES)	*Partnered with Jim Neidhart to defeat The British Bulldogs on January 26, 1987* *Partnered with Jim Neidhart to defeat Demolition on August 27, 1990*
WWE CHAMPION (5 TIMES)	*Defeated Ric Flair on October 12, 1992* *Defeated Yokozuna on March 20, 1994* *Defeated Diesel on November 19, 1995* *Defeated Undertaker, Stone Cold Steve Austin and Vader in a Fatal 4-Way Match on February 16, 1997* *Defeated Undertaker on August 3, 1997*

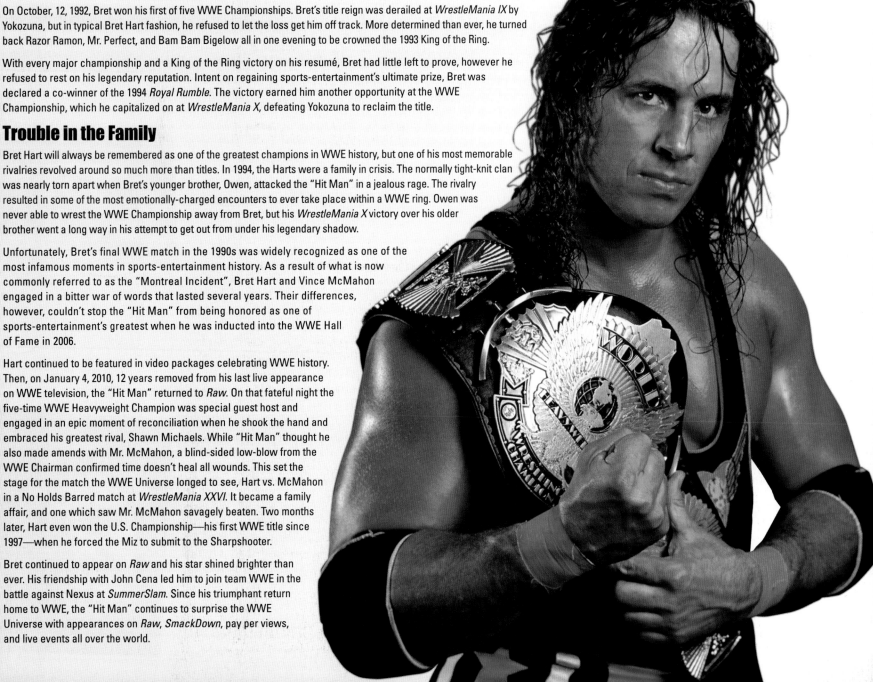

B

2010-

2000-09

1990-99

1980-89

1970-79

1960-69

BREAKINGPOINT

Sept 13 2009 Bell Centre; Montreal

Breaking Point was an event with two twists: first, its name chosen by the WWE Universe; second, many of the matches on the card could only be won via submission. *Breaking Point* matches included defenses of the Unified WWE Tag Team Championship, the United States Championship, and the ECW Championship.

The main events were defenses of the WWE and World Heavyweight Championships. WWE Champion Randy Orton faced John Cena in an I Quit Match, but was unable to count on outside help after Mr. McMahon threatened to take the title should anyone interfere on his behalf. In the end, John Cena forced "the Viper" to say "I quit" with a handcuff-aided STF. CM Punk left the event as World Heavyweight Champion after gaining victory in a controversy-filled match against Undertaker.

THE BRIAN KENDRICK HT: 5'8" WT: 184 lbs. FROM: Venice, California
SIGNATURE MOVE: Sliced Bread No. 2

TITLE HISTORY

WORLD TAG TEAM CHAMPION	*Partnered with Paul London to defeat Lance Cade & Trevor Murdoch on September 5, 2007*
WWE TAG TEAM CHAMPION	*Partnered with Paul London to defeat MNM on May 21, 2006*

A graduate of the Shawn Michaels Wrestling Academy, Brian Kendrick entered WWE with the proper fundamentals, a high threshold for pain, and the charismatic flare that only HBK could teach. In 2003, Brian debuted in WWE and wowed crowds with his aerial moves and speed. He soon found a tag team partner in fellow high-flyer Paul London. In early 2004, Kendrick left WWE to hone his skills overseas.

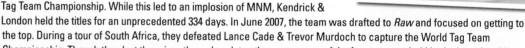

In September 2005, he returned to WWE and took aim at sports-entertainment's premier figures. Stronger, faster and tougher, Kendrick reunited with London and the two thrilled audiences. On May 21, 2006, they defeated MNM for the WWE Tag Team Championship. While this led to an implosion of MNM, Kendrick & London held the titles for an unprecedented 334 days. In June 2007, the team was drafted to *Raw* and focused on getting to the top. During a tour of South Africa, they defeated Lance Cade & Trevor Murdoch to capture the World Tag Team Championship. Though they lost the prizes three days later, they are on one of the few teams to hold both championships.

At the 2008 Supplemental Draft, Kendrick was sent back to *SmackDown* and unveiled a package fans never thought they'd see. With a new attitude, wardrobe, and bodyguard named Ezekiel, "The" Brian Kendrick displayed sneaky rule-breaker tactics and new dance moves Kendrick split from Ezekiel and returned to *Raw* with his body rockin' moves to focus on a singles career until his departure from WWE in 2009.

BRIAN PILLMAN HT: 6'0" WT: 227 lbs.
FROM: Cincinnati, Ohio

A former member of the Cincinnati Bengals, Brian Pillman turned to wrestling in 1986. No longer restricted by the shoulder pads and helmet, the unpredictable Superstar was able to unleash the real man lurking inside. The result: sports-entertainment's most notorious "Loose Cannon."

Armed with the training he received from Stu Hart, Pillman made his debut in Canada's Stampede Wrestling. Within a few short years, he cemented himself as one of the industry's premier high flyers, which caught the attention of WCW. As a member of WCW, Pillman used his acrobatic attack to claim two Light Heavyweight Championships and the WCW Tag Team Championship.

It wasn't until Pillman made his way to WWE in 1996 that fans began to see the true "Loose Cannon." Despite being sidelined with a severe ankle injury, Pillman managed to shock audiences with his unpredictable behavior.

Pillman's brief WWE in-ring career was equally controversial. Filled with an uncontrollable rage, he engaged in a memorable rivalry with the bizarre Goldust. Unfortunately, Pillman unexpectedly passed away soon after in Minnesota. His tragic death took away one of sports-entertainment's most colorful personalities.

BRISCO BROTHERS

MEMBERS: Gerald, Jack
COMBINED WT: 461 lbs.

Throughout sports-entertainment's rich history, there have been several famous brother tag team combinations. While they are all exceptional in their own right, Jack & Gerald Brisco are a cut above. The elder brother Jack was a stand-out amateur wrestler at Oklahoma State and is one of only three men to hold the NCAA Wrestling and NWA Championships. He made his pro debut in 1965 and went on to worldwide stardom. Gerald, like his brother Jack, knew success in the amateur ranks and won several AAU Tournaments. He was also a stand-out at Oklahoma State. Trained by brother, Jack, Gerald debuted in 1968 and went on to hold many titles throughout the NWA.

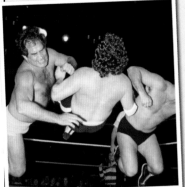

As a team during the 1970s, they displayed poetic continuity and superior ring strategy. Their dominance was shown in the ring as well as in their standing offer to any misguided challengers, "C'mon down! You know where the gold is!"

In 1984, the Brisco's made their much-anticipated WWE debut and did not disappoint. They raised the bar for tag team competition before retiring from the ring. Jack returned to Tampa, Florida and expanded their famous "Brisco Brothers Body Shop." Gerald became a confidant to Vince McMahon and during the late 1990s often appeared on television beside the Chairman with fellow associate Pat Patterson.

In March 2008, the Brisco Brothers reached the pinnacle of sports-entertainment when they were inducted in to WWE Hall of Fame. As individuals, they are two of the most decorated figures in all of sports-entertainment. Together, the Brisco Brothers are icons who epitomized the word "team" and are eternally revered as consummate professionals.

"THE BRITISH BULLDOG" DAVEY BOY SMITH

HT: 5'11" **WT:** 260 lbs.
FROM: Manchester, England
SIGNATURE MOVE: Powerslam

TITLE HISTORY	
EUROPEAN CHAMPION (2 TIMES)	*Defeated Owen Hart on February 26, 1997* *Defeated D-Lo Brown on October 28, 1999*
HARDCORE CHAMPION	*2 Times*
INTERCONTINENTAL CHAMPION	*Defeated Bret Hart on August 29, 1992*
WORLD TAG TEAM CHAMPION (2 TIMES)	*Partnered with Dynamite Kid to defeat Brutus Beefcake & Greg Valentine on April 7, 1986* *Partnered with Owen Hart to defeat The Smokin' Gunns on September 22, 1996*

WWE audiences first saw Davey Boy Smith in 1985 alongside his cousin, the Dynamite Kid. Together, they formed a revolutionary tag team, The British Bulldogs. They amazed audiences with their in-ring acrobatics and fluid teamwork. They won the World Tag Team Championship at *WrestleMania 2*, defeating the Dream Team (Brutus Beefcake & Greg Valentine). After a nine-month title reign they lost the titles in controversial fashion to the Hart Foundation.

In 1990, the protégé of mat legend Stu Hart returned as a singles wrestler and referred to himself as "The British Bulldog." Sporting the Union Jack, his blend of power, agility, and aerial moves made him a top attraction in North America and Europe. He faced his brother-in-law, Bret "Hit Man" Hart, in the main event of *SummerSlam 1992* for the Intercontinental Championship. In front of over 80,000 fans at Wembley Stadium, the British Bulldog emerged victorious in arguably the greatest match of his career. After a disappointing loss to Shawn Michaels on a November episode of *Saturday Night's Main Event,* he soon left WWE, but returned in 1993 to form The Allied Powers with Lex Luger.

After turning on his American ally, the Bulldog joined Camp Cornette. While teamed with another brother-in-law, Owen Hart, the duo won the World Tag Team Championship from the Smoking Gunns at *In Your House: Mind Games* in 1996. The Bulldog then took a bite out of the history books on February 26, 1997 in Berlin, Germany when he defeated Owen Hart in the tournament finals to crown the first European Champion. In late 1997, he joined Bret Hart, Owen Hart, Jim Neidhart, and Brian Pillman in the ever-dangerous Hart Foundation. After the infamous "Montreal Incident" where Shawn Michaels defeated Bret Hart amid high controversy at *Survivor Series 1997*, Bulldog followed the Bret and Neidhart to WCW in 1998. After leaving the organization, Bulldog returned to WWE in August 1999 and tangled with main event Superstars The Rock, Triple H, Mankind, and Big Show. Sadly in 2002, Davey Boy Smith passed away. The incredible performer's career will be fondly remembered.

BRITISH BULLDOGS

MEMBERS: Davey Boy Smith, Dynamite Kid
COMBINED WT: 471 lbs.   FROM: England

TITLE HISTORY

WORLD TAG TEAM CHAMPIONS	Defeated Brutus Beefcake & Greg Valentine on April 7, 1986

Behind the perfect combination of speed and power, the British Bulldogs became one of the most popular tag teams of their time. Originally competing in promotions throughout Canada and Japan, Dynamite Kid & Davey Boy Smith jumped to WWE in the mid-1980s and quickly gained tag-team success, as well as the hearts of the fans.

Shortly after making their WWE debut, the British Bulldogs, behind the tutelage of Capt. Lou Albano and rocker Ozzy Osbourne, defeated the Dream Team (Greg Valentine & Brutus Beefcake) for the World Tag Team Championship at *WrestleMania 2*. The popular duo maintained a strong hold of the titles for ten months before losing them to the Hart Foundation in January 1987. The match proved very costly, as some questionable officiating by Danny Davis also led to Dynamite Kid suffering serious injury.

Following the loss, the Bulldogs took some time off to rehab Dynamite Kid's injuries. When they returned, they immediately set their sights on gaining revenge on Davis. Teaming with Tito Santana, The Bulldogs sought vengeance at *WrestleMania III* when they battled Davis & the Hart Foundation. Unfortunately, the match didn't go in their favor, as the dastardly Davis weaseled his way to a win.

The Bulldogs' popularity reached new heights when they added mascot Matilda to the team. The lovable bulldog accompanied Dynamite Kid & Davey Boy Smith to ringside for all their matches and quickly became a fan favorite. Her popularity eventually drew ire of The Islanders, who dognapped the adorable pooch.

The Islanders' distasteful act lead the Bulldogs to another Six-Man Tag Team Match when they partnered with fellow animal lover Koko B. Ware to battle the dognappers and their manager Bobby Heenan at *WrestleMania IV*. Much like their *WrestleMania III* match, the Bulldogs were unable to secure victory. The Bulldogs struggled to get back on track following the *WrestleMania IV* loss, and disappeared from the WWE scene by 1989. Despite the woes they experienced late in their tenure, Dynamite Kid & Davey Boy Smith used a unique blend of quickness and strength to build an impressive legacy that is still admired today.

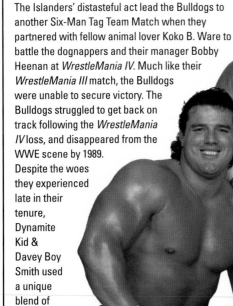

BROCK LESNAR 🇺🇸

HT: 6'3"   WT: 295 lbs.
FROM: Minneapolis, Minnesota
SIGNATURE MOVE: F5

TITLE HISTORY

WWE CHAMPION (3 TIMES)	Defeated The Rock on August 25, 2002 Defeated Kurt Angle on March 30, 2003 Defeated Kurt Angle on September 18, 2003

When Brock Lesnar entered WWE, he brought with him a championship amateur career and an overwhelming physique. The impressive combination caused many to believe they were looking at "The Next Big Thing." Over the course of his WWE career, Lesnar proved those predictions to be correct.

Under the tutelage of Paul Heyman, Lesnar made an immediate impact upon his 2002 debut. A mere three months into his career, he won the prestigious *King of the Ring* tournament. Two months later, he beat The Rock for the WWE Championship. In short, Lesnar accomplished more in six months than most Superstars do in an entire career.

Over the next two years, Lesnar continued to shine, especially against Undertaker. At *No Mercy 2002*, he defeated the "Deadman" inside the demonic Hell in a Cell. At the following year's event, Lesnar beat Undertaker in a Biker Chain Match. He even last eliminated the "Deadman" to win the 2003 *Royal Rumble*. With his victory in the *Royal Rumble*, Lesnar earned the opportunity to challenge Kurt Angle for the WWE Championship at *WrestleMania XIX*. Lesnar left WWE in 2004 to start an NFL career. While fans never saw him on the gridiron, he soon announced he was starting a career in mixed martial arts. Before illness derailed his career, fans were treated to a taste of his past in October 2010, when Brock engaged in a chilling stare down with the Undertaker after a bout. On April 2, 2012, Brock made a shocking return the night after *WrestleMania XXVIII* and attacked John Cena.

BRODUS CLAY 🇺🇸

HT: 6'7"   WT: 375 lbs.
FROM: Planet Funk
SIGNATURE MOVE: What the Funk?

As the only living, breathing, rompin', stompin', Funkasaurus in captivity, Brodus Clay brings a dangerous combination of domination and funk with him each time he enters the ring. With the beautiful Naomi and Cameron dancing at the big man's side, it's nearly impossible not to smile when Clay makes his way to the ring.

Clay's opponents, however, have very little to smile about. At nearly 400 pounds, the Funkasaurus is both an irresistible force and immovable object rolled into one mass of humanity. Making matters worse for his opposition, he couples his jaw-dropping girth with a speed and agility rarely found in men his size. This unique combination helped catapult Clay to victories over the likes of Drew McIntyre and Curt Hawkins upon his re-debut on *Raw* in 2012.

Prior to discovering his funky side, Clay was a Rookie on season four of *NXT*, where he grossed more than twice as many victories than any other rookie. As a result of his impressive won-loss record, Clay earned a spot in the season's finale.

Fellow Rookie Johnny Curtis eventually took home *NXT*'s top honors but that didn't stop Clay. The big man was quickly scooped up by Alberto Del Rio to serve as the Mexican Aristocrat's bodyguard. The role was not foreign to Clay, who served as Snoop Dogg's protection years earlier.

Simply protecting Del Rio eventually began to lose its luster for Clay, and it wasn't long before the rhythm took over his soul. Today the fun-loving Funkasaurus is one of the most popular and dominating Superstars in WWE.

THE BROOD

MEMBERS: David Heath (formerly known as Gangrel)
Edge & Christian, Matt & Jeff Hardy

In 1998, a mystical force appeared in World Wrestling Entertainment. Led by the David Heath, known in WWE as Gangrel, Edge & Christian often entered into WWE events rising from underground surrounded by a circle of flames. They crept to the ring as their leader sipped blood from his chalice and spit it out at the crowd. They often participated in bizarre rituals, intimidating and frightening the weak.

Opponents were viewed as enemies from another world and often victims to their bloodbaths, which occurred when the lights in the arena went out and a red light appeared. When the light came back the victim was laying in the ring covered in blood. In early 1999, they joined Undertaker's Ministry of Darkness.

The Brood left Undertaker's faction and battled the Hardy Boys. During one match, the brothers and their manager were doused in blood. As Edge & Christian grew as a tag team, they removed themselves from their leader's influence. For a brief period of time, Gangrel recruited Matt & Jeff Hardy, forming a New Brood, but it broke apart when the Hardys acquired a new manager. Both Edge & Christian and the Hardy Boys became two of WWE's most successful tag teams. David Heath faded from the scene until his 2007 return to at WWE's *Raw 15th Anniversary* special.

BROOKE

HT: 5'4" **FROM:** Houston, Texas

In 2006, Brooke saw the WWE Diva Search as her ticket to the big time. WWE, on the other hand, did not. She was cut from the competition just prior to the final eight hopefuls being announced.

Despite being eliminated, the aspiring Diva made a solid impression on WWE officials, who offered her a spot in their developmental program. After just a few months of training, the beautiful brunette made it to the big time when she debuted on *ECW* in January 2007. As a member of Extreme Exposé, Brooke performed seductive dance routines alongside Kelly Kelly and Layla. The threesome electrified male audiences and caught the eye of recording artist Timbaland, who placed the girls in his music video, "Throw it on Me".

THE BROOKLYN BRAWLER

HT: 6'0" **WT:** 248 lbs. **FROM:** Brooklyn, New York
SIGNATURE MOVE: Sidewalk Smash

From the rough streets of Brooklyn, New York, this Superstar was brought into WWE by Bobby "The Brain" Heenan. During a 1989 episode of *Prime Time Wrestling*, the Brooklyn Brawler made his presence felt when he jumped the Red Rooster and handed him a five boroughs beat-down.

The man from the County of Kings had a short-lived partnership with another New York City native, Bad News Brown. The Brawler also battled with Koko B. Ware after the fans voted for the two Superstars to lock up for Coliseum Video's *Fan Favorites* video cassette release.

The Brooklyn Brawler continued his street-fighting ways into the 1990s. He appeared on WWE television for the remainder of the decade and developed a reputation for showing up whenever he felt someone needed to get roughed up. You just never know when the Brawler will appear on *Raw* or *SmackDown* and take his rough-housing tactics to the next big Superstar.

BROTHER LOVE

Dressed in a white suit, the red-faced Brother Love claimed to preach the good word of love to WWE audiences of the late 1980s and early 1990s. The sight of him invoked thoughts of scandalous televangelists; despite nearly being booed out of every arena, he constantly used his annoying catchphrase to tell people how he felt: "I love you!"

Brother Love is best known for hosting a weekly interview segment appropriately named *The Brother Love Show*. He used the segment to verbally attack popular Superstars of the time. His long list of dissatisfied guests includes Hulk Hogan, Brutus Beefcake and Dusty Rhodes.

While Brother Love's antics on *The Brother Love Show* are widely chronicled by WWE historians, it's a lesser-known fact that might just be the preacher's ultimate career highlight. Amazingly, it was Brother Love, not Paul Bearer, who first introduced WWE audiences to Undertaker at *Survivor Series 1990*. He went on to manage the "Deadman" through February 1991, at which time he sold the future WWE Hall of Famer's contract to Bearer.

2010-
2000-09
1990-99
1980-89
1970-79
1960-69

THE BROTHERS OF DESTRUCTION
MEMBERS: Undertaker, Kane   **COMBINED WT:** 628 lbs.

TITLE HISTORY	
WORLD TAG TEAM CHAMPIONS (2 TIMES)	Defeated Edge & Christian on April 19, 2001 Defeated Kanyon & Diamond Dallas Page on August 19, 2001

When WWE first saw Undertaker and his half-brother in the ring, the two were bitter rivals and combatants in some of the most dangerous contests World Wrestling Entertainment has ever known.

Early showings of what they could be as a united force were first seen at the 2001 *Royal Rumble*. The powerful moves they used as individuals were now more deadly as double-team maneuvers. Enter the Brothers of Destruction. With their immense power, they crushed anyone who got in their way. The duo joined forces again in February and they beat Rikishi & Haku in a First Blood Match on *SmackDown*.

During their battles with Alliance members Diamond Dallas Page and Kanyon, they became the first team ever to unify the WWE and WCW Tag Team titles in a Steel Cage Match at *SummerSlam 2001*. Over the years, they have both reformed and reopened old battle wounds depending on where their path of destruction leads them.

Since they are family, they do tend to fight from time to time. However, history (and stretchers) have shown the worst beatings one could receive is when these brothers join forces. When you face the Brothers of Destruction, winning becomes a secondary concern to survival.

BRUISER BRODY 🇺🇸
HT: 6'8"   **WT:** 283 lbs.
FROM: Santa Fe, New Mexico
SIGNATURE MOVE: Knee Drop

Known for his wild hair, big bushy beard and bulging eyes, Bruiser Brody was a madman in the truest sense of the word. After 15 unpredictable years in the ring, the brawler earned the reputation as one of the toughest of his time, but instead will be remembered best by his tragic passing.

After making his professional debut in 1973, Brody became known as a bit of a nomad. Bouncing around from promotion to promotion, he never stayed in one place for very long. During his brief stints in WWE, WCCW, AWA, and the NWA, among other places, he took part in memorable battles against Andre the Giant, Abdullah the Butcher, Dick the Bruiser and the Von Erichs.

Internationally, Brody was seen as a legend, especially in Puerto Rico. Unfortunately, however, Puerto Rican rings would be the last he would ever compete in. In July 1988, Frank "Bruiser Brody" Goodish was stabbed to death in a locker room shower. Brody's impact and frenetic ring style live on in the memories of all who witnessed his mayhem.

Bruno Sammartino (see page 56)

BRUTE BERNARD 🍁
HT: 6'2"   **WT:** 250 lbs.
FROM: Montreal, Quebec, Canada

TITLE HISTORY	
UNITED STATES TAG TEAM CHAMPION	Partnered with Skull Murphy to defeat Buddy Austin & The Great Scott on May 16, 1963

A true Canadian wild man, Brute Bernard featured an uncontrollable, untamed ring style. Despite his unruly attitude, he always managed to find a tag team partner. In fact, many consider him to be one of the finest tag team wrestlers of his time.

The biggest win of Bernard's WWE career came in May 1963 when he teamed with Skull Murphy to defeat The Great Scott & Buddy Austin for the United States Tag Team Championship, the predecessor to today's World Tag Team Championship. The duo held the titles for six long months before finally being upended by Hall of Famers Gorilla Monsoon & Killer Kowalski. In addition to his union with Murphy, Bernard also formed successful tag teams with Larry Hamilton, The Angel, Jay York, and Mike Paidousis.

BRUTUS BEEFCAKE

HT: 6'4" **WT: 272 lbs.**
FROM: San Francisco, California
SIGNATURE MOVE: Sleeper

TITLE HISTORY

WORLD TAG TEAM CHAMPION	*Partnered with Greg Valentine to defeat Mike Rotundo & Barry Windham on August 24, 1985*

This extraordinary athlete debuted in 1984, managed by "Luscious" Johnny Valiant. This hated rulebreaker loved to strut and display his physical prowess in the ring while using a high-knee to put away opponents. As fans chanted "Fruitcake," he formed the vaunted Dream Team with Greg "The Hammer" Valentine. The arrogant pair won the

World Tag Team Championship when they defeated the U.S. Express. They held the titles until they were defeated by the British Bulldogs in a fast-paced thriller at *WrestleMania 2*. After the team disbanded at *Wrestlemania III*, audiences were introduced to WWE's new barber, and "Adorable" Adrian Adonis was the first customer.

With exciting new ring music, new ring attire, and steel shears, fans went wild as Brutus "The Barber" Beefcake took out opponents with his dreaded sleeper hold. Once they went to sleep, Brutus started struttin' and cuttin'. An intense rivalry with the Honky Tonk Man lead to an Intercontinental Championship Match at the inaugural *SummerSlam*. Sadly, Brutus never made the match as "Outlaw" Ron Bass attacked him days before the event.

He eventually returned and as the Mega-Powers exploded, "The Barber" came to the aid of Hulk Hogan. The two longtime friends battled Randy "Macho Man" Savage & Zeus in the *SummerSlam 1989* main event. In 1990, Brutus nearly lost his life in a parasailing accident. He received emergency surgery that lasted over seven hours. Eight titanium plates, 32 screws, 100 feet of steel wire, and a reconstructed skull later, the surgery's success was a miracle of medicine. He was told he'd never walk again but after months of physical rehabilitation, he returned to WWE and launched his talk show, *The Barber Shop*. When he was back at full strength, he formed the Mega-Maniacs with Hulk Hogan.

Today, Beefcake is the general manager at one of the largest gyms in New England and still makes select appearances on the independent circuit. Brutus' life is one of courage, commitment and desire. This legend is one of WWE's most beloved heroes and he has left his mark on the heads of opponents and in the hearts of fans.

BUDDY AUSTIN

HT: 6'2" **WT: 240 lbs.** **FROM: Lovejoy, Georgia**
SIGNATURE MOVE: Piledriver

Buddy Austin was a satanic Superstar who loved to be hated. And luckily for him, everybody hated him. After debuting in 1956, Austin quickly made a name for himself as the competitor with a lethal piledriver. Stories quickly began to spread across the United States about the up-and-comer with the career-ending maneuver.

TITLE HISTORY

UNITED STATES TAG TEAM CHAMPION	*Partnered with Great Scott to defeat Buddy Rogers & Johnny Barend on March 7, 1963*

As time passed, Austin's hit list was highlighted by the industry's top names, including WWE Hall of Famers Bobo Brazil and Pedro Morales. He beat both men for the WWA World Heavyweight Championship on separate occasions in 1966.

While in WWE, Austin briefly teamed with Great Scott to capture the United States Tag Team Championship from Buddy Rogers and Johnny Barend. They held the gold for more than one month before losing to Skull Murphy & Brute Bernard. Austin also formed several successful tag teams outside of WWE, including a union with Hall of Famer Freddie Blassie, which culminated in a WWA World Tag Team Championship reign in 1967.

BUDDY LANDELL

HT: 6'0" **WT: 220 lbs.** **FROM: Knoxville, Tennessee**
SIGNATURE MOVE: Figure-Four Leglock

Since 1979, Buddy Landell has traveled throughout the United States to become one of the ring's toughest and most accomplished veterans. In the mid 1980s, Landell became notorious throughout Tennessee and Jim Crockett Promotions. He continued to appear on independent cards through the early 1990s and saw success in Smoky Mountain Wrestling.

In December 1995, Landell debuted in WWE at *In Your House* against Ahmed Johnson. Over the next six years, Landell appeared sporadically for WWE in matches against Bob Holly, Matt Hardy, Bret "Hit Man" Hart, Edge, the Godfather and Triple H. He still makes appearances on the independent scene to show "he's still got it."

BRUNO SAMMARTINO

HT: 5'10"   **WT:** 265 lbs.   **FROM:** Abbruzi, Italy   **SIGNATURE MOVE:** Bearhug

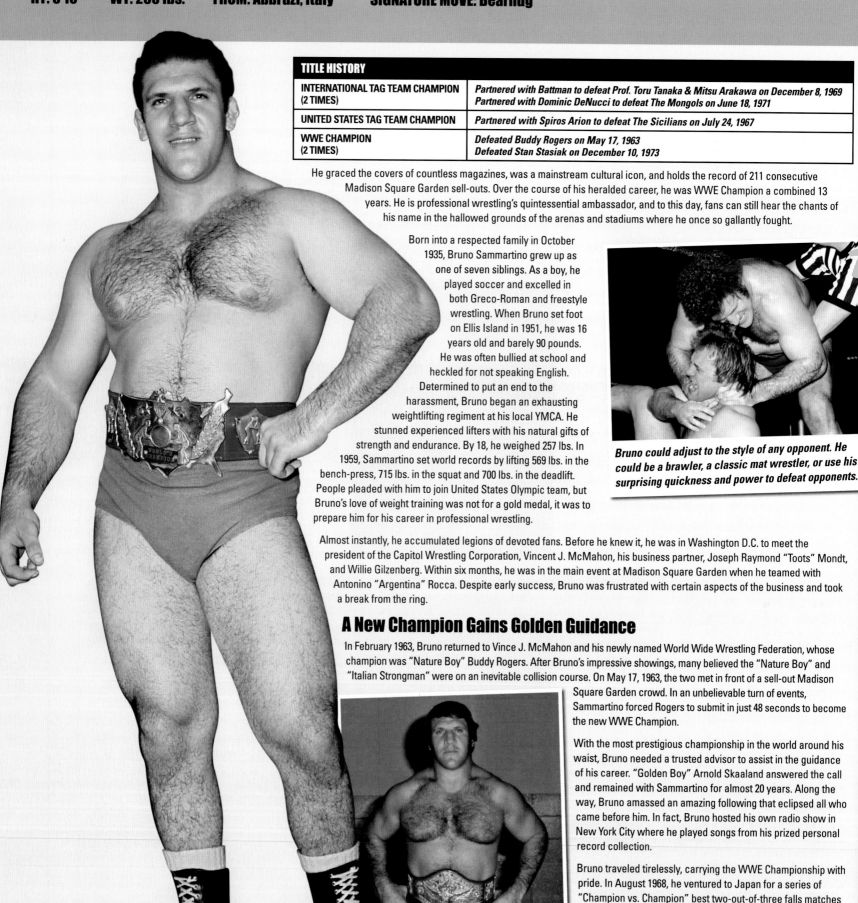

TITLE HISTORY	
INTERNATIONAL TAG TEAM CHAMPION (2 TIMES)	*Partnered with Battman to defeat Prof. Toru Tanaka & Mitsu Arakawa on December 8, 1969* *Partnered with Dominic DeNucci to defeat The Mongols on June 18, 1971*
UNITED STATES TAG TEAM CHAMPION	*Partnered with Spiros Arion to defeat The Sicilians on July 24, 1967*
WWE CHAMPION (2 TIMES)	*Defeated Buddy Rogers on May 17, 1963* *Defeated Stan Stasiak on December 10, 1973*

He graced the covers of countless magazines, was a mainstream cultural icon, and holds the record of 211 consecutive Madison Square Garden sell-outs. Over the course of his heralded career, he was WWE Champion a combined 13 years. He is professional wrestling's quintessential ambassador, and to this day, fans can still hear the chants of his name in the hallowed grounds of the arenas and stadiums where he once so gallantly fought.

Born into a respected family in October 1935, Bruno Sammartino grew up as one of seven siblings. As a boy, he played soccer and excelled in both Greco-Roman and freestyle wrestling. When Bruno set foot on Ellis Island in 1951, he was 16 years old and barely 90 pounds. He was often bullied at school and heckled for not speaking English. Determined to put an end to the harassment, Bruno began an exhausting weightlifting regiment at his local YMCA. He stunned experienced lifters with his natural gifts of strength and endurance. By 18, he weighed 257 lbs. In 1959, Sammartino set world records by lifting 569 lbs. in the bench-press, 715 lbs. in the squat and 700 lbs. in the deadlift. People pleaded with him to join United States Olympic team, but Bruno's love of weight training was not for a gold medal, it was to prepare him for his career in professional wrestling.

Bruno could adjust to the style of any opponent. He could be a brawler, a classic mat wrestler, or use his surprising quickness and power to defeat opponents.

Almost instantly, he accumulated legions of devoted fans. Before he knew it, he was in Washington D.C. to meet the president of the Capitol Wrestling Corporation, Vincent J. McMahon, his business partner, Joseph Raymond "Toots" Mondt, and Willie Gilzenberg. Within six months, he was in the main event at Madison Square Garden when he teamed with Antonino "Argentina" Rocca. Despite early success, Bruno was frustrated with certain aspects of the business and took a break from the ring.

A New Champion Gains Golden Guidance

In February 1963, Bruno returned to Vince J. McMahon and his newly named World Wide Wrestling Federation, whose champion was "Nature Boy" Buddy Rogers. After Bruno's impressive showings, many believed the "Nature Boy" and "Italian Strongman" were on an inevitable collision course. On May 17, 1963, the two met in front of a sell-out Madison Square Garden crowd. In an unbelievable turn of events, Sammartino forced Rogers to submit in just 48 seconds to become the new WWE Champion.

With the most prestigious championship in the world around his waist, Bruno needed a trusted advisor to assist in the guidance of his career. "Golden Boy" Arnold Skaaland answered the call and remained with Sammartino for almost 20 years. Along the way, Bruno amassed an amazing following that eclipsed all who came before him. In fact, Bruno hosted his own radio show in New York City where he played songs from his prized personal record collection.

Bruno traveled tirelessly, carrying the WWE Championship with pride. In August 1968, he ventured to Japan for a series of "Champion vs. Champion" best two-out-of-three falls matches against *puroresu* legend, Shohei "Giant" Baba. Bruno also teamed with former foe Skull Murphy and took on Baba with fellow Rikidozan protégé Antonio Inoki. Of all his challengers during the late 1960s, no one was more vicious than Killer Kowalski. The bouts between these men were not showcases of technical ring skill or displays of power, they were epic, blood-soaked battles. In 1969, the two combatants had a match that ended in pure bedlam in the main event of the only wrestling card in the history of Fenway Park in Boston.

Even though he was known as a singles Superstar, Bruno was also an excellent tag team competitor. On July 26, 1967, he teamed with Spiros Arion to defeat The Sicilians for the United States Tag Team Championship. Unfortunately, due to Sammartino's responsibilities as WWE Champion, he was forced to relinquish the title. To the delight of fans everywhere, this was not the only time Bruno held tag team gold. He won the International Tag Team Championship on December 8, 1969 with Gotham City's Battman, when the duo toppled Prof. Toru Tanaka & Mitsu Arakawa. Bruno continued to appear in tag bouts throughout his career with friends such as Bobo Brazil, Andre the Giant, Chief Jay Strongbow, Pedro Morales, and former enemy turned ally Gorilla Monsoon.

A Record Reign Ends

On January 18, 1971, "The Russian Bear" Ivan Koloff shocked the world when he defeated Sammartino at Madison Square Garden to win the WWE Championship. Bruno's record-setting reign of seven-years, eight months and one day was over. His return to the ring in 1972 began in Los Angeles, where he made a special appearance and won a 22-man Battle Royal. On September 30, 1972, at the original *Showdown At Shea*, Sammartino met friend, and then-champion Pedro Morales in a classic 1 hour, 18 minute contest made more incredible because it was contested on a rain-slicked mat. Despite the treacherous conditions, the showdown is considered one of the greatest, most technically sound wrestling matches of all time. The match ended in a draw due to Shea Stadium's curfew.

In 1973, Bruno returned to WWE to standing ovations throughout the region. On December 10, Sammartino made history when he became the first two-time WWE Champion as he defeated Stan "The Man" Stasiak. Due to the prestige Sammartino brought to wrestling's richest prize, rule-breakers from far and wide traveled to WWE in search of fame and fortune. The treacherous trio of The Grand Wizard and future WWE Hall of Famers, Capt. Lou Albano, and "Classy" Freddie Blassie continued to recruit new contenders from all corners of the Earth to dethrone Sammartino. As the

dishonorable threesome learned time-and-time again, the power and heart of Sammartino was too much for the wretched henchman they employed.

Sammartino's fame expanded during the 1970s, as he was featured on the *Famous Sports Legends* television program hosted by future Major League Baseball Hall of Famer, Johnny Bench. He also appeared on the NBC network late-night talk show *Tomorrow with Tom Snyder*.

Appearances on major national broadcasts encouraged more Superstars to set their sights set on the champion. In 1976, Ken Patera arrived in WWE and he was one of the few opponents who matched the strength and grappling technique of the champion. Fred Blassie brought in Stan "The Lariat" Hansen. During their championship match on April 26, Hansen broke Sammartino's neck with his dreaded Lariat clothesline. Driven by revenge, Bruno returned weeks later against doctor's orders to defeat Hansen at the second *Showdown At Shea* event.

On April 30, 1977, Bruno once again was the victim of in-ring controversy. In his title defense against "Superstar" Billy Graham, the self-proclaimed "Tower of Power" pinned Sammartino with his feet on the top rope for added (and illegal) leverage. The referee never saw it and awarded the title to Graham. Despite rematches, Sammartino couldn't regain what many felt was rightfully his. Bruno soon entered semi-retirement, where fans saw him travel the country in singles and tag team matches.

The Student Turns on the Teacher

Still the adored heroic figure, Bruno made the transition from the ring to the broadcast booth. Serving as color commentator on *Championship Wrestling* with Vince K. McMahon, Bruno once again was a fixture on WWE programming. In 1980, Bruno agreed to once again lace up his boots for a good-will, 15-minute exhibition contest with his former pupil, Larry Zbyszko. The match was a traditional exchange of holds and maneuvers until Zbyszko became frustrated with his mentor's effective counters and refusal to push the attack himself. The issue came to a boiling point as Sammartino inadvertently knocked Zbyszko out of the ring. When Bruno held the rope open for Larry to re-enter the ring, Zbyszko brutally attacked his teacher in a fit of rage, hitting him three times in the head with a ringside chair.

A Steel Cage Match was signed for the historic *Showdown At Shea III*. Bruno told his broadcast partner Vince McMahon in front of a live studio audience, "I'm going to destroy Larry Zbyszko." Though the match was a violent clash and both men's bodies were battered, Sammartino's resolve made him unstoppable. When it was all said and done, Sammartino walked through the cage door and proved he was indeed the master.

In 1984, Bruno decided to help guide the WWE career of his son, David. It didn't take long for the new generation of Superstars to challenge Bruno in hopes of making a name for themselves. The first contenders were "Rowdy" Roddy Piper and "Cowboy" Bob Orton. Bruno also had heated exchanges with Randy "Macho Man" Savage after his attack on Ricky Steamboat. As Sammartino gave fans a locker room report, Savage taunted both Steamboat and Sammartino. At his wit's end, Sammartino attacked Savage and had to be restrained.

The matches between Bruno and the then-Intercontinental Champion were so fierce, the score could only be settled in a Steel Cage with each man having a tag team partner. Bruno warned WWE officials and his fans that these matches were going to be brutal. He enlisted the help of Tito Santana to combat the attacks of Savage & "Adorable" Adrian Adonis. Bruno's last WWE match was when he teamed with then-WWE Champion Hulk Hogan. To fans, this was a dream team of professional wrestling's best from its past, present, and future as the two mega-heroes met the enormous pair of King Kong Bundy & One Man Gang. After their victory, Bruno continued his expert commentary alongside Vince McMahon until he left WWE in March 1988.

BUDDY ROGERS

HT: 6'0"   WT: 235 lbs.   FROM: Camden, New Jersey   SIGNATURE MOVE: Figure-Four Leglock

Being a WWE Superstar is an honor reserved for the world's most amazing athletes. Of these honored men, only a select few ever gain entry into the prestigious fraternity of WWE Champions. The brotherhood boasts such great names as Triple H, Ric Flair, and Superstar Billy Graham. While these men earned immortality, there was one man who blazed the trail they rode to greatness: "Nature Boy" Buddy Rogers.

TITLE HISTORY	
WWE CHAMPION	*Defeated Antonino Rocca in the finals of a tournament to crown the first WWE Champion on April 25, 1963*

Rogers' first career choice was that of a police officer. While enforcing the law proved to be an honorable profession, he yearned for the spotlight. With no professional experience to his credit, Rogers confronted New Jersey wrestling promoters Ray and Frank Hanley and demanded an opportunity to prove himself in the ring. Impressed by the youngster's aggressive behavior, they offered him twenty dollars and a match on the following evening's card. On July 4, 1939, Rogers made his debut with an easy victory.

"Nature Boy" Earns Gold

Rogers' early years in the ring were spent competing under several names, but in Texas in 1944 he settled on the name Buddy Rogers and added the nickname, "Nature Boy." With the new name came a new look and attitude, which included an arrogant air, blonde hair, tanned muscles, and a deliberately cocky strut. Decades later, the legendary Ric Flair patterned his entire persona after Rogers, right down to the signature figure-four leglock.

The new Rogers turned heads as he began to compile an impressive record. Shortly after becoming "Nature Boy," he carried his newfound success straight to the National Wrestling Alliance Texas Heavyweight Championship.

On January 1, 1950, "The Nature Boy" added to his legacy when he defeated Johnny Valentine in the finals of a tournament to crown the first-ever NWA United States Champion. He went on to hold the title for an unprecedented 11 years.

Territorial Conflict

As was normally the case in those days, Rogers bounced around from territory to territory, mainly working in the United States' Midwestern region. When he made trips to the Northeast, however, Rogers worked for Jack Pfefer until the promoter left the territory. With Pfefer out of the New York wrestling scene, Rogers was left without a Northeast promoter. The powerhouse promoting tandem of Vincent J. McMahon and Toots Mondt moved quickly to sign Rogers to Capitol Wrestling Corporation.

Shortly after aligning with Capitol Wrestling, Rogers captured the NWA Championship when he defeated Pat O'Connor in front of a record crowd at Chicago's Comiskey Park on June 30, 1961. After the victory the cocky Rogers grabbed the microphone and proclaimed, "to a nicer guy, it couldn't happen." It was this type of egotistical display that made the "Nature Boy" one of the most hated Superstars by both the fans and his fellow competitors.

Despite his conceited persona, Rogers had an amazing ability to fill arenas, especially after winning the NWA Championship. This proved to be huge for Capitol Wrestling, who controlled Rogers' schedule. Over the next two years, McMahon and Mondt sold out Madison Square Garden countless times behind Rogers' huge drawing power.

Rogers' lack of title defenses outside of the Northeast didn't sit well with the other NWA promoters. Eventually, the NWA collectively decided that having Rogers defend the title almost exclusively in the Northeast was bad for business. As a result of the decision, they contacted Lou Thesz to try to unseat Rogers. This caused a certain degree of conflict between Capitol Wrestling and the NWA, who eventually got their way when Thesz toppled Rogers for the title in Toronto on January 14, 1963.

1994

The Birth of WWE

Following the match, McMahon and Mondt refused to recognize the controversial title change, claiming that a championship cannot change hands during a one-fall match (a common rule at the time). To further illustrate their point, McMahon and Mondt withdrew Capitol Wrestling from the NWA to form their own wrestling promotion called the World Wide Wrestling Federation, which today's fans know as WWE.

In April 1963, McMahon and Mondt's new promotion was born with their hand-picked Superstar, Buddy Rogers, leading the way as champion. Fans instantly took to the new wrestling promotion, thanks in large part to the credibility Rogers brought as champion. While he held the championship for less than one month before making way for Bruno Sammartino, the "Nature Boy" truly blazed the trail for all the future WWE Champions that followed.

When his in-ring career ended, Buddy Rogers went on to host a popular interview segment called Rogers' Corner.

The great Buddy Rogers passed away on July 6, 1992, due to complications from a heart attack and multiple strokes. Rogers received the ultimate honor when he was posthumously inducted into the WWE Hall of Fame by then-WWE Champion Bret Hart in June 1994. The induction was a fitting honor to a man who was the first to hold the prestigious title known today as the WWE Championship.

A New Generation

Following the loss to Sammartino, Rogers quietly took a step back from his wrestling career to address his failing health. In the late- 1970s, he reemerged in the Mid-Atlantic wrestling territory to confront a young Ric Flair, who also claimed to be the "Nature Boy." Unfortunately for Rogers, he was unable to keep up with the younger Flair, as he fell to the future 16-time World Champion in July 1978.

In the early-1980s, Rogers made a brief return to WWE to manage the career of Jimmy "Superfly" Snuka. On rare occasions, he would even lace up his boots to compete with Snuka in tag action. However, after suffering a broken hip in a match against Capt. Lou Albano & Ray Stevens, the original "Nature Boy" decided his competitive days were finished.

2010-
2000-09
1990-99
1980-89
1970-79
1960-69

BUDDY ROSE

HT: 6'1"   WT: 271 lbs.
FROM: Las Vegas, Nevada
SIGNATURE MOVE: Las Vegas Jackpot

Shortly after making his 1973 debut, "Playboy" Buddy Rose was seen as one of the brightest up-and-coming stars of his time. Fast forward two decades and he was still competing in the ring, but by this time, Rose was universally scoffed for letting his figure grow to unhealthy proportions.

The young Rose was never short on arrogance. Born with a platinum spoon in his mouth, according to manager the Grand Wizard, Rose was afforded the finest things in life, including limousines and private jets. In the ring, however, he was anything but a preppy snob. In fact, his brutality made him one of the most feared Superstars of the early 1980s, and eventually lead to a series of WWE Championship opportunities against Bob Backlund.

Over time, Rose began to gain a considerable amount of weight. With each pound he packed on, the less intimidating he became. By the end of his career, he was relegated to comedy sketches. His most infamous scene portrayed him as the star of an infomercial for the Blow Away diet system. According to Blow Away, losing weight was a breeze. Rose's figure told another story.

BUDDY WOLFE

HT: 6'1"   WT: 260 lbs.   FROM: St. Cloud, Minnesota
SIGNATURE MOVE: Reverse Neck Breaker

A former professional football player in the Continental Football League, Buddy Wolfe hung up his cleats in 1968 to tackle a career in sports-entertainment. After training with Verne Gagne, Wolfe spent his early years competing in the Carolinas and Dallas, where he squared off against the likes of Fritz Von Erich, Wahoo McDaniel and Ole Anderson.

In 1972, Wolfe travelled north to begin competing for WWE. His earliest matches were against Blackjack Slade, El Olympico and Sonny King. Wolfe won them all and quickly earned an opportunity at Pedro Morales' coveted WWE Championship. Over the course of the next year, Wolfe and Morales battled over the WWE Title several times. Each time, though, Morales managed to walk away unscathed. The closest Wolfe came was in April 1973, but the match was forced to end prematurely when Wolfe began bleeding profusely from the forehead.

Wolfe is also known for facing Andre the Giant in the Hall of Famer's 1973 Madison Square Garden debut. Additionally, he fought boxing legend Muhammad Ali in an exhibition match in 1976.

BUGSY McGRAW

HT: 6'3"   WT: 301 lbs.   FROM: Lafayette, Indiana
SIGNATURE MOVE: Splash

Bugsy McGraw was certainly considered odd, even among his oftentimes off-color cohorts. If he wasn't wearing swimming goggles en route to the ring, he probably had on a big top hat or colorful scarves or maybe even all three. When it came to Bugsy McGraw, fans never really knew what to expect.

The words that came out of McGraw's mouth were equally incomprehensible. Much like the Ultimate Warrior years later, McGraw liked to break out into rants that made sense only to him. When he was done, he'd usually sprint around the ring with no true purpose.

While fans looked at McGraw quizzically, his opposition knew he was no laughing matter. Once the bell rang, the bearded behemoth was all business. Utilizing his signature splash, McGraw captured more than twenty NWA regional titles, including the Florida Heavyweight Championship, which he won from Don Muraco in 1980.

Later in his career, McGraw teamed with the evenly offbeat Jimmy Valiant. Together, the "Boogie Woogie Man" and McGraw electrified the Carolinas with their flamboyant approach to wrestling.

BULL BUCHANAN

HT: 6'7"   WT: 296 lbs.
FROM: Cobb County, Georgia
SIGNATURE MOVE: Scissors Kick

TITLE HISTORY

WORLD TAG TEAM CHAMPION	*Partnered with Goodfather to defeat The Hardy Boys on November 6, 2000*

A former prison guard, Bull Buchanan built his tough exterior while maintaining order in Georgia's most notorious penitentiaries. When pushing around hardened criminals became mundane for the near 300 pounder, he turned to the rough rings of WWE in 2000.

Originally the tag team partner of fellow prison guard Big Boss Man, Buchanan finally found the challenge he was looking for. The duo's brief time together was highlighted with many big wins, including a victory over The Godfather & D-Lo Brown at *WrestleMania 2000*.

Shortly after *WrestleMania*, Buchanan joined Steven Richards' Right to Censor campaign. Trading in his nightstick for a shirt and tie, the massive Superstar became a force in the tag ranks with partner The Goodfather. The converted tandem held the World Tag Team Championship for one month in late 2000.

BULL NAKANO

HT: 5'7"   FROM: Kawaguchi, Japan
SIGNATURE MOVE: Guillotine Legdrop

TITLE HISTORY

WOMEN'S CHAMPION	*Defeated Alundra Blayze on November 27, 1994*

A professional in Japan since the age of 15, Bull Nakano was a Women's Junior Champion in All-Japan Pro Wrestling. Her fame reached America and in March 1986 she debuted in World Wrestling Entertainment alongside the legendary Dump Masamoto.

In 1994, Nakano returned to WWE to win the only title that eluded her for her entire career. She battled with Alundra Blayze and in front of over 45,000 fans at Tokyo's Egg Dome, Nakano defeated Alundra to become WWE Women's Champion. She held the title for over four months until losing it back to Blayze. Nakano left WWE in 1995 and briefly appeared in WCW until she retired in 1997.

Bull Nakano will be forever remembered as one of the greatest female competitors of all time. Her dominance in the ring was a testament to her commitment to harnessing her talent to the utmost.

BULL ORTEGA

HT: 5'11"
WT: 300 lbs.

This pillar of power caught the eye of fan and foe alike during his 1966 WWE debut. After emerging victorious in a series of handicap matches, Bull Ortega was considered a serious WWE Championship contender. His offense was built around power and submission moves, but Bull Ortega also possessed deceptive speed.

When circumstances called for it, Bull Ortega joined forces with fellow rule-breakers of the era including Luke Graham, Bulldog Brower, Prof. Toru Tanaka, Tank Morgan, and future WWE Hall of Famer Baron Mikel Scicluna. Bull Ortega's toughest challenge came in the form of then-WWE Champion, Bruno Sammartino. Though he tried often, Ortega failed to defeat Sammartino for the title.

BULL RAMOS

HT: 6'0"   WT: 350 lbs.
FROM: Houston, Texas

"Apache" Bull Ramos was a proud Native American who put his wrestling skills on display all over the world. In addition to finding great success in American rings, Ramos used his massive size to dominate opponents in Korea, Australia, and Japan.

As a member of WWE, Ramos earned the unique distinction of competing in the old Madison Square Garden's final show, as well as the new Garden's first show. He successfully turned back Antonio Pugliese in the old Garden, but came up short in the new arena, losing to WWE Champion Bruno Sammartino.

After failing in several attempts to dethrone Sammartino, Ramos headed west where he was able to capture the NWA Pacific Northwest Tag Team Championship with WWE Hall of Famer Jesse Ventura.

BULLDOG BROWER

HT: 5'8"   WT: 270 lbs.   FROM: Hamilton, Ontario, Canada
SIGNATURE MOVE: The Brower Lock

This former chiropractic student started in Stampede Wrestling. Bulldog Brower was infamous all over the world as a one man riot in the ring. At one point he even tangled with Terrible Ted, the wrestling bear and body slammed the gargantuan Haystacks Calhoun! Often led to the ring by future WWE Hall of Famer Capt. Lou Albano, Brower feuded with Superstars throughout the mid 1960s and 1970s. Bower was known for his battles for the WWE Championship against Bruno Sammartino. Later in the decade he came within seconds of beating then-WWE Champion Bob Backlund.

Brower retired from active competition in 1988. On September 15, 1997 he passed away after complications following hip surgery. Bulldog Brower was as feared as anyone who ever laced up a pair of boots and is regarded as one of the original terrors of professional wrestling. In the time since his death both fans and his fellow Superstars have reminisced on his classic battles, terrorizing ring presence, and chilling interviews.

B

2010-

2000-09

1990-99

1980-89

1970-79

1960-69

BUSHWHACKERS

MEMBERS: Butch, Luke   COMBINED WT: 498 lbs.   FROM: New Zealand

Luke and Butch traveled to World Wrestling Entertainment by way of New Zealand in December 1988. As they came to the ring, they licked the heads of their adoring fans and affectionately yelled in their ears. Despised by opponents, the Bushwhackers made an immediate impact on the tag team ranks as they scored victories over the Bolsheviks, the Rougeaus, Brain Busters, and Powers of Pain.

Their unorthodox ring style combined primitive roughhousing with sophisticated tag team tactics. The duo used a wide array of double-team moves, including the devastating Double Gutbuster. The Bushwhackers also displayed an ability to fight any form of opponent, as shown in their battles with Rhythm & Blues, the Orient Express, Money Inc., and the Natural Disasters.

The Bushwhacker lifestyle was contagious and even caught the interest of "Mean" Gene Okerlund who traveled to New Zealand to conduct a special profile on the tandem. The team's meager accommodations in the outback initially made Gene reluctant to continue, but once he had their fresh Bushwhacker Buzzard off the grill he returned in traditional Bushwhacker garb of a black tank-top and camouflage pants and had to be carried away to the United States.

Luke & Butch are WWE Legends and one of the most beloved tag teams in sports-entertainment history. They are remembered as a fun-loving duo who took on all challengers and were masters of the unexpected.

BUTCH REED

HT: 6'2"   WT: 255 lbs.   FROM: Kansas City, Missouri

Originally a football player by trade, Butch Reed jumped to wrestling in 1978. While most footballer players find it difficult to make the transition to the ring, Reed picked up his new craft quickly, resulting in many claiming he was a "natural."

Reed's early days were spent competing in the Mid-South territory, but when he came up short in a Loser Leaves Town Match, the athletic Superstar was forced to find a new home. It didn't take long for Reed to land on his feet, as WWE officials had been watching him from afar and jumped at the opportunity to bring him in to the company.

With manager Slick by his side, Reed debuted in WWE in 1986 with a new look. He dyed his hair blonde, adopted "The Natural" nickname and developed an arrogant attitude. In the ring, though, he was still the same dominant force.

Reed's first big WWE win came at the expense of Koko B. Ware at *WrestleMania III*. The victory eventually landed Reed a series of Intercontinental Championship matches against Ricky Steamboat. Reed was ultimately unsuccessful in capturing the title, but didn't let that deter him from being a force in WWE. Later than year, he teamed with One Man Gang to sneak attack "Superstar" Billy Graham. The savage beating forced Graham into permanent retirement.

Reed left WWE in 1988, but would resurface in WCW as Ron Simmons' partner in the powerful tag team Doom, which won the WCW Tag Team Championship.

BUTCHER VACHON   HT: 6'2"   WT: 282 lbs.
FROM: Montreal, Quebec, Canada

Paul Vachon made his professional wrestling debut in 1957. Known as "Butcher," the crazed Canadian hoped to equal the success enjoyed by his older brother, Maurice "Mad Dog" Vachon.

After a few years competing on his own, "Butcher" united with his brother to form one of history's most unorthodox tandems. Known for their hardcore style, the Vachons terrorized their way to tag team titles across North America. Perhaps their most impressive reign came when they topped Dick the Bruiser & The Crusher for the AWA World Tag Team Championship in August 1969. "Butcher" and "Mad Dog" went on to hold the gold for an amazing 623 days.

In WWE, Butcher Vachon went toe-to-toe with many legendary names, including Sgt. Slaughter, Jimmy Snuka and Bob Backlund. Despite these great battles, it was his 1984 in-ring wedding for which he will most be remembered. With many of WWE's top Superstars serving as witnesses, Vachon and his bride Ophelia tied the knot in a ceremony that was ultimately marred by David Schultz' physical interference.

BUZZ SAWYER

HT: 5'9" **WT:** 240 lbs.
FROM: St. Petersburg, Florida

Always the first to remind fans of his greatness, Buzz Sawyer certainly never suffered from any self-esteem issues. Luckily for Sawyer, he was, as legendary announcer Gordon Solie put it, double-tough, making it easy for him to back up his boastful comments.

Sawyer's WWE career only consisted of a handful of matches, but outside of WWE, the man known as "Mad Dog" attained great success in many of the nation's southern territories, including Georgia Championship Wrestling and the Texas-based World Class Championship Wrestling.

While in Georgia, Sawyer turned back Tommy Rich to claim the NWA National Heavyweight Championship in May 1982. His time in the Lone Star State was highlighted by a lengthy reign as Texas Heavyweight Champion, which he captured from Brian Adias in July 1986. Over the course of his career, Sawyer engaged in memorable rivalries with some of the sport's greatest, including the Von Erichs, The Four Horsemen and Ronnie Garvin.

BUTTERBEAN

HT: 5'11" **WT:** 316 lbs.
FROM: Jasper, Alabama

A famous Toughman contest winner, boxer, and mixed martial-artist, Butterbean began boxing professionally in 1994. His loyal fan following grew and he made his first WWE appearance in 1997 when he defeated Marc Mero at *In Your House: Degeneration-X*. He returned in 1999 to win the Brawl For All Match against Bart Gunn at *WrestleMania XV*. Today, Butterbean continues to compete in organizations all over the world for boxing and mixed martial-arts.

bWo (BLUE WORLD ORDER)

MEMBERS: Big Stevie Cool, The Blue Guy, Hollywood Nova

During the height of the New World Order's popularity, a band of misfits joined forces to parody the powerful WCW faction in ECW. Known as the Blue World Order, each Superstar assumed the identity of an nWo member. As expected, the bWo garnered more laughs than victories, but that didn't stop them from hilariously mocking the nWo each week while brashly declaring, "We're taking over!"

Eight years after the bWo disbanded, the faction made an unexpected return at *ECW One Night Stand* in 2005. This time, the group found themselves right in the middle of all the hullabaloo. The bWo later earned a spot on *SmackDown* and an appearance at *The Great American Bash*.

Unfortunately for the bWo, their reunion tour did not last. One month into their run, Big Stevie Cool, The Blue Guy, and Hollywood Nova disbanded again.

BYRON SAXTON

HT: 6'2" **WT:** 219 lbs. **FROM:** Burke, Virginia

It's not a uncommon for a veteran Superstar to transition into the announce booth toward the end of his in-ring career. The most prominent examples of this include WWE Hall of Famers Gorilla Monsoon and Jerry "The King" Lawler. Byron Saxton, however, is taking the exact opposite career track.

Saxton made his debut as an ECW commentator in October 2009. The articulate newcomer stayed behind the announce booth until ECW closed its doors in early 2010.

The WWE Universe wasn't introduced to Saxton again until December 2010 when it was announced the former commentator would compete in season four of *WWE NXT*. With Chris Masters as his original Pro, and later Dolph Ziggler and Vickie Guerrero, the confident Rookie finished fourth in the competition.

Saxton received another opportunity at glory when he was chosen for *NXT Redemption*. This time, he displayed more of an edge and even turned on his Pro, Yoshi Tatsu. The new approach, however, did little to help Saxton, who was ultimately the second Rookie eliminated.

C

2010-

2000-09

1990-99

1980-89

1970-79

1960-69

THE CABINET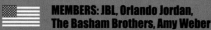

MEMBERS: JBL, Orlando Jordan, The Basham Brothers, Amy Weber

Shortly after John "Bradshaw" Layfield won the WWE Championship at *The Great American Bash 2004*, he employed Superstars to protect his interests and do his bidding inside and outside of the ring. The group operated like a corporation, with each member having a title and responsibilities. Orlando Jordan, the United States Champion, was the Chief of Staff. Doug & Danny Basham were the Secretaries of Defense and held the WWE Tag Team Championship. Amy Weber was the Image Consultant.

The group was defined by their brash behavior and the Longhorn pose, which was in homage to their leader. They bullied the *SmackDown* roster and clashed with the brand's top Superstars, and even clashed with ECW's Blue World Order. The Cabinet disbanded in the summer of 2005 when injuries forced JBL to take a break from in-ring competition.

CAMACHO

**HT: 6'2" WT: 230 lbs.
FROM: Juarez, Mexico**

Camacho credits longtime friend Hunico with saving his life back in the barrio where the two Superstars grew up. Years later, Camacho is returning the favor, ensuring that his vato is never roughed up by other WWE Superstars.

The street-tough Superstar's entrance is unlike any ever before seen in WWE. With Hunico standing on pegs on the back of his lowrider bicycle, Camacho slowly rolls to the ring with his signature scowl on his face. According to the two Superstars, the lowrider bicycle is an expression of their culture. They also build the bikes from scratch and each one costs thousands of dollars. Still relatively new to the WWE scene, Camacho has yet to show off much of his in-ring abilities. One thing's for certain, though; if his intimidating presence translates into victories, he will have a long and successful WWE career.

CAMP CORNETTE

MEMBERS: Vader, Owen Hart, British Bulldog

Loudmouth manager Jim Cornette's quest to dominate WWE during the mid-to-late 1990s largely depended on the success of three men: Vader, Owen Hart and British Bulldog. Collectively known as Camp Cornette, the trio was assembled with hopes of catapulting Cornette's managerial career to the WWE Championship, a status he formerly held while working with Yokozuna.

As the largest Superstar in the stable, Vader seemed the logical choice to bring the title to Cornette. After teaming with Hart & Bulldog to flatten WWE Champion Shawn Michaels and his partners, Sid & Ahmed Johnson, Vader was awarded a title opportunity against HBK.

Unfortunately for Camp Cornette, a WWE Championship reign was not in the cards, as Michaels defeated Vader at *SummerSlam 1996*. Both Hart and Bulldog also competed on the *SummerSlam* card; however, Cornette was too busy working with Vader to pay much attention to his other Superstars. The manager's disregard for their success eventually lead to the demise of Camp Cornette.

CANADIAN HEAVYWEIGHT CHAMPIONSHIP

The Canadian Heavyweight Championship was introduced in the summer of 1985 as World Wrestling Entertainment expanded its global reach into the provinces of Canada. The championship was awarded to Dino Bravo on August 1, 1985. Dino Bravo went on to defend the championship all over Canada during its brief existence. On January 6, 1986, the Canadian Heavyweight Championship was retired as Dino Bravo chose to concentrate on becoming World Wrestling Federation Champion.

THE CAN-AM CONNECTION

MEMBERS: Rick Martel, Tom Zenk   COMBINED WT: 471 lbs.

Take one of the top grapplers from Canada and add one of Minnesota's best athletes and you get the high-flying duo known as the Can-Am Connection. Rick Martel & Tom Zenk debuted in WWE in 1987 and became almost instant championship contenders after an impressive victory at *WrestleMania III* against the Magnificent Muraco & "Cowboy" Bob Orton.

The Can-Am Connection eventually earned a shot at the World Tag Team Championship. However, then-champions, the Hart Foundation, took out Zenk before the match started. Zenk never fully recovered from his injuries and disappeared from WWE. Martel, seeking revenge for the heinous action, recruited Tito Santana, and the pair competed under the name Strike Force. The Can-Am Connection enjoyed unprecedented success during their brief time together. Fans to this day wonder what might have been had the duo remained together.

CANDICE MICHELLE

HT: 5'7"   FROM: Milwaukee, Wisconsin
SIGNATURE MOVE: Candywrapper

TITLE HISTORY

WOMEN'S CHAMPION	*Defeated Melina on June 24, 2007*

When Candice Michelle arrived in WWE in 2004, few insiders expected her to be anything more than just a pretty face. Hearing the whispers, the determined Diva dedicated herself to proving her detractors wrong. Within three years of stepping foot in a ring for the first time, she reached the pinnacle of her profession, capturing the Women's Championship. She managed to keep the pretty face along the way, becoming a *Playboy* cover girl and star of several Super Bowl commercials.

Candice's WWE career nearly came to an end before it ever began. After failing to make the finals of the 2004 Diva Search, it appeared as though the beautiful brunette was at a career crossroads. Fortunately, WWE officials saw something they liked in her and offered a contract. At first, Candice's limited wrestling ability restricted her to non-competitive roles. While she enjoyed the attention she was garnering, Candice realized she was beginning to be regarded simply as eye candy.

Behind countless hours of training she undertook from former Four Horsemen enforcer Arn Anderson, Candice became a legitimate threat in the Women's Division by 2007. On June 24, she proved her worth when she defeated Melina for the coveted Women's Championship at *Vengeance*.

The win capped off Candice's amazing evolution into a dominant female force in the ring. All the while, she maintained an unmatched level of sensuality that eventually landed her on the cover of *Playboy*. On top of all this, Candice served as the popular girl in many controversial Go Daddy ads. She remined a top contender for the prestigious Women's Championship but a string of severe injuries forced her to leave the world of sports-entertainment sooner than expected.

CAPITOL PUNISHMENT

June 19 2011

Verizon Center - Washington, D.C.

The card at *Capitol Punishment* was dominated by singles matches between bitter rivals, including Rey Mysterio facing off against CM Punk, The Miz battling his former *NXT* rookie Alex Riley, and John Cena's successful defense of the WWE Championship. Cena defeated R-Truth, who had been disrespecting both the leader of the Cenation and the entire WWE Universe. Randy Orton was able to keep the World Heavyweight Championship with a victory over Christian, but two other titles changed hands during the night.

Ezekiel Jackson claimed the Intercontinental Championship when he forced his former Corre cohort, Wade Barrett, to submit to a backbreaker. Dolph Ziggler, with some help from Vickie Guerrero, put Kofi Kingston to sleep and left Washington, D.C. as the new United States Champion.

CARLITO

HT: 5'10"   WT: 220 lbs.   FROM: The Caribbean
SIGNATURE MOVE: The Backstabber

TITLE HISTORY

INTERCONTINENTAL CHAMPION	*Defeated Shelton Benjamin on June 21, 2005*
UNITED STATES CHAMPION	*Defeated John Cena on October 7, 2004*
WORLD TAG TEAM CHAMPION	*Partnered with Primo to defeat The Miz & John Morrison on April 5, 2009*
WWE TAG TEAM CHAMPION	*Partnered with Primo to defeat Curt Hawkins & Zack Ryder on September 26, 2008*

This brash second-generation Superstar had an unbelievable debut in October 2004 when he beat John Cena for the United States Championship on *SmackDown*. Carlito warned everyone that he spits in the face of people who don't want to be cool. Unfortunately, many Superstars failed to live up to his definition of cool. 2005 saw the debut of his talk segment *Carlito's Cabana,* where he disrespected guests and fans on a frequent basis.

After the Draft Lottery, Carlito brought his cool demeanor to *Raw* and again made an incredible debut when he beat Shelton Benjamin for the Intercontinental Championship. Though he lost it later in the year to "Nature Boy" Ric Flair, this bad apple remained a serious threat to any WWE champion. He also found time to kick it with the ladies as he developed a romance with Torrie Wilson.

In 2008, he returned to *SmackDown* and formed a championship combination with his brother, Primo. The brothers also won a match to unify the WWE and World Tag Team Championships at *WrestleMania XXV*. After losing the titles, Carlito turned on his brother and temporarily took on Rosa Mendes as a manager. Before his departure from WWE in 2010, Carlito served as a pro on the first season of *WWE NXT* and even reformed a tag team with his brother.

C

2010-
2000-09
1990-99
1980-89
1970-79
1960-69

CARLOS COLON

HT: 5'10"   **WT:** 246 lbs.
FROM: Santa Isabel, Puerto Rico

Puerto Rican fans recognize Carlos Colon as the founder and star of the World Wrestling Council promotion. While his in-ring dominance certainly leaves an impressive legacy, the legend of Carlos Colon amazingly continues to grow every time his two sons enter a WWE ring.

After spending the late 1960s competing in the Northeast territories of the United States, Colon retreated to his native Puerto Rico, where he became an iconic figure. Colon briefly competed in WWE during the early 1990s. The only high-profile account of his tenure was his participation in the 1993 *Royal Rumble*. Colon managed to eliminate Damian Damento from the contest before being tossed out by Yokozuna. Colon's greatest contributions to WWE would come more than 10 years later when his son Carlito made his WWE debut, followed by another son, Primo.

CAYLEN CROFT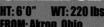

HT: 6'0"   **WT:** 220 lbs.
FROM: Akron, Ohio

Success came quickly for Caylen Croft. After ECW's New Superstar Initiative introduced audiences to the colorful competitor in December 2009, Croft, along with his longtime best friend and tag team partner Trent Barreta, racked up several impressive victories. Unfortunately for Croft, however, ECW ceased existing shortly after his debut; and with it went the new Superstar's success.

Following the end of ECW, Croft and Barreta shopped their talents to both *Raw* and *SmackDown*. The free agents ultimately signed with the Friday night brand, where they struggled mightily. In February 2010, Cryme Tyme became the first duo to pad their won-loss records courtesy of Croft & Barreta. Other teams soon followed, including The Hart Dynasty and MVP & JTG.

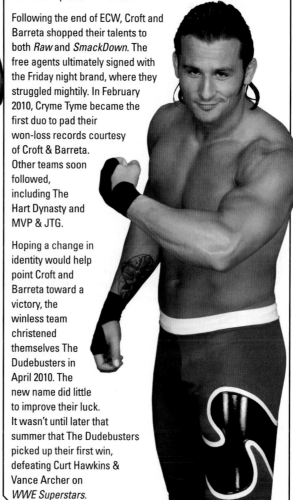

Hoping a change in identity would help point Croft and Barreta toward a victory, the winless team christened themselves The Dudebusters in April 2010. The new name did little to improve their luck. It wasn't until later that summer that The Dudebusters picked up their first win, defeating Curt Hawkins & Vance Archer on *WWE Superstars.*

CHARLIE FULTON

HT: 6'2"   **WT:** 246 lbs.
FROM: Marion, Ohio
SIGNATURE MOVE: Piledriver

Charlie Fulton kicked off his mat career in March 1968. But shortly after making his debut, the military draft forced the youngster to pack up his boots and enlist in the army. He served his country for several years before finally returning to the ring.

A skilled mat technician, Fulton spent the majority of the 1970s and early 1980s travelling from territory to territory. Texas. Montreal. Florida. Charlotte. Detroit. Tennessee. He competed in them all. Along the way, he stood across the ring from the greatest of all time, including Lou Thesz, Bruno Sammartino and Ric Flair.

One of Fulton's few tastes of gold came when he teamed with Bobby Mayne to defeat Ron Gibson and Stan Pulaski for the NWA Southern Tag Team Championship in June 1974. Fulton ventured to New York and WWE in the early 1980s. While there, he had many memorable battles with the likes of Tony Atlas, Rocky Johnson and S.D. Jones.

CHARLIE MINN

His tenure with WWE only lasted a few months, but Charlie Minn will always be remembered by longtime fans as the overly-excited announcer on *WWE Action Zone.*

Minn also brought a never-before-seen level of energy to WWE's Live Event News updates. As the segment's anchor, Minn enthusiastically alerted the WWE Universe to upcoming events in their area, complete with information on how to purchase tickets.

When he wasn't pushing ticket sales, Minn could also be seen interviewing Superstars. Unlike WWE Hall of Famer "Mean" Gene Okerlund, who conducted his interviews with a great deal of professionalism, Minn often appeared in awe of the Superstars he was interviewing.

Minn's WWE career came to a quick close in early 1995. After leaving the world of sports-entertainment, the animated announcer became a local sportscaster in several markets across the United States, including Fresno, Cleveland, Portland, Providence and Hartford. Minn also puts his talents to work as a part-time actor and filmmaker.

CHARLIE HAAS

HT: 6'2" **WT:** 242 lbs. **FROM:** Edmond, Oklahoma
SIGNATURE MOVE: Haas of Pain

TITLE HISTORY

WWE TAG TEAM CHAMPION (3 TIMES)	*Partnered with Shelton Benjamin to defeat Los Guerreros on February 6, 2003* *Partnered with Shelton Benjamin to defeat Eddie Guerrero & Tajiri on July 3, 2003* *Partnered with Rico to defeat Scotty 2 Hotty & Rikishi on April 22, 2004*

As a former two-time Big East amateur wrestling champion at Seton Hall University, Charlie Haas possesses technical grappling mastery that few can match. The result has been a successful WWE career, highlighted by several reigns atop the tag team division.

Haas made his debut on Dec. 26, 2002. Along with partner Shelton Benjamin, he was introduced as a member of Team Angle. His main responsibility was to ensure then-WWE Champion Kurt Angle would hold on to his title. Along the way, however, Haas & Benjamin won some gold of their own, defeating Los Guerreros for the WWE Tag Team Championship in February 2003.

The duo dubbed themselves the "World's Greatest Tag Team," but were forced to split in March 2004 when the WWE Draft sent Benjamin to *Raw*. Despite the separation, Haas sought another WWE Tag Team Championship. He formed an oddly successful team with the eccentric Rico. With Miss Jackie by their side, Haas & Rico defeated Rikishi & Scotty 2 Hotty for the titles in April 2004.

Haas departed from WWE in July 2005 and spent the next several months on the independent circuit, but hoped to return to WWE. He was given the chance on April 17, 2006 when he made his surprise return and defeated his former partner, Shelton Benjamin. In the summer of 2008, he took his career in an unexpected direction. He began to emulate WWE Legends and Superstars in the ring. These dead-ringer impersonations earned him a 2008 Slammy Award.

CHAVO GUERRERO

HT: 5'9" **WT:** 215 lbs. **FROM:** El Paso, Texas
SIGNATURE MOVE: Frog Splash

TITLE HISTORY

CRUISERWEIGHT CHAMPION (4 TIMES)	*Defeated Rey Mysterio on February 15, 2004* *Defeated Jacqueline on May 16, 2004* *Defeated Funaki on February 20, 2005* *Defeated Gregory Helms on February 18, 2007*
ECW CHAMPION	*Defeated CM Punk on January 22, 2008*
WWE TAG TEAM CHAMPION (2 TIMES)	*Partnered with Eddie Guerrero to defeat Edge & Rey Mysterio on November 17, 2002* *Partnered with Eddie Guerrero to defeat Shelton Benjamin & Charlie Haas on September 18, 2003*

As a member of the famed Guerrero family, Chavo Guerrero was born with sports-entertainment running through his veins. And after a childhood spent honing his skills in the family ring, the third-generation Superstar began to ply his trade professionally in Mexico and Japan during the mid-1990s.

Guerrero was introduced to American audiences in 1996, when he debuted in WCW. But it wasn't until 2001 that he truly began to shine as a member of the WWE roster.

In November 2002, Guerrero claimed his first of several championships in WWE when he teamed with his uncle, Eddie Guerrero, to capture the WWE Tag Team Titles. Guerrero continued to make his family proud over the next few years, winning the Cruiserweight Championship three times before inexplicably denouncing his family name. Claiming his Hispanic heritage was holding him back, Guerrero announced he was joining middle-class America under the new name of Kerwin White.

Chavo reclaimed the Guerrero name in November 2005, following the passing of his uncle, Eddie. Adopting the famed Frog Splash as his own, Guerrero went on to capture his fourth and final WWE Cruiserweight Championship in February 2007. He also defeated CM Punk in January 2008 to win the ECW Championship.

Guerrero was released from his WWE contract in June 2011, marking the end of his decade-long run with the recognized global leader in sports-entertainment.

1960-69
1970-79
1980-89
1990-99
2000-09
2010-

2010-
2000-09
1990-99
1980-89
1970-79
1960-69

CHAVO GUERRERO, SR.

HT: 5'11"   WT: 229 lbs.
FROM: El Paso, Texas

TITLE HISTORY

CRUISERWEIGHT CHAMPION	*Defeated Chavo Guerrero on May 20, 2004*

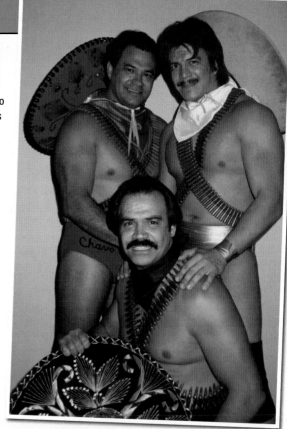

As the oldest son of wrestling great Gory Guerrero, Chavo Guerrero, Sr., was responsible for ushering in his family's second generation of Superstars, which also included Mando, Hector, and Eddie Guerrero.

A legend in Los Angeles, Chavo captured the territory's Americas Heavyweight Championship a record fifteen times during the 1970s and early 1980s. His record-breaking number of title reigns came at the expense of such great names as Ernie Ladd, Roddy Piper and Pat Patterson. He also claimed tag team gold with his father and brother Hector, among others.

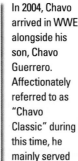

In 2004, Chavo arrived in WWE alongside his son, Chavo Guerrero. Affectionately referred to as "Chavo Classic" during this time, he mainly served as a mentor to his son. However, in May 2004, the elder Guerrero was uncharacteristically placed in a Triple Threat Match against his boy and Spike Dudley. In a shocking turn of events, Chavo Classic capitalized on a bizarre set of circumstances to defeat the younger Guerrero for the Cruiserweight Championship. He lost the title to Rey Mysterio one month later.

CHERRY

HT: 5'6"
FROM: The Other Side Of The Tracks

This sweetheart roller-skated into World Wrestling Entertainment in January 2007. On the arm of her boyfriend, Deuce, and her brother, Domino, this bubble-gum chewing babe was at ringside always ready to help her guys to win.

Her team ended the record-breaking reign of Brian Kendrick & Paul London, earning the WWE Tag Team Championship in the process. Eventually, the Diva traded in her roller skates for wrestling boots as she took on Victoria, Natayla and Michelle McCool. Unfortunately for Cherry, this venture into competition with the start of a fan following led to her being dumped by Deuce & Domino in favor of Maryse. Before it was all said and done, Cherry defeated Maryse on *SmackDown*.

In August 2008, Cherry returned to her side of the tracks and left WWE. Their may be other girls around, but none that can turn heads like Cherry.

CHIEF BIG HEART

FROM: Oklahoma
SIGNATURE MOVE: The Bow & Arrow

Adorned in an oversized Indian headdress and a long leather robe, Chief Big Heart usually made his way to the ring with a huge smile on his face. Once the bell rang, however, the proud Oklahoman concealed his jolly side and became all business in the ring.

Chief Big Heart's prime came in the late 1950s and early 1960s, where he formed several successful tag teams. His most prominent partners were Suni War Cloud, Red McIntyre and Chief Little Eagle. Chief Big Heart captured NWA tag team gold in Georgia with McIntyre and Little Eagle. He also paired with Little Eagle to win the Texas version of the NWA tag titles in April 1959.

As a singles competitor, Chief Big Heart briefly held the NWA Southern Heavyweight Championship when he defeated Jerry Graham for the gold on January 4, 1957. One week later, he lost the title back to Graham, thus ending his only taste of singles gold.

CHIEF JAY STRONGBOW

HT: 6'2" **WT:** 247 lbs. **FROM:** Pawhuska, Oklahoma **SIGNATURE MOVE:** Tomahawk Chop

TITLE HISTORY

WORLD TAG TEAM CHAMPION (4 TIMES)	Partnered with Sonny King to defeat Mikel Scicluna & King Curtis Iaukea on May 22, 1972
	Partnered with Billy White Wolf to win a three team tournament on December 7, 1976
	Partnered with Jules Strongbow to defeat Mr. Fuji & Mr. Saito June 28, 1982
	Partnered with Jules Strongbow to defeat Mr. Fuji & Mr. Saito October 26, 1982

This future WWE Hall of Famer's career began in 1947. Throughout the 1950s and '60s, he was one of the brightest stars in the NWA and held several singles and tag team titles around the southeastern United States. In 1970, Chief Jay Strongbow debuted in WWE and became an instant hero with his colorful Indian ring attire and high-flying attacks. The Chief fought rule-breakers such as Prof. Toru Tanaka, Waldo Von Erich, Ivan Koloff, Pampero Firpo, Tarzan Tyler, Crusher Verdu and future WWE Hall of Famers George "The Animal" Steele, Killer Kowalski, Eddie Graham, The Sheik, Johnny Rodz and Blackjack Mulligan.

With each Tomahawk Chop, Strongbow's popularity rose. In May 1972, he won his first of four World Tag Team Championships as he and Sonny King defeated future WWE Hall of Famer Baron Mike Scicluna & King Curtis Iaukea. Although Strongbow & King only held the title for one month, Chief loved being a part of a team and thrived on the fierce competition. Strongbow captured his second tag team championship in 1976 when he formed an alliance with fellow Native American warrior Chief Billy White Wolf. Their title reign was suddenly cut short when White Wolf suffered a career-ending neck injury at the hands of Ken Patera. Strongbow saught to avenge his partner's heartless attack. Back in singles action, Strongbow locked up with Stan "The Man" Stasiak, Tor Kamata, Spiros Arion, Baron Von Raschke and future WWE Hall of Famers Mr. Fuji and The Valiant Brothers.

Strongbow's violent battles against WWE's most vicious villains continued, and in 1979, he waged war on future WWE Hall of Famer Greg "The Hammer" Valentine. After Valentine broke Strongbow's leg, the Chief came back with a vengeance and settled their score in an Indian Strap Match at Madison Square Garden. In 1980, Strongbow took a brief hiatus from WWE and toured Puerto Rico. He was then brought into Georgia Championship Wrestling and joined another great, Chief Wahoo McDaniel. Strongbow returned to WWE in 1982 and formed another great tag team. This time, the men were bonded by blood and along with his brother, Jules, the pair from Pawhuska, Oklahoma defeated Mr. Fuji and Mr. Saito for the titles on June 28th. The Strongbows lost and regained the titles from Fuji & Saito later that year before they finally succumbed to future WWE Hall of Famers The Wild Samoans in 1983. Strongbow's remarkable popularity brought him to Hollywood, when he appeared in 1984's *Micki & Maude,* starring Dudley Moore.

The Chief retired from full-time action in 1985 and became a high-ranking member of the WWE front-office. Fans saw him return to television in 1994 when he mentored newcomer Tatanka in the young Native American's rivalry against Irwin R. Schyster. The relationship between the two Native Americans was so strong Chief gave Tatanka a sacred head dress in recognition of his WWE success. That June, Strongbow's unbelievable six-decade career was honored as Tatanka inducted him into the WWE Hall of Fame. Shortly thereafter, Strongbow put the world of sports-entertainment behind him and relocated to Georgia where he still lives today.

Chief Jay Strongbow is warmly remembered as one of the most beloved figures in WWE history. Many consider him the greatest Native American to ever step into the ring and not one with which to trifle. Strongbow was a hero in whom all WWE fans could believe.

Sadly, this legendary Superstar passed away on April 3, 2012.

CHIEF WHITE OWL 🇺🇸

HT: 5'10" **WT:** 230 lbs. **FROM:** Cherokee, North Carolina **SIGNATURE MOVE:** Tomahawk Chop

Chief White Owl, a proud Native American from the Cherokee Tribe, started his in-ring career in the mid-1950s. Utilizing a Tomahawk Chop as a finisher, his early career was highlighted by runs in several different territories, including Montreal, Florida, Pittsburgh, and even the Bahamas.

After making a name for himself in promotions worldwide, Chief White Owl briefly joined WWE, where he gained notoriety teaming with fellow Native Americans Wahoo McDaniel and Chief Big Heart. Madison Square Garden was the site of his greatest WWE victory, as he teamed with Big Heart to defeat Smasher Sloan & Waldo Von Erich in May 1965.

After leaving WWE, Chief White Owl went on to compete in Detroit before eventually landing with the Buffalo-based National Wrestling Federation.

CHRIS BENOIT 🍁

HT: 5'11" **WT:** 229 lbs. **FROM:** Edmonton, Alberta, Canada **SIGNATURE MOVE:** Crippler Crossface

TITLE HISTORY

INTERCONTINENTAL CHAMPION (4 TIMES)	*Defeated Kurt Angle on April 2, 2000* *Defeated Chris Jericho on May 8, 2000* *Defeated Billy Gunn on December 10, 2000* *Defeated Rob Van Dam on July 29, 2002*
UNITED STATES CHAMPION (3 TIMES)	*Defeated Orlando Jordan on August 21, 2005* *Defeated Booker T on February 19, 2006* *Defeated Mr. Kennedy on October 13, 2006*
WORLD HEAVYWEIGHT CHAMPION	*Defeated Triple H and Shawn Michaels in a Triple Threat Match on March 14, 2004*
WORLD TAG TEAM CHAMPION (3 TIMES)	*Partnered with Chris Jericho to defeat Stone Cold Steve Austin & Triple H on May 21, 2001* *Partnered with Edge to defeat Ric Flair & Batista on April 19, 2004* *Partnered with Edge to defeat Rob Conway & Sylvain Grenier on October 19, 2004*
WWE TAG TEAM CHAMPION	*Partnered with Kurt Angle to defeat Edge & Rey Mysterio on October 20, 2002*

When Chris Benoit was twelve years old he saw the Dynamite Kid perform in the ring. At that moment he dedicated himself to building his body for a career in sports-entertainment. After graduating high school in 1985, Chris pursued his dream and every week drove almost two-hundred miles to train in Stu Hart's famous Dungeon. Benoit worked tirelessly to learn this sacred art form and emulate Dynamite Kid's mannerisms and moves. Shortly thereafter he debuted in Calgary's Stampede Wrestling and in Japan.

By the early 1990s Benoit had a reputation as one of the world's greatest technical competitors. After he won Japan's prestigious Super J-Cup Tournament in 1994, he arrived in ECW where he had many memorable matches and held the ECW World Tag Team Championship with Dean Malenko. In October 1995 Benoit signed with World Championship Wrestling and was quickly recruited by future WWE Hall of Famer "Nature Boy" Ric Flair for a revival of The Four Horsemen. While Chris eventually held every championship the company had to offer, he knew what he truly wanted to achieve in sports-entertainment was unattainable in WCW.

In January 2000, he made a radical debut alongside future WWE Hall of Famer Eddie Guerrero, Dean Malenko, and Perry Saturn. In WWE Benoit competed against many of the best, including Stone Cold Steve Austin, The Rock, Undertaker, Kurt Angle, Chris Jericho, and Batista. In 2004, Benoit defied the odds when he bested twenty-nine other Superstars to win The Royal Rumble. This monumental accomplishment led him to fulfilling his destiny at *WrestleMania XX*, when he captured the World Heavyweight Championship in a Triple Threat Match versus Triple H and Shawn Michaels. After the realization of an eighteen-year dream, Benoit defended his championship against all challengers. While he lost the prestigious prize nine months later to Randy Orton at *SummerSlam*, Benoit remained a top contender for many of WWE's renowned championships.

Among the many skills Chris Jericho possesses is the ability to make a memorable first impression. His 1999 debut, which saw him revealed as the Superstar behind the mysterious millennium countdown clock, remains one of the most brilliant entrances of all time. And years later, Jericho managed to out-do himself when he returned in 2007 as the savior behind a cryptic binary code, and in 2012 when he mysteriously warned that the end begins on 1-2-12.

Prior to amazing WWE audiences, Jericho gained a cult-like following while competing in ECW and WCW. The earliest days of his career saw the Canadian Superstar typecast as a cruiserweight competitor. But after several successful runs with the promotion's Cruiserweight Title and the surfacing of an undeniably charismatic personality, the now-defunct promotion was forced to pay attention to the entertaining Jericho. He was soon elevated to more high-profile matches, but it was too late for WCW to retain his services. Jericho had his eyes on bigger and better opportunities. He was on his way to WWE.

"Welcome to *Raw* is Jericho!"

The move to WWE proved to be wise for Y2J. Moments after making his highly-anticipated debut in August 1999, Jericho found himself rubbing shoulders on television with sports-entertainment's biggest names, including The Rock, Big Show and Undertaker. He also captured his greatest recognition to date when he defeated Chyna to claim the Intercontinental Championship in December 1999. The victory marked the first of many WWE title reigns for Y2J.

In April 2000, Jericho's meteoric rise appeared to reach its apex when he defeated Triple H for the WWE Championship. Unfortuantely for Y2J, however, The Game used his stroke to get the decision reversed, resulting in the record books failing to recognize Jericho's career-changing victory.

The controversy surrounding Jericho's win over Triple H failed to derail the popular Superstar. In the months that followed, Y2J went on to reclaim the Intercontinental Championship, as well as capture the European, Hardcore and World Tag Team Titles. With so much gold to his credit, it was only a matter of time before Jericho was afforded another opportunity at the top prize.

CHRIS JERICHO 🍁

HT: 6'0" **WT:** 226 lbs. **FROM:** Winnipeg, Manitoba, Canada **SIGNATURE MOVE:** Codebreaker, Walls of Jericho, Lionsault

" BREAK THE WALLS DOWN "

TITLE HISTORY	
EUROPEAN CHAMPION	*Won a Triple Threat Match against Chris Benoit and Kurt Angle on April 2, 2000*
HARDCORE CHAMPION	*1 Time*
INTERCONTINENTAL CHAMPION (9 TIMES)	*Defeated Chyna on December 12, 1999* *Won a Triple Threat Match against Chyna and Hardcore Holly on January 23, 2000* *Defeated Chris Benoit on May 4, 2000* *Defeated Chris Benoit on January 21, 2001* *Defeated Rob Van Dam on September 16, 2002* *Defeated Rob Van Dam on October 27, 2003* *Defeated Christian on September 12, 2004* *Defeated Jeff Hardy on March 10, 2008* *Defeated Rey Mysterio on June 7, 2009*
WORLD HEAVYWEIGHT CHAMPION (3 TIMES)	*Won a Championship Scramble Match on September 7, 2008* *Defeated Batista on November 3, 2008* *Defeated Undertaker on February 21, 2010*
WORLD TAG TEAM CHAMPION (5 TIMES)	*Partnered with Chris Benoit to defeat Stone Cold Steve Austin & Triple H on May 21, 2001* *Partnered with The Rock to defeat The Dudley Boys on October 22, 2001* *Partnered with Christian to defeat Kane & The Hurricane on October 14, 2002* *Partnered with Edge to defeat Carlito & Primo on June 28, 2009* *Partnered with Big Show to defeat Cody Rhodes & Ted DiBiase on July 26, 2009*
WWE CHAMPION	*Defeated Stone Cold Steve Austin on December 9, 2001*
WWE TAG TEAM CHAMPION (2 TIMES)	*Partnered with Edge to defeat Carlito & Primo on June 28, 2009* *Partnered with Big Show to defeat Cody Rhodes & Ted DiBiase on July 26, 2009*

The Undisputed Champion

Jericho's chance at immortality came in December 2001, when WWE prepared to to unify the World and WWE Championships. To achieve such greatness, Y2J needed to get past both The Rock and Stone Cold Steve Austin. Amazingly, Jericho defeated both Superstars in one night to become the first-ever Undisputed WWE Champion.

Proving his victory wasn't a fluke, Jericho went on to once again defeat Rock and Austin in the weeks that followed. He also topped Kurt Angle, Tazz, Kane and others before finally losing the title to Triple H in the main event of *WrestleMania X8*.

Despite no longer possessing the WWE Championship, Jericho remained a prominent part of WWE's most high-profile matches, including an epic encounter against Shawn Michaels at *WrestleMania XIX* and the groundbreaking *WrestleMania 21* Money in the Bank Ladder Match. His WWE career, however, came to an abrupt halt when he lost a "You're Fired" Match to John Cena in August 2005.

With his WWE days seemingly behind him, the self-proclaimed "Ayatollah of Rock 'n' Rolla" released three rock albums with his band Fozzy. He also concentrated on acting and penned his autobiography, *A Lion's Tale: Around the World in Spandex*. All the while, though, Jericho's heart knew he would one day return to the ring.

In November 2007, Jericho finally returned to WWE in an attempt to "save us" from Randy Orton. He also captured the Intercontinental Championship on two separate occasions to increase his record number of reigns to nine. But perhaps the shining moment of Y2J's WWE return came in September 2008, when he emerged as a last-minute entrant and eventual victor in *Unforgiven*'s World Heavyweight Championship Scramble Match. The victory marked the first of three World Heavyweight Title reigns for Jericho over the next two years.

In an ironic twist, Jericho's second WWE run came to a screeching hault when the man he came to "save us" from, Randy Orton, punted Y2J in the head in September 2010.

Jericho spent the next year-plus void of any WWE action. Then in January 2012, he re-appeared out of the darkness wearing a jacket made of flashing neon lights. The WWE Universe rejoiced over the return of one of their heros. But when Jericho refused to speak to them for weeks, it was clear that the 2012 version was focused on CM Punk. The two battled at *WrestleMania XXVIII* and despite a loss, Jericho continued to taunt the Straight-Edge Superstar deeper into 2012.

C

2010-
2000-09
1990-99
1980-89
1970-79
1960-69

CHRIS MASTERS

HT: 6'4" **WT:** 275 lbs. **From:** Los Angeles, California
SIGNATURE MOVE: Master Lock

Chris Masters was introduced to fans in January 2005 through vignettes aired on *Monday Night Raw*. With a physique resembling ancient statues chiseled from stone, Masters dominated opponents with a variety of power moves and his debilitating version of the full nelson. He began the "Master Lock Challenge," where he offered $1,000 to anyone who could break the hold. The dollar amount grew each week and at its height, it was worth $20,000.

Though the Master Lock was broken on a few occasions, Masters cited outside interference and the challenge continued. It was officially broken by then-ECW Champion Bobby Lashley. During the June 2007 Draft, Masters was selected to *SmackDown*, where he appeared until he departed WWE that November. After honing his skills abroad, "The Masterpiece" returned to WWE in July 2009 with an even more powerful Master Lock. He soon found himself in the unfamiliar role of fan favorite, and received praise for having great matches on *Superstars*. While he was released in August 2011, history has shown "The Masterpiece" could become a fixture in WWE again.

CHRIS TOLOS

HT: 6'0" **WT:** 220 lbs. **FROM:** Hamilton, Ontario, Canada

TITLE HISTORY

UNITED STATES TAG TEAM CHAMPION	*Partnered with John Tolos to defeat Killer Kowalski & Gorilla Monsoon on December 28, 1963*

Decades after dominating the tag team scene in the 1950s and 1960s, Chris and John Tolos are still considered one of the greatest duos to ever come out of Canada. Known as The Canadian Wrecking Crew, the brothers captured titles all over North American wrestling territories, including Florida, Detroit and Toronto.

While in WWE, Chris, the older of the two brothers, helped lead the team to the United States Tag Team Championship. They defeated Hall of Famers Gorilla Monsoon & Killer Kowalski for the titles in December 1963.

Though primarily a tag team competitor, Chris, also known as "The Body", had a memorable 1968 rivalry with Mike DiBiase, father of WWE legend, Ted DiBiase.

CHRIS WALKER

FROM: Atlanta, Georgia

Chris Walker certainly had the look of a championship-caliber contender. His physique appeared as if it was carved out of granite, and he sported a long, curly, blonde mullet that was fitting for a competitor of the early 1990s. But after picking up two quick wins over Brooklyn Brawler and Kato, the muscular newcomer struggled to get his career back on track. Walker eventually disappeared from WWE in early 1992 after falling to The Warlord and Sid Justice.

Prior to WWE, Walker gained recognition in the Texas-based Global Wrestling Federation. While there, he teamed with Steve Simpson to defeat Scotty Anthony and Rip Rogers in a tournament finals match to crown the first-ever GWF Tag Team Champions in July 1991. They held the titles for four months before losing to the California Connection, John Tatum and Rod Price.

Walker briefly competed for Southern States Wrestling in the late 1990s. In March 1999, he defeated Heinrich Franz Keller to capture the now-defunct SSW International Cup.

CHRISTIAN

HT: 6'1"   WT: 212 lbs.   FROM: Toronto, Ontario, Canada
SIGNATURE MOVE: Killswitch

TITLE HISTORY

ECW CHAMPION (2 TIMES)	Defeated Jack Swagger on April 26, 2009 Defeated Tommy Dreamer on July 26, 2009
EUROPEAN CHAMPION	Defeated Bradshaw on November 1, 2001
HARDCORE CHAMPION	1 Time
INTERCONTINENTAL CHAMPION (3 TIMES)	Defeated Edge on September 23, 2001 Won a Battle Royal on May 18, 2003 Defeated Booker T on August 10, 2003
LIGHT HEAVYWEIGHT CHAMPION	Defeated Taka Michinoku on October 18, 1998
WORLD HEAVYWEIGHT CHAMPION (2 TIMES)	Defeated Alberto Del Rio on May 1, 2011 Defeated Randy Orton on July 17, 2011
WORLD TAG TEAM CHAMPION (9 TIMES)	Partnered with Edge to defeat The Dudley Boys on April 2, 2000 Partnered with Edge to defeat Too Cool on June 25, 2000 Partnered with Edge to defeat The Hardy Boys on October 22, 2000 Partnered with Edge to defeat Bull Buchanan & Goodfather on December 10, 2000 Partnered with Edge to defeat The Rock & Undertaker on December 21, 2000 Partnered with Edge to defeat The Hardy Boys on March 19, 2001 Partnered with Edge to defeat The Dudley Boys on April 1, 2001 Partnered with Lance Storm to defeat Hulk Hogan & Edge on July 21, 2002 Partnered with Chris Jericho to defeat Kane & The Hurricane on October 14, 2002

With more than a decade of service in WWE, Christian has literally grown up in front of the WWE Universe. His earliest days were spent as a young and brooding introvert, but as time passed, the Canadian Superstar grew into one of the most charismatic and highly-decorated competitors ever.

Success came quickly for Christian, who captured the Light Heavyweight Championship in his debut match in October 1998. From there, the young Superstar partnered with longtime friend Edge to form what would become one of the most revolutionary teams in history. Over the course of their pairing, Edge and Christian captured an amazing seven World Tag Team Title reigns.

The legacy of Edge and Christian isn't just about championship reigns; the awe-inspiring duo is also credited for their part in creating the popular TLC Match. Together, "E&C" turned back the Dudleys and Hardys in Triple Threat TLC Matches at both *SummerSlam 2000* and *WrestleMania X-Seven*.

Christian's singles career has proven equally successful. In addition to capturing the Intercontinental Championship, he has also proudly held the ECW and European Titles, among others. His greatest success, however, came in 2011 when he finally reached WWE's pinnacle.

After injury forced Edge to relinquish the World Heavyweight Championship in April 2011, Christian earned his opportunity at greatness when he battled Albert Del Rio at *Extreme Rules*. Competing in a Ladder Match, Christian scaled to the top of the sports-entertainment industry when he grabbed the gold and became World Heavyweight Champion.

Christian celebrated the monumentous win with Edge in the center of the ring. Unfortunately, however, the party didn't last long. Only a few days later, Randy Orton upended the new champ for the title. The loss sent Christian's "Peeps" into an uproar. They took their frustration to Twitter, where they flooded people's timelines with their displeasure.

Luckily for Christian's followers, the World Heavyweight Championship soon found its way back around the waist of "Captain Charisma." At *Money in the Bank* in July 2011, Christian defeated Orton to regain the gold and further cement his legacy as one of the greatest of his generation.

CHRISTOPHER NOWINSKI

HT: 6'5"   WT: 270 lbs.   From: Watertown, Massachusetts
SIGNATURE MOVE: Honor Roll

TITLE HISTORY

HARDCORE CHAMPION	2 Times

Christopher Nowinski is brilliant, and he's not afraid to remind you of it, either. The self-absorbed Harvard graduate first began annoying fans in 2001 as a cast member on *Tough Enough*. Nowinski failed to win the competition, but impressed officials enough to earn a WWE contract. As a member of the WWE roster, Nowinski's holier-than-thou attitude made him tough to like, but his abilities in the ring were undeniable.

By the end of his rookie campaign, Nowinski had scored major victories over his trainer, Al Snow, and *Tough Enough* champion Maven. Unfortunately, however, his promising career came to an abrupt halt when he retired due to post-concussion syndrome. Despite no longer being active in the ring, Nowinski remained a valuable part of the organization, serving as a political correspondent for *Smackdown Your Vote!*

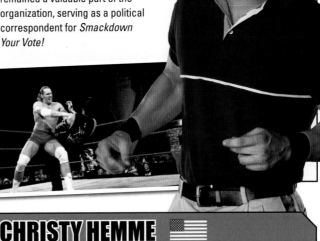

CHRISTY HEMME

HT: 5'5"   From: Los Angeles, California
SIGNATURE MOVE: Standing Split-legged Leg Drop

Christy Hemme's life changed forever when she was selected from over 7,000 women to become the first *Raw Diva Search* Winner. Christy's first taste of how life as a Diva would go was when she faced runner-up Carmella DeCesare in a Lingerie Pillow Fight at *Taboo Tuesday*.

Hemme became special guest ring announcer and timekeeper for some of WWE's biggest matches, and was also training for the ring with Lita. In April 2005, Christy landed on the cover of *Playboy*. The issue's success rubbed some of her fellow Divas the wrong way and she soon stood across the ring from her most vocal critic, Trish Stratus, at *WrestleMania 21*. Christy lost to the Women's Champion that night, but found some success while battling the likes of Victoria and Melina, before leaving World Wrestling Entertainment in December 2005.

CHUCK PALUMBO

HT: 6'7" WT: 280 lbs. FROM: San Diego, California
SIGNATURE MOVE: Full Throttle

TITLE HISTORY

| WORLD TAG TEAM CHAMPION (2 TIMES) | *Partnered with Billy Gunn to defeat Tazz & Spike Dudley on February 21, 2002* |
| | *Partnered with Billy Gunn to defeat Rico & Rikishi on June 6, 2002* |

Chuck Palumbo's WWE career is the story of two completely different Superstars. After Palumbo & Sean O'Haire lost the WCW Tag Team Championship in 2001, Palumbo found his career going nowhere fast. With nothing to lose, he formed a union with tag team specialist Billy Gunn. The result: the most controversial pairing in sports-entertainment history.

Billy & Chuck enjoyed two World Tag Team Championship reigns, but it was the flamboyant tandem's commitment ceremony that attracted the highest levels of national attention. Moments before officially becoming partners for life, though, Billy & Chuck revealed that the entire event was a hoax. The team split up soon after.

Three years later, Palumbo returned with a persona that more closely resembled his identity outside the ring, a leather-donned thrillseeker who is as comfortable speeding on a hog as he is pummeling opponents in the ring. Since he left active competition in late 2008, Chuck turned his passion for motorcycles and music into full-time pursuits.

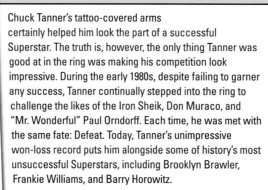

CHUCK TANNER

Chuck Tanner's tattoo-covered arms certainly helped him look the part of a successful Superstar. The truth is, however, the only thing Tanner was good at in the ring was making his competition look impressive. During the early 1980s, despite failing to garner any success, Tanner continually stepped into the ring to challenge the likes of the Iron Sheik, Don Muraco, and "Mr. Wonderful" Paul Orndorff. Each time, he was met with the same fate: Defeat. Today, Tanner's unimpressive won-loss record puts him alongside some of history's most unsuccessful Superstars, including Brooklyn Brawler, Frankie Williams, and Barry Horowitz.

CHYNA

HT: 5'10" FROM: Londonderry, New Hampshire

After her days in the Peace Corps, Chyna undertook grueling days of training at Killer Kowalski's Pro Wrestling School. At the time, no one thought they were witnessing the development of one of the most ground-breaking figures in sports-entertainment history. She was first seen on WWE programming coming from the crowd to assist Hunter Hearst Helmsley and became the famous enforcer for D-Generation X.

TITLE HISTORY

INTERCONTINENTAL CHAMPION (2 TIMES)	*Defeated Jeff Jarrett on October 17, 1999*
	Defeated Val Venis on August 27, 2000
WOMEN'S CHAMPION	*Defeated Ivory on April 1, 2001*

As Chyna broke away from the notorious faction her character became more defined and her star grew brighter as she became the first-ever female competitor in the *Royal Rumble*. In the ring, Chyna became known as "The 9th Wonder of The World." She made history at *No Mercy 1999* when she beat Jeff Jarrett to be crowned the first female Intercontinental Champion in World Wrestling Entertainment history!

The spotlight on her grew as she was a presenter at The MTV Movie Awards, released her own fitness video, and appeared on the television show *3rd Rock From The Sun*. In November of 2000 she made a splash as the covergirl of Playboy Magazine and broke all sales records previously held by the publication. In January of 2001 her remarkable life story hit print as her autobiography, *If They Only Knew* attacked the NY Times Bestseller list. Two months later she fulfilled another dream when she beat Ivory for the Women's Championship at *WrestleMania X-Seven*. Shortly thereafter, she was the host of *Robot Wars: Extreme Warriors*.

Since parting ways with WWE in November of 2001, she has remained in the public eye. Though her days in the ring appear to be behind her, the world will never forget her contributions to sports-entertainment as a Superstar, pop-culture figure and a woman. In her prime, she was an unstoppable force who opened a new realm for WWE Divas.

CLARENCE MASON

One of the most litigious human beings to ever practice law, Clarence Mason debuted on WWE television as the attorney for James E. Cornette. Mason made his presence immediately felt as he was able to regain the tag team titles lost the previous night at *In Your House* since Owen Hart, the Superstar pinned, was not recognized as a title holder in the match. Mason then contested every decision made that was not in the best interest of his clients and threatened lawsuits whenever possible. Mason was also known for hand delivering subpoenas to Superstars.

After his tenure with Camp Cornette he focused on the career of Crush. Mason soon guided the Nation of Domination until the group disbanded in the late 1990s. Mason then left WWE and opened his own law practice in south Florida. As he himself proclaimed, "Don't worry, Clarence Mason is on the scene, and justice will be served…" Mason will be forever remembered as one of the most controversial figures of the 1990s.

CM PUNK

HT: 6'2" **WT:** 218 lbs.
FROM: Chicago, Illinois
SIGNATURE MOVE: G.T.S. (Go To Sleep), Anaconda Vise

TITLE HISTORY

ECW CHAMPION	*Defeated John Morrison on September 1, 2007*
INTERCONTINENTAL CHAMPION	*Defeated William Regal on January 19, 2009*
WORLD HEAVYWEIGHT CHAMPION (3 TIMES)	*Defeated Edge on June 30, 2008* *Defeated Jeff Hardy on June 7, 2009* *Defeated Jeff Hardy on August 23, 2009*
WORLD TAG TEAM CHAMPION	*Partnered with Kofi Kingston to defeat Cody Rhodes & Ted DiBiase on October 27, 2008*
WWE CHAMPION (2 TIMES)	*Defeated John Cena on July 17, 2011* *Defeated Alberto Del Rio on November 20, 2011*

Since debuting in the summer of 2006, CM Punk has formed a cult-like following never before seen in WWE. And along the way, whether he's admired or abhorred, there has always been one constant surrounding the Second City Savior: Controversy.

Punk's controversial demeanor turned scandalous in the summer of 2011 when the Superstar threatened to leave the company with the WWE Championship following his title opportunity against John Cena at *Money in the Bank*. Prior to the match, Punk let a few verbal "pipe bombs" explode in the direction of WWE management, particularly Mr. McMahon. According to Punk's now-famous tirade, McMahon only makes money in spite of himself and surrounds himself with glad-handing, nonsensical yes-men like John Laurinaitis. Punk also took shots at McMahon's family, referring to Stephanie McMahon and Triple H as his "idiotic daughter and doofus son-in-law" respectively. This bold move did not earn him Employee of the Month status but certainly raised his profile to astonishing new heights.

As promised, Punk won the WWE Championship at *Money in the Bank* and immediately left the company, marking one of the most uncertain periods in WWE history. Punk later re-signed with WWE, stating he wanted to be a beacon of change within the sports-entertainment industry. And he equally yearned for the return of WWE ice cream bars.

Prior to the controversial summer of 2011, Punk used his power of persuasion and superior intellect to become one of the most influential leaders of his time. First as the prophetic head of the Straight Edge Society and later as the leader of the New Nexus, Punk had Superstars and fans alike flocking to him, hanging on his every word.

Punk has also proven to be equally successful in the ring. In addition to being a multiple-time WWE Champion, the Voice of the Voiceless has also captured two Money in the Bank briefcases. Both times, he used his guaranteed title opportunity to claim the World Heavyweight Championship, first from Edge in June 2008 and later from Jeff Hardy in June 2009. Punk is also a former ECW, Intercontinental and World Tag Team Champion.

1960-69
1970-79
1980-89
1990-99
2000-09
2010-

MERCHANDISE & MEMORABILIA

Whether it's clothing emblazoned with their favorite superstar's logo, trading cards, home videos, or action figures cast in the likenesses of the industry's greatest attractions, fans have always found a way to feel closer to their heroes of the ring. While far from a comprehensive list, the following pages provide a brief look at some of the items created by the WWE for its fans.

BRING THE ACTION INTO YOUR HOME

As great of an experience as live events are, you weren't able to watch you favorite matches over and over until the advent of the home video playe and Coliseum Home Video. Today, the video tape has given way to DVD Blu-ray and digital download but the excitement remains the same

From the first Coliseum release to today's productions from WWE Home Video, WWE collections have always been top-sellers.

WWE MAGAZINE

The printed programs from its first events were the earliest form of memorabilia from the WWE, but they're not the only printed items available. Since 1984, the WWE has produced a monthly or bi-monthly magazine, and also creates special editions of the magazine throughout the year. In 2008, the magazine broadened its readership by adding the WWE Kids Magazine, which hits newsstands four times per year.

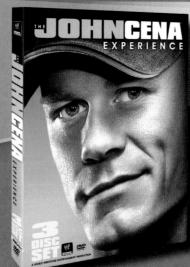

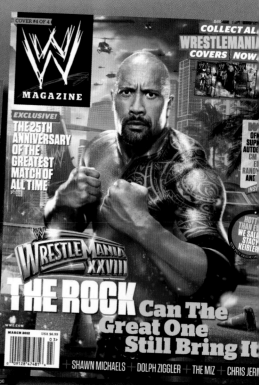

WWE TOYS

In 1984 World Wrestling Entertainment and LJN launched the first line of action figures. Fans around the world couldn't wait to get their hands on the first edition which included Hillbilly Jim, Hulk Hogan, Andre the Giant, Jimmy "Superfly" Snuka, Big John Studd, Junkyard Dog, the Iron Sheik, Nikolai Volkoff, and "Rowdy" Roddy Piper. Each Superstar came with a mini-poster, bio card, and accessories true to their larger than life personas like Cowboy Bob Orton's hat, Terry Funk's branding iron, and pets like Damien and Frankie. With the WWE ring also available fans could slam, zing and fling their favorite Superstars from pillar to post.

Since the initial toys were released, WWE has continued to build its presence in the toy aisle with additional figures and even entirely new toylines. Working with multiple companies over the past two decades has led to the creation of toys for fans of all ages. Here you see only a sampling of some of the latest true-to-life renderings from WWE and Mattel.

WEARING YOUR FAVORITE SUPERSTAR

While shirts are the most popular item, they're not the only option for fans who want to show support for their favorite Superstars. Pajamas, hats, headbands, and even armbands have been made available to WWE fans.

C
2010-
2000-09
1990-99
1980-89
1970-79
1960-69

THE COACH

After a making a career of bringing professional athletes across all sports to unprecedented heights, The Coach brought his combination of intellect and training techniques to WWE in 1991. The core of his belief system was simple: Win! Win! Win! However, it extended to underhanded tactics and rule-breaking where Coach could be heard yelling at ringside, "Discipline! Break their legs, smash their faces. The only people I want with me are winners!" His desire for victory also translated to him getting involved in the action when a referee's attention was diverted.

On an episode of *The Funeral Parlor*, Bobby Heenan introduced Coach as the new manager of then-Intercontinental Champion, Mr. Perfect. Heenan said he was retiring from managing to pursue broadcasting full-time. Under new management, Perfect thrived and proved that the Coach's strategies could, would, and did cross over to WWE. Coach decided to expand his talent pool and brought the Beverly Brothers into WWE. The Coach took his whistle and departed the company later that same year. Coach is remembered as one of the most intense and physical managers ever.

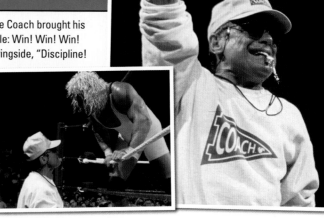

THE COBRA ● HT: 5'10" WT: 224 lbs.
FROM: Japan

Like many other masked Superstars of the 1980s, the Cobra was lightning quick with a strong aerial assault. Unlike his veiled

TITLE HISTORY	
JUNIOR HEAVYWEIGHT CHAMPION (2 TIMES)	Defeated Black Tiger on December 28, 1984 Defeated Hiro Saito on July 28, 1985

counterparts, the Cobra was quite a sharp-dressed man. The custom-made sports coat he wore to the ring went a long way in setting him apart from his masked colleagues.

One of the Cobra's first tastes of championship gold came in November 1983 when he defeated Davey Boy Smith for the National Wrestling Alliance Junior Heavyweight Championship. When the Dynamite Kid, Smith's future British Bulldogs partner, vacated the WWE Junior Heavyweight Championship one year later, the Cobra defeated Black Tiger to claim the title. The Cobra held the Junior Heavyweight Championship for five months before losing to Hiro Saito in Hiroshima, Japan. He eventually regained the title two months later, but was forced to vacate it when WWE discontinued recognizing the championship in October 1985.

CODY RHODES HT: 6'1" WT: 219 lbs.
FROM: Marietta, Georgia
SIGNATURE MOVE: Cross Rhodes

TITLE HISTORY	
INTERCONTINENTAL CHAMPION	Defeated Ezekiel Jackson on August 12, 2011
WORLD TAG TEAM CHAMPION (3 TIMES)	Partnered with Hardcore Holly to defeat Lance Cade & Trevor Murdoch on December 10, 2007 Partnered with Ted DiBiase to defeat Hardcore Holly on June 29, 2008 Partnered with Ted DiBiase to defeat Batista & John Cena on August 11, 2008
WWE TAG TEAM CHAMPION	Partnered with Drew McIntyre to defeat David Hart Smith & Tyson Kidd on September 19, 2010

The son of the legendary "American Dream" Dusty Rhodes, Cody was taught a route of patience had to be taken to become a WWE Superstar. Cody chose a different route when he turned his back on mentor, Hardcore Holly. A cocky Rhodes declared "When you're this good, you don't pay dues." The then-newcomer aligned himself with another young and dynamic Superstar, Ted DiBiase.

Backing their claims of greatness, the heirs of WWE Hall of Famers dominated the tag team scene during the second half of 2008. They even turned back John Cena & Batista for their second World Tag Team Championship. Their impressive performances led them to another Superstar with sports-entertainment in his blood, Randy Orton. With Orton as leader, the venomous ternion became known as Legacy. The brash attitude of each superstar clashed and at *WrestleMania XXVI*, the Legacy's met each other in a triple threat match.

In 2010, Cody traveled to *SmackDown* and won the WWE Tag Team Championship with Drew McIntyre. Shortly after being named "Most Handsome Superstar" in a Divas poll and adding "Dashing" to his name, he suffered a facial injury from the feet of Rey Mysterio. When Rhodes returned to the ring, he sported a protective mask and demanded audiences place brown paper bags over their heads to hide their offensive faces. Eventually Cody's face healed and he regained his former confidence. In August 2011, Rhodes captured his first individual prize, the Intercontinental Championship. Unfortunately for Rhodes, he chose to taunt Big Show in the months leading up to *WrestleMania XXVIII* and then lost the title to the "World's Largest Athlete" after being hit by a W.M.D.

COLIN DELANEY

HT: 5'9" WT: 172 lbs.
FROM: Rochester, New York

Perhaps the most persistent Superstar in WWE history, Colin Delaney continually climbed in the ring despite suffering devastating beatings from bigger foes, such as Big Daddy V, Mark Henry, and Kane. The punishment he received would have crippled a lesser man, but Delaney's heart would not let him quit. He finally picked up his first win when he teamed with his mentor, Tommy Dreamer, to defeat The Miz & John Morrison in February 2008.

Despite the victory, Delaney had yet to be offered a full-time contract. He finally earned his spot on the roster after defeating ECW general manager Armando Estrada in May. With job security in his back pocket, Delaney revealed his true colors when he turned on Dreamer at *The Great American Bash*. Dreamer eventually got his revenge, however, defeating his protégé in an Extreme Rules Match in August. Delaney left ECW a few days later.

COL. MUSTAFA

HT: 6'0" WT: 263 lbs.
FROM: Iraq
SIGNATURE MOVE: Camel Clutch

In 1991, the United States was in the midst of the Gulf War and WWE was under its own attack by one-time hero, Sgt. Slaughter. On March 30, 1991, Mustafa became the third member of Slaughter's despicable Triangle of Terror and showed his powerful, ruthless tactics in the ring.

During his campaign of terror in WWE, Mustafa attacked Superstars such as Undertaker, Big Boss Man, Koko B. Ware, "Hacksaw" Jim Duggan, and Bret "Hit Man" Hart. Mustafa was then part of the famous "Match Made In Hell" at *SummerSlam 1991* where he and cohorts Gen. Adnan and Sgt. Slaughter took on Hulk Hogan & Ultimate Warrior. By May 1992, Mustafa returned to the Middle East.

THE COLOSSAL CONNECTION

MEMBERS: Andre The Giant, Haku   COMBINED WT: 852 lbs.

TITLE HISTORY	
WORLD TAG TEAM CHAMPIONS	*Defeated Demolition on December 13, 1989*

In 1989, future WWE Hall of Famer Bobby "The Brain" Heenan unveiled his Colossal Connection at *Survivor Series*. They manhandled their opponents, and just weeks later, conquered Demolition to earn the World Tag Team Championship. During that time in WWE history, it was unheard of for Ax & Smash to be dominated in that fashion.

As champions, they were virtually unstoppable. As they entered a new decade, their stranglehold on the titles appeared to have no end in sight. However, after a botched double-team move led to Demolition regaining the tag titles at *WrestleMania VI*, "The Brain" lost his wits. After a slap in the face from his manager, Andre cleared the ring of his former family members, and the Colossal Connection was gone forever.

Despite a brief partnership, the Colossal Connection gave a glimpse of what can happen when two monsters are brought together by an individual obsessed with fame, power, and championships. If they hadn't self-destructed, there's no telling when the campaign of destruction would have ended.

CONOR O'BRIAN

HT: 6'3" WT: 247 lbs.   FROM: Grand Rapids, Michigan
SIGNATURE MOVE: Strychnine

Conor O'Brian toiled on the independent wrestling scene for ten long years before finally debuting on WWE television as a Rookie on *NXT* season four. When the rat-like competitor finally clawed his way out of the depths and into a WWE ring, he immediately began making up for lost time. In his debut match in December 2010, O'Brian teamed with his pro, Alberto Del Rio, to defeat Daniel Bryan & Derrick Bateman.

As season four progressed, O'Brian continued his dominance over Bateman, complete with two impressive victories. Despite his in-ring success, though, the Michigan native was not long for *NXT*. In January, he lost a match to his Pro's ring announcer, Ricardo Rodriguez, and was coincidentally eliminated later that same night.

Luckily for O'Brian, his ousting from season four didn't completely shatter his WWE dreams. In March 2011, *NXT Redemption* afforded the aspiring Superstar a second chance. With Vladimir Kozlov serving as his pro, O'Brian outlasted Lucky Cannon, Byron Saxton and Jacob Novak before finally being eliminated in week seventeen.

1960-69
1970-79
1980-89
1990-99
2000-09
2010-

THE CORPORATION

MEMBERS: Mr. McMahon, Shane McMahon, The Rock, Big Show, Big Boss Man, Ken Shamrock, Kane, Triple H, Chyna, Test, Shawn Michaels, Gerald Brisco, Pat Patterson, Sgt. Slaughter, Pete Gas, Rodney, Joey Abs

Leading up to *Survivor Series 1998*, Mr. McMahon began to surround himself with his own entourage of former Superstars, which consisted of Sgt. Slaughter, Gerald Brisco and Pat Patterson. The group had some influence, largely due to McMahon's powerful position within WWE, but lacked any real Superstar power. That all changed at *Survivor Series* when Mr. McMahon and his son Shane helped The Rock capture the WWE Championship, thus marking the official start of The Corporation.

With The Rock in the fold, The Corporation became an enticing destination for WWE Superstars with championship aspirations. They knew that with Mr. McMahon making the calls, they would be set up for instant greatness. Just as many predicted, The Corporation owned all the major titles in WWE by year's end (The Rock was WWE Champion, Ken Shamrock was Intercontinental Champion and Big Boss Man & Shamrock were World Tag Team Champions).

Though dominant in their rivalries with Stone Cold Steve Austin, Mankind and D-Generation X, The Corporation enjoyed only a brief existence. The beginning of the end came in April 1999 when Shane assumed leadership responsibilities after claiming his father had his priorities mixed up. According to the younger McMahon, Vince cared more about combating Undertaker's obsession with Shane's sister Stephanie than he did The Corporation. From that point, the male McMahons engaged in a bitter rivalry that eventually resulted in Shane merging his Corporation with Undertaker's Ministry of Darkness. The result was one super faction called The Corporate Ministry.

CORPORAL KIRSCHNER

HT: 6'2" WT: 263 lbs.
FROM: Fort Bragg, North Carolina
SIGNATURE MOVE: Corporal Clutch

A former member of the 82nd Airborne division of the U.S. Army, Corporal Kirschner fought for the American way inside and outside the ring. Prior to entering WWE, Kirschner developed a military style of combat while serving in the armed forces. When he debuted in 1985, he transferred that style into many rivalries with foreign Superstars, most notably Nikolai Volkoff. In fact, it was against the Russian powerhouse that Kirschner picked up his biggest win, besting Volkoff in a Flag Match at *WrestleMania 2*.

Unfortunately for Kirschner, victories were few and far between after *WrestleMania 2*. Following only moderate success against the likes of the Iron Sheik and "Adorable" Adrian Adonis, the Corporal turned his sights to the tag scene, teaming up with Danny Spivey. The duo, however, failed to make waves in the tag team division. Kirschner left WWE shortly after. Despite Kirschner's short stay in WWE, longtime fans will always look back at his tenure with great fondness, as it was difficult not to cheer for the tough serviceman who carried Old Glory to the ring.

THE CORRE

MEMBERS: Wade Barrett, Justin Gabriel, Heath Slater, Ezekiel Jackson

When Wade Barrett was replaced as Nexus leader in January 2011, new boss CM Punk demanded Justin Gabriel and Heath Slater go through an initiation to remain in the group. Rather than endure the humiliation, however, the original Nexus members jumped the *Raw* ship and joined Barrett on *SmackDown*.

Billing themselves as a leaderless group of equals, the former Nexus members soon welcomed Ezekiel Jackson into their pack and immediately became a force on *SmackDown*. Collectively known as The Corre, they quickly claimed gold when Gabriel and Slater defeated Santino Marella & Vladimir Kozlov for the tag titles in February 2011. The following month, Barrett brought the Intercontinental Title into the fold when he topped Kofi Kingston.

Despite their terrifying reign over much of *SmackDown*'s roster, The Corre started to become their own worst enemy following a *WrestleMania* loss to Big Show, Kane, Kingston & Marella. Soon Barrett and Jackson evolved into bitter enemies, battling over the Intercontinental Championship. Later, the group quietly disbanded after Barrett abandoned Gabriel and Slater during a *SmackDown* tag match.

"COWBOY" BOB ORTON

HT: 6'1" **WT: 242 lbs.**
FROM: Kansas City, Kansas
SIGNATURE MOVE: Superplex

"Cowboy" Bob Orton first appeared in WWE in 1982 managed by The Grand Wizard, and had battles against then-WWE Champion Bob Backlund. Orton returned to the NWA and made headlines when he and Dick Slater accepted $25,000 from Harley Race to end the career of "Nature Boy" Ric Flair.

The man credited with inventing the Superplex returned to WWE in the spring of 1984 to became bodyguard to "Rowdy" Roddy Piper. After his left forearm was broken in a match, Orton continued to compete with a cast. This was often the subject of controversy as "Cowboy" was accused of using it as a weapon well after the injury had healed. Though Orton was not an active participant at the original *WrestleMania*, no one made a bigger impact in the outcome of the match. As the corner man for "Hot Rod" and "Mr. Wonderful" Paul Orndorff, Orton attempted to hit Mr. T with the cast, but he missed and struck Orndorff instead, helping give Hulk Hogan & Mr. T the victory. Orton continued to back Piper through his *WrestleMania 2* boxing match against Mr. T, but when Piper changed his ways, Orton swore his allegiance to "Adorable" Adrian Adonis. The "Ace" also formed a successful tag team with the Magnificent Muraco with Mr. Fuji as their manager.

Orton remained active in a limited capacity for the remainder of the decade and began training his son, Randy, for a career in sports-entertainment. In February 2005, it was announced that "Ace's" heralded career would be honored with induction into the WWE Hall of Fame. During this time, he returned to WWE to manage his son in his rivalry against Undertaker.

"Cowboy" Bob Orton comes from one of the greatest families in professional wrestling history. One of the first Superstars to utilize the ropes for a finishing maneuver, Orton was an innovative technician in the ring and a hated villain. The Orton family legacy moves well into the 21st Century with his son, Randy. To those who oppose them, it feels like the "Age of Orton" is entering its eighth decade.

COWBOY LANG

HT: 4'0" **WT: 109 lbs.** **FROM: Calgary, Alberta, Canada**

For more than 30 years, Cowboy Lang was considered one of the world's premier midget wrestlers. Debuting in the mid-1960s at just 16 years old, Lang charged to the ring in his signature cowboy hat and boots.

Over the course of his successful career, Lang performed on some of the biggest cards of his time, including the American Wrestling Association's (AWA) WrestleRock on April 20, 1986. On this night, Lang teamed with Little Mr. T to defeat Lord Littlebrook & Little Tokyo.

Throughout Lang's career, Little Tokyo proved to be one of his most bitter rivals. The foes spent much of the early 1980s battling over the National Wrestling Alliance World Midget Championship, which they traded on two separate occasions.

CRAIG DeGEORGE

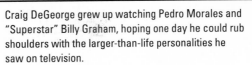

Craig DeGeorge grew up watching Pedro Morales and "Superstar" Billy Graham, hoping one day he could rub shoulders with the larger-than-life personalities he saw on television.

With aspirations of calling action from behind the microphone, DeGeorge enrolled in Syracuse University, where he earned a broadcast journalism degree. While at Syracuse, he served as the play-by-play announcer for Orangemen football and basketball, among other sports.

A few years after graduating in 1985, a young DeGeorge was brought into WWE as an announcer. While his stay only lasted a few years, DeGeorge did manage to leave a lasting impression. Fans today still talk about his rhythmically-challenged do-si-do with Hillbilly Jim.

After leaving WWE in the late 1980s, DeGeorge briefly called the action for the California-based Universal Wrestling Federation before leaving the sports-entertainment industry completely. He later moved on to the XFL, United Football League and Fox Sports Florida where he covers the Marlins and Panthers (under the name Craig Minervini).

C

2010-
2000-09
1990-99
1980-89
1970-79
1960-69

CRASH HOLLY

HT: 5'10" **WT:** Over 400 lbs. (alleged)
FROM: Mobile, Alabama
SIGNATURE MOVE: The Crash Course

TITLE HISTORY	
EUROPEAN CHAMPION	*Defeated William Regal on December 2, 2000*
HARDCORE CHAMPION	*22 Times*
LIGHT HEAVYWEIGHT CHAMPION	*Defeated Dean Malenko on March 15, 2001*
WORLD TAG TEAM CHAMPION	*Partnered with Hardcore Holly to defeat Mankind & The Rock on October 18, 1999*

Crash Holly could not be deterred from joining his cousin, Hardcore Holly, in WWE. He was also adamant about competing amongst sports-entertainment's greatest heavyweights. In 1999, Crash debuted on *Raw* and brought a scale with him to the ring to force opponents to prove they measured up. While he and his cousin often argued, they proved to be a formidable team when they could agree on the target of a famous Holly beatdown. This was no more evident than when they won the World Tag Team Championship from the Rock 'N' Sock Connection.

In 2000, he joined the Hardcore Division, and over the next three years became known as the Houdini of Hardcore. Crash wore the Hardcore Championship on over 20 occasions. Later in the year, he was accompanied to the ring by his cousin, Molly, and occassionally reformed his team with Hardcore Holly. Crash later added more trophies to his mantle when he won the Light Heavyweight title, and in 2001, he captured the European Championship. Crash continued to get in the face of all challengers no matter their size or reputation until he left the company in June 2003.

Sadly, in November 2003, Crash Holly passed away. He entertained millions with his performances in the ring and touched even more with his heart.

Cruiserweight Championship (see page 84)

CRUSH

HT: 6'6" **WT:** 315 lbs. **FROM:** Kona, Hawaii
SIGNATURE MOVE: The Skull Crush

In 1992, World Wrestling Entertainment was greeted by a happy man from the Hawaiian Islands with massive power named Kona Crush. Soon after his debut, he shortened his name to Crush and did exactly that to his opponents. He met Doink at *WrestleMania IX,* where audiences saw two Doinks attack Crush. After this match, his attitude changed and he fell under the dangerous influence of Mr. Fuji. Now using the heart punch to finish opponents, he attacked his former friend, Randy "Macho Man" Savage. The battles between the two raged on until their Falls Count Anywhere Match at *WrestleMania X.*

Crush returned to WWE in 1996. He was first a member of The Nation of Domination, but later formed the Disciples of the Apocalypse faction with Chainz, Skull & 8-Ball.

After he left WWE, he competed in WCW and Japan but a spinal injury forced him into retirement. Tragically, in August 2007, he passed away. Whether he was beloved or booed, this powerhouse was one of WWE's biggest Superstars of the 1990s.

"CRUSHER" JERRY BLACKWELL

HT: 5'9" **WT:** 473 lbs. **FROM:** Stone Mountain, Georgia
SIGNATURE MOVE: Big Splash

At nearly 500 pounds, Jerry Blackwell earned every bit of the nickname "The Mountain from Stone Mountain." But he wasn't just big, Blackwell also moved around the ring with the quickness of a cat, and often employed maneuvers only seen by men half his size.

Blackwell's WWE days were fleeting, but painful for those who got in his way, including S.D. Jones and Larry Zbyszko. After leaving the Northeast territory, the man known as the "Crusher" competed in the 1979 World's Strongest Man competition before finally nestling into a memorable AWA career.

Blackwell was showered with boos during the early part of his AWA tenure. But when Hulk Hogan left the territory in 1983, the AWA fans were left searching for somebody to cheer. They found that somebody in the massive frame of Jerry Blackwell. As the fans' hero, it was Blackwell's job to thwart the success of the territory's despised, such as King Kong Brody and Stan Hansen.

CRUSHER VERDU

HT: 5'10" **WT:** 275 lbs. **FROM:** Columbus, Ohio
SIGNATURE MOVE: Bear Hug

Known as "The Spanish Hercules", Crusher Verdu was an amateur wrestling champion and regarded as a powerhouse across Europe and the territories of the National Wrestling Alliance (NWA). When he entered the World Wide Wrestling Federation Superstars were placed on alert. Managed by the likes of Tony Angelo and Capt. Lou Albano, he stopped at nothing to reach the top. Although he was an almost instant contender for the WWE Championship—Verdu was driven to dethrone champion Bruno Sammartino—but never managed to beat the Italian Strongman.

Crusher Verdu retired from the ring in the early 1980s. To this day, when ring experts talk about all-time strongmen, "The Spanish Hercules" Crusher Verdu always makes the list!

CRYBABY CANNON

FROM: Montreal, Quebec, Canada

At 360 pounds, George "Crybaby" Cannon was a mountain of a man. Prior to his days inside the ring, Cannon parlayed his massive size into a successful football career, playing for the Canadian Football League's Regina Roughriders.

While his massive frame helped him earn many wins as a wrestler, Cannon gained most of his notoriety from being a manager. In addition to guiding the careers of the Mongols, he also managed the famed tag team The Fabulous Kangaroos. In 1983, Cannon struck a deal with Vince McMahon to help bring WWE to Detroit. This was just the beginning of WWE's national, and eventual global, dominance of the sports-entertainment scene.

CRYME TYME

MEMBERS: Shad, JTG   **COMBINED WT:** 530 lbs.   **FROM:** Brooklyn, New York

In an attempt to entertain WWE audiences, Cryme Tyme performed over-the-top parodies of the typical societal stereotypes they encountered during their lives, including stealing cars, televisions, wallets, and more.

In the ring, this duo from the county of Kings was all business. The perfect combination of speed and power, JTG & Shad threw down with WWE's best teams, as evidenced by their debut victory over Spirit Squad in October 2006. Their momentum carried over into their first pay-per-view match where they stole a win from the Highlanders, Lance Cade & Trevor Murdoch, and Charlie Haas & Viscera at *Cyber Sunday*.

In September 2007, Cryme Tyme took a six-month hiatus from WWE. When they returned in 2008, they picked up right where they left off. They even fought alongside John Cena during his war against JBL. Soon after moving to *SmackDown*, the Brooklyn boys were #1 contenders for the WWE Unified Tag Team Championship. After several unsuccessful attempts to win tag team gold, Shad brutally attacked his life-long friend. With their bond broken, Cryme Tyme disbanded in 2010.

CURT HAWKINS

HT: 6'1" **WT:** 221 lbs. **FROM:** Queens, New York
SIGNATURE MOVE: Hangman's Facebuster

TITLE HISTORY

WWE TAG TEAM CHAMPION	*Partnered with Zack Ryder to win a Fatal 4-Way Match on July 20, 2008*

The WWE Universe first learned what Curt Hawkins was capable of when he, along with Zack Ryder, cunningly helped Edge capture the World Heavyweight Championship at *Armageddon 2007*. Following the pay-per-view, the "Rated-R Entourage" of Hawkins and Ryder stayed by Edge's side, continually ensuring he kept a firm grasp on the gold. But it wasn't long before they had gold of their own.

Hawkins and Ryder captured the WWE Tag Team Championship in a Fatal 4-Way Match in July 2008. They held the titles for two months before losing to Carlito & Primo. A few months later, Hawkins disappeared for more than one year.

With Vance Archer as his partner, Hawkins returned to *SmackDown* in May 2010. The new tandem, known as the Gatecrashers, quickly made an impact, defeating MVP and Christian in tag action. However, as the year wore on, their momentum began to fade. They eventually took their frustrations out on each other, thus ending their union. No longer with Archer, Hawkins hopes to make a name for himself in *Raw*'s singles division.

CRUISERWEIGHT CHAMPIONSHIP

The WWE Cruiserweight Championship originated in World Championship Wrestling (WCW) in 1991. The title was designed to recognize sports-entertainment's top cruiserweights. However, the Cruiserweight Championship was forced to overcome several lofty obstacles early in its existence before finally achieving its level of prominence in WWE.

Less than one year after its inception, the Cruiserweight Championship was stripped from an injured Brad Armstrong, which resulted in a four-year hiatus. After the title made its return in 1996, cruiserweights like Dean Malenko and Rey Mysterio wowed audiences while rebuilding the championship's reputation.

WWE fans began to familiarize themselves with the Cruiserweight Championship in 2001 when Shane McMahon purchased WCW.

1991

October 27
Chattanooga, TN

In the finals of a tournament to crown the first-ever Cruiserweight Champion, Brian Pillman defeated Richard Morton.

December 25
Atlanta, GA

Jushin Liger defeated Brian Pillman

1992

February 29
Milwaukee, WI

Brian Pillman defeated Jushin Liger

June 20
Augusta, GA

Scotty Flamingo defeated Brian Pillman

July 5
Atlanta, GA

Brad Armstrong defeated Scotty Flamingo
An injury forced Brad Armstrong to vacate the Cruiserweight Championship in September 1992.

1996

March 20
Nagoya, Japan

Shinjiro Otani defeated Chris Benoit in the finals of a tournament to crown a new Cruiserweight Champion.

May 2
Orlando, FL

Dean Malenko defeated Shinjiro Otani

July 8
Orlando, FL

Rey Mysterio defeated Dean Malenko

October 27
Las Vegas, NV

Dean Malenko defeated Rey Mysterio

December 29
Nashville, TN

Ultimo Dragon defeated Dean Malenko

1997

January 22
Milwaukee, WI

Dean Malenko defeated Ultimo Dragon

February 24
San Francisco, CA

Syxx defeated Dean Malenko

June 28
Los Angeles, CA

Chris Jericho defeated Syxx

July 28
Charleston, WV

Alex Wright defeated Chris Jericho

August 16
Colorado Springs, CO

Chris Jericho defeated Alex Wright

September 14
Winston-Salem, NC

Eddie Guerrero defeated Chris Jericho

October 26
Las Vegas, NV

Rey Mysterio defeated Eddie Guerrero

November 10
Memphis, TN

Eddie Guerrero defeated Rey Mysterio

December 29
Baltimore, MD

Ultimo Dragon defeated Eddie Guerrero

1998

January 8
Daytona Beach, FL

Juventud Guerrera defeated Ultimo Dragon

January 15
Lakeland, FL

Rey Mysterio defeated Juventud Guerrera

January 24
Dayton, OH

Chris Jericho defeated Rey Mysterio

May 17
Worcester, MA

Dean Malenko defeated Chris Jericho
Dean Malenko was forced to vacate the championship because he wore a mask to the ring when he won the right to face Chris Jericho for the title.

June 14
Baltimore, MD

Chris Jericho defeated Dean Malenko

August 8
Sturgis, SD

Juventud Guerrera defeated Chris Jericho

September 14
Greenville, SC

Billy Kidman defeated Juventud Guerrera

November 16
Wichita, KS

Juventud Guerrera defeated Billy Kidman

November 22
Auburn Hills, MI

Billy Kidman defeated Juventud Guerrera

1999

March 15
Cincinnati, OH

Rey Mysterio defeated Billy Kidman

April 19
Gainesville, FL

Psicosis won a Fatal Four Way Match that also included Blitzkreig, Juventud Guerrera, and then-champion Rey Mysterio.

April 26
Fargo, ND

Rey Mysterio defeated Psicosis

August 19
Lubbock, TX

Lenny Lane defeated Rey Mysterio
WCW stripped Lenny Lane of the Cruiserweight Championship.

October 4
Kansas City, MO

Psicosis was awarded Cruiserweight Championship

October 4
Kansas City, MO

Disco Inferno defeated Psicosis

November 21
Toronto, Ontario

Evan Karagias defeated Disco Inferno

December 19
Washington, D.C.

Madusa defeated Evan Karagias

2000

January 16
Cincinnati, OH

Oklahoma defeated Madusa
Oklahoma was forced to vacate the Cruiserweight Championship after exceeding the weight limit.

February 20
San Francisco, CA

The Artist defeated Lash LeRoux in the finals of a tournament to crown a new Cruiserweight Champion.

March 30
Baltimore, MD

Billy Kidman defeated The Artist

March 31
Pittsburgh, PA

The Artist defeated Billy Kidman

▼

April 16
Chicago, IL

Chris Candido defeated Juventud Guerrera, Shannon Moore, Crowbar, Lash LeRoux, and The Artist to become the new titleholder.

▼

May 15
Biloxi, MS

Crowbar and Daffney beat Chris Candido and Tammy Sytch in a Mixed Tag Team Match to become co-holders of the Cruiserweight Championship.

▼

May 22
Grand Rapids, MI

Daffney defeated Crowbar

▼

June 6
Knoxville, TN

Lt. Loco defeated a Triple Threat Match that included Disco Inferno and then-champion Daffney.

▼

July 31
Cincinnati, OH

Lance Storm defeated Lt. Loco

▼

August 14
Kelowna, B.C.

Elix Skipper awarded Cruiserweight Championship by Lance Storm.

▼

October 2
San Francisco, CA

Mike Sanders defeated Elix Skipper

Mike Sanders and Kevin Nash beat Elix Skipper in a Handicap Match.

▼

December 4
Lincoln, NE

Chavo Guerrero defeated Mike Sanders

▼

2001

March 18
Jacksonville, FL

Shane Helms defeated Chavo Guerrero

▼

July 5
Tacoma, WA

Billy Kidman defeated Shane Helms

▼

July 30
Philadelphia, PA

X-Pac defeated Billy Kidman to unify the Light Heavyweight and Cruiserweight Championships.

▼

October 11
Moline, IL

Billy Kidman defeated X-Pac

▼

October 22
Kansas City, MO

Tajiri defeated Billy Kidman

▼

2002

April 4
Rochester, NY

Billy Kidman defeated Tajiri

▼

April 21
Kansas City, MO

Tajiri defeated Billy Kidman

▼

May 16
Montreal, Quebec

The Hurricane pinned Tajiri in a Triple Threat Match that also included Billy Kidman.

▼

June 23
Columbus, OH

Jamie Noble defeated The Hurricane

▼

November 17
New York, NY

Billy Kidman defeated Jamie Noble

▼

2003

February 23
Montreal, Quebec

Matt Hardy defeated Billy Kidman

▼

June 5
Anaheim, CA

Rey Mysterio defeated Matt Hardy

▼

September 25
Philadelphia, PA

Tajiri defeated Rey Mysterio

▼

2004

January 1
Washington, D.C.

Rey Mysterio defeated Tajiri

▼

February 15
San Francisco, CA

Chavo Guerrero defeated Rey Mysterio

▼

May 6
Tucson, AZ

Jacqueline defeated Chavo Guerrero

▼

May 16
Los Angeles, CA

Chavo Guerrero defeated Jacqueline

▼

May 20
Las Vegas, NV

Chavo Classic pinned Chavo Guerrero in a Triple Threat Match that also included Spike Dudley.

▼

June 17
Chicago, IL

Rey Mysterio defeated Chavo Classic

▼

July 29
Cincinnati, OH

Spike Dudley defeated Rey Mysterio

▼

December 12
Atlanta, GA

Funaki defeated Spike Dudley

▼

2005

February 20
Pittsburgh, PA

Chavo Guerrero last eliminated Paul London from an Elimination Match that also included Akio, Spike Dudley, Shannon Moore, and then-champion Funaki.

▼

March 31
Houston, TX

Paul London last eliminated Billy Kidman from an 8-man Battle Royal that also included Funaki, Scotty 2 Hotty, Akio, Nunzio, Spike Dudley, and then-champion Chavo Guerrero.

▼

August 6
Bridgeport, CT

Nunzio defeated Paul London

▼

October 9
Houston, TX

Juventud defeated Nunzio

▼

November 15
Rome, Italy

Nunzio defeated Juventud

▼

November 25
Sheffield, England

Juventud defeated Nunzio

▼

December 18
Providence, RI

Kid Kash defeated Juventud

▼

2006

January 29
Miami, FL

Gregory Helms pinned Funaki in a Cruiserweight Championship Invitational Match that also included Paul London, Jamie Noble, Nunzio, and then-champion Kid Kash.

▼

2007

February 18
Los Angeles, CA

Chavo Guerrero pinned Jimmy Wang Yang in a Cruiserweight Open that also included Daivari, Funaki, Shannon Moore, Scotty 2 Hotty, Jamie Noble, and then-champion Gregory Helms.

▼

July 22
San Jose, CA

Hornswoggle pinned Jamie Noble in a Cruiserweight Open that included Shannon Moore, Jimmy Wang Yang, Funaki, and then-champion Chavo Guerrero.

CYBER SUNDAY

Known as *Taboo Tuesday* for its first two years, *Cyber Sunday* gave WWE fans the opportunity to vote on virtually every aspect of the event.

October 19, 2004

Milwaukee, WI - Bradley Center

Main Event
Randy Orton defeated "Nature Boy" Ric Flair in a Steel Cage Match

▼

November 1, 2005

San Diego, CA - iPayOne Center

Main Event
World Heavyweight Champion John Cena defeated Shawn Michaels and Kurt Angle in a Triple Threat Match

▼

November 5, 2006

Cincinnati, OH - U.S. Bank Arena

Main Event
World Heavyweight Champion King Booker defeated WWE Champion John Cena and ECW Champion Big Show in a Triple Threat Match

▼

October 28, 2007

Washington, DC - Verizon Center

Main Event
World Heavyweight Champion Batista defeated Undertaker

▼

October 26, 2008

Phoenix, AZ - US Airways Center

Main Event
Batista defeated World Heavyweight Champion Chris Jericho. Stone Cold Steve Austin as the guest referee

DAIVARI

HT: 5'10" **WT:** 206 lbs.
FROM: Detroit, Michigan

Detroit native Daivari accused his fellow countrymen of racist activity toward him and other Arab-Americans. Clearly, his sentiments did not sit well with the melting pot of WWE fans, but that didn't stop him from continually spewing his unpopular opinions.

In the ring, Daivari's early days looked bright, especially after defeating Shawn Michaels in his singles debut in April 2005. When his partner, Muhammad Hassan, left WWE later that summer, his career was knocked off track and never fully recovered. Following Hassan's departure, Daivari focused mainly on managing. His list of clients included Kurt Angle, Mark Henry and The Great Khali.

DAMIAN DEMENTO

HT: 6'3" **WT:** 269 lbs.
FROM: The Outer Reaches Of Your Mind
SIGNATURE MOVE: Jumping Knee Drop

Demento and his odd forms of behavior inhabited WWE for the first time in October 1992. He prowled the rings, all the while speaking aloud to the voices speaking to him in his head. Demento disturbed all who watched him and battled the likes of Virgil, Bob Backlund, Tatanka and Tito Santana.

Despite Demento's peculiar persona, audiences became curious about what he would do next. In the ring, he saw continued success, which led him to the main event of the first ever *Monday Night Raw* against Undertaker. By the summer of 1994, Damian Demento left WWE.

DAN SEVERN

HT: 6'2" **WT:** 250 lbs.
FROM: Coldwater, Michigan

Walking to the ring in a plain grey T-shirt, Dan Severn appeared to be a no-frills Superstar. When the bell rang, he did little to change people's perception. His no-nonsense offensive onslaught was simple, and certainly made his deserving of the nickname "The Beast."

Upon entering WWE, Severn's résumé already included 85 wrestling titles, including the NWA Championship, which he actually brought with him to WWE. His long list of accolades, coupled with his Mixed Martial Arts submission style, made Severn a multi-faceted threat to the entire roster.

Following a fallout with Jim Cornette, Severn chose to find his own competition. The choice proved to be a wise decision, as his wars against Owen Hart will forever be remembered as some of his greatest WWE action. Unfortunately for Severn, however, a piledriver delivered by Hart caused a severe injury to his neck.

Severn's career never got back on track after the neck injury. As a result, some say his WWE days never lived up to their expectations. "The Beast's" success outside WWE, however, is something he can hang his hat on proudly.

DANIEL BRYAN

HT: 5'10" **WT:** 192 lbs. **FROM:** Aberdeen, Washington
SIGNATURE MOVE: LeBell Lock

TITLE HISTORY

UNITED STATES CHAMPION	Defeated The Miz on September 19, 2010
WORLD HEAVYWEIGHT CHAMPION	Defeated Big Show on December 18, 2011

After witnessing Daniel Bryan's sound offensive style in the ring, it should come as no surprise that he was trained by two all-time greats: Shawn Michaels and William Regal.

Armed with an invaluable education, Bryan took his game to multiple continents, including Asia and Australia, before finally appearing in a WWE ring in 2010. As a Rookie in the first-ever *NXT*, he was able to show a worldwide audience what Internet fans have been raving about for years.

Following *NXT*, Bryan was elevated to WWE's main stage as a member of Nexus. But before the renegade faction could catch steam, Bryan was gone from the group, as well as WWE, for several months. When he returned, Bryan was determined to make a name for himself as a singles star, and that's exactly what he did.

Upon returning, Bryan quickly captured the United States Championship from his former *NXT* Pro, The Miz. He later solidified his status as a singles star when he used his Money in the Bank briefcase to defeat Big Show for the coveted World Heavyweight Championship. His time as champion came to a painfully quick end at *WrestleMania XXVIII* where Sheamus took advantage of Bryan's uncharacteristic loss of focus and took the title after a record-breaking Championship match which lasted only 18 seconds.

DANNY DAVIS

HT: 6'0" **WT:** 180 lbs.
FROM: Dover, New Hampshire
SIGNATURE MOVE: Boston Crab

WWE audiences were introduced to Davis in the early 1980s as a referee. However, people uncovered a disturbing trend as Davis was seemingly becoming tolerant of rule-breaking tactics. Alleged offenses included making fast counts, not enforcing basic rules and turning a blind eye to the questionable activities.

In January 1987, he officiated the World Tag Team Championship Match between the Hart Foundation and British Bulldogs. Davis allowed extremely questionable double-team maneuvers from the Hart Foundation, which led to their victory to claim the titles. The outcome prompted Jack Tunney to launch an investigation, and Davis was soon suspended from officiating in WWE for life. Davis traded his referee's shirt for boots and became a WWE Superstar.

Davis became a member of the Hart Foundation and appeared at *WrestleMania III* and *IV* and the first two *Survivor Series* events. In 1989, Davis was reinstated as an official. He returned to the impartial ways of his early career and worked in WWE rings until the mid 1990s.

DANNY DORING

HT: 5'10" **WT:** 219 lbs.
FROM: Wildwood, New Jersey

Alongside partner Roadkill, Danny Doring has the honor of being one-half of the last-ever ECW Tag Team Champions. Unfortunately for Doring, however, that accolade failed to result in any WWE success. In fact, his entire WWE career only amounted to a handful of matches, none of which he won.

During 2004 and 2005, Doring made a few unsuccessful appearances on *Heat* and *Velocity*. Despite his losing record, he was awarded a contract to compete on WWE's reborn ECW brand. After losses to Mike Knox, Rob Van Dam and CM Punk, Doring was released from his contract in December 2006.

REFEREES

It takes a special person to stand up to the Superstars of the WWE. The hazards of this job include being on the receiving end of miss-timed maneuvers, falling victim to nefarious plots, and staying focused despite persistent distractions. Their uniforms have ranged from a blue button-up shirt with bow tie to black and white stripes to the many solid colors during the brand extension in the mid-2000s. However, for nearly 50 years WWE referees have worked hard to keep the action fair. To add to their challenge, WWE referees are not afforded the luxury of instant replay or second chances, but just as with every WWE Superstar in the ring, they do the best job possible.

WWE OFFICIALS FROM THE 1960s

Danny Bartfield

Dick Kroll

Fred Atkins

"Judo" Jack Terry

Mike Thanosoulos

WWE OFFICIALS FROM THE 1970s

Billy Caputo

Dick Woehrle

Dusty Feldbaumer

Eddie Gersh

Gilberto Roman

Harry Smythe

Jack Lotz

John Stanley

Lou Super

Mario Savoldi

Terry Yorkston

"Wee Willie" Webber

WWE OFFICIALS FROM THE 1980s

Danny Davis

Dave Hebner

Earl Hebner

Jim Korderas

Joey Marella

John Benello

John Reigler

Mike Figaroa

Mike Torres

Rita Marie

Teddy Long

Tim White

WWE OFFICIALS FROM THE 1990s

Jack Doan

Mike Chioda

Mike Sparks

WWE OFFICIALS FROM THE 2000s

Brian Hebner

Chad Patton

Charles Robinson

Chris Kay

John Cone

Mickie Henson

Nick Patrick

Scott Armstrong

WWE OFFICIALS FROM THE 2010s

Justin King

Rob Zapata

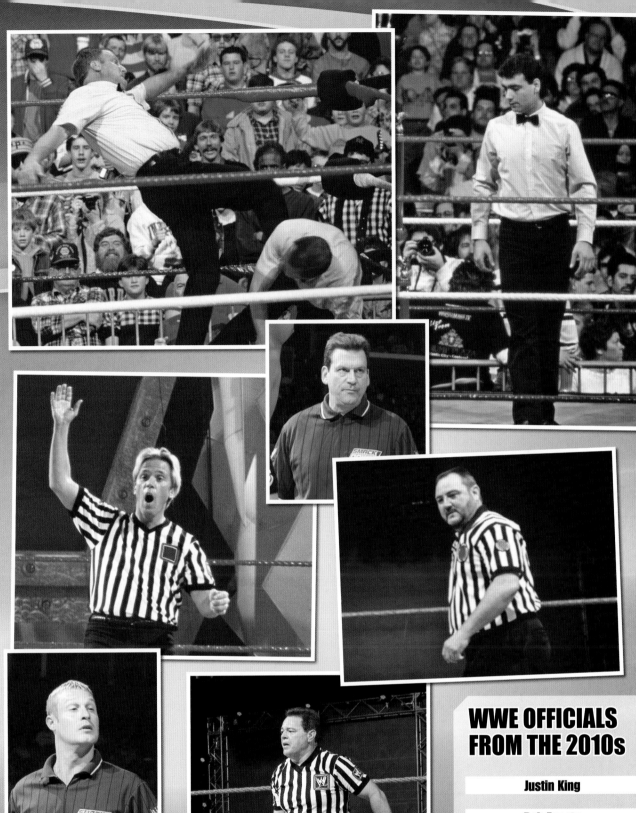

D

2010-

▲

2000-09

▲

1990-99

▲

1980-89

▲

1970-79

▲

1960-69

DANNY SPIVEY

HT: 6'8" **WT: 280 lbs.** **FROM: Tampa, Florida** **SIGNATURE MOVE: Bulldog**

In 1985, "Golden Boy" Danny Spivey made his WWE debut and soon became one half of the U.S. Express with Mike Rotundo. These two fan favorites came to the ring waving the Stars & Stripes. In 1988, Spivey left the company and toured with All-Japan Pro Wrestling and the World Wrestling Council in Puerto Rico.

Spivey spent the early 1990s in WCW, All-Japan Pro Wrestling and the Universal Wrestling Federation, where he was often known as "Dangerous" Danny Spivey. Spivey was forced to retire from the ring in the mid 1990s after a severe back injury. To this day, fans still talk about his successful runs as a tag team and singles competitor throughout the world.

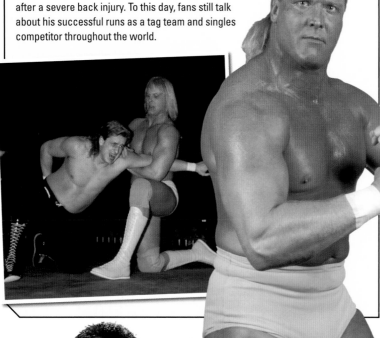

DARREN YOUNG

HT: 6'1" **WT: 242 lbs.** **FROM: Miami, Florida**
SIGNATURE MOVE: Fireman's Carry Gutbuster

As the self-proclaimed "South Beach party boy," the always flashy Darren Young lives for three things: Money, women and wrestling.

But Young wasn't always the entertaining character for which he has become known. Following his elimination from season one of *WWE NXT*, the young Superstar developed a no-nonsense personality as a founding member of Nexus. As a part of the rebellious faction, Young retired his signature pearly-white smile and began sporting a grimace while ganging up on WWE Superstars when they least expected it.

Nexus' style of gang warfare eventually turned its target on Young. Following a loss to John Cena on *Raw* in August 2010, he was attacked by his own running mates and exiled from the faction he helped build.

Young flew under the radar in early 2011 before returning to *NXT* for season five in March. While there, he was able to resurrect his smile, but still competes with the fierceness he displayed while in Nexus.

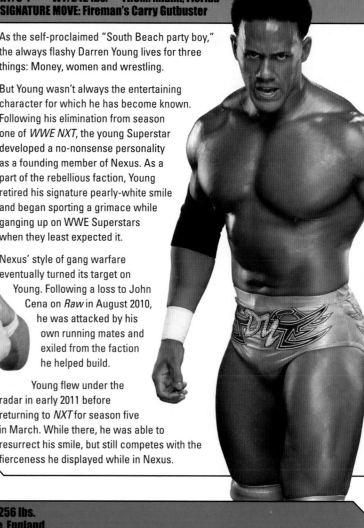

DAVE TAYLOR

HT: 6'3" **WT: 256 lbs.**
FROM: Yorkshire, England

Ten years after teaming with William Regal as the Blue Bloods in WCW, Dave Taylor reunited with his longtime friend and partner on *SmackDown* in October 2006. The brawling Brits made an instant impact, defeating Scotty 2 Hotty & Funaki in their debut, then toppled the mighty Bobby Lashley & Tatanka in their second match. The team's momentum eventually carried them to a Ladder Match for the WWE Tag Team Championship against Paul London & Brian Kendrick at *Armageddon 2006*. Taylor & Regal failed to capture the titles that night, but went a long way in solidifying their status in the tag ranks.

After the 2007 WWE Draft forced the successful British tandem to go their separate ways, Taylor briefly teamed with Paul Burchill before serving as Drew McIntyre's mentor.

DAVID HART SMITH

HT: 6'5" **WT: 260 lbs.** **FROM: Calgary, Alberta, Canada**
SIGNATURE MOVE: Running Powerslam

David Hart Smith was raised around some of the greatest figures to set foot

TITLE HISTORY	
WWE TAG TEAM CHAMPION	*Partnered with Tyson Kidd to defeat Big Show & The Miz on April 26, 2010*
WORLD TAG TEAM CHAMPION	*Partnered with Tyson Kidd to defeat Big Show & The Miz on April 26, 2010*

in the ring. His father was the British Bulldog, his uncles included Bret "Hit Man" Hart, Owen Hart, and Jim "The Anvil" Neidhart and his grandfather was Stu Hart. DH's offensive arsenal is a blend of moves for the new millennium and a tribute to his legendary father.

Smith debuted in Calgary as a professional at age 15 before setting off for appearances in Japan and England. In October 2007, DH appeared in WWE and defeated another Superstar from a famed bloodline, Carlito. He competed against the likes of "Hacksaw" Jim Duggan, Santino Marella, JBL, Umaga, and William Regal before being drafted to *SmackDown* in 2008. In 2010, he joined cousin Natalya and best friend Tyson Kidd to form the Hart Dynasty, which resulted in a Tag Team Championship. Since his WWE departure, he's competed in Japan and is training for a career in mixed martial arts under grappling legend, Billy Robinson.

DAVID OTUNGA

HT: 6'0" WT: 250 lbs.
FROM: Hollywood, California
SIGNATURE MOVE: Spinebuster

TITLE HISTORY

WWE TAG TEAM CHAMPION (2 TIMES)	Partnered with John Cena to defeat Drew McIntyre & Cody Rhodes on October 24, 2010 Partnered with Michael McGillicutty to defeat Big Show & Kane on May 23, 2011

David Otunga has it all: a chiseled physique, a beautiful fiancé in the Oscar-winning Jennifer Hudson, an A-list Hollywood lifestyle, a successful career and a powerful intelligence, evidenced by his Harvard Law School degree. When put together, these characteristics equate to a major force within the squared circle.

Originally *NXT*'s runner-up from season one, it wasn't until after the show's completion that Otunga truly started to shine. As a member of the controversial Nexus faction, the newcomer teamed with the rest of the *NXT* roster to strike fear into the WWE locker room. He also used his alliance with Wade Barrett and company to strong arm his way to two WWE Tag Team Title reigns. First, he and reluctant partner John Cena held the gold for one day in October 2010. Later, Otunga teamed with Michael McGillicutty to top Big Show & Kane in May 2011. With help from their Nexus cohorts, the duo held the titles for three months before losing to Air Boom.

In addition to competing in the ring, Otunga has also earned the role of official advisor to Senior Vice President of Talent Relations and Interim Raw General Manager John Laurinaitis. Aside from sipping large amounts of coffee, Otunga's responsibilities range from offering legal advice to delivering bad news to his fellow Superstars.

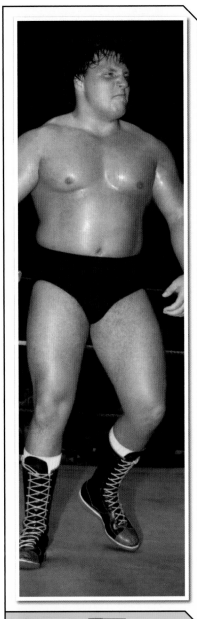

DAVID SAMMARTINO

HT: 5'8" WT: 252 lbs.
FROM: Pittsburg, Pennsylvania
SIGNATURE MOVE: Figure-Four Leg Lock

The son of former WWE Champion and all-time great Bruno Sammartino, young David dreamed about creating his own path to stardom. He began his career under the name Bruno Sammartino, Jr., but soon decided to adopt his birth name. In 1984, David entered WWE and pinned Jerry Valiant during his television debut. David enjoyed some success, and competed at the first *WrestleMania* against Brutus Beefcake.

In the summer of 1986, David left WWE and briefly appeared in the AWA. For the remainder of the 1980s, he traveled independent promotions throughout the United States. In 1990, he was part of the short-lived UWF, and in 1996, he was part of the WCW Cruiserweight Division.

Today, David is retired from the ring and has a successful Personal Training business in Georgia, where he resides with his family.

DAWN MARIE

HT: 5'7"
FROM: Rahway, New Jersey

The ring has seen its share of seductive women, but never before has a Diva used sex as a weapon as effectively, or lethally, as Dawn Marie. Over the course of her career, the manipulative brunette seduced countless male targets, both young and old.

Dawn Marie's greatest romantic exploit came in October 2002 when she fell for Al Wilson, the father of fellow Diva Torrie Wilson. Despite being half Wilson's age, Dawn Marie engaged in a passionate relationship with Torrie's dad, which did not sit well with Torrie. After just weeks together, the two lovebirds agreed to become husband and wife.

Dressed in nothing but their very revealing underwear, the couple was married in January 2003. Unfortunately, the wedding was one of the last times anybody would see Al Wilson alive, as Dawn Marie proved to be too much woman for him. His heart eventually gave out and he died on their honeymoon.

Proving a leopard never changes her spots, Dawn Marie was back at it the following year when her affair with Charlie Haas effectively ended his engagement to Miss Jackie. Luckily for all the WWE Superstars (and their fathers), the seductive Diva left WWE in shortly thereafter.

DEAN DOUGLAS

HT: 6'1" WT: 234 lbs. FROM: The University of Knowledge
SIGNATURE MOVE: Final Exam

TITLE HISTORY

INTERCONTINENTAL CHAMPION	Awarded championship when injuries forced Shawn Michaels to vacate the title on October 22, 1995

No other Superstar in the history of WWE had an easier route to the Intercontinental Championship than Dean Douglas. When injuries prevented Shawn Michaels from defending his title, it was simply handed over to Dean Douglas. Without even breaking a sweat, Douglas celebrated becoming the new Intercontinental Champion.

The celebration, however, didn't last long. Within moments of being awarded the title, Douglas was forced to defend it against Razor Ramon, who promptly defeated him and took the title.

Despite owning one of the least impressive Intercontinental Championship reigns in WWE history, the arrogant Douglas believed he had something he could teach all his fellow Superstars. Watching from his satellite classroom, he would grade the action he saw in the ring. Douglas proved to be a tough man to impress, as he never gave a favorable review. Some of the more notable Superstars Douglas offered failing grades to include The 1-2-3 Kid, Barry Horowitz and Shawn Michaels.

D

1960-69
1970-79
1980-89
1990-99
2000-09
2010-

91

DEAN HO

FROM: Hawaii
SIGNATURE MOVE: The Full Nelson

TITLE HISTORY

WORLD TAG TEAM CHAMPION	*Partnered with Tony Garea to defeat Prof. Toru Tanaka & Mr. Fuji on November 14, 1973*

This happy Hawaiian was a bodybuilder who won the "Mr. Hawaiian Islands" championship in 1956. In 1962, Dean Ho made his ring debut in the Pacific Northwest Wrestling territory, and for the next decade Ho appeared all over the Pacific Northwest and Hawaii.

In 1973, Dean debuted in WWE and tested his skills against the best and brightest. Dean Ho's in-ring style combined martial arts, grappling abilities, and aerial moves. He formed a popular tag team with Tony Garea, and the duo went on to hold the World Tag Team Championship for close to six months. Dean continued to appear on WWE until 1976. He then traveled to Georgia, San Francisco, and returned to Vancouver and Portland. He decided to hang up his boots in December 1983.

Today the happy Hawaiian lives in Vancouver, B.C. and owns a highly touted gourmet catering business. Dean Ho is recognized for all his in-ring accomplishments and versatility as well as a persona that influenced countless others that set foot in the ring after him.

DEAN MALENKO

HT: 5'10" **WT:** 212 lbs.
FROM: Tampa, Florida
SIGNATURE MOVE: Texas Cloverleaf

TITLE HISTORY

LIGHT HEAVYWEIGHT CHAMPION (2 TIMES)	*Defeated Essa Rios on March 13, 2000* *Defeated Scotty 2 Hotty on April 27, 2000*

Trained by his famous father, "Professor" Boris Malenko, Dean first consistently appeared on American television in his days with ECW, earning a reputation as a peerless technical competitor. In 1995, "The Man Of 1,000 Holds" moved on to WCW, where he held many championships.

In January 2000, Dean Malenko debuted on *Raw* as a part of the Radicalz. He made an immediate impact in the Light Heavyweight Division, defeating Essa Rios in March to become Light Heavyweight Champion, a title he held for most of the following year. In 2001, after a series of matches involving Divas and the Light Heavyweight Championship, Malenko retired from the ring and started work behind the scenes as a member of WWE's front office.

Over the years, he has been seen on WWE television breaking up wild melees. Don't let his time away from the ring fool you. He stays in ring shape, and if a Superstar goes too far during one of these wild brawls, they'll get taken down in the blink of an eye.

DEBRA

HT: 5'5" **FROM:** Tuscaloosa, Alabama

TITLE HISTORY

WOMEN'S CHAMPION	*Defeated Sable on May 10, 1999*

A former beauty pageant queen, Debra brought her award-winning looks to WCW in 1996. Alongside her then-husband Steve McMichael, the curvy blonde was originally seen as nothing more than eye candy. By the end of her career, however, she earned a reputation as one of the most powerful females of her time.

After a few years by McMichael's side, Debra jumped to WWE in 1998. At first glance, she gave the impression of a no-nonsense businesswoman. However, once she broke out of her shell, Debra revealed herself as quite an exhibitionist. In fact, it wasn't uncommon to see her remove her suits in an attempt to help her man at the time, Jeff Jarrett, pick up wins. This tactic also lead to Jerry Lawler's famous "puppies" catchphrase.

As a competitor, Debra didn't quite have the skills of a Fabulous Moolah, but that didn't stop her from capturing the Women's Championship, albeit on a technicality. In May 1999, Sable had disrobed Debra in an Evening Gown Match, thus winning the encounter. Commissioner Shawn Michaels saw things a bit differently, though. In his eyes, the winner should be the Diva left wearing nothing but her underwear. As a result, he reversed the decision and awarded the match and Women's Championship to Debra.

Debra was so inspired by HBK's leadership that night that she later went on to become Lieutenant Commissioner, thus proving herself as one of the most powerful females of her time.

DECEMBER TO DISMEMBER

Dec 03 2006
James Brown Arena; Atlanta, Georgia

December to Dismember included ECW veterans Tommy Dreamer, Balls Mahoney, and the FBI and other top Superstars like the Hardys, MNM, and Elijah Burke.

The main event was a bloody Extreme Elimination Chamber Match that locked ECW Champion Big Show, Bobby Lashley, Rob Van Dam, Hardcore Holly, Test, and CM Punk in the sadistic chamber. Bobby Lashley survived the extreme encounter (and Big Show's barbed wire bat!) to claim the ECW Title.

DEMOLITION

MEMBERS: Ax, Smash, Crush
COMBINED WT: 978 lbs.
FROM: Parts Unknown

TITLE HISTORY

WORLD TAG TEAM CHAMPIONS (3 TIMES)	Defeated Strike Force on March 27, 1988 Defeated Brain Busters on October 2, 1989 Defeated Andre the Giant & Haku on April 1, 1990

Originally looked upon by many as a cheap Road Warriors rip off, Demolition could have very easily folded under the weight of the naysayers. Instead, they combined their intimidating appearance with an aggressive in-ring style to dominate the WWE tag team scene for five years.

Clad in studded leather and colorful face paint, Ax & Smash made their WWE debut in 1987. With Mr. Fuji as their manager, Demolition destroyed their early competition, which consisted of some of the most popular tag teams of the time, including the British Bulldogs, Young Stallions, and Killer Bees.

The following year, Demolition carried their dominance into *WrestleMania IV* where they defeated Strike Force for the World Tag Team Championship. Behind the devastation of their Decapitation finisher, Ax and Smash held the titles for a record-breaking sixteen months.

In the midst of Demolition's epic World Tag Team Championship reign, the conniving Mr. Fuji turned his back on his clients to join forces with the Powers of Pain. Empathetic fans everywhere began to see Ax & Smash in a new light. Almost overnight, Demolition was transformed into the most popular tag team in WWE.

Demolition's dominance grew throughout 1990 when they added Crush as the team's third member. Younger and stronger, Crush served as the muscles for the already-forceful tag team. On several occasions, he also stepped in to help Smash through team's third reign as World Tag Team Champions.

By 1991, the trio began to fade, making way for such tag teams as The Nasty Boys and Road Warriors. Their final high-profile match came in a losing effort when they fell to international sensations Genichiro Tenryu & Koji Kitao at *WrestleMania VII*.

To this day, fans look back at Demolition's dominance over WWE as one of the most impressive displays in the history of tag team wrestling. Not bad for a team who were originally looked upon as copycats.

DERRICK BATEMAN 🇺🇸

HT: 6'0" **WT:** 224 lbs. **FROM:** Cleveland, Ohio

According to Derrick Bateman, there are no words in the dictionary that can accurately describe him, which is why he coined his own adjective to help explain who he is: "Man-tastic"

The off-the-wall Bateman made his WWE debut as a part of *NXT* season four in December 2010. It didn't take long for the WWE Universe to realize this Rookie wasn't playing with a full deck, especially after he introduced everybody to his fists, which he affectionately named Freedom and Justice.

Under Daniel Bryan's guidance, Bateman finished third in the *NXT* voting. Despite not winning, the colorful Clevelander learned an invaluable lesson in wrestling, particularly submission wrestling. But Bateman will tell you that he's not just about submission wrestling; he's also about "chicks and America."

Bateman returned to WWE for *NXT Redemption* in the summer of 2011. With Bryan once again serving as his pro, the confident Rookie is out to prove he has more "it" than any other competitor on *NXT*.

DESIREE PETERSON 🇩🇰

HT: 5'9" **FROM:** Copenhagen, Denmark

TITLE HISTORY

WOMEN'S TAG TEAM CHAMPION	Replaced Princess Victoria as Velvet McIntyre's partner in late 1984

Desiree Peterson made her professional debut against Velvet McIntyre in January 1983. Ironically, the two women would soon cross paths again; this time as partners. When McIntyre's tag-team partner, Princess Victoria, suffered a career-ending injury in late 1984, it was Peterson who filled in as her partner. For Peterson, it was like winning the lottery, as teaming with McIntyre also meant she assumed Victoria's role as one-half of the Women's Tag Team Champions.

When she wasn't defending the tag titles with McIntyre, Peterson made a name for herself competing in the women's singles division. There she battled many of sports-entertainment's most legendary female combatants, including Fabulous Moolah, Leilani Kai and Donna Christanello.

Peterson and McIntyre eventually lost their gold to The Glamour Girls in a rare match contested in Egypt in August 1985. The Denmark native left WWE immediately after the loss. She later returned in 1988 to challenge Sherri Martel for the Women's Championship. After failing to wrest the gold away from the now Hall of Famer, Peterson left WWE for good.

DEUCE & DOMINO

COMBINED WT: 730 lbs.
FROM: The Other Side of The Tracks

TITLE HISTORY

WWE TAG TEAM CHAMPIONS	*Defeated Paul London & Brian Kendrick on April 20, 2007*

Deuce & Domino made their WWE debut in 2007, claiming to be the biggest attraction in all of the past, present, and future. Led to the ring by Domino's sister, Cherry, the duo considered themselves God's gift to women.

Deuce & Domino shocked the world when they beat Brian Kendrick & Paul London for the WWE Tag Team Championship. They held the titles for four months, eventually losing to the combination of MVP & Matt Hardy. Cracks in the team began to show when Cherry started to run around with Michelle McCool. Deuce & Domino kicked her to the curb in favor of Maryse. Unfortunately for fans of these throwbacks, a lost match prompted a brawl between the pair, ending their partnership. In August 2008, Domino left WWE and Deuce tried his hand at singles competition.

D-GENERATION X

MEMBERS: Triple H, Shawn Michaels, Chyna, Road Dogg, Billy Gunn, X-Pac, Rick Rude

Throughout the storied history of WWE, there has never been a more controversial group of Superstars than D-Generation X. Their anti-establishment attitude made them an instant hit with fans, while cementing their legacy as the most defiant force in sports-entertainment.

Close friends Shawn Michaels and Triple H brought their notorious relationship to the fore in late 1997. Alongside bodyguard Chyna and "insurance policy" Rick Rude, the faction quickly claimed its first title when HBK defeated British Bulldog for the European Championship at *One Night Only*.

Over the years, DX has seen many different members. Regardless of the incarnation, they all shared the common desire to spit in the face of authority. An exception was made in the case of Commissioner Slaughter, where they were more concerned with avoiding the spit of authority.

At Odds with Authority

Shortly after the victory, DX began to unveil a sophomoric brand of humor that infuriated WWE Commissioner Sgt. Slaughter, but the more Slaughter tried to silence them, the louder they got. It wasn't long before they were mooning audiences and telling people to "Suck it!"

Despite their crude behavior, DX was becoming increasingly more popular and powerful. In November 1997, Michaels defeated Bret Hart for the WWE Championship in a highly controversial match at *Survivor Series*. With the victory came more arrogance and anarchy. In an attempt to sideline DX's chaotic behavior, Slaughter demanded Michaels and Triple H battle against each other on *Raw*. To ensure each man would compete to the fullest extent of his capabilities, Commissioner Slaughter put HBK's European Championship on the line. On the surface, Michaels and Triple H appeared concerned, but they ultimately spit in the face of Slaughter's authority when HBK simply laid down and allowed his partner to pin him for the title.

The lawlessness of D-Generation X seemed to come to an abrupt halt when injuries caused HBK to temporarily retire in early 1998. However, Triple H saw Michaels' injury as an opportunity to pick up the ball and run with it. He replaced Michaels in DX with three equally immature Superstars: Road Dogg, Billy Gunn, and longtime friend X-Pac.

The new DX never skipped a beat. Within days of their union, the revised faction invaded rival WCW's *Monday Nitro* telecast. Within weeks, they did the same to WCW headquarters in Atlanta. The stunts proved to be some of the most jaw-dropping events in sports-entertainment history.

The chaos continued into early 1999, but at *WrestleMania XV*, a shocking turn of events saw DX crumble to the ground. With X-Pac battling Shane McMahon, Triple H ran to the ring to presumably help his DX partner gain victory. Instead, he clobbered X-Pac, signifying the end of the popular faction.

The Rebirth of Rebellion

Eight years after the original DX disbanded, Triple H and Shawn Michaels began to hint at a possible reunion. Beginning at *WrestleMania 22*, both Superstars started to use the faction's signature crotch chop. The taunt went on for months, leaving fans to wonder if the duo would ever reunite. DX's founding fathers finally put the speculation to rest when they officially reformed the controversial faction in June 2006.

Fueled by the sole goal of embarrassing Mr. McMahon, Triple H and HBK used every childish trick in the book. The more immature the gag, the more cheers they heard from the fans. Much like in the faction's early days, they weren't afraid to be crude. DX's rivalry with Mr. McMahon culminated at *Unforgiven* when the Chairman teamed with his son Shane and Big Show to battle "The Game" and HBK in a Hell in a Cell Match. The controversial duo defeated McMahon's team, but the result was overshadowed by the image of DX shoving Mr. McMahon's head into Big Show's gigantic bare behind.

After the victory, D-Generation X changed targets and focused on Rated-RKO. The factional rivalry culminated in a *Survivor Series* match where Triple H and Shawn Michaels teamed up with the Hardy Boys and CM Punk to sweep Rated-RKO's team, 5-0. An injury to Triple H derailed the team for a few months and the duo focused on individual career goals but always reformed when the situation warranted it.

After a loss to Undertaker at *WrestleMania 23*, Shawn Michaels went on hiatus from WWE. At the same time, Triple H was battling the Legacy on his own and decided to search for his best friend. In some of the most entertaining segments in WWE television, Triple H found HBK serving blue-plate specials as a short-order cook. Triple H eventually convinced HBK to team up with him against Legacy at *SummerSlam* and again in subsequent events throughout 2009.

A triple threat match for the WWE Championship that pitted D-Generation X against each other and John Cena threatened to strain their relationship, but Triple H and HBK remained friends until their last televised match on March 1, 2010.

Though HBK has vowed to remain retired after his *WrestleMania XVI* loss to the Undertaker, as evidenced by a surprise appearance at 2010's *Tribute To The Troops*, and a WWE event in Dallas the next year, no one really knows when the music will hit, the green glow sticks will fly, and it will be time to once again break it down.

> *IF YOU'RE NOT DOWN WITH THAT, THEN WE GOT TWO WORDS FOR YOU!*

DIAMOND DALLAS PAGE 🇺🇸

HT: 6'5" **WT:** 248 lbs.
FROM: The Jersey Shore
SIGNATURE MOVE: Diamond Cutter

TITLE HISTORY

EUROPEAN CHAMPION	*Defeated Christian on January 31, 2002*
WORLD TAG TEAM CHAMPION	*Partnered with Kanyon to defeat The APA on August 9, 2001*

Diamond Dallas Page wasn't blessed with overwhelming strength or innate technical ability, but through magnetic charisma and unparalleled dedication to his craft, the New Jersey native became a champion.

With three WCW Championships to his credit, DDP made his WWE debut in 2001. Unlike his WCW days, however, he briefly chose to focus less on his in-ring success and more on stalking Undertaker's wife, Sara. For weeks, DDP sat outside the couple's ranch and videotaped her most intimate moments. Unfortunately for the WWE newcomer, as his obsession with the blonde beauty grew, so did Undertaker's ire. In the end, stalking Sara proved to be a poor decision. Not only did she eventually defeat DDP in August 2001, but Undertaker & Kane also took the World Tag Team Championship from him and his partner, Kanyon.

Despite his unsuccessful rivalry against Undertaker, DDP began to develop an overly optimistic attitude in 2002. Acting like a motivational speaker, he became famous for his cheerful catchphrase, "that's not a bad thing, that's a good thing." During this time, the positive Page also enjoyed some success in the ring, capturing the European Championship from Christian in January.

A few months after winning the European Championship, injury forced DDP to walk away from the ring. While his WWE days were not decorated with many highlights, his career was a major success.

D

2010-
2000-09
1990-99
1980-89
1970-79
1960-69

DICK MURDOCH

HT: 6'2" **WT:** 288 lbs. **FROM:** Waxahachie, Texas
SIGNATURE MOVE: Brainbuster

TITLE HISTORY

WORLD TAG TEAM CHAMPION	*Partnered with Adrian Adonis to defeat Tony Atlas & Rocky Johnson on April 17, 1984*

Murdoch began his career in the mid 1960s and learned his finishing move from the legendary "Killer" Karl Kox. For the next decade, he traveled the regions of the NWA and Japan. In 1983, the ruffian from the Lone Star State and partner Adrian Adonis brought their blend of grappling chaos to WWE. Together, they broke every rule in existence, and in April 1984, they defeated Rocky Johnson& Tony Atlas for the World Tag Team Championship.

In 1985, Murdoch left WWE and returned to the NWA as "Captain Redneck" and toured independent promotions in the United States and overseas. Murdoch made a surprise return appearance in WWE at the 1995 *Royal Rumble* and was one of the last Superstars in the ring before he was eliminated by Henry Godwinn. Sadly, Murdoch passed away in 1996. Murdoch pioneered a flying-fists style of raw-boned brawling never duplicated in the ring before or since.

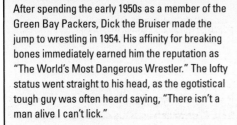

DICK SLATER

HT: 6'0" **WT:** 233 lbs.
FROM: Richmond, Virginia

Success followed Dick Slater everywhere he went, except to WWE. Known as "The Rebel" during his brief WWE run, Slater never seemed to get his career out of first gear. Elsewhere, however, the man known as "Dirty" Dick Slater cheated his way to an impressive won-loss record.

While competing for the National Wrestling Alliance, Slater captured many titles, including the Florida, Missouri, Georgia, Mid-Atlantic and Southeastern Heavyweight Championships, but it was the tag team title earned in World Championship Wrestling that gained him the most national exposure. In June 1992, Slater and his partner, The Barbarian, defeated the Fabulous Freebirds for the WCW United States Tag Team Championship. Three years later, he teamed with the rugged Bunkhouse Buck to take the WCW Tag Team Championship from Harlem Heat.

DICK THE BRUISER

HT: 6'1" **WT:** 261 lbs. **FROM:** Reno, Nevada
SIGNATURE MOVE: Top Rope Knee Drop

After spending the early 1950s as a member of the Green Bay Packers, Dick the Bruiser made the jump to wrestling in 1954. His affinity for breaking bones immediately earned him the reputation as "The World's Most Dangerous Wrestler." The lofty status went straight to his head, as the egotistical tough guy was often heard saying, "There isn't a man alive I can't lick."

Dick the Bruiser is most recognized for his efforts as a wrestler and promoter of the Indianapolis-based World Wrestling Association. While there, he became one of the game's greatest tag team competitors, capturing the promotion's tag titles 14 times with the likes of The Crusher, Bill Miller, and the legendary Bruno Sammartino.

In 1971, Dick the Bruiser found himself on the wrong side of one of history's most significant matches. With The Sheik as his partner, he came up short against Tarzan Tyler & Luke Graham in a match to declare the first-ever World Tag Team Champions in WWE history. Undeterred by the loss, The Bruiser went on to capture eight more tag team championships over the next 15 years.

While Dick the Bruiser is best remembered for being a noted tough man, many fail to credit him with one of the wittiest comments of all time. According to legend, The Bruiser is the first person to call Bobby Heenan "The Weasel." Decades later, Heenan still gets taunted by the derogatory nickname.

THE DICKS

MEMBERS: Chad Dick, James Dick
COMBINED WT: 430 lbs.

Clad in Chippendales outfits and carrying mirrors to the ring, Chad & James Dicks' pre-match ritual saw them strip down to their ring attire to what they believed was the delight of female fans.

Upon their debut in late 2005, the egotistical tandem scored a few big victories. It wasn't long before the WWE caught up to them, which resulted in a series of losses. In February 2006, the Dicks came up short in handicap action against Boogeyman. They were released from WWE immediately after.

DIESEL

HT: 6'10" WT: 328 lbs.
FROM: Detroit, Michigan
SIGNATURE MOVE: Jackkniffe Powerbomb

This giant began his WWE career in 1993 as the bodyguard of Shawn Michaels. At the 1994 *Royal Rumble,* WWE Superstars felt the force of diesel power when he eliminated seven men in under 18 minutes. That night showed that "Big Daddy Cool" was on his way to stardom.

TITLE HISTORY

INTERCONTINENTAL CHAMPION	*Defeated Razor Ramon on April 13, 1994*
WORLD TAG TEAM CHAMPION (2 TIMES)	*Partnered with Shawn Michaels to defeat The Headshrinkers on August 28, 1994* *Partnered with Shawn Michaels to defeat Owen Hart & Yokozuna on September 24, 1995*
WWE CHAMPION	*Defeated Bob Backlund on November 26, 1994*

On April 13, 1994, Diesel won his first major title when he defeated Razor Ramon for the Intercontinental Championship. While still champion, he teamed up with Shawn Michaels to capture the World Tag Team titles. He lost the Intercontinental Championship to Razor in a rematch at *SummerSlam* when Shawn Michaels' "Sweet Chin Music" was out of tune. Tensions grew between the partners, and it boiled up at *Survivor Series* when the two could no longer coexist and forfeited the World Tag Team Championship.

On November 26, 1994, Diesel made history at Madison Square Garden when he replaced an injured Bret "Hit Man" Hart and defeated Bob Backlund in eight seconds to become WWE Champion. With the fans behind him, "Big Daddy Cool's" championship reign lasted almost one full year and gave the title a stability it had not known since the days of Hulk Hogan and Randy "Macho Man" Savage.

Diesel reconnected with his friend Shawn Michaels after an attack by Sycho Sid. They joined forces as "The Dudes With Attitudes," and the duo enjoyed another World Tag Team Championship reign. Diesel continued to dominate in singles action until he met Undertaker at *WrestleMania XII.*

In 1996, Diesel left WWE and arrived on the set of *WCW Monday Nitro* under his real name, Kevin Nash. He formed the Outsiders with close friend Scott Hall, and the pair swore to take down WCW. Along with Hulk Hogan, they created the New World Order (nWo), and stayed with the company until 2001. Kevin Nash returned to WWE in February 2002, recreating the nWo with Hogan and Hall. After recovering from a severe injury, Nash returned as his own man in April 2003 to save old friend Shawn Michaels from a beating courtesy of Triple H, Chris Jericho, and Ric Flair. This led to many battles with former friend Triple H, including a Hell In A Cell Match at *Badd Blood.* Nash left WWE after his match at *SummerSlam* 2003 in the Elimination Chamber.

As rumors of retirement swirled, fifteen years removed from when the name was last heard, Diesel returned at the 2011 *Royal Rumble* to a deafening ovation. After he appeared at the Hall of Fame, this controversial figure raided the *SummerSlam* main event, which set-off an explosive series of encounters with Triple H.

DINK THE CLOWN

HT: 4'0" WT: 95 lbs. FROM: Parts Unknown
SIGNATURE MOVE: Cannonball

Presented as a gift to Doink the Clown, this sidekick packed quite a punch when called upon. Dink rarely left the side of Doink during the clown's days in WWE and gave splitting headaches to referees and opposing Superstars alike.

Dink joined his fellow clown in action against Bam Bam Bigelow & Luna Vachon. The four battled at *WrestleMania X* and from there the mischievous clowns took their act to the 1994 *Survivor Series.* In one of the most chaotic contests in WWE history, Dink teamed with Doink, Pink & Wink against Jerry "The King" Lawler and Queazy, Sleazy & Cheezy in a mixed tag team match. Dink followed his larger counterpart and exited WWE in 1995.

DINO BRAVO

HT: 6'0" WT: 248 lbs. FROM: Montreal, Quebec, Canada SIGNATURE MOVE: Side Suplex

TITLE HISTORY

CANADIAN HEAVYWEIGHT CHAMPION	*Awarded championship in August 1985*
WORLD TAG TEAM CHAMPION	*Partnered with Dominic DeNucci to defeat Prof. Toru Tanaka & Mr. Fuji on March 14, 1978*

Trained by Canadian legend Gino Brito, Dino Bravo began his in-ring career in 1970 and formed a popular tag team with his mentor, known as The Italian Connection. In 1978, Dino debuted in WWE and soon won the World Tag Team Championship with Dominic DeNucci. After a three month reign with the titles, Bravo competed in singles competition before he left the company in 1979. After a seven-year absence, Bravo returned to WWE and became the bleached blond associate of the Dream Team. He also joined forces with Greg Valentine in the New Dream Team.

For the remainder of his career, Bravo battled the biggest names in WWE both by himself and with the Canadian Earthquake. In the spring of 1992, he retired from active competition and opened a training school. Sadly, in March 1993, this Canadian legend died at his Montreal home. Whether he was a fan favorite or rule-breaker, Dino Bravo is remembered as one of the most powerful men in WWE history.

D
2010-
2000-09
1990-99
1980-89
1970-79
1960-69

THE DISCIPLES OF APOCALYPSE

MEMBERS: Crush, Chainz, Skull, 8-Ball

After being fired from the Nation of Domination, Crush formed a biker gang of Superstars he called the Disciples of Apocalypse. According to the former Nation member, DOA was a true brotherhood of Superstars who lived, rode and fought together. Fans expected greatness from Crush, Chainz, Skull & 8-Ball after they made their impressive debut in June 1997, but by the end of the year, Crush had left WWE and Chainz went on to pursue a singles career, leaving Skull & 8-Ball as the sole members of the faction.

As a tag team, Skull & 8-Ball engaged in an intense rivalry against the Legion of Doom. During this time, longtime LOD manager Paul Ellering actually turned on his team to join forces with DOA. The move will forever be remembered as one of the most shocking moments in tag team history.

With Ellering by their side, Skull & 8-Ball were able to turn back LOD at *Fully Loaded 1998*. Later that year, however, Droz teamed with LOD to get the ultimate measure of revenge on DOA & Ellering, defeating the trio at *Judgment Day*.

DIVAS CHAMPIONSHIP

Despite being just as athletic in the ring, *SmackDown*'s Divas spent years watching from the sidelines as *Raw*'s women competed over the Women's Championship. In the summer of 2008, *SmackDown* general manager Vickie Guerrero finally stood up for her brand when she introduced the Divas Championship. Michelle McCool became the first-ever Divas Champion when she defeated Natalya in a tournament final at *The Great American Bash* in 2008.

2008

July 20
Uniondale, NY

Michelle McCool defeated Natalya in the finals of a tournament to crown the inaugural Divas Champion

▼

December 26
Toronto, Onatario

Maryse defeated Michelle McCool

▼

2009

July 26
Philadelphia, PA

Mickie James defeated Maryse

▼

October 12
Indianapolis, IN

Jillian defeated Mickie James

▼

October 12
Indianapolis, IN

Melina defeated Jillian

Melina was forced to vacate the title due to injury.

▼

2010

February 22
Indianapolis, IN

Maryse defeated Gail Kim in the finals of a tournament to crown a new champion

▼

April 12
London, England

Eve defeated Maryse

▼

June 20
Uniondale, NY

Alicia Fox defeated Eve, Maryse and Gail Kim in a Fatal 4-Way Match

August 15
Los Angeles, CA

Melina defeated Alicia Fox

▼

September 19
Chicago, IL

Michelle McCool defeated Melina

Michelle McCool's victory unified the Divas and Women's Championships. In addition, Layla was named co-Champion meaning the title could be defended by either Michelle McCool or Layla

▼

November 21
Miami, FL

Natalya defeated Michelle McCool and Layla in a Handicap Match

▼

2011

January 30
Boston, MA

Eve defeated Natalya, Michelle McCool and Layla in a Fatal 4-Way Match

▼

April 11
Bridgeport, CT

Brie Bella defeated Eve

▼

June 20
Baltimore, MD

Kelly Kelly defeated Brie Bella

▼

October 2
New Orleans, LA

Beth Phoenix defeated Kelly Kelly

DJ GABRIEL

HT: 6'2"   WT: 252 lbs.   FROM: Wokingham, England
SIGNATURE MOVE: Flying European Uppercut

Thanks to Theodore Long's New Superstar Initiative, ECW was introduced to sports-entertainment's most questionable dancer since "Das Wunderkind" Alex Wright when DJ Gabriel debuted in November 2008. Displaying some fancy footwork, the new Superstar easily emerged victorious from his first-ever ECW match. Unquestionably, Gabriel's future was looking bright, which might explain his affinity for wearing shades to the ring.

With the beautiful Alicia Fox by his side, Gabriel went undefeated for the remainder of 2008, picking up quick wins over several inferior opponents. It wasn't until 2009 that Gabriel's competition finally started to pick up. He entered into a thrilling rivalry with fellow countryman Paul Burchill. In the end, Gabriel proved to be the top Brit.

Gabriel suffered his first loss in February 2009 when he fell victim to the massive Mark Henry and his devastating World's Strongest Slam. Shortly after the loss, Fox was drafted to *SmackDown*. Without his favorite dance partner by his side, Gabriel soon faded away from WWE.

D-LO BROWN

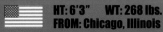 HT: 6'3"   WT: 268 lbs.
FROM: Chicago, Illinois

TITLE HISTORY

EUROPEAN CHAMPION (4 TIMES)	*Defeated Triple H on July 20, 1998* *Defeated X-Pac on October 5, 1998* *Defeated Mideon on July 25, 1999* *Defeated Mark Henry on September 26, 1999*
INTERCONTINENTAL CHAMPION	*Defeated Jeff Jarrett on July 26, 1999*

In 1997, Brown debuted in WWE as a member of the Nation of Domination, but he had a falling out with its leaders, first Faarooq, then The Rock. Amidst the turmoil within the ranks of the Nation, D-Lo defeated Triple H for the European Championship at *Fully Loaded 1998* and became the first Superstar to hold the European and Intercontinental Championships concurrently.

After a brief partnership with the Godfather, in 2000 D-Lo partnered with former Headbanger Chaz and formed Lo Down with their manager, Tiger Ali Singh. Later in 2002, D-Lo acquired the managerial services of Theodore R. Long and became part of his Thuggin' and Buggin' Enterprises, a group to fight the oppression within WWE. Soon after, D-Lo and WWE went their separate ways.

For the next four years, D-Lo competed on the independent scene and toured Japan. In June 2008, he briefly returned to WWE and reminded those who crossed his path that, "Chumps better recognize and become down with the Brown!" before returning to the North American independent circuit.

DOINK

HT: 5'10"   WT: 243 lbs.   FROM: Parts Unknown
SIGNATURE MOVE: The Whoopie Cushion

In late 1992, this clown brought his circus act to WWE. His mean-spirited pranks both in and out of the ring made him a prime target of competitors and audiences alike. At *WrestleMania IX,* he attacked Crush with the aid of an imposter, adding confusion to his cruel antics. Doink could not contain the joy he received by making others miserable.

After an incident with Jerry "The King" Lawler, fans began to embrace Doink, who displayed a softer side. His pranks brought out laughter from audiences and he introduced a sidekick, named Dink. The two battled Bam Bam Bigelow & Luna Vachon at *WrestleMania X.* At that year's *Survivor Series,* he assembled a crew of Dink, Wink, and Pink to battle Lawler's team of Queazy, Cheesy, and Sleazy. Although his appearances became less frequent, he still makes unexpected apperances. Though fans and Superstars didn't always appreciate his brand of humor, he always kept his opponents in stitches.

DOK HENDRIX

Put a microphone in front of Dok Hendrix and he could talk for hours. Amazingly, the only thing that was louder than this boisterous WWE announcer was his neon-colored suits. The energetic Hendrix began his WWE announcing career in 1995. His high-octane style propelled him to become a regular on such weekly WWE shows as *Superstars* and *Action Zone.* Hendrix even assumed color commentator duties for several pay-per-view matches.

In addition to sitting at the announce table, Hendrix also served as WWE's main interviewer, a role made famous years earlier by WWE Hall of Famer "Mean" Gene Okerlund. Hendrix's most famous interview occurred at the 1996 King of the Ring when he held the microphone for Stone Cold Steve Austin's now famous "Austin 3:16" rant.

DOLPH ZIGGLER

HT: 6'0"   WT: 213 lbs.   FROM: Hollywood, Florida
SIGNATURE MOVE: Zig Zag

Dolph Ziggler might just be the perfect WWE Superstar, at least that's what he wants you to believe. Blessed with amazing athleticism and an unmatched arrogance, the Florida native isn't afraid to show off his superiority in and out of the ring.

TITLE HISTORY

INTERCONTINENTAL CHAMPION	*Defeated Kofi Kingston on August 6, 2010*
UNITED STATES CHAMPION	*Defeated Kofi Kingston on June 19, 2011*
WORLD HEAVYWEIGHT CHAMPION	*Awarded championship on February 18, 2011*

Ziggler took great steps toward solidifying his cocky claims when he defeated Kofi Kingston for the Intercontinental Championship in August 2010. Over the course of the next five months, he turned back all comers, including Jack Swagger, Kaval and MVP.

In February 2011, Ziggler used his relationship with then-Acting *SmackDown* General Manager Vickie Guerrero to underhandedly back into a World Heavyweight Championship reign. But just minutes after Guerrero stripped Edge of the gold and awarded it to Ziggler, Theodore Long returned to his post atop *SmackDown* and demanded the new champ defend against the "Rated-R Superstar." Edge speared his way to victory and Ziggler will forever have one of history's shortest title reigns on his résumé.

Following the loss, Ziggler moved to *Raw* where he almost immediately regained his championship form by capturing the United States Title in June 2011. Ironically, the victory came over Kingston, the same Superstar he defeated for the Intercontinental Championship one year prior.

Over the course of his WWE career, Ziggler has continually proven that perfection is not just a catchphrase on a T-shirt. It's a way of life for the cocky Superstar.

2010-
2000-09
1990-99
1980-89
1970-79
1960-69

DOMINIC DeNUCCI

HT: 6'3" **WT:** 245 lbs. **FROM:** Pittsburgh, Pennsylvania
SIGNATURE MOVE: Airplane Spin

Dominic DeNucci debuted in WWE in 1965. Fans cheered his mat skills and strength while he fought for all that was honorable. DeNucci won his first major title in 1971 when he teamed with Bruno Sammartino to defeat the Mongols to capture the International Tag Team Championship. In 1975, he teamed with Victor Rivera to win the World Tag Team Championship. DeNucci earned a third reign with the World Tag Team titles in 1978, partnering with Dino Bravo.

In the mid-1980s, DeNucci retired from the ring. He opened a wrestling school in Freedom, Pennsylvania and trained the likes of hardcore legend Mick Foley, former ECW Champion Shane Douglas, and former WCW referee Brian Hildebrand.

TITLE HISTORY

INTERNATIONAL TAG TEAM CHAMPION	Partnered with Bruno Sammartino to defeat The Mongols on June 18, 1971
WORLD TAG TEAM CHAMPION (2 TIMES)	Partnered with Victor Rivera to defeat Jimmy & Johnny Valiant on May 13, 1975 Partnered with Dino Bravo to defeat Prof. Toru Tanaka & Mr. Fuji on March 14, 1978

DON KERNODLE

HT: 6'1" **WT:** 290 lbs.
FROM: Burlington, North Carolina

As part of the legendary Sgt. Slaughter's Cobra Corps faction, Don Kernodle's early years were filled with a great education and many victories. Known then as Pvt. Don Kernodle, the North Carolinian used what he learned from Slaughter to rise to the top of the National Wrestling Alliance tag team ranks with partner Pvt. Jim Nelson.

In 1983, Kernodle began a successful union with "Cowboy" Bob Orton, before ultimately turning his back on the United States to align himself with hated Russian Ivan Koloff. In May 1984, Kernodle & Koloff captured the NWA Mid-Atlantic Tag Team Championship.

In addition to wrestling, Kernodle's resume features a role in the 1978 motion picture *Paradise Alley*. He appropriately played a wrestler, alongside other Superstars such as Dick Murdoch, Ted DiBiase and Ray Stevens.

DON LEO JONATHAN

HT: 6'6" **WT:** 300 lbs.
FROM: Salt Lake City, Utah

Decades before high-flying action became the rage in sports-entertainment, Don Leo Jonathan was mesmerizing opponents with standing dropkicks, backflips, and even lofty leaps over the top rope. What made Jonathan's cat-like agility even more jaw-dropping was the fact that he was the size of a small tree at 6'6" and 300 pounds.

Over the course of his 30-year career, Jonathan competed all over the globe, including Europe, Canada, South Africa, Australia and Japan. Known as "The Mormon Giant," Jonathan enjoyed his greatest notoriety in the early 1970s while battling another colossal figure, Andre the Giant. In addition, Jonathan found great success competing in the tag team division with such partners as Jimmy Snuka, Haystacks Calhoun and Rocky Johnson.

DON MURACO

HT: 6'3" **WT:** 275 lbs. **FROM:** Sunset Beach, Hawaii

TITLE HISTORY

INTERCONTINENTAL CHAMPION	Defeated Pedro Morales on June 20, 1981 Defeated Pedro Morales on January 22, 1983

One of the most hated Superstars of the 1980s, Don Muraco was often showered with chants of "beach bum" while on his way to the ring. Once the bell rang, however, he proved to be anything but a bum. His technical mastery carried him to a Hall of Fame career, which was highlighted by two lengthy reigns as Intercontinental Champion.

Managed by The Grand Wizard, Muraco entered WWE in 1980. Dubbed "The Magnificent One," the cocky Superstar drew the fans' rage when he defeated the immensely popular Pedro Morales for the Intercontinental Championship in June 1981. Coincidentally, Morales was also the victim of Muraco's second Intercontinental Championship win in January 1983.

Muraco's second reign, which lasted a little more than one year, will forever be remembered by a title defense that many consider the greatest in Intercontinental Championship history. In October 1983, Muraco turned back challenger Jimmy "Superfly" Snuka in a grueling Madison Square Garden Steel Cage encounter. The result of the match, however, remains an afterthought. Instead, fans fondly recall Snuka executing his death-defying Superfly Splash from the top of the towering cage onto Muraco. Many Superstars credit the sight of Snuka flying through the air as their inspiration to enter sports-entertainment.

Muraco finally lost his title to Tito Santana in February 1984. Following the loss, "The Magnificent One" ascended to the top of the card, unsuccessfully challenging Hulk Hogan for the WWE Championship on several occasions.

In 1987, Muraco took on the managerial services of fellow Hall of Famer "Superstar" Billy Graham. With a newly chiseled physique, Muraco worked his way into the good graces of the fans.

The new-look Muraco competed in the main event of the first-ever *Survivor Series* before disappearing from WWE in 1988. Eight years later, he returned to the WWE scene to induct longtime rival Jimmy Snuka in the WWE Hall of Fame. Muraco's successes were later recognized with his own induction in 2004.

DON MURACO & "COWBOY" BOB ORTON
COMBINED WT: 512 lbs.

The devious Mr. Fuji used his resources to bring together the Magnificent Muraco and "Cowboy" Bob Orton in 1987. A tag team expert in his own right, Mr. Fuji taught both men the finer arts to tag team competition and how to sink to new lows to achieve victory.

Muraco & Orton were more than eager to display their new techniques, and along with Fuji, all three became quite efficient in brandishing a cane. Their rivalry with the Can-Am Connection culminated at the historic *WrestleMania III*. Though the rule-breakers didn't win, the largest live indoor audience in history watched them proudly show why they became one of the most abhorred tandems in WWE. The team continued to torment opponents and break the rules until the duo turned on each other in August.

DONNYBROOK THEATER

If you don't know what *Donnybrook Theatre* is, don't worry; you're not alone.

Created in 1995, *Donnybrook Theatre* was designed to feature WWE Superstars in comedic sketches, similar to how the 1985 cult favorite *Fuji Vice* was delivered.

The pilot episode of *Donnybrook Theatre* featured Yokozuna and his manager, WWE Hall of Famer Mr. Fuji, in a Wild West setting. Unfortunately for fans who like a good laugh, the sight of Yokozuna and Mr. Fuji in 10-gallon hats and cowboy boots never aired as planned, and production on *Donnybrook Theatre* was ceased followed the completion of the pilot.

More than ten years after the Wild West episode of *Donnybrook Theatre* was shot, WWE dusted off the old tapes and briefly placed it on their on-demand cable service. Those who were lucky enough to catch the quick airing now carry with them an unbelievable memory that will last a life time. Others are still searching for ways to somehow catch the elusive legend of *Donnybrook Theatre*.

DORY DIXON
HT: 5'9"   WT: 209 lbs.   FROM: Jamaica
SIGNATURE MOVE: Flying Bodyblock

Dory Dixon spent the early 1950s working as a physical education teacher. He never planned to become a professional wrestler, but a chance meeting with Mexican wrestling promoter Salvador Lutteroth changed everything.

Lutteroth persuaded Dixon to pursue a career in the ring, and in 1955, the former schoolteacher made his debut for Mexico's Empressa Mexicana de Lucha Libre. Dixon spent the majority of his career in Mexico, where he captured the NWA World Light Heavyweight Championship in February 1958. He held the title for nearly two years before losing to Ray Mendoza.

In the early 1960s, Dixon travelled to the United States, where he competed in the Texas and Los Angeles territories. He formed several successful tag teams with such partners as Pepper Gomez and Rito Romero. It was his union with Bobo Brazil, however, that is remembered most.

During his brief Northeast tenure, Dixon battled "Nature Boy" Buddy Rogers to draws on two separate occasions. He also competed on the same historic Madison Square Garden card that saw Bruno Sammartino defeat Rogers for the WWE Championship in 1963.

DORY FUNK, JR.

HT: 6'2"   WT: 240 lbs.   FROM: The Double Cross Ranch
SIGNATURE MOVE: Spinning Toe Hold

This second-generation competitor made his debut in 1963 after training from his famous father. In 1968, Dory, Jr. plied his trade in the NWA, where he enjoyed the second-longest reign as NWA Champion in history. During his travels, he invented the Texas Clover Leaf submission hold and Funk Forearm Uppercut.

In 1986, Dory ventured to WWE under his nickname, Hoss. He and brother Terry branded the logo of the Double Cross Ranch into the flesh of their beaten opponents. They engaged in a memorable rivalry with the Junkyard Dog that culminated in a Funk victory at *WrestleMania 2*. In 1994, the brothers moved to ECW. In 1996, Dory returned to WWE at the *Royal Rumble* and proved he could still put up a fierce fight.

In 1997, Dory opened the the Funkin' Conservatory to train future stars. Graduates of the school include the Hardy Boys, Edge and Mickie James. Dory's legacy was honored the night before *WrestleMania XXV*, when he took his rightful place in the WWE Hall of Fame.

D

1960-69 ▼
1970-79 ▼
1980-89 ▼
1990-99 ▼
2000-09 ▼
2010- ▼

2010-

2000-09

1990-99

1980-89

1970-79

1960-69

DOUG FURNAS & PHIL LAFON COMBINED WT: 484 lbs.

Years before making their WWE debut in 1996, Doug Furnas & Phil Lafon made a name for themselves in Japan and Mexico. While in Japan, the duo captured the AJPW All Asia Tag Team Championship five times. Over the course of their battles, they crossed paths with many names familiar to the WWE Universe, including Dynamite Kid and Johnny Ace (John Laurinaitis). Following Japan, Furnas and Lafon made a brief stop in Mexico, where they captured the UWA World Tag Team Championship twice.

In 1996, the highly decorated tag team traveled to the United States. They made a quick stop in ECW before debuting in WWE later in the year. At *Survivor Series 1996*, Furnas and Lafon outlasted British Bulldog, Owen Hart and the New Rockers to be their team's sole survivors.

Furnas & Lafon spent the early part of 1997 chasing the World Tag Team Championship. When they were unsuccessful in claiming the gold, they moved on to a brief rivalry with the Legion of Doom before leaving WWE in the summer of 1997.

"DR. D" DAVID SCHULTZ

HT: 6'6"   WT: 267 lbs.
FROM: Nashville, Tennessee
SIGNATURE MOVE:
Flying Corkscrew Elbow

Before his assault on the ranks of World Wrestling Entertainment, David Schultz was one of the most feared men in wrestling territories across North America. To Dr. D, matches were not contests to determine which opponent was the better man, they were personal wars where everything was on the line and no tactic was off-limits.

In 1984, Dr. D prescribed his form of pain on WWE Superstars and aligned himself with "Rowdy" Roddy Piper, "Mr. Wonderful" Paul Orndorff and "Cowboy" Bob Orton. As his reputation as one of the most dangerous men in WWE grew, his tenure with the company ended abruptly after a celebrated run-in with a news journalist while conducting a feature story on professional wrestling turned physical. "Dr. D" David Schultz will always be considered one of the ring's most dangerous figures who was always ready for a fight.

DOUG "GASHOUSE" GILBERT

FROM: Omaha, Nebraska   SIGNATURE MOVE: Top-Rope Backflip

Doug Gilbert was a barrel-chested brute of a man who first made a name for himself in the AWA during the early 1960s. Nicknamed "Gashouse," Gilbert's early AWA days were highlighted by three Midwest Tag Team Championship reigns with partner Reggie Parks. Over the course of their stints with the gold, Gilbert & Parks mainly clashed with future WWE Hall of Famers Bob Orton Sr. and Mad Dog Vachon.

Gilbert jumped to the NWA in the late 1960s. During this period, it wasn't uncommon to see the cocky competitor sit on his fallen opponent's chest, stroking his mustache while the referee counted to three. Overall, Gilbert staked claim to fourteen regional NWA championships, including three Georgia Heavyweight title victories (competing as The Professional).

When Gilbert made his way to WWE in the mid-1970s, his best years were already behind him. But that didn't stop him from competing in some thrilling matches against such luminaries as Bobo Brazil and Tony Garea.

DOUG GILBERT

HT: 6'0"   WT: 240 lbs.   FROM: Lexington, Tennessee
SIGNATURE MOVE: Piledriver

Following in the footsteps of his father, Tommy, and brother, "Hot Stuff" Eddie Gilbert, "Dangerous" Doug Gilbert debuted in 1986. Throughout the late 1980s and early 1990s, Doug competed in the United States, Puerto Rico and the NWA. As Doug's travels continued, he became well-versed in the hardcore style. In 1993, Doug was a member of the USWA and appeared on cards with several WWE Superstars. In 1996, Doug won a Royal Rumble-style match in Memphis. The winner of the match earned a spot in the WWE *Royal Rumble* weeks later in Fresno, CA.

Today, Doug still competes in the U.S., Puerto Rico and Japan. He has kept the Gilbert family name alive inside the ring and has added to its legacy.

THE DREAM TEAM

MEMBERS: Greg Valentine, Brutus Beefcake
COMBINED WT: 520 lbs.

TITLE HISTORY

WORLD TAG TEAM CHAMPIONS	Defeated Mike Rotundo & Barry Windham on August 24, 1985

The Dream Team consisted of an established, rugged second-generation Superstar and two-time Intercontinental Champion in Greg "The Hammer" Valentine, and a brash, powerful athlete in Brutus Beefcake whose strength was only second to his vanity. Managed by "Luscious" Johnny Valiant, this pair was considered championship contenders almost instantly as they squared off against the likes of The Killer Bees, Junkyard Dog & Jimmy "Superfly" Snuka, and Tito Santana & Pedro Morales. Valiant did an amazing job of bringing the two Superstars together and meshing their unique styles to translate into success. The despised Beefcake and Valentine reached the top when they defeated the U.S. Express for the World Tag Team Championship on August 24, 1985 at the Philadelphia Spectrum.

The Dream Team broke every rule in the book to maintain a stranglehold on the titles. The duo enjoyed an almost seven-month reign as World Tag Team Champions until they faced The British Bulldogs at *WrestleMania 2*. While they

continued to be threats within the tag team division, an associate was soon added in Canadian strongman Dino Bravo. Despite a win at *WrestleMania III* against the Rougeau Brothers, dissention within their ranks overflowed and Beefcake was left by himself in the ring. As Bravo became the new member of group, they were appropriately named the New Dream Team. Later that night Beefcake officially became a fan favorite as the "Barber" in him came out.

DREW MCINTYRE ✕

HT: 6'5"   **WT:** 254 lbs.   **FROM:** Ayre, Scotland
SIGNATURE MOVE: Future Shock DDT

TITLE HISTORY

INTERCONTINENTAL CHAMPION	Defeated John Morrison on December 13, 2009
WWE TAG TEAM CHAMPION	Partnered with Cody Rhodes to defeat The Hart Dynasty on September 19, 2010

Drew McIntyre has a bright future, partly because he is a skilled competitor, but mainly because WWE Chairman Mr. McMahon personally signed the Scottish Superstar in September 2009.

With the invaluable backing of Mr. McMahon, McIntyre earned the nickname "The Chosen One" and quickly set out to gain some gold. By the end of the year, the new Superstar had defeated John Morrison for the Intercontinental Championship at *WWE TLC 2009*. As champion, McIntyre acted as if he ran *SmackDown*. And in a way, with Mr. McMahon in his corner, he indirectly did. It wasn't uncommon to see decisions that didn't go in McIntyre's favor later reversed by the Chairman.

Not even Mr. McMahon could save "The Chosen One" from Kofi Kingston, who defeated McIntyre for the Intercontinental Championship in May 2010. The loss marked the end of his more than five-month reign, but more gold was right around the corner.

At *Night of Champions 2010*, McIntyre teamed with Cody Rhodes to capture the WWE Tag Team Championship in a thrilling Tag Team Turmoil Match.

DROZ 🇺🇸

HT: 6'4"   **WT:** 270 lbs.   **FROM:** Mays Landing, New Jersey
SIGNATURE MOVE: New Jersey Naptime

In the early 1990s, Darren Drozdov was one of the top NCAA football players in the United States. After a stint in the NFL, he trained for a life in the ring. After a short stay in ECW, Droz entered WWE in 1998 and caught the attention of Vince McMahon when he learned Droz could vomit on command. Droz's in-ring abilities caught the eye of the the Legion of Doom. When Droz donned spiked shoulder pads for the first time, a childhood dream was fulfilled. When the LOD went their separate ways, Droz formed an alliance with fellow pierced Superstar Albert.

Tragically on October 5, 1999, Droz suffered a career-ending injury in a match that has confined him to a wheelchair. Droz continues to contribute to WWE through his commentaries on WWE.com and in print. Droz remains the fun-loving individual who is loved by all who know him and he is determined to one day walk again.

2010-
▲
2000-09
▲
1990-99
▲
1980-89
1970-79
▲
▲
1960-69

THE DUDLEY BOYS

MEMBERS: D-Von, Bubba Ray   **COMBINED WT:** 565 lbs.

TITLE HISTORY

WORLD TAG TEAM CHAMPIONS (8 TIMES)	*Defeated the New Age Outlaws on February 27, 2000* *Defeated Edge & Christian on January 21, 2001* *Defeated Edge & Christian on March 19, 2001* *Defeated Chris Benoit & Chris Jericho on June 21, 2001* *Defeated Kane & Undertaker on September 17, 2001* *Defeated The Hardy Boys on November 18, 2001* *Defeated Lance Storm & William Regal on January 19, 2003* *Defeated Rene Dupree & Sylvain Grenier on September 21, 2003*
WWE TAG TEAM CHAMPIONS	*Defeated Charlie Haas & Rico on June 17, 2004*

Few teams revolutionized tag team wrestling more than The Dudleys, and none have achieved more success. In fact, they are the only tandem in sports-entertainment history to capture the ECW, WCW, and World tag titles.

Half-brothers D-Von & Bubba Ray Dudley first made a name for themselves competing in ECW during the late 1990s. While there, they earned a reputation as a hardcore powerhouse, as well as a record eight reigns with the promotion's tag titles.

In 1999, The Dudleys took their success to WWE where they gained instant national recognition. Within months, they were World Tag Team Champions. Furthermore, D-Von & Bubba Ray were painfully introducing a new brand of hardcore competition to WWE.

The Dudleys' penchant for driving opponents through wooden tables via the Dudley Death Drop paved the way for several groundbreaking matches. At the 2000 *Royal Rumble*, D-Von & Bubba Ray battled the Hardy Boys in the first-ever Tag Team Tables Match. The popularity of the carnage eventually raised the stakes to even more dangerous encounters. Later that year, they took part in the first-ever Tables, Ladders & Chairs Match against Edge & Christian and the Hardy Boys at *SummerSlam*. The same three teams battled in an epic TLC encore at *WrestleMania X-Seven*. Both matches were won by Edge & Christian.

D-Von & Bubba Ray added to their already-historic resume when they defeated Matt & Jeff Hardy for the WCW Tag Team Championship in October 2001. They would later unify the WCW and WWE World Tag Team Championships when they defeated the Hardy Boyz again at *Survivor Series*.

The unthinkable occurred in 2002 when the WWE Draft separated D-Von & Bubba Ray. On their own, the half-brothers failed to replicate the success they gained as a team. Luckily, their solo efforts only lasted eight months before they shockingly reunited at *Survivor Series*.

Together again, The Dudleys picked up right where they left off. By the time their WWE careers had ended, D-Von & Bubba Ray collected nine tag team championship reigns, as well as a legacy second to none.

DUKE "THE DUMPSTER" DROESE

HT: 6'6"   **WT:** 305 lbs.
FROM: Mount Trashmore, Florida

When it comes to taking out the trash, few Superstars did it with as much enthusiasm as Duke "The Dumpster" Droese. Originally a sanitation engineer by trade, Droese made the transition from his garbage route to the ring with one goal in mind: ridding WWE of its trash.

According to Droese, the Superstar with the most stink on him was Hunter Hearst-Helmsley, and it was against Helmsley that Droese picked up the biggest victory of his career. With the coveted No. 30 spot in the 1996 *Royal Rumble* on the line, Droese defeated the Greenwich blue blood via reverse decision.

Unfortunately for Droese, Helmsley went on to have one of the greatest careers of all time, while the sanitation engineer soon found himself back on his garbage route. Droese did, however, manage to make a brief but memorable return to the ring in 2001 when he competed in *WrestleMania X-Seven*'s Gimmick Battle Royal, which was ultimately won by former WWE Champion the Iron Sheik.

"THE AMERICAN DREAM" DUSTY RHODES

HT: 6'2"   WT: 275 lbs.   FROM: Austin, Texas   SIGNATURE MOVE: Bionic Elbow

The son of a plumber, Dusty Rhodes suffered from the crippling disease osteomyelitis, a bone affliction that prevented him from walking as a boy. As a man of the people, he possessed tremendous drive, courage and charisma that made him 275 pounds of blue-eyed soul who captivated an entire nation.

In September 1977, "The American Dream" came to WWE and waged war against then-WWE Champion "Superstar" Billy Graham. Their matches sold out Madison Square Garden and culminated in a Texas Bullrope Match. Dusty left and went on to great success in Florida and the Carolinas region, enjoying three reigns as NWA Champion. His epic struggle against the Four Horsemen in the mid-1980s is widely considered one of the greatest rivalries of all time.

In 1990, Rhodes returned to WWE as the blue-collar worker for the common man. In polka-dotted ring trunks with his valet Sapphire, his popularity reached its greatest heights as he engaged in bitter rivalries with the Big Boss Man, "Macho King" Randy Savage and "Million Dollar Man" Ted DiBiase. In the early 1990s, Dusty returned to WCW as a broadcaster. In 2000, he made a brief stop in ECW.

In 2005, he returned to WWE working behind the scenes. Even after five decades, he isn't afraid to step in the ring and show today's competitors how to mix it up, as witnessed at *WWE Homecoming*, *Survivor Series* in 2006 when he teamed with Ric Flair, Sgt. Slaughter & Ron Simmons, and his match with Randy Orton at 2007's *Great American Bash*. Rhodes continues to appear on WWE programming and even guest hosted *Raw* in 2009, despite at times breaking rules to help his son Cody. Today, "The Dream" works behind the scenes at WWE's developmental territory, FCW. Dusty Rhodes was the true working man's champion. As Cody said as he inducted Dusty into the WWE Hall of Fame in 2007, "He didn't need a 'Pit' or a 'Parlor,' all he needed was a mic." Dusty Rhodes has truly lived life at the end of a lightning bolt.

DUSTY WOLFE

HT: 5'11"   WT: 215 lbs.
FROM: San Antonio, Texas
SIGNATURE MOVE: Spinning Toe Hold

Wolfe started his career in his hometown of San Antonio. In 1984, he decided it was time to travel to territories in Kansas City, Memphis, Florida, and the Von Erich's World Class region. From there, Wolfe went to Puerto Rico and Hawaii, becoming skilled in various ring styles.

Dusty Wolfe debuted in WWE in 1987 and quickly became a staple on its televised programs. He traded blows with the likes of Jake "The Snake" Roberts, "Ravishing" Rick Rude, "Hacksaw" Jim Duggan, the Blue Blazer and the Junkyard Dog. In 1993, Wolfe left WWE and resumed his independent promotion travels in Puerto Rico, South Africa and Japan until 1996. For the next two years, he appeared in WCW before he resumed his mat career on the independent circuit.

A dream that began at 18 years of age turned into a 20-plus year career. When asked to summarize his career, Wolfe was once quoted as saying, "Getting in the ring was a privilege."

DYNAMITE KID

HT: 5'9"   WT: 225 lbs.   FROM: Manchester, England   SIGNATURE MOVE: Flying Headbutt

TITLE HISTORY	
JUNIOR HEAVYWEIGHT CHAMPION	*Defeated The Cobra on February 7, 1984*
WORLD TAG TEAM CHAMPION	*Partnered with Davey Boy Smith to defeat Brutus Beefcake & Greg Valentine on April 7, 1986*

Faster than greased lighting, as tough and technically sound as anyone to lace up a pair of boots, Dynamite Kid did it all in the ring. Dynamite Kid's innovative offensive moves influenced everyone who saw him in action.

Bruce Hart brought the Dynamite Kid to Stampede Wrestling after watching him in action in the late 1970s. In the early 1980s, Dynamite Kid was a top contender for the WWE Junior Heavyweight Championship. In his Madison Square Garden debut in 1982, he faced then-champion Tiger Mask. The bouts between the pair made headlines all over the world. Dynamite Kid eventually captured the Junior Heavyweight crown in February, 1984 when he defeated the Cobra.

Later that year, Dynamite Kid joined with Davey Boy Smith to form the British Bulldogs. With Lou Albano in their corner, they claimed the World Tag Team Championship at *WrestleMania 2*. After losing the titles to the Hart Foundation, the Bulldogs left WWE in November 1988.

Dynamite Kid retired from active competition in 1991, and released his autobiography titled *Pure Dynamite* in 1999. Dynamite Kid will be remembered as one of the most innovative, and possibly the greatest pound-for-pound, Superstars of all-time.

EARL MAYNARD

HT: 5'11" **WT:** 240 lbs. **FROM:** Barbados
SIGNATURE MOVE: Headbutt

As a boy growing up in Barbados, Earl Maynard had visions of greatness. Already a top bodybuilder, and member of the British Air Force, he wrestled as a means of staying in peak physical condition.

For two decades he pulled double-duty as a Superstar in both professional wrestling and body building. While in the World Wide Wrestling Federation, Maynard collided with the likes of future WWE Hall of Famers Baron Mikel Scicluna, Johnny Rodz, and Gorilla Monsoon.

In 1968, Earl added another element to his already versatile persona and made his silver screen debut in the feature film *Melinda*. He continued to appear in films for many years, and today he is a film producer/director. He's viewed as a legend in both the ring and bodybuilding circles.

EARTHQUAKE

HT: 6'7" **WT:** 468 lbs.
FROM: Vancouver, British Columbia, Canada
SIGNATURE MOVE: Earthquake Splash

TITLE HISTORY

WORLD TAG TEAM CHAMPION	*Partnered with Typhoon to defeat Money, Inc. on July 20, 1992*

With more than 450 pounds tacked to his enormous frame, Earthquake made arenas shake and Superstars tremble every time he walked the aisle. Behind the threat of his ring-rattling Earthquake Splash finisher, the massive Superstar was a perennial contender for every WWE title.

Disguised as a fan, Earthquake made his WWE debut in November 1989 when Jimmy Hart pulled him out of the audience to sit on Ultimate Warrior's back as the Superstar attempted pushups. Once in the ring, Earthquake revealed his allegiance to Hart by squashing the unexpected Warrior like a grape. From that point on, the

oversized Superstar proved himself as one of WWE's most dangerous competitors. His assaults were so severe, in fact, that many of his opponents were forced to leave the ring on a stretcher.

Earthquake quickly reached main event status after attacking Hulk Hogan on an edition of *The Brother Love Show*. The assault left the Hulkster's ribs severely injured and made Earthquake the target of the fans' hatred worldwide. Their rivalry culminated at *SummerSlam 1990* where Hogan earned a countout victory over the big man.

The following year, Earthquake teamed with Typhoon to form the colossal tag team known as the Natural Disasters. Together, they defeated Money Inc. to capture the World Tag Team Championship in July 1992.

THE EAST-WEST CONNECTION

MEMBERS: Adrian Adonis, Jesse "The Body" Ventura **COMBINED WT:** 580 lbs.

This team first formed in the late 1970s in Verne Gagne's AWA. Noticed by "Classy" Freddie Blassie, Adonis & Ventura were brought to WWE in 1981. With Blassie in their corner, they became prime-time players in WWE. Whether contending for the World Tag Team titles, or as individuals for the WWE Championship, the East-West Connection could beat you from any direction.

A combination of injuries and different goals led to their separation, though they remained close allies. Ventura went on to become one of the greatest color commentators ever and a 2004 WWE Hall of Fame inductee. Adonis transformed into one of WWE's most versatile and gifted performers. The legendary East-West Connection should always be included in a discussion of influential tag teams. Whether you approved of their practices or not, you can't deny their success.

The original ECW, a grassroots independent promotion that became a phenomenon in the Eastern United States, helped redefine sports-entertainment into what we see today. Housed in Philadelphia's ECW Arena, which was actually a bingo hall, Paul Heyman and Tod Gordon created a fertile breeding ground for many of the Superstars who are household names today. Caught in the crossfire between WWE and WCW during the infamous Monday Night Wars, ECW lost key talent to the larger promotions and struggled financially, eventually going out of business in 2001.

WWE acquired the assets to ECW in 2003. In 2005 under the WWE banner, the brand was gloriously resurrected at *ECW One Night Stand*, which was a tremendous success. One year later, ECW returned and became WWE's third active brand, and the brand flourished, once again serving as a proving ground of many of today's Superstars.

While the soldiers and battlegrounds may have changed, the revolutionary spirit behind ECW remained. Superstars like ECW Original Tommy Dreamer, Kane, Matt Hardy, Mark Henry, and Chavo Guerrero were established veterans that raised the level of competition in the new Land of Extreme. Young Superstars including CM Punk, The Miz, and John Morrison found their inner extreme and competed in some of the hardest fought bouts anywhere on the planet. The final episode of the WWE's incarnation of *ECW on Syfy* aired on February 16, 2010. At the conclusion of the show, the members of the ECW roster became free agents and were signed to *Raw* or *SmackDown*.

ECW CHAMPIONSHIP

When the ECW brand was relaunched in June, 2006, Paul Heyman awarded the championship to Rob Van Dam, who was also the reigning WWE Champion. During its four year run the ECW Championship was held by established Superstars and also served as a launching point for many WWE careers.

2006

June 13
Trenton, NJ

Rob Van Dam was named ECW Champion

July 4
Philadelphia, PA

Big Show defeated Rob Van Dam

December 3
Lowell, MA

Bobby Lashley pinned Big Show in an Extreme Elimination Chamber Match that also included Rob Van Dam, CM Punk, Test, and Hardcore Holly

2007

April 29
Atlanta, GA

Mr. McMahon defeated Bobby Lashley

June 3
Jacksonville, FL

Bobby Lashley defeated Mr. McMahon

On June 11, Bobby Lashley was stripped of the title when he was drafted to *Raw*.

June 25
Houston, TX

John Morrison defeated CM Punk

September 1
Cincinnati, OH

CM Punk defeated John Morrison

2008

January 22
Charlottesville, VA

Chavo Guerrero defeated CM Punk

March 30
Orlando, FL

Kane defeated Chavo Guerrero

June 29
Dallas, TX

Mark Henry defeated Kane

September 7
Cleveland, OH

Matt Hardy pinned the Miz in a Championship Scramble Match that also included Mark Henry, Finlay, and Chavo Guerrero.

2009

January 13
Sioux City, IA

Jack Swagger defeated Matt Hardy

April 26
Providence, RI

Christian defeated Jack Swagger

June 7
New Orleans, LA

Tommy Dreamer defeated Christian and Jack Swagger in a Triple Threat Match

July 26
Philadelphia, PA

Christian defeated Tommy Dreamer

2010

February 16
Kansas City, MO

Ezekiel Jackson defeated Christian

EDDIE GILBERT
HT: 5'10"   **WT:** 222 lbs.   **FROM:** Lexington, Kentucky   **SIGNATURE MOVE:** Hot Shot

Proudly nicknamed "Hot Stuff," Eddie Gilbert certainly had a high opinion of his in-ring abilities. Coming from the popular Gilbert wrestling family, he had every right to be a little cocky. Growing up, Eddie and brother Doug learned the business firsthand from their father, Tennessee wrestling great Tommy Gilbert.

Despite being remembered as one the South's greatest competitors, Gilbert's brief WWE career never really took off. He gained some notoriety as a protégé to WWE Champion Bob Backlund. The relationship, however, was short-lived and Gilbert soon returned to the South.

Gilbert owns the distinction of being involved in the first-ever NWA pay-per-view match. Teaming with Larry Zbyzsko & Rick Steiner, he battled Sting, Michael Hayes & Jimmy Garvin at *Starrcade 1987*. Over the next several years, Gilbert gained the reputation of coming up big when it counted, including several times against Jerry "The King" Lawler when the United States Wrestling Association Unified World Heavyweight Championship was on the line.

EDDIE GRAHAM
HT: 5'11"   **WT:** 215 lbs.   **FROM:** Tampa, Florida

WWE's national spotlight never really shined on Eddie Graham. But that doesn't mean he wasn't one of the most influential personalities of his time. Over the course of his 30-year career, Graham became known as a skilled competitor and brilliant promoter.

Early in his career, Graham teamed with his brother, Jerry, to capture the United States Tag Team Championship four times while competing in Vincent J. McMahon's Capitol Wrestling. The success led to great notoriety in the Northeast, but it wasn't until he moved to Florida in 1960 that Graham really began to come into his own.

By 1968, Graham had become a legend in Florida, but when a locker room window fell on his head, he was forced to sit on the sidelines for 15 months. Unable to compete, Graham still managed to make waves when he took over responsibilities of Championship Wrestling from Florida. As promoter of the popular territory, Graham built an impressive roster, which included such legends as Dusty Rhodes, Dory Funk, Jr. and Bruiser Brody.

Graham's power continued to grow in 1976 when he was elected president of the National Wrestling Alliance. While in office, he helped create the first-ever World title unification match, which pit NWA Champion Harley Race against WWE Champion "Superstar" Billy Graham. Health reasons forced Graham to step down from his post in 1978, officially marking the end of one of the most influential careers of his time.

E

1960-69
1970-79
1980-89
1990-99
2000-09
2010-

EDDIE GUERRERO

HALL OF FAME 2006

TITLE HISTORY

EUROPEAN CHAMPION (2 TIMES)	Defeated Chris Jericho on April 3, 2000 Defeated Test on April 1, 2001
INTERCONTINENTAL CHAMPION (2 TIMES)	Defeated Chyna on September 3, 2000 Defeated Rob Van Dam on April 21, 2002
UNITED STATES CHAMPION	Defeated Chris Benoit on July 27, 2003
WWE CHAMPION	Defeated Brock Lesnar on February 15, 2004
WWE TAG TEAM CHAMPION (4 TIMES)	Partnered with Chavo Guerrero to defeat Edge & Rey Mysterio on November 17, 2002 Partnered with Tajiri to defeat the World's Greatest Tag Team on May 18, 2003 Partnered with Chavo Guerrero to defeat the World's Greatest Tag Team on September 18, 2003 Partnered with Rey Mysterio to defeat the Basham Brothers on February 20, 2005

" LATINO HEAT "

The story of Eddie Guerrero is one of inspiration and heartbreak. After personal demons cost the second-generation Superstar his career and family, he dedicated himself to becoming clean and returning to society. The inspirational Guerrero eventually defeated his demons and returned to greatness. Tragically, however, Eddie Guerrero was taken from this world shortly after clawing his way back to the top of sports-entertainment.

Second Generation Superstar

As the son of influential Mexican wrestler Gory Guerrero, Eddie grew up in and around the business. From an early age, it was clear his passion was sports-entertainment. He spent most of his time in the family's wrestling ring, which was situated in the backyard. Before his fifth birthday, he was already delivering dropkicks to his older brothers.

Once he became old enough, Guerrero started competing professionally in Mexico and Japan. It wasn't until he began working for Extreme Championship Wrestling in 1995 that he gained any true exposure in the United States. While in ECW, Guerrero captured the Television Championship on two occasions, but it was classic matches against Dean Malenko that caught the eye of World Championship Wrestling (WCW) officials.

While things were going great for Guerrero inside the ring, his personal life was in severe jeopardy. In 1999, an impaired Guerrero nearly killed himself in a violent car wreck. Fortunately, Guerrero lived, but he failed to address the demons that were invading his life. In 2000, Guerrero moved to WWE where he gained instant notoriety as Chyna's fun-loving boyfriend. Affectionately referred to as "Latino Heat," Guerrero won the European and Intercontinental Championships within his first year with the company. Guerrero's in-ring success couldn't help fend off his personal demons. Addiction again caught up with him. This time, it cost him his wife and his job. He had hit rock bottom.

Turning Around His Life

Rather than slipping further into addiction, Guerrero used his recent woes to help drive him. He eventually crushed his demons, won back his wife and was given a second chance with WWE. The WWE Universe welcomed back the new Eddie Guerrero with open arms. Much like his first stint with the company, he compiled an impressive list of championships. In addition to becoming a four-time WWE Tag Team Champion, Guerrero had the honor of bringing the United States Championship back to prominence in 2003.

Guerrero's greatest in-ring conquest came in February 2004 when he defeated Brock Lesnar for the WWE Championship at *No Way Out*. The victory brought Guerrero full circle and completed his quest for redemption. As WWE Champion, Guerrero earned the ultimate opportunity of defending his title at *WrestleMania XX* at the famed Madison Square Garden. In the world of sports-entertainment, there is no greater honor. Guerrero seized the opportunity, defeating Kurt Angle to retain the title.

Guerrero's inspirational WWE Championship reign came to an end when John "Bradshaw" Layfield defeated him in a Texas Bull Rope Match at *The Great American Bash* in June 2004. Undeterred by the loss, Guerrero, as he had done so many times before, fought to regain his lofty status. By late 2005, he had solidified himself as a legitimate threat for the World Heavyweight Championship.

Eddie Guerrero celebrating his victory over Brock Lesnar.

A Tragic End

On November 13, 2005, Eddie Guerrero was found dead in his hotel room in Minneapolis. He was thirty-eight. In the days that followed, the entire wrestling world publicly mourned the tragic loss of an inspirational human being. In 2006, Guerrero took his rightful place in wrestling history when he was posthumously inducted into the WWE Hall of Fame. The night's celebration was proof that the great memories of Eddie Guerrero will live on forever.

Superstars gather in tribute to Eddie Guerrero.

Edge (see page 110)

EDGE & CHRISTIAN

COMBINED WT: 470 lbs.

TITLE HISTORY	
WORLD TAG TEAM CHAMPIONS (7 TIMES)	*Defeated The Dudley Boys on April 2, 2000* *Defeated Too Cool on June 25, 2000* *Defeated The Hardy Boys on October 22, 2000* *Defeated Bull Buchanan & Goodfather on December 10, 2000* *Defeated The Rock & Undertaker on December 21, 2000* *Defeated The Hardy Boys on March 19, 2001* *Defeated The Dudley Boys on April 1, 2001*

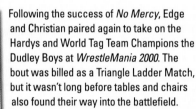

"For the benefit of those with flash photography," Edge and Christian would oftentimes strike a pre-match pose, allowing fans to snap a photograph of the seven-time World Tag Team Champions. With their oversized sunglasses and corny catchphrases, the charismatic combination always managed to get a reluctant laugh out of the fans who loved to hate them. In the ring, however, their offensive onslaught was no joke.

Edge and Christian first began to open eyes as a unit when they competed against Matt and Jeff Hardy in the Terri Invitational Tournament in 1999. The best-of-five series culminated in a *No Mercy* Ladder Match, which proved to be a precursor for the innovative action the proud Canadians would display in the years that followed.

Following the success of *No Mercy*, Edge and Christian paired again to take on the Hardys and World Tag Team Champions the Dudley Boys at *WrestleMania 2000*. The bout was billed as a Triangle Ladder Match, but it wasn't long before tables and chairs also found their way into the battlefield. Looking back, the historic *WrestleMania 2000* contest can be credited for the creation of the wildly popular Tables, Ladders and Chairs (TLC) Match. And more importantly for Edge and Christian, it also marked their first World Tag Team Championship victory.

Thanks in large part to two successful TLC Matches against the Dudleys and Hardys at *SummerSlam* and *WrestleMania X-Seven*, Edge and Christian cemented themselves as one of the greatest tag teams of all time. But as Edge began to breakout as a singles star, animosity found its way into the team. Jealousy eventually overtook Christian, who turned on his longtime partner in September 2001.

It took 10 long years, but in March 2011, Edge and Christian finally repaired their severed relationship when they teamed to defeat Alberto Del Rio & Brodus Clay. The two Superstars were inseparable over the next few weeks, but when injury pushed the Rated-R Superstar into early retirement, the team that totally reeked of awesomeness was forced to close the book on their historic pairing.

EDEN STILES

HT: 5'5"
FROM: Canton, Michigan

Eden Stiles' beauty is undeniable. With her seductive eyes, gorgeous smile and curvaceous frame, the former WWE announcer turns heads everywhere she goes. Naturally, Eden's pre-WWE days were spent modeling, where she became the focus of countless cameras, including those of Maxim Magazine. She also competed in many pageants, such as the popular Hawaiian Tropic competition. But being a lifelong athlete, Eden yearned for a career in the ring. And in 2011, the Michigan native took her first step toward becoming a Superstar when she began training at WWE's developmental facility, Florida Championship Wrestling.

After only a few months honing her skills, Eden was called up to the big stage when she debuted as the ring announcer for *WWE Superstars*. Her run on the globally-televised program was brief, however. Eden abruptly left WWE after only a few months. According to the dashing Diva's Twitter account, she left because the world was her oyster.

EDGE

HT: 6'5" WT: 250 lbs.
FROM: Toronto, Canada
SIGNATURE MOVE: Spear

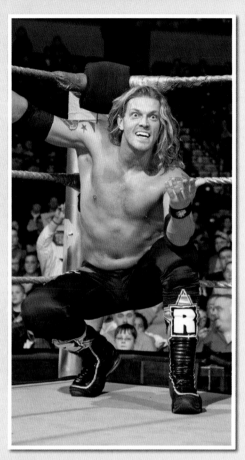

TITLE HISTORY

INTERCONTINENTAL CHAMPION (5 TIMES)	*Defeated Jeff Jarrett on July 24, 1999* *Defeated Lance Storm on August 19, 2001* *Defeated Christian on October 21, 2001* *Defeated Test on November 18, 2001* *Defeated Randy Orton on July 11, 2004*
UNITED STATES CHAMPION	*Defeated Kurt Angle on November 12, 2001*
WORLD HEAVYWEIGHT CHAMPION (7 TIMES)	*Defeated Undertaker on May 8, 2007* *Defeated Batista on December 16, 2007* *Defeated Undertaker on June 1, 2008* *Won an Elimination Chamber Match on February 15, 2009* *Defeated John Cena on April 26, 2009* *Won a Tables, Ladders & Chairs Match on December 19, 2010* *Defeated Dolph Ziggler on February 18, 2011*
WORLD TAG TEAM CHAMPION (12 TIMES)	*Partnered with Christian to defeat The Dudley Boys on April 2, 2000* *Partnered with Christian to defeat Too Cool on June 25, 2000* *Partnered with Christian to defeat The Hardy Boys on October 22, 2000* *Partnered with Christian to defeat Bull Buchanan & Goodfather on December 10, 2000* *Partnered with Christian to defeat The Rock & Undertaker on December 21, 2000* *Partnered with Christian to defeat The Hardy Boys on March 19, 2001* *Partnered with Christian to defeat The Dudley Boys on April 1, 2001* *Partnered with Hulk Hogan to defeat Billy & Chuck on July 4, 2002* *Partnered with Chris Benoit to defeat Ric Flair & Batista on April 19, 2004* *Partnered with Chris Benoit to defeat La Resistance on October 19, 2004* *Partnered with Randy Orton to defeat Ric Flair & "Rowdy" Roddy Piper on November 13, 2006* *Partnered with Chris Jericho to defeat Carlito & Primo on June 28, 2009*
WWE CHAMPION (4 TIMES)	*Defeated John Cena on January 8, 2006* *Won a Triple Threat Match against John Cena and Rob Van Dam on July 3, 2006* *Defeated Triple H on November 23, 2008* *Defeated Jeff Hardy on January 25, 2009*
WWE TAG TEAM CHAMPION (2 TIMES)	*Partnered with Rey Mysterio to defeat Kurt Angle & Chris Benoit on November 7, 2002* *Partnered with Chris Jericho to defeat Carlito & Primo on June 28, 2009*

WWE has been home to sports-entertainment's greatest Superstars, including Shawn Michaels, Ric Flair and The Rock. None of these men, however, have accumulated as many accolades as Edge. With more than 30 WWE titles to his credit, the "Rated-R Superstar" is the most decorated competitor of all time.

Edge's journey to greatness can be tracked all the way back to 1990. As a 16-year old, the future Hall of Famer sat in the crowd at Toronto's SkyDome to witness Ultimate Warrior challenge Hulk Hogan at *WrestleMania VI*. Surrounded by the pageantry of sports-entertainment's crown jewel, Edge vowed that night that he would one day headline *WrestleMania*.

You Think You Know Me

Eight long years later, which included an extended stay on the independent wrestling scene, Edge came one step closer to realizing his dream when he debuted in WWE. Shortly after his initial appearance, he teamed with longtime friend Christian to form one of the most successful pairings in tag-team history. Together, Edge and Christian captured seven World Tag Team Championships, while also revolutionizing the division with such innovations as the TLC Match.

As 2001 unfolded, the tag-team division proved unable to contain Edge's Superstardom. Starting with his King of the Ring crowning in June, the Toronto native began to show signs of being a main-event player. All the success, however, came at a price. A jealous Christian soon turned on Edge, marking the end of the popular pairing.

As a singles star, Edge quickly claimed the coveted Intercontinental Championship, a title he held proudly on five separate occasions. He also defeated Kurt Angle to capture the United States Championship in November 2001.

After proving himself as a legitimate Intercontinental Championship threat, Edge turned his attention on capturing sports-entertainment's richest prize. At *WrestleMania 21*, he moved one step closer when he won the Money in the Bank Ladder Match.

Edge toted his guaranteed title opportunity for nine long months before cashing in at *New Year's Revolution 2006*. At the event, John Cena retained the WWE Championship against five other Superstars in a grueling Elimination Chamber Match. Realizing Cena was at his weakest following the match, Edge wisely demanded his opportunity and defeated Cena to claim his first WWE Championship. The victory forever etched Edge's name next to the elite few that have owned the WWE Title, including his boyhood idol, Hulk Hogan.

The Ultimate Opportunist

Edge commemorated his victory by engaging in a live sex celebration with Lita the next night on *Raw*. The segment registered an amazing 5.2 rating, which was the highest for a *Raw* ending in more than two years. As a result of its popularity, Edge began touting himself as the most-watched WWE Champion of all time.

Edge added the World Heavyweight Championship to his résumé when he defeated Undertaker in May 2007. Like his first WWE Championship victory, the "Rated-R Superstar" took advantage of a beaten and battered Deadman to claim the title. As a result of his continued shrewd maneuvering, Edge was appropriately tagged with the "Ultimate Opportunist" moniker.

Undertaker later gained retribution for the loss when he defeated Edge for the gold at *WrestleMania XXIV*. For Edge, the loss was bittersweet. It clearly marked the end of his title reign, but the match was also the culmination of a nearly 20-year old dream to main event *WrestleMania*.

In January 2010, Edge bolstered his historic legacy when he last eliminated John Cena to win the *Royal Rumble*. With the victory, Edge became the only Superstar in history to have won the King of the Ring, Money in the Bank and Royal Rumble.

While Edge has been involved in a great number of rivalries, perhaps none was more personal than his clashes with Matt Hardy over his relationship with Lita.

Edge captured his eleventh and final World Title when he defeated Dolph Ziggler for the World Heavyweight Championship in February 2011. He carried the title into *WrestleMania XXVII* where he defeated Alberto Del Rio. At the time, the win appeared to be the latest in what many anticipated to be a lengthy reign. In reality, however, it proved to be Edge's final stand.

Shortly after *WrestleMania*, the "Rated-R Superstar" announced that injuries to his spine would prevent him from ever being medically cleared to compete again. As a result, Edge was forced into early retirement and fans were left with memories of the one of the greatest careers of all time.

On March 30, 2012 Edge's awesome career was capped off when he was inducted into the WWE Hall of Fame by his best friend, Christian.

2010-
2000-09
1990-99
1980-89
1970-79
1960-69

EDOUARD CARPENTIER

HT: 5'10" **WT:** 228 lbs.
FROM: Montreal, Quebec, Canada
SIGNATURE MOVE: Flying Head Scissors

Many WWE fans recognize Edouard Carpentier as the host of the company's French broadcast of WWE programming during the 1980s, but it was his awe-inspiring arsenal of high-flying ring action that endeared him to wrestling fans decades prior.

Dubbed "The Flying Frenchman", Carpentier's aerial assault left opponents' heads spinning. His acrobatic style eventually lead him to a reign as National Wrestling Alliance (NWA) Champion. He defeated the legendary Lou Thesz for the title in June 1957; but his reign was marred by controversy when the NWA later failed to recognized the victory after Carpentier's manager left the promotion. The incident will forever be remembered as one of the most controversial moments in the NWA's history.

EL OLYMPICO

HT: 5'9" **WT:** 234 lbs.
FROM: Mexico City, Mexico
SIGNATURE MOVE: Flying Cross Body

This high-flying masked man began his career in his homeland of Mexico and arrived in the World Wide Wrestling Federation in 1972. He became an instant fan-favorite with his mixture of high flying maneuvers and submission holds. El Olympico showcased his skills in front of a packed Shea Stadium at the 1972 *Showdown At Shea* as he defeated Chuck O'Connor.

The man from South of the border stood opposite side of the ring from greats including Dory Funk, Sr., Terry Funk, and future WWE Hall of Famers Greg "The Hammer" Valentine and Mr. Fuji. By the end of the 1970s, El Olympico returned to Mexico, but this virtuoso of *lucha libre* will always be fondly remembered as someone who upheld the tradition of Mexican wrestling no matter where the fight took him.

ELI COTTONWOOD

HT: 7'2" **WT:** 304 lbs.
FROM: River Falls, Wisconsin

At 7'2", it's no surprise that Eli Cottonwood achieved a successful basketball career, competing both collegiately at St. John's University in Minnesota and professionally in various leagues overseas. But the hardwood wasn't where Cottonwood wanted to make his name. Instead, he longed to be a WWE Superstar.

Cottonwood's opportunity at achieving his dream came in June 2010 when he debuted as a competitor on season two of *NXT*. With John Morrison as his Pro, the tree-like Rookie hoped he could become WWE's next breakout star. His quest started out well enough, picking up a victory in his debut match, then another over eventual *NXT* winner Kaval. But following a loss to Michael McGillicutty in July, Cottonwood's lofty hopes were chopped down to size when he was eliminated from competition. On his way out the door, the oversized hopeful took his frustrations out on his fellow *NXT* Rookies.

Following his elimination, Cottonwood made one more appearance on *NXT*, teaming with the other Rookies to attack Kaval after he was announced as the show's victor.

ELIJAH BURKE

HT: 6'1" **WT:** 235 lbs.
FROM: Jacksonville, Florida
SIGNATURE MOVE: The Elijah Express

Elijah Burke is a naturally gifted athlete who has won several tough man contests across the Eastern seaboard of the U.S. He also boasts an amateur boxing record of 103-1, with 102 KOs.

Elijah first appeared on *SmackDown* in July 2006. In November, he joined the ranks of ECW, where he disrespected the original ECW establishment, like Rob Van Dam, Sabu, Tommy Dreamer and the Sandman. The "Paragon of Virtue" formed a faction called the New Breed to battle the ECW Originals at *WrestleMania 23*. Burke also appeared in a battle royal at *WrestleMania XXIV* but was out of WWE before the end of 2008.

ELIMINATION chamber

Created by *Raw* general manager Eric Bischoff in 2002, an Elimination Chamber Match combines elements from *Royal Rumble*, *Survivor Series* and *War Games* matches into one steel structure. An Elimination Chamber Match starts with two Superstars in the ring. After a predetermined length of time, a new Superstar is released from a pod in the Chamber and enters the battle. The last Superstar standing is declared the winner.

In 2010, *Elimination Chamber* became an annual pay-per-view event which featured two Elimination Chamber Matches each year.

February 21, 2010

St. Louis, MO – Scottrade Center

Match for WWE Championship: John Cena last eliminated Triple H in a match that also included World Heavyweight Champion Sheamus, Ted DiBiase, Randy Orton and Kofi Kingston

Match for World Heavyweight Championship: Chris Jericho last eliminated WWE Champion Undertaker in a match that also included John Morrison, R-Truth, CM Punk and Rey Mysterio

▼

February 20, 2011

Oakland, CA - Oracle Arena

Match for World Heavyweight Championship: World Heavyweight Champion Edge last eliminated Rey Mysterio in a match that also included Wade Barrett, Big Show, Kane and Drew McIntrye

Match for shot at WWE Championship: John Cena last eliminated CM Punk in a match that also included John Morrison, Sheamus, Randy Orton and R-Truth

▼

February 19, 2012

Milwaukee, WI - Bradley Center

Match for World Heavyweight Championship: World Heavyweight Champion Daniel Bryan last eliminated Santino Marella in a match that also included Cody Rhodes, Wade Barrett, Big Show and Great Khali

Match for WWE Championship: WWE Champion CM Punk last eliminated The Miz in a match that also included R-Truth, Dolph Ziggler, Chris Jericho and Kofi Kingston

ELIMINATION

Decades after making her WWE debut, Elizabeth's impact is still being felt today. Appropriately dubbed the "First Lady of Sports-Entertainment," her gentle-yet-influential contributions helped pave the way for all the females that followed.

In 1985, WWE newcomer Randy "Macho Man" Savage set out on a search to find a manager. Nearly every personality with a manager's license threw his hat in the ring. In the end, Savage unveiled the beautiful Miss Elizabeth as his choice. Over the next seven years, Savage and Elizabeth's very public rollercoaster relationship provided fans with a soap-opera type romance never before seen in WWE.

Upon her debut, both fans and Superstars became smitten by her innocent smile and impeccable style. The admiration she received, however, didn't sit well with Savage. The jealous Superstar continually took his frustrations out on his harmless manager, despite the fact that she never acted on anybody's advances.

The always-classy Elizabeth took Savage's verbal attacks in stride. Instead of simply walking away, she stood by her man and helped guide him to greatness. In 1988, Elizabeth achieved the ultimate goal when she managed Savage to the WWE Championship at *WrestleMania IV*. The win made Elizabeth the first female to manage a WWE Champion.

Elizabeth's relationship with Savage reached its boiling point in 1989 when her friendship with Hulk Hogan sent Macho Man into a jealous rage. The couple split soon after, sending Elizabeth into a more private lifestyle and Savage into a working relationship with Sensational Sherri.

In 1991, after Savage lost a Retirement Match to Ultimate Warrior at *WrestleMania VII*, Elizabeth reemerged to save her man from an attacking Sherri. Following the save, Elizabeth and Savage shared a loving embrace that drew tears of happiness from nearly everybody watching.

The couple celebrated their love later that year when they married at *SummerSlam 1991*. The smile on Elizabeth's face told the entire story of a beautiful woman who finally found happiness in WWE.

E

2010-

2000-09

1990-99

1980-89

1970-79

1960-69

EPICO

HT: 6'2" **WT:** 217 lbs.
FROM: San Juan, Puerto Rico
SIGNATURE MOVE: Backstabber

TITLE HISTORY

WWE TAG TEAM CHAMPION	Partnered with Primo to defeat Air Boom on January 15, 2012

As the nephew of Puerto Rican wrestling legend Carlos Colon, Epico entered WWE with high expectations. But rather than crumble under the weight of the pressure, the multi-generational Superstar has proven to be one of Puerto Rico's greatest exports.

Epico's first order of business upon becoming a WWE Superstar in November 2011 was to help Hunico in his ongoing conflict with Sin Cara. Shortly after, Epico teamed with his cousin, Primo, and focused his efforts on making an impact in the tag-team division. As a unit, Epico and Primo enjoyed immediate success, defeating the Usos on an episode of *WWE Superstars*. But it wasn't until the tandem teamed up with the stunning Rosa that they realized their amazing potential.

In January 2012, Epico & Primo defeated Air Boom to claim the coveted WWE Tag Team Championship. Proving they were for real, the new titlists topped Air Boom again the next night to retain the gold.

ERIC BISCHOFF

HT: 5'10" **WT:** 195 lbs. **FROM:** Detroit, Michigan

Bischoff began his sports-entertainment career in August 1987 in the syndication and sales department for Verne Gagne's American Wrestling Association (AWA). He made the transition from behind the desk to behind the microphone and joined the long line of famous AWA announcers. In 1991, Eric Bischoff moved to World Championship Wrestling (WCW), where he began a complete overhaul of a fledgling division of Turner Broadcasting.

After he launched *WCW Monday Nitro* live in 1995, the face of sports-entertainment changed and The Monday Night Wars began. He signed major stars away from WWE, made innovations in how the product was presented, acquired talent from ECW and is credited for the creation of the nWo. Under Eric Bischoff's direction, WCW went from a perennial loss-leader to an over $300 million dollar sports-entertainment and broadcasting front-runner that won the ratings war 84 weeks in a row. When he left the company in 1999, he did so as the president of Turner/Time Warner's WCW Division.

Bischoff once again made sports-entertainment history in 2002 when he was introduced by Mr. McMahon as the new General Manager of *Raw*. No one in their wildest dreams thought this controversial figure who tried to put McMahon out of business would walk onto *Raw* and embrace the WWE Chairman and join forces with him.

As General Manager, Eric pushed his personal agenda and maintained his special gift of making enemies wherever he went. In 2006, his autobiography, *Controversy Creates Cash,* was released and sky-rocketed to *The New York Times Bestseller List.*

Despite the fact that Mr. Bischoff is likely not on top of many "most popular" lists, his achievements, business contributions, and success are indisputable. Sports-entertainment would not be where it is today without the drive, and commitment Eric Bischoff has displayed in his over 20-plus years in the sports-entertainment industry.

ERIC ESCOBAR

HT: 6'3"   WT: 246 lbs.   FROM: San Juan, Puerto Rico
SIGNATURE MOVE: Pure Escobar

After a brief hiatus, Vickie Guerrero returned to WWE in late 2009 to manage her new boyfriend, the considerably younger Eric Escobar. Being romantically linked to Guerrero instantly made Escobar one of WWE's most detested Superstars. But he didn't care. He knew that Guerrero's stroke in *SmackDown*'s front office could help him reach the top of the mountain.

Not surprisingly, Escobar was granted an opportunity at the Intercontinental Championship after only a handful of victories. Unfortunately for Escobar, his inexperience cost him and he was unable to dethrone John Morrison.

Vickie Guerrero was disgusted by Escobar's inability to beat Morrison. After berating him in the middle of the ring, she slapped her defeated boyfriend and ran off. Later, Escobar admitted to Guerrero that he was only in the relationship for the career benefits. But not even unearned title matches were enough to keep him around, he claimed. Escobar then dumped Guerrero, much to the delight of the WWE Universe.

Coincidentally, after breaking up with Guerrero, Escobar didn't last very long in WWE.

ERNEST "THE CAT" MILLER

HT: 6'2"   WT: 235 lbs.
FROM: Atlanta, Georgia

Fans who witnessed Ernest Miller's brief WWE in-ring career probably assume "The Cat" was a loudmouthed Superstar who was more concerned with dancing and having someone call his momma than actually competing. And they'd be right. In fact, at the 2004 *Royal Rumble*, Miller spent more time showing off his moves than he did competing. As a result, he was eliminated by Randy Orton mid-dance.

Miller's brief appearance accurately sums up much of his WWE tenure. It sums up the majority of his WCW career, as well. Unlike the WWE Universe, however, the WCW crowds ate up Miller's act. They jumped to their feet each time "The Cat" donned his patented ruby-red slippers and broke into dance. Even the original Godfather of Soul, James Brown, became a fan of Miller's moves, and at *SuperBrawl 2000*, the legendary singer/songwriter showed up to dance with "The Cat."

Miller's post-ring career has been highlighted by roles in several TV series and movies, including the critically acclaimed film *The Wrestler*. He is also a "three, three, three"-time world karate champion.

ERNIE LADD

HT: 6'9"
WT: 320 lbs.
FROM: New Orleans, Louisiana

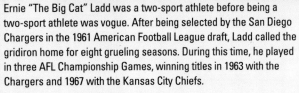

Ernie "The Big Cat" Ladd was a two-sport athlete before being a two-sport athlete was vogue. After being selected by the San Diego Chargers in the 1961 American Football League draft, Ladd called the gridiron home for eight grueling seasons. During this time, he played in three AFL Championship Games, winning titles in 1963 with the Chargers and 1967 with the Kansas City Chiefs.

While still an active member of the AFL, Ladd took part in a publicity stunt that saw him answer the challenge of several Los Angeles wrestlers. He went into the encounter assuming he would mop the floor with the smaller competition. Instead, they proved their dominance over Ladd, which eventually fueled the fire within "The Big Cat" to learn the craft of wrestling.

In the early 1960s, Ladd began wrestling in the Los Angeles area during AFL off-seasons. Behind the name he already built for himself on the field, he became an instant hit, as fans loved to hate the arrogant footballer-turned-wrestler.

Ladd landed in WWE in 1968. Guided by legendary manager The Grand Wizard, he became a perennial challenger for the promotion's top prize. And when he wasn't trying to claim the WWE Championship from Bruno Sammartino, he was engaging in memorable rivalries with fellow big men Andre the Giant, Gorilla Monsoon and Haystacks Calhoun.

When his in-ring career came to a close, Ladd remained a part of the wrestling community as a manager and color commentator. His most notable time behind the mic saw him call a portion of the action at *WrestleMania 2*.

In 1981, the San Diego Chargers recognized Ladd as a gridiron great when they inducted him into their Hall of Fame. His in-ring accomplishments were later honored when he was enshrined in the WWE Hall of Fame in 1995.

HALL of FAME
1995

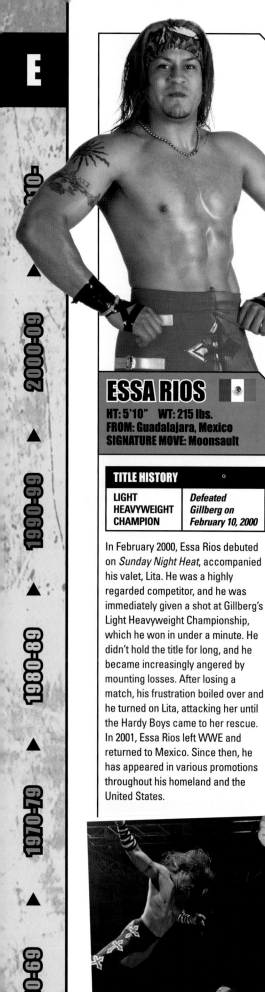

ESSA RIOS

HT: 5'10" WT: 215 lbs.
FROM: Guadalajara, Mexico
SIGNATURE MOVE: Moonsault

TITLE HISTORY

LIGHT HEAVYWEIGHT CHAMPION	Defeated Gillberg on February 10, 2000

In February 2000, Essa Rios debuted on *Sunday Night Heat*, accompanied his valet, Lita. He was a highly regarded competitor, and he was immediately given a shot at Gillberg's Light Heavyweight Championship, which he won in under a minute. He didn't hold the title for long, and he became increasingly angered by mounting losses. After losing a match, his frustration boiled over and he turned on Lita, attacking her until the Hardy Boys came to her rescue. In 2001, Essa Rios left WWE and returned to Mexico. Since then, he has appeared in various promotions throughout his homeland and the United States.

EUGENE 🇺🇸

HT: 6'1" WT: 225 lbs.
FROM: Louisville, Kentucky
SIGNATURE MOVE:
Special versions of other Superstar's moves

TITLE HISTORY

WORLD TAG TEAM CHAMPION	Partnered with William Regal to defeat Rob Conway & Sylvain Grenier on November 15, 2004

When Eugene first arrived on the WWE scene in April 2004, nobody would have predicted he'd become a future World Tag Team Champion. As the special-needs nephew of *Raw* General Manager Eric Bischoff, Eugene was seen by many as a non-threat. When the bell rang, Eugene proved to be a wrestling savant.

Using moves he learned while watching his favorite Superstars years earlier, Eugene was able to catch opponents off guard en route to an impressive early career. In addition to his expansive repertoire of moves, Eugene also possessed incredible strength.

Despite being a special Superstar, Eugene managed to earn major pay-per-view matches against the industry's greatest stars, including contests against Triple H and Kurt Angle on back-to-back *SummerSlam* cards. However, it was his teaming with William Regal that garnered the most success. In November 2004, the duo defeated La Resistance and Tajiri & Rhyno on *Raw* to capture the coveted World Tag Team Championship.

EUROPEAN CHAMPIONSHI

Introduced to WWE audiences in February 1997, the European Championship was wide recognized as a stepping-stone to greatness, as many of its holders went on to capture Championships later in their careers, including Triple H, Kurt Angle, and Eddie Guerrero.

After defeating Owen Hart in a tournament final, the British Bulldog was recognized as first-ever European Champion. His reign lasted more than 200 days, longer than any oth European Champion in history. The title was eventually vacated in July 2002 when Rob Dam defeated Jeff Hardy to unify the European and Intercontinental Championships.

1997

February 26
Berlin, Germany

British Bulldog defeated Owen Hart

In the finals of a tournament to crown the first-ever European Champion, British Bulldog defeated Owen Hart.

⬇

September 20
Birmingham, England

Shawn Michaels defeated British Bulldog

⬇

December 22
Lowell, MA

Triple H defeated Shawn Michaels

⬇

1998

January 22
Davis, CA

Owen Hart defeated Goldust

Owen Hart beat Goldust, who was dressed as then-champion Triple H, to win the European Championship. Despite Triple H not officially being involved in the match, Commissioner Sgt. Slaughter allowed the decision to stand.

⬇

March 16
Phoenix, AZ

Triple H defeated Owen Hart

⬇

July 20
Binghamton, NY

D-Lo Brown defeated Triple H

⬇

September 21
Sacramento, CA

X-Pac defeated D-Lo Brown

⬇

October 5
East Lansing, MI

D-Lo Brown defeated X-Pac

⬇

October 18
Chicago, IL

X-Pac defeated D-Lo Brown

⬇

1999

February 15
Birmingham, AL

Shane McMahon defeated X-Pac

Shane McMahon and Kane defeated X-Pac and Triple H when McMahon pinned X-Pac. Pre-match stipulations stated that if anybody pinned X-Pac, that man would be awarded the European Championship.

⬇

June 21
Memphis, TN

Mideon became European Champion

Mideon was declared European Champion after he found the title in Shane McMahon's bag.

⬇

July 25
Buffalo, NY

D-Lo Brown defeated Mideon

⬇

August 22
Minneapolis, MN

Jeff Jarrett defeated D-Lo Brown

⬇

August 23
Ames, IA

Mark Henry became European Champion

Jeff Jarrett awarded the European Championship to Mark Henry after he helped Jarrett defeat D-Lo Brown one night earlier.

⬇

September 26
Charlotte, NC

D-Lo Brown defeated Mark Henry

⬇

October 28
Springfield, MA

British Bulldog defeated D-Lo Brown

⬇

December 12
Fort Lauderdale, FL

Val Venis defeated British Bulldog

Val Venis pinned British Bulldog to win the European Championship in a Triple Threat Match that also included D'Lo Brown.

▼

2000

February 10
Austin, TX

Kurt Angle defeated Val Venis

▼

April 2
Anaheim, CA

Chris Jericho defeated Chris Benoit

Chris Jericho pinned Chris Benoit to win the European Championship in a Triple Threat Match that also included then-champion Kurt Angle.

▼

April 3
Los Angeles, CA

Eddie Guerrero defeated Chris Jericho

▼

July 23
Dallas, TX

Perry Saturn defeated Eddie Guerrero

▼

August 31
Fayetteville, NC

Al Snow defeated Perry Saturn

▼

October 16
Detroit, MI

William Regal defeated Al Snow

▼

December 2
Sheffield, England

Crash Holly defeated William Regal

▼

December 4
East Rutherford, NJ

William Regal defeated Crash Holly

▼

2001

January 22
Lafayette, LA

Test defeated William Regal

▼

April 1
Houston, TX

Eddie Guerrero defeated Test

▼

April 26
Denver, CO

Matt Hardy defeated Eddie Guerrero

▼

August 27
Grand Rapids, MI

The Hurricane defeated Matt Hardy

▼

October 22
Kansas City, MO

Bradshaw defeated The Hurricane

▼

November 1
Cincinnati, OH

Christian defeated Bradshaw

▼

2002

January 31
Norfolk, VA

Diamond Dallas Page defeated Christian

▼

March 21
Ottawa, Ontario

William Regal defeated Diamond Dallas Page

▼

April 8
Phoenix, AZ

Spike Dudley defeated William Regal

▼

May 6
Hartford, CT

William Regal defeated Spike Dudley

▼

July 8
Philadelphia, PA

Jeff Hardy defeated William Regal

Rob Van Dam defeated Jeff Hardy on July 21, 2002 to unify the European and Intercontinental Championships.

EVAN BOURNE

HT: 5'9" **WT:** 183 lbs. **FROM:** St. Louis, Missouri
SIGNATURE MOVE: Shooting Star Press

TITLE HISTORY

WWE TAG TEAM CHAMPION	*Partnered with Kofi Kingston to defeat David Otunga & Michael McGillicutty on August 22, 2011*

Evan Bourne idolized the likes of Rey Mysterio, Dean Malenko, Bret Hart and Eddie Guerrero. Evan also displayed a taste for hardcore as he also admired the brutal stylings of ECW Originals Rob Van Dam, Sabu and Tazz. Determined to bring something unique to sports-entertainment, Evan traveled the world and incorporated the techniques he learned from everywhere he competed. In June 2008, Evan arrived in ECW and amazed audiences with his array of high-flying maneuvers.

This man lives by a formula he has created that will ensure his WWE success for years to come: take one-third positive attitude, one-third technical brilliance, and three-thirds aerial magic and you get the Bourne Combination. Evan carried this philosophy with him to *Raw*, where he has become one of the brand's biggest Superstars. Early success on Monday nights has included competing in main events, representing the brand in *Money In the Bank* matches, and a WWE Tag Team Championship reign with another explosive high-flyer, Kofi Kingston.

EVE   **FROM: Los Angeles, California**

TITLE HISTORY

DIVAS CHAMPION (2 TIMES)	*Defeated Maryse on April 12, 2010* *Won a Fatal 4-Way Match on January 30, 2011*

This vision of beauty from the City of Angels is no stranger to the entertainment industry. A professional dancer well-versed in several styles, she was a member of the NBA's Los Angeles Clippers Spirit Dancers. Her moves were also featured on television programs including ABC's *Show Me the Money!*, *Days of our Lives*, and Damon Wayans' *The Underground*. While Eve is regarded as one of the sexiest women on television, she's also an intellectual and enjoys philosophical debates. Her mixture of beauty, power, and intelligence reached beyond the ropes as she trains in Gracie Jiu-Jitsu, and has appeared in Muscle and Fitness Magazine and as a contestant on *Deal or No Deal*.

Her unrelenting desire for excellence drove her to enter and win the 2007 Diva Search. On Feb. 1, 2008, she debuted on *SmackDown* and conducted an interview with Batista. After a 2009 move to *Raw*, Eve established herself as a top-notch competitor while facing the likes of Lay Cool, Maryse, the Bella Twins, Natalya, and Beth Phoenix. At the end of 2011, Eve began dating Zack Ryder after teaming with him in a match, though she later hinted at feelings for John Cena. In February 2012, the devious Diva admitted that her interest in both men was strictly for increased publicity. During the Team Teddy versus Team Johnny Match at *WrestleMania XXVIII*, Eve showed her true colors when she took out Ryder with a low blow.

E

1960-69 ▼
1970-79 ▼
1980-89 ▼
1990-99 ▼
2000-09 ▼
2010- ▼

2010-
2000-09
1990-99
1980-89
1970-79
1960-69

EVOLUTION

MEMBERS: "Nature Boy" Ric Flair, Triple H, Batista, Randy Orton

If someone combined the greatest in-ring competitor of all-time, the "King of Kings" and two bright, young Superstars, you would have Evolution. In 2003, "Nature Boy" Ric Flair, Triple H, Batista and third-generation Superstar Randy Orton formed a group that represented the evolution of sports-entertainment. This villainous group was led by Triple H, and with Ric Flair his second-in-command, the men used their experience and knowledge to their advantage. During its

existence, this group butted heads with Superstars of all types such as Shawn Michaels, Goldberg, Rob Van Dam, Mick Foley, Edge, and the Dudley Boys.

Evolution reached its apex when all four members held WWE championships. Triple H was the World Heavyweight Champion, Flair and Batista were World Tag Team Champions and Orton was the

Intercontinental Champion. When Randy Orton won the World Heavyweight Championship in August 2004, he was unceremoniously removed from the group. Batista later won the 2005 *Royal Rumble* and decided to challenge for Triple H's World Heavyweight Championship at *WrestleMania 21*, where the "Animal" won the title. At the *WWE Homecoming*, a returning Triple H turned on Flair and Evolution disbanded. On the *Raw 15th Anniversary*, this famous group had a reunion that saw Triple H, Ric Flair & Batista team up for a six-man match. When Randy Orton refused to rejoin his former stablemates, he opposed them with Edge & Umaga.

Evolution was about success, domination, and women. Since the group dissolved in 2005, "Nature Boy" Ric Flair was inducted into the WWE Hall of Fame, Triple H temporarily reformed D-Generation X and continues to wear a king's crown. Batista and Randy Orton are multi-time holders of the WWE and World Heavyweight Championships, respectively.

EXECUTIONER   FROM: Parts Unknown

After several grueling months of trying, Undertaker was finally on the verge of ridding WWE of his arch nemesis, Mankind, at *In Your House: Buried Alive*. However, before he could complete the job, a mysterious masked man attacked Undertaker from behind with a steel shovel. The masked monster, who was later revealed to be Paul Bearer's hired assassin known as the Executioner, then proceeded to bury the "Deadman" under six feet of soil.

Miraculously, Undertaker survived the burial and challenged the Executioner to a match at *In Your House: It's Time* in December 1996. Under "Armageddon Rules," Undertaker Tombstoned his way to victory. The Executioner was gone from WWE soon after.

THE EXECUTIONERS

MEMBERS: Executioner No. 1, Executioner No. 2, Executioner No. 3
COMBINED WT: 758 lbs.   FROM: Parts Unknown

TITLE HISTORY	
WORLD TAG TEAM CHAMPIONS	*Defeated Tony Parisi & Louis Cerdan on May 11, 1976*

Very little is known about The Executioners other than they were complete terrors in the ring. Hiding their faces with masks and replacing their names with numbers, Executioner No. 1 & Executioner No. 2 instilled the fear of the unknown into WWE in the mid-1970s.

In May 1976, The Executioners, who were managed by Capt. Lou Albano, reached the top of the tag division when they defeated Louis Cerdan & Tony Parisi for the World Tag Team Championship in Philadelphia. The mysterious duo held the titles for seven months before controversy caused them to lose the gold. By this time, the tag team had welcomed a third member into the fold, appropriately named Executioner No. 3. The new member participated in a title defense against Billy White Wolf & Chief Jay Strongbow. At the time, this was an illegal practice in WWE, resulting in The Executioners being stripped of the titles.

EXTREME EXPOSÉ

MEMBERS: Kelly Kelly, Layla, Brooke

The heart of this dance group and its extreme beginnings began as Kelly Kelly started her career in sports-entertainment in 2006 as part of ECW. In January 2007, Kelly returned to ECW and promised the Exposé would be back but that now she was bringing friends. The trio of Kelly, 2006 Diva Search winner Layla and Brooke danced in the ring with moves so hot the ring almost melted during their performances.

That August, the three Divas brought the extreme to *FHM* and appeared in an exclusive online pictorial that drove web traffic off the charts. Unfortunately for its devout followers, dissension amongst the Exposé members set in when chick magnet The Miz appeared on the ECW scene. In November, the group dissolved for good after Brooke parted ways with WWE while Kelly Kelly and Layla settled their differences in the ring.

EXTREME RULES

From the days of the original ECW where every match was waged in this manner, *WWE Extreme Rules* kicks the rules of traditional matches to the curb.

April 25, 2010

Baltimore, MD - 1st Mariner Arena

Main Event | WWE Champion John Cena defeated Batista in a Last Man Standing Match

June 7, 2009

New Orleans, LA - New Orleans Arena

Main Event | Jeff Hardy defeated World Heavyweight Champion Edge in a Ladder Match

May 1, 2011

Tampa, FL - St. Pete Times Forum

Main Event | John Cena defeated John Morrison and WWE Champion The Miz in a Triple Threat Steel Cage Match

EZEKIEL JACKSON

HT: 6'4" **WT:** 305 lbs. **FROM:** Harlem, New York **SIGNATURE MOVE:** The Book of Ezekiel

TITLE HISTORY	
ECW CHAMPION	*Defeated Christian on February 16, 2010*
INTERCONTINENTAL CHAMPION	*Defeated Wade Barrett on June 19, 2011*

A monstrous competitor who pulverizes opponents, Ezekiel Jackson made his WWE debut in July 2008 as the advisor to The Brian Kendrick. "The Personification of Domination" easily made the transition from advisor to willing participant in matches. His association with Kendrick ended when Ezekiel was drafted to ECW. While there, Jackson was a dominant force and guaranteed his inclusion in the annals of sports-entertainment history as the last man to hold the ECW Championship.

He next joined *SmackDown* and enlisted in Wade Barret's insidious faction, The Corre. After several months of service, Ezekiel found himself on the receiving end of a near career-ending attack by his former cohorts. Shrugging off any lasting effects of the attack, Jackson returned stronger, and as his own man. He met Wade Barret for the Intercontinental Championship at *Capitol Punishment* in 2011 and defeated his former leader via submission.

THE FABULOUS FREEBIRDS

MEMBERS: Michael Hayes, Terry Gordy, Buddy Roberts
COMBINED WT: 765 lbs.
FROM: Badstreet, Atlanta, Georgia

Michael "P.S." Hayes, Terry "Bam Bam" Gordy, and Buddy "Jack" Roberts truly were ahead of their time. Known as the Fabulous Freebirds, the threesome created a never-before-seen level of showmanship that is often emulated by today's Superstars. When it came to getting dirty, the Freebirds owned a gang-like mentality that could carry them through the toughest of wars.

While their WWE stay only lasted a few weeks, the Freebirds gained great success in other promotions throughout the United States. During the threesome's 1980s heyday, they held titles in the NWA, World Class, and UWF, among other territories.

In 1982, the Freebirds made history when they became the first-ever World Class Six-Man Tag Team Champions. Over the next six years, the trio engaged in one of the bloodiest rivalries of all time when they battled the Von Erichs for the titles. In all, the rivals traded the titles 10 times.

Outside the ring, the Freebirds gained the reputation as drinkers, rabble rousers, and even singers. At the height of the Rock 'n' Wrestling craze, Hayes became the first Superstar to record his own entrance theme, "Badstreet USA."

THE FABULOUS KANGAROOS

MEMBERS: Al Costello, Roy Heffernan, Don Kent

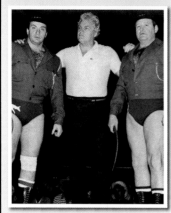

Many historians consider the original Fabulous Kangaroos, Al Costello & Roy Heffernan, to be the duo responsible for putting tag team competition on the map. Managed by Wild Red Berry, The Fabulous Kangaroos made their debut in the late 1950s. The Australian tandem quickly endeared themselves to New York City crowds by tossing boomerangs into the audience.

Costello & Heffernan enjoyed three runs as NWA United States Tag Team Champions before the World Wide Wrestling Federation claimed the titles as their own starting in 1963. Their final reign proved to be their most successful, as the Kangaroos maintained a firm grip on the titles for more than one year before finally losing to Johnny Valentine & Bob Ellis in January 1962. Shortly after the loss, Costello & Heffernan left WWE to work in various other United States territories, as well as Canada. The Fabulous Kangaroos did make a brief return in the early 1970s. This time, however, Heffernan was replaced by Don Kent.

FABULOUS MOOLAH

HT: 5'5"   FROM: Columbia, South Carolina   SIGNATURE MOVE: The Backbreaker

TITLE HISTORY	
WOMEN'S CHAMPION (4 TIMES)	*Defeated Judy Grable on September 18, 1956* *Defeated Wendi Richter on November 25, 1985* *Defeated Velvet McIntyre on July 9, 1986* *Defeated Ivory on October 17, 1999*

In 1949, fans saw a lovely valet in a leopard-skin skirt named Slave Girl Moolah. This vixen turned heads as she led the likes of "Nature Boy" Buddy Rogers to the ring. She was later trained by the most dominant female star of her generation, Mildred Burke. Now known as the Fabulous Moolah, she climbed the championship ladder, and in 1956, outlasted 12 other ladies to win the vacant Women's Championship. When she raised her arms in triumph with the championship, she took the first step toward an unprecedented 28-year championship dynasty. Her fame was immeasurable, as close friends Elvis Presley and Jerry Lee Lewis often attended her matches.

Moolah was unstoppable as she traveled the globe and defended her title. In 1972, her legend grew when she and Vince J. McMahon successfully lifted the ban that prohibited women from wrestling at Madison Square Garden. That September, she successfully defended her prize at the first-ever *Showdown At Shea* event against Debbie Johnson.

Decades of Domination

As The Fabulous One entered her fourth decade in the ring, a new era was dawning. In 1983, she signed an exclusive agreement with Vincent K. McMahon and her Women's title was a key component to WWE's national expansion. Moolah's historic title reign ended on July 23, 1984, when she met sensation Wendi Richter on MTV's broadcast of *The Brawl To End It All*. Filled with vengeful thoughts, Moolah ended the six-month reign of her new nemesis thanks to protégé, Lelani Kai. Moolah split time between managing her new Superstar and competing in the ring. She continued to battle Richter and pop star Cyndi Lauper, who helped launch the "Rock N' Wrestling Connection." Moolah regained her championship by deceptive means on November 25, 1985. Richter was signed to defend the title against the unknown Spider Lady. A hush fell over Madison Square Garden when the masked arachnid pinned their heroine. Fans were aghast when an enraged Richter ripped off Spider's mask and revealed it was Moolah. With the coveted prize around her waist, Moolah enjoyed a third title reign.

Moolah added another chapter to the WWE history books at *WrestleMania III* when she became the "Queen of WWE" as she accompanied "King" Harley Race and manager Bobby Heenan to the ring. Her championship campaign came to an end at the Sam Houston Coliseum on July 24, 1987, when she lost the gold to protégé "Sensational" Sherri Martel. That November, Moolah captained her team of Rockin' Robin, Velvet McIntyre & The Jumping Bomb Angels to victory in the inaugural *Survivor Series* over Martel, Lelani Kai, Judy Martin, Donna Christanello & Dawn Marie. As the year came to an end, Moolah disappeared from WWE.

In 1995, Moolah took her rightful place among the immortals as the first woman inducted into the WWE Hall of Fame. She shocked the world on October 17, 1999, when she returned to the ring in her 70s and defeated Ivory to capture her fourth Women's Championship, 43 years after she won her first Women's title. This unbelievable accomplishment made her the oldest champion in the history of sports-entertainment.

The spotlight continued to follow Moolah and in 2002 she authored her autobiography, *The Fabulous Moolah: First Goddess of the Squared Circle*. In September 2003, she became the first octogenarian to compete in a WWE ring when she defeated Victoria on her 80th birthday during *Monday Night Raw*. Over the next few years, she continued to appear on WWE programming, events, and pay-per-views. In 2004, she was prominently featured in the film documentary, *Lipstick and Dynamite* about the golden age of women's wrestling and was a guest on *The Tonight Show with Jay Leno*.

The Fabulous Moolah passed away on November 2, 2007 at the age of 84. Moolah will always be synonymous with success and is regarded as the undisputed icon of women's wrestling. This pioneer of sports-entertainment's period of domination as Woman's Champion is unmatched by any figure, in any sport, male or female.

At the height of the "Attitude" Era, Moolah returned to WWE programming with friend Mae Young.

THE FABULOUS ROUGEAU BROTHERS

MEMBERS: Jacques Rougeau, Raymond Rougeau
COMBINED WT: 472 lbs.
FROM: Montreal, Quebec, Canada

Trained by their legendary father, brothers Jacques Raymond were fixtures of the Montreal wrestling scene in the 1970s. The Fabulous Rougeau Brothers made their WWE debut in February 1986 and caught the eye of audiences from the opening bell with quick tags and smooth double-team moves.

In what was originally scheduled as a friendly exhibition match between top title contenders, the Rougeaus resorted to cheating in a victory over the Killer Bees. The once-honorable Rougeaus became condescending and smarmy, and they mocked the United States. To make matters worse, their new manager, Jimmy Hart, still had the Hart Foundation's contract and gave a percentage of their earnings to the Rougeaus as performance bonuses. In 1989, the Rougeaus engaged in a series of matches against the Rockers, which lead to a six-man clash at *SummerSlam*.

In 1990, Raymond was forced to retire due to injuries and became a broadcaster on WWE French television through 1998. Jacques returned to the company in 1993 as part of the Quebecers. Today, Raymond is a popular politician in Canada and Jacques runs a successful regional promotion and training academy in Montreal.

1960-69
1970-79
1980-89
1990-99
2000-09
2010-

FARMER PETE 🇨🇦

With his torn jeans, ragged hat and lucky horseshoe placed around his neck, Farmer Pete certainly looked as tough he spent plenty of time in the fields, which is surprising seeing as he dedicated much of his life to the ring.

A legend in Canada, the midget wrestler spent decades competing in the Ontario territory. When he wrestled in the United States, he worked in numerous regions, most notably Georgia. During the early 1950s, the Peach State was the site of Pete's memorable rivalries with Sky Low Low and Irish Jackie.

FBI (FULL BLOODED ITALIANS)

MEMBERS Nunzio, Chuck Palumbo, Johnny Stamboli, Tony Mamaluke, Trinity

A former member of ECW's Full Blooded Italians faction, Nunzio resurrected the group in WWE in 2003. With Chuck Palumbo and Johnny Stamboli also in the fold, the FBI, complete with every Italian stereotype, got off to a brilliant start when they whacked Nathan Jones just minutes before the start of *WrestleMania XIX*. Unfortunately for the FBI, that's where their highlights stopped.

In the following months, Nunzio, Palumbo & Stamboli fell to the likes of Billy Kidman, Booker T and an up-and-coming John Cena. By the end of 2004, the Italian trio quietly went their separate ways, but left behind a legacy WWE fans would rather "fuhgetabout." When ECW was revived by WWE in 2006, Nunzio briefly teamed again with Tony Mamaluke, with Trinity at their side.

FATAL 4 WAY — June 20 2010

Nassau Veterans Memorial Coliseum; Uniondale, NY

This one-of-a-kind event featured contests where four Superstars battled at one time. The first competitor to score a pinfall is declared the winner of the match, meaning a Champion could lose his or her title without being involved in the pinfall! The Divas Championship, World Heavyweight Championship, and WWE Championship were all on the line, and all three changed hands during the event.

In addition to the three Fatal 4-Way Matches during the night, the Intercontinental and United States Championships were put on the line, though the titles were successfully defended by Kofi Kingston and The Miz, respectively.

FATU 🇦🇸

HT: 6'1" **WT:** 282 lbs. **FROM:** The Isle of Samoa
SIGNATURE MOVE: Monster Splash

TITLE HISTORY

WORLD TAG TEAM CHAMPION	*Partnered with Samu to defeat The Quebecers on April 26, 1994*

First seen by most in the World Class region, Fatu was one half of the Samoan Swat Team with Samu. Under the tutelage of Paul E. Dangerously, they battled the likes of the Midnight Express, Doom, the Road Warriors and the Steiner Brothers as contenders for the WCW Tag Team Championship.

Samu and Fatu debuted in WWE in August 1992 as the feared Headshrinkers. The team reached the top of the mountain in April 1994 when they became World Tag Team Champions. The team disbanded in early 1995, but Fatu returned to WWE months later alone as a positive influence to fans everywhere against villains like Waylon Mercy, British Bulldog, Owen Hart, Hunter Hearst-Helmsley, Vader and King Kong Bundy. By April 1996, Fatu left WWE.

FINLAY

HT: 6'2"   WT: 233 lbs.
FROM: Belfast, Northern Ireland
SIGNATURE MOVE: Celtic Cross

TITLE HISTORY	
UNITED STATES CHAMPION	*Defeated Bobby Lashley on July 14, 2006*

For over 20 years, this third-generation bruiser from Belfast was known throughout Europe and Asia as one of the ring's most brutal competitors. He held 16 major championships before coming to the United States in 1996 as a member of WCW. In January 2006, Finlay debuted on *SmackDown*, and put WWE on notice that he loved to fight. With the help of his shillelagh, Finlay quickly established himself as the most vicious Superstar within the brand.

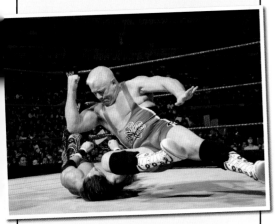

During his first year in WWE, Finlay managed to capture the United States Championship with an assist from Hornswoggle and his shillelagh. Recently, Finlay admitted that he was Hornswoggle's father. In 2008, Finlay and Hornswoggle were drafted into the ranks of ECW and immediately felt at home in the Land of Extreme. The Irish bruiser was a regular in ECW main events and challenged top Superstars like Tommy Dreamer, Christian, The Miz, and Jack Swagger. After a brief tenure on *SmackDown*, Finlay became a producer behind the scenes for WWE. In the spring of 2011, Finlay parted with the company and left his son behind. Personal feelings aside, one thing was certain when you met Finlay in the ring, you were in for the fight of your life!

FISHMAN

HT: 5'8"   WT: 220 lbs.
FROM: Torreon, Coahuila, Mexico

Fans in the United States may not recognize the name Fishman, but the successful Mexican grappler has a history that traces all the way back to the early days of the Light Heavyweight Championship, a period that pre-dates its official recognition by the WWE.

In 1981, WWE entered into a lengthy partnership with the Mexican-based Universal Wrestling Association. As part of the agreement, the UWA was entitled to defend the WWE Light Heavyweight Championship on its cards. In September 1981, the masked Fishman became the second competitor to ever hold the title when he defeated Perro Aguayo.

Fishman held the title for less than a month before losing it back to Aguayo. Five years later, Fishman captured the prestigious title again, this time from Villano III. Ironically, his second reign was also ended by Aguayo.

Fishman also gained great success competing for Empresa Mexicana de Lucha Libre. While there, he captured the Mexican National Welterweight Championship three times and the World Welterweight Championship once.

FLASH FUNK

HT: 5'11"   WT: 243 lbs.   FROM: Philadelphia, Pennsylvania
SIGNATURE MOVE: Funky Flash Splash

This veteran of WCW and ECW made his WWE debut at the 1996 *Survivor Series* as a member of Team Yokozuna. As he made his way to the ring accompanied by the Funkettes, the sell-out Madison Square Garden crowd knew this Superstar was unique. His aerial attacks were felt by many Superstars, including Hunter Hearst-Helmsley, Owen Hart, Mankind and Kane. In the spring of 1998, Flash Funk left WWE and split his time between ECW and Japan. He continued his journeys until 2006, when he briefly returned to WWE. Though he and WWE parted ways again, Flash Funk returned during the *Raw* 15th Anniversary broadcast and competed in the 15 Years of *Raw* Battle Royal.

The funk phenomenon continues to appear all over the world and flawlessly executes his version of the 450 Splash, known as the Funky Flash Splash. His days as a WWE Superstar are fondly remembered as Flash Funk was so funky, he showed everyone how to get up and boogie down!

"FLYIN'" FRED CURRY

HT: 5'11"   WT: 232 lbs.   FROM: Hartford, Connecticut
SIGNATURE MOVE: Dropkick

Trained by his father, "Wild Bull" Curry, "Flyin'" Fred Curry began his in-ring career in the early 1960s. Despite being considerably more mild mannered than his father, Fred spent much of his early years teaming with the elder Curry, who was known for his vicious attitude and wildly bushy eyebrows.

Curry's first taste of gold came with his dad as his tag team partner. In July 1964, the father-son combination topped Kurt & Karl von Stroheim to capture the NWA Texas International Tag Team Championship. They held the titles for two years before losing them back to the von Stroheims.

Over the course of his career, Curry claimed several other regional NWA tag titles with many notable partners, including Bobo Brazil and Fritz Von Erich. The high-flyer was also successful as a singles star. He won both the NWA Texas Junior Heavyweight Championship, as well as the NWA Hawaii Heavyweight Championship, which he claimed from the legendary Gene Kiniski.

F
1960-69
1970-79
1980-89
1990-99
2000-09
2010-

F

2010-
2000-09
1990-99
1980-89
1970-79
1960-69

FLYING NUNS
MEMBERS: Sister Angelica, Mother Smucker   COMBINED WT: 488 lbs.
FROM: A Tibetan order in the Himalayas

Looking to push the envelope for *Shotgun Saturday Night's* debut in January 1997, WWE made the controversial decision to book a male vs. female tag match. The Godwinns fit the bill for the male duo perfectly. The female team, however, was a little suspect. When Sister Angelica and Mother Smucker — collectively known as the Flying Nuns — made their way to the ring, people couldn't help but notice their goatees. Nevertheless, Angelica and Smucker competed in the match, claiming to be nuns from a Tibetan order.

Utilizing a little help from their manager, Brother Love, the Nuns earned the victory over the Godwinns that night. With the win, many assumed a blessed career was in the their future. But just one week after the match, Sister Angelica and Mother Smucker ran afoul of the law and were arrested.

Incidentally, the Headbangers filled in for the Nuns while they were incarcerated. Mosh & Thrasher went on to achieve great success in the tag division, while the Nuns were reportedly shipped back to Tibet.

FRANKIE KAZARIAN 🇺🇸
HT: 6'1"   WT: 210 lbs.   FROM: Anaheim, California

Frankie Kazarian was arrogant. He was abrasive. He was obnoxious. But most of all, Frankie Kazarian was confident. In fact, he was so confident that he billed himself as "the Future" of WWE after only his first match.

With his debut win over Nunzio in his back pocket, the conceited Kazarian looked to make good on his prediction. After wins over Scotty 2 Hotty, Funaki and Danny Doring on *Velocity*, fans were forced to take notice of the talented newcomer.

In August 2005, Kazarian carried his undefeated record into *Velocity* for his toughest challenge to date: Former WWE Tag Team and Cruiserweight Champion Paul London. Kazarian was able to beat London, and fans started to think that the cocky Superstar might be right. He might actually be the future of WWE.

Mysteriously, the undefeated Kazarian disappeared from WWE following his win over London. Despite claiming to be the future, the short-lived Superstar never appeared on *Raw*, *SmackDown* or a pay-per-view event.

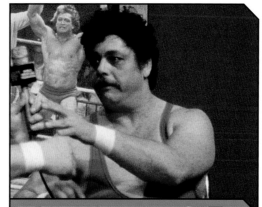

FRANKIE WILLIAMS 🇺🇸
HT: 5'9"   WT: 239 lbs.
FROM: Columbus, Ohio

This rugged competitor from the midwestern United States came to WWE in 1976. In one of his first matches, he took on "Nature Boy" Ric Flair at Madison Square Garden. This set the tone for a career of locking up with some of the greatest individuals in sports-entertainment.

For the next decade, Williams made it tough on opponents like Ken Patera, Baron Von Raschke, Spiros Arion, Ivan Koloff, Bulldog Brower, Nikolai Volkoff, Ernie Ladd and Greg "The Hammer" Valentine. Williams' highest profile battle came in March 1984 when he was a guest on *Piper's Pit* and was attacked by the "Hot Rod." This led to Williams being assaulted by Piper after defending his pride and honor. In 1991, Frankie Williams passed away after a battle with cancer. He will warmly be remembered as a fan favorite who fought with the heart of a lion and never gave up in the ring, no matter who opposed him.

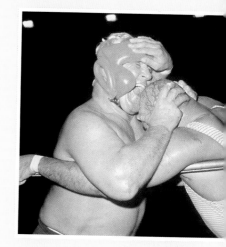

Freddie Blassie was a trusted member of the WWE family for more than 30 years. While the fans loved to hate him, everybody who knew him simply loved him.

Born in February 1918, Blassie grew up in St. Louis, where he initially developed his love for wrestling. After getting his feet wet competing in carnivals, he started working for several Midwest and Northeast promoters. While in the Northeast, he briefly wrestled for Jess McMahon, grandfather of WWE Chairman Vince McMahon.

The Classy Veteran

Blassie's budding wrestling career was temporarily derailed when the United States Navy called him to serve in World War II. After the war, in an attempt to capitalize on his Naval experience, he returned to the ring as "Sailor" Fred Blassie. The sailor persona didn't take off the way Blassie had hoped, as he seemed to garner more boos from the fans than his rule-breaking opponents. In what would prove to be a wise move, Blassie embraced their hatred. He ditched his sailor's cap, dyed his hair blonde and began insulting the fans. The result: "Classy" Freddie Blassie, one of the most hated Superstars of all time.

FREDDIE BLASSIE

HT: 5'10"   **WT: 220 lbs.**   **FROM: St. Louis, Missouri**

The ire Blassie drew from the fans is legendary and may never be duplicated. After being stabbed by angry fans more than 20 times and having acid thrown on him, he was eventually forced to travel with full security forces at all times.

Worldwide Notoriety

Throughout the 1950s, Blassie captured numerous championships while competing in the country's Southeast territories. He moved to Los Angeles in 1960, where he duplicated his success by capturing the World Wrestling Association Heavyweight Championship on four occasions. During this time, Blassie competed in a legendary battle with Japanese wrestler Rikidozan. According to legend, Blassie bloodied Rikidozan so badly that it caused several elderly Japanese fans to suffer heart attacks.

The popularity of the bloodbath earned Blassie an opportunity at Bruno Sammartino's WWE Championship in 1964. Unfortunately, Blassie's penchant for breaking the rules cost him the match. Several years later, he unsuccessfully challenged Pedro Morales for the WWE Championship as well.

Blassie's in-ring career began to slow down by the mid-1970s. Despite not being able to compete in the ring, he yearned to remain a part of the wrestling community. That's when Vincent J. McMahon hired Blassie to be a manager. He spent the next 13 years developing one of the most successful managerial careers in sports-entertainment history.

In September 1977, he guided Mr. Fuji & Professor Tanaka to the World Tag Team Championship. A few years later, he had the distinction of introducing a young Hulk Hogan to WWE audiences. Blassie's greatest success came while managing Iron Sheik. In December 1983, he was in Sheik's corner when the Iranian Superstar ended

Using his infamous cane as a weapon, Blassie lead many great Superstars to WWE prominence.

Bob Backlund's nearly six-year WWE Championship reign. The victory proved to be the biggest of any Blassie protégé.

In March 1985, Blassie became a part of history when he led Nikolai Volkoff & The Iron Sheik to the first-ever title change in *WrestleMania* history. In traditional Blassie fashion, he used his cane to help his duo turn back the U.S. Express for the World Tag Team Championship at the inaugural *WrestleMania*.

The following year, Blassie sold half interest in his stable of Superstars to managing newcomer Slick. Shortly after that, he decided to retire, awarding the "Doctor of Style" full control of his men.

When Blassie hung up his cane for good, the wrestling world lost one of its greatest entertainers. Despite their dislike for him, fans everywhere began to miss the days when legendary "Classy" Freddie Blassie would call them "pencil-neck geeks!"

FRENCHY MARTIN

HT: 6'2"   WT: 240 lbs.   FROM: Quebec City, Quebec
SIGNATURE MOVE: Knee Drop

Frenchy Martin started his in-ring career in 1971 in Quebec and soon traveled west to Stu Hart's Stampede Wrestling. From there, he found success in Puerto Rico and Japan in singles and tag team action. In 1986, Frenchy moved south to WWE.

After success as a competitor, Martin decided to share his wealth of knowledge as a manager, beginning in 1987 with "Canadian Strongman" Dino Bravo. Martin guided Bravo to championship contention and launched an anti-American campaign that revolved around the slogan, "USA Is Not Okay." Frenchy was also known to assist his client with a punch or kick when necessary. As he entered his third decade in sports-entertainment, he changed jobs and became a popular color commentator for WWE's French programming.

Today, Frenchy Martin trains budding Superstars in Canada. He will always remembered as one of sports-entertainment's most dangerous figures.

FRIAR FERGUSON

HT: 6'1"
WT: 385 lbs.

Unlike most men of the cloth, Friar Ferguson enjoyed inflicting pain on people. He loved it so much, in fact, that he oftentimes broke out into dance whenever he felled an opponent. His love for brutality wasn't the only characteristic that set him apart from his fellow religious servants. Unlike most friars, Ferguson completely ignored his vow of poverty, spending staggering amounts of money at the buffet line. At nearly 400 pounds, he was one of the largest Superstars of his time.

After only a few weeks, Ferguson disappeared from WWE, presumably to return to a life of preaching the good word.

FREDDY JOE FLOYD

HT: 6'1"   WT: 235 lbs.
FROM: Bowlegs, Oklahoma

Freddy Joe Floyd was a Southern boy trying to make good in the world of sports-entertainment. When he finally broke into WWE in the mid-1990s, he became an overnight sensation in his small hometown of Bowlegs, Oklahoma. Unfortunately, the admiration of his hometown did not equate to wins for Floyd. Week after week, Bowlegs residents would huddle around a small television only to watch their hero continually fall to the likes of Vader, Billy Gunn and the deranged Mankind.

The unrelenting Floyd kept battling, despite his unimpressive record. His perseverance finally paid off when he scored a count-out victory over Triple H, thanks in large part to interference by Mr. Perfect. When Floyd's singles career failed to take off, he tried his hand at tag team competition. With fellow journeyman Barry Horowitz by his side, the Southerner suffered a similar fate. By mid-1997, he had left WWE to return to Bowlegs.

FULLY LOADED

Fully Loaded was a short-lived annual pay-per-view that began as an *In Your House* event, but was eventually replaced by *Vengeance*.

July 26, 1998
Fresno, CA - Selland Arena

Main Event: Undertaker & Stone Cold Steve Austin defeated World Tag Team Champions Kane & Mankind

July 25, 1999
Buffalo, NY - Marine Midland Arena

Main Event: WWE Champion Stone Cold Steve Austin defeated Undertaker, First Blood Match

July 23, 2000
Dallas, TX - Reunion Arena

Main Event: WWE Champion The Rock defeated Chris Benoit

FUNAKI

HT: 5'7"   WT: 180 lbs.   FROM: Japan
SIGNATURE MOVE: Rising Sun

TITLE HISTORY

CRUISERWEIGHT CHAMPION	Defeated Spike Dudley on December 12, 2004
HARDCORE CHAMPION	1 Time

Funaki made his WWE debut 1998 as part of the hated Japanese faction Kaientai. Shortly after the stable of Superstars disbanded, fans had little choice but to cheer for Funaki, as he brought entire arenas to laughter with just one word – INDEED!

With the fans now by his side, Funaki's career began to build steam. At *WrestleMania 2000*, he managed to pin the monstrous Viscera to capture the Hardcore Championship.

Despite barely understanding a word of English, Funaki was tapped by Stephanie McMahon to become a backstage interviewer in 2002. The Japanese Superstar happily accepted the position and amazingly nicknamed himself "*SmackDown*'s No. 1 Announcer."

Funaki silenced his microphone in late 2004 in an attempt to gain more championship gold. He accomplished his goal when he toppled Spike Dudley at *Armageddon* to capture the Cruiserweight Championship. He held the title for two months before losing it to Chavo Guerrero. In the fall of 2010, he became Kung Fu Naki with a special set of strikes and holds. He took part in the *WrestleMania XXVI* Battle Royal, but left WWE shortly afterward.

THE FUNK BROTHERS

MEMBERS: Terry, Dory, Jimmy Jack
COMBINED WT: 587 lbs.

When it comes to being the roughest, toughest, meanest, and most technically gifted Superstars to compete in the ring, you'll be hard pressed to find many greater than the Funk Brothers. In 1985, Terry and Dory Funk were hired by Jimmy Hart and brought into WWE. The Amarillo ruffians obliged the "Mouth of the South" and administered beatings to dozens of Superstars over the next year, and branded their fallen foes with the Double-Cross Ranch logo.

While the Funks battled the likes of Ricky Steamboat, the British Bulldogs, Hulk Hogan, Pedro Morales and Paul Orndorff, their battles against Junkyard Dog remains one of the most violent times in WWE history and culminated in a tag team match at *WrestleMania 2*.

By summer of 1986, Terry left WWE, while Dory continued to appear briefly alongside younger brother, Jimmy Jack, before returning to the NWA and Japan. In the early 1990s, Terry and Dory appeared in ECW and cemented their iconic status throughout Asia. After more than 40 years captivating audiences, Terry and Dory's magnificent contributions were celebrated when they entered the WWE Hall of Fame in 2009.

FUZZY CUPID

HT: 4'0" **WT:** 86 lbs.
FROM: Newport, Rhode Island

When he was a young adult, Leon Stap took a trip to Texas that would forever change his life. While there, he attended a live wrestling event and immediately became amazed by the level of athleticism displayed by the midget wrestlers. He quickly sought out the show's promoter, asking him how he could get into wrestling. The promoter sent Stap to Detroit for training, and the rest is midget wrestling history.

After learning the ropes, Stap debuted in 1952 as Fuzzy Cupid. Although midget wrestling was extremely popular at this time, Cupid was one of the most unpopular Superstars in his division, as there wasn't a rule he wouldn't break.

Cupid earned his greatest success competing as a tag team with famed midget competitor Sky Low Low. Together, they ruled the Canadian midget tag team scene of the mid-1960s. Cupid & Sky Low Low also engaged in a short but memorable WWE rivalry with Tiny Tim & Pancho Lopez.

GAIL KIM

HT: 5'4" **FROM:** Toronto, Ontario, Canada
SIGNATURE MOVE: Top-Rope Hurricanrana

TITLE HISTORY

WOMEN'S CHAMPION	Defeated Jazz on June 30, 2003

She walked to the ring in sleek, long leather coats and sunglasses. Inside the ring, she used a mix of *lucha libre*, Japanese and Canadian grappling styles along with a variety of unique submission holds that left opponents broken and battered.

After vignettes aired on *Monday Night Raw,* this Maple-Leaf minx burst on the WWE scene and made history in her debut in June 2003. She won the Women's Championship when she bested seven other Divas in an over-the-top rope, Battle Royal. Gail lost the belt to the persistent Molly Holly one month later on *Raw*.

She spent the majority of the next year trying to regain the title, but was unsuccesful.

Gail briefly left WWE and returned in 2009. She became an immediate contender for the Divas Championship. During that time she grew close with Daniel Bryan, but their relationship did not sit well with his managers, the Bella Twins, which resulted in frequent confrontations between the women. Despite her best efforts, Gail was unable to reach her championship goals before parting with the company again in 2011.

GAMA SINGH

HT: 5'10" **WT:** 225 lbs.
FROM: Punjabi, India
SIGNATURE MOVE: Camel Clutch

Born in India, Gama Singh never fully achieved a solid reputation in the United States. He did, however, become a major draw for WWE during the promotion's international tours of the early-to-mid 1980s. Wrestling fans in such places as Australia, Kuwait, and Dubai came out in droves every time Singh was advertised to compete. His chief competition during this time was Roddy Piper.

He also had many memorable battles with Don Muraco and "Cowboy" Bob Orton. When not competing in WWE, Singh became very successful working for Stu Hart's Stampede Wrestling in Calgary.

DAVID HEATH (KNOWN IN WWE AS GANGREL)

HT: 6'1" **WT: 250 lbs.** **FROM: The Other Side of Darkness** **SIGNATURE MOVE: Blood Bath**

Being elevated through a ring of fire, David Heath, known as Gangrel in WWE, had one of the most ominous entrances ever. Once he hit the ring, the fang-toothed Superstar would sip from his medieval goblet and spew a blood-colored liquid into the crowd.

Despite targeting many of WWE's fan favorites, Gangrel's vampire-like appearance actually became appealing to many fans. Within weeks of his 1998 debut, he had acquired a strong cult following. His popularity grew even greater after forming an alliance with Edge & Christian.

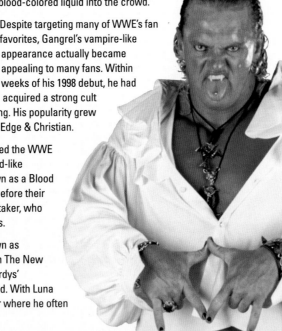

Known as The Brood, the goth trio vandalized the WWE roster, oftentimes soaking them with a blood-like substance. The event, which became known as a Blood Bath, struck fear into many. It wasn't long before their demonic behavior caught the eye of Undertaker, who recruited them into his Ministry of Darkness.

In August 1999, David Heath, formerly known as Gangrel, turned on Edge & Christian to form The New Brood with the Hardy Boys. Despite the Hardys' superior talent, the new union quickly fizzled. With Luna Vachon, he then set out on a singles career where he often appeared on *Heat* and *Jakked*.

GARY MICHAEL CAPETTA

As a child, Gary Michael Cappetta admired the work of ring announcers such as Jimmy Lennon, Sr., Buddy Wagner and "Friendly" Bob Freed. At a WWE show in 1974, Cappetta volunteered to be the ring announcer that evening and once his voice traveled through the arena, WWE knew they had their man for events in the New Jersey, Delaware and Pennsylvania areas.

The advent of cable television and home video resulted in Cappetta being the first wrestling ring announcer who enjoyed an international following. He continued to announce the biggest matches in the world until his departure from WWE in 1985. In 1989, he accepted an offer from WCW and appeared at all their major events. Since he was fluent in Spanish, Gary also commentated on WCW's Spanish telecasts before retiring in May 1995.

Capetta became a teacher, but still followed the industry he loved. He began work on his personal reflections from experiences in sports-entertainment and penned the autobiography *Bodyslams: Memoirs of a Wrestling Pitchman* to critical and commercial acclaim. The response was so great Cappetta adapted the work to a one-man stage show titled *Bodyslams & Beyond*.

GAVIN SPEARS

HT: 6'3" **WT: 225 lbs.** **FROM: Niagara Falls, Ontario, Canada**
SIGNATURE MOVE: Running Death Valley Driver

This Superstar is a man on a mission to prove he is the next in a long line of distinguished grapplers from the Great White North. Gavin Spears is accustomed to being the best at whatever endeavors he pursues. A top hockey player for over a decade, Spears decided to leave the rink and enter the ring following boyhood idols like "Ravishing" Rick Rude, "The Model" Rick Martel, Mr. Perfect and "Nature Boy" Ric Flair.

In August 2008, Spears debuted in WWE and announced he was the "Crown jewel of ECW's New Superstar Initiative." Spears enouraged others to study him to learn what wrestling was really about. While his claims were great, and the matches he had with the likes of Tommy Dreamer, Finlay, and Super Crazy were solid efforts, Spears' time in ECW did not pan out the way he had expected.

GENE KINISKI

HT: 6'4" **WT: 270 lbs.** **FROM: Edmonton, Alberta, Canada**
SIGNATURE MOVE: Backbreaker

One of the greatest athletes to ever come out of Canada, Gene Kiniski excelled in the Canadian Football League before turning down National Football League offers, choosing instead a life in the ring. Armed with the training he received from Tony Morelli and the legendary Dory Funk, Sr., Kiniski debuted in 1953. Within two years, he was challenging Lou Thesz for the NWA Championship. Still relatively green, Kiniski failed to wrest the title away from Thesz, but the two Superstars would meet again more than 10 years later.

TITLE HISTORY	
UNITED STATES TAG TEAM CHAMPION	*Partnered with Waldo Von Erich to defeat Dr. Jerry & Luke Graham on February 4, 1965*

In 1961, Kiniski defeated Verne Gagne to capture the AWA Championship. The victory gave him his first World title and opened the doors to several WWE Championship opportunities against Bruno Sammartino. At one point in 1964, Kiniski actually believed he defeated Sammartino for the title and left Madison Square Garden with the WWE Championship belt. Kiniski, though not the rightful champion, kept the title in his possession for nearly one month before losing to Sammartino in a rematch.

More than a decade after failing in his initial attempts to gain the NWA Championship, Kiniski beat the legendary Thesz for the title in January 1966. He held the championship for more than three years before being upended by Dory Funk, Jr. At the time of his defeat, Kiniski owned the second longest reign in NWA history, thus proving himself as one of the greatest competitors of all time.

GENE OKERLUND

"Mean" Gene Okerlund is arguably the most recognizable interviewer in the history of the ring. Over the course of his 30 years in wrestling, his pull-no-punches approach to interviewing resulted in revealing answers from the game's greatest, including Andre the Giant, Ric Flair and Hulk Hogan.

Okerlund's first big break came in the early 1970s, when he was tapped to serve as a temporary interviewer in the AWA. His line of questioning, however, was so impressive that he soon earned a full-time role behind the mic. While there, he interviewed many future WWE stars, such as Hulk Hogan and Bobby Heenan. It was during this period when Jesse Ventura gave him the moniker, "Mean" Gene, which took root and lasts to this day.

In 1984, Okerlund made the jump to WWE. It's here that he proved his esteemed place in ring lore. He also proved to be quite the vocalist, as it was his singing of the national anthem that kicked off the inaugural *WrestleMania*.

After nine years of asking WWE Superstars the tough questions, Okerlund headed to WCW in 1993. As a member of WCW's announce team, he served as the promotion's backstage interviewer during the height of the Monday Night Wars.

In April 2006, Okerlund was recognized as one of the greatest voices in WWE history when he was inducted into the WWE Hall of Fame by his close friend Hulk Hogan.

GENERAL ADNAN

HT: 6'0" **WT: 245 lbs.** **FROM: Iraq**

With the Gulf War foremost in the mind of every American, Iraqi sympathizer Sgt. Slaughter introduced WWE audiences to General Adnan in 1991. Striking an eerie resemblance to Saddam Hussein, Adnan was brought in to serve as Sgt. Slaughter's commanding officer. According to Slaughter, Adnan was a great military mind from a great military power, Iraq.

The defining moment of Adnan's WWE career saw the Iraqi holding a Hulk Hogan T-shirt while Sgt. Slaughter set it on fire. The blaze incited fans nationwide, as they recognized the Hulkster as the definitive American hero. In the ultimate sign of disrespect, Adnan simply laughed as the shirt went up in flames.

In addition to acting as manager, Adnan also competed in the ring alongside Col. Mustafa and Slaughter. Known as The Triangle of Terror, Adnan, Mustafa, and Slaughter headlined *SummerSlam 1991* when they battled Hulk Hogan & Ultimate Warrior. Dubbed "A Match Made in Hell", Hogan & Warrior turned back The Triangle in a thrilling main event. Afterward, Adnan & Mustafa publicly blamed Slaughter for the loss, marking the official end of The Triangle.

GENICHIRO TENRYU

HT: 6'1" **WT: 260 lbs.** **FROM: Katsuyama City, Japan**
SIGNATURE MOVE: Northern Lights Bomb

Genichiro Tenryu was a renowned sumo wrestler before he embarked on his career in sports-entertainment. In the early 1990s, Tenryu made several WWE appearances. His first official showing was at *WrestleMania VII* when he and partner Koji Katao demolished Demolition in less than five minutes. The next battle was in his homeland during the SWS/WWE series of co-promoted supershows. On the first night, he pinned Randy "Macho Man" Savage in front of a capacity Tokyo Dome crowd. One week later, he joined forces with Hulk Hogan in a battle against the Legion of Doom.

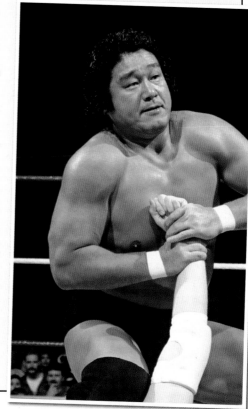

Tenryu competed in the 1993 and 1994 *Royal Rumble* before returning to his homeland. Genichiro Tenryu is regarded as one of the best competitors to emerge from Japan and is among a small group of men in the history of *puroresu* to hold pinfall victories over both Antonio Inoki and Shohei "Giant" Baba.

G

2010-
2000-09
1990-99
1980-89
1970-79
1960-69

"GENTLEMAN" JERRY VALIANT 🇺🇸

HT: 6'0" **FROM:** New York City, New York
SIGNATURE MOVE: Sleeper

TITLE HISTORY

WORLD TAG TEAM CHAMPION	Partnered with Johnny Valiant to defeat Tony Garea & Larry Zbyszko on March 6, 1979

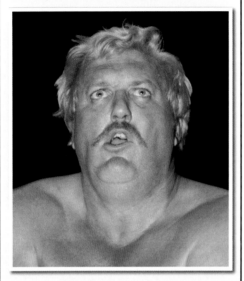

"Gentleman" Jerry Valiant debuted in February 1979 as the third brother of the famous Valiant family. Often accompanied to the ring by brother Jimmy and managed by Capt. Lou Albano, the "Gentleman" was dangerous on his own or teaming with his brothers. The Valiants were so hated that fans often attacked them before, during and after their matches. Often, they had great trouble leaving the venue at which they appeared.

One month into his WWE tenure, Jerry and brother Johhny bested Tony Garea & Larry Zbyszko to etch the Valiant name in the annuls of the WWE as World Tag Team Champions. They held the titles for more than seven months before losing them to Tito Santana & Ivan Putski. In 1980, the Valiants went their own way in the world of sports-entertainment. The big city slicker returned to WWE in singles action in 1983 and remained a despised Superstar until he departed from the company in 1986.

GEORGE SOUTH 🇺🇸

HT: 6'2" **WT:** 240 lbs. **FROM:** Atlanta, Georgia
SIGNATURE MOVE: The Claw Hold

A fixture of Jim Crockett Promotions in the early and mid 1980s, George South later plied his trade in the World Wrestling Federation and continued his rule-breaking ways against opponents like Ricky "The Dragon" Steamboat, The British Bulldogs, Koko B. Ware, Jake "The Snake" Roberts, and future WWE Hall of Famers including Tito Santana and the Junkyard Dog.

Today, George appears on the independent circuit and has his own wrestling school training prospective stars of tomorrow. Regardless of the year, fans never know when he's going to step through the ropes and bring an opponent to his limit.

GEORGE "THE ANIMAL" STEELE

Since its inception in 1963, WWE has been home to some of the most bizarre individuals to walk the earth. However, no one has proved to be more peculiar than WWE Hall of Famer George "The Animal" Steele. With his hirsute body, green tongue, and voracious appetite for turnbuckles, Steele's vicious assaults made him of one professional wrestling's most despised figures.

In the summer of 1968, this uncontrollable maniac debuted in WWE. To the horror of audiences, Steele attacked the likes of Eduard Carpentier, "Golden Boy" Arnold Skaaland, High Chief Peter Maivia and Chief Jay Strongbow. "The Animal's" most violent rivalry was with WWE Champion Bruno Sammartino. Steele stopped at nothing to maim the champion and rip away the prized title from him. No type of match settled the war as the two collided in Lumberjack, Stretcher, and Steel Cage matches and further, their Texas Death Match had to be officiated by boxing legend Joe Louis. For the entire decade "The Animal" was one of the most serious threats to the championship reigns of Sammartino, Pedro Morales, and Bob Backlund. Though his unorthodox behavior and bizarre outbursts frightened those around him, his Flying Hammerlock was a feared submission hold and could break an opponent's arm or separate a shoulder within seconds.

Steele's multitude of illegal tactics included unending biting fits, blatant chokes, scratching, clawing, and eye-rakes. George was also dubbed "The Master of the Foreign Object" as he had a propensity of hiding a foreign object somewhere on his person and accosted his opponents when the referee's attention was diverted. During this terror-filled time in history, Steele was guided by "Classy" Freddie Blassie, the Grand Wizard, Mr. Fuji,

and "Luscious" Johnny Valiant. George surprised the world in 1984 when he returned to WWE. After being abandoned by partners Iron Sheik and Nikolai Volkoff on *Saturday Night's Main Event*, Steele heard roars from the crowd alongside a re-hired Capt. Lou Albano. Despite being as unpredictable as ever, he became one of wrestling's most beloved figures.

HT: 6'1" WT: 275 lbs. FROM: Detroit, Michigan
SIGNATURE MOVE: The Flying Hammerlock

Green Tongue-tied in Love

In 1986 "The Animal" was in the middle of an intense, yet puzzling love triangle with then-Intercontinental Champion Randy "Macho Man" Savage and his manager, the lovely Miss Elizabeth. Steele and Savage clashed at *WrestleMania 2* and continued their violent encounters throughout WWE in a classic tale of "Beauty and The Beast." Instead of winning championship gold, George was more focused on carrying Miss Elizabeth in his arms and spending time with her. "The Animal" remained a nuisance to the "Macho Man" at *WrestleMania III* when he helped Ricky Steamboat beat Savage for the Intercontinental Championship. George continued to rip turnbuckles and opponents into the latter part of the 1980s. To add to his already perplexing persona, George was joined at ringside by friend and confidant, the puppet known as "Mine." Soon after, Steele disappeared from the WWE.

In 1994, George invaded Hollywood when he debuted in acclaimed director Tim Burton's Oscar-winning film, *Ed Wood*. Then, in typical "Animal" fashion, George astonished fans when he returned to WWE during the "Attitude Era" as a member of The Oddities.

The lore of George Steele becomes greater as time goes on. He is one of the most adored characters in the history of professional wrestling and an individual who entertained legions of fans wherever he went. What was truly remarkable about his legendary career was once eyes were on him, audiences were captivated

In 1995, George Steele's 40-year career and countless contributions were celebrated as he was inducted into the WWE Hall of Fame.

by him, and he didn't have to say one word. The wrestling world was never the same upon his entry or exit, and he'll always be one of the ring's most unique figures.

GEORGE WELLS
HT: 6'3" WT: 243 lbs. FROM: Oakland, California

An accomplished football player, George Wells was drafted by the Dallas Cowboys before taking his game to the Canadian Football League. After nearly a decade on the gridiron, he entered the wrestling arena, where he would later become famous for his run-in with Jake Roberts' famous snake.

After Roberts defeated Wells at *WrestleMania 2*, Jake's snake wrapped itself around the former football player's neck. The force of the attack caused Wells to foam from the mouth and fans worldwide to hide their eyes in fear. Wells' brief stay in WWE ended quickly after.

GIANT GONZALES
HT: 8'0" WT: 460 lbs. FROM: Argentina
SIGNATURE MOVE: Chokeslam

At a towering 8-feet tall, Giant Gonzales was one of the most impressive individuals to ever step foot in a WWE ring. Making his debut in January 1993, he immediately set his sights on Undertaker, eliminating him from the *Royal Rumble*. The move laid the foundation for a rivalry that lasted the entire length of Gonzales' WWE career.

At *WrestleMania IX*, the bitter feelings between the two giants nearly came to a premature end when Gonzales attacked Undertaker with a cloth soaked in chloroform. With Undertaker rendered motionless, many onlookers began to fear the worst. Miraculously, however, Undertaker rose to his feet and cleared the ring of his nemesis.

Following his assault on Undertaker, Gonzales tried to finish the job at *SummerSlam 1993* when he battled the "Deadman" in a Rest in Peace Match. Like *WrestleMania*, however, the result favored Undertaker. After the match, a frustrated Gonzales hit his smarmy manager, Harvey Wippleman, with his signature chokeslam. The attack immediately put the giant in the good graces of the fans. He didn't have long to enjoy it, though, as Gonzales was gone from WWE soon thereafter.

G

2010-

2000-09

1990-99

1980-89

1970-79

1960-69

GILLBERG

HT: 6'0"   WT: 227 lbs.   FROM: Atlanta, Georgia
SIGNATURE MOVE: The Jackhammer

TITLE HISTORY

| LIGHT HEAVYWEIGHT CHAMPION | Defeated Christian on November 19, 1998 |

The thunderous music, the blinding pyrotechnics, the remarkable physique, the tribal body art, and sports-entertainment's most incredible streak must mean only one Superstar is on the way to the ring: Gillberg! The only thing he has on his mind is "Who's first?"

This parody-phenom exploded onto the WWE scene during the height of the Monday Night Wars. While he started as a playful poke at then-WCW Champion, Goldberg, Gillberg soon shocked the world when he defeated Christian for the WWE Light Heavyweight Championship, a title he kept for nearly 15 months. Along the way, he joined forces with the vaunted J.O.B. Squad, who also doubled as his pyrotechnicians.

While Gillberg's appearances have dwindled in recent years, he still pops up from time to time, most recently during Raw's 15th Anniversary special, when he was quickly eliminated from a Battle Royal.

GINO BRITO

HT: 5'10"   WT: 240 lbs.
FROM: Montreal, Quebec, Canada

Prior to competing in the ring, Gino Brito worked for his father, promoter Jack Britton, in Montreal. Brito was responsible for escorting his family's famous stable of midget wrestlers from town to town. Once he became old enough, the fiery Italian Superstar hit the ring, teaming with best friend Tony Parisi.

Brito also competed under the name Louis Cerdan in the World Wide Wrestling Federation. With Parisi as his partner, Cerdan defeated The Blackjacks for the World Tag Team Championship in November 1975.

THE GLAMOUR GIRLS

MEMBERS: Judy Martin, Leilani Kai
COMBINED WT: 286 lbs.

TITLE HISTORY

| WOMEN'S TAG TEAM CHAMPIONS (2 TIMES) | Defeated Velvet McIntyre & Desiree Peterson on August 15, 1985
Defeated Jumping Bomb Angels on June 8, 1988 |

With long blonde hair and glittery gold tights, Judy Martin & Leilani Kai claimed to bring glamour to the Women's Division in the mid-to-late 1980s. They also brought winning. The egotistical duo, appropriately named The Glamour Girls, will be remembered as the only two-time WWE Women's Tag Team Champions.

Martin & Kai picked up their first tag titles in August 1985 at the expense of Velvet McIntyre & Desiree Peterson. With manager Jimmy Hart leading the way, The Glamour Girls held a firm grasp on the gold until January 1988 when the Jumping Bomb Angels upset them at the inaugural Royal Rumble.

After reclaiming the titles from the Jumping Bomb Angels in Japan, Martin & Kai returned to the United States, where they successfully defended the titles until the titles became defunct in 1989.

THE GOBBLEDY GOOKER

At the 1990 Survivor Series, a giant egg sat outside the Hartford Civic Center. "Mean" Gene Okerlund was determined to find out what was waiting inside. The weeks of speculation ended when the egg hatched and the Gobbledy Gooker emerged. Once in the ring, this agile cross between a human and a turkey shook a leg with dance moves, forward rolls and flips over the ropes.

The Gobbledy Gooker quietly vanished after its initial appearance, but just when the world thought it was safe from this avian anomaly, the Goobledy Gooker's feathered fury appeared at WrestleMania X-Seven's Gimmick Battle Royal. Unfortuantely, it was among the first contestants eliminated.

THE GODFATHER

HT: 6'6"   WT: 320 lbs.   FROM: The Red Light District
SIGNATURE MOVE: Pimp Drop, Ho Train

TITLE HISTORY

INTERCONTINENTAL CHAMPION	Defeated Goldust on April 12, 1999
WORLD TAG TEAM CHAMPION	Partnered with Bull Buchanan to defeat The Hardy Boys on November 6, 2000

WWE's popular "Attitude" Era was defined by the promotion's persistence to push the envelope. During this time, and while many Superstars were controversial, no Superstar ruffled more feathers than The Godfather.

A noted pimp, The Godfather was accompanied to the ring by a long line of scantily clad women he affectionately referred to as his "Ho Train." Despite being surrounded by miles of shapely curves, he somehow was under the impression that "pimpin' ain't easy."

In the ring, the normally fun-loving Superstar was all business. He defeated the likes of Faarooq, Marc Mero and Viscera on his way to becoming a legitimate threat to the Intercontinental Championship, which he captured when he defeated Goldust in April 1999. He went on to defend the title for six weeks before Jeff Jarrett upended him on an episode of *Raw*.

The Godfather's "Ho Train" was briefly derailed when he joined Steven Richards' Right to Censor crusade in 2000. While he did manage to claim the World Tag Team Championship under the RTC banner, fans couldn't come to grips with a WWE sans their favorite pimp. Luckily for everybody, The Godfather came to his senses and once again began keeping company with his lovely ladies in 2002.

THE GODWINNS 🇺🇸

MEMBERS: Phineas I., Henry O.   COMBINED WT: 576 lbs.
FROM: Bitters, Arkansas

TITLE HISTORY

WORLD TAG TEAM CHAMPIONS (2 TIMES)	Defeated The Bodydonnas on May 19, 1996 Defeated The Headbangers on October 5, 1997

These hog farmers brought their bucket of slop to WWE from Arkansas in the mid-1990s. Managed by Hillbilly Jim, Phineas and Henry brought the fighting style from the back of the barn into the ring. The good ol' boys scuffled with the likes of the Bodydonnas, the Smokin' Gunns and the New Rockers, and finished off opponents with the Slop Drop.

In April 1996, they became World Tag Team Champions, but their reign lasted a single week. During a match against the Legion of Doom, Henry was hit with a Doomsday Device, which resulted in a serious injury. That incident sparked a new attitude in the Godwinns. They dismissed Hillbilly Jim and attacked opponents with slop buckets. At *In Your House: Badd Blood* they defeated the Headbangers for a second run with the World Tag Team Championship, but fell two days later to Hawk & Animal.

Despite two titles reigns that were among the shortest in WWE history, the Godwinns are remembered for bringing their unique style to matches.

GOLDBERG 🇺🇸

HT: 6'4"   WT: 285 lbs.
FROM: Atlanta, Georgia
SIGNATURE MOVE: Jackhammer

A former member of the NFL's Atlanta Falcons, Goldberg turned to professional wrestling in 1997. What followed was the single most impressive rookie campaign in sports-entertainment history. With no experience and limited ability, Goldberg used his immense size to rack up an improbable 173-0 record. With each passing victory, the newcomer confidently questioned, "Who's next?"

TITLE HISTORY

WORLD HEAVYWEIGHT CHAMPION	Defeated Triple H on September 21, 2003

Goldberg's early WCW days saw him pick up wins over seasoned veterans such as Raven and Perry Saturn. It wasn't long before his impressive Jackhammer finisher started shooting him up the rankings. By the end of his first year in sports-entertainment, the undefeated Goldberg had captured the prestigious United States Championship.

Goldberg put his unbelievable streak on the line against Hollywood Hogan's WCW Championship on a July 1998 edition of *WCW Monday Nitro*. The dream continued for Goldberg that night, as he defeated the legendary Hulkster for the title. He went on to defend the championship for five months before losing both the title and his undefeated streak to Kevin Nash at *Starrcade 1998*.

WWE fans finally got their first glimpse of Goldberg when he made his highly anticipated debut with the company in March 2003. Much like his early days in WCW, his impact was immediate. The Rock, Chris Jericho, and Christian were just a few of the high-profile names that fell to Goldberg.

By July, Goldberg had his sights set on claiming the World Heavyweight Championship. Unlike his first WCW Championship victory, however, then-champion Triple H wasn't going to go down easy. To ensure he would continue to hold the gold, "The Game" had his Evolution stablemates watching his back.

After a few failed attempts at getting through Evolution, Goldberg put his career on the line against Triple H's title at *Unforgiven 2003*. In the end, it was Goldberg who walked away with the title. Unfortunately for the new champion, he failed to recreate the same magic he made while holding the WCW Championship. In his final match of what many might term a disappointing WWE career, Goldberg defeated Brock Lesnar at *WrestleMania XX*. Afterwards, guest referee Stone Cold Steve Austin delivered Stunners to both Goldberg and Lesnar.

THE GOLDEN TERROR

Despite the mystery surrounding The Golden Terror's career, records can accurately prove that he competed during the 1960s. He had a brief WWE stay that saw him fall to WWE Champion Bruno Sammartino on several different occasions. In addition to Sammartino, The Golden Terror's unimpressive won-loss record was also marred by Arnold Skaaland, Bobo Brazil, and Chief Wahoo McDaniel, among others.

After competing in WWE, The Golden Terror moved his mysterious mat game to Georgia where he formed regular tag teams with Butcher Vachon and George Harris. According to record books, The Golden Terror's time in Georgia was equally unsuccessful as his WWE days.

GOLDUST

HT: 6'6" **WT:** 260 lbs. **FROM:** Hollywood, California
SIGNATURE MOVE: Curtain Call

TITLE HISTORY

HARDCORE CHAMPION	*7 Times*
INTERCONTINENTAL CHAMPION (3 TIMES)	*Defeated Razor Ramon on January 21, 1996* *Defeated Savio Vega on April 1, 1996* *Defeated Road Dogg on March 29, 1999*
WORLD TAG TEAM CHAMPION	*Partnered with Booker T to defeat Christian & Chris Jericho on December 15, 2002*

Dressed in gold from head to toe, Goldust resembled an award statue more than he did a WWE Superstar, which is fitting considering his one-time fondness for quoting classic movies. What he loved more than the silver screen was a good game of psychological warfare. Playing off the homophobic fears of opponents, Goldust oftentimes made suggestive advances toward his foes, leaving them vulnerable for him to land his signature Curtain Call finisher.

While Goldust's showmanship was unparalleled, his in-ring skills were even greater. After all, he is the son of the great Dusty Rhodes. Within months of his debut, Goldust used his natural ability, as well as some mind games, to defeat Razor Ramon for the Intercontinental Championship. It was his first of three reigns with the prestigious title.

In late 1997, a confused Goldust left his "director" Marlena to become an even more bizarre Superstar referred to as The Artist Formerly Known as Goldust. With Luna Vachon by his side, he engaged in a brief rivalry with Marc Mero and Sable before finally coming to his senses and returning to the Goldust persona. Back in gold, Goldust spent the next several years struggling to regain the greatness of his early WWE days. In 2002, he finally returned to championship form when he teamed with Booker T to capture the World Tag Team Championship.

Since his 2008 return, this master of mind games is as active as ever. His autobiography *Cross Rhodes: Goldust, Out of the Darkness* was released, he enjoyed a televised wedding, and resumed the Rhodes/DiBiase family rivalry over the Million Dollar Championship.

Some fans may only recognize Gorilla Monsoon by the legendary words he spoke while announcing WWE action during the 1980s and 1990s. Lines such as "he's unloading the heavy artillery" and "the irresistible force meets the immovable object" made him a lovable legend, but it was his brute force in the ring decades prior that made him one of the most hated Superstars of his time.

Before entering the pro ranks, Gorilla Monsoon excelled as an amateur wrestler at Ithaca University. In fact, his accomplishments landed him induction into the school's Athletic Hall of Fame in 1973. After a successful collegiate career, Monsoon made the leap to the pros, defeating Pauncho Lopez in his 1959 debut. From that moment, it was clear the oversized savage would be a force to be reckoned with in the ring.

WWE Title Runs

In November 1963, Monsoon claimed his first WWE title when he teamed with Killer Kowalski to wrest the United States Tag Team Championship from Skull Murphy & Brute Bernard. Just days after the victory, Monsoon challenged Bruno Sammartino for the WWE Championship at Madison Square Garden. The now-famous encounter went to a 90-minute draw. Both Superstars later cited the match as the toughest of their respective careers.

The rule-breaking tandem of Monsoon & Kowalski lost their tag titles to the Tolos Brothers in December 1963. Monsoon eventually reclaimed gold, however, when he teamed with Bill Watts to defeat Gene Kiniski & Waldo Von Erich in April 1965.

GOON

HT: 6'1" **WT:** 250 lbs.
FROM: Duluth, Minnesota

Extended stays in the penalty box for slashing and high-sticking deemed the Goon too rough for the sport of hockey. After getting kicked off every team he played for, he finally took his brutal style of competition to the one place that welcomed rough-housing: WWE.

Clad in a complete hockey uniform, including skate-like boots, the Goon used hockey-style checks to put his opponents on ice. At *WrestleMania X-Seven*, he competed in the biggest match of his career when he participated in the famed Gimmick Battle Royal. Six years later, he returned to WWE to be a part of another Battle Royal during *Raw's* 15th Anniversary Special.

GORILLA MONSOON

HT: 6'7" WT: 401 lbs.

TITLE HISTORY

UNITED STATES TAG TEAM CHAMPION (2 TIMES)	Partnered with Killer Kowalski to defeat Skull Murphy & Brute Bernard on November 14, 1963 Partnered with Bill Watts to defeat Gene Kiniski & Waldo Von Erich on April 6, 1965

On a fateful night in 1969, Monsoon made the unlikely transition to one of wrestling's most-beloved figures when he found himself on the receiving end of a brutal attack at the hands of the hated Sheik. Former rival Bruno Sammartino ran to Monsoon's aid, signifying to the crowd that it was acceptable to cheer for the big man. As a fan favorite, Monsoon spent the rest of his legendary career battling the likes of "Superstar" Billy Graham and Ernie Ladd.

The most highly publicized event of Monsoon's career took place in 1976 when an arrogant Muhammad Ali tried to steal the spotlight from the wrestling action in the ring. Upset with the antics, Monsoon lifted Ali up into his signature airplane spin and dropped him to the ground. The move was front-page news across the nation.

In later years, Monsoon formed one of history's most popular announcing tandems when he teamed with Bobby Heenan.

A New Life Just Outside the Ring

After more than 20 years in the ring, Monsoon's competitive career came to an end when he lost a Retirement Match to Ken Patera in 1980. While the loss marked the end of a successful in-ring career for Monsoon, it also sparked the beginning of the next chapter of the big man's legendary story.

In 1982, WWE's new owner Vince McMahon (who actually bought a fraction of the company from Monsoon, among others) put the retired Superstar behind the announcers' table. In the years that followed, Monsoon's voice became synonymous with WWE's biggest matches. In addition to calling the action at the first-ever *WrestleMania*, Monsoon and his partner Jesse "The Body" Ventura were behind the mic for the epic *WresltleMania III* encounter between Andre the Giant and Hulk Hogan.

In 1994, Monsoon received the ultimate honor when he was inducted into the WWE Hall of Fame. However, unlike most Hall of Famers, he didn't retreat back into retirement. Monsoon stayed active behind the microphone before finally elevating his status to that of WWE President, a role he held for two years.

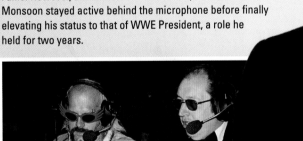

Monsoon made his final WWE appearance in 1999 when he served as a ringside judge as boxer Butterbean battled Bart Gunn in a Brawl For All Match at *WrestleMania XV*. The emotional ovation he received by the WWE fans in Philadelphia that night capped off an amazing career that may never be duplicated.

Robert "Gorilla Monsoon" Marella passed away later that year at the age of 62. He will forever be remembered as a true gentle giant who did it all in the world of sports-entertainment.

GRAN HAMADA

HT: 5'6" WT: 202 lbs.
FROM: Maebashi, Gunma, Japan

Gran Hamada has the great honor of being one-half of the only WWE Intercontinental Tag Team Champions. While competing in the Japanese-based Universal Wrestling Federation, Hamada and partner Perro Aguayo were awarded the titles in January 1991. As part of a working agreement with WWE, the UWF was empowered to defend the new tag titles on its cards. Unfortunately for Hamada & Aguayo, however, WWE and the UWF ended their relationship shortly after the titles were created. As a result, the Intercontinental Tag Team Championship was abandoned.

Hamada's Intercontinental Tag Team title reign was not the first time he benefited from a WWE international working agreement. In 1982, while competing for Mexico's Universal Wrestling Association, Hamada defeated Aguayo for the now-defunct WWE Light Heavyweight Championship. He repeated the act two years later to become a two-time Light Heavyweight Champion.

Hamada is hoping to become the patriarch of a long line of sports-entertainers. His daughters, Xochitl and Ayako, are also in the business.

G

1960-69
1970-79
1980-89
1990-99
2000-09
2010-

G

2010-
2000-09
1990-99
1980-89
1970-79
1960-69

GRAND MASTER SEXAY

 HT: 5'10" **WT:** 222 lbs. **FROM:** Memphis, Tennessee
SIGNATURE MOVE: Hip Hop Drop

TITLE HISTORY

WORLD TAG TEAM CHAMPION	*Partnered with Scotty Too Hotty to defeat Edge & Christian on May 29, 2000*

With their whacky ring gear and crazy dance routines, Grand Master Sexay and Scotty Too Hotty became one of WWE's most popular tag teams of the late 1990s and early 2000s.

Collectively known as Too Cool, the over-the-top tandem proved they were more than just two colorful cartoon-like characters when they defeated Edge and Christian for the World Tag Team Championship in May 2000. That same year, they also competed on the *WrestleMania 2000* card, where they teamed with Chyna to defeat The Radicalz in a Six-Person Intergender Tag Team Match.

Prior to teaming with Scotty Too Hotty, Grand Master Sexay was also known as Brian Christopher. Competing as Christopher, the dynamic Superstar reached the finals of the 1997 Light Heavyweight Championship tournament, where he ultimately fell to Taka Michinoku.

Following his release in 2001, Christopher made a handful of appearances on WWE television. His most notable return came in March 2011, where he verbally humiliated his father, Jerry "The King" Lawler, heading into the Hall of Famer's *WrestleMania* match with Michael Cole.

GRAND WIZARD

HALL OF FAME 1995

As a radio disc jockey in the 1960s, the Grand Wizard flipped phrases with the speed of an auctioneer and the eloquence of a beat poet. His sports-entertainment career began in Detroit's "Big Time Wrestling" promotion as he managed The Sheik. He became one of the first managers to physically insert himself into contests on his client's behalf.

Clad in a mish-mash of spangled attire, including a turban and wrap-around sunglasses, the Grand Wizard ominously walked to the ring with the presence of a giant. The mere sight of this man incited near riots throughout the northeastern United States. He possessed a vocabulary like no other and frightened all who listened to him. He could weave words into images of destruction, punctuated by the pain delivered by the ruthless men in his employ.

He made an instant impact on the WWE as his first protégé, Stan "The Man" Stasiak ended the historic WWE Championship reign of Pedro Morales in 1973. The Wizard put professional wrestling's richest prize around the waist of another one of his henchman in 1977 when "Superstar" Billy Graham defeated Sammartino. He also managed greats such as Pat Patterson, Ken Patera, and the Magnificent Muraco to the Intercontinental Championship.

He guided other notable figures, including Killer Kowalski, Mr. Fuji, "Big Cat" Ernie Ladd, Greg "The Hammer" Valentine, and "Cowboy" Bob Orton. He often conspired with "Classy" Freddie Blassie and Capt. Lou Albano to rid WWE of its greatest heroes. The Grand Wizard was always quick to remind the public, "It's hard to be humble when you're great!"

Sadly, on Oct. 12, 1983, this innovative sports-entertainment figure died after a heart attack. The Grand Wizard's immeasurable influence on the world of professional wrestling was finally put into perspective when he was posthumously inducted in the WWE Hall of Fame in 1995.

THE GREAT AMERICAN BASH

June 27, 2004
Norfolk, VA - Norfolk Scope

Main Event Undertaker defeated The Dudley Boys in a Concrete Crypt Handicap Match

July 24, 2005
Buffalo, NY - HSBC Arena

Main Event JBL defeated World Heavyweight Champion Batista

July 23, 2006
Indianapolis, IN - Conseco Fieldhouse

Main Event King Booker defeated World Heavyweight Champion Rey Mysterio

July 22, 2007
San Jose, CA - HP Pavilion

Main Event WWE Champion John Cena defeated Bobby Lashley

July 20, 2008
Uniondale, NY - Nassau Coliseum

Main Event WWE Champion Triple H defeated Edge

July 20, 2009
Sacramento, CA - ARCO Arena

Main Event WWE Champion Randy Orton defeated Triple H in a Three Stages of Hell Match

THE GREAT KABUKI

 HT: 5'10" WT: 240 lbs. FROM: Singapore
SIGNATURE MOVE: Thrust Kick

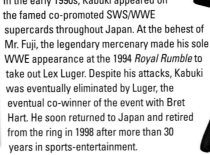

This martial-arts expert arrived in the United States in the 1970s. Long black hair and paint in the design of an ancient Japanese warrior combined to shroud the scarred features of his face, disfigured from hot coals in his youth. During his time in America, he appeared throughout the NWA and was the first to spit a secret green mist at his opponents.

In the early 1990s, Kabuki appeared on the famed co-promoted SWS/WWE supercards throughout Japan. At the behest of Mr. Fuji, the legendary mercenary made his sole WWE appearance at the 1994 *Royal Rumble* to take out Lex Luger. Despite his attacks, Kabuki was eventually eliminated by Luger, the eventual co-winner of the event with Bret Hart. He soon returned to Japan and retired from the ring in 1998 after more than 30 years in sports-entertainment.

The Great Kabuki set a standard that changed the face of sports-entertainment. His merciless attacks and style were influential in the development of future Superstars Killer Kahn and Tajiri.

THE GREAT KHALI

 HT: 7'3" WT: 420 lbs. FROM: India SIGNATURE MOVE: Vise Grip

TITLE HISTORY	
WORLD HEAVYWEIGHT CHAMPION	Won a 20-Man Battle Royal on July 17, 2007

Growing up in the deadly jungles of India, the Great Khali was forced to survive alongside tigers, pythons and Asiatic lions. Armed with nothing but his gigantic bare hands, the youngster fended off countless wildlife attacks while developing into one of the most destructive forces to walk the earth.

The "Punjabi Nightmare" made an instant impression on WWE audiences when he felled the legendary Undertaker with one mighty chop in his April 2006 debut. Never before had the "Deadman" been dropped so quickly. The impressive act served as a precursor of the terror that was about to hit the WWE locker room.

Within weeks of his debut, Khali used the devastating Punjabi Plunge and skull-crushing Vise Grip to defeat WWE's elite, including the World Heavyweight Champion at the time, Rey Mysterio, in non-title action. However, it wasn't until the summer of 2007 that the towering Superstar began to realize his full potential. When an injury forced Edge to vacate his World Heavyweight Championship, the giant Khali dominated a *SmackDown* Battle Royal to be crowned the new titleholder.

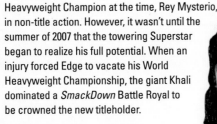

As time went on this "nightmare" transformed into a casanova and was dubbed "The Punjabi Playboy." This called for a weekly "Khali Kiss Cam" where women entered the ring and enjoyed a smooch from Khali. The decorated warrior soon added another prize to his collection when he won the *WrestleMania XXVII* inter-brand Battle Royal.

THE GREAT SASUKE

HT: 5'8" WT: 198 lbs.
FROM: Iwate, Japan
SIGNATURE MOVE: The Thunder Firebomb

Trained in Japan by the original Tiger Mask, Satoru Sayama, better known as the Great Sasuke, developed a stellar reputation throughout Japan in the early 1990s. The black-masked man impressed audiences throughout his native land with his deadly mixture of martial-arts, counter-attacks, aerial maneuvers, and toughness. In 1997, he appeared in ECW, oftentimes against Justin Credible. In July, he made his WWE debut at *In Your House: Canadian Stampede* against Taka Michinoku, but before the end of the year, his relationship with WWE came to an end and he returned to Japan.

Japanese audiences continued to marvel as Great Sasuke expanded his duties beyond the ring. In 2003, he became the first masked professional wrestler elected to a political office. His public duties haven't slowed him down, though, as he can still be seen today competing in Japan. The Great Sasuke is a highly decorated performer with countless championships in Light Heavyweight, Cruiserweight, and Welterweight divisions all over the world. He is a pioneer whose innovations will continue to inspire future Superstars.

THE GREAT HOSSEIN ARAB

HT: 6'0" WT: 258 lbs.
FROM: Tehran, Iran

The Great Hossein Arab didn't compete for WWE very long, but he certainly managed to leave a lasting impression. Alongside manager "Classy" Freddie Blassie, the proud Iranian arrived in 1979 and immediately pronounced his disdain for the United States and its people. He then focused his attention on destroying WWE's American Superstars.

Utilizing a healthy repertoire of suplexes and an impressive Greco-Roman style of offense, Arab regularly made short work of his opponents, which included Larry Zbyszko, Ted DiBiase and Chief Jay Strongbow. On the rare occasion he found himself in trouble, Arab would resort to using one of his controversial toe-curled boots as a weapon.

Arab's greatest WWE moment came at the famed Madison Square Garden when he won a Battle Royal to earn an opportunity at Bob Backlund's WWE Championship. With all of Iran rooting for him, Arab fell short of his goal to dethrone the champ.

THE GREAT SCOTT

WT: 225 lbs.
FROM: St. Andrews, Scotland

During the 1950s and 1960s, The Great Scott travelled to many of the United States' roughest wrestling territories looking for a fight. And behind the power of his pulverizing piledriver and dizzying Highland Fling, he usually won those fights.

TITLE HISTORY

UNITED STATES TAG TEAM CHAMPION	Partnered with Buddy Austin to defeat Buddy Rogers & Johnny Barend on March 7, 1963

The Great Scott defeated Johnny Valentine in May 1953 to claim the West Virginia Heavyweight Championship, the first of many titles for the Scottish competitor over the next decade. He then moved to Ohio, where he teamed with future WWE Champion and Hall of Famer "Nature Boy" Buddy Rogers to win the Midwest Wrestling Association American Tag Team titles three times. He also captured several tag team championships in the NWA with such partners as Bob Orton Sr. and Buddy Austin.

Over the course of his lengthy career, The Great Scott stood across the ring from some of the best of all time, including Bobo Brazil, Johnny Barend and Don Leo Jonathan.

GREG "THE HAMMER" VALENTINE

HT: 6'0" **WT:** 243 lbs.
FROM: Seattle, Washington
SIGNATURE MOVE: Figure Four Leglock

HALL OF FAME 2004

TITLE HISTORY

INTERCONTINENTAL CHAMPION	Defeated Tito Santana on September 24, 1984
WORLD TAG TEAM CHAMPION	Partnered with Brutus Beefcake to defeat Mike Rotundo & Barry Windham on August 24, 1985

The son of the legendary Johnny Valentine grew up around some of the greatest figures in the history of professional wrestling. Trained by the great Stu Hart and The Sheik, Greg Valentine honed his skills during the early 1970s. Valentine landed in Jim Crockett's Mid-Atlantic Championship Wrestling, where he won the NWA World Tag Team Championship with "Nature Boy" Ric Flair.

In 1981, Valentine appeared in WWE managed by The Grand Wizard, where he battled Bob Backlund and Chief Jay Strongbow. In 1984, Greg Valentine returned to the WWE sporting his new nickname, "The Hammer."

On September 24, 1984, he defeated Tito Santana for the Intercontinental Championship. After he lost the title back to Santana in July 1985 in a Steel Cage Match, Valentine destroyed the championship belt. He then formed a tag team with WWE up-and-comer Brutus Beefcake. Known as The Dream Team, they were managed by "Luscious" Johnny Valiant and on August 24, 1985 they defeated the U.S. Express for the World Tag Team Championship. Their seven-month title reign ended with a loss to the British Bulldogs at *WrestleMania 2*. After the duo split, he teamed with Dino Bravo as the New Dream Team. After a brief return to singles action, he joined forces with another former Intercontinental Champion, the Honky Tonk Man. Managed by "Mouth of the South" Jimmy Hart, the team became known as Rhythm and Blues.

In the 1990s, Valentine remained a contender for both the Intercontinental and WWE Championships. On March 13, 2004, his famed career was celebrated with an induction to the WWE Hall Of Fame. As he dedicated this unbelievable honor to his late father, Johnny, his sports-entertainment career came full circle.

GUILLOTINE GORDON

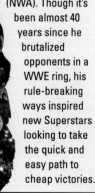

HT: 6'0" **WT:** 260 lbs.
SIGNATURE MOVE: Piledriver

Through the early to mid-1960s, this man received attention for taking rule-breaking to all-new lows in Georgia. In 1965, Guillotine Gordon brought his cut-and-slash style to WWE and made it difficult for anyone to prosper while he was in the ring.

A famous powerhouse and brawler, he battled the top Superstars of the era, including Angelo Savoldi, Smasher Sloan, Bulldog Brower, Spiros Arion and Carlos Colon. As his reputation grew and his regard for rules lessened, Gordon earned a shot at then-WWE Champion Bruno Sammartino in brawls throughout the Northeast.

In 1969, Guillotine Gordon left WWE and returned to the territories of the National Wrestling Alliance (NWA). Though it's been almost 40 years since he brutalized opponents in a WWE ring, his rule-breaking ways inspired new Superstars looking to take the quick and easy path to cheap victories.

THE GYMINI 🇺🇸

MEMBERS: Jesse, Jake   **COMBINED WT:** 608 lbs.

In January 2006, fitness guru Simon Dean introduced the world to two massive twins collectively known as the Gymini. For months, the only thing known about the tandem was their colossal size. After several victories on *SmackDown* and *Velocity*, the identical duo finally revealed themselves as Jesse & Jake. Despite the revelation, opponents and commentators still couldn't tell the two Superstars apart.

Luckily, confused onlookers didn't need to struggle with their identity for long. In May, just four months after their debut, The Gymini made their final WWE televised appearance.

GUNNER SCOTT 🇺🇸

HT: 6'0"   **WT:** 230 lbs.   **FROM:** Tulsa, Oklahoma   **SIGNATURE MOVE:** The Crowbar

In April 2006, Gunner Scott shocked the sports-entertainment world when he defeated Booker T in his *SmackDown* debut. Gunner continued to taste success in bouts against Simon Dean, Finlay, Orlando Jordan, Gregory Helms and Sylvester Terkay. His version of the dangerous fujiwara armbar known as the Crowbar showed he could mix it up in any situation versus virtually any opponent.

As Gunner's star was on the rise it suddenly burned out that June. After a match with Mr. Kennedy, The Great Khali planted Scott with a double choke throw and Daivari stuffed the young hopeful inside a body bag. That was the last anyone ever saw of Gunner Scott.

"HACKSAW" JIM DUGGAN 🇺🇸

HT: 6'3"   **WT:** 240 lbs.   **FROM:** Glen Falls, New York   **SIGNATURE MOVE:** Three Point Stance Clothesline

Above all else, "Hacksaw" Jim Duggan certainly knows how to withstand the test of time. The patriotic Superstar has an amazing thirty years of experience behind him, yet he still shows no sign of ever letting up.

After nearly ten years of competing in various smaller promotions, Duggan debuted in WWE in January 1987. He made his first major statement at *WrestleMania III*, attacking the Iron Sheik & Nikolai Volkoff during the singing of the Russian National Anthem. The act solidified Duggan's status as one of America's most patriotic Superstars. He even taped a small American flag to his signature 2x4.

The following year, Duggan made history when he last eliminated One Man Gang to win the first-ever *Royal Rumble* Match. The popularity of the event led WWE to creating an entire pay-per-view around the match the following January. One year later, Duggan claimed the *King of the Ring* crown from Haku. Again, the popular event would later become an annual pay-per-view extravaganza.

Behind the power of his devastating three-point stance clothesline, Duggan earned an opportunity at American turncoat Sgt. Slaughter's WWE Championship in 1991. Despite having Hulk Hogan in his corner, Duggan was unable to unseat the champ, but did earn a disqualification victory.

In 1994, Duggan jumped to WCW where he had a measure of success. While impressive, his greatest victory during his WCW stay came in 1998 when he defeated kidney cancer. The brave Duggan credits early detection, the grace of God and a superior medical team for saving his life.

With a new outlook on life, Duggan returned to WWE in 2005. Despite his best competitive days being behind him, he still managed to extract thunderous ovations from the WWE Universe. The night before *WrestleMania XXVII*, "Hacksaw" and his trusty 2x4 were welcomed to a place fitting for a former King, the WWE Hall of Fame. Win, lose, or draw, everyone knoww if you are to tangle with "Hacksaw," you better be ready for a fight, tough guy—"Hooooooooo!"

H
2010-
2000-09
1990-99
1980-89
1970-79
1960-69

HAITI KID FROM: Haiti

Haiti Kid's contributions to midget wrestling earned him great respect from Superstars of all sizes. In fact, many of the larger Superstars from the 1980s considered Haiti Kid a close friend, including Hillbilly Jim and Mr. T.

Prior to *WrestleMania 2*, however, Kid's alliance with Mr. T actually caused him great humiliation. Attempting to get under Mr. T's skin, "Rowdy" Roddy Piper abducted Kid and proceeded to cut his hair into a Mohawk. Afterward, Mr. T demanded that his little friend be in his corner at *WrestleMania 2* when he gained revenge on Piper.

The following year, Kid found himself in the center of one of the most infamous WrestleMania moments ever. With Hillbilly Jim & Little Beaver as his partners, he stepped in the ring to face King Kong Bundy, Lord Littlebrook & Little Tokyo. Unfortunately, when things started going poorly for Bundy, the big man took out his aggression on the smaller Beaver. At that point, Kid, along with the two other midgets and Hillbilly Jim, came to Beaver's aid. The image of friends and foes banding together to help Little Beaver will forever be remembered as an amazing *WrestleMania* memory.

HAKU

HT: 6'1"   WT: 275 lbs.
FROM: Isle of Tonga
SIGNATURE MOVE: Savate Kick

TITLE HISTORY

WORLD TAG TEAM CHAMPION	Partnered with Andre the Giant to defeat Demolition on December 13, 1989

This rugged Polynesian powerhouse was trained in sumo wrestling and many different martial-arts styles. WWE audiences first saw him in the mid 1980s as King Tonga. He made history on June 15, 1986, when he slammed Big John Studd during his "$15,000 Body Slam Challenge." He soon became known as Haku and joined with Tama to form the tag team combination known as The Islanders. During their match against the Can-Am Connection on *Superstars of Wrestling,* they fell under the influence of Bobby "The Brain" Heenan and became rule-breakers.

After the team parted ways, Haku remained a member of the Heenan Family and one of WWE's most feared men. In June 1988, the coronation of Haku was witnessed by all after he defeated "King" Harley Race. When he joined Andre the Giant as the Colossal Connection, the two dominated the tag team scene. They defeated Demolition on December 13, 1989 to become World Tag Team Champions. While they parted ways after their *WrestleMania VI* loss, Haku remained in WWE and briefly formed a team with the Barbarian. In late 1992 Haku left WWE.

In the mid 1990s, he appeared in WCW where he reunited with the Barbarian and formed the Faces of Fear. In 2001, Haku was announced as a contestant for the *Royal Rumble*. In early 2002, Haku left WWE and returned to the independent scene in the U.S. and Japan.

HAKUSHI

HT: 5'11"   WT: 238 lbs.   FROM: Japan

Well respected in his homeland of Japan for his innovative offense, Hakushi unleashed his unique in-ring style on WWE in 1995. With his skin covered in Japanese script from head to toe, he certainly drew the attention of fans. It was his combination of superior martial arts skills and amazing agility, however, that caught the eyes of his competition.

After impressive showings against then-unknown rookie Matt Hardy and Ricky Santana, Hakushi was catapulted into a high-profile rivalry against Bret "Hit Man" Hart. Against one of WWE's best, Hakushi certainly impressed many, despite coming up short at *In Your House* in May 1995.

Undeterred by the loss, Hakushi used his lightning-quick speed to upend the equally-fast 1-2-3 Kid at *SummerSlam 1995*. Initially, the win looked like the launching pad he needed to rise the WWE ranks. Inexplicably, however, he soon found himself involved with perennial loser Barry Horowitz. Hakushi's career never recovered.

In 1996, Hakushi became victimized by Justin "Hawk" Bradshaw's branding iron. Greatly embarrassed by the situation, the Japanese Superstar never showed his face in WWE again.

THE HANGMAN

HT: 6'3"   WT: 292 lbs.   FROM: Matane, Quebec, Canada   SIGNATURE MOVE: Bearhug

After his first matches, reports of this Canadian's vicious actions in the ring and his post-match treatment of defeated foes spread quickly across the globe. Dressed head-to-toe in black, the Hangman was prepared to take his rope to the United States after a brief tour of Japan.

In the late 1970s, he debuted in WWE with manager "Classy" Freddie Blassie in his corner. The Hangman sent chills through arenas, as he was known to hang defeated opponents over the top rope, with his noose pulled tight around their necks. After defeating Rene Goulet at *Showdown at Shea 1980*, the Hangman became a serious contender for the WWE Championship, then held by Bob Backlund.

By 1982, the Hangman left WWE and spread terror through promotions all over the world. In 1986, the Hangman hung up his boots and returned to Canada, but to this day, the feelings of dread left in his wake linger in all the arenas he visited.

HANS MORTIER

HT: 5'11" **WT:** 250 lbs. **FROM:** Nuremberg, Germany
SIGNATURE MOVE: The Full Nelson

Hans Mortier was a world-class bodybuilder before he entered the ring and was known by many as "The Great." A former European Champion, Mortier and his "unbreakable" full nelson arrived in WWE in 1968. Led to the ring by "Wild" Red Berry, he became an immediate threat to the title reign of then-WWE Champion, Bruno Sammartino. Mortier also teamed with his brother Max to wreak havoc on opposing tandems. His bouts for wrestling's richest prize against Sammartino were so physical the rivalry had to be settled in a Texas Death Match in Philadelphia. Hans Mortier will go down in wrestling lore as one of the most hated villains and biggest threats to Sammartino's WWE Championship.

HANS SCHMIDT

HT: 6'4" **WT:** 250 lbs.
FROM: Munich, Germany

Few Superstars attracted more hatred from the fans than Hans Schmidt. Known as the Teuton Terror, he stepped to the ring wearing a German World War II helmet, which enraged American audiences. Schmidt's brute, powerhouse ring style struck instant fear into his opponents. His complete disregard for the rules made it nearly impossible for referees to maintain order in his matches.

Schmidt captured several titles while competing for the National Wrestling Alliance (NWA). However, he was never able to score the big one, as his attempts to topple NWA Champion Lou Thesz fell short.

HARDCORE CHAMPIONSHIP

The Hardcore Championship not only broke all the rules, it took the rules and smashed them into thousands of little pieces. Ironically, that was the same concept behind the Hardcore Championship belt—an old WWE Championship belt that was broken into little pieces then taped back together.

The concept of the Hardcore Championship was unique as it catered to the no-holds-barred style of wrestling that was becoming increasingly popular in the late 1990s. In a Hardcore Championship title defense, anything and everything was legal, including the use of weapons and competing in locations outside the traditional arena. As the title started to take on a life of its own, so did its lack of rules. It wasn't long before the Hardcore Championship was being defended under 24/7 rules, meaning any Superstar could challenge the champion at any time of the day, as long as he (or she) had a referee with him (or her). The 24/7 rules resulted in an exorbitant amount of title changes. In fact, over its lifespan, which lasted less than four years, the Hardcore Championship changed hands more than 200 times!

The Hardcore Championship became defunct in August 2002, when Rob Van Dam defeated Tommy Dreamer to unify it with the Intercontinental Championship.

1998

November 2
Houston, TX

Mr. McMahon awarded Mankind the Hardcore Championship, crowning him the first-ever titleholder.

▼

November 30
Baltimore, MD

Big Boss Man defeated Mankind

▼

December 15
Spokane, WA

Road Dogg defeated Big Boss Man

Injury forced Road Dogg to vacate the Hardcore Championship in February 1999.

▼

1999

February 14
Memphis, TN

Hardcore Holly defeated Al Snow

▼

March 15
San Jose, CA

Billy Gunn defeated Hardcore Holly

▼

March 28
Philadelphia, PA

Hardcore Holly defeated Billy Gunn

▼

April 25
Providence, RI

Al Snow defeated Hardcore Holly

▼

July 25
Buffalo, NY

Big Boss Man defeated Al Snow

▼

August 22
Minneapolis, MN

Al Snow defeated Big Boss Man

▼

August 24
Kansas City, MO

Big Boss Man defeated Al Snow

▼

September 9
Albany, NY

British Bulldog defeated Big Boss Man

After defeating Big Boss Man for the Hardcore Championship, British Bulldog gave the title to Al Snow

▼

October 14
Birmingham, AL

Big Boss Man defeated Al Snow

▼

2000

January 17
New Haven, CT

Test defeated Big Boss Man

▼

February 24
Nashville, TN

Crash Holly defeated Test

▼

March 13
Newark, NJ

Pete Gas defeated Crash Holly
Crash Holly defeated Pete Gas

▼

April 2
Anaheim, CA

Tazz defeated Crash Holly
Viscera defeated Tazz
Funaki defeated Viscera
Rodney defeated Funaki
Joey Abs defeated Rodney
Thrasher defeated Joey Abs
Pete Gas defeated Thrasher
Tazz defeated Pete Gas
Crash Holly defeated Tazz
Hardcore Holly defeated Crash Holly

▼

April 3
Los Angeles, CA

Crash Holly defeated Hardcore Holly

▼

April 13
Tampa, FL

Perry Saturn defeated Crash Holly
Tazz defeated Perry Saturn
Crash Holly defeated Tazz

▼

April·24
Raleigh, NC

Matt Hardy defeated Crash Holly

April·27
Charlotte, NC

Crash Holly defeated Matt Hardy

May 6
London, England

British Bulldog defeated Crash Holly

May 11
New Haven, CT

Crash Holly defeated British Bulldog

May 15
Cleveland, OH

Godfather's Ho defeated Crash Holly
Crash Holly defeated Godfather's Ho

May 18
Detroit, MI

Gerald Brisco defeated Crash Holly

June 12
St. Louis, MO

Crash Holly defeated Gerald Brisco

June 19
Nashville, TN

Gerald Brisco defeated Crash Holly
Pat Patterson defeated Gerald Brisco

June 25
Boston, MA

Crash Holly defeated Pat Patterson

June·29
Hartford, CT

Steve Blackman defeated Crash Holly

July 2
Tampa, FL

Crash Holly defeated Steve Blackman
Steve Blackman defeated Crash Holly

August·21
Lafayette, LA

Shane McMahon defeated
Steve Blackman

August·27
Raleigh, NC

Steve Blackman defeated
Shane McMahon

September·24
Philadelphia, PA

Crash Holly defeated Steve Blackman
Perry Saturn defeated Crash Holly

December·22
Chattanooga, TN

Raven defeated Steve Blackman

2001

January·22
Lafayette, LA

Al Snow defeated Raven
Raven defeated Al Snow

February·3
Greensboro, NC

K-Kwick defeated Raven
Crash Holly defeated K-Kwick
Raven defeated Crash Holly

February·4
Columbia, SC

K-Kwick defeated Raven
Crash Holly defeated K-Kwick
Raven defeated Crash Holly

February·8
North Charleston, SC

Hardcore Holly defeated Raven
Raven defeated Hardcore Holly

February·10
St. Paul, MN

Hardcore Holly defeated Raven
Raven defeated Hardcore Holly

February·11
Boston, MA

Hardcore Holly defeated Raven
Al Snow defeated Hardcore Holly
Raven defeated Al Snow

February·17
Cedar Falls, IA

Steve Blackman defeated Raven
Raven defeated Steve Blackman

February·18
Cape Girardeau, MO

Steve Blackman defeated Raven
Raven defeated Steve Blackman

February·25
Las Vegas, NV

Billy Gunn defeated Raven
Raven defeated Billy Gunn
Big Show defeated Raven

March·19
Albany, NY

Raven defeated Big Show

April·1
Houston, TX

Kane defeated Raven

April·19
Nashville, TN

Rhyno defeated Kane

May·21
San Jose, CA

Big Show defeated Rhyno

May·28
Calgary, Alberta

Chris Jericho defeated Big Show
Rhyno defeated Chris Jericho

June·16
Baltimore, MD

Test defeated Rhyno

June·25
New York, NY

Rhyno defeated Test
Mike Awesome defeated Rhyno

July·12
Birmingham, AL

Jeff Hardy defeated Mike Awesome

July·22
Cleveland, OH

Rob Van Dam defeated Jeff Hardy

August·13
Chicago, IL

Jeff Hardy defeated Rob Van Dam

August·19
San Jose, CA

Rob Van Dam defeated Jeff Hardy

September·10
San Antonio, TX

Kurt Angle defeated Rob Van Dam
Rob Van Dam defeated Kurt Angle

December·9
San Diego, CA

Undertaker defeated Rob Van Dam

2002

February·7
Los Angeles, CA

Maven defeated Undertaker

February·28
Boston, MA

Goldust defeated Maven

March·11
Detroit, MI

Al Snow defeated Goldust

March·14
Cleveland, OH

Maven defeated Al Snow

March·17
Toronto, Ontario

Spike Dudley defeated Maven
The Hurricane defeated Spike Dudley
Mighty Molly defeated The Hurricane
Christian defeated Mighty Molly
Maven defeated Christian

March·28
Philadelphia, PA

Raven defeated Maven

April·1
Albany, NY

Bubba Ray Dudley defeated Raven

April·7
Denver, CO

William Regal defeated
Bubba Ray Dudley
Goldust defeated William Regal
Raven defeated Goldust
Bubba Ray Dudley defeated Raven

April 13
Odessa, TX

William Regal defeated Bubba Ray Dudley

Spike Dudley defeated William Regal

Goldust defeated Spike Dudley

Bubba Ray Dudley defeated Goldust

▼

April 14
Abilene, TX

William Regal defeated Bubba Ray Dudley

Spike Dudley defeated William Regal

Goldust defeated Spike Dudley

Bubba Ray Dudley defeated Goldust

▼

April 15
College Station, TX

Raven defeated Bubba Ray Dudley

Tommy Dreamer defeated Raven

Stevie Richards defeated Tommy Dreamer

Bubba Ray Dudley defeated Stevie Richards

▼

April 19
Uniondale, NY

Goldust defeated Bubba Ray Dudley

Raven defeated Goldust

Bubba Ray Dudley defeated Raven

▼

April 20
Des Moines, IA

Goldust defeated Bubba Ray Dudley

Raven defeated Goldust

Bubba Ray Dudley defeated Raven

▼

April 29
Buffalo, NY

Stevie Richards defeated Bubba Ray Dudley

▼

May 1
Cologne, Germany

Tommy Dreamer defeated Stevie Richards

Goldust defeated Tommy Dreamer

Stevie Richards defeated Goldust

▼

May 2
Glasgow, Scotland

Shawn Stasiak defeated Stevie Richards

Justin Credible defeated Shawn Stasiak

Crash Holly defeated Justin Credible

Stevie Richards defeated Crash Holly

Shawn Stasiak defeated Stevie Richards

Stevie Richards defeated Shawn Stasiak

▼

May 3
Birmingham, England

Crash Holly defeated Stevie Richards

Stevie Richards defeated Crash Holly

▼

May 4
London, England

Booker T defeated Stevie Richards

Crash Holly defeated Booker T

Booker T defeated Crash Holly

Stevie Richards defeated Booker T

▼

May 6
Hartford, CT

Bubba Ray Dudley defeated Stevie Richards

Raven defeated Bubba Ray Dudley

Justin Credible defeated Raven

Crash Holly defeated Justin Credible

Trish Stratus defeated Crash Holly

Stevie Richards defeated Trish Stratus

▼

May 25
Winnipeg, Manitoba

Tommy Dreamer defeated Stevie Richards

Raven defeated Tommy Dreamer

Stevie Richards defeated Raven

▼

May 26
Red Deer, Saskatchewan

Tommy Dreamer defeated Stevie Richards

Raven defeated Tommy Dreamer

Stevie Richards defeated Raven

▼

May 27
Edmonton, Alberta

Terri defeated Stevie Richards

Stevie Richards defeated Terri

▼

June 2
New Orleans, LA

Tommy Dreamer defeated Stevie Richards

Raven defeated Tommy Dreamer

Stevie Richards defeated Raven

▼

June 3
Dallas, TX

Bradshaw defeated Stevie Richards

▼

June 22
Cincinnati, OH

Raven defeated Bradshaw

Spike Dudley defeated Raven

Shawn Stasiak defeated Spike Dudley

Bradshaw defeated Shawn Stasiak

▼

June 28
Washington, DC

Shawn Stasiak defeated Bradshaw

Spike Dudley defeated Shawn Stasiak

Stevie Richards defeated Spike Dudley

Bradshaw defeated Stevie Richards

▼

June 29
New York, NY

Shawn Stasiak defeated Bradshaw

Spike Dudley defeated Shawn Stasiak

Stevie Richards defeated Spike Dudley

Bradshaw defeated Stevie Richards

▼

June 30
Uncasville, CT

Raven defeated Bradshaw

Crash Holly defeated Raven

Stevie Richards defeated Crash Holly

Bradshaw defeated Stevie Richards

▼

July 6
Frederick, MD

Stevie Richards defeated Bradshaw

Crash Holly defeated Stevie Richards

Christopher Nowinski defeated Crash Holly

Bradshaw defeated Christopher Nowinski

▼

July 7
Wildwood, NJ

Stevie Richards defeated Bradshaw

Crash Holly defeated Stevie Richards

Christopher Nowinski defeated Crash Holly

Bradshaw defeated Christopher Nowinski

▼

July 12
Lakeland, FL

Justin Credible defeated Bradshaw

Spike Dudley defeated Justin Credible

Big Show defeated Spike Dudley

Bradshaw defeated Big Show

▼

July 13
Daytona Beach, FL

Justin Credible defeated Bradshaw

Shawn Stasiak defeated Justin Credible

Bradshaw defeated Shawn Stasiak

▼

July 14
Bethlehem, PA

Justin Credible defeated Bradshaw

Shawn Stasiak defeated Justin Credible

Bradshaw defeated Shawn Stasiak

▼

July 15
East Rutherford, NJ

Johnny Stamboli defeated Bradshaw

Bradshaw defeated Johnny Stamboli

▼

July 26
Houston, TX

Raven defeated Bradshaw

Justin Credible defeated Raven

Shawn Stasiak defeated Justin Credible

Bradshaw defeated Shawn Stasiak

▼

July 27
San Antonio, TX

Raven defeated Bradshaw

Justin Credible defeated Raven

Shawn Stasiak defeated Justin Credible

Bradshaw defeated Shawn Stasiak

▼

July 28
Columbia, SC

Raven defeated Bradshaw

Justin Credible defeated Raven

Shawn Stasiak defeated Justin Credible

Bradshaw defeated Shawn Stasiak

▼

July 29
Greensboro, NC

Jeff Hardy defeated Bradshaw

Johnny Stamboli defeated Jeff Hardy

Tommy Dreamer defeated Johnny Stamboli

▼

August 3
Miami, FL

Bradshaw defeated Tommy Dreamer

Tommy Dreamer defeated Bradshaw

▼

August 4
Pittsburgh, PA

Bradshaw defeated Tommy Dreamer

Tommy Dreamer defeated Bradshaw

▼

August 9
Kelowna, British Columbia

Shawn Stasiak defeated Tommy Dreamer

Stevie Richards defeated Shawn Stasiak

Tommy Dreamer defeated Stevie Richards

▼

August 10
Kamloops, British Columbia

Shawn Stasiak defeated Tommy Dreamer

Stevie Richards defeated Shawn Stasiak

Tommy Dreamer defeated Stevie Richards

▼

August 11
Vancouver, British Columbia

Shawn Stasiak defeated Tommy Dreamer

Stevie Richards defeated Shawn Stasiak

Tommy Dreamer defeated Stevie Richards

▼

August 17
Terre Haute, IN

Raven defeated Tommy Dreamer

Shawn Stasiak defeated Raven

Tommy Dreamer defeated Shawn Stasiak

▼

August 18
Evansville, IN

Shawn Stasiak defeated Tommy Dreamer

Stevie Richards defeated Shawn Stasiak

Tommy Dreamer defeated Stevie Richards

▼

August 19
Norfolk, VA

Bradshaw defeated Tommy Dreamer

Crash Holly defeated Bradshaw

Tommy Dreamer defeated Crash Holly

▼

August 26
New York, NY

Rob Van Dam defeated Tommy Dreamer

Rob Van Dam beat Tommy Dreamer to unify the Hardcore and Intercontinental Championships.

H

2010-

2000-09

1990-99

1980-89

1970-79

1960-69

HARDCORE HOLLY

HT: 6'0" WT: 235 lbs.
FROM: Mobile, Alabama
SIGNATURE MOVE: Alabama Slam

TITLE HISTORY

HARDCORE CHAMPION	6 Times
WORLD TAG TEAM CHAMPION (3 TIMES)	*Partnered with 1-2-3 Kid to defeat Bam Bam Bigelow & Tatanka on January 22, 1995 Partnered with Crash Holly to defeat Mankind & The Rock on October 18, 1999 Partnered with Cody Rhodes to defeat Lance Cade & Trevor Murdoch on December 10, 2007*

Few Superstars can boast as lengthy a WWE career as Bob "Hardcore" Holly. During his 15 years with the company he saw it all, from the New Generation to the "Attitude" Era to the WCW Invasion. While many things changed over the course of his career, there was always one constant: Bob Holly equaled Hardcore. He was one of the leanest, meanest, roughest, and toughest Superstars to ever enter the squared circle.

The tough-as-nails Superstar earned his "Hardcore" moniker during the height of the Hardcore Division's popularity. Known for having no mercy in the ring, Holly brutalized his opponents on his way to six Hardcore Championship reigns. After the title became dormant, the "Alabama Slammer" still competed like the prize was on the line.

Over the years, Holly's hard-hitting ring style also translated to success in the tag team ranks. A three-time World Tag Team Champion, he captured the gold with partners 1-2-3 Kid, Crash Holly, and Cody Rhodes.

In 2001, the normally gruff Holly took a hiatus from the ring to teach WWE hopefuls on *Tough Enough*. Using tough love as his primary teaching tool, Holly molded several future Superstars. He remained true to his name throughout the decade before he hung up his boots in 2009.

THE HARDY BOYS

MEMBERS: Matt Hardy, Jeff Hardy   COMBINED WT: 461 lbs.

TITLE HISTORY

WORLD TAG TEAM CHAMPIONS (6 TIMES)	*Defeated The Acolytes on July 5, 1999 Defeated Edge & Christian on September 24, 2000 Defeated Edge & Christian on October 23, 2000 Defeated The Dudleys on March 5, 2001 Defeated Booker T & Test on November 12, 2001 Won a Tag Team Battle Royal on April 2, 2007*

In April 1999, the Hardy Boys acquired the guidance of the legendary Michael "P.S." Hayes.

Matt & Jeff Hardy became wrestling fanatics after they watched *WrestleMania IV*. As teenagers, they trained to wrestle on a trampoline and soon promoted their own wrestling shows at area high schools, outdoor fairs, and armories under their company name, OMEGA. This budding promotion also featured fellow future WWE Superstars Gregory Helms and Joey Mercury. The Hardys did anything to be involved with the wrestling business and their dream was to one day be World Tag Team Champions.

Matt & Jeff made their WWE debut in 1994 and were soon seen on *Monday Night Raw* against the WWE's top talent. In the late 1990s they began to be noticed for their agility, teamwork and resilience. Matt was the ring general who could beat you from the air or the ground. Jeff was the enigmatic figure and aerial daredevil who at any time, and from anywhere, could put away an opponent.

In April 1999, they acquired the guidance of the legendary Michael "P.S." Hayes. Their boyhood dream became reality when they defeated the APA for the World Tag Team Championship. To some, this would be the end, but for the Hardys, it was only the beginning.

The Hardys met with opponents who shared their desire to push the tag team division to the forefront of WWE. At *No Mercy 1999,* they had the first-ever tag team Ladder Match against Edge & Christian. At *WrestleMania 2000,* they met both Edge & Christian and the Dudley Boys in a Triple Threat Ladder Match. Months later at *SummerSlam,* the three teams squared off in the first–ever Tables, Ladders and Chairs (TLC) Match. During this time, the Hardys also added a third risk-taker to their group, Lita. The trio was inseparable and became known as Team Xtreme.

After years together, the Hardys went their own way to fulfill their individual dreams. In 2006, they reunited as part of Team DX at the *Survivor Series*. Amazingly, they won the World Tag Team Championship for the sixth time in 2007.

When focused on singles careers, the brothers had their share of rivalries and WWE title reigns. To the heartbreak of WWE Universe, the unthinkable took place when the brothers aimed their innovative offense towards one another in an Extreme Rules match at *WrestleMania XXV*. The rivalry extended to Stretcher and I Quit matches before they reconciled. Team Extreme faded from WWE after Jeff lost a "Loser Leaves WWE" steel cage match to CM Punk, and Matt parted with the company in October 2010.

THE HART DYNASTY

MEMBERS: Tyson Kidd, David Hart Smith, Natalya
FROM: Calgary, Alberta, Canada

TITLE HISTORY	
WWE TAG TEAM CHAMPIONS	*Defeated Big Show & The Miz on April 26, 2010*
WORLD TAG TEAM CHAMPIONS	*Defeated Big Show & The Miz on April 26, 2010*

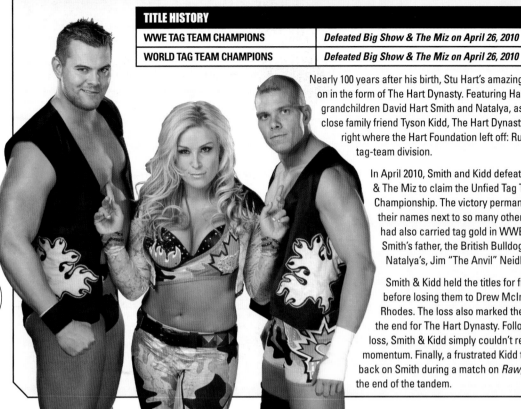

Nearly 100 years after his birth, Stu Hart's amazing legacy lived on in the form of The Hart Dynasty. Featuring Hart's grandchildren David Hart Smith and Natalya, as well as close family friend Tyson Kidd, The Hart Dynasty picked up right where the Hart Foundation left off: Ruling the tag-team division.

In April 2010, Smith and Kidd defeated Big Show & The Miz to claim the Unfied Tag Team Championship. The victory permanently etched their names next to so many other Harts that had also carried tag gold in WWE, including Smith's father, the British Bulldog, as well as Natalya's, Jim "The Anvil" Neidhart.

Smith & Kidd held the titles for five months before losing them to Drew McIntyre & Cody Rhodes. The loss also marked the beginning of the end for The Hart Dynasty. Following the loss, Smith & Kidd simply couldn't regain their momentum. Finally, a frustrated Kidd turned his back on Smith during a match on *Raw*, signifying the end of the tandem.

HARLEY RACE

HT: 6'1" **WT:** 253 lbs.
FROM: Kansas City, Missouri
SIGNATURE MOVE: Fisherman Suplex

Harley Race is the rare type of man who comes out of the womb ready to battle. He debuted in the ring as a teenager in the 1960s and formed a team with Larry "The Ax" Hennig. In 1967, Race authored an article in an issue of *Wrestling Revue* magazine titled "Why We Are The Greatest." The two parted ways toward the end of the decade and focused on singles careers.

During the 1970s and early 1980s, Race was the NWA's most commanding figure and held the NWA Championship eight times. Race's fame was so great he was even recognized by WWE and battled in historic unification matches with then-champions "Superstar" Billy Graham and Bob Backlund.

In 1986, he debuted in WWE with his impressive list of credentials and won an early version of the *King of the Ring* tournament. Now known as "King" Harley Race, he became a leading member of the Heenan Family and battled against Ricky "The Dragon" Steamboat, Hillbilly Jim, Tito Santana, Junkyard Dog and Hulk Hogan. After an injury in a match against Hogan, soon after, he lost his crown to Haku.

In 2004, Harley's iconic career was immortalized as he became a member of the WWE Hall of Fame on the eve of *WrestleMania XX*. With his intense interview style and rugged, technical presence in the ring, Harley Race will go down in history as one of the toughest men to ever walk the Earth.

THE HART FOUNDATION

MEMBERS: Bret "Hit Man" Hart, Jim "The Anvil" Neidhart, Owen Hart, Davey Boy Smith, Brian Pillman

TITLE HISTORY	
WORLD TAG TEAM CHAMPIONS (2 TIMES)	*Defeated The British Bulldogs on January 26, 1987 Defeated Demolition on August 27, 1990*

To fully appreciate The Hart Foundation's impact on sports-entertainment, you must travel through two decades of WWE action to examine its different incarnations.

Originally a tag team, The Hart Foundation debuted as a rule-breaking tandem in the mid-1980s. Bret "Hit Man" Hart provided the team's quickness and technical skill, while Jim "The Anvil" Neidhart served as the muscle. The duo, which was managed by Jimmy "Mouth of the South" Hart, enjoyed two World Tag Team Championship reigns. In January 1987, they defeated the British Bulldogs for their first. Three years later, they downed Demolition to reclaim the titles.

By the end of 1990, it was becoming evident that the "Hit Man" was destined for singles success. Following a loss to The Nasty Boys at *WrestleMania VII*, The Hart Foundation split and Bret went on to achieve legendary status as a singles competitor. Seven

years later, Hart & Neidhart reunited to wage war against the United States. This time, however, they welcomed Owen Hart, Davey Boy Smith, and Brian Pillman into the faction, bringing The Hart Foundation's membership up to five.

The new Hart Foundation, which was lead by then-WWE Champion Bret Hart, arrogantly waved Canadian and British flags, while denouncing the supposed immoral values of the United States. Their actions clearly infuriated American fans, but made The Hart Foundation heroes in Canada, which was the site of their greatest victory.

In front of a capacity crowd in Calgary's Saddledome, The Hart Foundation defeated Stone Cold Steve Austin, The Legion of Doom, Goldust & Ken Shamrock when Owen rolled up Stone Cold for the win. The Canadian crowd enthusiastically cheered their heroes, as numerous members of the Hart family celebrated in the ring.

H

2010-
2000-09
1990-99
1980-89
1970-79
1960-69

HARVEY WIPPLEMAN

FROM: Walls, Mississippi

TITLE HISTORY

WOMEN'S CHAMPION	*Defeated The Kat on January 31, 2000*

Despite being short in stature, Harvey Wippleman guided some of sports-entertainment's biggest Superstars. His list of oversized clients included Sid Justice, Giant Gonzales, Kamala, Adam Bomb, and even big Bertha Faye.

Wippleman's managerial prowess led his protégés to many high-profile encounters, including major *WrestleMania* matches. In the main event of *WrestleMania VIII*, he guided Sid Justice to a controversial disqualification loss to Hulk Hogan. One year later, at *WrestleMania IX*, Wippleman led the near 8-foot Giant Gonzales into battle against Undertaker.

Despite building a stable of some of the biggest horses in the game, Wippleman always had trouble winning titles for his clients. Then he met love interest Bertha Faye. Wippleman guided his girlfriend's career from the trailer park all the way up to the Women's Championship in 1995. The title was the only one Wippleman ever captured during his days as a WWE manager.

Five years after managing a Women's Champion, Wippleman actually won the title himself. Disguised as a female named Hervina, he defeated The Kat in a Lumberjill Snow Bunny Match to capture the title.

HAYSTACKS CALHOUN

HT: 6'4"   WT: 601 lbs.   FROM: Morgan's Corner, Arkansas   SIGNATURE MOVE: Big Splash

TITLE HISTORY

WORLD TAG TEAM CHAMPION	*Partnered with Tony Garea to defeat Prof. Toru Tanaka & Mr. Fuji on May 30, 1973*

Recognized by many as sports-entertainment's first giant, Haystacks Calhoun made his professional debut in the 1950s. His battles with fellow colossus, the over 700 pound Happy Humphrey gave new meaning to the term "when worlds collide." Crushing his way into the 1960s Calhoun was revered as a legend of the ring with his trademark beard, overalls and horse shoe around his neck.

In 1964 this happy behemoth debuted in World Wrestling Entertainment and became one of the most popular figures throughout the Northeast. Calhoun promised all "There are going to be a lot of pancakes around here before I get finished."

"'Stacks" formed a formidable team with Bobo Brazil and the duo were top contenders for the U.S. Tag Team Championship. By August 1965 Calhoun left the company and toured the United States and Canada. He returned to WWE in 1968 and picked up where he left off as one of the most popular Superstars in the region. In May, 1973 Calhoun and Tony Garea defeated Mr. Fuji & Prof. Toru Tanaka and became World Tag Team Champions.

Haystacks continued to amaze WWE audiences through 1979. In the 1980s he battled diabetes but sadly lost his battle in December 1989. Haystacks Calhoun's influence can still be felt today and he'll always be warmly remembered as one of the ring's most beloved heros and most sought after attractions.

THE HEADBANGERS

MEMBERS: Mosh, Thrasher   FROM: Mosh Pits Across America   COMBINED WT: 492 lbs.

TITLE HISTORY

WORLD TAG TEAM CHAMPIONS	*Won a Fatal Four-Way Match on September 7, 1997*

Mosh & Thrasher made their debut in 1997, sporting kilts (they claimed real mean wore skirts) and black face paint. The team blended speed and power to soften up their opponents, then finished them off with their signature Stage Dive move.

Their career reached its peak during *In Your House: Ground Zero* in a Fatal Four Way Elimination Match. After Dude Love and "Stone Cold" Steve Austin forfeited the World Tag Team Championships, Mosh & Thrasher outlasted the Godwinns, Legion of Doom and the Hart Foundation, with an assist from a Stunner courtesy of Stone Cold Steve Austin. They held the titles for close to one month before a disappointing loss to The Godwinns at *In Your House: Badd Blood*.

By late 2000, the metalheads parted ways and pursued individual careers within WWE. At times they entered what would be temporary partnerships, but couldn't duplicate past successes. By 2001, both had left WWE to compete in other promotions.

THE HEADSHRINKERS

MEMBERS: Samu, Fatu, Sionne

Samu & Fatu are proud members of a long line of savage Samoan Superstars to terrorize WWE. Collectively

TITLE HISTORY

WORLD TAG TEAM CHAMPIONS	*Defeated The Quebecers on April 26, 1994*

known as The Headshrinkers, the duo displayed a dangerous combination of size, agility and ferocity on their way to becoming one of the most feared tag teams of the mid-1990s.

Success didn't come quickly for The Headshrinkers. Managed by Afa, the tandem struggled to make a name for themselves during their first year with WWE. After competing in many non-descript matches against the likes of High Energy and the Steiner Brothers, the savage unit employed the services of legendary manager Capt. Lou Albano. The move proved to be the spark the team needed to succeed.

With the "Manager of Champions" leading the way, The Headshrinkers quickly became top contenders in the tag team division. In April 1994, they shot to the top when they defeated The Quebecers for the World Tag Team Championship. Over the course of the next four months, Samu & Fatu turned back all comers, including the Smoking Gunns and Yokozuna & Crush. Unfortunately for The Headshrinkers, their impressive reign was unexpectedly derailed when Shawn Michaels & Diesel defeated them in August.

Following the loss, a frustrated Samu left WWE. The massive Sionne briefly filled the vacancy, but the new version of The Headshrinkers simply could not recreate the magic. Fatu & Sionne split soon after.

HEATH SLATER

HT: 6'2" **WT:** 216 lbs. **FROM:** Pineville, West Virginia
SIGNATURE MOVE: Sweetness

TITLE HISTORY

WWE TAG TEAM CHAMPION (3 TIMES)	*Partnered with Justin Gabriel to defeat John Cena & David Otunga on October 25, 2010*
	Partnered with Justin Gabriel to defeat Santino Marella & Vladimir Kozlov on February 20, 2011
	Partnered with Justin Gabriel to defeat John Cena & The Miz on February 21, 2011

Despite being relatively new to WWE, Heath Slater walks around with an arrogance befitting of a multiple-time World champion with decades of experience. Luckily for him, he has the skills to back up his cocky claims in the ring.

Finding strength in numbers, Slater prefers to surround himself with equally talented Superstars. Following his run on season one of *NXT*, he immediately joined the rebel faction The Nexus, and then jumped to The Corre before finally forming a simple tag team with Justin Gabriel. Along the way, the self-proclaimed "One Man Rock Band" and Gabriel claimed the WWE Tag Team Championship several times.

The egotistical Slater eventually tired from sharing the spotlight with Gabriel. On July 15, 2011, he finally severed ties with his longtime partner, claiming Gabriel was holding his career back. Ironically, Gabriel defeated Slater that same night with a 450 splash. No longer surrounded by others, the "rock star without the instruments" must now prove he has what it takes to be a solo act.

THE HEART THROBS

MEMBERS: Antonio, Romeo

These heartbreakers entered WWE in 2005 and were so sexy they almost didn't know what to do with themselves. Antonio and Romeo wrapped up the attenion of the ladies in the audience with their charisma, and placed feathered boas around choice females to invite the ladies to dance in the ring with them after victories.

The Heart Throbs battled for tag team gold against the likes of William Regal & Tajiri, The Hurricane & Rosey, Lance Cade & Trevor Murdoch, Big Show & Kane, and Snitsky & Tomko. They also teamed with Victoria in intense mixed tag matches. In February 2006, the two self-proclaimed Don Juans left WWE.

THE HEAVENLY BODIES

MEMBERS: "Gigolo" Jimmy Del Ray, Tom Pritchard
COMBINED WT: 460 lbs.

In 1993, smooth operators "Gigolo" Jimmy Del Ray and Tom Pritchard came to WWE by way of Smoky Mountain Wrestling. Fans knew that with manager James E. Cornette in their corner, the duo would be a well-oiled machine with an innate mean streak.

Del Ray & Pritchard defeated team after team and soon ran up against the Smokin' Gunns and the Steiner Brothers. They demanded, and received, a shot at the World Tag Team Championship at *SummerSlam 1993*. While that encounter ended with a defeat, the Heavenly Bodies captured the Smoky Mountain Tag Team Championship a few months later at *Survivor Series*.

For the early portion of 1994, they appeared on WWE programming with the Smoky Mountain titles. In August 1995, Del Ray & Pritchard left WWE and briefly ventured to ECW. In 1996, however, the team went their separate ways.

THE HEENAN FAMILY

MEMBERS: Andre the Giant, Big John Studd, King Kong Bundy, Ken Patera, The Missing Link, Adrian Adonis, Paul Orndorff, Harley Race, Hercules, The Barbarian, Rick Rude, Haku, Tama, Brooklyn Brawler, Mr. Perfect, Red Rooster, Arn Anderson, Tully Blanchard

Though not related by blood, members of Bobby "The Brain" Heenan's stable of Superstars were so close he referred to them as family, The Heenan Family. The impressive ensemble traces its roots back to the early 1970s and the AWA. As a manager in the Minneapolis-based promotion, Heenan guided the careers of the territory's top names, including Nick Bockwinkel and "Cowboy" Bob Orton.

In 1984, Heenan moved to WWE, where he introduced his family approach to managing to his earliest clients, Ken Patera and Big John Studd. Within months of their union, Heenan had Studd challenging Hulk Hogan for the WWE Championship. Studd's main-event status caught the eye of many other Superstars who began to knock on Heenan's door. Before long, the manager's list of clients grew to epic proportions. Superstars such as King Kong Bundy and Harley Race were all clamoring to sign with Heenan.

The Family's biggest acquisition came in 1987 when Andre the Giant joined. Landing the massive Superstar proved to be a major coup for Heenan, who parlayed the signing into one of the biggest matches of all time: Hogan vs. Andre at *WrestleMania III*.

While Andre was unable to bring the WWE Championship to The Heenan Family, he did later team with Haku to claim the World Tag Team Championship. Heenan lead the Brain Busters to the same accolade in 1989. He also managed Rick Rude and Mr. Perfect to the Intercontinental Championship.

HEIDENREICH

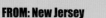

HT: 6'7"   WT: 285 lbs.   FROM: New Orleans, Louisiana
SIGNATURE MOVE: Cobra Clutch

Heidenreich's size certainly intimidated opponents, but it was the uncertainty of what was going on in his crazed

TITLE HISTORY	
WWE TAG TEAM CHAMPION	*Partnered with Animal to defeat MNM on July 25, 2005*

head that truly scared Superstars. With tattoos spread over his chiseled frame, Heidenreich was known for reciting cryptic poetry before attacking. Even more unnerving was the fact that nobody was safe from him, as Heidenreich was known to assault Superstars, announcers, and even fans.

In October 2004, Heidenreich cost Undertaker an opportunity at reclaiming the WWE Championship. Over the next several months, the Superstars faced off in several high-profile encounters. Unfortunately for Heidenreich, Undertaker bested him every bout, including a Casket Match at the 2005 *Royal Rumble*.

After failing to derail Undertaker, Heidenreich took a more fan-friendly approach to life. His poems, which he called "disasterpieces," softened in content, and he even began making friends with young WWE fans. The new-and-improved Heidenreich also began forming friendships with fellow Superstars, including Road Warrior Animal. Together, the duo defeated MNM to capture the WWE Tag Team Championship in July 2005.

HEIDI LEE MORGAN

FROM: New Jersey

An accomplished bodybuilder, Heidi Lee Morgan began her sports-entertainment career in 1987. Her high-flying offense and equally high blonde hair quickly caught the fans' attention.

Success came early for Morgan. With less than one year of professional experience, the New Jersey native battled former WWE Women's Champion Wendi Richter numerous times for independent promotions. Their rivalry was highlighted by a May 1987 Steel Cage Match, one of the first-ever cage matches featuring women in the United States.

Morgan turned her attention on the WWE Women's Championship in late 1993. In a tournament designed to crown a new titlist, she advanced to the final but lost to Alundra Blayze. After a few unsuccessful rematches, Morgan joined forces with Blayze to battle Luna Vachon & Bull Nakano before leaving WWE in 1994.

HELL IN A CELL

For over a decade, Hell In A Cell has been considered the most dangerous match in all of sports-entertainment. In this contest, regardless of the outcome, no Superstar leaves in the same condition in which he entered. Hell In A Cell made its debut at *In Your House: Badd Blood* in October 1997. The most memorable Hell In A Cell Match took place in 1998 when Undertaker launched Mankind off the top of the cage onto the Spanish announce table. Later in the match, Undertaker chokeslammed Mankind through the roof of the cage to the ring below.

After many years, the 20-foot steel enclosure required a redesign. In September 2006, Hell In A Cell became 3,500 square feet of steel beams. In 2009, *Hell In A Cell* became a yearly event which featured a Hell In A Cell Match as its main event.

October 4, 2009
Newark, NJ – The Prudential Center

Main Event Triple H & Shawn Michaels defeated Cody Rhodes & Ted DiBiase in a Hell In A Cell Match

October 3, 2010
Dallas, TX – American Airlines Arena

Main Event World Heavyweight Champion Kane defeated Undertaker in a Hell In A Cell Match

October 2, 2011
New Orleans, LA – New Orleans Arena

Main Event Alberto Del Rio defeated CM Punk and John Cena in a Triple Threat Hell In A Cell Match for the WWE Championship

HERCULES

HT: 6'1" **WT:** 270 lbs.
FROM: Tampa, Florida
SIGNATURE MOVE:
The Human Torture Rack

This stoic pillar of power came to World Wrestling Entertainment in 1986 managed by "Classy" Freddie Blassie. The strength of Hercules led him to numerous victories in a matter of minutes. He soon came to the ring with a steel chain around his neck which added intimidation to an already imposing figure. When his contract was acquired by Bobby "The Brain" Heenan, Hercules was more dangerous then ever.

He battled Billy Jack Haynes in a violent "Full Nelson Challenge" at *WrestleMania III*. At *WrestleMania IV*, Hercules was pitted against Ultimate Warrior. Hercules' rivalries with WWE's heroes continued until he became a victim of a plot himself in 1988 when "The Weasel" tried to sell him to "Million-Dollar Man" Ted DiBiase. With the fans behind him, Hercules battled Earthquake, Greg "The Hammer" Valentine, and Mr. Perfect. At the end 1990, Hercules formed the villainous Power & Glory with Paul Roma, managed by the "Doctor of Style" Slick. While they made for a formidable team, they separated after a series of disappointing defeats.

Hercules and WWE parted ways in 1991. He was seen through the decade in various promotions both in the United States and Japan displaying his raw power. Sadly, in March 2004, he passed away. This WWE Legend was one of the strongest and most intense competitors to ever ply his trade inside the ring.

HERCULES AYALA

HT: 6'1" **WT:** 265 lbs.
FROM: Puerto Rico

As a child on the tropical island of Puerto Rico, Hercules Ayala loved professional wrestling and his idol was island star, Hurricane Castillo. In his early 20s Ayala relocated to Boston where he met Angelo Savoldi. Ayala then landed in the World Wide Wrestling Federation shortly after his professional debut in 1971.

Ayala showed his skills and power all over the world. In Canada, Ayala was called "The Strongest Man In Wrestling" and ran roughshod through Stu Hart's Stampede territory where he tangled with Dynamite Kid, Davey Boy Smith, and future WWE Hall of Famers Harley Race and Bret "Hit Man" Hart. Ayala left the Stampede territory for a return to Puerto Rico one year before Vince McMahon took over the region's wrestling activities from his father.

HIGH ENERGY

MEMBERS: "The Rocket" Owen Hart, "The Birdman" Koko B. Ware
COMBINED WT: 456 lbs.

In 1992, Owen Hart and Koko B. Ware combined their abilities and threw fashion sense out the window. Decked out in fluorescent pants and checkered suspenders, the duo used speed and frequent tags to build momentum and dominate opponents.

High Energy took to the air in bouts against the best teams in WWE at the time, incluing the Headshrinkers and then-World Tag Team Champions, Money Inc. Unfortunately, just as High Energy was taking off, Owen Hart was sidelined with a serious knee injury. By the time he returned and was ready to once again take flight, Koko B. Ware was off flying high for other promotions. Fans of the colorful duo wish their partnership would have lasted longer, as the excitement they brought to WWE was unparalleled.

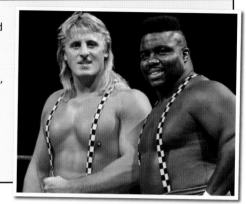

THE HIGHLANDERS

MEMBERS: Rory McAllister, Robbie McAllister
FROM: Oban, Scotland **COMBINED WT:** 470 lbs.

Rory & Robbie McAllister left their homes in the rugged Scottish Highlands in search of tag team gold. Since arriving in the United States in July 2006, however, they didn't have the easiest time adjusting to the American way of life.

When not attempting to figure out such technological advancements as a television or cell phones, the Highlanders were often found fending off WWE's top tag teams. Utilizing the Scot Drop, the fighting cousins picked up victories over The Spirit Squad, Lance Cade & Trevor Murdoch, and Paul London & Brian Kendrick.

Much like WWE Hall of Famer and fellow Scotsman "Rowdy" Roddy Piper, Rory & Robbie sported traditional plaid kilts to the ring. Many Americans scoffed at the sight of men in the pleated skirt-like garment, but The Highlanders enjoyed much success during their time in WWE.

THE HILLBILLIES

MEMBERS: Hillbilly Jim, Uncle Elmer,
Cousin Luke & Cousin Junior

Now don't go messin' with these country boys! Formed by Hillbilly Jim in 1985, the Hillbillies came to WWE to even the odds in Hillbilly Jim's battles against the Heenan Family, Jesse "The Body" Ventura, "Rowdy" Roddy Piper, "Cowboy" Bob Orton and Mr. Fuji and many others. Jim's relatives were a huge hit with audiences, as Elmer, Luke, and later, Junior battled in both singles and tag team action.

In one of the most touching moments in WWE history, Uncle Elmer was married on *Saturday Night's Main Event* despite the crude attempts by Piper to interrupt the ceremony. The reception was a star-studded event that included a poem recited by "Leapin'" Lanny Poffo and a surprise appearance from Tiny Tim.

By 1986, the cousins went back to the farm and Hillbilly Jim remained with the company. The Hillbillies will forever be remembered for putting smiles on the faces of fans wherever they traveled and weren't afraid to put a beating on no-good vermin either.

HILLBILLY JIM

HT: 6'7" **WT:** 285 lbs.
FROM: Mudlick, Kentucky
SIGNATURE MOVE: Bear Hug

At 6'7", it's hard not to notice Hillbilly Jim, especially when he's sitting in the front row. In late 1984, "Rowdy" Roddy Piper spotted the towering fan at a WWE Live Event and asked him to come on *Piper's Pit*. The arrogant "Hot Rod" mocked Jim's big bushy beard and denim overalls, but eventually offered to train him for a WWE career. Jim, despite wanting to start a ring career, declined the offer and chose to learn from Hulk Hogan instead.

After several weeks of training, the Kentucky native made his in-ring debut, defeating veteran Terry Gibbs with an impressive bear hug. The win marked the beginning of a long love affair between the fans and Hillbilly Jim. Audiences loved the country boy so much, in fact, that they began demanding more of him. Unable to keep up with the lofty demands, Hillbilly Jim introduced his equally lovable family members Uncle Elmer, Cousin Luke and Cousin Junior.

At *WrestleMania III*, Hillbilly Jim competed in the biggest match of his career when he teamed with midget wrestlers Little Beaver & Haiti Kid to battle King Kong Bundy and his pint-sized pals, Lord Littlebrook & Little Tokyo. The match was marred by controversy when the gigantic Bundy attacked Little Beaver. The sight of Hillbilly Jim carrying his limp little friend from the ring that night remains one of *WrestleMania*'s most memorable images.

HIRO SAITO

HT: 5'9" **WT:** 240 lbs.
FROM: Kawasaki, Japan

TITLE HISTORY

JUNIOR HEAVYWEIGHT CHAMPION	Defeated The Cobra on May 20, 1985

The sports-entertainment landscape changed dramatically when Kevin Nash, Scott Hall and Hulk Hogan formed the New World Order (nWo) in July 1996. In a matter of weeks, their buck-the-system attitude became vogue in locker rooms and a large portion of competitors longed to be in the renegade faction, including those in Japan.

Japanese Superstar Hiro Saito joined the controversial crew during its expansion into Asia. Known as nWo Japan, the group was led by Masahiro Chono and featured such members as Buff Bagwell, Scott Norton and Hiroyoshi Tenzan.

Years before Saito joined nWo Japan, he gained notoriety for his lengthy rivalry with The Cobra. In May 1985, Saito defeated The Cobra to claim the WWE Junior Heavyweight Championship. Two months later, he lost the title back to The Cobra in Osaka, Japan.

Saito was also an accomplished tag-team competitor. With Super Strong Machine as his partner, he won the International Wrestling Grand Prix Tag Team Championship in December 1990.

HISASHI SHINMA

A known figure for years within the world of Japanese *puroresu*, Hisashi Shinma began his tenure as WWE President in 1978. He set a tone of no nonsense leadership while making important strides to expand WWE's reach internationally. Shinma was instrumental in building many of the supercards that featured WWE Superstars and the best from New Japan Pro Wrestling, including the famous match that pit Muhammad Ali against Antonio Inoki. Hisashi was commonly seen at ringside impeccably dressed, making sure that WWE contests were filled with fighting spirit and its rules were always upheld.

Mr. Shinma honored the position with his wisdom, dignity and respect until 1984, when he was succeeded by Jack Tunney. Hisashi Shinma will be heralded as the man who upheld the standards of WWE at all costs, no matter what the circumstances were or what public pressures existed at the time.

HIROKO

FROM: The Land of the Rising Sun

Hell-bent on vengeance, Kenzo Suzuki and his valet, Hiroko, invaded *SmackDown* in the Summer of 2004. Clad in a Japanese kimono and sporting traditional white face makeup and red lipstick, Hiroko gave the impression of an unassuming geisha. In reality, though, she was a dangerous Diva with an unmatched temper.

Though her main responsibility was to second Suzuki to the ring and serve as his translator, Hiroko oftentimes stepped outside her job description to help her man achieve victory. It was not uncommon to see the devious geisha toss exotic powders into the eyes of Suzuki's opponents. Hiroko also proved to have a jealous side. The vindictive valet would regularly erupt into an uncontrollable rage any time Kenzo Suzuki's eye wandered toward the direction of another WWE Diva. During her time with WWE, Hiroko took her jealousy out on an unsuspecting Michelle McCool, and most notably Torrie Wilson. Both Suzuki and Hiroko were released from their WWE contracts in July 2005.

THE HOLLY COUSINS

MEMBERS: Crash, Hardcore, Molly
COMBINED WT: Over 800 lbs. (allegedly)

At first, Crash and Hardcore Holly constantly bickered about who was tougher, even when they were paired together in tag team matches. Calling themselves the "Superheavyweights," they insisted on competing only with the giants of sports-entertainment since they claimed a combined weight of allegedly over 800 lbs. Crash brought a scale to the ring with him to ensure that opponents measured up to the Superheavyweights' lofty standards.

TITLE HISTORY

WORLD TAG TEAM CHAMPIONS	Defeated The Rock 'N' Sock Connection on October 18, 1999

In October 1999, Crash and Hardcore Holly defeated the dysfunctional Rock 'N' Sock Connection to win the World Tag Team Championship. After losing the titles a month later, Crash and Hardcore remained top title contenders and even won a 16-team Battle Royal. In 2000, the beautiful and talented Molly Holly entered WWE and stepped right into family business. At *WrestleMania 2000,* Crash and Hardcore fought one another in addition to 11 other Superstars in a Hardcore Battle Royal.

While all three cousins went on to hold different titles during their respective stays in WWE, many fans would argue that this trio made the most magic when they appeared as a family.

HONKY TONK MAN

HT: 6'1" **WT: 243 lbs.** **FROM: Memphis, Tennessee** **SIGNATURE MOVE: Shake, Rattle, and Roll**

TITLE HISTORY

INTERCONTINENTAL CHAMPION	Defeated Ricky Steamboat on June 2, 1987

Many consider the Honky Tonk Man to be one of the greatest Superstars of the 1980s, including the Honky Tonk Man himself. Taking arrogance to a whole new level, it wasn't uncommon to hear the guitar-wielding Superstar remind audiences, "I'm cool, I'm cocky, I'm bad." Unfortunately for all the Honky Tonk Man detractors out there, of which there were plenty, he was everything he claimed to be.

With long sideburns and slicked-back hair, Honky Tonk Man rode into WWE in a pink Cadillac in 1986. Upon arriving, the Elvis look-alike expected to be showered with admiration. Instead, the fans vehemently despised the cocky newcomer. The boos, however, never deterred the Honky Tonk Man from succeeding in the ring. Alongside his manager "Colonel" Jimmy Hart, he set out on an impressive string of victories over WWE's most-noted Superstars, including his first big-name victim Jake "The Snake" Roberts at *WrestleMania III*.

Shortly after *WrestleMania*, the Honky Tonk Man defeated Ricky "The Dragon" Steamboat for the Intercontinental Championship in Buffalo, New York. The win proved historic, as he went on to hold the title for nearly fifteen months, longer than any other Superstar in history.

The Honky Tonk Man's record-breaking Intercontinental Championship reign came to an abrupt halt when Ultimate Warrior dethroned the titlist at *SummerSlam 1988* in a match that lasted a mere thirty seconds. Despite the humiliating loss, many consider the Honky Tonk Man to be exactly what he claimed to be: The greatest Intercontinental Champion of all-time.

Following his record-breaking reign, the Honky Tonk Man set out to create another record—a musical record. He teamed with Greg Valentine to form the singing duo known as Rhythm & Blues. At *WrestleMania VI*, much to the disgust of the sold-out SkyDome, they performed their single "Hunka, Hunka, Hunka Honky Love."

The twilight of the Honky Tonk Man's legendary career saw the singing Superstar contribute in several different capacities, including manager and commentator. Despite achieving moderate success in these new roles, however, fans everywhere will always remember him as the greatest Intercontinental Champion of all time.

HORNSWOGGLE

HT: 4'4" **WT: 135 lbs.**
FROM: Ireland **SIGNATURE MOVE: Tadpole Splash**

TITLE HISTORY

CRUISERWEIGHT CHAMPION	Defeated Chavo Guerrero on July 22, 2007

For a man so small in stature, Hornswoggle sure knows how to cause a huge commotion. Once revealed to be the illegitimate son of WWE Chairman Mr. McMahon, the pint-sized Superstar had the entire wrestling world buzzing over his newfound power. After only five months as a member of the McMahon family, JBL revealed the little guy was actually the son of Finlay.

The attention Hornswoggle garnered as a member of the McMahon family was not all that foreign to him. As a small person, he's used to people staring at him, especially when he's beating Superstars twice his size in the ring. He even turned back five of *SmackDown's* top names to capture the Cruiserweight Championship in July 2007. The victory put Hornswoggle on the same list with history's greatest cruiserweights. Despite his accomplishments in the ring, Hornswoggle considered his father's safety his main priority, whether he whacked an opponent with a shillelagh or delivered his signature Tadpole Splash.

Hornswoggle fulfilled a dream when he became the official mascot of D-Generation X. He continued to live large at 2011's *Royal Rumble* when he helped John Cena eliminate several Superstars and also served as Titus O'Neill's pro on *NXT: Redemption*. Thanks to Santa's stop on a special Holiday episode of *SmackDown*, the little Irishman now has the gift of speech.

Howard Finkel (see page 154)

HULK HOGAN

HT: 6'7"   **WT:** 303 lbs.   **FROM:** Venice Beach, California   **SIGNATURE MOVE:** Atomic Leg Drop

TITLE HISTORY

WORLD TAG TEAM CHAMPION	*Partnered with Edge to defeat Billy & Chuck on July 4, 2002*
WWE CHAMPION (6 TIMES)	*Defeated the Iron Sheik on January 23, 1984* *Defeated Randy Savage on April 2, 1989* *Defeated Sgt. Slaughter on March 24, 1991* *Defeated Undertaker on December 3, 1991* *Defeated Yokozuna on April 4, 1993* *Defeated Triple H on April 21, 2002*

Hulk Hogan, the most recognizable icon of professional wrestling, came from humble beginnings. During high school he had two passions: music and wrestling. He played in a string of bands within the bustling Tampa music scene. When he wasn't on stage, he was running to arenas to see his favorite stars of the ring. Once he saw "Superstar" Billy Graham jump on the middle turnbuckle and hit a double-bicep pose, the young Hogan knew his place was in the ring. One night after a concert he met the Briscos and soon introduced himself to Mike Graham. Graham arranged for Hogan to train with Japanese grappling master, Hiro Matsuda. After eighteen months of training he toured the Alabama, Pensacola, and Memphis territories.

An Early Taste of Mainstream Popularity

In 1978, Hulk Hogan debuted in the World Wide Wrestling Federation managed by "Classy" Freddie Blassie. Despite his questionable ways, he connected with the crowd at the 1980 *Showdown At Shea* when he met Andre the Giant in a wild bout. Against the wishes of Vince J. McMahon, Hogan left the company and appeared in *Rocky III* as "Thunderlips."

Hulk drifted to the AWA and though he resumed his rule-breaking ways, he quickly became a top contender to the AWA Championship. Hulk also traveled to Japan and defeated *puroresu* legend Antonio Inoki to become the first-ever IWGP Heavyweight Champion.

Hulkamania Runs Wild

Hulk Hogan returned to WWE in January 1984 and aided Bob Backlund against the Wild Samoans and Lou Albano. With the fans now behind him, Hulk was ready to catapult to the top of the ladder. Later that month, he replaced an injured Backlund and defeated the Iron Sheik for the WWE Championship. That night, dubbed "Super Monday," saw the birth of the most powerful force in the universe. Commentator Gorilla Monsoon perfectly proclaimed, "Hulkamania is here!"

The Hulkster became the voice of an entire generation. Hogan professed the importance of truth, training, saying your prayers, and eating your vitamins. By 1985, Hulk was splashed all over the mainstream media as he appeared on the *A-Team* and hosted *Saturday Night Live*.

The company's licensing and merchandising took the world by storm, spearheaded by the red and yellow of Hulkamania. The Hulkster had his own books, action figures, clothing line, workout set, vitamin pack, and an animated series titled *Hulk Hogan's Rock 'n' Wrestling*.

His success didn't sit well with Roddy Piper. In the main event of the first *WrestleMania*, Hogan and his partner, Mr. T, had Jimmy Snuka in their corner, while Piper had Paul Orndorff as his partner and "Cowboy" Bob Orton in their corner. Boxing legend Muhammad Ali was brought in as the special guest referee. The event was such a success that Hogan graced the cover of the April 29, 1985 issue of *Sports Illustrated*.

During a 1986 episode of *Saturday Night's Main Event* Hogan became the victim of a three-man attack by Don Muraco, Heenan, and King Kong Bundy. Despite missing than a month with broken ribs, and ignoring doctor's orders, Hogan defeated Bundy in a Steel Cage Match at *WrestleMania 2*.

WrestleMania III and a Million Dollar Threat

A giant threat to Hulk Hogan's career came from an unexpected source. Andre the Giant appeared on *Piper's Pit* with Bobby Heenan, and challenged Hogan to a WWE Championship match at *WrestleMania III*. Over 93,000 fans were on hand as the world's two most recognizable figures stood in the center of the ring. During the match, Hulk Hogan did the unthinkable and hoisted the 500–pound Andre the Giant and bodyslammed him. After Hulk Hogan's victory, which ended Andre's fifteen year undefeated streak, Hulkamaniacs all over the world rose to their feet in triumph.

In 1988, Hulk Hogan rejected the offers from "Million Dollar Man" Ted DiBiase to purchase the title, so DiBiase allied with Andre the Giant and Bobby Heenan. They plotted to dethrone the Hulkster during a nationally televised episode of *The Main Event* through subterfuge. With the plot uncovered, WWE president Jack Tunney declared the title vacant and that a new champion would be crowned in a tournament at *WrestleMania IV*. The quarterfinals match between Hogan and Andre ended in a double disqualification, so neither man was eligible to win the tournament.

The Rise and Fall of The Mega Powers

In the tournament finals, Hulk Hogan aided former foe, Randy "Macho Man" Savage against the "Million Dollar Man." The two Superstars became inseparable and soon Hulkamania and "Macho Madness" merged into the Mega Powers. Over the summer the Mega-Powers battled against Andre the Giant and Ted DiBiase, leading to clashes at the main event of the first *SummerSlam* and the 1988 *Survivor Series*.

Unfortunately, during *The Main Event* a series of misunderstandings between Hogan and Savage lead to the Macho Man slapping Hogan. After the match, the disagreement escalated and Macho Man blindsided Hulk Hogan. His former partner ignited the fuse that would lead to a colossal explosion at *WrestleMania V* where Hulk Hogan reclaimed the WWE Championship.

No Holds Barred

On June 2, 1989, the movie *No Holds Barred* opened and Hulk Hogan was the main attraction. The success of the picture led to a dispute with co-star Zeus. After a series of attacks on the Champion, Hulk Hogan and Brutus Beefcake defeated Zeus and Randy Savage at *SummerSlam '89*.

In the next decade, Hulk continued to star in feature films and commercials. After the Hulkster defeated Savage on *The Main Event* with special guest referee Buster Douglas, he moved on to other title contenders. At the 1990 *Royal Rumble* fate brought the two largest personas in the WWE nose-to-nose in the middle of the ring. The even exchange between Hogan and Ultimate Warrior had everyone on their feet. Even after the WWE Champion won his first Royal Rumble, the question remained if the two Superstars met, who would win? WWE answered the call and signed a Title Vs. Title match for the main event of *WrestleMania VI*.

Even though Hogan lost the WWE Championship to Ultimate Warrior that night, he exited with the grace of a true champion. He even joined Ultimate Warrior in victory at the 1990 *Survivor Series*, and in the Match Made in Hell at *SummerSlam '91*. Hogan went on to hold the WWE Championship three more times, and win a second Royal Rumble before leaving WWE to concentrate on raising his family and a movie career.

WCW AND THE nWo

In June 1994, Hogan was lured back to sports-entertainment by WCW. In July, he defeated Ric Flair to become WCW Champion. Despite holding the title on six separate occasions, his WCW tenure is remembered more for the shocking turn at *Bash At The Beach* in 1996, where Hogan revealed himself as the mystery partner of the Outsiders, Scott Hall and Kevin Nash.

As he turned his back on millions of Hulkamaniacs worldwide, "Hollywood" Hulk Hogan declared that the fans could "stick it" and formed the New World Order (nWo) with Hall and Nash.

After the 2002 *Royal Rumble*, the nWo were brought into WWE by Vince McMahon. The nWo's involvement in WWE reached its peak at *WrestleMania X-8*, Hogan's first appearance at the event in nine years, as Hollywood Hogan faced The Rock in a match labled Icon vs. Icon. Following that classic showdown, Hogan and The Rock shook hands and battled Scott Hall and Kevin Nash, who had turned their backs on Hogan.

Return to the Red and Yellow

Hulk removed the nWo attire and returned to the ring in the red and yellow of Hulkamania. With Hulkamania reinvigorated, the Hulkster found himself across the ring at *Backlash* from "The Game" Triple H. After a wild battle Hogan captured his sixth WWE Championship. Though the Hulkster lost the title to Undertaker at *Judgment Day*, he added a new prize to his collection when he won the World Tag Team Championship with Edge. Later in the year his autobiography titled *Hollywood Hulk Hogan* landed atop the *New York Times* Bestseller list. The next year he headlined *WrestleMania XIX* in a street fight against Mr. McMahon.

After being inducted in the Hall Of Fame at *WrestleMania 21*, Hulk saved Eugene from Muhammed Hassan and Daivari. Hogan was recruited by Shawn Michaels to eradicate the duo. On an episode of *Monday Night Raw,* Michaels suddenly turned on Hogan after they beat Kurt Angle & Carlito. HBK mocked sports-entertainment's most beloved figure, but Hulk Hogan had the last laugh and defeated the "Showstopper" in their Legend vs. Icon Match at *SummerSlam*.

Hogan also appeared at the *Raw Homecoming* in October 2005, battled Randy Orton at *SummerSlam 2006*, and saved Hornswoggle in 2008 from The Great Khali at the *Raw 15th Anniversary* broadcast.

In April 2005, Hulk Hogan's career was honored at the Hall Of Fame ceremony, where he was inducted by Sylvester Stallone.

The next year WWE released the *Hulk Hogan's Unreleased Collector's Series* DVD set, which featured rare and never-before-seen matches from the Hulkster's storied career.

HOWARD FINKEL

  FROM: New York, New York

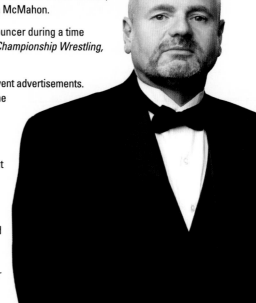

Howard Finkel began his career in the early 1970s as an usher at the New Haven Coliseum. After he persuaded his boss to contact WWE about holding events there, he met Vince McMahon, and by 1976 he was the ring announcer during WWE events at the venue. In 1980, Finkel became a full-time WWE employee and the first staff member of Titan Sports, hired by Vince and Linda McMahon.

As the company entered its critical phase of national expansion, Finkel was selected as the lead ring announcer during a time where WWE needed its own voice. Howard Finkel was heard everywhere – television programs such as *Championship Wrestling*, *Tuesday Night Titans*, *Superstars of Wrestling*, and *Saturday Night's Main Event*.

Finkel also appeared at untelevised stadium shows, pay-per-view events and provided voice-overs for live event advertisements. WWE was a global entity and Howard Finkel's distinctive delivery was recognized by fans in preparation of the incredible happenings that took place. Into the 1990s, fans and colleagues bestowed him the nickname "The Fink," and at *WrestleMania IX*, he was introduced as "Finkus Maximus." From 1993 to 1997, he was the ring announcer for the company's flagship program, *Monday Night Raw*.

Towards the late 1990s, Howard took on a lighter schedule and announced for live events while branching out to co-host the Internet program *WWE Byte This*. In August 2002, he entered into a dispute with up-and-coming ring announcer Lilian Garcia which turned physical. Unfortunately for "The Fink," he came up on the short end of the stick in an Evening Gown/Tuxedo Match for the right to be the *Raw* ring announcer.

Today, Finkel works behind the scenes, hosts the popular "Out Think The Fink" segment on WWE.com, and announces the Hall of Fame inductees at *WrestleMania*. In 2009, it was his turn to have his name announced as the night before *WrestleMania XXV*, he stepped into the WWE Hall of Fame. Howard is the only person to appear on camera at every *WrestleMania*. He still finds time for his old job. At 2011 *Survivor Series*, he appeared in front of a sold-out Madison Square Garden crowd as CM Punk's personal ring announcer for his WWE Championship match against Alberto Del Rio.

HUNICO

HT: 5'10" WT: 205 lbs.
FROM: Mexico City, Mexico
SIGNATURE MOVE: Senton Bomb

The WWE Universe caught Sin Cara fever in early 2011 when the high-flying, masked Superstar made his jaw-dropping debut. But after several months, fans began to question their allegiance to Sin Cara when he began to display an unbecoming change in attitude. There was a catch: It wasn't really Sin Cara under the mask. Instead, the Superstar who was turning fans off was really Hunico.

Following the revelation, Hunico and the original Sin Cara squared off in a Mask vs. Mask Match, which Hunico lost. As a result, the Mexican Superstar was forced to unmask and no longer compete as Sin Cara.

With Sin Cara behind him, an unmasked Hunico set out to make a name for himself. And to ensure there was no longer any ties to his earliest WWE days, he shelved much of his aerial offense in favor of a ground-and-pound style. He also employed the services of the menacing Camacho as his bodyguard. With the powerhouse watching his back, there's no telling how high Hunico's career can climb.

THE HURRICANE

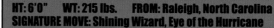

HT: 6'0" WT: 215 lbs. FROM: Raleigh, North Carolina
SIGNATURE MOVE: Shining Wizard, Eye of the Hurricane

TITLE HISTORY	
CRUISERWEIGHT CHAMPION (2 TIMES)	Defeated Tajiri on May 16, 2002 Defeated Kid Kash on January 29, 2006
EUROPEAN CHAMPION	Defeated Matt Hardy on August 27, 2001
HARDCORE CHAMPION	1 Time
WORLD TAG TEAM CHAMPION (2 TIMES)	Partnered with Kane to defeat Christian & Lance Storm on September 23, 2002 Partnered with Rosey to defeat La Resistance on May 1, 2005

Gregory Helms had visions of ruling the wrestling world and to be involved in the cosmos of superheroes. He first garnered attention in WCW as a top Cruiserweight and in fact, he was the Cruiserweight Champion when WWE purchased its competitor in 2001.

After WCW's Invasion, WWE audiences saw him backstage as a mild-mannered beat reporter for the Daily Globe. In times of peril, however, the crowd was warned: "Stand back, there's a Hurricane coming through!" As The Hurricane, Helms was a masked superhero who protected truth, justice, and the WWE way.

As a member of *SmackDown* in 2002, he captured the Cruiserweight Championship in a Triple Threat Match. Later that year, he arrived on *Raw* and formed an unlikely, yet successful, team with Kane. He shocked the WWE Universe on the March 10, 2003 edition of *Raw* when he pinned The Rock. He also enjoyed a successful association with Superhero-in-Training Rosey, and their super-sidekick Stacey, which led to a World Tag Team Championship reign.

In January 2006, The Hurricane jumped to *SmackDown*. Competing with a new attitude under his real name, Gregory Helms, he immediately captured the Cruiserweight Championship. His reign, which totaled a record thirteen months is widely recognized as the greatest of all-time. After a neck injury sidelined him for over a year, Helms returned to *SmackDown* and later answered the call to ECW, where he conducted backstage interviews for a brief time before parting ways with WWE.

HUSKY HARRIS

 HT: 6'2" **WT:** 300 lbs. **FROM:** Brooksville, Florida
SIGNATURE MOVE: Swinging Reverse STO

Unlike most second- and third-generation Superstars, Husky Harris refuses to use his family's fame to gain notoriety. He'd rather make a name for himself on his own. But it's hard to ignore his legendary bloodline. He's the grandson of Blackjack Mulligan, the nephew of Barry and Kendall Windham and the son of Mike Rotundo.

First appearing on WWE television as a part of *NXT*, Harris made it clear very quickly that he wasn't anything like his predecessors. He was as big as a tank and as fast as a Ferrari, and his unorthodox style was nothing ever before seen on his family tree. Following his time on *NXT*, Harris helped Wade Barrett defeat John Cena at *Hell in a Cell 2010*. In the weeks that followed, Harris continued to impress Barrett, resulting in induction into The Nexus. Harris remained an integral part of The Nexus through the end of the year. Then in January 2011, he was punted in the head by Randy Orton. The impact of the blow was so great that Harris never returned to the notorious faction.

IN YOUR HOUSE

IN YOUR HOUSE 1
May 14, 1995
Nashville, TN
Nashville Municipal Auditorium

Main Event: WWE Champion Diesel defeated Sycho Sid

2: THE LUMBERJACKS
July 23, 1995
Nashville, TN
Nashville Municipal Auditorium

Main Event: WWE Champion Diesel defeated Sycho Sid, Lumberjack Match

3: TRIPLE HEADER
September 24, 1995
Saginaw, MI
Saginaw Civic Center

Main Event: WWE Champion Diesel & Intercontinental Champion Shawn Michaels defeated British Bulldog & Yokozuna

4: GREAT WHITE NORTH
October 22, 1995
Winnipeg, Manitoba
Winnipeg Arena

Main Event: British Bulldog defeated WWE Champion Diesel

5: SEASON'S BEATINGS
December 17, 1995
Hershey, PA
Hersheypark Arena

Main Event: WWE Champion Bret "Hit Man" Hart defeated British Bulldog

6: RAGE IN THE CAGE
February 18, 1996
Louisville, KY
Louisville Gardens

Main Event: WWE Champion Bret "Hit Man" Hart defeated Diesel, Steel Cage Match

7: GOOD FRIENDS, BETTER ENEMIES
April 28, 1996
Omaha, NE
Omaha Civic Center

Main Event: WWE Champion Shawn Michaels defeated Diesel, No Holds Barred Match

8: BEWARE OF DOG
May 26, 1996
Florence, SC
Florence Civic Center

Main Event: WWE Champion Shawn Michaels vs. British Bulldog. Went to No Contest

May 28, 1996
North Charleston, SC
North Charleston Coliseum

Main Event: Undertaker defeated Intercontinental Champion Goldust, Casket Match

9: INTERNATIONAL INCIDENT
July 21, 1996
Vancouver, BC
General Motors Place

Main Event: Vader, Owen Hart & British Bulldog defeated WWE Champion Shawn Michaels, Intercontinental Champion Ahmed Johnson & Sycho Sid

10: MIND GAMES
September 22, 1996
Philadelphia, PA
CoreStates Center

Main Event: WWE Champion Shawn Michaels defeated Mankind

11: BURIED ALIVE
October 20, 1996
Indianapolis, IN
Market Square Arena

Main Event: Undertaker defeated Mankind, Buried Alive Match

12: IT'S TIME
December 15, 1996
West Palm Beach, FL
West Palm Beach Auditorium

Main Event: WWE Champion Sycho Sid defeated Bret "Hit Man" Hart

13: FINAL FOUR
February 16, 1997
Chattanooga, TN
UTC Arena

Main Event: Bret "Hit Man" Hart defeated Undertaker, Stone Cold Steve Austin and Vader, Vacant WWE Championship Four Corners Elimination Match

14: REVENGE OF THE UNDERTAKER
April 20, 1997
Rochester, NY
War Memorial Auditorium

Main Event: Stone Cold Steve Austin defeated Bret "Hit Man" Hart

15: A COLD DAY IN HELL
May 11, 1997
Richmond, VA
Richmond Coliseum

Main Event: WWE Champion Undertaker defeated Stone Cold Steve Austin

16: CANADIAN STAMPEDE
July 6, 1997
Calgary, Alberta
Saddledome

Main Event: Bret "Hit Man" Hart, Jim Neidhart, Brian Pillman, Owen Hart & British Bulldog defeated Stone Cold Steve Austin, Goldust, Ken Shamrock & Legion of Doom

17: GROUND ZERO
September 7, 1997
Louisville, KY
Louisville Gardens

Main Event: Shawn Michaels vs. Undertaker. Went to No Contest

18: BADD BLOOD
October 5, 1997
St. Louis, MO
Kiel Center

Main Event: Shawn Michaels defeated Undertaker, Hell In A Cell Match

19: DEGENERATION-X
December 7, 1997
Springfield, MA
Springfield Civic Center

Main Event: Ken Shamrock defeated WWE Champion Shawn Michaels

20: NO WAY OUT OF TEXAS
February 15, 1998
Houston, TX
Compaq Center

Main Event: Stone Cold Steve Austin, Cactus Jack, Chainsaw Charlie & Owen Hart defeated Triple H, Billy Gunn, Road Dogg & Savio Vega

21: UNFORGIVEN
April 26, 1998
Greensboro, NC
Greensboro Coliseum

Main Event: Dude Love defeated WWE Champion Stone Cold Steve Austin

22: OVER THE EDGE
May 31, 1998
Milwaukee, WI
Wisconsin Center Arena

Main Event: WWE Champion Stone Cold Steve Austin defeated Dude Love, No Disqualification Falls Count Anywhere Match, Mr. McMahon as guest referee

23: FULLY LOADED
July 26, 1998
Fresno, CA
Selland Arena

Main Event: Undertaker & Stone Cold Steve Austin defeated World Tag Team Champions Kane & Mankind

24: BREAKDOWN
September 27, 1998
Hamilton, Ontario
Copps Coliseum

Main Event: Undertaker and Kane defeated WWE Champion Stone Cold Steve Austin, Triple Threat Match

25: JUDGMENT DAY
October 18, 1998
Rosemont, IL
Rosemont Horizon

Main Event: Kane vs. Undertaker. Went to No Contest, Stone Cold Steve Austin as guest referee

26: ROCK BOTTOM
December 13, 1998
Vancouver, British Columbia
General Motors Place

Main Event: Stone Cold Steve Austin defeated Undertaker, Buried Alive Match

27: ST. VALENTINE'S DAY MASSACRE
February 14, 1999
Memphis, TN
The Pyramid

Main Event: Stone Cold Steve Austin defeated Mr. McMahon, Steel Cage Match

28: BACKLASH
April 25, 1999
Providence, RI
Providence Civic Center

Main Event: WWE Champion Stone Cold Steve Austin defeated The Rock, Shane McMahon as guest referee

INTERCONTINENTAL CHAMPIONSHIP

After unifying the North and South American Championships in September 1979, Pat Patterson was recognized as the first-ever Intercontinental Champion. Patterson's impressive resumé prior to becoming Intercontinental Champion gave the title instant credibility. However, nobody could have predicted that the Intercontinental Championship would eventually become one of the most prestigious titles in sports-entertainment history.

Over the next several decades, many future Hall of Famers went on to prove their greatness with the Intercontinental Championship strapped around their waist, including Greg "The Hammer" Valentine, Mr. Perfect, and "Rowdy" Roddy Piper. Several others used the title to propel themselves to World Championship reigns, including Shawn Michaels, Stone Cold Steve Austin, and The Rock.

1981
June 20
Philadelphia, PA

Don Muraco defeated Pedro Morales

November 23
New York, NY

Pedro Morales defeated Don Muraco

1984
February 11
Boston, MA

Tito Santana defeated Don Muraco

1986
February 8
Boston, MA

Randy Savage defeated Tito Santana

September 24
London, Ontario

Greg Valentine defeated Tito Santana

1979
September 1
Rio de Janeiro

Pat Patterson becomes Intercontinental Champion

After winning a tournament in Rio de Janeiro, Pat Patterson unified the North and South American Championships to become the first-ever Intercontinental Champion.

1980
April 21, 1980
New York, NY

Ken Patera defeated Pat Patterson

December 8
New York, NY

Pedro Morales defeated Ken Patera

1983
January 22
New York, NY

Don Muraco defeated Pedro Morales

1987
March 29
Pontiac, MI

Ricky Steamboat defeated Randy Savage

June 2
Buffalo, NY

Honky Tonk Man defeated Ricky Steamboat

1985
July 6
Baltimore, MD

Tito Santana defeated Greg Valentine

1988

August 29
New York, NY

Ultimate Warrior defeated Honky Tonk Man

▼

1989

April 2
Atlantic City, NJ

Rick Rude defeated Ultimate Warrior

▼

August 28
East Rutherford, NJ

Ultimate Warrior defeated Rick Rude

Ultimate Warrior vacated the Intercontinental Championship shortly after defeating Hulk Hogan for the WWE Championship in April 1990

▼

1990

April 23
Austin, TX

Mr. Perfect defeated Tito Santana in the finals of a tournament to crown a new Intercontinental Champion.

▼

August 27
Philadelphia, PA

Texas Tornado defeated Mr. Perfect

▼

November 19
Rochester, NY

Mr. Perfect defeated Texas Tornado

▼

1991

August 26
New York, NY

Bret Hart defeated Mr. Perfect

▼

1992

January 17
Springfield, MA

The Mountie defeated Bret Hart

▼

January 19
Albany, NY

Roddy Piper defeated The Mountie

▼

April 5
Indianapolis, IN

Bret Hart defeated Roddy Piper

▼

August 29
London, England

British Bulldog defeated Bret Hart

▼

October 27
Terre Haute, IN

Shawn Michaels defeated British Bulldog

▼

1993

May 17
New York, NY

Marty Jannetty defeated Shawn Michaels

▼

June 6
Albany, NY

Shawn Michaels defeated Marty Jannetty

After failing to defend the Intercontinental Championship for 30 days, Shawn Michaels was stripped of the title

▼

September 27
New Haven, CT

Razor Ramon defeated Rick Martel

After being the last two Superstars standing in a Battle Royal, Razor Ramon and Rick Martel squared off to crown a new Intercontinental Champion

▼

1994
April 13

August 29
Chicago, IL

Razor Ramon defeated Diesel

▼

1995

January 22
Tampa, FL

Jeff Jarrett defeated Razor Ramon

Jeff Jarrett was stripped of the Intercontinental Championship on April 26 after a title defense against Bob Holly ended in controversy.

▼

April 26
Moline, IL

Jeff Jarrett defeated Bob Holly to reclaim the vacated title

▼

May 19
Montreal, Quebec

Razor Ramon defeated Jeff Jarrett

▼

May 22
Trios-Rivieres, Quebec

Jeff Jarrett defeated Razor Ramon

▼

July 23
Nashville, TN

Shawn Michaels defeated Jeff Jarrett

Injuries forced Shawn Michaels to relinquish the Intercontinental

October 22
Winnipeg, Manitoba

Dean Douglas is awarded Intercontinental Championship

October 22
Winnipeg, Manitoba

Razor Ramon defeated Dean Douglas

1996

January 21
Fresno, CA

Goldust defeated Razor Ramon

Goldust was stripped of the Intercontinental Championship after a title defense against Savio Vega ended in controversy

April 1
San Bernardino, CA

Goldust defeated Savio Vega

June 23
Milwaukee, WI

Ahmed Johnson defeated Goldust

Injuries forced Ahmed Johnson to relinquish the Intercontinental Championship on August 12

September 23
Hershey, PA

Marc Mero defeated Faarooq in the finals of a tournament to crown a new Intercontinental Champion

October 21
Fort Wayne, IN

Hunter Hearst Helmsley defeated Marc Mero

1997

February 13
Lowell, MA

Rocky Maivia defeated Hunter Hearst Helmsley

April 28
Omaha, NE

Owen Hart defeated Rocky Maivia

August 3
East Rutherford, NJ

Stone Cold Steve Austin defeated Owen Hart

Shortly after winning the Intercontinental Championship, injuries forced Stone Cold Steve Austin to relinquish the title

October 5
St. Louis, MO

Owen Hart defeated Faarooq in the finals of a tournament to crown a new Intercontinental Champion

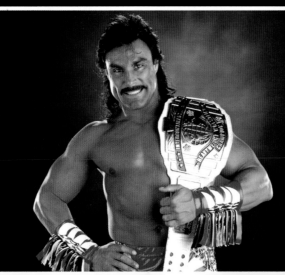

November 9
Montreal, Quebec

Stone Cold Steve Austin defeated Owen Hart

Stone Cold Steve Austin vacated the Championship by throwing the title belt into a river

December 8
Portland, ME

The Rock was awarded the Intercontinental Champion

1998

August 30
New York, NY

Triple H defeated The Rock

Injuries forced Triple H to relinquish the Intercontinental Championship on October 9

October 12
Uniondale, NY

Ken Shamrock defeated X-Pac in the finals of a tournament to crown a new Intercontinental Champion

1999

February 14
Memphis, TN

Val Venis defeated Ken Shamrock

March 15
San Jose, CA

Road Dogg defeated Val Venis

March 29
East Rutherford, NJ

Goldust defeated Road Dogg

April 12
Detroit, MI

The Godfather defeated Goldust

May 31
Moline, IL

Jeff Jarrett defeated The Godfather

July 24
Toronto, Ontario

Edge defeated Jeff Jarrett

July 25
Buffalo, NY

Jeff Jarrett defeated Edge

▼

July 26
Dayton, OH

D'Lo Brown defeated Jeff Jarrett

▼

August 22
Minneapolis, MN

Jeff Jarrett defeated D'Lo Brown

▼

October 17
Cleveland, OH

Chyna defeated Jeff Jarrett

▼

December 12
Sunrise, FL

Chris Jericho defeated Chyna

Chris Jericho and Chyna were declared co-Intercontinental Champions on January 3, after a match between the two ended in a double pinfall

▼

2000

January 23
New York, NY

Chris Jericho defeated Chyna and Hardcore Holly in a Triple Threat Match

▼

February 27
Hartford, CT

Kurt Angle defeated Chris Jericho

▼

April 2
Anaheim, CA

Chris Benoit defeated Chris Jericho and Kurt Angle in a Triple Threat Match

▼

May 4
Richmond, VA

Chris Jericho defeated Chris Benoit

▼

May 8
Uniondale, NY

Chris Benoit defeated Chris Jericho

▼

Memphis, TN

Rikishi defeated Chris Benoit

▼

July 6
Ft. Lauderdale, FL

Val Venis defeated Rikishi

▼

August 27
Raleigh, NC

Chyna and Eddie Guerrero defeated Val Venis and Trish Stratus in a Mixed-Tag Team Match where the winner of the match would be declared Intercontinental Champion; Chyna pinned Trish Stratus to win the title

▼

September 3
Knoxville, TN

Eddie Guerrero defeated Chyna and Kurt Angle in a Triple Threat Match

▼

November 23
Sunrise, FL

Billy Gunn defeated Eddie Guerrero

▼

December 10
Birmingham, AL

Chris Benoit defeated Billy Gunn

▼

2001

January 21
New Orleans, LA

Chris Jericho defeated Chris Benoit

▼

April 5
Oklahoma City, OK

Triple H defeated Chris Jericho

▼

April 12
Philadelphia, PA

Jeff Hardy defeated Triple H

▼

April 16
Knoxville, TN

Triple H defeated Jeff Hardy

▼

Sacramento, CA

Kane defeated Triple H

▼

June 28
New York, NY

Albert defeated Kane

▼

July 23
Buffalo, NY

Lance Storm defeated Albert

▼

August 19
San Jose, CA

Edge defeated Lance Storm

▼

September 23
Pittsburgh, PA

Christian defeated Edge

▼

October 21
St. Louis, MO

Edge defeated Christian

▼

November 5
Uniondale, NY

Test defeated Edge

▼

November 18
Greensboro, NC

Edge defeated Test

Edge unified the Intercontinental and United States Championships

▼

2002

January 20
Atlanta, GA

William Regal defeated Edge

▼

March 17
Toronto, Ontario

Rob Van Dam defeated William Regal

▼

Kansas City, MO

Eddie Guerrero defeated Rob Van Dam

▼

May 27
Edmonton, Alberta

Rob Van Dam defeated Eddie Guerrero

▼

July 29
Greensboro, NC

Chris Benoit defeated Rob Van Dam

▼

August 25
Uniondale, NY

Rob Van Dam defeated Chris Benoit

▼

September 16
Denver, CO

Chris Jericho defeated Rob Van Dam

▼

September 30
Houston, TX

Kane defeated Chris Jericho

▼

October 20
Little Rock, AR

Triple H defeated Kane

Triple H unified the World Heavyweight Championship with the Intercontinental Championship; the Intercontinental Title remained inactive until May 2003

▼

2003

May 18
Charlotte, NC

Christian last eliminated Booker T in a Battle Royal to crown the new Intercontinental Champion

▼

July 7
Montreal, Quebec

Booker T defeated Christian

▼

August 10
Des Moines, IA

Christian defeated Booker T

▼

September 29
Chicago, IL

Rob Van Dam defeated Christian

▼

October 27
Fayetteville, NC

Chris Jericho defeated Rob Van Dam

▼

October 27
Fayetteville, NC

Rob Van Dam defeated Chris Jericho

▼

December 14
Orlando, FL

Randy Orton defeated Rob Van Dam

▼

2004

July 11
Hartford, CT

Edge defeated Randy Orton

Injuries forced Edge to relinquish the Intercontinental Championship in September 2004

▼

September 12
Portland, OR

Chris Jericho defeated Christian in a Ladder Match to crown a new Intercontinental Champion.

▼

October 19
Milwaukee, WI

Shelton Benjamin defeated Chris Jericho

▼

2005

June 21
Phoenix, AZ

Carlito defeated Shelton Benjamin

▼

September 19
Oklahoma, City, OK

Ric Flair defeated Carlito

▼

2006

February 20
Trenton, NJ

Shelton Benjamin defeated Ric Flair

▼

April 30
Lexington, KY

Rob Van Dam defeated Shelton Benjamin

▼

May 15
Lubbock, TX

Shelton Benjamin, Chris Masters & Triple H battled John Cena & Rob Van Dam in a 3-on-2 Handicap Texas Tornado Match. Pre-match stipulations stated that if any member of Benjamin's team defeated John Cena or Rob Van Dam, they would win that Superstar's Championship; Benjamin pinned Rob Van Dam to win the Intercontinental Championship

▼

June 25
Charlotte, NC

Johnny Nitro defeated Shelton Benjamin and Carlito in a Triple Threat Match

▼

October 2
Topeka, KS

Jeff Hardy defeated Johnny Nitro

▼

November 6
Columbus, OH

Johnny Nitro defeated Jeff Hardy

▼

November 13
Manchester, England

Jeff Hardy defeated Johnny Nitro

▼

2007

February 19
Bakersfield, CA

Umaga defeated Jeff Hardy

▼

April 16
Milan, Italy

Santino Marella defeated Umaga

▼

July 2
Dallas, TX

Umaga defeated Santino Marella

▼

September 3
Columbus, OH

Jeff Hardy defeated Umaga

▼

2008

March 10
Milwaukee, WI

Chris Jericho defeated Jeff Hardy

▼

June 29
Dallas, TX

Kofi Kingston defeated Chris Jericho

▼

August 17
Indianapolis, IN

Santino Marella & Beth Phoenix defeated Kofi Kingston & Mickie James in an Intergender Winners-Take-All Tag Team Match

▼

November 10
Manchester, England

William Regal defeated Santino Marella

▼

2009

January 19
Chicago, IL

CM Punk defeated William Regal

▼

March 9
Jacksonville, FL

JBL defeated CM Punk

▼

April 5
Houston, TX

Rey Mysterio defeated JBL

▼

June 7
New Orleans, LA

Chris Jericho defeated Rey Mysterio

▼

June 28
Sacramento, CA

Rey Mysterio defeated Chris Jericho

▼

September 4
Cleveland, OH

John Morrison defeated Rey Mysterio

▼

December 13
San Antonio, TX

Drew McIntyre defeated John Morrison

▼

2010

May 23
Detroit, MI

Kofi Kingston defeated Drew McIntyre

▼

August 6
Laredo, TX

Dolph Ziggler defeated Kofi Kingston

▼

2011

January 7
Tucson, AZ

ofi Kingston defeated
olph Ziggler

▼

March 25
Columbus, OH

Vade Barrett defeated
Kofi Kingston

▼

June 19
Washington, D.C.

zekiel Jackson defeated
Vade Barrett

▼

August 12
Sacramento, CA

Cody Rhodes defeated
Ezekiel Jackson

▼

2012

April 1
Miami, FL

Big Show defeated Cody Rhodes

INVASION

July 22 2001 **Gund Arena;
Cleveland, Ohio**

or decades, sports-entertainment fans dreamed of what would happen if Superstars from their favorite
romotion crossed over and battled competitors from a rival organization. In 2001, those dreams became a
eality when WWE squared off against the WCW/ECW Alliance at the *Invasion* pay-per-view.

he wheels for the historic event were set in motion when Shane McMahon purchased WCW in March
001. Shane's sister, Stephanie, later assumed control of ECW. The siblings then combined forces to create
he Alliance, a mega-promotion, whose sole goal was to put Mr. McMahon and WWE out of business.

he two forces finally collided in July 2001, at the *Invasion* pay-per-view. Team WWE (Stone Cold Steve
ustin, Chris Jericho, Undertaker, Kane, Kurt Angle) looked to be in control of the main event but in a shocking
evelopment, Stone Cold turned on his team late in the match, allowing the win to go to Team Alliance (Booker
, Diamond Dallas Page, the Dudley Boys, Rhyno). Other highlights included Rob Van Dam defeating Hardcore
hampion Jeff Hardy, Tajiri beating Tazz, and Edge & Christian topping Lance Storm & Mike Awesome.

IRISH JACKIE 🇮🇪

Prior to entering WWE, midget wrestler Irish Jackie
struggled to make it big while competing in Southern
wrestling territories. For much of the 1950s, he fell short
against the likes of Little Beaver and Pee Wee James.
After moving north to WWE in the 1960s, Irish Jackie
began to find his winning ways. He wowed Northern
audiences alongside his new partner the Jamaica Kid.
The famed Boston Garden was the scene of many of the
team's victories over rivals Sky Low Low & Little Brutus.
Irish Jackie also had many remarkable battles against
Sonny Boy Cassidy in the late 1960s.

"IRON" MIKE SHARPE 🇨🇦

HT: 6'4" **WT: 283 lbs.**
FROM: Hamilton, Ontario, Canada
SIGNATURE MOVE: Forearm Smash

A second-generation Superstar, "Iron" Mike Sharpe was a
rough and tough customer who proclaimed himself
"Canada's Greatest Athlete." He was first seen by WWE
audiences in the early 1980s managed by Lou Albano.

During the mid 1980s, Sharpe traveled through Canada and
Japan before returning to WWE programming. Sharpe
always attributed his success to himself, but others
attributed it to the controversial black armpad that covered
his right forearm.

"Iron" Mike Sharp retired in 1995. Today he owns and
operates Iron Mike Sharpe's School of Pro-Wrestling in
Asbury Park, NJ. There's no official word on whether or not
students receive a black forearm band upon graduation.

IRON SHEIK

HT: 6'0"   **WT: 258 lbs.**   **FROM: Tehran, Iran**   **SIGNATURE MOVE: Camel Clutch**

TITLE HISTORY	
WORLD TAG TEAM CHAMPION	Partnered with Nikolai Volkoff to defeat Mike Rotundo & Barry Windham on March 31, 1985
WWE CHAMPION	Defeated Bob Backlund on December 26, 1983

" IRAN NUMBER ONE! IRON SHEIK NUMBER ONE! "

The Iron Sheik is remembered as one of the most loathed villains in the history of the ring. His mixture of technical ring skill, charisma and athleticism brought terror to WWE and its fans to heights that may never be seen again. Whether he was in singles or tag team competition, one word can be used to describe the Iron Sheik: dangerous.

As a member of the Iranian Army, this man became a national wrestling champion and later the bodyguard for Mohammed Reza Pahlavi, the Shah of Iran. He was an alternate on the 1968 Iranian Olympic wrestling team and a two-time Asian freestyle champion. In 1970, he risked his life and defected to the United States, where he won several AAU Championships. His impressive credentials led him to the coaching staff of the 1972 U.S. Olympic team, and, in 1973, he was trained for a career in the ring by future WWE Hall of Famer Verne Gagne.

In 1979, the Iron Sheik entered WWE swinging his Persian Clubs. In his Madison Square Garden debut, he won a 20-man over-the-top-rope battle royal and earned a WWE Championship Match in that night's main event against Bob Backlund. After that bout, he tied-up with the likes of Bruno Sammartino, Antonio Inoki, Ted DiBiase, Dominic DeNucci and future WWE Hall of Famers Chief Jay Strongbow, Gorilla Monsoon and Tito Santana. He left WWE in 1980 and toured the Southeastern territories of the NWA.

While he toured the United States and exuded anti-American rhetoric, the terror from Tehran became known as a cold blooded rule-breaker, a premier ring technician and "The Master of the Suplex."

In the fall of 1983, the Iron Sheik, with "Classy" Freddie Blassie as his manager, returned to WWE. Sheik waved the flag of his home nation as he shouted, "Iran Number One!"

At Odds with America's Champions

The Sheik attacked the company's most beloved heroes with his controversial loaded boot and forced them to submit with his dangerous Camel Clutch. On December 26, 1983, Sheik won the WWE Championship amidst a sea of controversy when Bob Backlund's manager, future WWE Hall of Famer Arnold Skaaland, threw in the towel as the injured champion was trapped in the Camel Clutch. But his title reign would be short lived. Replacing an injured Backlund, Hulk Hogan defeated Sheik for the WWE Championship on January 23, 1984, at Madison Square Garden. Despite the loss, the Iron Sheik was part of the match that catapulted professional wrestling into the age of sports-entertainment. Enraged in defeat, the Sheik started a war with another American hero, future WWE Hall of Famer Sgt. Slaughter. These bloody battles spread across America and came to a head at the "World's Most Famous Arena." On June 16, 1984, Sheik and Slaughter used Madison Square Garden as their battlefield in a legendary Boot Camp Match that gave new meaning to the word "violence."

The Iron Sheik entered the tag team division and formed an alliance with another future WWE Hall of Famer, Nikolai Volkoff. With the "Hollywood Fashion Plate" Blassie at ringside, the duo became World Tag Team Champions when they defeated the U.S. Express at the first-ever *WrestleMania*. Though Sheik & Volkoff lost the titles back to Windham & Rotundo that June in Poughkeepsie, NY, they remained a lethal team.

The Iron Sheik returned to singles action and fought to the finals of the first-ever *King Of The Ring* tournament against future WWE Hall of Famer, the Magnificent Muraco. At *WrestleMania III,* he and Volkoff reunited with new manager Slick and fought The Killer Bees in a melee that was interrupted by "Hacksaw" Jim Duggan.

In 1997, the man from Tehran returned to WWE as the manager of The Sultan. He then came back at *WrestleMania X-Seven* and won the over-the-top-rope Gimmick Battle Royal, but not before reigniting his rivalry with Sgt. Slaughter. The night before *WrestleMania 21,* the Iron Sheik was inducted into the WWE Hall of Fame. Today, the Sheik tours the world attending autograph conventions and training sessions.

IRON SHEIK & NIKOLAI VOLKOFF

COMBINED WT: 571 lbs.

TITLE HISTORY

WORLD TAG TEAM CHAMPIONS	Defeated Mike Rotundo & Barry Windham on March 31, 1985

Separately, the Iron Sheik and Nikolai Volkoff were quite a force to be reckoned with in the ring. Together, however, they were nearly unstoppable. Both members of "Classy" Freddie Blassie's stable of Superstars, the Iron Sheik & Nikolai Volkoff began teaming with each other in 1984. The foreign rule-breakers instantly became recognized as the time's most-hated tag team. The fans learned to loathe them even more when Volkoff demanded arenas all across the United States stand for the singing of the Russian national anthem. When Volkoff was done serenading the fans, The Iron Sheik would famously remind everybody, "Russia, number one. Iran, number one, U.S.A., pooey!"

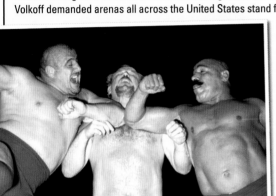

At the inaugural *WrestleMania* in 1985, the Iron Sheik & Nikolai Volkoff used some help from their manager's infamous cane to defeat the U.S. Express for the World Tag Team Championship. The victory marked the first-ever title change in *WrestleMania* history. The duo went on to hold the titles for nearly three months before Mike Rotundo & Barry Windham reclaimed the gold in Poughkeepsie, New York.

Following the loss, the Iron Sheik & Nikolai Volkoff temporarily set out on singles careers, which was highlighted by the big Russian's patriotic rivalry with American hero Corporal Kirschner.

By 1987, Blassie had sold interest in his stable of Superstars to "The Doctor of Style" Slick. The new manager reunited Iron Sheik & Nikolai Volkoff for a brief run that saw the foreigners defeat The Killer Bees at *WrestleMania III*. Slick eventually aligned Volkoff with fellow Russian Boris Zhukov to form The Bolsheviks. The move effectively marked the end of the successful tag team. Both The Iron Sheik and Nikolai Volkoff were honored with induction into the WWE Hall of Fame in 2005.

IRWIN R. SCHYSTER

HT: 6'3"   WT: 248 lbs.   FROM: Washington, D.C.
SIGNATURE MOVE: The Write-Off

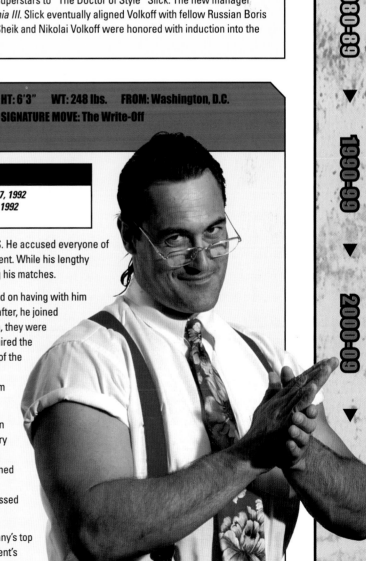

TITLE HISTORY

WORLD TAG TEAM CHAMPION (3 TIMES)	Partnered with Million Dollar Man to defeat The Legion of Doom on February 7, 1992 Partnered with Million Dollar Man to defeat Natural Disasters on October 13, 1992 Partnered with Million Dollar Man to defeat The Steiners on June 16, 1993

In 1991, World Wrestling Entertainment was antagonized by one Mr. Irwin R. Schyster, commonly known as I.R.S. He accused everyone of being worthless tax cheats and reminded everyone of their duty to pay their taxes to the United States government. While his lengthy diatribes upheld the United States tax laws, he had no problem whatsoever in breaking the rules of WWE during his matches.

This technically sound competitor was not afraid to wallop opponents with his trusty briefcase, which he insisted on having with him at all times. Schyster made it to the finals of the 1991 *King of the Ring,* where he met Bret "Hit Man" Hart. Soon after, he joined forces with another Superstar who was infatuated with money, "Million Dollar Man" Ted DiBiase. As a tag team, they were known as Money, Inc. They took out an insurance policy and acquired the managerial services of "Mouth of the South" Jimmy Hart. As one of the the most cunning duos to ever set foot in a ring, Money Inc. soon had their first taste of WWE gold after winning the World Tag Team Championship on February 7, 1992.

When the team parted ways, I.R.S. returned to singles competition and was one of the early fixtures of *Monday Night Raw.* With every match, he proved why he was a top contender for both the WWE Championship and Intercontinental Championship. In 1994, he joined the ranks of the Million Dollar Corporation. Schyster knew no boundries as he interfered in Undertaker's matches and repossessed sacred grave sites until their match at the 1995 *Royal Rumble*.

During his WWE tenure, Irwin R. Schyster was one of the company's top talents and a versatile Superstar who could adjust to any opponent's fighting style. When he appears today, it shows that no matter what time of year it is, or how much money you have in the bank, you're never safe from the tax man.

2010-
2000-09
1990-99
1980-89
1970-79
1960-69

ISAAC YANKEM DDS

HT: 6'10" **WT:** 300 lbs. **FROM:** Decatur, Illinois
SIGNATURE MOVE: DDS

Isaac Yankem was one of the least liked Superstars in WWE history. Despite his lack of popularity, however, the evil dentist claimed to be a walking public service announcement. According to Yankem, he let his teeth deteriorate to show the "rotten-teethed idiots" what can happen if they don't practice oral hygiene. The message didn't connect with the fans of WWE, but the malodorous effect it had on his opponents was brilliant.

Jerry Lawler introduced Yankem to WWE audiences in the summer of 1995. As "The King's" personal dentist, Yankem's sole purpose was to extract pain (and teeth) from Lawler's prime rival, Bret Hart. When Yankem and Hart finally squared off at *SummerSlam 1995*, a victory was not the dentist's prime objective. Instead, Yankem set out to permanently end Hart's career. He nearly accomplished his goal when he wrapped Hart's neck between two ring ropes. Luckily for Bret, WWE officials broke up the horrifying scene before permanent damage could be done.

THE ISLANDERS

MEMBERS: Haku, Tama
COMBINED WT: 501 lbs.

Haku & Tama wanted to achieve success through dedication, hard work and honesty. They displayed these traits throughout their matches in the mid-1980s. After *WrestleMania III* they were signed to compete against the popular Can-Am Connection on *Superstars of Wrestling*. What was supposed to be a contest between sportsman turned into a vicious attack as Haku & Tama became clients of Bobby "The Brain" Heenan and his family. With a newfound aggression, they ruthlessly took aim at anyone pointed out by Bobby Heenan. They showed their true devotion to "The Brain" when they dog-knapped Matilda, the mascot of the British Bulldogs. The Bulldogs, along with Koko B. Ware, punished the transgression at *WrestleMania IV*. The abduction went down as one of the most heartless acts in WWE history.

The Islanders soon went separate ways. Tama left WWE in April 1988. Haku soon became "King" Haku and reigned as a World Tag Team Champion as a part of the Colossal Connection.

THE ITALIAN STALLION

HT: 6'3" **WT:** 260 lbs. **FROM:** Naples, Italy
SIGNATURE MOVE: Powerslam

A storied amateur athlete, the Italian Stallion immigrated to the United States from Naples, Italy. He entered sports-entertainment in 1983 and spent his formative years in Jim Crockett Promotions. During his time there, he appeared at the first Jim Crockett, Sr. Memorial Cup Tag Team Tournament in 1986, as well as *Clash of Champions IV*.

In 1990, the Stallion wanted to test his mettle against WWE's Superstars. He appeared on broadcasts of *Superstars of Wrestling* and *Wrestling Challenge* facing the Honky Tonk Man, Shawn Michaels and Greg "The Hammer" Valentine.

In 1995, Stallion left WWE and spent time among independents promotions in the Southeastern part of the United States. After returning to his adopted home in North Carolina, he opened a training school with George South. Noted alumni from their academy are R-Truth, as well as Jeff and Matt Hardy.

IVAN KOLOFF

HT: 6'1" **WT:** 298 lbs. **FROM:** Moscow, Russia
SIGNATURE MOVE: Bearhug

TITLE HISTORY

WWE CHAMPION	*Defeated Bruno Sammartino on January 18, 1971*

At a time when tension between the United States and Soviet Union was at its height, Russian powerhouse Ivan Koloff proved to be the ultimate threat to American wrestling fans' in-ring heroes. Known as "The Russian Bear," Koloff joined WWE in 1970, under the tutelage of manager Lou Albano. The sight of him struck communistic fears into American fans, but it was his dreaded bear hug and knee drop that frightened the WWE locker room.

Within months of Koloff's debut, fans had their greatest fear realized when "the Russian Bear" handily defeated their champion of nearly eight years, Bruno

Sammartino. A stunned Madison Square Garden crowd watched in disbelief as their hero's shoulders were pinned to the mat for seemingly the longest three seconds in sports-entertainment history. After the match, the ring announcer refused to announce Koloff as the winner, fearing a riot might ensue.

A mere three weeks into his shocking championship reign, Koloff crossed paths with a hungry Pedro Morales. Much to the fans' delight, Morales beat Koloff for the WWE Championship, marking the end of the most terrifying title reign to date.

Shortly after the loss, Koloff disappeared from the WWE scene, only to return periodically during the 1970s and 1980s to challenge Sammartino and Bob Backlund. When he wasn't making rare WWE appearances, "the Russian Bear" was gaining tag team notoriety in the Mid-Atlantic territory. His impressive list of partners includes Ray Stevens, Krusher Khruschev, Dick Murdoch, and nephew Nikita Koloff.

At age fifty, Koloff took his game to the budding Eastern Championship Wrestling. His popular past and memorable matches with Jimmy Snuka and Sandman helped the promotion build the foundation for what would later be recognized as the hardcore powerhouse Extreme Championship Wrestling.

IVAN PUTSKI

HT: 5'10" **WT:** 245 lbs.
FROM: Krakow, Poland
SIGNATURE MOVE: The Polish Hammer

Hall of Fame 1995

TITLE HISTORY

WORLD TAG TEAM CHAMPION	*Partnered with Tito Santana to defeat Johnny & Jerry Valiant on October 22, 1979*

In 1976, World Wrestling Entertainment was introduced to the phenomenon known as "Polish Power." As a former professional body builder, Ivan Putski possessed great strength and a fire that burned to rid WWE of its questionable elements. He was the first Polish Superstar and with his success and charisma became one of the top names in WWE. He took the fight to individuals such as Crusher Blackwell, Bruiser Brody, Stan Hansen, Ivan Koloff, Spiros Arion, and Baron Mikel Scicluna. Putski's feats of strength continued to garner attention and he competed in the 1978 World's Strongest Man Competition. As his following grew, Putski began to speak more English to his legion of fans, sang his favorite Polish songs and professed the importance of "Polish Power" after his matches.

On October 22, 1979, Putski teamed Tito Santana to defeat Johnny and Jerry Valiant to win the World Tag Team Championship. The duo complemented each other perfectly and held the belts for months before losing to the Wild Samoans. As "Polish Power" entered the 1980s, he remained a huge star.

In 1995, Ivan took his rightful place amongst sports-entertainment's elite when he was enshrined in the WWE Hall of Fame. "Polish Power" made his triumphant return to WWE television in 1997 when he appeared alongside his son Scott on *Monday Night Raw* and tangled with Jerry "The King" Lawler and Brian Christopher.

Ivan Putski is one of professional wrestling's most admired individuals whose fame transcended ethnicities and broke down geographic barriers. For this, everyone loves "Polish Power!"

I

1960-69
1970-79
1980-89
1990-99
2000-09
2010-

I

2010-

2000-09

1990-99

1980-89

1970-79

1960-69

IVORY

HT: 5'5" **FROM:** Seattle, Washington
SIGNATURE MOVE: Poison Ivy

TITLE HISTORY

WOMEN'S CHAMPION (3 TIMES)	*Defeated Debra on June 14, 1999* *Defeated Fabulous Moolah on October 25, 1999* *Defeated Lita on November 2, 2000*

If someone wants excellent ring skills, a fabulous physique and a mean streak that turns smiles into frowns, look no further than this former WWE Diva. She first appeared on WWE programming in 1999 as the Valentine's Day gift from D-Lo Brown to tag partner Mark Henry. Trained by Mexican legend Mondo Guerrero, it didn't take Ivory long to challenge the Divas in the ring.

After capturing the Women's Championship on an episode of *Monday Night Raw*, she participated in the first-ever Women's Hardcore match against Tori. She held the prized championship for four months before a loss to Fabulous Moolah at *No Mercy*.

Something in Ivory snapped after the loss, and she soon joined the Right To Censor. Her clothing now consisted of ankle-length skirts, a button-down white shirt, modest black heels and her hair worn up in a tightly wrapped bun. She enjoyed success as part of the group, winning the Women's Championship two more times.

After the Right to Censor disbanded, Ivory became a trainer on the second season of *WWE Tough Enough,* then traded in her ring gear for a microphone as the co-host of the now-defunct *WWE Experience*.

JACK KORPELA

A longtime fan of WWE, Jack Korpela remembers the exact day he fell in love with the sports-entertainment industry. It was April 2, 1989. On this day, he witnessed future WWE Hall of Famers Mr. Perfect, Shawn Michaels and Bret "Hit Man" Hart compete at *WrestleMania V*.

With hopes of one day sitting in the same seat as his hero, legendary announcer Gorilla Monsoon, Korpela enrolled in the University of Florida, where he earned a degree in journalism and communications. His education helped propel him to a motorsports commentator position with ESPN2. He held the role until 2006, when he got the call from WWE.

Korpela called the action on such shows as *NXT* and *WWE Superstars*. He was also seen on the international hit programs *WWE Experience, After Burn* and *This Week in WWE*.

JACK SWAGGER

 HT: 6'4" **WT:** 263 lbs. **FROM:** Perry, Oklahoma
SIGNATURE MOVE: Swagger Bomb

TITLE HISTORY

ECW CHAMPION	*Defeated Matt Hardy on January 13, 2009*
UNITED STATES CHAMPION	*Defeated Zack Ryder on January 16, 2012*
WORLD HEAVYWEIGHT CHAMPION	*Defeated Chris Jericho on April 2, 2010*

The charismatic Jack Swagger caught the eye of ECW general manager Theodore Long in September 2008, and the GM signed the self-proclaimed "All American American" as a part of his New Superstar Initiative. The move proved to be just the break Swagger needed, as he hasn't looked back since making his impressive debut.

Swagger's cocky smile and arrogant strut make him tough to cheer for, but fans can't help but appreciate his confidence. After only weeks in the promotion, Swagger stood up to ECW legend Tommy Dreamer. Within his first year in the Land of Extreme, Swagger defeated Matt Hardy to win the ECW Championship. With a 2009 move to *Raw*, the "All American American" became one of the most despised villains in WWE whose stock shot through the roof when he won the final Money In The Bank Ladder Match at *WrestleMania XXVI*. He carefully chose his time to cash-in his World Heavyweight Championship opportunity, and five days from his *WrestleMania* victory he defeated an injured and stunned Chris Jericho.

Swagger's stellar amateur background and signature mean streak has established him as one of the most dangerous Superstars in WWE. His association with Vickie Guerrero and Dolph Zigler have made him more loathsome to fans, but what people despise most is that his Swagger Bomb and Ankle Lock are able to defeat opponents at virtually anytime he chooses. That's just how the "All American American" likes it.

JACK TUNNEY

He wasn't a muscle man. He didn't possess cat-like quickness, and he never owned a devastating offensive arsenal. Despite these perceived shortcomings, Jack Tunney was one of the most feared men in all of sports-entertainment during the 1980s and 1990s.

As WWE President, Tunney was one of the most respected authoritative figures of his time. Usually ruling from afar, unlike many of today's leaders, he only showed up when matters became too heavy for his referees to police. This style of leadership proved to be fruitful, as his tenure saw few controversies. When things did get ugly, however, you could bet Tunney would mete out punishment with an iron fist.

To this day, many of Tunney's decisions are looked back upon with great fondness. In 1986, the WWE President was forced to make a difficult decision when one of his top draws, Andre the Giant, failed to show at several of his contracted appearances. Seeing Andre's absence as an insult to the paying fans, Tunney suspended the popular "Eighth Wonder of the World" from competitive action.

A few months later, Tunney made a similar ruling when he suspended rogue official Danny Davis for life, following the referee's blatant bias towards rule breakers.

Perhaps Tunney's toughest decision came when a series of controversial matches between Hulk Hogan and Undertaker forced the President to vacate the WWE Championship in 1991. The ruling eventually lead to the WWE Championship being on the line at the 1992 *Royal Rumble*, which was won by Ric Flair.

As is normally the case with any administration, Tunney's time in office did see some controversial rulings. When Bret Hart and Lex Luger were simultaneously last eliminated from the 1994 *Royal Rumble*, rather than sending the two Superstars into the ring to declare a definitive winner, Tunney announced them as co-winners. He then ruled that both men would receive an opportunity at the WWE Championship at *WrestleMania X*, but not before confusing everybody with talk of a coin toss, "suitable competition" and guest referees.

Despite the rare miscue, Tunney's time in office will forever be looked upon as time when Superstars actually feared their boss and lawlessness was unacceptable.

JACKIE GAYDA

HT: 5'7"   FROM: Cleveland, Ohio
SIGNATURE MOVE: Neckbreaker

Jackie Gayda's determination, strength, and in-ring ability led to her becoming the co-winner of the second season of *Tough Enough*. Before she knew it, Miss Jackie was strutting her stuff on *Raw* and *SmackDown* with the most beautiful and dangerous females in all of sports-entertainment.

In 2003, she added valet to her resumé when she began to accompany Rico to the ring, and later in her career she managed Rico & Charlie Haas to the WWE Tag Team Championship. Jackie became fond of interfering on her team's behalf, so they fought in mixed tag matches. On her own, she locked up with Trish Stratus and Lita and became a contender for the Women's Championship. At *WrestleMania XX*, she partnered with Stacy Keibler against Torrie Wilson & Sable in a Playboy Evening Gown Match. Jackie left WWE in June 2005 and spent a brief time on the independent scene before retiring from the ring.

JACOB NOVAK

HT: 6'5"   WT: 257 lbs.   FROM: Kent, Washington
SIGNATURE MOVE: Big Boot

In sports-entertainment, a certain prestige is associated with Superstars who are the first to accomplish something. Unless, of course, you're Jacob Novak, who owns the dreadful distinction of being the first person eliminated from both *NXT* seasons four and five.

With Dolph Ziggler serving as his Pro, Novak debuted in December 2010 and immediately lost to Johnny Curtis in his debut match. Despite the defeat, Novak remained extremely confident, and sometimes arrogant. He avenged the loss to Curtis with a win later in the month.

Later in the season, Ziggler became dissatisfied with Novak's potential and traded the Rookie to Chris Masters for Byron Saxton. That same night, Novak was eliminated from *NXT* competition.

Novak returned for season five of *NXT* in March 2011. JTG served as his Pro, but not even the energetic tag-team specialist could help Novak survive the first round of eliminations. Novak was later released from his WWE contract in June 2011.

J

2010-
▲
2000-09
▲
1990-99
▲
1980-89
▲
1970-79
▲
1960-69

JACQUELINE 🇺🇸

HT: 5'3"   FROM: Dallas, Texas

TITLE HISTORY

CRUISERWEIGHT CHAMPION	Defeated Chavo Guerrero on May 6, 2004
WOMEN'S CHAMPION (2 TIME)	Defeated Sable on September 21, 1998 Defeated Hervina on February 3, 2000

Over the course of her WWE career, Jacqueline had the unique distinction of being equally successful against both male and female Superstars. In fact, her impressive record against the men of WWE actually carried her to the male-dominated Cruiserweight Championship. The bombshell from Dallas defeated Chavo Guerrero in May 2004 to become the only woman in WWE history to ever hold the gold.

Jacqueline's Cruiserweight Championship proved to be the final highlight of her brilliant six-year WWE run. It also served as a golden bookend to a career that took off after capturing the Women's Championship mere months after making her debut.

The period between Jacqueline's high-profile debut and ground-breaking finale was filled with one memorable moment after another. The feisty Diva will forever be remembered for her involvement in the all-female faction Pretty Mean Sisters. Affectionately referred to as P.M.S., Jacqueline, alongside Terri and Ryan Shamrock, preyed on the male Superstars of WWE, usually making them their love slaves. A list of their ultimate conquests includes D-Lo Brown and Mark Henry.

JAKE "THE SNAKE" ROBERTS

> ❝ IF YOU KEEP PLAYING WITH SNAKES, SOON YOU'LL GET BIT.

The son of the legendary Grizzly Smith, Jake Roberts' career in professional wrestling began in Louisiana as a referee. He traveled throughout the Southeastern United States and Calgary's Stampede Wrestling, gaining the reputation of being a superior technician and ring psychologist. Along the way, he invented one of the most lethal moves in the history of sports-entertainment, the DDT.

Jake "the Snake" Roberts debuted in WWE in 1986 alongside his python, Damien, who was often restless inside his burlap sack during Jake's matches. After a DDT, Jake often brought out Damien and dropped the snake on his fallen opponents.

From the start of his WWE career, Jake was often at the center of intense rivalries. In one of his first matches, Jake delivered a DDT to Ricky "the Dragon" Steamboat on concrete during *Saturday Night's Main Event*. The assault left Steamboat unconscious and sparked a bitter rivalry that lead to a Snake Pit Match at *The Big Event* in Toronto.

Jake shook up the early days of the married life of Randy Savage and Elizabeth. He presented the couple with a king cobra who leapt up and bit the "Macho Man."

Jake Roberts quickly became known for cryptic interviews that sent chills down the spines of all of saw them. His speaking acumen convinced WWE to give him his own talk show segment which he called *The Snake Pit*. During an episode of *The Snake Pit*, Jake was attacked by the Honky Tonk Man, who smashed a guitar over Jake's head. The heinous action lead to a match at *WrestleMania III*. His victory there changed the attitude of fans, and suddenly capacity crowds were calling for Jake's signature DDT.

Jake was featured at *WrestleMania* for the next several years, incluing a match against Andre the Giant at *WrestleMania V* and a Blindfold Match against Rick "the Model" Martel at *WrestleMania VII* after Roberts was blinded by Martel's signature cologne, Arrogance.

Getting Personal

The intesity of those rivalries could not compare to the emotions generated by personal attacks against those closest to Jake. "Ravishing" Rick Rude would often select a female fan from the audience for a post-match kiss. One night, he picked Jake's wife, who refused to participate. After a slap and a shove, Jake arrived to defend his wife. Roberts and Rude engaged in a brutal war that lasted several months and was exacerbated each time Rude's wrestling trunks bore a likeness of Roberts' wife.

Damien was the target of another Superstar who tried to attack Jake by proxy. The behemoth Earthquake crushed Damien while Jake watched helplessly, tangled in the ring ropes. After the loss of his snake, Roberts went back home to Stone Mountain, Georgia. When Roberts finally returned, he unveiled a monstrous python he called Lucifer.

After revealing that Lucifer was Damien's older brother, a demonic-looking Roberts boldly claimed his new snake was the devil himself. Coincidentally, Roberts began to display a darker persona after the debut of Lucifer. His return to the darkside was just as mysterious as his sudden disappearance from WWE after his *Wrestlemania VIII* match against Undertaker.

"The Snake" spent the next few years in seclusion, but returned at the 1996 *Royal Rumble*. While Jake struck fear into the hearts of a new generation, he met his match in Stone Cold Steve Austin at the *King Of The Ring* finals. Austin's victory gave rise to the era of Stone Cold and arguably sports-entertainment's most famous chapter and verse, "Austin 3:16."

Jake again vanished from WWE in 1997, and rumors swirled as to his whereabouts. Jake made an incredible return on the March 14, 2005 episode of *Monday Night Raw* and warned "Legend Killer" Randy Orton about the fear one feels when facing Undertaker at *WrestleMania*. That November, WWE released the retrospective DVD titled, *Jake The Snake Roberts: Pick Your Poison* to sate the public's ravenous apetite for the history of the man whose methods changed the face of sports-entertainment.

HT: 6'6"   WT: 249 lbs.
FROM: Stone Mountain, Georgia
SIGNATURE MOVE: The DDT

JAMAICA KID

HT: 4'4"   WT: 94 lbs.   FROM: Jamaica
SIGNATURE MOVE: Jumping Headbutt

An outstanding export from the island of the Greater Antilles, Jamaica Kid arrived in the World Wide Wrestling Federation in the summer of 1964. For over a decade he was a mainstay with a jumping headbutt that stopped most of his foes dead in their tracks. His matches were filled with action and entertained audiences wherever he appeared.

Jamaica's battles with the likes of Sky Low Low, Fuzzy Cupid, Billy the Kid, Farmer Pete, Little Brutus, Frenchy Lamont, Pee Wee Adams and Dirty Morgan helped put the midget division on the map. He had a steady array of tag team partners that included Little Beaver, Tiny Tim, Irish Jackie, Sonny Boy Cassidy, Pancho Lopez, Cowboy Bradley, and Little Louie. These bouts were as unpredictable and exciting as anything ever seen in the ring.

JAMES DUDLEY

HALL OF FAME
1994

Although he spent more time behind the scenes than in front of capacity crowds, James Dudley was one of the most important and influential men in sports-entertainment history. WWE Chairman Vince K. McMahon once said, "Had there been no James Dudley, the WWE possibly wouldn't exist as it does today."

Before he played an integral role in the success of WWE, James Dudley was a catcher for the Baltimore Elite Giants of the Negro League. When his playing days were over, he looked toward a career that matched the thrill of being on the baseball diamond. In the early 1940s, he started as an employee of Jess McMahon, and ultimately became a trusted associate of Vincent J. McMahon. History was made in 1956 when Vince, Sr., appointed Dudley manager of Turner Arena in Washington, D.C., making Dudley the first African-American to run a major arena in the United States.

Dudley's keen business acumen allowed Vince McMahon to concentrate on growing his business to other areas. As WWE's reach expanded, Dudley's job responsibilities continued to grow. By 1980, he retired and became a valued consultant to Vince K. McMahon. In 1994, Dudley was included in the first full-class of sports-entertainment immortals in the WWE Hall of Fame.

On June 1, 2004, Dudley passed away at the age of 93. He was more than a valued employee to several generations of McMahons. He was a cherished friend and made a lasting impact on everyone around him.

JAMIE

HT: 5'4"
FROM: Sarasota, Florida

Jamie made her debut as the sexy ring announcer for the second season of *NXT* in June 2010. While showing off her exceptional vocal talents, the blonde bombshell developed a craving to compete in the ring. And when the season came to a close, it was announced that she would try her hand at becoming WWE's next breakout Diva during season three of *NXT*.

With a background that includes karate, boxing, weightlifting and modeling, Jamie appeared to be one of the favorites heading into the competition. She even defeated Aksana in her debut match in September 2010 and later went on to team with Kelly Kelly and Naomi to top eventual *NXT* champion Kaitlyn, Layla and Michelle McCool. Unfortunately for Jamie, her undefeated record failed to impress the Pros, and the beautiful Jamie was the first Diva-wannabe eliminated from competition.

Despite being eliminated, Jamie graciously returned for the *NXT* season finale to offer her support for fellow Rookie Naomi.

J

1960-69
1970-79
1980-89
1990-99
2000-09
2010-

J

2010-

▲

2000-09

▲

1990-99

▲

1980-89

▲

1970-79

▲

1960-69

JAMIE NOBLE

HT: 5'9"   WT: 202 lbs.   FROM: Hanover, West Virginia
SIGNATURE MOVE: Modified Dragon Sleeper

TITLE HISTORY

CRUISERWEIGHT CHAMPION	*Defeated The Hurricane on June 23, 2002*

Jamie Noble is the exact opposite of many of the country boys that have competed in World Wrestling Entertainment since its inception. Raised in the trailer parks of West Virginia, Noble will do anything in his matches to get what he wants.

He won the Cruiserweight Championship from The Hurricane at the 2002 *King of the Ring* and enjoyed an almost five-month title reign. After a one year hiatus, Noble returned as part of the short-lived team, the Pitbulls. While on *SmackDown,* he fought the likes of Rey Mysterio, Jimmy Wang Yang, Shannon Moore and Hornswoggle. He began hearing cheers from the crowd when he came to the aid of Diva Michelle McCool to protect her from Chuck Palumbo.

In November 2009 Noble's near 15-year career in sports-entertainment ended abruptly after he suffered a severe back injury. During his career, Noble was known for impulsive, unpredictable behavior. Today, Noble instills that tenacity in his students at WWE's developmental territory, Florida Championship Wrestling.

JAMISON

Jamison told everybody he was an "everyday, ordinary kind of guy," but in reality, the best word to accurately describe this socially challenged boy of a man is "nerd."

Redeeming qualities were certainly lost on Jamison. He didn't have a job. He didn't have a girlfriend. And he didn't even have a place to live until his step-cousin Francesca gave him a room in her house. Despite all his shortcomings, though, Jamison regularly found his way onto WWE television during the late 1980s and early 1990s.

During his stay with WWE, Jamison somehow managed to consistently irritate Bobby "The Brain" Heenan. Each time, the WWE Hall of Famer responded by tossing insults the nerdy uber-fan's way.

Jamison also became the target of a Viking ritual at the hands of The Berzerker. During the event, The Berzerker attempted to burn Jamison at the stake. Luckily for the lovable loser, The Berzerker failed to figure out the lighter. Jamison eventually found an equally odd pairing to hang out with when he briefly managed the Bushwhackers.

JAZZ

HT: 5'4"
FROM: New Orleans, Louisiana

TITLE HISTORY

WOMEN'S CHAMPION (2 TIMES)	*Defeated Trish Stratus on February 4, 2002* *Defeated Trish Stratus on April 27, 2003*

With washboard abs and muscles on top of muscles, Jazz was one of WWE's most-feared Divas between 2001 and 2004. The tattooed powerhouse debuted on one of WWE's biggest stages when she competed in a Six-Pack Challenge at the 2001 *Survivor Series*. The encounter whet her appetite for championship glory, and in February 2002, she defeated Trish Stratus for the Women's Championship.

After a successful championship stint, Jazz took on Theodore Long as her manager. With Long leading her career, Jazz was able to upend Stratus a second time for the title at *Backlash 2003*. She held the championship for two months before losing it to Gail Kim in a Divas Battle Royal. Jazz left WWE a few months later.

Jazz returned in June 2006 when she represented ECW in a match against Women's Champion Mickie James. Jazz came up short in her attempt to topple James, and was never seen on WWE television again.

JEAN PIERRE LaFITTE

HT: 6'1"   WT: 235 lbs.   FROM: New Orleans, Louisiana

An ancestor of the infamous LaFitte family of pirates, Jean Pierre LaFitte made his WWE debut in 1995. His goal was to exact revenge on the United States, starting with WWE Superstars, for the Embargo Act of 1807 that forced his family out of New Orleans.

With a patch over his right eye, LaFitte showed all of the characteristics of an evil pirate, including thievery. His most-noted victim was Bret Hart, from who he stole his signature leather jacket and sunglasses. Unfortunately for LaFitte, Hart gained revenge when he defeated him at *In Your House* in September 1995. LaFitte left WWE shortly after the loss.

JEFF HARDY

HT: 6'1" WT: 225 lbs. FROM: Cameron, North Carolina
SIGNATURE MOVE: Swanton Bomb

TITLE HISTORY

EUROPEAN CHAMPION	*Defeated Spike Dudley on July 8, 2002*
HARDCORE CHAMPION	*3 Times*
INTERCONTINENTAL CHAMPION (4 TIMES)	*Defeated Triple H on April 12, 2001* *Defeated Johnny Nitro on October 2, 2006* *Defeated Johnny Nitro on November 13, 2006* *Defeated Umaga on September 3, 2007*
LIGHT HEAVYWEIGHT CHAMPION	*Defeated Jerry Lynn on June 7, 2001*
WWE CHAMPION	*Won a Triple Threat Match against Triple H and Edge on December 14, 2008*
WORLD TAG TEAM CHAMPION (6 TIMES)	*Partnered with Matt Hardy to defeat The Acolytes on July 5, 1999* *Partnered with Matt Hardy to defeat Edge & Christian on September 24, 2000* *Partnered with Matt Hardy to defeat Edge & Christian on October 23, 2000* *Partnered with Matt Hardy to defeat The Dudleys on March 5, 2001* *Partnered with Matt Hardy to defeat Booker T & Test on November 12, 2001* *Partnered with Matt Hardy to win a Tag Team Battle Royal on April 2, 2007*
WORLD HEAVYWEIGHT CHAMPION (2 TIMES)	*Defeated Edge on June 7, 2009* *Defeated CM Punk on July 26, 2009*

Alongside his brother Matt, Jeff first began making a name for himself in 1998. Known as the Hardy Boys, Jeff & Matt spent the next few years redefining the art of tag team competition. Their battles with the Dudley Boys and Edge & Christian, particularly their TLC Matches, featured truly groundbreaking action that today's tag teams strive to recreate.

On his own, Hardy proved to be a true artist. Using the ring as his canvas, Hardy executed his awe-inspiring Swanton Bomb to create the ultimate portrait of success. A multiple-time Intercontinental Champion, Hardy finally rose to main-event status in 2008 when he challenged Randy Orton for the WWE Championship at the *Royal Rumble*. Jeff finally reached the top of the mountain in December, 2008 when he pinned Edge during a Triple Threat Match at *Armageddon*. One month later at the *Royal Rumble* Jeff suffered incredible loss when brother Matt drove a stake in the heart of his family and cost Jeff the WWE Championship. Left with no alternative, Jeff fought his brother in a string of violent encounters. Thankfully the charismatic enigma and his brother made amends. On August 28, 2009, the 15-year relationship Jeff enjoyed with WWE came to an end after he lost a "Loser Leaves WWE" Steel Cage Match to CM Punk on *SmackDown*.

JEFF JARRETT

HT: 6'0" WT: 230 lbs. FROM: Nashville, Tennessee
SIGNATURE MOVE: Figure-Four Leglock

TITLE HISTORY

EUROPEAN CHAMPION	*Defeated D-Lo Brown on August 22, 1999*
INTERCONTINENTAL CHAMPION (6 TIMES)	*Defeated Razor Ramon on January 22, 1995* *Defeated Bob Holly on April 26, 1995* *Defeated Razor Ramon on May 22, 1995* *Defeated The Godfather on May 31, 1999* *Defeated Edge on July 25, 1999* *Defeated D-Lo Brown on August 22, 1999*
WORLD TAG TEAM CHAMPION	*Partnered with Owen Hart to defeat Big Boss Man & Ken Shamrock on January 25, 1999*

Jarrett debuted in WWE as a flashy country music star in 1994. While "Double J" didn't quite make it to the top of Nashville with his single *With My Baby Tonight,* he did become Intercontinental Champion for the first time at the 1995 *Royal Rumble*. Over the next four months, he held that title twice more before he left WWE in 1996.

Jarrett then appeared in WCW and became a United States Champion as well as member of the famed Four Horsemen. In 1997, he returned to WWE where he ditched the country-western scene and lived by the motto/warning, "Don't Piss Me Off." As he returned to Intercontinental glory, he reunited with longtime associate Debra. With her considerable assets added to his formidable arsenal, Jeff then formed a well-known tandem with Owen Hart. He also had memorable battles against Chyna, who defeated him in a "Good Housekeeping Match" for the Intercontinental prize at *No Mercy*. Jarrett parted ways with WWE again and returned to WCW where he proclaimed himself "The Chosen One." He remained with the organization, where he became WCW Champion, until it closed in March 2001.

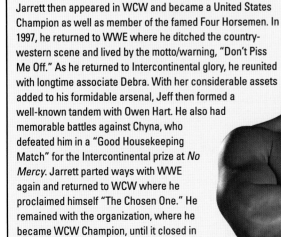

JEFF JARRETT & OWEN HART

COMBINED WT: 457 lbs.

TITLE HISTORY

WORLD TAG TEAM CHAMPIONS	*Defeated Big Boss Man & Ken Shamrock on January 25, 1999*

The most successful tag teams historically combine opposing styles in an effort to form the most well-rounded unit possible. Jeff Jarrett & Owen Hart, on the other hand, fused their like styles into one technically sound team. The rare pairing proved fruitful, as they owned the tag scene during their brief time together. Of course, it didn't hurt that they had the bosomy Debra by their side, either.

The former Intercontinental Champions began teaming together in late 1998. During this time, Hart was going through a bit of an identity crisis, which resulted in him occasionally donning his Blue Blazer mask. Claiming to be a superhero, Hart believed his true identity was concealed, but in reality, the entire world knew it was him under the mask, especially when the Blazer would team with Jeff Jarrett (Hart's tag team partner).

After teaming with Jarrett as the Blue Blazer for several tag team matches, Hart dropped his masked persona to defeat Big Boss Man & Ken Shamrock for the World Tag Team Championship in January 1999. The crafty combination of Jarrett & Hart went on an impressive winning streak that saw them topple such teams as the Public Enemy and Legion of Doom during their four-month reign.

After losing the titles in April, Hart reverted back to his Blue Blazer persona, but that didn't stop him from conveniently showing up by the side of Jarrett.

J

2010-

2000-09

1990-99

1980-89

1970-79

1960-69

JERRY LAWLER "THE KING"

HT: 6'0" WT: 243 lbs.
FROM: Memphis, Tennessee
SIGNATURE MOVE: Piledriver

HALL OF FAME 2007

Jerry Lawler first became involved with professional wrestling when his caricutures were discovered by famous announcer Lance Russell. Trained by "Fabulous" Jackie Fargo, Lawler went on to become a legend in the Mid-South and Memphis territories during the 1970s and 1980s. His most well-known rivalry actually began outside of the ring. In the early 1980s, the war of words between Lawler and Andy Kaufman became mainstream news when as guests on *The David Letterman Show,* Lawler slapped Kaufman out of his chair and sent the Hollywood star into an obscenity-laced tirade. The rivalry was recreated by Hollywood in 1999, as "The King" made his silver-screen debut in *Man On The Moon,* a movie based on Kaufman's life.

Though he held numerous regional championships, his shining moment in the ring came on May 9, 1988 when he beat Curt Hennig for the AWA Championship. Lawler later unified the title when he defeated legend Kerry Von Erich for his World Class Championship.

In 1993, Lawler debuted in WWE as an announcer. Lawler has been a long-time announcer for *Monday Night Raw* and along with partner Jim Ross, has changed the face of television broadcasting. He also enjoyed his own talk show segment appropriately called, *The King's Court.* His outspoken attitude as a commentator lead to heated matches with Bret "Hit Man" Hart. This war raged on until their "Kiss My Foot" Match at the 1995 *King of the Ring.*

Lawler also garnered media attention when he took aim at an entire promotion during ECW's first invasion of WWE. Lawler's crown continued to shine in 2002 when his autobiography titled, *It's Good To Be King… Sometimes* became one of the best-selling WWE books of all-time.

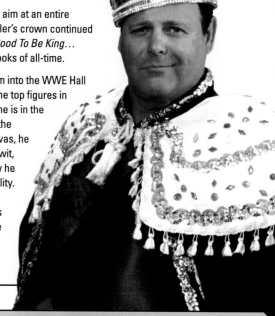

In 2007, Lawler's friend William Shatner inducted him into the WWE Hall of Fame. Jerry "The King" Lawler has been one of the top figures in sports-entertainment for almost 40 years. Whether he is in the ring dropping a fist from the middle rope, or behind the broadcast booth eagerly volunteering to help the Divas, he has entertained millions all over the world with this wit, creativity and charisma."The King" is proud to show he can still bring the fight to any voluble WWE personality. After he came within inches of winning the WWE Championship from The Miz, Lawler competed in his first *WrestleMania* match against Michael Cole. The "Voice of WWE" ultimately learned you don't mess with wrestling royalty whose trophy case includes over 140 championships.

JERRY GRAHAM

HT: 5'10" WT: 245 lbs.
FROM: Phoenix, Arizona

TITLE HISTORY

UNITED STATES TAG TEAM CHAMPION	*Partnered with Luke Graham to defeat Don McClarity & Vittoro Apollo on June 6, 1964*

A member of the famed Graham family, Dr. Jerry Graham was a noted troublemaker in and out of the ring. When the madman wasn't wreaking havoc with brothers Crazy Luke, Eddie, and "Superstar" Billy Graham in the ring, he was butting heads with law enforcement all over the nation.

Graham won tag team titles in six different promotions over the course of his career. His first taste of success came in 1955 when he teamed with Don McIntyre to topple Bill & Fred Blassie for the Georgia version of the NWA Tag Team Championship. Over the next 20 years, Graham formed championship teams with Abdullah the Butcher, Jim Wright, and brother Eddie. He even captured the WWE United States Tag Team titles with brother Luke in June 1964.

While Graham's main source of fame came from his action in between the ropes, his run-ins with the law are simply legendary. Following the passing of his mother, Graham broke into the morgue to steal her corpse. In doing so, he assaulted several morgue workers and security. A few years later, the police picked him up after he was seen shooting the lights out at a Utah house of worship. According to legend, Graham maintained his outlaw-like attitude even while spending his final days in hospice.

JERRY LYNN

HT: 5'11" WT: 212 lbs. FROM: Minneapolis, Minnesota
SIGNATURE MOVE: Cradle Piledriver

TITLE HISTORY

LIGHT HEAVYWEIGHT CHAMPION	*Defeated Crash Holly on April 29, 2001*

Jerry Lynn began his career in the late 1980s, and as his reputation began to grow, he made appearances in WCW and WWE, where he participated in the Light Heavyweight Championship tournament. Lynn's next stop was ECW and a slew of matches with Rob Van Dam that were considered classics amongst the ECW faithful. In the weeks and months that followed ECW's closure, Jerry explored his options and felt he needed to prove himself where the world would be watching.

In April 2001, Lynn returned to WWE and had his debut match on *Sunday Night Heat.* In his return, the former ECW Champion pinned Crash Holly and won the prized Light Heavyweight championship that eluded him four years prior. Unfortunately, Lynn lost the title a little over one month later to a driven Jeff Hardy. Lynn renewed his rivalry against Rob Van Dam, but he suffered a torn patella and parted ways with the company in February 2002.

JESSE & FESTUS

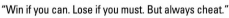

COMBINED WT: 501 lbs.

Much like the legendary Hillbilly Jim before them, Jesse & Festus were a couple of country boys you didn't go messin' with. Jesse, the brains of the operation, brought to the ring an accomplished amateur background, while Festus, the team's brawn, inexplicably transformed from a gentle giant into a beast every time he heard the ring bell sound.

After making their WWE debut in October 2007, Jesse & Festus made short work of many of the top units in ECW and on *SmackDown*, including then-WWE Tag Team Champions The Miz & John Morrison in non-title action in early 2008. The duo remained championship contenders through the year but tag team gold was ultimately not meant to be. The team disbanded soon after when Festus was drafted to *Raw*.

JESSE "THE BODY" VENTURA

HT: 6'2"   WT: 245 lbs.   FROM: Brooklyn Park, Minnesota

HALL OF FAME 2004

"Win if you can. Lose if you must. But always cheat."

Luckily for residents of Minnesota, Jesse Ventura didn't employ his famous phrase while serving as their governor. He did, however, live by the motto during his days in the ring.

After a successful stint with the American Wrestling Association (AWA), Ventura, whose impressive build earned him the nickname "The Body," entered WWE in the early 1980s. As a member of the East-West Connection tag team (with Adrian Adonis), he nearly claimed the World Tag Team Championship on several occasions.

Ventura's colorful singles career mirrored his tag days, as he came close to claiming the WWE Championship from Bob Backlund, but was never able to seal the deal. A second opportunity at the title came Ventura's way when he was scheduled to challenge Hulk Hogan in 1984. Unfortunately, health issues prevented "The Body" from taking part in the match. He later retired to the broadcast booth.

As a commentator, Ventura sat ringside for some of WWE's biggest matches, including the *WrestleMania III* encounter between Hogan and Andre the Giant. Just like his days in the ring, Ventura pulled no punches when it came to voicing his opinions. This bold attitude served as the perfect complement to his legendary partner Gorilla Monsoon's more direct approach to announcing.

Blessed with a magnetic personality, Ventura made the natural progression into Hollywood in 1987. His list of credits include box-office hits *Predator*, *The Running Man* and *Demolition Man*. Ventura's career took an unexpected turn in 1990 when he won the race for mayor of Brooklyn Park, Minnesota. Eight years later, he rose all the way up to the office of governor, where he was affectionately known as Jesse "The Governing Body" Ventura.

In 2004, Ventura's accomplishments in and out of the ring were honored when he was inducted into the WWE Hall of Fame.

JÉSUS

HT: 6'3"   WT: 262 lbs.
FROM:: Puerto Rico

The latter portions of 2004 were not kind to John Cena, thanks in large part to the actions of Jésus. Serving as Carlito's bodyguard, the ruthless Superstar made an instant impact by allegedly attacking Cena in a Boston nightclub. The severity of the assault cost Cena more than one month of his career.

When Cena finally returned, Jésus picked up right where he left off, nearly crippling the Superstar with a vicious attack to the kidney. Following the assault, Jésus proudly paraded about with Cena's signature chain around his neck. It served as a reminder that Jésus' ferocity was as advertised.

The Jésus-Cena rivalry came to a head at *Armageddon 2004* when the two Superstars squared off in a Street Fight. With the United States Championship on the line, challenger Jésus focused much of his attack on Cena's injured kidney region. Miraculously, though, the champ overcame the odds and pinned Jésus following an Attitude Adjustment. The result of the match proved that Cena was, indeed, superior to Jésus, who was never heard from again.

WWE ON TV

WWE Championship Wrestling

Years Broadcast: 1978 - 1986

Championship Wrestling was the first-ever nationally syndicated WWE television program. With Vince McMahon as the voice of the program, the show featured in-ring action from promotion's top stars.

WWE All-Star Wrestling

Years Broadcast: Mid-1970s - 1986

Featuring matches between the era's top Superstars and lesser-known competitors, *All-Star Wrestling* was not all that different from other sports-entertainment shows of its time. Very often, however, *All-Star Wrestling* also served as a home for big announcements. In January 1984, Gene Okerlund broke the news that Hulk Hogan was named the No. 1 contender for the WWE Championship. He later went on the defeat the Iron Sheik for the title and become one of the greatest champions in WWE history.

Years Broadcast: 1983 - 1994

Airing on the USA Network, *All-American Wrestling* featured exclusive WWE action during its first several years of existence. As the 1990s rolled around, however, the show served mainly as a vehicle to show highlights from the past week of WWE action.

Tuesday Night Titans

Years Broadcast: 1984 - 1986
See page 350

Years Broadcast: 1985-1993

A weekly two-hour show hosted mainly by Bobby Heenan and Gorilla Monsoon, *Prime Time Wrestling* featured matches from arenas across the country. In 1991, the show's format was slightly altered to include a live studio audience. By the end of the year, however, the show changed again. This time, it featured roundtable discussions lead by Vince McMahon.

Years Broadcast: 1985 - PRESENT
See page 225

Years Broadcast: 1986 - 1995

A weekly syndicated show, *Wrestling Spotlight* served dual purposes by recapping recent WWE action and featuring exclusive matches. The show was hosted from a studio Sean Mooney and Sherri Martel, among others.

WRESTLING CHALLENGE

Years Broadcast: 1986 - 1996

Wrestling Challenge was a weekly syndicated show hosted at various times by Gorilla Monsoon, Tony Schiavone, Jim Ross, Bobby Heenan, and Stan Lane, among others. For much of its existence, the show featured exclusive matches. However, in the mid-1990s, *Wrestling Challenge* became a highlight show hosted by Dok Hendrix and Mr. Perfect.

WWE Superstars of Wrestling

Years Broadcast: 1986 - 2001

A program that set the early standard for sports-entertainment television, this show featured an amazing three-man booth of Vince McMahon, "The Living Legend" Bruno Sammartino, and Jesse "the Body" Ventura. Championship matches, intense interview segments, and updates in the newsroom from all WWE happenings around the globe courtesy of "Mean" Gene Okerlund. Over the years, many different hosts called the action including "Rowdy" Roddy Piper, Bobby "The Brain" Heenan, Mr. Perfect, Johnny Polo, Dok Hendrix, Jim Ross, and Jim Cornette among others.

Years Broadcast: 1993 - Present
See page 278

WWE Mania

Years Broadcast: 1993 - 1997

During the mid-to-late 1990s, the USA Network's weekend programming included *WWE Mania*, a weekly highlight show hosted by Todd Pettengill and Stephanie Wiand.

WWE Sunday Night Slam

Years Broadcast: 1994 - 1995

Much like the popular *Free For All* program, *Sunday Night Slam* previewed the action fans could expect to see on WWE's monthly pay-per-views.

WWE Action Zone

Years Broadcast: 1994 - 1996

The earliest days of *Action Zone* featured exclusive in-ring competition from WWE's top Superstars, including Bret Hart defending the WWE Championship against Owen Hart on the show's premiere episode. By the end of its second year, however, *Action Zone* became a highlight show hosted by Todd Pettengill and Dok Hendrix.

WWE Free For All

Years Broadcast: 1996 - 1998

During the mid-to-late 1990s *Free For All* counted down the final thirty minutes before the start of each monthly pay-per-view. In addition to recapping the stories that lead up to the event, *Free For All* also featured exclusive live matches. The most notable *Free For All* match saw the Bodydonnas topple the Godwinns for the World Tag Team Championship just minutes before the official start of *WrestleMania XII*.

Years Broadcast: 1996 - 2001

Hosted by Todd Pettengill and Sunny (and later Michael Cole) *Livewire* was originally a live call-in show where fans were given the opportunity to interact with their favorite Superstars. Towards the end of the show's existence, it dropped its interactivity in favor of highlights.

Years Broadcast: 1997 - 1999

The edgy content found on *Shotgun Saturday Night* epitomized WWE's popular Attitude Era. Emanating from nightclubs rather than arenas, the show featured some of the 1990s most controversial moments.

Years Broadcast: 1998 –2008

Heat saw many different looks and feels over the course of its ten-year existence. The show's formats included matches and interviews, music videos, recapping events, and previews of upcoming pay-per-views.

Years Broadcast: 1999 - PRESENT
See page 318

Years Broadcast: 1999 - 2002

Airing Saturday afternoons in syndication, *Metal* featured in-ring WWE action. Kevin Kelly and Dr. Tom Prichard called the matches from ringside.

JAKKED

Years Broadcast: 1999 - 2002
Airing Saturday nights in syndication, *Jakked* featured in-ring WWE action. Over the course of the show's history, matches were called by Michael Cole, Michael Hayes, and Jonathan Coachman.

Years Broadcast: 2001 - 2002
Telecast live from WWE studios in Connecticut, *Excess* was touted as the premiere show for TNN's Slammin' Saturday Night lineup of programming. The show's format featured two hours of highlights and interviews, as well as the opportunity for fans to call in and talk to their favorite Superstars.

Years Broadcast 2001 – 2004; 2011 – Present
See page 347

Years Broadcast: 2002 - 2004
Hosted by "Mean" Gene Okerlund, *Confidential* was known for pulling the curtain back to allow fans see inside the sports-entertainment industry. The show touched on topics previously considered taboo, including the truth behind the Montreal Incident and Stone Cold Steve Austin's highly-publicized departure from WWE in 2002.

Years Broadcast: 2002 - 2005
A weekend syndication show, *AfterBurn* highlighted the past week's high points from *SmackDown* and *Velocity*, including matches and interviews.

Years Broadcast: 2002 - 2005
A weekly syndicated magazine show, *Bottom Line* looked back at the week that was on *Monday Night Raw* and *Heat*. Marc Loyd served as the show's main host; Jonathan Coachman and Todd Grisham also briefly held the honors.

Years Broadcast: 2002 – 2006
Much like *Heat* did for *Raw*, *Velocity* served as platform to highlight the recent action on *SmackDown*, as well as feature exclusive matches involving the brand's Superstars. In 2005, the show moved from television screens to computer monitors when it began streaming over WWE.com.

Years Broadcast: 2003 – Present
A patriotic television event like no other, *Tribute To The Troops* is one of the ways WWE supports the U.S. Military and says "Thank you." This annual event has been broadcast from Iraq, Afghanistan and military bases across the United States. Featuring incredible matches, soldiers have also been treated to WWE Hall of Famer appearances, as well as star-studded guests from Hollywood, the world of music, and special video messages from U.S. Presidents George W. Bush and Barack Obama.

Years Broadcast: 2004 - Present
Originally hosted by Todd Grisham and Ivory, *WWE Experience* began as a one-hour recap of the week that was in WWE. The show also took viewers behind the scenes to see Superstars' favorite activities outside the ring. The show went off the air in the United States when *WWE A.M. Raw* made its debut but it continues to appear on television stations around the world. Josh Matthews and Jack Korpella also served as hosts for *WWE Experience* but Matt Striker has filled that role since November 2011.

Years Broadcast: 2004 - Present
As the name suggests, *24/7 Classics On Demand* is WWE's video on demand subscription service. It features approximately forty hours of new programming each month, pulling memorable events in sports-entertainment history from its gigantic library, which includes action from WCW, AWA, ECW, WCCW and other promotions.

Years Broadcast: 2005 - Present
A.M. Raw condenses the most recent two hours of *Monday Night Raw* into a fast-paced sixty minutes of action. The highlight show also features a continuous ticker at the bottom of the screen where fans can catch up on the latest WWE news and test their knowledge with trivia and fun facts.

Years Broadcast: 2006 – 2010
See page 106

WWE Madison Square Garden Classics

Years Broadcast: 2006 – 2009
Aired Wednesday nights on the MSG Network, Madison Square Garden Classics looked back at the greatest matches to ever take place in the "World's Most Famous Arena."

Years Broadcast: 2008 – Present
Hosted by "Mean" Gene Okerlund, *Vintage Collection* is an overseas sensation and features classic matches from WWE's expansive library.

Years Broadcast: 2009 - Present
A weekly show with lineage to the original Superstars of Wrestling, Superstars features competitors from all WWE brand locker rooms. A place where heated rivalries continue and are conceived, audiences never know when a new champion will be crowned and when new wars will be waged.

Years Broadcast: 2010 – Present
See page 405

J

2010-

2000-09

1990-99

1980-89

1970-79

1960-69

JILLIAN

HT: 5'6"   FROM: Los Angeles, California
SIGNATURE MOVE: The High Note

TITLE HISTORY

DIVAS CHAMPION	*Defeated Mickie James on October 12, 2009*

This Diva first appeared in late 2005 as a "fixer" for MNM. She was later seen at the side of business mogul John "Bradshaw" Layfield. Within a short period, Jillian made it clear that if she was at ringside, then she would make her presence felt and her voice heard.

At *No Way Out* in 2007, Jillian proudly made her WWE singing debut and though her lead vocals were greeted by a chorus of boos, she was motivated to become the greatest pop recording artist on the planet. In the ring, she became a top contender for the Women's Championship. In December 2007, she released her debut album titled, *A Jingle With Jillian*. This collection of her favorite Christmas tunes was a hit with fans.

In October of 2009, Jillian reached the crescendo of her career when she defeated Mickie James for the Divas Championship. Though the tone-deaf Diva lost the title to Melina immediately afterwards, being WWE champion for even just a few moments is more than most will ever accomplish in their career.

JIM CORNETTE

FROM: Louisville, Kentucky

One of the most controversial and outspoken men in sports-entertainment history, James E. Cornette first rose to prominence as a manager of the Midnight Express in the NWA. With his always-present tennis racket, he managed both iterations of the Midnight Express to the NWA Tag Team Championship and United States Tag Team Championship. In 1991, he left WCW and started the influential regional promotional known as Smoky Mountain Wrestling. As his mouth moved faster than ever, Cornette and his tennis racket traveled north.

In 1993, he debuted in WWE and was appointed to be the United States spokesperson for then-WWE Champion Yokozuna. In 1996, he created Camp Cornette with the British Bulldog, Owen Hart and Vader. As the Monday Night Wars were fought Cornette's keen sports-entertainment perspective were aired during *Raw*. A mastermind, Cornette led an NWA invasion of WWE in 1998 and introduced fans to the New Midnight Express. WWE utilized Cornette's expertise in developing talent and made him an important part to their development system. He made a surprise appearance at *WrestleMania X-7*, competing in the Gimmick Battle Royal.

In 2005, Cornette and WWE ended their 12-year relationship. Fans and Superstars will never forget this momma's boy's mouth, his tennis racket, or his countless contributions to furthering the future of sports-entertainment.

JIM "THE ANVIL" NEIDHART

HT: 6'2"   WT: 281 lbs.
FROM: Reno, Nevada
SIGNATURE MOVE: Anvil Flattener

TITLE HISTORY

WORLD TAG TEAM CHAMPION (2 TIMES)	*Partnered with Bret Hart to defeat The British Bulldogs on January 26, 1987* *Partnered with Bret Hart to defeat Demolition on August 27, 1990*

His menacing laugh, barrel chest and pointy goatee made Jim Neidhart one of the most recognizable Superstars of the 1980s and 1990s, but it was his efforts as a member of the Hart Foundation that made him one of the most feared competitors of his time.

Following very intensive training from Stu Hart in the legendary Dungeon, Neidhart got his start competing in Calgary's Stampede Wrestling. For the next few years, he gained great experience competing alongside Canada's best. However, it was the nickname he earned during this time that proved most valuable. After Stu Hart paid him $500 to enter (and win) a local anvil-throwing contest, Helen Hart started calling him "The Anvil." The nickname has stuck with him ever since.

In the early 1980s, Neidhart moved to WWE after Vince McMahon purchased Stampede Wrestling. A few months into his tenure, he began teaming with Bret Hart. Managed by Jimmy Hart, the team became known as the Hart Foundation and would go on to become one of history's most successful teams.

After the Hart Foundation broke up in the early 1990s, Neidhart began to team with Bret's brother, Owen. Initially, the duo achieved lackluster results and soon separated, but they later reunited when "The Anvil" helped Owen win the 1994 *King of the Ring*. Together, they spent the next six months trying to expel former ally Bret "Hit Man" Hart from WWE. Like most family quarrels, this was eventually resolved. "The Anvil" later reunited with the "Hit Man" and joined a reformed Hart Foundation. While Jim has let the WWE spotlight drift to his daughter, Natalya, he still makes rare appearances such as at the *Raw 15th Anniversary* battle royal.

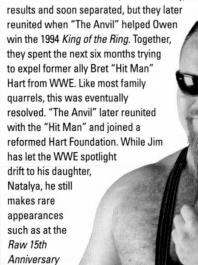

JIM POWERS

HT: 6'1"   WT: 235 lbs.
FROM: New York City
SIGNATURE MOVE: Powerslam

Trained by Big John Studd, Jim Powers made his WWE debut in 1984. With his good looks and physique, Powers was an instant hit with the women in the WWE audience. He was quickly recognized as an outstanding competitor who excited crowds all over the world. He first took to the mat as a singles competitor, but started a search for a partner as 1986 came to a close.

In March 1987, Jim Powers & Paul Roma formed the Young Stallions. A young, gutsy duo whose theme song *Crank It Up* prepared the audience for their fast-paced, high-flying style that featured quick tags and thrilling double-team maneuvers. Unfortunately, the team's inability to capture World Tag Team gold by 1989 resulted in a bad split. Powers resumed his singles career and appeared at WWE events through 1994 before leaving for WCW, where he wrapped up his career in sports-entertainment.

JIM ROSS

FROM: Westville, Oklahoma

> ## IT'S GOING TO BE A SLOBBERKKNOCKER!

As the man under the black Resistol cowboy hat travels to the next sold-out WWE event, he prepares to entertain millions of fans worldwide on television every week. On a rare occasion, a quiet moment will present itself and a memory from his incredible thirty-five year career will enter into his mind.

Jim Ross grew up idolizing men like his father, John Wayne, and Mickey Mantle. His excursion into sports-entertainment began in 1974 working for LeRoy McGuirk. The 22 year old was not only the driver for the legendary, legally blind promoter, but also a referee who maintained order in the Tulsa territory. From there Jim worked for "Cowboy" Bill Watts and became the voice for Mid-South Wrestling and its Power Pro television program, which later became the Universal Wrestling Federation. As the UWF was purchased by Jim Crockett Promotions, Ross became the lead play-by-play announcer for the National Wrestling Alliance. Corporate buyouts in the 1980s continued when Ted Turner purchased the business from the Crocketts and launched World Championship Wrestling (WCW). Jim's body of work grew when he became nationally recognized as the voice of the NFL's Atlanta Falcons. All the while, he worked to get to the big time and become internationally known.

After a nineteen year journey Jim Ross made it to sports-entertainment's premier entity and debuted at *WrestleMania IX*. Alongside Randy "Macho Man" Savage and Bobby Heenan, Ross called the action at the "World's Largest Toga Party." His broadcast duties expanded in 1994 when he was the host of WWE Radio and heard on *Monday Night Raw, Action Zone,* and *Shotgun Saturday Night.*

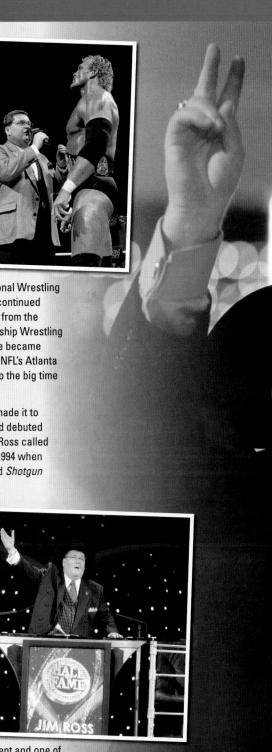

Business is about to pick up here."

In 1997, Ross became one-half of what would be a future WWE Hall of Fame broadcast team, as he and Jerry Lawler were the voices of *Monday Night Raw.* The voice of Jim Ross and his partner chronicled the conflict that became known as "The Monday Night Wars." More times than not, if an important moment took place in the ring, the good ol' boy from Oklahoma made the call. During his famed career, Jim at times has had to reluctantly leave the broadcast booth and knock the taste out of someone's mouth to the pleasure of WWE audiences. During this era, J.R.'s fame led him to the silver screen in 1999 when he appeared in the critically acclaimed *Man on the Moon.* As J.R. continued to broaden the scope of announcing as the voice of *Monday Night Raw*, he brought his many talents to the world of publishing in 2003 when he penned his top-selling cookbook titled, *J.R.'s Cookbook: True Ringside Tales, BBQ, and Down-Home Recipes.*

Jim Ross is considered an esteemed authority on the history of sports-entertainment and one of the most inventive broadcast personalities ever. In 2007, Ross traveled to the world of higher learning and gave lectures at MIT about the global phenomenon of professional wrestling. Days later, Ross entered the chamber of immortals as he was inducted into the WWE Hall of Fame. Later, based on the resounding success of his barbecue product line he opened "J.R.'s Family Bar-B-Q Restaurants" in his home state of Oklahoma.

After the 2008 Draft, Ross brought his Hall of Fame voice to *SmackDown* and brings that big game feel to every broadcast. Over time, prominent figures have given their own commentary regarding "The Voice of WWE." Triple H said, "There is no else I'd rather have call my match than Jim Ross." WWE Hall of Famer "Nature Boy" Ric Flair added, "A lot of people are good, few are great. Jim Ross is great." Perhaps no words ring truer than those of Stone Cold Steve Austin, "Jim Ross is the best ever, end of story."

Jim Ross is a WWE institution and is the soundtrack to the greatest moments in sports-entertainment history. He was blessed with the unique gift to paint wonderful murals of imagery with speech.

J
2010-
2000-09
1990-99
1980-89
1970-79
1960-69

JIM YOUNG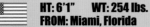

HT: 6'1" **WT:** 254 lbs.
FROM: Miami, Florida

With his big, burly moustache and long curly brown hair, Jim Young reminded many wrestling fans of Magnum T.A. Unfortunately, however, Young's appearance is the only characteristic he shared with the NWA legend. During his WWE tenure of the early-to-mid 1980s, Young lost more often than not. The WWE Superstars who regularly bettered their record against the Florida native included Don Muraco, Big John Studd, The Missing Link and "Dr. D" David Schultz.

JIMMY JACK FUNK

HT: 6'0" **WT:** 242 lbs.
FROM: Amarillo, Texas
SIGNATURE MOVE: Bulldog

Jimmy Jack Funk was crazy, even by Funk standards.

For decades, fans feared the wild Funk brothers. Hailing from Amarillo, Texas, Terry and Hoss made a career out of their maniacal in-ring actions. Little did anybody know, however, that there was a younger Funk back home at the Double Cross Ranch who was even crazier. In 1986, Terry and Hoss finally introduced WWE audiences to Jimmy Jack, their uncontrollable and unpredictable brother.

Managed by Jimmy Hart, Jimmy Jack kept with the Funk ways by wearing a cowboy hat and boots to the ring. In addition to this classic Funk garb, he also sported a mask over his eyes and noose around his neck.

According to the Funks, Jimmy Jack was an amazing amateur wrestler who only missed competing in the Olympics because of the American boycott of the Moscow Games in 1980. Unfortunately for Jimmy Jack, his supposed amateur success never equated to wins in a WWE ring, as he frequently fell short in matches against the likes of Blackjack Mulligan and Hillbilly Jim.

JIMMY HART

FROM: Memphis, Tennessee

HALL OF FAME 2005

When it comes to managers in sports-entertainment, few can outshine the accomplishments of "Mouth of the South" Jimmy Hart. His sports-entertainment career began when he met Jerry "The King" Lawler and started work in the Memphis Wrestling territory. He first gained notoriety being the manager for the comedian Andy Kaufman in his battles with the King of Memphis.

Jimmy Hart arrived in WWE in 1985 just prior to the groundbreaking first *WrestleMania*. His first of many clients included King Kong Bundy and then-Intercontinental Champion, Greg "The Hammer" Valentine. Hart became known as a manager who quickly changed the fortunes of a given Superstar, causing chaotic scenes with the greatest of ease, and for his megaphone. He was known to scream instructions to his protégés and snide remarks toward their opponents, the officials and fans. Hart's amplified voice was so piercing that during televised broadcasts, "The Mouth" could be heard by the audience watching at home. This communication piece also came in handy as a weapon to change the outcome of many matches.

Giants, technical standouts, brawlers, monsters, law enforcers, tag teams — "The Mouth" managed them all. He managed dangerous teams like the Funk Brothers and led The Hart Foundation, Nasty Boys, the Natural Disasters, and Money Inc. to the World Tag Team Championship. In addition to the "The Hammer," Jimmy also managed the Honky Tonk Man and The Mountie to the Intercontinental Championship. Jimmy's managerial genius extended to the Women's ranks as he managed the Glamour Girls to the WWE Women's Tag Team Championship. He capped off his WWE career in style in 1993 when he managed Hulk Hogan to his fifth WWE Championship.

In 1994, Jimmy took his megaphone South and landed in WCW with his close friend, Hulk Hogan. During his time in WCW, he continued to write entrance themes as well as perform invaluable duties behind the scenes.

In 2005, the "Mouth of the South's" exceptional career was honored as he was inducted into the WWE Hall of Fame. This unforgettable figure still appears for WWE and is one of the most loved characters in the history of sports-entertainment.

JIMMY "SUPERFLY" SNUKA

HT: 5'10"   **WT:** 235 lbs.   **FROM:** The Figi Islands   **SIGNATURE MOVE:** Superfly Splash

No nickname in sports-entertainment history has been more appropriately assigned than "Superfly." Gliding through the sky, Jimmy Snuka used his aerial theatrics to amaze audiences and inspire countless future Superstars.

As a young boy growing up on the islands of Fiji, Snuka perfected his Superfly Splash by diving off cliffs. In 1969, he took his awe-inspiring leap to Hawaii where he made his professional debut. Not long after his first match, Snuka moved to the mainland and began competing in the Pacific Northwest.

In the late 1970s, Snuka traveled to the Mid-Atlantic territory where news of his gravity-defying Superfly Splash began to circulate around the United States. Fans nationwide wanted to witness the move firsthand. They finally got the opportunity in 1982 when Snuka signed on with WWE.

Flying High in the WWE

Within weeks of his debut, Snuka soared straight to main events. Behind manager Capt. Lou Albano, the savage newcomer earned several opportunities at Bob Backlund's WWE Championship. Their most notable encounter took place at Madison Square Garden. With the WWE Championship within reach, Snuka climbed to the top of the 15-foot steel cage and dove straight down toward Backlund's body. Unfortunately for Snuka, the champion narrowly escaped the Superfly Splash. The stunt cost Snuka the match, but remains one of the most memorable moments of all time.

After Albano failed to deliver the championship to Snuka, the high-flying Superstar began to take the advice of the legendary Buddy Rogers, who told "Superfly" that his manager was stealing from him. Snuka immediately fired Albano and took Rogers on as his new manager. The move ignited one of the most brutal rivalries of the 1980s. Looking for revenge, Albano sent his new protégé, Ray Stevens, after Snuka. The two Superstars bled buckets over the course of their intense rivalry.

In 1983, Snuka focused his attention on attaining the Intercontinental Championship from Don Muraco. Much like his quest for the WWE Championship, Snuka's road to glory went through a Steel Cage Match. This time, "Superfly" landed his breath-taking leap from the top of the steel structure. Unfortunately, the match had already ended in Muraco's favor at the time of aerial assault. While Snuka failed to pry the Intercontinental Championship away that night, he did successfully inspire a young Mick Foley who was watching from the third row. In his 1999 autobiography, *Have a Nice Day!*, Foley called the leap, "The most impressive sight I've ever seen."

Piper's Pit Ambush

Snuka's amazing Superfly Splash from the top of the cage instantly made him WWE's most popular Superstar, which naturally made him the target of the time's least popular competitor, "Rowdy" Roddy Piper. In 1984, the loudmouth Scot invited the soft-spoken Snuka to be a guest on *Piper's Pit.* "Superfly" obliged, but was prepared to be the object of a verbal assault, as was usually the case when fan favorites visited the *Pit.* Instead, Snuka was brutally attacked by a coconut-wielding Piper. The mugging was so vicious that the two Superstars actually tore the *Piper's Pit* set to the ground. Decades later, the attack is widely acknowledged as the most infamous moment in *Piper's Pit* history.

Following the incident, Snuka volunteered to be in the corner of Hulk Hogan & Mr. T when they battled Piper & Paul Orndorff in the main event of the first-ever *WrestleMania.* After the event, "Superfly" made appearances in other territorites (he was the first champion recognized by the group that would one day become Extreme Championship Wrestling) and with WWE before entering into semi-retirement in 1994.

Snuka's sports-entertainment accomplishments were recognized by WWE when they inducted him into the Hall of Fame in 1996. On the night following the ceremony, "Superfly" donned his leopard-print trunks for one more leap through the MSG skies at *Survivor Series* as the Mystery Partner for Yokozuna's team. Since then, the Fijian continues to appear on WWE television including returns to the ring in 2005 at *Taboo Tuesday,* 2007's *Vengeance: Night of Champions,* and as a surprise entrant in the 2008 *Royal Rumble.* Most recently, "Superfly" returned to the *WrestleMania* stage with "Rowdy" Roddy Piper and Ricky "The Dragon" Steamboat in a battle versus Chris Jericho.

2010-
2000-09
1990-99
1980-89
1970-79
1960-69

JINDER MAHAL

HT: 6'5"   WT: 222 lbs.   FROM: Punjab, India
SIGNATURE MOVE: Full Nelson Slam

As a successful movie studio executive in India, Jinder Mahal was accustomed to people following his orders. And when he came to WWE in the spring of 2011, he demanded the same level of respect, particularly from The Great Khali.

Mahal began playing games with The Great Khali's mind, claiming Ranjin Singh turned the giant from a main-event World Heavyweight Champion into a comedic sideshow. The wealthy newcomer eventually twisted Khali's emotions to the breaking point, convincing the oversized Superstar to turn on Singh and join forces with him.

Together, Mahal and Khali looked unstoppable. But after only a few months, Khali finally realized he was being used. When this happened, the former World Heavyweight Champion turned on Mahal, much to the delight of the WWE Universe.

The arrogant newcomer brushed off Khali's betrayal, claiming he didn't need the big man to gain notoriety. Whether or not that is true remains to be seen.

J.O.B. SQUAD

MEMBERS: Al Snow, Hardcore Holly, Scorpio, Gillberg, The Blue Meanie

Headed by Al Snow, the J.O.B. Squad banded together in 1998 after coming to the realization that they weren't getting a proper exposure in a high-profile storyline. They accepted their spots on the roster, and even developed the catchphrase "pin me, pay me," meaning they would put up with losing, just as long as they were paid.

Ironically, shortly after coming together, each member of the J.O.B. Squad began to experience great success. In fact, during their brief stay together, the J.O.B. Squad captured three championships; Gillberg became Light Heavyweight Champion and both Al Snow and Hardcore Holly won the Hardcore Championship.

JIMMY WANG YANG

HT: 5'9"   WT: 206 lbs.
FROM: Austell, Georgia
SIGNATURE MOVE: Corkscrew 450 Splash

In August 2006, this newcomer appeared on *SmackDown* and showed he's not the one to ask where to find good Chinese food. Jimmy Wang Yang could not be more proud of his affinity for anything country. With a fusion of martial-arts and good old fashioned Southern rough-housing, Jimmy Wang Yang became one of the premier Cruiserweights in the world.

JOE McHUGH

Over the years, it has become commonplace to see ring announcers put their own spin on Superstar introductions. Howard Finkel. Lilian Garcia. Tony Chimel. They all did it. But perhaps no ring announcer in sports-entertainment history has put as big of a personalized stamp on introductions as Joe McHugh.

As an announcer in the 1970s, McHugh introduced some of WWE's greatest names, including Pat Patterson, Pedro Morals and Jimmy "Superfly" Snuka. But because McHugh's style incorporated an overemphasis on enunciating (as well as sometimes adding new syllables), the names normally came out sounding a bit different. As an example, he would introduce Snuka as "Jim-eee Super-Fa-Ly Sanooka."

McHugh's unique style of ring announcing usually resulted in elongated introductions. But fans didn't mind the delay. They found his distinctive vocals to be entertaining and often imitated him throughout each introduction.

Over the course of his career, McHugh also announced more than 10,000 boxing matches. He passed away in 1993 at the age of 88.

The black cowboy-hat wearing Superstar was a favorite of the WWE Universe. His walk to the ring as country tunes filled arenas got crowds on their feet as he took on challengers of all shapes and sizes. Jimmy was not the stereotypical redneck, and brought a style all his own to WWE rings.

JOE TURCO

WT: 237 lbs.
FROM: Catania, Sicily

With his unruly hair, bushy goatee and dark hooded cape, Joe Turco was one of the most fearsome looking opponents of all time. Then the bell rang. Unfortunately for Turco, his in-ring abilities failed to match his terrifying appearance.

Nicknamed the "Continental Nobleman," Turco competed for WWE in the late 1960s and early 1970s. Fans loved to boo the unsuccessful Superstar; and each time that they did, he responded with several rude hand gestures. Eventually, Turco started to become more known for the entertaining way in which he responded to fans than his athleticism.

Turco often teamed with the equally unsuccessful Pancho Valdez. They hoped that through a combined effort they could rise up the card. They didn't.

In 1975, Turco received the opportunity of his career when he challenged WWE Hall of Famer Mil Mascaras for the now-defunct IWA International Championship. As expected, though, Mascaras proved superior after Turco submitted to a modified abdominal stretch.

JOEY ABS

HT: 6'3" **WT:** 277 lbs.
FROM: Greenwich, Connecticut

When the Mean Street Posse walked the affluent streets of Greenwich, Connecticut, they made their fellow sweater-vest-wearing neighbors tremble in fear. When they appeared in WWE in 1999, however, they failed to induce the same trepidation. Instead, the WWE Superstars simply looked down upon them as Shane McMahon's bratty friends. At least that's how they saw Pete Gas and Rodney. Joey Abs was a different story.

TITLE HISTORY	
HARDCORE CHAMPION	1 Time

As the biggest and baddest member of the Mean Street Posse, Abs picked up significantly more victories than his stablemates, but that wasn't really saying much, considering their lackluster won-loss record. Abs did, however, manage to permanently etch his name into the WWE records book when he captured the Hardcore Championship at *WrestleMania 2000*. In typical Mean Street Posse fashion, he lost the gold only seconds after capturing it.

JOEY MAGGS

HT: 6'0" **WT:** 235 lbs.
FROM: Baltimore, Maryland

Joey Maggs was never the biggest Superstar on the card, but what he lacked in size, he made up for in quickness. Dubbed "Jumping" Joey Maggs, the Superstar from Baltimore used his speed to bounce around the ring and dizzy his opponents.

People began to take notice of Maggs while he was competing in the United States Wrestling Association. Maggs soon left for the bright lights of WCW, once earning a shot at Steve Austin's WCW Television Championship at *Clash of the Champions* in 1992. Through the rest of the 1990s, he joined WWE, appearing on the television shows *Prime Time Wrestling* and *Monday Night Raw*.

JOEY MERCURY

HT: 5'9" **WT:** 212 lbs.
FROM: Los Angeles, California

TITLE HISTORY	
WWE TAG TEAM CHAMPION (3 TIMES)	*Partnered with John Morrison to defeat Rey Mysterio & Eddie Guerrero on April 21, 2005* *Partnered with John Morrison to defeat Animal & Heidenreich on October 28, 2005* *Partnered with John Morrison to defeat Batista & Rey Mysterio on December 30, 2005*

Only a handful of Superstars can say they won gold in their first-ever WWE match. Joey Mercury is one of the elite few. In April 2005, Mercury debuted alongside Johnny Nitro to defeat the reigning WWE Tag Team Champions, Eddie Guerrero & Rey Mysterio. The win shocked the WWE Universe, but for the cocky newcomers, claiming the gold was a mere formality.

With Melina as their manager, Mercury & Nitro went on to enjoy three tag title reigns. Despite their success in the tag division, perhaps Mercury's most memorable moment came in a losing effort. While competing in a Fatal 4-Way Ladder Match at *Armageddon 2006*, the arrogant Superstar was nailed in the face with a ladder, resulting in a completely shattered nose. Shortly after, Mercury left WWE for several years.

In April 2010, a masked man emerged from under the ring to help CM Punk in a match against Mysterio. It was later revealed that the man under the mask was the Straight Edge Society's newest member, Joey Mercury.

J

2010-

2000-09

1990-99

1980-89

1970-79

1960-69

JOHN "BRADSHAW" LAYFIELD

HT: 6'6"   WT: 290 lbs.
FROM: New York, New York
SIGNATURE MOVE: Clothesline From Hell

TITLE HISTORY	
EUROPEAN CHAMPION	*Defeated The Hurricane on October 22, 2001*
HARDCORE CHAMPION	*17 Times*
INTERCONTINENTAL CHAMPION	*Defeated CM Punk on March 9, 2009*
UNITED STATES CHAMPION	*Defeated Chris Benoit on April 2, 2006*
WWE CHAMPION	*Defeated Eddie Guerrero on June 27, 2004*
WORLD TAG TEAM CHAMPION (3 TIMES)	*Partnered with Faarooq to defeat Kane & X-Pac on May 31, 1999* *Partnered with Faarooq to defeat The Hardy Boys on July 25, 1999* *Partnered with Faarooq to defeat The Dudley Boys on July 9, 2001*

JOEY STYLES 🇺🇸

With knowledge of the industry matched by very few, and his trademark call, "Oh My God!", Joey Styles will be forever associated with the rise of ECW. During an internship at *Pro Wrestling Illustrated*, he met Paul Heyman, who soon took over Eastern Championship Wrestling. Joey Styles was Heyman's choice to serve as its television commentator, where his insight and distinctive voice provided the perfect accompaniment as the promotion transitioned to Extreme Championship Wrestling.

Styles made history during ECW's *Barely Legal* as he became the first announcer to call a live pay-per-view broadcast without the use of a full-time color commentator. From June 1993 to January 2001, Styles performed play-by-play on pay-per-views, television programs, home videos and video games while also working on a plethora of other projects for the company.

After ECW went out of business, Joey Styles was out of the public eye until June 2005, when the revolution was revived at *One Night Stand*. His performance exceeded expectations and he soon joined the WWE as a full-time announcer on *Monday Night Raw*. His tenure included fulfilling a lifelong dream of calling a match at *WrestleMania.* Styles vocally and publicly quit *Raw*, but returned to ECW when WWE relaunched the brand.

Joey Styles retired from announcing in 2008 and became the Director of Digital Media Content at WWE.com, where he also hosts a weekly feature known as the *Oh My God! Moment of the Week.*

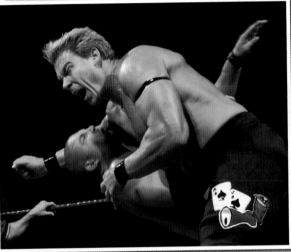

Whether it's on Wall Street or in a Street Fight, John "Bradshaw" Layfield is a dangerous man. The self-made millionaire's investing acumen has earned him the reputation of a stock market genius, while his devastating Clothesline From Hell propelled him to the top of WWE.

Following a brief professional football career, JBL invested his attention on entering sports-entertainment. After a few years competing on the independent circuit, he made the leap to WWE. Over the next eight years, he proved himself as one of the toughest Superstars around. But it wasn't until he began to publicize his impressive portfolio in March 2004 that he gained greatness.

Claiming to be a great American, the new JBL focused his energies on many of the United States' political matters, including illegal immigrants. His bold statements drew the attention of then-WWE Champion Eddie Guerrero. The two Superstars quickly engaged in a memorable rivalry that saw JBL claim the WWE Championship from Guerrero in June 2004.

Despite holding the WWE Championship, JBL sought even more power. To ensure he would have complete control over *SmackDown*, he formed a strong cabinet of Superstars around him. With Chief of Staff Orlando Jordan and Secretaries of Defense Danny & Doug Basham by his side, JBL went on to become the longest-reigning WWE Champion in *SmackDown* history.

In May 2006, JBL's in-ring career seemingly came to an end when a defeat at the hands of Rey Mysterio forced him into early retirement. Instead of retreating back to Wall Street after the loss, he donned a headset and became *SmackDown's* color commentator, alongside play-by-play man Michael Cole. JBL remained a fixture at the announce booth until Chris Jericho lured him out of retirement in December 2007.

Back in the ring, the self-proclaimed "Wrestling God" picked up right where he left off. He even managed to gain a level of retribution from the man who took his WWE Championship from him when he defeated John Cena in a New York City Parking Lot Brawl at The Great American Bash in July 2008.

Nothing exhibited JBL's shrewd business practices like when he forced Shawn Michaels to work for him after HBK lost his family savings during America's financial crisis. Layfield enjoyed one last taste of WWE gold when he defeated CM Punk for the Intercontinental Championship in March of 2009.

John Cena (see page 184)

JOHN "BRADSHAW" LAYFIELD™

JOHN LAURINAITIS

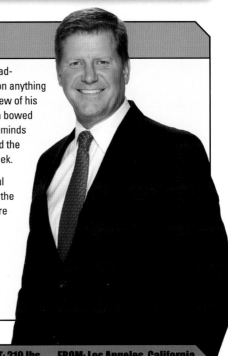

CM Punk will tell you that John Laurinaitis is nothing more than a glad-handing, nonsensical yes man with a propensity to tell Mr. McMahon anything he wants to hear. Laurinaitis, however, has a considerably higher view of his position within WWE, and he's not afraid to share it with you. With a bowed chest and what some equate to an arrogant smirk, he continually reminds people that he's *the* Executive Vice President of Talent Relations and the man with his finger on what you watch on WWE television each week.

Prior to being named to one of sports-entertainment's most powerful positions, Laurinaitis was an accomplished competitor. Throughout the 1980s and 1990s, he competed in the United States and Japan, where he claimed several tag team championship reigns.

After retiring from the ring in 2000, Laurinaitis began his front office career in the talent relations department of WCW. When the now-defunct promotion was acquired by WWE in 2001, Laurinaitis jumped to Mr. McMahon's company, where he quickly became one of the Chairman's most trusted associates.

JOHN MORRISON

HT: 6'2"   **WT: 219 lbs.**   **FROM: Los Angeles, California**
SIGNATURE MOVE: Moonlight Drive, Starship Pain

TITLE HISTORY

ECW CHAMPION	*Defeated CM Punk on June 25, 2007*
INTERCONTINENTAL CHAMPION (3 TIMES)	*Defeated Shelton Benjamin on June 25, 2006* *Defeated Jeff Hardy on November 6, 2006* *Defeated Rey Mysterio on September 4, 2009*
WORLD TAG TEAM CHAMPION	*Partnered with The Miz to defeat CM Punk & Kofi Kingston on December 13, 2008*
WWE TAG TEAM CHAMPION (4 TIMES)	*Partnered with Joey Mercury to defeat Rey Mysterio & Eddie Guerrero on April 21, 2005* *Partnered with Joey Mercury to defeat Animal & Heidenreich on October 28, 2005* *Partnered with Joey Mercury to defeat Batista & Rey Mysterio on December 30, 2005* *Partnered with The Miz to defeat MVP & Matt Hardy on November 16, 2007*

For much of his WWE career, John Morrison's arrogant attitude made him tough to like. You just couldn't tell him that; his warped impression of himself had him believing the earth is covered with Morrison Followers (or MoFos, as he calls them) who eagerly awaited the weekly installments of *The Dirt Sheet*.

Ever since Morrison's *SmackDown* debut in April 2005 (as Johnny Nitro), gold gravitated to his waist. A multiple-time Intercontinental and WWE Tag Team Champion, it wasn't until he was drafted to ECW in June 2007 that Morrison truly took his game to the next level. Within one week of his arrival on the extreme brand, the self-appointed "Tuesday Night Delight" defeated CM Punk for the vacant ECW Championship. Over the next several months, Morrison defeated Punk time and time again before the challenger finally defeated him in September.

In typical Morrison fashion, he wasn't without gold for long. In November, he teamed with then rival The Miz to capture the WWE Tag Team Championship from Matt Hardy & MVP. After the victory, the two conceited Superstars realized they had more in common than originally thought and went on to enjoy a lengthy eight-month reign.

The partnership ended when The Miz moved to *Raw*, and Morrison took to the air on *SmackDown*. On September 4th, Morrison won the Intercontinental Championship from Rey Mysterio. The Shaman of Sexy then fist-pumped his way to top pop-culture status when he joined WWE legend Trish Stratus and *Jersey Shore* star Snooki in a mixed tag match at *WrestleMania XXVII* against Lay Cool & Dolph Ziggler.

The last time he was seen, Morrison fell victim to a ghastly attack from former partner, The Miz. As a capacity crowd sat in silence, Morrison was carried out on a stretcher by emergency medical technicians. Fans hold hope that the Guru of Greatness will make a full recovery.

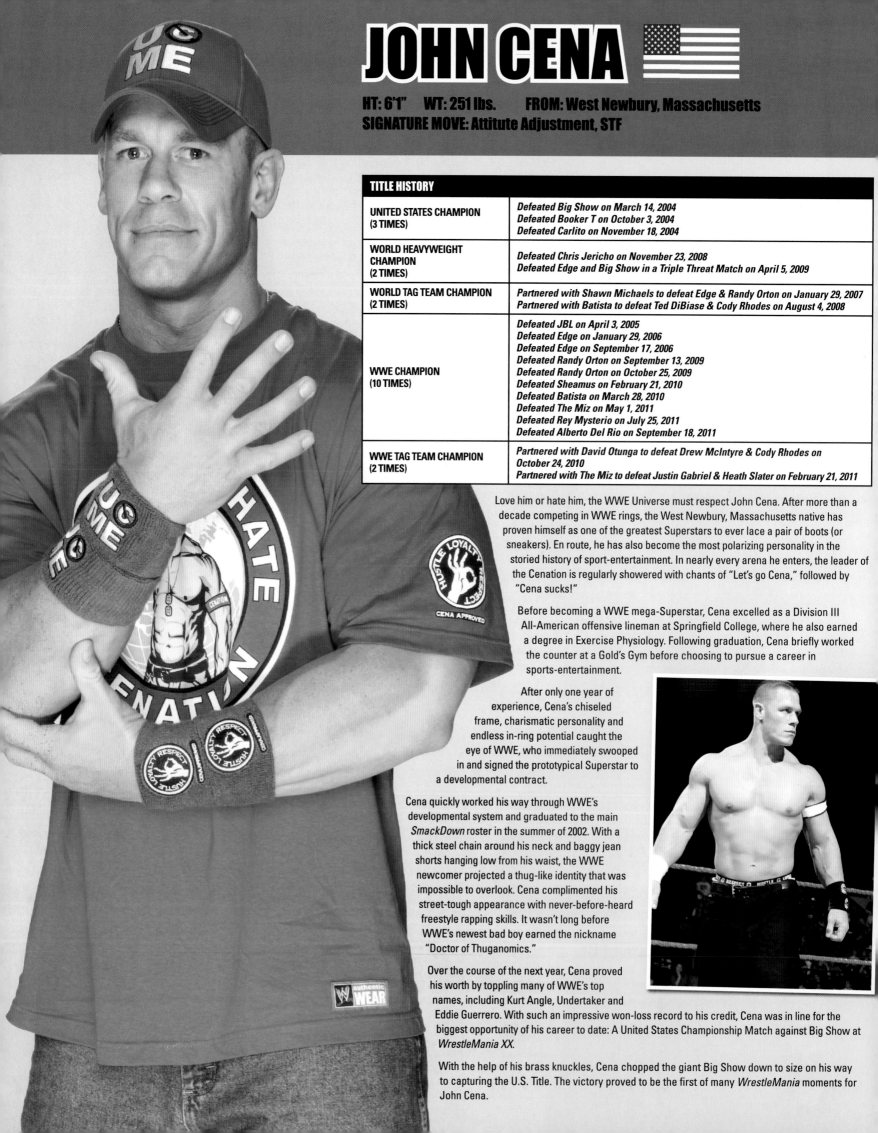

JOHN CENA

HT: 6'1" **WT:** 251 lbs. **FROM:** West Newbury, Massachusetts
SIGNATURE MOVE: Attitude Adjustment, STF

TITLE HISTORY

UNITED STATES CHAMPION (3 TIMES)	*Defeated Big Show on March 14, 2004* *Defeated Booker T on October 3, 2004* *Defeated Carlito on November 18, 2004*
WORLD HEAVYWEIGHT CHAMPION (2 TIMES)	*Defeated Chris Jericho on November 23, 2008* *Defeated Edge and Big Show in a Triple Threat Match on April 5, 2009*
WORLD TAG TEAM CHAMPION (2 TIMES)	*Partnered with Shawn Michaels to defeat Edge & Randy Orton on January 29, 2007* *Partnered with Batista to defeat Ted DiBiase & Cody Rhodes on August 4, 2008*
WWE CHAMPION (10 TIMES)	*Defeated JBL on April 3, 2005* *Defeated Edge on January 29, 2006* *Defeated Edge on September 17, 2006* *Defeated Randy Orton on September 13, 2009* *Defeated Randy Orton on October 25, 2009* *Defeated Sheamus on February 21, 2010* *Defeated Batista on March 28, 2010* *Defeated The Miz on May 1, 2011* *Defeated Rey Mysterio on July 25, 2011* *Defeated Alberto Del Rio on September 18, 2011*
WWE TAG TEAM CHAMPION (2 TIMES)	*Partnered with David Otunga to defeat Drew McIntyre & Cody Rhodes on October 24, 2010* *Partnered with The Miz to defeat Justin Gabriel & Heath Slater on February 21, 2011*

Love him or hate him, the WWE Universe must respect John Cena. After more than a decade competing in WWE rings, the West Newbury, Massachusetts native has proven himself as one of the greatest Superstars to ever lace a pair of boots (or sneakers). En route, he has also become the most polarizing personality in the storied history of sport-entertainment. In nearly every arena he enters, the leader of the Cenation is regularly showered with chants of "Let's go Cena," followed by "Cena sucks!"

Before becoming a WWE mega-Superstar, Cena excelled as a Division III All-American offensive lineman at Springfield College, where he also earned a degree in Exercise Physiology. Following graduation, Cena briefly worked the counter at a Gold's Gym before choosing to pursue a career in sports-entertainment.

After only one year of experience, Cena's chiseled frame, charismatic personality and endless in-ring potential caught the eye of WWE, who immediately swooped in and signed the prototypical Superstar to a developmental contract.

Cena quickly worked his way through WWE's developmental system and graduated to the main *SmackDown* roster in the summer of 2002. With a thick steel chain around his neck and baggy jean shorts hanging low from his waist, the WWE newcomer projected a thug-like identity that was impossible to overlook. Cena complimented his street-tough appearance with never-before-heard freestyle rapping skills. It wasn't long before WWE's newest bad boy earned the nickname "Doctor of Thuganomics."

Over the course of the next year, Cena proved his worth by toppling many of WWE's top names, including Kurt Angle, Undertaker and Eddie Guerrero. With such an impressive won-loss record to his credit, Cena was in line for the biggest opportunity of his career to date: A United States Championship Match against Big Show at *WrestleMania XX.*

With the help of his brass knuckles, Cena chopped the giant Big Show down to size on his way to capturing the U.S. Title. The victory proved to be the first of many *WrestleMania* moments for John Cena.

John Cena displayed his versatility again on October 13, 2006, when he entered the world of Hollywood and starred in **The Marine.**

By 2005, there was no denying Cena his time to shine as WWE's top star. Early in the year, he defeated Orlando Jordan, Booker T, and Kurt Angle in a No. 1 Contender's tournament. The victory earned Cena an opportunity at JBL's WWE Championship on the grandest stage of them all, *WrestleMania 21*.

With a sold-out Staples Center in his corner, Cena permanently etched his name in the annals of sports-entertainment when he dropped JBL with an Attitude Adjustment to claim the WWE Championship. To prove his reign was no fluke, the new champ followed his *WrestleMania* victory with another win over JBL at *Judgment Day*. This time, Cena did it in one of history's most gruesome "I Quit" Matches.

With the WWE Championship strapped firmly around his waist, Cena's star began to shoot higher and faster than any other Superstar in recent memory. Before long, the champ's time was in high demand. When he wasn't competing in the ring, he was making personal appearances; and when he wasn't making personal appearances, he was training or traveling or in the recording studio making his debut album, *You Can't See Me*, which debuted at No. 15 on the *Billboard* charts.

Through it all, Cena also managed to find time to redesign the WWE Championship from its traditional look into what is regularly referred to as the "spinner belt." Wrestling traditionalists gasped at the idea of altering sports-entertainment's most elite championship but Cena simply shrugs off the naysayers, claiming the business is evolutionary and must move forward to survive. His defense: Go back and watch an old match from the 1950s and compare it to today's action. It's evolved; so should the title.

Cena proudly carried the WWE Championship into 2006. His first big test came at January's *New Year's Revolution* when he defended the gold against Kurt Angle, Shawn Michaels, Kane, Carlito, and Chris Masters in an unforgiving Elimination Chamber. Despite having the odds stacked firmly against him, Cena never backed down and walked away from the grueling half-hour affair with the win.

Shortly after the match, however, a beaten and battered Cena was forced to defend the title yet again when Edge emerged to cash in his Money in the Bank briefcase. The exhausted champ was no match for the well-rested Rated-R Superstar. Less than two minutes into the contest, Cena and his title reign fell victim to Edge's lethal spear.

For Cena, the loss marked the end of his amazing nine-month reign atop WWE. Luckily for him, however, he only had to wait three weeks before gaining revenge on Edge and reclaiming the title at the *Royal Rumble*.

Around the same time, the movement that has become known as the "Cena divide" began to gain steam. Some of the Cena cheers transformed into boos. But the more anti-Cena fans booed, the more Cena supporters cheered. It eventually turned into a giant circle of deafening sentiment, both for and against, showering down on the champ.

In June 2006, however, there was no circle of sentiment. When Cena defended the WWE Championship against Rob Van Dam at *One Night Stand* in front of a venomous ECW crowd, there was only one reaction Cena elicited: "Cena sucks!" The ECW faithful were so anti-Cena that they even rejected the champ's merchandise when he threw it into the crowd as a souvenir.

Cena suffered a discouraging loss at *One Night Stand* but it failed to derail him. By year's end, he reclaimed the WWE Title for a third time. He went on to hold the gold longer than anybody in many years. In the past three decades, Only Hulk Hogan's 1984 WWE Championship reign exceeded Cena's 380 days.

Unfortunately for Cena, a torn right pectoral tendon put a premature end to his epic title reign. The injury required surgery and a six-month rehabilitation period. But after only three months, a determined Cena made a shocking return to win the 2008 *Royal Rumble*. The win not only added "*Royal Rumble* winner" to his accomplishments, but also led to a WWE Championship Match at *WrestleMania XXIV* against champion Randy Orton and Triple H.

Cena was unable to regain the gold at *WrestleMania XXIV* and later that same year, a herniated disc delayed his continued pursuit to return to the top. When Cena finally returned in November 2011, he made a huge splash by doing something he had never done before: He won the World Heavyweight Championship by defeating Chris Jericho at *Survivor Series*.

Cena topped Edge and Big Show at *WrestleMania XXV* to tack a second World Heavyweight Championship reign to his credit before turning his attention back to the WWE Title. In September 2009—three years after last losing the WWE Championship—Cena turned back Orton in a thrilling "I Quit" Match to finally regain the title.

The victory gave Cena his fourth reign with the WWE Championship. Reign No. 5 also came at Orton's expense, while a victory over Sheamus awarded Cena his sixth run at the top. *WrestleMania XXVI* was the historic backdrop for Cena's thrilling victory over Batista and his seventh WWE Title reign.

With plans of tying Triple H's then-record of eight WWE Championship reigns, Cena challenged The Miz for the gold at *WrestleMania XXVII*. But the event's host, The Rock, had other plans for Cena. Toward the end of the match, Rock flattened Cena with a Rock Bottom, allowing The Miz to pick up the win. The controversial conclusion to the match set the wheels in motion for the epic year-long rivalry with The Rock, which culminated in a match at *WrestleMania XXVIII*.

Before squaring off with The Rock, however, Cena finally wrested the title away from The Miz in May 2011. Later that year, he topped Rey Mysterio to claim his record-breaking ninth WWE Title. Cena padded his record to ten reigns at the expense of Alberto Del Rio.

Despite all his championship success, Cena wanted nothing more than to defeat The Rock in a "Once in a Lifetime" encounter at *WrestleMania XXVIII*. In the months leading up to the epic matchup, each Superstar tossed psyche-crushing barbs at the other but neither man backed down. As *WrestleMania* approached, it became clear that neither man would be broken by mere words. Their score was to be settled in the ring.

Unfortunately for Cena, The Rock got the best of him at *WrestleMania*. Like a man, however, Cena dusted himself off and accepted defeat the next night on *Raw*. Members of Cenation applauded their leader's humility and recognize that regardless of the outcome of any one match, John Cena is, and always will be, one of the greatest Superstars of all time.

JOHN MORRISON & THE MIZ

COMBINED WT: 439 lbs.

TITLE HISTORY

WORLD TAG TEAM CHAMPIONS	Defeated CM Punk & Kofi Kingston on December 13, 2008
WWE TAG TEAM CHAMPIONS	Defeated MVP & Matt Hardy on November 16, 2007

John Morrison & The Miz might just be the most self-centered tag team in sports-entertainment history. Respectively known as "The Shaman of Sexy" and "The Chick Magnet", Morrison & Miz's larger-than-life egos drew instant ire from audiences. Unfortunately for the fans who loved to hate them, the arrogant tandem was as good as they were narcissistic.

In November 2007, the egotistical Superstars took full advantage of the *SmackDown/ECW* working agreement, which allowed talent to cross from brand to brand, when they jumped to the Friday night show to upend Matt Hardy & Montel Vontavious Porter for the WWE Tag Team Championship. After the win, Morrison & Miz successfully defended the titles against both rosters of Superstars, including Jesse & Festus, CM Punk & Kane and the father-son duo of Finlay & Hornswoggle at *Night of Champions* in June 2008.

While they saw incredible success in the ring, they also became media sensations outside of it for their award-winning WWE.com webcast, *The Dirt Sheet*. This weekly program saw both Superstars mock their most recent challengers as well as pop-culture figures. This team fell apart when The Miz was drafted to *Raw* as part of the 2009 Supplemental Draft. In a show of his awesome-ness and loyalty to himself mentality, The Miz attacked Morrison once the move was official.

JOHN TOLOS

HT: 6'2" WT: 240 lbs. FROM: Hamilton, Ontario, Canada
SIGNATURE MOVE: Knuckle Corkscrew

TITLE HISTORY

UNITED STATES TAG TEAM CHAMPION	Partnered with Chris Tolos to defeat Killer Kowalski & Gorilla Monsoon on December 28, 1963

"Golden Greek" John Tolos was one of the biggest stars in all of professional wrestling. At one time he held five territory Championships simultaneously and appeared on television wearing all the belts. He and his brother Chris, known as the Canadian Wrecking Crew dissected opponents and won tag team championships wherever they traveled. On December 28, 1963 they defeated future WWE Hall of Famers Killer Kowalski & Gorilla Monsoon for the United States Tag Team Championship. John Tolos was also a major contender to the WWE Championship held at the time by Bruno Sammartino.

Whether he appeared in tag team matches with his brother Chris, or in singles competition, the "Golden Greek" helped change the face of wrestling. His villainous ways continue to influence rule-breakers all over the world. His famous proclamation can still be heard today: "The only way to spell wrestling is T-O-L-O-S!" The wrestilng world suffered a tremendous loss on May 21, 2009 when John Tolos passed away at the age of 78.

JOHNNY BAREND

HT: 6'1" WT: 230 lbs. FROM: Rochester, New York SIGNATURE MOVE: Atomic Drop

TITLE HISTORY

U.S.A. HEAVYWEIGHT CHAMPION	Defeated Bobo Brazil on June 8, 1963

Johnny Barend began his ring career after wrestling in the U.S. Navy during World War II. His earliest matches emanated from the New York territory, mainly Buffalo, with a few stops at the famed Madison Square Garden. He later moved to California, where he gained great success as a tag team specialist. He and Enrique Torres defeated Gene Kiniski & James Blears for the San Francisco NWA World Tag Team Championship in July 1955. The win marked his first of many tag title reigns with nine separate partners.

Despite his increasing success rate in California, Barend chose to take his game to Hawaii in the 1960s. The decision proved to be a wise one. While in Hawaii, Barend became a true legend. Each week, more than half the island would turn on their television sets just to see the charismatic and crazy Barend compete. Equally entertaining were his wild interview segments, which he conducted from a casket inside a smoke-filled room. Few people actually understood what the wild man was saying, but that helped add to his allure.

JOHNNY CURTIS

HT: 6'4" WT: 244 lbs. FROM: Westbrook, Maine

Longtime fan Johnny Curtis achieved his dream of becoming a WWE Superstar when he won season four of *NXT*. As a result of his victory, he and his Pro, R-Truth, were awarded an opportunity at the WWE Tag Team Championship. Unfortunately for Curtis, though, R-Truth refused to take part in the match.

The unpredictable Superstar has a knack for taking any situation and turning it into a play on words. For example, in anticipation for his *SmackDown* debut, he sarcastically told the WWE Universe he'd be able to "cut the mustard" before also declaring that he'd "take the cake."

Curtis' clever forecasting proved incorrect. When he finally did make his debut, the Maine native lost to Mark Henry in less than one minute. Following the loss, Curtis only appeared on *SmackDown* sparingly, which resulted in him developing "a chip on his shoulder." Curtis admits that his shenanigans may result in him "painting himself in a corner," but he doesn't seem to care.

JOHNNY DeFAZIO

FROM: Pittsburgh, Pennsylvania

A native of Pittsburgh, "Jumpin'" Johnny DeFazio started his wrestling career competing for his hometown's Studio Wrestling promotion in the 1960s. While he enjoyed great success in Pittsburgh, DeFazio will forever be remembered for being WWE's first-ever Junior Heavyweight Champion. He went on to win the now-defunct title four times, a record that will never be broken.

TITLE HISTORY

JUNIOR HEAVYWEIGHT CHAMPION	*Recognized as first Junior Heavyweight Champion in 1967*
INTERNATIONAL TAG TEAM CHAMPION	*Partnered with Bepo Mongol to defeat Luke Graham & Tarzan Tyler on December 18, 1971*

In addition to his four runs as Junior Heavyweight Champion, DeFazio went on to form several winning tag teams, including unions with Ace Freeman and Geto Mongol. But it was his teaming with Bepo Mongol that garnered the most success. DeFazio & Bepo defeated Luke Graham & Tarzan Tyler in New York City for the International Tag Team Championship in late November 1971.

Prior to retiring in the mid-1980s, DeFazio engaged in many brutal battles with rivals Sgt. Slaughter and Bobby Duncum.

JOHNNY PARISI

**HT: 5'10" WT: 247 lbs.
FROM: Long Island, New York**

According to second-generation Superstar Johnny Parisi, "it ain't easy being Parisi."

The frustrated Parisi made the above declaration after an embarrassing losing streak resulted in the WWE Universe booing him wildly. Rather than silence them with his work in the ring, however, he grabbed a microphone and demanded their respect. He didn't get it. But what he did get was a one-on-one battle with Kane. The "Big Red Monster" batted Parisi around like a cat playing with a defeated mouse. After a few minutes, he finally put the dejected Superstar out of his misery with a devastating chokeslam.

Kane's painful assault was just one example of what had become commonplace toward the end of Parisi's stint with WWE. Other Superstars bolstering their records at the expense of Parisi include Chavo Guerrero, Ron Simmons and The Hurricane. In June 2006, Parisi was released from his WWE contract after less than one year of service.

JOHNNY POLO

This preppy, pompous brat joined WWE in May 1993. He debuted as a manager and became one of the most despised figures in all of WWE. He began his managerial career leading Adam Bomb to the ring, and later managed of the Quebecers to three reigns as World Tag Team Champions. Polo also spent some time in the ring facing stars such as X-Pac (as 1-2-3 Kid), Marty Jannetty, Virgil and Doink. In 1994, he even faced-off against one-time client, Adam Bomb.

Polo's eloquent motor mouth led him behind the broadcast booth as he appeared on Coliseum Home Video releases, *Monday Night Raw*, Radio WWE and a co-host of *All-American Wrestling*. Johnny took his ball and went home in October 1994.

World Wrestling Entertainment Superstars and fans do their best to forget Johnny Polo and the sound of his antagonizing voice. However, one can't argue the success he enjoyed in his relatively brief time with the company.

JOHNNY POWERS

**HT: 6'4" WT: 265 lbs. FROM: Hamilton, Ontario, Canada
SIGNATURE MOVE: Powerlock**

On more than one occasion, Johnny Powers came within milliseconds from dethroning longtime WWE Champion Bruno Sammartino. Had things played out just a little differently, fans today would look back at Powers' career as one of the greatest ever. Instead, Powers now has little to show for his brief WWE stay.

Powers used the Powerlock (a version of the figure four leglock) to turn back opponents in many Northern wrestling territories. He defeated the legendary Freddie Blassie and Johnny Valentine to gain championship on two separate occasions.

JOHNNY RODZ

**HT: 5'8" WT: 239 lbs. FROM: New York, New York
SIGNATURE MOVE: Falling Headbutt**

Widely recognized as the hardest working man in sports-entertainment, "The Unpredictable" Johnny Rodz used his undying passion to compete to earn the respect of his peers. Unfortunately for Rodz, however, his hard work rarely resulted in victories, as the New York City native lost more matches than he won.

Despite his unenviable won-loss record, Rodz earned the ultimate honor of being inducted into the WWE Hall of Fame in 1996. Brooklyn Brawler, a fellow New Yorker who also lost more matches than he won, inducted Rodz during an emotional ceremony in the Big Apple.

After retiring from the ring in the mid-1980s, Rodz began training the Superstars of tomorrow. Using the gritty Gleason's Gym as a training facility, Rodz harnassed his unorthodox style to teach aspiring competitors respect for the game. Many of his pupils went on to enjoy high-profile WWE careers, including Tommy Dreamer, Tazz and Matt Striker.

JOHNNY VALENTINE

HT: 6'4"   WT: 255 lbs.
FROM: Seattle, Washington
SIGNATURE MOVE: Atomic Skull Crusher

TITLE HISTORY

UNITED STATES TAG TEAM CHAMPION	*Partnered with Antonio Pugliese to defeat Dr. Bill Miller & Dan Miller on February 21, 1966*

With tanned skin, sculpted frame and bleached-blonde hair, Johnny Valentine certainly had the look of a successful professional wrestler. Calling himself "Handsome," Valentine's arrogant attitude made him one of the most hated men in wrestling for close to three decades.

Valentine started competing in Argentina in 1947, but soon afterward, he was back in the United States where he began to build one of the game's greatest legacies. With more than fifty different National Wrestling Alliance titles to his credit, few can match his success in the ring.

In July 1975, Valentine defeated Harley Race for the United States Championship. Well into his third decade of competition, the victory proved Valentine as a timeless talent with plenty of fight left in him. Unfortunately, a mere three months after capturing the title, Johnny Valentine's life would tragically change forever when he was involved in a plane crash. The impact from the accident, which also involved Ric Flair, David Crockett, Tim Woods, and Bob Bruggers, left Valentine partially paralyzed.

No longer able to compete in the ring, Valentine watched from the sidelines with great pride as his son, Greg "The Hammer" Valentine, carried the family name throughout his Hall of Fame career.

JOHNNY VALIANT HT: 6'4"   WT: 245 lbs.
FROM: New York City

TITLE HISTORY

WORLD TAG TEAM CHAMPION (2 TIME)	*Partnered with Jimmy Valiant to defeat Tony Garea & Dean Ho on May 8, 1974* *Partnered with Jerry Valiant to defeat Tony Garea & Larry Zbyszko on March 6, 1979*

One of the most colorful Superstars of his time, "Luscious" Johnny Valiant drew the attention of fans with his outrageous outfits and boisterous personality. However, what really caught the eye of his competition was his rugged in-ring skills, particularly in the tag team ranks.

After heeding the advice given to him by the legendary Bruno Sammartino, Valiant embarked on his Hall of Fame career in 1967. He spent a few years bouncing around as a singles competitor before finally deciding to try his hand in the tag team division with his brother "Handsome" Jimmy Valiant. Together, the Valiants found their niche and over the next decade, the duo cemented their legacy as one of the greatest brother tandems to ever compete.

In May 1974, the Valiant Brothers defeated Tony Garea & Don Ho in Hamburg, PA, to capture the coveted World Tag Team Championship. For more than a year, the flamboyant combination successfully defended the titles before finally being upended by Victor Rivera & Dominic DeNucci. At the time, their reign was recognized as the longest in WWE tag team history.

Following his in-ring career, Valiant turned his efforts toward managing. After a brief stint guiding the career of a young Hulk Hogan in the AWA, "Lucious" Johnny jumped back to WWE, where he led Brutus Beefcake & Greg Valentine to the World Tag Team Championship.

JONATHAN COACHMAN

In 2000, Jonathan Coachman became a regular member of the WWE broadcast team as he conducted backstage interviews and wrap-up segments. Coachman was an energetic young reporter who often entertained WWE fans with his antics during interviews. His segments with The Rock became immensely popular as the "Brahma Bull" often forced him to sing, dance and smile for the camera after multiple insults.

Coachman worked his way into announcing duties, first on *Sunday Night Heat* with Al Snow, and in 2005, Coachman became a full-time *Raw* announcer alongside Jim Ross and Jerry Lawler. He also co-hosted the first-ever WWE Diva Search and "CoachCast" on WWE.com. Coachman also found time to compete in the ring, including appearances at *Backlash 2004* and *Taboo Tuesday* in 2005.

After first acting as an executive assistant to the McMahon family, Coachman traded general manager duties with William Regal from August to October of 2007. Coach's final role with WWE was as a part of the *SmackDown* announce team with Michael Cole. Jonathan Coachman departed WWE on amicable terms in spring, 2008 to allow him to focus on his other sports broadcast interests.

JOS LeDUC HT: 6'1"   WT: 280 lbs.   FROM: Godbout, Quebec
SIGNATURE MOVE: One-Armed Backbreaker

During an interview, Jos LeDuc once said, "When I'm breathing, I make things happen..." This was a concise summation of what turned into a storied four decade career. Trained in Judo, Jos LeDuc received his degree in ring arts from Calgary's Stu Hart. In the early 1970s the lumberjack appeared on World Wide Wrestling Federation cards in singles action, and in tags with brother, Paul, as well as other partners. During this time LeDuc also sparked a bloody rivalry against Bruno Sammartino over the WWE Championship.

In 1988 he re-emerged in WWE under the guidance of Frenchy Martin. He also appeared in Hulk Hogan's 1989 film *No Holds Barred* and continued to destroy opponents until his retirement in 1995. While visiting family in 1999, this wrestling legend passed away due to complications from diabetes. Jos LeDuc created his own path to stardom and will always be regarded as one of the most feared, and wild Superstars to set foot in the ring.

JOSE ESTRADA

FROM: Brooklyn, New York

TITLE HISTORY

JUNIOR HEAVYWEIGHT CHAMPION	Defeated Tony Garea on January 20, 1978

While competing in the United States, the proud Puerto Rican Jose Estrada called Brooklyn, NY, home. His WWE career was highlighted by a three-day Junior Heavyweight Championship reign (as Carlos Jose Estrada) in January 1978. Three days later, he lost the title to Japanese star Tatsumi Fujinami. Estrada was never able to reclaim the prize.

Much of Estrada's WWE in-ring action took place inside the famed Madison Square Garden. It was there that he engaged in many encounters against the likes of Greg Gagne and Outback Jack. Estrada also owns the dubious distinction of falling to the legendary Kerry Von Erich in the fabled Texan's MSG debut.

Back in his native Puerto Rico, Estrada honed his craft competing for the World Wrestling Council. Estrada is also the father of former WWE Superstar Jose Estrada, Jr.

JOSE LOTHARIO

HT: 5'7"   WT: 245 lbs.
FROM: San Antonio, Texas

Jose Lothario debuted in the ring during the mid 1960s. Lothario became a hero to millions throughout the southern United States in the territories of the NWA and in Mexico. He also spent time in successful tag teams with Dory Funk, Jr., Mil Mascaras, Chief Wahoo McDaniel, Eddie Graham, Ivan Putski and Rocky Johnson.

Many WWE fans saw him for the first time in August 1987 at the retirement show for legendary promoter Paul Boesch. Jose was in the corner of Tito Santana & Mil Mascaras. In 1996, he appeared in WWE as the manager to his protégé, Shawn Michaels, in his quest for the WWE Championship. Lothario also teamed with his star pupil against members of Camp Cornette. He even stepped into the ring with James E. Cornette at *In Your House: Mind Games*.

By early 1997, Jose returned to San Antonio and shared his love of the action in the ring with students. Lothario will be remembered as a hero in the ring and an excellent teacher.

JOSE LUIS RIVERA

HT: 6'3"   WT: 231 lbs.
FROM: Puerto Rico
SIGNATURE MOVE: Boston Crab

Jose Luis Rivera comes from a long line of Latin grapplers and graced the WWE from 1984 until 1990. With a background including boxing, Jose rarely hesitated to resort to fisticuffs when necessary. During a 1986 episode of *Piper's Pit,* Roddy Piper expressed doubt in Rivera's abilities in the ring and mocked his Spanish accent. Although Jose was unable to best the loudmouth and his bodyguard in the end, both found out that Jose Luis Rivera had an unwaivering will and an excess of courage.

During his six-year career in WWE, Jose Luis Rivera's actions in the ring left everyone from Puerto Rico with a feeling of pride due to his toughness and fighting spirit.

JOSEPH RAYMOND "TOOTS" MONDT

A young Joe Mondt subscribed to a wrestling correspondence course offered by the renowned "Farmer" Burns and honed his "hooking" skills, which is the ability to apply crippling submission holds. Mondt became part of a traveling show and was discovered by the man whose correspondence course led him to the sport and gave him his nickname, "Toots."

Professional wrestling changed forever in 1919 when Mondt met promoter Billy Sandow and legendary grappler Ed "Strangler" Lewis. This triumvirate became known as the Gold Dust Trio. "Toots" had a vision to change the way professional wrestling, as a product, was presented to the public. To make it more entertaining, he introduced "Slam Bang Western Wrestling" which was a style that mixed kicking, strikes, and various forms of contact to generate more excitement. He developed the concept of time limit matches and a package wrestling show that was a program with rivalries between participants with "good guys" and "bad guys."

By the end of the 1940s, "Toots" had positioned himself as the undisputed czar of wrestling in the Northeast section of the United States. In the 1950s, Mondt's stranglehold on the Northeast was contested by a promoter with strong ties to the television industry, Vincent J. McMahon. At the same time McMahon courted Mondt's top attraction, Antonino "Argentina" Rocca. He was running shows at Madison Square Garden.

The two former rivals soon became allies and they broke away from the NWA to form the WWE in 1963. By 1969, a number of health issues forced Toots to retire. On June 11, 1976, Mondt passed away at age 82.

JOSH MATHEWS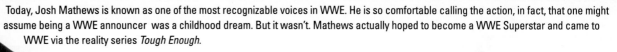

Today, Josh Mathews is known as one of the most recognizable voices in WWE. He is so comfortable calling the action, in fact, that one might assume being a WWE announcer was a childhood dream. But it wasn't. Mathews actually hoped to become a WWE Superstar and came to WWE via the reality series *Tough Enough*.

After nearly winning *Tough Enough*, Mathews traded in his ring gear for a microphone. His initial WWE responsibilities included conducting backstage interviews for *SmackDown* and hosting WWE.com's *Byte This!* Web cast.

Mathews has since grown into more high-profile positions, including commentating on *Raw* and *SmackDown*. He even called the action at *WrestleMania XXVII* before Stone Cold Steve Austin ended his night with a jaw-rattling Stunner.

Though his in-ring aspirations are firmly behind him, Mathews did reach deep into his bag of *Tough Enough* tricks in 2004 to compete in a pair of matches. First, he teamed with Booker T to defeat JBL & Orlando Jordan. And later, he defeated Jordan solo. With an impressive 2-0 record, Mathews then hung up his boots for good.

JOY GIOVANNI

HT: 5'4"
FROM: Boston, Massachusetts

Joy Giovanni's curvaceous frame first caught the attention of the WWE Universe in 2004 when the Boston native competed in the $250,000 *Raw* Diva Search. She failed to win the competition, but WWE officials recognized the power of her healing hands and hired her to be a massage therapist later that year.

Shortly after being hired, Joy and her close friend, Big Show, engaged in a rivalry with fellow Diva Search contestant Amy Weber and JBL. Things turned disturbing when Weber and JBL kidnapped Joy, tied her up, gagged her and left her in the trunk of a limo. The emotional kidnapping failed to derail Joy. The following month, at *No Way Out*, she won the 2005 Rookie Diva of the Year contest, turning back Michelle McCool, Rochelle and Lauren. Unfortunately for Joy, the *No Way Out* victory failed to catapult her career. She left WWE a few months later.

JTG

HT: 6'2"   WT: 232 lbs.   FROM: Brooklyn, New York
SIGNATURE MOVE: The Shout Out

Hold on to your valuables, it's JTG. The street-tough Brooklyn brawler isn't above stealing anybody's belongings and selling it for "money, money — yeah, yeah."

JTG debuted as a member of Cryme Tyme in October 2006. In their first-ever match, the popular tag team defeated the then-World Tag Team Champions, the Spirit Squad, in a non-title match on *Raw*. Cryme Tyme's success spilled over to pay-per-views, where they picked up victories at both *Cyber Sunday 2006* and *New Year's Revolution 2007*. All the while, they kept an eye out for any items they could swipe from their opponents.

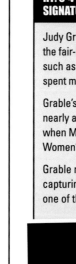

In 2009, Cryme Tyme was drafted to *SmackDown,* where they enjoyed early success before ultimately breaking up after a disappointing loss caused Shad Gaspard to turn on JTG. The resilient JTG eventually gained retribution, however, when he defeated Shad in a Strap Match at *Extreme Rules 2010*.

JTG also served as Jacob Novak's Pro on *NXT Redemption*. Unfortunately, Novak was unable to absorb his Pro's advice and was the first Rookie eliminated.

Judgment Day (see page 191)

JUDY GRABLE

HT: 5'4"   FROM: Bremerton, Washington
SIGNATURE MOVE: Dropkick

Judy Grable was one of sports-entertainment's first sex symbols. Debuting in 1938, the fair-haired femme excited male audiences decades before blonde bombshells such as Torrie Wilson and Trish Stratus. Unlike Torrie and Trish, however, Grable spent most of her career as a noted rule breaker, which incited most fans.

Grable's greatest rivalry came against the Fabulous Moolah. The two women spent nearly a decade battling each other. Their most memorable encounter came in 1956 when Moolah defeated Grable in the finals of a tournament to crown the first-ever Women's Champion. Moolah went on to hold the title for nearly thirty years.

Grable retired from the ring shortly after her 1956 loss to Moolah. Despite never capturing the WWE Women's Championship, she will forever be remembered as one of the true trailblazers of female wrestling.

Judgment DAY

October 18, 1998

Rosemont, IL - Rosemont Horizon

Event: Kane vs. Undertaker, went to No Contest, Stone Cold Steve Austin as guest referee

May 21, 2000

Louisville, KY - Freedom Hall

Event: Triple H defeated WWE Champion The Rock in a 60-Minute WWE Iron Man Match

May 20, 2001

Sacramento, CA - Arco Arena

Event: WWE Champion Stone Cold Steve Austin defeated Undertaker, No Holds Barred Match

May 19, 2002

Nashville, TN - Gaylord Entertainment Center

Event: Undertaker defeated WWE Champion Hulk Hogan

May 18, 2003

Charlotte, NC - Charlotte Coliseum

Event: WWE Champion Brock Lesnar defeated Big Show in a Stretcher Match

May 16, 2004

Los Angeles, CA - STAPLES Center

Main Event: JBL defeated WWE Champion Eddie Guerrero

May 22, 2005

Minneapolis, MN - Target Center

Main Event: WWE Champion John Cena defeated JBL in an "I Quit" Match

May 21, 2006

Phoenix, AZ - US Airways Center

Main Event: World Heavyweight Champion Rey Mysterio defeated JBL

May 20, 2007

St. Louis, MO - Scottrade Center

Main Event: WWE Champion John Cena defeated The Great Khali

May 18, 2008

Omaha, NE - Qwest Center

Main Event: WWE Champion Triple H defeated Randy Orton, Steel Cage Match

May 17, 2009

Rosemont, IL - Allstate Arena

Main Event: World Heavyweight Champion Edge defeated Jeff Hardy

---

JUDY MARTIN

HT: 5'6"
SIGNATURE MOVE: Powerbomb

TITLE HISTORY

WOMEN'S TAG TEAM CHAMPION (2 TIMES)	*Partnered with Leilani Kai to defeat Velvet McIntyre & Desiree Peterson on August 15, 1984* *Partnered with Leilani Kai to defeat the Jumping Bomb Angels on June 8, 1988*

One of the toughest women to enter WWE, Judy Martin first appeared in WWE in 1979 in singles and tag team action. She became regular partners with Leilani Kai and fought the likes of Donna Christianello, Joyce Grable, Desiree Peterson and Fabulous Moolah.

During the mid-1980s, Martin became a threat to the title reign of then Women's Champion Wendi Richter. In 1987, she reunited with Kai to form the Glamour Girls and with Jimmy Hart in their corner, the team won the Women's Tag Team Championship. Martin remained a contender for the singles title until she left the company in 1989.

THE JUMPING BOMB ANGELS

MEMBERS: Noriyo Tateno, Itsuki Yamazaki   FROM: Tokyo, Japan

TITLE HISTORY

WOMEN'S TAG TEAM CHAMPIONS	*Defeated The Glamour Girls on January 24, 1988*

Just as summer 1987 got underway, Noriyo Tateno & Itsuki Yamazaki came to WWE and heated up the Women's Division. Once the bell rang, the Jumping Bomb Angels used fast tags, quick countermoves, and impressive acrobatics that all translated into high-power offense.

As members of Fabulous Moolah's team at the first *Survivor Series,* they emerged the sole survivors. At the 1988 *Royal Rumble,* they captured tag team gold in a thrilling two-out-of-three falls bout. As they proudly defended the titles, Tateno & Yamazaki became heroes to female fans across the United States and the world. After their title reign came to an end, the duo went their separate ways.

While they were together, they lifted fans to their feet and dropped opponents to the canvas in all four corners of the Earth. In the process, they changed the face of women's wrestling forever.

1960-69
1970-79
1980-89
1990-99
2000-09
2010-

JUNIOR HEAVYWEIGHT CHAMPIONSHIP

The now-defunct Junior Heavyweight Championship was a precursor to the more recent Cruiserweight Championship. Designed to recognize the achievements of Superstars 220 lbs. and under, names like Black Tiger, Tiger Mask, and Dynamite Kid all enjoyed reigns as Junior Heavyweight Champion. The lighter Superstars thrilled audiences with their quick-paced action until 1985 when the title was vacated.

Early records of the championship offer conflicting reports but between 1967 and 1972, the title was traded multiple times between Johnny De Fazio and Jackie Nichols. The championship was inactive from De Fazio's retirement in 1972 until 1978.

1978

January 20
Uniondale, NY

Carlos Estrada defeated Tony Garea

▼

January 23
New York, NY

Tatsumi Fujinami defeated Jose Estrada

▼

1979

October 2
Osaka, Japan

Ryuma Go defeated Tatsumi Fujinami

October 4
Tokyo, Japan

Tatsumi Fujinami defeated Ryuma Go

Tatsumi Fujinami vacated the Junior Heavyweight Championship in December 1981 after entering the heavyweight division.

1982

January 1
Tokyo, Japan

Tiger Mask defeated Dynamite Kid in a match to crown a new Junior Heavyweight Champion.

Injury forced Tiger Mask to vacate the title in April 1982.

May 6
Fukuoka, Japan

Black Tiger defeated Gran Hamada in a match to crown a new Junior Heavyweight Champion.

▼

May 26
Osaka, Japan

Tiger Mask defeated Black Tiger

Injury forced Tiger Mask to vacate the Junior Heavyweight Championship on April 3, 1983.

1983

June 13
Mexico City, Mexico

Tiger Mask defeated Fishman in a match to crown a new Junior Heavyweight Champion.

Tiger Mask vacated the title after retiring in August 1983.

1984

February 7
Tokyo, Japan

Dynamite Kid defeated The Cobra in a match to crown a new Junior Heavyweight Champion.

Dynamite Kid vacated the title in November 1984.

December 28
New York, NY

The Cobra defeated Black Tiger in a match to crown a new Junior Heavyweight Champion.

▼

1985

May 20
Hiroshima, Japan

Hiro Saito defeated The Cobra

▼

July 20
Osaka, Japan

The Cobra defeated Hiro Saito

JUNKYARD DOG

HT: 6'3" **WT:** 280 lbs.
FROM: Charlotte, North Carolina
SIGNATURE MOVE: Powerslam

In 1984, Junkyard Dog became an instant star in WWE. As WWE entered its phase of national expansion, JYD was featured in toy and merchandise lines and even sang his own hit entrance theme, *Grab Them Cakes.* Whether it was his rolling headbutt or his patented powerslam, opponents knew Junkyard Dog's bite was just as bad as his bark.

Junkyard Dog appealed to fans of all ages and walks of life, and he brought children from the audience in the ring to dance with him. JYD's battles with the Funks, Adrian Adonis, "Rowdy" Roddy Piper, "Cowboy" Bob Orton and the Magnificent Muraco were all of epic proportions. None of those battles were as personal as his rivalry against "King" Harley Race as they fought tooth-and-nail at *WrestleMania III.* Junkyard Dog continued to bring fans to a fever pitch and met "Ravishing" Rick Rude at the very first *SummerSlam* at Madison Square Garden. Regrettably, the Dog and WWE parted ways in November 1988.

Before the end of the year, he returned to his home area and WCW. Soon after, he left the company and competed on the independent scene through the mid 1990s. In May 1998, he was honored as a hardcore legend at ECW's *Wrestlepalooza* and once again ruled the ring as fans chanted his name. Tragically, just weeks later, he was involved in a fatal one-car accident while driving home from his daughter's high school graduation.

On March 14, 2004, Junkyard Dog's extraordinary career came full circle as he was posthumously inducted into the WWE Hall of Fame the night before *WrestleMania XX.* With his daughter LaToya on hand to accept the honor, she told touching stories of how her father loved his fans and WWE. No matter where in the world that Junkyard Dog appeared, one thing was for sure: fans of all ages, color, and creeds were going to be on their feet as one raucous force as their hero rocked the ring.

JUSTIN "HAWK" BRADSHAW

HT: 6'6" **WT:** 309 lbs.
FROM: Roscoe, Texas
SIGNATURE MOVE: Lariat Clothesline

During his WWE debut in 1996, Justin "Hawk" Bradshaw immediately reminded audiences of past rugged Texans Dick Murdoch and Stan Hansen. Like the Lone Star State Superstars before him, his nasty demeanor and immense size made him an instant threat to the entire WWE locker room.

JUST JOE

HT: 6'4" **WT:** 252 lbs.
FROM: Toronto, Ontario, Canada

During the latter half of 2000, a mysterious man began to show up backstage at WWE events. When the Superstars asked him who he was, he simply told them that he was Joe, Just Joe. The man with no last name was an unpopular presence backstage. He was always stirring the pot, telling people that others were talking trash about them. On the rare occasion Joe stepped into the ring, he proved to be just as unsuccessful as he was unpopular. He routinely lost to the likes of Essa Rios, Steve Blackman, and even Brooklyn Brawler. By 2001, Joe had quietly disappeared from WWE.

After defeating a foe, Bradshaw oftentimes used his personalized JB branding iron to mark and embarrass his victim. In fact, Hakushi was so embarrassed after being branded in March 1996 that he never showed his face in WWE again. One week later, Fatu fell victim to the branding iron just moments before being flattened by Bradshaw's signature lariat clothesline in a match that lasted only eight seconds.

With his manager Zebekiah Blu by his side, Bradshaw dominated WWE rings through the beginning of 1997. He later went on to form the New Blackjacks with Barry Windham.

JUSTIN CREDIBLE

HT: 6'0" **WT:** 225 lbs.
FROM: Ozone Park, New York
SIGNATURE MOVE: That's Incredible

TITLE HISTORY

HARDCORE CHAMPION	8 Times

This ego-maniac came to the original ECW with a chip on his shoulder and a Singapore cane in his hand. His finishing manuever, "That's Incredible" was a spinning Tombstone Piledriver that planted his opponent's head on the mat and brought him much success in the world of sports-entertainment. He formed "The Impact Players" with Lance Storm and proceeded to hold multiple titles in ECW before leaving the company in 2001.

After joining WWE, Justin Credible became a member of X-Factor, then joined the ECW/WCW Alliance. Before he left the company in 2003, he was able to capture the Hardcore Championship on several, albeit brief, occassions. Justin returned to WWE in 2006 as part of the new ECW and tangled with CM Punk before he parted ways with the company that September.

JUSTIN GABRIEL

HT: 6'1" **WT:** 213 lbs.
FROM: Cape Town, South Africa
SIGNATURE MOVE: 450 Splash

TITLE HISTORY

WWE TAG TEAM CHAMPION (3 TIMES)	*Partnered with Heath Slater to defeat John Cena & David Otunga on October 25, 2010 Partnered with Heath Slater to defeat Santino Marella & Vladimir Kozlov on February 20, 2011 Partnered with Heath Slater to defeat John Cena & The Miz on February 21, 2011*

Don't let Justin Gabriel's boyish good looks fool you. He's actually one of the most dangerous competitors in WWE, complete with a repertoire that features lightning-fast speed and amazing aerial skills.

Following his run on *NXT*, Gabriel joined the show's other Rookies to form The Nexus. While in the renegade faction, the South African Superstar teamed with Heath Slater to defeat fellow Nexus members David Otunga & John Cena for the WWE Tag Team Championship. In reality, though, the titles were essentially handed to Gabriel & Slater after Nexus leader Wade Barrett ordered Otunga to lose.

When Barrett was replaced as head of The Nexus in January 2011, Gabriel & Slater followed him to *SmackDown* where they formed The Corre. While members of the new faction, Gabriel & Slater went on to claim the WWE tag titles two more times. But after a series of losses to the Usos in the summer of 2011, a frustrated Slater turned on his partner. The betrayal had little impact on Gabriel, who quickly gained revenge by beating his former partner on *SmackDown*.

FAN SIGNS

Outside of The Rock facing Mankind at *Halftime Heat*, WWE events are never complete without fans. These days, part of the WWE fan experience is boldly sharing your opinion on a store-bought piece of poster board covered in permanent marker. Fan signs started to make appearances as WWE blanketed the world with its television programming in the 1980s. When *Monday Night Raw* started to air, the phenomenon exploded to what is seen today at each WWE event. From proclamations of support for a favored Superstar to shocking statements that straddle the line of good taste, WWE fans are never afraid to show the world what's on their minds.

2010-

2000-09

1990-99

1980-89

1970-79

1960-69

JUSTIN ROBERTS

As a child growing up in the Windy City, Justin Roberts loved watching WWE and dreamed of one day being under those bright lights himself. When he was 16, Justin started working for local wrestling events and became comfortable in front of various size crowds. After he graduated from the University of Arizona, Roberts auditioned for WWE and began his sports-entertainment career in 2002 filling in during *Raw* and *SmackDown* events. Two years later, he found himself a full-time member of WWE.

Roberts developed an impressive body of work on *SmackDown* that eventually brought him to Monday nights. His resilience was tested in June 2010 when he fell victim to a vicious Nexus attack. Today, he's the man with the microphone on *Raw*, and the sole figure in the ring that calls the combatants to battle at the "Showcase of the Immortals", *WrestleMania*.

KAIENTAI
MEMBERS: Taka Michinoku, Funaki, Mens Teioh, Dick Togo, Yamaguchi-San
FROM: Japan

Funaki, Mens Teioh, and Dick Togo were first introduced to American audiences when they attacked Taka Michinoku in March 1998. Managed by Yamaguchi-San, the group known as Kaientai wowed fans with their rapid-fire offensive onslaught.

Shortly after Kaientai's debut, it was learned that Yamaguchi-San's wife was having an affair with Val Venis. This lead to one of the most infamous moments in WWE history, as Yamaguchi-San threatened revenge, telling Venis, "I choppy choppy your pee pee."

The following week, Venis tagged with Michinoku to battle Kaientai. During the match, however, Michinoku turned on his partner and helped Yamaguchi attempt to make good on his promise. Luckily for Venis, Yamaguchi-San's aim wasn't very good.

With Michinoku in the fold, Kaientai became even more dangerous. Though short in stature, the faction boasted huge levels of confidence. Unfortunately, the promising Japanese faction didn't last long as Teioh, Togo, and Yamaguchi-San left WWE in late 1998. Their departure left Michinoku and Funaki as the sole members of the faction. The pair wasted little time showing WWE audiences the true meaning of EVIL. INDEED!

KAITLYN
HT: 5'6"
FROM: Houston, Texas

The WWE Universe recognizes the curvaceous Kaitlyn as one of *SmackDown*'s top Divas. But if it wasn't for an off-camera altercation, her road to WWE would have detoured and fans might never have gotten to appreciate her athleticism.

Heading into season three of *NXT*, Vickie Guerrero was slated to serve as Pro for Aloisia. But in the days leading up to the premiere, the two ladies had a behind-the-scenes argument that led to Guerrero firing the Rookie. The dismissal left an opening that Kaitlyn happily filled.

Despite being a last-minute replacement, Kaitlyn performed like she had been training for *NXT* all along. And after more than three months of grueling competition, the beautiful Texas native was announced the winner of *NXT* and WWE's next breakout Diva.

Theodore Long signed Kaitlyn to a *SmackDown* contract following her *NXT* victory. As a member of the Friday night brand, she partnered with A.J. to form the popular tag team The Chickbusters.

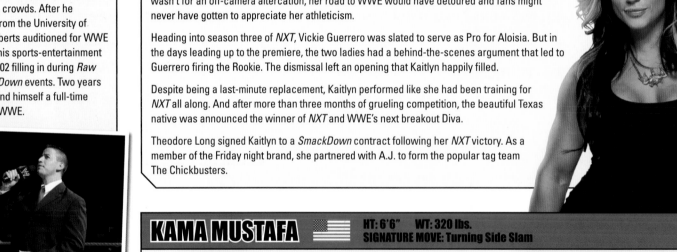

KAMA MUSTAFA
HT: 6'6" **WT:** 320 lbs.
SIGNATURE MOVE: Turning Side Slam

Originally known as the "Supreme Fighting Machine" of Ted DiBiase's Million Dollar Corporation, this enforcer met Undertaker in a Casket Match at *SummerSlam 1995*. In early 1997, Kama became a member of the Nation of Domination where his vicious fighting style aided the Nation in their battles against the Legion of Doom, Ken Shamrock, Ahmed Johnson, the Disciples of the Apocalypse, Los Boriquas, and D-Generation X.

During 1998, the Nation of Domination's leadership changed hands and Kama decided to part ways with the militant faction.

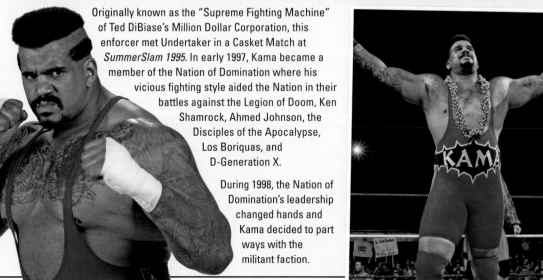

KAMALA 🇺🇬

HT: 6'7" **WT:** 380 lbs. **FROM:** Uganda
SIGNATURE MOVE: Big Splash

Hailing from the Ugandan jungle, Kamala is recognized as one of history's most frightening Superstars. Believe it or not, his overwhelming size might not have been his scariest trait. Some Superstars are on record by saying they feared the inability to read his simple mind most.

Lead to the ring by his handler Kim Chee, the Ugandan Giant never seemingly possessed the intellect required to communicate with fellow Superstars or referees. Instead, he let his savage beatings do the talking for him. His impressive list of victims eventually put him in line for a series of WWE Championship opportunities against Hulk Hogan in 1986 and 1987. The big man failed to capitalize on the opportunities and left WWE soon after.

In 1992, Kamala re-emerged from the dark jungles of Uganda. This time, he was recruited by Harvey Wippleman to take down Undertaker. Like so many before him, the Ugandan Giant was unable to defeat the "Deadman." After losing to Undertaker in WWE's first-ever Casket Match (known then as a Coffin Match), Kamala became the target of inhumane abuse from his handlers. Luckily for Kamala, Reverend Slick was there to save the giant. For the remainder of Kamala's career, Slick chose to treat him as a man, not a savage. Unfortunately, the new approach didn't result in many wins.

Kane (see page 198)

KANYON 🇺🇸

HT: 6'4" **WT:** 245 lbs. **FROM:** Queens, New York
SIGNATURE MOVE: The Flatliner

TITLE HISTORY

UNITED STATES CHAMPION	*Given title by Booker T on July 26, 2001*
WORLD TAG TEAM CHAMPION	*Partnered with Diamond Dallas Page to defeat the APA on August 9, 2001*

"Who's better than Kanyon?"

Don't answer that. It's the rhetorical question that the confident Kanyon often asked the WWE Universe before his matches. Of course, his arrogance rubbed fans the wrong way. But in Kanyon's mind, he had every right to brag.

After a successful WCW career, Kanyon entered WWE in 2001 as a member of The Alliance, a group of former WCW and ECW stars whose mission was to destroy WWE from within. Shortly after his debut, Kanyon was given the United States Championship when then-champ and fellow Alliance member Booker T simply handed it to him. Despite not winning the title in an athletic contest, Kanyon quickly anointed himself the Alliance MVP.

Kanyon added more gold to his trophy case when he teamed with Diamond Dallas Page to defeat the APA for the World Tag Team Championship in August 2001.

At *Survivor Series 2001*, The Alliance lost to Team WWE, resulting in all members of the losing faction being fired. Kanyon, an innovative offensive competitor in the ring, eventually made a brief return in 2003, competing mainly on *Velocity*.

KARL GOTCH 🇩🇪

HT: 6'1" **WT:** 245 lbs. **FROM:** Germany
SIGNATURE MOVE: German Suplex

TITLE HISTORY

WORLD TAG TEAM CHAMPION	*Partnered with Rene Goulet to defeat Luke Graham & Tarzan Tyler on December 6, 1971*

A bona fide tough man, Karl Gotch began his amateur wrestling career in Hamburg, Germany, at the ripe age of 9. He perfected his craft over the next fifteen years, resulting in a spot in the 1948 Olympics in London. Following the Olympic games, Gotch turned to the pro circuit, spending much of his early days competing in Europe.

In 1959, Gotch moved his skills to the United States. According to legend, many U.S. promoters feared booking him due to his overly-aggressive style in the ring. Even the great "Nature Boy" Buddy Rogers supposedly feared stepping in the ring with Gotch.

When he did convince promoters to use him, Gotch proved to be near unstoppable in the ring. In 1961, he captured his first major singles title when he defeated Don Leo Jonathan for the Ohio version of the AWA Championship. He held the title for two years before finally losing to the legendary Lou Thesz.

Gotch's WWE career was fleeting, but did result in a championship reign. In December 1971, the mighty German teamed with Rene Goulet to become the second World Tag Team Champions in WWE history.

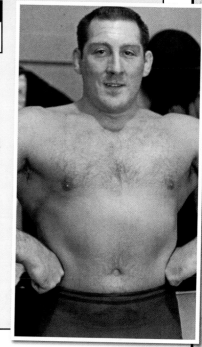

KARL VON HESS 🇩🇪

HT: 5'10" **WT:** 220 lbs. **FROM:** Germany
SIGNATURE MOVE: The Claw

During the mid-1950s, this vile Nazi sympathizer caused near riots whenever he appeared in Vincent J. McMahon's Capitol Wrestling Company. In 1963, Hess continued the tradition in World Wrestling Entertainment. This incredible physical specimen battled the best Superstars of the era, including "Golden Boy" Arnold Skaaland, and Antonino "Argentina" Rocca.

Von Hess quickly became known as the worst type of villain and reminded audiences of a darker period in the world's history. By the late 1960s he left the world of sports entertainment to the joy of all who saw him compete, or fell victim to his brutal attacks.

KANE

HT: 7'0"   **WT: 323 lbs.**   **FROM: Parts Unknown**   **SIGNATURE MOVE: Chokeslam, Tombstone Piledriver**

" *THE BIG RED MONSTER* "

TITLE HISTORY	
ECW CHAMPION	*Defeated Chavo Guerrero on March 30, 2008*
HARDCORE CHAMPION	*1 Time*
INTERCONTINENTAL CHAMPION (2 TIMES)	*Defeated Triple H on May 20, 2001* *Defeated Chris Jericho on September 30, 2002*
WORLD TAG TEAM CHAMPION (9 TIMES)	*Partnered with Mankind to defeat the New Age Outlaws on July 13, 1998* *Partnered with Mankind to defeat Stone Cold Steve Austin & Undertaker on August 10, 1998* *Partnered with X-Pac to defeat Owen Hart & Jeff Jarrett on March 30, 1999* *Partnered with X-Pac to defeat The Acolytes on August 9, 1999* *Partnered with Undertaker to defeat Edge & Christian on April 19, 2001* *Partnered with Undertaker to defeat Kanyon & Diamond Dallas Page on August 19, 2001* *Partnered with The Hurricane to defeat Christian & Lance Storm on September 23, 2002* *Partnered with Rob Van Dam to defeat Lance Storm & Chief Morley on March 31, 2003* *Partnered with Big Show to defeat Lance Cade & Trevor Murdoch on November 1, 2005*
WORLD HEAVYWEIGHT CHAMPION	*Defeated Rey Mysterio on July 18, 2010*
WWE CHAMPION	*Defeated Stone Cold Steve Austin on June 28, 1998*
WWE TAG TEAM CHAMPION	*Partnered with Big Show to defeat Justin Gabriel & Heath Slater on April 22, 2011*

No WWE superstar has had a tougher or darker road than Kane. The "Big Red Monster" had to overcome physical deformity, emotional scarring, and the inability to speak just to reach WWE, yet Kane has remained a fixture in WWE for well over a decade. During that time, Kane's actions often jump from heroic to villanous as the tortured psyche of a man who struggles to keep his inner demons at bay, but has also followed their orders with a menacing grin plastered on his face.

Big Red Debut

Throughout 1997, Paul Bearer provided frightening descriptions and dire predictions that Undertaker's half-brother, long thought dead, was on his way to exact his revenge. For years, the "Phenom" thought Kane had perished in a fire that also claimed the lives of Undertaker's mother and father. Audiences first laid eyes on the masked Kane at *Badd Blood* in October 1997 where he tore the door off the Hell in a Cell ring to confront Undertaker. After a brief stand-off, Kane used a crushing Tombstone Piledriver on Undertaker and left him unconscious in the ring.

While Undertaker initially refused to fight his own flesh and blood, the brothers met at *WrestleMania XIV*. It was a match WWE officials hesitated to sanction due to the enmity the superstars had for each other, and it marked the first of many emotional battles between the half-brothers. They competed in Inferno Matches, which saw Kane set ablaze and forced to relive the horrors of his childhood.

One of Kane's greatest victories came at the 1998 King of the Ring where he defeated Stone Cold Steve Austin for the WWE Championship in a controversial First Blood Match.

Newfound Allies and the Brothers of Destruction

Kane found other opponents and allies while battling his half-brother, and is one of the most successful competitors in the tag team ranks in WWE history. Kane teamed up with Mankind for his first run as a WWE Tag Team champion, and has also won titles with Big Show, The Hurricane, and Rob Van Dam in his corner.

An improbable partnership with X-Pac during 1999 took Kane down an unfamiliar path at the time, that of a fan favorite. He even found his first love in then-DX valet Tori, and the world heared him speak without the aid of a voicebox. The duo held the World Tag Team Championship twice, but the partnership dissolved when X-Pac and Tori turned on Kane. Kane managed to get a measure of revenge against his former partner at *WrestleMania 2000*.

For Undertaker and Kane, time has both healed the wounds of their past and also ripped them open fresh again. The warring brothers occasionally find it within themselves to operate together when they aren't actively trying to destroy each other. Teaming up as the Brothers of Destruction, they captured the World Tag Team Championship twice. They even jointly held the WWE and WCW tag team crowns during the 2001 Alliance Invasion and are nearly unstoppable when the wounds of the past don't drive them apart.

The Mask of Kane

The emotional scarring Kane suffered following the horrific fire of his childhood caused him to hide behind a mysterious red and black mask. Kane used the mask as a psychological crutch, suppressing his pain, and hiding from the ridicule of others. However, after losing a World Championship vs. Mask match against Triple H, the "Big Red Monster" was forced to remove his mask and face the world. No longer hiding behind the mask, Kane proved to be more emotionally unstable. The troubled superstar went on a rampage, highlighted by setting Jim Ross on fire, delivering a Tombstone Piledriver to then-WWE CEO Linda McMahon on the *Raw* stage, electrocuting Shane McMahon, and rekindling the violent rivalry with his brother at *WrestleMania XX*.

In the ring, he remained equally destructive while fighting off the challenge of an imposter in 2006, spread fear and darkness on *SmackDown*, and won the ECW Championship in record time at *WrestleMania XXIV*. Kane has competed in a few Money in the Bank matches, but his victory at the 2010 edition allowed him to defeat Rey Mysterio later that same night to claim the World Heavyweight Championship.

Kane began 2011 on a high note. He partnered with Big Show to take on The Corre, then claimed the WWE Tag Team Championship in April. However, after losing a Street Fight against Randy Orton, Kane was attacked by Mark Henry and suffered a fractured fibula which left Kane out of action for months.

Toward the end of 2011, chilling vignettes aired around the world, heralding the return of a masked Kane. Now known as "The Devil's Favorite Demon," Kane set his sights initially on John Cena, but quickly turned his attention to Randy Orton in 2012. Kane claimed he needed to purge the memory of the handshake with "The Apex Predator" after their Street Fight. Their rivalry resulted in a match at *WrestleMania XXVIII*, which Kane won.

KATIE LEA BURCHILL 🇬🇧

FROM: Chelsea, England

As the little sister to Paul Burchill, Katie Lea loved nothing more than to see her "most brutal, most vicious, most beautiful" brother destroy his competition. In fact, the sinister sibling seemed to become inexplicably happy when brother Paul inflicted pain on opponents.

In the ring, Katie Lea was no stranger to handing out punishment while battling both men and women. During her WWE career, she faced off against opponents like The Bella Twins, Eve Torres, Mickie James, Alicia Fox, and Kelly Kelly.

KATIE VICK

Many WWE Superstars have used head games to gain the psychological advantage over an opponent. Triple H took the tactic to the extreme when he accused Kane of murder in October 2002. According to "The Game," Kane killed a girl named Katie Vick after the car he was driving swerved off the road. To make matters worse, "The Game" claimed Kane took physical advantage of Vick afterward that same night.

With hopes of putting the entire ordeal behind him, Kane admitted to being behind the wheel the night Vick died, but the "Big Red Monster" claimed it was an accident. With everything out in the open, the saga should have gone away. However, Triple H took the heinous exploit to an unimaginable level when he presented a mock video of the girl's wake.

The disgusting display will forever go down as one of the most controversial moments in WWE history. While it offended many, the ploy was successful in getting inside Kane's head. At *No Mercy 2002*, "The Game" defeated Kane to unify the Intercontinental and World Heavyweight Championships.

KAVAL 🇺🇸

HT: 5'8"   WT: 174 lbs.
FROM: Brooklyn, New York
SIGNATURE MOVE: The Warrior's Way

Kaval made his professional debut in 1998. Over the following 12 years, he competed all over the world, earning a reputation as one of the most no-nonsense competitors around. It was this all-business attitude that made his pairing with Lay-Cool on the second season of *NXT* so entertaining.

Michelle McCool and Layla couldn't be more opposite than Kaval. Their in-your-face, obnoxious personalities are everything the laid-back Kaval is not. Despite their differences, Lay-Cool's guidance helped the Internet sensation win *NXT* in August 2010.

Following his *NXT* victory, Kaval began his quest to become WWE's next breakout star as a member of the *SmackDown* roster. Unfortunately for Kaval, however, the competition on the Friday night brand proved tougher than expected. He lost his debut match to Drew McIntyre in September 2010, followed by more losses at the hands of Chavo Guerrero, Tyler Reks and Jack Swagger. Kaval didn't pick up his first victory until November, when he topped Dolph Ziggler on *SmackDown*. Unable to maintain the momentum following the Ziggler victory, Kaval left WWE soon after.

KC JAMES & IDOL STEVENS

COMBINED WT: 470 lbs.

For a few months in 2006, KC James & Idol Stevens were the hottest tag team on *SmackDown*. Managed by Michelle McCool, the young tandem defeated Scotty 2 Hotty & Funaki in their August debut. The momentum of their initial victory carried James & Stevens to a shocking non-title win over WWE Tag Team Champions Paul London & Brian Kendrick a few days later.

With a victory over the WWE Tag Team Champions to their credit, James & Stevens became an overnight success. Over the next few weeks, their wins started to mount up and at *No Mercy 2006*, they were awarded an opportunity at London & Kendrick's titles. James & Stevens came up short in their attempt to claim the gold. Shortly after the pay-per-view loss, the duo disappeared just as quickly as they exploded onto the scene.

KELLY KELLY

FROM: Jacksonville, Florida

TITLE HISTORY	
DIVAS CHAMPION	*Defeated Brie Bella on June 20, 2011*

Kelly Kelly has never been afraid of showing off her assets. After debuting in ECW in June 2006, the beautiful blonde gained instant popularity with her *Kelly's Exposé* segment. Unfortunately, her then-boyfriend, Mike Knox, failed to see the fun and constantly interrupted Kelly. After an ugly breakup with Knox, Kelly performed as a member of Extreme Exposé, a dancing trio that also included ECW Divas Layla and Brooke.

Over the next two years she became a respected competitor within championship ranks taking on the likes of Maryse, Natalya, Beth Phoenix, Lay Cool, and Vickie Guerrero. 2011 proved to a breakout year for Kelly. She was drafted back to *Raw* in April, on June 20th she won her first WWE Divas Championship, she was voted #82 in *Maxim's* Top 100 list, was ranked 15th Best Female Singles Wrestler in *Pro Wrestling Illustrated's PWI Female 50*, and she graced the cover of *Maxim's* December issue.

Kelly is the most adored Diva in WWE today. Her presence is requested at conventions, late night talk shows, and charity events all over the world. After years of training, her inherent toughness, athleticism, and beauty are now fused with excellent in-ring ability. This top female figure is bringing opponents and audiences to their knees, and you could be next.

KEN PATERA

HT: 6'1"   WT: 267 lbs.   FROM: Portland, Oregon
SIGNATURE MOVE: Full Nelson

TITLE HISTORY	
INTERCONTINENTAL CHAMPION	*Defeated Pat Patterson on April 21, 1980*

Ken Patera was a world-class powerlifter who won four gold medals at the 1971 Pan-Am Games and a bronze medal at the 1972 Olympics. After training with Verne Gagne, Patera debuted for the AWA in 1973 and quickly became one of its most dangerous rule-breakers.

Patera came to World Wrestling Entertainment in 1977 and stalked then-champion Bruno Sammartino. That year he competed in several of the World's Strongest Man Competitions and ended the career of Chief Billy White Wolf with his swinging neckbreaker. Patera was voted "Most Hated Wrestler" by *Pro Wrestling Illustrated*. In 1980, he defeated Pat Patterson to become the second Intercontinental Champion. His motto was "Win if you can, lose if you must, but always cheat."

After a hiatus from WWE, he returned in 1987 as an Olympic hero determined to rid the world of his former manager. Coliseum Video released *The Ken Patera Story* in 1988, but Patera left WWE shortly afterward.

Ken Patera will always be remembered as one of sports-entertainment's most decorated and powerful performers. Whether a dastardly rule-breaker or determined American hero he entertained fans everywhere.

KEN SHAMROCK

HT: 6'1" **WT:** 243 lbs.
FROM: Sacramento, California
SIGNATURE MOVE: Ankle Lock

TITLE HISTORY

INTERCONTINENTAL CHAMPION	Defeated X-Pac on October 12, 1998
WORLD TAG TEAM CHAMPION	Partnered with Big Boss Man to defeat the New Age Outlaws on December 14, 1998

Over the past fifteen years, many men have attempted a jump to WWE from the world of mixed martial arts. Only one man, however, was able to do it with great success. That would be "The World's Most Dangerous Man," Ken Shamrock.

Shamrock's first role in WWE was that of special guest referee for Stone Cold Steve Austin's epic "I Quit" Match against Bret "Hit Man" Hart at *WrestleMania 13*. Following *WrestleMania*, Shamrock made his own in-ring debut, destroying Vernon White. The convincing victory introduced the MMA legend as a legitimate threat in WWE.

In June 1998, Shamrock achieved his first major WWE accolade when he defeated The Rock to win the prestigious *King of the Ring* tournament. Later that year, he used the ankle lock to breeze through yet another tournament. This time, the prize was the coveted Intercontinental Championship.

With the Intercontinental Championship in his possession, Shamrock eyed even more gold. Teaming with fellow Corporation member Big Boss Man, he accomplished his goal when the duo defeated the New Age Outlaws for the World Tag Team Championship in December 1998.

After less than three years in WWE, Shamrock left to restart his MMA career. While his sports-entertainment tenure was brief, it certainly proved memorable.

KENNY DYKSTRA

HT: 6'4" **WT:** 240 lbs. **FROM:** Worcester, Massachusetts
SIGNATURE MOVE: Guillotine Leg Drop

TITLE HISTORY

WORLD TAG TEAM CHAMPION	Defeated Big Show & Kane as part of the Spirit Squad on April 3, 2006

This gifted Superstar first appeared on the WWE scene in later 2005 and became part of the golden quintet known as the Spirit Squad. Brazen on the mic and versatile in the ring, Kenny waisted no time making his mark against Ric Flair, Jeff Hardy, Carlito, CM Punk and Rey Mysterio. The night after *WrestleMania 22*, Kenny & Mikey shocked the sports-entertainment world when they beat Big Show & Kane and became World Tag Team Champions. After a seven-month reign they lost to the legendary team of "Nature Boy" Ric Flair and "Rowdy" Roddy Piper.

During the 2007 Supplemental Draft, Kenny was sent to *SmackDown* and gave the program one of WWE's brashest young Superstars. He competed on the Friday night show until he parted ways with WWE in late 2008.

THE KENTUCKIANS

MEMBERS: Grizzly Smith, Luke Brown
COMBINED WT: 620 lbs.

These good old boys from Kentucky brought a different style to World Wrestling Entertainment when they arrived in 1964. Grizzly Smith and Luke Brown were a colorful pair who brought fans to their feet in battles with the Graham Brothers, Hans & Max Mortier, Magnificent Maurice & Boris Malenko, and Killer Kowalski & Gorilla Monsoon. The team from Kentucky went on to hold numerous championships in NWA territories around the United States.

The Kentuckians are remembered as one of the most beloved tag teams in professional wrestling history and were popular figures in the early days of World Wrestling Entertainment.

KENZO SUZUKI

HT: 6'3" **WT:** 250 lbs. **FROM:** The Land of the Rising Sun
SIGNATURE MOVE: Claw Leg Sweep

TITLE HISTORY

WWE TAG TEAM CHAMPION	Partnered with René Duprée to defeat Billy Kidman & Paul London on September 9, 2004

Alongside his geisha valet, Hiroko, Kenzo Suzuki debuted in WWE in June 2004 as a member of the *SmackDown* roster. Claiming to be fueled by hate and hungry for redemption, the new Superstar from the "Land of the Rising Sun" made short work of veteran Scotty 2 Hotty.

The martial-arts expert followed his debut victory with equally impressive wins over Billy Gunn and Spike Dudley. Along the way, the man who claimed his mission was vengeance and purpose was conquest never cracked a smile. Then he met René Duprée.

After teaming with Duprée, Suzuki's serious side began to slowly fade. But that didn't mean he was less aggressive in the ring. In fact, the duo even captured the WWE Tag Team Championship in September 2004, at the expense of Billy Kidman & Paul London.

Prior to leaving WWE in 2005, Suzuki tried to make amends with the fans in the United States by claiming he loved the country. He even loved its women, particularly Torrie Wilson.

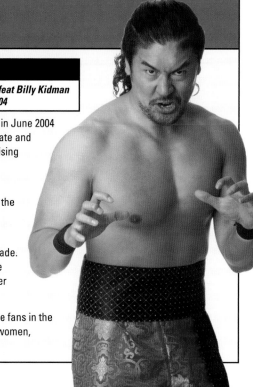

K

2010-

2000-09

1990-99

1980-89

1970-79

1960-69

KERRY VON ERICH

HT: 6'2"   WT: 254 lbs.
FROM: Denton, Texas
SIGNATURE MOVES: The Claw; Discus Punch

TITLE HISTORY	
INTERCONTINENTAL CHAMPION	Defeated Mr. Perfect on August 27, 1990

Years before ever competing in his first WWE match, the "Texas Tornado" Kerry Von Erich had already taken the wrestling world by storm. As a member of the famed Von Erich family, Kerry was a huge star in many Southern wrestling territories, most notably the World Class region in Texas. In fact, six years before touching down in WWE, he defeated the legendary Ric Flair for the NWA Championship at Texas Stadium.

When he finally made his WWE debut in July 1990, Von Erich's powerful, unpredictable and devastating past earned him the moniker the "Texas Tornado". He used his family's famed claw, coupled with a devastating discus punch, to tear through the WWE roster. His immediate impact earned him an Intercontinental Championship shot less than one month into his WWE tenure. He capitalized on his opportunity, defeating Mr. Perfect for the title at *SummerSlam*.

Three months after winning the Intercontinental Championship, Von Erich lost the title back to Mr. Perfect. The loss failed to set him off course, though, as he spent the next two years competing on some of the biggest cards of the time, including *WrestleMania VII*, where he defeated Dino Bravo.

On April 4, 2009, the Von Erich family's amazing accomplishments brought them to the WWE Hall of Fame. Shortly thereafter fans rejoiced as for the first time in 20 years, Kerry's likeness returned to the world of action figures as part of Mattel's WWE Legends Series.

KEVIN KELLY

After earning a degree in communications from Florida State University, longtime sports-entertainment fan Kevin Kelly began his journey to WWE when he debuted as a ring announcer for the International Wrestling Federation in 1991. After several years honing his skills behind the microphone, Kelly was finally brought into WWE in 1996.

Over the course of his seven-year stay with WWE, Kelly held numerous job responsibilities, both in front of and behind the camera. But most fans remember him for his humorous and ongoing battle with The Rock, where Kelly was not-so-affectionately dubbed "Hermie" by "The Great One."

In addition to sitting alongside Michael Cole to call the action on Monday nights, Kelly also served as a backstage interviewer for *Raw* and *SmackDown*. Additionally, he spent many years hosting WWE.com's long-running and controversial webcast, *Byte This!*

Behind the scenes, Kelly worked in WWE's talent relations and magazine departments for several years before departing from the company in 2003.

KEVIN SULLIVAN  HT: 5'11"   WT: 235 lbs.   FROM: Boston, Massachusetts
SIGNATURE MOVE: Spinning Toe Hold

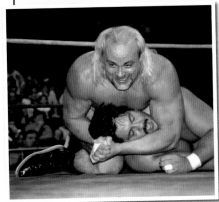

This respectable sportsman from Boston began his career in the mid-1970s defending the rules of the ring. He valiantly faced the likes of Tor Kamata, Crusher Blackwell, Bruiser Brody, and Nikolai Volkoff.

Into the early 1980s, he underwent a drastic change and became one of the darkest villains in the National Wrestling Alliance. He was described by opponents as the devil incarnate and later became known as "the Taskmaster." He ended his career in the mid-1990s with World Championship Wrestling.

KEVIN THORN  HT: 6'3"   WT: 270 lbs.
SIGNATURE MOVE: Original Sin Modified Neckbreaker

Kevin Thorn and his valet Ariel celebrated the vampire lifestyle during their time in ECW. Their dark, gothic appearances intimidated audiences, but it was Thorn's extensive history of frequenting the globe's greatest fight clubs that frightened his opponents.

Thorn began seeking the blood of ECW Superstars in the summer of 2006. His first victims were ECW mainstays Tommy Dreamer and Stevie Richards. Later that year, he picked up the biggest win of his career when he teamed with Ariel to defeat Mike Knox & Kelly Kelly at *December to Dismember*.

As 2006 came to a close, Thorn and several other young Superstars began making an impact in ECW. In February, the upstarts officially formed a faction called the New Breed. With fellow New Breed

members Matt Striker, Elijah Burke, and Marcus Cor Von by his side, Thorn battled ECW Originals Dreamer, Rob Van Dam, Sabu, and Sandman in front of more than 80,000 fans at *WrestleMania 23*. Thorn's team came up short, but the match remains one of the brightest moments of his career.

KID KASH 🇺🇸

HT: 5'9"   WT: 200 lbs
FROM: Johnson City, Tennessee
SIGNATURE MOVE: Dead Level

TITLE HISTORY

CRUISERWEIGHT CHAMPION	Defeated Juventud on December 18, 2005

A former Television Champion in the original ECW, Kid Kash jumped to WWE in June 2005. In his debut match on *Heat*, the cruiserweight came up short against the lightning-quick Tajiri. The loss proved costly to Kash, who failed to see any more time on WWE television for several months.

Shortly after re-emerging on the WWE scene, Kash began to make quick work of *SmackDown's* top cruiserweights, including Paul London, Scotty 2 Hotty, and Super Crazy. At *Armageddon 2005*, he defeated Juventud for the Cruiserweight Championship.

Following his reign as Cruiserweight Champion, Kash briefly teamed with Jamie Noble. Collectively known as The Pitbulls, Kash & Noble displayed an unorthodox style that oftentimes saw them bite their opponents. The Pitbulls were challengers for the WWE Tag Team Championship but failed to win the titles. The team split upon Kid Kash's departure from WWE in 2006.

KHARMA 🇺🇸

HT: 5'11"

Kharma is not your typical Diva. At nearly 300 pounds, she is a mountain of a woman who provides a terrifying presence never before seen in the Divas division.

The callous Kharma begin mysteriously popping up on WWE television in April 2011, when videos of her laughing sinisterly while dismembering pretty little dolls aired throughout arenas. Without even opening her mouth or stepping foot in a ring, Kharma was letting every Diva know that things were about to change.

Kharma finally debuted at *Extreme Rules 2011*, when she brutally attacked Michelle McCool following her match. For the next several weeks, she continued her assault on the Divas division, attacking Maryse, Eve and Layla, among others.

THE KILLER BEES 🇺🇸

MEMBERS: B. Brian Blair & Jumpin' Jim Brunzell
COMBINED WT: 465 lbs.

The Killer Bees buzzed into WWE in 1985 and took the tag team division on an exciting ride. The Bees used outstanding teamwork and high-flying manuevers to establish themselves as one of the top teams in all of World Wrestling Entertainment.

When opponents would come at the duo with under-handed tricks, the Killer Bees would often resort to "masked confusion" where they would don matching masks and switch places in the ring without making tags. At the inaugural *Survivor Series* the Bees and Young Stallions were the survivors of their tag team match.

The team split up when B. Brian Blair left the company, with Jumpin' Jim departing shortly thereafter. Fans will always remember the Killer Bees for their exciting matches, high-energy and innovations to tag team wrestling.

KILLER KHAN 🇲🇳

HT: 6'5"   WT: 310 lbs.   FROM: Upper Mongolia
SIGNATURE MOVE: Top Rope Knee Drop

This former Superstar debuted in the 1970s while frightening audiences and opponents wherever he appeared. In 1980, Khan debuted in WWE with "Classy" Freddie Blassie at his side. Khan also teamed with George "The Animal" Steele from time to time.

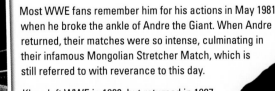

Most WWE fans remember him for his actions in May 1981 when he broke the ankle of Andre the Giant. When Andre returned, their matches were so intense, culminating in their infamous Mongolian Stretcher Match, which is still referred to with reverance to this day.

Khan left WWE in 1982, but returned in 1987 with Mr. Fuji leading him into battle. Killer Kahn went barefoot, utilized a sumo-inspired pre-match ritual and spewed green mist into the eyes of his opponents. In 1988, he returned to Mongolia and today resides in Japan. Memories of Killer Kahn and his violent acts in the ring will continue to haunt fans and Superstars for decades to come.

KILLER KOWALSKI

HT: 6'7" **WT: 280 lbs.** **FROM: Windsor, Ontario, Canada** **SIGNATURE MOVE: Stomach Claw**

TITLE HISTORY

UNITED STATES TAG TEAM CHAMPION	Partnered with Gorilla Monsoon to defeat Skull Murphy & Brute Bernard on November 14, 1963

This remarkable athlete made his professional in-ring debut in 1947 as Tarzan Kowalski. Over the next seven years, he captured several regional singles and tag team titles in multiple NWA territories. In 1950, he defeated the Texas Tag Team Champions in a handicap match by himself! In January 1953, Kowalski made history when he appeared in the first match televised in Canada.

After an incident involving Kowalski left his opponent short one ear, he became the most despised man in all of professional wrestling. Fans' anger was so intense he required police escorts to and from the ring to ensure their safety. In 1957, he arrived in Vince McMahon Sr.'s Capitol Wrestling Corporation and displayed his bloodthirsty tendencies. Kowalski returned in 1963 and began a relentless pursuit of the WWE Championship. He became one of the greatest threats to Bruno Sammartino's reign. That November, he formed one of the most dominating teams in WWE history with Gorilla Monsoon. The two monsters beat Skull Murphy & Brute Bernard to become United States Tag Team Champions. Kowalski also traveled to Japan and had a series of matches with Shoehi "Giant" Baba that were televised throughout the entire country.

Kowalski worked sparodically with the McMahon-led company over the following years, and in 1974 he concluded his battles against Bruno Sammartino in a Texas Death Match. In 1976, Kowalski and Big John Studd concealed their identities and competed as the Executioners.

In 1977, this legend retired from active competition and opened "Killer Kowalski's School of Professional Wrestling." For the first time in decades, he was able to show people his passions outside the ring. He became a philanthropist working for children with special needs as well as a renowned photographer. In 2001, he published a collection of his photos.

In 1996, he was inducted by one of his pupils, Triple H, into the WWE Hall of Fame. Kowalski was honored again in 2007 when he was inducted into the National Polish-American Sports Hall of Fame. On August 30, 2008, Kowalski passed away at 81. Killer Kowalski was one of the true pioneers of professional wrestling, and one of its first mainstream celebrities.

KIM CHEE

An expert handler of wild animals, this masked man's identity became a topic of conversation when he arrived in WWE in 1986. As part of the contingent that came with Kamala "the Ugandan Giant" to the ring, Kim Chee was the only individual that could communicate with Kamala and curtail his behavior. Given his unique talents, he was an invaluable asset to managers who wanted the giant as part of their stable of WWE Superstars.

Kim Chee was also willing to interfere in a match on Kamala's behalf if it was deemed necessary. Though they have spent periods of time apart, history has shown that if you see Kim Chee, Kamala is not too far behind. The identity and origin of this individual remains a mystery that will probably remain unsolved.

KING CURTIS IAUKEA

HT: 6'3"   WT: 290 lbs.
FROM: Honolulu, Hawaii
SIGNATURE MOVE: Splash

TITLE HISTORY

WORLD TAG TEAM CHAMPION	Partnered with Baron Mikel Scicluna to defeat Karl Gotch & Rene Goulet on February 1, 1972

King Curtis Iaukea began his illustrious professional wrestling career in the early 1960s, competing mainly for promotions in Australia and his home state of Hawaii. Despite his blatant disregard for the rules and his unkempt appearance, audiences in both locales accepted him with great fondness.

The mighty Hawaiian didn't spend much time in WWE, but he did manage to gain great success during his brief stint with the promotion. In February 1972, Iaukea teamed with Baron Mikel Scicluna to defeat Karl Gotch & Rene Goulet for the World Tag Team Championship. With Lou Albano as their manager, Iaukea & Scicluna held the gold for more than three months before being dethroned by Chief Jay Strongbow & Sonny King.

Using a flattening splash to finish off his foes, Iaukea eventually compiled enough victories to earn an opportunity at the coveted WWE Championship, held at the time by Pedro Morales. Unfortunately for the King, he was unable to unseat Morales. He left WWE soon after.

KING KONG BUNDY

HT: 6'4"   WT: 485 lbs.   FROM: Atlantic City, New Jersey   SIGNATURE MOVE: Avalanche Splash

The rules of the ring are simple. To defeat your opponent via pinfall, you must keep his shoulders on the mat for three seconds. Unless, of course, you're King Kong Bundy. The massive Bundy pummeled his opponents so severely that he demanded referees count all the way up to five. The stunt was the ultimate slap in the face of his foes and went a long way in intimidating future competition.

Originally managed by Jimmy "The Mouth of the South" Hart, Bundy used the inaugural *WrestleMania* as the site of his first commanding victory. In a matter of a mere nine seconds, the man appropriately dubbed "The Walking Condominium," crushed veteran S.D. Jones. The victory opened the eyes of everybody associated with WWE, including Bobby "The Brain" Heenan, who acquired Bundy from Hart shortly after *WrestleMania*.

Under Heenan's tutelage, Bundy set his sights on ridding WWE of Hulk Hogan. He nearly accomplished his goal when he ambushed Hulk Hogan on *Saturday Night's Main Event* in December 1985. With help from Don Muraco, Bundy delivered several rib-crushing splashes that almost ended Hogan's career.

The Hulkster eventually recovered and put his WWE Championship on the line against Bundy in a Steel Cage Match at *WrestleMania 2*. The match, which Hogan won, is still *WrestleMania's* only steel cage main event.

Bundy's string of memorable *WrestleMania* moments continued the following year when he nearly splattered midget wrestler Little Beaver all over the canvas. Luckily, the other midgets involved in the match saved Beaver from a certain demise.

Following the events of *WrestleMania III*, Bundy took a six-year hiatus from WWE. When he returned however, he found himself involved in yet another high-profile *WrestleMania* encounter. In 1995, Bundy attempted to become the first Superstar to put a blemish on Undertaker's legendary *WrestleMania* winning streak. Unfortunately for the big man, he went the way of so many other greats that have unsuccessfully tried to bury the "Deadman." Bundy disappeared shortly after *WrestleMania XI*, marking the end of an imposing WWE career.

KING KONG BUNDY & BIG JOHN STUDD

COMBINED WT: 822 lbs.

Paired up in 1985 by Bobby "the Brain" Heenan, this colossal combination's first target was the only WWE Superstar larger than them, Andre the Giant. In August 1985, Bundy interfered in Studd's singles match against Andre. The unwarranted attack left the Eighth Wonder of the World with an injured sternum and set the stage for a lengthy rivalry. Unfortunately for Bundy & Studd, Andre proved his superiority by beating the team numerous times with various partners, including Hulk Hogan, Hillbilly Jim, and Junkyard Dog.

In 1986, Bundy & Studd got back on the winning track, turning back smaller teams such as the Killer Bees. However, just when momentum seemed to be on their side, Andre derailed them again. Disguised as a masked Superstar called Giant Machine, Andre picked up where he left off, making Bundy & Studd's life miserable. Studd left WWE the following year, marking the end of the gigantic tag team.

KING OF THE RING

King of the Ring began as a one night, single-elimination tournament in 1985. In 1993, *King of the Ring* became a yearly pay-per-view event which featured the tournament of the same name. After 2002, the tournament was put on hiatus for a few years. It was revived in 2006 on *SmackDown* but the tournament took place over a month instead of a single day. In 2008, *Raw* hosted a one night tournament but Superstars from *SmackDown* and *ECW* were invited to participate.

PAY-PER-VIEW EVENTS

June 13, 1993
Dayton, OH - Nutter Center

Main Event: Bret "Hit Man" Hart defeated Bam Bam Bigelow, King of the Ring finals

June 19, 1994
Baltimore, MD - Baltimore Arena

Main Event: "Rowdy" Roddy Piper defeated Jerry "The King" Lawler

June 25, 1995
Philadelphia, PA - The Spectrum

Main Event: WWE Champion Diesel & Bam Bam Bigelow defeated Tatanka & Sycho Sid

June 23, 1996
Milwaukee, WI - MECCA Arena

Main Event: WWE Champion Shawn Michaels defeated British Bulldog

June 8, 1997
Providence, RI - Providence Civic Center

Main Event: WWE Champion Undertaker defeated Faarooq

June 28, 1998
Pittsburgh, PA - The Civic Arena

Main Event: Kane defeated WWE Champion Stone Cold Steve Austin, First Blood Match

June 27, 1999
Greensboro, NC - Greensboro Coliseum

Main Event: Shane McMahon & Mr. McMahon defeated Stone Cold Steve Austin, Ladder Match

June 25, 2000
Boston, MA - FleetCenter

Main Event: The Rock, Kane & Undertaker defeated WWE Champion Triple H, Shane McMahon & Mr. McMahon

June 24, 2001
East Rutherford, NJ - Continental Airlines Arena

Main Event: WWE Champion Stone Cold Steve Austin defeated Chris Benoit & Chris Jericho, Triple Threat Match

June 23, 2002
Columbus, OH - Nationwide Arena

Main Event: WWE Champion Undertaker defeated Triple H

KING OF THE RING CHRONOLOGY

1985: Don Muraco
1986: Harley Race
1987: Randy Savage
1988: Ted DiBiase
1989: Tito Santana
1990: No Tournament

1991: Bret "Hit Man" Hart
1992: No Tournament
1993: Bret "Hit Man" Hart
1994: Owen Hart
1995: Mabel

1996: Stone Cold Steve Austin
1997: Hunter Hearst-Helmsley
1998: Ken Shamrock
1999: Billy Gunn
2000: Kurt Angle

2001: Edge
2002: Brock Lesnar
2003: No Tournament
2004: No Tournament
2005: No Tournament

2006: Booker T
2007: No Tournament
2008: William Regal
2009: No Tournament
2010: Sheamus

KIZARNY
HT: 6'2"   **WT:** 236 lbs.
FROM: Wizard Beach

There's strange, and then there's Kizarny.

The Superstar from Wizard Beach joined the carnival after running away from home as a child. It was here that he developed characteristics not typical of anybody anywhere ever. He became a fire-eater, befriended bearded ladies, developed a disturbing love for pain and began speaking in carny, which is an antiquated secret language impossible for the normal population to understand.

Kizarny joined WWE in early 2009, defeating Montel Vontavious Porter in his debut match on *SmackDown*. The overly inked Superstar looked to have a limitless future, but following his elimination in a Battle Royal the following month on *SmackDown*, Kizarny mysteriously disappeared from WWE, much to the delight of those petrified by the carnival freak's behavior.

THE KLIQ
MEMBERS: Shawn Michaels, Diesel, Razor Ramon, Triple H, X-Pac

Though never acknowledged as a legitimate on-air faction, the Kliq was perhaps one of the most powerful WWE forces during the mid-1990s. Comprised of Shawn Michaels, Diesel, Razor Ramon, Triple H, and X-Pac (as 1-2-3 Kid), the Kliq was a group that used their popularity and power to make demands from WWE's top decision makers.

The Kliq made their first public appearance at Madison Square Garden in 1996. With Diesel and Ramon about to leave WWE for rival WCW, members of the backstage faction joined in an unscheduled heartfelt embrace in the middle of the ring. The move, which is commonly referred to as the "Curtain Call," infuriated Vince McMahon. Years later, The Kliq's "Curtain Call" remains one of sports-entertainment's most controversial moments. Proving once again that anything can happen in WWE, a second "Curtain Call" took place almost 15 years later during the closing moments of Shawn Michaels' WWE Hall of Fame induction.

K

2010-
2000-09
1990-99
1980-89
1970-79
1960-69

KLONDIKE BILL 🇺🇸

HT: 6'0"   **WT:** 365 lbs.
FROM: Kodiak Island, Alaska
SIGNATURE MOVE: Bear Hug

After a successful amateur wrestling career, Bill Solowekyo turned to Stu Hart's legendary Dungeon to prepare him for the pro ranks. After amazing the hard-to-impress Hart with his toughness, Solowekyo donned a pair of worn blue jeans, tied a tattered white rope around his waist and adopted the name Klondike Bill. The rest is Canadian wrestling history.

Billed from Kodiak Island, Alaska, Klondike Bill amazed crowds throughout Canada with his superhuman strength and his firm bear hug finisher and was a threat to nearly every champion. Shockingly, however, Klondike Bill only captured one crown while competing in Canada.

Klondike Bill also brought his game to the United States where he was equally feared. While competing in the United States, he enjoyed two National Wrestling Alliance Tag Team Championship reigns with partners Nelson Royal and Luke Brown.

KOFI KINGSTON ⭐

HT: 6'0"   **WT:** 218 lbs.   **FROM:** Ghana, West Africa
SIGNATURE MOVE: Trouble in Paradise

TITLE HISTORY	
INTERCONTINENTAL CHAMPION (3 TIMES)	*Defeated Chris Jericho on June 29, 2008* *Defeated Drew McIntyre on May 23, 2010* *Defeated Dolph Ziggler on January 7, 2011*
UNITED STATES CHAMPION (2 TIMES)	*Defeated Montel Vontavious Porter on June 1, 2009* *Defeated Sheamus on May 5, 2011*
WORLD TAG TEAM CHAMPION	*Partnered with CM Punk to defeat Cody Rhodes & Ted DiBiase on October 27, 2008*
WWE TAG TEAM CHAMPION	*Partnered with Evan Bourne to defeat David Otunga & Michael McGillicutty on August 22, 2011*

Kofi Kingston burst onto the WWE scene in January 2008. He stood out instantly, with his unique abilities, wide smile, and seemingly boundless enthusiasm. In June, Kofi was drafted to *Raw* and in his first match on the brand, he claimed his first piece of WWE gold when he defeated Chris Jericho for the Intercontinental Championship at *Night of Champions*. Kingston is heralded as a master of forward momentum and one of WWE's most popular Superstars. The "Boom Squad" leader has captivated the WWE Universe like never before with his peerless attack from high above the mat while chants of "BOOM! BOOM! BOOM!" resound in venues all over the world.

After stand-out performances in Money In The Bank contests, Kofi recaptured the Intercontinental Championship in early 2011. After so many individual accomplishment, Kofi turned to the tag team ranks. A partnership with CM Punk in 2010 resulted in a championship, while teaming with Evan Bourne to form Air Boom brought some prestige back to the tag team division. The frequent flyers managed to defeat David Otunga & Michael McGillicutty for the WWE Tag Team Championship in August 2011 and held the titles for almost five months.

KOKO B. WARE 🇺🇸

HALL OF FAME 2009

HT: 5'7"   **WT:** 228 lbs.   **FROM:** Union City, Tennessee
SIGNATURE MOVE: Ghostbuster

Starting in 1986, competitors in WWE were dazzled by the high-flying attacks of Koko B. Ware. With the help of his macaw, Frankie, he taught fans all over the world how to do the "Birdman" dance. In the ring, Koko B. Ware dazed opponents with his unmatched flying dropkick, then finished off matches with his version of a brainbuster, known as the Ghostbuster

Koko and Frankie were immortalized in 1987 when they became part of the famed WWE action-figure line from LJN Toys. That year he also sang the lead on the title track to WWE's platinum-selling album *Piledriver*. Koko joined forces with "The Rocket" Owen Hart to form High-Energy in 1992. That next year Koko was again part of history when he had the first-ever match on *Monday Night Raw* against Yokozuna. Koko left World Wrestling Entertainment in 1994. After more than a

decade away from WWE television he appeared in the Legends Ceremony at the October 2005 *WWE Raw Homecoming* and weeks later returned to the ring on *Heat* against Rob Conway.

"KRIPPLER" KARL KOVACS 🇺🇸

HT: 6'2"   **WT:** 290 lbs.
FROM: Minneapolis, Minnesota

Given his brief stay in WWE during the early 1970s, many of today's fans don't recognize the name "Krippler" Karl Kovacs. The name Stan "Killer" Kowalski, however, has a rich past.

Following his debut in the 1950s, Kowalski made a name for himself competing mainly in Minnesota and Ohio. But when he came to WWE later in his career, he changed his name to "Krippler" Karl Kovacs, presumably to avoid confusion with the great Walter "Killer" Kowalski, with whom Kovacs periodically teamed.

As Stan Kowalski, the Minnesota native has the distinction of being one-half of the first-ever AWA World Tag Team Champions. Collectively known as Murder, Inc., he and Tiny Mills were awarded the gold in August 1960 after the AWA withdrew from the NWA.

Kowalski later teamed with Bob Geigel to capture a second AWA World Tag Team Championship, at the expense of Larry "The Axe" Hennig & Duke Hoffman. They held the titles for nearly two months before losing to Art and Stan Neilson.

KRISTAL

FROM: Los Angeles, California

After an eye-opening appearance in the 2005 *Raw* Diva Search, Kristal was welcomed into WWE as a member of the *SmackDown* broadcast team. While she shined in her role as an interviewer, it quickly became clear that the fiery Diva needed to be in the ring.

Upon making her in-ring debut in early 2006, Kristal engaged in bitter rivalries with Jillian Hall and Ashley. The three Divas squared off in several contests over the course of the year, including a Bra & Panties Match at *The Great American Bash*, which also featured Michelle McCool.

In 2007, Kristal began a torrid love affair with the considerably older Theodore Long. Those watching from afar assumed Kristal was merely after the *SmackDown* General Manager's power. But Long failed to see it that way and eventually asked for Kristal's hand in marriage.

The odd pairing planned a beautiful ceremony for the September 21, 2007 edition of *SmackDown*. Unfortunately, however, tragedy struck when a Theodore Long heart attack cut the ceremony short. Kristal was released from WWE shortly after.

KRONIK

MEMBERS: Brian Adams, Bryan Clark
COMBINED WEIGHT: 573 lbs.

When Steven Richards began to verbally assault Undertaker in September 2001, fans everywhere assumed the former Right To Censor leader had lost his mind. In reality, however, he was simply luring in Undertaker so that his newest acquisition, Kronik, could attack from behind.

Shortly after their debut, Kronik, which consisted of former WCW Tag Team Champions Brian Adams & Bryan Clark, targeted Undertaker once again. This time, they cost Undertaker & Kane the World Tag Team Championship. At *Unforgiven 2001*, the Brothers of Destruction finally gained revenge when they decisively defeated Kronik in tag action. A few days later, Adams & Clark were released from WWE. In all, their WWE tenure lasted less than one month.

KURT ANGLE

HT: 6'0"   **WT:** 250 lbs.
FROM: Pittsburg, Pennsylvania
SIGNATURE MOVE: Ankle Lock

TITLE HISTORY

EUROPEAN CHAMPION	*Defeated Val Venis on February 10, 2000*
HARDCORE CHAMPION	*1 Time*
INTERCONTINENTAL CHAMPION	*Defeated Chris Jericho on Febuary 27, 2000*
UNITED STATES CHAMPION	*Defeated Rhyno on October 22, 2001*
WORLD HEAVYWEIGHT CHAMPION	*Won a Battle Royal on January 10, 2006*
WWE TAG TEAM CHAMPION	*Partnered with Chris Benoit to defeat Edge & Rey Mysterio on October 20, 2002*
WWE CHAMPION (4 TIMES)	*Defeated The Rock October 22, 2000* *Defeated Stone Cold Steve Austin on September 23, 2001* *Defeated Big Show on December 15, 2002* *Defeated Brock Lesnar on July 27, 2003*

From the day he was born, Kurt Angle's life was about proving that he was the absolute best in whatever he did. Years of dedication led to a gold medal in freestyle wrestling at the 1996 Summer Games. Kurt decided to enter sports-entertainment, and he knew that if he was to succeed he needed to take a serious approach. After Angle graduated from the world-renowned Funkin' Conservatory, he debuted in World Wrestling Entertainment in 2000.

In February, he defeated Val Venis for the European Championship on *SmackDown,* and days later beat Chris Jericho for the Intercontinental Title at *No Way Out*. In October, he defeated The Rock at *No Mercy* for his first WWE Championship. Angle showed he was for real when he defeated Stone Cold Steve Austin, The Rock, Undertaker, Triple H and Rikishi in a Hell in a Cell Match at *Armageddon*.

In 2001, Angle's incredible achievements continued as he won the *King of the Ring* tournament, penned his autobiography, *It's True, It's True,* and was inducted into the National Amateur Wrestling Hall of Fame. Over the next five years, Kurt had famous battles against the likes of Chris Jericho, Shawn Michaels, John Cena, Rey Mysterio, Eddie Guerrero, Hulk Hogan and "Nature Boy" Ric Flair.

After being on both *Raw* and *SmackDown* brands, Angle was drafted to ECW in the spring of 2006 and defeated Randy Orton at *One Night Stand*. Kurt Angle is one of the most decorated athletes in the history of sports-entertainment. His list of victories reads like a Who's Who of legends. No one will likely ever be able to match his intensity, integrity and intelligence. He can make you tap out from any position within seconds. Oh, it's true!

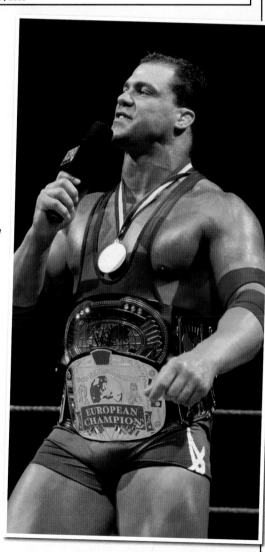

KWANG

HT: 5'11" WT: 248 lbs. FROM: Japan
SIGNATURE MOVE: Super Spin Kick

In 1994, World Wrestling Entertainment was infiltrated by a martial-arts expert named Kwang. Managed by Harvey Whippleman, Kwang was known for his disregard for rules, and for using a mysterious Asian mist that was often used to blind opponents.

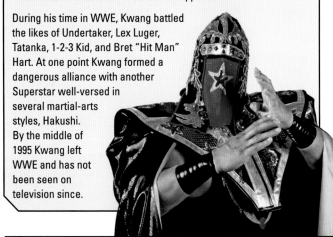

During his time in WWE, Kwang battled the likes of Undertaker, Lex Luger, Tatanka, 1-2-3 Kid, and Bret "Hit Man" Hart. At one point Kwang formed a dangerous alliance with another Superstar well-versed in several martial-arts styles, Hakushi. By the middle of 1995 Kwang left WWE and has not been seen on television since.

KYO DAI

MEMBERS:
Tajiri, Akio, Sakoda

Some sports-entertainment factions are so great that they will undoubtedly transcend generations. Among the most prevalent are the Four Horsemen, D-Generation X and the New World Order. Others, however, were so fleeting that there's barely evidence of their existence. Kyo Dai falls into this category.

During Tajiri's Cruiserweight Championship defense against Rey Mysterio at *No Mercy 2003*, the "Japanese Buzzsaw" received some surprising support when what appeared to be two fans jumped the guardrail to help him pick up the win. It was later learned that the two collaborators weren't fans at all — they were Akio & Sakoda.

Over the next few weeks, Tajiri, Akio & Sakoda worked together to ensure their superiority over *SmackDown*'s other cruiserweights. But after a while, Tajiri slowly started to fade from the trio, leaving Akio & Sakoda to compete as a tag team. The Akio-Sakoda union eventually fizzled as well when Sakoda was released from WWE in the summer of 2004.

LA FAMILIA

MEMBERS: Edge, Vickie Guerrero, Zack Ryder, Curt Hawkins, Bam Neely, Chavo Guerrero

Few things in life are more intoxicating than power, as evidenced by the torrid love affair between Vickie Guerrero and Edge. After all, it wasn't long after Guerrero assumed power of *SmackDown* that the Rated-R Superstar expressed his love for the considerably older General Manager.

Shortly after the unconventional couple made their romance public, Vickie's nephew, Chavo Guerrero, expressed great displeasure with his aunt's choice of a beau. But Chavo eventually came around after Edge helped him capture the ECW Championship. With Chavo in the fold, the roots of La Familia began to embed themselves into the WWE landscape.

With Zack Ryder, Curt Hawkins and Bam Neely rounding out the sextet, La Familia became one of the most powerful forces in recent WWE history. Combined, they used Vickie's stroke to claim the WWE, World Heavyweight, ECW and WWE Tag Team Championship. Eventually, the stresses of being in such a high-profile position caused Vickie to resign her role as GM. No longer wielding any power, Vickie was quickly dumped by Edge, thus marking the official end of La Familia.

LA RESISTANCE

MEMBERS: Sylvain Grenier, Rene Dupree, Robert Conway
COMBINED WT: 727 lbs. FROM: Quebec, Canada

TITLE HISTORY

WORLD TAG TEAM CHAMPIONS (4 TIMES)	*Defeated Kane & Rob Van Dam on June 15, 2003* *Defeated Chris Benoit & Edge on May 31, 2004* *Defeated Chris Benoit on November 1, 2004* *Defeated William Regal & Coach on January 16, 2005*

For a little more than two years, the French Canadian combination of Sylvain Grenier, Rene Dupree & Robert Conway dominated the WWE tag team scene.

Dubbed La Resistance, Grenier & Dupree immediately opened eyes when they attacked Scott Steiner during their April 2003 debut. Less than two months later, they had the World Tag Team Championship strapped around their waists. Using a whiplash side slam finisher known as Au Revoir, La Resistance turned back all comers. However, they needed a little help from an American to get past the Dudley Boys. At *SummerSlam 2003*, the faction's newest member, turncoat Robert Conway, attacked D-Von & Bubba Ray, allowing La Resistance to pick up the win.

In the months that followed, the three-man faction utilized their numbers advantage to succeed in WWE's competitive tag team ranks. With Conway in the fold, La Resistance appeared unstoppable until Dupree was unexpectedly drafted to *SmackDown* in March 2004.

With Grenier & Conway holding down the fort, many insiders predicted doom for La Resistance. However, the new duo proved to be even more successful than the original, earning three more championship reigns.

LANCE CADE

HT: 6'5" WT: 262 lbs.
FROM: Nashville, Tennessee

TITLE HISTORY

WORLD TAG TEAM CHAMPION (3 TIMES)	*Partnered with Trevor Murdoch to defeat The Hurricane & Rosey on September 18, 2005* *Partnered with Trevor Murdoch to defeat The Hardy Boys on June 4, 2007* *Partnered with Trevor Murdoch to defeat Paul London & Brian Kendrick on September 8, 2007*

Lance Cade received his first big break in September 2005. Teaming with Trevor Murdoch, the duo defeated The Hurricane & Rosey in their first *Raw* match. A few weeks later, they used the momentum from that win to capture the World Tag Team Championship. The rugged Southerners held the titles for close to two months before losing to Big Show & Kane. After the loss, Cade & Murdoch chose to split amicably, an amazing feat considering tag teams rarely break on good terms.

On his own, Cade struggled to find his way. And after six long months of non-descript matches, he finally chose to reform his union with Murdoch. The decision to reunite proved advantageous, as two more championship reigns soon followed. After an uncharacteristic losing streak plagued the team in May 2008, Cade took out his frustrations on Murdoch, officially marking the end of the successful tandem.

Cade's second attempt at singles success got off to a much more positive start. Rather than sitting back and waiting for the spotlight to come to him, Cade went out and grabbed it for himself. Cade became a close of associate of Chris Jericho and attacked the likes of John Cena, Batista and legends Shawn Michaels and Triple H. Sadly, Lance Cade passed away in August 2010.

LANCE CADE & TREVOR MURDOCH
COMBINED WT: 501 lbs.

TITLE HISTORY

WORLD TAG TEAM CHAMPIONS (3 TIMES)	*Defeated The Hurricane & Rosey on September 18, 2005* *Defeated The Hardy Boys on June 4, 2007* *Defeated Paul London & Brian Kendrick on September 8, 2007*

This cowboy and truck driving tough guy used a blend of down-home fightin' and power to quickly make an impact *Raw*. Shortly after their debut, everyone learned that Cade was trained by Shawn Michaels while Murdoch was trained by Harley Race.

The two captured the World Tag Team Championship from The Hurricane & Rosey at *Unforgiven 2005*. Shortly after their title loss to Big Show & Kane at *Taboo Tuesday* they parted ways to focus on singles careers. They reformed in 2007 for the *Raw* tag team Battle Royal, showing a new regard for sportsmanship. They went on to hold the tag team titles facing teams like the Hardys, Paul London & Brian Kendrick, and Hardcore Holly & Cody Rhodes. Their relationship slowly unraveled, ultimately leading to Lance Cade turning on his longtime partner in early 2008.

LANCE CASSIDY
HT: 6'1"   WT: 232 lbs.   FROM: Texas
SIGNATURE MOVE: Top Rope Clothesline

Over the course of sports-entertainment, there have been many cowboys that have made the successful transition to the ring. Names such as Dick Murdoch, Blackjack Mulligan and Terry Funk immediately come to mind. Lance Cassidy may never appear on that legendary list, but in late 1992, the gun-slinging Cassidy used his patented top-rope clothesline to earn victories over Terry Taylor, Brooklyn Brawler and Skinner. Unfortunately for Cassidy, that's where the success stopped. By 1993, only a few months into his WWE career, he left the rigors of the ring to return to his ranch.

LANCE STORM
HT: 6'0"   WT: 231 lbs.   FROM: Calgary... Alberta, Canada
SIGNATURE MOVE: Canadian Crab

TITLE HISTORY

INTERCONTINENTAL CHAMPION	*Defeated Albert on July 23, 2001*
WORLD TAG TEAM CHAMPION (4 TIMES)	*Partnered with Christian to defeat Hollywood Hogan & Edge on July 21, 2002* *Partnered with William Regal to defeat Booker T & Goldust on January 6, 2003* *Partnered with William Regal to defeat The Dudley Boys on January 20, 2003* *With partner Chief Morley, awarded the championship on March 24, 2003*

A graduate of Stu Hart's Dungeon, Lance Storm first made waves in Canada and Japan before he arrived in Smokey Mountain Wrestling, where he teamed with Chris Jericho as the Thrillseekers. He soon moved to ECW and formed the Impact Players with Justin Credible. He didn't claim to be the whole show, just the best part of it. In June 2000, Storm went to World Championship Wrestling and held multiple titles shortly after making his debut. Fans were treated to a preview of what was to come in WWE after Storm renamed each belt to suit a Canadian champion.

Storm landed in WWE in 2001, first as part of the Alliance, then as part of the hated Un-Americans group with Christian, Test, and William Regal. Storm enjoyed a few Tag Team Championship runs with his Un-American partners, but ultimately the group split after a string of losses.

His last match for WWE was at the first *One Night Stand* against former partner Chris Jericho. He semi-retired from active ring competition in 2007. Today this technically gifted athlete trains prospects for a career in the ring at the Storm Wrestling Academy.

LANNY POFFO
HT: 6'0"   WT: 236 lbs.   FROM: Downers Grove, Illinois
SIGNATURE MOVE: Honor Roll

Lanny Poffo has the unique distinction of being one of WWE's most-admired Superstars, as well as one of the most despised. Affectionately known as "Leaping" Lanny, Poffo amazed audiences with his high-flying ability. Many credit him for introducing the moonsault to American arenas in the mid-1980s. Additionally, Poffo's arsenal of aerial attacks included a breathtaking backflip off the top rope, which some consider a precursor to today's Swanton Bomb.

Poffo complemented his remarkable wrestling talent with an aptitude for writing poetry. Prior to each match, he would recite one of his witty limericks before throwing Frisbees out to the crowd. Poffo's rhymes made him one of the most-beloved Superstars of his time.

In 1989, Poffo's poetry began to take a hurtful twist. The once fun-loving Superstar started to use his words to verbally attack the fans and their favorites, such as Hulk Hogan. Claiming to possess superior intellect, Poffo renamed himself The Genius. He would go on to become one of the most hated Superstars of his time.

LARRY "THE AXE" HENNIG

HT: 6'1"   **WT:** 275 lbs.   **FROM:** Robbinsdale, Minnesota

More recent WWE fans might only recognize Larry "The Ax" Hennig as the father of Mr. Perfect. Longtime fans know him as one of the toughest Superstars of the 1960s and 1970s. Following a championship high school wrestling career, Hennig was awarded a scholarship to compete at the University of Minnesota. Though he never cashed in on his full scholarship, he used the opportunity to develop impeccable amateur skills, which he later brought to the professional ranks.

Debuting in the early 1960s, Hennig quickly established himself as a tag-team specialist. His earliest partners were Duke Hoffman and The Viking; both pairings resulted in title reigns. However, it wasn't until he formed a union with the legendary Harley Race that Hennig truly began to be recognized as a true ring warrior. The duo won their first tag titles (AWA) in 1965. Over the next two years, the powerhouse team would go on to claim three more reigns in two separate promotions. An unfortunate knee injury knocked Hennig out of action in 1967, thus marking the end of the momentum he gained while teaming with Race.

Late in his career, Hennig experienced the greatest thrill a wrestling father could imagine when he teamed with his son, WWE Hall of Famer Curt Hennig, to capture the NWA Pacific Northwest Tag Team Championship.

LARRY SHARPE

FROM: New Jersey

Larry Sharpe joined WWE in 1974 after a successful amateur wrestling career, which ultimately resulted in an induction into the New Jersey College Hall of Fame. However, Sharpe was unable to reclaim the magic he created on the amateur level. He then went on to look for success in other wrestling promotions, including Stampede Wrestling. While a member of Stu Hart's Stampede promotion, Sharpe captured the International Tag Team Championship with his partner Ripper Collins.

Despite moderate success in the ring, Sharpe is most known for training many of the sport's top names, including Big Show, Bam Bam Bigelow, and Kevin Von Erich.

LARRY ZBYSZKO

HT: 5'9"   **WT:** 233 lbs.   **FROM:** Pittsburgh, Pennsylvania
SIGNATURE MOVE: Piledriver

TITLE HISTORY

WORLD TAG TEAM CHAMPION	Partnered with Tony Garea to defeat the Yukon Lumberjacks on November 21, 1978

After growing up as a close family friend of Bruno Sammartino, Larry Zbyszko became his protégé in 1972. Audiences loved his excellent technical skills and sportsmanship, and the fire he displayed when getting back at an opponent for breaking the rules.

Zbyszko left the WWE breifly, but returned in 1976. In 1978, he teamed with Tony Garea to become a World Tag Team Champion. At the end of the decade, Zbyszko's frustration as being known chiefly as Sammartino's pupil boiled over, and he attacked his teacher during a technical exhibition. The attack lead to a Steel Cage Match at the 1980 *Showdown At Shea*. The attack is remembered as one of the most shocking acts of betrayal in sports-entertainment.

He soon left WWE but excelled at every stop he made, from the AWA to WCW. After retiring from active competition, he became an announcer for WCW until it closed its doors in 2001.

LAUREN MAYHEW

FROM: Tampa, Florida

Lauren Mayhew is no stranger to the spotlight. She began her entertainment career in 1998, when she appeared as Marah Lewis on the hit daytime soap *Guiding Light*. She was then cast to appear on several other television series, such as *Law & Order*, *CSI: Crime Scene Investigation* and *CSI: Miami* before landing a role in the straight-to-DVD movie *American Pie Presents: Band Camp*.

As a singer, Mayhew was a member of the all-girl group PYT (Prove Yourself True). The quartet split in 2002, but not before appearing live on the Super Bowl XXXV pregame show and touring with Britney Spears, Destiny's Child and 'N Sync.

In October 2009, Mayhew took her talents to WWE, where she served as the ring announcer for ECW. She also sang the National Anthem prior to the start of each WWE event. Mayhew's stay with WWE was a short one. In November 2009, just weeks after making her debut, Mayhew and WWE parted ways.

LAYLA

HT: 5'3" **FROM:** Miami, Florida

TITLE HISTORY

WOMEN'S CHAMPION	Defeated Beth Phoenix on May 14, 2010

This fiery WWE Diva was a dancer for the NBA's Miami Heat before she won the 2006 *Diva Search*. She made her first WWE appearance at *SummerSlam*. Layla brought her unreal appeal to *SmackDown* before she joined ECW. In ECW, Layla joined Kelly Kelly and Brooke to form the tantalizing Extreme Exposé. After the trio acrimoniously dissolved their partnership, Layla was drafted to *Raw* during the 2008 Supplemental Draft. When she joined forces with Michelle McCool in 2009, Layla found her greatest success. Known as Team Lay-Cool, the duo terrorized other Divas and became Women's Champion when Layla pinned Beth Phoenix in a Handicap Match. In October 2010, Layla was in Michelle McCool's corner during when she successfully unified the Women's and Divas Championships. The loss of the Divas Championship at the *Royal Rumble* in 2011 split the team, and an injury forced Layla to take time away from the ring.

Since her WWE debut, Layla has experienced mainstream attention including features in *King*, *JET*, *Smooth* and *FHM* in addition to appearing on *Family Feud* and *Project Runway*. In April 2008, she was also a featured trainer on *Celebrity Fit Club Boot Camp*.

LEE WONG **FROM:** Hong Kong

Lee Wong from Hong Kong was on the wrong side of nearly every match in which he competed. He began his WWE career in the early 1970s, where he regularly fattened the wallets of future WWE Hall of Famers Killer Kowalski, George "The Animal" Steele and Mr. Fuji.

After WWE, Wong travelled down the East Coast. Competitors from each territory along the way welcomed him with open arms. He eventually reached Florida, where he made the Sunshine State's stars look good before turning around and returning to WWE.

Wong's second tour of duty with WWE was much like his first: Unsuccessful. By this time, he appeared to beef up his martial arts repertoire, but his karate chops rarely succeeded in eliciting fear from his foes. Instead, Blackjack Mulligan, Pedro Morales, "The Russian Bear" Ivan Koloff and the rest of the WWE locker room simply saw Wong as another win on their resumé.

THE LEGACY

MEMBERS: Randy Orton, Cody Rhodes, Ted DiBiase

A generation ago, "Cowboy" Bob Orton, Dusty Rhodes and Ted DiBiase travelled the globe, earning their reputations as some of the toughest men to ever lace up a pair of boots. Fast forward a few decades and these legends were enshrined in WWE Hall of Fame, but their sons—Randy Orton, Cody Rhodes and Ted DiBiase—attempted to carry on their family legacies.

Collectively known as Legacy, Orton, Rhodes and DiBiase all possess the same superior ring skills as their fathers before them. Just in case members of the WWE Universe forgot that fact, Legacy was happy to remind people of their natural abilities, raw aggression and disregard for the rules. It was this unmatched level of arrogance that helped the trio become one of the least-liked groups in WWE.

Unfortunately for their detractors, Legacy's success in the ring could not be questioned. During their year-plus together, the multi-generational trio racked up a near spotless win-loss record, particularly their leader, Orton, who claimed three WWE Championship reigns.

In early 2010, a series of miscues by Rhodes and DiBiase cost Orton some high-profile matches. Not long after, the once-powerful faction began to crumble. Finally at *WrestleMania XXVI*, all three Legacy members squared off in a Triple Threat Match, with Orton emerging victorious.

Legion of Doom (see page 214)

LEILANI KAI

HT: 5'7" **FROM:** Hawaii
SIGNATURE MOVE: Aloha Splash

TITLE HISTORY

WOMEN'S WORLD TAG TEAM CHAMPION (2 TIMES)	*Partnered with Judy Martin to defeat Velvet McIntyre & Desiree Peterson on August 15, 1985* *Partnered with Judy Martin to defeat the Jumping Bomb Angels on June 8, 1988*
WOMEN'S CHAMPION	*Defeated Wendi Richter on February 18, 1985*

Competitors don't come much tougher than this woman from Hawaii. Trained by Fabulous Moolah, she began her career in local promotions in the mid-1970s. In 1977, she joined WWE and became an instant contender for the championship held by her teacher.

In 1985, she beat Wendi Richter at *The War To Settle The Score* for the Women's Championship. Shortly after her loss to Richter at *WrestleMania*, Kai formed a team with another Moolah protégé, Judy Martin. Known as the Glamour Girls, Kai and Martin defeated Velvet McIntyre & Desiree Peterson in a wild championship bout in Cairo, Egypt. When they returned to America, they found a new manager in "Mouth of the South" Jimmy Hart. The Girls traded title reigns with the Jumping Bomb Angels until retiring as the champions in 1989. Leilani left WWE, but returned briefly in 1994. She competed in World Championship Wrestling until the late 1990s, and today she remains active in the independent scene all over the world.

1960-69 ▼ 1970-79 ▼ 1980-89 ▼ 1990-99 ▼ 2000-09 ▼ 2010-

LEGION OF DOOM

MEMBERS: Hawk, Animal, Paul Ellering   **COMBINED WT:** 530 lbs.

TITLE HISTORY

WORLD TAG TEAM CHAMPIONS (2 TIMES)	Defeated The Nasty Boys on August 26, 1991 Defeated The Godwinns on October 7, 1997

The Legion of Doom snacked on danger and dined on death for nearly two decades. Along the way, the face-painted Superstars earned a reputation as history's most influential tag team.

Hawk & Animal first came together in 1983 as part of "Precious" Paul Ellering's nine-man stable, the Legion of Doom. The duo's dominance eventually earned them sole ownership of the L.O.D. name. Behind the power of their devastating Doomsday Device—a clothesline delivered by Hawk to a battered opponent sitting on Animal's shoulders—L.O.D. became a world-renowned force before first setting their feet in a WWE ring in 1990.

L.O.D. made an immediate impact upon their arrival, helping the Hart Foundation capture the World Tag Team Championship from Demolition. Over the course of the next year, Hawk & Animal made quick work of such teams as Power & Glory and the Orient Express. Their dominance eventually lead them past the Nasty Boys at *SummerSlam 1991*, earning the duo their first taste of the World Tag Team Championship.

Hawk & Animal quietly left WWE in 1992, only to make a shocking return five years later. Many feared the 1997 version of L.O.D. were too long in the tooth to compete with the promotion's younger teams. They quickly put those fears to rest when they defeated the Godwinns to reclaim the World Tag Team Championship. They held the titles for nearly two months before losing them to the up-and-coming New Age Outlaws.

Following the loss, Hawk & Animal slightly reinvented themselves as L.O.D. 2000. Led by the lovely Sunny, the recharged duo picked up their final major victory when they won the *WrestleMania XIV* Tag Team Battle Royal.

The Legion of Doom that fans recognized as the greatest tag team of all time came to a tragic end when Michael "Hawk" Hegstrand passed away in October 2003. Since that time, Animal has attempted to recreate the magic he made with Hawk, including a WWE Tag Team Championship reign with Heidenreich, but there was only one duo that can make entire arenas stand up in unison and scream, "Oh, what a rush!"

LENA YADA

HT: 5'4"   **FROM:** Honolulu, Hawaii

Lena Yada was a 2007 Diva Search contestant who turned backstage interviewer for ECW. The self-proclaimed "Asian Sensation" was familiar with life in the public eye before her career in sports-entertainment.

In addition to competing as a professional surfer, Lena assembled an impressive acting resume with movie credits that included a role in the box-office hit *I Now Pronounce You Chuck & Larry*. She also landed an appearance on the popular Baywatch parody, *Son of the Beach*. A fitness fanatic, Lena has also used her toned frame to open eyes in many swimsuit competitions. Although her WWE tenure lasted less than one year, she certainly made a lasting impression on the WWE Universe.

LES THORNTON

HT: 5'9"   **WT:** 225 lbs.   **FROM:** Manchester, England

WWE record books are not filled with Les Thornton accomplishments, but that doesn't mean he wasn't a success in the ring. Prior to defining himself as a tough-as-nails Superstar from England, Thornton excelled as a boxer in the British Navy, as well as a professional rugby player. After making his sports-entertainment debut in the late 1950s, Thornton toured the globe, earning the respect of foreign fans. Beirut, New Zealand, Germany and Australia are just a few of the territories he dominated before moving on to North America.

When Thornton arrived in Canada, he began competing for Stu Hart's Stampede Wrestling promotion. While there, he captured the North American Heavyweight Championship twice. Thornton didn't compete for WWE until the latter days of his career. During the infancy of WWE's global dominance, the organization recognized Thornton as a Superstar with great international influence. WWE quickly made Thornton a focal point of its overseas tours of the mid-1980s.

LEX LUGER

HT: 6'6" WT: 275 lbs.
FROM: Chicago, Illinois
SIGNATURE MOVE: Running Forearm; Human Torture Rack

After a series of injuries forced him to leave pro football, Lex Luger trained with Hiro Matsuda to learn the art of the ring. Following a celebrated stint in WCW, WWE fans first saw Lex Luger as part of the World Bodybuilding Federation. Luger was officially unveiled at the 1993 *Royal Rumble* as "The Narcissist." He became on one of the most hated Superstars in WWE as before every match he posed in front of full-body mirrors.

That summer, Luger shocked the world on America's birthday. After numerous WWE Superstars and professional athletes failed to slam then-WWE Champion Yokozuna, Luger flew in via helicopter onto the deck of the USS Intrepid to answer the call. In a Herculean display of strength, Luger lifted and slammed the 600-plus pound champion. As everyone in attendance rejoiced, the days of "The Narcissist" were gone and WWE's "American Original" had arrived.

Covered in the red, white and blue of the USA, Luger embarked on the "Lex Express," a nationwide bus tour during which he campaigned for a shot at the WWE Championship. Millions of fans from far and wide answered the call to support him. Lex received a shot at Yokozuna's title at *SummerSlam 1993*, but Luger won by countout, and the title remained with the giant sumo. Luger wasn't done with Yokozuna, however. Luger and Bret "Hit Man" Hart were declared co-winners of the 1994 *Royal Rumble*. They both had a chance to capture the WWE Championship from Yokozuna at *WrestleMania X*. Unfortunately for Lex, the title wasn't in the cards, as Hart defeated Yokozuna for the title.

He went on to form a popular team with the British Bulldog, dubbed The Allied Powers. The duo faced off against the Million-Dollar Corporation and were considered top contenders for the World Tag Team Championship. In September 1995, Lex suddenly left WWE, making a shocking appearance on the initial episode of *WCW Monday Nitro,* which was widely acknowledged as the first major salvo of the Monday Night War.

LIGHT HEAVYWEIGHT CHAMPIONSHIP

The now-defunct Light Heavyweight championship was initially awared in 1997 at a tournament during the *In Your House: Degeneration X* Pay Per View. Eight of the greatest Light Heavyweights in the world competed. Taka Michinoku, Brian Christopher, Super Loco, and Águila were among the participants. During its existence the Light Heavyweight Championship changed hands 13 times, totaling 11 different champions including Christian, Jeff Hardy, Dean Malenko, X-Pac, and Taijiri.

1997

December 7
Springfield, MA

Taka Michinoku defeated Brian Christopher in the finals of the Light Heavyweight tournament

▼

1998

October 18
Rosemont, IL

Christian defeated Taka Michinoku

▼

November 19
Columbus, OH

Gillberg defeated Christian

▼

2000

February 10
Austin, TX

Essa Rios defeated Gillberg

▼

March 13
East Rutherford, NJ

Dean Malenko defeated Essa Rios

▼

April 17
State College, PA

Scotty 2 Hotty defeated Dean Malenko

▼

April 27
Charlotte, NC

Dean Malenko defeated Scotty 2 Hotty

▼

2001

March 15
Anaheim, CA

Crash Holly defeated Dean Malenko

▼

April 29
Chicago, IL

Jerry Lynn defeated Crash Holly

▼

June 7
Grand Forks, ND

Jeff Hardy defeated Jerry Lynn

▼

June 25
New York, NY

X-Pac defeated Jeff Hardy

▼

August 6
Anaheim, CA

Taijiri defeated X-Pac

▼

August 19
San Jose, CA

X-Pac defeated Taijiri

The title was abandoned in 2001 when WWE put the WCW/ECW Alliance out of business. The WCW Cruiserweight Championship was then adopted as the WWE Cruiserweight Championship.

2010-
2000-09
1990-99
1980-89
1970-79
1960-69

LILIAN GARCIA

Lilian Garcia has done the ring announcing for some of sports-entertainment's most historic matches. Along the way, her melodious tone has become synonymous with the success of WWE's flagship program, *Monday Night Raw*.

In addition to announcing, Lilian is an accomplished vocalist. Prior to each *Raw*, the beautiful Diva showed off her talents with an emotional rendition of *The Star-Spangled Banner*. She has also opened up for many professional sports teams, including the New York Jets and Phoenix Suns. The popularity of her amazing voice eventually lead to the production of her own album, *¡Quiero Vivir!*, which was released in October 2007.

Being as talented as Lilian is, it was only a matter of time before a WWE Superstar made a pass at her. In May 2005, the inevitable occurred when the mighty Viscera proclaimed his love for the ring announcer. On the surface, Lilian and Big Vis didn't look like the prototypical couple; but inside, they shared a deep connection. Or so Lilian thought. In June, a smitten Lilian proposed marriage to her man. She was ultimately heartbroken when he chose to be with The Godfather's ladies rather than marry her. After a remarkable 10-year career with WWE, Lilian bid farewell to her fans on September 21, 2009. Thankfully, this turned out to be a two year sabbatical and this Diva's angelic voice, returned to WWE rings on *SmackDown*.

LINDA McMAHON

Born in New Bern, North Carolina, Linda Marie Edwards was a Southern belle like no other. She was a member of the Girl Scouts of America, an honor student who enjoyed sports and a part of her church choir. One day after service, she met a young Vince McMahon, and it was love at first sight. When the two wed in 1966, Vince promised her two things, "I'll always love you, and there will never be a dull moment." Vince quickly learned that was going to be a two-way street.

After she graduated from East Carolina University, the McMahons moved to Washington, DC. In 1979, Linda and Vince relocated to Massachusetts and created Titan Sports. After purchasing the Cape Cod Coliseum, they promoted various events, from professional wrestling to rock concerts and professional hockey. In 1980, they incorporated Titan Sports, and in 1982, bought Capitol Wrestling Corporation from Vince's father. Linda and Vince gave World Wrestling Entertainment the opportunity to be seen beyond the geographic region of the Northeast and marketed as the premier form of entertainment.

Their revolutionary approach helped cultivate WWE's broader appeal, which led to syndication and later national and international television contracts. The McMahons ran these activities concurrently with new branding and trademarking initiatives that put World Wrestling Entertainment in a class by itself.

Linda negotiated and implemented WWE's first-ever licensing contract with then-industry leading toy company LJN to produce the WWE Superstar action figures. Today, that product line is considered a classic within the toy business and is sought-after by collectors. She also managed the development of WWE publications, and in the beginning wrote a majority of the articles. This foresight, drive and success were a harbinger of the multi-million dollar revenue streams that Linda would go on to create for the company. In 1993, she became President of WWE and in 1997, was made its Chief Executive Officer. Under Linda's leadership, the company continued to prosper. In October 1999, WWE undertook a successful initial public offering and today trades on the New York Stock Exchange.

In addition to her brilliant business accomplishments and performance in front of the camera, Linda was instrumental in nurturing WWE's community and charitable pursuits.

She spearheaded the creation of WWE's Get R.E.A.L. educational programs, as well as the company's nationwide WrestleMania Reading Challenge. She also led the development of WWE's Smackdown Your Vote! with partners including the League of Women Voters, the National Association of Secretaries of State, and the Harvard Institute of Politics.

In recognition for work over the past 20 years to support children, The Make-A-Wish Foundation awarded WWE its highest honor, the Chris Grecius Award in 2004. In honor of the company's efforts for over two decades, Linda was appointed to The Make-A-Wish Foundation of America National Advisory Council in 2005.

From: Greenwich, Connecticut

During the "Attitude" Era, WWE programming became a family affair. As her husband and two children, Shane and Stephanie, ran roughshod throughout the company, Linda was often the sensible voice of reason who upheld the honor of World Wrestling Entertainment and kept the family in line. Although at times it was a struggle to maintain order, she always achieved her goal.

She is also a major supporter of The Starlight Foundation Research Foundation and the USO. In addition, Linda served as the Honorary Corporate Chair of the Multiple Myeloma Research Foundation and on the Governor's Council for the World Special Olympics. Linda continues to be a visionary in the world of philanthropy and business.

In 2007, she was named one of Multichannel News' Wonder Woman award recipients, recognizing her accomplishments with WWE and as a leader in the U.S. cable television industry. Linda also guided the strategic direction of World Wrestling Entertainment's content and products that were distributed on a global basis via broadcast, syndication and cable television, publications, mobile phones, and the Internet. Other key businesses areas included licensing, merchandising, home video, e-commerce, and catalog sales.

For over three decades, the work of Linda McMahon was a critical component to the success of a company that was once run out of a basement with a staff of two. Now, it is an integrated, multi-billion dollar, publicly traded media giant. While the McMahon family shares a sense of pride in World Wrestling Entertainment, Linda McMahon was the power behind the throne until Fall, 2009. It was then she announced she was leaving WWE in the capable hands of its executive team to follow another life-long passion, public service. Since then, Linda has dedicated her professional life to the people of her home-state of Connecticut, improving its local economy and overall quality of life.

While her day-to-day work in WWE is behind her, Linda's ground-breaking achievements while shaping a global entertainment entity should inspire generations to come.

LITA

HT: 5'6"
FROM: Sanford, North Carolina
SIGNATURE MOVE: Litacanrana

TITLE HISTORY

WOMEN'S CHAMPION (4 TIMES)	Defeated Stephanie McMahon on August 21, 2000 Defeated Trish Stratus on December 6, 2004 Defeated Mickie James on August 14, 2006 Defeated Mickie James on November 5, 2006

When Lita first arrived in WWE, she became instantly recognizable by her fiery red hair, gigantic shoulder tattoo, and high-flying ring presence. By the time she left, however, Lita was widely known for her lewd actions and questionable behavior.

Lita joined WWE in 2000 and quickly made a name for herself as the valet of Essa Rios. However, when jealousy drove a wedge between the two, she shifted her allegiances to the Hardy Boys. Known as Team Xtreme, the threesome went on to wow crowds with their acrobatic offense for nearly five years. During this period, Lita also developed a romantic relationship with Matt Hardy.

As an in-ring competitor, Lita enjoyed four reigns as Women's Champion. Her first came at the expense of Stephanie McMahon-Helmsley in August 2000. The match, which was officiated over by The Rock, was the first *Raw* main event to feature competition from the Women's Division.

Lita's meteoric rise to the top came crashing down in 2002 when she suffered a neck injury while shooting scenes for FOX's *Dark Angel*. The injury proved so severe that major surgery was required, which forced Lita out of action for a year and a half.

In 2004, Lita became the object of Kane's sadistic desires. When she refused to give in to his advances, he began tormenting her boyfriend, Matt Hardy. Fearing for Matt's wellbeing, Lita eventually caved in to Kane's demands as a way to halt the monster's constant attacks. However, this was just the first of two indiscretions she hoped Matt would never discover.

The following year, Lita began a romantic relationship with Edge while she was still involved with Matt. When it became public, the three Superstars engaged in the ugliest love triangle in sports-entertainment history. To make matters worse for the broken-hearted Matt, Lita and Edge continually flaunted their love for the entire world to see. They even engaged in a highly publicized celebration following Edge's WWE Championship victory in January 2006.

Lita left WWE following a loss to Mickie James at *Survivor Series* 2006. It was a bittersweet moment for the Diva, as she was finally given the opportunity to keep her private life out of the spotlight.

LITTLE BEAVER

HT: 4'6"   WT: 60 lbs.   From: Quebec, Canada
SIGNATURE MOVE: Dropkick

In 1948, Little Beaver made his debut, sporting a mohawk and a full-length headdress. He became one of the most popular Superstars in the world and in 1963 he joined WWE. His battles with rival Sky Low Low made headlines in wrestling publications everywhere. In September 1972, Little Beaver teamed with Little Louie against Sonny Boy Hayes and Pee Wee Adams at the first-ever *Showdown At Shea*.

The highest and lowest points of his career may have come in the same night. At *WrestleMania III* he teamed with Hillbilly Jim and Haiti Kid in a mixed tag against King Kong Bundy, Lord Littlebrook, and Little Tokyo but received an elbow drop from King Kong Bundy. Little Beaver never competed again.

In December 1996, Little Beaver passed away at 61 years old.

L

2010-

2000-09

1990-99

1980-89

1970-79

1960-69

LITTLE BOOGEYMAN

From: The Bottomless Pit
SIGNATURE MOVE:
Pump Handle Slam

This little worm eater appeared in WWE alongside his larger counterpart in 2007 during the Boogeyman's rivalry with Finlay. "Little Boogey" was brought to the world of sports-entertainment to counter the presence of Hornswoggle. As the two beings from the Bottomless Pit battled Ireland's toughest sons, the shorter version showed he was just as disgusting and just as dangerous in the ring.

History has shown that the Superstars of WWE are never safe as long as the Boogeyman is around. Where he dwells, this frightening miniature sidekick is somewhere close.

LITTLE BRUTUS

Little Brutus competed in WWE's Northeast territory during midget wrestling's surge in popularity in the 1960s. During this time, he wrestled mainly as a tag team competitor, alongside Sky Low Low, Billy the Kid and Butch Cassidy. Chief rival Jamaica Kid normally upended the bearded Brutus during these encounters. In October 1969, Brutus gained the ultimate revenge when he defeated Jamaica Kid in one-on-one action in Boston.

After his in-ring career came to a close, Little Brutus turned to training future midget wrestlers. His most noted pupil was Dink the Clown.

LITTLE TOKYO HT: 4'7"   WT: 45 lbs.
SIGNATURE MOVE: Flying Chop

One of the most successful midget stars of the ring during the 1970s and 1980s, Little Tokyo took WWE by storm in 1975 and performed in packed arenas all over the northeast section of the United States.

Over the years Tokyo developed an intense rivalry with Cowboy Lang over who was the best midget wrestler in the world. As sports-entertainment grew, Little Tokyo was there to do his part, appearing at *WrestleMania III* in the mixed tag match with King Kong Bundy and Lord Littlebrook to square-off against Hillbilly Jim, Little Beaver and Haiti Kid.

Few Superstars in any era of any physical stature enjoyed the years of success that Little Tokyo did. He is remembered fondly as a gifted performer who withstood the test of time.

LO DOWN MEMBERS: D-Lo Brown, Chaz
COMBINED WEIGHT: 511 lbs.

Prior to 2000, both D-Lo Brown and Chaz enjoyed championship-caliber WWE careers. When they decided to unite as Lo Down in July 2000, fans everywhere assumed the same level of success would follow the talented tandem. It didn't.

Shortly after forming Lo Down, D-Lo & Chaz employed the managerial services of Tiger Ali Singh. The duo began to dress like their manager, complete with turbans. Their won-loss record also resembled that of Singh's, which wasn't very impressive.

Lo Down's biggest win came at the expense of Kaientai. Competing on *Heat*, D-Lo & Chaz turned back the Japanese combination to earn a spot in the 2001 *Royal Rumble*. However, they never made it to the *Royal Rumble*. Instead, comedian Drew Carey took their spot.

LORD ALFRED HAYES   HT: 5'9"   WT: 238 lbs.   FROM: Windermere, England
SIGNATURE MOVE: London Bridge

When he debuted in WWE in 1982, he was retired form the active competition. In his earlier years, Lord Alfred Hayes was known throughout Europe, Japan and parts of the National Wrestling Alliance as a dangerous grappler and crafty champion.

WWE audiences first saw the Lord as Vince McMahon's partner in crime on the hit talk show *Tuesday Night Titans*. From there Alfred's pleasant demeanor became regularly seen on WWE programming as he served as a backstage interview correspondent, introductory announcer and color commentator. As WWE's business expanded their home video business exploded and Lord Alfred was a major part of several of the products released during that time. Hayes continued his excellent work into the 1990s as he was seen on early episodes of *Monday Night Raw*. In 1995, Alfred and WWE parted ways after a successful partnership that lasted over a decade.

He retired from sports-entertainment and quietly enjoyed the fruits of his labor in his adopted home state of Texas. Sadly, in July 2005 this WWE legend passed away at his home. Lord Alfred Hayes spent decades as one of the top figures in sports-entertainment, whether it was in the ring or behind the microphone.

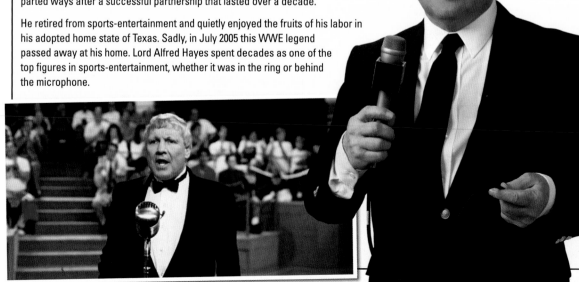

LORD LITTLEBROOK

HT: 4'4" WT: 108 lbs.
FROM: London, England

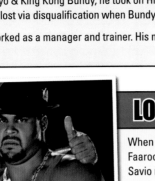

Hailing from London, England, Lord Littlebrook possessed many of the same noble qualities today's fans see in William Regal, only much less annoying. Complete with his monocle and plaid jacket, the midget wrestler looked every bit the part of a proper Englishman.

While competing in the United States, Littlebrook managed to capture the NWA World Midget Championship in 1966. He also garnered much attention during his days in the AWA. However, it was his *WrestleMania III* match that will always remain Littlebrook's ultimate highlight. Teaming with Little Tokyo & King Kong Bundy, he took on Hillbilly Jim and his midget friends, Haiti Kid & Little Beaver. In the end, Littlebrook's team lost via disqualification when Bundy inexplicably attacked Beaver.

After his in-ring career came to an end, Littlebrook worked as a manager and trainer. His most noted pupil, Butch Reed, also competed at *WrestleMania III*.

LOS BORICUAS

MEMBERS: Savio Vega, Miguel Perez, Jose Estrada Jr., Jesus Castillo

When Superstar Savio Vega was physically removed from the Nation of Domination by Faarooq he was driven to seek out for revenge. When he returned in the summer of 1997, Savio made it clear that he was not alone. The four man gang from Puerto Rico then rushed the ring in a brawl that ended up involving Los Boricuas, the Nation of Domination and the Disciples of Apocalypse.

All four men were driven to beat on anyone who stepped to them in and out of the ring. Los Boricuas took on LOD 2000, the New Blackjacks, the Headbangers and D-Generation X while pursuing tag team and singles championships. In June 1998, the Boricuas went their separate ways. While each member has seen success in their own rights elsewhere, Los Boricuas will be remembered as one of the most dangerous groups in WWE during the late 1990s.

LOS CONQUISTADORS

Men underneath gold masks entered World Wrestling Entertainment in 1987. They were conquerors of the ring in other parts of the world but traveled to WWE to face the best tag teams in the world. Their disregard for the rules did not win them any fans and in most instances it did not help win matches either. Their win/loss record was not a true indicator of their abilities in the ring and they were always considered a dangerous tag team.

The Conquistadors gave a glimpse of their old world form at the inaugural *Survivor Series* when they were the last team fighting for victory. Though they went down in a losing effort, that impressive showing kept them in the World Tag Team Title hunt.

Since their departure in the late 1980s the masked men have made sporadic appearances in WWE, even as recently as 2003. Both fans and Superstars alike have questions whether or not these recent appearances are the originals or other Superstars assuming the golden identities for nefarious purposes.

LOS GUERREROS

MEMBERS: Eddie Guerrero, Chavo Guerrero   COMBINED WT: 441 lbs.
FROM: El Paso, Texas

TITLE HISTORY

WWE TAG TEAM CHAMPIONS (2 TIMES)	*Defeated Edge & Rey Mysterio on November 17, 2002* *Defeated Shelton Benjamin & Charlie Haas on September 18, 2003*

They lie. They cheat. They steal. Despite their immoral qualities, Los Guerreros were one of the most popular tag teams of their time.

Eddie Guerrero started teaming with his nephew, Chavo, during the summer of 2002. After cheating their way to victory over many of *SmackDown*'s finest tag teams, they were entered into a tournament to crown the first-ever WWE Tag Team Champions. Unfortunately for Los Guerreros, they fell short in the semifinals.

Eddie & Chavo rebounded from the defeat well. Only one month after the loss, they found themselves on top of the tag team mountain when they won a Triple Threat Match to capture the titles at *Survivor Series 2002*. They went on to hold the gold for three months before losing to Shelton Benjamin & Charlie Haas.

The dastardly uncle-nephew combination enjoyed one more reign atop the tag division before Chavo brutally attacked Eddie in January 2004, signifying the end of the adored Los Guerreros. After the breakup, both Guerreros went on to lie, cheat, and steal their way to great singles success.

LOU ALBANO

HT: 5'10"
WT: 350 lbs.
FROM: Carmel, New York

TITLE HISTORY

UNITED STATES TAG TEAM CHAMPION	Partnered with Tony Altomare to defeat Spiros Arion & Arnold Skaaland on July 10, 1967

Capt. Lou Albano was a short, round man with limited wrestling ability, but that didn't stop him from becoming one of the greatest entertainers the industry has ever seen. After a brilliant five decades in the wrestling business, the eccentric Albano will forever be remembered for managing an unprecedented number of champions, an amazing speaking ability and, believe it or not, rubber bands hanging from his face.

Albano originally hoped to make a name for himself as a boxer, but after promoter Willy Gilzenberg refused to use him due to his short stature, he turned his efforts toward professional wrestling. After being trained by the legendary Arnold Skaaland and Soldier Barry, Albano began his professional career competing in front of miniscule audiences around the New York area. He eventually worked up to more prestigious promotions in Canada and Chicago. While in the Windy City, Albano began teaming with fellow Italian Tony Altomare. Collectively known as the Sicilians, Albano & Altomare attracted great controversy due to their mafia innuendos.

A Managerial Move

In 1967, The Sicilians jumped to WWE where they immediately claimed the United States Tag Team Championship from Spiros Arion & Arnold Skaaland. Despite his success in the tag ranks, it was clear that Albano's wrestling skills were not going to carry him much further. So rather than settle for a career of mediocrity, Albano made the decision to jump into the managerial ranks. The move proved to be a wise one, as Albano spent the next quarter-century cementing his legacy as one of the greatest wrestling managers ever.

Albano's first client was the powerhouse Crusher Verdu. Like Albano, Verdu never seemed destined for greatness, but with Albano leading the way, he eventually earned an opportunity at Bruno Sammartino's WWE Championship. Unfortunately, Verdu failed in his attempts to unseat Sammartino, but glory was right around the corner for Albano.

In January 1971, Albano's protégé Ivan Koloff ended one of history's greatest title reigns when he defeated Sammartino for the WWE Championship. The win ended Sammartino's nearly eight-year run at the top and catapulted Albano straight to the top of the managerial ranks.

The Golden Touch

In the years that followed, Albano also lead many of WWE's most hated Superstars to the Intercontinental Championship. Pat Patterson, Don Muraco, and Greg Valentine all employed the services of Albano en route to claiming the Intercontinental title.

Despite all his success guiding Superstars to singles titles, Albano's greatest managerial accomplishments are from his time spent in the tag team ranks. Over the course of his career, Albano lead an amazing 17 teams to tag team titles, more than any other man in sports-entertainment history. His list of championship duos includes such legendary teams as the Valiant Brothers, the Blackjacks, the Wild Samoans, and the British Bulldogs.

Albano also helped launch the "Rock 'n' Wrestling Connection" that took America by storm in the mid-1980s. His famed friendship with rocker Cyndi Lauper landed him in the *Girls Just Want to Have Fun* music video. In turn, Lauper appeared on several WWE televised events, including the first-ever *WrestleMania*. The on-air chemistry between Albano and Lauper made national news and eventually helped propel WWE into the mainstream.

Albano took his rightful place alongside wrestling's greatest when he was inducted into the WWE Hall of Fame in 1996. The honor was the ultimate sign of respect for an amazing entertainer who was often imitated, but never duplicated.

Sadly, the world lost one of its most influential performers on October 14, 2009 when Lou passed away at the age of 76. He's survived by his loving family, friends, and a performance portfolio that's unmatched within the realms of sports-entertainment.

LOU THESZ

HT: 6'2" **WT:** 225 lbs.
FROM: St. Louis, Missouri
SIGNATURE MOVE: Lou Thesz Press

Lou Thesz debuted in St. Louis at age 16. Trained by Ray Steele and Greek Olympian George Tragos, Thesz later studied under Ad Santel to learn painful submission locks. In December 1937 he became the youngest World Heavyweight Champion in history at 21 years of age. Thesz also had historic encounters with "Nature Boy" Buddy Rogers in early 1963, which influenced the formation of the World Wide Wrestling Federation.

Thesz continued to compete throughout the 1970s all over the world as a featured competitor and special guest referee. During the 1980s he made appearances for World Wrestling Entertainment, most notably in November 1987 when he emerged the victor in a Legends Battle Royal.

Remarkably, Thesz wrestled his last match on December 26, 1990 in Japan against former student, Masahiro Chono for New Japan Pro Wrestling. He was 74 years old and became the only man to wrestle in seven different decades. Thesz was honored at *Badd Blood* along with other NWA Legends from the St. Louis area like Sam Muchnick, the Funks, Gene Kiniski, Jack Brisco, and Harley Race.

Sadly on April 28, 2002 one of professional wrestling's founding fathers passed away at 86.

LOUIE SPICOLLI

HT: 5'11" **WT:** 258 lbs.
FROM: Los Angeles, California
SIGNATURE MOVE: Spicolli Driver

After he developed a steady following in Mexico and independent promotions throughout the United States, Louie Spicolli made his WWE debut in 1988 and continued to appear intermittently in WWE through the mid 1990s.

In 1996 he debuted in Extreme Championship Wrestling and butted heads with the Innovator of Violence and ECW Original, Tommy Dreamer. After leaving ECW in 1997 he appeared in World Championship Wrestling and was an associate of the New World Order. Spicolli will always be remembered as a gifted Superstar who gave his all whenever in the ring.

LOUIS CERDAN

HT: 5'10" **WT:** 240 lbs. **FROM:** Montreal, Quebec, Canada
SIGNATURE MOVE: Figure-Four Leglock

TITLE HISTORY

WORLD TAG TEAM CHAMPION	Partnered with Tony Parisi to defeat The Blackjacks on November 8, 1975

This French-Canadian began his WWE career in 1966 and was a close friend to then World Champion Bruno Sammartino. For three years, Cerdan showed his fire in the ring, but in 1969 Cerdan left WWE and returned to Canada. In 1974, Cerdan made a glorious return to WWE, teaming with close friend Tony Parisi. In November 1975, the duo defeated the Blackjacks to become World Tag Team Champions. They defended the belts for six months until they crossed paths with the Executioners in May 1976. Cerdan soon left World Wrestling Entertainment and returned to the rings of the Great White North, where he retired after a stellar 25-year career.

LUCKY CANNON

HT: 6'5" **WT:** 238 lbs. **FROM:** New Port Richey, Florida
SIGNATURE MOVE: Lucky Break

How do you get a name like "Lucky?" For Lucky Cannon, unfortunately, it came the hard way.

In 2004, the future *NXT* Rookie's life changed when he was viciously attacked and hit in the back of the head with a lead pipe. The assault left Cannon comatose for three weeks. When he awoke, he had lost his memory, as well as his ability to speak and walk. But he was lucky to be alive.

After a tireless rehabilitation period, Cannon set his mind on becoming a WWE Superstar. He came one step closer to his dream when he was tapped to be a Rookie on season two of *NXT*. With Mark Henry as his Pro, Cannon was able to pick up a handful of tag-team victories, but was ultimately unable to get over the hump. He was the third Rookie eliminated from competition.

In March 2011, Cannon returned to *NXT* for season five. Again, he was the third Rookie eliminated.

LUDVIG BORGA

HT: 6'3" **WT:** 275 lbs.
FROM: Helsinki, Finland
SIGNATURE MOVE:
Human Torture Rack

This Finish powerhouse burst on the scene into World Wrestling Entertainment in 1993. The monster Borga squashed his opponents and showed little respect for the WWE rulebook. Fans quickly came to despise this individual and his spread of anti-American sentiment which resulted in him butting heads with "All-American" Lex Luger.

Borga often withstood the attacks made by many opponents. After picking up a win at *SummerSlam* against Marty Jannetty, he ended the two year undefeated streak of Tatanka, pinning him with one finger.

In early 1994 Borga left World Wrestling Entertainment to travel to Japan. He embarked on a successful professional boxing career, fighting both in the United States and Europe. In recent years he has entered the political arena in his homeland on Finland.

LUKE GALLOWS

HT: 6'7" **WT:** 291 lbs.
SIGNATURE MOVE: Gallows Pole

Festus walked around WWE in a near-comatose state for almost two years. Most found his unresponsiveness to be somewhat entertaining. But not CM Punk. The "Straight Edge Superstar" saw a man struggling with torturous drug abuse and neglect.

In November 2009, Festus revealed that he had been suffering from an apparent addiction to pain medication, which CM Punk helped him overcome. With his dark past behind him, the formerly irregular Superstar transformed into one of the most aggressive and menacing forces of his time: Luke Gallows.

As Gallows, the reformed competitor found a new beginning as the muscle behind Punk's Straight Edge Society, which also included Serena and Joseph Mercury. Additionally, Gallows in-ring victims included some of WWE's brightest stars, such as Rey Mysterio and Matt Hardy.

Gallows eventually lost his spot in the Straight Edge Society when Punk knocked him out with the GTS following an embarrassing loss to Big Show in September 2010. Leaderless, Gallows disappeared from WWE soon after.

LUKE GRAHAM

HT: 6'1" **WT:** 219 lbs.
FROM: Charlotte, North Carolina

TITLE HISTORY	
INTERNATIONAL TAG TEAM CHAMPION	*Partnered with Tarzan Tyler to defeat The Mongols on November 12, 1971*
UNITED STATES TAG TEAM CHAMPION	*Partnered with Jerry Graham to defeat Don McClairty & Argentina Apollo on June 6, 1964*
WORLD TAG TEAM CHAMPION	*Partnered with Tarzan Tyler to defeat Dick the Bruiser & The Sheik on June 3, 1971*

"Crazy" Luke Graham comes from a long line of Grahams who thrived inside the ring. His brothers are Dr. Jerry Graham and WWE Hall of Famers "Superstar "Billy Graham and Eddie Graham. Following them into the business were five of their sons, bringing the multi-generational clan to a total of nine.

Graham began teaming with his brother, Jerry, in Canada in 1963. It was during this time that fans began to recognize him as slightly deranged. Despite his efforts to convince them otherwise, Graham was constantly being called "crazy" by the fans. Infuriated by the chants, the bleached-blond Superstar would oftentimes hold his hands over his ears to drown out the sound, but that only made the crowds chant louder.

Graham's greatest singles success came in 1965 when he won the prestigious WWA Heavyweight Championship from Pedro Morales. The victory proved to be a shining point in Graham's career, but paled in comparison to the groundbreaking win he would earn six years later in WWE.

In June 1971, with Tarzan Tyler as his partner, Graham turned back The Sheik & Dick the Bruiser to become one-half of WWE's first-ever World Tag Team Champions. The historic duo held the gold proudly for six months, paving the way for all the great teams that followed, including the Road Warriors, Hart Foundation, and Hardy Boys.

LUKE GRAHAM & TARZAN TYLER

COMBINED WT: 560 lbs.

TITLE HISTORY	
INTERNATIONAL TAG TEAM CHAMPIONS	*Defeated The Mongols on November 12, 1971*
WORLD TAG TEAM CHAMPIONS	*Defeated Dick the Bruiser & The Sheik on June 3, 1971*

All the great teams that have proudly worn the World Tag Team Championship over the past four decades have one trailblazing tandem to thank for building the titles's strong foundation. On a historic evening in June 1971, Luke Graham & Tarzan Tyler defeated The Sheik & Dick the Bruiser to become the first-ever World Tag Team Champions.

In the six months that followed, Graham & Tyler fended off various combinations of WWE's best. Pedro Morales, Dominic DeNucci, and Chief Jay Strongbow all wanted the new titles wrapped around their waists, but it was Karl Gotch & Rene Goulet who finally unseated the champs in December 1971.

In addition to the World Tag Team Championship, Graham & Tyler also held the now-defunct International Tag Team Championship in late 1971. They went their separate ways shortly after losing their titles, but will forever be remembered as the first in a long line of historic teams to be called champions.

LUNA VACHON 🍁

HT: 5'6"
FROM: Montreal, Quebec, Canada
SIGNATURE MOVE: Luna Eclipse

Boasting names like "The Butcher," "The Mad Dog," and Vivian, the Vachon family spread fear among Superstars for decades. Luna wanted to follow in their footsteps, and after being trained by her aunt and Fabulous Moolah, she made her debuted in Florida in 1986.

In 1993, she brought a unique style to World Wrestling Entertainment, joining forces first with "the Heartbreak Kid" Shawn Michaels, and later "the Beast From The East" Bam Bam Bigelow. She guided Bigelow through his rivalry with Doink, and his sidekick Dink, that led to their match at *WrestleMania X*.

After brief stops in ECW and WCW, Luna returned to WWE in 1997 and managed "the Artist Formerly Known as Goldust." During this time she was involved in a mixed-tag match at *WrestleMania XIII*. Luna later joined the Oddities while on the chase for the Women's Championship.

Luna Vachon left WWE in 2000, but will be remembered for proudly carrying her family legacy into the next millennium. Tragically, Luna Vachon passed away in August, 2010.

LUTHER REIGNS 🇺🇸

HT: 6'5"   WT: 295 lbs.   FROM: Phoenix, Arizona
SIGNATURE MOVE: Reign of Terror

Kurt Angle introduced the world to Luther Reigns in April 2004. With Angle then laid up in a wheelchair, Reigns was hired to be the then-*SmackDown* General Manager's assistant. Essentially, he was brought on board to help Angle get around and aid in certain business dealings. But at nearly 300 pounds, it was only a matter of time before Reigns ditched his suit and began an in-ring career.

After decimating Funaki in his debut, Reigns earned a pay-per-view match against Charlie Haas at *The Great American Bash*. Like Funaki, Haas found himself overmatched by Reigns' impressive power.

Reigns formed a tag team with Mark Jindrak in September 2004. In one of their most memorable moments, the duo distracted Big Show long enough for Angle to chop down "The World's Largest Athlete" with a tranquilizer dart. While out, the trio of Superstars celebrated their conquest by shaving Big Show's head bald.

Prior to his WWE release in May 2005, Reigns stood across the ring from some of the greatest, including Eddie Guerrero, Undertaker and John Cena.

MABEL 🇺🇸

HT: 6'9"   WT: 525 lbs.   FROM: Harlem, New York
SIGNATURE MOVE: Big Splash

TITLE HISTORY

WORLD TAG TEAM CHAMPION	Partnered with Mo to defeat The Quebecers on March 29, 1994

The massive Mabel made his WWE debut in 1993 as a member of the rapping tag team Men on a Mission. Managed by Oscar, Mabel and his partner, Mo, hoped their success inside the ring would serve as a positive influence to inner-city youths struggling to decipher right from wrong.

For the better part of their first year, the duo easily destroyed smaller competition. Their colossal success eventually earned them an opportunity at The Quebecers' World tag titles at *WrestleMania X*. The rapping tandem was unable to walk away with the win, but did manage to capture the titles just days later when they defeated The Quebecers in England. Unfortunately for Mabel & Mo, they lost the titles two days later.

Men on a Mission struggled to get on a winning streak following their championship loss. Their inconsistency lasted for more than one year before they finally developed an unpopular mean streak. Immediately after dismissing the fans' opinions of him, Mabel went on an incredible winning streak, which ultimately resulted in him winning the 1995 *King of the Ring* tournament. As King, he found himself competing in main events all over the world. He even challenged Diesel for the WWE Championship at *SummerSlam*.

THE MACHINES

MEMBERS: Giant Machine, Super Machine, Big Machine

As controversy surrounded the suspension of Andre The Giant in 1986, "Mean" Gene Okerlund traveled to Japan on special assignment. His mission was to find the team that was rumored to be coming to WWE. He found Giant Machine and Big Machine, who were fluent in English and received double master's degrees from the University of Tokyo in Education and Business Administration.

When they debuted alongside Super Machine in a six-man bout, they had a combined weight of 1,129 lbs. Bobby "The Brain" Heenan began a relentless campaign to prove that Giant Machine was actually the suspended Andre The Giant. The Machines often faced against Heenan Family members, sometimes with the aid of additional Machines that bore striking resemblances to other Superstars.

By the end of 1986 the Machines disappeared from WWE. The identities of these men remains one of World Wrestling Entertainment's unsolved mysteries.

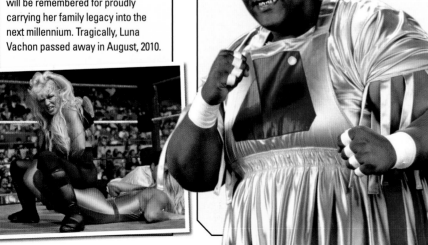

M

1960-69
1970-79
1980-89
1990-99
2000-09
2010-

M

2010-
2000-09
1990-99
1980-89
1970-79
1960-6

MAD DOG VACHON

HT: 5'7" **WT: 230 lbs.** **FROM: Montreal, Quebec, Canada**
SIGNATURE MOVE: Piledriver

At only 5'7", Mad Dog Vachon was oftentimes at a disadvantage well before the opening bell ever rang. What he lacked in size, he more than made up for in determination. The savage sparkplug was known for going at his opposition with ruthless aggression. On the rare occasion he found himself on the wrong end of a beating, he'd usually resort to biting, which made Vachon one of the most hated villains of his time.

The unofficial leader of the Vachon wrestling family, the rabid Mad Dog found his greatest success competing in the AWA. Shortly after his 1986 retirement from the ring, Vachon became the victim of a horrible hit and run accident. He luckily survived the tragedy, but lost his leg in the process. Nearly one decade after the accident, WWE honored Vachon at an *In Your House* pay-per-view. During the show, Diesel actually tore Vachon's prosthetic leg from his body to use as a weapon against Shawn Michaels. The act remains one of the most infamous moments in WWE history. This Olympian and former AWA World Heavyweight Champion received the ultimate honor on March 27, 2010 when he was inducted into the WWE Hall of Fame.

MAD MAXINE
HT: 6'4"

Though she only competed in a handful of WWE matches, Mad Maxine will forever be remembered as one of the most frightening females to ever lace a pair of boots. Standing at an astonishing 6'4" (6'7" if you include her bright green Mohawk in the measurement) and sporting demonic eye makeup, Maxine instilled instant fear into her competition.

Brought into WWE by Fabulous Moolah, Maxine's sole responsibility was to strip Wendi Richter of the Women's Championship. However, before the highly anticipated encounter could ever take place, Maxine mysteriously left WWE.

MAE YOUNG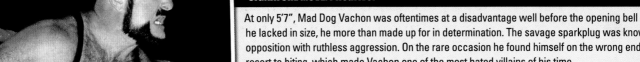

FROM: Sand Springs, Oklahoma

Mae Young has been an influential force in sports-entertainment for seventy years. Yes, you read that right. Seventy years.

A former member of her high school's boys' wrestling team, Young made her professional debut in 1939. Although she was only fifteen years old at the time, Young proved herself as a tough-as-nails competitor. In the decades that followed, Young's efforts helped pave the way for future female Superstars such as The Fabulous Moolah and Judy Grable. Her success eventually lead her to becoming the first United States Women's Champion.

In addition to achieving great in-ring success, Young is known as one of the most influential trainers of both male and female Superstars. Her most noted pupil was perhaps the greatest women's wrestler of all time, The Fabulous Moolah. She also helped mold the early career of Ric "The Equalizer" Drasin, the former lead guitarist of The Hollywood Vines.

Today's WWE fans best recognize Young as the fearless senior citizen who always seems to attract controversy. Her most exposing moment occurred at the 2000 *Royal Rumble* when she flashed a packed Madison Square Garden crowd.

Despite her advanced age, Young isn't afraid to mix it up in the ring. Unfortunately, however, her attempts at physicality usually land her in enormous amounts of trouble. It's not uncommon to see Young flattened by both men and women less than half her age. She was even sent off the stage and through a wooden table at the hands of Bubba Ray Dudley.

In 2008, Young's contributions to women's wrestling were recognized when she was inducted into the WWE Hall of Fame, alongside other great females The Fabulous Moolah and Sherri Martel. Mae continues to appear on WWE television just when you least expect it. She was the guest time keeper for the 25 Diva Battle Royal at *WrestleMania XXV*, 2010's "Old School" *Raw* broadcast, *WrestleMania XXVII*, and even locked lips with The Rock on a May 2011 episode of *Raw*.

MAGNIFICENT MAURICE

Long before "Adorable" Adrian Adonis and Lenny Lane pranced around wrestling rings in an effete fashion, Magnificent Maurice flashed a flamboyant charisma second to none. Maurice oftentimes utilized outrageous antics to get inside his opponents' heads. From there, it was easy for him to take advantage of his mystified foes, en route to victory.

Managed by the equally charismatic Grand Wizard, Maurice took part in many memorable rivalries over the years, including contests against such legends as Bobo Brazil, Pedro Morales, and Bruno Sammartino. Tragically, Magnificent Maurice's life was cut short when he was killed in an airplane crash in January 1974.

THE MAIN EVENT

After the entertainment world saw the incredible success generated by the WWE events *The Brawl To End It All* and *The War To Settle The Score* on MTV, television executives were eager to work with World Wrestling Entertainment. As the revolution known as sports-entertainment began to assault pop culture, NBC and WWE announced that professional wrestling was returning to network television for the first time in decades.

The inaugural episode of *Saturday Night's Main Event* aired on May 11, 1985 from The Nassau Coliseum in Uniondale, NY. That evening fans saw a lineup that included George "The Animal" Steele, The Iron Sheik, Nikolai Volkoff, Junkyard Dog, Fabulous Moolah, "Cowboy" Bob Orton and Hulk Hogan. A new ratings record was set on the March 14, 1987 show that saw Hulk Hogan and Andre the Giant engaged in hostile contact for the first time in a 20-man over-the-top rope Battle Royal right before their monumental clash at *WrestleMania III*.

One of the most memorable moments of **Main Event's first run in the 1980s** was Hulk Hogan losing the WWE Championship, then discovering that the referee who counted him out was paid off by "Million Dollar Man" Ted DiBiase.

The success of the show was so great that in 1988 NBC began to air prime time broadcasts on Friday nights called, *The Main Event*. That first event saw Andre The Giant end the championship reign of Hulk Hogan in a rematch from *WrestleMania III*. WWE changed networks in 1991 and FOX aired both *Saturday Night's Main Event* and *The Main Event* specials in 1992 before it left the airwaves after a historic eight-year run.

In March 2006, WWE and *Saturday Night's Main Event* made its amazing return to network television. Audiences saw a beer drinking contest between Stone Cold Steve Austin and JBL, a Street Fight with Shane McMahon and Shawn Michaels, plus the battle of *WrestleMania* main eventers as John Cena & Triple H teamed against Kurt Angle, Rey Mysterio & Randy Orton. In August 2008, WWE showed again what sports-entertainment is all about as main event caliber bouts that featured Edge, John Cena, Batista, JBL and more were combined with a special appearance by actress Jenny McCarthy.

The Main Event thrilled like no other program on network television and is a show dear to people's hearts. In 2009, WWE Home Video released a special collector's DVD set on the history of this ground-breaking program.

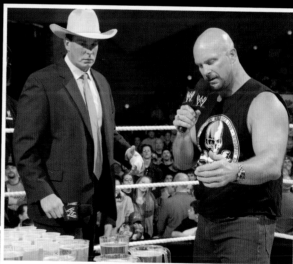

In addition to the more traditional contests shown on the March 2006 show, fans were treated a beer drinking contest between Stone Cold Steve Austin and JBL.

MAN MOUNTAIN MIKE 🇺🇸

HT: 6'4"   **WT:** 600 lbs.
SIGNATURE MOVE: Big Splash

Perhaps no Superstar in sports-entertainment history was more appropriately named than Man Mountain Mike. At an amazing 600 pounds, he was a mountain of a man. After making his debut in 1968, Man Mountain Mike formed a feared tag team with fellow big man Haystacks Calhoun. Together, the pair tipped the scales at more than 1,200 pounds.

With so much weight tacked on to his enormous frame, Man Mountain Mike was nearly impossible to toss over the top rope, which is why Championship Wrestling from Florida billed him as "The Acknowledged King of Battle Royals." While in Los Angeles, Man Mountain Mike teamed with Butcher Brannigan to crush Dr. Wagner & Angel Blanco for the NWA Americas Tag Team Championship in August 1974. They held the titles for two weeks before losing to Porkchop Cash & Victor Rivera.

Man Mountain Mike competed for WWE briefly during the mid-1970s. His stay is most remembered for his teaming with fellow big man Jerry "Crusher" Blackwell.

MAN MOUNTAIN 🇺🇸 ROCK

HT: 6'6"   **WT:** 350 lbs.
SIGNATURE MOVE: Front-Face Suplex

A former All-American wreslter, Man Mountain Rock ripped into WWE in 1995. Man Mountain Rock played his six-string electric guitar before bouts and rocked the crowd with his hard licks and opponents with his mix of power and surprising agility.

The man with tie-dye ring attire unleashed force to villains like Brooklyn Brawler, Kwang, Jean-Pierre LaFitte, Tatanka, Mantaur, Dean Douglas and Bob Backlund. By October 1995, Man Mountain Rock left WWE. Today, he is involved in making motion pictures, but WWE fans will always remember him as the tie-dye Superstar who rocked the house wherever he appeared.

MANTAUR 🇬🇷   **HT:** 6'0"   **WT:** 401 lbs.
FROM: The Isle of Crete

Mantaur is widely considered one of the most unorthodox competitors in WWE history. With his life-sized bull carcass costume and animalistic characteristics, the mighty Superstar was impossible to control, even by his own manager Jim Cornette.

Upon his January 1995 debut, Mantaur made quick work of several lesser-known Superstars. As the weeks passed, the WWE locker room began to outsmart the animal. It wasn't long before the likes of Bret "Hit Man" Hart, Razor Ramon and Man Mountain Rock were pinning his shoulders to the mat. Eventually, the ring proved too wild for Mantaur, who left WWE by year's end.

MANU 🇺🇸

HT: 6'2"   **WT:** 290 lbs.   **FROM:** Lehigh Valley, Pennsylvania
SIGNATURE MOVE: Lights Out

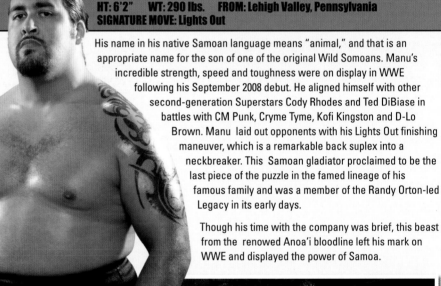

His name in his native Samoan language means "animal," and that is an appropriate name for the son of one of the original Wild Somoans. Manu's incredible strength, speed and toughness were on display in WWE following his September 2008 debut. He aligned himself with other second-generation Superstars Cody Rhodes and Ted DiBiase in battles with CM Punk, Cryme Tyme, Kofi Kingston and D-Lo Brown. Manu laid out opponents with his Lights Out finishing maneuver, which is a remarkable back suplex into a neckbreaker. This Samoan gladiator proclaimed to be the last piece of the puzzle in the famed lineage of his famous family and was a member of the Randy Orton-led Legacy in its early days.

Though his time with the company was brief, this beast from the renowed Anoa'i bloodline left his mark on WWE and displayed the power of Samoa.

MANUEL SOTO 🇵🇷   **HT:** 5'9"   **WT:** 230 lbs.
FROM: Puerto Rico

Manuel Soto was a no-nonsense competitor whose one goal was to use his superior technical ability to walk away with the winner's portion of the purse.

Soto competed mainly on the West Coast, as well as Georgia (under the identity of Cyclone Soto). While in Los Angeles, the Puerto Rican star teamed with the popular Porkchop Cash to wrest away the NWA Americas Tag Team Championship from Goliath & Black Gordman in July 1974. They held the titles for more than a month before losing to Angel Blanco & Dr. Wagner.

In August 1974, Soto defeated Mr. California for the Beat the Champ Television title. He only held the gold for one week before being beat himself. Some historical records refuse to recognize the reign.

Soto enjoyed a short stay in WWE during the mid 1970s. While there, he inspired much of the Puerto Rican fan base of the Northeast with his in-ring ability. One of his greatest victories came over future WWE Hall of Famer "The Unpredictable" Johnny Rodz at Madison Square Garden in 1976.

MARC MERO

HT: 6'1" WT: 235 lbs.
FROM: Macon, Georgia
SIGNATURE MOVE: Merosault

TITLE HISTORY

INTERCONTINENTAL CHAMPION	Defeated Faarooq on September 23, 1996

Few Superstars have made their debut at sports-entertainment's greatest spectacle. At *WrestleMania XII* the world saw what Marc Mero was all about when he came to the aid of Sable, who was being berated by Hunter-Heart Helmsley.

An appreciative Sable led him to the ring as he fought WWE's infamous Superstars. Within a year of his debut, he defeated Faarooq in a tournament final to become the new Intercontinental Champion.

After he recovered from a severe knee-injury he returned in 1997, claiming he was "Marvelous." With Sable on her way to mega-stardom, Mero grew jealous of the attention and the two violently parted ways. During the remainder of his WWE career, Mero retained the managerial services of Jacqueline and the duo often were at odds with Sable until Marc Mero left the company in 1999.

MARCUS COR VON

HT: 6'1" WT: 265 lbs.
FROM: Detroit, Michigan
SIGNATURE MOVE: Pounce

Marcus Cor Von made his WWE debut in January 2007 on ECW. According to Mr. McMahon, the presence of Superstars like Cor Von exemplified the future of the ECW brand. Shortly after his debut, "The Alpha Male" joined forces with fellow upstarts Elijah Burke, Matt Striker and Kevin Thorn. Collectively known as the New Breed, the young stable of Superstars took exception to the veteran presence of Rob Van Dam, Tommy Dreamer, Sandman, and Sabu, also known as the ECW Originals.

At *WrestleMania 23*, Cor Von and his fellow New Breeders came up short against the Originals in an Eight Man Tag Team Match. Following the loss, Cor Von spent the majority of the next few months looking to avenge the *WrestleMania* defeat. Unfortunately, however, he failed to appear on ECW television after June and left WWE a few months later.

MARIA

FROM: Chicago, Illinois

World Wrestling Entertainment audiences were first wowed by this beauty when she participated in the 2004 *Raw* Diva Search. She soon began hosting the popular "WWE Kiss Cam" segments and became a backstage correspondent during *Monday Night Raw*. In 2005, she proved she wasn't just another pretty face when she won her first official match, beating Christy Hemme in a Lingerie Pillow Fight on *Raw*.

Maria continued to step between the ropes, facing competition such as Melina, Victoria and Torrie Wilson. She even ended the undefeated streak of "The Glamazon" Beth Phoenix. Maria also appeared in many magazines that feature the most beautiful women in the world and appeared on television shows that included *Family Feud*, *Project Runway*, *Sunset Tan*, and *Celebrity Apprentice*. The delightful diva added another highlight to her sports-entertainment career in 2009 when she was voted WWE Diva of the Year. The former beauty queen made a lasting impression on the sports-entertainment industry and today can be seen on the independent circuit around the United States as she launches a music recording career.

MARIANNA

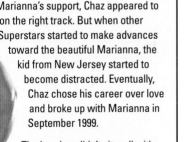

Frustrated with the way in which he was portrayed in the past, Chaz denounced all his previous identities, which included Headbanger Mosh and Beaver Cleavage, in the summer of 1999. According to Chaz, he was just a kid from New Jersey and he was inspired to start being himself by his girlfriend Marianna.

With Marianna's support, Chaz appeared to be on the right track. But when other Superstars started to make advances toward the beautiful Marianna, the kid from New Jersey started to become distracted. Eventually, Chaz chose his career over love and broke up with Marianna in September 1999.

The breakup didn't sit well with Marianna. In an attempt to get back at her former boyfriend, she showed up on *Raw* with a black eye, claiming she was the victim of domestic violence. She later had Chaz arrested for the offense.

With the help of GTV, it was revealed that Marianna's black eye was actually just makeup. When authorities learned of this, they released Chaz and took her into custody instead.

INTERVIEW SEGMENTS

THE BARBER SHOP

In 1991, Brutus "The Barber" Beefcake introduced audiences to the place where he would regularly "cut and strut." *The Barber Shop* became one of the most popular talk show segments in WWE, as Superstars were answering questions, and at times being held accountable for their actions by one of their own. Whether it was a showdown between The Nasty Boys and The Legion of Doom, or Ted DiBiase's Million Dollar Team, fans were guaranteed to see something exciting take place when the Shop opened for business.

The show's most talked-about moment came in January 1992, when Shawn Michaels threw partner Marty Jannetty through the *Barber Shop's* glass window and ended the almost decade-long partnership of The Rockers. Later that year, the show set was destroyed by a crazed Sid Justice after he decided the time for answering questions regarding his deeds toward Hulk Hogan was over.

THE BODY SHOP

Even after injuries sidelined Jesse "The Body" Ventura's in-ring career, the charismatic Superstar remained a pivotal personality on WWE television. Using a makeshift gym as a set, Ventura welcomed WWE's most hated Superstars to *The Body Shop*. Week after week, the likes of Randy "Macho Man" Savage and Bobby "The Brain" Heenan appeared to spew their oft-unpopular opinions, as Ventura sat back and agreed with every word.

In late 1985, "Magnificent" Don Muraco assumed hosting duties of *The Body Shop*. Despite having a new host, the interviews remained equally biased towards WWE's villains. One of *The Body Shop's* most memorable moments saw Freddie Blassie shock the world when he revealed he had sold half of his stable of Superstars to WWE newcomer, the "Doctor of Style" Slick.

THE BROTHER LOVE SHOW

Despite its host professing an annoying level of affection for everybody, love certainly was not in the air at *The Brother Love Show*. The weekly interview segment debuted in 1988 and provided a platform for WWE's most controversial Superstars to voice their unpopular opinions. *The Brother Love Show* also served as the scene of some of WWE's most memorable moments. In 1990, Earthquake's brutal attack on Hulk Hogan ignited one of the hottest rivalries of the summer. The following year, Brother Love introduced the world to Paul Bearer, who assumed managerial control of Undertaker.

In March 1991, Brother Love welcomed Ultimate Warrior to the set. At the time, Ultimate Warrior was preparing for his Retirement Match against Randy Savage at *WrestleMania VII*. As a warm-up, he decided to start sending people into retirement right then and there. He proceeded to destroy *The Brother Love Show* set, officially marking the end of the interview segment.

CARLITO'S CABANA

Decked out in beach chairs, buckets of apples and oversized sun umbrellas, *Carlito's Cabana* certainly appeared to be a cool place. That is, until its host opened his mouth. Claiming to be the authority on all things cool, Carlito started hosting his own interview segment in April 2005. When he wasn't bragging, Carlito welcomed some of WWE's biggest names to his set. Hulk Hogan's appearance on July 4, 2005 resulted in one of the biggest matches of Carlito's career. Kurt Angle interrupted the interview, and the result was a tag team match between Carlito & Angle and Hogan & Shawn Michaels. During its run, the notable guests on *Carlito's Cabana* included Mr. McMahon, Eddie Guerrero and *Piper's Pit* host "Rowdy" Roddy Piper.

THE CUTTING EDGE

In 2005, Edge joined the fraternity of noted WWE loudmouths when he was given his own interview segment, *The Cutting Edge*. The "Rated-R Superstar" used his time with the microphone to incite fans with his unpopular opinions. In March 2006, *The Cutting Edge* turned hardcore when Edge welcomed Mick Foley to a special *Saturday Night's Main Event* edition of the segment.

In the years that followed, the "Ultimate Opportunist" used *The Cutting Edge* as his platform to assault anyone who did not share his views on sports-entertainment. Sometimes what began as a verbal onslaught, ended in physical assault, with the distinguished host usually getting the better of the exchange. Although Edge retired from in-ring action in 2011, the WWE Universe still looks forward to the next episode. Stay tuned, Edgeheads!

THE FUNERAL PARLOR

Hosted by Paul Bearer, *The Funeral Parlor* was the most frightening talk show segment in WWE history. During its run which began in 1991, *The Funeral Parlor* lured the enemies of Undertaker and Paul Bearer into its dark chamber. This show was specifically intended to give people a glimpse into the world of Undertaker and his morbid keeper. During its time on the air WWE Superstars, Legends, and Hall of Famers made their way through it. Although some have still not returned...

THE FLOWER SHOP

When Adrian Adonis traded in his leather jacket for pink tights and eye makeup, he also added to his reputation as one of history's most antagonizing loudmouths. Rather than try to silence the opinionated Superstar, WWE gave him his own interview segment. Each week, the "Adorable One" welcomed Superstars to his set, which he decorated with hundreds of flowers. Serving as a replacement for *Piper's Pit*, *The Flower Shop* debuted in 1986 and served as a platform for the host to berate fan favorite Superstars and stoke the egos of rulebreakers. When Piper returned to WWE in August 1986, a showdown between *The Flower Shop* and *Piper's Pit* was inevitable. When Roddy Piper verbally assaulted Adonis and his new bodyguard, "Cowboy" Bob Orton, the duo from *The Flower Shop* responded with a beatdown. The following week, Piper retaliated by destroying *The Flower Shop* with a baseball bat. The actions ultimately resulted in a Hair vs. Hair Match at *WrestleMania III*.

HEARTBREAK HOTEL

In 1994 Shawn Michaels, the Heartbreak Kid, opened the *Heartbreak Hotel* to the biggest names in WWE. Superstars such as Bret Hart, Mr. Perfect, and Owen Hart all visited the swanky set decorated with a heart-shaped bed, a flashing neon sign and a luminescent lamp.

With Diesel at his side, Shawn Michaels left the light on for his guests to speak their mind or air their differences, as was the case when Million Dollar Man and Paul Bearer offered conflicting reports about the status of Undertaker. Each visit to the *Heartbreak Hotel* concluded with HBK reminding the WWE Universe to "Turn out the lights, it's check out time."

HIGHLIGHT REEL

Chris Jericho is rarely at a loss for words, as evidenced by his reoccurring interview segment, *The Highlight Reel*. Debuting on *Raw* in April 2003, *The Highlight Reel* was Y2J's "cooler and more entertaining" answer to *Piper's Pit*, which had resurfaced on *SmackDown* earlier in the month.

The pull-no-punches approach to interviewing laid the groundwork for what would go on to become one of the most entertaining interview segments in WWE history. Shortly after *The Highlight Reel's* debut, Y2J introduced his "obscenely and obesely expensive" Jeritron 5000, which was later renamed the Jeritron 3000 and Jeritron 6000 in HD. In June 2008, it was destroyed when Y2J drove Shawn Michaels' head through the plasma screen. One month after destroying the Jeritron 5000, Jericho shelved *The Highlight Reel*, claiming he no longer wanted to be seen as the fans' party host for the new millennium. When Jericho returned in 2010 and again in 2012, he brought back *The Hightlight Reel* to use as a platform to address the WWE Universe.

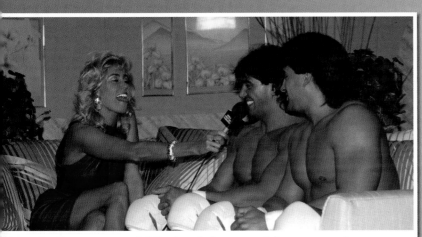

Many other Superstars were briefly given their own special segments such as Blackjack's Barbeque with Blackjack Mulligan, the Abraham Washington Show, Missy's Manor hosted by Missy Hyatt, and Victory Corner presented by Robert Debord.

KING'S COURT

Jerry "The King" Lawler has often been recognized as the game's greatest antagonist, particularly when he had a microphone in his hand. As the host of *King's Court* in the 1990s, the loud-mouthed Lawler was given plenty of time to speak. When he wasn't verbally assaulting capacity crowds worldwide, "The King" used his Court to dive deep into the minds of WWE's top Superstars and even interviewed WWE President Jack Tunney in 1993. In one of the most memorable *King's Court* episodes, Lawler welcomed actor William Shatner to his show in 1995. The *Star Trek* legend believed he was there to promote his new show, *TekWar*. But after Lawler threatened him, Shatner's goal quickly shifted to attacking and ultimately embarrassing "The King."

PEEP SHOW

Claiming to be hotter than Jerry Springer, Christian used the *Peep Show* to get to the bottom of the most probing questions surrounding WWE Superstars. For the 2005 debut (not counting the night in 2003 when he took over the *Highlight Reel*), Christian welcomed both Rey Mysterio and Eddie Guerrero during the height of their custody battle over Mysterio's son, Dominic.

The *Peep Show* went dark following the Superstar's departure from WWE in late 2005, but the show "by the peeps, for the peeps" was revived when Christian returned to WWE in 2009. Over the course of the next few years, Christian interviewed the likes of Jack Swagger, Matt Hardy and Alberto Del Rio. He even attempted to teach Hornswoggle how to speak Canadian on an episode of the *Peep Show*!

PIPER'S PIT

In 1984, WWE executives gave noted loudmouth "Rowdy" Roddy Piper a microphone and the platform to say whatever was in his mind. The move resulted in the creation of *Piper's Pit*, the most vitriolic interview segment in sports-entertainment history. Early in the segment's existence, Piper lured Jimmy "Superfly" Snuka to the *Pit* where he proceeded to savagely beat him with a coconut.

In the years that followed, many other fan favorites became victimized on the set of *Piper's Pit*. In the weeks leading up to Piper's boxing match with Mr. T at *WrestleMania 2*, Piper and his bodyguard, "Cowboy" Bob Orton, abducted the actor's friend, Haiti Kid, then dragged him to the *Piper's Pit* set where they forcefully shaved his head to resemble Mr. T's unique look.

The most-noted moment in *Piper's Pit* history also helped set the stage for arguably WWE's greatest match. In early 1987, whispers of an alliance between Andre the Giant and Bobby "The Brain" Heenan began to circulate. The alleged union would assuredly mark the end of Andre's well-publicized friendship with Hulk Hogan. Unable to accept the rumors, Hulk Hogan appeared on *Piper's Pit* in an attempt to learn the truth. Hogan's worst fears were confirmed when Andre tore Hogan's *Hulkamania* T-shirt and crucifix from his body.

The *Piper's Pit* set is still dusted off for use on WWE's biggest events, including *WrestleMania V* (with guest Morton Downey, Jr.) and *WrestleMania 21* (with guest Stone Cold Steve Austin).

ROGERS' CORNER

"Nature Boy" Buddy Rogers was one of the greatest performers sports-entertainment will ever know. Rogers returned to WWE in 1982 and debuted his talk show segment *Rogers' Corner*. *Rogers' Corner* was where Superstars discussed their careers, and shared their opinions and future intentions with the great "Nature Boy."

THE SNAKE PIT

In September 1986 audiences were treated to the twisted prophecies of a man who walked in eternal darkness. Jake "the Snake" Roberts invited all to come into his pit.

Roberts always professed that the DDT is like life, cruel but fair. Many times he showed audiences around the globe we were living in his world. By July 1987 "the Snake" decided

to solely focus on dominating WWE rings. Fans and Superstars alike will forever recall the words of Roberts spoken from his pulpit, "We're not born from the original sins, but we may well be the original sinners. Enter the Snake Pit if you dare..."

VIP LOUNGE

With its expensive leather sofas, black carpeting and velvet ropes, the *VIP Lounge* was considered an elite interview segment. Hosted by MVP, the show debuted in 2007 and welcomed some of WWE's top names, including Triple H, Chris Jericho and Ric Flair. The appeal of *VIP Lounge* extended outside of the WWE Universe. In September 2009, renowned civil rights activist Al Sharpton used the *VIP Lounge* to promote education reform in the United States. In August 2010, Jack Swagger defeated MVP for the right to host a future edition of the *VIP Lounge*. As expected, the "All-American American" turned the once prestigious segment into a glorified trophy case, which prompted MVP to rush to the set and destroy Swagger's awards.

M

2010-
2000-09
1990-99
1980-89
1970-79
1960-69

MARIO MANCINI

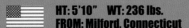

HT: 5'10" WT: 236 lbs.
FROM: Milford, Connecticut

In the world of sports-entertainment, it's generally believed that in order to be successful, a Superstar must possess at least some sort of charisma and/or muscle. Mario Mancini displayed neither. But he was recognized as one of the most resilient Superstars of all time. Despite losing nearly every match in which he ever competed, Mancini kept coming back for more.

Still a teenager, Mancini debuted in WWE in 1984. Looking back, the man from Milford, Connecticut, could've used some more seasoning, as he quickly became cannon fodder for the likes of Greg "The Hammer" Valentine, the Iron Sheik, "Mr. Wonderful" Paul Orndorff and anybody else WWE put him in the ring against.

Unfortunately for Mancini, more experience didn't necessarily mean more wins. Instead, as the decade wore on, he helped a new crop of Superstars look good, including Bad News Brown, "Million Dollar Man" Ted DiBiase and the Honky Tonk Man.

MARK HENRY

HT: 6'1" WT: 392 lbs.
FROM: Silsbee, Texas
SIGNATURE MOVE: World's Strongest Slam

With more than a decade of WWE experience to his credit, Mark Henry has seen his share of professional ups and downs.

TITLE HISTORY

ECW CHAMPION	*Defeated Kane on June 29, 2008*
EUROPEAN CHAMPION	*Awarded title by Jeff Jarrett on August 23, 1999*
WORLD HEAVYWEIGHT CHAMPION	*Defeated Randy Orton on September 18, 2011*

After a high-profile weightlifting career where he participated in the 1992 and 1996 Summer Games, Mark Henry entered WWE in 1996 to much fanfare, but an unfortunate barrage of injuries sidelined him for the majority of his early years.

In 2006, long after nearly every sports-entertainment insider had written him off, Henry returned to the ring more determined than ever. He spent the next year competing in high-profile matches against WWE's top names and even challenged the legendary Undertaker to a Casket Match at *WrestleMania 22.*

In 2008, Henry's career continued its meteoric rise when he was drafted to ECW in June. Just days after making the move, he defeated Kane and Big Show at *Night of Champions* to capture the ECW Championship. Shortly after the victory, Henry aligned himself with Tony Atlas. With the historic powerhouse in his corner, Henry appeared more unstoppable than ever.

In the summer of 2009 "The World's Strongest Man" returned to *Raw* and soon became a fan-favorite. The cheers from the WWE Universe led him to form a popular tag team with MVP. With his popularity at its greatest height, Henry was drafted to *SmackDown*. Sadly for his fans, frustration from a WWE Championship drought reached its breaking point and Henry viciously mowed down down anyone in his path as he freely appeared on *Raw* and *SmackDown*. He carved a path of destruction and followed it to a victory over Randy Orton at 2011's *Night of Champions* and the World Heavyweight Championship. Throughout 2011, he engaged in one of the most vicious conflicts in WWE history with the Big Show. The highlight of this conflict came at *Vengeance 2011*, when a thunderous superplex caused the entire ring to collapse under the weight of the two behemoths.

MARK JINDRAK

HT: 6'7" WT: 305 lbs. FROM: Atlanta, Georgia
SIGNATURE MOVE: Mark of Excellence

Trained in WCW's Power Plant by Paul Orndorff, Mark Jindrak began his career in WCW as part of the Natural Born Thrillers. When the company was purchased by WWE in March 2001, he was soon seen on WWE programming as a member of the Alliance.

After the Alliance dissolved, Jindrak returned to WWE in late 2002 in matches against Raven and Justin Credible. During 2004, he teamed with Garrison Cade and saw action against La Resistance, Evolution and the Dudley Boys. In March 2004, he debuted on *SmackDown* and became so impressed with himself he referred to himself as "the Reflection of Perfection." With Teddy Long in his corner, Jindrak fought Billy Gunn, Rey Mysterio, Hardcore Holly, Funaki, Charlie Haas and Rob Van Dam. Shortly after these bouts, he aligned himself with Kurt Angle and Luther Reigns before being drafted to *Raw* in June 2005. That July, Jindrak left WWE, but still appears on cards in Japan and Mexico.

MARK YOUNG

With solid bloodlines, and well schooled in the grappling arts, Mark Young debuted in WWE in 1986. Over the next four years, he took on the most dangerous rule-breakers sports-entertainment has ever seen. Young was a capable competitor who could mix it up between the ropes with any opponent.

His foes included Jimmy Jack Funk, Barry O, Dino Bravo, Boris Zhukov, Earthquake and Mr. Perfect. He teamed with a number of Superstars against teams like the Islanders, Demolition, the Fabulous Rougeau Brothers, the Brain Busters, Rhythm & Blues and the Orient Express.

By September 1990, Young left WWE and toured Asia. In the early 1990s, Young retired from the ring but will be remembered as a man who took on anybody at any time.

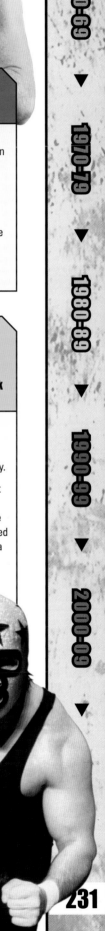

MARTY JANNETTY

HT: 5'11"   **WT:** 234 lbs.
FROM: Columbus, Georgia
SIGNATURE MOVE: Rocker Dropper

TITLE HISTORY

INTERCONTINENTAL CHAMPION	Defeated Shawn Michaels on May 17, 1993
WORLD TAG TEAM CHAMPION	Partnered with 1-2-3 Kid to defeat The Quebecers on January 10, 1994

Marty Jannetty made his in-ring debut in 1984 and soon met another future star, Shawn Michaels. The two formed a popular duo known as The Midnight Rockers and exploded onto the tag team scene in the AWA. In June 1988, the Rockers skyrocketed to instant fame in WWE. With incredible speed, agility, quickness and continuity, Jannetty and Michaels were considered by many as uncrowned World Tag Team Champions. Inseparable for years, Jannetty and Michaels began to drift apart. Audiences witnessed a violent split on a January 1992 episode of *The Barber Shop* when Michaels put Jannetty through the Shop's glass window.

Once Jannetty returned, the former friends traded Intercontinental Championship reigns. In January 1994 Jannetty teamed with 1-2-3 Kid to capture the World Tag Team Championship. Marty continued to appear in WWE throughout 1996 before leaving the company. In 2005, Janetty returned to team with Michaels again for a single match against La Resistance. Since then Jannetty has appeared in WWE on several occasions, most notably the 15th Anniversary episode of *Raw*.

MARYSE

HT: 5'8"   **FROM:** Montreal, Quebec, Canada
SIGNATURE MOVE: French Kiss

TITLE HISTORY

DIVAS CHAMPION (2 TIMES)	Defeated Michelle McCool on December 26, 2008 Defeated Gail Kim on February 22, 2010

This French-Canadian Diva was first noticed when she won the 2003 Miss Hawaiian Tropic Canada competition. Over the next few years she appeared in the pages of ten different issues of *Playboy* Magazine, and graced three covers. A finalist in the 2006 *Raw Diva Search*, Maryse gave WWE audiences a sample of her seductive methods in May 2008 when she stole Deuce and Domino away from their manager, Cherry. Once she entered active competition, she used the French Kiss, her devastating version of the DDT, to put down her competition. On December 26, 2008 she became the second Divas Champion in WWE history and ruled the division for eight months.

After a second stint as Divas Champion in 2010, her appreciation for precious metals and rare stones led her the French Canadian to appoint herself the executive assistant to Million Dollar Champion, Ted DiBiase. This glamorous material girl and "sexiest of the sexy" was last seen as co-host of *NXT* being lavished with gifts from the always charming Hornswoggle.

MASCARITA SAGRADA

FROM: Mexico   **SIGNATURE MOVE:** Missile Dropkick

A legend in Mexico, this masked Lucha Libre star was known in Mexico and WCW before his debut in WWE on the first episode of *Shotgun Saturday Night* in 1997. The daredevil went undefeated in his first tour of duty with World Wrestling Entertainment.

In 2005, he returned to WWE as part of the newly-launched Juniors Division. Sagrada picked-up where he left off and dominated his opponents. Though he left WWE in March 2006, he is one of few Superstars to go undefeated during his tenure with the company.

THE MASKED SUPERSTAR

HT: 6'3"   **WT:** 291 lbs.   **FROM:** New York, New York
SIGNATURE MOVE: Swinging Neckbreaker

The Masked Superstar was as mean as he was mysterious. Hiding behind a star-covered mask, the oversized Superstar broke every rule in the book to earn several high-profile encounters during his brief WWE stay.

The man behind the mask received his first opportunity at WWE immortality in 1983 when he challenged Bob Backlund for the WWE Championship at Madison Square Garden. On this night, the Masked Superstar accomplished what few were able to do when he defeated Backlund via countout. Unfortunately for the Masked Superstar, WWE titles cannot change hands on a countout.

Still searching for that elusive title, the Masked Superstar earned another opportunity at the WWE title when he challenged newly crowned titleholder Hulk Hogan in early 1984. Again, he was unable to walk away with the title, as he was disqualified for using a foreign object.

While championship glory escaped The Masked Superstar during his WWE career, he did gain great success in his previous years. Among his many accolades, The Masked Superstar was a four-time Georgia Championship Wrestling Heavyweight Champion.

MASON RYAN

HT: 6'5"   WT: 289 lbs.
FROM: Cardiff, Wales
SIGNATURE MOVE: Swinging Side Slam

When CM Punk was looking for muscle to add to his New Nexus faction, he turned to the 6'5", nearly 300-pound powerhouse Mason Ryan.

One of the most physically imposing Superstars in recent memory, Ryan made an immediate impact when he defeated R-Truth via submission in his debut match in February 2011. After the bell rang, however, it was quickly learned that Ryan didn't care about wins and losses. Instead, he was out to maim people. With R-Truth still suffering from the loss, Ryan

continued his punishing assault. As a result, the referee had no choice but to reverse his decision and award the match to Truth via disqualification.

Ryan continued to plow through the *Raw* roster until an injury sidelined him later that same summer. After several

months away, the monster from Wales returned to the ring in September 2011 to apparently help Vickie Guerrero's clients, Jack Swagger and Dolph Ziggler, in six-man tag action. But instead of aiding the arrogant duo, Ryan turned on them, much to the delight of the WWE Universe.

MATT BORNE

HT: 6'0"   WT: 241 lbs.
FROM: Portland, Oregon

Second-generation Superstar Matt Borne grew up watching his father, "Tough" Tony Borne, dominate the Pacific Northwest tag team scene during the 1960s. In the early 1980s, Matt followed in dad's footsteps, capturing the territory's tag titles on four separate occasions.

In 1985, just a few years into his career, Borne competed in the biggest match of his career when he battled Ricky "The Dragon" Steamboat at Madison Square Garden at the first-ever *WrestleMania*. Borne failed to pick up a victory against the legendary Steamboat, but will forever be linked to the historic start of sports-entertainment's crown jewel.

MATT HARDY

HT: 6'2"   WT: 236 lbs.   FROM: Cameron, North Carolina
SIGNATURE MOVE: Twist of Fate

TITLE HISTORY

CRUISERWEIGHT CHAMPION	*Defeated Billy Kidman on February 23, 2003*
ECW CHAMPION	*Won a Championship Scramble on September 7, 2008*
EUROPEAN CHAMPION	*Defeated Eddie Guerrero on April 26, 2001*
HARDCORE CHAMPION	*1 Time*
UNITED STATES CHAMPION	*Defeated MVP on April 27, 2008*
WORLD TAG TEAM CHAMPION (6 TIMES)	*Partnered with Jeff Hardy to defeat The Acolytes on July 5, 1999* *Partnered with Jeff Hardy to defeat Edge & Christian on September 24, 2000* *Partnered with Jeff Hardy to defeat Edge & Christian on October 23, 2000* *Partnered with Jeff Hardy to defeat The Dudleys on March 5, 2001* *Partnered with Jeff Hardy to defeat Booker T & Test on November 12, 2001* *Partnered with Jeff Hardy to win a Tag Team Battle Royal on April 2, 2007*
WWE TAG TEAM CHAMPION	*Partnered with MVP to defeat Deuce & Domino on August 31, 2007*

At the time of his debut, Matt Hardy was seen as nothing more than a scrawny kid that WWE's top Superstars could prove their worth against. Refusing to be held down, however, Matt, alongside his brother, Jeff, soon proved himself as a legitimate force in the tag team ranks. In fact, many of today's wrestling insiders credit The Hardy Boys for revolutionizing the art of tag team competition.

During his climb to the top, Hardy fell madly in love with WWE Diva Lita. The two shared a long relationship until it was revealed that the fiery redhead was cheating on him with his friend, Edge. Hardy was released from his WWE contract shortly after and many assumed the final chapter of his career had been written. Hardy, on the other hand, saw things a bit differently.

Hardy actually showed up on WWE television and attacked Edge. The popularity of the rebellious act forced WWE to re-sign Matt. Over the next several years, the resilient Hardy achieved great success when he captured the United States Championship, and his first World singles title, the ECW Championship.

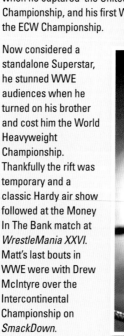

Now considered a standalone Superstar, he stunned WWE audiences when he turned on his brother and cost him the World Heavyweight Championship. Thankfully the rift was temporary and a classic Hardy air show followed at the Money In The Bank match at *WrestleMania XXVI*. Matt's last bouts in WWE were with Drew McIntyre over the Intercontinental Championship on *SmackDown*.

MATT MORGAN

HT: 6'10" **WT:** 328 lbs.
FROM: Fairfield, Connecticut
SIGNATURE MOVE:
Vertical Suplex Side Slam

When *SmackDown* general manager Paul Heyman formed Team Lesnar in late 2003, it was with the hope of creating one of the most physically imposing factions of all time. And he certainly succeeded. Led by then-WWE Champion Brock Lesnar, the group consisted of Nathan Jones, Big Show, A-Train and the nearly 7-foot tall newcomer Matt Morgan.

The monstrous Morgan spent the remainder of the year protecting Lesnar's reign, as well as flattening the likes of Funaki and Shannon Moore in the ring. But when the calendar turned to 2004, injury forced Morgan out of action for several months.

When Morgan returned in April 2005, it was learned that the oversized Superstar had acquired a speech impediment. Despite his stuttering, Morgan was still a force in the ring. So much so, in fact, that Carlito hired the big man to serve as his bodyguard.

Morgan watched Carlito's back for one month before the Caribbean Superstar was drafted *Raw*. Following the draft, Morgan slowly faded from the WWE scene.

MATT STRIKER 🇺🇸

HT: 5'10" **WT:** 224 lbs.
FROM: Bayside, New York

As Matt Striker molded young minds as a member of the New York City school system, he also fostered his love of sports-entertainment. To prepare himself for a life in the ring, he studied with Johnny Rodz at Gleason's Gym underneath the Brooklyn Bridge.

Matt continued to teach as his sports-entertainment career started to build, until he participated in the Angle Invitational on *Raw* the same night after calling in sick from his teaching job. When he was forced to resign, it sparked a national media frenzy.

Though he may have received detention from school, the controversy launched his WWE career. In 2007, he joined ECW's New Breed in their mission to rid sports-entertainment of the ECW Originals. Striker created his own "Striker Match" which prohibits eye-gouging, hair pulling, top rope maneuvers, and the use of obscene language. In addition to his talk show segment, *Matt Striker's Classroom*, he also served as manager for Big Daddy V and an announcer for ECW. Striker quickly came into his own and won the Slammy Award with Todd Grisham for "Announce Team of the Year." Today, Striker is the host of *NXT* and is at the heart of WWE's newswire, conducting important interviews from the field.

MAVEN 🇺🇸

HT: 6'2" **WT:** 220 lbs. **FROM:** Chantilly, Virginia
SIGNATURE MOVE: Halo DDT

TITLE HISTORY	
HARDCORE CHAMPION	3 Times

Originally a schoolteacher, Maven received the opportunity of a lifetime when he was chosen to participate in the WWE reality program, *Tough Enough*. After being crowned the first-ever male champion in this show's history, he was awarded a contract and immediately began his professional career. Unfortunately for the newcomer, his lack of experience cost him, as he lost several of his early matches against more seasoned competitors such as Tazz and Chris Jericho.

Despite coming up short in his early days, Maven persevered. By 2002, the former schoolteacher was beaming with confidence. He used his newfound self-assurance to eliminate the legendary Undertaker from the 2002 *Royal Rumble*. A few weeks later, he defeated the "Deadman" for the Hardcore Championship.

In November 2004, Maven parlayed an impressive *Survivor Series* appearance into a World Heavyweight Championship opportunity against Triple H. Unfortunately for the youngster, he was unsuccessful in his bid to uncrown "The Game." Shortly after the loss, fans turned against Maven when he attacked the endearing Eugene. The former *Tough Enough* champion left WWE later that year.

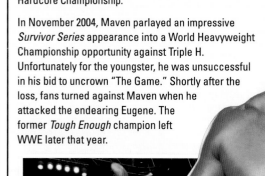

MAX MINI 🇲🇽

HT: 3'7" **WT:** 83 lbs.
FROM: Mexico

Billed as "The World's Smallest Athlete," the masked Max Mini first caught the imagination of the WWE Universe in late 1997. Despite his diminutive stature — even within WWE's mini division — Max Mini was not afraid to mix it up in the ring. And with his high-flying, have-no-fear attitude, he proved to be 83 pounds of pure excitement.

Max Mini's popularity led to a string of high-profile pay-per-view matches. At *Ground Zero* in September 1997, he defeated El Torito in singles action. He then teamed with Nova the following month to top Tarantula & Mosaic at *Badd Blood*. And in January 1998, he was part of a six-man team that defeated Battalion, El Torito & Tarantula at the *Royal Rumble*.

When he wasn't wowing audiences in the ring, Max Mini became the obsession of El Tigre, the host of WWE.com's *Code Rojo* Web cast. During each show, it wasn't uncommon to see El Tigre spend at least a portion of the episode chasing Max Mini throughout the arena.

M

2010-
2000-09
1990-99
1980-89
1970-79
1960-69

MAX MOON

HT: 5'10"   WT: 240 lbs.   FROM: Outer Space
SIGNATURE MOVE: Spinning Flying Body Press

World Wrestling Entertainment was invaded by a space traveler wearing a blue-armored suit in 1992. Max Moon defeated Supestars like the Brooklyn Brawler, Terry Taylor, Skinner, and Repo Man while enjoying a good measure of success. He continued to impress crowds wherever he appeared and became a contender to the Intercontinental Championship, held at that time by "The Heartbreak Kid" Shawn Michaels.

After a strong showing during a 1993 WWE European Tour, this cyborg from another galaxy has not been seen in World Wrestling Entertainment.

MAXINE

HT: 5'4"
FROM: Tampa, Florida

According to Maxine, being sexy can only get you so far, which is why the power-obsessed Florida native also employs characteristics of cockiness, confidence, intelligence and a touch of class.

With Alicia Fox serving as her Pro, Maxine debuted as a Rookie on the third season of *NXT*. Despite having a well-qualified Diva showing her the ropes, the former model failed to impress the judges. After just nine weeks, she was eliminated from competition.

Maxine's self-professed claim to be on top in WWE didn't end with *NXT* season three. In August 2011, the exiled Diva wannabe returned to *NXT* season five as the love interest of Rookie Derrick Bateman. As Bateman's girlfriend, Maxine made it a point to interfere in her man's matches when she believes he needs the help. She's also not afraid to join in the action herself, having challenged A.J. and Kaitlyn on numerous occasions. In October 2011, Maxine's relationship with Bateman was taken to the next level when the lovebirds got engaged on an episode of *NXT*.

MEAN STREET POSSE

MEMBERS: Pete Gas, Rodney, Joey Abs
FROM: Greenwich, Connecticut

Hailing from the "mean streets" of ritzy Greenwich, Connecticut, Pete Gas, Rodney, and Joey Abs may very well be the only three people in the history of the world to claim they are tough while wearing argyle sweater vests.

Prior to ever stepping foot in a WWE ring, the Mean Street Posse told tall tales of ruling the affluent streets of their hometown. Unfortunately for the Posse, childhood friends of Shane McMahon, their supposed toughness did not equate to success in WWE. Despite their inability to backup their boasts, all three Mean Street Posse members managed to permanently etch their names into the WWE record books when they briefly held (and quickly lost) the Hardcore Championship at *WrestleMania 2000*.

The Mean Street Posse faded from the WWE scene in 2001, but rest assured that patrons of Papyrus stationary store on Greenwich Avenue are shaking in their loafers at thought of Pete Gas, Rodney, & Joey Abs taking back the neighborhood.

MEAT

HT: 6'4"   WT: 250 lbs.
SIGNATURE MOVE: Meat Grinder

Meat appeared as the submissive boy-toy to Terri and Jacqueline of Pretty Mean Sisters in 1999. A natural in the ring with an incredible physique, the man known as Meat displayed his abilities against Test, the Blue Meanie, Ken Shamrock, The Road Dogg, Val Venis, Kurt Angle, Billy Gunn, and The Godfather.

Pleasing Terri and Jacqueline took both a physical and mental toll on him. After ending his association with both Divas, Meat began using his real name, Shawn Stasiak. He left World Wrestling Entertainment by the end of 1999. He debuted in World Championship Wrestling shortly afterward, and returned to WWE in 2001 as part of the Alliance.

MEGA MANIACS

MEMBERS: Hulk Hogan, Brutus Beefcake
COMBINED WT: 573 lbs

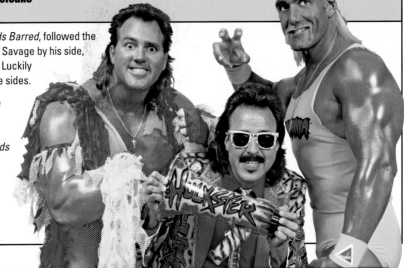

In the ultimate example of life imitating art, Zeus, Hulk Hogan's rival in the film *No Holds Barred*, followed the Hulkster from Hollywood to WWE. With former WWE Champion Randy "Macho Man" Savage by his side, it appeared as though nothing could stop Zeus from ending Hogan's illustrious career. Luckily for the Hulkster, longtime friend Brutus "The Barber" Beefcake stepped up to even the sides.

Collectively known as the Mega Maniacs, Hogan & Beefcake proved their dominance when they defeated Zeus & Savage at *SummerSlam 1989*. However, the devious duo simply would not go away. The two teams finally decided to settle the score in December 1989. In a unique pay-per-view event that also saw the airing of the *No Holds Barred* movie, the Mega Maniacs once again toppled Zeus & Savage, this time in a steel cage.

Several years later, the Mega Maniacs reunited to challenge Money, Inc. for the World Tag Team Championship at *WrestleMania IX*. They were unable to claim the titles after being disqualified for using Beefcake's titanium mask as a weapon.

THE MEGA POWERS

MEMBERS: Randy Savage, Hulk Hogan
COMBINED WT: 548 lbs

The two biggest Superstars in WWE during the late 1980s were undoubtedly Randy "Macho Man" Savage and Hulk Hogan. Alone, they possessed great power within the promotion. Together, however, they took that control to a whole new level, proving themselves as Mega Powers. Former rivals, Savage and Hogan patched up their differences when Miss Elizabeth persuaded "The Hulkster" to save "Macho Man" from a beating at the hands of Honky Tonk Man and The Hart Foundation. After Hogan cleared the ring of Savage's foes, the former adversaries shook hands, signifying the start of a powerful new friendship.

The new relationship helped Savage greatly, as he used help from Hogan to defeat Ted DiBiase to claim the WWE Championship at *WrestleMania IV*. Seeking retribution, DiBiase and Andre the Giant later double teamed "Macho Man," which prompted the new WWE Champion to challenge his two attackers to a tag team match at *SummerSlam 1988*. Savage later revealed his partner to be his friend Hogan.

In a match billed as "The Mega Powers vs. The Mega Bucks," Savage &

Hogan defeated DiBiase & Andre after Elizabeth removed her skirt to distract the opposition. Just when it appeared things couldn't be going any better for the Mega Powers, Savage began to develop an intense feeling of jealously over Elizabeth's friendship with Hogan. As a result, a paranoid "Macho Man" began to slowly pull back from his friendship with Hogan. Their relationship finally dissolved in early 1989 when Savage brutally attacked Hogan in the locker room following their match against The Twin Towers on *The Main Event*.

The unwarranted attack set the stage for the historic Savage vs. Hogan WWE Championship Match at *WrestleMania V*. Billed as "The Mega Powers Explode," the encounter was the culmination of a rollercoaster friendship that lasted more than one year. In the end, it was Hogan dropping his signature leg drop across the throat of Savage to claim his second WWE Championship.

MELINA

HT: 5'4" **FROM:** Los Angeles, California
SIGNATURE MOVE: California Dream

TITLE HISTORY

DIVAS CHAMPION (2 TIMES)	Defeated Jillian on October 12, 2009 Defeated Alicia Fox on August 15, 2010
WOMEN'S CHAMPION (3 TIMES)	Defeated Mickie James on February 19, 2007 Defeated Mickie James on April 24, 2007 Defeated Beth Phoenix January 25, 2009

This former fashion model first made a name for herself in April 2005 when she guided fellow socialites Johnny Nitro & Joey Mercury to the WWE Tag Team Championship. During their reign, MNM (Melina, Nitro, Mercury) annoyed fans with their constant namedropping. According to the threesome, Paris Hilton and Kevin Federline were just a few of their high-profile Hollywood friends.

Melina's managerial credits also included leading Nitro to the Intercontinental Championship. Despite her impressive efforts outside the ring, it was the Diva's moves in between the ropes that had industry insiders and fans buzzing. In early 2007, Melina dedicated herself to becoming a force in the then- Women's Division. Within weeks, she accomplished her goal when she defeated Mickie James for the Women's Championship. Her successful reign was highlighted by a *WrestleMania 23* victory over Ashley in a Lumberjill Match. Despite losing the championship two months later to James, Melina won it back that very night and went on to a total of three Women's Championship reigns. The beauty from the City of Angels made history when she competed in the first ever women's "I Quit Match" against rival Beth Phoenix.

In October 2009, Melina became one of the few Diva's to hold both the Women's and Divas titles.

M

2010-

2000-09

1990-99

1980-89

1970-79

1960-69

MEN ON A MISSION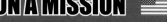

MEMBERS: Mo, Oscar, Mabel   **COMBINED WT: 770 lbs.**

TITLE HISTORY

WORLD TAG TEAM CHAMPIONS	Defeated The Quebecers on March 29, 1994

Managed by Oscar, Men On A Mission were a mammoth team that presented many match-up challenges for their opposition. At 300 lbs, Mo was larger than most opponents, but was nearly 200 lbs lighter than his partner, Mable. Both Superstars were light on their feet and performed double-team moves that wowed audiences. They perfected their style and in March, 1994 defeated the Quebecers for the World Tag Team Championship.

Mable won the 1995 *King of the Ring*. With Mable's crown, Mo became Sir Mo and was in Mable's corner for a match against Diesel for the WWE Heavyweight Championship. Both men took their mission elsewhere as they left WWE in 1996.

Men On A Mission were one of the more popular attractions of the WWE during the mid 1990s. They rocked the ring and their foes with an imposing physical presence that has rarely been seen in the ring.

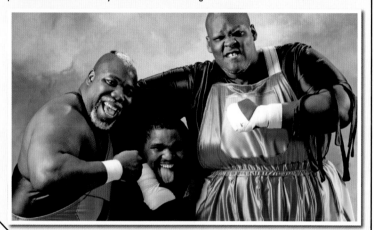

THE MEXICOOLS   **MEMBERS: Juventud Guerrera, Psicosis, Super Crazy**

In 2005, these three crossed the border on their tricked-out John Deere tractors and rolled right into *SmackDown*. Their inspirational leader Juventud declared they were the true Mexican luchadores and superior Mexicools. The angry trio constantly interfered in matches on *SmackDown* and faced other factions such as the bWo and the Full Blooded Italians.

Along the way Juventud won the Cruiserweight Championship of the World and gave the group instant credibility among WWE Superstars. In addition, Psicosis and Super Crazy were contenders for the WWE Tag Team Championship. Guerrera lost his Cruiserweight crown and eventually left WWE in January 2006. Psicosis and Super Crazy continued to team but soon disbanded when Psicosis left WWE later in the year.

MICHAEL BOLLEA   HT: 6'2" WT: 255 lbs. FROM: Tampa, Florida
SIGNATURE MOVE: Full Nelson Slam

Powerful, agile, and tough as nails, Michael Bollea was a promising up-and-comer during the early 1990s. It didn't matter who he faced in the ring, he viewed all opponents the same, as the enemy. A brief run in Japan caught the attention of WWE, who were impressed with Bollea's intimidating, rugged demeanor. By 1998 he changed locations and appeared in WCW. In his time there, he was a part of Raven's Flock and the nWo. He remained with WCW until 2000 when he returned to the independent scene.

Michael Cole (see page 237)

MICHAEL McGILLICUTTY   HT: 6'3" WT: 227 lbs. FROM: Champlin, Minnesota
SIGNATURE MOVE: McGillicutter

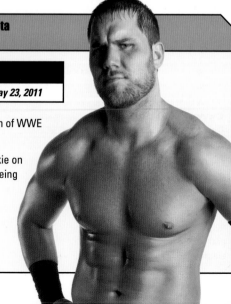

When your father is one of the best of all time, following in his footsteps could be a rather

TITLE HISTORY

WWE TAG TEAM CHAMPION	Partnered with David Otunga to defeat Big Show & Kane on May 23, 2011

daunting task. For better or worse, Michael McGillicutty is faced with such a mission and then some. Not only is he the son of WWE Hall of Famer "Mr. Perfect" Curt Hennig, but he's also the grandson of the legendary Larry "The Axe" Hennig.

Despite the tough road placed in front of him, McGillicutty has persevered. He first appeared on WWE television as a Rookie on season two of *NXT*. With Kofi Kingston as his Pro, the third-generation Superstar made it all the way to the finals, before being selected as runner-up to Kaval.

Refusing to be denied a spot in the family business, McGillicutty returned in October 2010, helping Wade Barrett defeat John Cena at *Hell in a Cell*. From there, he continued to impress Barrett until he was rewarded with a spot in The Nexus. As a member of The Nexus, McGillicutty teamed with David Otunga to capture the WWE Tag Team Championship in May 2011.

MICHAEL COLE

Starting his sports-entertainment career in 1997, Cole's earliest assignments saw him hosting such programs as *Livewire* and *Shotgun Saturday Night*. After cutting his teeth on these now-defunct shows, he landed the role of *SmackDown*'s lead announcer in 1999. Over the following nine years, Cole sat beside numerous color commentators, but eventually proved himself as the true voice of the popular brand.

In June 2008, Cole was surprisingly drafted to WWE's flagship program, *Monday Night Raw*. Within weeks of his debut, he found himself right in the thick of things. Not only did the monstrous Kane viciously attack him, but the new *Raw* announcer also teamed up with broadcast partner and WWE Hall of Famer Jerry "The King" Lawler to challenge for the World Tag Team Championship.

While he continued to call the action on Monday nights, in early 2010 Michael became the commentator for WWE's new program, *NXT*. Early into the show's inaugural season, he showed a different side of his personality by taunting then-WWE rookie, Daniel Bryan. On *Raw*, he smugly accepted one of the most unpopular roles in recent WWE history, the official spokesperson for the Anonymous *Raw* General Manager.

That fall, Michael interfered in Jerry "The King" Lawler's match with The Miz and prevented his broadcast partner from becoming WWE Heavyweight Champion. To save himself from Lawler's wrath, Cole started announced both *Raw* and

SmackDown from inside a protective glass booth which he called the Cole Mine. During his war with "The King," Cole sunk so low he brought Lawler's son and former Superstar, Brian Christopher to *Raw* to make hateful remarks about his father. All of this led to match between Cole and "The King" at *WrestleMania XXVII*. Despite his plan of a handpicked referee being spoiled, Cole ultimately emerged the victor via disqualification.

A two-time Slammy Award winner, the "Voice of WWE" continues to applaud the awful acts of WWE's most horrible rule-breakers. Michael Cole is hell-bent on becoming a WWE institution, whether the WWE Universe approves of it or not.

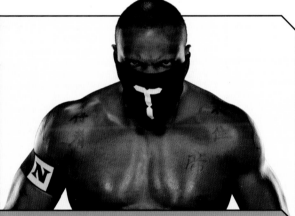

MICHAEL TARVER

HT: 6'3" **WT: 250 lbs.** **FROM: Akron, Ohio**
SIGNATURE MOVE: Tarver's Lightning

"With a single strike, I can knock out any man in 1.9 seconds," claimed a cocky Michael Tarver heading into season one of *WWE NXT*. Luckily for the other seven competitors on the show, Tarver proved to be more bark than bite.

After sporting a less-than-impressive won-loss record and refusing to participate in mandatory challenges, Tarver was cut from *NXT* during the first round of eliminations. The dismissal, however, did not spell the end for the aspiring WWE Superstar. Shortly after season one of *NXT* ended, all eight competitors united to form The Nexus, one of WWE's most rebellious factions in recent memory.

The Nexus targeted WWE's most popular Superstars, namely John Cena, who Tarver and his stablemates battled in a 7-on-7 Elimination Tag Team Match at *SummerSlam 2010*. The thrilling contest featured more than 30 minutes of action, but Tarver's participation lasted less than four minutes. He was quickly eliminated by John Morrison after being hit with Starship Pain.

MICHELLE McCOOL

HT: 5'10"
FROM: Palatka, Florida

TITLE HISTORY	
DIVAS CHAMPION (2 TIMES)	Defeated Natalya on July 20, 2008 Defeated Melina on September 19, 2010
WOMEN'S CHAMPION (2 TIMES)	Defeated Melina on June 28, 2009 Defeated Mickie James on February 26, 2010

Michelle McCool took her first step towards realizing her dreams when she entered the *2004 Diva Search*. Although she didn't win the competition, her beauty and athleticism caught the attention of WWE officials, who offered her a contract. The former schoolteacher spent her early WWE days on the sidelines as a fitness trainer and manager, but her exceptional athleticism allowed her to step into the ring, and excel within it. In 2008, she defeated Natalya at *The Great American Bash* to become the first-ever Divas Champion.

After a five-month reign, she she lost to Maryse, which resulted in McCool going from America's sweetheart to mean girl #1. The following year at *The Great American Bash* Michelle made history when she defeated Melina to become the first Diva to hold both Championships. McCool made another historical "twin" moment when she formed Lay-Cool with Layla, and delcared that any championships held by the team would be jointly defended. At *Night of Champions 2010*, Michelle pinned Melina in a Lumberjill Match to unify the Women's and Divas Championships. In 2011, McCool and Layla's relationship had deteriorated, and the pair met in a Loser Leaves WWE match at *Extreme Rules*. McCool lost the match, and hasn't been seen on WWE programming since.

MICK FOLEY

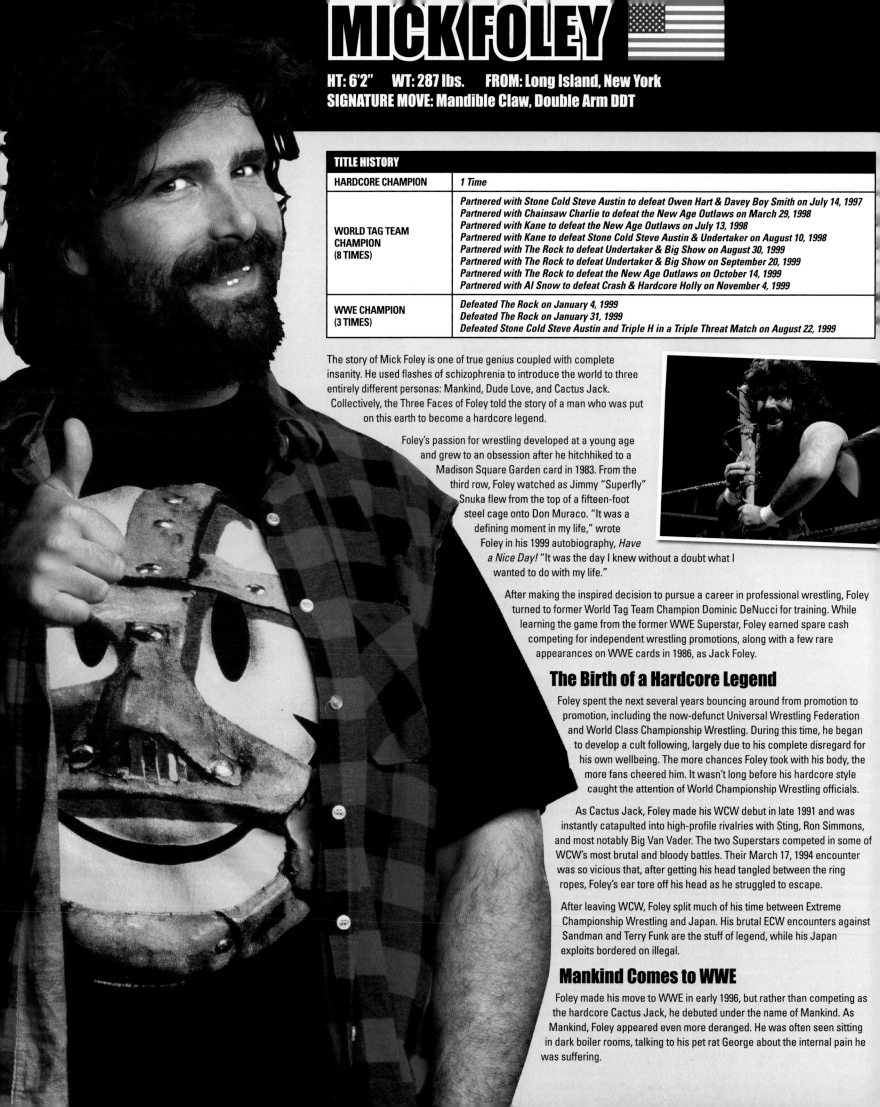

HT: 6'2"   **WT:** 287 lbs.   **FROM:** Long Island, New York
SIGNATURE MOVE: Mandible Claw, Double Arm DDT

TITLE HISTORY	
HARDCORE CHAMPION	*1 Time*
WORLD TAG TEAM CHAMPION (8 TIMES)	*Partnered with Stone Cold Steve Austin to defeat Owen Hart & Davey Boy Smith on July 14, 1997* *Partnered with Chainsaw Charlie to defeat the New Age Outlaws on March 29, 1998* *Partnered with Kane to defeat the New Age Outlaws on July 13, 1998* *Partnered with Kane to defeat Stone Cold Steve Austin & Undertaker on August 10, 1998* *Partnered with The Rock to defeat Undertaker & Big Show on August 30, 1999* *Partnered with The Rock to defeat Undertaker & Big Show on September 20, 1999* *Partnered with The Rock to defeat the New Age Outlaws on October 14, 1999* *Partnered with Al Snow to defeat Crash & Hardcore Holly on November 4, 1999*
WWE CHAMPION (3 TIMES)	*Defeated The Rock on January 4, 1999* *Defeated The Rock on January 31, 1999* *Defeated Stone Cold Steve Austin and Triple H in a Triple Threat Match on August 22, 1999*

The story of Mick Foley is one of true genius coupled with complete insanity. He used flashes of schizophrenia to introduce the world to three entirely different personas: Mankind, Dude Love, and Cactus Jack. Collectively, the Three Faces of Foley told the story of a man who was put on this earth to become a hardcore legend.

Foley's passion for wrestling developed at a young age and grew to an obsession after he hitchhiked to a Madison Square Garden card in 1983. From the third row, Foley watched as Jimmy "Superfly" Snuka flew from the top of a fifteen-foot steel cage onto Don Muraco. "It was a defining moment in my life," wrote Foley in his 1999 autobiography, *Have a Nice Day!* "It was the day I knew without a doubt what I wanted to do with my life."

After making the inspired decision to pursue a career in professional wrestling, Foley turned to former World Tag Team Champion Dominic DeNucci for training. While learning the game from the former WWE Superstar, Foley earned spare cash competing for independent wrestling promotions, along with a few rare appearances on WWE cards in 1986, as Jack Foley.

The Birth of a Hardcore Legend

Foley spent the next several years bouncing around from promotion to promotion, including the now-defunct Universal Wrestling Federation and World Class Championship Wrestling. During this time, he began to develop a cult following, largely due to his complete disregard for his own wellbeing. The more chances Foley took with his body, the more fans cheered him. It wasn't long before his hardcore style caught the attention of World Championship Wrestling officials.

As Cactus Jack, Foley made his WCW debut in late 1991 and was instantly catapulted into high-profile rivalries with Sting, Ron Simmons, and most notably Big Van Vader. The two Superstars competed in some of WCW's most brutal and bloody battles. Their March 17, 1994 encounter was so vicious that, after getting his head tangled between the ring ropes, Foley's ear tore off his head as he struggled to escape.

After leaving WCW, Foley split much of his time between Extreme Championship Wrestling and Japan. His brutal ECW encounters against Sandman and Terry Funk are the stuff of legend, while his Japan exploits bordered on illegal.

Mankind Comes to WWE

Foley made his move to WWE in early 1996, but rather than competing as the hardcore Cactus Jack, he debuted under the name of Mankind. As Mankind, Foley appeared even more deranged. He was often seen sitting in dark boiler rooms, talking to his pet rat George about the internal pain he was suffering.

Using his dreaded Mandible Claw, Mankind made short work of his early competition. The victories put him in perfect position to move up the WWE ladder. To prove his worth, Mankind soon targeted one of WWE's most successful Superstars, Undertaker. The two men spent a year competing in such revolutionary encounters as the Boiler Room Brawl and Buried Alive Match.

By mid-1997, Mankind was a bona fide main eventer. His in-ring conquests carried him to WWE Championship opportunities against Shawn Michaels, Sycho Sid, and Undertaker. He even fought to the finals of the 1997 *King of the Ring* tournament. Despite all his successes, he couldn't garner the admiration of the WWE fans. That all changed when Jim Ross began a series of probing interviews with the deranged Mankind.

The Third Face of Foley

Ross' questioning revealed that a young Foley produced home videos of himself as a character called Dude Love, Foley's fun-loving alter-ego. Fans became instantly enthralled by the hippy persona, and were pleasantly shocked when he made his

in-ring debut as Stone Cold Steve Austin's tag team partner in July 1997. The tie-dye-clad Dude Love & Stone Cold went on to defeat Owen Hart & British Bulldog for the World Tag Team Championship, Foley's first WWE title.

For the next several months, Foley kept his opponents on their toes, as they were never quite sure which persona they were going to face, Mankind or Dude Love. Foley took the confusion a

step further in September 1997 when a vignette aired featuring Mankind and Dude Love actually talking to each other about who should face Triple H that night. In the end, they decided neither persona should face "The Game." Instead, they chose Foley's third face, Cactus Jack, to do the honors. The match marked the WWE debut of Foley's popular hardcore character.

In January 1998, Foley made history by competing in the *Royal Rumble* as all three personas. At *WrestleMania XIV*, Foley, as Cactus Jack, teamed with longtime friend Terry Funk, who competed as Chainsaw Charlie, to wrest the World Tag Team Championship belts from the New Age Outlaws in a Dumpster Match.

Hell in a Cell

Foley's popularity reached iconic status in June 1998 when, as Mankind, he faced Undertaker in a Hell in a Cell Match. In one of the most shocking moments in sports-entertainment history, Mankind was tossed off the top of the demonic structure down to the arena floor. The blood-curdling sight caused announcer Jim Ross to scream the now-famous words, "Good God Almighty! They've killed him! With God as my witness, he is broken in half!" As if the sixteen-foot fall wasn't enough, Mankind was later thrown through the top of the cell, all the way down to the ring. A steel chair followed

his descent, hitting him in the face upon impact.

In typical Foley fashion, the hardcore Superstar continued to evolve his in-ring personalities. In late 1998, Mankind went through significant changes and became a sensation with the fans, especially after debuting his sock puppet, Mr. Socko. Unfortunately for Mankind, he was as gullible as he was goofy. After accepting the newly-created Hardcore Championship as a gift from Mr. McMahon in November 1998, Mankind looked up to the WWE Chairman as a father figure. The diabolical Mr. McMahon took full advantage of this, luring the naïve Mankind close to him, then screwing him over in the finals of the WWE Championship tournament at *Survivor Series*.

Bang bang! During his infamous Japanese days, it was not uncommon to see Foley victimized by such weapons as shards of glass, baseball bats, thumbtacks, barbed wire, and even C-4 explosives.

WWE Champion

Within weeks of his heartbreaking loss at *Survivor Series*, he gained the ultimate revenge when he upended The Rock to capture the WWE Championship on January 4, 1999. The victory saw "Mrs. Foley's baby boy" realize a boyhood dream that many assumed impossible to accomplish. The Mankind-Rock rivalry resulted in a series of brutal and bloody matches. Perhaps their most unsightly encounter occurred at the *Royal Rumble* where The Rock smashed Mankind's skull with seemingly countless steel chair shots. The force of The Rock's swings eventually rendered Mankind unconscious. Mankind reclaimed the title one week later during halftime of Super Bowl XXXIII.

Despite being nearly comatose at the hands of The Rock, Mankind found it within himself to forgive his foe and form a popular tag team known as The Rock & Sock Connection. The duo defeated Undertaker & Big Show for the World Tag Team Championship in August 1999, the first of three reigns for the combination. Mankind later presented his partner with a "This is Your Life" walk down memory lane, one of the most memorable and popular segments in *Monday Night Raw* history.

Foley captured his third and final WWE Championship when he defeated Triple H and Stone Cold Steve Austin at *SummerSlam 1999*. His reign lasted only twenty-four hours, but his rivalry with Triple H was merely beginning. The two battled for the WWE Championship in the main event of the 2000 *Royal Rumble*, and Foley put his career on the line for a final title opportunity at *No Way Out*. He lost in a brutal Hell in a Cell encounter with "The Game", but was granted a spot in the main event of *WrestleMania 2000*. The contest, which was the culmination of a fifteen-year dream for Foley, saw the hardcore Superstar compete in a Fatal Four Way Elimination Match against Triple H, The Rock, and Big Show.

With his in-ring days nestled away in the history books, Foley focused much of his attention on his budding writing career. He is largely recognized for his best-selling autobiographical efforts *Have a Nice Day! Foley is Good,* and *The Hardcore Diaries* but has also penned many children's books, as well as adult fiction. Foley also periodically assumed several roles on WWE television, most notably that of commissioner, referee, and announcer. He even made a few rare returns to the ring, including a brutal Hardcore Match against Edge at *WrestleMania 22*.

The icon of sports-entertainment and the literary world showed the WWE Universe he's never short on surprises when he made his WWE television return on the November 14, 2011 episode of *Raw*. Foley reconnected with friend John Cena in the ring and reprised his role of Master of Ceremonies for another round of *This Is Your Life*. Though it didn't end the way Foley had planned, the WWE Universe was just happy to witness his return. Now back among sports-entertainment's elite, the world is asking, "What will Mrs. Foley's baby boy do next?"

M

2010-

2000-09

1990-99

1980-89

1970-79

1960-69

MICKIE JAMES 🇺🇸

HT: 5'4"   **FROM: Richmond, Virginia**
SIGNATURE MOVE: Mick Kick

TITLE HISTORY

DIVAS CHAMPION	Defeated Maryse on July 26, 2009
WOMEN'S CHAMPION (5 TIMES)	Defeated Trish Stratus on April 2, 2006 Defeated Lita on November 26, 2006 Defeated Melina on April 24, 2007 Defeated Beth Phoenix on April 14, 2008 Defeated Michelle McCool on January 31, 2010

Mickie first introduced herself to WWE audiences in October 2005 when she ran to the ring to save her idol Trish Stratus from a vicious attack at the hands of Victoria. Over the next several months, the two Divas enjoyed a close friendship, but when Trish started to feel smothered by Mickie's admiration, the alliance turned sour and the girls engaged in a bitter rivalry. Their battles reached a peak at *WrestleMania 22* when Mickie defeated Trish for her first Women's Championship.

The following year, Melina emerged as Mickie's chief nemesis. The two Divas spent the first four months of 2007 battling over the Women's Championship, a title they traded three times during this period. Unfortunately for Mickie, one of her championship reigns lasted mere minutes.

Despite the short reign, Mickie remained a top Diva and added another prize to her collection in June 2009 when she defeated Maryse for the Divas Championship. Upon her *SmackDown* arrival, James found herself in battle with Lay-Cool in a war over words and WWE gold. Her Friday nights were filled with battles against the likes of Alicia Fox, Maryse, and Vickie Guerrero, and she also found time to form a tremendous team with an unlikely ally, Beth Phoenix.

Shortly thereafter Mickie left the ring to become a country music star. This gorgeous little lady represented the new generation of Diva in WWE with her marvelous beauty and wonderful fighting spirit.

MIDEON 🇺🇸   HT: 6'3"   WT: 288 lbs.

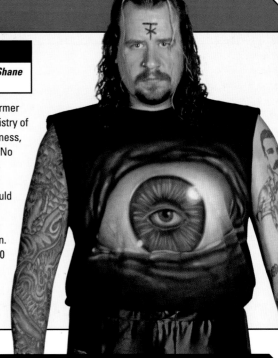

TITLE HISTORY

EUROPEAN CHAMPION	*Awarded championship by Shane McMahon on June 21, 1999*

In January 1999, a grim ceremony transformed a former hillbilly into Mideon, a member of Undertaker's Ministry of Darkness. During his time with the Ministry of Darkness, Mideon often teamed up with the gigantic Viscera. No other Superstar in WWE history had an easier time acquiring a championship in WWE than Mideon. In June 1999 Mideon asked Shane McMahon if he could have the European Championship. When Shane O' Mac told him he could do what he wanted, Mideon took the prize but lost it a month later to D-Lo Brown. After a brief hiatus from the ring, he returned in 2000 as Naked Mideon, wearing only a thong and fanny pack. Fans at live events attended by Mideon during this time likely saw more of the Superstar than they really wanted.

MIGHTY IGOR 🇺🇸   FROM: Dearborn, Michigan
SIGNATURE MOVE: Bearhug

Prior to entering the world of sports-entertainment, Mighty Igor gained fame as an accomplished body builder. His immense size made him a force in the ring; but it was his pre-match antics that oftentimes gave him the psychological advantage well before ever locking horns, as Mighty Igor was known to show off by having cinder blocks broken over his head with a sledgehammer.

Appropriately referred to as the "World's Strongest Wrestler," Mighty Igor's greatest accomplishment came when he overpowered the great Mad Dog Vachon for the AWA Championship. He only held the title for one week before losing it back to Vachon, but he will forever be remembered alongside such great former AWA Champions as Verne Gagne, Nick Bockwinkel and Jerry "The King" Lawler.

Utilizing a bearhug finisher that sucked the life from his foes, Mighty Igor crossed paths with many of the industry's finest over the course of his thirty-year career. Some of his most notable rivalries include The Sheik, The Masked Superstar and Jos LeDuc.

MIGUEL PEREZ 🇵🇷   HT: 6'1"   WT: 238 lbs.   FROM: Puerto Rico
SIGNATURE MOVE: Sunset Flip

During the late 1950s Miguel Perez, shot to stardom as one-half of one of the most successful tag teams in sports-entertainment history. Along with Antonino "Argentia" Rocca, the two Superstars were main event attractions throughout the eastern seaboard for Vincent J. McMahon's Capitol Sports. Rocca and Perez were heroes everywhere as fans admired their heart, desire, and fire in the ring.

Perez stayed with McMahon when Capitol Sports became the World Wide Wrestling Federation and battled "Nature Boy" Buddy Rogers for the Heavyweight Championship. In 1968 Perez left the company and appeared in Puerto Rico where he reunited with Rocca for a time before retiring from action in 1979. For decades Miguel Perez was considered the greatest Superstar to emerge from Puerto Rico.

MIKE ADAMLE 🇺🇸

After career as a player in the NFL, Mike Adamle enjoyed a thirty year run in sports broadcasting, both as a studio host and sideline reporter. In 1989, he became the host of the ground-breaking "American Gladiators" program and remained with them until 1996. He was also part of the XFL broadcast team and covered the 2000 and 2004 Summer Olympic Games.

In 2008, Adamle felt it was time for a change. He kicked off his new career in sports-entertainment at the *Royal Rumble*, then went on to conduct interviews on *Raw*. That April he debuted on ECW before he eventually walked off the set with broadcast partner Tazz. Fans began to jeer the sight of Adamle, but they had know idea what was in store.

That July saw one of the most shocking events in *Raw* history when Shane McMahon promoted Mike Adamle to General Manager. During his tenure, broadcasts of WWE's flagship program were dubbed "Adamle Originals." Neither WWE fans nor its Superstars had any idea of what to expect each week. Though he resigned his post in November 2008, General Manager Adamle brought a fresh perspective to WWE during this time.

MIKE AWESOME 🇺🇸

HT: 6'6" **WT:** 292 lbs.
FROM: Tampa, Florida
SIGNATURE MOVE: Awesome Bomb

TITLE HISTORY

HARDCORE CHAMPION	1 Time

Mike Awesome had the strength to powerbomb virtually any opponent and the agility to clear the top rope while nailing opponents with a plancha. A dominant champion in ECW and Japan, Awesome sparked controversy in the beginning of the new millennium when he jumped to WCW while still reigning as ECW Champion. This resulted in Awesome, under contract with WCW, meeting Tazz, under contract with WWE, for the ECW title at an ECW live event.

Awesome remained with WCW until the company was purchased by WWE in March 2001. In June, Awesome made his WWE debut and defeated Rhyno for the Hardcore Championship, making him the first WCW wrestler to win a championship in WWE.

After time in independent promotions and Japan, Awesome returned to WWE in 2005 at *ECW One Night Stand*. The roof of The Hammerstein Ballroom almost blew off as Awesome warred with old nemesis Masato Tanaka. Tragically, in February 2007 Mike Awesome passed away. This dynamic competitor will always be regarded as one of the most agile big men the world has ever seen.

MIKE KNOX 🇺🇸

HT: 6'6" **WT:** 293 lbs.
FROM: Phoenix, Arizona
SIGNATURE MOVE:
Spinning Reverse STO

Proving you only get one chance to make a good first impression, Mike Knox's extreme unpopularity can be traced back to his initial appearance, which saw him prevent then-girlfriend Kelly Kelly from disrobing for the ECW fans. From that moment on, Knox had a tough time gaining any fans, but that hasn't seemed to bother the near 300-pound monster, as he became more focused on inflicting pain than making friends.

Just months into his career, the vicious Knox joined forces with Rated-RKO to battle Team DX at *Survivor Series* 2006. The momentum of the high-profile encounter catapulted the bushy-bearded Superstar to several victories over some of ECW's longtime favorites, including Tommy Dreamer, Stevie Richards, and Balls Mahoney. During the spring of 2009 Knox moved to *SmackDown* and *Superstars* and showed his passion for inflicting pain onto others. Before parting ways with WWE in April 2010, Knox took part in the 26 Man, Over-The-Top Battle Royal at *WrestleMania XXVI*.

MIKE McGUIRK 🇺🇸

Years before Lilian Garcia's voice became a staple on *Monday Night Raw*, the lovely Mike McGuirk introduced capacity crowds to such WWE Superstars as Hulk Hogan, Jake "The Snake" Roberts and "Hacksaw" Jim Duggan.

As a female ring announcer in the late 1980s, McGuirk oftentimes had a difficult time fitting into the male-dominated industry. On more than one occasion, the blonde voice of WWE became the target of Bobby "The Brain" Heenan's verbal barbs, but it was Harvey Wippleman and Big Bully Busick who frightened McGuirk the most. On an episode of *Wrestling Challenge*, Wippleman and The Bully verbally harassed McGuirk to the point of tears. Luckily, Sid Justice ran to the ring to fend off the frightened female's offenders.

In addition to her ring announcing duties, McGuirk also worked as a commentator on WWE's *All-American Wrestling* television program.

M

1960-69
1970-79
1980-89
1990-99
2000-09
2010-

241

MIL MASCARAS

HT: 5'11" WT: 245 lbs.
FROM: Mexico City, Mexico
SIGNATURE MOVE: Plancha

Mil Mascaras is arguably the most admired masked wrestler of all time. Despite his immense popularity, however, he is difficult to identify upon appearance alone, as Mascaras rarely wears the same mask twice. Once the bell rings, however, "The Man of 1,000 Masks" has a style that is unmistakable.

Shortly after debuting in the mid-1960s, Mascaras began utilizing a high-flying style not normally associated with men of his size. His expansive repertoire of planchas and flying bodyblocks made him an instant success in Mexico. After becoming a national sensation in his homeland, Mascaras took his game international, most notably Japan and the United States, where he continued to excel.

Mascaras' reputation preceded him on his way to WWE. As a result, he was instantly propelled into main event status upon debuting. In addition to a memorable rivalry with Ernie Ladd, Mascaras challenged "Superstar" Billy Graham for the WWE Championship in 1977.

Mascaras' final in-ring WWE appearance came at the 1997 *Royal Rumble*. The masked man's unfamiliarity with the rules of the Rumble ultimately cost him, as he eliminated himself after leaping off the top rope to the outside.

MILLION DOLLAR CHAMPIONSHIP

Perhaps the most controversial Championship in the history of sports-entertainment, the Million Dollar Championship was conceived by "Million Dollar Man" Ted DiBiase when he could neither buy the World Heavyweight Championship nor defeat then-champion, Hulk Hogan. This championship was never officially acknowledged by the WWE.

1989
March 4
Binghamton, NY

"Million Dollar Man" Ted DiBiase crowned himself Champion during an episode of *The Brother Love Show*.

1991
August 26
New York, NY

Vigril defeated "Million Dollar Man" Ted DiBiase.

November 24
Utica, NY

"Million Dollar Man" Ted DiBiase defeated Virgil via Pinfall.

From February 7, 1992 until January 8, 1996 The Million Dollar Championship was dormant.

1996
January 8
Newark, DE

"Million Dollar Man" Ted DiBiase awarded the Million Dollar Championship to his protégé, The Ringmaster.

May 28
North Charleston, SC

The Ringmaster lost a Caribbean Strap Match to Savio Vega. As a result, "Million Dollar Man" Ted DiBiase had to leave World Wrestling Entertainment.

2010
April 5
Moline, IL

The heir to the "Million Dollar Man's" fortune, Ted DiBiase was handed the championship. He gave up the title on November 15 and it hasn't been seen since.

MILLION DOLLAR CORPORATION

MEMBERS: Nikolai Volkoff, Irwin R. Schyster, King Kong Bundy, Bam Bam Bigelow, Tatanka, 1-2-3 Kid, Sycho Sid, Xanta Klaus

When "Million Dollar Man" Ted DiBiase became a manager in 1994 he was determined to acquire Superstars like he acquired assets in the business world. His first recruits were former tag team partner I.R.S. and Nikolai Volkoff. When DiBiae wanted a Superstar he more often than not persuaded them to join by interfering in their matches on their behalf and luring them with large sums of money.

If a recruited Superstar did not join the Million Dollar Corporation, they were considered an enemy of the Million Dollar Corporation. The group disbanded in 1994 after "The Ringmaster" Steve Austin lost to Savio Vega, thus eliminating the "Million Dollar Man" from World Wrestling Entertainment.

"MILLION DOLLAR MAN" TED DiBIASE

HT: 6'1" **WT: 260 lbs.** **FROM: Palm Beach, Florida** **SIGNATURE MOVE: Million Dollar Dream**

TITLE HISTORY

WORLD TAG TEAM CHAMPION (3 TIMES)	Partnered with Irwin R. Schyster to defeat The Legion of Doom on February 7, 1992 Partnered with Irwin R. Schyster to defeat The Natural Disasters on October 13, 1992 Partnered with Irwin R. Schyster to defeat The Steiners on June 16, 1993

Ted DiBiase used his never-ending bankroll to acquire the world's most lavish possessions. He had mansions, fur coats, servants, limousines, and private jets. He even used his funds to nearly purchase the WWE Championship. In short, his spending was the stuff of legend, the legend of the "Million Dollar Man."

The obnoxiously rich Superstar first made a name for himself in 1987 when he made his now-famous claim that everybody had a price. Proving his point, DiBiase often gave fans large sums of money to perform demeaning tasks such as barking like a dog and kissing his feet.

In one of the most infamous moments in WWE history, DiBiase funded a complex ploy designed to put the WWE Championship around his waist. Prior to Andre the Giant's WWE Championship Match against Hulk Hogan in February 1988 at *The Main Event*, the "Million Dollar Man" paid Andre to hand over the championship if he won. To better Andre's chances of beating Hogan, DiBiase abducted the match's referee and replaced him with a man he paid to have plastic surgery to look like the referee. The substitute referee made several questionable calls, including the decisive pin itself, which resulted in Andre winning the WWE Championship. After the match, Andre handed the title over to DiBiase as planned. The devious scheme worked perfectly, with the exception of one thing: President Jack Tunney refused to recognize the title change.

After his failed attempts at claiming the WWE Championship, DiBiase used his impressive bank account to create his own title. In 1989, he debuted the Million Dollar Championship, a multi-million dollar prize covered in diamonds. DiBiase wore the title proudly, despite the fact that WWE refused to recognize it as an official championship.

Lost in all the talk of money is the fact that DiBiase was also an accomplished competitor. Alongside Irwin R. Schyster, DiBiase claimed three World Tag Team Championships. Toward the end of his career, DiBiase used his finances become a powerful manager. His legendary reputation as a free spender helped him lure many of the game's top names, including Sycho Sid and Steve Austin.

MINISTRY OF DARKNESS

MEMBERS: Undertaker, The Acolytes, Mideon, Edge, Christian, Gangrel, Viscera, Paul Bearer

After more than two years apart, Undertaker and Paul Bearer reconciled in early 1999 to form the most sinister faction in WWE history. Known as The Ministry of Darkness, the group threatened to unleash a never-before-seen plague on WWE. With Faarooq & Bradshaw already in tow, Undertaker performed a series of sadistic rituals to initiate the remaining members of the group, which consisted of Mideon, Viscera and the Brood. As a collective unit, the Ministry claimed to take orders from a "higher power," who ordered them to mentally and emotionally cripple Mr. McMahon.

The Ministry knew no boundaries when it came to their war against McMahon. They even took their devious assault to the WWE owner's private estate, where they left a burning Undertaker symbol in the yard. However, their most offensive attack came when the "Deadman" abducted McMahon's daughter. With Stephanie in custody, Undertaker threatened to join her in unholy matrimony if McMahon failed to hand over control of WWE. Luckily for Stephanie, Stone Cold Steve Austin saved her from the darkness.

In April 1999, the Ministry became even more powerful when they joined forces with the Corporation. The merger certainly proved to be a shock to fans, but the biggest surprise was yet to come. In June, The Ministry finally revealed the identity of the "higher power." The world watched in complete disbelief as Mr. McMahon exposed himself as the mastermind behind the entire ploy.

MISS KITTY

HT: 5'3" **FROM: Menphis, Tennessee**
SIGNATURE MOVE: Stinkface

TITLE HISTORY

WOMEN'S CHAMPION	Defeated Ivory on December 12, 1999

This sweet femme debuted in August 1999 on an episode of *Monday Night Raw* as an assistant to Debra, manager of Jeff Jarrett. Audiences then saw her become the sidekick to Chyna. Before the end of the year, she stripped Ivory out of her gown and became Women's Champion in a Swimming Pool Evening Gown Match at *Armageddon '99*. After her win, she spread the word that she would know be known as "The Kat."

Despite losing the title shortly after winning it, she appeared at *WrestleMania 2000* and at a Thong Stink Face Match at *SummerSlam*. In early 2001, she took exception to the group known as Right to Censor, and created the Right to Nudity group to oppose it. Unfortunately, after her team lost a match at *No Way Out*, the Kat was forced to join the Right to Censor. After a single appearance with Right to Censor, Kat parted ways the WWE.

MISSING LINK

HT: 6'2" WT: 250 lbs. FROM: Parts Unknown
SIGNATURE MOVE: Diving Headbutt

One of the original oddities of sports-entertainment, the Missing Link first appeared in WWE in May 1985. He baffled audiences and Superstars with his confusing brand of violence that usually involved using his own body. Missing Link's incredible power and speed was attributed to his hunting and consumption of wild animals. Missing Link's outward appearance was so shocking it even caught the eye of *Sports Illustrated*.

Managed by Bobby Heenan and later Jimmy Hart, Missing Link was almost impossible to control. He often bashed his own head with chairs to regain his composure and grabbed the back of his hair for added force when executing one of his trademark headbutts. He only knew how to do one thing: attack anyone who stood in front of him. By the end of the year, Missing Link left WWE and traveled to World Class Championship Wrestling and Universal Wrestling Federation. He vanished after 1987 and remained in retirement until 2004 when he remerged on the independent scene. In 2006 his autobiography, *Bang Your Head: The Real Story of the Missing Link* was released. Sadly in 2007 the Missing Link passed away after a long battle with cancer.

MITSU ARAKAWA

HT: 5'10" WT: 240 lbs.
FROM: Japan SIGNATURE MOVE: Iron Claw

TITLE HISTORY

INTERNATIONAL TAG TEAM CHAMPION	Partnered with Prof. Toru Tanaka to win a tournament on June 1, 1969

Mitsu Arakawa wasn't very well liked by his fellow Superstars. Whether it was a result of his consistent, illegal use of salt as a weapon or his dreaded Iron Claw, his colleagues practically refused to get in the ring with him. The fans weren't too fond of him either. In fact, many consider Arakawa to be one of the most hated villains of the 1960s.

In an attempt to avoid squaring off against him, many Superstars actually aligned themselves with Arakawa instead. Over the course of his career, he became known as one of the most sought after tag team partners in the business. His pairings resulted in ten tag team championship reigns over fifteen years. He even teamed with Prof. Toru Tanaka to capture the WWE International Tag Team Championship in June 1969. They held the titles for six months before losing to Bruno Sammartino & Battman.

THE MIZ

HT: 6'1" WT: 231 lbs.
FROM: Cleveland, Ohio
SIGNATURE MOVE: Skull-Crushing Finale

TITLE HISTORY

UNITED STATES CHAMPION	Defeated Kofi Kingston on October 5, 2009 Defeated R-Truth on June 14, 2010
WORLD TAG TEAM CHAMPION (2 TIMES)	Partnered with John Morrison to defeat CM Punk & Kofi Kingston on December 13, 2008 Partnered with Big Show to defeat D-Generation X on February 8, 2010
WWE CHAMPION	Defeated Randy Orton on November 22, 2010
WWE TAG TEAM CHAMPION (3 TIMES)	Partnered with John Morrison to defeat MVP & Matt Hardy on November 16, 2007 Partnered with Big Show to defeat D-Generation X on February 8, 2010 Partnered with John Cena to defeat Justin Gabriel & Heath Slater on February 21, 2011

When The Miz first arrived in WWE as a *Tough Enough* contestant in 2004, most assumed he was nothing more than a reality-television star looking to score another 15 minutes of fame. Those people were dead wrong. Fast forward just a few years and The Miz has become an elite Superstar, unleashing his arrogant brand of awesome all over WWE.

Miz first proved his naysayers wrong when he teamed with John Morrison to capture the WWE Tag Team Titles in November 2007. As champions, not only did Miz and Morrison rule the tag division for eight long months, but they also debuted *The Dirt Sheet*, a WWE.com segment used to ridicule other Superstars. Today, many view *The Dirt Sheet* as the coming-out party for Miz's now-famous charismatic personality.

Miz and Morrison's greatness in the ring was recognized at the 2008 Slammy Awards when they were crowned Tag Team of the Year. Despite their dominance, however, singles success was right around the corner for the Cleveland native.

The Miz moved from ECW to *Raw* in the spring of 2009. As a member of WWE's flagship program, the smug Superstar developed a more aggressive style in the ring. The change helped catapult him to multiple singles accomplishments, starting with the United States Championship in October 2009.

With Tag Team and U.S. Championships already to his credit, The Miz turned his attention to owning the most prized accolade in all of sports-entertainment, the WWE Championship. In July 2010, he moved one step closer to realizing this goal when he turned back seven other Superstars to claim the Money in the Bank briefcase.

Over the next four months, The Miz patiently assessed the championship scene, waiting for the perfect time to cash in his guaranteed title opportunity. Finally, in November 2010, Miz picked off a weakened Randy Orton on *Raw* to capture the coveted WWE Championship.

As champion, Miz soared to the top of the sports-entertainment industry. For the following five-plus months, he main evented nearly every show, including *WrestleMania XXVII*, where he defeated John Cena.

MNM
MEMBERS: Joey Mercury, Johnny Nitro, Melina

TITLE HISTORY

WWE TAG TEAM CHAMPIONS (3 TIMES)	Defeated Rey Mysterio & Eddie Guerrero on April 21, 2005 Defeated Animal & Heidenreich on October 28, 2005 Defeated Batista & Rey Mysterio on December 30, 2005

Unlike many young newcomers, the bright lights of WWE failed to intimidate the self-proclaimed A-List celebrities MNM. With paparazzi commonplace in their everyday lives, Joey Mercury, Johnny Nitro & Melina were accustomed to the media frenzy associated with WWE. As a result, they were able to make an instant impact upon their debut. In fact, Mercury & Nitro captured the WWE Tag Team Championship in their first match in April 2005.

Over the next year, the duo claimed the tag titles a total of three times, proving themselves as one of *SmackDown*'s greatest teams. Unfortunately, things went sour for the red-carpet trio in May 2005 when Melina & Nitro viciously attacked Mercury following a loss. Shortly after their assault, Nitro & Melina left *SmackDown* for *Raw*. As a member of the *Raw* roster, Nitro achieved great solo success, including two reigns as Intercontinental Champion.

In true Hollywood fashion, MNM premiered their thrilling sequel in November 2006 when they reunited to challenge The Hardy Boys. Unfortunately for Mercury & Nitro, they were unable to duplicate the greatness of their first blockbuster. They went their separate ways soon after.

MOLLY HOLLY
HT: 5'4" FROM: Mobile, Alabama
SIGNATURE MOVE: Molly Go-Round

In 2000, the time had come for this Diva to be with her older cousins, Crash and Hardcore, in the ring. Molly started off battling Trish Stratus, but a relationship with Spike Dudley captured her attention for a time. Molly later became a super-hero alongside The Hurricane, but dissolved the partnership when she had the opportunity to take his Hardcore Championship.

TITLE HISTORY

HARDCORE CHAMPION	1 Time
WOMEN'S CHAMPION (2 TIMES)	Defeated Trish Stratus on June 23, 2002 Defeated Gail Kim on July 28, 2003

Molly soon separated herself from the rest of the Divas, claiming that she was pure, wholesome, and better than any other Diva in the ring. Molly backed up her claim in 2002 at *King of the Ring* when she defeated Trish Stratus for the Women's Championship. After losing the title at *Unforgiven* in the same year, she managed to capture the title again in 2003. She lost in 2004 to Victoria, and the women met in a Hair vs. Title match at *WrestleMania XX*, which ended with Molly getting her head shaved. Molly left WWE in 2005, but still appears at independent events. She also devotes her time to charity work for causes important to her.

MOMMA BENJAMIN

Momma Benjamin first appeared on *Raw* as son Shelton was in the middle of a losing streak that carried over from 2005 to 2006. Momma said to him, "You're going to be a champion if I have to beat you down to make it happen." Remembering experiences from his childhood Shelton toughened up and did what was necessary to make his momma happy. She began to challenge other Superstars on her boy's behalf, and even assisted him from time to time. Momma eventually led Shelton to the Intercontinental Championship in a victory over Ric Flair. Weeks later Shelton announced that the woman who brought him into this world left WWE to undergo corrective heart surgery. Since her procedure, she stayed away, and allowed her boy find his own way in the ring again.

2010-
2000-09
1990-99
1980-89
1970-79
1960-69

Money in the Bank began as a special match at *WrestleMania 21* but has grown into a standalone event. In an otherwise standard Ladder Match, a briefcase is suspended over the ring. It contains a contract for a World Championship Match of the winner's choice anytime between that night and the following year's *WrestleMania*. The matches have included anywhere from six to eight participants spanning all WWE brands.

WrestleMania 21 (2005)

2005 match during *WrestleMania 21* for a shot at the WWE Championship

WINNER: EDGE

WrestleMania 22 (2006)

2006 match during *WrestleMania 22* for a shot at either the WWE or World Heavyweight Championship

WINNER: ROB VAN DAM

WrestleMania 23 (2007)

2007 match at *WrestleMania 23* for a shot at any WWE Championship

WINNER: MR. KENNEDY

WrestleMania XXIV (2008)

2008 match at *WrestleMania XXIV* for a shot at any WWE Championship

WINNER: CM PUNK

WrestleMania XXV (2009)

2009 match at *WrestleMania XXV* match for a shot at any WWE Championship

WINNER: CM PUNK

WrestleMania XXVI (2010)

2010 match at *WrestleMania XXVI* for a shot at any WWE Championship

WINNER: JACK SWAGGER

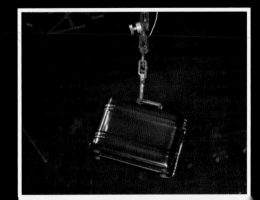

July 18, 2010

Kansas City, MO - Sprint Center

Money In The Bank Ladder Match for a shot at the World Heavyweight Championship

WINNER: KANE

Money In The Bank Ladder Match for a shot at the WWE Championship

WINNER: THE MIZ

July 17, 2011

Rosemont, IL Allstate Arena

Money In The Bank Ladder Match for a shot at the World Heavyweight Championship

WINNER: DANIEL BRYAN

Money In The Bank Ladder Match for a shot at the WWE Championship

WINNER: ALBERTO DEL RIO

MONEY, INC.

MEMBERS: Ted DiBiase, Irwin R. Schyster
COMBINED WT: 508 lbs.

TITLE HISTORY	
WORLD TAG TEAM CHAMPIONS (3 TIMES)	*Defeated The Legion of Doom on Febuary 7, 1992 Defeated Natural Disasters on October 13, 1992 Defeated The Steiners on June 16, 1993*

Among the many derogatory things you could say about Ted DiBiase is that he is arrogant, demeaning and obnoxious. One thing you can't call him is a cheat. Otherwise, why would he choose to keep company with noted tax accountant Irwin R. Schyster?

DiBiase & Schyster first began competing as a unit in February 1992. With Jimmy "The Mouth of the South" Hart as their manager, the money-hungry duo known as Money, Inc. gained instant success, capturing the World Tag Team Championship from the Legion of Doom shortly after their formation. The win ruffled the feathers of another team managed by Hart, the Natural Disasters, who believed their manager should have placed them into the championship match instead. The contention set off a fiery rivalry between the two teams.

After five months of successfully fending off Earthquake & Typhoon, Money, Inc. finally fell to the mammoth tag team in July 1992. The loss failed to set DiBiase & Schyster back, however, as they quickly reclaimed the titles a few months later. The victory gave them their second of three World Tag Team Championship reigns.

Following DiBiase's retirement in 1993, the affluent duo remained close business partners. When the "Million-Dollar Man" set out to manage his own stable of Superstars, he pinpointed I.R.S. as one of his crown jewels.

THE MONGOLIAN STOMPER

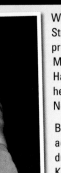

HT: 6'1" **WT:** 260 lbs.
FROM: Mongolia

While most WWE fans may not be overly familiar with the Mongolian Stomper, his résumé boasts more than fifty championship reigns from promotions all over North America. The chiseled Superstar from Mongolia achieved his greatest notoriety while competing for Stu Hart's Stampede Wrestling in Calgary, Alberta, Canada. While there, he engaged in heated rivalries with Bad News Allen (known as Bad News Brown to WWE fans) and a very young Bret Hart.

Between reigns atop Stampede Wrestling, the Mongolian Stomper achieved great success in the United States. On several occasions during the 1960s and 1970s, he nearly defeated Lou Thesz, Gene Kiniski and Harley Race for the NWA Championship.

THE MONGOLS

MEMBERS: Bepo, Geto **WT:** 578 lbs.

TITLE HISTORY

INTERNATIONAL TAG TEAM CHAMPIONS (2 TIMES)	*Defeated Victor Rivera & Tony Marino on June 15, 1970 Defeated Bruno Sammartino & Dominic DeNucci on July 2, 1971*

These hideous beasts were first seen in wrestling rings in Canada as part of Stu Hart's Stampede Wrestling. By the late 1960's, they were part of World Wrestling Entertainment and the first clients of Lou Albano. When the bell rang Bepo and Geto shredded opponents with their strong double-team moves and illegal tactics.

In June 1970 the pair captured the International Tag Team Championship during their Madison Square Garden debut. With the precursor to the World Tag Team Championship around their waist, the Mongols left WWE in 1971 and took the belts with them. WWE held a tournament that saw "Crazy" Luke Graham & Tarzan Tyler win on November 12, 1971. Graham & Tyler beat the Mongols at a later date, ending any question of who were the real tag team champions. After the defeat the Mongols parted ways.

MOONDOG MAYNE

HT: 6'0" **WT:** 275 lbs. **FROM:** Crabtree, Oregon
SIGNATURE MOVE: The Bone Smash

Mayne was a crazed competitor who was unpredictable both in and out of the ring. Moondog was known for howling and chomping on pieces of broken glass during his interviews. His unorthodox means of dissecting opponents included biting them, raking their eyes, and he even took beverages from those sitting in the audience and dumped them in the face of his opponent.

Moondog debuted in WWE in 1972 and quickly set to eradicate the company's top Superstars. Mayne's "blood-eat-blood" mentality also led to many victories in Battle Royals before leaving the company in late 1973. He took his brawling ways to the west coast of the United States and became a threat everywhere he appeared. Tragically in August 1978, Moondaog Mayne was killed in an automobile accident.

THE MOONDOGS

MEMBERS: Rex, Spot, King
FROM: Parts Unknown

TITLE HISTORY

WORLD TAG TEAM CHAMPIONS	*Defeated Tony Garea & Rick Martel on March 17, 1981*

Although unorthodox in appearance, the Moondogs were one of the most skilled tag teams of the early 1980s. Managed by Capt. Lou Albano, the barrel-chested combination was known for its shaggy hair, ripped jeans and habit of gnawing on large animal bones.

Rex & King proved their bark was as big as their bite when they beat Tony Garea & Rick Martel for the World Tag Team Championship in March 1981. A few months into their reign, however, King established himself as the runt of the litter when he ran away from WWE completely. Rex, however, filled the vacancy with another Moondog, Spot, and the duo went on to successfully defend the tag titles for two more months.

After losing the World Tag Team Championship back to Garea & Martel in July 1981, Rex & Spot struggled to regain their momentum. The wild duo eventually moved on to moderately successful singles careers.

1960-69
1970-79
1980-89
1990-99
2000-09
2010-

2010-

2000-09

1990-99

1980-89

1970-79

1960-69

"THE MOOSE" FRANK MONROE 🍁

WT: 295 lbs.   FROM: Canada

When you hail from Canada and weigh close to 300 pounds, you have every right to call yourself "The Moose." And that's exactly what Frank Monroe did as a member of the WWE roster in the late 1970s and early 1980s.

Unfortunately, unlike most moose, with their menacing antlers and barrel chests, Monroe failed to strike fear in his opponents. And rather than use his immense size to his advantage, Monroe gained a reputation for being more of a brawler, whose offense comprised mainly of punches and kicks.

Monroe's opposition usually had the big man well scouted. They would wait for him to miss an ill-timed punch, and then attack when his weight forced him to lose his balance. Because of this, many of Monroe's matches lasted less than three minutes. In fact, in 1979, future WWE Hall of Famer Tony Atlas beat "The Moose" in less than one minute. Other Superstars benefiting from Monroe's inferior skills include Tito Santana, Ted DiBiase and Pedro Morales.

MORDECAI

HT: 6'3"   WT: 270 lbs.
SIGNATURE MOVE: Crucifix Powerbomb

According to Mordecai, sin eats away at the soul of society like a ravenous cancer, devouring it until there's nothing left but a black hole of despair. And from that hole, the mysterious Superstar emerged. Clad in pure white, Mordecai made his debut at the *Judgment Day 2004*, soundly defeating Scotty 2 Hotty. From there, he turned his attention on the rest of the *SmackDown* locker room, threatening to make them pay for their sins.

Utilizing a slow and deliberate offensive style, the mysterious man punished Billy Kidman and Akio before defeating veteran Hardcore Holly at *The Great American Bash*. With a perfect record, including two pay-per-view victories over established Superstars, Mordecai went into battle against Rey Mysterio on a July 2004 edition of *SmackDown*. Given his impressive start, many assumed the newcomer could beat the then-Cruiserweight Champion. But it wasn't to be. Mysterio defeated Mordecai and the mysterious Superstar was never heard from again.

MOUNTIE 🍁

HT: 6'1"   WT: 257 lbs.
FROM: Montreal, Quebec, Canada
SIGNATURE MOVE:
Carotid Control Technique

TITLE HISTORY	
INTERCONTINENTAL CHAMPION	Defeated Bret Hart on January 17, 1992

A former member of the Royal Canadian Mounted Police, this Superstar debuted in WWE in 1991. Despite claims that the world was his jurisdiction and that he upheld international law and order, the Mountie often broke the rules to earn his victories. To add insult to injury, he often handcuffed fallen opponents to the ring ropes and tasered them with his shock stick.

Big Boss Man took exception to his methods and the two former law enforcers battled for months, culminating in a Jailhouse Match at *SummerSlam 1991* with the stipulation that the loser would spend the night in a New York City jail. The Mountie lost the match and was taken away by New York's Finest.

In January 1992, the Mountie caught Bret Hart on an off night and captured the Intercontinental Championship, but held the title for only two days. By the end of 1992, the Mountie was gone from WWE, but fans will always remember him and his vow to always get his man!

MR. FUJI

In 1972, Mr. Fuji arrived in World Wrestling Entertainment managed by the Grand Wizard. He quickly became known for secretly hiding bags of ceremonial Japanese salt on his person and throwing it into the eyes of opponents. He allied himself with the dreaded Prof. Toru Tanaka, and on June 27, 1972, they began their first of three World Tag Team Championship reigns. After losing the titles for the second time, Fuji & Tanaka left WWE and stormed into the NWA, where they won numerous regional tag team championships.

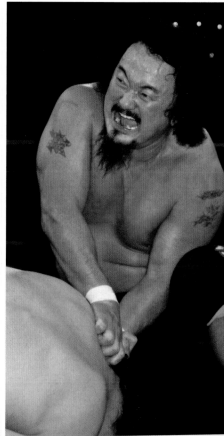

	HT: 5'10" WT: 270 lbs.
	FROM: Osaka, Japan
	SIGNATURE MOVE: Bonzai Drop

TITLE HISTORY

| WORLD TAG TEAM CHAMPION (5 TIMES) | Partnered with Prof. Toru Tanaka to defeat Chief Jay Strongbow & Sonny King on June 27, 1972
Partnered with Prof. Toru Tanaka to defeat Tony Garea & Haystacks Calhoun on September 11, 1973
Partnered with Prof. Toru Tanaka to defeat Tony Garea & Larry Zbyszko on September 27, 1977
Partnered with Mr. Saito to defeat Tony Garea & Rick Martel on October 13, 1981
Partnered with Mr. Saito to defeat Jules Strongbow & Chief Jay Strongbow on July 13, 1982 |

In 1977, they returned with "Classy" Freddie Blassie as their new manager. Though their final championship reign ended on March 14, 1978, they remained one of wrestling's most feared teams until they separated in 1979. Fuji reappeared in WWE in 1981 with a new partner, Mr. Saito. Managed by Capt. Lou Albano, they enjoyed two reigns as World Tag Team Champions. Either alone or with a partner, Mr. Fuji was regarded as one of the world's most dangerous men and one who could not be trusted under any circumstances.

In 1985, Fuji started to dress in a black tuxedo and black top hat, carried a cane and embarked on his managerial career. Fuji also ventured into acting and received critical acclaim for his work on *Tuesday Night Titans* in the landmark skits *Fuji General* and *Fuji Vice*. At *WrestleMania IV*, he led Demolition to the World tag team titles for his first championship as a manager.

After managing multiple teams to great success, Fuji introduced the intimidating Yokozuna to WWE in 1992, then led him straight to the top of sports-entertainment. At *WrestleMania IX*, Yokozuna, with Mr. Fuji in his corner, defeated Bret Hart for the WWE Championship. Despite losing the title in a challenge to Hulk Hogan moments later, Yokozuna regained the prize at the *King of the Ring*. The devious one left WWE in 1995, but reappeared for the last time at *WrestleMania XII* with Yokozuna.

On the eve of *WrestleMania 23*, Mr. Fuji joined the WWE Hall of Fame. Mr. Fuji is one of the rare legendary figures of WWE that had as much success out of the ring as he did in it.

MR. HUGHES 🇺🇸

HT: 6'6" WT: 330 lbs. FROM: Kansas City, Missouri
SIGNATURE MOVE: Powerslam

The scowl on his face said it all; Mr. Hughes was one mean dude. He certainly proved this during his three brief stints with WWE. Decked in dress pants, a button-down shirt and suspenders, Mr. Hughes made his WWE debut alongside manager Harvey Wippleman in 1993. After making an immediate impact by stealing Undertaker's signature urn, the colossal Hughes spent the next several weeks tearing through many lesser-known Superstars. Surprisingly, however, Mr. Hughes made a quick exit from WWE in the summer of 1993.

Four years after mysteriously leaving WWE, Mr. Hughes made his return as the bodyguard to Hunter Hearst-Helmsley, but he again disappeared just as quickly as he came in. In 1999, a more svelte looking Hughes reemerged as Chris Jericho's bodyguard. The no-nonsense Superstar instantly earned his money, helping Y2J defeat rival Ken Shamrock in a First Blood Match in September. In typical Hughes fashion, however, the big man once again disappeared from WWE approximately one month later.

MR. KENNEDY 🇺🇸

HT: 6'2" WT: 235 lbs. FROM: Green Bay, Wisconsin
SIGNATURE MOVE: Mic Check

TITLE HISTORY

UNITED STATES CHAMPION	Defeated Finlay and Bobby Lashley in a Triple Threat Match on September 1, 2006

After serving in the United States military, Mr. Kennedy hit the independent wrestling scene and chased his dream. When he entered the ranks of WWE in 2005, he marched to the beat of his own drum. He tangled with the likes of Undertaker, Rey Mysterio, Batista, and Shawn Michaels. His first taste of WWE gold came on September 1, 2006 when he won the United States Championship in a Triple Threat Match against Finlay and Bobby Lashley.

Kennedy kept rolling and became "Mr. Money In the Bank" at *WrestleMania 23*. In 2008 he was drafted to *Raw* where he continued to verbally and physically assault WWE Superstars and later turned his efforts to the *SmackDown* roster. The next year Kennedy made his Hollywood debut in the anticipated sequel to 2001's *Behind Enemy Lines* with *Behind Enemy Lines: Colombia*. That spring he parted with the company and returned to independent cards in Puerto Rico and the United States.

2010-
2000-09
1990-99
1980-89
1970-79
1960-69

MR. PERFECT

HT: 6'3"   **WT:** 257 lbs.
FROM: Robbinsdale, Minnesota
SIGNATURE MOVE: Perfectplex

HALL OF FAME 2007

Athletically, there wasn't anything Curt Hennig couldn't do. He could hit a home run, sink a forty-foot putt and even catch his own Hail Mary football pass. Basically, he was perfect in every way. He was Mr. Perfect.

TITLE HISTORY

INTERCONTINENTAL CHAMPION (2 TIMES)	Defeated Tito Santana on April 23, 1990 Defeated Texas Tornado on November 19, 1990

Following a successful stint in the American Wrestling Association (AWA), Curt Hennig, the son of wrestler Larry "The Axe" Hennig, first started making a name for himself as WWE's Mr. Perfect in 1988. His first year with the company was highlighted by convincing victories over Superstars such as Red Rooster and Koko B. Ware.

By April 1990, Mr. Perfect's superior technical wrestling ability earned him a spot in a tournament designed to crown a new Intercontinental Champion. In the finals, the master of the Perfectplex turned back Tito Santana to capture his first of two Intercontinental titles. While others have held the championship longer, many consider Mr. Perfect to be the greatest Intercontinental Champion of all time.

Injuries unfortunately sidelined Mr. Perfect through much of his prime, but he didn't let that stop him from gaining a prominent role within WWE. In addition to working as color commentator for many WWE television programs, he also served as Ric Flair's advisor during his initial stint with the company.

Hennig dropped his Mr. Perfect persona in 1997 to embark on a three-year run with World Championship Wrestling (WCW). While there, he became a member of two of the most influential factions of all time, the Four Horsemen and the New World Order.

Perfection returned to WWE in 2002 when Hennig competed in the *Royal Rumble*. Looking like the Mr. Perfect of old, he impressed many as one of the final four participants in the match.

Curt Hennig passed away on February 10, 2003. Four years later, he took his rightful place alongside sports-entertainment's greats when he was posthumously inducted into the WWE Hall of Fame, a perfect honor for an absolutely perfect competitor.

MR. SAITO

HT: 5'11"   **WT:** 265 lbs.   **FROM:** Tokyo, Japan
SIGNATURE MOVE: Saito Suplex

TITLE HISTORY

WORLD TAG TEAM CHAMPION (2 TIMES)	Partnered with Mr. Fuji to defeat Tony Garea & Rick Martel on October 13, 1981 Partnered with Mr. Fuji to defeat Jules Strongbow & Chief Jay Strongbow on July 13, 1982

A former Japanese Olympian, Mr. Saito was admired within amateur wrestling circles for his superior technical skills. When it came to his professional career, he refused to rest solely on his previous laurels. Instead, Saito developed a punishing high-impact offense, coupled with a complete disregard for the rules, which helped round out his impressive repertoire.

Mr. Saito's impressive list of NWA championship partners includes Ivan Koloff, Mr. Sato, and Gene Kiniski. However, it wasn't until 1981 that he reached the pinnacle of tag team wrestling. Moving to WWE and teaming with Mr. Fuji, Saito captured the World Tag Team Championship from Tony Garea & Rick Martel in Allentown, Pennsylvania. Sans a few weeks in the summer of 1982, the devious tandem held the titles for more than one year. Following his stay in WWE, Saito took his talents to Japan, where he proved himself as a force in both the tag team and singles ranks.

MR. T

HT: 5'10"   **WT:** 236 lbs.
FROM: Chicago, Illinois

Mr. T's sports-entertainment career only consisted of a handful of appearances, but don't let the low number of times he stepped in the ring fool you, as the former *A-Team* star always found himself in the middle of some of the biggest moments in WWE history.

In 1985, Mr. T teamed with friend Hulk Hogan to help usher in *WrestleMania*. The popularity of their main event victory over "Rowdy" Roddy Piper & "Mr. Wonderful" Paul Orndorff helped propel WWE to an international sensation.

The following year, Mr. T used the fame he gained as Clubber Lang in *Rocky III* to secure a Boxing Match against Piper at *WrestleMania 2*. Mr. T's boxing prowess proved superior, as he defeated "Hot Rod" via disqualification.

Nearly a decade later, Mr. T returned to the ring to serve as the special guest referee in the WCW Championship Match between Hogan and Ric Flair. In the end, Mr. T raised the Hulkster's hand in victory. As a result of the pre-match stipulations, the legendary Flair was forced into early— and temporary—retirement.

MUFFY MOWER

Muffy Mower learned the hard way that insulting fans and co-workers is not the way to achieve job security.

After being introduced as Stephanie McMahon-Helmsley's personal trainer in 2000, Mower began spreading her health tips to anybody she came across, even if they didn't ask for them. During the few times she appeared on WWE television, she would regularly tell the audience that they needed to come to terms with the fact that they were fat and out of shape. She would then urge them to get on their feet for an arena-wide aerobic workout. The irritated crowds rarely cooperated.

To give Mower credit, she clearly knew what was needed to create a healthy body. The blonde bombshell, though annoying, sported an amazingly fit body. She proudly wore washboard abs and had nearly no body fat. Mower's shenanigans grew tired after only a few appearances. She quickly faded from WWE television.

MUHAMMAD HASSAN

HT: 6'2" **WT:** 245 lbs. **FROM:** Detroit, Michigan
SIGNATURE MOVE: Camel Clutch

In 2004, this man with Middle Eastern ancestry entered WWE alongside his spokesperson, Daivari. He often interrupted the interview segments of others and verbally accosted Jim Ross and Jerry "The King" Lawler over their characterizations of him.

Hassan was last seen at the 2005 *Great American Bash* and was powerbombed through the stage by Undertaker. Muhammad Hassan will go down in WWE history books as one of the most controversial figures to appear in the company.

MR. WRESTLING II

HT: 5'11" **WT:** 236 lbs.
FROM: Atlanta, Georgia
SIGNATURE MOVE: Running High Knee

Mr. Wrestling II was one of the most popular Superstars of the Southern territories during the 1970s and early 1980s. Spending the majority of his time in Georgia and Florida, the mysterious masked Superstar solidified himself as a force in both the singles and tag team ranks.

As a solo competitor, Mr. Wrestling II used his signature running high knee to claim an astonishing ten NWA Georgia Heavyweight Championships. He also won the NWA Florida Heavyweight Championship twice. A World Championship reign escaped Mr. Wrestling II during his illustrious career, but he did manage to battle NWA Champion Jack Brisco to several breathtaking draws during the 1970s.

Mr. Wrestling II was no stranger to tag team gold either. Among many of the partners the masked man captured tag titles with were Mr. Wrestling I, Tony Atlas and "Cowboy" Bob Orton. Mr. Wrestling II's impressive career began to wind down toward the mid-1980s. In 1993, he was honored with induction into the short-lived WCW Hall of Fame.

MVP

HT: 6'3" **WT:** 252 lbs. **FROM:** Miami, Florida
SIGNATURE MOVE: Playmaker

TITLE HISTORY	
UNITED STATES CHAMPION (2 TIMES)	*Defeated Chris Benoit on May 20, 2007* *Defeated Shelton Benjamin on March 20, 2009*
WWE TAG TEAM CHAMPION	*Partnered with Matt Hardy to defeat Deuce & Domino on August 31, 2007*

After MVP signed the most lucrative deal in *SmackDown* history in 2006, many fans expected the new Superstar to be all talk, but the Miami native proved to be the real deal. MVP captured the United States Championship in May 2007. As champion, he did everything

in his power to ensure the title would remain around his waist, including befriending possible threats. In August 2007, he teamed with rival Matt Hardy in an attempt to keep his foe from challenging for the prize. In an unusual development, the odd couple actually won the WWE Tag Team Championship in August 2007.

Unfortunately for MVP, his plan was flawed. In April 2008, after an ugly split between the two, Hardy beat MVP for the United States Championship. Upon being drafted to *Raw* in 2009, he formed a popular tag team with "The World's Strongest Man," Mark Henry. However, the supplemental draft that year sent him back to *SmackDown*. Once there, he vied for the Intercontinental Championship and was part of the victorious Team Mysterio at the 2010 *Survivor Series*.

MYSTERY MAN

In July 1991, Mystery Man appeared in the ring, but exited as quickly as he entered. Dressed in black with his face covered, no one has learned how this individual came to WWE or why he was there. Ominous symbols were seen on his ring attire and fur covered his hands, arms, head and back.

Mystery Man is one of the Superstars in WWE's storied history whose name was a literal description of his persona. Could he have returned to WWE with a new name? Did he leave sports-entertainment and establish himself in another profession? Is he a fan sitting next to you at a WWE event? The answer may never be known.

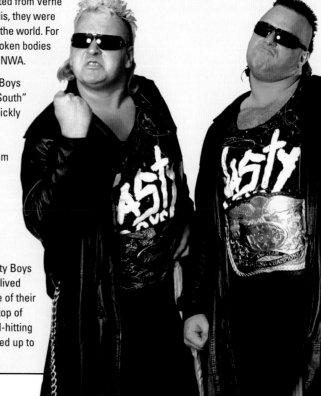

NAILZ

HT: 6'5" **WT:** 302 lbs.
FROM: Department of Corrections

After serving hard time in a Cobb County jail, Nailz made a beeline for WWE, where he immediately attacked his former prison guard, Big Boss Man. The ex-convict was so intent on exacting revenge from Boss Man, in fact, that he didn't even bother to change out of his orange prison jumpsuit. Instead, he wore the state-issued garb throughout the entirety of his brief WWE career.

The hardened criminal picked up his first major victory when he made short work of Virgil at *SummerSlam 1992*. Three months later, he finally had the opportunity to gain the upper hand from his former prison guard when the two Superstars battled in a Nightstick Match at *Survivor Series*. Boss Man ultimately proved his dominance that night and Nailz disappeared from WWE shortly after.

NAOMI

HT: 5'5" **FROM:** Orlando, Florida

Sporting a personality just as colorful as her neon ring gear, Naomi burst onto the scene as Kelly Kelly's energetic Rookie on season three of *WWE NXT*. Wasting no time, she made an immediate impact by not only winning a Capture the Flag competition, but also teaming with her Pro to defeat Alicia Fox & Maxine.

In her quest to become WWE's next breakout Diva, Naomi made it all the way to the finals of *NXT*, but was ultimately beaten out by Vickie Guerrero's Rookie, Kaitlyn.

Prior to NXT, Naomi entertained basketball fans as a dancer for the NBA's Orlando Magic. She also toured the world as a backup dancer for various hip hop acts, including the Grammy-nominated Flo Rida.

When Naomi was young, she dreamed of one day becoming a WWE Diva. Despite falling short on *NXT*, the athletically gifted Diva-hopeful showed enough desire and promise that her dream is now at hand.

THE NASTY BOYS

MEMBERS: Brian Knobbs, Jerry Saggs
COMBINED WT: 546 lbs.

When you take a trip to Nastyville you're travelling to one of the toughest places on Earth. After Knobbs and Saggs graduated from Verne Gagne's wrestling school in Minneapolis, they were prepared to face the best tag teams in the world. For their warm-up act, they left a trail of broken bodies in the AWA, Memphis, Florida, and the NWA.

In 1991 WWE got "Nastisized" as the Boys made their debut with "Mouth of the South" Jimmy Hart as their manager. They quickly rose up the ranks and in their *WrestleMania* debut defeated the Hart Foundation for the World Tag Team Championship. Shortly after losing their titles to the Legion of Doom, they left WWE for World Championship Wrestling.

In 1996 Saggs was forced out of the action for a number of years due to a serious neck injury. However, the Nasty Boys reunited in 2001 as a part of the short-lived XWF organization. Through the course of their careers, the Nasty Boys reached the top of the AWA, WCW, and WWE. Their hard-hitting style became legendary as the duo lived up to their Nasty name.

TITLE HISTORY	
WORLD TAG TEAM CHAMPIONS	*Defeated The Hart Foundation on March 24, 1991*

NATALYA

HT: 5'6"   FROM: Calgary... Alberta, Canada
SIGNATURE MOVE: Sharpshooter

She is a descendant of sports-entertainment royalty, as well as a graduate of the famous Hart Dungeon. Daughter of Jim "The Anvil" Neidhart, Natalya is also well versed in amateur wrestling and mixed martial arts.

TITLE HISTORY	
DIVAS CHAMPION	*Defeated Lay-Cool in a Handicap Match on November 21, 2010*

She debuted in memorable fashion on the April 4, 2008 edition of *SmackDown* when she came from the crowd and aided Victoria against Michelle McCool and Cherry. She spent many months under the tutelage of the "Black Widow" and expanded her rule-breaking abilities. In 2009, Natalya left Victoria behind and formed the Hart Dynasty with Tyson Kidd and cousin, DH Smith.

After the group split, the third-generation star set her sights on the prestigious Divas Championship. As Natalya became the #1 contender, her overwhelming popularity did not sit well with certain Divas, especially the co-championship duo of Lay-Cool. Calgary's favorite daughter was often the target of harassment and beatings from the "Flawless" pair. At the 2010 *Survivor Series*, Natalya bested both motor-mouthed Divas in a handicap match to claim the Divas Championship.

A new year brought a new attitude and Natalya's alliance with "Glamazon" Beth Phoenix resulted in heartless attacks of many other Divas. Natalya feels she's the ultimate embodiment of the brains, beauty, and brawn in this new era of "pin-up strong" Divas.

NATHAN JONES

HT: 6'10"   WT: 305 lbs.   FROM: Australia
SIGNATURE MOVE: Gutwrench Suplex

Formerly one of Australia's most wanted fugitives, Nathan Jones spent 10 years in prison for his part in eight armed robberies. When he was released, the "Colossus of Boggo Road" found an outlet for his aggression in the WWE ring.

The untamed Jones was scheduled to make his WWE debut alongside Undertaker at *WrestleMania XIX*. But when Big Show and A-Train attacked the big man prior to the match, the "American Bad Ass" was forced to compete solo and Jones' debut was pushed back.

Jones finally debuted in April 2003, defeating the veteran Bill DeMott in less than two minutes. Looking unstoppable, the mighty Australian went into action against Nunzio the following week. Unfortunately for Jones, that's where his momentum stopped. The Full Blooded Italians shattered Jones' ankle with the ring steps, causing him to miss several months of action.

Jones returned to the ring in October 2003 as a member of Team Lesnar. But just one month after his return, he was gone from WWE.

NATION OF DOMINATION

MEMBERS: Faarooq, The Rock, Kama, The Godfather, D-Lo Brown, Owen Hart, Crush, Savio Vega, Ahmed Johnson, Mark Henry, Clarence Mason, J.C. Ice, Wolfie D

Led by Faarooq, The Nation of Domination was a militant group assembled to fight for the rights of black Superstars. Claiming to be held back due to the color of their skin, the controversial faction set out to gain equality "by any means necessary."

The earliest version of group contained Crush, Savio Vega, D-Lo Brown, PG-13, and Clarence Mason. When they failed to help Faarooq defeat Undertaker for the WWE Championship, the leader fired all of them, with the exception of D-Lo Brown. The new-look Nation was filled with Superstars that shared Faarooq's twisted visions: Kama, The Rock and Mark Henry.

The Nation claimed its first piece of gold in December 1997 when The Rock was awarded the Intercontinental Championship after Stone Cold Steve Austin refused to defend the title. As the faction's only titleholder, the cocky Rock slowly began to extract leadership responsibilities from Faarooq, before finally kicking him out of the Nation altogether in early 1998.

Under The Rock's leadership, the Nation developed a more hip quality. No longer mad at the world, various members were allowed to show their true personalities. The most notable change saw Kama transform into the fun-loving pimp Godfather.

By the end of 1998, the Godfather left the Nation to pursue his budding pimping career. Shortly after that, The Rock's ego grew to epic proportions, forcing Brown and Henry to attack their leader, thus ending the Nation's existence.

N

1960-69
1970-79
1980-89
1990-99
2000-09
2010-

NATURAL DISASTERS

MEMBERS: Earthquake, Typhoon
COMBINED WT: 846 lbs.

TITLE HISTORY

WORLD TAG TEAM CHAMPIONS	Defeated Money, Inc. on July 20, 1992

At a time when most WWE tag teams topped out at 500 pounds, Earthquake & Typhoon joined forces to create a near half-ton of total destruction. Appropriately named the Natural Disasters, the colossal duo stormed through their competition with the greatest of ease.

Prior to the Natural Disasters' formation, Typhoon spent many years competing as the hugely popular Tugboat. In 1991, he revealed a darker side when he turned on his friends, the Bushwhackers, to align himself with the hated Earthquake. Together, the Natural Disasters left such destruction in their wake that a wrecking ball would cringe.

In January 1992, Earthquake & Typhoon scored a major countout victory over the World Tag Team Champions, the Legion of Doom. By all accounts, the win should have put the Natural Disasters in line for another opportunity at the titles, but their manager Jimmy Hart put Money, Inc. in the ring with the champs instead. The move infuriated the oversized tag team, who immediately fired "The Mouth of the South." The bold move made Earthquake & Typhoon instant fan favorites and also propelled them into a heated rivalry with the new champs, DiBiase & Schyster.

The Natural Disasters gained a level of revenge when they defeated Money, Inc. for the titles in July 1992. Unfortunately, they only held the championship for three months before losing them back to DiBiase & Schyster in October.

NEW AGE OUTLAWS

MEMBERS: "Road Dogg" Jesse James, "Bad Ass" Billy Gunn   **COMBINED WT:** 548 lbs.

TITLE HISTORY

WORLD TAG TEAM CHAMPIONS (5 TIMES)	Defeated The Legion of Doom on November 24, 1997 Defeated Cactus Jack & Chainsaw Charlie on March 30, 1998 Defeated Mankind on August 30, 1998 Defeated The Rock 'N' Sock Connection on September 23, 1999 Defeated Mankind & Al Snow on November 8, 1999

"Oh...you didn't know?"

This famous introduction brought capacity crowds around the world to their feet. In a case of good enemies, better friends, the two former rivals became a team in 1997. When Billy laid out his then-manager, the Honky Tonk Man, with a guitar, the spirit of the New Age Outlaws was born and tag team competition was about to change forever.

The New Age Outlaws became known for their abilities and antics both in and out of the ring. They quickly took aim at the top and stole the spiked shoulder pads of The Legion of Doom to get a shot at the World Tag Team Championship. Their strategy worked when they defeated Animal & Hawk for the titles.

The Outlaws then showed their mean streak when they locked Cactus Jack and Terry Funk in a dumpster and pushed the dumpster off the *Raw* stage. Their handiwork began to catch the interest of Shawn Michaels and Hunter Hearst-Helmsley as they were set to defend their titles at *WrestleMania XIV*. Though they lost to Cactus Jack & Chainsaw Charlie, they regained the titles the next night in a steel cage with a little help from their new friends.

This collaboration marked the second incarnation of D-Generation X and the Outlaws helped build the group's legacy. Though differences caused them to split in 1999, "Road Dogg" and Billy reformed to show they were still the best against the Rock 'N' Sock Connection, Edge & Christian, the Hollys, and the Dudley Boys. James & Gunn rode with DX for the final time in 2000 when they faced The Radicalz in eight-man action on *Monday Night Raw*.

Soon after, "Road Dogg" and Billy Gunn went their separate ways. Though they saw success apart, it paled in comparison to when they wreaked havoc together. The New Age Outlaws were a major attraction during WWE's Attitude Era.

THE NEW BLACKJACKS

MEMBERS: Blackjack Windham, Blackjack Bradshaw   **COMBINED WT:** 565 lbs.

The tag team division in World Wrestling Entertainment was given a loud wake-up call in 1998. With classic rough-house tactics matched with innovative power moves the cowboys in black became serious contenders for the World Tag Team Championship from the get-go.

The New Blackjacks had showdowns with the Godwinns, Faarooq & Kama, and the New Age Outlaws. This iteration of the classic duo did not last long. Blackjack Windham turned on Bradshaw before the end of 1998 to join Jim Cornette's collection of NWA stars.

Even though the team lasted a short period of time, Windham & Bradshaw brought traditional Texas brutality back to the ring. Their stint as the New Blackjacks paid homage to the originals and celebrated the team's legacy in sports-entertainment.

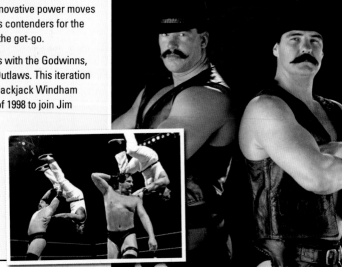

NEW DREAM TEAM

Contrary to popular belief, new doesn't always mean improved. Following a *WrestleMania III* argument between original Dream Team members Brutus Beefcake and Greg Valentine, Beefcake was unceremoniously ousted from the unit and replaced with Dino Bravo. The new union, however, failed to reach the same level of success as the original duo, who once ruled WWE as World Tag Team Champions.

Managed by "Luscious" Johnny Valiant, the New Dream Team saw its greatest success early on. After several impressive showings against the Islanders, Valentine & Bravo were granted an opportunity for the Hart Foundation's World Tag Team titles. The new combination failed to capture the gold, however, and quickly slipped into obscurity. Shortly after the loss, Valentine & Bravo agreed to go their separate ways.

THE NEW FOUNDATION

MEMBERS: Owen Hart, Jim "The Anvil" Neidhart
COMBINED WT: 508 lbs.

Jim Neidhart was left at a career crossroads after his tag team partner, Bret Hart, left The Hart Foundation to pursue singles success. Rather than attempting to find similar solo greatness, Neidhart looked to Bret's younger brother, Owen Hart, to fill the void left by the "Hit Man." Together, Owen & "The Anvil "adopted the name The New Foundation.

Owen's collective body of work proves that he was one of the industry's greatest tag team competitors. His impressive résumé boasts World Tag Team Championship reigns with partners Yokozuna, British Bulldog and Jeff Jarrett. On the flip side, Neidhart will forever be remembered as one-half of one of the greatest tag teams ever assembled. Together, however, The New Foundation failed to get out of the starting block.

Luckily for both Superstars, their amazing success at other points in their respective careers far overshadows The New Foundation's checkerboard ring gear and unimpressive record. Years after The New Foundation crumbled, Neidhart stood by Owen's side as the young Hart claimed the 1994 *King of the Ring* crown.

NEW MIDNIGHT EXPRESS

MEMBERS: Bob Holly, Bart Gunn   **COMBINED WT:** 493 lbs.

During the 1980s, manager James E. Cornette led The Midnight Express, a constantly evolving tag team consisting of such Superstars as "Beautiful" Bobby Eaton, "Sweet" Stan Lane and "Loverboy" Dennis Condrey, to tag team greatness in the NWA. A decade later, Cornette recreated the egotistical team in WWE. This time, though, he replaced its aging members with the considerably younger Bob Holly and Bart Gunn.

Known as The New Midnight Express, Holly & Gunn adopted nicknames fitting of the 1980s squad. Holly became "Bodacious" Bob, while Gunn went by "Bombastic" Bart. The name changes, however, did little in the way of creating success. The duo failed to make any real waves in WWE. Their highest-profile encounter came at *WrestleMania XV*, where they competed in the Tag Team Battle Royal, which was ultimately won by LOD 2000. By the end of 1998, less than one year into their existence, The New Midnight Express went their separate ways.

THE NEW ROCKERS

MEMBERS: Marty Jannetty, Leif Cassidy
COMBINED WT: 468 lbs.

The familiar rock n' roll theme that echoed in arenas all over the world during the late 1980s and early 1990s played again in 1996. World Wrestling Entertainment saw the thrilling tag team duo of original Rocker Marty Jannetty and newcomer Leif Cassidy take on all of the WWE's top duo's including the Godwinns, the Bodydonnas, the Smoking Gunns, and the Bushwhackers. Marty and Leif stayed true to the Rocker tradition of excellent continuity and double-team moves, and a finishing move that is still regarded as one of the most dangerous in WWE history. Despite only a brief time together, the New Rockers added another element to the legacy of the famed tandem and proved that they were in charge whenever they stepped in the ring.

N

1960-69 ▼
1970-79 ▼
1980-89 ▼
1990-99 ▼
2000-09 ▼
2010- ▼

HALL OF FAME

WORLD WRESTLING ENTERTAINMENT

On the eve of *WrestleMania*, WWE proudly honors the legends of yesteryear with induction into the prestigious Hall of Fame.

Started in 1993, the Hall of Fame is the ultimate honor for any Superstar who has ever stepped foot in a WWE ring. To be recognized means a Superstar is among the absolute elite of all time. Over the years, only the greatest have gained entry into the hallowed Hall.

CLASS OF 1993

Andre the Giant

CLASS OF 1994

Arnold Skaaland

Bobo Brazil

Buddy Rogers

Freddie Blassie

Chief Jay Strongbow

Gorilla Monsoon

James Dudley

CLASS OF 1995

Antonino Rocca

Ernie Ladd

Fabulous Moolah

George "The Animal" Steele

The Grand Wizard

Ivan Putski

Pedro Morales

CLASS OF 1996

Baron Mikel Scicluna

"Captain" Lou Albano

Jimmy "Superfly" Snuka

Johnny Rodz

Killer Kowalski

Pat Patterson

The Valiant Brothers

Vincent J. McMahon

CLASS OF 2004

Big John Studd

Bobby "The Brain" Heenan

Don Muraco

Greg "The Hammer" Valentine

Harley Race

Jesse "The Body" Ventura

Junkyard Dog

Pete Rose

Sgt. Slaughter

"Superstar" Billy Graham

Tito Santana

CLASS OF 2005

"Cowboy" Bob Orton

Hulk Hogan

The Iron Sheik

Jimmy Hart

Nikolai Volkoff

Paul Orndorff

"Rowdy" Roddy Piper

CLASS OF 2006

The Blackjacks

Bret "Hit Man" Hart

Eddie Guerrero

"Mean" Gene Okurlund

"Sensational" Sherri

Tony Atlas

Verne Gagne

William Perry

CLASS OF 2007

Dusty Rhodes

Jerry "The King" Lawler

Jim Ross

Mr. Fuji

"Mr. Perfect" Curt Hennig

Nick Bockwinkel

The Sheik

The Wild Samoans

CLASS OF 2008

The Brisco Brothers

Eddie Graham

Gordon Solie

"High Chief" Peter Maivia

Mae Young

Ric Flair

Rocky Johnson

CLASS OF 2009

Bill Watts

The Funks

Howard Finkel

Koko B. Ware

Ricky "The Dragon" Steamboat

Stone Cold Steve Austin

The Von Erichs

CLASS OF 2010

Antonio Inoki

Bob Uecker

Gorgeous George

Maurice "Mad Dog" Vachon

Stu Hart

"Million Dollar Man" Ted DiBiase

Wendi Richter

CLASS OF 2011

Abdullah the Butcher

"Bullet" Bob Armstrong

Drew Carey

"Hacksaw" Jim Duggan

Road Warriors w/ Paul Ellering

Shawn Michaels

Sunny

CLASS OF 2012

Edge

Four Horsemen

Mike Tyson

Mil Mascaras

Ron Simmons

Yokozuna

2010-
2000-09
1990-99
1980-89
1970-79
1960-69

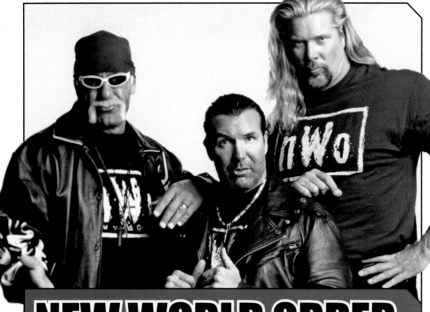

NEW WORLD ORDER

MEMBERS: Hollywood Hogan, Kevin Nash, Scott Hall, Big Show, X-Pac, Shawn Michaels, Booker T

There are a few things you can say about Mr. McMahon with complete certainty. He's a sports-entertainment icon. He's a brilliant businessman. He possesses superior physical strength. He's also made emotional decisions that lead others to question his sanity.

The Chairman's questionable decision-making reached epic proportions in 2002 when rival Ric Flair assumed a leadership role within WWE. With the "Nature Boy" calling the shots, McMahon slipped into an uncontrollable depression, which caused him to diagnose WWE with, as he termed it, terminal cancer.

Unable to sit back and watch somebody else kill his creation, McMahon took matters into his own hands. With tears flowing from his eyes, a maniacal McMahon announced he was going to inject WWE with a lethal dose of poison, thus destroying the promotion before anybody else could. That lethal dose of poison? The New World Order (nWo).

In years prior to WWE's injection, the nWo ravaged WCW to the brink of destruction. Sporting more than twenty members, the rebellious faction turned a once profitable organization into a land of lawlessness. McMahon hoped the original members — Hollywood Hogan, Kevin Nash and Scott Hall — would do the same for WWE.

When the nWo arrived, they immediately targeted WWE's biggest names, Stone Cold Steve Austin and The Rock. In typical nWo fashion, they spray painted their initials onto Stone Cold's back, then used a gigantic tractor trailer to crush an ambulance carrying The Rock. The stunts set the stage for two huge *WrestleMania X8* matches.

The nWo saw *WrestleMania* as their opportunity to chop down WWE's two most popular stars. By night's end, however, Stone Cold had defeated Hall, and The Rock beat Hogan. Realizing things weren't going as planned, Hall and Nash attacked Hogan, marking the end of his nWo involvement.

By all accounts, the nWo's *WrestleMania* efforts were seen as a colossal failure. In the months that followed, Hall & Nash attempted to recreate their WCW magic by recruiting ex-nWo members Big Show and X-Pac, as well as Booker T and Shawn Michaels, but their attempts proved futile and the faction soon disbanded.

NEW YEAR'S REVOLUTION

January 9, 2005

San Juan, PR - Coliseo de Puerto Rico

Main Event: Triple H defeated Edge, Chris Benoit, Chris Jericho, Batista, and Randy Orton in an Elimination Chamber Match

January 8, 2006

Albany, NY - Pepsi Arena

Main Event: WWE Champion John Cena defeated Carlito, Chris Masters, Kane, Kurt Angle, and Shawn Michaels in an Elimination Chamber Match

January 7, 2007

Kansas City, MO - Kemper Arena

Main Event: WWE Champion John Cena defeated Umaga

NEXUS

MEMBERS: Wade Barrett, CM Punk, Justin Gabriel, Heath Slater, David Otunga, Skip Sheffield, Daniel Bryan, Michael Tarver, Darren Young, Michael McGillicutty, Husky Harris, Mason Ryan, John Cena

During *NXT*'s first season, eight Rookies battled relentlessly for the right to be called WWE's next breakout star. But once it was over, those eight men united to form Nexus, one of the most destructive forces in WWE history.

Led by Wade Barrett, Nexus shocked the sports-entertainment world when they invaded a June 2010 *Raw* main event between John Cena and CM Punk. The result of the invasion was pure devastation, as every soul in their wake was left a beaten and battered mess. They even destroyed the announce table, ring and anything else in their way.

Over the next few months, Nexus performed some of the most detestable acts imaginable, including viciously attacking Ricky Steamboat, Bret Hart and Mr. McMahon. Through it all, however, their main target was Cena.

In December 2010, Punk seized power of Nexus from Barrett. Despite the new leadership, the group still had a bull's eye on Cena's back. And in July 2011, Punk penned the final chapter in the Nexus-versus-Cena rivalry when he defeated his nemesis for the WWE Championship.

NICOLE BASS

HT: 6'2"
FROM: New York, New York

During her short WWE career, Nicole Bass proved to be a legitimate force in the Women's division, although you wouldn't think it by looking at her. The massive Diva made her debut in March 1999, helping Sable defend the Women's Championship against Tori at *WrestleMania XV*. From there, she went on to manhandle nearly every female on the WWE roster, including Ivory, Debra and Jacqueline. Before she could string together any major victories, Bass abruptly disappeared from the WWE scene.

NIDIA

HT: 5'6"
FROM: Mayaguez, Puerto Rico

A co-winner of the first season of *Tough Enough,* this former Diva debuted on *SmackDown* in 2002 and was revealed as the person sending letters to The Hurricane. Nidia began as a valet to her boyfriend, Jamie Noble, and demonstrated that behind every great man is an even better woman.

In time she also proved that her win on *Tough Enough* was no fluke in bouts against Torrie Wilson, Gail Kim, Dawn Marie, and Jazz. Considered a top contender for the Women's Championship, Nidia upped the ante when she showed her sexy side in the video release *Divas: Desert Heat.* In the spring of 2004 Nidia became a member of *Raw* but by November she left the company and retired from sports-entertainment shortly thereafter.

July 26, 2009

Philadelphia, PA - Wachovia Center

Main Event | Jeff Hardy defeated World Heavyweight Champion CM Punk

▼

September 19, 2010

Rosemont, IL - Allstate Arena

Main Event | Randy Orton last eliminated WWE Champion Sheamus in a Six-Pack Challenge Elimination Match that also included Chris Jericho, John Cena, Wade Barrett and Edge

▼

September 18, 2011

Buffalo, NY - First Niagara Center

Main Event | WWE COO Triple H defeated CM Punk in a No Disqualification Match

June 24, 2007

Houston, TX - Toyota Center

Main Event | WWE Champion John Cena defeated Booker T, Mick Foley, Randy Orton, and Bobby Lashley in a WWE Championship Challenge

▼

June 29, 2008

Dallas, TX - American Airlines Center

Main Event | WWE Champion Triple H defeated John Cena

▼

In 2007, *Vengeance* was subtitled *Night of Champions* as every match at the event was a title defense. In 2008, *Vengeance* was dropped from the event's title, and *Night of Champions* continued to serve up a night filled with champions battling top contenders. With few exceptions, that has been the case at every *Night of Champions* event since.

Nikolai Volkoff (see page 260)

 WWE **No Mercy**

October 9, 2005

Houston, TX
Toyota Center

Main Event | World Heavyweight Champion Batista defeated Eddie Guerrero

▼

October 8, 2006

Raleigh, NC
RBC Center

Main Event | World Heavyweight Champion King Booker defeated Bobby Lashley, Finlay and Batista, Fatal 4-Way Match

▼

October 7, 2007

Rosemont, IL
Allstate Arena

Main Event | Randy Orton defeated WWE Champion Triple H, Last Man Standing Match

▼

October 5, 2008

Portland, OR
Rose Gardens

Main Event | World Heavyweight Champion Chris Jericho defeated Shawn Michaels, Ladder Match

October 17, 1999

Cleveland, OH
Gund Arena

Main Event | WWE Champion Triple H defeated Stone Cold Steve Austin, Anything Goes Match

▼

October 22, 2000

Albany, NY
Pepsi Arena

Main Event | Kurt Angle defeated WWE Champion The Rock

▼

October 21, 2001

St. Louis, MO
Savvis Center

Main Event | WWE Champion Stone Cold Steve Austin defeated Kurt Angle and Rob Van Dam, Triple Threat Match

October 20, 2002

Little Rock, AR
Alltel Arena

Main Event | WWE Champion Brock Lesnar defeated Undertaker, Hell In A Cell Match

▼

October 19, 2003

Baltimore, MD
1st Mariner Arena

Main Event | WWE Champion Brock Lesnar defeated Undertaker, Biker Chain Match

▼

October 3, 2004

East Rutherford, NJ
Continental Airlines Arena

Main Event | WWE Champion JBL defeated Undertaker, Last Ride Match

1960-69
▼
1970-79
▼
1980-89
▼
1990-99
▼
2000-09
▼
2010-

NIKOLAI VOLKOFF

HT: 6'4" WT: 313 lbs. FROM: The Soviet Union SIGNATURE MOVE: The Russian Backbreaker

During his days behind the Iron Curtain, Nikolai Volkoff was a world-class amateur wrestler and bodybuilder. While attending a 1968 weightlifting competition in Vienna, Austria, Nikolai risked his life and said goodbye to everything he knew when he defected from the Soviet Union. He traveled to Calgary, Alberta, Canada and was trained for a life in the ring by legend Stu Hart. In 1970, Volkoff came to America with $50.00 in his pocket and one suit.

TITLE HISTORY	
WORLD TAG TEAM CHAMPION	*Partnered with the Iron Sheik to defeat Mike Rotundo & Barry Windham on March 31, 1985*

By 1974, Volkoff was a huge draw. A match against Bruno Sammartino broke the live gate attendance record at Madison Square Garden. During the mid 1970s, the hated Volkoff was involved in a near riot as he was discovered along with Killer Kowalski and Big John Studd to be part of the tag team championship tandem of the Executioners. After the deceptive trio was stripped of the titles, Volkoff split time between WWE, Japan and the regional territories of the NWA.

In 1984, Nikolai returned to WWE as the first protégé of "Classy" Freddie Blassie. Blassie paired Volkoff with another anti-American rule-breaker, the Iron Sheik. As the duo spread panic throughout the United States, they became top contenders for the World Tag Team Championship. During the first championship match of the first *WrestleMania*, they defeated the U.S. Express and left New York City as champions. Their success continued to grow and on May 10, 1985 they appeared on the very first episode of *Saturday Night's Main Event*.

Volkoff brought the hammer and sickle of the Soviet Union with him wherever he went and demanded everyone stand as he sang the Russian National Anthem before each match.

Following the loss of the title belts in June 1985, Nikolai focused on a return to singles action. On the October 3, 1985 episode of *Saturday Night's Main Event,* two Cold War Superpowers clashed when Nikolai challenged Hulk Hogan to a Flag Match for the WWE Championship. Volkoff then sparked a rivalry against former United States Armed Forces member Corporal Kirschner in a series of Flag Matches. After the retirement of Blassie, the managerial contractual rights for Volkoff and Iron Sheik were sold to WWE newcomer, Slick. After the "Doctor of Style" led them to a reunion at *WrestleMania III* against the Killer Bees, Nikolai and his Iranian ally soon parted ways.

Volkoff then aligned himself with another Russian monster, Boris Zhukov. With Slick in their corner, the two referred to themselves as the Bolsheviks. They were top tag title contenders and appeared at the first two *Survivor Series* events. The Russians had a violent split at *WrestleMania VI* after a humiliating 19-second loss to the Hart Foundation. As the former comrades battled, WWE fans witnessed the birth of a patriot.

During an episode of *The Brother Love Show,* newfound-friend "Hacksaw" Jim Duggan adopted Nikolai as a brother and they formed a team with the stars and stripes of the USA as their inspiration. Nikolai was then awarded a Medal of Honor from the National Boy Scouts for his contribution to world peace. Their winning ways continued as they toppled The Orient Express at *SummerSlam 1990*. Nikolai became a member of Duggan's victorious Alliance team at that November's *Survivor Series*. The two then took aim at Sgt. Slaughter when he turned his back on his country and became an Iraqi sympathizer during The Gulf War. Shortly afterward, Volkoff entered semi-retirement.

In 1995, Nikolai returned to WWE and broke the hearts of fans when he joined Ted DiBiase's Million Dollar Corporation as a low-level henchman for the greedy faction. Volkoff also appeared at *WrestleMania X-Seven's* Gimmick Battle Royal and since then has appeared sporadically on WWE programming. In 2005, Nikolai's remarkable five-decade career was celebrated when he was inducted into the WWE Hall of Fame alongside several of his contemporaries, including former partner, the Iron Sheik.

Nikolai's combination of raw power and stunning agility were ahead of its time. He enraged fans all over the world and was a serious threat to the WWE Championship reigns of men like Bruno Sammartino, Bob Backlund, and Hulk Hogan. Nikolai Volkoff undoubtedly contributed to the bright future of WWE and will be heralded as one of the greatest villains of all time. Now, please rise for the singing of the Russian National Anthem...

NO WAY OUT

The first *No Way Out* was an *In Your House* event that took place in 1998, then became a regular pay per view event two years later. After consecutive years where the main events featured Elimination Chamber Matches, *No Way Out* was replaced by the *Elimination Chamber* pay per view.

February 15, 1998
Houston, TX
Compaq Center

Main Event: Stone Cold Steve Austin, Cactus Jack, Chainsaw Charlie & Owen Hart defeated Triple H, Billy Gunn, Road Dogg & Savio Vega

February 27, 2000
Hartford, CT
Hartford Civic Center

Main Event: WWE Champion Triple H defeated Cactus Jack, Hell In A Cell Match

February 25, 2001
Las Vegas, NV
Thomas & Mack Center

Main Event: The Rock defeated WWE Champion Kurt Angle

February 17, 2002
Milwaukee, WI
Bradley Center

Main Event: WWE Champion Chris Jericho defeated Stone Cold Steve Austin

February 23, 2003
Montreal, Quebec, Canada
Bell Centre

Main Event: The Rock defeated Hulk Hogan

February 15, 2004
San Francisco, CA
Cow Palace

Main Event: Eddie Guerrero defeated WWE Champion Brock Lesnar

February 20, 2005
Pittsburgh, PA
Mellon Arena

Main Event: WWE Champion JBL defeated Big Show, Barbed Wire Steel Cage Match

February 19, 2006
Baltimore, MD
1st Mariner Arena

Main Event: World Heavyweight Champion Kurt Angle defeated Undertaker

February 18, 2007
Los Angeles, CA
Staples Center

Main Event: WWE Champion John Cena & Shawn Michaels defeated World Heavyweight Champion Batista & Undertaker

February 17, 2008
Las Vegas, NV
Thomas & Mack Center

Main Event: Triple H defeated Jeff Hardy, Shawn Michaels, JBL, Chris Jericho and Umaga in an Elimination Chamber Match

February 15, 2009
Seattle, WA
Key Arena

Main Event: Edge defeated World Heavyweight Champion John Cena, Rey Mysterio, Chris Jericho, Mike Knox and Kane in an Elimination Chamber Match

NORTH AMERICAN HEAVYWEIGHT CHAMPIONSHIP

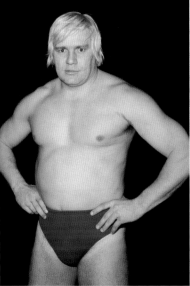

Pat Patterson defeated Ted Dibiase in Allentown, PA on June 19, 1979. On September 1, 1979, Pat Patterson participated in a tournament held in Rio de Janiero, Brazil. His victory at the tournament unified the North American and South American Heavyweight Championships into the Intercontinental Championship. In November, 1979, Japanese wrestling star Seiji Sakaguchi resurrected the championship in Japan and defended the title until it was officially retired in April of 1981.

Despite being short-lived, the North American Heavyweight Championship is viewed by many historians as an important prize. In March 1979, after weeks of deliberation, the World Wrestling Entertainment Championship committee awarded Ted DiBiase the North American Heavyweight Championship.

NUNZIO

HT: 5'7" **WT:** 170 lbs. **FROM:** Rockland County, New York
SIGNATURE MOVE: The Sicilian Slice

TITLE HISTORY

CRUISERWEIGHT CHAMPION (2 TIMES)	Defeated Paul London on August 6, 2005 Defeated Juventud on November 15, 2005

To sports-entertainment fans of the extreme, this former Superstar looks familiar because in the mid-1990s he was a member of the Full Blooded Italians in the original ECW. Though the cultural make-up of the faction changed over time, he remained a constant and was a two-time ECW World Tag Team Champion with partners Tracy Smothers and Tony Mamaluke.

The fierce Nunzio debuted on SmackDown in 2002 and established himself as one of the most dangerous cruiserweights around. After a brief reformation of the FBI, he continued to challenge for cruiserweight gold. Nunzio had a reunion with the original FBI at 2005's ECW *One Night Stand*. On August 6, 2005 he defeated Paul London for the Cruiserweight Championship. In 2006, Nunzio went to the new ECW. Over time, attempts to pump new life into the FBI met little success and in August 2008 Nunzio left World Wrestling Entertainment, although he briefly resurfaced as a referee in 2011.

1960-69 ▼ 1970-79 ▼ 1980-89 ▼ 1990-99 ▼ 2000-09 ▼ 2010-

O

2010-

2000-09

1990-99

1980-89

1970-79

1960-69

THE ODDITIES

MEMBERS: Giant Silva, Kurrgan, Golga, Insane Clown Posse, George "The Animal" Steele, Luna, Sable

All too often, today's judgmental society shuns individuals who may be deemed a little different. In 1998, however, a band of misfits made huge efforts towards reversing the norm when Golga, Kurrgan, and Giant Silva rallied together to form The Oddities.

Each member of The Oddities suffered from their own social shortcomings: The intellectually unstable Golga was forced to wear a mask to hide his deformed face, Kurrgan scared young children with his tree-like height and poor fashion sense, and Giant Silva, who was even taller than Kurrgan, was plain inaudible when he spoke. Despite these perceived handicaps, The Oddities proved that it was acceptable to cheer for a bunch of self-proclaimed sideshow freaks.

While fun-loving outside the ring, The Oddities were all business once the bell rang. Their most high-profile victory came at *SummerSlam 1998* when they overmatched the smaller Kaientai faction. After the match, the oddballs celebrated with their equally bizarre friends, Luna and the Insane Clown Posse, as well as a packed Madison Square Garden crowd.

In late 1998, Golga, Kurrgan, and Giant Silva were joined by the original oddity, George "The Animal" Steele. With the Hall of Famer by their side, The Oddities enjoyed their greatest success. Despite their newfound popularity, the curious combination disappeared from WWE soon after.

ONE MAN GANG

HT: 6'9"   WT: 450 lbs.
FROM: Halsted Street, Chicago, Illinois
SIGNATURE MOVE: 747 Splash

In 1987, the "Dr. of Style" Slick brought one of the largest monsters to enter World Wrestling Entertainment. His destructive work was already known throughout the country, but the One Man Gang could not resist the opportunity for his dirty work to receive global exposure. The master of the 747 Splash was on a mission, and that mission was to destroy Hulkamania and all of those who supported it.

As One Man Gang pulled out all the stops in his matches, he began to show subtle signs of changes in behavior. In 1988 "Mean" Gene Okerlund went on special assignment to find out what was going down. Slick orchestrated a startling transformation and brought the spirit of Africa to WWE. As the lyrics of *Jive Soul Bro* pumped through his boom-box the man once known as One Man Gang was reborn and became Akeem, "the African Dream." He may have sported a new name, but his dedication to dismembering opponents never waivered.

He soon formed one-half of the largest teams in the history of sports-entertainment when he joined Big Boss Man to become the Twin Towers. These giants became obsessed with ending the careers of The Mega-Powers. Their attempts proved futile, and by the end of 1990, Akeem left WWE.

For the rest of the decade, One Man Gang made appearances in WCW, ECW, and in Japan. His last WWE appearance was in 2001 at the Gimmick Battle Royal during *WrestleMania X-7*. Whether he appeared as One Man Gang, or his soul brother #1 alter-ego Akeem, he was always an intimidating force in the ring.

The original *One Night Stand* was a tribute to the original ECW, and took on a life of its own as an annual WWE event. In 2009, *One Night Stand* was replaced by *Extreme Rules*.

June 12, 2005

New York, NY - Hammerstein Ballroom

| Main Event | The Dudley Boys defeated Tommy Dreamer & Sandman |

June 11, 2006

New York, NY - Hammerstein Ballroom

| Main Event | Rob Van Dam defeated WWE Champion John Cena, Extreme Rules Match |

June 3, 2007

Jacksonville, FL - Veterans Memorial Arena

| Main Event | WWE Champion John Cena defeated The Great Khali, Falls Count Anywhere Match |

June 1, 2008

San Diego, CA - San Diego Sports Arena

| Main Event | Edge defeated Undertaker in a TLC Match for the vacant World Heavyweight Championship |

ORIENT EXPRESS

MEMBERS: Sato, Tanaka, Kato

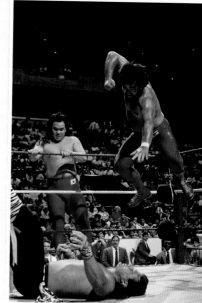

In 1990, Mr. Fuji hand-picked the most deadly assassins from his homeland to spread terror amongst the world's greatest tag teams. Sato and Tanaka debuted on *Superstars of Wrestling* and mixed under-handed tactics with martial-arts expertise. The duo met the Rockers at *WrestleMania VI* and stole a count-out victory with assistance from their ceremonial salt. The Orient Express also took on Demolition, Hacksaw Jim Duggan & Nikolai Volkoff, the Hart Foundation and the Legion of Doom. At *Survivor Series* they were hired by Sgt. Slaughter for his team of "Mercenaries."

Shortly after Sato returned to Japan, a third member was brought to the United States, Kato. This masked man brought power and speed to complement Tanaka's skills. By early 1992 the Orient Express returned to Japan. That was a day that WWE fans and Superstars rejoiced as they were finally safe from Fuji-orchestrated attacks at the hands of his ruthless tandem.

ORLANDO JORDAN

HT: 6'4"   WT: 257 lbs.   FROM: Miami, Florida
SIGNATURE MOVE: Black Out

TITLE HISTORY	
UNITED STATES CHAMPION	*Defeated John Cena on March 3, 2005*

For a brief period of time, Orlando Jordan was one of the most powerful Superstars on *SmackDown*. After aligning himself with JBL in August 2004, the Miami native quickly began to reap the benefits of making company with the WWE Champion. Serving as JBL's Chief of Staff, he found himself thrust into many high-profile matches.

In March 2005, Jordan picked up the biggest win of his career when he toppled John Cena on *SmackDown* to capture the coveted United States Championship. He went on to successfully defend the gold against *SmackDown*'s greatest for more than five months.

Shortly after Jordan's United States Championship reign came to an end, so did his alliance with JBL. With the self-proclaimed "Wrestling God" no longer watching his back, Jordan struggled to find his way. By mid-2006, Jordan was gone from WWE completely.

OTTO VON HELLER

WT: 260 lbs.
FROM: Germany

Wrestling's rulebook is filled with hundreds of rules. Otto Von Heller broke them all. Known for his villainous tactics, the big German made a name for himself within WWE as one of the most dangerous men of the 1970s. And he certainly looked the part. His bald head, dark goatee, cold eyes and black cape always gave Von Heller the psychological advantage well before the bell even rang.

During his WWE tenure, Von Heller crossed paths with some of his era's best, including Bruno Sammartino, Haystacks Calhoun and Pedro Morales.

Von Heller's post-WWE career was highlighted by a successful pairing with fellow countryman Karl Von Steiger. In May 1975, the duo defeated Jackie Fargo and George Gulas for the NWA Mid-America Tag Team Championship. Von Heller and Von Steiger beat the same pairing again in August. This time to claim the NWA Mid-America United States Tag Team Championship. Sandwiched between the two victories was a reign with the NWA Southern Tag Team Championship, a title they also captured a second time the following summer.

OUTBACK JACK

HT: 6'5"   WT: 300 lbs.   FROM: Humpty Doo, Australia
SIGNATURE MOVE: The Boomerang

In 1987 WWE welcomed a bushman from Australia's Northern Territory. Thanks to the survival skills learned after years with the Aborigines, Outback feared nothing—not even a saltwater croc! To prepare fans for his arrival video segments showed Jack in the Australian outback, training for his much anticipated debut.

When it came time to step through the ropes Outback Jack did not disappoint. The Boomerang, a modified version of the dangerous Enzui Lariat, put all Superstars on notice. Australia's favorite son battled against the likes of Barry Horowitz, "Iron" Mike Sharpe, Jim "The Anvil" Neidhart, "Million Dollar Man" Ted DiBiase and "Ravishing" Rick Rude.

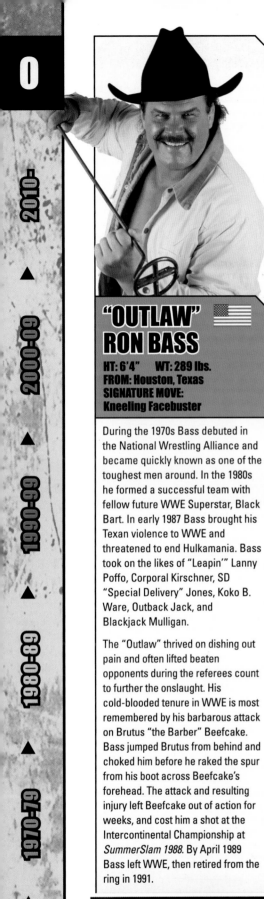

2010-
2000-09
1990-99
1980-89
1970-79
1960-69

"OUTLAW" RON BASS

HT: 6'4" WT: 289 lbs.
FROM: Houston, Texas
SIGNATURE MOVE:
Kneeling Facebuster

During the 1970s Bass debuted in the National Wrestling Alliance and became quickly known as one of the toughest men around. In the 1980s he formed a successful team with fellow future WWE Superstar, Black Bart. In early 1987 Bass brought his Texan violence to WWE and threatened to end Hulkamania. Bass took on the likes of "Leapin'" Lanny Poffo, Corporal Kirschner, SD "Special Delivery" Jones, Koko B. Ware, Outback Jack, and Blackjack Mulligan.

The "Outlaw" thrived on dishing out pain and often lifted beaten opponents during the referees count to further the onslaught. His cold-blooded tenure in WWE is most remembered by his barbarous attack on Brutus "the Barber" Beefcake. Bass jumped Brutus from behind and choked him before he raked the spur from his boot across Beefcake's forehead. The attack and resulting injury left Beefcake out of action for weeks, and cost him a shot at the Intercontinental Championship at *SummerSlam 1988*. By April 1989 Bass left WWE, then retired from the ring in 1991.

May 23, 2010

Detroit, MI - Joe Louis Arena

| Main Event | WWE Champion John Cena defeated Batista in an "I Quit" Match |

▼

May 22, 2011

Seattle, WA - KeyArena

| Main Event | WWE Champion John Cena defeated The Miz in an "I Quit" Match |

OWEN HART

HT: 5'10" WT: 227 lbs.
FROM: Calgary, Alberta, Canada
SIGNATURE MOVE: Sharpshooter

TITLE HISTORY

EUROPEAN CHAMPION	*Defeated Goldust on January 22, 1998*
INTERCONTINENTAL CHAMPION (2 TIMES)	*Defeated Rocky Maivia on April 28, 1997* *Defeated Faarooq on October 5, 1997*
WORLD TAG TEAM CHAMPION (4 TIMES)	*Partnered with Yokozuna to defeat The Smokin' Gunns on April 2, 1995* *Championships returned to Owen Hart & Yokozuna on September 25, 1995* *Partnered with Davey Boy Smith to defeat The Smokin' Gunns on September 22, 1996* *Partnered with Jeff Jarrett to defeat Big Boss Man & Ken Shamrock on January 25, 1999*

Growing up in the famed Hart wrestling family, Owen Hart could have relied on the clan's storied reputation to open doors for him. Rather than ride his family's name to the top, he paved his own path to greatness by developing one of the most technically sound offensive arsenals of all time.

THE BLUE BLAZER

In August 1988, the Blue Blazer lit up rings with a never-before-seen blend of aerial assaults, speed, and expert grappling techniques. The masked superhero moved as if he was from another galaxy and immediately brought fans to their feet before each match as he landed in the ring via a top rope Moonsault.

At the second *Survivor Series* he was part of the winning team captained by the Ultimate Warrior. At *Wrestlemania V*, Blue Blazer had a match with Mr. Perfect that kept fans on the edge of their seats. He vanished from the WWE in 1989, but returned in the 1990s to remind fans to train, say their prayers, and drink their milk.

Owen's career skyrocketed in 1994 after turning on his brother, Bret. The move proved unpopular with fans, but ultimately served as a launching pad for the younger Hart to finally break free from his sibling's overwhelming shadow. Owen finally accomplished his goal when he defeated Bret in their classic *WrestleMania X* showdown.

Following his victory over Bret, Owen began to compile an impressive list of accolades, starting with the *King of the Ring* crown in June 1994, capturing the European Championship, and two reigns as Intercontinental Champion.

Despite drawing the wrath of fans for his in-ring trickery, Owen developed a respectable reputation among his fellow Superstars. In fact, his impeccable approach to performing made him a popular tag team partner among his peers.

A tragic accident claimed the life of Owen Hart on May 23, 1999. The loss of such a great man has left a void that can never be filled. The memory of Owen's technical brilliance inside the ring and his kind, jovial nature out of it will endure in the hearts and minds of WWE fans everywhere.

OWEN HART & YOKOZUNA ★ ●

COMBINED WT: 827 lbs.

TITLE HISTORY

WORLD TAG TEAM CHAMPIONS (2 TIMES)	Defeated The Smokin' Gunns on April 2, 1995. Championships returned to Owen Hart & Yokozuna on September 25, 1995

Hart announced Yokozuna as his mystery partner just moments before challenging the Smokin' Gunns for the World Tag Team Championship at *WrestleMania XI*. Though they had no experience working together as a team, Hart & Yokozuna used their size advantage to unseat the longtime partners. Over the next five months, Hart and Yokozuna turned back all challengers.

When Owen Hart was supposedly unable to compete at *In Your House III*, Davey Boy Smith stepped in as Yokozuna's partner against WWE Champion Diesel & Intercontinental Champion Shawn Michaels. Towards the latter stages of the match, however, Hart actually interjected himself into the match. Diesel then pinned Hart and the referee awarded the World Tag Team Championship to the challengers.

The next night, Hart & Yokozuna's lawyer Clarence Mason claimed the titles could not change hands because Hart was not a legal participant in the match. The persuasive Mason eventually got his way and the titles were given back to Hart & Yokozuna. However, the emotional rollercoaster of the past twenty-four hours took its toll on the team, as they lost the titles to the Smokin' Gunns approximately one hour later. Following the loss, Yokozuna focused his attention on a singles career, while Hart formed a successful team with Davey Boy Smith.

OX BAKER   HT: 6'5"   WT: 311 lbs.   FROM: Iowa
SIGNATURE MOVE: Heart Punch

Ox Baker was unorthodox in every way, from his insatiable thirst to hurt people right down to his appearance, which featured long, curly eyebrows and an even longer mustache. Behind the power of his legendary heart punch, which was sometimes referred to as a "Hurt Punch," Baker immobilized some of sports-entertainment's greatest names, including Bruiser Brody, Harley Race and a young Hulk Hogan. Along the way, he compiled an impressive list of championships. While competing in Puerto Rico, he turned back the native hero Carlos Colon to claim both the WWC Universal Heavyweight and Puerto Rico Heavyweight Championships. He also topped The Sheik for Detroit's United States Championship in September 1977.

Tag team success was not foreign to the oversized Ox Baker. Teaming with such greats as "Superstar" Billy Graham, Ole Anderson and Chuck O'Connor, he captured eight tag title reigns over the course of his amazing career.

Outside the ring, Baker appeared in *Escape from New York*, *Blood Circus* and *I Like to Hurt People*, as well as other movies and television shows.

PALMER CANON   HT: 6'4"   WT: 260 lbs.
FROM: Portland, Maine

By August 2005, Theodore Long had more than one full year under his belt as *SmackDown* General Manager. Despite his successes at the helm, Network executives felt it necessary to send one of their own, Palmer Canon, to *SmackDown* to ensure the show ran smoothly.

It didn't take long for Canon to prove he had very little knowledge of the sports-entertainment industry. But despite his inability to properly produce *SmackDown*, the arrogant executive continually made decisions that undermined Long's authority, including canceling a Lingerie Pillow Fight between Christy Hemme and Stacy Keibler.

Canon's eye for talent proved to be just as poor as his matchmaking skills. As part of his New Talent Initiative, Canon introduced the WWE Universe to such underwhelming talents as The Dicks and The Juniors. As expected, none of Canon's signings made a lasting mark on the *SmackDown* roster.

After only a few months, Canon finally realized he was in over his head. The Network executive eventually backed off, allowing Long to do his job on his own.

PAMPERO FIRPO   HT: 5'9"   WT: 225 lbs.   FROM: Buenos Aires, Argentina
SIGNATURE MOVE: El Garfio

Pampero Firpo was one of the original horrors of sports-entertainment. The mighty madman from the pampas of Argentina first appeared on the scene in the early 1950s. As if he was summoned from the Stone Age, Firpo's body was covered in his natural fur, while a bushy beard and wild hair obscured his head.

In 1960 he appeared in Capitol Wrestling Company and became known as a loathsome figure who was more concerned with hurting an opponent than winning a match. The wild bull vanished from the Northeast territory and traveled throughout the National Wrestling Alliance. The peculiar Pampero re-appeared in WWE in 1972 and once again took aim at fan-favorites. Firpo often screamed during his matches and became the first figure to coin the phrase "Ohh yeah!" during his fits of rage in-and-out of the ring. He departed again for the NWA where his wild wrath continued to earn him regional championships. His last match of public record was in October 1986 for Carlos Colon's WWC promotion in Puerto Rico. There was never any love lost between this deranged individual and other Superstars. Today words like "extreme" and "hardcore" would be used to describe Firpo's ring style and behavior.

P

1960-69
1970-79
1980-89
1990-99
2000-09
2010-

P

2010-

2000-09

1990-99

1980-89

1970-79

1960-69

PAPA SHANGO

HT: 6'6"   WT: 330 lbs.
FROM: Parts Unknown
SIGNATURE MOVE:
Shoulder Breaker

A master of voodoo, Papa Shango first began casting his mysterious spells in 1992. With a menacing skull painted over his entire face and a terrifying threat of black magic, the bizarre Superstar quickly became one of the most feared men on the WWE roster.

Though Papa Shango's time in WWE only lasted a little more than a year, he will forever be remembered for the reign of terror he unleashed on many of the promotion's biggest names, including Ultimate Warrior. Showing no fear of the former WWE Champion, Shango unleashed several supernatural spells that forced Ultimate Warrior to mysteriously double over in pain and excrete an ominous black liquid from his skull.

Unfortunately for Papa Shango, his dark voodoo rarely translated into wins. Despite standing 6'6" and possessing a devastating shoulder breaker, Shango struggled against WWE's top-tier talent. Tito Santana, Bob Backlund, and Bret "Hit Man" Hart all picked up victories over Shango during his short tenure. In April 1993, Papa Shango strangely disappeared from the WWE scene. While nobody is certain of his whereabouts, it's safe to say the entire locker room was happy to see him go.

PAT BARRETT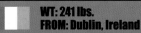

WT: 241 lbs.
FROM: Dublin, Ireland

TITLE HISTORY

WORLD TAG TEAM CHAMPIONS	*Replaced Victor Rivera as Dominic DeNucci's partner in May, 1975*

For "Irish" Pat Barrett, Victor Rivera's loss was his gain. In May 1975, Rivera teamed with Dominic DeNucci to win the World Tag Team Championship. But only four weeks into the reign, Rivera abruptly left WWE, leaving his half of the coveted titles behind.

After an extensive search, DeNucci chose Barrett as his new partner. As a result, the Irish Superstar had inherited one-half of the tag titles and will forever be listed alongside sports-entertainment's greatest tag teams. Barrett's WWE career also featured a run at Bruno Sammartino's WWE Championship. However, much like nearly everybody else who tried, he was never able to defeat the popular Italian Superstar for the gold.

Outside the Northeast territory, Barrett claimed several tag championships, including Vancouver's NWA Canadian Tag Team Titles with both Don Leo Jonathan and Tom Geohagen. He also defeated Bull Ramos to capture the NWA Americas Heavyweight Championship in August 1979.

PAT PATTERSON

HT: 6'1"   WT: 237 lbs.
FROM: Montreal, Quebec, Canada

HALL OF FAME 1996

TITLE HISTORY

HARDCORE CHAMPION	*1 Time*
INTERCONTINENTAL CHAMPION	*Unified North American and South American Championships on September 1, 1979*

After an accomplished twenty years competing in Montreal, San Francisco, and the Minneapolis-based AWA, Pat Patterson made his WWE debut in 1979. What followed was one of the most remarkable Hall of Fame careers of all time.

Shortly after entering WWE, Patterson made history when he won a September 1979 tournament to become the first-ever Intercontinental Champion. He held the title proudly for seven months before losing to Ken Patera in New York City. Many credit Patterson's tireless efforts in the ring for adding legitimacy to the title during its infancy.

After solidifying the Intercontinental Championship's strong foundation, Patterson engaged in one of WWE's most brutal rivalries. For much of 1981, Patterson and Sgt. Slaughter bled buckets during a vicious series of Boot Camp Matches. Their bloody rivalry culminated in the famed Madison Square Garden when Patterson defeated Slaughter in an Alley Fight that is considered one of the most brutal matches in WWE history. After hanging up his boots in 1984, Patterson continued to be a prominent WWE force working as an announcer and official. As a respected decision-maker, Patterson is credited with creating the Royal Rumble Match.

THE PATRIOT

HT: 6'5"   WT: 275 lbs.   FROM: Columbia, South Carolina
SIGNATURE MOVE: Patriot Missile

This man who bore the Stars N' Stripes of the USA began his career in the early 1990's. While he made a name for himself within regional circles and even won the 1991 "Most Inspirational Wrestler of The Year Award" from *Pro Wrestling Illustrated*, he wanted to take his message of freedom to the masses.

The Patriot made his WWE debut in July, 1997 and defended the honor of America in every match. He rose through the ranks quickly and won a 20-man over-the-top-rope battle royal. The highlight of his WWE career was when he pinned Bret "Hit Man" Hart on the July 28th episode of *Monday Night Raw*. Unfortunately later that year he suffered a severe back injury that forced him to retire from the ring. Though his time in the spotlight was brief, the Patriot fought for all that was good about the American way. The fans of WWE will never forget his spirit and how he inspired everyone to be the best American they can be.

PAUL BURCHILL

HT: 6'4"   **WT: 247 lbs.**   **FROM: Chelsea, England**
SIGNATURE MOVE: Reverse Swinging Neckbreaker

This Superstar was introduced to World Wrestling Entertainment by mentor William Regal on *SmackDown*. Regal trained this British bruiser in the grappling arts and various methods of submission wrestling to be prepared for the numerous fighting styles he would encounter in WWE.

The fury Burchill displayed in matches against the likes of Super Crazy, Mr. Kennedy, Jeff Hardy, and Kofi Kingston earned him the moniker "the Ripper." After recovering from injuries, Burchill debuted on *Raw* in February 2008 alongside his sister, the beautiful and sadistic Katie Lea. The English rulebreaker inflicted excruciating pain on some of the biggest names in sports-entertainment. By year's end, he found himself in ECW against Gregory Helms butting heads over the backstage interviewer's true identity. In the winter of 2010, Burchill was released from WWE shortly after The Land of Extreme closed its doors for the final time.

PAUL ELLERING

Despite a brief WWE tenure, Paul Ellering will be remembered by sports-entertainment fans around the world as the loud-mouthed manager of arguably the greatest tag team of all time, Legion of Doom.

Ellering introduced himself to WWE fans in 1992 when he reunited with Hawk & Animal following a brief separation. Unfortunately, the reunion didn't go quite as planned. Ellering failed to gain fans after showing up at ringside with a ventriloquist dummy named Rocco. He left WWE shortly after his debut.

Six years later, Ellering's popularity sank even more when he returned to WWE to manage LOD's chief rivals, the Disciples of Apocalypse. Ellering successfully led his new duo to victory over LOD at *Fully Loaded* in July 1998. A few months later, however, Hawk & Animal teamed with Droz to get their revenge when they defeated Ellering & DOA at *Judgment Day*.

Unfortunately, Ellering's time in WWE failed to mirror the amazing success he achieved as LOD's longtime friend and manager. Ellering's unmatched intellect and guidance of Hawk and Animal during their rise to worldwide domination in the 1980s was honored the night before *WrestleMania XXVII*. In an emotional induction ceremony the LOD accepted their final accolade, taking their places in the WWE Hall of Fame.

PAUL BEARER

In the words of WWE Chairman Vince McMahon, "Paul Bearer is the most unique manager in the history of the business." That's exactly what fans discovered as this creepy individual made his way to World Wrestling Entertainment in 1991. Taking over the managerial duties of Undertaker from Brother Love, this licensed mortician was the keeper of the urn from which the "Deadman" drew a mysterious power. Bearer was also often the first one seen coming through the curtain as the frightening chords of Undertaker's music haunted venues around the world.

Bearer and Undertaker embarked on a campaign of destruction, targetting WWE Superstars. The duo often reached mainstream media as seen during appearances on the *Live With Regis & Kathy Lee* television program. Paul also utilized WWE programming for his own cryptic predictions on the talk segment, *The Funeral Parlor*. The famous funeral director was also a key contributor and architect for WWE's scariest type of encounter, the Casket Match. Over the years, Bearer had periods away from the "Deadman" and managed those who opposed him such as Mankind, the Executioner, Vader and introduced the world to Undertaker's brother, Kane.

After an extended sabbatical from WWE, Bearer made his historic return to accompany Undertaker at *WrestleMania XX* as he fought Kane. Months later at *The Great American Bash*, Bearer was victimized by Paul Heyman. As the fate of the legendary urn rested in Heyman's hands and Undertaker faced the Dudley Boys, Bearer was encased in glass with cement up to his chest. After Undertaker's victory, he was left no choice but to pull the lever and cover his longtime manager in cement. The keeper of the urn vanished for years but made a shocking appearance in September 2010 when Bearer returned to *SmackDown*. Once again the mortician was at the side of Undertaker as the "Deadman" battled his brother. The reunion proved to be short-lived as in the chaos of a Hell In A Cell match Bearer entered the cage and blinded Undertaker with a beam of light from the urn. Bearer was last seen tied and bound as collateral in Kane's battle with "The Rated-R Superstar" Edge.

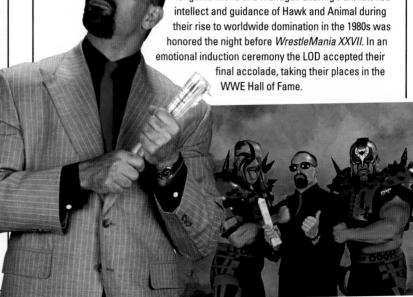

P

1960-69 ▼
1970-79 ▼
1980-89 ▼
1990-99 ▼
2000-09 ▼
2010- ▼

PAUL HEYMAN

Perhaps no personality in the history of the ring was more anti-establishment than Paul Heyman. Whether it was as Paul E. Dangerously, the manager, or as a general manager or even a promoter, the rebellious New Yorker's counterculture approach to the industry made him one of the most controversial figures of all time.

After breaking into the business as a photographer, Heyman's big break came in the mid-1980s when he landed a managerial job. His first high-profile clients were Tommy Rich and Austin Idol. Over the course of his managerial career, the diabolical Heyman went on to represent many of the game's greatest names, including a young Steve Austin.

Heyman's career took a fateful turn in 1993 when he took his managerial game to Eastern Championship Wrestling. Within months of his arrival, Heyman became one of the most powerful personalities backstage, and the promotion was renamed Extreme Championship Wrestling. By the end of 1996, he had secured full control of the promotion from then-owner Tod Gordon. Under Heyman, ECW mixed hardcore action and fast-paced technical grappling with popular music to North American fans.

Despite its popularity, financial woes ultimately claimed ECW in 2001. Following its closing, Heyman emerged in WWE, where he served as an announcer, manager and even General Manager of *SmackDown*. After the success of ECW *One Night Stand* pay-per-views in 2005 and 2006, Mr. McMahon had no choice but to reinvent the brand with Heyman back at the controls. The "Messiah of ECW" spent the next several months rebuilding his creation. Heyman quietly left sports-entertainment soon thereafter. Since his time away from the squared circle, the once "Evil Genius" remains involved in the enertainment industry and has remained a close associate of Brock Lesnar.

PAUL LONDON 🇺🇸

HT: 5'10"   **WT:** 195 lbs.   **FROM:** Austin, Texas
SIGNATURE MOVE: 450 Splash

TITLE HISTORY

CRUISERWEIGHT CHAMPION	*Won an 8-Man Battle Royal on March 31, 2005*
WORLD TAG TEAM CHAMPION	*Partnered with Brian Kendrick to defeat Lance Cade & Trevor Murdoch on September 5, 2007*
WWE TAG TEAM CHAMPION (2 TIMES)	*Partnered with Billy Kidman to defeat the Dudley Boys on July 8, 2004 Partnered with Brian Kendrick to defeat MNM on May 21, 2006*

This eccentric high-flyer is as innovative in the ring as it gets. Audiences have been captivated by this Superstar since his October 2003 debut. London is known for innovative moves like the "Dropsault" (a Moonsault and a Drop-Kick), "Mushroom Stomp" (where he leaps from the middle rope over a charging opponent, then presses his feet off their back, pushing them into the corner and then lands on his feet), and the 450 Splash.

In July 2004 he and Billy Kidman defeated the Dudley Boys to become WWE Tag Team Champions. They held the titles for two months before he set his sights on the singles ranks. In March 2005 he won an 8-Man Cruiserweight Battle Royal on *SmackDown*. London then formed one of the greatest teams in WWE history with fellow high-flyer Brian Kendrick and the two captured the WWE Tag Team Titles in May, 2006. Their reign lasted a record 334 days as champions. London's partner eventually turned his back on him, and he was drafted #1 to *Raw* in the 2007 Supplemental Draft. London continued to amaze WWE live and television audiences with his high-risk offense until he parted from the company in November 2008.

PAUL LONDON & 🇺🇸
BRIAN KENDRICK

COMBINED WT: 380 lbs.

TITLE HISTORY

WORLD TAG TEAM CHAMPIONS	*Defeated Lance Cade & Trevor Murdoch on September 5, 2007*
WWE TAG TEAM CHAMPIONS	*Defeated MNM on May 21, 2006*

London & Kendrick briefly worked together in 2003, but it wasn't until they reunited in 2005 that the high-flying tandem began to realize their true potential. Sporting theatrical masks, the eccentric duo made short work of many tag teams on *SmackDown*. Despite their impressive record, London & Kendrick weren't afforded an opportunity at true glory until the following year.

Starting in February 2006, London & Kendrick tore off five straight non-title victories over WWE Tag Team Champions MNM. Finally, at *Judgment Day 2006*, they upended the champs when it counted, giving London his second reign with the tile and Kendrick his first. They went on to hold the gold for nearly one year, longer than any other *SmackDown* team in history.

London & Kendrick were drafted from *SmackDown* to *Raw* in June 2007. The new address failed to slow the quick combination, who picked up where they left off when they captured the World Tag Team Championship while on tour in South Africa. Despite a brief title reign, the two remained one of the top tag teams in the world. Though they hit a rough patch when Kendrick walked out on his longtime partner, the duo resolved their differences and continued to bring the WWE Universe to its feet. The team succumbed to the WWE draft, and split when Kendrick was moved to *SmackDown* in June 2008.

PAUL ORNDORFF

HT: 6'0" **WT:** 252 lbs.
FROM: Brandon, Florida
SIGNATURE MOVE: Piledriver

"Mr. Wonderful" was an amazing athlete even before he trained for a career in sports-entertainment. A student of Hiro Matsuda, Orndorff applied what he learned in the NWA and was quickly noticed for his intensity, skill, and devastating piledriver.

Orndorff made his WWE debut in 1984. He associated with the likes of "Dr. D" David Schultz, "Rowdy" Roddy Piper, and "Cowboy" Bob Orton. Orndorff was selected to participate in the main event of the original *WrestleMania* against Hulk Hogan & Mr.T. His team would lose the match after an Orton miscue, and in the months following, Piper and Orton deserted him in the ring. He formed a bond with the Hulkster but eventually double-crossed the WWE Champion and ignited one of the most physical rivalries wrestling has ever seen. Their encounter in front of 76,000 fans at Toronto's CNE Stadium left no clear winner, so they met inside a 15-foot high Steel Cage in January 1987 on *Saturday Night's Main Event.*

Orndorff took a hiatus from the ring and returned with Sir Oliver Humperdink guiding his career. One of the first things he did was reconcile with Hogan and was a member of his team at the first-ever *Survivor Series.*

In 1990 he appeared in World Championship Wrestling, but a serious neck injury forced Orndorff to retire in 1996. He then became the lead trainer for WCW's Power Plant before retiring in 2000. The night before *WrestleMania 21,* the three decade career of "Mr. Wonderful" was honored as he was inducted into the WWE Hall of Fame.

PAUL ROMA

HT: 5'11" **WT:** 235 lbs. **FROM:** Kensington, New York
SIGNATURE MOVE: Flying Cross Body

This Superstar was first seen by WWE audiences in 1984, and his impressive physique and good looks quickly brought him a great deal of attention. He also became known for throwing one of the greatest dropkicks in all of sports-entertainment. In 1987 Roma became one-half of an exciting duo known as the Young Stallions. Roma and partner Jim Powers were top contenders for the World Tag Team Championship and, along with the Killer Bees, were the sole survivors at the inaugural *Survivor Series.*

The team disbanded in 1990 when Roma changed his ways and formed Power & Glory with Hercules, but that team disbanded in late 1991. Roma shocked the wrestling world in 1993 when he debuted in WCW as the fourth member of the legendary stable, the Four Horsemen. He left WCW in 1995 and after a brief return to WWE in 1997, Roma retired from the ring to pursue other interests. Today he trains ring hopefuls at his wrestling school in Connecticut.

PEDRO MORALES

HT: 5'1"
WT: 240 lbs.
FROM: Culebra, Puerto Rico

While rarely mentioned in the same breath as Bruno Sammartino, Hulk Hogan, or Triple H, Pedro Morales'
accomplishments

TITLE HISTORY

INTERCONTINENTAL CHAMPION (2 TIMES)	*Defeated Ken Patera on December 8, 1980* *Defeated Don Muraco on November 23, 1981*
U.S.A. HEAVYWEIGHT CHAMPION	*Defeated Freddie Blassie in the finals of a tournament on January 7, 1971*
WORLD TAG TEAM CHAMPION	*Partnered with Bob Backlund to defeat The Samoans on August 9, 1980*
WWE CHAMPION	*Defeated Ivan Koloff on February 8, 1971*

are the equal of any Superstar to ever lace a pair of boots. Over the course of his nearly thirty years in the ring, the Puerto Rican legend captured the WWE, World Tag Team and Intercontinental Championships, making him the first-ever Triple Crown Champion.

Morales made his professional debut in 1959. Still only a teenager, he spent much of his time competing on smaller cards around the New York area. It wasn't until 1963 that he made his Madison Square Garden debut, teaming with his boyhood hero Miguel Perez. As he slowly started to make a name for himself, it wasn't long before promotions nationwide were looking to add him to their rosters.

Morales eventually settled in Los Angeles and in 1971, he jumped to WWE, making his debut on the same card that saw Sammartino's nearly eight-year WWE Championship reign come to an end. A mere three weeks later, Morales defeated Ivan Koloff to claim the WWE Championship, an honor he held for nearly three years. Only Sammartino, Hogan and Bob Backlund held the championship longer.

With the title in his grasp, Morales became a hero to the large number of Puerto Rican fans living in the Northeast. In August 1980, he gave his passionate fan base even more reason to celebrate when he teamed with Bob Backlund to capture the World Tag Team Championship. Later that year, he completed the trifecta when he won his first of two Intercontinental Championships. The win made Morales the first-ever Triple Crown Champion, paving the way for future champions such as Bret Hart, Shawn Michaels, and Edge.

In 1995, Morales was honored as one of WWE's all-time elite when he was inducted into the WWE Hall of Fame by fellow Puerto Rican Superstar Savio Vega.

1960-69
1970-79
1980-89
1990-99
2000-09
2010-

2010-
2000-09
1990-99
1980-89
1970-79
1960-69

PERCY WATSON

HT: 6'6"   WT: 245 lbs.
FROM: South Beach, Miami, Florida
SIGNATURE MOVE: The Percycution

"Showtime" Percy Watson paired with WWE Pro MVP for season two of *WWE NXT*. With the former United States Champion guiding the way, the energetic and eccentric Rookie showed signs of being one of the season's top contenders, but was eliminated midway through the competition. More recently, Watson resurfaced as the tag team partner of fellow Superstar hopeful Titus O'Neil on *NXT Redemption*.

When he's not competing in the ring, Watson is often found living it up on the Miami club scene. The self-professed "South Beach Party Boy" loves to party, and he also loves to feature the moves he learns on the dance floor in the ring.

Prior to *NXT*, Percy Watson excelled on the gridiron as a member of the NFL's Green Bay Packers and Washington Redskins. He also attended West Carolina University, where he graduated with a bachelor's degree in computer information systems. (That must explain the glasses.)

PERRY SATURN

HT: 5'10"   WT: 241 lbs.   FROM: Boston, Massachusetts
SIGNATURE MOVE: Death Valley Driver

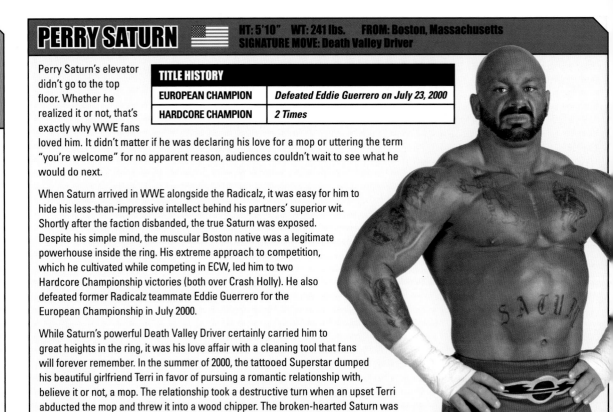

Perry Saturn's elevator didn't go to the top floor. Whether he realized it or not, that's exactly why WWE fans loved him. It didn't matter if he was declaring his love for a mop or uttering the term "you're welcome" for no apparent reason, audiences couldn't wait to see what he would do next.

TITLE HISTORY	
EUROPEAN CHAMPION	*Defeated Eddie Guerrero on July 23, 2000*
HARDCORE CHAMPION	*2 Times*

When Saturn arrived in WWE alongside the Radicalz, it was easy for him to hide his less-than-impressive intellect behind his partners' superior wit. Shortly after the faction disbanded, the true Saturn was exposed. Despite his simple mind, the muscular Boston native was a legitimate powerhouse inside the ring. His extreme approach to competition, which he cultivated while competing in ECW, led him to two Hardcore Championship victories (both over Crash Holly). He also defeated former Radicalz teammate Eddie Guerrero for the European Championship in July 2000.

While Saturn's powerful Death Valley Driver certainly carried him to great heights in the ring, it was his love affair with a cleaning tool that fans will forever remember. In the summer of 2000, the tattooed Superstar dumped his beautiful girlfriend Terri in favor of pursuing a romantic relationship with, believe it or not, a mop. The relationship took a destructive turn when an upset Terri abducted the mop and threw it into a wood chipper. The broken-hearted Saturn was never able to rebound from the loss and left WWE the following year.

PETE DOHERTY

WT: 232 lbs.
FROM: Dorchester, Massachusetts

Pete Doherty was the anti-Goldberg. Instead of racking up one of sports-entertainment's most enviable winning streaks, the Superstar known as the "Duke of Dorchester" owned one of the game's most unenviable losing streaks. In fact, during the mid 1980s, Doherty competed in more than 300 matches without a single win. It wasn't until 1987 when the Massachusetts native finally defeated Lanny Poffo in his hometown Boston Garden.

Unfortunately for "The Duke," his win over Poffo failed to ignite a white-hot winning streak. Instead, he went right back to losing to the likes of King Kong Bundy, Special Delivery Jones and Andre the Giant. Despite his lackluster record, however, Doherty always maintained a big smile, sans several teeth.

Doherty gave announcing a try after taking a break from full-time competition in the late 1980s. But much like his in-ring career, "The Duke" couldn't seem to make it work. He left WWE soon after.

During the twilight of his career, Doherty made occasional appearances on the Northeast's independent wrestling scene.

PETE SANCHEZ

HT: 6'0"   WT: 279 lbs.   FROM: San Juan, Puerto Rico
SIGNATURE MOVE: Cannonball

A popular figure from the early days of World Wrestling Entertainment, Pete Sanchez was known throughout the northeast as a fiery competitor who excelled in both singles and tag team competition. Through the 1960s and 1970s Sanchez took on the likes of Crusher Verdu, the Mongols, Pampero Firpo, Stan "The Man" Stasiak, Gorilla Monsoon, Blackjack Mulligan and "Superstar" Billy Graham. He even locked-up with Ric Flair in the "Nature Boy's" WWE and Madison Square Garden debut in 1976.

Pete Sanchez continued to appear on WWE events until 1992 and remained one of the most respected journeymen to compete in the ring. Along with his opponents, Sanchez helped build the foundation to what today is the greatest sports-entertainment company in the world. With a career that spanned nearly three decades, Pete Sanchez's longevity in World Wrestling Entertainment is an accomplishment matched by few Superstars.

PETER MAIVIA

HT: 5'9" WT: 275 lbs. FROM: The Isle of Samoa
SIGNATURE MOVE: Samoan Stump Puller

Sports-entertainment has had several influential families that have produced great competitors. Perhaps none is greater than the dynasty of High Chief Peter Maivia whose wrestling family includes his blood brothers in the Anoa'i family, his son-in-law Rocky Johnson, and his grandson, The Rock.

In early 1960, Peter moved to New Zealand to train under Steve Rickard. Maivia's charisma, toughness, power, and surprising speed led him to many championships throughout the South Pacific. Maivia also made time for Hollywood as he appeared in the 1967 James Bond film, *You Only Live Twice.* He arrived on the American mainland in 1970. He held different versions of the NWA World Tag Team Titles with Chief Billy White Wolf, Ray Stevens, and Pat Patterson.

After a brief stop in Texas, Maivia debuted in the WWE in 1977. Fans were drawn to his ring presence and the ancient Samoan tribal tattoos that covered most of his body. Maivia was a genuine Samoan High Chief and fought for the pride of his people every time he entered the ring. In 1978 Maivia broke the hearts of people everywhere when he turned on friends Chief Jay Strongbow and Bob Backlund. Managed by "Classy" Freddie Blassie, Maivia became one of the most despised men in all of sports-entertainment.

Sadly, Maivia was diagnosed with cancer in 1981, and tragically passed away in June 1982 at the age of 45. Peter Maivia created a legacy that inspired an entire culture and brought sports-entertainment some of its most storied warriors. What he began continues to live on today in the mind, body, and spirit of both his people and his fans around the world.

PEZ WHATLEY

HT: 5'10" WT: 245 lbs. FROM: Chattanooga, Tennessee
SIGNATURE MOVE: The Flying Headbutt

This Superstar and "Pistol" was the first-ever African American amateur wrestler at the University of Tennessee at Chattanooga. Whatley made his WWE debut in 1990 and brought the fight to Superstars like "Ravishing" Rick Rude, "Million Dollar Man" Ted DiBiase, Tito Santana, "Rowdy" Roddy Piper, and Mr. Perfect. Pez left WWE in March of 1991 and returned to the ring in Japan and Amercian independents before landing in WCW. He retired from active competition in 1995 and became a trainer at WCW's Power Plant.

Sadly, in January 2005 Pez passed away following complications from a heart attack. Pez Whatley will be regarded as one of the toughest and most entertaining individuals in all of sports-entertainment history.

PHANTASIO

HT: 6'3"
WT: 235 lbs.

A master illusionist, Phantasio made his WWE debut on *Wrestling Challenge* in July 1995. Following a few awe-inspiring magic tricks, the WWE newcomer made short work of his opposition, Tony DeVito. After the match, the magic continued when Phantasio mysteriously removed the referee's striped underwear, despite the fact that the official was still wearing his pants.

With a 1-0 professional record to his credit, Phantasio strangely disappeared from WWE, never to be seen again. Legend claims he was the victim of a magic trick gone bad.

PG-13

MEMBERS: J.C. Ice, Wolfie D
COMBINED WT: 410 lbs.

As members of the original Nation of Domination, J.C. Ice and Wolfie D had one job: Recite threatening rap lyrics while Faarooq, D-Lo Brown and the rest of the Nation made their way to the ring.

On rare occasions, PG-13 would put their microphones down long enough to actually compete in the ring. But at a total combined weight of just over 400 pounds, they proved to be a less-than-formidable duo.

Outside of WWE, J.C. Ice and Wolfie D were able to attain great success as a tag team, particularly in the Memphis-based United States Wrestling Association. From 1993 to 1997, the undersized rappers claimed the organization's World Tag Team Championship 15 times, beating teams that included Tommy Rich, Terry Gordy and Brian Christopher along the way.

PG-13 made a few appearances in WCW during the promotion's waning days. Competing mainly on *Thunder*, they squared off against the likes of Three Count and the David Flair & Crowbar pairing.

P

1960-69
1970-79
1980-89
1990-99
2000-09
2010-

P

2010-

2000-09

1990-99

1980-89

1970-79

1960-69

THE PITBULLS

MEMBERS: Kid Kash, Jamie Noble
COMBINED WT: 402 lbs.

In June 2006 two former Cruiserweight Champions joined forces to ambush the tag team division on *SmackDown*. Wearing dog collars, barking, biting opponents, and attacking anything that moved in the ring, these Pitbulls were vicious and out for blood. In addition to an aggressive style, Kash and Noble displayed great speed and teamwork while showing no regard for the rules of the ring.

They battled the Mexicools and then-WWE Tag Team Champions Brian Kendrick & Paul London, and in a brief period of time became top title contenders. The Pitbulls went their own way that September when Kid Kash left World Wrestling Entertainment. While some fans are disappointed that the team never realized their full potential, tag teams throughout World Wrestling Entertainment are happy they no longer have to worry about the bite of the Pitbulls.

PJ WALKER

HT: 6'0"   WT: 229 lbs.   FROM: New York City
SIGNATURE MOVE: Superkick

Identified as a top prospect in the early 1990s, PJ Walker was seen on *Monday Night Raw*, and *Wrestling Challenge*. Walker was an accomplished grappler with speed, grit, and superior ring technique thanks to his training in Stu Hart's Dungeon.

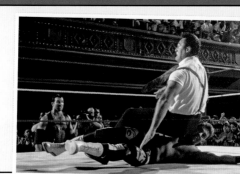

As fans chanted his name, PJ took on anyone who had an open contract including Diesel, Yokozuna, Jeff Jarrett, Bam Bam Bigleow, and Undertaker. The highlight of his WWE tenure was when he beat Irwin R. Schyster on *Raw*. Walker left World Wrestling Entertainment in early 1994 to pursue other professional endeavors.

PMS

MEMBERS: Terri, Jacqueline, Ryan Shamrock

Fresh off unsuccessful romances with Marc Mero and Goldust, respectively, Jacqueline and Terri joined forces in November 1998 to exact revenge on WWE's male Superstars. Calling themselves Pretty Mean Sisters, or PMS, they used their sensuality as a weapon, using their curves, sex appeal, and questionable tactics to get what they wanted from male Superstars.

Val Venis, the duo's first victim, was told he had impregnated Terri. The shocking news caused the former adult film star to run for the hills. However, PMS was not done milking the pregnancy for all it was worth. Shortly after Terri announced she was with child, D-Lo Brown accidentally knocked the mother-to-be off the ring apron, causing her to miscarry (it was later revealed that she was never pregnant in the first place). As payback, PMS forced Brown to be their servant.

The following year, Ryan Shamrock joined the sexually charged faction. Together, the threesome adopted Meat as their sex slave. They worked the young Superstar so hard that he was too exhausted when it came time to compete, which might explain his lackluster won-loss record.

POWER & GLORY

MEMBERS: Hercules, Paul Roma
COMBINED WT: 519 lbs.

The "Dr. Of Style" Slick brought a new era to tag team wrestling in July 1990 when the mighty Hercules (who represented power) and Paul Roma (glory) looked for guidance as these two rule-breakers told off fans and former friends and lived by the motto: nice guys finish last.

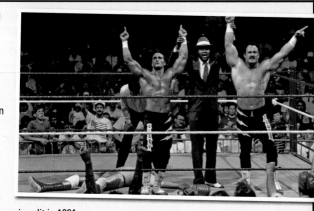

Hercules and Roma were devastating together in the ring as they battled for supremacy and the World Tag Team Championship. They clashed with the likes of the Rockers, the Hart Foundation, and the Legion of Doom. Power & Glory often teamed in six-man action with another Slick client, the Warlord. After disappointing losses and mounting frustration the pair split in 1991.

POWERS OF PAIN

MEMBERS: Warlord, Barbarian
COMBINED WT: 618 lbs.

The story of the Powers of Pain is puzzling, at best. They had the look. They had the size. They even had the speed. But with all these physical gifts, it is surprising that the sum of it all didn't equate to championships.

Warlord & Barbarian joined WWE in 1988, following a very successful year competing in NWA's Mid-Atlantic territory. Managed by the Baron (Baron von Raschke), the Powers of Pain quickly became favorites with the fans, who were enamored by the team's immense size and colorful face paint. The team's popularity propelled them into a lengthy rivalry with the World Tag Team Champions, Demolition.

Following several unsuccessful attempts to wrest the gold away from Ax & Smash, the Powers of Pain lured Mr. Fuji to their side. Bringing the devious manager into their camp proved unpopular with the fans, but Warlord & Barbarian saw it as an opportunity to capture the elusive World Tag Team Championship. Unfortunately, however, not even the great Mr. Fuji could lead the Powers of Pain to the titles. In 1990, after failing to achieving any success with Warlord & Barbarian, Fuji sold them separately to Slick and Bobby "The Brain" Heenan respectively. The sale marked the end of the Powers of Pain.

PRIMO

HT: 5'10" WT: 218 lbs.
FROM: San Juan, Puerto Rico

TITLE HISTORY

WORLD TAG TEAM CHAMPION	*Partnered with Carlito to defeat John Morrison & The Miz on April 5, 2009*
WWE TAG TEAM CHAMPION (2 TIMES)	*Partnered with Carlito to defeat Curt Hawkins & Zack Ryder on September 26, 2008* *Partnered with Epico to defeat Air Boom on January 15, 2012*

Primo has some huge shoes to fill. Not only is he the younger brother of former WWE Superstar Carlito, but he's also the son of Puerto Rican wrestling legend Carlos Colon. The success he's experienced during his WWE career proves he's unfazed by the pressure.

It didn't take long for Primo to prove his worth in WWE. Only one month after making his successful debut against Charlie Haas in August 2008, the agile Puerto Rican Superstar teamed with his brother to capture the WWE Tag Team Championship from Zack Ryder & Curt Hawkins. In the wake of losing the titles, Primo found himself the victim of an attack from his brother. Despite the turn, Primo decided to soon rejoin Carlito and the Colon's became feared rule-breakers.

In battles with the likes of Sin Cara, Zack Ryder, Randy Orton, and Santino Marella, Primo sent a message that he's after WWE gold. Early in 2012, alongside his cousin, Epico, he shocked the WWE Universe by taking down Air Boom to reclaim the WWE Tag Team Championship.

PRINCESS VICTORIA

HT: 5'8"
FROM: Canada

TITLE HISTORY

WOMEN'S TAG TEAM CHAMPION	*Partnered with Velvet McIntyre and awarded Tag Team Championship in May 1983*

Even the greatest of champions loses their title eventually. Unless, of course, you're Princess Victoria.

With Velvet McIntyre as her partner, Princess Victoria proudly represented WWE as one-half of the first-ever Women's Tag Team Champions. But in September 1984, the popular trailblazer to today's Divas suffered a broken neck, thanks to a Despina Mantagus piledriver inside Philadelphia's famed Spectrum. The unfortunate injury effectively ended her promising career. As a result, Princess Victoria was never able to complete her tag title reign with McIntyre. She was later replaced by Desiree Peterson.

Immediately prior to WWE, Princess Victoria and McIntyre were recognized by the NWA as the promotion's Women's Tag Team Champions. They defeated Joyce Grable and future WWE Hall of Famer Wendi Richter for the titles in 1983. Princess Victoria held the same titles with Sabrina one year earlier. That victory also came at the expense of Grable and Richter.

PROF. TORU TANAKA

HT: 5'11" WT: 280 lbs.
FROM: Hiroshima, Japan

TITLE HISTORY

INTERNATIONAL TAG TEAM CHAMPION	*Partnered with Mitsu Arakawa to win a tournament on June 1, 1969*
WORLD TAG TEAM CHAMPION (3 TIMES)	*Partnered with Mr. Fuji to defeat Chief Jay Strongbow & Sonny King on June 27, 1972* *Partnered with Mr. Fuji to defeat Tony Garea & Haystacks Calhoun on September 11, 1973* *Partnered with Mr. Fuji to defeat Tony Garea & Larry Zbyszko on September 27, 1977*

Famed manager Wild Red Berry lured Japanese powerhouse Prof. Toru Tanaka to the United States in the late 1960s. Tanaka was immediately looked upon as one of the most hated Superstars of his time, but the barrel-chested Superstar from the Land of the Rising Sun reveled in his role as the evil foreigner. In fact, he oftentimes intentionally incited fans by using ceremonial Japanese salts as a weapon.

Tanaka achieved most of his notoriety competing in the tag team ranks. With Mr. Fuji as his partner, Tanaka became a three-time World Tag Team Champion. The duo's first and lengthiest reign came after defeating Chief Jay Strongbow & Sonny King in June 1972. They went on to hold the titles for nearly one year.

As a singles competitor, Tanaka earned opportunities against WWE Champions Bruno Sammartino, Pedro Morales and Bob Backlund. After retiring from the ring in the early 1980s, the Superstar parlayed his natural charisma into a successful movie career. *Pee-wee's Big Adventure*, *The Running Man* and *The Last Action Hero* are just a few of the box-office hits in which Tanaka appeared.

2010-
2000-09
1990-99
1980-89
1970-79
1960-69

PUBLIC ENEMY

MEMBERS:
Johnny Grunge, Flyboy Rocco
FROM: South Philly
COMBINED WT: 487 lbs.

Johnny Grunge and Flyboy Rocco lived by one simple philosophy: If it ain't broke, break it! Collectively known as Public Enemy, Grunge and Rocco had an affinity for destruction, particularly when it came to tables. In fact, the duo from South Philly commonly carried tables to the ring with the sole intention of sending their opposition through the wooden structure.

Upon arriving in WWE in 1999, Public Enemy earned an early disqualification victory over The Brood on *Raw*. Unfortunately for Grunge and Rocco, that's where the winning stopped. They soon found themselves on the wrong end of matches against the Hardys, Owen Hart & Jeff Jarrett, and APA, who boast they ran Public Enemy out of WWE only a few months after their debut.

Prior to WWE, Grunge and Rocco made a name for themselves obliterating the competition in ECW. Four ECW Tag Team Championship reigns later, they jumped to WCW, where they claimed the WCW Tag Team Titles from Harlem Heat in September 1996.

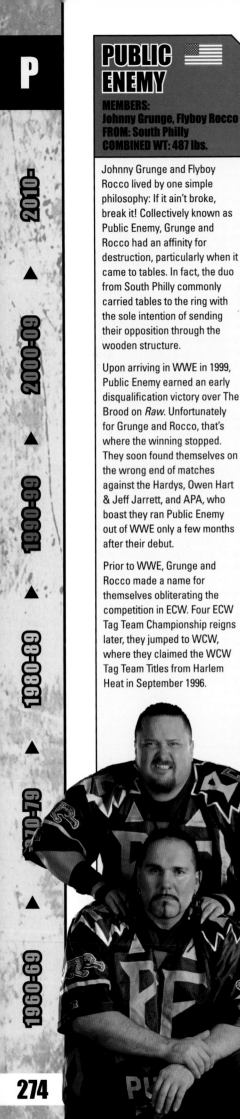

"THE PUG" ALEX PORTEAU

HT: 5'10" **WT:** 226 lbs. **FROM:** New Orleans, Louisiana
SIGNATURE MOVE: The Pugbomb

From The Big Easy, Alex Porteau started his career in the late 1980s in Fritz Von Erich's World Class Championship Wrestling. After a short tenure in World Championship Wrestling he spent the early 1990s in the GWF and Carlos Colon's World Wrestling Council. Porteau's power and technical skills earned him the opportunity to grapple with the best sports-entertainment had to offer.

In 1996 "the Pug" debuted in World Wrestling Entertainment as was a quick hit with fans everywhere. Alex battled all comers including Goldust, Mankind, Faarooq, Justin Bradshaw, the Sultan, Aldo Montoya, and Vader. He was a top contender for the Intercontinental Championship until he left WWE in early 1997. Since, then he has appeared on wrestling cards in United States, Puerto Rico, and Japan.

THE QUEBECERS

MEMBERS: Jacques, Pierre
COMBINED WT: 479 lbs.

Managed by the obnoxious Johnny Polo, the Quebecers entered the WWE ranks in 1993. They quickly became title contenders known for their rule-breaking ways, their manager interfering in matches, and their abilities in the ring.

TITLE HISTORY	
WORLD TAG TEAM CHAMPIONS (3 TIMES)	*Defeated The Steiners on September 13, 1993* *Defeated Marty Jannetty & 1-2-3 Kid on January 17, 1994* *Defeated Men on a Mission on March 31, 1994*

On an episode of *Monday Night Raw* they challenged the Steiner Brothers for the World Tag Team Championship under Province of Quebec Rules, which meant that the titles could change hands even on a disqualification. That minor change resulted in a victory when Scott Steiner lost his cool and nailed Johnny Polo with a hockey stick.

They held the titles until January 1994, and would hold them two more times before splitting in 1994 after a disappointing loss to the Headshrinkers. In the following two year span, both men left the WWE. They returned in 1998 where they competed in the Tag Team Battle Royal at *WrestleMania XIV*.

"QUICKDRAW" RICK McGRAW

HT: 5'7" **WT:** 235 lbs.
FROM: Charlotte, North Carolina

After a career as a stand-out talent in the Florida and Mid-South territories during the mid-1970's, Rick McGraw debuted in World Wrestling Entertainment in May 1980. His explosive style and power made him an instant hit with the fans. Weeks later he debuted at Madison Square Garden and that energy carried him to the August *Showdown At Shea* where he locked-up with Greg Gagne.

McGraw often teamed with Steve Travis and with Andre the Giant on two occassions, against the Moondogs and the Wild Samoans. On his own "Quickdraw" faced the likes of Ken Patera, Bulldog Brower, Tor Kamata, Killer Kahn, Johnny Rodz, Baron Mikel Scicluna and Harley Race.

Tragically as McGraw's star was on the rise he passed away in November 1985. To wrestling fans, Rick McGraw will always be the energetic "Quickdraw" who brought fans to their feet and never backed down from a challenge.

RAD RADFORD

HT: 5'11" **WT:** 264 lbs.
FROM: Seattle, Washington
SIGNATURE MOVE:
Northern Lights Suplex

In 1995, Rad Radford left his home in Seattle to become a WWE Superstar. As a fan of grunge bands, the flannel-clad Superstar certainly beat to his own drum. Inside the ring, he was just as sound as the most accomplished Superstar on the roster.

Armed with a devastating Northern Lights Suplex finisher, Radford picked up many wins early in his WWE stay. However, he wanted to be known for more than just victories— he also desired an amazing physique. That's when he turned to Skip & Sunny of the Bodydonnas. The fitness gurus agreed to take Radford on as a Bodydonna-in-training, but eventually fired the rotund Superstar after he failed to make any progress. Radford left WWE soon after.

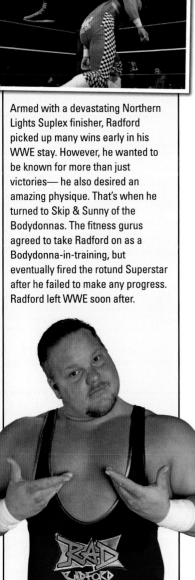

THE RADICALZ

MEMBERS: Chris Benoit, Eddie Guerrero, Dean Malenko, Perry Saturn

It's the story of one of the most-noted talent jumps in history, as Eddie Guerrero, Chris Benoit, Dean Malenko, and Perry Saturn moved en masse from WCW to WWE. Collectively known as the Radicalz, Benoit, Guerrero, Malenko, and Saturn became greatly displeased with WCW's lackluster direction in 2000. Despite Benoit being recognized as WCW Champion, the group opted to leave WCW in favor of WWE. The quartet's earliest appearances saw them sitting in the front row at WWE events, but it wasn't long before they jumped the barrier between the ring and fans to embark on their own dreams of superstardom.

Individually, each member of the Radicalz enjoyed championship-filled careers. Together, however, their success was fleeting, as the group broke apart within months of their formation. Over the next few years, the Radicalz would go on to reunite on rare occasions, including *Survivor Series 2000* where they turned back the team of Road Dogg, Billy Gunn, K-Kwik & Chyna.

Randy Orton (see page 276)   *Randy Savage (see page 277)*

RANJIN SINGH

When the Punjabi Nightmare, the Great Khali, speaks people listen. The problem is many are unable to understand what he is saying. Enter Ranjin Singh who first appeared in WWE in the summer of 2007. As Khali's chief communicator, Ranjin sang the 7-foot monster's praises and echoed every roar of danger that comes from the behemoth's mouth.

With such an important position and his own arrogance, Singh became one of the most despised individuals in sports-entertainment. Over time the WWE Universe began to applaud Ranjin and the Great Khali, who was now known as the "Punjabi Playboy." In 2008, Ranjin seized opportunity and premiered the "Khali Kiss Cam," which gave female fans the opportunity to share a kiss with India's national hero.

Though Singh and Khali were estranged in 2011 due to the meddlesome Jinder Mahal, he and Khali rebuilt their relationship. They are poised to once again send shockwaves through WWE with their doctrine of destruction.

RAVEN

HT: 6'1" **WT:** 235 lbs. **FROM:** The Bowery
SIGNATURE MOVE: Evenflow DDT

TITLE HISTORY

HARDCORE CHAMPION	26 Times

Despite a privileged childhood, Raven grew to be a very troubled adult. Suffering from deep mental anguish, he used the memories of what he believed was a turbulent past as the inspiration to create a disturbing career.

During the mid-to-late 1990s, Raven was recognized as one of sports-entertainment's up-and-coming stars. His dark persona intrigued fans, while his in-ring ability carried him to many prestigious accolades, including the ECW Championship and United States Championship. His successes eventually caught the eye of WWE officials, who lured him into their fold in 2000.

As a WWE Superstar, big things were expected from Raven. Unfortunately, however, he was only able to achieve mediocre success while competing on the big stage. His greatest claim to fame during his WWE tenure was capturing the Hardcore Championship a record 26 times, although many of his reigns only lasted a few minutes.

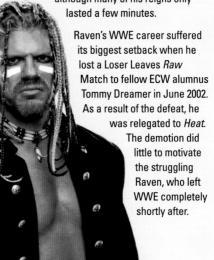

Raven's WWE career suffered its biggest setback when he lost a Loser Leaves *Raw* Match to fellow ECW alumnus Tommy Dreamer in June 2002. As a result of the defeat, he was relegated to *Heat*. The demotion did little to motivate the struggling Raven, who left WWE completely shortly after.

RANDY ORTON

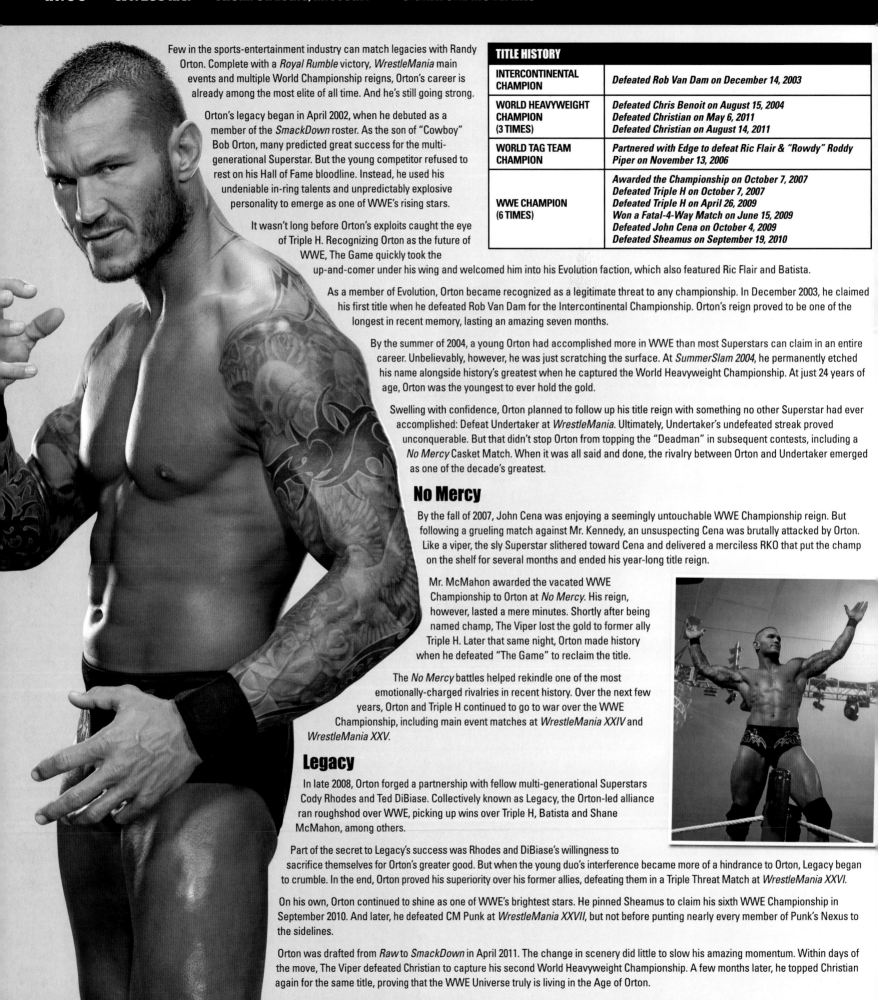

THE APEX PREDATOR

HT: 6'5" **WT: 235 lbs.** **FROM: St. Louis, Missouri** **SIGNATURE MOVE: RKO**

Few in the sports-entertainment industry can match legacies with Randy Orton. Complete with a *Royal Rumble* victory, *WrestleMania* main events and multiple World Championship reigns, Orton's career is already among the most elite of all time. And he's still going strong.

Orton's legacy began in April 2002, when he debuted as a member of the *SmackDown* roster. As the son of "Cowboy" Bob Orton, many predicted great success for the multi-generational Superstar. But the young competitor refused to rest on his Hall of Fame bloodline. Instead, he used his undeniable in-ring talents and unpredictably explosive personality to emerge as one of WWE's rising stars.

It wasn't long before Orton's exploits caught the eye of Triple H. Recognizing Orton as the future of WWE, The Game quickly took the up-and-comer under his wing and welcomed him into his Evolution faction, which also featured Ric Flair and Batista.

TITLE HISTORY	
INTERCONTINENTAL CHAMPION	*Defeated Rob Van Dam on December 14, 2003*
WORLD HEAVYWEIGHT CHAMPION (3 TIMES)	*Defeated Chris Benoit on August 15, 2004* *Defeated Christian on May 6, 2011* *Defeated Christian on August 14, 2011*
WORLD TAG TEAM CHAMPION	*Partnered with Edge to defeat Ric Flair & "Rowdy" Roddy Piper on November 13, 2006*
WWE CHAMPION (6 TIMES)	*Awarded the Championship on October 7, 2007* *Defeated Triple H on October 7, 2007* *Defeated Triple H on April 26, 2009* *Won a Fatal-4-Way Match on June 15, 2009* *Defeated John Cena on October 4, 2009* *Defeated Sheamus on September 19, 2010*

As a member of Evolution, Orton became recognized as a legitimate threat to any championship. In December 2003, he claimed his first title when he defeated Rob Van Dam for the Intercontinental Championship. Orton's reign proved to be one of the longest in recent memory, lasting an amazing seven months.

By the summer of 2004, a young Orton had accomplished more in WWE than most Superstars can claim in an entire career. Unbelievably, however, he was just scratching the surface. At *SummerSlam 2004*, he permanently etched his name alongside history's greatest when he captured the World Heavyweight Championship. At just 24 years of age, Orton was the youngest to ever hold the gold.

Swelling with confidence, Orton planned to follow up his title reign with something no other Superstar had ever accomplished: Defeat Undertaker at *WrestleMania*. Ultimately, Undertaker's undefeated streak proved unconquerable. But that didn't stop Orton from topping the "Deadman" in subsequent contests, including a *No Mercy* Casket Match. When it was all said and done, the rivalry between Orton and Undertaker emerged as one of the decade's greatest.

No Mercy

By the fall of 2007, John Cena was enjoying a seemingly untouchable WWE Championship reign. But following a grueling match against Mr. Kennedy, an unsuspecting Cena was brutally attacked by Orton. Like a viper, the sly Superstar slithered toward Cena and delivered a merciless RKO that put the champ on the shelf for several months and ended his year-long title reign.

Mr. McMahon awarded the vacated WWE Championship to Orton at *No Mercy*. His reign, however, lasted a mere minutes. Shortly after being named champ, The Viper lost the gold to former ally Triple H. Later that same night, Orton made history when he defeated "The Game" to reclaim the title.

The *No Mercy* battles helped rekindle one of the most emotionally-charged rivalries in recent history. Over the next few years, Orton and Triple H continued to go to war over the WWE Championship, including main event matches at *WrestleMania XXIV* and *WrestleMania XXV*.

Legacy

In late 2008, Orton forged a partnership with fellow multi-generational Superstars Cody Rhodes and Ted DiBiase. Collectively known as Legacy, the Orton-led alliance ran roughshod over WWE, picking up wins over Triple H, Batista and Shane McMahon, among others.

Part of the secret to Legacy's success was Rhodes and DiBiase's willingness to sacrifice themselves for Orton's greater good. But when the young duo's interference became more of a hindrance to Orton, Legacy began to crumble. In the end, Orton proved his superiority over his former allies, defeating them in a Triple Threat Match at *WrestleMania XXVI*.

On his own, Orton continued to shine as one of WWE's brightest stars. He pinned Sheamus to claim his sixth WWE Championship in September 2010. And later, he defeated CM Punk at *WrestleMania XXVII*, but not before punting nearly every member of Punk's Nexus to the sidelines.

Orton was drafted from *Raw* to *SmackDown* in April 2011. The change in scenery did little to slow his amazing momentum. Within days of the move, The Viper defeated Christian to capture his second World Heavyweight Championship. A few months later, he topped Christian again for the same title, proving that the WWE Universe truly is living in the Age of Orton.

RANDY "MACHO MAN" SAVAGE

HT: 6'2" **WT:** 237 lbs. **FROM:** Sarasota, Florida **SIGNATURE MOVE:** Flying Elbow Drop

This unmistakable second-generation competitor began his full-time sports-entertainment career in 1979 after years as a Major League Baseball catching prospect.

Randy "Macho Man" Savage debuted in World Wrestling Entertainment in 1985 with "Classy" Freddie Blassie, Bobby "the Brain" Heenan, "Mouth of the South" Jimmy Hart, and Mr. Fuji vying to be his manager. He shocked the world when he signed with the unknown Miss Elizabeth. Savage came to the ring to the song *Pomp and Circumstance,* dressed in extravagant sequined robes, headbands, and wrap-around sunglasses. The "Macho Man" served notice to all that he was an elite talent when as he reached the finals of the company's first pay-per-view event, *The Wrestling Classic.*

On February 8, 1986, he used a foreign object to defeat Tito Santana for the Intercontinental Championship. The "Macho Man" did everything imaginable to keep his championship, even if it meant putting Miss Elizabeth in front of him. Savage's next opponent was more interested in his gorgeous manager than defeating him in the ring. George "the Animal" Steele entered into a string of violent matches that resulted in Savage leaving *WrestleMania 2* victorious.

In November 1986, "Macho Madness" took a dangerous turn when he crushed the larynx of Ricky Steamboat with the timekeeper's bell and put him out of commission for months. Upon Steamboat's return, a championship rematch was signed for *WrestleMania III.* Despite the fact that Savage lost, this contest is regarded as one of the greatest matches in sports-entertainment history.

Months after this epic battle, Savage was the victim of an attack by the Honky Tonk Man and the Hart Foundation. When this included an assault on Miss Elizabeth, one of the most thrilling moments in WWE history followed as "Macho Madness" and Hulkamania joined forces. As Randy mowed through the WWE Championship tournament at *WrestleMania IV,* the Hulkster came to ringside for the tournament final to watch Savage's back. With a capacity crowd on its feet, "Macho Man" dropped his famous elbow on "Million-Dollar Man" Ted DiBiase and became the WWE Champion.

Sadly, miscommunication and misunderstandings led to Savage attacking Hulk Hogan in the locker room after their match against the Twin Towers on *The Main Event.* This resulted in the Mega Powers exploding at *WrestleMania V.* In one of the more hotly anticipated matches in *WrestleMania* history, Hogan defeated Savage for the title.

Macho Royalty

Savage began the new decade with a new valet, Sensational Sherri. The two became royalty when he beat "King" Duggan and became the "Macho King." After a series of matches against Dusty Rhodes, Savage turned his attention to Ultimate Warrior. The two met in a Retirement Match at *WrestleMania VII,* which Savage lost. Sherri attacked her fallen client, but was chased off by a returning Miss Elizabeth. The two reunited in a wash of emotion and a "Match Made in Heaven" was set for *SummerSlam 1991.* A heartfelt ceremony turned frightful when Jake Roberts presented them a wrapped gift that contained a deadly king cobra which bit Savage. After being reinstated by Jack Tunney, Savage defeated Roberts on *Saturday Night's Main Event.*

Savage was once again tested as Ric Flair made scandalous remarks about a one-time relationship with Miss Elizabeth. At *WrestleMania VIII,* "Macho Man" not only cleared the name of his wife, but defeated Flair to become WWE Champion for the second time. Randy then made the move to the broadcast booth for WWE programs, including the first episode of *Monday Night Raw* and *WrestleMania IX.* At *WrestleMania X,* he defeated former pupil Crush in a "Falls Count Anywhere" Match.

In 1995, he traveled to World Championship Wrestling where he became a four-time WCW Champion before leaving the company in 1999. Randy later invaded the mainstream when he made his Hollywood debut as "Bonesaw McGraw" in the 2002 blockbuster *Spiderman.* In 2003, he released his rap album *Be a Man.* In 2010, "Macho Man" was included as a part of Mattel's WWE Legends Series, his first WWE figure in over 15 years.

Randy "Macho Man" Savage is revered as one of the greatest figures in all of sports-entertainment and a true legend in the ring. Savage combined unparalleled charisma, Sadly, on May 20, 2011 Randy Savage suffered a heart attack while driving his car and passed away. Randy "Macho Man" Savage remains one of the greatest figures in all of sports-entertainment and a true legend in the ring. Savage combined unparalleled athleticism, charisma, determination, and skill to dominate opponents and amaze fans worldwide.

> " OH YEAH! "

TITLE HISTORY	
INTERCONTINENTAL CHAMPION	Defeated Tito Santana on February 8, 1986
WWE CHAMPION (2 TIMES)	Defeated Ted DiBiase on March 27, 1988 Defeated Ric Flair on April 5, 1992

"Ravishing" Rick Rude (see page 280)

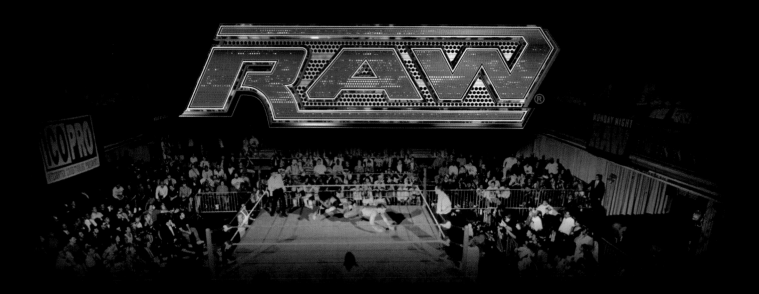

On January 11, 1993 WWE made sports-entertainment history. As a raucous crowd filled The Manhattan Center, *Raw* made its one-hour debut. The three-man broadcast team of Vince McMahon, Randy "Macho Man" Savage, and Rob Bartlett called the action and brought the excitement to viewers everywhere.

After its first year, *Raw* was such a hit that fans demanded the show tour the United States. WWE obliged and hit the road selling out arenas coast-to-coast every week. Whether it was the "Loser Leaves WWE" match with "Nature Boy" Ric Flair and Mr. Perfect, an unknown "Kid" defeating Razor Ramon and adding 1-2-3 to his name, or Leslie Nielsen scanning the globe for the real Undertaker, *Raw* quickly earned a reputation as a place where anything could happen. Its tagline of "Uncut, Uncensored and Uncooked" described the action of the Superstars who emerged on sports-entertainment's most prominent stage.

Sports-entertainment evolved during the mid-1990s and *Raw* led the way. Its success on Mondays reached new heights and extended to the world of interactive software in 1994 with the release of the first *Monday Night Raw* video game. *Raw* provided drama and excitement weekly, and even included comedic moments, including a 1995 edition of *The King's Court* when William Shatner showed-off his self-defense techniques against Jerry "The King" Lawler.

The Monday Night War Begins

Witnessing WWE's success, media mogul Ted Turner decided to air *WCW Monday Nitro* starting in September, 1995. Competition remained fierce, with *Nitro* going to a two hour broadcast in 1996, and *Raw* following suit in February 1997. Shortly thereafter, the WWE Championship changed hands for the first time on the program when Sycho Sid defeated Bret "Hit Man" Hart. The next week the action went to the land of extreme with the original ECW Invasion when Paul Heyman, the Eliminators, Tazz, Tommy Dreamer, Sabu, the Dudley Boys, and the bWo invaded the Manhattan Center.

WWE expanded its global reach with the introduction of its first new title since the Intercontinental Championship. At the end of a tournament, the British Bulldog defeated Owen Hart for the European Championship on the March 3, 1997 episode of *Raw*.

However, with a seemingly endless budget and questionable tactics, WCW was winning the ratings war. As WWE fought for its life, it turned to younger Superstars like Stone Cold Steve Austin, The Rock, Mankind, Undertaker, and D-Generation X to carry *Raw* to ratings dominance. On September 27, *Raw* emanated for the first time from Madison Square Garden and showcased Stone Cold Steve Austin hitting Vince McMahon with a Stone Cold Stunner which ignited the Austin vs. McMahon conflict. The year ended with an exclusive, controversial Vince McMahon interview relating the events that led up to what has been dubbed "The Montreal Incident" and the departure of Bret Hart from WWE.

The Attitude Era

As *Monday Night Raw* celebrated its fifth anniversary, the battle with WCW continued. Many within WWE felt *Raw* would eventually unseat *Nitro* and regain the top spot of sports-entertainment television ratings. Stone Cold Steve Austin kicked off 1998 by interrupting Vince McMahon's important announcement and came face-to-face with former heavyweight boxing champion "Iron" Mike Tyson. All hell broke loose after

Austin gave the self-proclaimed "Baddest Man on the Planet" the Stone Cold Salute. In the aftermath all that could be heard was a vexed Vince McMahon yelling, "You ruined it damnit!" In the wake of the departure of Shawn Michaels after *WrestleMania XIV*, D-Generation X began a new era under the leadership of Triple H and his right-hand man, X-Pac.

On April 13, 1998 WWE won its first battle in the ratings war since 1996. Audiences were geared up for the first-ever match between the Chairman and the "Texas Rattlesnake." As the bell was about to ring, Dude Love brought the festivities to a screeching halt thanks to his Mandible Claw. In the following weeks DX showed why they ruled sports-entertainment when they invaded *WCW Monday Nitro*. DX also took on The Nation of Domination when they mocked the entire group during a memorable edition of *Raw*.

In September, Stone Cold Steve Austin barreled through the gates of Detroit's Joe Louis Arena to get at his nemesis, Mr. McMahon. Austin arrived on a Zamboni, then launched himself over the top rope onto Mr. McMahon. Even being restrained and handcuffed by police didn't stop the former WWE Champion as he continued to lunge at the WWE Chairman. While recovering from the injuries, Mr. McMahon's hospital suite was visited by Mankind, who introduced the world to Mr. Socko just before Stone Cold Steve Austin administered his form of alternative medicine. Just when it seemed the Austin-McMahon rivalry couldn't get any hotter, something new would occur to worsen their already acrimonious relationship. The "Texas Rattlesnake" filled Mr. McMahon's prized $60,000 Corvette with cement one night, then left the Chairman in urine-soaked slacks laid-out in the center of the ring courtesy of "BANG 3:16" on another.

The May 10, 1999 episode of *Raw* was seen by over 8 million viewers and is among the highest-rated episodes in the distinguished history of the program. After the McMahon family suffered at the hands of Undertaker and the mysterious Higher Power, Vince proved that he would sacrifice anything to get the "Texas Rattlesnake," even his own daughter.

As the year 2000 approached, the WWE Universe was greeted by a countdown clock which marked the debut of "Y2J" Chris Jericho, who interrupted The Rock to announce that "*Raw* Is Jericho!" *Raw* set another ratings record in September when "Rock: This Is Your Life" became the highest-rated segment in *Monday Night Raw* history. Despite Mick Foley's

The Monday Night War Concludes

By the time the calendar hit the year 2000, WWE reigned supreme in the Monday Night Wars. On March 26, 2001 an event no one could have foreseen just two years earlier took place when Mr. McMahon informed television audiences that he was about to purchase World Championship Wrestling, and that the fate of the company rested in his hands. The czar of sports-entertainment added that *Monday Night Raw* and *WCW Monday Nitro* would be simulcast. However, the McMahon that shocked everyone was Shane. When his music hit, it was not in Cleveland for *Raw* but instead he was at Panama City on *Nitro*. He confirmed the contract to purchase WCW did indeed have the name McMahon on it, but it read Shane McMahon. The resulting bad blood between family members led to an invasion of WWE.

In 2002, WWE Superstars and fans braced themselves for the triumphant return of Triple H at Madison Square Garden. After eight months of grueling physical rehabilitation to repair a torn quadriceps, the "Cerebral Assassin" announced his entry into the *Royal Rumble*. The next month, the past and present clashed when Hollywood Hogan and The Rock stood eye-to-eye in the middle of the ring and set their historic *"Icon vs. Icon"* Match for *WrestleMania X8*. In March, WWE underwent a brand division where *Raw* and *SmackDown* became their own entities under the WWE banner.

Operating within its own rules and bylaws, *Raw* instituted the position of General Manager to make the important decisions and guide the brand. Superstars who filled the role included WWE Hall of Famer "Nature Boy" Ric Flair, Stone Cold Steve Austin & Mick Foley in cooperative efforts, Mr. McMahon, Jonathan Coachman, William Regal, and Mike Adamle. In July, Mr. McMahon made a surprise announcement and introduced the new *Raw* General Manager, former WCW-boss Eric Bischoff. A hush formed over the crowd as the one-time bitter competitors embraced. The former President of WCW listed his personal examples of ruthless aggression and guaranteed to put the "E" in WWE.

Over the years, *Raw* survived invasions from ECW, The Alliance, and the nWo, though no invasion was as destructive as the time the *NXT* rookies banded together and trashed *Raw*. Proving nothing could keep it down, *Raw* endured and celebrated episode 900 on August 30, and even went *"Old School Raw"* on November 15. For an evening, fans had the opportunity to travel back in time with the original *Raw* set including the red, white, and blue ring ropes and classic WWE logos. The show included appearances from "Mean" Gene Okerlund, Sgt. Slaughter, the Million Dollar Man, Mae Young, "Cowboy" Bob Orton, Jimmy "Superfly" Snuka, "Hacksaw" Jim Duggan, and Iron Sheik among others.

An Electrifying Host Announcement

The WWE Universe was overjoyed by the 2011 return of The Rock, who agreed to act as the host of *WrestleMania*. Even after *WrestleMania XXVII* took place, "The Great One" continued to trade verbal jabs with John Cena. Not one to be left out of the spotlight, CM Punk interrupted an edition of *Raw Roulette* to demand his due respect and recognition. The Straight Edge Superstar laid out his grievances directly to the WWE Universe despite malfunctioning microphones and suspensions.

The rest of 2011 was marked by change and upheaval. In August, the name of the show changed to the *Raw Supershow* where competitors from both *Raw* and *SmackDown* battled one another in contests normally reserved for pay-per-view events. Triple H became Chief Operating Officer of WWE but a vote of no confidence resulted in the introduction of WWE's Executive Vice President of Talent Relations, and Interim *Raw* General Manager, Mr. John Laurinaitis.

Today, this iconic television program continues to innovate and brings the Superstars of WWE into homes all over the world. *Raw* features more than sixty Superstars on its roster and WWE programming averages nearly 12 million viewers every week. It's the longest running episodic television program in history; in July 2012, it celebrated episode 1,000. For nearly 20 years, *Raw* has brought laughs, tears, and audiences to their feet as the world's greatest sports-entertainers ply their trade with no reruns, no do-overs and no off-season.

Celebrating 15 Years

On October 23, 2006 *Raw* aired its 700th episode, making it the longest running weekly entertainment show without a hiatus, in the history of American broadcast television. On December 10, 2007 the show-of-shows celebrated its 15th Anniversary with a three-hour spectacular that saw the return of Stone Cold Steve Austin, Mankind, Hulk Hogan, Sunny, The Godfather, "Million Dollar Man" Ted DiBiase, Trish Stratus, and Howard Finkel.

In 2008, WWE embraced high-definition television and introduced an all-new set for *Raw*. Late in 2008, WWE celebrated the 800th episode of *Raw* with a three-hour episode. For a brief period of 2009, Donald Trump owned *Raw* but WWE Chairman Vince McMahon reacquired it a short time later and announced a "guest star" initiative. The WWE Universe experienced something new each week when Guest Hosts set matches and maintained order. Many stars from other media took on the role, including Hugh Jackman, Bradley Cooper, Jeremy Piven, Shaquille O'Neal, Seth Green, ZZ Top, Snoop Dogg, William Shatner, Mark Cuban, and The Muppets.

2010 began with the shocking return of Bret "Hit Man" Hart after an absence of thirteen years from WWE programming. Two months later, D-Generation X made their final appearance in tag action. 2010 also marked the debut of the Anonymous Raw General Manager, a figure of authority whose identity remained a mystery and made proclamations via email read by Michael Cole.

R

2010-
▲
2000-09
▲
1990-99
▲
1980-89
▲
1970-79
▲
1960-69

"RAVISHING" RICK RUDE

HT: 6'3" WT: 252 lbs.
FROM: Robbinsdale, Minnesota
SIGNATURE MOVE: The Rude Awakening

TITLE HISTORY

INTERCONTINENTAL CHAMPION	Defeated Ultimate Warrior on April 2, 1989

This former National Arm Wrestling Champion was seen in several regional wrestling promotions including Minnesota, Canada, Georgia, Memphis and Florida in the early 1980s. In 1985, he traveled to Fritz Von Erich's World Class Championship Wrestling. After World Class withdrew from the NWA, this villain became its first Heavyweight Champion.

In 1987, the self-proclaimed "Sexiest Man Alive" debuted in WWE as a member of the Heenan Family. In his mind, the era of "The Ravishing One" arrived as he grabbed the microphone before matches and demeaned fans and invited them to observe what a real man looked like. After victories courtesy of the "Rude Awakening" neckbreaker, Rick selected a woman from the crowd and administered his other version of this maneuver, a kiss that often left the ladies breathless on the mat.

As his unrelenting vanity rolled through WWE, he won the Jesse "The Body" award at that year's Slammy's. Rude held the Intercontinental Championship twice, trading it with Ultimate Warrior. Shortly after their main event match inside a 15-foot high Steel Cage at *SummerSlam 1990* for the WWE Championship, Rude left WWE.

Rude bounced between promotions and countries for a few years, but then displayed a penchant for doing the unexpected. First, he arrived in ECW in 1996 during Jerry "The King" Lawler's crusade against the renegade promotion. In 1997, he re-emerged in WWE as the insurance policy for DX. As The Monday Night Wars continued, Rude made history that November when he appeared on *Raw* as a member of D-Generation X and on *WCW Monday Nitro* as a member of the nWo in the same evening!

Sadly, as he trained for a comeback to the ring, this true WWE legend passed away in 1999. "Ravishing" Rick Rude was one of the most infamous villains of all-time and possessed an incredible physique by any standards. His reputation as an incredible athlete, premier ring competitor, and heartbreaker of the ladies proceeded him wherever he went in the world. To those who knew him and to those who watched him, Rick Rude was simply "Ravishing."

RAY "THE CRIPPLER" STEVENS

HT: 5'8" WT: 235 lbs. FROM: San Francisco, California SIGNATURE MOVE: Bombs Away Knee-Drop

The man who first became known as "The Blonde Bomber" began his career in 1950. Stevens' early dastardly acts made him one of the most loathed men in the business. However, by the mid 1960s he teamed with Pat Patterson to form one of the most revered tag teams in history, the Blonde Bombers.

TITLE HISTORY

U.S.A. HEAVYWEIGHT CHAMPION	Defeated Bobo Brazil on June 18, 1967

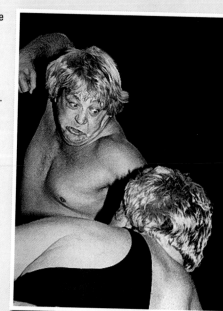

In the 1970s Stevens spent most of his time in the AWA and NWA before heading to World Wrestling Entertainment in 1980. Ray had the distinction of having co-managers in Lou Albano and "Classy" Freddie Blassie. He showed how he got his nickname when he viciously attacked Jimmy "Superfly" Snuka and administered two piledrivers to him on the concrete floor after Snuka was declared a free man on *Rogers' Corner*. Stevens soon returned to the AWA as a competitor and broadcaster until he retired in 1992. On April 5, 1995 Stevens' impact was recognized when the mayors of San Francisco and Oakland jointly declared it "Ray Stevens Day."

In May 1996, one of sports-entertainment's true pioneers passed away at his California home. Ray Stevens left a lasting impression within the world of sports-entertainment. He was master at his craft and consummate performer.

RAZOR RAMON

HT: 6'7" WT: 287 lbs.
FROM: Miami, Florida
SIGNATURE MOVE: Razor's Edge

TITLE HISTORY

INTERCONTINENTAL CHAMPION (4 TIMES)	**Defeated Rick Martel on September 27, 1993** **Defeated Diesel on August 29, 1994** **Defeated Jeff Jarrett on May 19, 1995** **Defeated Dean Douglas on October 22, 1995**

During his introductory interviews in 1992, Razor Ramon proclaimed that he was the only real man in the WWE and that if you wanted to be like Razor, you had to do like Razor and take whatever you want. Known as "The Bad Guy," Ramon was both hated for his attitude and respected for his abilities in the ring.

Despite his impressive win-loss record, Razor Ramon may be best remembered for being the victim of one of the greatest upsets in WWE history. The unknown Kid (who later became known as X-Pac) scored an improbable victory over Razor on *Monday Night Raw*. Despite the loss, Razor and the Kid bonded and started to compete as a tag team, much to the delight of WWE fans.

Over the rest of Razor Ramon's WWE tenure, he held the Intercontinental Championship multiple times and often faced off against Shawn Michaels. At *WrestleMania X* "The Bad Guy" defeated "The Heartbreak Kid" in a legendary Ladder Match regarded by many as one of the greatest sports-entertainment moments in history.

In 1996 Razor Ramon left WWE and signed with WCW. He appeared under his real name, Scott Hall, alongside Kevin Nash and Hulk Hogan. The trio formed the nWo and changed the face of sports-entertainment forever. After his time in WCW, Hall made stops in ECW and in Japan, then briefly reformed the nWo in WWE in 2002. Whether the tooth-pick is being flicked from Razor Ramon or Scott Hall, people know they just got hit with a little bit of his oozing machismo.

REBECCA DiPIETRO

The WWE Universe first laid eyes on the curvaceous Rebecca DiPietro during the 2006 *Raw* Diva Search. The contest was ultimately won by Layla, but Rebecca managed to outlast eventual Diva Maryse before being sent home herself.

Later in 2006, Rebecca returned to WWE as the extreme backstage interviewer for ECW. She only held the position briefly before being released by WWE, but during her time, she managed to ask the tough questions to such ECW Superstars as Bobby Lashley, Big Show and Rob Van Dam.

Rebecca enjoyed a successful modeling career prior to entering the sports-entertainment world. She has appeared in the pages of Maxim and Stuff magazines, among others. She also landed on the small screen as a part of E! Entertainment Television's *Wild On…* series and gained notoriety as the 2005 Miss Hawaiian Tropic USA, an accomplishment also held by former WWE Diva Ashley Massaro in 2002. Since leaving WWE, Rebecca won the Miss MET-RX Model Search in 2008.

RED BASTIEN

HT: 6'0" WT: 190 lbs.
FROM: Bottineau, North Dakota

At just 16, Red Bastien developed a love for fighting while wrestling and boxing in carnivals. Before he could turn his passion into a career, Bastien was drafted into the Navy. He spent his time in the military beefing up for what he hoped would be a profitable professional career. By the time his commitment to the Navy was finished, he had added 30 pounds to his frame, which was greatly needed considering he was considerably smaller than most pros.

As a professional, Bastien was dedicated to constantly improving his craft. Over time, he eventually became recognized as one of the game's toughest men. He then combined his rugged persona with lightning-fast speed, which he acquired while training with noted Mexican speed merchant Manuel Barintez.

Bastien's career took him all over the world, but it was in the United States that he gained his greatest fame, especially in the tag team ranks. Teaming with his brother Lou, he enjoyed five tag team title reigns. In later years, he went on to form championship combinations with several other Superstars, including Hercules Cortez, who he won the AWA Tag Team Championship with in May 1971.

RENE DUPREE

HT: 6'3" WT: 260 lbs. FROM: Paris, France
SIGNATURE MOVE: Dupree Bomb

TITLE HISTORY

WORLD TAG TEAM CHAMPION	**Partnered with Sylvain Grenier to defeat Kane & Rob Van Dam on June 15, 2003**
WWE TAG TEAM CHAMPION	**Partnered with Kenzo Suzuki to defeat Billy Kidman & Paul London on September 9, 2004**

Nobody loved Rene Dupree more than, well, Rene Dupree. The cocky Superstar believed he was greatest Superstar to ever grace a WWE ring. Unfortunately for his detractors, Dupree's early ring efforts certainly backed his boasts. In June 2003, a little more than a month after his in-ring debut, Dupree and his partner, Sylvain Grenier, defeated Kane & Rob Van Dam to capture the World Tag Team Championship. The victory proved historic, as it put Dupree in the record books as the youngest tag champ in WWE history (at 19 years old). Collectively known as La Resistance, Dupree & Grenier dominated the *Raw* tag team division until he was drafted to *SmackDown* in March 2004.

As a member of *SmackDown*, Dupree continued his tag team excellence; this time with partner Kenzo Suzuki. The new duo defeated Billy Kidman & Paul London for the WWE Tag Team Championship in September 2004. They held the titles for three months before losing to Rey Mysterio & RVD. Following the loss, Dupree struggled to get back on track. He bounced around from *SmackDown* to *Raw* to *ECW on Syfy* before finally being released from WWE in July 2007.

R

1960-69
1970-79
1980-89
1990-99
2000-09
2010-

R

2010-

2000-09

1990-99

1980-89

1970-79

1960-69

RENE GOULET

HT: 6'0"   WT: 236 lbs.
FROM: Nice, France
SIGNATURE MOVE: Claw

TITLE HISTORY

WORLD TAG TEAM CHAMPION	Partnered with Karl Gotch to defeat Luke Graham & Tarzan Tyler on December 6, 1971

By the time WWE's mainstream boom of the 1980s came along, Rene Goulet's glory days were behind him. The self-proclaimed No. 1 Frenchman spent much of the Hulkamania era falling to up-and-coming fan favorites such as "Leaping" Lanny Poffo and Hillbilly Jim, but longtime WWE fans actually remember Goulet as a serious threat to all titleholders during the 1970s.

Goulet formed a formidable tandem with fellow foreigner Karl Gotch of Germany in 1971. Together, they defeated Luke Graham & Tarzan Tyler to become the second-ever World Tag Team Champions in December 1971. Fans and insiders alike predicted a lengthy reign for Goulet & Gotch. Surprisingly, however, they were unseated by Baron Mikel Scicluna & King Curtis only two months later.

After the loss, Goulet left WWE to tour the globe. He competed in Japan, Australia and Germany before returning to WWE in the early 1980s. Unfortunately by this time, the aged "Master of the Claw" he rarely had the opportunity to apply his feared finisher.

RENO RIGGINS

HT: 5'10"   WT: 226 lbs.   FROM: Las Vegas, Nevada

Reno Riggins won countless matches over the course of his career. It just so happens, however, that none of them were in WWE. As a WWE Superstar during the late 1980s and early 1990s, Riggins was regularly seen on the losing end of matches against the likes of Randy "Macho Man" Savage, Honky Tonk Man and the mighty One Man Gang.

Riggins had considerably better success competing outside the WWE ring. While wrestling for various Tennessee promotions, the Nevada native engaged in bitter rivalries with Wolfie D, Flash Flanagan and Brian Christopher, who he defeated to claim the USWA Southern Heavyweight Championship in August 1992.

Riggins briefly retired from the ring in 1995, only to return again later in the decade. When he came back, he formed a successful tag team with Steve Dunn. Together, the combination claimed three NWA North American Tag Team Title reigns and one run with the NWA World Tag Team Championship.

REPO MAN

HT: 6'2"   WT: 290 lbs.
SIGNATURE MOVE: The Crowbar

In 1991, this Superstar was introduced to WWE audiences in vignettes that showed him repossessing cars from garages and parking lots. His services were retained by "Million Dollar Man" Ted DiBiase to acquire the Million Dollar Championship from DiBiase's former bodyguard, Virgil.

The man with his black mask and bull rope terrorized fans and Superstars like Big Boss Man, British Bulldog, "Hacksaw" Jim Duggan, Tito Santana, Jimmy "Superfly" Snuka, Sgt. Slaughter and "Rowdy" Roddy Piper until he left World Wrestling Entertainment in Spring 1993.

In recent years Repo Man has resurfaced in WWE most notably at *WrestleMania X-Seven* in the Gimmick Battle Royal and in December 2007 for the *Raw 15th Anniversary* special. The imprint this individual left on WWE is as permanent as the tire tracks on his ring attire. The Repo Man will always be right around the corner. It's just a matter of if you see him or not.

HT: 5'6"   WT: 175 lbs.
FROM: San Diego, California
SIGNATURE MOVE: 619, West Coast Pop

" THE ULTIMATE UNDERDOG "

At 5'6" and 175 pounds, Rey Mysterio is often considered WWE's ultimate underdog. Despite his size disadvantage, it's not uncommon to see the masked marvel chop his opposition down to size at a dizzying pace. Utilizing a repertoire that features a unique combination of high flying and heavy impact, Mysterio has established himself as one sports-entertainment's premier Superstars.

Mysterio's earliest years were spent perfecting his Lucha Libre style on cards across Mexico. After more than five years battling the likes of Juventud Guerrera and Psicosis, the young high-flyer finally caught the eye of ECW's Paul Heyman, who introduced North American fans to Mysterio in 1995.

Word of Mysterio's innovative offense began to stretch past ECW's Philadelphia footprint; and it wasn't long before the San Diego native was scooped up by national powerhouse WCW. Within weeks of his June 1996 debut, Mysterio picked off Dean Malenko to capture the coveted Cruiserweight Championship. The win marked Mysterio's first of a record eight reigns with the title (WCW and WWE combined).

Mysterio made his WWE debut in July 2002, and as expected, cemented himself as a top threat in the cruiserweight division. He also started to show signs of becoming a main-event star. Shortly after his debut, the Master of the 619 captured the WWE Tag Team Championship with Edge; and as time went on, he partnered with other main eventers to claim gold, including Rob Van Dam, Batista and longtime friend Eddie Guerrero.

Following Guerrero's tragic passing in 2005, Mysterio focused his efforts on honoring his friend by winning the World Championship. He took the first step in realizing his goal when he last eliminated Randy Orton to win the 2006 *Royal Rumble*.

REY MYSTERIO ![US Flag]

TITLE HISTORY

CRUISERWEIGHT CHAMPION (3 TIMES)	*Defeated Matt Hardy on June 5, 2003* *Defeated Tajiri on January 1, 2004* *Defeated Chavo Guerrero, Sr. on June 17, 2004*
INTERCONTINENTAL CHAMPION (2 TIMES)	*Defeated JBL on April 5, 2009* *Defeated Chris Jericho on June 28, 2009*
WORLD HEAVYWEIGHT CHAMPION (2 TIMES)	*Defeated Randy Orton on April 2, 2006* *Won a Fatal 4-Way Match on June 20, 2010*
WWE CHAMPION	*Defeated The Miz in the finals of a tournament on July 25, 2011*
WWE TAG TEAM CHAMPION (4 TIMES)	*Partnered with Edge to defeat Kurt Angle & Chris Benoit on November 7, 2002* *Partnered with Rob Van Dam to defeat Kenzo Suzuki & Rene Dupree on December 9, 2004* *Partnered with Eddie Guerrero to defeat the Basham Brothers on February 20, 2005* *Partnered with Batista to defeat MNM on December 16, 2005*

Then at *WrestleMania 22*, Mysterio accomplished the unthinkable when he defeated Kurt Angle and Orton to win the World Championship. Following the match, Mysterio celebrated his victory with Guerrero's family. The image of him embracing Chavo and Vickie Guerrero on the *WrestleMania* stage remains one of the most emotional scenes in WWE history.

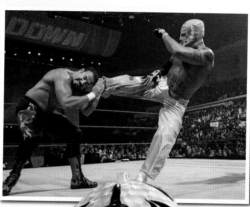

Ironically, it would also be Chavo Guerrero who cost Mysterio his World Championship three months later. Fueled by jealousy, Guerrero turned on Mysterio at *The Great American Bash*, allowing King Booker to walk away with the gold. Over the course of the next year-plus, Mysterio repeatedly gained retribution from his former friend, including at *No Mercy 2006* and *SummerSlam 2007*.

Mysterio joined elite company in April 2009, when he became just the 21st Superstar to win WWE's Triple Crown. The honor came at the expense of John Bradshaw Layfield, who Mysterio trounced in a matter of seconds to claim the Intercontinental Title. A few months later, Mysterio became a two-time Intercontinental Champion when he defeated Chris Jericho to regain the gold in a Mask vs. Title Match.

In June 2010, Mysterio outlasted *SmackDown*'s best when he won a Battle Royal for the right to challenge for the World Championship. Mysterio was given his opportunity at *Fatal 4-Way*, where he turned back CM Punk, Big Show and defending champ Jack Swagger to win the World Title for a second time. He held the gold for four weeks before Kane cashed in his Money in the Bank briefcase and defeated a weakened Mysterio for the title.

The longtime *SmackDown* Superstar moved to *Raw* in April 2011, courtesy of the annual WWE Draft. As a member of the Monday night brand, Mysterio continued to prove himself as an elite Superstar. Just months into his stay, the Master of the 619 defeated The Miz in a tournament finals to capture his first-ever WWE Championship. As a result of the victory, Mysterio became one of the elite few to have held both the World and WWE Titles.

More than 20 years after his first match, Mysterio continues to prove his skeptics wrong. And with multiple World Championship reigns, amazing *WrestleMania* moments and a *Royal Rumble* victory to his credit, the ultimate underdog continues to prove he truly is the "Biggest Little Man."

RHYNO ![US Flag]

HT: 5'10" WT: 275 lbs.
FROM: Detroit, Michigan
SIGNATURE MOVE: Gore

TITLE HISTORY

HARDCORE CHAMPION	*3 Times*
UNITED STATES CHAMPION	*Defeated Tajiri on September 23, 2001*

Billed as half man and half beast, Rhyno entered WWE in 2001 with the distinction of being the original ECW's final champion. His reputation preceding him, fans demanded he live up to his lofty hardcore reputation. Refusing to disappoint WWE's rabid fans, Rhyno immediately proved he was extreme when he defeated the mighty Kane for the Hardcore Championship on *SmackDown*. He went on to win the title two more times during his WWE tenure, once from Chris Jericho and once from Test.

In July 2001, Rhyno reverted back to his ECW roots when he joined forces with Stephanie and Shane McMahon's Alliance of ECW and WCW Superstars. As a member of The Alliance, Rhyno became Stephanie's pet, largely because he refused to allow Y2J to verbally berate her. The rivalry lead to a *SummerSlam* showdown between the two Superstars. Despite coming out on the losing end, the match is widely regarded as a highlight of Rhyno's WWE career. Undeterred by the loss, the "Man-Beast" defeated Tajiri the following month for the United States Championship.

Proving he will always be tied to the original ECW, Rhyno's final WWE appearance took place at *One Night Stand* in 2005. He battled Sabu in a thrilling throwback to his hardcore days.

1960-69
1970-79
1980-89
1990-99
2000-09
2010-

R

2010-
2000-09
1990-99
1980-89
1970-79
1960-69

RHYTHM & BLUES

MEMBERS: Honky Tonk Man, Greg Valentine
COMBINED WT: 514 lbs.

Former Intercontinental Champions Honky Tonk Man & Greg Valentine joined forces in 1989 to help manager Jimmy Hart in his battle against the Hart Foundation. Though not officially recognized as Rhythm & Blues yet, the duo battled Bret Hart & Jim Neidhart at *WrestleMania V*. The Hart Foundation walked away victorious that night, but it didn't deter Honky Tonk Man & Valentine from continuing to make music together.

A few months after the loss, Valentine began his transformation from a no-nonsense professional to Elvis look-alike. He dyed his hair jet black, donned oversized sunglasses and began carrying around a classic guitar. With the makeover complete, Valentine officially joined forces with Honky Tonk Man and Rhythm & Blues was born.

The tone-deaf duo appeared to care more about their fledgling music careers than they did about competing in the ring. As a result, Rhythm & Blues failed to score any major hits in the tag ranks. They did, however, manage to debut their single "Hunka, Hunka, Honky Love" at *WrestleMania VI*. Unfortunately for Honky Tonk Man & Valentine, the Bushwhackers crashed the performance, destroying their guitars.

Ric Flair (see page 286)

RICARDO RODRIGUEZ
HT: 6'0"
WT: 225 lbs.

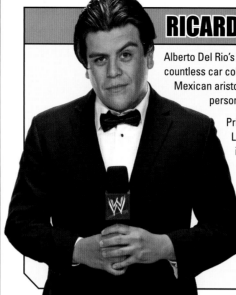

Alberto Del Rio's riches have bought him many envied possessions, including a countless car collection, several palatial estates and extravagant watches. The Mexican aristocrat's impressive bank account also pays the way for his own personal ring announcer, Ricardo Rodriguez.

Prior to Del Rio making his way to the ring in one of his custom Lamborghinis or Maybachs, the arrogant Superstar is always introduced by the distinctive voice of the well-dressed Rodriguez. Clad in a black tuxedo and sporting a perfectly-parted head of hair, the custom ring announcer always adds a little punch when pronouncing his boss' name, complete with an emphasis on rolling the Rs in "Rio."

Unlike most ring announcers, whose job inevitably takes a break between bells, Rodriguez is equally as busy during Del Rio's matches. If the referee's attention is distracted, you can bet he'll find a way to interfere in the match on Del Rio's behalf.

RICK MARTEL

HT: 6'0" **WT:** 230 lbs.
FROM: Montreal, Quebec, Canada

TITLE HISTORY

WORLD TAG TEAM CHAMPION (3 TIMES)	Partnered with Tony Garea to defeat the Wild Samoans on November 8, 1980 Partnered with Tony Garea to defeat the Moondogs on July 21, 1981 Partnered with Tito Santana to defeat the Hart Foundation on October 27, 1987

In an ironic twist, Rick Martel didn't develop his arrogant behavior until later in his career. By that time, however, the matches he had every right to brag about were well behind him. As a result, the Rick Martel most WWE fans choose to remember with great fondness is the modest man who let his in-ring skills do the talking for him.

The earliest days of Martel's career saw the Canadian-born Superstar honing his craft all over the world, including Puerto Rico and New Zealand. It wasn't until 1980 that joined WWE, the promotion that would play home to Martel's greatest successes. Within months of his debut, Martel reunited with Tony Garea, a former partner from his days in New Zealand, to capture the World Tag Team Championship from the Wild Samoans in Philadelphia. It was the first of two championship reigns for the tandem.

Shortly after losing the titles for the final time, Martel left WWE in favor of a singles career in the American Wrestling Association (AWA). Following an amazing nineteen-month reign as AWA Champion, Martel made his return to WWE and tag-team competition in 1987. After a brief union with Tom Zenk, he settled in alongside Tito Santana as one-half of Strike Force. The new duo found immediate success, capturing the World Tag Team Championship from The Hart Foundation in October. It was Martel's third run with the prestigious titles.

Strike Force's success was unexpectedly derailed when Martel accused Santana of riding his coattails. The accusation was uncharacteristic for Martel and helped pave the way for the arrogant Superstar he would soon become.

On his own, Martel began to display a cocky side never before seen by WWE fans. It wasn't long before the smug Superstar began to call himself "The Model." Perhaps Martel's most notorious moment as "The Model" came in 1990 when he temporarily blinded Jake Roberts after spraying him with his signature Arrogance cologne. The incident eventually lead to the famous *WrestleMania VII* Blindfold Match, which Roberts won.

RICKY "THE DRAGON" STEAMBOAT

HT: 5'10" WT: 235 lbs. FROM: Honolulu, Hawaii

TITLE HISTORY

INTERCONTINENTAL CHAMPION	Defeated Randy Savage on March 29, 1987

Ricky Steamboat had a unique career that saw him spend his prime bouncing around from promotion to promotion. Despite never staying in one place for very long, "The Dragon" became immensely popular, thanks in large part to his involvement in what many consider the greatest match in sports-entertainment history, and firmly established himself among the all-time greats.

After successful stints in the AWA and NWA, Steamboat arrived in WWE in 1985. Within months of his debut, "The Dragon" earned a spot on the inaugural *WrestleMania* card, defeating Matt Borne with a flying crossbody. Following *WrestleMania*, Steamboat successfully proved his worth against Jake "The Snake" Roberts and fellow Hawaiian Don Muraco.

WWE's championship committee finally took note of Steamboat's success and afforded him an opportunity at Randy Savage's Intercontinental Championship in late 1986. Unfortunately for Steamboat, the match ended when "Macho Man" savagely crushed the challenger's larynx with the ring bell from the top rope. The heinous act not only kept Steamboat from competing for months, but also threatened his chances of ever speaking again.

Luckily for "The Dragon," he was able to make a full recovery. With revenge occupying his every thought, Steamboat challenged Savage for the Intercontinental Championship at *WrestleMania III*. In the end, it was Steamboat gaining the ultimate measure of retribution, defeating "Macho Man" for the title in a match many believe to be the greatest of all time.

The following year, Steamboat returned to the NWA, where he battled Ric Flair in arguably the greatest series of matches ever witnessed, and enjoyed a three-month reign as NWA Champion. Steamboat briefly rejoined WWE in 1991. While he failed to recreate the same in-ring success as his initial WWE run, "The Dragon" did manage to amaze crowds with his fire-breathing pre-match rituals.

Steamboat's in-ring days came to an end in 1994. Following his retirement, he settled into a backstage producer role with WWE. "The Dragon's" three-decade career was commemorated when he entered the WWE Hall of Fame in 2009. The next day he returned to the *WrestleMania* stage alongside Roddy Piper and Jimmy Snuka to face Chris Jericho. In 2010, WWE released *Ricky Steamboat: The Life Story of the Dragon* on DVD. Steamboat continues to work with WWE and his position allows him to disseminate his years of superior wrestling knowledge to the Superstars of today.

RICKY ORTIZ

HT: 6'3" WT: 246 lbs.
FROM: Paradise Valley, Arizona
SIGNATURE MOVE: The Big O

As a child growing up in Paradise Valley, the imagination of Ricky Ortiz was consumed with another man from the Arizona desert, "Superstar" Billy Graham. A stand-out four sport athlete, Ortiz dreamed of being part of WWE. When ECW General Manager Theodore Long launched his "New Superstar Initiative" the powerful, charismatic Ortiz debuted in the Land of Extreme in July 2008.

After an impressive debut victory over Armondo Estrada, Ortiz faced the likes of Carlito, Gavin Spears, and Chavo Guerrero. His career was built on discipline, self-reliance, courage, and an unmatched energy and the fans were strongly behind him. Ortiz moved to *SmackDown* in April 2009 and was viewed as a promising young Superstar in the company. His impressive string of matches came to an abrupt end four months later when he squared-off against The Great Khali in a lop-sided losing effort.

RICO

HT: 6'0" WT: 238 lbs. FROM: Las Vegas, Nevada
SIGNATURE MOVE: Spinning Roundhouse Kick

In an industry overflowing with masculinity, Rico oozed femininity. And it worked for him. Clad in leopard print and sporting perfectly coiffed hair, Rico made his WWE debut in early 2002 as Billy and Chuck's overly-effeminate stylist. But simply making the then-World Tag Team Champions look good wasn't his only job responsibility. When needed, the surreptitiously tough Superstar also interfered to ensure the gold stayed with his guys.

TITLE HISTORY

WORLD TAG TEAM CHAMPION	Partnered with Rikishi to defeat Billy & Chuck on May 19, 2002
WWE TAG TEAM CHAMPION	Partnered with Charlie Haas to defeat Scotty 2 Hotty & Rikishi on April 22, 2004

At *Judgment Day 2002*, Rico became the reluctant tag-team partner of Rikishi. Together, they actually defeated the stylist's allies for the World Tag Team Championship. Being the good friend that he was, however, Rico later helped Billy and Chuck regain the gold from him and Rikishi.

Rico jumped from *SmackDown* to *Raw* in late 2002, where he briefly managed 3-Minute Warning. He would eventually head back to Friday nights via the 2004 Draft Lottery. Upon returning, he made an immediate impact by defeating Scotty 2 Hotty & Rikishi to claim the WWE Tag Team Championship with partner Charlie Haas.

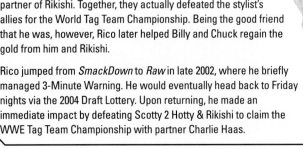

1960-69 ▼ 1970-79 ▼ 1980-89 ▼ 1990-99 ▼ 2000-09 ▼ 2010-

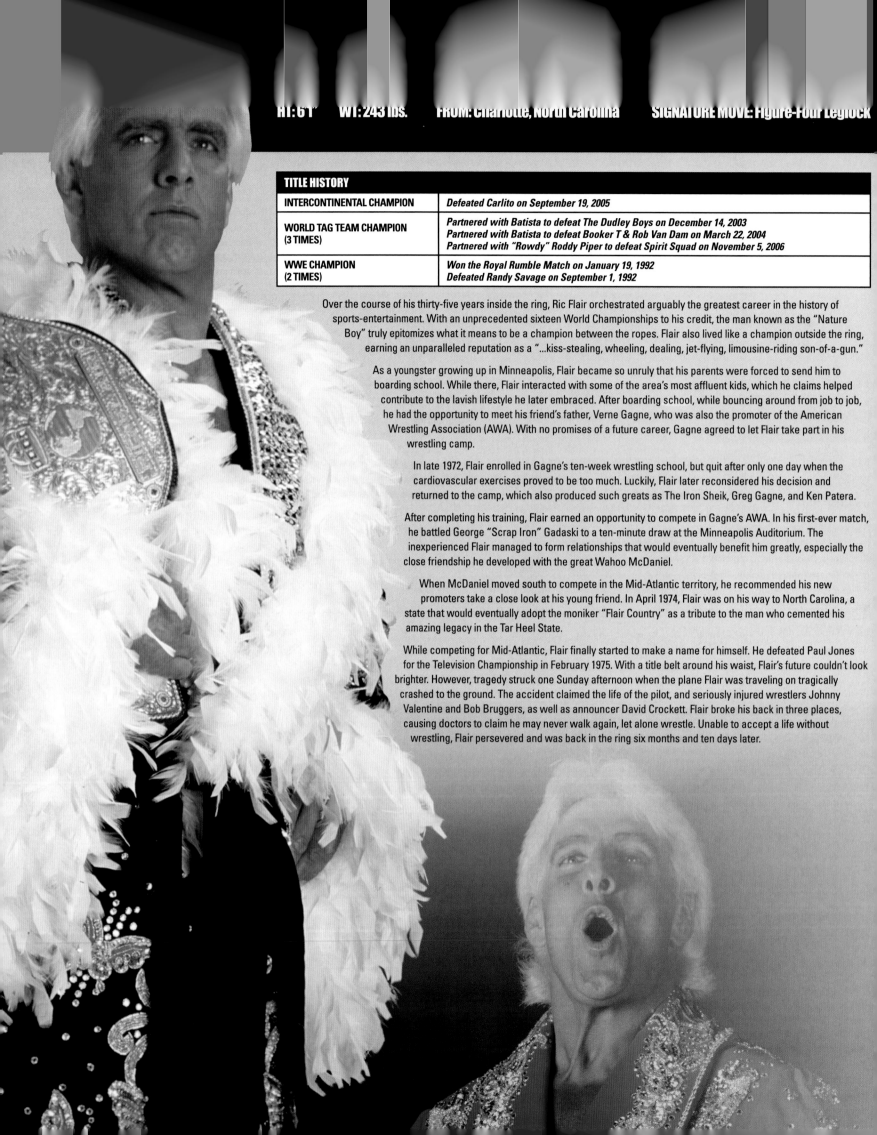

TITLE HISTORY

INTERCONTINENTAL CHAMPION	*Defeated Carlito on September 19, 2005*
WORLD TAG TEAM CHAMPION (3 TIMES)	*Partnered with Batista to defeat The Dudley Boys on December 14, 2003* *Partnered with Batista to defeat Booker T & Rob Van Dam on March 22, 2004* *Partnered with "Rowdy" Roddy Piper to defeat Spirit Squad on November 5, 2006*
WWE CHAMPION (2 TIMES)	*Won the Royal Rumble Match on January 19, 1992* *Defeated Randy Savage on September 1, 1992*

Over the course of his thirty-five years inside the ring, Ric Flair orchestrated arguably the greatest career in the history of sports-entertainment. With an unprecedented sixteen World Championships to his credit, the man known as the "Nature Boy" truly epitomizes what it means to be a champion between the ropes. Flair also lived like a champion outside the ring, earning an unparalleled reputation as a "...kiss-stealing, wheeling, dealing, jet-flying, limousine-riding son-of-a-gun."

As a youngster growing up in Minneapolis, Flair became so unruly that his parents were forced to send him to boarding school. While there, Flair interacted with some of the area's most affluent kids, which he claims helped contribute to the lavish lifestyle he later embraced. After boarding school, while bouncing around from job to job, he had the opportunity to meet his friend's father, Verne Gagne, who was also the promoter of the American Wrestling Association (AWA). With no promises of a future career, Gagne agreed to let Flair take part in his wrestling camp.

In late 1972, Flair enrolled in Gagne's ten-week wrestling school, but quit after only one day when the cardiovascular exercises proved to be too much. Luckily, Flair later reconsidered his decision and returned to the camp, which also produced such greats as The Iron Sheik, Greg Gagne, and Ken Patera.

After completing his training, Flair earned an opportunity to compete in Gagne's AWA. In his first-ever match, he battled George "Scrap Iron" Gadaski to a ten-minute draw at the Minneapolis Auditorium. The inexperienced Flair managed to form relationships that would eventually benefit him greatly, especially the close friendship he developed with the great Wahoo McDaniel.

When McDaniel moved south to compete in the Mid-Atlantic territory, he recommended his new promoters take a close look at his young friend. In April 1974, Flair was on his way to North Carolina, a state that would eventually adopt the moniker "Flair Country" as a tribute to the man who cemented his amazing legacy in the Tar Heel State.

While competing for Mid-Atlantic, Flair finally started to make a name for himself. He defeated Paul Jones for the Television Championship in February 1975. With a title belt around his waist, Flair's future couldn't look brighter. However, tragedy struck one Sunday afternoon when the plane Flair was traveling on tragically crashed to the ground. The accident claimed the life of the pilot, and seriously injured wrestlers Johnny Valentine and Bob Bruggers, as well as announcer David Crockett. Flair broke his back in three places, causing doctors to claim he may never walk again, let alone wrestle. Unable to accept a life without wrestling, Flair persevered and was back in the ring six months and ten days later.

The Nature Boy

Flair adopted a new style upon returning to the ring. Following the advice of George Scott, he patterned his persona after the legendary Buddy Rogers. He even adopted Rogers' nickname, "Nature Boy." As the "Nature Boy," Flair demonstrated an unquenchable thirst for the best the world had to offer.

Life was also good for Flair inside the ring. After capturing numerous titles, including the prestigious United States Championship, Flair reached the sports-entertainment pinnacle when he defeated Dusty Rhodes for the National Wrestling Alliance (NWA) Championship on September 17, 1981. The victory put Flair on the map as one of the time's most accomplished competitors. However, after touring the globe and competing against such legends as Harley Race, Kerry Von Erich, and Ricky Steamboat every single night, Flair proved himself as one of the greatest Superstars in the world.

The Four Horsemen

In 1986, Flair made a decision that would forever alter the face of sports-entertainment, when he aligned himself with Tully Blanchard, Arn Anderson, Ole Anderson, and J.J. Dillon. Collectively known as The Four Horsemen, the well-dressed faction of bullies controlled the gold in the Mid-Atlantic territory. Blanchard held the United States Championship, the Andersons controlled the NWA Tag Team Championship, while Flair maintained a stranglehold on the NWA Championship. The unstoppable unit plowed through their competition, laying the groundwork for future great factions, such as the New World Order and D-Generation X.

By decade's end, Flair had become a multiple-time NWA Champion. If had decided to retire then, he would have walked away as one of the finest to ever step foot in a ring. However, there was plenty more for the "Nature Boy" to accomplish. Surprisingly, however, he was forced to find a new place of employment for the next chapter of his legendary story.

The "Real World Heavyweight Champion"

After Ted Turner purchased Jim Crockett Promotions and renamed it World Championship Wrestling, the billionaire made a series of questionable decisions that rubbed his competitors the wrong way, including hiring Jim Herd to run the wrestling operation. Unable to accept Herd's decisions and perceived disrespect of the industry, Flair left WCW. The wrestling world was sent into a frenzy when Bobby Heenan announced to the world on *Wrestling Challenge* that a great champion was on his way to WWE and then displayed the WCW Championship belt, shocking millions of viewers. Flair soon debuted on WWE television with the WCW Championship belt in tow, claiming to be the "real World Champion." Flair displayed the title proudly, while fans and Superstars alike observed in utter disbelief.

For years, fans and experts wondered how a match between Flair and Hulk Hogan, the two greatest competitors of their era, would play out. Fans would savor pondering a question that looked like it would never be answered. With Flair in WWE, however, such fantasy became reality.

A mere three months after making his WWE debut, Flair put any doubt surrounding his championship claims to rest when he captured the WWE Championship by winning the 1992 *Royal Rumble*. Flair's victory put him in elite company, as he joined another "Nature Boy," Buddy Rogers, as the only men to capture both the NWA and WWE Championships. Flair enjoyed a second WWE Championship reign before finally falling to former confidant Mr. Perfect in a Loser Leaves WWE Match in January 1993.

"The Dirtiest Player in the Game" gets an assist from Mr. Perfect.

Back in World Championship Wrestling

Following the loss, Flair returned to WCW and picked up right where he left off. He defeated Vader at *Starrcade 1993* to reclaim the WCW Championship, which was followed by an impressive win over Sting months later. Hulk Hogan and Flair renewed their epic rivalry at the 1994 *Bash at the Beach*. Though the result was not in Flair's favor, the star-studded encounter, which featured Shaquille O'Neal in Hogan's corner, will forever be remembered as one of sports-entertainment's most historic matches.

Despite going on to reclaim his WCW Championship and eventually reunite the Four Horsemen, internal politics caused Flair to become disenchanted with WCW. He spent the final years of the promotion's existence extremely unhappy. By the time WCW closed its doors, Flair's heart had already left the great sport he spent decades loving.

New Life in WWE

When WWE purchased WCW, Flair's passion for competition quickly resurfaced. Now over 50 years old, the "Nature Boy" miraculously located the fountain of youth and sipped from it for the following seven years.

Perhaps Flair's greatest accomplishment during his second WWE run was his union with Triple H, Batista, and Randy Orton. Collectively known as Evolution, the faction was built using ideologies borrowed from The Four Horsemen. During their successful time together, the well-dressed stable controlled WWE's championship scene. Years later, both Batista and Orton credited Flair's guidance with helping them achieve World Championship status.

Flair's unprecedented in-ring career came to an end on March 30, 2008. One day after being the first active Superstar ever inducted into the WWE Hall of Fame, Shawn Michaels defeated the "Nature Boy" at *WrestleMania XXIV*. The historic match officially signified the end of an era that can never be duplicated.

Flair made a second trip to the Hall of Fame in 2012 when he was inducted as a member of The Four Horsemen.

Hogan and Flair battled in sold-out arenas across the country, and while they thrilled fans, a clear winner was never determined.

RIGHT TO CENSOR

MEMBERS: Steven Richards, Val Venis, The Goodfather, Bull Buchanon, Ivory

In the summer of 2000 World Wrestling Entertainment was raided by a self-righteous collection of transformed Superstars that had more conviction for convenience than all politicians put together. Spear-headed by Steven Richards, this faction brainwashed those who one-time loved the pageantry and glitz of sports-entertainment into believing life was about a tireless campaign to cover-up Divas and remove weapons from the ringside area during matches.

Despite their unpopular acts they did achieve success in the ring as Ivory became Women's Champion in November 2000. Days later Bull Buchanon and The Goodfather became World Tag Team Champions. However, everyone started to tire of their pontification and WWE had enough of Right To Censor. Each member lost their match at *WrestleMania X-Seven* and soon after a Last Ride from Undertaker on their leader, they disappeared from WWE television.

Though fans may be reluctant to admit it, Right To Censor sent the following message to the self-proclaimed moralists of society: perhaps before proclaiming how everyone else should live, they take a long look at themselves.

RIKISHI

HT: 6'1" WT: 423 lbs.
FROM: Samoa   SIGNATURE MOVE: Stinkface

TITLE HISTORY

INTERCONTINENTAL CHAMPION	*Defeated Chris Benoit on June 22, 2000*
WORLD TAG TEAM CHAMPION	*Partnered with Rico to defeat Billy & Chuck on May 19, 2002*
WWE TAG TEAM CHAMPION	*Partnered with Scotty 2 Hotty to defeat the Basham Brothers on February 5, 2004*

The fans' love affair with Rikishi was similar to a ride on a wild rollercoaster. One minute, his fun-loving persona carried them to great heights; the next, his reprehensible actions brought them crashing down, only to be thrust back up again when he had a change of heart.

Despite wearing a revealing thong to the ring, the massive Rikishi immediately won over fans upon his debut in 1999. Alongside Too Cool, the Samoan Superstar oftentimes broke out into a contagious dance that always got audiences moving their feet. His popularity eventually lead to an Intercontinental Championship reign in June 2000.

Rikishi's approval rating took a huge hit in late 2000 when it was revealed that he ran over Stone Cold Steve Austin with a car. While the vicious attack certainly put the big man in bad standing with the fans, it also helped catapult him to main event status. Over the next few months, Rikishi found himself across the ring from many of WWE's all-time greats, including The Rock, Undertaker and Stone Cold Steve Austin.

Toward the end 2001, Rikishi began to slowly regain the fans' trust. Then in December, he completely won them over when he performed one of the most disgusting acts ever seen on television. With the hated Mr. McMahon sitting battered in the corner of the ring, Rikishi delivered a gag-inducing Stinkface to the WWE Chairman.

"ROAD DOGG" JESSE JAMES

TITLE HISTORY

INTERCONTINENTAL CHAMPION	*Defeated Val Venis on March 15, 1999*
HARDCORE CHAMPION	*1 Time*
WORLD TAG TEAM CHAMPION (5 TIMES)	*Partnered with Billy Gunn to defeat The Legion of Doom on November 24, 1997 Partnered with Billy Gunn to defeat Cactus Jack & Chainsaw Charlie on March 30, 1998 Partnered with Billy Gunn to defeat Mankind on August 30, 1998 Partnered with Billy Gunn to defeat The Rock 'N' Sock Connection on September 23, 1999 Partnered with Billy Gunn to defeat Mankind & Al Snow on November 8, 1999*

As Jeff Jarrett's personal roadie, Jesse James did everything in his power to make his boss look good, including sing for him. In 1995, Jarrett began serenading WWE audiences with his single *With My Baby Tonight*. However, it was later learned that Double J was lip-syncing the song that was actually performed by James.

Once credit to the song went to James, the young upstart's career began to skyrocket. In 1997, he reinvented himself as the Road Dogg and began to team with Billy Gunn. Collectively known as the New Age Outlaws, Dogg & Gunn went on to become members of the rebellious D-Generation X faction and one of the most successful tag teams in WWE history, capturing the World Tag Team Championship on five occasions.

ROADKILL

HT: 6'0" **WT:** 323 lbs.
FROM: Lancaster, Pennsylvania

Roadkill can count his number of WWE televised appearances on one hand. Outside of a few losing efforts on *Velocity* and the reborn ECW in 2006, the "Angry Amish Warrior" doesn't have much WWE experience. However, he can certainly look back at his efforts in the original ECW with great fondness.

While competing in the original ECW, Roadkill formed an unlikely, yet successful tandem, with Danny Doring. In December 2000, Roadkill & Doring bested Tony Mamaluke & Little Guido for the ECW Tag Team Championship. The duo remained champions until the promotion closed its doors in the spring of 2001.

HT: 6'1" **WT:** 241 lbs.
FROM: Music City, USA
SIGNATURE MOVE: Shake, Rattle, and Roll

On his own, Road Dogg proved to be just as rabid. In addition to being the third in a long line of Superstars to hold the Hardcore Championship, he also topped Val Venis in March 1999 to become Intercontinental Champion.

Ten years removed from his last appearance on WWE television, the "D-O-Double-G" returned in 2011 on the evening before *WrestleMania XXVII* when he inducted his father, "Bullet" Bob Armstrong into the WWE Hall of Fame. Months later, James was a presenter at the Slammy Awards. Now, he's moved behind the scenes as a producer for WWE, and was also a surprise entrant in the 2012 *Royal Rumble*.

ROB BARTLETT

Vince McMahon, Randy "Macho Man" Savage and comedian Rob Bartlett will forever be linked as the first-ever announce team for the longest running weekly episodic television show in history, *Monday Night Raw*.

Few sports-entertainment fans knew who Bartlett was when *Raw* first went on the air in January 1993. But given the excitement surrounding the groundbreaking live show, they were willing to give him a chance. Then he spoke. In his very first statement on WWE TV, Bartlett unknowingly misidentified the legendary Yokozuna as "Yokozuma," before then claiming the future WWE Champion was "the guy who's got that diaper." It was all downhill from there.

Bartlett was gone from WWE three months after his debut. Following his departure, the comedian continued his standup act and also began a career as a stage actor. His Broadway credits include *More to Love* and *Little Shop of Horrors*. Bartlett is also known for his semi-regular appearances on his longtime friend Don Imus' radio programs.

ROBERT CONWAY

HT: 6'2" **WT:** 230 lbs. **FROM:** Atlantic City, New Jersey
SIGNATURE MOVE: Neckbreaker

TITLE HISTORY	
WORLD TAG TEAM CHAMPION (3 TIMES)	*Partnered with Sylvain Grenier to defeat Chris Benoit & Edge on May 31, 2004* *Partnered with Sylvain Grenier to defeat Chris Benoit on November 1, 2004* *Partnered with Sylvain Grenier to defeat William Regal & Coach on January 16, 2005*

After brief appearances with the WWE, Conway made his presence felt in August 2003 when he disguised himself as a US serviceman and attacked the Dudley Boys to reveal himself as the third member of La Resistance. Conway turned on his native USA and was introduced as being from the Province of Quebec. He formed a dangerous tag team with Sylvain Grenier and won the World Tag Team Championship on three separate occasions. The two rule-breakers parted ways in 2005 when they couldn't keep their egos in check. Conway returned to singles competition and later became part of the anti-ECW crusade. He started to refer to himself as "Con Man," but his fast talk got him in hot water during the WWE Homecoming. After interrupting a Legends Ceremony, Conway felt the effects of the Von Erich Claw followed by a "Superfly" Splash.

Conway spent much of 2006 on the end of a horrid losing streak. In January 2007, he proclaimed he would quit if he didn't defeat Jeff Hardy. After a disappointing twelve second loss, WWE Chairman Mr. McMahon appeared and fired Conway on the spot.

R

1960-69
1970-79
1980-89
1990-99
2000-09
2010-

ROB VAN DAM

HT: 6'0" **WT:** 235 lbs. **FROM:** Battle Creek, Michigan
SIGNATURE MOVE: Five-Star Frog Splash

TITLE HISTORY

ECW CHAMPION	*Named ECW Champion on debut of ECW on Sci Fi on June 13, 2006*
EUROPEAN CHAMPION	*Defeated Jeff Hardy to unify European and Intercontinental Championships on July 22, 2002*
INTERCONTINENTAL CHAMPION (6 TIMES)	*Defeated William Regal on March 17, 2002* *Defeated Eddie Guerrero on May 27, 2002* *Defeated Chris Benoit on August 25, 2002* *Defeated Christian on September 29, 2003* *Defeated Chris Jericho on October 27, 2003* *Defeated Shelton Benjamin on April 30, 2006*
HARDCORE CHAMPION	*4 Times*
WORLD TAG TEAM CHAMPION (2 TIMES)	*Partnered with Kane to defeat Lance Storm & Chief Morley on March 31, 2003* *Partnered with Booker T to defeat Ric Flair & Batista on February 16, 2004*
WWE CHAMPION	*Defeated John Cena on June 11, 2006*
WWE TAG TEAM CHAMPION	*Partnered with Rey Mysterio to defeat Kenzo Suzuki & Rene Dupree on December 9, 2004*

Considered by many to be sports-entertainment's ultimate risk taker, Rob Van Dam utilized a lethal combination of acrobatic offense and martial arts to mold a WWE career that was truly "one of a kind."

A standout in ECW, "Mr. Monday Night" made his highly-anticipated WWE debut in 2001. Although a member of The Alliance at the time, he managed to gain the admiration of the fans through his awe-inspiring aerial assault, which was highlighted by electrifying moves such as the Van Terminator, Rolling Thunder and Five-Star Frog Splash. It wasn't long before Van Dam's innovative offense was driving him to championship opportunities.

RVD won his first major piece of WWE hardware at *WrestleMania X8* when he beat William Regal for the Intercontinental Championship. Subsequent victories saw him claim nearly every other singles championship in WWE, including the now-defunct European and Hardcore championships. He also proved to be a force in the tag team ranks, winning titles with partners Kane, Booker T and Rey Mysterio.

In 2006, RVD's career finally reached the pinnacle so many predicted when he won the thrilling Money in the Bank Ladder Match at *WrestleMania 22*. As "Mr. Money in the Bank," RVD was afforded the opportunity to challenge for a World Championship at the time and location of his choosing. He chose wisely.

In front of a large ECW fan base at *One Night Stand*, RVD challenged the normally popular John Cena for the WWE Championship. The ECW faithful nearly booed Cena out of the arena, but not before RVD could defeat him for the WWE Championship first. A few days later, Paul Heyman also awarded the rechristened ECW Championship to RVD, making him the first Superstar to hold both titles simultaneously.

RVD quietly left WWE in the summer of 2007. While he no longer entertains WWE audiences, many fans look back at his time on *Raw*, *SmackDown,* and especially in ECW with great fondness. In fact, some might say he was the "Whole Dam Show."

The Rock (see page 292)

ROCK 'N' SOCK CONNECTION

MEMBERS: The Rock, Mankind
COMBINED WT: 562 lbs.

TITLE HISTORY

WORLD TAG TEAM CHAMPIONS (3 TIMES)	*Defeated Undertaker & Big Show on August 30, 1999* *Defeated Undertaker & Big Show on September 20, 1999* *Defeated the New Age Outlaws on October 14, 1999*

Know your role, and have a nice day.

What do you get when you a take third-generation Superstar and a Hardcore Legend? The Rock 'N' Sock Connection. These two gifted performers and former adversaries were brought together by chance in August 1999 after Undertaker and Big Show attacked The Rock. As success helped grow the unlikely pair grew closer, Mankind wanted to surprise his new friend that September. On what would be a ratings record-setting segment on *Monday Night Raw,* Mankind treated The Rock to a special *"This is Your Life."*

While The Rock grew tired of the team and accused Mankind of stealing his catchphrases and signature moves, their was always something about the odd couple that brought a smile to his face. Even after Mankind wrongfully accused "The Great One" of throwing his New York Times best-seller, *Have A Nice Day,* in the trash and letting him defend the World Tag Team Championship on his own, they were always able to get back on the same page. The popular tandem reunited from time-to-time as called for up until Mick Foley's brief retirement from the ring in 2000.

THE ROCKERS

MEMBERS: Shawn Michaels, Marty Jannetty   **COMBINED WT:** 455 lbs.

The Rockers are seen by many as the greatest tag team never to win titles in WWE. While this is an astonishing fact, it's even harder to grasp the idea that Shawn Michaels & Marty Jannetty almost never had an opportunity to prove themselves in WWE.

After opening eyes while competing as the Midnight Rockers in the AWA, Michaels & Jannetty made the move to WWE in 1987. The good-looking tandem had dreams of dominating the stacked tag division. WWE, however, didn't share the same dream and fired the youngsters after only two weeks.

With their tails between their legs, Michaels & Jannetty left, never knowing if they would get another opportunity at greatness. The high-flying duo continued to work on their game for the better part of a year before WWE officials agreed to give them another look. By the summer of 1988, Michaels & Jannetty re-debuted as the Rockers, and the rest is sports-entertainment history.

The Rockers achieved early success, turning back such highly celebrated duos as the Brain Busters and the Rougeau Brothers. By 1990, their incredible teamwork earned them the reputation of tag team specialists. However, despite all their wins, they were never given a serious opportunity to claim the World Tag Team Championship.

In October 1990, the Rockers were finally granted a high-profile championship shot against The Hart Foundation at *Saturday Night's Main Event*. The match proved to be one of the most controversial tag team encounters of all time, as the Rockers actually left the arena that night with the titles. The championship switch, however, was later stricken from the record after the match was ruled unsafe, due to a ring rope breaking during the bout.

That was the closest the Rockers ever came to claiming the World Tag Team Championship. By 1992, Michaels believed he had outgrown his role in The Rockers. To prove his point, he kicked his longtime partner through the window of *The Barber Shop*, thus signifying the end of the popular tag team. But in recent years, the duo has reunited on occasion, giving fans a glimpse at what made the Rockers such a groundbreaking and memorable tandem.

When all hope was lost for Foley, who was outnumbered in his fight against Evolution, the three-time World Tag Team Champions reformed on sports-entertainment's most famed stage for the last time at *WrestleMania XX*. The packed Madison Square Garden crowd saw the Rock 'N' Sock Connection battle "Nature Boy" Ric Flair, Batista & Randy Orton in a Handicap Match.

This duo ignited World Wrestling Entertainment and continuously showed that no matter the odds, the Rock 'N' Sock Connection could come together at any given time and take care of business. To this day, audiences fondly recall their thrilling matches and entertaining interviews.

ROCKIN' ROBIN

HT: 5'7"   **FROM:** Charlotte, North Carolina
SIGNATURE MOVE: Bulldog

TITLE HISTORY	
WOMEN'S CHAMPION	*Defeated Sherri Martel on October 7, 1988*

Rockin' Robin made her WWE debut on one of the biggest stages possible when she joined the Fabulous Moolah's stable to turn back Sensational Sherri and her team of Divas at the 1987 *Survivor Series*.

The athletic brunette spent the next several months utilizing her devastating bulldog finisher to open the eyes of WWE officials. After racking up an impressive won-loss record, Robin finally earned an opportunity at the Women's Championship. Capitalizing on her big break, she upended Sherri for the gold in France in October 1988.

Proving her championship victory was no fluke, Robin handily defeated challenger Judy Martin at the 1989 *Royal Rumble*. A few months later, she established herself as a multi-talented Diva when she opened *WrestleMania V* with a stirring rendition of "America the Beautiful."

Robin remained Women's Champion until she left WWE in 1990. As a result of her departure, WWE deemed the title inactive until 1993.

THE ROCK

HT: 6'5"   **WT:** 275 lbs.   **FROM:** Miami, Florida   **SIGNATURE MOVE:** The People's Elbow

TITLE HISTORY	
INTERCONTINENTAL CHAMPION (2 TIMES)	*Defeated Hunter Hearst Helmsley on February 13, 1997* *Defeated Stone Cold Steve Austin on December 8, 1997*
WORLD TAG TEAM CHAMPION (5 TIMES)	*Partnered with Mankind to defeat Undertaker & Big Show on August 30, 1999* *Partnered with Mankind to defeat Undertaker & Big Show on September 20, 1999* *Partnered with Mankind to defeat the New Age Outlaws on October 14, 1999* *Partnered with Undertaker to defeat Edge & Christian on December 18, 2000* *Partnered with Chris Jericho to defeat The Dudley Boys on October 22, 2001*
WWE CHAMPION (7 TIMES)	*Defeated Mankind on November 15, 1998* *Defeated Mankind on January 24, 1999* *Defeated Mankind on February 15, 1999* *Defeated Triple H on April 30, 2000* *Defeated Triple H on June 25, 2000* *Defeated Kurt Angle on February 25, 2001* *Defeated Undertaker on July 21, 2002*

Dwayne Johnson grew up in a family of wrestling royalty. His father, future WWE Hall of Famer Rocky Johnson, was one of the most popular Superstars in the industry. His maternal grandfather, future WWE Hall of Famer High Chief Peter Maivia, was the patriarch of the famous Maivia family, one of professional wrestling's toughest competitors who also appeared in the 1967 James Bond classic, *You Only Live Twice.*

Because he idolized his father, grandfather and WWE Hall of Famers Andre The Giant, Hulk Hogan, Jimmy "Superfly" Snuka, and "Nature Boy" Ric Flair, it was only natural Dwayne thought about a life in both sports and entertainment. After a childhood of mischief, Dwayne was an All-American on the gridiron at Freedom High School in Bethlehem, PA. The young Johnson went on to the University of Miami and in 1991 was part of the Hurricanes NCAA Championship team. After a brief career in the Canadian Football League, Johnson entered the industry in which his family played such a significant role for so many decades. Trained by his father, along with Pat Patterson, Dwayne exceeded all expectations and soon cut his teeth in the United States Wrestling Association. While there, he learned his craft and stared across the ring at Jerry Lawler.

A Rocky Start

At the 1996 *Survivor Series,* a capacity Madison Square Garden crowd witnessed this first third-generation Superstar make his way to the ring. As a tribute to his grandfather and father, he chose the name Rocky Maivia. As the next Maivia emerged the sole survivor, this Superstar was set to take the sports-entertainment world by storm. Within three months of his debut, Rocky captured the Intercontinental Championship when he defeated Hunter Hearst-Helmsley on a special episode of *Thursday Raw.*

As the tone of sports-entertainment changed, the fans' cheers suddenly turned to jeers as they chanted "Rocky Sucks" and "Die Rocky Die." Shortening his name to "The Rock" and referring to himself in the third person, he became one of the most detested figures in all of WWE and a member of The Nation of Domination. The anger from the fans fueled his fire to succeed, and his undiluted arrogance enraged crowds everywhere. The Rock dubbed himself "The People's Champion" and made it clear he would reach the top of World Wrestling Entertainment by any means necessary. The Rock soon physically removed Faarooq as Nation leader and became the self-appointed ruler of The Nation, citing the term leader was beneath him. In the summer of 1998, The Nation began a fierce rivalry against D-Generation X to decide which was the dominant faction in WWE. The two leaders met in the King of the Ring tournament. After The Rock pinned rival Triple H, both crews threw fists of fury as pure bedlam flooded the ring.

The Rock's career gained momentum and he left The Nation to construct his own path to glory. He invited all Superstars to "Go One-on-One with The Great One," and in the process became the object of Mr. McMahon's intense scrutiny.

"The People's Champion" went into the *Survivor Series'* 16-man tournament for the WWE Championship a heavy favorite. In the tournament finals against Mankind, the 26-year-old showed the perseverance and poise of a seasoned veteran. After he locked-in the Sharpshooter, the bell unexpectedly rang and their collusion became known. The McMahons courted The Rock and made "The People's Champion," "The Corporate Champion." A confused Mankind got his final explanation courtesy of a blindside beating by the newly crowned champion.

This event led to a string of classic clashes between the two, and though Mankind temporarily regained the championship, the sight of a jubilant Mankind brought out an even more barbarous "Brahma Bull." Their most sadistic bout was the Last Man Standing Match at the *St. Valentine's Day Massacre*. When neither man answered the ten-count, the match was ruled a draw and they met the next night on *Raw* in a Ladder Match, won by The Rock. Afterward, "The Most Electrifying Man in Sports-Entertainment" put his problems with Mankind behind him and focused on a new enemy.

At *WrestleMania XV*, the "Great One" took on the anti-establishment Stone Cold Steve Austin for the WWE Championship. The carnage in Philadelphia proved to be the beginning of one of the greatest rivalries in WWE history. Despite a loss to the "Texas Rattlesnake," The Rock truly became "The People's Champion" when he left The Corporation and went his own way. As the mystique of The Rock grew, audiences continued to marvel at his undeniable charisma and wildly

entertaining interview segments. As he entered the summer of 1999, he resumed war with a familiar foe, Triple H. When former enemy Mankind was looking for a friend, he treated The Rock to a parade of his past on an episode of "Rock: This is Your Life." In the process, the two joined forces as The Rock N' Sock Connection and surprised everyone with their continuity and resolve when they defeated Undertaker & Big Show for the World Tag Team Championship.

The Great One At #1

After he won the 2000 *Royal Rumble*, The Rock's popularity rose to new heights each week on WWE programming. He wrote his autobiography, *The Rock Says, which* reached No. 1 on the prestigious New York Times Bestseller List. He hosted *Saturday Night Live,* gave a special address at the Republican National Convention, and appeared in hip-hop legend Wyclef Jean's famous video, "It Doesn't Matter". By 2001, The Rock was considered an absolute multimedia superstar as he appeared in the feature film, *The Mummy Returns* and later starred in its highly successful prequel, *The Scorpion King,* which was commemorated with a wax statue of "The Great One" at Madame Tussaud's famous gallery in New York City.

Of course, The Rock didn't sever his ties with WWE during this time. The Rock secured the fate of World Wrestling Entertainment at the 2001 *Survivor Series* as he captained Team WWE and destroyed The Alliance. This defense of his first love became indisputable in February 2002, when WWE was injected with the lethal poison of the nWo. The path taken by Hogan, Hall, and Nash left The Rock no choice but to do what was needed for the company's survival.

The Rock challenging someone to go one-on-one with the Great One.

As millions (and millions) of The Rock's fans continued to smell what he was cookin', his opponents headed down Jabroni Drive, hung a left on Know Your Role Boulevard, and were checked directly into the Smackdown Hotel.

At *Wrestlemania X-8,* he defeated Hollywood Hulk Hogan in their epic fantasy turned reality Icon vs. Icon Match. In 2003, The Rock's Hollywood stock continued to rise, but he may have saved his greatest act for *WrestleMania XIX,* when he defeated his long-time nemesis Stone Cold Steve Austin.

The Rock returned to Hollywood for *The Rundown* with Christopher Walken, but returned to WWE in 2004 to reform the Rock N' Sock Connection, and battle Evolution at *WrestleMania XX.* The Rock's international following grew and he continued to electrify movie screens as the main draw in multiple Hollywood blockbusters.

After three years away from WWE, The Rock appeared on *Monday Night Raw* in a taped segment where he gave his prediction to the Battle of The Billionaires Match at *WrestleMania 23.* In 2008, he returned to induct his father, Rocky Johnson, and late grandfather, High Chief Peter Maivia, into the WWE Hall of Fame.

Over the next three years the Great One continued to build on his impressive list of film credits. Working with such names as Mark Wahlberg, Samuel L. Jackson, Vin Diesel, Will Ferrell, Steve Carrell, Anne Hathaway and Bruce Willis, he developed into one of the biggest stars in the world. He also continued his philanthropic works, helping at-risk and terminally ill children through the Dwayne Johnson Rock Foundation.

Finally, The Rock Has Come Back..!

The WWE Universe discovered on the February 14, 2011 edition of *Raw* that the most electrifying man in all of entertainment would be the host of *WrestleMania XXVII.* The Brahma Bull also made it known he planned to bring it to John Cena after "The Champ" made disparaging remarks about him.

The Rock laying the smackdown…trending worldwide.

At *WrestleMania XXVII,* the Jabroni beating, pie eating, trailblazing, eyebrow raising Team Bring It captain electrified the event and became involved in the ending of the WWE Championship match between The Miz and John Cena. The next night on *Raw* John Cena challenged The Rock to a match at *WrestleMania XXVIII* in The Rock's hometown of Miami.

For the rest of 2011, The Rock and John Cena traded verbal jabs even when they were forced to team up at the 2011 *Survivor Series.* While the duo rarely saw eye-to-eye, they put aside their differences long enough to defeat The Miz & R-Truth.

On Sunday April 1, 2012 The Rock returned to Miami and battled John Cena in the main event of *WrestleMania XXVIII.* Over 78,000 people witnessed thirty grueling minutes of back-and-forth action between two Superstars who each defined an era of WWE history. In the end, The Rock emerged triumphant in the "Once in a Lifetime" confrontation, then basked in the adulation of his hometown fans.

ROCKY JOHNSON

HT: 6'2"   WT: 243 lbs.   FROM: Toronto, Ontario, Canada
SIGNATURE MOVE: The Dropkick

HALL of FAME 2008

TITLE HISTORY

WORLD TAG TEAM CHAMPION	*Partnered with Tony Atlas to defeat The Samoans on November 15, 1983*

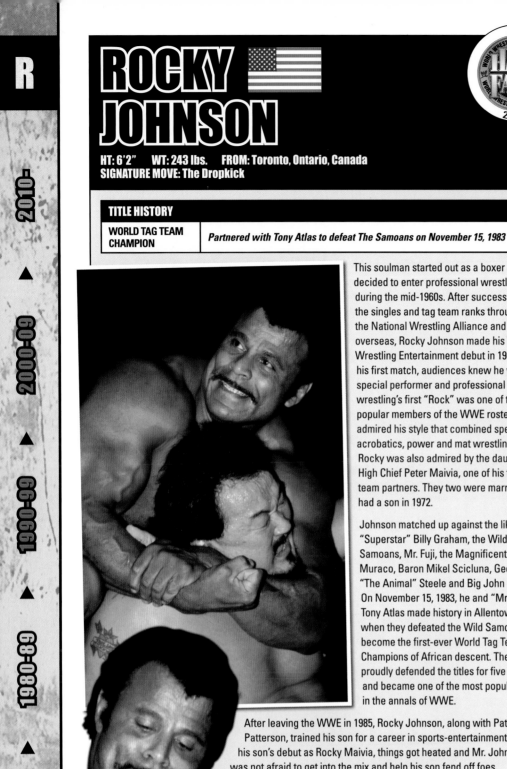

This soulman started out as a boxer and decided to enter professional wrestling during the mid-1960s. After success in both the singles and tag team ranks throughout the National Wrestling Alliance and overseas, Rocky Johnson made his World Wrestling Entertainment debut in 1983. From his first match, audiences knew he was a special performer and professional wrestling's first "Rock" was one of the most popular members of the WWE roster. Fans admired his style that combined speed, acrobatics, power and mat wrestling. Rocky was also admired by the daughter of High Chief Peter Maivia, one of his tag team partners. They two were married, and had a son in 1972.

Johnson matched up against the likes of "Superstar" Billy Graham, the Wild Samoans, Mr. Fuji, the Magnificent Muraco, Baron Mikel Scicluna, George "The Animal" Steele and Big John Studd. On November 15, 1983, he and "Mr. USA" Tony Atlas made history in Allentown, PA when they defeated the Wild Samoans to become the first-ever World Tag Team Champions of African descent. They proudly defended the titles for five months and became one of the most popular duos in the annals of WWE.

After leaving the WWE in 1985, Rocky Johnson, along with Pat Patterson, trained his son for a career in sports-entertainment. During his son's debut as Rocky Maivia, things got heated and Mr. Johnson was not afraid to get into the mix and help his son fend off foes.

The night before *WrestleMania XXIV*, the career that was fueled by courage and desire was immortalized when Rocky Johnson was inducted into the WWE Hall of Fame by his son, now known as The Rock.

RODNEY MACK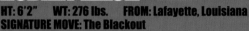

HT: 6'2"   WT: 276 lbs.   FROM: Lafayette, Louisiana
SIGNATURE MOVE: The Blackout

Claiming "the man" was holding him down, Rodney Mack made his *Raw* debut in February 2003, alongside manager Theodore Long. With Long leading the way, Mack ran over veteran Al Snow like a truck in his first-ever match.

In an attempt to break free from the supposed shackles placed on him by "the man," Mack soon instituted a "Five-Minute, White-Boy Challenge." As the title suggests, Mack guaranteed he could defeat any Caucasian competitor in under five minutes.

Mack made good on his promise for several weeks, albeit against considerably weaker competition. Then, when *Raw* went to Madison Square Garden in June 2003, the undefeated Superstar was finally met with a "white boy" worthy of the challenge: Goldberg. A mere 26 seconds into the match, Mack had fallen victim to the Jackhammer, en route to his first loss. Following the defeat, Mack went on to compete mainly as a tag-team competitor with partners Mark Henry and Christopher Nowinski.

RON SHAW

WT: 265 lbs.   FROM: Philadelphia, Pennsylvania

Ivan Putski. Ricky Steamboat. Hillbilly Jim. Tito Santana. The Iron Sheik. Ron Shaw wrestled them all, and lost each and every time. He was even defeated by Salvatore Bellomo.

Despite his lackluster record, Shaw continued to compete, hoping one day his luck would change. And it did once. While squaring off against David Sammartino in Philadelphia's famed Spectrum, the hometown boy miraculously mustered up enough confidence to bodyslam the second-generation Superstar an amazing 15 times. He then locked Sammartino into a bear hug. The strength of the submission maneuver eventually forced Sammartino to give up, giving Shaw an extremely rare victory.

Luck nearly found its way to Shaw again in July 1984, when the Philadelphia native took part in a Battle Royal on the historic MTV broadcast of *The Brawl to End It All*. Shaw outlasted 17 other Superstars to become one of the final three combatants, but he was eventually eliminated by Rene Goulet. Antonio Inoki was later declared the victor.

RON "FAAROOQ" SIMMONS

HT: 6'2"   WT: 260 lbs.
FROM: Warner Robins, Georgia

WWE HALL OF FAME 2012

TITLE HISTORY

WORLD TAG TEAM CHAMPION (3 TIMES)	Partnered with Bradshaw to defeat Kane & X-Pac on May 31, 1999
	Partnered with Bradshaw to defeat The Hardy Boys on July 25, 1999
	Partnered with Bradshaw to defeat The Dudley Boys on July 9, 2001

Following a Hall of Fame football career at Florida State University, Ron Simmons made the jump to the ring in 1986. What followed was a groundbreaking career that saw the African-American Superstar break down all color barriers to reach the pinnacle.

Simmons first made a name for himself competing in WCW during the late 1980s and early 1990s. As a member of the intimidating tag team Doom, he is recognized as one-half of the promotion's first-ever World Tag Team Champions. Led by manager Theodore Long, Doom held the titles for nine months before losing to the Fabulous Freebirds in February 1991.

In August 1992, Simmons made history when he defeated Vader for the WCW Championship. The landmark victory made Simmons the first African-American World Champion of any major promotion. He held the title for five months before losing it back to Vader.

Simmons underwent an identity change in 1996 when he debuted in WWE under the name Faarooq. With his new moniker, Simmons gained great fame, first as the leader of The Nation of Domination, and later as a three-time World Tag Team Champion with Bradshaw.

Faarooq disappeared from the WWE scene in 2004, but Ron Simmons did not. Reverting back to his original name, Simmons slipped into semi-retirement. He is now best known popping up at the most opportune times to say his signature catchphrase: Damn!

RONNIE GARVIN

HT: 5'10"   WT: 242 lbs.   FROM: Charlotte, North Carolina
SIGNATURE MOVE: Figure-Four Leglock

Before ever stepping foot in a WWE ring, "Rugged" Ronnie Garvin spent more than two decades proving himself as one of the game's toughest competitors. At just 5'10", the smaller Garvin was forced to work overtime to gain success against larger rivals such as Dusty Rhodes and the Road Warriors. In the end, however, his dedication to his craft paid off, as Garvin claimed more than 30 titles over the course of his career, including the prestigious NWA Championship.

Garvin made his WWE debut in 1988 to much fanfare. Almost immediately after entering the promotion, he found himself in a bitter rivalry with the similarly styled Greg Valentine. For nearly one year, the two Superstars battled over which had the greater Figure Four Leglock. Garvin eventually proved superiority when he defeated Valentine in a Submission Match at the 1990 *Royal Rumble*.

Garvin subtly retired shortly after his *Royal Rumble* victory. Despite his quiet exit from the game, fans will forever remember the thunderous thump his "hands of stone" would leave on an opponent's chest.

ROSA MENDES

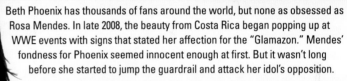

HT: 5'9"
FROM: San Jose, Costa Rica

Beth Phoenix has thousands of fans around the world, but none as obsessed as Rosa Mendes. In late 2008, the beauty from Costa Rica began popping up at WWE events with signs that stated her affection for the "Glamazon." Mendes' fondness for Phoenix seemed innocent enough at first. But it wasn't long before she started to jump the guardrail and attack her idol's opposition.

Mendes' obsession could've turned ugly, but rather than shun her crazed fan, Phoenix made the unorthodox decision to actually bring her closer. As Phoenix's intern, Mendes earned a first-hand education in competing in the Divas division.

In October 2009, Mendes moved from *Raw* to ECW, where she began a torrid relationship with Zack Ryder. The two up-and-comers dated until Mendes was shipped to *SmackDown* in the spring of 2010. While on *SmackDown*, Mendes' tireless work with a Shake-Weight was recognized when she was presented with the prestigious 2010 Slammy Award for Best Use of Exercise Equipment.

ROSEY

HT: 6'7"   WT: 420 lbs.   FROM: San Francisco, California
SIGNATURE MOVE: Super-Hero Slam

TITLE HISTORY

WORLD TAG TEAM CHAMPION	Partnered with The Hurricane to defeat La Resistance on May 1, 2005

This former Superstar began his WWE career, along with his brother Jamal, as a hired gun for Eric Bischoff as a part of 3-Minute Warning. After their act was given the axe, his natural abilities in the ring caught they eye of WWE's resident super-hero and soon the Samoan Superstar began a special type of training.

In the summer of 2004, Rosey was a changed man. He had a new outlook on life, new ring attire and a new purpose. Together with The Hurricane they were the super-heroes the world needed. At *Backlash 2005* their combined strength pushed them past Lance Cade and Trevor Murdoch to become World Tag Team Champions. After Cade and Murdoch won the titles back the team entered a terrible losing streak and broke apart when The Hurricane decided to ditch his super-hero persona. Rosey departed from World Wrestling Entertainment soon after, in March 2006.

"ROWDY" RODDY PIPER

HT: 6'2"   **WT: 230 lbs.**   **FROM: Glasgow, Scotland**   **SIGNATURE MOVE: Sleeper**

Roddy Piper debuted at the Winnipeg Arena as the youngest competitor to ever set foot in the ring. Ten seconds after the bell rang, he was defeated by legend Larry Hennig. That night began his initiation into the sacred fraternity of the ring.

TITLE HISTORY	
INTERCONTINENTAL CHAMPION	*Defeated The Mountie on January 19, 1992*
WORLD TAG TEAM CHAMPION	*Partnered with Ric Flair to defeat Spirit Squad on November 5, 2006*

In 1984, "Rowdy" Roddy Piper entered WWE with his kilt, bagpipes, and irascible manner. As manager to "Dr. D" David Schultz and "Mr. Wonderful" Paul Orndorff, Piper incited audiences and Superstars alike from ringside and was never shy about inserting himself into a match. "Hot Rod" pushed the limits of what was considered decent and his appearances in the ring required WWE to employ a police presence at every arena he visited. Roddy evoked such anger from people he hired "Cowboy" Bob Orton as a bodyguard.

Determined to show the world that when he spoke people listened, he introduced a revolutionary segment to WWE programming called *Piper's Pit*. Whether he pulled the microphone away from a guest as they answered a question or blindsided a guest with an unprovoked attack, his segment was a breeding ground for confrontation. This was never clearer than when he humiliated Jimmy "Superfly" Snuka and viciously broke a coconut over his head.

Piper hit his stride during 1985's Rock N' Wrestling Connection. Piper ruined Capt. Lou Albano's Gold Record award ceremony, kicked Cyndi Lauper in the head and knocked out her manager, David Wolff. This heinous act put all eyes on the first *WrestleMania*'s main event as Piper & "Mr. Wonderful" squared-off against Mr. T and then-WWE Champion Hulk Hogan. With the world watching perhaps the biggest match of all time, Piper stayed true to form when he deserted his partner and laid-out referee Pat Patterson during his Madison Square Garden exit with bodyguard in tow. The lack of respect between Piper and Mr. T carried through to the next year and the two met in a boxing match at *WrestleMania 2*. Piper's war with Hulk Hogan led to attendance reaching unprecedented numbers.

Months later, Piper returned to WWE and changed his villainous ways. He soon entered into a debate with "Adorable" Adrian Adonis over which was the better show, *Piper's Pit* or *The Flower Shop*. After an attack by Adonis, a Hair vs. Hair Match was set for *WrestleMania III*. Billed as Piper's final match, Roddy defeated his foe with the help of Brutus Beefcake. When they shaved Adrian's head and revived him, the colorful Adonis darted out of the ring.

Piper exited the WWE in a blaze of glory, but went directly to the silver screen in November 1988 in John Carpenter's sci-fi classic *They Live*. Flooded with movie offers, Piper yearned for the energy that only WWE could provide. At *WrestleMania V,* he silenced big mouth Brother Love and drove Morton Downey, Jr. from the ring. With Piper hotter than ever, Superstars such as "Ravishing" Rick Rude, "Million Dollar Man" Ted DiBiase, Dino Bravo, and Bad News Brown looked to use him as a stepping stone to stardom. Piper's conflict with Brown culminated at *WrestleMania VI*. Still an expert psychologist, Piper raced through the SkyDome to the ring with half of his body painted black.

In 1991, Roddy brought his brand of mayhem to the broadcast position on *Prime Time Wrestling* and pay-per-view events. On January 19, 1992, he won his first major title in WWE by defeating the Mountie for the Intercontinental Championship. He lost the title to Bret "Hit Man" Hart a few months later at *WrestleMania VIII*.

By the mid-1990s, Roddy was a bona fide leading man in Hollywood and one of WWE's most popular Superstars. Whether he was a surprise special guest referee at *WrestleMania X*, or involved in a Backlot Brawl with Goldust at *WrestleMania XII*, "Hot Rod" brought audiences to their feet.

After a seven-year absence, Piper stunned WWE audiences in 2003 when he returned at *WrestleMania XIX* during the Street Fight between Hulk Hogan and Mr. McMahon. On April 2, 2005, he was enshrined into the WWE Hall of Fame. The next night, at *WrestleMania 21,* he hosted a special *Piper's Pit* with guest Stone Cold Steve Austin. Since then, Piper has continued to appear on WWE programming and even captured the World Tag Team Championship on November 5, 2006 with "Nature Boy" Ric Flair. Three years later Piper was part of the team that taught Chris Jericho a wrestling lesson after he blatantly disrespected the legends of sports-entertainment. In 2010, Roddy inducted his friend, Wendi Richter, into the WWE Hall of Fame.

The WWE Universe even enjoyed a revival of *Piper's Pit*, where WWE Superstars attempt to resolve their differences and receive a reality check from the Hall of Famer at the same time. The "Hot Rod" also stays busy as co-host of *WWE Vintage* with "Mean" Gene Okerlund.

" *I GUARANTEE YOU THIS, MY NAME IS "ROWDY" RODDY PIPER AND YOU AIN'T SEEN NOTHING YET!*

ROYAL RUMBLE

For 25 years, the Royal Rumble has proven to be one of the WWE Universe's most anticipated events. And with an opportunity to main event *WrestleMania* on the line, WWE Superstars share the same enthusiasm for the annual match. The list of past winners reads like a "Who's Who" of sports-entertainment, including Hulk Hogan, Bret Hart, Ric Flair, Shawn Michaels, Stone Cold Steve Austin, and even Mr. McMahon himself.

January 29, 2006
Miami, FL
American Airlines Arena

Royal Rumble Winner
Rey Mysterio

January 24, 1988
Hamilton, Ontario, Canada
Copps Coliseum

Royal Rumble Winner
"Hacksaw" Jim Duggan

January 22, 1994
Providence, RI
Providence Civic Center

Royal Rumble Winners
Bret "Hit Man" Hart and Lex Luger

January 23, 2000
New York, NY
Madison Square Garden

Royal Rumble Winner
The Rock

January 28, 2007
San Antonio, TX
AT&T Center

Royal Rumble Winner
Undertaker

January 15, 1989
Houston, TX
The Summit

Royal Rumble Winner
Big John Studd

January 22, 1995
Tampa, FL
USF Sun Dome

Royal Rumble Winner
Shawn Michaels

January 21, 2001
New Orleans, LA
New Orleans Arena

Royal Rumble Winner
Stone Cold Steve Austin

January 27, 2008
New York, NY
Madison Square Garden

Royal Rumble Winner
John Cena

January 21, 1990
Orlando, FL
Orlando Arena

Royal Rumble Winner
Hulk Hogan

January 21, 1996
Fresno, CA
Selland Arena

Royal Rumble Winner
Shawn Michaels

January 20, 2002
Atlanta, GA
Philips Arena

Royal Rumble Winner
Triple H

January 25, 2009
Detroit, MI
Joe Louis Arena

Royal Rumble Winner
Randy Orton

January 19, 1991
Miami, FL
Miami Arena

Royal Rumble Winner
Hulk Hogan

January 19, 1997
San Antonio, TX
Alamodome

Royal Rumble Winner
Stone Cold Steve Austin

January 19, 2003
Boston, MA
Fleet Center

Royal Rumble Winner
Brock Lesnar

January 31, 2010
Atlanta, GA
Philips Arena

Royal Rumble Winner
Edge

January 19, 1992
Albany, NY
Knickerbocker Arena

Royal Rumble Winner
Ric Flair

January 18, 1998
San Jose, CA
San Jose Arena

Royal Rumble Winner
Stone Cold Steve Austin

January 24, 2004
Philadelphia, PA
Wachovia Center

Royal Rumble Winner
Chris Benoit

January 27, 2011
Boston, MA
TD Garden

Royal Rumble Winner
Alberto Del Rio

January 24, 1993
Sacramento, CA
ARCO Arena

Royal Rumble Winner
Yokozuna

January 24, 1999
Anaheim, CA
Arrowhead Pond

Royal Rumble Winner
Mr. McMahon

January 30, 2005
Fresno, CA
Save Mart Arena

Royal Rumble Winner
Batista

January 29, 2012
St. Lous, MO
Scottrade Center

Royal Rumble Winner
Sheamus

R-TRUTH

HT: 6'2"   WT: 228 lbs.
FROM: Charlotte, North Carolina
SIGNATURE MOVE: Lie Detector

TITLE HISTORY	
HARDCORE CHAMPION	2 Times
UNITED STATES CHAMPION	Defeated The Miz on May 24, 2010

"The truth shall set you free..." Growing up on the rough streets of Charlotte, North Carolina, R-Truth chose a life of crime. His imprudence ultimately landed him behind bars. Once a free man, R-Truth recognized the wrongs of his past and considered himself a stronger man after paying his debt to society.

R-Truth first appeared in WWE in 1999 alongside Road Dogg as K-Kwik. After six years away from WWE the reformed Superstar returned in 2008 with an optimism and charismatic rap flow that spread throughout arenas all over the world. His unparalleled agility and athleticism inside the ring made him an instant fan favorite and legitimate championship threat. In the spring of 2010, R-Truth let everyone know what's up when he won the United States Championship and became a contender for the WWE Heavyweight Championship.

After being within heartbeats of claiming sports-entertainment's richest prize, R-Truth accused WWE, its Superstars, and fans of conspiring against him. His belief was so strong he turned on John Morrison, interrupted Mr. McMahon and Stone Cold Steve Austin while dressed in a Confederate uniform, and formed a team with The Miz known as Awesome Truth.

Truth has returned to his fan-friendly ways and embraces all the Little Jimmy's around the world. But foes beware, because you're gonna get got!

RUE DeBONA

The WWE Universe remembers Rue DeBona as the host of such weekly shows as *After Burn* in 2003 and '04. But the brunette bombshell actually became accustomed to the spotlight well before joining the esteemed WWE broadcast team.

As a member of the all-girl group Boy Krazy, DeBona scored a hit single with "That's What Love Can Do" in 1993. That same year, she also appeared on Disney Channel's *The All New Mickey Mouse Club*, which also featured future A-list celebrities Ryan Gosling, Justin Timberlake and Britney Spears, among others.

DeBona has appeared in several films following her brief WWE career. She is most known for her role as Emily in Steven Seagal's 2008 straight-to-DVD action movie *Pistol Whipped*. She was also the face of the now-defunct television network VOOM.

Despite having a fleeting WWE career, DeBona's peppy personality and natural beauty has left an impression on the WWE Universe that will not soon be forgotten.

RYAN BRADDOCK

HT: 6'4"   WT: 262 lbs.
FROM: Chicago, Illinois
SIGNATURE MOVE: Lariat

Rough, tough and ready for anything, this young Superstar showed his lack of fear in his WWE debut against Big Show. Ryan Braddock employed an aggressive style of fighting while facing *SmackDown* Superstars of various shapes and sizes.

This tough guy from the South Side of Chicago bruised competition in contests as part of ECW and on *SmackDown* in his search for WWE championships, but he wasn't able to capture any titles during his brief time in WWE.

RYAN SHAMROCK

HT: 5'6"   FROM: Sacramento, California

With her quiet demeanor and innocent smile, Ryan Shamrock certainly played the part of a proper young woman. In reality, Ken Shamrock's little sister was anything but pure. Just weeks after making her first WWE appearance, Ryan was co-starring in Val Venis' latest flick, *Sister Act*. Proving her act of indiscretion was not a momentary lapse of judgment, the leggy blonde later intentionally left the blinds to her SkyDome hotel room open so that *Raw* fans could witness the couple in their most intimate moments. In typical fashion, Val Venis eventually kicked young Ryan to the curb. Refusing to be a victim, the jilted Diva later joined forces with Terri and Jacqueline in the male-bashing faction Pretty Mean Sisters. As a member of PMS, Ryan used her sexuality to get whatever she wanted from the male WWE Superstars.

RYUMA GO

FROM: Japan

TITLE HISTORY

JUNIOR HEAVYWEIGHT CHAMPION	*Defeated Tatsumi Fujinami on October 2, 1979*

While competing for New Japan Pro Wrestling in the late 1970s, Ryuma Go experienced a whirlwind two days that will forever link him to WWE. On October 2, 1979, the powerful Go ended Tatsumi Fujinami's amazing 600-plus day reign with the WWE Junior Heavyweight Championship when he defeated the legend in Osaka, Japan. Go enjoyed the now-defunct title for two quick days before losing it back to Fujinami in a match contested in Tokyo, Japan. Fujinami went on to hold the gold for nearly 800 more days.

In addition to his days in NJPW, Go travelled the globe, competing mainly in Canada, Germany and the United States. Over the course of his travels, he captured the NWA Beat the Champ Television Title, the NWA Americas Tag Team Championship twice and became one of two teams to ever hold the short-lived CWIA International Tag Team Championship.

He also started Pioneer Senshi, one of the first independent promotions in Japan.

SABA SIMBA

HT: 6'2"   **WT:** 250 lbs.
FROM: Africa

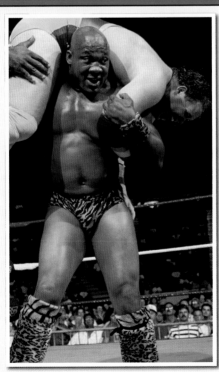

In the early 1990s, a mountain of a man emerged on the WWE scene under the moniker of Saba Simba. Clad in a giant feather headdress and leopard print tights, Saba Simba was billed as an African tribal warrior. He struggled to pick up wins and was gone from WWE, but not before he was able to compete in the 1991 *Royal Rumble*.

SABLE

HT: 5'6"   **FROM:** Jacksonville, Florida   **SIGNATURE MOVE:** Sable Bomb

Although women competed for decades in WWE rings before her, Sable is considered by many as a pioneer. Behind her amazing athleticism and spine-jarring Sable Bomb, the blonde bombshell became the sixteenth Women's Champion in WWE history. Despite her impressive in-ring accolades, however, Sable will be long remembered for being the first of many beautiful Divas to bare all in *Playboy*.

TITLE HISTORY

WOMEN'S CHAMPION	*Defeated Jacqueline on November 15, 1998*

Sable's earliest WWE days were spent by the side of Hunter Hearst-Helmsley, but when he began to mistreat the fair-haired Diva, her husband, Marc Mero, ran to her aid. For the better part of the next two years, the loving couple shared a strong bond both on and off the air.

By 1998, the spotlight began to shine brightest on Sable, leaving Mero's star to fade. Jealous of his wife's popularity, Mero tried everything in his power to dim her bright career and hide her voluptuous curves. His attempts eventually backfired when Sable escaped from his grasp, delivering a Sable Bomb in the process.

Sable then went on to achieve never-before-seen success. Her first step toward greatness was capturing the Women's Championship from Mero's new lady, Jacqueline. In the months that followed, the new champ rode her popularity all the way to Hollywood, landing guest roles on a few television programs.

Sable's inevitable break into mainstream came when she landed the cover of *Playboy* in April 1999. The overwhelming success of her spread led to two more covers, but more importantly, helped pave the way for future Divas. Sable made a shocking return to WWE in 2003, where she was featured in another *Playboy* spread—this time with Torrie.

2010-

2000-09

1990-99

1980-89

1970-79

1960-69

"SAILOR" ART THOMAS

HT: 6'6" **WT:** 265 lbs. **FROM:** Fitchburg, Wisconsin
SIGNATURE MOVE: Bearhug

A chiseled giant of the ring with 20-inch biceps, "Sailor" Art Thomas was a member of the United States Navy before he began his sports-entertainment career in 1943. During the 1950s Thomas became one of the most beloved performers in the world and one of the first Superstars of African descent.

In the early 1960s Thomas contended for the NWA Heavyweight Championship held at the time by "Nature Boy" Boddy Rogers. In 1963 Thomas made his WWE debut dazzling the fans in the northeast with his physique, power, and quickness. For the next seven years "Sailor" appeared for WWE in singles competition and formed thrilling tandems with Bruno Sammartino and Bobo Brazil.

He continued his sports-entertainment career until his retirement early in the 1980's. Sadly, this cultural icon and legend of the ring passed away in 2003. "Sailor" Art Thomas was a hero to all and touched fans throughout the world over the course of his career.

SABU

HT: 6'0" **WT:** 235 lbs.
FROM: Bombay, Michigan
SIGNATURE MOVE:
Arabian Facebuster

Trained by his Hall of Fame uncle, the Sheik, Sabu knew no fear inside the ring. Possessing a complete disregard for his own wellbeing, the maniacal Superstar gained a cult-like following while competing in ECW in the mid-to-late 1990s.

Over the course of his lengthy ECW career, Sabu captured every piece of hardware the promotion offered, including three reigns with the prestigious ECW Championship. Despite his golden resumé, Sabu is best remembered for the abundance of injuries he suffered. Sliced open by barbed wire and shards of broken tables, his scarred body proudly displays permanent memories of his vicious battles.

Sabu competed at *ECW One Night Stand* in June 2006. Battling Rey Mysterio for the World Heavyweight Championship, he used his extreme style of competition to take the WWE Superstar to the limit. In the end, the match was declared a no-contest after both men crashed through a table, rendering them unable to compete.

Following the success of his *One Night Stand* appearance, Sabu entered WWE's revived version of ECW. He used the brand's premiere episode to reintroduce himself as one of ECW's supreme Superstars, winning an Extreme Battle Royal to earn the right to challenge John Cena for the WWE Championship at *Vengeance*. He ultimately lost to Cena, but successfully reminded fans that he was the "Suicidal, Homicidal, Genocidal, Death-Defying Maniac."

SALVATORE BELLAMO

HT: 6'2" **WT:** 290 lbs.
FROM: Italy
SIGNATURE MOVE: Running Splash

Known as the "Wildman", Italian Superstar Salvatore Bellomo gained moderate WWE success upon his arrival in the early 1980s. During this time, his greatest claim to fame was filling in for his injured friend Junkyard Dog on an in-ring edition of *Piper's Pit*. As a guest of "Rowdy" Roddy Piper, Bellomo was the target of severe verbal barbs from both Piper and "Mr. Wonderful" Paul Orndorff. Finally, after the verbal attack turned physical, the injured JYD dragged himself to the ring to fend off Bellomo's adversaries.

After his WWE days came to a close, Bellomo brought his signature running splash finisher to ECW. As a member of the Philadelphia-based promotion, the "Wildman" became a brief member of the Full Blooded Italians stable. With his in-ring days behind him, Bellomo now works in Belgium as a trainer to Superstars of tomorrow.

SALVATORE SINCERE

HT: 6'3" **WT:** 262 lbs.
FROM: Philadelphia, Pennsylvania
SIGNATURE MOVE: Sincerely Yours

Arrogant, charismatic and with a bodybuilder's physique, Salvatore Sincere entered WWE in 1996. Sincere battled Superstars such as Barry Horowitz, Savio Vega, Rocky Maivia, Jake "The Snake" Roberts, Shawn Michaels, and Undertaker. While battilng over the services of Sable, Marc Mero revealed Salvatore's real name was Tom Brandi, which lead to Salvatore often using that name while competing until he left WWE in April 1998.

Whichever name was announced to audiences, whether a villain or fan favorite, this rugged soldier brought the same grit and fight to the ring. Today, he still appears at independent events all over the United States.

SAM HOUSTON

HT: 6'1" **WT:** 227 lbs.
FROM: Waco, Texas

Sam Houston liked to dance just as much as he liked to wrestle. Upon his debut in 1987, he caught the attention of fans with his pre-match dance steps. Once the bell rang, he was all business.

Houston's WWE career was highlighted by decisive victories in rivalries with Barry Horowitz and Danny Davis. Unfortunately, he had trouble keeping up with WWE's more skilled competitors. Houston did, however, compete in the first-ever *Royal Rumble* in 1988. He was also a member of Ultimate Warrior's *Survivor Series* team later that year.

SAMU

HT: 6'4" **WT:** 260 lbs. **FROM:** Isle of Samoa
SIGNATURE MOVE: Flying Head-Butt

TITLE HISTORY

WORLD TAG TEAM CHAMPION	Partnered with Fatu to defeat The Quebecers on April 26, 1994

This young monster appeared in Canada, Puerto Rico, and elsewhere in the United States, managed by the ever-agitating Paul E. Dangerously. In 1992, Samu and his cousin Fatu entered WWE under the name the Headshrinkers. Managed by Afa and later co-managed by Lou Albano. They won the World Tag Team Championship in April 1994, but lost them in August. Soon after their title run, Samu left the company. In 1996 he appeared in Extreme Championship Wrestling and remains active on the Independent scene.

SAMULA

HT: 6'4" **WT:** 260 lbs.
FROM: Isle of Samoa

TITLE HISTORY

WORLD TAG TEAM CHAMPION	Joined World Tag Team Champions, The Wild Samoans, when Sika was injured.

Samula comes from a long line of successful Samoan Superstars. As a member of the famed Anoa'i family, which also includes Afa, Sika, Peter Maivia, and The Rock, Samula was born into wrestling greatness.

At the young age of 20, Samula was thrust into the WWE spotlight. With his Uncle Sika sidelined by injury, Samula became the third member of the legendary Wild Samoans tag team. While Sika rehabbed his injury, Samula teamed with his father, Afa, to help defend the World Tag Team Championship. Samula also gained some success as a singles Superstar before finally leaving WWE in 1985.

THE SANDMAN

HT: 6'4" **WT:** 240 lbs. **FROM:** Philadelphia, Pennsylvania
SIGNATURE MOVE: The White Russian Legsweep

This Singapore Cane swingin', cigarette smokin', beer-chuggin' maniac was one of the primary reasons the "E" stood for Extreme in ECW. In his six years with ECW he was a five-time ECW Champion and Tag Team Champion. The Sandman was also seen by WWE audiences during ECW's first invasion of WWE in 1996. In 1999 Sandman left the world of barbed-wire and blood and went to WCW but returned home by the end of the year. After ECW's closure in 2001 he toured the globe.

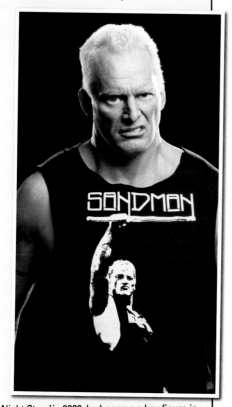

When the hardcore revolution arose from the ashes in 2005, culminating at *ECW One Night Stand*, the Sandman made a dramatic entrance, highlighted by the entire arena singing along with his entrance music, Sandman flattening a can against his head, and Joey Styles noting, "He's already busted open, and the match hasn't begun yet!" After appearing at *One Night Stand* in 2006, he became a key figure in WWE's re-launch of ECW. As a part of the ECW Originals, he stood victorious in the ring at *WrestleMania 23* after defeating the New Breed. That June, he became the first ECW Original to be drafted away from the brand to *Raw,* where he appeared until he left WWE in September 2007.

SANTINO MARELLA

HT: 5'10" **WT:** 227 lbs. **FROM:** Calabria, Italy
SIGNATURE MOVE: The Cobra

TITLE HISTORY

INTERCONTINENTAL CHAMPION (2 TIMES)	Defeated Umaga on April 16, 2007 Defeated Kofi Kingston on August 17, 2008
WWE TAG TEAM CHAMPION	Partnered with Vladimir Kozlov to defeat Justin Gabriel & Heath Slater on December 6, 2010
UNITED STATES CHAMPION	Defeated Jack Swagger March 5, 2012

Santino Marella turned a front row seat into a golden opportunity when he answered Mr. McMahon's challenge for any WWE fan to step into the ring with Intercontinental Champion Umaga. In one of the most improbable moments in WWE history, Marella defeated Umaga for the title.

Unforunately, his initial momentum began to disappear and with each loss, an ugly side of Marella's personality slowly emerged. Despite his annoyingly insecure attitude, Marella managed to catch the eye of Maria. The two quickly engaged in an intense affair, though Maria's success and feature in Playboy magazine ultimately proved to be too much for Marella to handle. Santino then sought comfort in the arms of Beth Phoenix, who carried him to the Intercontinental Championship at *SummerSlam* in 2008. Calabria's son and his "Glamarella" were WWE's power couple. The passionate romance abruptly ended when it was discovered that Marella, disguised as Santina eliminated Beth from the Divas Battle Royal at *WrestleMania XXV.*

After his partnership with Vladimir Kozlov resulted in a brief WWE Tag Team Championship stint, Santino returned to singles action and won the heart of the once cold Tamina. At the 2012 *Royal Rumble*, the present met the past when Marella's Cobra collided with Mick Foley's legendary Mr. Socko.

Santino remains a beloved WWE Superstar. He's proud to be Italian, and proud to be, as he once declared himself, the Champion of Planet Earth.

S

2010-
2000-09
1990-99
1980-89
1970-79
1960-69

SAPPHIRE

In 1989, longtime fan Sapphire bought a ticket to a WWE live event that changed her life forever. While sitting ringside, the superfan was spotted by WWE Superstar Dusty Rhodes. Admiring her enthusiasm, the "American Dream" pulled her from her seat and took her on as his valet.

As Rhodes' second, Sapphire escorted her man to the ring and sat ringside while he climbed the WWE ladder. As a sign of loyalty to Rhodes, she even wore matching yellow polka dots. As time went on, Sapphire's involvement increased. It wasn't long before the onetime fan soon became an in-ring competitor. At *WrestleMania VI*, Sapphire teamed with Rhodes to defeat Randy Savage & Sensational Sherri in WWE's first-ever Mixed Tag Team Match.

In the summer of 1990, Sapphire began to receive extravagant gifts from an unknown source. Week after week, she was seen with new diamond rings, bracelets and necklaces. She claimed she had no idea where the gifts were coming from. At *SummerSlam 1990*, Sapphire proved that everybody has a price for the "Million Dollar Man" when she turned her back on Rhodes to join forces with Ted DiBiase.

SAVANNAH

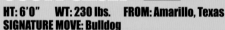

Savannah made her WWE debut in September 2009, as a part of the ECW broadcast team. As the brand's chief backstage interviewer, she was tasked with asking the tough questions to ECW Superstars Zack Ryder, Vance Archer and Christian, among others.

In November 2009, Lauren Mayhew's departure from ECW opened the door for Savannah to step in as the brand's official ring announcer, a job also previously held by Justin Roberts and Tony Chimel. When *ECW on Syfy* made way for the debut of WWE's groundbreaking show *NXT*, Savannah used her experience to serve as the new show's ring announcer.

Savannah was released from her WWE contract in June 2010. Outside of WWE, Savannah's stunning good looks helped launch a successful modeling career. She was also a cheerleader for the British Columbia Lions of the Canadian Football League. Additionally, she once walked away with cash and prizes from the television game show *Let's Make A Deal*, starring host Wayne Brady.

SAVIO VEGA

HT: 5'11" **WT:** 260 lbs. **FROM:** South Bronx, New York
SIGNATURE MOVE: Spinning Heel Kick

Savio Vega made a big splash in his debut at May 1995's *In Your House*. After saving Razor Ramon from a brutal beating at the hands of Jeff Jarrett and The Roadie, the two became tag team partners. After Razor Ramon left WWE, Vega continued to make an impression within the singles ranks against the likes of Hunter Hearst-Helmsley and Steve Austin, then known as the Ringmaster.

In 1997 he briefly joined the Nation of Domination, but after he was forcibly expelled, Vega created a group of his own, Los Baricuas. Vega also competed in 1998's *Brawl For All* Tournament before leaving World Wrestling Entertainment later in the year. He returned to his homeland of Puerto Rico where he has been a huge star since his early days in sports entertainment.

SCOTT CASEY

HT: 6'0" **WT:** 230 lbs. **FROM:** Amarillo, Texas
SIGNATURE MOVE: Bulldog

Trained by the legendary Dory Funk, Sr., Scott Casey showcased his talents in various promotions worldwide over the course of his thirty years in the ring. The rugged Texan's days of constantly bouncing around finally settled, however, when he signed a WWE contract in 1987.

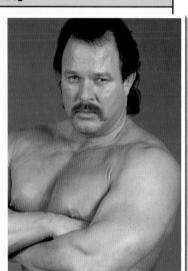

Casey's greatest WWE highlight saw him team with "Hacksaw" Jim Duggan, Jake "The Snake" Roberts, Tito Santana & Ken Patera at the 1988 *Survivor Series*. After a brutal thirty-minute battle, Casey's team succumbed to the mighty combination of Andre the Giant, "Ravishing" Rick Rude, Mr. Perfect, Dino Bravo & Harley Race. Casey failed to achieve much success after *Survivor Series*, but will forever have the memory of competing alongside many future Hall of Famers on one of the biggest stages around. After retiring from WWE in 1990, Casey began working as a trainer to future Superstars. He is credited for helping shape the career of a young Booker T.

SCOTT PUTSKI

HT: 5'9" **WT:** 275 lbs. **FROM:** Austin, Texas
SIGNATURE MOVE: Polish Hammer

Scott Putski grew up in the sports-entertainment world of his father "Polish Power" Ivan Putski. In the early 1990s, Scott began his professional career and even toured Japan. In 1997, Scott Putski debuted in WWE on *Monday Night Raw* and had fans on their feet once his name was announced. His rivalry against Brian Christopher escalated to a father and son affair. On an episode of *Raw,* father and son teams of Scott Putski & "Polish Power" Ivan Putski clashed against Christopher & Jerry "The King" Lawler. Scott soon left WWE and appeared in WCW in 1998 before returning to the North American independent scene.

SCOTT STANFORD

Scott Stanford joined WWE in 2009 and instantly became recognizable worldwide as the voice behind several of WWE's International television shows, including *The Bottom Line* and *WWE Superstars*. Stanford also teamed with fellow commentator Jack Korpela to preview each pay-per-view on WWE's popular countdown show, *Free For All*.

Despite his busy workload, Stanford has found time to appear as a regular on Zack Ryder's hit weekly web show, *Z! True Long Island Story*.

Prior to joining WWE, Stanford was best known for his work as a sports anchor in the New York market. The four-time Emmy Award-winning sportscaster covered the Yankees and Giants for such networks as WNBC, WWOR and WNYW. Along the way, he also showed his lighter side while taking part in comedic features on girls roller derby, kickball and sumo wrestling, among others.

Stanford's history also includes radio. As the full-time afternoon sports anchor for WCBS Newsradio 880 in New York, he was twice honored with the AIR Award, which recognizes the best radio sports anchor in the market.

SCOTT STEINER 🇺🇸

HT: 6'1" WT: 265 lbs.
FROM: Detroit, Michigan
SIGNATURE MOVE: Steiner Recliner

TITLE HISTORY

WORLD TAG TEAM CHAMPION (2 TIMES)	*Partnered with Rick Steiner to defeat Money, Inc. on June 14, 1993* *Partnered with Rick Steiner to defeat Money, Inc. on June 19, 1993*

Scott Steiner was an All-American in freestyle wrestling at the University of Michigan. He was trained for a career in the pro ranks by The Sheik. After working for local promotions in 1986, he joined his older brother Rick in Jim Crockett Promotions.

From 1992 to 1994 they appeared in World Wrestling Entertainment and became World Tag Team Champions as well as wrestled on the debut episode of *Monday Night Raw* in 1993. After a short stay in ECW the brothers returned to WCW in 1996. Soon they reclaimed the WCW Tag Team Titles, but Scott turned on his brother and joined the nWo as the genetic freak, "Big Poppa Pump."

Steiner shined on his own and won virtually every WCW Championship before it shutdown in March of 2001. Steiner rejoined WWE at the 2002 *Survivor Series*. The General Managers of *SmackDown* and *Raw* vied for him, with Eric Bischoff eventually signing him to *Raw*. Steiner became a top challenger for the World Heavyweight Championship held by Triple H. Though trumping "The Game" in pose-downs and arm-wrestling contests, Steiner was unable to get the title away from him. In 2004 Steiner and WWE parted ways. He remains active, and occasionally reunites with his brother. No matter where he goes, he always gives a shout-out to all his freaks. In the words of the man with the largest arms in the world, "Holla if ya hear me!"

SCOTTY 2 HOTTY 🇺🇸

HT: 5'9" WT: 209 lbs. FROM: Westbrook, Maine
SIGNATURE MOVE: The Worm

TITLE HISTORY

LIGHT HEAVYWEIGHT CHAMPION	*Defeated Dean Malenko on April 17, 2000*
WORLD TAG TEAM CHAMPION	*Partnered with Grand Master Sexay to defeat Edge & Christian on May 29, 2000*
WWE TAG TEAM CHAMPION	*Partnered with Rikishi to defeat the Basham Brothers on February 5, 2004*

No, Scotty 2 Hotty didn't stick his finger in a light socket. He actually styled his hair like that intentionally. No, he never got dressed in the dark. He purposely decked himself out in blinding neon attire. While the common man may choose to do things a bit more conventionally, Scotty's colorful personality was the driving force behind his success.

After several non-descript years competing in WWE, Scotty's fortunes changed when he was randomly paired with Grandmaster Sexay to compete in *WrestleMania XIV*'s Tag Team Battle Royal. The new pairing liked each other so much they couldn't stop showing their affection for each other. Eventually, they molded themselves into Too Cool, an over-the-top hip-hop tandem severely short on hip.

Despite their inability to act even remotely cool, Too Cool emerged as fan favorites. With close friend Rikishi by their side, the threesome regularly broke into dance routines that always brought the fans to their feet. The team's popularity reached even greater heights when they defeated Edge & Christian for the World Tag Team Championship in May 2000. Several years later, Scotty would team with Rikishi to claim SmackDown's WWE Tag Team Championship.

On his own, Scotty was equally impressive. Using his popular Worm signature move, he successfully turned back noted rivals Billy Gunn, Crash Holly, and D'Lo Brown. He even defeated Dean Malenko for the Light Heavyweight Championship in April 2000.

2010-
2000-09
1990-99
1980-89
1970-79
1960-69

SD "SPECIAL DELIVERY" JONES

HT: 6'1"   WT: 265 lbs.   FROM: Antigua in the West Indies
SIGNATURE MOVE: Jumping Headbutt

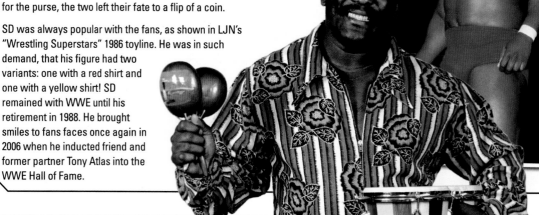

SD Jones was energy-personified and fans loved him from his first appearances in the mid-1970s. Into the 1980s SD teamed with "Mr. USA" Tony Atlas and contended for the World Tag Team Championship. One of the moments that defined SD as a man was when he and friend Tony Atlas were the final two men in a battle royal. Instead of fighting it out for the purse, the two left their fate to a flip of a coin.

SD was always popular with the fans, as shown in LJN's "Wrestling Superstars" 1986 toyline. He was in such demand, that his figure had two variants: one with a red shirt and one with a yellow shirt! SD remained with WWE until his retirement in 1988. He brought smiles to fans faces once again in 2006 when he inducted friend and former partner Tony Atlas into the WWE Hall of Fame.

SCOTTY GOLDMAN

HT: 6'1"   WT: 242 lbs.
FROM: Deerfield, Illinios

Week after week, Scotty Goldman fell in fast fashion to gigantic Superstars like the Great Khali, Vladimir Kozlov, and Umaga. Despite the brutal beatings, Goldman always accepted the outcomes with a smile. In fact, in his relatively short period of time in WWE, the happy-go-lucky Superstar made a name for himself as a bit of a joker. Since words like "boom" and "pow" were stitched onto his singlet, he resembled more of a walking comic book page than someone in ring gear. The young Superstar also hosted the popular *What's Crackin' with Scotty Goldman* on WWE.com, where he regularly discussed the art of wrestling.

SEAN MOONEY

Over the course of his five-year WWE career, Sean Mooney performed nearly every broadcast duty available. Upon debuting in 1988, he served as host for such shows as *WWE Wrestling Challenge*. He also teamed with the legendary Lord Alfred Hayes to host many of WWE's popular Coliseum Home Video releases.

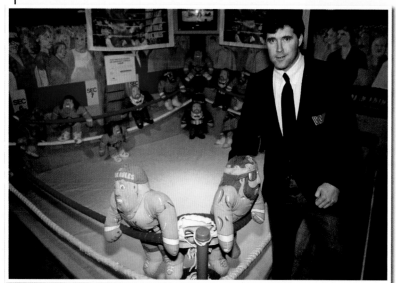

As a play-by-play announcer, Mooney's call of the action could be heard on *Prime Time Wrestling*, among other shows. He also served as a backstage interviewer for WWE's pay-per-views.

Prior to parting ways with the company in 1993, Mooney achieved the distinction of being the first-ever voice to *Monday Night Raw*, as he welcomed viewers to the live broadcast before throwing the announcing duties to Vince McMahon, Randy "Macho Man" Savage and Rob Bartlett.

During his WWE tenure, Mooney was often confused with his identical twin siblings Ian and Betty, who often appeared on *Wrestling Spotlight* and *Prime Time Wrestling* respectively.

SEAN O'HAIRE

HT: 6'6"   WT: 274 lbs.   FROM: Hilton Head, South Carolina
SIGNATURE MOVE: Cruel Intentions

As one-half of the WCW Tag Team Champions with Chuck Palumbo, Sean O'Haire invaded WWE with a giant chip on his shoulder. But it wasn't long before he learned that WWE wasn't "where the big *boys* played." Shortly after his debut, O'Haire and his partner Palumbo lost their tag titles to Undertaker & Kane.

O'Haire took a brief hiatus following the loss. During his time away, the muscular Superstar became a master of mind games, urging people to commit such regretful acts as adultery, tax fraud and law breaking.

Unfortunately for O'Haire, his dastardly game of devil's advocate only got him so far. Realizing he needed an education in being evil, he employed the managerial services of "Rowdy" Roddy Piper. With the WWE Hall of Famer leading the way, O'Haire picked up major victories over Eddie Guerrero, Rikishi and Mr. America.

Piper temporarily left WWE in June 2003, leaving O'Haire to go at it alone. Unable to retain Piper's education, he began to fall on hard times. O'Haire was later released in April 2004.

SEIJI SAKAGUCHI

HT: 6'5" **WT:** 290 lbs.
FROM: Japan

When Pat Patterson unified the North and South American Championships to become the first-ever Intercontinental Champion in 1979, it was believed WWE fans would never again see the short-lived North American Title. But a few short months after the unification, Japanese sensation Seiji Sakaguchi resurrected the gold and proudly defended it for nearly 500 days before the title was finally retired for good in 1981.

Sakaguchi also had a successful run with the NWA, a promotion which recognized him as its president in 1992 and 1993. As a competitor, he captured the Los Angeles/Japan version of the NWA North American Tag Team Championship twice (with Antonio Inoki and Strong Kobayahsi). He was also a two-time NWA United National Champion, defeating King Krow in January 1972 and The Sheik in September of the same year. Additionally, Sakaguchi held the NWA International and Polynesian Pacific Tag Team Championships.

Despite hanging up his boots in 1990, Sakaguchi made one return to the ring in 2003, when he teamed with Masahiro Chono to battle Yoshihiro Takayama and Shinya Makabe.

Sgt. Slaughter (see page 306)

SHAD GASPARD

HT: 6'7" **WT:** 295 lbs.
FROM: Brooklyn, New York

Shad Gaspard and JTG were great friends and an even better tag team. Collectively known as Cryme Tyme, the duo spent years turning back WWE's top teams, including the Self-Proclaimed World's Greatest Tag Team and Lance Cade and Trevor Murdoch.

But after losing a match to John Morrison & R-Truth in April 2010, a frustrated Gaspard severed all ties with his longtime friend when he blasted him with a big boot to the face. According to Gaspard, it was time for him to stand up, break out and take what he deserved. And to do so, he believed he needed to eliminate JTG.

Gaspard's time to shine came when he challenged his former partner to a Strap Match at *Extreme Rules 2010.* Given his excessive size advantage, many assumed Gaspard would make short work of JTG. But in the end, it was JTG proving his superiority over Gaspard, much to the surprise of many. Gaspard never fully rebounded from the loss and was released from WWE later that year.

SERENA

Prior to meeting CM Punk, Serena claimed that years of pill addiction had her questioning her worth. But that all changed in January 2010, when the troubled beauty washed away a lifetime of suffering by pledging allegiance to the Straight Edge Society.

After accepting CM Punk as her savior, Serena did as all disciples of "The Second City Savior" do: She had her head shaved bald. Throughout the entire appearance-altering process, Serena proudly wore a smile that told a story of relief and recovery.

After adopting the straight edge movement, Serena regularly sacrificed her own safety for the betterment of the Straight Edge Society. As a result, she became one of Punk's most trusted allies. But when the supposedly-cured Serena was seen drinking alcohol in July 2010, her spot within the controversial faction came into question.

Punk ultimately forgave Serena for her wrongdoing, much to the disdain of fellow Straight Edge Society member Luke Gallows. After the incident, much hostility followed Serena until her release from WWE in August 2010.

THE SHADOW

As Vincent J. McMahon and "Toots" Mondt transformed Capitol Wrestling Corporation into WWE, a kinetic energy spread through the entire wrestling world. As grapplers from all over vied for employment, one surfaced with an unknown origin with an unknown identity and an unknown past. All he went by was the Shadow.

This stealth-like individual was a hazard to opposing Superstars like Miguel Perez, Bruno Sammartino, Pedro Morales, Bobo Brazil, and Gorilla Monsoon. During this time Shadow also joined forces with other dangerous figures like Dr. Jerry Graham and Hans Mortier. By the end of 1963 the Shadow disappeared into thin air. It has been over 45 years since the silhouette of this man was seen in a wrestling ring. Or has it appeared again and no one knew it?

The Shadow's influence lingered after his last appearance as nearly two decades later a tag team emerged from nowhere and called themselves the Shadows. The duo took on the likes of the Young Stallions and the Fabulous Rougeau Brothers during their brief time in WWE.

S

1960-69
1970-79
1980-89
1990-99
2000-09
2010-

SGT. SLAUGHTER

" AT-TEN-HUT "

HT: 6'6"   **WT: 305 lbs.**   **FROM: Paris Island, South Carolina**   **SIGNATURE MOVE: Cobra Clutch**

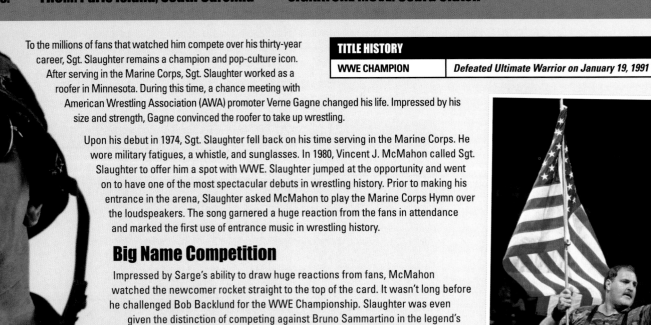

To the millions of fans that watched him compete over his thirty-year career, Sgt. Slaughter remains a champion and pop-culture icon. After serving in the Marine Corps, Sgt. Slaughter worked as a roofer in Minnesota. During this time, a chance meeting with American Wrestling Association (AWA) promoter Verne Gagne changed his life. Impressed by his size and strength, Gagne convinced the roofer to take up wrestling.

Upon his debut in 1974, Sgt. Slaughter fell back on his time serving in the Marine Corps. He wore military fatigues, a whistle, and sunglasses. In 1980, Vincent J. McMahon called Sgt. Slaughter to offer him a spot with WWE. Slaughter jumped at the opportunity and went on to have one of the most spectacular debuts in wrestling history. Prior to making his entrance in the arena, Slaughter asked McMahon to play the Marine Corps Hymn over the loudspeakers. The song garnered a huge reaction from the fans in attendance and marked the first use of entrance music in wrestling history.

Big Name Competition

Impressed by Sarge's ability to draw huge reactions from fans, McMahon watched the newcomer rocket straight to the top of the card. It wasn't long before he challenged Bob Backlund for the WWE Championship. Slaughter was even given the distinction of competing against Bruno Sammartino in the legend's final Madison Square Garden match.

Under the guidance of famed manager the Grand Wizard, Slaughter engaged in a brutal and bloody rivalry with Pat Patterson. In truly revolutionary fashion, the two Superstars battled for bragging rights in an infamous Alley Fight at Madison Square Garden that did not feature a referee. The match came to a stunning conclusion when the Grand Wizard, fearing the worst for his battered protégé, threw in the towel.

In early 1984, WWE fans began to recognize Slaughter as a hero when he stood up to the Iron Sheik and his manager "Ayatollah" Freddie Blassie. The Sarge's patriotic change of heart marked the end of an epic love-hate relationship between Slaughter and the fans. It also sparked the beginning of an amazing rivalry with the Iron Sheik that sold out arenas across the country.

A Real American Hero?

Shortly after his rivalry with the Iron Sheik, Slaughter left WWE. The decision to return to Minnesota caused Slaughter to miss out on the nationwide phenomenon WWE became in the mid-1980s. Ironically, the Sarge gained national exposure of his own when he became the spokesperson for the G.I. Joe line of toys. The new role saw the Sarge become a household name while being featured in cartoons, comic books, and as multiple action figures.

Slaughter made his return to WWE in 1990. When news of his comeback began to circulate, fans couldn't wait to once again cheer their hero. Unfortunately, Slaughter gave them no reason to celebrate, as he denounced his country to become an Iraqi sympathizer. The move shocked WWE fans, who needed a hero during the tumultuous times of the Persian Gulf War.

Matters became worse for the American fans when Slaughter defeated Ultimate Warrior for the coveted WWE Championship at the *Royal Rumble* in 1991. The victory resulted in Slaughter becoming even more hated than he was during his early days in sports-entertainment. It wasn't long before his family was receiving death threats.

Luckily, American hero Hulk Hogan saved the day when he defeated Slaughter for the WWE Championship at *WrestleMania VII.* Following the loss, Slaughter begged for his country back. The fans ultimately forgave the Marine Corps drill sergeant, who was given the opportunity to finish his competitive career with the support of his fans.

After retirement, Slaughter assumed several prominent roles within WWE, including Commissioner and road producer. In 2004, he was recognized with induction into the WWE Hall of Fame, a fitting honor for a man who was both a wrestling great and real American hero.

Since his induction into the WWE Hall of Fame, the Sarge remains active behind the scenes in WWE, and on occasion has stepped through the ropes to lock disrespectful maggots in the Cobra Clutch. Some of his more recent in-ring moments include a 2006 appearance alongside "Nature Boy" Ric Flair, Ron Simmons, and "The American Dream" Dusty Rhodes at the *Survivor Series,* taking part in the *Raw 15th Anniversary* Battle Royal, a dance-off on the 800th episode of *Raw,* and 2010's *Old School Raw* where he saw action versus Alberto Del Rio. Slaughter also had a memorable cameo on *Tosh.0* where he clotheslined the host, Daniel Tosh, out of his shoes.

SHANE DOUGLAS

HT: 6'1"   WT: 241 lbs.   FROM: Pittsburgh, Pennsylvania
SIGNATURE MOVE: Belly-to-Belly Suplex

Trained by Dominic DeNucci, Douglas first made a name for himself in the Universal Wrestling Federation. Shane Douglas was a fan favorite who was highly regarded for his exciting, high-flying style and tough as nails, never say die attitude.

In the spring of 1990 Shane Douglas debuted in WWE and impressed fans in bouts against Buddy Rose, Brooklyn Brawler, Haku, Dino Bravo, Barbarian, Undertaker and Greg Valentine. While he contended for the Intercontinental Championship, his resiliency was best shown during the *1991 Royal Rumble,* when he lasted almost 30 minutes before being eliminated. By August 1991, Shane left the company but stayed busy in the ring in other promotions.

In 1994, after winning a Three Way Dance against Terry Funk and Sabu, Shane Douglas threw down his newly won NWA Championship. Douglas was immediately named champion of the upstart ECW promotion, which began the movement that made the group a grassroots phenomenon.

Shane McMahon (see page 308)

SHANIQUA

When Linda Miles won the second season of *WWE Tough Enough,* many assumed she would have a bright career ahead of her. But Miles saw things differently. Proving bright and cheery wasn't for her, the *Tough Enough* champ unleashed a dark and masochistic side as the manager of the Basham Brothers.

Miles' 2003 union with Danny and Doug Basham was accompanied by a name change. Now known as Shaniqua, the amazon-like Diva began to dress in all-leather and carried a whip, which let everybody know, particularly the Bashams, that she wasn't afraid to get rough, either in or out of the ring.

Later that year, a Clothesline From Hell at the hands of JBL temporarily sidelined Shaniqua. When she returned, her low-cut leather ring gear revealed that the clothesline resulted in extreme and permanent swelling in her chest region. But she didn't seem to mind, and neither did the Bashams, who couldn't keep their eyes off her supposedly-injured area.

SHANNON MOORE

HT: 5'9"   WT: 207 lbs.   FROM: Whispering Pines, North Carolina   SIGNATURE MOVE: The Halo

Originally introduced to wrestling by childhood friends The Hardy Boys, this former Superstar appeared in their North Carolina-based OMEGA promotion. Moore debuted in WWE in 2002 and soon became a devout follower of Matt Hardy's way of life known as "Mattitude." As a follower (called an "MF'er") Moore appeared at ringside for Hardy's matches. Moore found a subordinate of his own, who was known as a "Moore-On."

After Hardy and Shannon parted he took on a variety of opponents and participated in the Cruiserweight Open at *WrestleMania XX.* In 2005 he tapped into the punk in him and rocked-out in several locations with his mohawk haircut, elaborate body art and piercings. The self-labeled "Prince of Punk" spread his messages of non-conformity to WWE fans. After spending much of 2005 making appearances on the independant circuit, Moore returned to WWE in 2006 as part of ECW before moving to *SmackDown.* Leaving the "Prince of Punk" in his past, he remained a consistent contender for the Cruiserweight Championship.

SHANE MCMAHON

HT: 6'2"   **WT: 236 lbs.**   **FROM: Greenwich, Connecticut**   **SIGNATURE MOVE: Coast-To-Coast**

Most individuals would collapse under the pressure of being the son of a famous father. This dynamic figure thrives on it. Shane McMahon dreamed of one day following in the extraordinary path walked by his father, grandfather, and great grandfather in the amazing world of sports-entertainment. It was commonplace in the McMahon household for Shane to share a meal or conversation with the pioneers and legends of the business. His childhood experiences were unique as he carried the bags of Superstars from the locker room and appeared in WWE merchandise catalogues. As an adolescent, Shane spent school vacations and summers stocking the company warehouse, and was a member of the ring crew as well as a referee and an announcer.

After he graduated from Boston University in 1993, Shane furthered his experience into the various levels of World Wrestling Entertainment business. The fourth generation McMahon needed to work harder than everyone else and studied the intricacies of television production, sales, marketing, and international business development. In 1998 he was a driving force in the company's new exploration into the world of digital media and led the team that launched WWE.com, which today exceeds 14.5 million monthly unique visitors worldwide.

TITLE HISTORY	
EUROPEAN CHAMPION	*Defeated X-Pac on February 15, 1999*
HARDCORE CHAMPION	*1 Time*

This time in Shane's career brought about interesting circumstances. While he was building an impressive resumé amongst the top professionals in the industry, he also began to entertain audiences in the ring as well as became a creative contributor. As the rivalry between his father and Stone Cold Steve Austin defined the Attitude Era, Shane was often involved in defending the McMahon name and adopted the alias, Shane-O-Mac. While he later became a critical member of the Corporation, he made history on the February 15, 1999 episode of *Monday Night Raw* when he became the first McMahon to capture a WWE championship by covering X-Pac for the European title. Shane battled with X-Pac for the European prize and though he held the European Championship for almost two months, he retired it on an episode of *Sunday Night Heat.* While he continued to appear in the corners of his associates and as a special guest referee, Shane mixed it up in the ring with the likes of Triple H, Mankind, Ken Shamrock, and Test. The master of the Greenwich Street Fight ended 1999 by winning the prestigious Rookie of the Year Award from *Pro Wrestling Illustrated.*

WCW Under New Ownership

In 2001 Shane rocked the foundation of sports-entertainment when he announced that he purchased the shares of rival World Championship Wrestling (WCW). The brash McMahon rode that momentum into the granddaddy of them all and beat his father at *WrestleMania X-7* in a Street Fight. Shortly after Shane led the invasion of WWE and came extremely close to ruling the world of sports-entertainment.

In 2003 he returned to the public eye in the wake of his father's match with Hulk Hogan at *WrestleMania XIX.* That July he began his tenure as Executive Vice President of WWE Global Media, overseeing international TV distribution, live event bookings, digital media, consumer

SHARMELL 🇺🇸

Formerly a member of WCW's Nitro Girls dance team, Sharmell waited four years after WCW closed its doors before making her WWE debut in 2005. Once she got there, she quickly made up for lost time, stopping at nothing to ensure a victory for her man, Booker T.

While she certainly wasn't known for her in-ring prowess, Sharmell did manage to land a match on the biggest card of 2006. At *WrestleMania 22*, she teamed with Booker to battle Boogeyman in a Handicap Match. The loving couple not only walked away with the loss that night, but Sharmell also left the event with a lingering taste of worms in her mouth.

Sharmell failed to let the *WrestleMania 22* defeat derail her man. The following month, she lead him to victory in the *King of the Ring* tournament, which was immediately followed by a World Heavyweight Championship victory over Rey Mysterio at *The Great American Bash*.

Shawn Michaels (see page 310)

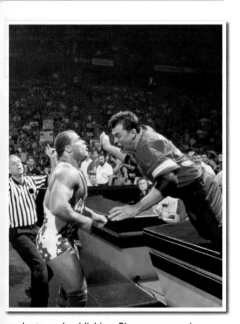

Shane avenged Kane's senseless attack on his mother, Linda, in a Last Man Standing Match at Unforgiven and in the first-ever Ambulance Match at Survivor Series.

products, and publishing. Shane once again performed multiple tasks as he wiped the mat with Eric Bischoff at *SummerSlam*, and danced with Chris Jericho.

Just as his father took WWE from a regional operation to a national enterprise recognized around the world, Shane expanded WWE's global business and contributed to its North American success. While honoring the legacies of those before him, Shane was dedicated to blazing his own trail into the annals of sports-entertainment. With the additional responsibilities behind the scenes, Shane was rarely seen on television, but he found the time to help his family when The Legacy caused problems for the McMahons throughout 2008 and 2009. Shane left WWE in January 2010 in order to pursue other business opportunities.

SHEAMUS

HT: 6'4" **WT:** 267 lbs. **FROM:** Dublin, Ireland
SIGNATURE MOVE: High Cross

TITLE HISTORY	
UNITED STATES CHAMPION	*Defeated Daniel Bryan on March 14, 2011*
WWE CHAMPION (2 TIME)	*Defeated John Cena on December 13, 2009* *Won a Fatal 4-Way Match on June 20, 2010*
WORLD HEAVYWEIGHT CHAMPION	*Defeated Daniel Bryan on April 1, 2012*

Over the course of his relatively young career, Sheamus has created a legacy that would make most veterans envious. Since debuting in 2009, the Celtic Warrior has already staked claim to the WWE Championship, United States Championship and King of the Ring crown. And he's not done yet.

After a few months of annihilating ECW's locker room, Sheamus moved to *Raw*, where he truly began to shine. In September, he won a Battle Royal to earn an opportunity at John Cena's WWE Championship at *WWE TLC*. Competing in a Tables Match, the Great White sent Cena sailing through an unforgiving table to claim his first WWE Title.

As the first-ever Irish born WWE Champion, Sheamus proudly defended the gold for two months before losing at *Elimination Chamber*. But it wouldn't be long before the fiery-haired Superstar would stake claim to the gold once again. In June 2010, he turned back Cena, Edge and Randy Orton to become a two-time titlist.

Sheamus continued to cement his place in history when he defeated John Morrison in the finals of a 16-Superstar tournament to become *King of the Ring*. The win placed him in an elite fraternity with other past Kings, including Bret Hart, Steve Austin and Triple H.

In March 2011, Sheamus defeated Daniel Bryan for the U.S. Championship. During his reign, he was drafted from *Raw* to *SmackDown*, where he evolved into one of WWE's most popular Superstars.

Having firmly cemented himself as a fan favorite, Sheamus carried his momentum from the previous year into the 2012 Royal Rumble, where he outlasted 29 other competitors to add yet another milestone to his ever-expanding career résumé.

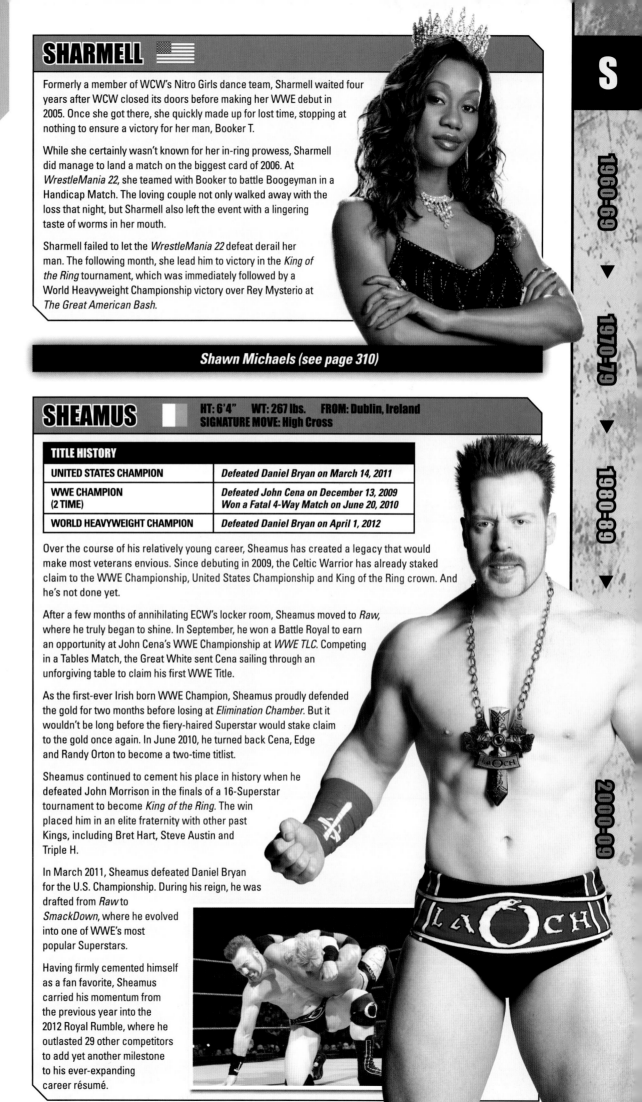

SHAWN MICHAELS

HT: 6'1" **WT: 225 lbs.** **FROM: San Antonio, Texas** **SIGNATURE MOVE: Sweet Chin Music**

TITLE HISTORY

EUROPEAN CHAMPION	*Defeated British Bulldog on September 20, 1997*
INTERCONTINENTAL CHAMPION (3 TIMES)	*Defeated British Bulldog on October 27, 1992* *Defeated Marty Jannetty on June 6, 1993* *Defeated Jeff Jarrett on July 23, 1995*
WORLD HEAVYWEIGHT CHAMPION	*Won an Elimination Chamber Match on November 17, 2002*
WORLD TAG TEAM CHAMPION (5 TIMES)	*Partnered with Diesel to defeat The Headshrinkers on August 28, 1994* *Partnered with Diesel to defeat Owen Hart & Yokozuna on September 24, 1995* *Partnered with Stone Cold Steve Austin to defeat Owen Hart & Davey Boy Smith on May 25, 1997* *Partnered with John Cena to defeat Edge & Randy Orton on January 29, 2007* *Partnered with Triple H to defeat Chris Jericho & Big Show on December 13, 2009*
WWE CHAMPION (3 TIMES)	*Defeated Bret Hart on March 31, 1996* *Defeated Sid on January 19, 1997* *Defeated Bret Hart on November 9, 1997*
WWE TAG TEAM CHAMPION	*Partnered with Triple H to defeat Chris Jericho & Big Show on December 13, 2009*

In a world where nicknames get thrown around fairly liberally, Shawn Michaels has earned many monikers that can never be disputed: "The Showstopper." "The Headliner." "The Main Event." "The Icon." "Mr. *WrestleMania*."

Shawn Michaels and his tag team partner, Marty Jannetty, first appeared in WWE in 1987. Known as the Midnight Rockers, the high-flying duo had grand visions of taking over WWE's tag team scene. WWE, however, saw things a bit differently, as they fired the team after only two weeks. Michaels & Jannetty never gave up on their dream of competing for WWE. The following year, they were given another opportunity. This time, they took advantage of the situation. After dropping the word "Midnight" from their name, the Rockers took WWE by storm, proving themselves as true tag team specialists.

Barber Shop Break-Up

By 1992, Michaels believed his union with Jannetty was holding him back from true greatness. So he severed their relationship in one of the most memorable scenes in WWE history. While guests on Brutus Beefcake's *Barber Shop*, Michaels superkicked Jannetty straight through a window. The kick marked the end of the popular tag team and the beginning of an iconic singles career.

On his own, the egotistical Michaels adopted the nickname "The Heartbreak Kid." With Sensational Sherri by his side stroking his ego, HBK went on an unbelievable tear that saw him capture his first WWE title when he defeated British Bulldog for the Intercontinental Championship in October 1992. The win over Bulldog marked the first of three Intercontinental Championship reigns for Michaels. Over the course of these reigns, HBK competed in some of WWE's most athletic and dangerous encounters, including the landmark *WrestleMania X* Ladder Match against Razor Ramon. With each passing match, it became more obvious that he was destined for greatness.

A Childhood Dream Realized

In January 1996, he last eliminated Diesel to become a back-to-back *Royal Rumble* winner. The victory put HBK back in the main event of *WrestleMania* and gave him the opportunity to accomplish his boyhood dream of becoming WWE Champion. At *WrestleMania XII*, he faced Bret "Hit Man" Hart in a grueling 60-minute Iron Man Match that required sudden-death overtime to deliver a conclusive winner. Michaels scored the win after landing Sweet Chin Music and became WWE Champion.

In 1997, Michaels teamed with longtime friend Triple H to form the most controversial faction in WWE history, D-Generation X. Together, HBK and Triple H spat in the face of authority while their unparalleled popularity set the bar for all future factions. As a member of DX, HBK captured the European Championship, making him the first-ever Grand Slam Champion in WWE history (he held the WWE, Intercontinental, World Tag Team, and European titles during his career), but it was a WWE Championship victory over Bret Hart at *Survivor Series 1997* that will be forever remembered for its controversial conclusion. With Hart caught in a Sharpshooter, the referee called for the bell, despite the fact that the "Hit Man" never submitted. The "Montreal Incident" remains arguably the most infamous event in WWE history.

Retirement?
No, Rejuvenation!

Back injuries forced Michaels into early retirement in 1998. During this time, he became a spiritual person, which helped him overcome his personal demons. He also used this time to rest his battered back. By 2002, a reinvigorated HBK had the itch to compete again.

When he returned, Michaels found himself embedded in a bloody rivalry against former friend Triple H. Amazingly, he showed no sign of ring rust, defeating "The Game" at *SummerSlam 2002*. A few months later, Michaels last eliminated Triple H in an unforgiving Elimination Chamber Match that saw HBK claim the World Heavyweight Championship.

Over the next several years, the renewed Michaels worked effortlessly to recreate the magic of his earlier years. In typical HBK fashion, he found himself in the spotlight of WWE's biggest matches, including his match at *WrestleMania XXIV* where he sent Ric Flair into retirement. Michaels spent the rest of 2008 battling Flair's former protégé, Batista, then engaging Chris Jericho in an incredibly personal rivalry that saw Michaels thrown through the Jeritron 6000. HBK ended the year in a financial hole and was forced to work for JBL until he defeated the former world champion in an All or Nothing Match at 2009's *No Way Out*.

The Showstopper's final steps into the Hall of Fame

Shawn Michaels looked back on his historic career, then pondered his future, and realized only one thing remained for him to do: defeat Undertaker at *WrestleMania*. At *WrestleMania XXV* HBK and "The Deadman" engaged in a spectacular contest. Though HBK came within inches of victory, he failed to end Undertaker's undefeated *WrestleMania* streak.

Michaels took some time away from WWE after the loss; however, when longtime friend and D-Generation X cohort Triple H needed a partner to take on The Legacy at *SummerSlam*, he sought out HBK. Triple H found him working in a cafeteria, and worked to convince him to return to the ring. The reformed D-Generation X stayed together through the summer and fall, and managed to capture the Unified Tag Team Championship. During his time as Tag Team Champion, Shawn Michaels reconciled with Bret Hart, healing a wound ripped open nearly fifteen years earlier in Montreal.

After D-Generation X lost the Tag Team titles, Michaels demanded a rematch with Undertaker at *WrestleMania XXVI*. In order to secure the match, Michaels put his career on the line. With no disqualifications, and no count-outs, the battle lines were drawn for a "Streak vs. Career" Match. Michaels was unable to overcome three Tombstone Piledrivers and the man known as "Mr. WrestleMania" lost his final match as a Superstar in the WWE. Less than 24 hours later, "The Heartbreak Kid" gave a touching farewell on *Raw*.

On the eve of *WrestleMania XXVII*, in front of a capacity crowd, Shawn Michaels' brilliant, quarter-century career was recognized with induction into the WWE Hall of Fame. Always the "Showstopper" Michaels and Triple H surprised the WWE Universe with a reunion of the Kliq when Kevin Nash and X-Pac joined them on stage. While his competetive days are behind him, Shawn Michaels still makes appearances on WWE programming to the delight of his fans worldwide. In 2012, Shawn Michaels became involved in another *WrestleMania* match involving the Undertaker. At *WrestleMania XXVIII*, "The Heartbreak Kid" donned a striped shirt and officiated the match that became known as the "End of an Era" when Undertaker defeated Triple H in a Hell In A Cell Match.

THE SHEIK

HT: 5'11" WT: 250 lbs.
FROM: The Syrian Desert

A true pioneer of hardcore wrestling, The Sheik left a legacy that fans are reminded of every time a Superstar breaks a table or swings a flaming baseball bat. Considered by many as the father of extreme, many believe there never would have been an ECW without his vicious vision.

TITLE HISTORY

U.S.A. HEAVYWEIGHT CHAMPION (2 TIMES)	Defeated Bobo Brazil on September 22, 1967 Defeated Bobo Brazil on January 20, 1969

Using anything he could get his hands on as a weapon, The Sheik made a name for himself competing in Detroit, Toronto, and Japan. While wrestling in the Midwest, he began a bitter rivalry with Bobo Brazil, which lasted more than thirty years. Over the course of their bloody rivalry, The Sheik captured the now-defunct WWE U.S.A. Heavyweight Championship twice.

Amazingly, The Sheik managed to wrestle into the 1990s, despite already celebrating his seventieth birthday. The twilight of his hardcore career saw him compete in many classic ECW encounters against Kevin Sullivan and Tazz, who would later go on to become a heated rival of Sabu, The Sheik's nephew. In 2007, The Sheik's innovative approach to hardcore competition was recognized with induction into the WWE Hall of Fame.

SHELTON BENJAMIN

HT: 6'2" WT: 248 lbs.
FROM: Orangeburg, South Carolina
SIGNATURE MOVE: T-Bone Suplex

Shelton Benjamin claims to be sports-entertainment's "Gold Standard." By looking at his in-ring exploits and championships résumé, it's hard to argue against that claim. After refusing to fall into the dangerous drug scene of Orangeburg, SC, Benjamin attended the University of Minnesota, where he became a national amateur wrestling powerhouse. Following graduation, he parlayed his college success into a WWE contract, thus fulfilling a lifelong dream of becoming a WWE Superstar.

TITLE HISTORY

INTERCONTINENTAL CHAMPION (3 TIMES)	Defeated Chris Jericho on October 19, 2004 Defeated Ric Flair on February 20, 2006 Defeated Rob Van Dam on May 15, 2006
UNITED STATES CHAMPION	Defeated Matt Hardy on July 20, 2008
WWE TAG TEAM CHAMPION (2 TIMES)	Partnered with Charlie Haas to defeat Los Guerreros on February 6, 2003 Partnered with Charlie Haas to defeat Eddie Guerrero & Tajiri on July 3, 2003

Alongside partner Charlie Haas, Benjamin debuted in December 2002 as a part of the powerful Team Angle faction. In less than two months, Benjamin & Haas proved their dominance, defeating Los Guerreros for the WWE Tag Team Championship. Dubbing themselves as "The World's Greatest Tag Team," they would go on to capture the titles one more time before the WWE Draft sent Benjamin to *Raw*, which forced the athletic tandem to split.

With a shocking victory over Triple H in his debut match, Benjamin's *Raw* career had an electric start. The victory put the newcomer on the map as one of the brand's top singles stars. It also opened the eyes of many WWE fans, who voted Benjamin into *Taboo Tuesday*'s Intercontinental Championship Match. Taking full advantage of the opportunity, Benjamin defeated Chris Jericho to capture his first WWE singles title.

In November 2007, following an impressive *Raw* career, Benjamin jumped to ECW. Benjamin used his time in ECW to cement his status as one of history's most athletic competitors. His breathtaking efforts in the *WrestleMania XXIV* Money in the Bank Ladder Match will live on highlight reels for generations to come.

Just when it seemed Benjamin was hitting his ECW stride, the 2008 WWE Draft once again sent the Superstar packing. In typical Shelton Benjamin fashion, however, he refused to be deterred by the move. Within one month of his debut, Benjamin defeated Matt Hardy to claim the United States Championship.

Over the years, Benjamin developed a swagger. He combined unparalleled athleticism, ring technique, and a penchant for making powerful first impressions. Benjamin also became a favorite of spectators during the *Money In The Bank* contests as he took the concept of in-ring flight to new levels.

SHERRI MARTEL

HT: 5'7"   FROM: New Orleans, Louisiana   SIGNATURE MOVE: Sleeper

TITLE HISTORY

WOMEN'S CHAMPION	*Defeated Fabulous Moolah on July 24, 1987*

World Wrestling Entertainment turned "Sensational" when Sherri debuted on July 24, 1987 and pinned her mentor, the Fabulous Moolah, for the WWE Women's Championship. As champion, Sherri successfully defended her crown for over 15 months against challengers such as Velvet McIntyre, Angie Minelli, Desiree Peterson, and Debbie Combs. Sherri also continued to battle Moolah and the two captained opposing teams at the first *Survivor Series*. She was finally dethroned in October 1988 in Paris, France by Rockin' Robin.

Sherri transitioned to managing some of WWE's most infamous rule-breakers in the early 1990s. Her first client was Randy "Macho Man" Savage. When he pinned "King Hacksaw" Jim Duggan, Savage became a King and Sherri, his Queen. In 1991 "Million Dollar Man" Ted DiBiase enlisted her expert services and later a new bad boy signed her, "The Heartbreak Kid" Shawn Michaels. In 1993, Sherri left WWE.

Later in the year and into 1994, she toured the independent circuit. That spring, she signed a contract with WCW and became "Sensuous" Sherri at the side of "Nature Boy" Ric Flair in his war against Sting and Hulk Hogan. Later she became "Sister" Sherri and guided Harlem Heat to an amazing seven World Tag Team Championship reigns before leaving the company in the summer of 1997.

In 2005, she returned to WWE on *SmackDown* during the Shawn Michaels/Kurt Angle conflict. On April 1, 2006, the 30 year career of the girl whose dream began with a ring of a bell in a barn was celebrated as she was inducted into the WWE Hall of Fame by DiBiase.

Sadly, Sherri passed away in June 2007 while visiting her mother in Alabama. This pioneer was as tough as nails, but those around her remember her for her big heart. Sensational Sherri is the only woman to ever hold both AWA and WWE Women's titles and was a legitimate force in-and-out of the ring. She was the forerunner to the WWE Divas of today and her legacy lives on through them. DiBiase described her—and all who knew her remember her—as "truly priceless."

SHOHEI "GIANT" BABA

HT: 6'10"   WT: 310 lbs.   FROM: Sanjo, Nigata, Japan
SIGNATURE MOVE: Running Yakuza Kick

When a shoulder injury ended his baseball career, Giant Baba looked to make a name for himself in the ring. In 1959 he trained alongside Antonio Inoki with the founding father of *puroresu*, Rikidozan. Both future legends debuted in September, 1959 and dominated the Japanese scene for the next thirty years. He debuted in WWE in 1964, challenging Champion Bruno Sammartino for the Heavyweight Championship.

Over the next decade, Baba competed against the biggest names in sports-entertainment all over the world. In December 1974, Baba defeated Jack Brisco to become the first-ever Japanese NWA Heavyweight Champion. Baba made history in 1975 when he faced Bruno Sammartino in a "Champion vs. Champion" bout marking the first time the WWE Championship was defended in Japan.

In January 1990 Vince McMahon appeared at an All-Japan event at Korauken Hall and announced a Wrestling Summit at Tokyo's Egg Dome featuring WWE, and the biggest names in Japan. Baba was instrumental in co-promoting shows with WWE in Japan and teamed with Andre The Giant to defeat Demolition.

On January 31, 1999 this legend passed away days after his 61st birthday. Shohei "Giant" Baba was one of sports-entertainment's leading ambassadors and brightest stars who was honored by all those who knew him in Japan and around the world.

SHOWDOWN AT SHEA

Showdown At Shea was a series of three supercards held at Shea Stadium. Each event had at least two title matches, while the undercard was filled with the biggest names in wrestling.

September 30, 1972

Main Event	WWE Champion Pedro Morales and Bruno Sammartino battled to a draw (curfew)

June 25, 1976

Main Event	Andre the Giant defeated Chuck Wepner via countout in a Wrestler vs. Boxer Match Antonio Inoki fought Muhammad Ali to a draw in a Wrestler versus Boxer Match

August 9, 1980

Main Event	Bruno Sammartino defeated Larry Zbyszko in a Steel Cage Match

SID JUSTICE 🇺🇸

HT: 6'8" **WT:** 320 lbs.
FROM: West Memphia, Arkansas
SIGNATURE MOVE: Powerbomb

TITLE HISTORY	
WWE CHAMPION	*Defeated Shawn Michaels on November 17, 1996* *Defeated Bret Hart on February 17, 1997*

An early master of the chokeslam and powerbomb, this monster first appeared in WCW as Sid Vicious. Shortly after his 1991 debut in WWE as Sid Justice, he was announced as the special guest referee for the main event match at *SummerSlam 1991*. While he appeared to be on the side of Hulk Hogan, fans caught a glimpse of his true nature at the 1992 *Royal Rumble* when he eliminated Hogan in hopes of capturing the WWE Championship. They met at *WrestleMania VIII* as part of the double main event. After the encounter, Sid abruptly left WWE and soon returned to World Championship Wrestling.

In 1995 he resurfaced as Sycho Sid, the new bodyguard for Shawn Michaels. After a mishap cost his boss the WWE Championship, Sid attacked Michaels the next night on *Raw* when he was told his services were no longer needed. After his tenure with Ted DiBiase's Million Dollar Corporation, Sid was not seen in WWE again until June 1996. He patched things up with HBK and teamed with him and Ahmed Johnson against Camp Cornette. Sid captured the WWE Championship on two different occassions, but his second reign ended at the hands of Undertaker at *WrestleMania 13*. Sid departed WWE in 1996, then shocked the sports-entertainment world in 1998 when he stopped in ECW before going to World Championship Wrestling, where he held different championships. Although a horrific injury halted his career for a few years, he has been a fixture on the independent scene since 2004.

SIM SNUKA 🇬🇧🇫🇯

HT: 6'1" **WT:** 234 lbs.
FROM: The Fiji Islands

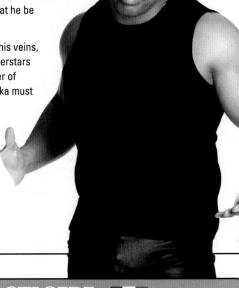

Following a successful run with partner Domino in *SmackDown*'s tag-team division, Deuce was shipped to *Raw* in June 2008, via the annual WWE Draft Lottery. Upon arrival, the new *Raw* Superstar revealed that he was the son of WWE Hall of Famer Jimmy "Superfly" Snuka and demanded that he be recognized by his real name, Sim Snuka.

With decades of sports-entertainment history flowing through his veins, Snuka yearned to join forces with other multi-generational Superstars Cody Rhodes, Ted DiBiase, Manu and Randy Orton as a member of Legacy. But as leader of the elite faction, Orton demanded Snuka must first pass a series of tests in order to gain entry.

Snuka ultimately failed to pass Orton's tests, and as a result, was denied a spot in Legacy. A frustrated Snuka attempted to exact revenge on Orton, but was ultimately thwarted by Rhodes and DiBiase.

Snuka's presence on WWE television diminished greatly following his bid to join Legacy. And in June 2009, the second-generation Superstar was released from his WWE contract.

SIMON DEAN 🇺🇸

HT: 5'10" **WT:** 210 lbs.
FROM: Clearwater, Florida
SIGNATURE MOVE: Simonizer

Fitness guru Simon Dean first began shilling his Simon System to WWE viewers in late 2004. Decked out in bright purple, the annoying salesman claimed his "patented" system could transform any couch potato into a lean, mean, fighting machine.

Despite purchasing valuable advertising time on WWE television, Dean's infomercials failed to turn the Simon System into a profitable product. As sales for the system sank, so did Dean's career. It wasn't long before the unsuccessful salesman began losing to nearly every Superstar he faced, including Gunnar Scott, Tatanka and the dress-wearing Vito.

Realizing his in-ring career wasn't taking off like he hoped, Dean turned to managing in 2006. Unfortunately, however, his protégés, the Gymini, were just as unsuccessful in the ring as he was. Dean finally walked away from the ring completely later that year.

SIN CARA 🇲🇽

HT: 5'7" **WT:** 180 lbs.
FROM: Mexico City, Mexico
SIGNATURE MOVE: Moonsault Side Slam

Sin Cara made his WWE debut in the spring of 2011, following nearly 15 years of cementing himself as a lucha libre legend in Mexico. The WWE Universe quickly became enamored by the masked man from Mexico City and his high-flying offense.

Over the next few months, Sin Cara picked up big victories over the likes of Sheamus, Jack Swagger and Daniel Bryan. Despite his success, the Superstar mysteriously stated that he needed to be more aggressive.

The comment seemed uncharacteristic of the Sin Cara the WWE Universe learned to love. But as weeks passed, it was revealed that there was a Sin Cara imposter, which made it impossible for fans to detect which one was real.

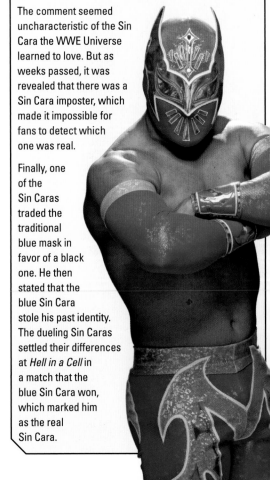

Finally, one of the Sin Caras traded the traditional blue mask in favor of a black one. He then stated that the blue Sin Cara stole his past identity. The dueling Sin Caras settled their differences at *Hell in a Cell* in a match that the blue Sin Cara won, which marked him as the real Sin Cara.

SIR OLIVER HUMPERDINK

With his long red beard, bright flowing hair and outrageously colored suits, Sir Oliver Humperdink became one of the game's most easily recognized managers. While his WWE timeline only spanned one year, Humperdink's flamboyant persona left a lasting impression that will be remembered for generations.

His biggest win as a manager came when he was awarded the services of Bam Bam Bigelow in 1987. Bigelow was easily the largest Superstar in Humperdink's stable, which also housed Hall of Famer "Mr. Wonderful" Paul Orndorff. In November 1987, Humperdink led his duo into action in the first-ever *Survivor Series* pay-per-view main event. Bigelow & Orndorff teamed with WWE Champion Hulk Hogan, Don Muraco, & Ken Patera to take on Andre the Giant, Rick Rude, Butch Reed, One Man Gang, & King Kong Bundy. Andre last eliminated Bigelow to pick up the victory for his squad. By 1988, Humperdink had left WWE in favor of a managerial career in the NWA. While there, he guided the careers of the Fabulous Freebirds, among others.

SIVI AFI

HT: 5'11" **WT:** 248 lbs. **FROM:** The Isle of Samoa
SIGNATURE MOVE: High Cross Body

Claiming to be the cousin of WWE Hall of Famer Jimmy "Superfly" Snuka, Sivi Afi made his debut appearance on WWE television in January 1986, defeating the masked Gladiator. Like Snuka, Afi competed barefoot and employed a dizzying style of high-flying offense.

In the months following his debut, Afi successfully turned back such Superstars as Rene Goulet, Moondog Spot and Paul Roma. But as the calendar approached 1987, the Samoan Superstar's luck began to sink. Honky Tonk Man, Randy "Macho Man" Savage, Harley Race and a host of others regularly defeated the bewildered Afi.

Afi became recognized as a Samoan High Chief in 1988. With the acknowledgement came the traditional tribal tattoos indicative of such lofty status, as well as a new attitude. With Bobby "The Brain" Heenan serving as his manager, High Chief Afi briefly joined Tama and Haku as a member of the hated Islanders.

Following his WWE career, Afi worked as a Hollywood stuntman and a celebrity bodyguard.

SKANDOR AKBAR

HT: 6'2" **WT:** 242 lbs.
SIGNATURE MOVE: Camel Clutch

General Skandor Akbar competed professionally for nearly 15 years, including a brief WWE run in the late 1970s, but will forever be remembered for his decades of managerial service to some of the greatest names to ever run through the South.

Akbar's blatant disregard for the rules propelled him to become one of World Class Championship Wrestling's most hated personalities. But he didn't care; his rebellious style, which included the dangerous use of fireballs, resulted in wins for his stable of Superstars, which he affectionately referred to as Devastation, Inc. It also resulted in threats on his life, which required the detested manager to often wear a bullet-proof vest while accompanying his Superstars to the ring.

Over the course of his legendary managerial career, Akbar lead the way for some of history's top draws, including WWE Hall of Famer Abdullah the Butcher, King Kong Bundy, "Dr. Death" Steve Williams and a mysteriously-masked phenom known as The Punisher.

SKINNER

HT: 6'0" **WT:** 215 lbs. **FROM:** The Everglades
SIGNATURE MOVE: Gatorbreaker

Skinner emerged from the sawgrass prairies of one of the world's most diverse eco-regions as a man who survived dangerous encounters with the dangerous predators that inhabit the Everglades.

Skinner entered WWE in 1991 and he immediately set to taking down Superstars like he did alligators back in Florida. Audiences witnessed Skinner brawl with Undertaker, Tatanka, Crush, Sid, Ultimate Warrior, and Mr. Perfect. Although Skinner was a contender for both the Intercontinental and WWE Championships he was not interested in material prizes. His trophy was taking something from a fallen opponent and keeping it to show his superior fighting skill.

In 1993 Skinner returned to the Everglades and his familiar wild surroundings. He reappeared in October 2005 for *WWE Raw Homecoming* and then again in 2007 for the *Raw 15th Anniversary*. Skinner remains one of WWE's most unusual Superstars nearly two decades after his debut.

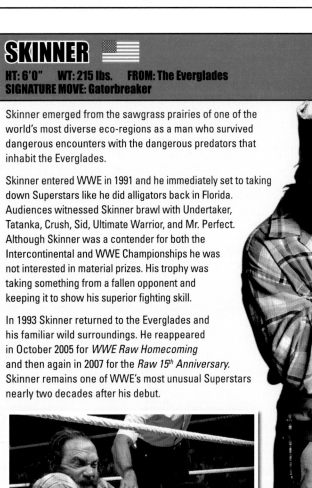

SKULL MURPHY

HT: 6'1" **WT:** 265 lbs. **FROM:** Hamilton, Ontario, Canada
SIGNATURE MOVE: Heart Punch

TITLE HISTORY	
UNITED STATES TAG TEAM CHAMPION	*Partnered with Brute Bernard to defeat Buddy Austin & the Great Scott on May 16, 1963*

Long before Stone Cold Steve Austin made the bald head a widely recognized fashion of the ring, John Joseph Murphy proudly sported the hairless cranium. The Canadian Superstar, however, didn't have much of a choice, as a childhood disease left him permanently hairless. Murphy chose to embrace the unique trait, though; he even adopted the moniker "Skull."

As Skull Murphy, the bald Superstar became one of the ring's most hated personalities during the 1950s and 1960s. Utilizing a devastating heart punch, Murphy was able to claim many NWA singles titles, but it was in the tag team ranks that he gained his greatest notoriety.

As a 14-time tag team titlist, Murphy was accustomed to wearing gold around his waist. His most prestigious victory came in May 1963 when he teamed with Brute Bernard to defeat Buddy Austin & Great Scott for the United States Tag Team Championship. They held the titles for six months before being unseated by WWE Hall of Famers Killer Kowalski & Gorilla Monsoon.

SKY LOW LOW

HT: 3'7" **WT:** 86 lbs.
FROM: Montreal, Quebec, Canada
SIGNATURE MOVE: Hanging Vertical Suplex

Always in impeccable physical condition, Sky Low Low was revered as "the Little Atlas of the Wrestling World." His performances became legendary; he fought in front of Queen Elizabeth of the United Kingdom and King Farouk of Egypt. Sky Low Low amazed fans by standing on top of his head without using his hands for balance.

Sky Low Low's mixture of strength, speed, and devilish tactics brought him great success in the ring. He was the first-ever NWA Midget World Champion, capturing the title in 1949. He made his WWE debut in 1963, where he battled the likes of Little Beaver, Farmer Pete, Tiny Tim, Pancho Lopez, The Jamaica Kid, Irish Jackie and Cowboy Bradley.

His career continued for decades, reaching the Hulkamania era. He even appeared in the classic Mixed-Tag Match at *WrestleMania III*. Sadly in November 1998 this sports-entertainment pioneer passed away. Sky Low Low was a special type of performer with an endless imagination that always brought audiences to their feet.

SKIP SHEFFIELD

HT: 6'4" **WT:** 291 lbs.
FROM: College Station, Texas
SIGNATURE MOVE: Running Lariat

As a Rookie on the first season of *NXT*, Skip Sheffield became known as the Cornfed Meathead, who goes to the ring full throttle. And his combination of muscle and hustle coupled with his signature catchphrase "yep, yep, yep, what it do," proved that Sheffield knew wins and putting smiles on fans' faces were equal parts of the job.

In the summer of 2010, Sheffield joined his fellow *NXT* Rookies in the creation of one of WWE's most feared factions, Nexus. As a member of the renegade group, Sheffield shelved his fun-loving side in favor of a more ruthless brand of domination. Alongside leader Wade Barrett, the Texas native took part in systematically dismantling WWE's foundation, including brutal attacks on Chairman Mr. McMahon, Hall of Famer Ricky "The Dragon" Steamboat and Superstar John Cena.

Sheffield headlined *SummerSlam 2010* when he teamed with his Nexus cohorts to battle Team WWE in an Elimination Tag Team Match. During the contest, he eliminated both John Morrison and R-Truth before ultimately exiting at the hands of Edge.

SLAM MASTER J

HT: 5'9" **WT:** 210 lbs. **FROM:** The ATL

Representing the ATL, or Atlanta to most people, Slam Master J spent the majority of his brief *SmackDown* career trying to impress Cryme Tyme. Hoping he would get to roll with JTG and Shad, Slam Master set out on a crusade to prove he was street tough. His antics included vandalizing Theodore Long's office, stealing DVDs and generally speaking in an urban vernacular incomprehensible by anybody within earshot.

Sporting a skull cap and oversized jeans, Slam Master J made his *SmackDown* in-ring debut against Charlie Haas in the summer of 2009. He picked up the impressive win over the former tag champ, but was unable to keep the momentum going, as he followed the victory up with disappointing performances against Dolph Ziggler and Kane.

Hoping his family's history of success in tag-team competition would rub off (his father is Terry Gordy of the Fabulous Freebirds), Slam Master formed a partnership with Jimmy Wang Yang in late 2009. The odd pairing, however, failed to mirror the Freebirds' success. Slam Master J was gone from WWE soon after.

THE SLAMMY AWARDS

Much like the television industry does with the popular Emmy Awards, WWE rewards excellence in sports-entertainment with their annual Slammy Awards. The prestigious awards ceremony, which was created by the Academy of Wrestling Arts & Science, can be traced all the way back to 1986. The inaugural ceremony focused largely on the musical efforts on *The Wrestling Album*. The night's big winner was Junkyard Dog, who walked away with the award for Best Single Performer.

The following year, the Slammys altered its categories to include the mat, as well as music. In the end, few remembered the winners and losers. Instead, the 1987 Slammy Awards are mainly remembered for Mr. McMahon's now-embarrassing rendition of *Stand Back*. McMahon's musical act almost single-handedly sent the Slammys into a nine-year hiatus. When it finally returned in 1996, however, some of WWE's all-time greatest names walked away with golden statuettes, including Shawn Michaels, Bret Hart, and Freddie Blassie, who was honored with the Lifetime Achievement Award.

In 1997, Arnold Skaaland followed Blassie's lead when he too was given the Lifetime Achievement Award. Other 1997 winners include Rocky Maivia for Best Sensation and Sable for Best Dressed and Miss Slammy. Following the 1997 ceremony, The Slammy Awards took another hiatus, but the prestigious honor returned in 2008. For the first time ever, the new millennium version of the Slammys included fan voting on WWE.com.

SLICK

While his academic record may dispute it, Slick arrived in WWE in 1986 claiming to be a doctor. A "Doctor of Style," that is. The impeccably dressed manager introduced himself to WWE audiences when he dipped into his "pockets of green" to purchase half interest in the legendary "Classy" Freddie Blassie's stable of Superstars. The innovative merger gave the newcomer instant credibility, as he was thrust into the spotlight alongside such greats as Iron Sheik and Nikolai Volkoff. He eventually added Butch Reed to his list of clients before finally assuming full ownership of Blassie's crop. Within months, the "Doctor of Style" assembled one of the most dominant forces in WWE.

Always looking to make a buck, Slick became a popular recording artist in 1987. With his hit single, *Jive Soul Bro*, Slick attempted to convince everybody that he was an honest man. His claims fell on deaf ears among the fans of WWE.

In the early 1990s, Slick took an unexpected leave of absence from WWE. When he returned, the normally fast-talking manager was barely recognizable. Instead of his traditional claims of greatness, the manager presented a more reserved personality. Renamed Reverend Slick, he preached the importance of good over evil.

SmackDown (see page 318)

SMASHER SLOAN

 WT: 275 lbs.
FROM: Butte, Montana

TITLE HISTORY

UNITED STATES TAG TEAM CHAMPION	*Partnered with Baron Mikel Scicluna to defeat Antonio Pugliese & Johnny Valentine on September 22, 1966*

Son of wrestler Whitey Whitler, Smasher Sloan made his professional debut in 1965. Shortly after becoming a pro, the second-generation Superstar teamed with Baron Mikel Scicluna to defeat Johnny Valentine & Antonio Pugliese in controversial fashion to claim the United States Tag Team Championship. They held the titles for two months before losing the gold back to Pugliese and his new tag team partner, Spiros Arion.

After losing the titles, Sloan left WWE to compete in various other North American promotions. When he was unable to recreate the success he found in WWE, he began to compete under a mask using several different monikers, including The Beast.

Sloan made a brief and unsuccessful return to WWE in 1972. Competing mainly as a singles Superstar, he failed to become a legitimate force in the promotion. Sloan retired from wrestling shortly after.

S

1960-69
1970-79
1980-89
1990-99
2000-09
2010-

For more than a decade, *SmackDown* has served as a two-hour, weekly extravaganza where classic rivalries are conceived and Superstars are created. WWE Superstars know that when they step through the blue ropes, they're entering the ring to perform on one of sports-entertainment's brightest stages.

SmackDown made its debut in 1999 as a one-time special but it was such a hit that it became a weekly program. Its first episode featured Big Show, Mankind, the New Age Outlaws, Triple H, The Rock, Stone Cold Steve Austin, and Undertaker.

The title for **SmackDown** *was inspired by one of The Rock's catchphrases; the "Brahma Bull" often referred to* **SmackDown** *as "The Rock's Show."*

In early 2002, WWE underwent a brand division and *SmackDown* became its own entity with exclusive Superstars, championships, management, magazine, announcers, and pay-per-view events. The hit program's strong lineage of leaders includes Stephanie McMahon, Paul Heyman, Kurt Angle, Theodore Long, and Vickie Guerrero.

While initially the Undisputed WWE Champion and Women's Champion were to defend their titles on both shows, then-champion Brock Lesnar defied the decree and made his title exclusive to *SmackDown*. *Raw* created its own title, the World Heavyweight Championship, and the Women's Championship became exclusive to the Monday night program. As a result of the Brand Division, WWE implemented an annual Draft Lottery, where members of their respective rosters could be exchanged.

On April 20, 2007 *SmackDown* celebrated its 400th episode. That October, *SmackDown* and *ECW on Syfy* instituted a talent exchange where Superstars would appear on both brands. The next year was filled with exciting developments, beginning with the

In June, the landscape changed as the Draft Lottery sent Triple H and Jim Ross to Friday nights. It was not long after that Michelle McCool became the first-ever Divas Champion and Tazz joined J.R. at the broadcast booth.

In the spring of 2009 SmackDown aired its 500th episode. The show's decade of dazzling action was honored when WWE Home Video released *The Best of SmackDown 10th Anniversary*. During this time the brand's Superstars put aside their personal differences and, over the next two years, focused on victory over *Raw* at *Bragging Rights*.

In a milestone year, *SmackDown* audiences witnessed incredible confrontations, such as Jeff Hardy battling his brother, Matt, in a Stretcher Match. They also saw D-Generation X, Undertaker and John Cena align against Legacy and CM Punk. The rollercoaster ride of emotions for the fans continued when Batista shockingly turned on his longtime friend, Rey Mysterio who he blamed for a loss in a Fatal 4-Way Match.

During all the years of incredible contests, championship victories, and rivalries one figure embodied the *SmackDown* brand like no one else: "The Rated-R Superstar" Edge. Edge's body of work included thrilling bouts against Undertaker, Big Show, Rey Mysterio, Jeff Hardy, Chris Jericho, and Kane, while often crossing the line between fan favorite and reviled rule-breaker.

In recent years, waves of fresh talent appeared on *SmackDown* including Superstars like Dolph Ziggler, Jack Swagger, Wade Barrett, Cody Rhodes, and Drew McIntyre. Daniel Bryan made arguably the biggest splash in recent memory when he won the Money In The Bank Ladder Match, then cashed it in to claim the World Heavyweight Championship.

Fierce competition is not limited to just the men in the locker room. Starting from the foundation created by female competitors of previous generations, WWE Divas including Mickie James, the Bella Twins, LayCool, Eve, Natalya, Maryse, and Beth Phoenix have added prestige to the Divas division with outstanding in-ring performances.

Audiences also saw the transformation of a Superstar who was always known as the World's Strongest Man. Mark Henry became World Heavyweight Champion fifteen years after his WWE debut. In battles with Randy Orton and Big Show, Mark Henry established himself as one of the most intimidating figures in *SmackDown* history, and created the Hall of Pain.

SmackDown is the second longest running episodic television program in American history. It may have begun as an electrifying catchphrase, but it has become synonymous with Friday night excitement. *SmackDown* is the one of the brightest stages

THE SMOKIN' GUNNS

MEMBERS: Billy, Bart
COMBINED WT: 534 lbs.

TITLE HISTORY

WORLD TAG TEAM CHAMPIONS (3 TIMES)	Defeated 1-2-3 Kid & Bob Holly on January 23, 1995 Defeated Owen Hart & Yokozuna on September 25, 1995 Defeated The Godwinns on May 26, 1996

These cowboys arrived in WWE in 1993 and were an instant sensation. At that year's *King of the Ring* they joined the Steiner Brothers to defeat the Headshrinkers and Money Inc. The Smokin' Gunns climbed the tag team championship ladder while fans everywhere cheered their appearances. At the 1994 *Survivor Series* they joined Lex Luger's "Guts & Glory" team to battle Ted DiBiase's Million Dollar Corporation.

In January 1995 Billy and Bart defeated Bob "Spark Plug" Holly and 1-2-3 Kid to become World Tag Team Champions. Although they lost the belts at *WrestleMania XI*, they regained the titles in September. Unfortunately, Billy suffered a serious neck injury and they were forced to forfeit the belts.

After Billy recovered, the Gunn's refocused their efforts. With an assist from Sunny, the duo won their third World Tag Team Championship from the Godwinns at *In Your House 8: Beware of Dog*. Sunny joined the brothers, adding her considerable experience as a manager to the team. Unfortunately, her presence became a mixed blessing, as she was the cause of infighting between the brothers. They split in October 1996 when Billy walked out on Bart.

SNITSKY

HT: 6'8" **WT:** 307 lbs. **FROM:** Nesquehoning, Pennsylvania
SIGNATURE MOVE: Pump Handle Slam

While this deranged monster was not runway model material, he was perfect for the world of WWE. Well, perfect for himself, but the exact opposite for the audiences he terrified and Superstars he met. In 2004, Snitsky debuted and displayed his sadistic tendencies against the likes of John Cena, Kane, and Big Show. In 2007, he moved to ECW and bludgeoned CM Punk, Balls Mahoney, Matt Striker, and even took Hardcore Holly out of action by breaking his arm. Snitsky lurked in WWE for a few years, but was last seen on *Raw*. He'd often test his ability to harm anyone he encountered. Such behavior gave this monster true pleasure.

SONNY BOY HAYES

HT: 4'6"
WT: 76 lbs.

Sonny Boy Hayes brought experience, toughness and heart to WWE's midget wrestling ranks in 1967. His matches against the likes of Little Beaver, Sky Low Low, Little Boy Blue, Little Tokyo, Lord Littlebrook, Little John, Tiger Jackson, and Butch Cassidy were filled with non-stop action.

While mainly known as a singles competitor, Hayes teamed with Superstars like Cowboy Bradley, Haiti Kid, Farmer Jerome, Tahiti Kid and Poncho Boy. At one time he was a co-holder of the briefly sanctioned NWA Midget World Tag Team Championship with partner Little Louie, which was defended occasionally on WWE cards.

SONNY KING

Sonny King arrived in WWE in 1971 and showed from the start that he was ready for anything. During the early portion of 1972 he teamed up with Chief Jay

TITLE HISTORY

WORLD TAG TEAM CHAMPION	Partnered with Chief Jay Strongbow to defeat Baron Mikel Scicluna & King Curtis on May 22, 1972

Strongbow. In May, 1972 the duo won the World Tag Team Championships at Madison Square Garden. King and Strongbow defended the belts for one month until they were defeated by Prof. Toru Tanaka & Mr. Fuji. By spring 1973 King left the company but remained a force throughout the territories of the National Wrestling Alliance. In the early 1980s he became a manager and shared his methods of success with up-and-coming competitors. WWE fans will always remember him as a great singles contender and part of one of the most popular teams of the 1970s.

2010-
2000-09
1990-99
1980-89
1970-79
1960-69

SPIKE DUDLEY

HT: 5'8" **WT:** 150 lbs.
FROM: New York City
SIGNATURE MOVE: Dudley Dog

TITLE HISTORY

CRUISERWEIGHT CHAMPION	*Defeated Rey Mysterio on July 29, 2004*
EUROPEAN CHAMPION	*Defeated William Regal on April 8, 2002*
HARDCORE CHAMPION	*7 Times*
WORLD TAG TEAM CHAMPION	*Partnered with Tazz to defeat The Dudley Boys on January 7, 2002*

As the runt of the Dudley litter, Spike Dudley entered WWE with very low expectations, but over the course of his career, the half-brother of Bubba Ray and D-Von Dudley proved that size doesn't matter.

Spike made an immediate impact when he helped his brothers defeat Edge & Christian for the World Tag Team Championship in March 2001. Unfortunately, the brotherly love didn't last long, as he eventually turned his back on his brothers and the ECW-WCW Alliance to stay by the side of his girlfriend Molly Holly and WWE. His decision to follow his heart resulted in a bitter Dudley family feud. Teaming with Tazz, Spike eventually gained the ultimate retribution over his bullying brothers when he pinned Bubba Ray to gain his brothers' cherished World Tag Team Championship.

In addition to his success in the tag team division, Spike also achieved notoriety as a singles competitor. Not only did he capture both the European and Hardcore Championships, but he also defeated Rey Mysterio for the Cruiserweight Championship in July 2004.

SPIKE HUBER

HT: 5'9" **WT:** 235 lbs.
FROM: Indianapolis, Indiana

Spike Huber was a scientific wrestler, who plied his trade the world over. But he's best known for his time spent competing in the Indianapolis-based World Wrestling Association, which was owned and operated by his father-in-law, the legendary Dick The Bruiser.

While in WWA, Huber earned a reputation as a tag-team specialist. He won the organization's World Tag Team Championship five times with three different partners (Dick The Bruiser, Wilbur Snyder and Steve Regal). He also defeated Bobby Colt to capture the WWA World Heavyweight Championship in January 1984. Huber held the title for several months before reportedly having a falling out with his father-in-law, which resulted in the end of his WWA tenure.

Huber joined WWE during the promotion's national expansion of the mid 1980s. He had early success over the likes of Dennis Stamp, Max Blue and Billy Travis. He eventually formed a short-lived tag team with Brian Blair, who later became one-half of the popular Killer Bees duo.

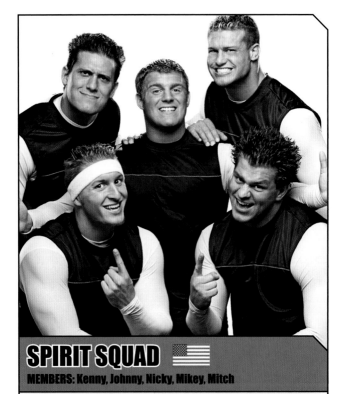

SPIRIT SQUAD

MEMBERS: Kenny, Johnny, Nicky, Mikey, Mitch

TITLE HISTORY

WORLD TAG TEAM CHAMPIONS	*Defeated Big Show & Kane on April 3, 2006*

In a locker room overflowing with testosterone, Spirit Squad knew they would have difficulty fitting in. So rather than making futile attempts at changing people's opinions of them, the male cheerleaders chose to focus on the one thing they could control: their actions in the ring.

The quintet of Superstars first began annoying fans with their uncoordinated routines in January 2006. Lacking self-awareness, the group believed their horrible chants were brilliant. Spirit Squad's talents in the ring, however, were amazing. Within months of their debut, the high-flyers defeated Kane & Big Show for the World Tag Team Championship.

Despite their comical exterior, Spirit Squad possessed a vicious mean streak. In May 2006, all five members of the crew nearly crippled Shawn Michaels when they targeted his knee with a steel chair. Luckily for HBK, Triple H saved him from certain doom. The rescue served as a launching pad for a D-Generation X revival, and landing the cheerleaders in a bitter rivalry with the reunited faction.

In late 2006, Spirit Squad hit an uncharacteristic losing streak. Cryme Tyme, Eugene, Sgt. Slaughter and a whole host of others lined up to topple the annoying faction. Finally at *Cyber Sunday*, Ric Flair & "Rowdy" Roddy Piper defeated the group to capture the World Tag Team Championship. Shortly after the loss, longtime rivals DX packed Spirit Squad into a shipping crate and sent them off to OVW in Louisville, KY.

SPIROS ARION

HT: 6'5" **WT:** 260 lbs. **FROM:** Athens, Greece
SIGNATURE MOVE: Atomic Drop

TITLE HISTORY

UNITED STATES TAG TEAM CHAMPION (2 TIMES)	*Partnered with Tony Parisi to defeat Smasher Sloan & Baron Mikel Scicluna on December 8, 1966* *Partnered with Bruno Sammartino to defeat Lou Albano & Tony Altomare on July 24, 1967*

The man known throughout the world as "the Iron Greek" appeared in WWE rings in 1966. Spiros Arion's fiery Mediterranean nature made him one of the most popular Superstars in the northeast as he squared off against Angelo Savoldi, Tony Nero, Smasher Sloan, and Tank Morgan. In December, 1966 he won his first championship in WWE when he and Antonio Pugliese won the United States Tag Team Championship. In 1967 Arion's close friendship with Bruno Sammartino led to another United States Tag Team reign.

Over the next few years Arion traveled the globe, then returned to WWE in 1974. Sadly, Spiros turned on his mentor and fell under the sinister influence of "Classy" Freddie Blassie. Filled with hate the once heroic Greek gladiator became a treacherous and crafty villain aligned with slime such as the Wolfman, Bobby Duncum, and Waldo Von Erich.

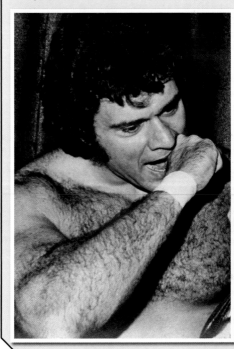

THE SPOILER

HT: 6'4" **WT:** 293 lbs.
FROM: Parts Unknown
SIGNATURE MOVE: Iron Claw

Don Jardine made his in-ring debut at the young age of 15. He spent more than ten years competing under his given name, as well such aliases as The Butcher and Sonny Cooper. Then in 1967, famed promoter Fritz Von Erich gave him the name "The Spoiler." From there, Jardine went on to become one of the most well-known masked Superstars of all time.

The Spoiler was a double threat in the ring. At 6'4" and nearly 300 pounds, he possessed immense strength. But he was also very athletic for a man of his size. In fact, The Spoiler perfected the top-rope walk decades before Undertaker made it popular in WWE rings.

As a member of WWE, The Spoiler used his feared Iron Claw to eventually earn an opportunity at Pedro Morales' WWE Championship. He was unable to unseat the champ, but the match will forever hold historical significance, as The Spoiler was forced to compete without his trademark mask due to Madison Square Garden regulations.

STACY KEIBLER

HT: 5'11"
FROM: Baltimore, Maryland

At more than 41 inches in length, Stacy Keibler's legs seem to go on forever. Just like her entrance theme suggested, she certainly knows how to use them. A former Baltimore Ravens cheerleader, Stacy broke into sports-entertainment by winning a WCW contest designed to find a new Nitro Girl. Within months of her debut, it was clear that the leggy Diva was destined to become so much more than a member

of an ensemble dance team. She soon broke free from the Nitro Girls to become the valet Miss Hancock.

Following WWE's acquisition of WCW, Stacy remained loyal to her roots and joined The Alliance. While the faction of WCW and ECW Superstars was universally despised, WWE fans found it hard to boo the beautiful newcomer, especially after seeing her during the *Invasion* pay-per-view.

Stacy's early managerial efforts saw her guide the careers of Bubba Ray and D-Von Dudley. Known as the "Duchess of Dudleyville," she often distracted her team's opposition. The sexy ploy carried the Dudleys to numerous victories, but when it finally resulted in a loss for Bubba Ray & D-Von, the team drove the Diva through a table, signifying the end of their relationship.

Stacy's managerial career also landed her by the side of Scott Steiner and Test, but it was her in-ring action that truly excited audiences. In March 2004, she competed in the biggest match of her career when she participated in *WrestleMania XX*'s Playboy Evening Gown Match. Despite never having graced the pages of *Playboy* (she's rumored to have declined numerous invitations), Stacy's participation made it one of the event's most memorable matches.

The popularity Stacy gained while competing in WWE rings eventually led her to a career in Hollywood. Her most well-known role saw the Diva dance all the way to the final episode of ABC's hit series *Dancing with the Stars*. She also landed recurring roles on *George Lopez* and *What About Brian*.

THE STALKER

HT: 6'6" **WT:** 274 lbs.
FROM: The Environment
SIGNATURE MOVE: Superplex

In August 1996 World Wrestling Entertainment began to air videos showing a man who could see you, but go unseen. Wearing camouflage, the Stalker hunted Superstars such as Goldust, Faarooq, Justin Bradshaw, Hunter Hearst-Helmsley, Stone Cold Steve Austin, the Goon and Jerry "The King" Lawler.

Shortly after his pay-per-view debut at the 1996 *Survivor Series* he disappeared from WWE. Anything could happen when he was in the ring and for all anyone knows he could be watching you right now, waiting for the right moment to strike.

STAN HANSEN 🇺🇸

HT: 6'4" **WT:** 321 lbs.
FROM: Borger, Texas
SIGNATURE MOVE: The Lariat

Stan Hansen began wrestling in the early 1970s in Amarillo. In 1976 the double-tough roughneck arrived in WWE, courtesy "Classy" Freddie Blassie, who was trying to eliminate Bruno Sammartino. On April 26th in the main event at Madison Square Garden he broke Sammartino's neck when he connected with his Lariat clothesline.

After this brutal attack, Hansen gained a reputation as a vicious bounty hunter. Though they settled their score at the *Showdown At Shea,* more despicable attacks took place against the likes of Ivan Putski, Andre The Giant, and Gorilla Monsoon.

Hansen returned to WWE in 1981 and hunted the WWE and Intercontinental Titles, calling out respective champions Bob Backlund and Pedro Morales. He left WWE in 1982 and spent time in Georgia, the AWA and Japan.

In April 1990 Hansen fought Hulk Hogan in the main event of the Wrestling Summit. He briefly appeared in WCW and even stopped in ECW in 1993. For the first time in nearly 30 years, "The Lariat" appeared on WWE television in 2010. He didn't decapitate an opponent with his dreaded clothesline, but he did induct longtime adversary turned friend Antonio Inoki into the WWE Hall of Fame. Stan Hansen was a rare individual whose home territory was the world. The bad man from Borger left a legacy that may never be duplicated.

STAN LANE 🇺🇸

HT: 6'1" **WT:** 230 lbs.
FROM: Pensacola, Florida

Members of the WWE Universe might only recognize Stan Lane for his brief run as an announcer on *WWE Superstars* during the mid 1990s. But in the two decades preceding his time behind the microphone, "Sweet" Stan excelled as one-half of three of the greatest tag teams around: The Fabulous Ones, The Midnight Express and The Heavenly Bodies.

Trained by Ric Flair, Lane debuted in 1974, but didn't truly break out until he teamed with Steve Keirn to form The Fabulous Ones. Together, they captured more than 20 tag titles from promotions across North America, including the AWA Southern Tag Team Championship 15 times.

Lane later teamed with Bobby Eaton as a member of The Midnight Express. Among their accomplishments include a reign with the prestigious NWA World Tag Team Championship in late 1988.

In the 1990s, Lane teamed with Tom Prichard to create The Heavenly Bodies. The duo earned the distinction of being the first-ever Smokey Mountain Wrestling Tag Team Champions in April 1992. They went on to win the gold four more times.

STAN STASIAK 🇺🇸

HT: 6'4" **WT:** 270 lbs.
FROM: Buzzard Creek, Oregon
SIGNATURE MOVE: Heart Punch

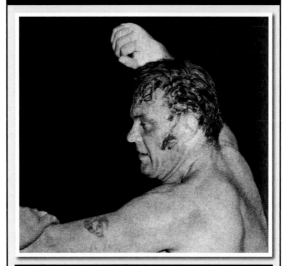

TITLE HISTORY	
WWE CHAMPION	*Defeated Pedro Morales on December 1, 1973*

Stan Stasiak's name will never be mentioned alongside the greats that held the WWE Championship, but his nine-day stint with the prestigious title is recognized as one of the promotion's most significant reigns, as it served as an historic bridge between Pedro Morales and Bruno Sammartino's lengthy runs with the title.

Stasiak made his professional debut in Quebec, Canada, in 1958. Known for his long sideburns and rugged offensive approach, he quickly earned the moniker "The Crusher." Over the next several years, he bounced back and forth between territories in Canada and the United States' Pacific Northwest. During this time, Stasiak became known for his paralyzing heart punch, but it wasn't until he took his game to the Northeast that he truly became immortal.

In December 1973, Stan "The Man" forever cemented his name in sports-entertainment lore when he defeated Pedro Morales for the WWE Championship in Philadelphia, PA. The victory made him the fifth champion in WWE history; and while his reign only lasted a little more than a week, he spent the rest of his life being recognized as one of the few Superstars lucky enough to have reached the sport's zenith.

STEINER BROTHERS 🇺🇸

MEMBERS: Rick, Scott   **COMBINED WT:** 510 lbs.

TITLE HISTORY	
WORLD TAG TEAM CHAMPIONS (2 TIMES)	*Defeated Money, Inc. on June 14, 1993* *Defeated Money, Inc. on June 19, 1993*

These superior athletes and All-Americans from the University of Michigan began teaming professionally in the National Wrestling Alliance, and also toured Japan. In late 1992 the brothers made their debut in WWE, where they showcased their unmatched teamwork and technical prowess. In 1993, they appeared on the debut episode of *Monday Night Raw,* beat the Beverly Brothers at the *Royal Rumble* and defeated the Headshrinkers at *WrestleMania IX.* Their year hit its peak in June when they defeated Money Inc. for the World Tag Team Championships.

After trading the titles with Money Inc., then losing them to the Quebecers in a bizarre "Province of Quebec" rules match, the Steiners left WWE. The brothers appeared in ECW in 1995, and WCW until 1998. During a WCW Tag Team Title defense, Scott turned his back on Rick and joined the nWo. In recent years, the Steiner Brothers have made up and sometimes appear together in promotions around the world. A good sign for a team that will go down as one of the most dominant and technically gifted tag teams in sports-entertainment's history.

STEPHANIE McMAHON

![US Flag]

FROM: Greenwich, Connecticut

Proving the apple doesn't fall far from the tree, Stephanie McMahon has transformed herself into one of the most powerful personalities in sports-entertainment. With an intoxicating combination of beauty and brains, she demands nothing short of excellence. If she doesn't get it from others, Stephanie isn't afraid to step in the ring and beat it out of somebody, much like her father, WWE Chairman Vince McMahon.

Stephanie was introduced to WWE in early 1999 when the sadistic Undertaker abducted her as a means to get to her father. With the innocent Stephanie firmly in his possession, the "Deadman" arranged for a ceremony that would forever lock the two in unholy matrimony. Luckily for Stephanie, an unlikely hero made the save when noted McMahon nemesis Stone Cold Steve Austin ran to the ring and attacked Undertaker.

Love Life Put to the Test

Following the horrifying Undertaker incident, Stephanie found love in the form of a WWE Superstar, Test. The relationship helped put a smile back on her face, but also managed to infuriate her protective older brother, Shane. Looking out for what he believed were his sister's best interests, Shane attempted to put an end to the fiery love affair when he battled Test in a Love Her or Leave Her Match at *SummerSlam 1999*. In the end, Test won the match and the right to continue his romance with Stephanie.

The strong bond between Stephanie and Test eventually led to an engagement. The young lovers planned to wed in November 1999, but just before they could exchange vows, one Superstar made a very revealing objection. Armed with video evidence, Triple H exposed the shocking truth that Stephanie was already a married woman.

In an attempt to salvage his daughter's good name, an irate Mr. McMahon battled Triple H at *Armageddon* in December 1999. Unfortunately for the WWE Chairman, however, "The Game" wasn't his only opponent that night, as his daughter shocked the sports-entertainment world when she helped Triple H defeat her father. After the match, Stephanie jumped into the arms of her husband, proving the two had been in cahoots all along.

McMahon-Helmsley Era

Together, Stephanie and Triple H went on to become one of the most power-hungry couples ever. The husband-and-wife team began a ruthless dictatorship that controlled all of WWE. Abusing their power as much as possible, they were both conveniently placed in situations that would benefit them most. As a result, it wasn't long before Triple H had regained the WWE Championship, and Stephanie claimed the Women's Championship.

In July 2001, Stephanie elevated the rivalry with her father to new heights. After already breaking his heart in 1999, Stephanie revealed herself as the new owner of ECW, which she merged with her brother's WCW to form The Alliance. Stephanie and Shane's goal was simple: Put their father and WWE out of business forever.

The Alliance began as a very serious threat to Mr. McMahon's empire, as many of his major Superstars jumped ship to Stephanie's camp, including Stone Cold and William Regal. In the end, however, The Alliance was forced to disband when they were defeated by Team WWE at *Survivor Series 2001*.

With the loss, Stephanie was finally forced out of sports-entertainment, or so it seemed. In January 2002, she used a faux pregnancy to weasel her way back into WWE, alongside her husband, Triple H. Her plan eventually backfired, however, when "The Game" learned of the hoax. Following the emotional rollercoaster, an enraged Triple H demanded a divorce from his conniving wife.

Back in Power

In July 2002, Stephanie returned to prominence when she took over the reigns of *SmackDown*. As the brand's General Manager, she acquired some of sports-entertainment's biggest names, including Hulk Hogan, Brock Lesnar, and Undertaker. She is also credited with creating the WWE Tag Team Championship and resurrecting the prestigious United States Championship.

Stephanie's time in office came to a painful end when she lost an "I Quit" Match to her father at *No Mercy 2003*. While she refused to submit to her father, the match ultimately ended when Stephanie's mother, Linda, couldn't bear to watch the brutality any longer. As a result, she threw in the towel, signifying the end of Stephanie's time on *SmackDown*. Following the loss, Stephanie limited her public appearances in favor of assuming several executive roles behind the scenes. On occasion, however, she reappears when the situation calls for a strong leader. One of her more memorable returns to WWE programming took place during Triple H's war with Randy Orton and Legacy.

Today Stephanie is responsible for all the creative development in WWE as it pertains to television and pay-per-view programming, print, digital, and social media content. In 2009 and 2011, she was recognized as one of the "Most Powerful Woman in Cable" by CableFAX magazine. She is also a proud member of the Board of Directors for the USO Metropolitan Washington.

2010-

2000-09

1990-99

1980-89

1970-79

1960-69

STEPHANIE WIAND

Stephanie Wiand is best known as the super-hyper cohost of *WWE Mania* during the mid 1990s. Alongside Todd Pettengill, her main responsibility was to recap the week that was in WWE. Heading into the first-ever *In Your House* pay-per-view event in May 1995, Wiand proved she was ahead of her time when she toured a beautiful new house, which would eventually be given away to a lucky member of the WWE Universe. Years later, networks such as HGTV and MTV would also begin touring houses, using the same template laid out by Wiand.

Wiand remained a member of the entertainment industry following her brief run with WWE. In 1998, she appeared as a nurse in two episodes of *The Bold and the Beautiful*. She later appeared in the short-lived television series *Afterworld*. And most recently, she wrote, produced and appeared in the sci-fi comedy *Revenge of the Bimbot Zombie Killers*. Despite all this, though, WWE fans will always remember Wiand fondly as Pettengill's over-caffeinated sidekick.

STEVE BLACKMAN HT: 6'2" WT: 245 lbs.
FROM: Annville, Pennsylvania

When Steve Blackman walked to the ring with his eskrima and kendo sticks in hand, everybody knew danger lurked ahead, but it was Blackman's bare hands and mastery of martial arts more than anything else that earned him the nickname "the Lethal Weapon."

TITLE HISTORY	
HARDCORE CHAMPION	*6 Times*

Blackman's no-nonsense approach to competition made him a natural fit for WWE's hardcore division, as there were few Superstars that could match his intensity and training with martial arts weaponry. One thing Blackman couldn't combat, however, was being out-manned. In August 2000, "the Lethal Weapon" lost his Hardcore Championship to Shane McMahon when the WWE heir enlisted the help of several other Superstars to help his cause. Later that month at *SummerSlam*, Blackman regained the title after knocking McMahon off the top of the TitanTron onto the arena floor approximately fifty feet below. Blackman then jumped off the structure onto McMahon's limp body for the win. The image of "the Lethal Weapon" flying through the air remains one of Blackman's greatest career highlights.

STEVE "DR. DEATH" WILLIAMS HT: 6'1" WT: 285 lbs. FROM: Norman, Oklahoma
SIGNATURE MOVE: Oklahoma Stampede

Steve Williams was an All-American in amateur wrestling and football at the University of Oklahoma. After training by "Cowboy" Bill Watts, Dr. Death became famous all over North America and Japan, winning titles at virtually every stop he made.

In 1998 Williams arrived in sports-entertainment's most competitive landscape, WWE. He was an early favorite to win the Brawl For All Tournament, but he suffered a severe hamstring tear. He returned in 1999 alongside Jim Ross, but soon left for WCW and Japan. In 2006, Williams made surprise appearances for WWE after a heroic fight against throat cancer.

2007 was a huge year for Williams. He was inducted into the George Tragos/Lou Thesz Professional Wrestling Hall of Fame and penned his inspirational autobiography titled *"How Dr. Death Became Dr. Life."* Sadly, on December 29, 2009 this legendary athlete's life was cut short when the cancer he valiantly battled for years returned. Steve Williams' influence on the gridiron and inside the ring will be surpassed only by his love of life, family, and friends.

STEVIE RICHARDS HT: 6'2" WT: 230 lbs. FROM: Philadelphia, Pennsylvania
SIGNATURE MOVE: Stevie Kick

Often referred to as a clueless putz, Stevie Richards must've done something right, as many experts give him partial credit for the early success of ECW. In fact, Richards owns the distinction of competing in ECW's first-ever match, battling Jimmy Jannetty to a twenty-minute draw in 1992.

TITLE HISTORY	
HARDCORE CHAMPION	*21 Times*

Following an eventful ECW career, Stevie Richards briefly competed in WCW before ultimately landing in WWE. He spent his earliest WWE days mocking fellow Superstars, *a la* his popular bWo persona from ECW. After poking fun at the likes of Dude Love, Richards made a shocking transformation. He traded in his cutoff jean shorts for more formal attire and became leader of Right to Censor. As the head of RTC, Steven Richards protested against WWE's risqué content.

Luckily for his fans, the movement lasted less than a year. After the faction broke up, Richards returned to the extreme style of competition that initially gained him great fame. In April 2002, he defeated fellow ECW alumnus Tommy Dreamer for the Hardcore Championship. It was his first of twenty-one reigns with the title. Only Crash Holly and Raven boast more reigns than Richards.

After the retirement of the Hardcore Championship, Richards became a regular on *Heat*. He took full advantage of his opportunity and even proclaimed himself Heat's General Manger, though he was never officially appointed the role. WWE audiences saw Richards return to his extreme roots during 2005's rebirth of ECW. He donned the colors of the bWo for *One Night Stand* and in conflicts with the Mexicools. In addition to his time on *SmackDown* in 2007, Stevie had on-again-off-again alliances with his fellow ECW Originals as well as highly contested bouts against CM Punk.

STRAIGHT EDGE SOCIETY

MEMBERS: CM Punk, Luke Gallows, Serena, Joseph Mercury

CM Punk doesn't smoke. He doesn't drink. He doesn't do drugs. And in late 2009, the "Second-City Savior" began obsessively preaching these lifestyle choices, much to the chagrin of the WWE Universe. Claiming he was the role model the world needed, Punk began compiling disciples to help him in his crusade against drugs and alcohol. His first convert was Luke Gallows, who Punk saved from a supposed prescription pain pill addiction. The prophetic leader then rescued fan Serena and Superstar Joseph Mercury.

Collectively known as the Straight Edge Society, the foursome spent the next several months promoting abstinence and discipline. Then in July, Serena was caught drinking and the foundation of the faction began to crack. Serena was temporarily permitted to stay in the group before eventually being dismissed completely. Not long after that, Punk blamed Gallows for a loss to Big Show in a Handicap Match. Frustrated, Punk nailed his disciple with thunderous GTS, marking the end of the Straight Edge Society.

STRIKE FORCE

MEMBERS: Tito Santana, Rick Martel
COMBINED WT: 460 lbs.

TITLE HISTORY	
WORLD TAG TEAM CHAMPIONS	*Defeated The Hart Foundation on October 27, 1987*

Prior to joining forces, both Tito Santana and Rick Martel enjoyed successful singles career, which is why it was no surprise to see them achieve greatness as a unit. They first began teaming together in 1987 after Santana ran to the ring to save Martel from a double-team attack at the hands of the Islanders. From that point on, they became known as Strike Force, a good looking tandem whose sound technical skills carried all the way to the top of the tag team division.

After defeating the Hart Foundation for the World Tag Team Championship in October 1987, Strike Force looked nearly unstoppable. Many predicted a lengthy reign for the duo, but after only five months with the gold, the impact of Mr. Fuji's cane caused Santana & Martel to lose their titles to Demolition at *WrestleMania IV*. The loss proved to be a major setback for the popular tag team, as they struggled to regain their momentum.

After a brief hiatus, Strike Force reunited to battle the Brain Busters at *WrestleMania V*. In a shocking turn of events, Martel turned on his partner during the match, marking the official end of Strike Force. Over the next several years, the two Superstars engaged in an emotional rivalry that never saw a clear-cut winner declared.

STRONG KOBAYASHI

 HT: 6'2" WT: 275 lbs.
FROM: Japan

For a period of time in the 1970s, the International Wrestling Alliance World Heavyweight Championship was considered to be the premiere title in all of Japan, thanks in large part to the tireless effort of one of its greatest titleholders, Strong Kobayashi.

Ironically, Kobayashi first staked claim to the title after beating Dr. Bill Miller in Minnesota in June 1971. He then brought the title back to Japan, where he defended it proudly for more than two years before losing to Wahoo McDaniel in Tokushima, Katsuura. McDaniel only held the title for a few weeks before Kobayashi wrestled it away from him in a match contested in Tokyo.

Kobayashi vacated the IWA World Heavyweight Championship in February 1974 when he left the promotion to compete for New Japan Pro Wrestling. Kobayashi later traveled to the United States, where he competed for WWE. His success, however, failed to follow him overseas. He regularly lost to the likes of SD Jones, Tony Garea and a very young Curt Hennig.

THE STRONGBOWS

 MEMBERS: Chief Jay, Jules

TITLE HISTORY	
WORLD TAG TEAM CHAMPIONS (2 TIMES)	*Defeated Mr. Fuji & Mr. Saito on June 28, 1982* *Defeated Mr. Fuji & Mr. Saito on October 26, 1982*

In 1982 Chief Jay Strongbow tapped his brother Jules for help to face WWE's rule-breakers and bring audiences to their feet. Their high-flying moves, ground-attacks, and double-team actions paved the road of their success. In June 1982 they defeated Mr. Fuji and Mr. Saito for the World Tag Team Championship. Over the next few months they traded title reigns with the hired Japanese guns. Their final title reign ended in March 1983 when they lost to the Wild Samoans. Shortly after the loss the Chief retired from the ring and Jules left WWE and spent the rest of his career competing on the Independent scene.

The Strongbows are warmly remembered as two of the most honorable heroes in WWE history and an exciting duo. When great brother tag team combinations are mentioned, Chief Jay and Jules Strongbow undoubtedly make the list!

THE SULTAN

HT: 6'3" WT: 295 lbs. FROM: The Middle East
SIGNATURE MOVE: Camel Clutch

When this former masked Superstar was first seen in 1997 some experts speculated that his face was deformed. After his impressive debut win against Jake "The Snake" Roberts, the focus was off of his mask and turned to his dangerous array of maneuvers in the ring. Mentored by the Iron Sheik and Mr. Bob Backlund, Sultan was well versed in submission wrestling, mat techniques, and rule-breaking.

Although he met foes like Phineas Godwinn, Yokozuna, Goldust, Undertaker and Bret Hart, Sultan's greatest battle was with Rocky Maivia over the Intercontinental Championship. The two Superstars settled their score at *WrestleMania 13*. By early 1998 Sultan returned to the home of the one-time Persian Empire and has not been on World Wrestling Entertainment programming since.

1960-69
1970-79
1980-89
1990-99
2000-09
2010-

STONE COLD STEVE AUSTIN

HT: 6'2" **WT: 252 lbs.** **FROM: Victoria, Texas** **SIGNATURE MOVE: Stone Cold Stunner**

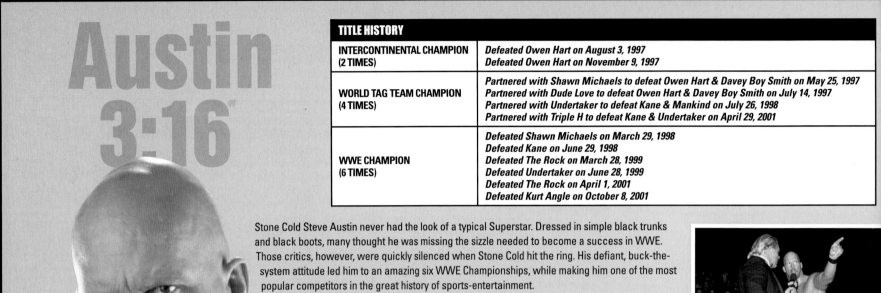

Austin 3:16

TITLE HISTORY	
INTERCONTINENTAL CHAMPION (2 TIMES)	*Defeated Owen Hart on August 3, 1997* *Defeated Owen Hart on November 9, 1997*
WORLD TAG TEAM CHAMPION (4 TIMES)	*Partnered with Shawn Michaels to defeat Owen Hart & Davey Boy Smith on May 25, 1997* *Partnered with Dude Love to defeat Owen Hart & Davey Boy Smith on July 14, 1997* *Partnered with Undertaker to defeat Kane & Mankind on July 26, 1998* *Partnered with Triple H to defeat Kane & Undertaker on April 29, 2001*
WWE CHAMPION (6 TIMES)	*Defeated Shawn Michaels on March 29, 1998* *Defeated Kane on June 29, 1998* *Defeated The Rock on March 28, 1999* *Defeated Undertaker on June 28, 1999* *Defeated The Rock on April 1, 2001* *Defeated Kurt Angle on October 8, 2001*

Stone Cold Steve Austin never had the look of a typical Superstar. Dressed in simple black trunks and black boots, many thought he was missing the sizzle needed to become a success in WWE. Those critics, however, were quickly silenced when Stone Cold hit the ring. His defiant, buck-the-system attitude led him to an amazing six WWE Championships, while making him one of the most popular competitors in the great history of sports-entertainment.

A little more than a year after his professional debut, Austin made the gigantic leap to WCW. Under the name of "Stunning" Steve Austin, the relatively inexperienced youngster from Texas found instant success, defeating Bobby Eaton for the WCW Television Championship in June 1991. Over the next four years, Austin went on to capture the United States Championship, and WCW Tag Team Championship with Brian Pillman. Despite all of Austin's success in the ring, the head of WCW, Eric Bischoff, didn't see him as a marketable commodity. After Austin injured himself while competing in Japan, Bischoff picked up the phone and fired him.

From ECW to WWE

Austin was unemployed for approximately 24 hours before ECW's Paul Heyman called him with a job offer. Still injured, Austin couldn't compete in the ring, but that didn't faze Heyman. Instead, he gave Austin a microphone and simply told him to talk. What followed were some of the most emotionally charged promos sports-entertainment has ever seen. Austin's anti-WCW tirades entertained the ECW fans, but more importantly, they were his first opportunity to truly voice his opinions on-air, and served as a preview to his future in WWE, which soon came calling for Austin.

"You sit there and you thump your bible, you say your prayers, and it didn't get yo anywhere. Talk about your Psalms, talk about John 3:16; Austin 3:16 says I just whipped your ass."

In January 1996, competing under the moniker of the Ringmaster, Austin made his WWE debut, handily defeating Matt Hardy. With Ted DiBiase as his manager, the Ringmaster immediately began to butt heads with Savio Vega. After a win at *WrestleMania XII*, the Ringmaster successfully turned back Vega, but then, in a shocking turn of events, the Ringmaster later lost a Strap Match to Vega, which resulted in DiBiase losing his job.

With his manager fired, it seemed as though Austin's career was about to suffer another debilitating setback, but a determined Austin refused to be held back any longer, and he soon turned the negative into a huge positive. With nobody at his side telling him what to do, Austin was able to rid himself of the Ringmaster name and rebuild his image on his own terms. The result: Stone Cold Steve Austin.

Pay Per View Victories

It didn't take long for Stone Cold to prove he was the "toughest S.O.B." in all of WWE. Just one month after remaking his image, Austin defeated Jake Roberts to become the 1996 WWE King of the Ring. After the match, Austin made a victory speech that would forever change the face of sports-entertainment.

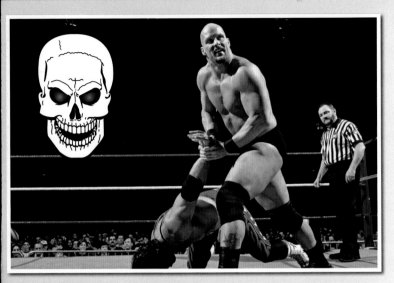

Austin's post-match rant was an instant rage. Within days, Austin 3:16 T-shirts were everywhere. Stone Cold fans soon started dressing like their hero, making it impossible to walk through the mall without seeing a bald-headed, goatee-wearing fan in jeans and a black T-shirt. Not since Hulkamania had WWE been taken over by such a phenomenon.

As a result of his *King of the Ring* victory, Stone Cold was afforded opportunities that were denied him while in WCW, which lead to friction between him and Bret "Hit Man" Hart. After last eliminating Hart to win the 1997 *Royal Rumble*, Stone Cold squared off against his rival in a Submission Match at *WrestleMania 13*. While the result did not go in his favor, the sight of Stone Cold profusely bleeding to the point of losing consciousness proved to be one of the most memorable images in WWE history.

Several other members of the famed Hart family muscled their way into the historic rivalry, including Bret's brother Owen. While competing against the younger Hart at *SummerSlam 1997*, Stone Cold suffered a career-threatening injury when a piledriver delivered by Owen broke his neck. Miraculously, Austin was able to recover just enough to roll Owen up for the win and the Intercontinental Championship. Unfortunately for Stone Cold, the severity of his injury forced him to relinquish the title. Upon returning to the ring later that year, however, Stone Cold gained retribution by defeating Owen to become a two-time Intercontinental Champion.

At the *D-Generation X* pay-per-view in December 1997, Stone Cold defeated The Rock to retain his title. By all accounts, the victory should have silenced The Rock's quest to become Intercontinental Champion. The next night on *Raw*, however, Mr. McMahon demanded Stone Cold defend his title against the same man he defeated twenty-four hours earlier. When a defiant Austin refused to give in to McMahon's demands, the Chairman of WWE stripped Stone Cold of the Intercontinental Championship. A fired-up Austin responded by knocking Mr. McMahon out of the ring, officially igniting one of the greatest rivalries in the history of sports-entertainment—Stone Cold vs. Mr. McMahon.

The Attitude Era Personified

After winning the 1998 *Royal Rumble*, Stone Cold challenged Shawn Michaels for the WWE Championship in the main event of *WrestleMania XIV*. With Mike Tyson serving as the match's special enforcer, Austin floored HBK with his signature Stone Cold Stunner. Three seconds later, Stone Cold was celebrating his first of six WWE Championship reigns in front of a capacity crowd in Boston's FleetCenter.

The victory infuriated Mr. McMahon, who now had a beer-drinking, middle-finger gesturing Superstar representing his company as its champion. Unable to stand by and allow Stone Cold to act in such a rebellious fashion, McMahon demanded that the new titleholder act more like a "corporate champion". The authority-defying Austin had other plans, however. In typical Stone Cold fashion, he delivered a Stunner to his boss and continued to drink beers while flipping the middle finger.

Stone Cold and Mr. McMahon continued their heated rivalry for the better part of the next three years. However, in April 2001, Austin did the unthinkable. While competing against The Rock at *WrestleMania X-Seven*, Stone Cold actually aligned himself with the man he tried to destroy for so many years. With assistance from Mr. McMahon, Austin defeated The Rock for the WWE Championship that fateful night. After the match, the former rivals actually shook hands and shared a beer.

Stone Cold's shocking allegiance to Mr. McMahon left his dedicated followers scratching their heads while attempting to digest their hero's heinous actions. Just when it appeared as though things couldn't get any worse, Stone Cold dropped another bomb three months later when he turned his back on the entire WWE locker room to join the WCW/ECW Alliance.

Stone Cold's defection from WWE ultimately proved to be an unsuccessful venture. After the Alliance was forced to disband, he found himself right back on the WWE roster. The fans were happy to see him back, but unsure about whether they could trust him again. Stone Cold quickly put all their misgivings to rest the best way he knew how: attacking Mr. McMahon.

Post-Wrestling Career

Chronic neck injuries began to take their toll on Stone Cold Steve Austin in 2002. After taking off the second half of the year, he returned to WWE in 2003 to battle The Rock at *WrestleMania XIX*. Despite a valiant effort, Austin came up short in what was ultimately his final official WWE match.

Stone Cold's in-ring career may be behind him, but he still manages to steal the spotlight every time he steps foot inside a WWE arena. While serving as guest referee for the Goldberg vs. Brock Lesnar *WrestleMania XX* match, Austin received one of the loudest ovations of the night after delivering the Stunner to both Goldberg and Lesnar. The following year at *WrestleMania 21*, Carlito and "Rowdy" Roddy Piper suffered the same fate. At *WrestleMania 23*, Stone Cold even Stunned billionaire Donald Trump.

Hollywood and the Hall of Fame

As his time in the ring ended, Stone Cold started to branch out into other forms of entertainment. He appeared in a handful of television programs and made his big screen acting debut in the 2005 remake of *The Longest Yard*. In 2007, Austin was cast as the lead in *The Condemned*, one of the first movies produced by WWE Films (now WWE Studios). Stone Cold's drawing power also landed him a role in Sylvester Stallone's big budget, star-filled, adrenaline rush of a movie, 2010's *The Expendables*.

While acting took up a good deal of his time, Stone Cold still found time for the WWE Universe. While he made appearances at WWE events, none could measure up to the night before *WrestleMania XXV*, when the "Texas Rattlesnake" was inducted into the WWE Hall of Fame. To emphasize the importance of Stone Cold Steve Austin's contribution to WWE and his impact on the industry as a whole, he was inducted by Vince McMahon, the chairman of WWE and the man who was often at odds with Austin during his career.

In 2011, Stone Cold served as the head trainer and host for a new season of *Tough Enough*, and also served as a host and general manager of *Raw* on multiple occasions. Regardless of the reason for his appearance, when that glass breaks and his music hits, the WWE Universe roars its approval for one of the greatest Superstars of all time.

SummerSlam

S

2010-
2000-09
1990-99
1980-89
1970-79
1960-69

328

August 29, 1988

New York, NY
Madison Square Garden

Main Event: Mega Powers (Hulk Hogan & Randy "Macho Man" Savage (with Miss Elizabeth)) defeated Mega Bucks ("Million Dollar Man" Ted DiBiase & Andre The Giant (with Virgil & Bobby Heenan))

August 28, 1989

East Rutherford, NJ
The Meadowlands Arena

Main Event: Hulk Hogan & Brutus "The Barber" Beefcake (with Miss Elizabeth) defeated Randy "Macho Man" Savage & Zeus (with Sensational Sherri)

August 27, 1990

Philadelphia, PA
The Spectrum

Main Event: WWE Champion Ultimate Warrior defeated "Ravishing" Rick Rude in a Steel Cage Match

August 26, 1991

New York, NY
Madison Square Garden

Main Event: Hulk Hogan & Ultimate Warrior defeated Sgt. Slaughter, Colonel Mustafa, & Gen. Adnan in the Match Made In Hell (Handicap Tag Team Match with Sid Justice as guest referee)

August 29, 1992

London, England
Wembley Stadium

Main Event: British Bulldog defeated Intercontinental Champion Bret "Hit Man" Hart

August 30, 1993

Auburn Hills, MI
The Palace At Auburn Hills

Main Event: Lex Luger defeated WWE Champion Yokozuna (with Mr. Fuji & Jim Cornette) via count out

August 29, 1994

Chicago, IL
The United Center

Main Event: Undertaker (with Paul Bearer) defeated "Undertaker" (with "Million Dollar Man" Ted DiBiase)

August 27, 1995

Pittsburgh, CA
Pittsburgh Civic Arena

Main Event: WWE Champion Diesel defeated King Mabel (with Sir Mo)

August 18, 1996

Cleveland, OH
Gund Arena

Main Event: WWE Champion Shawn Michaels (with Jose Lothario) defeated Vader (with Jim Cornette)

August 3, 1997

East Rutherford, NJ
Continental Airlines Arena

Main Event: Bret "Hit Man" Hart defeated WWE Champion Undertaker with Shawn Michaels as guest referee

August 30, 1998

New York, NY
Madison Square Garden

Main Event: WWE Champion Stone Cold Steve Austin defeated Undertaker

August 22, 1999

Minneapolis, MN
Target Center

Main Event: Mankind defeated Triple H (with Chyna) and WWE Champion Stone Cold Steve Austin in a Triple Threat Match with Jesse "The Body" Ventura as guest referee

August 27, 2000

Raleigh, NC
Raleigh Entertainment and Sports Arena

Main Event: WWE Champion The Rock defeated Kurt Angle and Triple H in a Triple Threat Match

August 29, 2001

San Jose, CA
Compaq Center

Main Event: **WCW:** The Rock defeated WCW Champion Booker T (with Shane McMahon)
WWE: Kurt Angle defeated WWE Champion Stone Cold Steve Austin via Disqualification

August 25, 2002

Uniondale, NY
Nassau Coliseum

Main Event: Brock Lesnar (with Paul Heyman) defeated WWE Champion The Rock

August 24, 2003

Phoenix, AZ
America West Arena

Main Event: **SmackDown:** WWE Champion Kurt Angle defeated Brock Lesnar via submission
Raw: World Heavyweight Champion Triple H (with Ric Flair) defeated Kevin Nash, Goldberg, Chris Jericho, Randy Orton, and Shawn Michaels in an Elimination Chamber Match

August 15, 2004

Toronto, ON
Air Canada Centre

Main Event: **SmackDown:** WWE Champion JBL (with Orlando Jordan) defeated Undertaker via disqualification
Raw: Randy Orton defeated World Heavyweight Champion Chris Benoit

August 21, 2005

Washington, D.C.
MCI Center

Main Event: Hulk Hogan defeated Shawn Michaels

August 20, 2006

Boston, MA
TD Banknorth Garden

Main Event: WWE Champion Edge (with Lita) defeated John Cena

August 26, 2007

East Rutherford, NJ
Continental Airlines Arena

Main Event: WWE Champion John Cena defeated Randy Orton

August 17, 2008

Indianapolis, IN
Conseco Fieldhouse

Main Event: Undertaker defeated Edge in a Hell In A Cell Match

August 23, 2009

Los Angeles, CA
Staples Center

Main Event: CM Punk defeated WWE Champion Jeff Hardy in a Tables, Ladders, and Chairs Match

August 15, 2010

Los Angeles, CA
Staples Center

Main Event: Team WWE defeated The Nexus in a seven-on-seven elimination match

August 14, 2011

Los Angeles, CA
Staples Center

Main Event: CM Punk defeated John Cena in a WWE Championship Unification Match with guest referee Triple H

SUNNY

A life-long fan, Sunny did everything she could to learn the art of managing within the world of sports-entertainment. One day she got a call that made all of her dreams come true. This ground-breaker began her sports-entertainment career in Smokey Mountain Wrestling in the early 1990s.

In the summer of 1995, Sunny debuted as the manager of fellow Bodydonna, Skip. This fabulous female shined brighter than any before her as audiences were captivated by her striking beauty, charisma, and confidently energetic persona. As her career expanded Sunny was a broadcast correspondent, a ring announcer, color commentator, and ambassador during her time with WWE. There was nothing Sunny couldn't do and she was more than happy to remind people of that whenever she had the opportunity. In 1996 Sunny brought Faarooq to WWE, was the most downloaded woman on America Online, and won two Slammy Awards.

After guiding Skip and his brother Zip to the tag team titles at *WrestleMania XII*, Sunny left the team behind after they lost to the Godwinns a few months later. Sunny's stay with the Godwinns came to a sudden halt when she helped the Smokin' Gunns win the match and claim the World Tag Team Championship. However, she caused problems between the brothers which ultimately led to losing the belts to Owen Hart & Yokozuna.

In 1998, she rejuvenated the Legion of Doom and re-christened them L.O.D. 2000 as they won the Tag Team Battle Royal at *WrestleMania XIV*. She left WWE later in 1998, but resurfaced in ECW and WCW over the next few years before taking a break from sports-entertainment in 2001.

During the *Raw 15th Anniversary* the original Diva appeared on WWE television for the first time in almost a decade, as her theme song *I Know You Want Me* sent shivers down the spines of the male fans around the world. The tingles returned when she appeared as part of the *"Miss WrestleMania"* 25-Diva Battle Royal at *WrestleMania XXV*.

Two years later her ground-breaking career was recognized when, in an incredible show of respect, the innovative blonde was inducted into the WWE Hall of Fame by the entire Divas roster. Without this vivacious performer's beauty, intellect, and talent, the term "WWE Diva" may not exist today.

SUPER CRAZY

HT: 5'8" **WT:** 200 lbs. **FROM:** Tulancingo, Hidalgo, Mexico
SIGNATURE MOVE: Moonsault

He's super. He's crazy. He's Super Crazy.

The appropriately named Super Crazy was inked to a WWE contract after executing an insane moonsault off the second balcony of New York's Hammerstein Ballroom at *ECW One Night Stand*. Alongside Juventud and Psicosis, Super Crazy made his WWE debut as a member of the Mexicools faction. Despite being rule breakers in the ring, the Mexicools' high-flying style made them instant fan favorites.

In late 2006, Super Crazy left *SmackDown* in favor of a singles career on *Raw*. The extreme luchador made an instant impact, defeating Chris Masters several times within his first month on the roster. After a year of impressing *Raw* audiences in singles matches, Super Crazy returned to tag action, teaming with the legendary "Hacksaw" Jim Duggan in late 2007.

The next year, Super Crazy was shipped from *Raw* to *ECW on SyFy* in the 2008 Supplemental Draft. The move sent him back to the rings of The Land of the Extreme, where he first made a name for himself ten years earlier.

The insane luchador battled the likes of The Miz, Chavo Guerrero, John Morrison, and "The" Brian Kendrick. Super Crazy parted with WWE by year's end and returned to the rings of Mexico.

"SUPERSTAR" BILLY GRAHAM

HT: 6'4"   WT: 275 lbs.
FROM: Paradise Valley, Arizona
SIGNATURE MOVE: Bearhug

I AM THE REFLECTION OF PERFECTION. I AM THE SENSATION OF THE NATION. THE NUMBER-ONE CREATION.

TITLE HISTORY

WWE CHAMPION	*Defeated Bruno Sammartino on April 30, 1977*

As a high-school track and field star, "Superstar" Billy Graham held national records for discus and shot-put events and was groomed for the 1964 Olympic Games. After he won the Teenage Mr. America contest, Graham landed in Santa Monica in 1968 and trained at the original Gold's Gym with future movie star and Governor of California, Arnold Schwarzenegger. After attempts at pro football left him uninspired, Graham traveled to Calgary, Alberta, Canada, and trained with the legendary Stu Hart.

In 1975 "Superstar" Billy Graham debuted in World Wrestling Entertainment determined to take Earth on a magnificent vision quest. Wearing a psychedelic kaleidoscope of tie-dye outfits, feathered boas, sunglasses and a sun-kissed tan, Graham was the finest physical specimen the world had ever seen. He possessed a physique chiseled from granite and a cornucopia of catchphrases that were so innovative, people wrote down his words to study and recite them as if they were their own. Brought to the ring by the Grand Wizard, Graham hunted then-champion Bruno Sammartino for wrestling's richest honor. On April 30, 1977, Graham met Sammartino for the WWE Championship in Baltimore, Maryland, where both men fought beyond the brink of exhaustion. As Sammartino barraged Graham in the corner, the challenger moved with the cunning of a viper. Graham swept Sammartino's feet out from under him, pinned his shoulders to the mat and put his feet on the top rope for added (and illegal) leverage to win the WWE Championship. The entire professional wrestling industry changed as "Superstar" held its most prestigious trophy and transcended pop culture.

Six months later, Graham had a series of title matches against Dusty Rhodes that sold out Madison Square Garden and electrified the wrestling world. On February 20, 1978, Graham's feet once again changed history as he lost the WWE Championship to Bob Backlund despite Graham's foot being on the bottom rope as the referee counted three. Devastated in defeat, Billy took a sabbatical from competition and returned to Arizona. During this fall from grace, he became detached from reality and spiraled into the dangerous world of drug abuse.

"Superstar" Billy Graham possessed a physique chiseled from granite and a cornucopia of catchphrases that were so innovative, people wrote down his words to study and recite them as if they were their own.

In 1982, Graham returned to WWE as a martial arts expert with a new look, complete with shaved head, black mustache and black karate pants. Once again managed by the Grand Wizard, Graham chased Backlund in unsuccessful attempts to regain the WWE Championship. A dejected Graham left WWE again and briefly appeared in the NWA. While there, he brought back the popular Technicolor appearance and poetic flow with a new two-toned goatee. In 1987, "Superstar" made his triumphant WWE return to swarms of adoring fans.

Unfortunately, years of competition had taken its toll and Graham was in dire need of hip replacement surgery. He returned to the ring for a short time before his litany of injuries forced him to leave the ring permanently. With the desire to inspire, Graham managed fellow future WWE Hall of Famer Don Muraco and was his inspiration for a newfound attitude. Graham also used his gift of gab in the broadcast booth and provided commentary for *SummerSlam 1988*. Sadly, Graham's body continued to break down and he was no longer physically able to perform for the company in any capacity. Graham was forced to leave the profession he so dearly loved at age 45. While on the outside looking in, WWE experienced extraordinary success. "Superstar" once again battled depression, bitterness, and drug addition. The once admired sports-entertainment visionary was trapped underneath a mountainous valley of regret and anger.

Soon, Graham was facing another obstacle as he was in dire need of a liver replacement. Things looked so grim, he considered planning his own funeral in 2002, but luckily, a suitable donor was found. As he enjoyed a new lease on life, Graham was invigorated like never before and started his crusade for organ donor awareness. After being estranged from WWE for 14 years, Graham had a joyous reunion with Vince McMahon backstage at *SummerSlam 2003*. In March 2004, Graham finally found his rightful place in history alongside the immortals of sports-entertainment when he was inducted into the WWE Hall of Fame. To the delight of his fans, he continues to appear on WWE programming and in January 2006, he penned his autobiography titled, *Tangled Ropes*.

There was never a finer physical specimen or as masterful a communicator than "Superstar" Billy Graham. He was the ultimate entertainer and an original like no other who defeated all contenders and pretenders. Graham's unparalleled influence and success touched generations as seen with future WWE Hall of Famers Hulk Hogan and Jesse "The Body" Ventura. The only question that remains is how great could he have been if he blessed us with his presence 20 years later?

SURVIVOR SERIES

November 26, 1987

Richfield, OH
Richfield Coliseum

Main Event
Andre the Giant, One Man Gang, King Kong Bundy, "The Natural" Butch Reed & "Ravishing" Rick Rude versus Hulk Hogan, Paul Orndorff, Don Muraco, Ken Patera & Bam Bam Bigelow
Sole Survivor: Andre the Giant

November 24, 1988

Richfield, OH
Richfield Coliseum

Main Event
Hulk Hogan, "Macho Man" Randy Savage, Hercules, Koko B. Ware & Hillbilly Jim versus "Million Dollar Man" Ted DiBiase, Akeem, Big Boss Man, Haku & Red Rooster
Survivors: Hulk Hogan and "Macho Man" Randy Savage

November 23, 1989

Rosemont, IL
The Rosemont Horizon

Main Event
The Ultimate Warriors (Ultimate Warrior, Jim Neidhart, & the Rockers) versus the Heenan Family (Andre the Giant, Bobby Heenan, Haku, & Arn Anderson)
Sole Survivor: Ultimate Warrior

November 22, 1990

Hartford, CT
Hartford Civic Center

Main Event
Hulk Hogan, Ultimate Warrior & Tito Santana versus "The Model" Rick Martel, Power & Glory, the Warlord & "Million Dollar Man" Ted DiBiase, in a Survivors Match
Survivors: Ultimate Warrior and Hulk Hogan

November 27, 1991

Detroit, MI
Joe Louis Arena

Main Event
Undertaker (with Paul Bearer) defeated WWE Champion Hulk Hogan

November 25, 1992

Richmond, OH
Richfield Coliseum

Main Event
WWE Champion Bret "Hit Man" Hart defeated Shawn Michaels via Submission

November 24, 1993

Boston, MA
Boston Garden

Main Event
The All Americans (Lex Luger, the Steiner Brothers & Undertaker) versus The Foreign Fanatics (Quebecer Jacques, Yokozuna, Ludvig Borga & Crush)
Sole Survivor: Lex Luger

November 23, 1994

San Antonio, TX
Freeman Coliseum

Main Event
Undertaker (with Paul Bearer) defeated Yokozuna (with Mr. Fuji & Jim Cornette) in a Casket Match

November 19, 1995

Landover, MD
U.S. Air Arena

Main Event
Bret "Hit Man" Hart defeated WWE Champion Diesel in a No Disqualification Match

November 17, 1996

New York, NY
Madison Square Garden

Main Event
Sid defeated WWE Champion Shawn Michaels (with Jose Lothario)

November 9, 1997

Montreal, Quebec Canada
Molson Centre

Main Event
Shawn Michaels defeated WWE Champion Bret Hart via Submission

November 15, 1998

St. Louis, MO
Kiel Center

Main Event
The Rock defeated Mankind in the WWE Championship Tournament Finals

November 14, 1999

Detroit, MI
Joe Louis Arena

Main Event
Big Show defeated The Rock and Triple H, Triple Threat Match for the WWE Championship

November 19, 2000

Tampa, FL
Ice Palace

Main Event
Stone Cold Steve Austin versus Triple H, No Disqualification Match went to a No Contest after Stone Cold Steve Austin used a forklift

November 18, 2001

Greensboro, NC
Greensboro Coliseum

Main Event
WWE (The Rock, Chris Jericho, Big Show, Kane & Undertaker) versus The Alliance (Stone Cold Steve Austin, Kurt Angle, Shane McMahon, Booker T & Rob Van Dam) in an Elimination Match
Sole Survivor: The Rock

November 17, 2002

New York, NY
Madison Square Garden

Main Event
SmackDown: Big Show defeated WWE Champion Brock Lesnar
Raw: Shawn Michaels defeated World Heavyweight Champion Triple H, Booker T, Rob Van Dam, Chris Jericho, and Kane, in an Elimination Chamber Match for the World Heavyweight Championship

November 16, 2003

Dallas, TX
American Airlines Center

Main Event
World Heavyweight Champion Goldberg defeated Triple H (with Ric Flair)

November 14, 2004

Cleveland, OH
Gund Arena

Main Event
SmackDown: Eddie Guerrero, Rob Van Dam, Big Show & John Cena versus Kurt Angle, Mark Jindrak, Luther Reigns & Carlito
Survivors: Eddie Guerrero, Big Show and John Cena
Raw: Randy Orton, Chris Benoit, Chris Jericho & Maven versus Triple H (w/ Ric Flair), Batista, Edge & Snitsky
Sole Survivor: Randy Orton

November 27, 2005

Detroit, MI
Joe Louis Arena

Main Event
Team SmackDown (Batista, Rey Mysterio, JBL, Bobby Lashley & Randy Orton) versus **Team Raw** (Shawn Michaels, Kane, Big Show, Carlito & Chris Masters) in a Classic Survivor Series Match
Sole Survivor: Randy Orton

November 26, 2006

Philadelphia, PA
Wachovia Center

Main Event
Batista defeated World Heavyweight Champion King Booker (with Queen Sharmell)

November 18, 2007

Miami, FL
American Airlines Arena

Main Event
World Heavyweight Champion Batista defeated Undertaker, in a Hell In A Cell Match

November 23, 2008

Boston, MA
TD Banknorth Garden

Main Event
John Cena defeated World Heavyweight Champion Chris Jericho

November 22, 2009

Washinton, D.C.
Verizon Center

Main Event
WWE Champion John Cena defeated Triple H and Shawn Michaels in a Triple Threat Match

November 21, 2010

Miami, FL
American Airlines Arena

Main Event
WWE Champion Randy Orton defeated Wade Barrett in a Pinfall and Submissions Only Match with John Cena as referee

November 20, 2011

New York, NY
Madison Square Garden

Main Event
The Rock & John Cena defeated The Miz & R-Truth

S

2010-
2000-09
1990-99
1980-89
1970-79
1960-69

SWEDE HANSON

HT: 6'5" **WT:** 307 lbs. **FROM:** Slaughter Creek, North Carolina
SIGNATURE MOVE: Bearhug

A former Golden Gloves competitor, this giant was trained by the legendary George Tragos and debuted in Vincent J. McMahon's Capitol Wrestling in the late 1950s, often facing off against Bruno Sammartino. In the early 1960s, Swede ventured to Jim Crockett Promotions where he was part of one of the most famous tandems in professional wrestling history with Rip Hawk. In 1979 the man known as "Big Swede" returned to World Wrestling Entertainment, managed by Freddy Blassie. He reignited his battle with Bruno Sammartino and warred with Ivan Putski, Chief Jay Strongbow, Gorilla Monsoon, Andre the Giant, Tito Santana and Pedro Morales, but his main objective was to end the Heavyweight Championship reign of Bob Backlund. Swede remained with WWE until 1985. He retired from the ring one year later.

Swede Hanson passed away in 2002. His career was legendary and spanned four decades. Tough guys may come and go as time continues on but no one will ever forget the "Big Swede."

SWEET DADDY SIKI

HT: 5'10" **WT:** 245 lbs.
FROM: Montgomery, Texas

Sweet Daddy Siki was born in Texas, but cemented his legacy while competing north of the border in Canada. After several non-descript years of competing in New Mexico, Los Angeles, and Japan, Siki moved to Toronto where he became one of the country's most admired Superstars of the 1960s and 1970s.

While competing for Calgary's Stampede Wrestling, Siki defeated Dave Ruhl to capture the organization's North American Heavyweight Championship in September 1970. He held the title for six months before being toppled by the great Abdullah the Butcher.

During the twilight of his career, Siki began to train future competitors out of Sully's Gym in Toronto. During this time, he helped shape the career of a very young Edge. The "Rated-R Superstar" later went on to achieve amazing success as both a WWE Champion and World Heavyweight Champion.

SWS / WWE SUPERCARDS

In 1990 and 1991, WWE teamed up with Super World of Sports, a Japanese promotion, to hold a series of events that often saw WWE competitors facing an opponent from Japan.

WRESTLING SUMMIT
April 13, 1990

Tokyo Dome - Tokyo, Japan

Main Event: Shohei "Giant" Baba & Andre the Giant defeated Demolition in a Non-Title Special Tag Team Challenge Match

WRESTLEFEST
March 30, 1991

Tokyo Dome - Tokyo, Japan

Main Event: The Legion of Doom defeated Hulk Hogan & Genichiro Tenryu in a Special Tag Team Challenge Match

SUPERWRESTLE
December 12, 1991

Tokyo Dome - Tokyo, Japan

Main Event: Hulk Hogan defeated Genichiro Tenryu in a Special Challenge Match

SYLVAIN GRENIER

HT: 6'0" **WT:** 250 lbs.
FROM: Montreal, Quebec, Canada
SIGNATURE MOVE: 3 Seconds of Fame

TITLE HISTORY	
WORLD TAG TEAM CHAMPION (4 TIMES)	Partnered with Rene Dupree to defeat Kane & Rob Van Dam on June 15, 2003 Partnered with Rob Conway to defeat Chris Benoit & Edge on May 31, 2004 Partnered with Rob Conway to defeat Chris Benoit on November 1, 2004 Partnered with Rob Conway to defeat William Regal & Coach on January 16, 2005

After a chance meeting in Florida with Pat Patterson, Grenier changed from a supermodel to a sports-entertainer. After being trained by the legendary Dory Funk, Jr. and Rocky Johnson, Grenier made his WWE debut at *No Way Out 2003* as the referee in The Rock versus Hulk Hogan match. After an appearance at *WrestleMania XIX* as the referee for Mr. McMahon, the self-proclaimed prized treasure of North America soon formed the French elitist group known as La Resistance with Renee Dupree. In June, he and Dupree defeated Rob Van Dam & Kane to capture the World Tag Team Championship.

Towards the end of the year Sylvain suffered a severe neck injury, but he returned to WWE in March 2004 and rejoined La Resistance. In August 2005 Grenier became a member of *SmackDown* and the Ambassador to Quebec. He briefly changed his name to Sylvain and took aim at people's lack of fashion sense. In February 2007 Grenier briefly reunited with Dupree in ECW before he ultimately parted ways with WWE that August.

TAJIRI

HT: 5'9" **WT:** 205 lbs. **FROM:** Japan
SIGNATURE MOVE: Tarantula

TITLE HISTORY

CRUISERWEIGHT CHAMPION (3 TIMES)	*Defeated Billy Kidman on October 22, 2001* *Defeated Billy Kidman on April 21, 2002* *Defeated Rey Mysterio on September 25, 2003*
LIGHT HEAVYWEIGHT CHAMPION	*Defeated X-Pac on August 6, 2001*
UNITED STATES CHAMPION	*Defeated Chris Kanyon on September 10, 2001*
WORLD TAG TEAM CHAMPION	*Partnered with William Regal to defeat La Resistance on February 7, 2005*
WWE TAG TEAM CHAMPION	*Partnered with Eddie Guerrero to defeat the World's Greatest Tag Team on May 18, 2003*

After nearly a decade of professional experience in Japan and Mexico, Tajiri graced American rings with his lightning quick offense in 1998. As a member of Paul Heyman's ECW, he quickly reminded fans of fellow Japanese export Great Muta with his flying somersaults, roundhouse kicks, and mysterious mist.

When financial woes forced ECW's doors to close in 2001, Tajiri followed many of his colleagues in signing with WWE. Initially, he served as the comedic sidekick to WWE Commissioner William Regal. Despite never speaking English, Tajiri exhibited a hilarious sense of humor, but there was nothing funny about his in-ring skills.

His signature Tarantula and hand spring back elbow smash struck fear into the locker room. If the ref wasn't looking, the "Japanese Buzzsaw" was never above spitting a blinding green mist into the eyes of his competition. His combination of talent and a little rule breaking propelled Tajiri to numerous singles titles, including four combined runs with the now-defunct Cruiserweight and Light Heavyweight Championships.

Over the course of his five-year stay with WWE, Tajiri was also considered a top tag team talent. In May 2003, he teamed with Eddie Guerrero to claim the WWE Tag Team Championship from Shelton Benjamin & Charlie Haas. A few years later, alongside longtime associate William Regal, he bested La Resistance for the World Tag Team Titles in his home country of Japan. Tajiri last competed for WWE at *One Night Stand* in 2006 before he returned to action in his home country. After an appearance at a 2008 WWE event in Tokyo, the WWE Universe still waits for the "Japanese Buzzsaw" to reemerge.

SYLVESTER TERKAY

HT: 6'6" **WT:** 320 lbs.
FROM: Big Bear, California

An accomplished mixed martial artist, Sylvester Terkay made the jump to sports-entertainment in July 2006. With corner man Elijah Burke backing him, the Superstar dubbed "the Man Bear" made quick work of his fellow *SmackDown* Superstars, including Matt Hardy and Tatanka.

In November 2006, Terkay left *SmackDown* in favor of the competition found on ECW. The move proved to be a mistake, as his initial ECW match also marked his first-ever loss. Outside of a victory at *December to Dismember*, "the Man Bear" struggled to make waves as a member of the ECW roster.

TAKA MICHINOKU

HT: 5'8" **WT:** 201 lbs. **FROM:** Iwate, Japan
SIGNATURE MOVE: Michinoku Driver

TITLE HISTORY

LIGHT HEAVYWEIGHT CHAMPION	*Defeated Brian Christopher in the finals of a Light Heavyweight Tournament on December 7, 1997*

Trained by the legendary Great Sasuke, Taka Michinoku first arrived in the United States courtesy the bWo and ECW. A master of high-flying assaults, martial-arts, lucha libre, and grappling, he collected his share of admirers.

At *In Your House: Calgary Stampede* Taka made his debut in a thrilling contest against his mentor. In December, 1997 Michinoku defeated Brian Christopher to become the first WWE Light Heavyweight Champion in the finals of a tournament. Taka set a new championship standard as he defended the prize for more than 10 months before losing it to Christian.

Around this time he turned on partner Val Venis and joined the ranks of Kaientai, most often working with Funaki. Taka continued to appear in WWE into 2002 before returning to Japan where he remains one of the country's most popular Superstars. Taka Michinoku will be remembered by WWE audiences as one who took the Light Heavyweight Championship to new heights and brought a special brand of evil to the ring, indeed!

TAMINA SNUKA

HT: 5'9"
FROM: The Pacific Islands

Tamina boasts a unique blend of beauty, brawn and familial wrestling lineage that no other Diva can match. The daughter of WWE Hall of Famer Jimmy "Superfly" Snuka, Tamina debuted alongside fellow second-generation Superstars Jimmy and Jey Uso in May 2010. Together, the trio of Superstars claimed they were created for one purpose, to dominate. And that's exactly what they did to all three members of The Hart Dynasty. Over the next few weeks, Tamina and the Usos traded victories with The Hart Dynasty in Six-Person Tag Team Matches.

Later in the year, Tamina developed a budding romance with fellow *Raw* Superstar Santino Marella. During this time, the second-generation Diva split time between the Usos and Marella. She was even in her man's corner when he teamed with Vladimir Kozlov to capture the WWE Tag Team Championship.

Tamina was drafted to *SmackDown* in April 2011. She spent the following few months battling Kaitlyn and A.J. in the brand's Divas division and would later become a consistent presence in the in the Divas Championship picture.

TANK MORGAN

Fans who witnessed the beatings delivered by Tank Morgan may forever hold the images of his battered opponents in their minds. The opponents who took the beatings likely relive them in their worst nightmares. A detested villain, Morgan barreled into WWE in October 1966. He used power, agility, and cunning to further his ambitions to destroy his competition. His brutal, but effective methods made him a top challenger for the Heavyweight Championship held by Bruno Sammartino. The two Superstars brawled throughout the northeast and pushed one another to the limit of their physical endurance.

Though Tank never held the championship, he continued to ruin the lives of WWE heroes on his own as well as with associates of the treacherous sort, such as Luke Graham, Bull Ortega, Smasher Sloan, Gorilla Monsoon, and Baron Mikel Scicluna. Morgan left WWE in 1967 and toured the National Wrestling Alliance, developing a soft-spot in his blackheart for its Hawaiian territory.

TARZAN TYLER

HT: 6'3"   **WT:** 270 lbs.
FROM: Miami Beach, Florida

TITLE HISTORY	
INTERNATIONAL TAG TEAM CHAMPION	*Partnered with Luke Graham to defeat The Mongols on November 12, 1971*
WORLD TAG TEAM CHAMPION	*Partnered with Luke Graham to defeat Dick the Bruiser & The Sheik on June 3, 1971*

After nearly one decade of competing in Canadian wrestling rings, Tarzan Tyler took his game to the United States during the 1960s. Clad in multi-colored trunks and sporting bleached blonde hair, Tyler would incite the crowds by breaking nearly every rule in the book. For years, fans suspected he illegally loaded his boots, making them nearly lethal weapons. Referees, however, were unable to confirm the allegations.

As a singles star, Tyler engaged in many world championship rivalries. In the early 1960s, he challenged American Wrestling Association Champion Verne Gagne for the title on numerous occasions. Later, Tyler tried to wrest the National Wrestling Alliance Title from champions Lou Thesz and Dory Funk Jr. Tyler's greatest claim to fame came as a tag competitor. Teaming with "Crazy" Luke Graham, he turned back Dick the Bruiser & The Sheik in June 1971 to become WWE's first-ever World Tag Team Champions.

TATANKA

HT: 6'2"   **WT:** 285 lbs.   **FROM:** Pembroke, North Carolina
SIGNATURE MOVE: The Indian Death Drop

This Native American warrior was a renowned body builder before he entered the ring. After winning several bodybuilding competitions along the east coast of the United States, he trained at Larry Sharpe's Monster Factory.

After appearing in regional promotions, Tatanka came to WWE in 1992. Pushed by his Lumbee tribe war cry, his opponents knew that when he went on his war dance, it marked the beginning of the end for them. He enjoyed a lengthy undefeated streak where he didn't suffer a loss until September 1993 after Ludvig Borga used a steel chair on Tatanka's back when the referee was distracted.

Tatanka earned so much respect that Chief Jay Strongbow became his mentor and presented him with a Lumbee tribe chief headdress. Unfortunately, something in Tatanka snapped at *SummerSlam 1994* when he turned on Lex Luger and joined the Million Dollar Corporation. In 1995 Tatanka left WWE to take care of his family, but he made a surprise return at the 1996 *Royal Rumble*. Afterwards, Tatanka departed WWE again, and spent the next ten years on the independent scene. He made an amazing return to *Raw* in 2005 and for the next two years reminded audiences of the warrior he always was.

TATSUMI FUJINAMI

HT: 6'0"   WT: 238 lbs.   FROM: Oita, Japan
SIGNATURE MOVE: Dragon Sleeper

TITLE HISTORY

INTERNATIONAL TAG TEAM CHAMPION	*Partnered with Kengo Kumura to defeat Adrian Adonis & Dick Murdoch in the finals of a tournament on May 24, 1985*
INTERNATIONAL HEAVYWEIGHT CHAMPION (2 TIMES)	*Defeated Gino Brito on August 30, 1982 Defeated Riki Choshu on August 4, 1983*
JUNIOR HEAVYWEIGHT CHAMPION (2 TIMES)	*Defeated Jose Estrada on January 23, 1978 Defeated Ryma Go on October 4, 1979*

Tatsumi Fujinami's career started in 1971. His intensity and superior technical abilities quickly earned him the nickname "the Dragon." He developed revolutionary moves including the Dragon Sleeper, Dragon Suplex, and Dragon Backbreaker. In the late 1970s Fujinami arrived in North America competing in Mexico and Jim Crockett Promotions before his WWE debut in 1976. He defeated Jose Estrada in his debut to become WWE Light Heavyweight Champion.

Fujinami's fame brought him to the 1980 *Showdown At Shea* where he defeated Lucha Libre legend Chavo Guerrero. In August, 1982 Fujinami defeated Gino Brito to capture the prized International Heavyweight Championship with its lineage dating back to Antonino "Argentina" Rocca. Fujinami made headlines in the United States when he opposed "Nature Boy" Ric Flair for a historic "Champion vs. Champion" match at the first-ever WCW *SuperBrawl* in 1991.

Fujinami continues to be active in Japan, and has even started his own promotion. Tatsumi Fujinami is one of the greatest legends to ever do battle in professional wrestling on any continent and his influence goes beyond time periods and cultures.

TAZZ

HT: 5'9"   WT: 240 lbs.
FROM: Red Hook Section of Brooklyn

During his days in the ring, Tazz was widely regarded as one of the most dangerous competitors of his time. Though undersized by most standards, his offensive attack was pure dynamite.

TITLE HISTORY

HARDCORE CHAMPION	*3 Times*
WORLD TAG TEAM CHAMPION	*Partnered with Spike Dudley to defeat The Dudley Boys on January 7, 2002*

Known as "the Human Suplex Machine," Tazz's rise to the top started in 1993 when he joined ECW. Over the next six years, he defined himself as a true ECW icon, winning every piece of hardware the promotion offered. He even proudly carried his own FTW Championship, a title he created in 1998. He was known to challenge opponents to "...win if you can; survive if I let you."

Tazz made his WWE debut in 1999, beating the undefeated Kurt Angle. The win started Tazz's WWE career on the right foot, but little did anybody realize the extreme Superstar still had some ECW fight left in him. A few months after his WWE debut, Tazz returned to ECW and defeated Mike Awesome for the ECW Championship. The victory was truly historic, considering Tazz, under contract with WWE at the time, defeated Mike Awesome, a Superstar employed by WCW.

Towards the end of his in-ring career, Tazz began serving as a part-time commentator on *Sunday Night Heat*. His tell-it-like-it-is approach to announcing made him popular with the fans and it wasn't long before he was the permanent color commentator on *SmackDown*.

Proving he could do just about anything, Tazz added trainer to his impressive list of accomplishments. In 2001, he joined the cast of *Tough Enough* and trained aspiring Superstars including Christopher Nowinski and Josh Mathews. The man who brought the phrase "Tap Out" to sports-entertainment made a final return to the ring when he forced Jerry "The King" Lawler to submit at *One Night Stand* in 2006. Tazz remained one of the most popular broadcasters on television until he parted ways with WWE three years later.

TED ARCIDI

HT: 5'11"   WT: 285 lbs.
FROM: Boston, Massachusetts

The sports-entertainment world has seen many Superstars falsely claim to be the world's strongest man. In 1985, Ted Arcidi proved his bold assertion when he became the first human being to ever bench press more than seven-hundred pounds. The awesome Arcidi put up 705 pounds, breaking the world record once held by Bruno Sammartino.

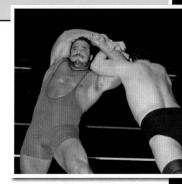

The record-breaking feat caught the eyes of WWE officials, who quickly signed Arcidi to a contract. Within moments of the ink drying, the solid block of a man took to the ring. Arcidi quickly engaged in rivalries with fellow toughmen Hercules and Big John Studd.

Arcidi's impressive strength earned him a spot in the famed WWE/NFL Battle Royal at *WrestleMania 2*. While he didn't win the competition, he did impress those watching, as it took the combination of Hillbilly Jim, B. Brian Blair and Danny Spivey to eliminate him.

T

1960-69
1970-79
1980-89
1990-99
2000-09
2010-

2010-
2000-09
1990-99
1980-89
1970-79
1960-69

TED DiBIASE

HT: 6'3"   WT: 235 lbs.
FROM: Palm Springs, Florida
SIGNATURE MOVE: Cobra Clutch Legsweep

TITLE HISTORY

WORLD TAG TEAM CHAMPION (2 TIMES)	Partnered with Cody Rhodes to defeat Hardcore Holly on June 29, 2008 Partnered with Cody Rhodes to defeat Batista & John Cena on August 11, 2008

While growing up, Ted DiBiase watched his father the "Million Dollar Man" prove that everyone has a price. He started to dream of taking the DiBiase name into the next millennium. After graduating college in 2005, Ted began training under Harley Race.

By 2007 Ted was generating a buzz in the WWE developmental system. In May 2008, the third generation Superstar made his debut on *Raw* and guaranteed he would become a champion in his first match. At *Night of Champions*, he delivered when Cody Rhodes turned on his partner Hardcore Holly and joined DiBiase to capture the World Tag Team Championship. In addition to Rhodes, DiBiase aligned himself with other men of distinguished sports-entertainment lineages including Manu and Randy Orton, calling themselves the Legacy. Proclaiming they were "Born Better," DiBiase became a hated villain as he aided Randy Orton in stalking WWE's most respected figures. Persistent in-fighting led to the break-up of this group. On the July 6, 2009 episode of *Raw*, DiBiase showed he was set for stardom as his own man during a match versus Randy Orton.

DiBiase then made the move to Hollywood. Soon after an appearance on *The Tonight Show with Conan O' Brien*, Ted made his movie debut in *The Marine 2*. "The Fortunate Son" had the Million Dollar Championship and a bountiful trust fund bestowed upon him by his father, the Million Dollar Man. He briefly employed his father's former assistant, Virgil, but replaced him with the dazzling Maryse.

DiBiase moved to *SmackDown* in April 2011 where he battled alongside, then against, Cody Rhodes. DiBiase gave up the Million Dollar Championship and found himself in a strange position, a favorite of the WWE Universe. Later in 2011, he began to host "DiBiase Posse" tailgating parties before WWE events. Ted DiBiase is a naturally gifted Superstars who gives his all in his matches, and whose devout following grows with every "DiBiase Posse" party.

TEKNO TEAM 2000 🇺🇸

MEMBERS: Travis, Troy
COMBINED WT: 480 lbs.

Following successful collegiate football careers with the University of Louisville, Travis and Troy reunited in 1995 to compete in WWE's heated tag team division. Dressed in shiny silver jackets and ultramodern elbow and knee pads, the agile duo claimed to be the team of the future. Unfortunately for them, their record said otherwise.

After picking up easy victories over combinations such as Brooklyn Brawler & Barry Horowitz, Travis & Troy found defeating the Smoking Gunns and other top-notch tandems quite difficult. In 1996, the futuristic tag team disappeared from WWE completely.

TENNESSEE LEE 🇺🇸

When you're the star of the magnitude that Jeff Jarrett thought he was in 1998, you need to have a strong support system around you. For Double J, his support included Southern Justice serving as his bodyguards and Tennessee Lee working as Jarrett's promoter and manager.

With his 10-gallon hat, cowboy boots and distinct southern accent, Tennessee Lee was easily recognizable as the irritating figure alongside Jarrett. Unlike most, however, Double J wasn't annoyed by Tennessee Lee, especially considering the manager oftentimes interfered to ensure his man would pick up the win.

In the summer of 1998, Tennessee Lee's interference started to become somewhat clumsy. Rather than helping Jarrett, the overzealous manager was actually costing his man matches. Finally, after Droz dropped Jarrett on an episode of *Sunday Night Heat*, Jarrett and Southern Justice delivered a vicious beat down to Tennessee Lee, marking the end of their short-lived business agreement. A deflated Tennessee Lee disappeared from WWE shortly after.

TERRI RUNNELS 🇺🇸

HT: 5'0"
FROM: Gainesville, Florida

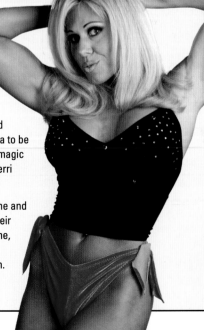

Movie buff Goldust introduced the world to his leading lady at the 1996 *Royal Rumble*. Calling herself Marlena, she sat in her director's chair and watched her masterpiece unfold, as Goldust beat Razor Ramon for the Intercontinental Championship. In the months that followed, the bizarre duo pushed the limits of acceptable social behavior, including public displays of affection and posing almost completely nude for *Raw Magazine*. Unfortunately for Marlena, what she assumed to be a storybook romance revealed itself as horror in November 1997. While a stipulation forced Marlena to be by the side of Brian Pillman for thirty days, Goldust was out making magic with the exotic Luna. The affair crushed Marlena's spirit, but gave Terri Runnels new life.

With "Marlena" a distant memory, Terri joined forces with Jacqueline and Ryan Shamrock to form Pretty Mean Sisters. Together, PMS used their sexuality to prey on WWE's male Superstars. Despite her petite frame, Terri held her own in the ring, highlighted by her greatest victory at *WrestleMania 2000* when she defeated the Kat in one-on-one action. During her time with WWE, Terri, also known as the Horny Little She-Devil, worked as a backstage interviewer and manager.

TERRY DANIELS

HT: 5'10" WT: 225 lbs.
FROM: Amarillo, Texas

As the first inductee into Sgt. Slaughter's elite Cobra Corps, a young Terry Daniels was immediately thrust into high-profile matches upon making his WWE debut in 1984. In fact, with little ring experience under his belt, the former Marine Private teamed with his Hall of Fame leader to challenge Dick Murdoch & Adrian Adonis for the World Tag Team Championship on the historic *Brawl to End It All* card from Madison Square Garden. Daniels competed again that night in a 20-man over-the-top-rope Battle Royal, which was won by Antonio Inoki.

Unfortunately for Daniels, the *Brawl to End It All* is where the Texas native's WWE career peaked. For the remainder of the decade and into the early 1990s, Daniels regularly found himself on the wrong side of decisions against the likes of George "The Animal" Steele, Iron Sheik and "Ravishing" Rick Rude. One of Daniels few wins on record came in August 1984, when he defeated Fred Marzino via pinfall at MSG.

TERRY FUNK

HALL OF FAME 2009

HT: 6'1" WT: 247 lbs. FROM: The Double Cross Ranch, Amarillo, Texas

TITLE HISTORY

WORLD TAG TEAM CHAMPION	*Partnered with Mick Foley to defeat the New Age Outlaws on March 29, 1998*

A man sees the world through a different set of eyes when growing up on the Double-Cross Ranch. Raised in a wrestling family, Terry Funk wanted to follow the career path of his famous father Dory Funk Sr. and brother, Dory Funk Jr. In 1965, Terry was regarded as one of the brightest stars in the National Wrestling Alliance. He combined rough housing, mat skills, and a mean streak a mile wide to become a legend in North America and Japan. In 1985 Terry came to WWE with his brothers, Dory and Jimmy Jack. In the late 1980s, he returned to the NWA for a classic "I Quit" Match with "Nature Boy" Ric Flair.

As the 1990s began, Funk became the backbone of the upstart ECW promotion, leading the revolution in sports-entertainment. In 1998, Funk joined his friend Mick Foley in WWE, and captured the World Tag Team Championships under their demented alter-egos, Chainsaw Charlie and Cactus Jack.

As the years went on this legend of sports-entertainment just got tougher and crazier. After penning his autobiography, *Terry Funk: More Than Just Hardcore* in 2005, he returned to WWE for *One Night Stand* in 2006 to join Tommy Dreamer & Beulah against Mick Foley, Edge & Lita.

After more than forty years of telling tales of terror throughout the world, the Hardcore Icon's career was honored in 2009. Alongside brother, Dory, Terry entered the WWE Hall of Fame. He regularly shows he's still "middle-aged and crazy" at events throughout North America and Japan.

Some Superstars graduated from The School of Hard Knocks; Terry Funk, who's meaner than a Texas rattlesnake, tougher than shoe leather, and more dangerous than a hallow-eyed scorpion, built that institution brick-by-brick with his bare hands.

TERRY GIBBS

HT: 6'0" WT: 240 lbs.
FROM: Tampa, Florida
SIGNATURE MOVE: Inverted Atomic Drop

This tough customer was known in regions within the National Wrestling Alliance and Puerto Rico's World Wrestling Council before his WWE debut in November 1984. Over the next four years Terry Gibbs was then seen against the premiere Superstars on programs like *Championship Wrestling, All-Star Wrestling,* and *Prime-Time Wrestling* .

Gibbs took on individuals like Mr. Wrestling II, Hillbilly Jim, SD Jones, Barry Windham, Ultimate Warrior and Hulk Hogan. By the late 1980s Gibbs left WWE and returned to the Independent scene. Terry Gibbs was one of the fixtures of WWE programming during the early days of Hulkamania and will be remembered as a rule-breaker who would do anything to win a match.

TERRY TAYLOR

HT: 6'1"   WT: 225 lbs.   FROM: Vero Beach, Florida
SIGNATURE MOVE: Scorpion Death Lock

This Superstar began his career in the late 1970s and made his WWE debut in October 1980, defeating Jose Estrada. Over the next eight years he expanded and honed his abilities in various territories in North America before returning to World Wrestling Entertainment in 1988. In his first match back, he attacked partner Sam Houston after a loss to Los Conquistadors.

Soon Taylor became a member of the Heenan Family and was greeted by jeers from fans at every turn. In 1989 he appeared as "the Red Rooster" but quickly grew tired of Bobby "The Brain" Heenan's verbal abuse. After facing the Brooklyn Brawler in a series of matches, he left WWE in June 1990. Taylor spent the next few years in WCW, and held various titles during his time there.

In 1992 he returned to WWE as "Terrific" Terry Taylor and used a new move to put away opponents, the Gutwrench Sit-out Powerbomb. Taylor also became a broadcaster for WWE television before he left the company again in 1993. After his departure from WWE, Taylor shifted his focus from in-ring work to calling the action and interviewing Superstars. In 1998, he returned to WWE to conduct backstage interviews but departed for WCW when he was given the opportunity to host *WCW Saturday Night*.

During competetive prime, Terry Taylor was a versatile performer with a great deal of technical wrestling ability as well as the gift of gab when given the microphone.

TEST

HT: 6'6"   WT: 285 lbs.   FROM: Toronto, Ontario, Canada
SIGNATURE MOVE: Big Boot

TITLE HISTORY	
EUROPEAN CHAMPION	Defeated William Regal on January 22, 2001
HARDCORE CHAMPION	2 Times
INTERCONTINENTAL CHAMPION	Defeated Edge on November 5, 2001
WORLD TAG TEAM CHAMPION	Partnered with Booker T to defeat The Rock & Chris Jericho on November 1, 2001

Test was proof that it paid to be in the right place at the right time. In late 1998, the oversized Canadian caught the eyes of WWE officials when he was working as a bodyguard for Mötley Crüe, and was soon signed to a contract.

Mixing business with pleasure, Test eventually fell for Stephanie McMahon. The affair infuriated the male McMahons, and at *SummerSlam 1999*, Test was forced to fight for his love against older brother Shane, but Test's adoration for Stephanie carried him to victory. Despite the win, things quickly turned ugly for the young lovers when Stephanie concocted a devious plan to leave Test and marry Triple H.

Refusing to be derailed by a broken heart, Test persevered. Over the next several years, he engaged in many high-profile encounters. His most notable match took place at *Survivor Series 2001* where he unsuccessfully defended his Intercontinental Championship against Edge's United States Title in a Unification Match. Test's WWE career also saw him capture the European and Hardcore Championships, as well as the World Tag Team Titles with Booker T.

After time away from WWE he returned to the pinnacle of sports-entertainment in 2006. Bringing his amazing power to ECW, Test battled ECW Originals Rob Van Dam, Sabu, Sandman, and Tommy Dreamer. His impressive showings earned him a shot at then-ECW Champion Bobby Lashley and the two clashed in several highly-contested encounters. He soon parted with WWE and toured independent cards around the world before he announced his retiremet from the ring. Sadly, Andrew "Test" Martin passed away in March 2009.

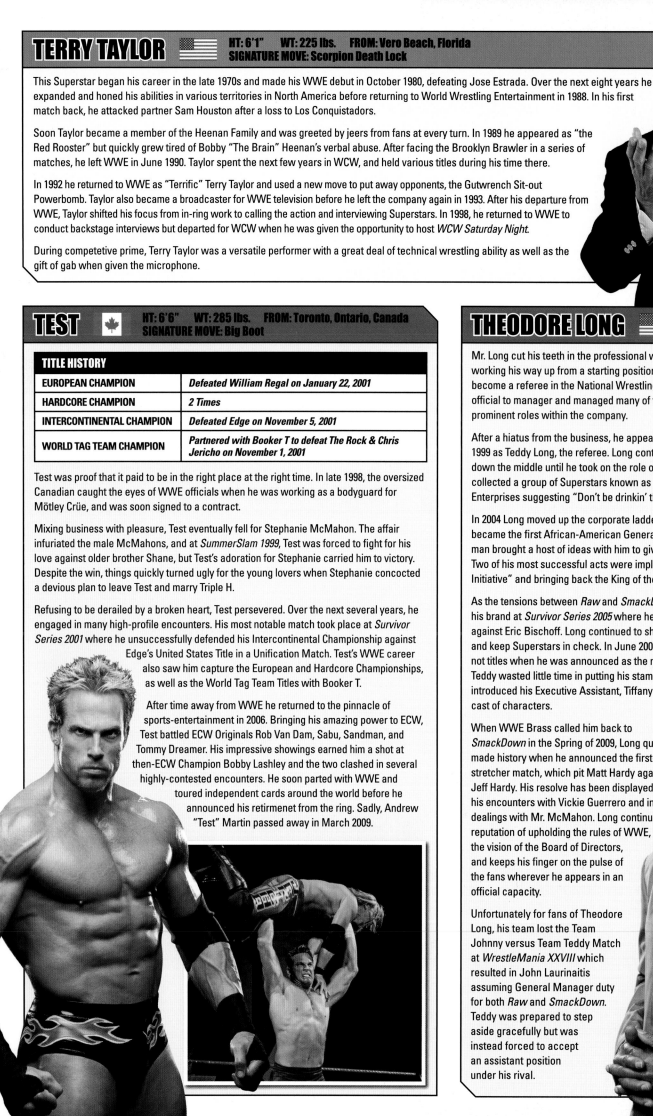

THEODORE LONG

Mr. Long cut his teeth in the professional wrestling business working his way up from a starting position with the ring crew to become a referee in the National Wrestling Alliance. He went from ring official to manager and managed many of the organizations top stars to prominent roles within the company.

After a hiatus from the business, he appeared on WWE programming in 1999 as Teddy Long, the referee. Long continued to call the action straight down the middle until he took on the role of conspirator. He quickly collected a group of Superstars known as "Thuggin' & Buggin' " Enterprises suggesting "Don't be drinkin' that hatorade."

In 2004 Long moved up the corporate ladder, and made history when he became the first African-American General Manager of *SmackDown*. The man brought a host of ideas with him to give the fans what they wanted. Two of his most successful acts were implementing the "New Talent Initiative" and bringing back the King of the Ring Tournament.

As the tensions between *Raw* and *SmackDown* arose, Long represented his brand at *Survivor Series 2005* where he won the "Battle of the GM's" against Eric Bischoff. Long continued to shake things up on Friday nights and keep Superstars in check. In June 2008 he changed work nights but not titles when he was announced as the new General Manager of ECW. Teddy wasted little time in putting his stamp on the innovative brand and introduced his Executive Assistant, Tiffany while dealing with its eclectic cast of characters.

When WWE Brass called him back to *SmackDown* in the Spring of 2009, Long quickly made history when he announced the first-ever stretcher match, which pit Matt Hardy against Jeff Hardy. His resolve has been displayed in his encounters with Vickie Guerrero and in his dealings with Mr. McMahon. Long continues his reputation of upholding the rules of WWE, the vision of the Board of Directors, and keeps his finger on the pulse of the fans wherever he appears in an official capacity.

Unfortunately for fans of Theodore Long, his team lost the Team Johnny versus Team Teddy Match at *WrestleMania XXVIII* which resulted in John Laurinaitis assuming General Manager duty for both *Raw* and *SmackDown*. Teddy was prepared to step aside gracefully but was instead forced to accept an assistant position under his rival.

THIS TUESDAY IN TEXAS

Dec 03 1991
Freeman Coliseum; San Antonio, TX

Following Undertaker's controversial WWE Championship victory over Hulk Hogan at Survivor Series 1991, WWE President Jack Tunney called for an immediate rematch. Unable to wait for January's *Royal Rumble*, he created the impromptu *This Tuesday in Texas* event, which was held on December 3, 1991.

Ironically, the Undertaker-Hogan rematch proved to be just as controversial as their *Survivor Series* encounter. The match fell apart when Tunney, who was seated ringside to ensure justice, was inadvertently knocked out. With Tunney unconscious, action quickly got out of hand, highlighted by Hogan temporarily blinding Undertaker with the ashes from the "Deadman's" signature urn. In the end, it was Hogan picking up the win, but Tunney later declared the WWE championship vacant due to the madness that arose during the match. The following month, Ric Flair outlasted 29 other Superstars to win the *Royal Rumble* and the vacant WWE Championship.

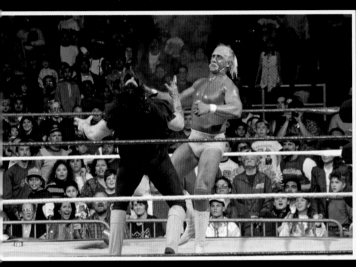

This Tuesday in Texas also featured the emotional return of Randy "Macho Man" Savage. Following his *WrestleMania VII* loss to Ultimate Warrior, Savage had been forced into an early retirement. However, when Jake "the Snake" Roberts pushed his venomous cobra on the "Macho Man," Tunney had no choice but to reinstate Savage for a *This Tuesday in Texas* encounter. In the record books, Savage earned the pinfall victory, but Roberts walked away with the psychological win. After the match, "the Snake" delivered three DDTs to his opponent. He then forced Elizabeth to beg for her man's safety before grabbing her by the hair and slapping her across the face.

In other *This Tuesday in Texas* action, Intercontinental Champion Bret Hart successfully defended his title against the undefeated Skinner, Ted DiBiase teamed with Repo Man to defeat Virgil & Tito Santana, and Davey Boy Smith beat the Warlord via pinfall.

Following the event, WWE did not hold another Tuesday night pay-per-view until the interactive *Taboo Tuesday* in 2004.

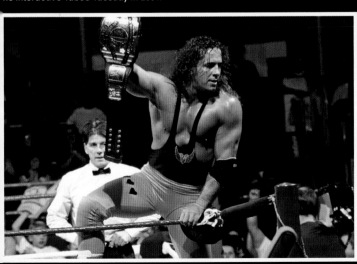

TIFFANY 🇺🇸
HT: 5'6"
FROM: New Orleans, Louisiana

This beautiful Diva debuted in WWE in 2008 as the Executive Assistant to ECW General Manager Theodore Long. Her acumen for business, marketing, and maintaining strong relationships made her a valued employee.

Tiffany utilized all of her attributes to make an impact wherever she went in WWE. Her ability to make tough decisions quickly gained her a following from the WWE Universe and the respect of Superstars. Her professional demeanor and razor sharp wit was a tremendous aid for Theodore Long as he revolutionized ECW. She eventually became the General Manager of the Land of Extreme and helped transition Superstar contracts when the brand closed and its talent was drafted to *Raw* or *SmackDown*.

In the spring of 2010 the dynamic executive turned competitor on *SmackDown*. As Beth Phoenix and Kelly Kelly stood by her side, Tiffany squared off against Lay-Cool and became a contender for the Women's Championship.

TIGER ALI SINGH 🇮🇳
HT: 6'5"   WT: 275 lbs.
FROM: The Continent of Asia
SIGNATURE MOVE: Reverse Neck Breaker

Considering his familial ties to the sports-entertainment industry, one would assume Tiger Ali Singh would understand the concept of respect. Unfortunately, however, the apple fell very far from the legendary Tiger Jeet Singh's tree, because the only thing his son, Tiger Ali Singh, respected was his money.

Tiger Ali Singh succeeded in hiding his true persona during the early portion of his WWE career. But after winning WWE's second-annual Kuwaiti Cup Invitational in April 1997, the second-generation Superstar began to reveal his true colors. It wasn't long before he began bragging about his riches. With his servant, Babu, by his side, he would regularly offer piles of cash to any American fan willing to perform humiliating tasks.

In the ring, Tiger Ali Singh successfully turned back such Superstars as Al Snow and Gillberg before focusing his efforts on managing. In 2000, he briefly guided the careers of Lo Down (Chaz and D-Lo Brown) before being released from WWE in 2002.

2010-
2000-09
1990-99
1980-89
1970-79
1960-69

TIGER CHUNG LEE

HT: 6'4"   WT: 289 lbs.
FROM: Korea

A master of martial arts, Tiger Chung Lee made a name for himself early on in his career while competing in Japan. While there, he and tag team partner Kintaro Ohki traded the All Japan International Tag Team Championship twice with Giant Baba & Jumbo Tsuruta.

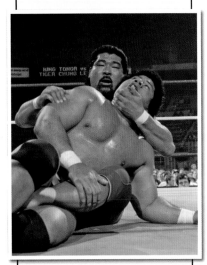

After losing the titles for the final time in May 1978, Tiger Chung Lee made his way to the United States where he briefly wrestled for the National Wrestling Alliance before finally landing in WWE.

Affectionately referred to as "the Chunger" by WWE Hall of Famer Gorilla Monsoon, Tiger Chung Lee proved his toughness almost immediately when he broke solid bricks on live television using only his bare hands. Unfortunately, his toughness failed to translate into victories, as Tiger Chung Lee oftentimes walked away from his WWE matches with the loser's share of the purse.

TIGER JEET SINGH

HT: 6'3"   WT: 265 lbs.
FROM: Punjab, India
SIGNATURE MOVE: Tiger Claw

Tiger Jeet Singh was a famous bodybuilder in his native India before he emigrated to Canada in 1965. Over the next few years, he became one of the most feared men of the ring. His match in 1967 at the Maple Leaf Gardens against Bruno Sammartino was such a huge draw that thousands of fans were turned away after the arena reached its capacity.

For the next three decades, Tiger Jeet Singh continued to maul opponents all over the world while appearing on cards with WWE Superstars. His popularity was greatest in Japan, where he fought in the IWA "King of the Death Match" tournament with fellow Superstars Terry Funk, Cactus Jack, and Terry "Bam Bam" Gordy.

Singh appeared in the crowd at *SummerSlam 1997* alongside his son, Tiger Ali Singh. Tiger Jeet managed his son into the Attitude Era before returning to terrorize foes overseas. Today, he remains one of the greatest figures in all of Japan and an influence to all rule-breakers who step into the ring.

TIGER MASK

HT: 5'8"   WT: 198 lbs.   FROM: Japan
SIGNATURE MOVE: Tiger Suplex

TITLE HISTORY	
JUNIOR HEAVYWEIGHT CHAMPION (3 TIMES)	*Defeated Dynamite Kid on January 1, 1982* *Defeated Black Tiger on May 26, 1982* *Defeated Fishman on June 13, 1983*

Originally a Japanese comic book superhero, Tiger Mask came to life in 1981 when he debuted in New Japan Pro Wrestling. With superior mat skills and high-flying aerial assaults, the furry masked Superstar was a legitimate double threat in the ring.

Tiger Mask's legendary rivalries with fellow technicians Bret Hart and Chris Adams made news all over the world, but it was his battles with Dynamite Kid that resonated most. In January 1982, he defeated Dynamite Kid in Japan to capture the WWE Junior Heavyweight Championship. Over the next several years, the two Superstars engaged in a global battle for junior heavyweight supremacy. In all, Tiger Mask held the title three times during the course of their epic rivalry.

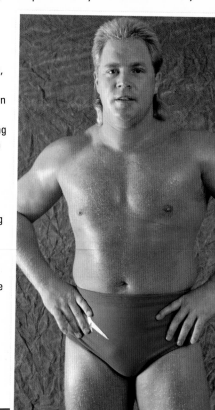

Tiger Mask simply wowed American audiences during his rare United States appearances. Never before had they seen such innovative high-flying offense. Some even say his unique approach helped motivate many of the today's Superstars, including Rey Mysterio.

By the mid-1980s, Tiger Mask lost his passion to compete. Still relatively young at the time, he walked away from the sport at the height of his popularity. Over the next several years, many Japanese Superstars donned the furry mask, claiming to be Tiger Mask. However, true sports-entertainment historians only recognize the original as the true Tiger Mask.

TIM HORNER

HT: 5'10"   WT: 230 lbs.
FROM: Morristown, Tennessee

As one half of the Lightning Express with partner Brad Armstrong, Tim Horner made a name for himself as a tag team specialist early in his career. After only a brief time together, the young team topped Rip Rogers & Ted Oates to win the NWA National Tag Team Championship in November 1984. Later that month, however, Lightning Express was forced to relinquish the gold when an injury prevented Horner from defending. Years later, the Lighting Express would strike again when Horner and Armstrong defeated Sting and Rick Steiner for the UWF World Tag Team Championship. They held the titles for five months before being upended by the Sheepherders.

As a singles competitor, "White Lightning" Tim Horner attempted to make a name for himself inside WWE and WCW rings. But he soon learned that the competition was too great. The Tennessee native regularly lost to the likes of Barry Windham, Paul Orndorff and Randy "Macho Man" Savage.

TITO SANTANA

HT: 6'2" **WT:** 234 lbs.
FROM: Tocula, Mexico
SIGNATURE MOVE: Flying Forearm

TITLE HISTORY

INTERCONTINENTAL CHAMPION (2 TIMES)	Defeated Don Muraco on February 11, 1984 Defeated Greg Valentine on July 6, 1985
WORLD TAG TEAM CHAMPION (2 TIMES)	Partnered with Ivan Putski to defeat Johnny Valiant & Jerry Valiant on October 22, 1979 Partnered with Rick Martel to defeat The Hart Foundation on October 27, 1987

A two-time Intercontinental and World Tag Team Champion, Tito Santana pieced together an impressive career that spanned decades. Along the way, he displayed class and a sound technical ability that made him one of the game's elite.

While Santana is most recognized for the success he experienced during the 1980s, his first taste of WWE superstardom actually came in the late 1970s. During a brief stay with the promotion, he teamed with Ivan Putski to claim the World Tag Team Championship from the Valiant Brothers. Santana & Putski held the titles for close to six months before losing to The Samoans. Following the loss, Santana took an extended leave from WWE.

In 1983, Santana returned to WWE and immediately found himself back in the title hunt. This time, he had eyes for Don Muraco's Intercontinental Championship. After a few unsuccessful tries, Santana was finally able to end Muraco's lengthy reign in February 1984. The win gave Santana his first of two Intercontinental Championships.

Between runs with the Intercontinental Championship, Santana made history when he defeated The Executioner in the first-ever *WrestleMania* match. He went on to earn a spot on the first nine *WrestleMania* cards (although his *WrestleMania IX* match was untelevised). Only Hulk Hogan can make the same claim.

Santana returned to his tag team roots in 1987, teaming with fellow fan favorite Rick Martel. Known as Strike Force, the duo defeated the Hart Foundation for the World Tag Team Championship in October. The popular tag team operated as a successful unit until April 1989 when Martel turned on Santana at *WrestleMania V*.

Following Strike Force's untimely demise, Santana adopted a bullfighting persona. Aptly named El Matador, Santana enjoyed a bit of a resurgence to his maturing career. El Matador's highest-profile encounter came at *WrestleMania VIII* when he fell to an up-and-coming Shawn Michaels.

In 2004, Santana assumed his rightful place alongside sports-entertainment's greatest when he was inducted into the WWE Hall of Fame.

TITUS O'NEIL

HT: 6'6" **WT:** 270 lbs. **FROM:** Live Oak, Florida
SIGNATURE MOVE: Clash of the Titus

Titus O'Neil is one of the most physically gifted Rookies *NXT* has ever produced. But the WWE Universe almost never got to realize this after his performance on the show's second season. Despite having the successful Zack Ryder as his Pro, the former University of Florida football star was the first person eliminated from competition.

Luckily for O'Neil, he was afforded an opportunity at redemption when he was announced as a Rookie for season five of *NXT*. Promising to show more of the true Titus O'Neil this time around, the 270-pound mammoth has proven he has what it takes to be WWE's next breakout star, thanks in large part to the strong leadership skills of his Pro, Hornswoggle. Along the way, he has laid waste to fellow Rookies Lucky Cannon and Darren Young, as well as WWE Superstar JTG. Prior to a career in the ring, O'Neil excelled as a professional football player in the Arena Football League.

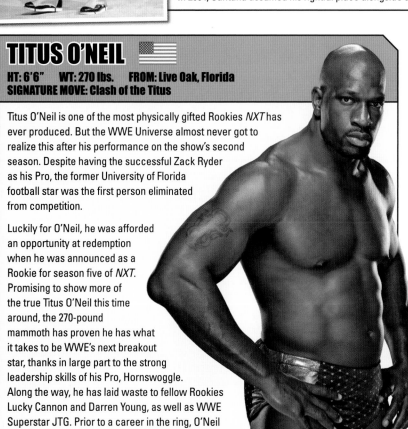

TL HOPPER

HT: 5'10"
WT: 235 lbs.

This plumber-turned-performer first appeared in World Wreslting Entertainment in 1996. His appearances in the ring were heralded by the sound of a flushing toilet, and he never strayed far from Betsy, his beloved plunger. During his tenure with WWE, he battled the likes of the Stalker, Aldo Montoya, the Bushwhackers, Marc Mero, and the Godwinns. He was also involved in a match where he teamed up with Billy Gunn to face Bart Gunn & Freddie Joe Floyd after the Smokin' Gunns' tumultuous split. After less than a year competing in WWE, TL Hopper left the the company to return to his former profession.

T

1960-69
1970-79
1980-89
1990-99
2000-09
2010-

The Tables, Ladders and Chairs Match provides some of the most exciting and death-defying moments in sports-entertainment. The object of a TLC Match is to ascend to the top of the ladder and capture the item that hangs from the ceiling before your opponent can do the same. As TLC Matches grew in popularity, the WWE Board of Directors created a yearly event, starting in 2009, featuring one or more of these dangerous components.

December 13, 2009

San Antonio, TX – AT&T Center

Main Event D-Generation X defeated WWE Tag Team Champions Chris Jericho & The Big Show in a Tables, Ladders, and Chairs Match

December 19, 2010

Houston, TX – Toyota Center

Main Event John Cena defeated Wade Barrett in a Chairs Match

December 18, 2011

Baltimore, MD – 1st Mariner Arena

Main Event WWE Champion CM Punk defeated The Miz and Alberto Del Rio in a Triple Threat Tables, Ladders, and Chairs Match

TODD GRISHAM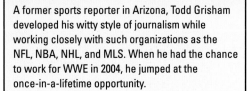

A former sports reporter in Arizona, Todd Grisham developed his witty style of journalism while working closely with such organizations as the NFL, NBA, NHL, and MLS. When he had the chance to work for WWE in 2004, he jumped at the once-in-a-lifetime opportunity.

As a member of WWE's esteemed announce team, Grisham did it all. He was best known for his hard-hitting line of questioning as *Raw*'s backstage interviewer, but also served on the now-defunct *Heat* as play-by-play man and hosted WWE.com's webcast *Byte This!*

But it was when this native of Bay Minette, Alabama became the lead announcer for *ECW on Syfy* he truly developed his own following. His broadcasting style became so popular with the WWE Universe Grisham remained the backstage interviewer for *Raw*, teamed with Tazz and later Josh Mathews on ECW, and commentated with WWE Hall of Famer, Jim Ross on *SmackDown*.

Todd also stood behind the podium and hosted WWE's 2009 Hall of Fame induction ceremony. He soon reunited with Mathews as the lead announcer on *NXT*. Grisham left WWE in August 2011, and started working for ESPN shortly afterward.

TODD PETTENGILL

Todd Pettengill debuted in WWE in early 1993, and over the next five years, he performed nearly every task imaginable to a sports-entertainment broadcaster and then some.

Some of Pettengill's more unorthodox job responsibilities included interviewing Superstars at *WrestleMania IX* while wearing a toga, providing fans with tips for all types of video games (not just WWE) and giving away a house to a lucky member of the WWE Universe. But perhaps his most memorable performance came at the prestigious 1996 Slammy Awards ceremony, where the always-smiley announcer sang the show's opening number. Much like Neil Patrick Harris, Ricky Gervais or any other of today's award-show hosts, Pettengill used his song to poke fun at WWE's most prominent Superstars, including Shawn Michaels, Ultimate Warrior and Triple H.

Pettengill has also found fame outside the squared circle as the co-host of WPLJ's hit morning radio show, *The Big Show*, which can be heard in the New York market.

TOM MAGEE

HT: 6'5" **WT:** 275 lbs.
FROM: Winnipeg, Manitoba, Canada

Holding a black belt in karate, and world titles in competitive bodybuilding, Tom Magee trained for the ring with the incomparable Stu Hart. After appearing in Japan, Magee took his impressive physique and charisma to WWE.

Magee debuted in World Wrestling Entertainment in 1986 and jumped right into the mix taking on Jimmy Jack Funk, Terry Gibbs, Tiger Chung Lee, Ron Bass, Barry O, Iron Mike Sharpe and Bret "Hit Man" Hart. Magee left WWE in 1990 and pursued a career as an actor. Today, he lends his training expertise to bodybuilding hopefuls.

TOMMY DREAMER

HT: 6'2" **WT:** 265 lbs. **FROM:** Yonkers, New York
SIGNATURE MOVE: The Dreamer DDT

TITLE HISTORY

ECW CHAMPION	*Defeated Christian and Jack Swagger in a Triple Threat Match on June 7, 2009*
HARDCORE CHAMPION	*14 Times*

From the moment he saw Jimmy "Superfly" Snuka dive from the top of the cage at Madison Square Garden, all this kid from Yonkers wanted to do was wrestle. After training from Johnny Rodz, Dreamer became one of the primary forces that changed the E in ECW from Eastern to Extreme. Known as "the Innovator of Violence" Dreamer often turned the ring into a blood-stained battleground. Dreamer faithfully remained with the company until it closed in 2001.

That July, Dreamer and fellow Extremist Rob Van Dam debuted on Raw and fired the first shot in ECW's second invasion of WWE. When he joined the WWE roster, he became one of the Hardcore Division's toughest competitors and went on to be a 14-time Hardcore Champion. He played a huge role in the first two *One Night Stand* events. At *WrestleMania 23*, Tommy survived the war with The New Breed as over 80,000 fans chanted, "ECW! ECW!"

Tommy competed for the final time in an ECW ring in December 2009. He remains synonymous with ECW and is regarded as one of the toughest, most respected competitors ever to step between the ropes. Tommy Dreamer sacrificed his blood throughout his storied career and is the only man to hold the ECW Championship in the original promotion and WWE's extreme reincarnation.

THE TONGA KID

HT: 6'3" **WT:** 225 lbs.
FROM: The Isle of Tonga
SIGNATURE MOVE:
Flying Headbutt

This son of Samoa from the Isle of Tonga flew into WWE in August 1983. The cousin of Jimmy "Superfly" Snuka, the Kid took to the air against Mr. Fuji, Iron Sheik, "Mr. Wonderful" Paul Orndorff, "Cowboy" Bob Orton and "Rowdy" Roddy Piper.

The Kid also joined forces with his famous cousin and electrified audiences with their high-flying moves and exciting style. In 1986 he formed an awesome tag team combination with King Tonga which became known as the Islanders.

TONY ALTOMARE

HT: 5'11" **WT:** 265 lbs.
FROM: Stamford, Connecticut

TITLE HISTORY

UNITED STATES TAG TEAM CHAMPION	*Partnered with Lou Albano to defeat Spiros Arion & Arnold Skaaland on July 10, 1967*

An Italian tough guy, Tony Altomare is best remembered as part of the Sicilians tag team. With Lou Albano as his partner, Altomare spun a convincing tale about being a part of the mafia. He was so believable, in fact, that mobsters hunted him down in the 1960s to tell him to give up the façade.

In July 1967, Altomare & Albano defeated Spiros Arion & Arnold Skaaland to capture the WWE United States Tag Team Championship. They held the titles for only two weeks before losing to Arion and his new partner, Bruno Sammartino.

Shortly after the loss, Albano hung up his boots and began managing. This left Altomare to fend for himself. On his own, the Italian Superstar's star began to fade. As the losses began to pile up, he started to investigate other ways to earn a living. He briefly served as a referee and a trainer. One of his most noted pupils was Steve Blackman.

TONY ATLAS

HT: 6'2" **WT:** 250 lbs. **FROM:** Roanoke, Virginia
SIGNATURE MOVE: Gorilla Press Slam

TITLE HISTORY

WORLD TAG TEAM CHAMPION	*Partnered with Rocky Johnson to defeat The Samoans on November 15, 1983*

A former bodybuilder, Tony Atlas possessed one of the most impressive physiques to ever grace a WWE ring. Known as "Mr. USA," he used his great strength to break through color barriers and become a true WWE legend.

Atlas made his professional debut in 1974. Despite having little experience to draw upon, his early days were filled with numerous NWA regional championships. By the early 1980s, he had properly honed his skills, developed a powerful Gorilla Press Slam and moved up north to WWE.

The WWE fans quickly took to the sculpted newcomer. Behind the support of their vociferous cheers, Atlas began to rack up an impressive winning streak, which included a pinfall victory over Hulk Hogan. In November 1983, he made sports-entertainment history when he teamed with Rocky Johnson to become the first African-Americans to capture the World Tag Team Championship. They held the titles for five months before losing to Adrian Adonis & Dick Murdoch.

Following the loss, Atlas became a bit of a nomad, competing for several smaller wrestling promotions such as World Class Championship Wrestling and the American Wrestling Federation.

In 2006, Atlas' efforts toward equality in sports-entertainment were recognized with induction into the WWE Hall of Fame. Despite the honor, "Mr. USA" refused to retreat into retirement. Instead, he continued to compete on independent wrestling cards and eventually worked his way back to WWE. In 2008, he revealed himself as the manager of ECW Champion Mark Henry. For the first time in his WWE career, he found himself on the wrong side of the fans' admiration. However, the lack of cheers didn't stop Atlas from guiding Henry toward the same level of greatness Tony achieved during the prime of his career. While in The Land of Extreme Atlas even returned to the ring on occasion. The man known as "Mr. USA" was last seen on 2010's *Old School Raw* and will be remembered for his combination of incredible strength, speed, and charisma.

TONY CHIMEL

Tony Chimel is best recognized as the former ring announcer for *ECW on Syfy*, but his sports-entertainment career started long before the extreme brand even came into existence. Back in the early 1980s, Chimel parlayed his friendship with Gorilla Monsoon's son into a job setting up wrestling rings. Then in 1999, he permanently moved in front of the cameras when he defeated legendary ring announcer Howard Finkel for the right to introduce *SmackDown*'s Superstars. Chimel spent the next eight years on *SmackDown* before taking his game to ECW in September 2007. When ECW closed its doors, Chimel returned to the familiar surroundings of *SmackDown*. Tony's trademark energy and delivery got the WWE Universe ready for the action that awaited them at events all over the world. He briefly left announcing in 2011 for a role with the company behind the scenes, but has returned to the ring as the announcer for *NXT*.

TONY GAREA

HT: 6'2" WT: 246 lbs. FROM: Auckland, New Zealand
SIGNATURE MOVE: The Octopus Hold

TITLE HISTORY

WORLD TAG TEAM CHAMPION (5 TIMES)	Partnered with Haystacks Calhoun to defeat Professor Tanaka & Mr. Fuji on May 30, 1973 Partnered with Dean Ho to defeat Professor Tanaka & Mr. Fuji on November 14, 1973 Partnered with Larry Zbyszko to defeat The Yukon Lumberjacks on November 21, 1978 Partnered with Rick Martel to defeat The Samoans on November 8, 1980 Partnered with Rick Martel to defeat The Moondogs on July 21, 1981

This sensational athlete debuted in World Wrestling Entertainment in 1972. His accomplishments within the ranks of tag team wrestling set him apart from every other Superstar before or since. In May 1973 the former Rugby player and giant Haystacks Calhoun defeated Prof. Toru Tanaka & Mr. Fuji. Over the next eight years Garea enlisted other great men like Dean Ho, Larry Zbyszko, and Rick Martel to capture tag team gold against the likes of the Valiant Brothers, the Yukon Lumberjacks, the Wild Samoans, and the Moondogs.

Garea continued his in-ring career until his retirement from the ring in 1986. During this time he also dabbled in announcing as a commentator alongside Vince McMahon on episodes of *Championship Wrestling*. Garea then made the transition to WWE's front office and was often seen breaking apart violent brawls on WWE programming. Today he is still a valued WWE employee who is often out scouting for the next WWE Superstar.

In his career, Garea was a five-time World Tag Team Champion, and his success with partner Rick Martel was celebrated in June 2007 at *Vengeance: Night of Champions*. Tony Garea will go down in WWE history as a legend of tag team wrestling and one of its most decorated competitors. His abilities and heart made him a favorite among fans, and a difficult individual for opposing Superstars to beat.

TONY MAMALUKE

HT: 5'10" WT: 150 lbs. FROM: Bensonhurst, Brooklyn
SIGNATURE MOVE: Sicilian Stretch

After a brief stint in WCW, Tony Mamaluke made his mark in ECW as part of the Full Blooded Italians. He became ECW World Tag Team Champions with Little Guido and remained a star until ECW closed its doors in March 2001.

Tony spent the next few years appearing at independent events throughout the United States. In 2005 he appeared with the FBI at *ECW One Night Stand*. When WWE relaunched ECW, Mamaluke was a part of it and after *One Night Stand 2006* he was seen on *ECW On Syfy* fighting the likes of Sabu, Test, and Mike Knox. In January 2007 Mamaluke and World Wrestling Entertainment severed ties and he returned to the independent circuit where he can be seen competing today.

TONY MARINO

HT: 5'10" WT: 240 lbs. FROM: New York
SIGNATURE MOVE: Abdominal Stretch

TITLE HISTORY

INTERNATIONAL TAG TEAM CHAMPION	Began partnering with Victor Rivera to defend the titles in early 1970

Tony Marino began his professional wrestling career in the mid 1960s. Shortly after his debut, he began competing for WWE, mainly on the promotion's Pittsburgh cards. It was during this period that he started to don a dark mask and call himself Battman, based on the popular superhero, Batman.

With two WWE International Tag Team Championship reigns under his belt (one was credited to Battman), Marino left WWE in the early 1970s and embarked on a 15-year career with the NWA. He found his greatest success teaming with Fred Curry. Together, the duo claimed the Detroit version of the promotion's World Tag Team Championship four times. Marino also won the same titles with future WWE Hall of Famer Bobo Brazil on three separate occasions.

Marino's only singles title came at the expense of the legendary Sheik. He beat the madman for the Detroit version of the NWA United States Championship in March 1974. He held the gold for two weeks before losing back to The Sheik.

TONY PARISI

HT: 5'11" **WT:** 241 lbs.
FROM: Cozena, Italy

Early in his WWE career, Tony Parisi, then known as Antonio Pugliese, was billed as the cousin of the legendary Bruno Sammartino. The family ties helped lend legitimacy to the newcomer's career and

TITLE HISTORY

UNITED STATES TAG TEAM CHAMPION (2 TIMES)	Partnered with Johnny Valentine to defeat Dan Miller & Dr. Bill Miller on February 21, 1966 Partnered with Spiros Arion to defeat Baron Mikel Scicluna & Smasher Sloan on December 8, 1966
WORLD TAG TEAM CHAMPION	Partnered with Louis Cerdan to defeat The Blackjacks on November 8, 1975

within weeks of his 1966 debut, the proud Italian was co-holder of the now-defunct United States Tag Team Championship with Johnny Valentine.

In mid-1967, Parisi left WWE to compete in various territories throughout the United States and Australia. When he finally returned several years later, he periodically teamed with Sammartino before forming a championship combination with Louis Cerdan. The new pairing defeated the Blackjacks for the World Tag Team Championship in November 1975. They held the titles for six months before being upended by The Executioners.

TONY SCHIAVONE

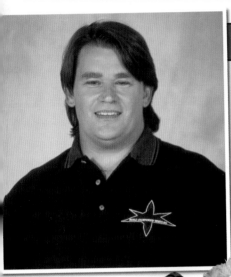

With 20 years behind the microphone, Tony Schiavone became one of the most recognizable sports-entertainment voices of the late 1980s and 1990s. Despite his years of tireless service, Schiavone will forever be remembered most for a poor choice of words during a pivotal moment of the WWE-WCW Monday Night Wars.

On January 4, 1999, while serving as the lead announcer of *Monday Nitro*, Schiavone spoiled the results of a pre-taped WWE Championship Match on *Raw*:

"Tonight, fans, Mick Foley, who wrestled here as Cactus Jack and now wrestles in WWE as Mankind, will win the WWE Title," said Schiavone before sarcastically proclaiming, "That'll put some butts in the seats."

The move backfired when a large portion of WCW's viewers switched over to see Foley win the WWE Championship. Many believe Schiavone was simply following the orders of WCW boss Eric Bischoff when he revealed the results. Regardless, WWE won the ratings war that night and never looked back. Prior to his run with WCW, Schiavone briefly called WWE's action in 1989 and 1990.

TOO COOL

MEMBERS: Scotty 2 Hotty, "Grand Master Sexay" Brian Christopher
COMBINED WT: 433 lbs.

TITLE HISTORY

WORLD TAG TEAM CHAMPIONS	Defeated Edge & Christian on May 29, 2000

In the late 1990's Scotty 2 Hotty and Grand Master Sexay were a pair of hip-hoppers who stood out from the pack who called themselves Too Much. In 2000, after taking on the name Too Cool, they were joined by Rikishi and became a three-man squad that was a huge hit with fans who cheered as much for the trio's wins as they did their post-match celebratory dance.

In May, 2000 Too Cool showed they were too good when they defeated Edge & Christian to became World Tag Team Champions. Though Rikishi eventually left to follow a darker path, Scotty and Grand Master continued to thrill until 2001 when Brian Christopher and WWE parted ways. Rikishi and Scotty reunited in 2004 and managed to capture the WWE Tag Team Championship for a brief time.

TOR KAMATA

HT: 6'3" **WT:** 350 lbs. **FROM:** The South Pacific Islands
SIGNATURE MOVE: Big Splash

Tor Kamata toured the globe many times over during the course of his thirty-year career, but it was his time spent in Canada's Stampede Wrestling that fans will remember most. While competing for Stampede Wrestling, the hated Tor Kamata, who often used salt as a weapon to blind his foes, captured the prestigious North American Heavyweight Championship on three separate occasions. He also teamed with Sugi Siti to win the promotion's International Tag Team Championship in February 1972.

Later that year, Kamata competed in one of sports-entertainment's first Ladder Matches. With Cowboy Dan Kroffat as his opponent, Kamata did everything in his power to claw his way up the ladder towards the bag of money. In the end, it was Kroffat who walked away the winner. In the late 1970s, Kamata joined WWE under the tutelage of Freddie Blassie. His brief WWE career was highlighted by several memorable matches with an up-and-coming Bob Backlund.

1960-69
1970-79
1980-89
1990-99
2000-09
2010-

T

2010-
2000-09
1990-99
1980-89
1970-79
1960-69

TORRIE WILSON 🇺🇸 FROM: Boise, Idaho

This WWE Diva grew up a competitive athlete and dancer. She was passionate about nutrition and fitness and in 1998 won the prestigious Miss Galaxy competition.

Torrie began her career in sports-entertainment with WCW in 1999 and was a manager through late 2000. Torrie joined the WCW invasion of WWE in June of 2001, and first appeared on *SmackDown* in a segment with WWE Chairman Vince McMahon. Her in-ring debut was in a Bra and Panties Match, teaming with Stacy Kiebler against Lita and Trish Stratus at *Invasion*.

Despite being a part of the enemy, this breathtaking blonde became an instant sensation with audiences all over the globe. She returned to managing when she aligned herself with "Japanese Buzzsaw" Tajiri. From there she moved on to more Diva-centric pursuits like ruling Lingerie, Bra and Panties, and Paddle On A Pole Matches.

In May of 2003 Torrie adorned the cover of Playboy and set a new standard of beauty for the classic magazine. As the issue achieved

incredible success, she returned to the cover for a second time in March of 2004. On this occasion however she brought a partner in crime with her, the intoxicating Sable.

Torrie's fame continued to skyrocket during 2005 when she joined *Raw* and participated in Mixed Tag, Evening Gown, Kimono, Santa's Little Helper, and Lumberjill Matches. In June 2006, she defeated Candice Michelle in the first-ever Wet & Wild Match where the winner graced the cover of WWE's Summer Special Magazine. Torrie followed that pictorial in September by gracing the cover of FHM Magazine.

Wilson went from cover girl to calendar girl in FHM's 2007 Calendar. She was also listed in its *Sexiest Women In The World* issue. Torrie entered the fashion world when she unveiled her own clothing line called "Officially Jaded."

To the sadness of her fans worldwide, Torrie and WWE parted ways in May 2008. Torrie Wilson will forever be remembered for her charisma, athleticism, and dedication to sports-entertainment.

TORI 🇺🇸

HT: 5'9"
FROM: Portland, Oregon
SIGNATURE MOVE: Tori-Plex

This former Diva morphed from a bodybuilder into a wrestling machine and burst into the spotlight in 1998. Tori faced the likes of Luna, Jacqueline, and Sable and also showed her skills in Mixed Tag matches with partners Val Venis and Al Snow before going after Ivory's Women's Championship.

In late 1999 Tori became romantically involved with "the Big Red Monster" Kane but eventually left him for high-flying bad boy, X-Pac. Her ring savvy later served her well as she became a trainer on the first season of *Tough Enough*. By 2001 Tori left World Wrestling Entertainment. Today she is a yoga guru and makes the occasional appearance on the independent wrestling scene.

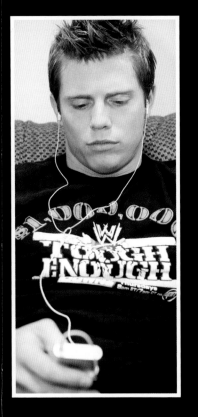

TOUGH ENOUGH®

Want to know what it's like to try to become a WWE Superstar? Do you think you have what it takes to be a part of the greatest sports-entertainment company in the history of human civilization? In June 2001 fans of sports-entertainment had the opportunity to enter a competition-based television program. Over 4,000 audition tapes were sent into WWE and from that enormous pool, 230 individuals were invited to New York. There were 13 finalists selected to compete in the inaugural season. They were trained by an expert staff led by Al Snow and included Tori, Jacqueline and Tazz. *Tough Enough* took a big step up for its *SmackDown*-exclusive 2004 season when the prize WWE contract was worth up to $1,000,000.

Tough Enough went off the air for the rest of the decade but made a huge return in 2011 the night after *WrestleMania XXVII*. For the show's big return, WWE called on Stone Cold Steve Austin to host the show and serve as the head trainer. His hand-selected training team included Booker T, Trish Stratus and Bill DeMott. Nine men and five women, including a former Miss USA from Michigan, competed for a WWE contract. Each week the prospective Superstars went through rigorous training, competed against each other in physical challenges and were surprised by weekly visits from the biggest names in WWE.

Winners

Season 1:
Maven Huffman & Nidia Guenard

Season 2: *Linda Miles & Jackie Gayda*

Season 3:
John Hennigan & Matt Cappotelli

Season 4: *Daniel Puder*

Season 5: *Andy Leavine*

TRENT BARRETA

HT: 6'2"   WT: 195 lbs.   FROM: Mount Sinai, New York
SIGNATURE MOVE: Dudebuster DDT

The WWE Universe can thank ECW's New Superstar Initiative for introducing them to the ever exciting Trent Barreta. Alongside lifelong best friend and tag-team partner Caylen Croft, Barreta emerged victorious in the pair's debut match in December 2009. Together, Barreta and Croft continued their hot streak until ECW closed its doors for good in February 2010.

Both Barreta and Croft were highly sought-after free agents following ECW's final show. In the end, the duo decided to sign with *Friday Night SmackDown*, where they competed as The Dudebusters for several months until Croft's release from WWE in late 2010.

On his own, Baretta has adjusted rather nicely to singles action. Competing mainly on *WWE Superstars*, the up-and-comer's matches have become "can't miss." And behind the force of his feared Dudebuster DDT, the New York native has earned victories over the likes of Tyson Kidd and Curt Hawkins. He's also found ways to eke out wins against former Intercontinental Champions Goldust and Drew McIntyre.

TRINITY 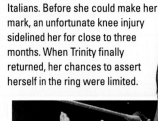   FROM: Long Island, New York

You didn't have to look hard to see that Trinity was a dangerous Diva. With peaking biceps and yellow police tape strapped across her sculpted chest, it was practically written all over her. The stuntwoman-turned-Diva made her debut in June 2006 as the manager of ECW's Full Blooded Italians. Before she could make her mark, an unfortunate knee injury sidelined her for close to three months. When Trinity finally returned, her chances to assert herself in the ring were limited.

T

1960-69
1970-79
1980-89
1990-99
2000-09
2010

TRIPLE H

HT: 6'4" **WT:** 260 lbs. **FROM:** Greenwich, Connecticut **SIGNATURE MOVE:** Pedigree

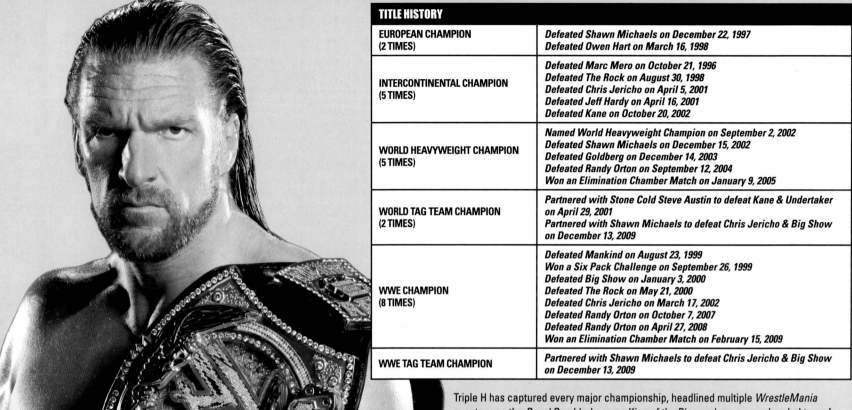

TITLE HISTORY	
EUROPEAN CHAMPION (2 TIMES)	*Defeated Shawn Michaels on December 22, 1997* *Defeated Owen Hart on March 16, 1998*
INTERCONTINENTAL CHAMPION (5 TIMES)	*Defeated Marc Mero on October 21, 1996* *Defeated The Rock on August 30, 1998* *Defeated Chris Jericho on April 5, 2001* *Defeated Jeff Hardy on April 16, 2001* *Defeated Kane on October 20, 2002*
WORLD HEAVYWEIGHT CHAMPION (5 TIMES)	*Named World Heavyweight Champion on September 2, 2002* *Defeated Shawn Michaels on December 15, 2002* *Defeated Goldberg on December 14, 2003* *Defeated Randy Orton on September 12, 2004* *Won an Elimination Chamber Match on January 9, 2005*
WORLD TAG TEAM CHAMPION (2 TIMES)	*Partnered with Stone Cold Steve Austin to defeat Kane & Undertaker on April 29, 2001* *Partnered with Shawn Michaels to defeat Chris Jericho & Big Show on December 13, 2009*
WWE CHAMPION (8 TIMES)	*Defeated Mankind on August 23, 1999* *Won a Six Pack Challenge on September 26, 1999* *Defeated Big Show on January 3, 2000* *Defeated The Rock on May 21, 2000* *Defeated Chris Jericho on March 17, 2002* *Defeated Randy Orton on October 7, 2007* *Defeated Randy Orton on April 27, 2008* *Won an Elimination Chamber Match on February 15, 2009*
WWE TAG TEAM CHAMPION	*Partnered with Shawn Michaels to defeat Chris Jericho & Big Show on December 13, 2009*

Triple H has captured every major championship, headlined multiple *WrestleMania* events, won the *Royal Rumble*, become King of the Ring and even spearheaded two of WWE's most influential factions. However, these achievements didn't happen by chance. They are the result of an unparalleled commitment to excellence that propelled Triple H past controversy and career-threatening injuries to become one of the greatest of all time.

Triple H was a lanky 135 pounds at the age of 14 when he received a gym membership that would change his life forever. Over the next several years, Triple H committed himself to becoming bigger and stronger. His dedication eventually led to numerous bodybuilding crowns.

Looking for advice on breaking into wrestling, Triple H turned to former Superstar Ted Arcidi. The two men developed a friendship while working out together at the same gym in New Hampshire. Arcidi pointed Triple H in the direction of Killer Kowalski, who agreed to train him.

After one year of working with Kowalski, Triple H competed on an independent wrestling card that happened to have a legend quietly sitting in the stands. As a favor to Big John Studd, Pat Patterson went to the event to scout out one of Studd's protégés. While he was there, however, Patterson couldn't help but be amazed by the skill of Triple H.

WWE Comes Calling

Triple H was thrilled by Patterson's compliments, but knew he still had some seasoning to do. However, it didn't take long for word of his outstanding matches, which included a stint in WCW, to reach Vince McMahon, who signed the young star.

Outside the ring, Helmsley began to form close bonds with several of his fellow Superstars, most notably Shawn Michaels, Kevin Nash (known then as Diesel) and Scott Hall (known then as Razor Ramon), the group became known as "The Kliq." On their final night together in Madison Square Garden (Hall and Nash were on their way to join WCW), all four members of "The Kliq" shared a heartfelt embrace in the center of the ring. The controversial stunt infuriated Mr. McMahon. As a result, McMahon punished Helmsley, relegating him to near-meaningless matches.

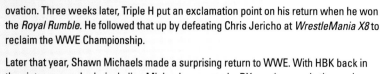

Lesser Superstars would never have rebounded from McMahon's wrath, but Helmsley refused to stay down, using his in-ring talent to force his way back to the top. Five months after the MSG incident, Helmsley defeated Marc Mero for the first of many singles titles in WWE.

By 1997, the successful Helmsley became the target of many Superstars. To combat their attacks, he employed the services of a muscle-bound bodyguard. *Her* name was Chyna. With his new enforcer watching his back, Helmsley continued to post impressive wins.

Forming D-Generation X

As 1997 continued to roll on, Helmsley began to shed his American blue blood persona and WWE fans were shocked at what they saw. The one-time snob transformed into one of the most rebellious Superstars in history. By the end of September, Triple H moved his backstage friendship with Shawn Michaels in front of the television cameras. Together, they pushed the envelope and formed one of the most notorious factions of all time: D-Generation X.

The Game a.k.a. The Cerebral Assassin

Less than five months after turning his back on DX at *WrestleMania XV*, Triple H reached the summit of the sports-entertainment world when he defeated Mankind for the WWE Championship. By the end of the year, the cerebral Triple H managed to advance his career and personal life in one fell swoop when he married Mr. McMahon's daughter, Stephanie. The announcement of their union sickened the WWE Chairman, especially after learning "The Game" apparently drugged his little girl to get her to go through with the ceremony.

Mr. McMahon had one opportunity to make everything right for his daughter when he battled Triple H at *Armageddon*. Just when it appeared as though the Chairman was going to clear his daughter's good name, however, Stephanie shocked the world by attacking her own father and running into the arms her new husband. What followed was the infamous McMahon-Helmsley Era, one of the most blatant abuses of power in sports-entertainment history. With Stephanie at his side, Triple H was able to piece together an impressive string of victories, including a *WrestleMania 2000* win over Big Show, The Rock, and Mick Foley in a Four Corners Match.

Proving anything can happen in WWE, Triple H teamed with the unlikeliest of Superstars when he joined forces with longtime rival Stone Cold Steve Austin in 2001. Collectively known as "The Two-Man Power Trip," Triple H and Stone Cold controlled the championship scene at the time, as Triple H once again wore the Intercontinental title, while Austin was WWE Champion. They also defeated Kane & Undertaker for the World Tag Team Championship in April 2001.

The End of "The Game"?

The golden duo seemed almost unstoppable, until Triple H suffered a career-threatening injury when his left quadriceps tore completely off the bone during a tag team match. The severity of the injury caused noted orthopedic surgeon Dr. James Andrews to predict the end of "The Game's" career. Triple H refused believe Andrews' prognosis and began an exhausting eight months of rehabilitation.

"The Game" made his highly-anticipated return at Madison Square Garden in January 2002. The WWE crowd in attendance welcomed him back with a sustained standing

ovation. Three weeks later, Triple H put an exclamation point on his return when he won the *Royal Rumble*. He followed that up by defeating Chris Jericho at *WrestleMania X8* to reclaim the WWE Championship.

Later that year, Shawn Michaels made a surprising return to WWE. With HBK back in the picture, everybody, including Michaels, assumed a DX reunion was in the works. "The Game," however, saw things a bit differently. The former friends met in a series of memorable battles, including a bloody Three Stages of Hell Match at *Armageddon* that saw Triple H defeat HBK to reclaim the World Heavyweight Championship.

The Evolution of Sports-Entertainment

Triple H accomplished a lifelong dream when he joined forces with childhood hero, Ric Flair, to form Evolution in early 2003. With Batista and Randy Orton, the well-dressed stable had the feel of a present-day Four Horsemen. At *Armageddon 2003*, they proved their greatness when all four members walked away with a title.

The following year, the original D-Generation X (Triple H and Shawn Michaels) made their triumphant WWE return. In typical DX fashion, the duo targeted authority, most notably Mr. McMahon.

Unfortunately, Triple H suffered another debilitating setback when he tore his right quadriceps in January 2007. With nothing left to prove, Triple H could have easily walked away from sports-entertainment following the injury. Instead, after willing himself through eight grueling months of rehabilitation, he returned to the ring and defeated King Booker and didn't stop there. By the end of 2009 Triple H added to his already impressive résumé with two more WWE Championships, setting a then-record eight total WWE Championship reigns.

New Enemies and Old Friends

During an intense rivalry with Randy Orton and Legacy, Triple H realized he couldn't face them alone and set out to enlist his best friend, Shawn Michaels, to reform D-Generation X. The duo faced Legacy in heated contests and then defeated Chris Jericho & Big Show in a title match at *TLC: Tables, Ladders, and Chairs* in 2009, resulting in the first WWE Tag Team Championship for the longtime friends.

In early 2010, Triple H found himself battling Sheamus, a relative newcomer to WWE who had already captured the WWE Championship. The two met at *WrestleMania XXVI* after Triple H cost Sheamus his championship in an Elimination Chamber Match and Sheamus later retaliated. A win by Triple H did not settle matters as the two were scheduled to meet again at *Extreme Rules*. Sheamus viciously attacked Triple H before their match and knocked "The Game" out of action until 2011. When Triple H returned, he gained a measure of revenge by putting Sheamus through a table with a Pedigree. After settling things with the "Celtic Warrior", Triple H turned his attention to Undertaker, the Superstar who sent Shawn Michaels into retirement.

At *WrestleMania XXVII*, "The Game" met Undertaker in a No Holds Barred match. Though Undertaker's streak remained intact, "The Deadman" had to be carted from the ring. The next day on *Raw*, Triple H promised that when the Undertaker returns, "He'll be waiting." He then went unseen for months but reappeared on a July episode of *Raw* on behalf of the WWE Board of Directors. After he relieved Vince McMahon of his duties, it was announced "The King of Kings" was entering the corporate world as WWE's new Chief Operating Officer. His new role had its share of memorable moments, including multiple confrontations with his old friend, Kevin Nash.

Triple H's early 2012 appearance on *Raw* was interrupted by Undertaker who goaded "The Game" into a rematch at *WrestleMania XXVIII*. In a contest befitting the end of an era, Triple H and Undertaker battered each other for thirty minutes before Triple H lost to "The Deadman." In a show of mutual respect, the two men supported each other as they departed the ring.

TRISH STRATUS

FROM: Toronto, Ontario, Canada
SIGNATURE MOVE: Stratusfaction

TITLE HISTORY	
HARDCORE CHAMPION	1 Time
WOMEN'S CHAMPION (7 TIMES)	Won a Six-Way Match on November 18, 2001 Defeated Jazz on May 13, 2002 Defeated Molly Holly on September 22, 2002 Defeated Victoria on March 30, 2003 Defeated Victoria on June 13, 2004 Defeated Lita on January 9, 2005 Defeated Lita on September 17, 2006

Her beauty was astonishing; combined with her strength and natural athleticism, Trish Stratus redifined WWE Diva for a new generation. She began her career as a top fitness model, appearing in many magazines. She grew up as a fan of sports-entertainment, and after college, she attended Ron Hutchison's wrestling school to pursue a dream.

She made her debut on *Sunday Night Heat* in March of 2000. She became the manager of Test & Albert, and Val Venis. After she parted with her stable of Superstars, she became involved with WWE Chairman Vince McMahon in an affair that did not sit well with other members of his family, particularly his daughter. The tension between mistress and daughter reached a boiling point at 2001's *No Way Out*. When Stephanie emerged victorious, Vince turned on Trish the next night on *Raw*. Trish had her revenge at *WrestleMania X-Seven* when she wheeled Linda McMahon to ringside for the Father vs. Son Streetfight between Shane and Vince, costing Vince the match.

Trish began to focus on competition within the women's division. At the 2001 *Survivor Series* she won her first (of seven) Women's Championships in the Six-Pack Challenge. After she lost three months later to Jazz at *No Way Out*, she managed to briefly hold the Hardcore Championship.

Over the next few years Trish evolved as a performer and her dedication and hard work were recognized by fans when she was voted WWE.com *Babe of the Year* from 2002-2004. She was voted Diva of the Decade at *Raw's 10th Anniversary* in 2003, as well as 2000-2009 "Woman of the Decade" by Pro Wrestling Illustrated.

In October 2005 Trish met her biggest fan in Mickie James. As James' friendship turned to infatuation, she turned on Trish and defeated her for the Women's Championship at *WrestleMania 22*. In August of 2006 Trish signed a contract to face Lita for the Women's Championship at *Unforgiven* after confirming that it would be her final match. With Toronto's Air Canada Centre chanting her name, Trish forced Lita to submit to the finishing move made famous by Bret "Hit Man" Hart, the Sharpshooter. An emotional Trish bid her devoted fans farewell and her storied WWE career came to a close.

Thankfully, Stratus continues to make appearances on WWE programming. She teamed with John Cena against Santino Marella and Beth Phoenix on *Raw*. She acted as guest host for WWE's flagship program in 2009, and took part in a match at *WrestleMania XXVII*. "Stone Cold" Steve Austin hand-selected Trish as one of the expert trainers on the 2011 edition of *Tough Enough*.

During her time in WWE, Trish Stratus redefined "Diva" and took the women's division to all-new levels. Her formula for success was simple: 33% Beauty + 34% Brains + 33% Brawn = 100% Stratusfaction guaranteed.

THE TRUTH COMMISSION

MEMBERS: The Jackyl, Kurrgan the Interrogator, Recon, Sniper, Tank, The Commandant

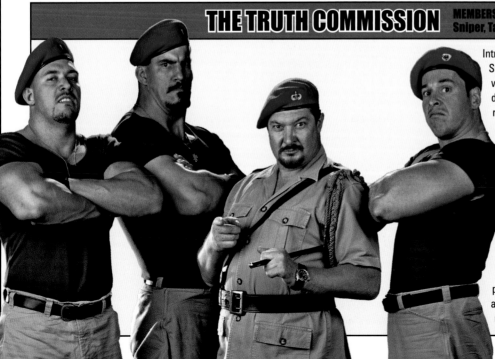

Introduced to WWE audiences by the Commandant in 1997, Recon, Sniper, Tank & Kurrgan displayed a style of South African guerilla warfare that struck fear into the WWE locker room. Shortly after their debut, however, the frightening faction went through a bit of restructuring when the Jackyl assumed leadership responsibilities from the Commandant, and Tank was relieved of his duties. The new-look Truth Commission proved to be equally as dangerous as the original.

At a towering seven-foot tall, Kurrgan proved to be the monster solo Superstar of the group, while Recon & Sniper competed mainly as a tag team. The entire Commission managed to make a rare appearance as an entire unit at the 1997 *Survivor Series* when they defeated the Disciples of Apocalypse.

Despite their success at *Survivor Series*, the Truth Commission struggled in the early parts of 1998. Unhappy with his team's performance, the Jackyl frequently ordered the monstrous Kurrgan to attack Recon & Sniper. The infighting eventually proved to be too much, as the faction slowly crumbled.

TUESDAY NIGHT TITANS

One of the major contributors to WWE forging into the uncharted waters of sports-entertainment in 1984 was a program that breathed a breath of fresh air into a classic television format. With host Vince McMahon and faithful sidekick Lord Alfred Hayes, *Tuesday Night Titans* brought audiences the lives of their most beloved and despised WWE Superstars both in and out of the ring.

In front of a live studio audience, McMahon and Hayes took fans on a wild ride that included Superstar interviews, action in the ring and countless golden moments including the Hart Foundation on "The Mating Game," the wedding of Paul "Butcher" Vachon, Kamala eating a live chicken and Mr. Fuji and the Magnificent Muraco starring in "Fuji Vice" and "Fuji General." Other memorable episodes saw "This is Your Life" with Nikolai Volkoff, "Baffle The Brain" with Bobby Heenan and "Rowdy" Roddy Piper become the ultimate Scrooge as Roddy Ebenezer Piper.

Considered by many as classic television, TNT showed that anything can and often would happen in World Wrestling Entertainment. Over time one word has consistently been used to describe this show of shows: EXPLOSIVE!

TUGBOAT
HT: 6'3" **WT:** 384 lbs.
SIGNATURE MOVE: Big Splash

In 1990 World Wrestling Entertainment was visited by the gargantuan Tugboat Thomas. After a few dominating victories, he dropped the Thomas and went just by Tugboat. His cheery demeanor and warm ways towards friends made Tugboat seem like a big teddy bear to WWE audiences, but he was a beast to those who broke the rules and took shortcuts to win. Tugboat was a good friend of Hulk Hogan and helped out in the clashes with Earthquake and "Mouth of the South" Jimmy Hart.

In 1991, the unthinkable took place when Tugboat turned on the Bushwhackers in a six-man tag match against the Nasty Boys and Earthquake. His new attitude called for a new name, so Tugboat rechristened himself Typhoon and joined Earthquake to form the Natural Disasters, a team that left destruction in its wake for the two years they were partners. By the mid 1990s, Typoon decided to leave behind sports-entertainment, but reappeared as Tugboat at the Gimmick Battle Royal held during *WrestleMania X-Seven*.

THE TWIN TOWERS
MEMBERS: Akeem, Big Boss Man
COMBINED WT: 800 lbs.

In 1988, Slick brought together his two largest Superstars to form one colossal team he called the Twin Towers. Over the next year, the mighty Akeem & Big Boss Man used their overwhelming size to manhandle WWE's smaller competition.

Alone, Akeem and Boss Man weren't going to win any popularity contests. Together, they were even more hated, especially after they handcuffed Hulk Hogan to a ring post at *Survivor Series 1988* and proceeded to beat him. Following the savage attack, the Twin Towers engaged in a high-profile rivalry with the Hulkster and his newfound friend, Randy Savage.

Unfortunately for Akeem & Boss Man, the popular pairing of Hogan & Savage proved superior when they defeated the oversized team on NBC's *The Main Event* in February 1989. While discouraging, the loss failed to set back the Twin Towers. They rebounded nicely with a major victory over The Rockers on the year's biggest stage, *WrestleMania V*.

As 1989 came to a close, Boss Man became unhappy with Slick's handling of the team. Akeem, on the other hand, didn't share the same feelings. Their disagreement eventually led to a complete breakup when Boss Man attacked his partner. Following their inevitable dissolution, Boss Man defeated Akeem at *WrestleMania VI*. The victory won over the fans, as Boss Man went on to enjoy an amazing WWE career. Akeem never recovered from the loss and was gone from WWE shortly after.

TYLER REKS
HT: 6'5" **WT:** 246 lbs. **FROM:** Parts Unknown
SIGNATURE MOVE: Burning Hammer

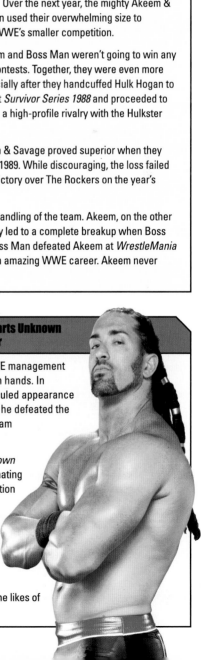

After a brief run in ECW, the intimidating Tyler Reks believed WWE management was holding him back. So he decided to take matters into his own hands. In October 2010, the dark and brooding Superstar made an unscheduled appearance on *SmackDown* and immediately targeted Kaval. Within minutes, he defeated the *NXT* season two champion and as a result, earned his spot on Team SmackDown at *Bragging Rights*.

Despite being a loner at heart, Reks worked well with his *SmackDown* cohorts, which included Big Show and Alberto Del Rio. After eliminating *Raw*'s Santino Marella from competition, the "Dreadlocked Demolition Man" was finally ousted at the hands of Sheamus. In the end, however, it was Reks' team of *SmackDown* Superstars who took home the prestigious *Bragging Rights* trophy.

The following month, Reks joined Del Rio's *Survivor Series* team in an unsuccessful battle against Team Mysterio. After the annual November pay-per-view, Reks continued to display his intense brand of terror on *WWE Superstars*, where he victimized the likes of Chris Masters, JTG and Curt Hawkins.

TYSON KIDD

HT: 5'10"   WT: 195 lbs.   FROM: Calgary, Alberta, Canada
SIGNATURE MOVE: Sharpshooter

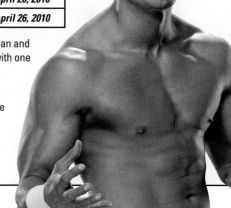

The lineage of the historic Hart Family Dungeon dates back to the 1940s. Over the

TITLE HISTORY

| WORLD TAG TEAM CHAMPION | Partnered with David Hart Smith to defeat Big Show & The Miz on April 26, 2010 |
| WWE TAG TEAM CHAMPION | Partnered with David Hart Smith to defeat Big Show & The Miz on April 26, 2010 |

course if its existence, the facility produced some of sports-entertainment's greatest names, including Bret Hart, Brian Pillman and "Superstar" Billy Graham. Decades later, when the Dungeon finally closed its doors, it left the sports-entertainment world with one final graduate: Tyson Kidd.

With huge shoes to fill, Kidd debuted in WWE in early 2009. Upon arriving, he almost immediately joined forces with Hart family members David Hart Smith and Natalya. Collectively known as The Hart Dynasty, the trio set out to prove they were worthy of being in the same class as their legendary forefathers.

Behind Kidd's superior technical style, The Hart Dynasty quickly proved their worth by defeated The Miz & Big Show for the Unified Tag Team Championship in April 2010. Hoping to make a name for himself as a singles star, Kidd broke out on his own in late 2010. Since then, he has successfully topped the likes of Trent Barreta and Yoshi Tatsu.

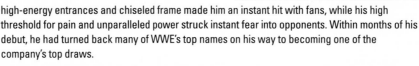

TYSON TOMKO

HT: 6'6"   WT: 275 lbs.   FROM: Jacksonville, Florida
SIGNATURE MOVE: Big Boot

If there's a problem, Tyson Tomko could solve it. Introduced to WWE fans in April 2004, the behemoth known as the "Problem Solver" was brought in by Christian with the purpose of protecting "Captain Charisma" and his beautiful girlfriend Trish Stratus against Chris Jericho. A man of few words, Tomko used his unique appearance to intimidate fellow Superstars. In addition to sporting a bald skull and pointy goatee, his entire upper body was covered in tattoos. Coupled with his immense size, Tomko truly was an unmistakable figure.

In January 2005, Tomko teamed with Christian to challenge William Regal & Eugene for the World Tag Team Championship. A reign atop the tag scene was not to be, however, as Eugene rolled Tomko up to retain the titles. It was the closest the tattooed Superstar came to claiming a WWE championship.

After Christian was drafted to *SmackDown* in June 2005, Tomko went on to gain moderate success on *Raw*. Using his big boot to literally knock opponents unconscious, he racked up an impressive string of victories. Tomko eventually went on to form a tag team with Snitsky before leaving WWE in the spring of 2006.

ULTIMATE WARRIOR

HT: 62"   WT: 280 lbs.
FROM: Parts Unknown

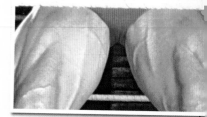

TITLE HISTORY

| INTERCONTINENTAL CHAMPION (2 TIMES) | Defeated Honky Tonk Man on August 29, 1988
Defeated Rick Rude on August 28, 1989 |
| WWE CHAMPION | Defeated Hulk Hogan on April 1, 1990 |

With unmatched energy, Ultimate Warrior exploded on the WWE scene in 1987. In record time, the face-painted Superstar became a household name and sports-entertainment icon. Ultimate Warrior had a natural charisma that was undeniable. His

high-energy entrances and chiseled frame made him an instant hit with fans, while his high threshold for pain and unparalleled power struck instant fear into opponents. Within months of his debut, he had turned back many of WWE's top names on his way to becoming one of the company's top draws.

At *SummerSlam 1988*, Ultimate Warrior ended Honky Tonk Man's record fifteen-month Intercontinental Championship reign when he toppled the titleholder in a mere thirty seconds. The dominant victory proved that nobody was safe from the Ultimate Warrior's intensity. With the Intercontinental Championship around his waist, the Ultimate Warrior became one of WWE's most marketable Superstars. It wasn't long before arenas were filled with Ultimate Warrior T-shirts; fans even began to paint their faces like their eccentric hero.

Ultimate Warrior's superhuman strength carried him to a nearly eight-month Intercontinental Championship reign. It eventually took outside interference from Bobby "The Brain" Heenan for "Ravishing" Rick Rude to wrest the title from Ultimate Warrior at *WrestleMania V*. He later reclaimed the gold from Rude at *SummerSlam 1989*.

Ultimate Warrior's second stint with the Intercontinental Championship proved to be even more popular with the fans, setting the stage for an inevitable showdown with WWE Champion Hulk Hogan. WWE's two most popular Superstars finally met at *WrestleMania VI* in an historic encounter dubbed The Ultimate Challenge. With both titles on the line, Ultimate Warrior defeated Hogan in front of more than 67,000 screaming fans in Toronto's SkyDome. The victory was capped off by an amazing fireworks display, a precursor to the pyrotechnics seen on a weekly basis on today's WWE television.

Following the WrestleMania win, Ultimate Warrior spent the next nine months proudly defending the WWE Championship. His whirlwind reign was eventually silenced when Sgt. Slaughter, with some help from Randy Savage, defeated him at the 1991 *Royal Rumble*. Rather than set his sights on reclaiming the prize, Ultimate Warrior focused his attention on gaining revenge from Savage. He finally accomplished the ultimate retribution when he defeated Savage in a Retirement Match at *WrestleMania VII*.

UMAGA

HT: 6'4" **WT: 350 lbs.** **FROM: The Isle of Samoa**
SIGNATURE MOVE: Samoan Spike

TITLE HISTORY

INTERCONTINENTAL CHAMPION (2 TIMES)	Defeated Jeff Hardy on February 19, 2007 Defeated Santino Marella on July 2, 2007

The Samoan Bulldozer, Umaga, was a giant who combined savagery, raw power, and incredible speed. His earliest appearances in WWE were overseen by Armando Alejandro Estrada, who would later become General Manager of ECW. After his debut in 2006, Umaga immediately set his sights on the best in the business, "Nature Boy" Ric Flair. Umaga then went weeks without being pinned and became the #1 contender for John Cena's WWE Championship.

On Feburary 19, 2007 Umaga was named the representative of Mr. McMahon for the Battle of the Billionaires Match at *WresteMania 23*. That same night he crushed Jeff Hardy to become the Intercontinental Champion. At *Backlash*, Umaga teamed with Mr. McMahon again. When the duo defeated the team of Bobby Lashley & Shane McMahon, the WWE Chairman became the new ECW Champion.

The Samoan Bulldozer continued to target WWE's most beloved heroes and later clashed with Batisa at *WrestleMania XXIV* in one of the most physical encounters in recent memory. As a member of *SmackDown*, Umaga showed no regard for humanity and displayed his Samoan savagery in famous bouts with CM Punk.

The monster from the legendary Anoa'i family soon left WWE and toured the globe on independent cards before his untimely passing on December 4, 2009.

ULTIMO DRAGON

HT: 5'8" **WT: 185 lbs.**
FROM: Nagoya, Japan
SIGNATURE MOVE: Asai DDT

Born Yoshihiro Asai, Ultimo Dragon became such an international superstar during his time in Japan and Mexico that the sports-entertainment world named the Asai moonsault after him. In 2003, the masked Superstar took his amazing legacy with him to WWE, where he competed mainly in the cruiserweight division.

As the final student of the legendary Bruce Lee, Ultimo Dragon, which translates to "Last Dragon," coupled a dizzying martial arts repertoire with his daredevil style of high-flying offense. It was this unforgettable pairing that made him such a threat during his brief WWE tenure.

Prior to WWE, Ultimo Dragon became one of the world's most decorated Superstars. At one point, he even held ten championships at the same time. His most successful United States run came as a member of WCW. While there, he defeated Eddie Guerrero and Dean Malenko to become a two-time Cruiserweight Champion. He was also a two-time Television Champion, at the expense of Lord Steven Regal and Prince Iaukea.

THE UN-AMERICANS

MEMBERS: Lance Storm, Christian, Test, William Regal

TITLE HISTORY

WORLD TAG TEAM CHAMPIONS	Defeated Edge & Hollywood Hogan on July 21, 2002

Led by Lance Storm, this collection of resident malcontents formed in June 2002 on *SmackDown*. Claiming that Canadians have been discriminated against in World Wrestling Entertainment since the company's early days, this group spewed anti-American rhetoric wherever they traveled. Their antics were hammered home in the ring as they failingly attempted on several occasions to burn the American flag. The Un-Americans' plans were thwarted by the likes of Booker T., Goldust, Bradshaw, Kane, Rey Mysterio, Rikishi, Edge, Undertaker, and Hulk Hogan.

The group did see success as Christian & Lance Storm captured the World Tag Team Championship on July 21, 2002 from Edge & Hollywood Hogan. They held the title for two months and the group experienced added power from WWE gold. However, when they lost the titles two months later the team eventually crumbled.

UNCLE ELMER

HT: 6'10" **WT: 430 lbs.** **FROM: Mississippi**
SIGNATURE MOVE: Big Splash

Uncle Elmer was a simple man. The only things he needed to be happy were a good meal and the affection of his family. He loved those around him so much, in fact, that he would unleash his mass on any Superstar that threatened to mess with them.

Introduced to WWE audiences in 1985, Uncle Elmer proudly stood by the side of his nephew, Hillbilly Jim, and later Cousin Luke and Cousin Junior. As far as technical wrestling skills were concerned, the big man didn't necessarily have any. Furthermore, he was as slow as a turtle, but he did possess a more than 400-pound frame that struck fear into his competition. His size was such a factor, in fact, that he once beat an opponent in just six seconds after dropping all his weight on him.

In a world where weddings rarely go as planned, Uncle Elmer actually pulled it off when he married his longtime girlfriend Joyce on *Saturday Night's Main Event* in October 1985. The nuptials feature some major star power, as Elmer's wedding party consisted of both Hulk Hogan and Andre the Giant. The following year, the newlywed competed in the biggest match of his career when he lost to Adrian Adonis at *WrestleMania 2*. Shortly afterwards, he retreated back to his bride and farm in Mississippi.

Uncle Zebakiah (see page 358)

1960-69
1970-79
1980-89
1990-99
2000-09
2010-

UNDERTAKER

HT: 6'10½" **WT: 295 lbs.** **FROM: Death Valley** **SIGNATURE MOVE: Tombstone Piledriver**

TITLE HISTORY

HARDCORE CHAMPION	*1 Time*
WORLD HEAVYWEIGHT CHAMPION (3 TIMES)	*Defeated Batista on April 1, 2007* *Defeated Edge on March 30, 2008* *Defeated CM Punk on October 4, 2009*
WORLD TAG TEAM CHAMPION (6 TIMES)	*Partnered with Stone Cold Steve Austin to defeat Kane & Mankind on July 26, 1998* *Partnered with Big Show to defeat Kane & X-Pac on August 22, 1999* *Partnered with Big Show to defeat Mankind & The Rock on September 9, 1999* *Partnered with The Rock to defeat Edge & Christian on December 18, 2000* *Partnered with Kane to defeat Edge & Christian on April 19, 2001* *Partnered with Kane to defeat Chris Kanyon & Diamond Dallas Page on August 19, 2001*
WWE CHAMPION (4 TIMES)	*Defeated Hulk Hogan on November 27, 1991* *Defeated Sycho Sid on March 23, 1997* *Defeated Stone Cold Steve Austin on May 23, 1999* *Defeated Hulk Hogan on May 19, 2002*

From darkness, he emerged to build a dynasty second to none. He is the "Deadman." He is the "Phenom." He is the "Lord of Darkness." He is Undertaker. The mysterious Superstar from Death Valley was unveiled to WWE audiences at the 1990 *Survivor Series*. Over the next two decades, the "Deadman's" domination in the ring led to multiple World Championships, as well as an unblemished *WrestleMania* record.

Deadman Walking

The first chapter in Undertaker's remarkable *WrestleMania* epic was penned in Los Angeles in 1991. Under the tutelage of new manager Paul Bearer, the "Phenom" destroyed Jimmy "Superfly" Snuka. The victory marked his first *WrestleMania* win, and also catapulted the "Deadman" straight to main-event status.

Undertaker spent the next several months using caskets and his mysteriously powerful urn to exploit his opponents' fear of their own mortality. He tore through every Superstar put in his path and in November 1991, at *Survivor Series*, he defeated Hulk Hogan for the WWE Championship. Ric Flair's interference in Undertaker's WWE Championship victory ultimately caused President Jack Tunney to order a rematch at *This Tuesday in Texas*. Hogan wound up walking away from the event with the WWE Championship, but the controversial conclusion to the match caused Tunney to later vacate the title.

Following his WWE Championship reign, Undertaker faced a series of colossal competitors looking to rid WWE of the "Deadman." The four-hundred pound Kamala nearly accomplished the task during WWE's first-ever Coffin Match at the 1992 *Survivor Series*. Undertaker was able to avoid Kamala's offensive onslaught en route to picking up the ground-breaking win. The following year, the "Phenom" toppled the near eight-foot Giant Gonzalez at *WrestleMania IX*.

Two Undertakers!

Many believed Undertaker had finally met his match when he squared off against WWE Champion Yokozuna at the 1994 *Royal Rumble*. The encounter saw Undertaker victimized by not only the mighty Yokozuna, but a posse of oversized Superstars, including Bam Bam Bigelow and Diesel. Many assumed the defeat, which saw Undertaker stuffed into a ringside casket, meant the demise of the "Deadman." However, as Yokozuna's gang pushed the casket up the aisle, an eerie smoke began to fill the arena, followed by the familiar gong of Undertaker's entrance theme. The "Deadman" then appeared on the TitanTron to proclaim, "I will not rest in peace."

Both the Million Dollar Man and Paul Bearer claimed to have found Undertaker in the summer of 1994. The two men agreed to have their Undertakers square off against each other at *SummerSlam*. In the end, Bearer's Undertaker proved to be the real "Phenom," defeating DiBiase's fake after hitting him with three Tombstone Piledrivers.

Undertaker's 1994 disappearance caused him to miss *WrestleMania X*, but his dark dominance returned the following year when he defeated the massive King Kong Bundy in Hartford, Connecticut. The following year, he handily defeated Diesel.

Following his defeat of Diesel, Undertaker became the target of WWE newcomer Mankind. Their intense rivalry sparked the advent of two revolutionary match types, the Boiler Room Brawl and Buried Alive Match. It also marked the shocking end to one of the closest alliances of all time when Paul Bearer clobbered Undertaker with his urn at *SummerSlam 1996*.

Despite losing his manager to Mankind, Undertaker continued to post an impressive record, which earned him a WWE Championship opportunity against Sycho Sid at *WrestleMania 13*.

Following a skull-crushing Tombstone, the "Phenom" covered Sid to reclaim the title he lost more than five years earlier. The victory catapulted Undertaker back to the top of the sports-entertainment scene. He spent the next five months successfully defending the title against the likes of Stone Cold Steve Austin and Vader.

Family Ties

An errant steel chair shot at the hands of special referee Shawn Michaels allowed Bret "Hit Man" Hart to dethrone Undertaker at *SummerSlam 1997*. Yearning for revenge, the "Deadman" shifted his focus from the WWE Championship scene to destroying HBK. After a series of inconclusive contests, the two Superstars agreed to settle the score in the first-ever Hell In A Cell Match at *Badd Blood*. Once locked inside the satanic structure, Undertaker released all his frustrations on Michaels, but just when it appeared as though victory was certain, Undertaker came face to face with a familiar figure from the past that cost him the match: Kane.

In the months leading up to Kane's shocking debut, Paul Bearer, in an attempt to blackmail Undertaker, threatened to uncover a disturbing secret from the "Deadman's" past. When Undertaker refused to give in to the demands, Bearer finally revealed that the "Phenom" set fire to his family's funeral parlor twenty years earlier, killing his mother and father. Undertaker assumed his younger brother also perished in the fire. At *Badd Blood*, Undertaker's assumption proved to be dead wrong, as his disfigured sibling appeared from out of nowhere to attack him.

In the months following the shocking revelation, Undertaker refused to step in the ring with his flesh and blood. However, after Kane attempted to send him to a fiery grave at the 1998 *Royal Rumble*, Undertaker had no choice but to respond with force. The two brothers finally squared off at *WrestleMania XIV*. Undertaker won the emotional battle, but the war between the two was just heating up. Undertaker and Kane went on to engage in some of the most bitter battles ever seen, including several Inferno Matches.

By 1999, Undertaker adopted an even darker, more demonic demeanor. He also made the unpopular decision to reconcile with Paul Bearer to form the Ministry of Darkness. Claiming to serve a "higher power", Undertaker unleashed a never-before-seen assault on the entire WWE. Nobody was safe from the "Deadman's" wicked wrath, not even Stephanie McMahon, who was abducted by Undertaker. Luckily for Stephanie, Stone Cold Steve Austin rescued her from further assault. The heroics, however, landed Stone Cold in a WWE Championship defense against Undertaker the following month.

A Fresh Start

Leaving his "Deadman" persona in the dust, he reemerged at *Judgment Day* riding a motorcycle. Recognized as the "American Bad Ass," the new Undertaker was equally imposing. Following an impressive victory over Triple H at *WrestleMania X-Seven*, Undertaker formed an alliance with Kane. Known as the Brothers of Destruction, the duo spent the next several months dominating the tag team scene.

More than a decade after defeating Hulk Hogan for his first WWE Championship, Undertaker challenged the Hulkster for the same prize at *Judgment Day 2002*. Much like that fateful night back in November 1991, he used a steel chair to claim the title from Hogan.

The fiery family hostility between Undertaker and Kane reignited in late 2003. This time, however, Kane appeared to walk away the victor when he helped Mr. McMahon bury his brother alive at *Survivor Series*. As mounds of dirt covered Undertaker's seemingly lifeless body, many assumed they had finally seen the end of Undertaker.

The Deadman Returns

Proving you can't kill what's already dead, Undertaker made his triumphant return to WWE at *WrestleMania XX*. He defeated Kane to improve his *WrestleMania* record to an astonishing 12-0. The "Phenom's" iconic status made him the perfect target for the brash youngster Randy Orton. The third-generation Superstar saw Undertaker's spotless *WrestleMania* record as an opportunity to permanently etch his name into the WWE history books. Unfortunately for the self-appointed "Legend Killer", he became unlucky victim number thirteen.

By 2007, there were two glaring holes on the Undertaker's impressive resumé: He had never won a *Royal Rumble* or captured the World Heavyweight Championship. In January 2007, he filled in one hole when he last eliminated Shawn Michaels to win the *Royal Rumble*. Winning that match allowed him to meet Batista at *WrestleMania 23* for the World Heavyweight Championship, which he won after a Tombstone Piledriver. Undertaker duplicated his efforts the following year when he toppled Edge at *WrestleMania XXIV* to become a two-time World Heavyweight Champion.

His time with the title was cut short when Vickie Guerrero declared Undertaker's submission hold, Hell's Gate, illegal. Edge and Undertaker battled over the World Heavyweight Championship multiple times but nothing was resolved until *One Night Stand* in June. Edge won the match with an assist from La Familia, which resulted in Undertaker being forced out of WWE. Fortunately for the WWE Universe, Edge and Vickie had a bitter falling out, resulting in Vickie reinstituting Undertaker two months later.

The Streak Put In Jeopardy

Over the course of sixteen *WrestleMania* appearances, Undertaker had never tasted defeat. However, Shawn Michaels claimed Undertaker had never defeated him in a singles match and demanded a shot at *WrestleMania XXV*. In what is widely considered one of the most epic matches in WWE history, Undertaker won the encounter to run his record to 17-0, then went on to claim the World Heavyweight Championship from CM Punk later in the year. Undertaker defended the title against CM Punk and Batista but lost it to Chris Jericho when Shawn Michaels, demanding a second chance at Undertaker's *WrestleMania* streak, interfered in the match. Undertaker ultimately agreed to the match, but with one stipulation: if Shawn Michaels lost, he must retire. The "Career versus Streak" Match took place at *WrestleMania XXVI*. In the end, Undertaker put Michaels through hell and sent him into retirement.

Shortly after his victory over Shawn Michaels, Undertaker was out of action after he was attacked by an unknown assailant. Kane and Rey Mysterio each blamed the other, but the truth came to light when Undertaker returned at *SummerSlam* and was attacked by Kane. The two eventually met in a Buried Alive Match at *Hell In A Cell* where Paul Bearer and the Nexus helped Kane bury Undertaker, who then wasn't seen for months.

The End of an Era

Hints of Undertaker's return first appeared during the 2011 *Royal Rumble*. His return on February 21 was interrupted by Triple H, making his first appearance in nearly a year. Following in the footsteps of his friend, Shawn Michaels, "The Game" sought to end Undertaker's *WrestleMania* winning streak. The No-Holds Barred Match between WWE's two "Last Outlaws" at *WrestleMania XXVII* ended in win for Undertaker, but he left the ring on a stretcher while Triple H walked out under his own power.

Undertaker vanished from the WWE Universe for the rest of 2011, returning in January 2012 to demand a rematch against an initially-reluctant Triple H. The two met at *WrestleMania XXVIII* in a Hell In A Cell Match refereed by Shawn Michaels. The brutal encounter left both men bloodied and battered, but in the end Undertaker claimed victory and pushed his streak to 20-0. When it came time to leave the ring, all three men supported each other and walked into the night, together, symbolizing the "End of an Era."

20-0: THE STREAK

Twenty times in his career, Undertaker has appeared on the biggest stage of sports-entertainment. Twenty times the night ended with Undertaker's arm raised in victory. *WrestleMania* is known as the Showcase of the Immortals, and no Superstar has made a greater claim to immortality than Undertaker and his 20-0 *WrestleMania* undefeated streak.

WRESTLEMANIA VII
Los Angeles, California

Defeated Jimmy "Superfly" Snuka

WRESTLEMANIA VIII
Indianapolis, Indiana

Defeated Jake "the Snake" Roberts

WRESTLEMANIA IX
Las Vegas, Nevada

Defeated Giant Gonzalez (won via DQ)

WRESTLEMANIA XI
Hartford, Connecticut

Defeated King Kong Bundy

WRESTLEMANIA XII
Anaheim, California

Defeated Diesel

WRESTLEMANIA 13
Chicago, Illinois

Defeated WWE Champion Sycho Sid

WRESTLEMANIA XIV
Boston, Massachusetts

Defeated Kane

WRESTLEMANIA XV
Philadelphia, Pennsylvania

Defeated Big Boss Man,
Hell in a Cell Match

WRESTLEMANIA X-SEVEN
Houston, Texas

Defeated Triple H

WRESTLEMANIA X8
Toronto, Ontario

Defeated Ric Flair,
No Disqualification Match

WRESTLEMANIA XIX
Seattle, Washington

Defeated A-Train & Big Show,
Handicap Match

WRESTLEMANIA XX
New York, New York

Defeated Kane

WRESTLEMANIA 21
Los Angeles, California

Defeated Randy Orton

WRESTLEMANIA 22
Rosemont, Illinois

Defeated Mark Henry, Casket Match

WRESTLEMANIA 23
Detroit, Michigan

Defeated World Heavyweight
Champion Batista

WRESTLEMANIA XXIV
Orlando, Florida

Defeated World Heavyweight
Champion Edge

WRESTLEMANIA 25
Houston, Texas

Defeated Shawn Michaels

WRESTLEMANIA XXVI
Glendale, Arizona

Defeated Shawn Michaels,
Streak versus Career Match

WRESTLEMANIA XXVII
Atlanta, Georgia

Defeated Triple H,
No Holds Barred Match

WRESTLEMANIA XXVIII
Miami, Florida

Defeated Triple H,
End of an Era Hell in a Cell Match

U

2010-
2000-09
1990-99
1980-89
1970-79
1960-69

UNCLE ZEBAKIAH

This managerial ruffian first appeared in World Wrestling Entertainment in 1995 as the manager of Jacob and Eli Blu. Zebakiah was an ultimate strategist who preached the importance of rule-breaking and permanently hurting opponents. He also had no issue with interfering on behalf of his team as they became top contenders for the World Tag Team Championship.

When they Blu Brothers left the company in 1996, Zebakiah brought in one of the hardest-hitting Superstars to ever enter the ring, Justin "Hawk" Bradshaw. As Zebakiah led Bradshaw to the ring with whip and bull-rope they were branding opponents as the Texan became a top contender for both the Intercontinental and Heavyweight Championships. In late 1996 Uncle Zebakiah returned to the mountains and has not been seen in World Wrestling Entertainment since.

UNFORGIVEN

April 26, 1998

Greensboro, North Carolina
Greensboro Coliseum

Main Event: Dude Love defeated WWE Champion Stone Cold Steve Austin by Disqualification

September 26, 1999

Charlotte, North Carolina
Charlotte Coliseum

Main Event: Triple H defeated The Rock, Mankind, Big Show, British Bulldog, and Kane in a Six Pack Challenge Match for the vacant WWE Championship

September 24, 2000

Philadelphia, Pennsylvania
First Union Center

Main Event: The Rock (Champion) defeated Chris Benoit, Undertaker, and Kane in a Fatal Four Way for the WWE Championship

September 23, 2001

Pittsburgh, Pennsylvania
Mellon Arena

Main Event: Kurt Angle defeated WWE Champion Stone Cold Steve Austin

September 22, 2002

Los Angeles, California
Staples Center

Main Event: WWE Champion Brock Lesnar fought Undertaker to a Double Disqualification

September 21, 2003

Hershey, Pennsylvania
Giant Center

Main Event: Goldberg defeated World Heavyweight Champion Triple H

September 12, 2004

Portland, Oregon
Rose Garden

Main Event: Triple H defeated World Heavyweight Champion Randy Orton

September 18, 2005

Oklahoma City, Oklahoma
Ford Center

Main Event: Kurt Angle defeated WWE Champion John Cena by Disqualification

September 17, 2006

Toronto, Ontario, Canada
Air Canada Centre

Main Event: John Cena defeated WWE Champion Edge in a Tables, Ladders & Chairs Match

September 16, 2007

Memphis, Tennessee
FedEx Forum

Main Event: Undertaker defeated Mark Henry

September 7, 2008

Cleveland, Ohio
Quicken Loans Arena

Main Event: Championship Scramble Matches for the ECW, WWE, and World Heavyweight Championships

THE UNION   MEMBERS: Mankind, Big Show, Ken Shamrock, Test

People all over the world hate their bosses. They huddle in corners of the office and whisper about how unfairly they're treated or how little they're compensated. Rarely do these employees have the courage to voice their feelings aloud to their superiors. When four WWE Superstars felt this way, however, they refused to sit back silently. Instead, they formed a union and waged war on their boss.

In May 1999, former Corporation members Mankind, Big Show, Ken Shamrock, and Test banded together to form the "Union of People You Oughta Respect, Son". According to Mankind, the initials of The Union spelled out U.P.Y.O.U.R.S., a blatant sign of disrespect for their former boss, Shane McMahon. Upon their debut, the 2x4-carrying Superstars immediately engaged in a rivalry with Shane's Corporate Ministry.

The Union was able to gain some of the respect they were looking for when they defeated Corporate Ministry members Big Boss Man, Viscera, Faarooq & Bradshaw at the *Over The Edge* pay-per-view. The stable silently disbanded shortly after the win.

UNITED STATES CHAMPIONSHIP

Today's fans recognize the United States Championship as the title defended in WWE arenas by the likes of Kofi Kingston, Sheamus and Jack Swagger. However, what many might not realize is that the United States Championship had its start in the NWA in 1975.

Harley Race, Terry Funk, Magnum T. A. and a host of other legendary names drove the highways of the southern United States in the 1970s and 1980s, defending the title in small arenas in Florida, North Carolina and Virginia. When the championship became exclusive to World Championship Wrestling in 1991, it was defended nationwide by Sting, Rick Rude, and Dustin Rhodes.

The United States Championship appeared in WWE with the purchase of WCW in 2001. Unfortunately, fans had less than one year to truly appreciate the title, as it was unified with the Intercontinental Championship when Edge defeated Test in November 2001. In July 2003, Stephanie McMahon restored the historic championship in a tournament which saw Eddie Guerrero emerge victorious.

1975

January 1
Tallahassee, FL

Harley Race defeated Johnny Weaver in the finals of a tournament to crown a United States Champion

▼

July 3
Greensboro, NC

Johnny Valentine defeated Harley Race

Injuries forced Johnny Valentine to vacate the United States Championship in October 1975

▼

November 9
Greensboro, NC

Terry Funk defeated Paul Jones in the finals of a tournament to crown a new United States Champion

▼

November 27
Greensboro, NC

Paul Jones defeated Terry Funk

▼

1976

March 13
Greensboro, NC

Blackjack Mulligan defeated Paul Jones

▼

October 16
Greensboro, NC

Paul Jones defeated Blackjack Mulligan

▼

December 15
Greensboro, NC

Blackjack Mulligan defeated Paul Jones

▼

1977

July 7
Norfolk, VA

Bobo Brazil defeated Blackjack Mulligan

▼

July 29
Norfolk, VA

Ric Flair defeated Bobo Brazil

▼

October 23
Greensboro, NC

Ricky Steamboat defeated Ric Flair

▼

1978

January 1
Greensboro, NC

Blackjack Mulligan defeated Ricky Steamboat

▼

March 19
Greensboro, NC

Mr. Wrestling defeated Blackjack Mulligan

▼

April 9
Greensboro, NC

Ric Flair defeated Mr. Wrestling

▼

December 18
Toronto, Ontario

Ricky Steamboat defeated Ric Flair

▼

1979

April 1
Greensboro, NC

Ric Flair defeated Ricky Steamboat

After winning the NWA World Tag Team Championship in August 1979, Ric Flair was forced to vacate the United States Championship

▼

September 1
Charlotte, NC

Jimmy Snuka defeated Ricky Steamboat in the finals of a tournament to crown a new United States Champion

▼

1980

April 19
Greensboro, NC

Ric Flair defeated Jimmy Snuka

▼

1981

January 27
Raleigh, NC

Roddy Piper defeated Ric Flair

▼

August 8
Greensboro, NC

Wahoo McDaniel defeated Roddy Piper

Injury forced Wahoo McDaniel to vacate the United States Championship in September 1981

▼

October 4
Charlotte, NC

Sgt. Slaughter defeated Ricky Steamboat in the finals of a tournament to crown a new United States Champion

▼

1982

May 21
Richmond, VA

Wahoo McDaniel defeated St. Slaughter

Injury forced Wahoo McDaniel to vacate the United States Championship

▼

June 7
Greensville, SC

Sgt. Slaughter is awarded United States Championship

▼

August 22
Charlotte, NC

Wahoo McDaniel defeated Sgt. Slaughter

▼

November 4
Norfolk, VA

Greg Valentine defeated Wahoo McDaniel

▼

1983

April 16
Greensboro, NC

Roddy Piper defeated Greg Valentine

▼

Greensboro, NC

Greg Valentine defeated
Roddy Piper

▼

December 14
Shelby, NC

Dick Slater defeated Greg Valentine

▼

1984
April 21
Greensboro, NC

Ricky Steamboat defeated
Dick Slater

▼

June 24
Greensboro, NC

Wahoo McDaniel defeated Ricky
Steamboat

Wahoo McDaniel was forced to
vacate the United States
Championship after Tully Blanchard
interfered in McDaniel's match

▼

October 7
Charlotte, NC

Wahoo McDaniel defeated Manny
Fernandez in the finals of a
tournament to crown a new United
States Champion

▼

1985
March 23 1985
Charlotte, NC

Magnum T.A. defeated
Wahoo McDaniel

▼

Charlotte, NC

Tully Blanchard defeated
Magnum T.A

▼

November 28
Greensboro, NC

Magnum T.A. defeated
Tully Blanchard

Magnum T.A. was stripped of the
United States Championship in
May 1985 after attacking NWA
President Bob Geigel

▼

1986
August 17
Charlotte, NC

Nikita Koloff defeated Magnum T.A
in the finals of a tournament to
crown a new United States
Champion

▼

1987
July 11
Greensboro, NC

Lex Luger defeated Nikita Koloff

▼

November 26
Chicago, IL

Dusty Rhodes defeated Lex Luger

Dusty Rhodes was stripped of
the United States Championship
in April 1987 after attacking
Jim Crockett

▼

1988
May 13
Houston, TX

Barry Windham defeated Nikita
Koloff in the finals of a tournament
to crown a new United States
Champion

▼

1989
February 20
Chicago, IL

Lex Luger defeated Barry Windham

▼

March 7
Nashville, TN

Michael Hayes defeated Lex Luger

▼

March 22
Bluefield, WV

Lex Luger defeated Michael Hayes

▼

1990
October 27
Chicago, IL

Stan Hansen defeated Lex Luger

▼

December 16
St. Louis, MO

Lex Luger defeated Stan Hansen

Lex Luger vacated the United States
Championship on July 14 after
winning the WCW Championship

▼

1991
August 25
Atlanta, GA

Sting defeated Steve Austin in the
finals of a tournament to crown a
new United States Champion

▼

November 19
Savannah, GA

Rick Rude defeated Sting

Injury forced Rick Rude to vacate
the United States Championship in
December 1992

▼

1993
January 11
Atlanta, GA

Dustin Rhodes defeated Ricky
Steamboat

Rhodes was forced to vacate the
title in May 1993 after a title
defense against Rick Rude ended in
a double pinfall

▼

August 30
Atlanta, GA

Dustin Rhodes defeated Rick Rude
in a match for the vacant United
States Championship

▼

December 27
Charlotte, NC

Steve Austin defeated Dustin Rhodes

▼

1994
August 24
Cedar Rapids, IA

Ricky Steamboat defeated
Steve Austin

Injury forced Ricky Steamboat to
vacate the United States
Championship

▼

September 18
Roanoke, VA

Steve Austin is awarded the United
States Championship

▼

September 18
Roanoke, VA

Jim Duggan defeated Steve Austin

Nashville, TN

1995
June 18
Dayton, OH

Sting defeated Meng in the finals
of a tournament to crown a new
United States Champion

▼

November 13
Tokyo, Japan

Kensuke Sasaki defeated Sting

▼

December 27
Nashville, TN

One Man Gang defeated
Kensuke Sasaki

▼

1996
January 29
Canton, OH

Konnan defeated One Man Gang

▼

July 7
Daytona Beach, FL

Ric Flair defeated Konnan

Injury forced Ric Flair to vacate the
United States Championship in
September 1996

▼

December 29
Nashville, TN

Eddie Guerrero defeated Diamond
Dallas Page in the finals of a
tournament to crown a new United
States Champion

▼

1997
March 16
Charleston, SC

Dean Malenko defeated
Eddie Guerrero

▼

June 9
Boston, MA

Jeff Jarrett defeated Dean Malenko

▼

August 21
Nashville, TN

Steve McMichael defeated Jeff Jarrett

▼

September 15
Charlotte, NC

Curt Hennig defeated Steve McMichael

▼

December 28
Washington, DC

Diamond Dallas Page defeated Curt Hennig

▼

1998

April 19
Denver, CO

Raven defeated Diamond Dallas Page

▼

April 20
Colorado Springs, CO

Goldberg defeated Raven

Goldberg vacated the United States Championship on July 6 after winning the WCW Championship

▼

July 20
Salt Lake City, UT

Bret Hart defeated Diamond Dallas Page in a match to determine a new United States Champion

▼

August 10
Rapid City, SD

Lex Luger defeated Bret Hart

▼

August 13
Fargo, ND

Bret Hart defeated Lex Luger

▼

October 26
Phoenix, AZ

Diamond Dallas Page defeated Bret Hart

▼

November 30
Chattanooga, TN

Bret Hart defeated Diamond Dallas Page

▼

1999

February 8
Buffalo, NY

Roddy Piper defeated Bret Hart

▼

February 21
Oakland, CA

Scott Hall defeated Roddy Piper

WCW President Ric Flair stripped Scott Hall of the United States Championship on March 18

▼

April 11
Tacoma, WA

Scott Steiner defeated Booker T in the finals of a tournament to crown a new United States Champion

WCW President Ric Flair stripped Scott Steiner of the United States Championship on July 5

July 5
Atlanta, GA

David Flair is awarded the United States Championship

▼

August 9
Boise, ID

Chris Benoit defeated David Flair

▼

September 12
Winston-Salem, NC

Sid Vicious defeated Chris Benoit

▼

October 24
Las Vegas, NV

Goldberg defeated Sid Vicious

▼

October 25
Phoenix, AZ

Bret Hart defeated Goldberg

▼

November 8
Indianapolis, IN

Scott Hall defeated Bret Hart, Goldberg and Sid Vicious in a Ladder Match

Injury forced Scott Hall to vacate the United States Championship on December 19

▼

December 19
Washington, DC

Chris Benoit is awarded the United States Championship

▼

December 20
Baltimore, MD

Jeff Jarrett defeated Chris Benoit

Injury forced Jeff Jarrett to vacate the United States Championship in January 2000

▼

2000

January 17
Columbus, OH

Jeff Jarrett is awarded the United States Championship

Jeff Jarrett was stripped of the title on April 10, when WCW heads Vince Russo and Eric Bischoff vacated all titles

▼

April 16
Chicago, IL

Scott Steiner defeated Sting in the finals of a tournament to crown a new United States Champion

After using a banned maneuver in a match, Steiner was stripped of the title by WCW Commissioner Ernest Miller on July 9

▼

July 18
Auburn Hills, MI

Lance Storm defeated Mike Awesome in the finals of a tournament to crown a new United States Champion

▼

September 22
Amarillo, TX

Terry Funk defeated Lance Storm

▼

September 23
Lubbock, TX

Lance Storm defeated Terry Funk

▼

October 29
Las Vegas, NV

Gen. Rection defeated Jim Duggan and Lance Storm in a Handicap Match

▼

November 13
London, England

Lance Storm defeated Gen. Rection

▼

November 26
Milwaukee, WI

Gen. Rection defeated Lance Storm

▼

2001

January 14
Indianapolis, IN

Shane Douglas defeated Gen. Rection

▼

February 5
Tupelo, MS

Rick Steiner defeated Shane Douglas

▼

March 18
Jacksonville, FL

Booker T defeated Rick Steiner

▼

July 26
Pittsburgh, PA

Kanyon is awarded the United States Championship by then-champion Booker T

▼

September 10
San Antonio, TX

Tajiri defeated Kanyon

▼

September 23
Pittsburgh, PA

Rhyno defeated Tajiri

▼

October 22
Kansas City, MO

Kurt Angle defeated Rhyno

November 12
Boston, MA

Edge defeated Kurt Angle

Edge unified the United States and Intercontinental Championships. The title was declared inactive until July 2003

2003

July 27
Denver, CO

Eddie Guerrero defeated Chris Benoit in the finals of a tournament to crown a new United States Champion

October 19
Baltimore, MD

Big Show defeated Eddie Guerrero

2004

March 14
New York, NY

John Cena defeated Big Show

John Cena was stripped of the United States Championship in July 2004

July 29
Cincinnati, OH

Booker T last eliminated Rob Van Dam in an 8-man Elimination Match that also included Billy Gunn, Rene Dupree, Kenzo Suzuki, John Cena, Charlie Haas, and Luther Reigns

October 3
East Rutherford, NJ

John Cena defeated Booker T

October 7
Boston, MA

Carlito defeated John Cena

November 18
Dayton, OH

John Cena defeated Carlito

2005

March 3
Albany, NY

Orlando Jordan defeated John Cena

August 21
Washington, DC

Chris Benoit defeated Orlando Jordan

October 21
Reno, NV

Booker T defeated Chris Benoit

Booker T was forced to vacate the United States Championship after a title defense against Chris Benoit ended with a double pinfall

2006

January 13
Philadelphia, PA

Booker T defeated Chris Benoit

Substituting for Booker T, Randy Orton beat Chris Benoit. As a result, Booker T was named new United States Champion

February 19
Baltimore, MD

Chris Benoit defeated Booker T

April 2
Chicago, IL

JBL defeated Chris Benoit

May 26
Bakersfield, CA

Bobby Lashley defeated JBL

July 14
Minneapolis, MN

Finlay defeated Bobby Lashley

September 1
Reading, PA

Mr. Kennedy defeated Bobby Lashley and Finlay in a Triple Threat Match

October 13
Jacksonville, FL

Chris Benoit defeated Mr. Kennedy

2007

May 20
St. Louis, MO

Montel Vontavious Porter defeated Chris Benoit

2008

April 27
Baltimore, MD

Matt Hardy defeated Montel Vontavious Porter

July 20
Uniondale, NY

Shelton Benjamin defeated Matt Hardy

2009

March 20
Corpus Christi, TX

Montel Vontavious Porter defeated Shelton Benjamin

June 1
Birmingham, AL

Kofi Kingston defeated Montel Vontavious Porter

October 5
Wilkes-Barre, PA

The Miz defeated Kofi Kingston

2010

May 17
Toronto, Ontario

Bret Hart defeated The Miz

Bret Hart vacated the title in May, 2010

May 24
Toledo, OH

R-Truth defeated The Miz in a match for the vacant United States Championship

June 14
Charlotte, NC

The Miz defeated R-Truth

September 19
Chicago, IL

Daniel Bryan defeated The Miz

2011

March 14
St. Louis, MO

Sheamus defeated Daniel Bryan

May 1
Tampa, FL

Kofi Kingston defeated Sheamus

June 19
Washington, D.C

Dolph Ziggler defeated Kofi Kingston

December 18
Baltimore, MD

Zack Ryder defeated Dolph Ziggler

2012

January 16
Anaheim, CA

Jack Swagger defeated Zack Ryder

March 5
Boston, MA

Santino Marella defeated Jack Swagger

THE U.S. EXPRESS

MEMBERS: Barry Windham, Mike Rotundo
COMBINED WT: 505 lbs.

TITLE HISTORY

WORLD TAG TEAM CHAMPIONS (2 TIMES)	Defeated Adrian Adonis & Dick Murdock on January 21, 1985 Defeated Iron Sheik & Nikolai Volkoff on June 17, 1985

Blessed with boy-next-door good looks, Barry Windham & Mike Rotundo teamed up in 1984 and quickly became America's sweethearts. Collectively referred to as the U.S. Express, they became known for fending off WWE's most devious Superstars.

A mere three months after making their WWE debut, the U.S. Express defeated Adrian Adonis & Dick Murdoch to win the World Tag Team Championship. Following the win, the patriotic pairing began to use Rick Derringer's single *Real American* as their theme song. Hulk Hogan would later adopt the song as his own, using it for the majority of his career.

Behind some outside interference from "Classy" Freddie Blassie, the U.S. Express lost their titles to Iron Sheik & Nikolai Volkoff at the inaugural *WrestleMania*. Unable to stand by and allow the rule-breaking Iranian and Russian parade around the United States with the gold, Windham & Rotunda focused on exacting revenge. They finally accomplished their goal in June 1985 when they regained the titles from their rivals.

Later that year, Windham left WWE to return to the Florida territories. The U.S. Express would reunite more than twenty years later, though, when they signed on to battle Sheik & Volkoff in a *WrestleMania* rematch. Unfortunately, the match never got underway, as Jillian interrupted to sing *Born in the U.S.A.*

THE USOS

MEMBERS: Jimmy Uso, Jey Uso
COMBINED WT: 479 lbs.
FROM: San Francisco, California

Jimmy and Jey Uso are the latest in a long line of successful Samoan WWE Superstars. As members of the famed Anoa'i family, the twins' bloodlines include DNA from some of sports-entertainment's greatest, including father Rikishi, The Rock and great uncles The Wild Samoans.

As a tribute to their descendants, the Usos' pre-match ritual regularly includes the Siva Tau, a Samoan war dance that was performed by their ancestors prior to entering into battle. The Siva Tau's main purpose is to strike fear into the opposition, which helps give the Usos the advantage well before the opening bell rings.

As a unit, Jimmy and Jey Uso have earned WWE Tag Team Championship opportunities on several high-profile cards, including *Money in the Bank* and *Night of Champions* in 2010. Along the way, they have turned back such teams as The Hart Dynasty and Vladimir Kozlov & Santino Marella. They even own a win over the mighty Mark Henry in a Handicap Match.

VADER

HT: 6'5" **WT:** 450 lbs.
FROM: The Rocky Mountains
SIGNATURE MOVE: Vader Splash, Vader Bomb

Before ever stepping foot in a WWE ring, the man they call Vader earned a worldwide reputation as a bona fide tough man. At well over four hundred pounds, he possessed the power of a super heavyweight, while also owning the unbelievable ability to fly through the air like a cruiserweight.

The three-time WCW Champion made his WWE debut at the 1996 *Royal Rumble*. Despite being eliminated by Shawn Michaels, Vader made an impressive showing, eliminating an impressive list of Superstars. Following his debut, the mastodon assaulted both Superstars and WWE officials. He even attacked WWE President Gorilla Monsoon, which earned him a brief suspension.

Upon returning to the ring, Vader's path of destruction left many of WWE's biggest names laying in his wake, including Yokozuna, Razor Ramon and Sycho Sid. His impressive victories over WWE's elite eventually earned him a WWE Championship match against Shawn Michaels at *SummerSlam*. Vader defeated the champ at the event, but the victory came by countout, which meant the title could not change hands. Realizing is client would not be awarded the gold, Jim Cornette demanded the match be restarted. Vader won again, this time by disqualification. As expected, Cornette cried for another restart, which he received. However, this time HBK defeated Vader via pinfall to mark the official end to the wild encounter.

The following year, Vader traded in Cornette for Paul Bearer. The move proved to be a wise one, as his new manager helped him gain a huge victory over the legendary Undertaker at the 1997 *Royal Rumble*. Bearer also paired Vader up with Mankind in an attempt to claim tag team gold. The duo nearly dethroned Owen Hart & Davey Boy Smith at *WrestleMania 13*, but fell just short after the match was declared a double countout. Following losses to Edge and Bradshaw in late 1998, Vader disappeared from the WWE scene for many years.

VAL VENIS

HT: 6'4" WT: 245 lbs.
FROM: Las Vegas, Nevada
SIGNATURE MOVE: Money Shot

TITLE HISTORY

EUROPEAN CHAMPION	Defeated British Bulldog on December 12, 1999
INTERCONTINENTAL CHAMPION (2 TIMES)	Defeated Ken Shamrock on February 14, 1999 Defeated Rikishi on July 6, 2000
WORLD TAG TEAM CHAMPION	Named Lance Storm's partner when William Regal suffered an injury on March 24, 2003

"Hello Ladies!"

Val Venis made his debut with a towel around his waist and gyrations before his matches that left female fans in a hypnotic trance. The Big Valbowski often made waves in WWE by seducing the wives and sisters of other Superstars and managers. His actions resulted in battles against Kaientai, Goldust, and Ken Shamrock.

At *St. Valentine's Day Massacre* Venis, with an assist from Billy Gunn, defeated Ken Shamrock for the Intercontinental Title. Val Venis claimed his other singles title at *Armageddon 1999*. He defeated British Bulldog and D-Lo Brown in a Triple Threat Match to win the European Championship.

In 2000, Venis became the antithesis of his former self when he joined the Right To Censor. After the group fell apart and he took some time away from WWE, Val returned as the Chief of Staff to *Raw* GM Eric Bischoff. Not wanting the association with Bischoff to tarnish the name he cultivated earlier in his career, he operated under the name Chief Morley.

Working as an authority figure ultimately left Val unsatisfied, so he returned to his true calling, making the ladies swoon while showing off his impressive in-ring repertoire.

THE VALIANT BROTHERS

MEMBERS: Jimmy Valiant, Johnny Valiant, Jerry Valiant
COMBINED WT: 490 lbs.

HALL OF FAME 1996

TITLE HISTORY

| WORLD TAG TEAM CHAMPIONS (2 TIMES) | Defeated Tony Garea & Dean Ho on May 8, 1974 Defeated Tony Garea & Larry Zbyszko on March 6, 1979 |

"Handsome" Jimmy & "Luscious" Johnny Valiant were two of the most charismatic characters of the 1970s. With their bleached blond hair and outrageous ring attire, they had a magnetic personality that made them tough not to like, even though you weren't supposed to.

Jimmy's career kicked off in 1964. Johnny followed the lead, making his debut in 1967. Initially singles stars, the brothers turned to tag team competition at the turn of the decade. They gained some level of success early, capturing a title while competing in Indianapolis.

The flamboyant duo made their WWE debut in early 1974. Within days of their arrival, they defeated Dean Ho & Tony Garea for the World Tag Team Championship. They would go on to hold the titles for more than one year, longer than any other tandem at that time. Demolition's reign of the late 1980s is the only one to top Jimmy & Johnny in length.

After a brief hiatus, The Valiants returned to WWE in 1978. This time, however, Jimmy stepped aside and brother "Gentleman" Jerry stepped in. With Jimmy serving as manager, Johnny & Jerry defeated Larry Zbyzsko & Tony Garea for the World Tag Team Championship in March 1979.

Jimmy & Johnny Valiant took their rightful place alongside the all-time best when they were inducted into the WWE Hall of Fame in 1996.

VANCE ARCHER

HT: 6'9" WT: 272 lbs. FROM: Dallas, Texas
SIGNATURE MOVE: Inverted DDT

Introduced as a part of ECW's New Superstar Initiative in late 2009, Vance Archer debuted with one simple goal: Make sure something bad happened to his opponents. If Archer was successful in achieving his goal, he knew that he would one day reach the top of ECW, while painting his self-proclaimed masterpiece of agony along the way.

The majority of Archer's childhood was spent fighting on the rough streets of Dallas, where he developed a penchant for pain. As a result, he was able to compartmentalize much of the abuse inflicted on him in the ring, en route to slowly and methodically dismantling the ECW roster. Along the way, he earned impressive victories over such stars as Goldust and ECW Original Tommy Dreamer.

When ECW ended in early 2010, Archer took his skills to *SmackDown*. While there, he formed a short-lived tag team with Curt Hawkins. But unlike his stay in ECW, Archer was unable to intimidate members of the Friday night brand. He was eventually released from WWE later that year.

VELVET McINTYRE

HT: 5'9" WT: 143 lbs. FROM: County Cork, Ireland

TITLE HISTORY

| WOMEN'S CHAMPION | Defeated Fabulous Moolah on July 3, 1986 |
| WOMEN'S WORLD TAG TEAM CHAMPION | Partnered with Princess Victoria and awarded championship in May 1983 |

Over the course of her nearly-20-year career, Velvet McIntyre established herself as one of the most successful female competitors of all time.

With Princess Victoria as her partner, McIntyre entered WWE in 1984 and immediately became recognized as one-half of the promotion's first-ever Women's Tag Team Champions. Later that same year, a career-ending injury forced Princess Victoria aside, allowing Desiree Peterson to slide in as McIntyre's championship partner. In all, McIntyre held the gold for more than one year before losing to The Glamour Girls in Egypt.

McIntyre's trophy case did sit empty for long. After unsuccessfully unseating Women's Champion Fabulous Moolah in the Chicago portion of *WrestleMania 2*, the Irish-born Superstar finally claimed the gold from the future Hall of Famer in July 1986. She held the championship for six days before losing it back to Moolah in Sydney, Australia.

McIntyre's impressive resume also includes a match at the first-ever *Survivor Series*, where she teamed with former nemesis Moolah to defeat the squad captained by Sherri Martel.

The first *Vengeance* event featured a tournament to unify the WWE Championship and the WCW Championship which arrived in WWE earlier in the year when WWE acquired WCW. In 2007, the event became *Vengeance: Night of Champions* (see *Night of Champions*) then the Vengeance was dropped. In 2011, *Vengeance* made its return as a pay-per-view event.

December 9, 2001
San Diego, CA
San Diego Sports Arena

Main Event
Chris Jericho defeated Stone Cold Steven Austin in a World Heavyweight Championship Unification Match

July 21, 2002
Detroit, MI
Joe Louis Arena

Main Event
The Rock defeated WWE Champion Undertaker and Kurt Angle in a Triple Threat Match

July 27, 2003
Denver, CO
Pepsi Arena

Main Event
Kurt Angle defeated Big Show, and WWE Champion Brock Lesnar in a Triple Threat, No Disqualification Match

July 11, 2004
Hartford, CT
Hartford Civic Center

Main Event
World Heavyweight Champion Chris Benoit defeated Triple H

June 26, 2005
Las Vegas, NV
Thomas & Mack Center

Main Event
World Heavyweight Champion Batista defeated Triple H in Hell In A Cell Match

June 25, 2006
Charlotte, NC
Charlotte Bobcats Arena

Main Event
D-Generation X defeated the Spirit Squad in a 5-On-2 Handicap, Non-Title Match

October 23, 2011
San Antonio, TX
AT & T Center

Main Event
WWE Champion Alberto Del Rio defeated John Cena in a Last Man Standing Match

NIGHT OF CHAMPIONS

VERNE GAGNE

HT: 5'11"   WT: 215 lbs.
FROM: Robbinsdale, Minnesota
SIGNATURE MOVE: Gagne Sleeper Hold

Verne Gagne was one of the top amateur athletes in the United States during the 1940s. At the University of Minnesota he was a four-time Big Ten Conference Champion and a two-time NCAA National Champion, and held a spot on the 1948 Olympic team. After a short tenure with the Green Bay Packers, Gagne entered sports-entertainment in 1950. His first major championship was the NWA World Junior Heavyweight Championship.

During the 1960s, while still active in the ring, Verne became a promoter and eventual owner of the AWA, leading it to new heights. From 1972 to 1979 Verne made special appearances for World Wrestling Entertainment in Madison Square Garden and battled Eddie Graham, Mr. Fuji, The Valiant Brothers, and Nikolai Volkoff. In 1981, Verne retired from the ring but did lace-up the boots on occasion if foes overstepped their bounds. Throughout his career, Verne honed many budding Superstars' in-ring talents and the list of individuals he taught reads like a veritable Who's Who of sports-entertainment.

In 1991 the AWA closed its doors after an astonishing 31 years of operation. Verne has enjoyed life away from the ring but was called back under the bright lights in April 2006 when he was enshrined amongst the immortals in the WWE Hall of Fame.

Verne Gagne dedicated his life to the advancement of sports-entertainment. Over his four decades in the business, he showed that he was a dynamic performer in the ring, and an inventive business mind behind the scenes.

VICKIE GUERRERO

As the widow of WWE Hall of Famer Eddie Guerrero, Vickie Guerrero was a beloved figure when she entered WWE. It wasn't long, however, before she revealed a darker side. Fans everywhere were shocked when Vickie turned into a power-hungry witch who would stop at nothing to get what she wants.

Vickie became a regular on WWE television during the emotional rivalry between Rey Mysterio and Chavo Guerrero in 2006. Appearing as a neutral party, she pleaded with them to call a truce. However, she later aligned with her nephew to defeat Mysterio.

In May 2007, Vickie was awarded the position of *SmackDown*'s Assistant General Manager. She eventually gained full control when her boss, Theodore Long, suffered a heart attack. As a protégé of the popular Long, Vickie slowly began to regain the fans' trust again. Vickie, however, then revealed a torrid tryst with Edge. The cunning GM proceeded to abuse her power to ensure the "Rated-R Superstar" would become World Heavyweight Champion.

With championship gold strapped around her lover's waist, Vickie began to build a powerful faction around her known as La Familia. Vickie continued to gain more power and satisfy her own agenda, while at the same time inciting WWE audiences with her shrieking "Excuse Me!!" catchphrase echoing from the rafters. After she split with Edge, a romance with Dolph Ziggler blossomed into a professional relationship. With Vickie at his side, Ziggler became one of the most impressive U.S. Champions in recent years. Envious of such success, Jack Swagger pleaded with Vickie to add him to her client list.

She's seen action at *Extreme Rules* 2009 in a Hog Pen Match, and tangled with Trish Stratus, Hornswoggle, and ex-lover Edge. Vickie's tagged with LayCool, and even donned the referee uniform all just to get what she wants. She's a Miss WrestleMania, General Manager, an *NXT* Pro, and now the premiere manager in WWE. Due to the tactics she employs, the WWE Universe regularly greets her with a cascade of boos. This Cougar doesn't care, she is out to make WWE her personal playground.

VICTOR RIVERA

HT: 6'2" **WT:** 240 lbs.
FROM: Puerto Rico
SIGNATURE MOVE: Cannonball

TITLE HISTORY

INTERNATIONAL TAG TEAM CHAMPION	*Named Tony Marino's partner on December 12, 1969*
WORLD TAG TEAM CHAMPION	*Partnered with Dominic DeNucci to defeat Jimmy Valiant & Johnny Valiant on May 13, 1975*

Victor Rivera arrived in WWE in 1964. With his reputation as a defender of all things positive and just, Rivera became a hero to all audiences during his wars with Dr. Jerry & "Crazy" Luke Graham, Hans Mortier, Gorilla Monsoon and Eddie Graham. Over the years he worked with partners like Bruno Sammartino, Haystacks Calhoun, and Spiros Arion. In December, 1969 Rivera claimed half the International Tag Team Championship with partner Tony Marino.

Rivera also traveled the National Wrestling Alliance in the early 1970s, mainly in the Los Angeles Territory. In March 1975 Victor worked with Dominic DeNucci to defeat the Valiant Brothers for the World Tag Team Championship. Rivera split time for the rest of the decade in the NWA and WWE and made his last WWE appearance in 1989. Victor Rivera will be remembered forever by fans as a beloved champion who fought on the side of good for three decades.

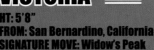

VICTORIA

HT: 5'8"
FROM: San Bernardino, California
SIGNATURE MOVE: Widow's Peak

TITLE HISTORY

WOMEN'S CHAMPION (2 TIMES)	*Defeated Trish Stratus on November 17, 2002 Defeated Molly Holly on February 23, 2004*

In 2002, WWE was introduced to Victoria, who quickly proved she was a different type of Diva. She gained notoriety when she nailed Trish Stratus in the back with a steel chair. That November, she beat Trish for the Women's Championship and held the prize for almost five months, often with the help of Steven Richards.

Almost a year after winning her first championship this dangerous black widow kept spun her web of pain in the first-ever Women's Steel Cage Match where she defeated Lita. Victoria's winning ways continued for many months, including a second title run that started in February 2004. That March, Victoria faced Molly Holly in a Hair vs. Title match at *WrestleMania XX*.

In June of 2007 Victoria found herself on *SmackDown* where she was one of of the top challengers for the Divas Championship. She remained a feared member of the Divas roster until she retired from the ring in January 2009. She made a surprise one night return for the "Miss WrestleMania" Divas Battle Royal at *WrestleMania XXV*.

During her days in the ring, this mixed martial artist earned a reputation for crushing any Diva that was foolish enough to oppose her using whatever methods she felt was necessary.

The global phenomenon known today as WWE would not exist had it not been for Vincent J. McMahon. The father of current WWE Chairman Vincent K. McMahon, the elder McMahon used his keen business acumen and unparalleled passion for wrestling to lay the groundwork for what would become the most successful sports-entertainment company in the history of the world.

The son of Rose and Jess McMahon, Vincent J. was born on July 6, 1915 in Harlem. He spent much of his childhood roaming the backstage hallways of Madison Square Garden while his father Jess, an accomplished boxing promoter, booked the famed arena with some of the era's biggest names, including Jack Johnson, Jack Delaney, and Paul Berlenbach.

In the early 1930s, Vince's father took an uncharacteristic step back from the boxing world to focus his attention on promoting wrestling events. Little did anybody know at the time that Jess's decision would greatly impact generations of McMahons to follow, as well as millions of wrestling fans.

Vince had his first taste of working in the business in 1935 when he began promoting fights out of Hempstead, Long Island. Unfortunately for the up-and-coming promoter, his career was put on hold before it ever took off when he was shipped to North Carolina to serve in the Coast Guard. While there, he met and married a young girl named Vicki. While the marriage didn't last long, they did have two sons together, Vincent and Rod.

Following his divorce, Vince was eager to get back into the wrestling business in a major way. However, successful promoter Toots Mondt controlled the New York territory, so Vince was forced to take his ambition elsewhere. He eventually settled on Washington, D.C.

Capitol Wrestling Corporation

Upon arrival, Vince purchased a small dilapidated venue he later called Capitol Arena; and on January 7, 1953, he put on the first-ever Capitol Wrestling Corporation event. Like most startups, Capitol Wrestling experienced its share of growing pains, but the company took its first real step towards greatness when Vince decided to embrace television, a new technology at the time.

On January 5, 1956, Capitol Wrestling produced its first-ever television program. The show was an instant hit. Within six months, Capitol Wrestling was in high demand as far north as the prestigious New York market, which was controlled by Mondt at the time. Some of the regular weekly viewers of Capitol Wrestling included General Douglas MacArthur and former First Lady Bess Truman.

VINCENT J. MCMAHON 🇺🇸

FROM: New York, New York

Proving that timing is everything, Vince miraculously was able to promote Capitol Wrestling shows at Madison Square Garden while Mondt had his promoter's license temporarily suspended. Vince's wrestling product was an instant hit with Northeast fans, which infuriated Mondt and many other of the area's promoters. While those promoters were busy pouting, Vince used his television product to take over the territory.

Forging an Alliance

By 1960, Vince was the sole survivor of the promoters' battle for the Northeast. Vince welcomed former adversary Mondt into Capitol Wrestling as a partner. In what would eventually prove to be one of the most important talent signings in sports-entertainment history, Capitol Wrestling assumed the booking rights to Buddy Rogers in 1960. One year later, Rogers captured the National Wrestling Alliance (NWA) Championship. The victory provided an amazing opportunity for Vince to use Rogers' drawing power to sell out Madison Square Garden time after time. Realizing he had a hot commodity on his hands, Vince also only allowed Rogers to defend his title outside of the Northeast on very rare occasions. This didn't sit well with the other NWA promoters, who eventually demanded Rogers cease his reign. The promoters got their wish when Lou Thesz defeated Rogers for the title in Toronto on January 24, 1963.

World Wide Wrestling Federation

Vince refused to recognize the title change, claiming a championship could not change hands during a one-fall match (championship matches were traditionally two-out-of-three falls at this time). To further show his dissatisfaction, Vince made the perilous decision to withdraw Capitol Wrestling from the NWA and start his own independent wrestling promotion. Shortly thereafter, the World Wide Wrestling Federation was born, and Buddy Rogers was its first champion.

After buying out Mondt in 1969, Vince proved his generosity by splitting his former partner's shares and offering them to longtime confidants Gorilla Monsoon, Arnold Skaaland, and Phil Zacko. Together, they brought professional wrestling into the 1970s and ushered in such legendary names as Andre the Giant, Pedro Morales, and "Superstar" Billy Graham.

After nearly 50 years in the business, Vince decided it was time to retire in 1982. The successful promoter planned on passing on the company to Monsoon, but his ambitious son Vincent K. had other plans. Just prior to Monsoon assuming leadership, the young McMahon convinced his father and his partners to sell the entire company to him.

Over the next several years, Vince watched his son incorporate the same formula for success he used when taking over the Northeast decades prior. The only difference was that Vincent K. wasn't interested in simply ruling a single territory. Instead, the determined entrepreneur intended on taking over the entire nation, and eventually the globe.

The young McMahon's plans to put other wrestling promotions out of business originally didn't sit well with his father, who grew up in a business that only knew separate territories. Furthermore, the elder McMahon had friends in many of the other territories his son planned on taking over. As a result, the father-son duo butted heads over the company's future on several occasions. In the end, after seeing his son gain amazing success in a short period of time, Vince came around and offered his support to Vincent K.

On January 23, 1984, Vince walked the halls of his home away from home, Madison Square Garden, for the final time. In the main event of the evening, a young newcomer called Hulk Hogan defeated the Iron Sheik for the WWE Championship. A proud Vince watched as The Hulkster's victory instantly ushered in his son's new vision of sports-entertainment.

On May 27, 1984, Vincent J. McMahon passed away after a battle with pancreatic cancer. He was 68.

In the months following Vince's death, Vincent K. took his company to heights never imagined before, thanks in large part to the unbelievable success of the first-ever *WrestleMania* at Madison Square Garden. Like his father before him, Vincent K. also embraced technological advances when he made his product available on pay-per-view. These early moves help build the foundation for today's sports-entertainment empire known as WWE, but none of it would have been possible had it not been for the foresight and groundwork put in place by the father of WWE, Vincent J. McMahon.

VINCENT K. MCMAHON

HT: 6'2"   **WT: 248 lbs.**   **FROM: Greenwich, Connecticut**   **SIGNATURE MOVE: Power Walk**

Vince McMahon did not meet his biological father until the age of 12, an event that would forever change the direction of his life. From that day, he became enamored with professional wrestling. However, the elder McMahon wanted his son to become either a physician or attorney and sent a protesting Vince to military school. As Vince grew up, major career influences continued to be the wrestling kind. He even patterned himself after the extravagant Superstar, Dr. Jerry Graham and at one point bleached his hair blond to duplicate the looks of the good doctor. After graduating from college, he married the love of his life and entrepreneurial muse Linda Marie Edwards. Vince's unwavering ambition propelled him to do everything he could to get into the business he prized above all else. His father did everything he could to keep him out. After a few years as a reluctant traveling salesman, Vince's dream finally came true.

In 1971, Vince McMahon had one chance to prove himself in the arena he longed to enter. Failure would put him out of the business forever; success meant a ticket to the main event. Thankfully, his effort in Bangor, Maine was a huge success, and Vince became the third generation McMahon promoter. As he learned the ropes of the business, another opportunity came his way in 1972. Right before a show was to go on the air, then-announcer Ray Morgan tried to hold up the McMahons for more money. The elder McMahon promptly showed Ray the way out. As the door closed for Mr. Morgan, it opened for the young Vince McMahon, and he became the new voice of WWE. As hundreds of thousands of fans watched every week on television, few people knew the major role Vince was playing behind the scenes. For the remainder of the 1970s he was a driving force behind the company's success, responsible for an almost quadruple increase in its television syndication. Vince's innovative implementation of his father's business formula prepared him to turn the corner, and catapult the company into the era of sports-entertainment.

TITLE HISTORY	
ECW CHAMPION	*Defeated Bobby Lashley on April 29, 2007*
WWE CHAMPION	*Defeated Triple H on September 16, 1999*

Titan Sports and Hulkamania

In 1980, the entrepreneurial McMahon edged toward the pinnacle as he incorporated Titan Sports. In 1982, he and his wife, Linda, acquired Capital Wrestling Company shares, taking control of World Wrestling Entertainment, and ultimately changing the model of the professional wrestling business. Vince adopted the formula his father created for dominance in the Northeast section of the United States and began implementing key initiatives to expand the company's reach. As he took the first steps toward expansion, Vince approached many of the members of the old wrestling territory fiefdoms and offered them buy-outs. Set in their ways and resting on past laurels, they laughed him out of their offices. They didn't see that the days of great moments in the ring being confined to a specific geographic area were quickly coming to an end. In a classic example of "He who laughs last, laughs loudest," Vince flexed his entrepreneurial muscle and assembled a world-class roster of Superstars. His vision of global expansion was complete when he orchestrated the return of the 6'7", 303 lbs. Hulk Hogan. Audiences were captivated by Hogan, and with McMahon as the brains, and Hulk Hogan providing the brawn, the two made an unstoppable team. As every ring of the bell brought an amazing match, World Wrestling Entertainment steamrolled through the United States, breaking down the imaginary walls that had protected the territory system against legitimate competition for decades.

In 1985, with Hulkamania running wild, and wrestling experiencing its second "Golden Age," the driven McMahon rolled the dice and bet it all on a one-time experiment called *WrestleMania*. This star-studded event garnered global attention as it featured Muhammad Ali, Liberace, The Rockettes, Billy Martin, and Mr. T. The happening became an annual phenomenon, and today *WrestleMania* is considered the greatest sports-entertainment spectacle on Earth. After the success of *WrestleMania*, McMahon brought WWE to network television with a bi-monthly replacement for *Saturday Night Live* called *Saturday Night's Main Event*. A company that was once a successful regional entity was now a global entertainment powerhouse. WWE exploded with television programs, pay-per-view events, a monthly magazine, home video, action figures, official Superstar merchandise, and interactive video game software. The era of sports-entertainment had arrived and tens of millions of fans around the globe were watching World Wrestling Entertainment with an indescribable fervor.

" NO CHANCE IN HELL! "

In 1987 he achieved the unthinkable and packed 93,173 fans into the Pontiac Silverdome to see Hulk Hogan battle Andre the Giant for the WWE Championship in the main event of *WrestleMania III*. As Hogan took his step towards immortality, WWE solidified its position as the premiere sports-entertainment company in the world.

Sports-Entertainment, Live on TV!

As McMahon and his Superstars marched into the 1990s setting records for live crowd attendance, pay-per-view buy rate revenue, cable television ratings, and licensed merchandise sales, McMahon once again changed the face of broadcast television. In January 1993, he launched *Monday Night Raw*. In 1995, media magnate Ted Turner chose to go head-to-head with Vince McMahon and broadcast his competing *WCW Monday Nitro* during the same time-slot on his own network, which lead to the Monday Night Wars.

After a number of duplicitous gambits and billions of dollars, World Championship Wrestling (WCW) became a formidable opponent, and took the lead in the sports-

entertainment television ratings. Now Vince was fighting for his company and his livelihood. He reinvented and reconfigured his entrepreneurial game plan, adding a new persona to the mix. Once again, he would literally and figuratively change the face of sports-entertainment.

At the 1997 *Survivor Series*, in the wake of "The Montreal Incident," Vince wiped Bret "Hit Man" Hart's spit off his face and in that one fell swoop, Vince McMahon, the broadcaster, morphed into "Mr. McMahon," and an infamous, wicked character was born. Since Vince always believed adaptation is the key to survival, the Attitude Era bombarded television sets everywhere and a rivalry between "Mr. McMahon" and Stone Cold Steve Austin propelled WWE to fantastical heights. Now Vince McMahon was recognized for his maniacal acts in the ring, as well as for his dramatic business accomplishments outside it. In 1999, World Wrestling Entertainment made history when it became a publicly traded company. Now that its fans could truly be part of the company's success, WWE proved that it ruled Wall Street and the world.

A New Millenium

In March 2001, the WWE emerged as the victor of the Monday Night Wars after the McMahon family acquired WCW. In November 2001, riding the wave of success from earlier in the year, Vince created a club that required a specific act to join. Unlike other groups characterized by prestige and distinction, the Vince McMahon Kiss My Ass Club was designed for individuals to kiss the Chairman's bare posterior or suffer the threat of suspension or termination.

Vince started the year 2003 on a crusade to kill the cultural ideology he helped create—the red and yellow of Hulkamania. This led to a Street Fight at *WrestleMania XIX* between the Chairman and future WWE Hall of Famer. This flight of fisticuffs was 20 years in the making and as the bell rang, the line between entertainment and reality was obliterated. As two decades of history blended into one historic moment the two men annihilated each other and donned the proverbial crimson mask. This battle showed once again that "Mr. McMahon" will do anything to entertain the fans. On September 18, the entrepreneurial pioneer in promoting, television, marketing, and business took his rightful place —next to his father—among the greatest figures of the world's most famous arena. Inducted in by his children Shane and Stephanie, Vince McMahon became a member of the Madison Square Garden Hall of Fame. In March 2008 Vince joined entertainment immortals when he received a star on the Hollywood Walk of Fame.

The first months of 2009 were troubled times for Mr. McMahon. Randy Orton waged a one-man war against the McMahon family, attacking Vince, Shane and Stephanie because of his rivalry with Vince's son-in-law, Triple H. The night after *WrestleMania XXV* the Chairman booked himself, son Shane, and "The Game" in a six-man match against Randy Orton and Legacy. The troubles continued into June when Vince McMahon sold *Monday Night Raw* to Donald Trump, though he bought it back—for twice as much—the following week.

In January 2010, the Chairman shocked the sports-entertainment world when Bret "Hit Man" Hart returned to WWE television for the first time in over a decade. Hart was the guest host for *Monday Night Raw* and was looking for closure with Mr. McMahon after the 1997 Montreal Incident. Instead, Mr. McMahon left the "Hit Man" doubled over in pain after a surprise kick to the stomach. The end result was a No Holds Barred Match between Mr. McMahon and Hart at *WrestleMania XXVI*. After losing to the "Hit Man", Mr. McMahon retired from in-ring competition.

Vince McMahon still appears on WWE programming to make important announcements, such as The Rock as the host of *WrestleMania XXVII* and the winner of *Tough Enough*. He also stepped in during the conflict between CM Punk and John Cena over the WWE Championship. The Chairman has also been embroiled in a corporate struggle involving the Board of Directors and son-in-law, Triple H over who should oversee the day-to-day operations of *Raw*. After four months, Mr. McMahon returned, removed Triple H from his position and named John Laurinaitis as interim general manager.

Vince McMahon remains on the cutting edge of entertainment. The company he created has grown into a global entity with offices in New York, Los Angeles, London, Mumbai, Istanbul, Shanghai, Singapore and Tokyo. The constant forward thinker, in December 2011, WWE received Mashable Awards for "Digital Company of the Year" and "Must Follow Brand on Social Media."

Despite all the accolades, there is another side of the WWE Chairman: his boundless philanthropy and patriotism. Vince McMahon works with the Special Olympics. He launched a non-partisan campaign to help Americans register to vote. He hosts a yearly show dedicated to the people serving in the armed forces and along with his wife, Linda, he is on the Honorary National Board of The Make-A-Wish Foundation. For the WWE Chairman, it's not just about giving back. It's about leading by example.

V

2010-

2000-

1990-99

1980-89

1970-79

1960-69

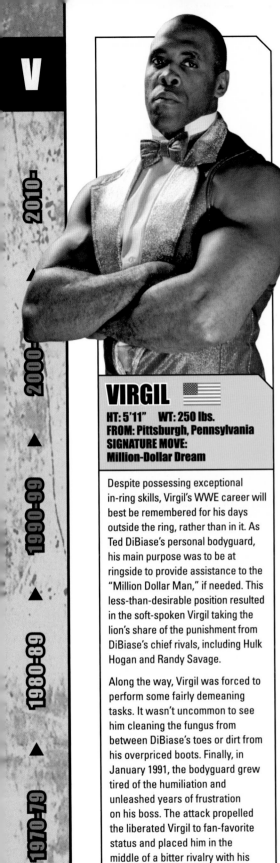

VIRGIL

HT: 5'11" WT: 250 lbs.
FROM: Pittsburgh, Pennsylvania
SIGNATURE MOVE:
Million-Dollar Dream

Despite possessing exceptional in-ring skills, Virgil's WWE career will best be remembered for his days outside the ring, rather than in it. As Ted DiBiase's personal bodyguard, his main purpose was to be at ringside to provide assistance to the "Million Dollar Man," if needed. This less-than-desirable position resulted in the soft-spoken Virgil taking the lion's share of the punishment from DiBiase's chief rivals, including Hulk Hogan and Randy Savage.

Along the way, Virgil was forced to perform some fairly demeaning tasks. It wasn't uncommon to see him cleaning the fungus from between DiBiase's toes or dirt from his overpriced boots. Finally, in January 1991, the bodyguard grew tired of the humiliation and unleashed years of frustration on his boss. The attack propelled the liberated Virgil to fan-favorite status and placed him in the middle of a bitter rivalry with his former employer.

Armed with the training he received from "Rowdy" Roddy Piper, Virgil earned the biggest victory of his career when he defeated DiBiase for the Million Dollar Championship at *SummerSlam 1991*. Following the win, Virgil managed to maintain his high level of popularity, but struggled to reach the same level of success in the ring. He finally left WWE in 1994, but made a surprise appearance in May 2010 when the Million Dollar Championship made a brief return to WWE.

VIRGIL THE KENTUCKY BUTCHER

 HT: 6'5" WT: 290 lbs.
FROM: Hamilton, Ontario, Canada

Virgil the Kentucky Butcher brought an impressive Canadian won-loss record with him when he entered WWE in the mid-1960s. His reputation earned him instant respect in the United States, where he almost immediately moved to the top of the card. After turning back Hall-of-Famer Arnold Skaaland several times, Virgil was awarded an opportunity at Bruno Sammartino's WWE Championship. He was unsuccessful in his quest to dethrone Sammartino, but did earn several rematches. Unfortunately for Virgil, he fell short in all attempts to claim Sammartino's title.

VISCERA

HT: 6'9" WT: 450 lbs.
SIGNATURE MOVE: Viscera Drop

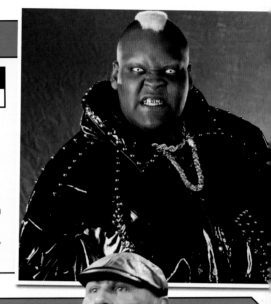

In 1998, this giant Superstar became an unwilling member of Undertaker's Ministry of Darkness.

TITLE HISTORY	
HARDCORE CHAMPION	1 Time

Viscera abused opponents with a methodical style that utilized his size and brute strength. He worked with the Acolytes to eliminate any individuals who tried to hinder Undertaker's work. After breaking free of Undertaker's control, Viscera vanished in 2000.

Upon his return a few years later, parts of his personality that were previously dormant bubbled to the surface and he soon became known as "the World's Biggest Love Machine." He pursued a few Divas, but focused his attention on Lilian Garcia. He teamed briefly with Val Venis, and later Charlie Haas but ultimately both partnerships dissolved.

VITO

HT: 6'2" WT: 250 lbs. FROM: Little Italy, Manhattan
SIGNATURE MOVE: Code of Silence

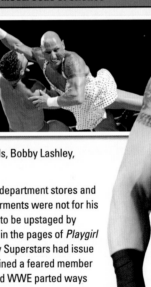

A veteran of the ring who handed out beatings in ECW and WCW, this hard-headed Italian debuted in WWE in August 2005. Trained by Johnny Rodz, Vito teamed with Nunzio and locked up with Charlie Haas, the Mexicools, Steven Richards, Bobby Lashley, Tatanka, Matt Hardy and Funaki.

In June 2006 Vito began frequenting department stores and purchasing dresses. These lovely garments were not for his lady friends, but for himself. Not one to be upstaged by Divas doing pictorals, Vito appeared in the pages of *Playgirl* magazine in April 2007. Though many Superstars had issue wrestling a cross-dresser, Vito remained a feared member of the *SmackDown* roster until he and WWE parted ways late in 2007.

VIVIAN VACHON

 **HT: 5'7"**
FROM: Montreal, Quebec, Canada

Wrestling flowed through Vivian Vachon's veins. As the sister of legendary Superstars Mad Dog and Butcher Vachon, competing in the ring was her main focus from a young age. Still a teenager, Vivian made her professional debut in the late 1960s. A few years later, she gained her greatest accolade when she captured the AWA Women's Championship in November 1971.

Many consider Vivian to be one of the supreme female competitors of the 1970s, despite the fact that she retired midway through the decade. Vachon made a brief return to the ring in 1986 when she toured Japan with brother Mad Dog. Adding acting to her resume, Vivian also starred in the 1975 motion picture *Wrestling Queen*.

VLADIMIR KOZLOV

HT: 6'8"   WT: 302 lbs.
FROM: Moscow, Russia

TITLE HISTORY

WWE TAG TEAM CHAMPION	Partnered with Santino Marella to defeat Heath Slater & Justin Gabriel on December 6, 2010

Judo, sambo, and kickboxing are just a few of the fighting styles Vladimir Kozlov perfected prior to his WWE debut in April 2008. This experience, coupled with his massive three hundred pound frame, earned him his "Moscow Mauler" moniker. After spending the first few months of his WWE career decimating SmackDown Superstars, Kozlov demanded better competition. Armed with his patented battering ram head butt, the mighty Russian targeted WWE's top stars.

With a fearless attitude and multiple offensive weapons, Kozlov ambushed anyone that held WWE gold and soon attacked ECW. The "Mauler" then made his Raw debut in 2010. After an unlikely string of events, he formed a team with Santino Marella. Initially not expected to have much success, they were the most entertaining duo in WWE. They even hosted a Monday night tea party for guest Sheamus and won the WWE Tag Team Championships that December.

Kozlov helped tackle the Corre at WrestleMania XVII and continued to be a popular Superstar. After he was a Pro on NXT Redemption, Vladimir suddenly disappeared from WWE after his leg was savagely attacked by Mark Henry.

WADE BARRETT

    HT: 6'7"   WT: 246 lbs.   FROM: Manchester, England
SIGNATURE MOVE: Wasteland

TITLE HISTORY

INTERCONTINENTAL CHAMPION	Defeated Kofi Kingston on March 25, 2011

As the first-ever winner of NXT, Wade Barrett was billed as WWE's next breakout star. But nobody realized just how fast he would become one of sports-entertainment's most-feared forces. Less than one week after being crowned NXT champion, Barrett joined forces with his fellow Rookies to demolish Raw and its main event, featuring John Cena and CM Punk. Like a pack of rabid dogs, the Barrett-led barrage destroyed everything in its path, including the ring.

Collectively known as Nexus, Barrett's crew of renegades spent the next several months targeting only the most prevalent personalities, including Bret Hart, Ricky Steamboat and Mr. McMahon.

In 2011, Barrett jumped to SmackDown, where he teamed with Justin Gabriel, Heath Slater and Ezekiel Jackson to form The Corre. The equally rebellious faction owned Friday nights during its six-month run. Along the way, Barrett claimed the Intercontinental Championship from Kofi Kingston in March 2011.

Now on his own, the young Superstar has launched his "Barrett Barrage," where he claims the arena is his battlefield and his opponents are mere casualties of war.

WAHOO McDANIEL

   HT: 6'2"   WT: 265 lbs.   FROM: Midland, Texas
SIGNATURE MOVE: Tomahawk Chop

A former football player, most notably with the New York Jets and Miami Dolphins, Wahoo McDaniel first began his in-ring career in the 1960s during the off-season. It wasn't until his time on the gridiron ended that the proud Native American began to cement his legacy as one of the toughest men to grace the ring.

Trained by the legendary Dory Funk, Sr., McDaniel rarely competed in WWE. Choosing to leave the Northeast territory to fellow Native American Chief Jay Strongbow, McDaniel instead spent the majority of his career in the Mid-Atlantic region. Armed with a devastating chop, a move perfected by various Indian Superstars, he battled many of the region's top names, including Ric Flair, Johnny Valentine, and Dory Funk, Jr.

In August 1981, "The Chief" defeated Roddy Piper for the United States Championship. Unfortunately, an injury at the hands of Abdullah the Butcher forced McDaniel to vacate the championship shortly after his victory. Over the next three years, however, he went on to capture the title four more times.

WALDO VON ERICH

HT: 6'0"   WT: 260 lbs.   FROM: Germany
SIGNATURE MOVE: Blitzkrieg

TITLE HISTORY

UNITED STATES TAG TEAM CHAMPION	Partnered with Gene Kiniski to defeat Jerry Graham & Luke Graham on February 4, 1965

When this merciless remnant of the Third Reich entered WWE in 1963 audiences throughout the northeastern United States were horrified. The brother of Fritz Von Erich, Waldo operated in the ring with a controlled fury that ended careers of countless heroes. People watched in fear as Von Erich threatened favorite son Bruno Sammartino in sold-out arenas from Maine to Washington DC.

In 1965 Waldo teamed with Gene Kiniski and defeated Dr. Jerry & "Crazy" Luke Graham to capture the WWE United States Tag Team Championship. Even after he lost the title, Von Erich continued his assault and recruited "Classy" Freddie Blassie as his manager in battles against Chief Jay Strongbow and Andre the Giant. Waldo Von Erich retired from the ring in 1979, but will be remembered as a dangerous threats to any champion in any era.

W

1960-69
1970-79
1980-89
1990-99
2000-09
2010-

THE WARLORD

HT: 6'5"   **WT:** 323 lbs.
FROM: Parts Unknown
SIGNATURE MOVE: Full Nelson

Few teams in WWE history could match strength with colossal duo of Warlord & Barbarian. Collectively known as The Powers of Pain, the muscular tandem amazed audiences with their incredible athleticism and frightening face paint.

After tangling with legendary tag teams The Hart Foundation and Demolition, including a failed attempt at unseating Ax & Smash for the World Tag Team Championship at *WrestleMania V*, The Powers of Pain went their separate ways. With manager Slick guiding him, Warlord's singles career looked bright early on. He even defeated former Intercontinental Champion Tito Santana at *SummerSlam 1990*. Unfortunately, however, that's where the success stopped.

Over the next several years, Warlord found himself on the wrong end of rivalries with "Texas Tornado" Kerry Von Erich and fellow strongman British Bulldog. Despite coming up short, however, Warlord did push Bulldog to the limit during their encounter at *WrestleMania VII*.

WAYLON MERCY

HT: 6'7"   **WT:** 290 lbs.
SIGNATURE MOVE: Sleeperhold

A man of few words but a variety of violent actions, Waylon Mercy came to WWE in 1995. He claimed to be a peaceful person and friend to all mankind. During his slow walk to the ring he shook hands with fans, ring announcers, referees, and opponents alike with an eerily calm demeanor. His interviews sent chills down people's spines as he stated, "Lives are gonna be in Waylon Mercy's hands."

When the bell rang Waylon became a man possessed and attacked opponents in a fit of rage. By October of that year Waylon was forced to leave the ring after feeling the bone-crushing effects from Diesel's Jacknife Powerbomb. Waylon Mercy was not a man to be trusted, associated with, or challenged. He could snap at the slightest move or word and make people pay dearly for such offenses.

WELL DUNN

MEMBERS: Timothy Well, Steve Dunn
COMBINED WT: 470 lbs.

A well known team in the southeastern United States, Timothy Well & Steven Dunn debuted in the big time in the summer of 1993. Determined to show their talents where the world could see them, Well Dunn combined excellent tag team wrestling with relentless rule-breaking tactics, along with their always irritating manager, Harvey Wippleman.

The duo attacked the likes of the Smokin' Gunns, Men On A Mission, the Bushwhackers, 1-2-3 Kid & Bob "Spark Plugg" Holly, the Headshrinkers and the Allied Powers. Despite being contenders for WWE tag team gold, they were never able to win the prizes and left the company in the spring of 1995. As the duo soon went their separate ways, Dunn joined WCW and was in the ring the night Scott Hall made his historic debut on *Nitro*. Well Dunn briefly reunited on the independent circuit in the late 1990s. Sadly, on March 22, 2009, after years of declining health, Steve Doll (Dunn) passed away.

Wendi Richter (see page 373)

WHO

WT: Who Knows What
FROM: Who Knows Where

More than 50 years after comedians Abbott and Costello famously wondered "who" was on first base, the mysterious athlete finally fled the baseball diamond in favor of a career in sports-entertainment. Known simply as Who, the masked Superstar began his brief and befuddling WWE career in 1996. With his anvil-shaped chest and impressive wrestling acumen, Who immediately struck fear into the WWE locker room.

He also confused broadcasters greatly. Typical banter during a Who match:

Vince McMahon: The question is who is in the ring?

Mr. Perfect: Exactly, Who is in the ring.

Jim Ross: Who's the referee for this match?

Perfect: No, Who's wrestling.

Luckily, the WWE broadcast team didn't have to fumble over Who's identity for long. After coming up short against the likes of Savio Vega and Jake "The Snake" Roberts, Who realized he didn't have the heart to be a WWE Superstar. He soon left WWE and retreated back to his home in Who Knows Where.

WENDI RICHTER

HT: 5'8"
FROM: Dallas, Texas
SIGNATURE MOVE: Swinging Arm Wrench

Wendi Richter came to WWE in 1984 and was an exciting addition to the WWE roster, boasting an impressive combination of size, agility, and power. She took audiences on a thrilling ride when she joined forces with Cyndi Lauper to form a ground-breaking alliance called "the Rock N' Wrestling Connection." Wendi Richter became a pop-culture phenomenon during WWE's growth into a global brand of sports-entertainment.

TITLE HISTORY

WOMEN'S CHAMPION (2 TIMES)	Defeated Fabulous Moolah on July 23, 1984 Defeated Lelani Kai on March 31, 1985

On July 23, 1984 Wendi ended the three-decade championship reign of her former mentor, Fabulous Moolah at *The Brawl To End It All*. Despite losing to Leilani Kai, Wendi Richter remained the main attraction in the women's division. Their rematch, won by Richter, took place at the first *WrestleMania*.

Wendi lost the title in controversial fashion to the Spider, who was revealed to be Fabulous Moolah.

The loss devastated her, and it proved to be Wendi Richters last match in WWE. In the following years Wendi toured North America, Japan, and Puerto Rico. She also briefly competed in the AWA but soon after stepped away from the ring. In 2010, audiences saw her on WWE television for the first time in more than 25 years when her sports-entertainment career was celebrated at the WWE Hall of Fame ceremonies.

WILD RED BERRY

FROM: Pittsburg, Kansas

Boxer-turned-wrestler Red Berry had a reputation for being a bit outrageous. In fact, it was his unorthodox style that eventually lead to his nickname. After spending three days in a tree outside Memorial Hall in Kansas, the local newspaper dubbed Berry a "wild man." The description was perfect, and Wild Red Berry was born.

Standing only 5'8", Berry had to find creative ways to win his matches, which is why he oftentimes turned to rule breaking. His defiant in-ring actions made him one of the most hated Superstars of the 1930s, 1940s and 1950s. Berry didn't care, as his disregard for authority eventually lead him to more than fifteen championship reigns over the course of his lengthy career.

Berry continued his deviant behavior long after his in-ring career came to a close. As manager to such top stars as Gorilla Monsoon, the Fabulous Kangaroos and Bull Ramos, Berry was not above using his signature cane as a weapon.

THE WILD SAMOANS

MEMBERS: Afa, Sika   COMBINED WT: 645 lbs.

TITLE HISTORY

WORLD TAG TEAM CHAMPIONS (3 TIMES)	Defeated Ivan Putski & Tito Santana on April 12, 1980 Defeated Tony Garea & Rene Goulet on September 9, 1980 Defeated The Strongbows on March 8, 1983

In the early 1970s, Afa started training with his uncle, High Chief Peter Maivia, and Rocky Johnson. Afa took what he learned and trained his brother, Sika. From there the two began a 30 year reign of terror that may never be duplicated. They tore through Stu Hart's Stampede Wrestling as well as the territories of the NWA.

In the fall of 1979, the Samoans were brought to World Wrestling Entertainment by Capt. Lou Albano. Afa & Sika ripped apart opponents and were so dominant that even as individuals they were both contenders for the WWE Championship. On April 12, 1980, they defeated "Polish Power" Ivan Putski & Tito Santana for their first World Tag Team Championship. They held the titles for five months until at the 1980 mega-event *Showdown at Shea,* the dream team of WWE Champion Bob Backlund & Pedro Morales beat them in a Best 2-out-of-3 Falls contest. The duo had to vacate the titles because of a rule at the time that didn't allow Backlund to hold two championships simultaneously. A tournament was arranged to crown new champs, and the Samoans defeated Tony Garea & Rene Goulet to regain the World Tag Team titles. After a loss to Garea & Rick Martel, they soon departed from WWE.

For the next two years, they dominated the Mid-South and Mid-Atlantic Wrestling scenes. However, after a call from Albano, the Wild Samoans were back in WWE frightening audiences, speaking in ancient Samoan tongues, and consuming raw fish. Their third and final title reign came at the expense of Jay & Jules Strongbow in March 1983. By 1984, they left the company.

Sika briefly returned as a singles competitor in 1992. Afa returned to co-manage The Headshrinkers with Capt. Lou, guiding them to the World Tag Team Championship. Shortly after he left WWE, Afa opened The Wild Samoan Training Center, and today it is regarded as one of the premiere wrestling schools in the world.

WrestleMania 23 saw the Wild Samoans take their rightful place among the immortals of sports-entertainment when they were inducted into the WWE Hall of Fame.

WILLIAM REGAL

HT: 6'2" **WT:** 240 lbs. **FROM:** Blackpool, England
SIGNATURE MOVE: Regal Stretch

A former King of the Ring, William Regal looks down upon the WWE roster as a group of filthy peasants. Rather than carry himself as a true monarch, the smug Superstar has proven to be nothing but a royal pain.

Luckily for Regal, he backs up his arrogant behavior with superior in-ring skills, which he developed as a teenager while competing in carnivals across the United Kingdom. By the time he reached WWE in mid-1998, he had already established himself as a legitimate technical threat in his home country of England, as well as WCW. If for some reason his natural ability failed to carry him to victory, the sly Brit was never above dipping into his tights to grab his deadly set of brass knuckles.

TITLE HISTORY

EUROPEAN CHAMPION (4 TIMES)	*Defeated Al Snow on October 16, 2000* *Defeated Crash Holly on December 4, 2000* *Defeated Diamond Dallas Page on March 21, 2002* *Defeated Spike Dudley on May 6, 2002*
HARDCORE CHAMPION	*3 Times*
INTERCONTINENTAL CHAMPION (2 TIMES)	*Defeated Edge on January 20, 2002* *Defeated Santino Marella on November 10, 2008*
WORLD TAG TEAM CHAMPION (4 TIMES)	*Partnered with Lance Storm to defeat Booker T & Goldust on January 6, 2003* *Partnered with Lance Storm to defeat The Dudley Boys on January 20, 2003* *Partnered with Eugene to defeat La Resistance on November 15, 2004* *Partnered with Tajiri to defeat La Resistance on February 7, 2005*

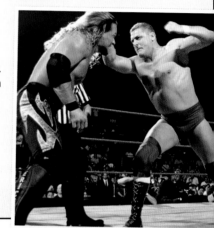

Over the course of his career, Regal has assumed numerous leadership responsibilities, including WWE Commissioner and Raw General Manager. However, it's his championship resume that's most impressive. In addition to runs with the now-defunct European and Hardcore Championships, he defeated Edge to capture the prestigious Intercontinental Championship at *Royal Rumble 2002*. He is also a noted tag team competitor, winning titles with partners Lance Storm, Eugene and Tajiri. Regal joined the WWE incarnation of ECW and was a top challenger for its title. The WWE Universe has also witnessed him leading competitors to the ring, acting as a Pro on *NXT*, and happily expressing his elitist views as a guest commentator.

WILLIE GILZENBERG

In the early 1960s Vince McMahon, Sr. and his partners were looking to break Capitol Wrestling free from the National Wrestling Alliance. One of the key figures in this transformation was an individual who had a reputation as a sharp businessman and a pioneering promoter. When McMahon needed a savvy administrator to handle dealing with promoters, venue executives, the public and his vast array of Superstars, Willie Gilzenberg was the man for the job.

Willie was a successful promoter based out of Newark, New Jersey. As McMahon's first President, Gilzenberg influenced the careers of some of the most pivotal figures in sports-entertainment such as Antonino "Argentina" Rocca, "Nature Boy" Buddy Rogers, Bruno Sammartino and Swede Hanson.

Sadly on November 15, 1978 this innovator of great attractions passed away. Willie Gilzenberg set the standard for the on-air positions of authority seen for decades on WWE programming.

THE WIZARD

His brutally scarred forehead served as a reminder of the bloody battles he competed in during his days as an active competitor; but while the cavernous ditches in The Wizard's skull were certainly disturbing, it was his relationships with the wild Kamala and Sika that freaked out fans the most.

For a brief period of time during the mid-1980s, the four-hundred-pound manager not only served as Kamala and Sika's representation, but more importantly their voices. While the untamed Superstars shouted unintelligible noises, The Wizard stood by their side to translate their offensive words.

Unlike the Grand Wizard (the Hall of Fame manager with whom he is oftentimes confused), The Wizard failed to bring his protégés to great success. After a brief stint by the sides of Kamala and Sika, he disappeared from the WWE scene.

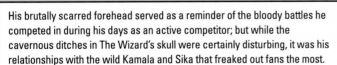

THE WOLFMAN

HT: 6'2" **WT:** 260 lbs.
FROM: The Wilds of Canada
SIGNATURE MOVE: Hanging Neckbreaker

Ushered to the ring on a chain by Lou Albano, this Superstar debuted in 1970, and appeared to be half man and half beast. According to his manager, he was raised amongst the wolves of the Great White North. Once he was released from his chain the Wolfman's behavior could not be predicted and his animalistic tendencies were only controllable by Albano.

After many of his victories, television stations throughout the northeast demanded that WWE place a large X on the screen due to Wolfman's proclivity for chewing on fallen opponents and ring ropes. These disturbing acts along with lunging at referees frightened all who witnessed them and stayed in the backs of the minds of his opponents. By the late 1970s Wolfman fled WWE and returned to the Canadian wilderness. It has been over 30 years since he has been seen by humans and his location remains unknown.

WOMEN'S CHAMPIONSHIP

This prestigious prize was regarded as the pinnacle of female wrestling for more than 50 years. The championship's first title-holder, Fabulous Moolah is considered the most successful, with an almost three decade title reign. During its existence incredible performers like Wendi Richter, Chyna, Trish Stratus, Lita, Maryse, and many other great names have enjoyed reigns atop the women's division.

1956
September 18
Baltimore, MD

Fabulous Moolah defeated Judy Grable in the finals of a tournament to crown a new Women's Champion

▼

1984
July 23
New York, NY

Wendi Richter defeated Fabulous Moolah

▼

1985
February 18
New York, NY

Lelani Kai defeated Wendi Richter

▼

March 31
New York, NY

Wendi Richter defeated Lelani Kai

▼

November 25
New York, NY

Fabulous Moolah defeated Wendi Richter

▼

1986
July 3
Brisbane, Australia

Velvet McIntyre defeated Fabulous Moolah

▼

July 9
Sydney, Australia

Fabulous Moolah defeated Velvet McIntyre

▼

1987
July 24
Houston, TX

Sherri Martel defeated Fabulous Moolah

▼

1988
October 7
Paris, France

Rockin' Robin defeated Sheri Martel

Rockin' Robin held the Women's Championship until 1990 when the title was deemed inactive

▼

1993
December 13
Poughkeepsie, NY

Alundra Blayze defeated Heidi Lee Morgan in the finals of a tournament to crown a new Women's Champion

▼

1994
November 27
Tokyo, Japan

Bull Nakano defeated Alundra Blayze

▼

1995
April 3
Poughkeepsie, NY

Alundra Blayze defeated Bull Nakano

▼

August 27
Pittsburgh, PA

Bertha Faye defeated Alundra Blayze

▼

October 23
Brandon, Manitoba

Alundra Blayze defeated Bertha Faye

The Women's Championship was deemed inactive in December 1995 after Alundra Blayze left WWE

1998
September 21
Sacramento, CA

Jacqueline defeated Sable in a match to crown a new Women's Champion

▼

November 15
St. Louis, MO

Sable defeated Jacqueline

▼

1999
May 10
Orlando, FL

Debra defeated Sable

▼

June 14
Worcester, MA

Ivory defeated Debra

▼

October 17
Cleveland, OH

Fabulous Moolah defeated Ivory

▼

October 25
Providence, RI

Ivory defeated Fabulous Moolah

▼

December 12
Sunrise, FL

The Kat defeated Ivory, Jacqueline, and B.B. in an Evening Gown in a Pool Match

▼

2000
January 31
Pittsburgh, PA

Hervina defeated The Kat

▼

February 3
Detroit, MI

Jacqueline defeated Hervina

▼

March 30
San Antonio, TX

Stephanie McMahon defeated Jacqueline

▼

August 21
Lafayette, LA

Lita defeated Stephanie McMahon

▼

November 2
Rochester, NY

Ivory defeated Lita, Trish Stratus and Jacqueline in a Fatal Four Way Match

▼

WOMEN'S CHAMPIONSHIP TIMELINE

2001

April 1
Houston, TX

Chyna defeated Ivory

Chyna was stripped of the Women's Championship upon leaving WWE in November 2001

November 18
Greensboro, NC

Trish Stratus defeated Ivory, Jazz, Jacqueline, Molly Holly, and Lita in a Six-Pack Challenge Match

2002

February 4
Las Vegas, NV

Jazz defeated Trish Stratus

May 13
Toronto, Ontario

Trish Stratus & Bubba Ray Dudley defeated Jazz & Steven Richards in a Mixed Gender Tag Team Match with the stipulation that if Trish Stratus pinned Jazz, then she would win the Women's Championship

June 23
Columbus, OH

Molly Holly defeated Trish Stratus

September 22
Los Angeles, CA

Trish Stratus defeated Molly Holly

November 17
New York, NY

Victoria defeated Trish Stratus

2003

March 30
Seattle, WA

Trish Stratus defeated Victoria and

April 27
Worcester, MA

Jazz defeated Trish Stratus

June 30
Buffalo, NY

Gail Kim last eliminated Victoria in a 7-Diva Battle Royal that also included Molly Holly, Trish Stratus, Ivory, Jacqueline and Jazz

July 28
Colorado Springs, CO

Molly Holly defeated Gail Kim

2004

February 23
Omaha, NE

Victoria last eliminated Lita to become Women's Champion in a Fatal Four Way Elimination Match that also included Jazz and Molly Holly

June 13
Columbus, OH

Trish Stratus defeated Lita, Gail Kim and Victoria in a Fatal Four Way Match

December 6
Charlotte, NC

Lita defeated Trish Stratus

2005

January 9
Puerto Rico

Trish Stratus defeated Lita

2006

April 2
Chicago, IL

Mickie James defeated Trish Stratus

August 14
Charlottesville, VA

Lita defeated Mickie James

September 17
Toronto, Ontario

Trish Stratus defeated Lita

Trish Stratus retired after the match, vacating the Women's Championship

November 5
Cincinnati, OH

Lita defeated Mickie James in the finals of a tournament to crown a new Women's Champion

November 26
Philadelphia, PA

2007

February 19
Bakersfield, CA

Melina defeated Mickie James

April 24
Paris, France

Mickie James defeated Melina and Victoria in a Triple Threat Match

April 24
Paris, France

Melina defeated Mickie James

June 24
Houston, TX

Candice defeated Melina

October 7
Chicago, IL

Beth Phoenix defeated Candice

2008

April 14
London, England

Mickie James defeated Beth Phoenix

August 17
Indianapolis, IN

Santino Marella & Beth Phoenix defeated Kofi Kingston & Mickie James in an Intergender Winners-Take-All Match

2009

January 25
Detroit, MI

Melina defeated Beth Phoenix

June 28
Sacramento, CA

Michelle McCool defeated Melina

2010

January 31
Atlanta, GA

Mickie James defeated Michelle McCool

February 26
Milwaukee, WI

Michelle McCool defeated Mickie James

April 25
Baltimore, MD

Beth Phoenix defeated Michelle McCool

May 14
Buffalo, NY

Layla defeated Beth Phoenix in a Handicap Tornado Match that also included Michelle McCool

September 19
Rosemont, IL

Michelle McCool defeated Melina

Michelle McCool unified the Divas Championship and the Women's Championship at *Night of Champions*; the Women's Championship was declared inactive as a result

WOMEN'S WORLD TAG TEAM CHAMPIONSHIP

The Women's World Tag Team Championship provided some of the greatest bouts in tag team wrestling history. World Wrestling Federation rings all over the world saw these femme fatales clash to capture tag team gold.

1983
May 1
Calgary, Alberta

Velvet McIntyre & Princess Victoria are recognized as Champions

In late 1983 Princess Victoria gives her half of the championship to Desiree Peterson

1985
August 15
Cairo, Egypt

The Glamour Girls defeated Velvet McIntyre & Desiree Peterson

1988
January 24
Hamilton, Ontario

The Jumping Bomb Angels defeated The Glamour Girls in a Best 2-out-of-3 Falls Match

June 8
Omiya, Japan

The Glamour Girls defeated The Jumping Bomb Angels

The Women's Tag Team Championship was retired in 1989

WORLD HEAVYWEIGHT CHAMPIONSHIP

For close to four decades, WWE recognized only one World Champion. However, when then-WWE Champion Brock Lesnar chose to become exclusive to *SmackDown* in 2002, *Raw* was left without a top Superstar. General Manager Eric Bischoff quickly rectified the situation by dusting off the old WCW Championship and bringing it to *Raw*. He awarded the gold to Triple H, making him the first-ever World Heavyweight Champion in WWE history.

The World Heavyweight Championship remained *Raw*'s top prize until June 2005 when then-champ Batista was drafted to *SmackDown*. The change in scenery had no ill-effect on the title's prestige, as many of *SmackDown*'s top names went on to capture to gold, including Undertaker, Kurt Angle, and Edge. This prestigious championship remains a heavily sought-after trophy and has been in the possession of Superstars including Chris Jericho, Kane, Mark Henry, Big Show, Rey Mysterio, and Daniel Bryan.

2002
September 2
Milwaukee, WI

Triple H was awarded the World Heavyweight Championship by *Raw* General Manager Eric Bischoff

November 11
New York, NY

Shawn Michaels last eliminated Triple H to win the World Heavyweight Championship in an Elimination Chamber Match that also included Chris Jericho, Kane, Booker T and Rob Van Dam

December 15
Fort Lauderdale FL

Triple H defeated Shawn Michaels

2003
September 21
Hershey, PA

Goldberg defeated Triple H

December 14
Orlando, FL

Triple H defeated Goldberg in a Triple Threat Match that also included Kane

2004
March 14
New York, NY

Chris Benoit defeated Triple H in a Triple Threat Match that also included Shawn Michaels

August 15
Toronto, Ontario

Randy Orton defeated Chris Benoit

September 12
Portland, OR

Triple H defeated Randy Orton

Eric Bischoff declared the World Heavyweight Championship vacant in December, 2004 after a controversial ending to a title defense

2005
January 9
Puerto Rico

Triple H last eliminated Randy Orton in an Elimination Chamber Match that also included Edge, Chris Benoit, Chris Jericho and Batista

April 3
Los Angeles, CA

2006
January 10
Philadelphia, PA

Kurt Angle won a Battle Royal to become the World Heavyweight Champion

April 2
Chicago, IL

Rey Mysterio defeated Randy Orton

July 23
Indianapolis, IN

King Booker defeated Rey Mysterio

November 26
Philadelphia, PA

Batista defeated King Booker

2007

May 8
Pittsburgh, PA

Edge defeated Undertaker

An injury forced Edge to vacate the title in July, 2007

July 17
Laredo, TX

The Great Khali won a Battle Royal to become the World Heavyweight Champion

September 16
Memphis, TN

Batista defeated the Great Khali in a Triple Threat Match that also included Rey Mysterio

December 16
Pittsburgh, PA

Edge defeated Batista in a Triple Threat Match that also included Undertaker

2008

March 30
Orlando, FL

Undertaker defeated Edge

Vickie Guerrero stripped Undertaker of the World Heavyweight Championship in May, 2008

June 1
San Diego, CA

Edge defeated Undertaker in a TLC Match

June 30
Oklahoma City, OK

CM Punk defeated Edge

September 7
Cleveland, OH

Chris Jericho defeated Kane in a Championship Scramble Match that also included Batista, JBL and Rey Mysterio

October 26
Tampa, FL

Batista defeated Chris Jericho

November 3
Boston, MA

Chris Jericho defeated Batista

November 23
Boston, MA

John Cena defeated Chris Jericho

2009

February 15
Seattle, WA

Edge last eliminated Rey Mysterio in an Elimination Chamber match that also included WWE Champion John Cena, Chris Jericho, Mike Knox and Kane

April 5
Houston, TX

John Cena defeated World Heavyweight Champion Edge and Big Show in a Triple Threat Match

---

April 26
Providence, RI

Edge defeated John Cena

June 7
New Orleans, LA

Jeff Hardy defeated Edge

June 7
New Orleans, LA

CM Punk defeated Jeff Hardy

July 26
Philadelphia, PA

Jeff Hardy defeated CM Punk

August 23
Los Angeles, CA

CM Punk defeated Jeff Hardy

October 4
Newark, NJ

Undertaker defeated CM Punk

2010

February 21
St. Louis, MO

Chris Jericho defeated Undertaker

April 2
Las Vegas, NV

Jack Swagger defeated Chris Jericho

June 20
Uniondale, NY

Rey Mysterio defeated Jack Swagger, CM Punk and Big Show in a Fatal 4-Way Match

July 18
Kansas City, MO

Kane defeated Rey Mysterio

December 19
Houston, TX

Edge defeated Kane, Rey Mysterio and Albert Del Rio in a Tables, Ladders & Chairs Match

Edge was stripped of the title in February, 2011 after using a move banned by *SmackDown* General Manager, Vickie Guerrero

---

2011

February 18
San Diego, CA

Dolph Ziggler was awarded the World Heavyweight Title

February 18
San Diego, CA

Edge defeated Dolph Ziggler

Edge gave up the title when injuries forced him to retire in April, 2011

May 1
Tampa, FL

Christian defeated Alberto Del Rio

May 6
Orlando, FL

Randy Orton defeated Christian

July 17
Chicago, IL

Christian defeated Randy Orton

August 14
Los Angeles, CA

Randy Orton defeated Christian

September 18
Buffalo, NY

Mark Henry defeated Randy Orton

December 18
Baltimore, MD

Big Show defeated Mark Henry

December 18
Baltimore, MD

Daniel Bryan defeated Big Show

2012

April 1
Miami, FL

Sheamus defeated Daniel Bryan

WORLD MARTIAL ARTS HEAVYWEIGHT CHAMPIONSHIP

The Martial Arts Heavyweight Championship was awarded to Japanese *Puroresu* legend Antonio Inoki by Vincent J. McMahon. The belt was defended all over the world until 1985, when it solely appeared in Japan. This championship was for skilled competitors with specialties in a variety of fighting disciplines.

1978
December 18
New York, NY

Antonio Inoki made his debut with the championship and successfully defended the title against Texas Red at Madison Square Garden

▼

1989
April 24
Tokyo, Japan

Shota Chochoshivili defeated Antonio Inoki

▼

May 25
Osaka, Japan

Antonio Inoki defeated Shota Chochoshivili

The championship would be retired by Antonio Inoki during the middle of his second title reign. However, in 1990 a new championship was created by New Japan Pro Wrestling called The Greatest 18 Championship. This title was represented with the same Martial Arts Heavyweight Championship belt that was given to Inoki in 1978 by Vince McMahon, Sr.

WORLD TAG TEAM CHAMPIONSHIP

The original tag team prize in WWE, the World Tag Team Championship was first awarded in 1971 and was later unified with the WWE Tag Team Championship at *WrestleMania 25*. Some legends are linked to its lineage, and other legends were created while defending these prestigious belts.

In its first decade of existence, Hall of Famers like The Blackjacks and The Valiants battled over the championship before passing the torch to teams like Demolition and The Hart Foundation, who dominated the tag team scene in the 1980s. The memorable matches between these teams caught the attention of many young, aspiring Superstars. Teams like the Hardy Boys, Edge & Christian and the Dudley Boys were living their lifelong dreams as World Tag Team Champions.

1971
June 3
New Orleans, LA

Luke Graham & Tarzan Tyler defeated Dick the Bruiser & The Sheik in the finals of a tournament to crown World Tag Team Champions

▼

December 6
New York, NY

Karl Gotch & Rene Goulet defeated Luke Graham & Tarzan Tyler

▼

1972
February 1
Philadelphia, PA

Mikel Scicluna & King Curtis defeated Karl Gotch & Rene Goulet

▼

May 22
New York, NY

Chief Jay Strongbow & Sonny King defeated Mikel Scicluna & King Curtis

▼

June 27

1973
May 30
Hamburg, PA

Tony Garea & Haystacks Calhoun defeated Professor Tanaka & Mr. Fuji

▼

September 11
Philadelphia, PA

Professor Tanaka & Mr. Fuji defeated Tony Garea & Haystacks Calhoun

▼

November 14
Hamburg, PA

Tony Garea & Dean Ho defeated Professor Tanaka & Mr. Fuji

▼

1974
May 8
Hamburg, PA

Jimmy & Johnny Valiant defeated Tony Garea & Dean Ho

▼

1975
May 13
Philadelphia, PA

Victor Rivera & Dominic DeNucci defeated Jimmy & Johnny Valiant. Pat Barrett became Dominic DeNucci's partner when Victor Rivera left the WWE in June 1975

▼

August 26
Philadelphia, PA

The Blackjacks defeated Dominic DeNucci & Pat Barrett

▼

November 8
Philadelphia, PA

Tony Parisi & Louis Cerdan defeated The Blackjacks

▼

1976
May 11
Philadelphia, PA

The Executioners defeated Tony Parisi & Louis Cerdan

The Executioners were stripped of the World Tag Team Championship in December 1976 when they illegally used a third Executioner

December 7
Philadelphia, PA

Chief Jay Strongbow & Billy White Wolf won a three-team tournament to capture the World Tag Team Championship

Injury forced Strongbow & White Wolf to vacate the titles in August 1977

▼

1977
September 27
Philadelphia, PA

Professor Tanaka & Mr. Fuji

1978

March 14
Philadelphia, PA

Dino Bravo & Dominic DeNucci defeated Professor Tanaka & Mr. Fuji

June 26
New York, NY

The Yukon Lumberjacks defeated Dino Bravo & Dominic DeNucci

November 21
Allentown, PA

Tony Garea & Larry Zbyszko defeated The Yukon Lumberjacks

1979

March 6
Allentown, PA

Johnny & Jerry Valiant defeated Tony Garea & Larry Zbyszko

October 22
New York, NY

Ivan Putski & Tito Santana defeated Johnny & Jerry Valiant

1980

April 12
Philadelphia, PA

The Samoans defeated Ivan Putski & Tito Santana

August 9
New York, NY

Bob Backlund & Pedro Morales defeated The Samoans

Shortly after winning the World Tag Team Championship, Bob Backlund & Perdro Morales were forced to vacate the title due to Backlund already holding the WWE Championship

September 9
Allentown, PA

The Samoans defeated Tony Garea & Rene Goulet in the finals of a tournament to crown new World Tag Team Champions

November 8
Philadelphia, PA

Tony Garea & Rick Martel defeated The Samoans

1981

Mach 17
Allentown, PA

The Moondogs defeated Tony Garea & Rick Martel

July 21
Allentown, PA

Tony Garea & Rick Martel defeated The Moondogs

October 13
Allentown, PA

Mr. Fuji & Mr. Saito defeated Tony Garea & Rick Martel

1982

June 28
New York, NY

Jules & Chief Jay Strongbow defeated Mr. Fuji & Mr. Saito

July 13
Allentown, PA

Mr. Fuji & Mr. Saito defeated Jules & Chief Jay Strongbow

October 26
Allentown, PA

Jules & Chief Jay Strongbow defeated Mr. Fuji & Mr. Saito

1983

March 8
Allentown, PA

The Samoans defeated Jules & Chief Jay Strongbow

November 15
Allentown, PA

Tony Atlas & Rocky Johnson defeated The Samoans

1984

April 17
Hamburg, PA

Adrian Adonis & Dick Murdoch defeated Tony Atlas & Rocky Johnson

---

1985

January 21
Hartford, CT

Mike Rotundo & Barry Windham defeated Adrian Adonis & Dick Murdoch

March 31
New York, NY

The Iron Sheik & Nikolai Volkoff defeated Mike Rotundo & Barry Windham

June 17
Poughkeepsie, NY

Mike Rotundo & Barry Windham defeated The Iron Sheik & Nikolai Volkoff

August 24
Philadelphia, PA

Brutus Beefcake & Greg Valentine defeated Mike Rotundo & Barry Windham

1986

April 7
Rosemont, IL

The British Bulldogs defeated Brutus Beefcake & Greg Valentine

---

1987

January 26
Tampa, FL

The Hart Foundation defeated The British Bulldogs

October 27
Syracuse, NY

Strike Force defeated The Hart Foundation

1988

March 27
Atlantic City, NJ

Demolition defeated Strike Force

1989

July 18
Worcester, MA

Brain Busters defeated Demolition

October 2
Wheeling, WV

Demolition defeated Brain Busters

December 13
Huntsville, AL

Andre the Giant & Haku defeated Demolition

1990

April 1
Toronto, Ontario

Demolition defeated
Andre the Giant & Haku

August 27
Philadelphia, PA

The Hart Foundation defeated
Demolition

1991

March 24
Los Angeles, CA

The Nasty Boys defeated
The Hart Foundation

August 26
New York, NY

The Legion of Doom defeated
The Nasty Boys

1992

February 7
Denver, CO

Money, Inc. defeated
The Legion of Doom

July 20
Worcester, MA

Natural Disasters defeated
Money, Inc.

October 13
Regina, Saskatchewan

Money, Inc. defeated
Natural Disasters

1993

June 14
Columbus, OH

The Steiners defeated Money, Inc.

June 16
Rockford, IL

Money, Inc. defeated The Steiners

June 19
St. Louis, MO

The Steiners defeated Money, Inc.

September 13
New York, NY

The Quebecers defeated
The Steiners

1994

January 10
Richmond, VA

Marty Jannetty & 1-2-3 Kid
defeated The Quebecers

January 17
New York, NY

The Quebecers defeated
Marty Jannetty & 1-2-3 Kid

March 29
London, England

Men on a Mission defeated
The Quebecers

March 31
Sheffield, England

The Quebecers defeated
Men on a Mission

April 26
Burlington, VT

The Headshrinkers defeated
The Quebecers

August 28
Indianapolis, IN

Diesel & Shawn Michaels defeated
The Headshrinkers

Diesel & Shawn Michaels were
forced to vacate the World Tag
Team Championship on November
23, 1994, after they were unable to
co-exist as a team

1995

January 22
Tampa, FL

Bob Holly & 1-2-3 Kid defeated
Bam Bam Bigelow & Tatanka in the
finals of a tournament to become
new World Tag Team Champions

January 23
Palmetto, FL

The Smokin' Gunns defeated
Bob Holly & 1-2-3 Kid

April 2
Hartford, CT

Owen Hart & Yokozuna defeated
The Smokin' Gunns

September 24
Saginaw, MI

Diesel & Shawn Michaels defeated
Owen Hart & Yokozuna

The World Tag Team Championship
was returned to Owen Hart &
Yokozuna after their lawyer
threatened legal action

September 25
Grand Rapids, MI

The Smokin' Gunns defeated Owen
Hart & Yokozuna

An injury to Billy Gunn's neck
forced the Smokin' Gunns to vacate
the World Tag Team Championship
in February, 1996

1996

March 31
Anaheim, CA

The Bodydonnas defeated The
Godwinns in the finals of a
tournament to become new World
Tag Team Champions

May 19
New York, NY

The Godwinns defeated
The Bodydonnas

May 26
Florence, SC

The Smokin' Gunns defeated
The Godwinns

September 22
Philadelphia, PA

Owen Hart & Davey Boy Smith
defeated The Smokin' Gunns

1997

May 25
Evansville, IN

Stone Cold Steve Austin & Shawn
Michaels defeated Owen Hart &
Davey Boy Smith

An injury to Shawn Michaels
forced Stone Cold Steve Austin &
Shawn Michaels to vacate the
World Tag Team Championship in
July 1997

July 14
San Antonio, TX

Stone Cold Steve Austin & Dude
Love defeated Owen Hart & Davey
Boy Smith in match to determine
new World Tag Team Champions

An injury to Austin's neck forced
the duo to vacate the titles in
September 1997

September 7
Louisville, KY

The Headbangers last eliminated
Owen Hart & Davey Boy Smith to
win the World Tag Team
Championship in a Fatal Four-Way
Elimination Match that also
included The Legion of Doom and
The Godwinns

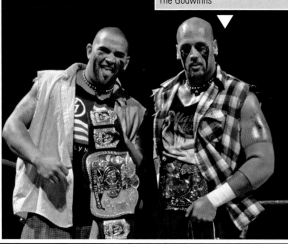

October 5
St. Louis, MO

The Godwinns defeated The Headbangers

▼

October 7
Topeka, KS

The Legion of Doom defeated The Godwinns

▼

November 24
Fayetteville, NC

The New Age Outlaws defeated The Legion of Doom

▼

1998

March 29
Boston, MA

Cactus Jack & Chainsaw Charlie defeated the New Age Outlaws

Cactus Jack & Chainsaw Charlie were forced to vacate the World Tag Team Championship due to a controversial ending to their title victory

▼

March 30
Albany, NY

The New Age Outlaws defeated Cactus Jack & Chainsaw Charlie in a Steel Cage Match

▼

July 13
East Rutherford, NJ

Kane & Mankind defeated New Age Outlaws

▼

July 26
Fresno, CA

Stone Cold Steve Austin & Undertaker defeated Kane & Mankind

▼

August 10
Omaha, NE

Kane & Mankind last eliminated Stone Cold Steve Austin & Undertaker to win the World Tag Team Championship in a Fatal Four-Way Match that also included the New Age Outlaws and The Rock & D'Lo Brown

▼

August 30
New York, NY

The New Age Outlaws defeated Mankind

▼

December 14
Tacoma, WA

Big Boss Man & Ken Shamrock defeated the New Age Outlaws

▼

1999

January 25
Phoenix, AZ

Owen Hart & Jeff Jarrett defeated Big Boss Man & Ken Shamrock

▼

March 30
Uniondale, NY

Kane & X-Pac defeated Owen Hart & Jeff Jarrett

▼

May 31
Moline, IL

The Acolytes defeated Kane & X-Pac

▼

July 5
Fayetteville, NC

The Hardy Boys defeated The Acolytes

▼

July 25
Buffalo, NY

The Acolytes defeated The Hardy Boys & Michael Hayes

▼

August 9
Rosemont, IL

Kane & X-Pac defeated The Acolytes

▼

August 22
Minneapolis, MN

Undertaker & Big Show defeated Kane & X-Pac

▼

August 30
Boston, MA

Mankind & The Rock defeated Undertaker & Big Show

▼

September 9
Albany, NY

Undertaker & Big Show defeated Mankind & The Rock

▼

September 20
Houston, TX

Mankind & The Rock defeated Undertaker & Big Show

▼

September 23
Dallas, TX

The New Age Outlaws defeated Mankind & The Rock

▼

October 14
Birmingham, AL

Mankind & The Rock defeated the New Age Outlaws

▼

October 18
Columbus, OH

Crash & Hardcore Holly defeated Mankind & The Rock

▼

November 4
Philadelphia, PA

Mankind & Al Snow defeated Crash & Hardcore Holly

▼

November 8
State College, PA

The New Age Outlaws defeated Mankind & Al Snow

▼

2000

February 27
Hartford, CT

The Dudley Boys defeated New Age Outlaws

▼

April 2
Anaheim, CA

Edge & Christian defeated the Dudley Boys and the Hardy Boys in a Triple Threat Ladder Match

▼

May 29
Vancouver, British Columbia

Too Cool defeated Edge & Christian

▼

June 25
Boston, MA

Edge & Christian last eliminated Too Cool to win the World Tag Team Championship in Four Corners Elimination Match that also included the Hardy Boys and Test & Albert

▼

September 24
Philadelphia, PA

The Hardy Boys defeated Edge & Christian

▼

October 22
Albany, NY

Edge & Christian defeated the Hardy Boys

▼

October 23
Hartford, CT

The Hardy Boys defeated Edge & Christian

▼

November 6
Houston, TX

Bull Buchanan & Goodfather defeated the Hardy Boys

▼

December 10
Birmingham, AL

Edge & Christian last eliminated the Dudley Boys in a Four Corners Match that also included Road Dogg & K-Kwik and Bull Buchanan & Goodfather

▼

December 18
Greenville, SC

The Rock & Undertaker defeated Edge & Christian

▼

December 21
Charlotte, NC

Edge & Christian defeated The Rock & Undertaker

2001

January 21
New Orleans, LA

The Dudley Boys defeated Edge & Christian

March 5
Washington, D.C.

The Hardy Boys defeated the Dudley Boys

March 19
Albany, NY

Edge & Christian defeated the Hardy Boys

March 19
Albany, NY

The Dudley Boys defeated Edge & Christian

April 1
Houston, TX

Edge & Christian defeated the Dudley Boys and the Hardy Boys in a Tables, Ladders and Chairs Match

April 19
Nashville, TN

Undertaker & Kane defeated Edge & Christian

April 29
Chicago, IL

Stone Cold Steve Austin & Triple H defeated Undertaker & Kane

May 21
San Jose, CA

Chris Benoit & Chris Jericho defeated Stone Cold Steve Austin & Triple H

June 21
Orlando, FL

The Dudley Boys defeated Chris Benoit & Chris Jericho

July 9
Atlanta, GA

The APA defeated The Dudley Boys

August 9
Los Angeles, CA

Kanyon & Diamond Dallas Page defeated The APA

August 19
San Jose, CA

Undertaker & Kane defeated Kanyon & Diamond Dallas Page

September 17
Nashville, TN

The Dudley Boys defeated Undertaker & Kane

October 22
Kansas City, MO

The Rock & Chris Jericho defeated The Dudley Boys

November 1
Cincinnati, OH

Booker T & Test defeated The Rock & Chris Jericho

November 12
Boston, MA

The Hardy Boys defeated Booker T & Test

November 18
Greensboro, NC

The Dudley Boys defeated the Hardy Boys

The Dudley Boys beat the Hardy Boys in a Steel Cage Match to unify the World and WCW Tag Team Championships

---

2002

January 7
New York, NY

Tazz & Spike Dudley defeated The Dudley Boys

February 21
Rockford, IL

Billy & Chuck defeated Tazz & Spike Dudley

May 19
Nashville, TN

Rico & Rikishi defeated Billy & Chuck

June 6
Oklahoma City, OK

Billy & Chuck defeated Rico & Rikishi

July 4
Boston, MA

Hulk Hogan & Edge defeated Billy & Chuck

July 21
Detroit, MI

Christian & Lance Storm defeated Hulk Hogan & Edge

September 23
Anaheim, CA

Kane & the Hurricane defeated Christian & Lance Storm

October 14
Montreal, Quebec

Christian & Chris Jericho defeated Kane & the Hurricane

December 15
Fort Lauderdale, FL

Booker T & Goldust last eliminated Christian & Chris Jericho to win the World Tag Team Championship in a Fatal Four Way Elimination Match that also included the Dudley Boys and Lance Storm & William Regal

---

2003

January 6
Phoenix, AZ

William Regal & Lance Storm defeated Booker T & Goldust

January 19
Boston, MA

The Dudley Boys defeated William Regal & Lance Storm

January 20
Providence, RI

William Regal & Lance Storm defeated the Dudley Boys

An injury to William Regal forced him to vacate the World Tag Team Championship on in March, 2003

March 24
Sacramento, CA

Lance Storm & Chief Morley are awarded the World Tag Team Championship

March 31
Seattle, WA

Kane & Rob Van Dam last eliminated Lance Storm & Chief Morley in an Elimination Match that also included the Dudley Boys

June 15
Houston, TX

Sylvain Grenier & Rene Dupree defeated Kane & Rob Van Dam

September 21
Hershey, PA

The Dudley Boys defeated Sylvain Grenier, Rene Dupree & Rob Conway

December 14
Orlando, FL

Ric Flair & Batista last eliminated the Dudley Boys to win the World Tag Team Championship in a Tag Team Turmoil Match that also included the Hurricane & Rosey, Mark Jindrak & Garrison Cade, La Resistance, Val Venis & Lance Storm and Scott Steiner & Test

---

2004

February 16
Bakersfield, CA

Booker T & Rob Van Dam defeated Ric Flair & Batista

March 22
Detroit, MI

Ric Flair & Batista defeated Booker T & Rob Van Dam

April 19
Calgary, Alberta

Chris Benoit & Edge defeated Ric Flair & Batista

May 31
Montreal, Quebec

Sylvain Grenier & Rob Conway defeated Chris Benoit & Edge

October 19
Milwaukee, WI

Chris Benoit & Edge defeated Sylvain Grenier & Rob Conway

November 1
Peoria, IL

Sylvain Grenier & Rob Conway defeated Chris Benoit

November 15
Indianapolis, IN

Eugene & William Regal beat Sylvain Grenier & Rob Conway to win the World Tag Team Championship in an Elimination Match that also included Rhyno & Tajiri

2005

January 16
Winnipeg, Manitoba

Sylvain Grenier & Rob Conway defeated William Regal & Jonathan Coachman, who was filling in for an injured Eugene

Tajiri & William Regal defeated Sylvain Grenier & Rob Conway

▼

May 1
Manchester, NH

The Hurricane & Rosey defeated Sylvain Grenier & Rob Conway in a Tag Team Turmoil Match that also included The Heart Throbs, Simon Dean & Maven and Tajiri & William Regal

▼

September 18
Oklahoma City, OK

Lance Cade & Trevor Murdoch defeated The Hurricane & Rosey

▼

November 1
San Diego, CA

Big Show & Kane defeated Lance Cade & Trevor Murdoch

▼

2006

April 3
Chicago, IL

Spirit Squad defeated Big Show & Kane

▼

Ric Flair & Roddy Piper defeated Spirit Squad

▼

November 13
Manchester, England

Edge & Randy Orton defeated Ric Flair & Roddy Piper

▼

2007

January 29
Dallas, TX

John Cena & Shawn Michaels defeated Edge & Randy Orton

▼

April 2
Dayton, OH

The Hardy Boys last eliminated Lance Cade & Trevor Murdoch in a 10-team Battle Royal that also included Tommy Dreamer & Sandman, Brian Kendrick & Paul London, William Regal & Dave Taylor, Chavo Guerrero & Gregory Helms, Johnny Nitro & The Miz, Viscera & Val Venis, Kevin Thorn & Marcus Cor Von and John Cena & Shawn Michaels

▼

Lance Cade & Trevor Murdoch defeated the Hardy Boys

▼

September 5
Cape Town, South Africa

Paul London & Brian Kendrick defeated Lance Cade & Trevor Murdoch

▼

September 8
Johannesburg, South Africa

Lance Cade & Trevor Murdoch defeated Paul London & Brian Kendrick

▼

December 10
Bridgeport, CT

Cody Rhodes & Hardcore Holly defeated Lance Cade & Trevor Murdoch

▼

2008

June 29
Dallas, TX

Cody Rhodes & Ted DiBiase defeated Hardcore Holly

▼

Batista & John Cena defeated Cody Rhodes & Ted DiBiase

▼

August 11
Richmond, VA

Cody Rhodes & Ted DiBiase defeated Batista & John Cena

▼

October 27
Tucson, AZ

CM Punk & Kofi Kingston defeated Cody Rhodes & Ted DiBiase

▼

December 13
Hamilton, Ontario

The Miz & John Morrison defeated CM Punk & Kofi Kingston

▼

2009

April 5
Houston, TX

Carlito & Primo defeated The Miz & John Morrison to unify the World and WWE Tag Team Championships

▼

Edge & Chris Jericho defeated Carlito & Primo

▼

July 26
Philadelphia, PA

Big Show & Chris Jericho defeated Ted DiBiase & Cody Rhodes

▼

December 13
San Antonio, TX

D-Generation X defeated Big Show & Chris Jericho

▼

2010

February 8
Lafayette, LA

The Miz & Big Show defeated D-Generation X

▼

April 26
Richmond, VA

The Hart Dynasty defeated The Miz & Big Show

In August 2010, the new WWE Tag Team title belts were awarded to the Hart Dynasty and the World Tag Team championship was retired

---

WORLD WIDE WRESTLING FEDERATION INTERNATIONAL HEAVYWEIGHT CHAMPIONSHIP

One of professional wrestling's first prizes recognized globally, this championship traces its history to the National Wrestling Alliance and Vince McMahon, Sr.'s Capitol Wrestling.

WWE Hall of Famer Atonino "Argentina" Rocca was the first title holder and with every contest, set the standard for all future champions.

1959

July
New York, NY

Antonino "Argentina" Rocca defeated "Nature Boy" Buddy Rogers in the tournament finals

In 1963, the championship was declared inactive. After nearly 20 years of being dormant, the title resurfaced in 1982

▼

1982

August 1
Buffalo, NY

Tony Parisi reinstated the championship and begins defending it

▼

August
Buffalo, NY

Gino Brito defeated Tony Parisi

▼

August 30
New York, NY

Tatsumi Fujinamia defeated Gino Brito

▼

1983

April 3
Tokyo, Japan

Riki Choshu defeated Tatsumi Fujinami

▼

August 4
Tokyo, Japan

Tatsumi Fujinamia defeated Riki Choshu

Fujinami won the match by countout but refused to accept the belt; Choshu was denied entry into Canada for the rematch

▼

August 12
Calgary, Alberta, Canada

Tatsumi Fujinami recognized as champion

After months without a title defense the championship was considered vacant

▼

1984

March 25
New York, NY

Akira Maeda defeated Pierre Lefebvre

Maeda returned to Japan that April and defended the title until mid-July. Then-UWF President, and former WWE President, Hisashi Shinma moved to All-Japan Pro Wrestling, ending the relationship between the UWF and WWE, thus making the championship inactive.

WORLD WIDE WRESTLING FEDERATION INTERNATIONAL TAG TEAM CHAMPIONSHIP

This tag team championship was the precursor to the most prestigious prize in all of tag team wrestling, the World Tag Team Championship.

1969

June 1
Osaka, Japan

Prof. Toru Tanaka & Mitsu Arakawa won a tournament to be crowned the first World Wide Wrestling Federation International Tag Team Champions

▼

December 8
Pittsburgh, PA

Bruno Sammartino & Battman defeated Prof. Toru Tanaka & Mitsu Arakawa

Victor Rivera replaced Bruno Sammartino as Tony Marino's (Battman) new partner on December 12

▼

1970

June 15
New York, NY

The Mongols defeated Victor Rivera & Tony Marino in a Best 2-out-of-3 Falls Match

▼

1971

June 18
Pittsburgh, PA

Bruno Sammartino & Dominic DeNucci defeated The Mongols

▼

July 2
New York, NY

The Mongols defeated Bruno Sammartino & Dominic DeNucci

▼

November 12
New York, NY

Luke Graham & Tarzan Tyler defeated The Mongols

▼

December 18
Pittsburgh, PA

Bepo Mongol & Johnny DeFazio defeated Luke Graham & Tarzan Tyler

In 1972, the titles were vacated and inactive for the next decade

▼

1985

May 24
Kobe, Japan

Tatsumi Fujinami & Kengo Kimura defeated Adrian Adonis & Dick Murdoch in the tournament finals to crown new champions. The titles were almost exclusively defended in Japan for the remainder of the year before being retired

WORLD WIDE WRESTLING FEDERATION UNITED STATES HEAVYWEIGHT CHAMPIONSHIP

The World Wide Wrestling Federation United States Heavyweight Championship was the company's first iteration of a United States title and was passionately battled for during its existence. From 1963 to 1977, this championship was held by names such as WWE Hall of Famers Bobo Brazil, The Sheik, and Pedro Morales.

1963

Bobo Brazil is recognized as the first United States Heavyweight Champion

▼

1963

June 8
Philadelphia, PA

Johnny Barend defeated Bobo Brazil

▼

July 9
Philadelphia, PA

Bobo Brazil defeated Johnny Barend

▼

1967

June 18

Ray Stevens defeated Bobo Brazil

▼

August 24
Trenton, NJ

Bobo Brazil defeated Ray Stevens

▼

September 22
Salisbury, MD

The Sheik defeated Bobo Brazil

▼

1968

November 25
Washington, D.C.

Bobo Brazil defeated The Sheik

▼

1969

January 20
Boston, MA

The Sheik defeated Bobo Brazil

▼

February 10
Washington, D.C.

Bobo Brazil defeated The Shiek

▼

1971

January
Los Angeles, CA

Pedro Morales defeated Fred Blassie in the finals of a tournament

On February 8, 1971, Pedro Morales forfeited the title when he became the World Wide Wrestling Federation Heavyweight Champion

▼

February 15

Bobo Brazil was recognized as champion and would go on to hold the championship until it was removed from the World Wide Wrestling Federation

WORLD WIDE WRESTLING FEDERATION UNITED STATES TAG TEAM CHAMPIONSHIP

This tag team championship traces its lineage back to the Northeast territory of the National Wrestling Alliance. In 1963, the championship became a part of the World Wide Wrestling Federation and was held by a number of teams, including WWE Hall of Famers Killer Kowalski & Gorilla Monsoon, Dr. Jerry & Luke Graham, The Sicilians, and Bruno Sammartino & Spiros Arion before being retired in 1967.

1963

March 7
Washington, D.C.

Buddy Austin & The Great Scott defeated "Nature Boy" Buddy Rogers & Johnny Barend

Buddy Austin & The Great Scott won a Best 2-out-of-3 Falls Match; Austin replaced The Great Scott's original partner who was injured while losing the first fall

May 16
Washington, D.C.

Skull Murphy & Brute Bernard defeated Buddy Austin & The Great Scott

November 14
Washington, D.C.

Killer Kowalski & Gorilla Monsoon defeated Skull Murphy & Brute Bernard

December 28
Teaneck, N.J.

Chris & John Tolos defeated Killer Kowalski & Gorilla Monsoon

1964

February 16
New Haven, CT

Don McClarity & Vittorio Apollo defeated Chris & John Tolos

June 6
Washington, D.C.

Dr. Jerry & Luke Graham defeated Don McClarity & Vittorio Apollo

1965

February 4
Washington, D.C.

Gene Kiniski & Waldo Von Erich defeated Dr. Jerry & Luke Graham

April 6
Washington, D.C.

Gorilla Monsoon & Cowboy Bill Watts defeated Gene Kiniski & Waldo Von Erich

August 7
Washington, D.C.

Dr. Bill Miller & Dan Miller defeated Gorilla Monsoon & Cowboy Bill Watts

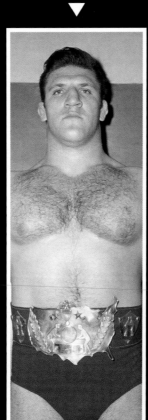

1966

February 21
New York, NY

Antonio Pugliese & Johnny Valentine defeated Dr. Bill Miller & Dan Miller

September 22
Washington, D.C.

Baron Mikel Scicluna & Smasher Sloan defeated Antonio Pugliese & Johnny Valentine

December 8
Washington, D.C.

Spiros Arion & Antonio Pugliese defeated Baron Mikel Scicluna & Smasher Sloan

In June 1967, Antonio Pugliese abruptly left the United States; Sprios Arion selected Arnold Skaaland as his new tag team partner to defend the championship

1967

July 10
Atlantic City, N.J.

The Sicilians defeated Spiros Arion & Arnold Skaaland

July 24
Atlantic City, N.J.

Bruno Sammartino & Spiros Arion defeated The Sicilians

In late 1967, Bruno Sammartino vacated his half of the championship to concentrate on his WWE Champion title defenses; the United States Tag Team Championship would remain vacant and eventually vanish from the World Wide Wrestling Federation

THE WORLD'S GREATEST TAG TEAM

MEMBERS: Shelton Benjamin, Charlie Haas
COMBINED WT: 497 lbs.

TITLE HISTORY	
WWE TAG TEAM CHAMPIONS (2 TIMES)	Defeated Los Guerreros on February 6, 2003 Defeated Eddie Guerrero & Tajiri on July 3, 2003

The exchanging of gifts continued for Kurt Angle on the day after Christmas 2002. It was on this day that Paul Heyman presented the former gold medalist with the athletic tandem of Shelton Benjamin & Charlie Haas, collectively known as Team Angle. Their main responsibility was to help Angle retain his WWE Championship at all costs. The duo, however, was able to capture titles of their own when they defeated Los Guerreros for the WWE Tag Team Championship in February 2003.

After losing the titles back to Eddie Guerrero and his new partner Tajiri in May 2003, Team Angle found themselves in an uncharacteristic slump. As a result, Angle fired them as his associates. On their own, Benjamin & Haas dubbed themselves The World's Greatest Tag Team, and quickly duplicated their earlier success when they regained the WWE Tag Team Championship from Guerrero & Tajiri.

The duo was forced to go their separate ways when Benjamin was sent to *Raw* via the WWE Draft in March 2004. They briefly reformed a few years later on *Raw* and though they split and competed on separate brands, Benjamin and Haas reunited on *SmackDown* before they parted ways with WWE in 2010. Today, fans can see them on independent cards across North America.

World Wrestling Entertainment approached a pivotal time in its existence. To make the crucial turn to sports-entertainment complete, Vince McMahon rolled the dice. If he was to succeed in turning his WWE into an international entity, the initial *WrestleMania* needed to be a hit. This was a closed-circuit spectacle that saw the greatest Superstars in sports-entertainment meet in the legendary Madison Square Garden. In addition, celebrities such as Billy Martin, Liberace, the Rockettes, and Muhammad Ali contributed in turning the wrestling event into a spectacle.

Over twenty-five years later, it's safe to say the gamble paid off and the world of sports-entertainment has never been the same.

MATCH RESULTS

Tito Santana defeated the Executioner

David Sammartino (with Bruno Sammartino) versus Brutus Beefcake (with "Luscious" Johnny Valiant) went to a no contest

Ricky "The Dragon" Steamboat defeated Matt Borne

King Kong Bundy (with Jimmy Hart) defeated SD "Special Delivery" Jones

Bodyslam Challenge

Andre the Giant defeated Big John Studd

Intercontinental Championship Match

Junkyard Dog defeated Intercontinental Champion Greg "the Hammer" Valentine (with Jimmy Hart) via count-out

World Tag Team Championship Match

Nikolai Volkoff & Iron Sheik (with "Classy" Freddie Blassie) defeated World Tag Team Champions US Express (with Lou Albano) to become new champions

Women's Championship Match

Wendi Richter (with Cyndi Lauper) defeated Women's Champion Leilani Kai (with Fabulous Moolah) to become new champion

Main Event

Hulk Hogan & Mr. T (with Jimmy "Superfly" Snuka) defeated "Rowdy" Roddy Piper & "Mr. Wonderful" Paul Orndorff (with "Cowboy" Bob Orton)

Apr 07 1986

Nassau Veterans Memorial Coliseum; Uniondale, NY
The Rosemont Horizon; Rosemont, IL
The Sports Arena; Los Angeles, CA

The unbelievable response to *WrestleMania* left WWE no choice but to make it an annual extravaganza. The stakes were raised as this event emanated from three locations simultaneously across the United States. After Ray Charles sang "America the Beautiful" to kick off the event, audiences saw a match decided with the sweet science, a battle royal with WWE and NFL Superstars, and the first *WrestleMania* title defense inside a 15-foot high Steel Cage!

MATCH RESULTS

"Mr. Wonderful" Paul Orndorff versus the Magnificent Muraco (with Mr. Fuji) went to a double count-out

Intercontinental Championship Match

Intercontinental Champion Randy "Macho Man" Savage (with Elizabeth) defeated George "the Animal" Steele

Jake "The Snake" Roberts defeated George Wells

Boxing Match

Mr. T (with Joe Frazier and Haiti Kid) defeated "Rowdy" Roddy Piper (with "Cowboy" Bob Orton) by Disqualification

Women's Championship Match

The Fabulous Moolah defeated Women's Champion Velvet McIntyre to become new champion

Flag Match

Corporal Kirchner defeated Nikolai Volkoff (with "Classy" Freddie Blassie)

WWE and NFL Battle Royal

Andre the Giant was the last man standing. The other entrants were Jimbo Covert (Chicago Bears), Pedro Morales, Tony Atlas, Ted Arcidi, Harvey Martin (Dallas Cowboys), Dan Spivey, Hillbilly Jim, King Tonga, Iron Sheik, Ernie Holmes (Pittsburgh Steelers), Big John Studd, B. Brian Blair, Jumpin' Jim Brunzell, Bill Fralic (Atlanta Falcons), Bret "Hit Man" Hart, Jim "the Anvil" Neidhart, Russ Francis (San Francisco 49ers), Bruno Sammartino, and William "Refrigerator" Perry (Chicago Bears)

World Tag Team Championship Match

The British Bulldogs (with Captain Lou Albano and Ozzy Osbourne) defeated World Tag Team Champions the Dream Team (with "Luscious" Johnny Valiant) to become new champions

Ricky "The Dragon" Steamboat defeated Hercules

"Adorable" Adrian Adonis (with Jimmy Hart) defeated Uncle Elmer

Terry & Hoss Funk (with Jimmy Hart) defeated Tito Santana & Junkyard Dog

Steel Cage Match for the WWE Championship

WWE Champion Hulk Hogan defeated King Kong Bundy (with Bobby "The Brain" Heenan)

As WWE set a new indoor attendance record of 93,173 it proved that it was "Bigger, Better & Badder" than any other sports-entertainment company past or present. It continued its tradition of star-studded happenings as "the Queen of Soul" Aretha Franklin kicked off the historic day with her rendition of "America The Beautiful." The scores that were to be settled received global media attention, and Superstars became legends as they battled on this epic occasion.

MATCH RESULTS

Can Am Connection defeated "Cowboy" Bob Orton & The Magnificent Muraco (with Mr. Fuji)

Full Nelson Challenge

Billy Jack Haynes versus Hercules (with Bobby "the Brain" Heenan) went to a double count-out

Hillbilly Jim, Little Beaver, & Haiti Kid defeated King Kong Bundy, Lord Littlebrook, & Little Tokyo by Disqualification

"Loser Must Bow" Match

"King" Harley Race (with Bobby Heenan and Fabulous Moolah) defeated Junkyard Dog

The Dream Team (with "Luscious" Johnny Valiant & Dino Bravo) defeated The Rougeau Brothers

Hair vs. Hair Match

"Rowdy" Roddy Piper defeated "Adorable" Adrian Adonis (with Jimmy Hart)

The Hart Foundation & "Dangerous" Danny Davis (with Jimmy Hart) defeated The British Bulldogs & Tito Santana

"The Natural" Butch Reed (with Slick) defeated Koko B. Ware

Intercontinental Championship Match

Ricky "the Dragon" Steamboat (with George "the Animal" Steele) defeated Intercontinental Champion Randy "Macho Man" Savage (with Elizabeth) to become new champion

Honky Tonk Man (with Jimmy Hart) defeated Jake "the Snake" Roberts (with Alice Cooper)

Nikolai Volkoff & Iron Sheik (with Slick) defeated Killer Bees by Disqualification

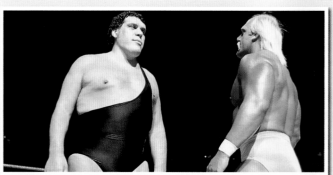

WWE Championship Match

WWE Champion Hulk Hogan defeated Andre the Giant (with Bobby Heenan)

Where there's chaos, there's opportunity. The fate of sports-entertainment's richest prize hung in the balance as the vacant WWE Championship was to be awarded at the end of a one-night tournament. The biggest names in sports-entertainment gathered for the event, but only one would emerge from Atlantic City the new undisputed Champion of the World!

MATCH RESULTS

Battle Royal

Bad News Brown defeated Bret "Hit Man" Hart, Jim "The Anvil" Neidhart, Jim Powers, Paul Roma, Sika, "Dangerous" Danny Davis, Sam Houston, Hillbilly Jim, B. Brian Blair, Jumpin' Jim Brunzell, Ray Rougeau, Jacques Rougeau, Junkyard Dog, Ken Patera, Ron Bass, "King" Harley Race, Nikolai Volkoff, Boris Zhukov, and George "The Animal" Steele

Ultimate Warrior defeated Hercules (with Bobby "The Brain" Heenan)

Intercontinental Championship Match

Brutus "the Barber" Beefcake defeated Intercontinental Champion Honky Tonk Man (with Jimmy Hart and Peggy Sue) by Disqualification

The Islanders & Bobby Heenan defeated the British Bulldogs & Koko B. Ware (with Matilda)

World Tag Team Championship Match

Demolition (with Mr. Fuji) defeated World Tag Team Champions Strike Force to become new champions

WWE Championship Tournament

Round One Matches

"Million Dollar Man" Ted DiBiase (with Virgil and Andre The Giant) defeated "Hacksaw" Jim Duggan

Don "the Rock" Muraco (with "Superstar" Billy Graham) defeated Dino Bravo (with Frenchy Martin) by Disqualification

Greg "the Hammer" Valentine (with Jimmy Hart) defeated Ricky "The Dragon" Steamboat

Randy "Macho Man" Savage (with Elizabeth) defeated "The Natural" Butch Reed (with Slick)

One Man Gang (with Slick) defeated Bam Bam Bigelow (with Sir Oliver Humperdink)

"Ravishing" Rick Rude (with Bobby Heenan) vs. Jake "The Snake" Roberts went to a draw

Round Two Matches

Hulk Hogan vs. Andre The Giant (with Bobby "The Brain" Heenan, "Million Dollar Man" Ted DiBiase and Virgil) ended in a Double Disqualification

"Million Dollar Man" Ted DiBiase (with Virgil) defeated Don "the Rock" Muraco (with "Superstar" Billy Graham)

Randy "Macho Man" Savage (with Elizabeth) defeated Greg "the Hammer" Valentine (with Jimmy Hart)

Round Three Match

Randy "Macho Man" Savage (with Elizabeth) defeated One Man Gang (with Slick) by Disqualification

WWE Championship Tournament Final Match

Randy "Macho Man" Savage (with Elizabeth & Hulk Hogan) defeated "Million Dollar Man" Ted DiBiase (with Virgil & Andre the Giant) to become new champion

Over 19,000 fans attended the event, and millions around the world tuned in to see WWE legends go to war. The main event featured Hulk Hogan and Randy "Macho Man" Savage, who once battled together as the Mega-Powers, face off for Savage's WWE Championship. *WrestleMania IV* and *WrestleMania V* remain the only *WrestleMania* events to date that have originated from the same venue in consecutive years.

MATCH RESULTS

Hercules defeated "King" Haku (with Bobby "the Brain" Heenan)

The Twin Towers (with Slick) defeated The Rockers

"Million Dollar Man" Ted DiBiase (with Virgil) versus Brutus "the Barber" Beefcake ended in a double count-out

The Bushwhackers defeated the Fabulous Rougeau Brothers (with Jimmy Hart)

Mr. Perfect defeated Blue Blazer

Handicap Match for the World Tag Team Championship

World Tag Team Champions Demolition defeated Powers of Pain & Mr. Fuji

Dino Bravo (with Frenchy Martin) defeated "Rugged" Ronnie Garvin

The Brain Busters (with Bobby Heenan) defeated Strike Force

Jake "the Snake" Roberts defeated Andre the Giant (with Bobby Heenan) by Disqualification, Big John Studd as guest referee

The Hart Foundation defeated Rhythm & Blues (with Jimmy Hart)

Intercontinental Championship Match

"Ravishing" Rick Rude (with Bobby Heenan) defeated Intercontinental Champion Ultimate Warrior to become new champion

Bad News Brown versus "Hacksaw" Jim Duggan ended in a no contest

Red Rooster defeated Bobby Heenan (with the Brooklyn Brawler)

WWE Championship Match

Hulk Hogan defeated WWE Champion Randy "Macho Man" Savage with Elizabeth in a neutral corner to become new champion

WRESTLEMANIA VI — Apr 01 1990 — Toronto SkyDome; Toronto, Ontario, Canada

The first *WrestleMania* of the 1990s brought about many firsts for the world's greatest annual entertainment event. This was the first time *WrestleMania* was held outside the United States, the first time the main event saw a "Title versus Title" bout, and the first time two fan favorites clashed as 67,678 fans traveled to SkyDome and to witness "The Ultimate Challenge."

MATCH RESULTS

"The Model" Rick Martel defeated Koko B. Ware

World Tag Team Championship Match

Demolition defeated World Tag Team Champions Colossal Connection (with Bobby "the Brain" Heenan) to become new champions

Earthquake (with Jimmy Hart) defeated Hercules

Brutus "the Barber" Beefcake defeated Mr. Perfect (with The Genius)

"Rowdy" Roddy Piper versus Bad News Brown went to a no contest

The Hart Foundation defeated the Bolsheviks

The Barbarian (with Bobby Heenan) defeated Tito Santana

Mixed Tag Team Match

Dusty Rhodes & Sapphire (with Elizabeth) defeated Randy "Macho King" Savage & Queen Sherri

The Orient Express (with Mr. Fuji) defeated The Rockers by count-out

"Hacksaw" Jim Duggan defeated Dino Bravo (with Earthquake)

Million Dollar Championship Match

Million Dollar Champion "Million Dollar Man" Ted DiBiase (with Virgil) defeated Jake "the Snake" Roberts by count-out

Big Boss Man defeated Akeem (with Slick)

"Ravishing" Rick Rude (with Bobby Heenan) defeated Jimmy "Superfly" Snuka

Title vs. Title Match

Intercontinental Champion Ultimate Warrior defeated WWE Champion Hulk Hogan to retain Intercontinental Championship and become new WWE Champion

The United States of America was at war and the WWE Championship was in the hands of an enemy sympathizer. Patriots everywhere pulled for Hulk Hogan once again to be the hero and bring sports-entertainment's richest prize back home. This historic event also saw the first-ever Blindfold Match, a King's career on the line, and as "the Eighth Wonder of the World" made his final *WrestleMania* appearance, Undertaker made his debut.

MATCH RESULTS

The Rockers defeated Haku & The Barbarian (with Bobby "the Brain" Heenan)

Texas Tornado defeated Dino Bravo

British Bulldog defeated Warlord (with Slick)

World Tag Team Championship Match

The Nasty Boys (with Jimmy Hart) defeated World Tag Team Champions the Hart Foundation to become new champions

Blindfold Match

Jake "the Snake" Roberts defeated "The Model" Rick Martel

Undertaker (with Paul Bearer) defeated Jimmy "Superfly" Snuka

Retirement Match

Ultimate Warrior defeated Randy "Macho King" Savage (with Queen Sherri)

Genichiro Tenryu & Koji Kitao defeated Demolition

Intercontinental Championship Match

Big Boss Man defeated Intercontinental Champion Mr. Perfect (with Bobby Heenan) by Disqualification

Earthquake defeated Greg "the Hammer" Valentine

Legion of Doom defeated Power & Glory (with Slick)

Virgil (with "Rowdy" Roddy Piper) defeated "Million Dollar Man" Ted DiBiase by count-out

The Mountie (with Jimmy Hart) defeated Tito Santana

WWE Championship Match

Hulk Hogan defeated WWE Champion Sgt. Slaughter (with General Adnan) to become new champion

---

Apr 05 1992 — Hoosier Dome; Indianapolis, IN

Over 62,000 crazed fans flocked to the Hoosier Dome to see the first *WrestleMania* featuring a double main-event. While the "Macho Man" fought to clear the name of the one he loved and become a two-time WWE Champion, Hulk Hogan defended WWE against the Superstar who sought to rule the world. In the end, audiences were jolted to their feet as they saw the return of Ultimate Warrior.

MATCH RESULTS

Shawn Michaels (with Sensational Sherri) defeated "El Matador" Tito Santana

Undertaker (with Paul Bearer) defeated Jake "the Snake" Roberts

First Main Event— WWE Championship Match

Randy "Macho Man" Savage (with Elizabeth) defeated WWE Champion "Nature Boy" Ric Flair (with Mr. Perfect) to become new champion

Tatanka defeated "The Model" Rick Martel

World Tag Team Championship Match

Natural Disasters defeated World Tag Team Champions Money Inc. (with Jimmy Hart) by count-out

Owen Hart defeated Skinner

Second Main Event

Hulk Hogan defeated Sid Justice (with Harvey Wippleman) by Disqualification

Intercontinental Championship Match

Bret "Hit Man" Hart defeated Intercontinental Champion "Rowdy" Roddy Piper to become new champion

"Hacksaw" Jim Duggan, Sgt. Slaughter, Virgil & Big Boss Man defeated The Mountie, Repo Man & Nasty Boys (with Jimmy Hart)

WrestleMania IX

The ninth annual *WrestleMania* was the first to be held outdoors and hosted the world's biggest Toga Party. "The Brain" entered Caesars Palace on a camel, Jim Ross made his WWE debut dressed in a toga, and fans heard the voice of Finkus Maximus announce Superstars on their way to the ring. Who would leave the Greco-Roman coliseum victorious? Could the Mega-Maniacs get revenge on Money Inc? Could anyone stand up to the seemingly unstoppable Japanese force of Yokozuna?

MATCH RESULTS

Intercontinental Championship Match

Tatanka defeated Intercontinental Champion Shawn Michaels (with Luna Vachon) by count-out

The Steiner Brothers defeated the Headshrinkers (with Afa)

Doink defeated Crush

Razor Ramon defeated Bob Backlund

World Tag Team Championship Match

World Tag Team Champions Money Inc. defeated Hulk Hogan & Brutus "the Barber" Beefcake (with Jimmy Hart) by disqualification

"The Narcissist" Lex Luger defeated Mr. Perfect

Undertaker (with Paul Bearer) defeated Giant Gonzales (with Harvey Wippleman) by disqualification

WWE Championship Match[1]

Yokozuna (with Mr. Fuji & Jim Cornette) defeated WWE Champion Bret "Hit Man" Hart to become new champion

[1]After the match, Hulk Hogan defeated Yokozuna to become new champion

Mar 20 1994 **Madison Square Garden; New York, NY**

WrestleMania X

The event celebrating a decade of sports-entertainment dominance took place back where it all began as *WrestleMania X* returned to Madison Square Garden. This event exceeded all expectations as fans witnessed a unique mixed tag match, an all-out brawl, and the ladder match that set the standard for all future encounters of its kind.

MATCH RESULTS

Owen Hart defeated Bret "Hit Man" Hart

Mixed Tag Team Match

Bam Bam Bigelow & Luna Vachon defeated Doink & Dink

Falls Count Anywhere Match

Randy "Macho Man" Savage defeated Crush (with Mr. Fuji)

Women's Championship Match

Women's Champion Alundra Blayze defeated Leilani Kai

WWE Championship Match

Yokozuna (Champion, with Mr. Fuji and Jim Cornette) defeated Lex Luger by disqualification, with special guest referee, Mr. Perfect

Ladder Match for the Intercontinental Championship

Intercontinental Champion Razor Ramon defeated Shawn Michaels

World Tag Team Championship Match

Men on a Mission (with Oscar) defeated World Tag Team Champions the Quebecers (with Johnny Polo) by count-out

Earthquake defeated Adam Bomb (with Harvey Wippleman)

WWE Championship Match

Bret "Hit Man" Hart defeated WWE Champion Yokozuna (with Mr. Fuji & Jim Cornette) to become new champion

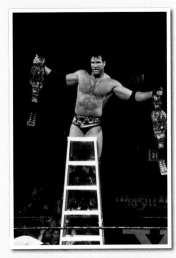

The only *WrestleMania* to be held in WWE's home state continued the tradition of an awesome array of contests and celebrities. With stars in attendance, from Pamela Anderson and Jenny McCarthy to hip-hop legends Salt-N-Pepa, millions tuned in all over the world to see the WWE Championship on the line, a Superstar quit and a type of main event that will never be duplicated.

MATCH RESULTS

Lex Luger & British Bulldog defeated Eli & Jacob Blu (with Uncle Zebekiah)

Intercontinental Championship Match

Razor Ramon (with 1-2-3 Kid) defeated Jeff Jarrett (with the Roadie) by disqualification

Undertaker (with Paul Bearer) defeated King Kong Bundy (with "Million Dollar Man" Ted DiBiase)

World Tag Team Championship Match

Owen Hart & Yokozuna (with Mr. Fuji & Jim Cornette) defeated World Tag Team Champions Smokin' Gunns to become new champions

I Quit Match

Bret "Hit Man" Hart defeated Bob Backlund

WWE Championship Match

WWE Champion Diesel defeated Shawn Michaels to retain

Lawrence Taylor (with Ken Norton, Jr., Carl Banks, Rickey Jackson, Steve McMichael, Chris Spielman, & Reggie White) defeated Bam Bam Bigelow (with the Million Dollar Corporation)

Following in *WrestleMania* tradition, the bar for the world's greatest entertainment spectacle was raised as WWE legends returned, and two Superstars solidified their legendary status in a 60 Minute Iron Man Match. The capacity crowd at Arrowhead Pond also saw the *WrestleMania* debuts of Steve Austin and Triple H, a sign that an era filled with attitude was on the horizon.

MATCH RESULTS

Owen Hart, British Bulldog, & Vader (with Jim Cornette) defeated Yokozuna, Jake "the Snake" Roberts, & Ahmed Johnson

Hollywood Backlot Brawl

"Rowdy" Roddy Piper defeated Goldust (with Marlena)

The Ringmaster (with "Million Dollar Man" Ted DiBiase) defeated Savio Vega

Ultimate Warrior defeated Hunter Hearst Helmsley (with Sable)

Undertaker (with Paul Bearer) defeated Diesel

Iron Man Match for the WWE Championship

Shawn Michaels (with Jose Lothario) defeated WWE Champion Bret "Hit Man" Hart in overtime to become new champion

Eleven years after hosting a portion of *WrestleMania 2*, Chicago's Rosemont Horizon was once again the site of sports-entertainment's annual crown jewel in 1997. The 18,197 in attendance witnessed a Submission Match that will be remembered as one of the greatest battles of all time. Trapped in the Sharpshooter, Stone Cold refused to submit to his rival, even with blood spewing from his forehead. Austin refused to give up, but the blood loss became too great for him to overcome and he passed out.

MATCH RESULTS

No. 1 Contenders Tag Team Fatal Four Way Elimination Match

The Headbangers defeated the Godwinns (with Hillbilly Jim), the New Blackjacks, and Phil Lafon & Doug Furnas

Intercontinental Championship Match

Intercontinental Champion Rocky Maivia defeated the Sultan (with Bob Backlund & Iron Sheik) to retain

Hunter Hearst-Helmsley (with Chyna) defeated Goldust (with Marlena)

World Tag Team Championship Match

World Tag Team Champions Owen Hart & British Bulldog vs. Mankind & Vader went to a double countout

WWE Championship Match

Undertaker defeated WWE Champion Sycho Sid to become WWE Champion

Submission Match

Bret "Hit Man" Hart defeated Stone Cold Steve Austin, with Special Guest Referee Ken Shamrock

Chicago Street Fight

Ahmed Johnson & Legion of Doom defeated the Nation of Domination

---

Tagged "DX-raided," *WrestleMania XIV* was supposed to be the site of D-Generation X's greatest triumph. With special enforcer Mike Tyson already announcing his allegiance to Shawn Michaels heading into the WWE Championship Match, it looked like an HBK win was a mere formality. With Austin's dream just three seconds away, Tyson hit the ring to make the three count and officially usher in the Austin era. Also, the 19,028 on hand saw Kane and Undertaker's first encounter. Prior to the match, guest ring announcer Pete Rose poked fun at the Boston crowd for the Red Sox inability to win a World Series. His words not only angered the crowd, but set something off in Kane, who delivered a Tombstone to baseball's all-time hits leader.

MATCH RESULTS

Tag Team Battle Royal

Legion of Doom (with Sunny) defeated Savio Vega & Miguel Perez, Jose Estrada & Jesus Castillo, New Midnight Express, Truth Commission, Bradshaw & Chainz, D-Lo Brown & Mark Henry, the Quebecers, Rock n' Roll Express, Faarooq & Kama, the Headbangers, Scott Taylor & Brian Christopher, the Godwinns, and D.O.A.

Light Heavyweight Championship Match

Light Heavyweight Champion Taka Michinoku defeated Aguila

European Championship Match

European Champion Triple H defeated Owen Hart

Mixed Tag Team Match

Marc Mero & Sable defeated The Artist Formerly Known as Goldust & Luna

Intercontinental Championship Match

Intercontinental Champion The Rock (with the Nation of Domination) defeated Ken Shamrock via disqualification

Dumpster Match for the World Tag Team Championship

Cactus Jack & Terry Funk defeated World Tag Team Champions New Age Outlaws to become new champions

Undertaker defeated Kane

WWE Championship Match

Stone Cold Steve Austin defeated WWE Champion Shawn Michaels to become new champion

Despite Stone Cold Steve Austin's unparalleled popularity, Mr. McMahon failed to recognize him as a worthy representative of WWE. In September 1998, he declared the title vacant after Stone Cold Steve Austin had been simultaneously pinned by Undertaker and Kane. At *WrestleMania XV*, the 19,514 fans inside the First Union Center watched Stone Cold Steve Austin face The Rock. *WrestleMania XV* also hosted arguably the most one-sided match to ever take place in a WWE ring as Bart Gunn, who won the Brawl For All Tournament, faced Butterbean, with boxing great Vinny Pazienza serving as referee. Elsewhere, Pete Rose sought revenge from Kane for his *WrestleMania XIV* humiliation. Things didn't go as planned, and the "Big Red Monster" planted Rose with a Tombstone for the second year in a row.

MATCH RESULTS

Triple Threat Match for the Hardcore Championship

Hardcore Holly defeated Al Snow and Hardcore Champion Billy Gunn to become new champion

World Tag Team Championship Match

World Tag Team Champions Owen Hart & Jeff Jarrett (with Debra) defeated D-Lo Brown & Test (with Ivory)

Brawl For All

Butterbean defeated Bart Gunn by knockout, with guest referee Vinny Pazienza

Referee Match

Mankind defeated Big Show via disqualification to become referee for main event

Fatal Four Way Match for the Intercontinental Championship

Intercontinental Champion Road Dogg defeated Val Venis, Ken Shamrock and Goldust (with Blue Meanie & Ryan Shamrock)

Kane defeated Triple H via disqualification

Women's Championship Match

Women's Champion Sable defeated Tori

European Championship Match

European Champion Shane McMahon defeated X-Pac

Hell in a Cell Match

Undertaker (with Paul Bearer) defeated Big Boss Man

WWE Championship Match

Stone Cold Steve Austin defeated WWE Champion The Rock to become new champion

---

Apr 02 2000 Arrowhead Pond; Anaheim, CA

With a McMahon in every corner for the main event and 19,776 fans in attendance, the WWE Championship Match at *WrestleMania 2000* certainly had the makings of a volatile situation. Accompanied by Stephanie, WWE Champion Triple H defended his title against The Rock (with Vince), Big Show (with Shane), and Mick Foley (with Linda) in a Fatal Four Way Elimination Match. However, the World Tag Team Championship Match stole the show. The champion Dudley Boys battled Edge & Christian and the Hardy Boys in a thrilling Ladder Match. Throughout the epic encounter, tables and chairs also made their way into the fray, leading many to consider this encounter the precursor to the famed TLC Match.

MATCH RESULTS

Big Boss Man & Bull Buchanan defeated The Godfather & D-Lo Brown (with Ice-T)

Hardcore Battle Royal

Hardcore Holly was the final winner of the Hardcore Championship Battle Royal, which also included Hardcore Champion Crash Holly, Viscera, Tazz, Kaientei, Mean Street Posse, the Headbangers, and the Acolytes

Test & Albert (with Trish Stratus) defeated Al Snow & Steve Blackman (with Chester McCheeserton)

Ladder Match for the World Tag Team Championship

Edge & Christian defeated the Hardy Boys and the Dudley Boys to become new champions

Catfight

Terri defeated the Kat

Too Cool & Chyna defeated the Radicalz

Two-Fall Triple Threat Match for the Intercontinental & European Championships

Chris Benoit defeated Chris Jericho and Intercontinental Champion Kurt Angle to become new Intercontinental Champion

Chris Jericho defeated Chris Benoit and European Champion Kurt Angle to become new European Champion

Kane & Rikishi defeated Road Dogg & X-Pac

Fatal Four Way Elimination Match for the WWE Championship

WWE Champion Triple H (with Stephanie McMahon) defeated The Rock (with Mr. McMahon), Mick Foley (with Linda McMahon), and Big Show (with Shane McMahon)

Apr 01 2001 — **Astrodome; Houston, TX**

As *WrestleMania* transformed into a true global phenomenon, Mr. McMahon watched from the sidelines as the sport's greatest became legends at the extravaganza he created. In 2001, he decided it was his turn to step into the ring. In the midst of a bitter divorce from his wife Linda, Mr. McMahon began a very public love affair with Trish Stratus. Viewing the relationship as the ultimate sign of disrespect, son Shane challenged his father to a Street Fight. For the second year in a row, Edge & Christian captured the World Tag Team Championship in an epic encounter. In front of 67,925 fans, they successfully out-climbed the Hardy Boys and Dudley Boys to become unofficial Kings of the TLC Match.

MATCH RESULTS

Intercontinental Championship Match

Intercontinental Champion Chris Jericho defeated William Regal

Bradshaw, Faarooq & Tazz defeated Right to Censor

Triple Threat Match for the Hardcore Championship

Kane defeated Big Show and Hardcore Champion Raven to become new champion

European Championship Match

Eddie Guerrero defeated European Champion Test to become new champion

Kurt Angle defeated Chris Benoit

Women's Championship Match

Chyna defeated Women's Champion Ivory to become new champion

Street Fight

Shane McMahon defeated Mr. McMahon, with special guest referee, Mick Foley

TLC Match for the World Tag Team Championship

Edge & Christian defeated the Hardy Boys and World Tag Team Champions the Dudley Boys to become new champions

Gimmick Battle Royal

Iron Sheik defeated Nikolai Volkoff, Kamala, Doink, Repo Man, Brother Love, The Bushwhackers, Jim Cornette, Duke "The Dumpster" Droese, Tugboat, Sgt. Slaughter, Kim Chee, One Man Gang, Hillbilly Jim, The Goon, Michael Hayes, Gobbledy Gooker, and Earthquake

Undertaker defeated Triple H

WWE Championship Match

Stone Cold Steve Austin defeated WWE Champion The Rock to become new champion

---

Mar 17 2002 — **Toronto SkyDome; Toronto, Ontario, Canada**

For the second time in WWE history, *WrestleMania* went international when the eighteenth annual event took place in front of 68,237 fans inside Toronto's SkyDome. Nine years after making his last *WrestleMania* appearance, Hulk Hogan returned to the spotlight to battle The Rock. *WrestleMania X8* proved to be a tough night for the nWo. Not only did Hogan falter, but Scott Hall also came up short in his contest against Stone Cold Steve Austin. By the end of the night, the nWo was a mere shell of itself, as Hall and Kevin Nash attacked Hogan, officially marking the beginning of the end for the feared faction.

MATCH RESULTS

Intercontinental Championship Match

Rob Van Dam defeated Intercontinental Champion William Regal to become new champion

European Championship Match

European Champion Diamond Dallas Page defeated Christian

Hardcore Championship

Utilizing the 24/7 rule, Spike Dudley, The Hurricane, Mighty Molly, Maven, and Christian all scored pinfalls to win the Hardcore Championship during the night

Kurt Angle defeated Kane

Undertaker defeated Ric Flair

Edge defeated Booker T

Stone Cold Steve Austin defeated Scott Hall (with Kevin Nash)

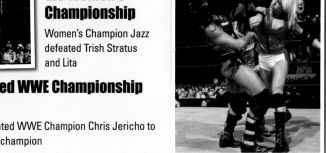

Fatal Four Way Elimination Match for the World Tag Team Championship

World Tag Team Champions Billy & Chuck defeated the Hardy Boys, the Dudley Boys, and the APA

Icon vs. Icon Match

The Rock defeated Hulk Hogan

Triple Threat Match for the Women's Championship

Women's Champion Jazz defeated Trish Stratus and Lita

Undisputed WWE Championship Match

Triple H defeated WWE Champion Chris Jericho to become new champion

WRESTLEMANIA XIX

In 2003, one of the greatest *WrestleMania* rivalries continued when The Rock squared off against Stone Cold Steve Austin for the third time. On the eve of the epic encounter, a combination of anxiety, nerves, and heart palpitations hospitalized the "Texas Rattlesnake." Despite waking up that morning in a hospital bed, Stone Cold battled the Rock in front of 54,097, but in the end, it was Austin falling to three Rock Bottoms.

In the months leading up to *WrestleMania XIX*, Hulk Hogan and Mr. McMahon engaged in a bitter rivalry over which man was most responsible for WWE's enormous success. In a battle for bragging rights, the two powerful personalities faced off in a Street Fight. *WrestleMania XIX* also marked the first time that both the World Heavyweight and WWE Championships were contested in the same *WrestleMania*. While Triple H retained his title, Brock Lesnar delivered a now-infamous Shooting Star Press to top Kurt Angle for the WWE Championship.

MATCH RESULTS

Cruiserweight Championship Match

Cruiserweight Champion Matt Hardy defeated Rey Mysterio

Handicap Match

Undertaker defeated A-Train & Big Show

Triple Threat Match for the Women's Championship

Trish Stratus defeated Jazz and Women's Champion Victoria to become new champion

Triple Threat Match for the World Tag Team Championship

World Tag Team Champions Team Angle defeated Los Guerreros and Chris Benoit & Rhyno to retain

Shawn Michaels defeated Chris Jericho

Cat Fight

Stacy Keibler, Torrie Wilson and the Miller Light Cat Fight Girls battled to a no contest

World Heavyweight Championship Match

World Heavyweight Champion Triple H defeated Booker T

Street Fight

Hulk Hogan defeated Mr. McMahon

The Rock defeated Stone Cold Steve Austin

WWE Championship Match

Brock Lesnar defeated WWE Champion Kurt Angle to become new champion

---

WRESTLEMANIA XX

With over 20,000 fans on hand on its twentieth anniversary, *WrestleMania* returned to Madison Square Garden, the home of the inaugural *WrestleMania*. *WrestleMania XX* was John Cena's *WrestleMania* debut, and the site of the start of his first title reign. It was also the last time Goldberg would compete in a WWE ring. Prior to their match, fans caught wind that both Goldberg and Lesnar would be leaving WWE following *WrestleMania*. To the delight of fans, the real highlight came after the bout when special referee Stone Cold Steve Austin hit both men with a Stone Cold Stunner.

MATCH RESULTS

United States Championship Match

John Cena defeated United States Champion Big Show to become new champion

Fatal Four Way Match for the World Tag Team Championship

World Tag Team Champions Booker T & Rob Van Dam defeated the Dudley Boys, La Resistance, and Mark Jindrak & Garrison Cade to retain

Handicap Match

Batista, Randy Orton, & Ric Flair defeated The Rock & Mick Foley

Playboy Evening Gown Match

Sable & Torrie Wilson defeated Stacy Keibler & Miss Jackie

Cruiserweight Open for the Cruiserweight Championship

Ultimo Dragon defeated Shannon Moore; Jamie Noble defeated Ultimo Dragon; Jamie Noble defeated Funaki; Jamie Noble defeated Nunzio; Billy Kidman defeated Jamie Noble; Rey Mysterio defeated Billy Kidman; Rey Mysterio defeated Tajiri; Cruiserweight Champion Chavo Guerrero defeated Rey Mysterio

Goldberg defeated Brock Lesnar, with guest referee Stone Cold Steve Austin

Fatal Four Way Match for the WWE Tag Team Championship

WWE Tag Team Champions Scotty 2 Hotty & Rikishi defeated APA, World's Greatest Tag Team, and the Basham Brothers

Women's Championship Match

Women's Champion Victoria defeated Molly Holly

WWE Championship Match

WWE Champion Eddie Guerrero defeated Kurt Angle

Undertaker defeated Kane

Triple Threat Match for the World Heavyweight Championship

Chris Benoit defeated Shawn Michaels and World Heavyweight Champion Triple H to become new champion

WrestleMania 21

Apr 03 2005 Staples Center; Los Angeles, CA

Emanating from Los Angeles, California, *WrestleMania 21* was aptly tagged "*WrestleMania* Goes Hollywood." Even with celebrities Sylvester Stallone, Carmen Electra, and Adam Sandler among the 20,193 in attendance, the true stars of the night were Batista and John Cena. After his 2005 *Royal Rumble* victory, Batista shocked the wrestling world when he chose to battle fellow Evolution member Triple H for the World Heavyweight Championship. John Cena claimed his first world title in WWE, allowing him to usher in the modern "spinner" championship belt that is seen today. *WrestleMania 21* also marked the beginning of the annual tradition known as the Money in the Bank Ladder Match. Big Show took part in a *WrestleMania* first when he signed on to compete in a Sumo Match against the famed Akebono.

MATCH RESULTS

Rey Mysterio defeated Eddie Guerrero

Money in the Bank Ladder Match

Edge defeated Chris Benoit, Chris Jericho, Christian, Kane, and Shelton Benjamin

Legend vs. Legend Killer Match

Undertaker defeated Randy Orton

Women's Championship Match

Women's Champion Trish Stratus defeated Christy Hemme

Kurt Angle defeated Shawn Michaels

Sumo Match

Akebono defeated Big Show

WWE Championship Match

John Cena defeated WWE Championship JBL to become new champion

World Heavyweight Championship Match

Batista defeated World Heavyweight Champion Triple H to become new champion

---

BIG TIME WrestleMania 22

Apr 02 2006 Allstate Arena; Rosemont, IL

Despite being one of the smallest Superstars on the WWE roster, Rey Mysterio took the event's "Big Time" theme literally. Competing in a World Heavyweight Championship Triple Threat Match against Kurt Angle and Randy Orton, the undersized underdog won the title. After defeating Big Show and Rob Van Dam in the *Road to WrestleMania* Tournament, momentum was clearly on Triple H's side heading into his WWE Championship Match with John Cena. Shockingly, so was half of the crowd, as the normally-popular Cena was booed by a good portion of the 17,159 fans in attendance.

MATCH RESULTS

World Tag Team Championship Match

World Tag Team Champions Big Show & Kane defeated Carlito & Chris Masters

Money in the Bank Ladder Match

Rob Van Dam defeated Ric Flair, Finlay, Shelton Benjamin, Bobby Lashley, and Matt Hardy

United States Championship Match

JBL defeated United States Champion Chris Benoit to become new champion

Hardcore Match

Edge (with Lita) defeated Mick Foley

Handicap Match

Boogeyman defeated Booker T & Sharmell

Women's Championship Match

Mickie James defeated Women's Champion Trish Stratus to become new champion

Casket Match

Undertaker defeated Mark Henry

No Holds Barred Match

Shawn Michaels defeated Mr. McMahon

Triple Threat Match for the World Heavyweight Championship

Rey Mysterio defeated Randy Orton and World Heavyweight Champion Kurt Angle to become new champion

Playboy Pillow Fight

Torrie Wilson defeated Candice Michelle

WWE Championship Match

WWE Champion John Cena defeated Triple H

The "Battle of the Billionaires" ruled the mainstream media heading into *WrestleMania 23*. With every major news outlet keeping a sharp eye on WWE, both Donald Trump and Mr. McMahon agreed to put their signature heads of hair on the line in front of over 80,000 fans at Detroit's Ford Field. For the second straight year, WWE Champion John Cena walked into the *WrestleMania* main event facing a divided crowd, as he took on the iconic Shawn Michaels. Elsewhere, Undertaker advanced his perfect *WrestleMania* record to 15-0 when he defeated Batista for the World Heavyweight Championship.

MATCH RESULTS

Money in the Bank Ladder Match

Mr. Kennedy defeated CM Punk, King Booker, Edge, Randy Orton, Finlay, Matt Hardy, and Jeff Hardy

The Great Khali defeated Kane

United States Championship Match

United States Champion Chris Benoit defeated Montel Vontavious Porter

World Heavyweight Championship Match

Undertaker defeated World Heavyweight Champion Batista to become new champion

The ECW Originals (Tommy Dreamer, Sandman, Sabu & Rob Van Dam) defeated the New Breed (Elijah Burke, Marcus Cor Von, Matt Striker & Kevin Thorn)

Battle of the Billionaires, Hair vs. Hair Match

Bobby Lashley (representing Donald Trump) defeated Umaga (representing Mr. McMahon), with guest referee, Stone Cold Steve Austin

Lumberjill Match for the Women's Championship

Women's Champion Melina defeated Ashley

WWE Championship Match

WWE Champion John Cena defeated Shawn Michaels

Mar 30 2008 — Citrus Bowl; Orlando, FL

WRESTLEMANIA XXIV

Held outdoors in Orlando's famed Citrus Bowl, *WrestleMania XXIV* proved to be the "Biggest *WrestleMania* Under the Sun." Unfortunately for Ric Flair, it also marked the day the sun set on his legendary WWE career. After a loss to Shawn Michaels, a tearful Flair thanked the fans and his family for their decades of support before riding off into the sunset. Three years after falling to Akebono in a sumo match, Big Show stepped out of his traditional wrestling arena yet again, this time to battle acclaimed boxer Floyd "Money" Mayweather.

MATCH RESULTS

Belfast Brawl

JBL defeated Finlay

Money in the Bank Ladder Match

CM Punk defeated Chris Jericho, Carlito, Montel Vontavious Porter, Shelton Benjamin, John Morrison, and Mr. Kennedy

Battle for Brand Supremacy

Batista defeated Umaga

ECW Championship Match

Kane defeated ECW Champion Chavo Guerrero to become new champion

Career Threatening Match

Shawn Michaels defeated Ric Flair

BunnyMania Lumberjill Match

Melina & Beth Phoenix defeated Maria & Ashley

Triple Threat Match for the WWE Championship

WWE Champion Randy Orton defeated Triple H and John Cena

The Biggest vs. The Best

Floyd "Money" Mayweather defeated Big Show via knockout

World Heavyweight Championship Match

Undertaker defeated World Heavyweight Champion Edge to become new champion

WRESTLEMANIA 25TH ANNIVERSARY

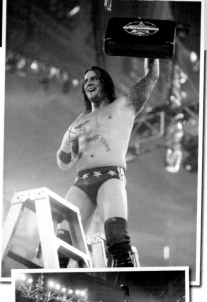

The 25th anniversary of sports-entertainment's crown jewel served as the perfect event to host what many consider the greatest match of all time: Undertaker versus Shawn Michaels. Also at *WrestleMania 25*, CM Punk became the first Superstar to win back-to-back Money in the Bank Ladder Matches when he outclimbed seven other Superstars to claim the prestigious briefcase.

Despite heading into *WrestleMania 25* as the Intercontinental Champion, JBL experienced one of the lowest nights of his amazing career when he lost to Rey Mysterio in less than 30 seconds.

Triple H's victory over Randy Orton proved extra sweet for "The Game", who was also defending the honor of the McMahon family. In the weeks leading up to the event, The Viper victimized Stephanie, Shane and Mr. McMahon.

MATCH RESULTS

Money in the Bank Ladder Match

CM Punk defeated Mark Henry, Kane, Montel Vontavious Porter, Kofi Kingston, Christian, Shelton Benjamin and Finlay

Miss WrestleMania Battle Royal

Santina Marella last eliminated Beth Phoenix and Melina

Handicap Elimination Match

Chris Jericho defeated Ricky Steamboat, Roddy Piper and Jimmy Snuka

Extreme Rules Match

Matt Hardy defeated Jeff Hardy

Intercontinental Championship Match

Rey Mysterio defeated Intercontinental Champion JBL to become new champion

Undertaker defeated Shawn Michaels

World Heavyweight Championship Triple Threat Match

John Cena defeated Big Show and World Heavyweight Champion Edge to become new champion

WWE Championship Match

WWE Champion Triple H defeated Randy Orton

WRESTLEMANIA XXVI

Mar 28 2010 University of Phoenix Stadium; Glendale, AZ

More than 72,000 members of the WWE Universe converged on University of Phoenix Stadium to witness the most anticipated rematch in *WrestleMania* history: Undertaker vs. Shawn Michaels. Stating he would retire if he couldn't beat the "Deadman," Michaels walked into the night's main event confident he could snap Undertaker's 17-match *WrestleMania* winning streak.

Also at *WrestleMania XXVI*, Bret Hart healed a wound that had been open for 12 years when he forced Mr. McMahon to submit to his signature Sharpshooter. The victory put an exclamation point on the final chapter of a book that began at *Survivor Series 1997*.

MATCH RESULTS

Unified Tag Team Championship Match

Unified Tag Team Champions The Miz & Big Show defeated John Morrison & R-Truth

Triple Threat Match

Randy Orton defeated Cody Rhodes and Ted DiBiase

Money in the Bank Ladder Match

Jack Swagger defeated Kane, Shelton Benjamin, Dolph Ziggler, Drew McIntyre, Christian, Montel Vontavious Porter, Kofi Kingston, Evan Bourne and Matt Hardy

Triple H defeated Sheamus

Rey Mysterio defeated CM Punk

No Holds Barred Lumberjack Match

Bret "Hit Man" Hart defeated Mr. McMahon

WWE Championship Match

John Cena defeated WWE Champion Batista to become new champion

Streak vs. Career Match

Undertaker defeated Shawn Michaels

World Heavyweight Championship Match

World Heavyweight Champion Chris Jericho defeated Edge

Michelle McCool, Layla, Vickie Guerrero, Alicia Fox & Maryse defeated Beth Phoenix, Eve, Mickie James, Kelly Kelly & Gail Kim

Hosted by The Rock, *WrestleMania XXVII* proved to be the most electrifying *WrestleMania* to date. For the first time in *WrestleMania*'s rich history, the WWE Championship Match appeared to end in a double countout when both The Miz and John Cena were unable to answer the referee's 10 count. Refusing to let such a monumental match end in a disappointing fashion, The Rock demanded that the contest continue until a winner was declared. Moments after the match restarted, the "Great One" flattened Cena with a Rock Bottom, allowing The Miz to easily cover his opponent for the win. Proving he's an equal-opportunity ass kicker, The Rock later laid Miz out with a People's Elbow.

WrestleMania XXVII also featured an epic showdown between two of the greatest of all time. Triple H met Undertaker in a No Holds Barred Match. In the weeks leading up to the event, The Game became obsessed with burying the undefeated WrestleMania record of the "Deadman."

After winning the 2011 *Royal Rumble*, Alberto Del Rio believed it was his destiny to walk out of *WrestleMania XXVII* as the World Heavyweight Champion. Edge, however, saw things a bit differently.

MATCH RESULTS
World Heavyweight Championship Match

World Heavyweight Champion Edge defeated Alberto Del Rio

Cody Rhodes defeated Rey Mysterio

Big Show, Kane, Santino Marella & Kofi Kingston defeated The Corre (Wade Barrett, Justin Gabriel, Heath Slater & Ezekiel Jackson)

Randy Orton defeated CM Punk

Michael Cole defeated Jerry "The King" Lawler

No Holds Barred Match

Undertaker defeated Triple H

John Morrison, Trish Stratus & Snooki defeated Dolph Ziggler, Michelle McCool & Layla

WWE Championship Match

WWE Champion The Miz defeated John Cena

Apr 01 2012 — **Sun Life Stadium; Miami Gardens, FL**

For nearly three decades, *WrestleMania* has been the site of sports-entertainment's most historic matches. In keeping with the tradition *WrestleMania XXVIII* produced a main event that was not only historic, but also a "Once in a Lifetime" affair when The Rock met John Cena in front of more than 78,000 screaming members of the WWE Universe. Also on the line was the position of General Manager for *Raw* and *SmackDown*, as teams representing John Laurinaitis and Teddy Long met to see who would helm both shows.

Other clashes on the card included Triple H seeking to end Undertaker's *WrestleMania* streak inside Hell In A Cell. Sheamus used his *Royal Rumble* victory to challenge World Heavyweight Champion Daniel Bryan. Big Show's *WrestleMania* past was the subject of ridicule from Cody Rhodes, and the two met for the Intercontinental Title. CM Punk and Chris Jericho each claimed be "The Best in the World" and clashed over CM Punk's WWE Championship.

MATCH RESULTS
World Heavyweight Championship Match

Sheamus defeated World Heavyweight Champion Daniel Bryan to become new champion

Kane defeated Randy Orton

Intercontinental Championship Match

Big Show defeated Intercontinental Champion Cody Rhodes to become new champion

Kelly Kelly & Maria Menounos defeated Beth Phoenix & Eve

Hell In A Cell Match

Undertaker defeated Triple H, with guest referee Shawn Michaels

Twelve-Man Tag Team Match

Team Johnny (David Otunga, The Miz, Mark Henry, Dolph Ziggler, Jack Swagger & Drew McIntyre) defeated Team Teddy (Santino Marella, Booker T, R-Truth, Kofi Kingston, Zack Ryder & The Great Khali)

WWE Championship Match

WWE Champion CM Punk defeated Chris Jericho

"Once in a Lifetime" Match

The Rock defeated John Cena

THE WRESTLING CLASSIC

The *Wrestling Classic*, also known as WrestleVision, was the first pay per view event WWE made available on a large scale (*WrestleMania* came first but was available in a limited number of markets). The Wrestling Classic is also the name of the tournament that took place at the event. Sixteen Superstars (Adrian Adonis, Corporal Kirschner, Dynamite Kid, Nikolai Volkoff, Randy Savage, Ivan Putski, Ricky Steamboat, Davey Boy Smith, Junkyard Dog, Iron Sheik, Moondog Spot, Terry Funk, Tito Santana, the Magnificent Muraco, Paul Orndorff, & "Cowboy" Bob Orton) began the night. Junkyard Dog emerged victorious over Randy Savage at the end of the tournament with a hard-fought count-out victory.

The only match of the night that did not involve the tournament was a WWE Championship Match between Hulk Hogan and "Rowdy" Roddy Piper, who lost after being disqualified due to the interference of "Cowboy" Bob Orton.

WWE CHAMPIONSHIP

Widely recognized as the top prize in all of sports-entertainment, the WWE Championship began its historic existence on April 29, 1963, when Buddy Rogers defeated Antonino Rocca in the finals of a tournament to crown the first-ever titleholder.

Many memorable reigns followed Rogers' inaugural tour of duty with the WWE Championship, but none were as lengthy as Bruno Sammartino's first run with the title. Sammartino defeated Rogers on May 17, 1963, and went on to hold the gold until January 18, 1971, when he was finally upended by Ivan Koloff. Sammartino's reign of nearly eight years is a record many sports-entertainment insiders believe will never be broken.

The WWE Championship reached iconic levels in January 1984, when Hulk Hogan won the title from The Iron Sheik. Almost immediately after Hogan strapped the gold around his waist for the first time, Hulkamania began to take over the nation. It wasn't long before kids across the United States starting donning Hogan's signature headband, while The Hulkster found himself on countless magazine covers, including *Sports Illustrated*.

In the years that followed, such great names as Ric Flair Bret Hart, and Shawn Michaels climbed the elusive WWE Championship mountain. In March 1998, the defiant Stone Cold Steve Austin captured the WWE Championship and brought the title to heights once thought unimaginable. His popularity quickly became a global phenomenon, as fans the world over tuned into RAW at record rates to watch the working man's champion.

Stone Cold Steve Austin's championship days ended in September 2001, but Superstars like The Rock, Triple H, and John Cena worked long and hard to maintain the WWE Championship's remarkable reputation.

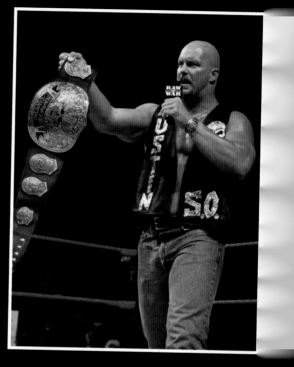

1963
April 25
Rio de Janeiro

Buddy Rogers defeated Antonino Rocca in the finals of a tournament to be crowned the first-ever WWE Champion

▼

May 17
New York, NY

Bruno Sammartino defeated Buddy Rogers

▼

1971
January 18
New York, NY

Ivan Koloff defeated Bruno Sammartino

1973
December 1
Philadelphia, PA

Stan Stasiak defeated Pedro Morales

▼

December 10
New York, NY

Bruno Sammartino defeated Stan Stasiak

▼

1977
April 30
Baltimore, MD

Superstar Billy Graham defeated Bruno Sammartino

▼

1983
December 26
New York, NY

The Iron Sheik defeated Bob Backlund

▼

1984
January 23
New York, NY

Hulk Hogan defeated the Iron Sheik

▼

1988
February 5
Indianapolis, IN

Andre the Giant defeated

March 27
Atlantic City, NJ

Randy Savage defeated Ted DiBiase in the finals of a 14-man tournament to crown a new WWE Champion

▼

1989
April 2
Atlantic City, NJ

Hulk Hogan defeated Randy Savage

▼

1990
April 1
Toronto, Ontario

Ultimate Warrior defeated Hulk Hogan

1991
January 19
Miami, FL

Sgt. Slaughter defeated Ultimate Warrior

▼

March 24
Los Angeles, CA

Hulk Hogan defeated Sgt. Slaughter

▼

November 27
Detroit, MI

Undertaker defeated Hulk Hogan

▼

December 3
San Antonio, TX

Hulk Hogan defeated Undertaker

1992
January 19
Albany, NY

Ric Flair last eliminated Sid Justice to win the Royal Rumble and the WWE Championship

▼

April 5
Indianapolis, IN

Randy Savage defeated Ric Flair

▼

September 1
Hershey, PA

Ric Flair defeated Randy Savage

▼

October 12
Saskatoon, Saskatchewan

Bret Hart defeated Ric Flair

1993
April 4
Las Vegas, NV

Yokozuna defeated Bret Hart

▼

April 4
Las Vegas, NV

Hulk Hogan defeated Yokozuna

June 13
Dayton, OH

Yokozuna defeated Hulk Hogan

▼

1994
March 20
New York, NY

Bret Hart defeated Yokozuna

▼

November 23
San Antonio, TX

Bob Backlund defeated Bret Hart

▼

November 26
New York, NY

Diesel defeated Bob Backlund

▼

1995
November 19
Landover, MD

Bret Hart defeated Diesel

▼

1996
March 31
Anaheim, CA

November 17
New York, NY

Sid defeated Shawn Michaels

▼

1997
January 19
San Antonio, TX

Shawn Michaels defeated Sid

Injuries forced Shawn Michaels to vacate the title shortly after his victory

▼

February 16
Chattanooga, TN

Bret Hart last eliminated Undertaker in a Fatal Four-Way Match that also included Vader and Stone Cold Steve Austin

▼

February 17
Nashville, TN

Sid defeated Bret Hart

▼

March 23
Chicago, IL

Undertaker defeated Sid

▼

August 3
East Rutherford, NJ

Bret Hart defeated Undertaker

▼

November 9
Montreal, Quebec

Shawn Michaels defeated Bret Hart

▼

1998
March 29
Boston, MA

Stone Cold Steve Austin defeated Shawn Michaels

▼

June 28
Pittsburgh, PA

Kane defeated Stone Cold Steve Austin

▼

June 29
Cleveland, OH

Stone Cold Steve Austin defeated Kane

Mr. McMahon vacated the title in September, 1998 after a controversial ending to a Triple Threat Match featuring Stone Cold Steve Austin, Undertaker, and Kane

▼

November 15
St. Louis, MO

The Rock defeated Mankind in the finals of a 14-man tournament to crown a new WWE Champion

▼

1999
January 4
Worcester, MA

Mankind defeated The Rock

▼

January 24
Anaheim, CA

The Rock defeated Mankind

▼

January 31
Tucson, AZ

Mankind defeated The Rock

▼

February 15
Birmingham, AL

The Rock defeated Mankind

▼

March 28
Philadelphia, PA

Stone Cold Steve Austin defeated The Rock

▼

May 23
Kansas City, MO

Undertaker defeated Stone Cold Steve Austin

▼

June 28
Charlotte, NC

Stone Cold Steve Austin defeated Undertaker

▼

August 22
Minneapolis, MN

Mankind defeated Stone Cold Steve Austin in a Triple Threat Match that also included Triple H

▼

August 23
Ames, IA

Triple H defeated Mankind

▼

Mr. McMahon defeated Triple H

Mr. McMahon vacates the title in September, 1999

▼

September 26
Charlotte, NC

Triple H defeated The Rock in a Six-Pack Challenge Match that also included Mankind, British Bulldog, Big Show, and Kane

▼

November 14
Detroit, MI

Big Show defeated Triple H in a Triple Threat Match that also included The Rock

2000

January 3
Miami, FL

Triple H defeated Big Show

▼

April 30
Washington, DC

The Rock defeated Triple H

▼

May 21
Louisville, KY

Triple H defeated The Rock

▼

June 25
Boston, MA

The Rock becomes WWE Champion

The Rock, Undertaker & Kane met Triple H, Shane McMahon & Mr. McMahon in a six-man tag team match with a pre-match stipulation which stated that if anybody on Triple H's team lost, he would lose the WWE Championship; The Rock pinned Mr. McMahon to win the title

▼

October 22
Albany, NY

Kurt Angle defeated The Rock

▼

2001

February 25
Las Vegas, NV

The Rock defeated Kurt Angle

▼

April 1
Houston, TX

Stone Cold Steve Austin defeated The Rock

▼

September 23
Pittsburgh, PA

Kurt Angle defeated Stone Cold Steve Austin

▼

October 8
Indianapolis, IN

Stone Cold Steve Austin defeated Kurt Angle

▼

December 9
San Diego, CA

Chris Jericho defeated Stone Cold Steve Austin

▼

2002

March 17
Toronto, Ontario

Triple H defeated Chris Jericho

▼

April 21
Kansas City, MO

Hulk Hogan defeated Triple H

▼

May 19
Nashville, TN

Undertaker defeated Hulk Hogan

▼

July 21
Detroit, MI

The Rock defeated Kurt Angle and Undertaker in a Triple Threat Match

▼

August 25
Uniondale, NY

Brock Lesnar defeated The Rock

▼

November 17
New York, NY

Big Show defeated Brock Lesnar

▼

December 15
Fort Lauderdale, FL

Kurt Angle defeated Big Show

▼

2003

March 30
Seattle, WA

Brock Lesnar defeated Kurt Angle

▼

July 27
Denver, CO

Kurt Angle defeated Brock Lesnar and Big Show in a Triple Threat Match

▼

September 18
Raleigh, NC

Brock Lesnar defeated Kurt Angle

▼

2004

February 15
San Francisco, CA

Eddie Guerrero defeated Brock Lesnar

▼

June 27
Norfolk, VA

JBL defeated Eddie Guerrero

▼

2005

April 3
Los Angeles, CA

John Cena defeated JBL

▼

2006

January 8
Albany, NY

Edge defeated John Cena

▼

January 29
Miami, FL

John Cena defeated Edge

▼

June 11
New York, NY

Rob Van Dam defeated John Cena

▼

July 3
Philadelphia, PA

Edge defeated Rob Van Dam and John Cena in a Triple Threat Match

▼

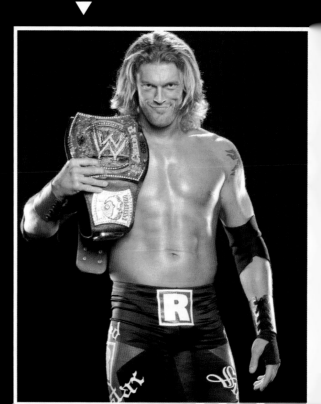

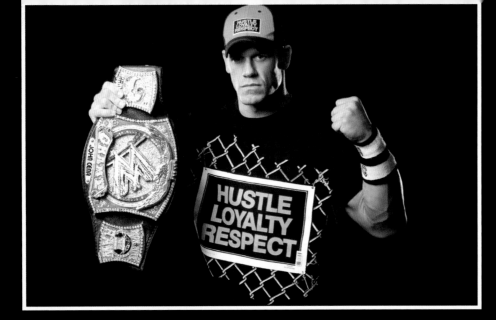

September 17
Toronto, Ontario

John Cena defeated Edge

Injuries forced John Cena to vacate the Championship

▼

2007

October 7
Chicago, IL

Randy Orton is awarded the WWE Championship

▼

October 7
Chicago, IL

Triple H defeated Randy Orton

▼

October 7
Chicago, IL

Randy Orton defeated Triple H

▼

2008

April 27
Baltimore, MD

Triple H defeated Randy Orton, John Cena and JBL in a Fatal 4-Way Match

▼

November 23
Boston, MA

Edge defeated Triple H

▼

December 14
Buffalo, NY

Jeff Hardy defeated Edge

▼

2009

January 25
Detroit, MI

Edge defeated Jeff Hardy

▼

February 15
Seattle, WA

Triple H last eliminated Undertaker in an Elimination Chamber Match that also included Jeff Hardy, Big Show, Vladimir Kozlov, and WWE Champion Edge

▼

April 26
Providence, RI

Randy Orton defeated Triple H

▼

June 7
New Orleans, LA

Batista defeated Randy Orton

Injuries forced Batista to vacate the title shortly after winning it

▼

June 15
Charlotte, NC

Randy Orton defeated Triple H, John Cena and Big Show in a Fatal 4-Way Match

▼

September 13
Montreal, Quebec

John Cena defeated Randy Orton

▼

October 4
Newark, NJ

Randy Orton defeated John Cena

▼

October 25
Pittsburgh, PA

John Cena defeated Randy Orton

▼

December 13
San Antonio, TX

Sheamus defeated John Cena

▼

2010

February 21
St. Louis, MO

John Cena defeated Sheamus

▼

February 21
St. Louis, MO

Batista defeated John Cena

▼

March 28
Phoenix, AZ

John Cena defeated Batista

▼

June 20
Uniondale, NY

Sheamus defeated John Cena, Randy Orton and Edge in a Fatal 4-Way Match

▼

September 19
Chicago, IL

Randy Orton defeated Sheamus

▼

November 22
Orlando, FL

The Miz defeated Randy Orton

▼

2011

May 1
Tampa, FL

John Cena defeated The Miz

▼

July 17
Chicago, IL

CM Punk defeated John Cena

CM Punk's WWE contract expired shortly after winning the title, so a tournament was held to determine a new champion

▼

July 25
Hampton, VA

Rey Mysterio defeated The Miz in the finals of the tournament

▼

July 25
Hampton, VA

John Cena defeated Rey Mysterio

CM Punk defeated John Cena in a WWE Championship Unification Match at *SummerSlam* on August 14, 2011

▼

August 14
Los Angeles, CA

Alberto Del Rio defeated CM Punk

▼

September 18
Buffalo, NY

John Cena defeated Alberto Del Rio

▼

October 2
New Orleans, LA

Alberto Del Rio defeated CM Punk and John Cena in a Triple Threat Hell In A Cell Match

▼

November 20
New York, NY

CM Punk defeated Alberto Del Rio

▼

Started in 2003, the WWE Diva Search was an annual competition designed to give smart, beautiful and powerful females the life-changing opportunity of becoming a WWE Diva.

2003

Unlike the more recent Diva Search contests, the inaugural event was held exclusively on WWE.com. Thousands of girls from all over the world sent their photos. In the end, the crown went to Canada's Jaime Koeppe.

2005

Won by Ashley Massaro, the finals of the 2005 Diva Search also featured future WWE Diva Kristal.

2004

Won by Christy Hemme, the finals of the 2004 Diva Search also featured future WWE Divas Joy Giovanni, Amy Weber, Michelle McCool and Maria. Following the contest, McCool went on to become a two-time Women's and Divas Champion.

2006

Won by Layla, the finals of the 2006 Diva Search also featured future WWE Divas Maryse, Rosa Mendes and Rebecca DiPietro. Following the contest, Layla went on to become the first-ever British-born Women's Champion.

2007

Won by Eve, the finals of the 2007 Diva Search also fe future WWE Divas Lena Yada and Tiffany.

In February 2010, following the closing of ECW, WWE announced the debut of the groundbreaking new show *WWE NXT*. This next generation of sports entertainment programming features a batch of well-established WWE Superstars, known as Pros, mentoring a crop of young and hungry Rookies, itching to become WWE Superstars.

Each week's episode emanates from a live arena and features the *NXT* Rookies competing against each other in a series of matches, as well as challenges. In the end, the Pro's Poll reveals which Rookies will fall by the wayside and which will go on to become WWE's next breakout star.

Season One: February 23 - June 1, 2010

ROOKIE	PRO	ELIMINATED
WADE BARRETT	*Chris Jericho*	*Winner*
DAVID OTUNGA	*R-Truth*	*Week 15*
JUSTIN GABRIEL	*Matt Hardy*	*Week 15*
HEATH SLATER	*Christian*	*Week 14*
DARREN YOUNG	*CM Punk*	*Week 13*
SKIP SHEFFIELD	*William Regal*	*Week 12*
MICHAEL TARVER	*Carlito*	*Week 12*
DANIEL BRYAN	*The Miz*	*Week 12*

Season Two: June 8 - August 31, 2010

ROOKIE	PRO	ELIMINATED
KAVAL	*Lay-Cool*	*Winner*
MICHAEL McGILLICUTTY	*Kofi Kingston*	*Week 13*
ALEX RILEY	*The Miz*	*Week 13*
HUSKY HARRIS	*Cody Rhodes*	*Week 11*
PERCY WATSON	*MVP*	*Week 11*
LUCKY CANNON	*Mark Henry*	*Week 10*
ELI COTTONWOOD	*John Morrison*	*Week 8*
TITUS O'NEIL	*Zack Ryder*	*Week 4*

Season Four: December 7 - March 1, 2011

ROOKIE	PRO	ELIMINATED
JOHNNY CURTIS	*R-Truth*	*Winner*
BRODUS CLAY	*Alberto Del Rio/Ted DiBiase*	*Week 13*
DERRICK BATEMAN	*Daniel Bryan*	*Week 12*
BYRON SAXTON	*Dolph Ziggler/Chris Masters*	*Week 10*
CONOR O'BRIAN	*Alberto Del Rio*	*Week 7*
JACOB NOVAK	*Chris Masters/Dolph Ziggler*	*Week 5*

Season Three: September 7 - November 30, 2010

ROOKIE	PRO	ELIMINATED
KAITLYN	*Vickie Guerrero*	*Winner*
NAOMI	*Kelly Kelly*	*Week 13*
A.J.	*Primo*	*Week 12*
AKSANA	*Goldust*	*Week 11*
MAXINE	*Alicia Fox*	*Week 9*
JAMIE	*The Bellas*	*Week 5*

Season Five: March 8, 2011 -

ROOKIE	PRO	ELIMINATED
TITUS O'NEIL	*Hornswoggle*	*TBD*
DARREN YOUNG	*Chavo Guerrero*	*TBD*
DERRICK BATEMAN	*Daniel Bryan*	*TBD*
CONOR O'BRIAN	*Vladimir Kozlov*	*Week 17*
LUCKY CANNON	*Tyson Kidd*	*Week 15*
BYRON SAXTON	*Yoshi Tatsu*	*Week 13*
JACOB NOVAK	*JTG*	*Week 11*

WWE TAG TEAM CHAMPIONSHIP

Once it was decided by WWE brass in 2002 that the World Tag Team Championship would be exclusive to *Raw*, *SmackDown* General Manager Stephanie McMahon created her own version of the Tag Team Championship. She stated that the first team to wear these prestigious belts could only do so if they survived a brutal tournament. Since that historic tournament several outstanding tag teams claimed this prominent championship including the Dudley Boys, Los Guerreros, the World's Greatest Tag Team, and John Morrison & The Miz.

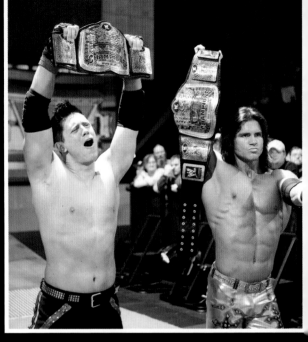

2002

October 20
Little Rock, AR

Kurt Angle & Chris Benoit defeated Edge & Rey Mysterio in the finals of tournament to crown the first-ever WWE Tag Team Champions

November 7
Manchester, NH

Edge & Rey Mysterio defeated Kurt Angle & Chris Benoit

November 17
New York, NY

Los Guerreros defeated Edge & Rey Mysterio

2003

February 6
Philadelphia, PA

The World's Greatest Tag Team defeated Los Guerreros

May 18
Charlotte, NC

Eddie Guerrero & Tajiri defeated The World's Greatest Tag Team

July 3
Rochester, NY

The World's Greatest Tag Team defeated Eddie Guerrero & Tajiri

September 18
Raleigh, NC

Los Guerreros defeated the World's Greatest Tag Team

October 23
Albany, NY

The Basham Brothers defeated Los Guerreros

2004

February 5
Cleveland, OH

Scotty 2 Hotty & Rikishi defeated the Basham Brothers

April 22
Kelowna, BC

Charlie Haas & Rico defeated Scotty 2 Hotty & Rikishi

June 17
Chicago, IL

The Dudley Boys defeated Charlie Haas & Rico

July 8
Winnipeg, Manitoba

Billy Kidman & Paul London defeated the Dudley Boys

September 9
Tulsa, OK

Kenzo Suzuki & Rene Dupree defeated Billy Kidman & Paul London

December 9
Greenville, SC

Rob Van Dam & Rey Mysterio defeated Kenzo Suzuki & Rene Dupree

2005

January 13
Tampa, FL

The Basham Brothers defeated Rob Van Dam & Rey Mysterio

February 20
Pittsburgh, PA

Rey Mysterio & Eddie Guerrero defeated the Basham Brothers

April 21
New York, NY

MNM defeated Rey Mysterio & Eddie Guerrero

July 25
Buffalo, NY

Road Warrior Animal & Heidenreich defeated MNM

October 28
San Francisco, CA

MNM defeated Road Warrior Animal & Heidenreich

December 16
Springfield, MA

Batista & Rey Mysterio defeated MNM

December 30
Uncasville, CT

MNM defeated Batista & Rey Mysterio

2006

May 21
Phoenix, AZ

Brian Kendrick & Paul London defeated MNM

2007

April 20
Milan, Italy

Deuce & Domino defeated Brian Kendrick & Paul London

August 31
Albany, NY

MVP & Matt Hardy defeated Deuce & Domino

November 16
Wichita, KS

John Morrison & The Miz defeated MVP & Matt Hardy

2008

July 20
Uniondale, NY

Curt Hawkins & Zack Ryder defeated Deuce & Domino

September 26
Columbus, OH

Carlito & Primo defeated Curt Hawkins & Zack Ryder

2009

April 5
Houston, TX

Carlito & Primo defeated The Miz & John Morrison

Carlito & Primo unified the World and WWE Tag Team Championships into the Unified Tag Team Title

June 28
Sacramento, CA

Edge & Chris Jericho defeated Carlito & Primo

Big Show teamed up with Chris Jericho when injury forced Edge to vacate his half of the gold

July 26
Philadelphia, PA

Chris Jericho & Big Show defeated Ted DiBiase & Cody Rhodes

December 13
San Antonio, TX

D-Generation X defeated Chris Jericho & Big Show

2010

February 8
Lafayette, LA

The Miz & Big Show defeated D-Generation X

April 26
Richmond, VA

The Hart Dynasty defeated Big Show & The Miz

The Hart Dynasty is recognized as the final World Tag Team Championship team, as the titles were retired during this reign. They continued to reign as WWE Tag Team Champions.

September 19
Chicago, IL

Drew McIntyre & Cody Rhodes defeated The Hart Dynasty

October 24
Minneapolis, MN

John Cena & David Otunga defeated

October 25
Green Bay, WI

Justin Gabriel & Heath Slater defeated John Cena & David Otunga

▼

December 6
Louisville, KY

Santino Marella & Vladimir Kozlov defeated Justin Gabriel & Heath Slater

▼

2011

February 20
Oakland, CA

Justin Gabriel & Heath Slater defeated Santino Marella & Vladimir Kozlov

▼

February 21
Fresno, CA

John Cena & The Miz defeated Justin Gabriel & Heath Slater

▼

February 21
Fresno, CA

Justin Gabriel & Heath Slater defeated John Cena & The Miz

▼

April 22
London, England

Big Show & Kane defeated Justin Gabriel & Heath Slater

▼

May 23
Portland, OR

David Otunga & Michael McGillicutty defeat Big Show & Kane

▼

August 22
Edmonton, Alberta

Kofi Kingston & Evan Bourne defeated David Otunga & Michael McGillicutty

▼

2012

January 15
Oakland, CA

Primo & Epico defeated Kofi Kingston & Evan Bourne

XANTA CLAUS

HT: 6'2"   WT: 305 lbs.   FROM: The South Pole
SIGNATURE MOVE: Nutcracker Suite

During the December 17, 1995 *In Your House* Pay-Per-View it appeared that Santa Claus was giving gifts to young fans around the ring with the help of Savio Vega. The "Million Dollar Man" Ted DiBiase then appeared and disparaged both Santa and his helper. Just as his verbal exchange with Vega ended, the Million Dollar Man's twisted sense of holiday gift giving presented itself. Suddenly, Santa attacked Savio Vega and viciously beat him in front of the capacity crowd.

Thanks to Jim Ross, audiences soon learned that this individual claimed to be the twin brother of Santa Claus and went by the name "Xanta Claus." He hailed from the South Pole, stole presents from good children and used underhanded maneuvers to put away opponents. While Xanta Claus had a brief tenure in the WWE history, his despicable actions during his television debut made a lasting impression.

X-FACTOR

MEMBERS: X-Pac, Albert, Justin Credible
COMBINED WT: 775 lbs.

X-Factor may not sit atop historians' lists of greatest factions of all time, but what many fail to remember is the rapid rate in which the group snatched up championships. In all, X-Factor compiled an astonishing four championship reigns during their brief eight-month union.

The leader of the group, X-Pac, enjoyed two Light Heavyweight Championship reigns before unifying the title with the Cruiserweight Championship in July 2001. Albert attained the group's greatest success when he used his patented Baldo Bomb to defeat Kane for the Intercontinental Championship in June 2001. Finally, the faction's most extreme Superstar, Justin Credible, was a perennial contender for the Hardcore Championship, which he eventually captured eight times after X-Factor split up.

Together, X-Factor's biggest victory came when they defeated Bubba Ray, D-Von & Spike Dudley at *Backlash 2001*. The faction began to slowly crumble after Credible left X-Pac & Albert to join forces with the WCW/ECW Alliance.

X-PAC

HT: 6'1"   WT: 212 lbs.
FROM: Minneapolis, Minnesota
SIGNATURE MOVE: 1-2-3 Kick

TITLE HISTORY

CRUISERWEIGHT CHAMPION	*Defeated Billy Kidman on July 30, 2001*
EUROPEAN CHAMPION (2 TIMES)	*Defeated D-Lo Brown on September 21, 1998* *Defeated D-Lo Brown on October 18, 1998*
LIGHT HEAVYWEIGHT CHAMPION (2 TIMES)	*Defeated Jeff Hardy on June 25, 2001* *Defeated Tajiri on August 19, 2001*
WORLD TAG TEAM CHAMPION (4 TIMES)	*Partnered with Marty Jannetty to defeat The Quebecers on January 10, 1994* *Partnered with Bob Holly to defeat Bam Bam Bigelow & Tatanka on January 22, 1995* *Partnered with Kane to defeat Owen Hart & Jeff Jarrett on March 30, 1999* *Partnered with Kane to defeat The Acolytes on August 9, 1999*

Making his WWE debut in the spring of 1993 as the Kid, he made an immediate impact during an episode of *Monday Night Raw* when he beat Razor Ramon. Renamed the 1-2-3 Kid, he teamed with Marty Jannetty to win the World Tag Team Championship. Sadly, WWE's shy hero soon took a new career direction as a member of Ted DiBiase's Million Dollar Corporation.

In late 1996, the 1-2-3 Kid left WWE and stunned audiences when he appeared in the front row of an episode of *WCW Monday Nitro,* calling himself Syxx. In March 1998, his contract was suddenly terminated, but he didn't stay gone for long. During an episode of *Monday Night Raw*, Triple H introduced the latest recruit to DX, X-Pac. Though later Triple H turned on him, which caused a split within DX, X-Pac later rejoined the group. Partnering with Kane, the duo won the World Tag Team Championship. When he returned from injury, DX had dissolved and in 2001 he formed the short-lived X-Factor with Justin Credible and Albert.

He was the only Superstar to wear both the WCW Cruiserweight and WWE Light Heavyweight championships at once after he defeated Billy Kidman. Plagued by injuries, X-Pac was out of action and released from WWE that August. When he recovered he brought his mix of martial arts and aerial maneuvers to arenas all over the world.

He made a surprising return to WWE in April 2011 at the end of Shawn Michaels' WWE Hall of Fame induction speech, along with other Kliq members Triple H and Kevin Nash.

Y

2010-

2000-09

1990-99

1980-89

1970-79

1960-69

YOKOZUNA

HT: 6'4"   WT: 600 lbs.
FROM: The Land of the Rising Sun
SIGNATURE MOVE: Bonzai Drop

HALL OF FAME 2012

TITLE HISTORY

WORLD TAG TEAM CHAMPION (2 TIMES)	*Partnered with Owen Hart to defeat The Smokin' Gunns on April 2, 1995* *Along with Owen Hart, awarded championship on September 25, 1995*
WWE CHAMPION (2 TIMES)	*Defeated Bret Hart on April 4, 1993* *Defeated Hulk Hogan on June 13, 1993*

When Yokozuna first entered a WWE ring in October 1992, every Superstar was forced to take notice of the massive newcomer. A mountain of a man, he used his unbelievable size to flatten his foes. To make matters worse for his challengers, Yokozuna complemented his enormous frame with an amazing agility rarely found in big men.

Yokozuna's impact was immediate. In fact, shortly after his debut, the sumo Superstar muscled his way to main event status when he last eliminated Randy Savage to win the 1993 *Royal Rumble*. The victory earned Yokozuna a shot at Bret Hart's WWE Championship at *WrestleMania IX*. With a little help from his crafty manager, Mr. Fuji, Yokozuna upended Hart to claim his first WWE Championship.

Unfortunately for Yokozuna, his reign would prove to be one of the shortest of all time as Hulk Hogan defeated the new champion a mere minutes after he beat Hart for the title. Yokozuna was able to avenge his loss, however, when he defeated "The Hulkster" to regain the WWE Championship at the 1993 *King of the Ring*. This time, Yokozuna kept a firm grasp on the gold for an amazing 280 days.

In addition to his dominance as a singles competitor, Yokozuna also found great success in the tag team ranks. With Owen Hart as his partner, Yokozuna enjoyed two reigns atop the WWE tag team division.

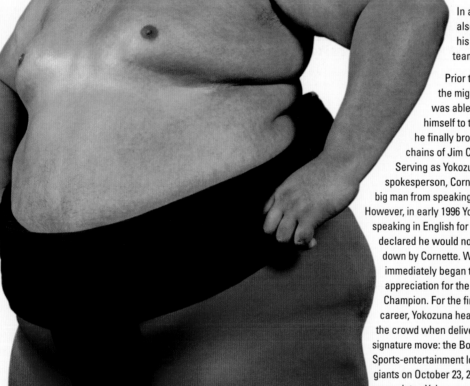

Prior to leaving WWE, the mighty Yokozuna was able to endear himself to the fans when he finally broke free from the chains of Jim Cornette. Serving as Yokozuna's American spokesperson, Cornette forbade the big man from speaking for himself. However, in early 1996 Yokozuna, speaking in English for the first time declared he would no longer be held down by Cornette. WWE fans immediately began to show appreciation for the former WWE Champion. For the first time in his career, Yokozuna heard cheers from the crowd when delivering his signature move: the Bonzai Drop. Sports-entertainment lost one of its giants on October 23, 2000 when Yokozuna passed away at the age of 34. Nearly twelve years later, Yokozuna was inducted into the WWE Hall of Fame in a touching ceremony involving his close-knit, extended family.

YOSHI TATSU

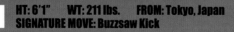

HT: 6'1"   WT: 211 lbs.   FROM: Tokyo, Japan
SIGNATURE MOVE: Buzzsaw Kick

Behind an arsenal of high-impact kicks, Yoshi Tatsu immediately became one of sports-entertainment's most exciting Superstars upon making his debut in ECW in June 2009. During his tenure in ECW, the man from the "Land of the Rising Sun" successfully turned back many of the brand's top stars, including Shelton Benjamin, Jack Swagger and William Regal.

Tatsu eventually became a free agent when ECW ceased operations in February 2010. After a brief courting period, the Japanese Superstar signed with *Raw*, but was soon shipped to *SmackDown* via the 2010 WWE Draft Lottery.

As a *SmackDown* Superstar, Tatsu used his educated feet to outsmart the likes of Zack Ryder and Primo. He later served as Byron Saxton's Pro on *NXT* season five. Under Tatsu's tutelage, Saxton lasted until Week 13 until finally being eliminated from competition. Despite his Rookie's ousting, however, Tatsu stuck around *NXT* to battle Tyson Kidd in a thrilling rivalry that culminated with a Necklace on a Pole Match, which Tatsu won.

THE YOUNG STALLIONS

MEMBERS: Paul Roma, Jim Powers   COMBINED WT: 481 lbs.

No strangers to WWE audiences, these two former singles competitors joined forces in the late 1980s. As a cohesive unit, Roma & Powers were an exciting combination during one of the greatest eras of tag team wrestling. They battled the Hart Foundation over the rights of use to the theme song *Crank It Up*, when Jimmy Hart claimed the tune was intended for his men.

The shining moment for the Young Stallions came at the 1987 *Survivor Series* when, along with the Killer Bees, they were the sole survivors in the tag team elimination match. They also appeared in the 20-Man Over the Top Rope Battle Royal at *WrestleMania IV* before taking on top teams like the Brain Busters, the Fabulous Rougeaus and the Twin Towers.

Unfortunately for their fans, mounting losses turned frustration into fighting and the Stallions fell apart. Paul Roma became a member of Power & Glory while Jim Powers returned to singles action.

THE YUKON LUMBERJACKS

MEMBERS: Eric, Pierre   COMBINED WT: 551 lbs.
FROM: The Yukon

TITLE HISTORY

WORLD TAG TEAM CHAMPIONS	*Defeated Dominic DeNucci & Dino Bravo on June 26, 1978*

Managed by Capt. Lou Albano, the Yukon Lumberjacks spent a brief, but successful time competing in WWE. Eric & Pierre made their WWE debut in 1978. Shortly after their initial appearance, the bearded duo defeated the legendary Dominic DeNucci & Dino Bravo in New York City to capture the World Tag Team Championship. Behind Eric's devastating big boot and Pierre's Cobra Clutch, the Yukon Lumberjacks sawed through all challengers before finally losing the titles to Tony Garea & Larry Zbyszko in November 1978.

The Yukon Lumberjacks split up shortly after losing the World Tag Team Championship. Eric went on to compete for various southern United States promotions, while Pierre achieved most of his notoriety wrestling in Canada.

ZACK RYDER

HT: 6'2"   WT: 214 lbs.   FROM: Long Island, New York
SIGNATURE MOVE: Rough Ryder

TITLE HISTORY

UNITED STATES CHAMPION	*Defeated Dolph Ziggler on December 18, 2011*
WWE TAG TEAM CHAMPION	*Partnered with Curt Hawkins to win a Fatal 4-Way Match on July 20, 2008*

In the long and storied history of sports-entertainment, few Superstars have forced their way into the spotlight as effectively as Zack Ryder. Feeling overlooked by WWE management, the spiked-hair Superstar took to YouTube to vent his frustrations and display his wildly charismatic side. In a matter of weeks, Ryder's *Z! True Long Island Story* web show caused an unforeseeable groundswell of support.

It wasn't long before "We want Ryder" chants and "Ryder=Ratings" signs began to overwhelm arenas. WWE had no choice; thanks to his powerful grassroots efforts, Ryder was thrust into the spotlight. The self-proclaimed WWE Internet Champion was soon sharing the same ring with the likes of John Cena and The Miz. He even had Hollywood heavyweight Hugh Jackman in his corner for a match against Dolph Ziggler.

Members of WWE management weren't the only ones forced to take notice of Ryder's social media prowess. In 2011, *Sports Illustrated* named @ZackRyder one of the most influential Twitter accounts in all of sports.

ZACH GOWEN

HT: 6'1"   WT: 169 lbs.
FROM: Flint, Michigan
SIGNATURE MOVE: Unisault

When Zach Gowen was eight years old he lost his left leg to cancer. He was a WWE fan and dreamed of meeting Hulk Hogan. Through the years Zach followed sports-entertainment and became an amateur wrestler in high school. In May 2003, his life-long dream came true when he appeared on *SmackDown* and held the American Flag for Mr. America. He intervened on America's behalf when he was jumped by Roddy Piper and Sean O' Haire. Piper exposed Zach's condition when he pulled off his prosthetic limb.

Zach's spent a year in WWE fending off Big Show, Brock Lesnar, and the manipulative Mr. McMahon. In early 2004, Zach and World Wrestling Entertainment parted ways, but he was recognized for his achievements by *Pro Wrestling Illustrated* who named Zach the 2003 "Rookie of the Year" and "Most Inspirational Wrestler of the Year."

ZEUS

HT: 6'5"   WT: 300 lbs.
FROM: Parts Unknown

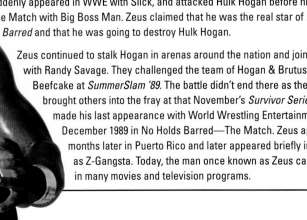

During the filming of *No Holds Barred* reports spread that tensions were high on the set between Hulk Hogan and the man known as "the Human Wrecking Machine," Zeus. In the spring of 1989 Zeus suddenly appeared in WWE with Slick, and attacked Hulk Hogan before his Steel Cage Match with Big Boss Man. Zeus claimed that he was the real star of *No Holds Barred* and that he was going to destroy Hulk Hogan.

Zeus continued to stalk Hogan in arenas around the nation and joined forces with Randy Savage. They challenged the team of Hogan & Brutus Beefcake at *SummerSlam '89*. The battle didn't end there as the four men brought others into the fray at that November's *Survivor Series*. Zeus made his last appearance with World Wrestling Entertainment in December 1989 in No Holds Barred—The Match. Zeus appeared months later in Puerto Rico and later appeared briefly in WCW as Z-Gangsta. Today, the man once known as Zeus can be seen in many movies and television programs.

INDEX